THE GREAT

CONTEMPORARY

ISSUES

THE PRESIDENCY

THE GREAT CONTEMPORARY ISSUES

OTHER BOOKS IN THE SERIES

DRUGS
Introduction by J. Anthony Lukas
THE MASS MEDIA AND POLITICS
Introduction by Walter Cronkite
CHINA
O. Edmund Clubb, *Advisory Editor*
LABOR AND MANAGEMENT
Richard B. Morris, *Advisory Editor*
WOMEN: THEIR CHANGING ROLES
Elizabeth Janeway, *Advisory Editor*
BLACK AFRICA
Hollis R. Lynch, *Advisory Editor*
EDUCATION, U.S.A.
James Cass, *Advisory Editor*
VALUES AMERICANS LIVE BY
Garry Wills, *Advisory Editor*
CRIME AND JUSTICE
Ramsey Clark, *Advisory Editor*

1975 PUBLICATIONS
POPULAR CULTURE
David Manning White, *Advisory Editor*
FOOD AND POPULATION: THE WORLD IN CRISIS
Sen. George McGovern, *Advisory Editor*
U.S. AND WORLD ECONOMY
Leonard Silk, *Advisory Editor*
SCIENCE IN THE TWENTIETH CENTURY
Walter Sullivan, *Advisory Editor*

THE GREAT
CONTEMPORARY
ISSUES

THE PRESIDENCY

The New York Times

ARNO PRESS

NEW YORK/1975

GEORGE E. REEDY

Advisory Editor

Library of Congress Cataloging in Publication Data
Main entry under title:
The Presidency.
(The Great contemporary issues)
"A Hudson group book."
Articles from the New York times.
Bibliography: p.
Includes index.
1. Presidents—United States—Addresses, essays, lectures. 2. United States—Politics and government—20th century—Addresses, essays, lectures.
I. Reedy, George E., 1917 - II. New York times.
III. Series.
JK511.P77 353.03'13 74-7766
ISBN 0-405-04169-1
Manufactured in the United States of America by Arno Press, Inc.

The editors express special thanks to The Associated Press, United Press International, and Reuters for permission to include in this series of books a number of dispatches originally distributed by those news services.

A HUDSON GROUP BOOK
Edited by Joanne Soderman

Contents

Publisher's Note About the Series

It would take even an accomplished speed-reader, moving at full throttle, some three and a half solid hours a day to work his way through all the news *The New York Times* prints. The sad irony, of course, is that even such indefatigable devotion to life's carnival would scarcely assure a decent understanding of what it was really all about. For even the most dutiful reader might easily overlook an occasional long-range trend of importance, or perhaps some of the fragile, elusive relationships between events that sometimes turn out to be more significant than the events themselves.

This is why "The Great Contemporary Issues" was created—to help make sense out of some of the major forces and counterforces at large in today's world. The philosophical conviction behind the series is a simple one: that the past not only can illuminate the present but must. ("Continuity with the past," declared Oliver Wendell Holmes, "is a necessity, not a duty.") Each book in the series, therefore, has as its subject some central issue of our time that needs to be viewed in the context of its antecedents if it is to be fully understood. By showing, through a substantial selection of contemporary accounts from *The New York Times*, the evolution of a subject and its significance, each book in the series offers a perspective that is available in no other way. For while most books on contemporary affairs specialize, for excellent reasons, in predigested facts and neatly drawn conclusions, the books in this series allow the reader to draw his own conclusions on the basis of the facts as they appeared at virtually the moment of their occurrence. This is not to argue that there is no place for events recollected in tranquility; it is simply to say that when fresh, raw truths are allowed to speak for themselves, some quite distinct values often emerge.

"The Great Contemporary Issues" inevitably encompasses a substantial amount of history. In order to explore their subjects fully, some of the books go back a century or more. Yet their fundamental theme is not the past but the present. In this series the past is of significance insofar as it suggests how we got where we are today. These books, therefore, do not always treat a subject in a purely chronological way. Rather, their material is arranged to point up trends and interrelationships that the editors believe are more illuminating than a chronological listing would be.

'The Great Contemporary Issues" series will ultimately constitute an encyclopedic library of today's major issues. Long before editorial work on the first volume had even begun, some fifty specific titles had already been either scheduled for definite publication or listed as candidates. Since then, events have prompted the inclusion of a number of additional titles, and the editors are, moreover, alert not only for new issues as they emerge but also for issues whose development may call for the publication of sequel volumes. We will, of course, also welcome readers' suggestions for future topics.

Introduction

No matter what happens in the next quarter century, the last 75 years have certainly justified naming this the Century of the Presidency. The title does not mean that they were happy times for individual presidents. Some of them—notably Woodrow Wilson, Herbert Hoover, Lyndon B. Johnson and Richard M. Nixon—ended their terms on notes of tragedy. Nor should the title be construed as indicating that the White House was occupied by an unbroken succession of giants. Some of them—especially William Howard Taft and Calvin Coolidge—made scarcely a ripple, and Warren G. Harding is remembered only for the acrid odor of cheap cigar smoke in the back rooms where "the boys" cut their deals. But despite the fates of the men who held the job, the office itself amassed unprecedented power and became not only the pinnacle of the American political structure but the focal point of our nation's life.

In the nineteenth century the presidency was not like that. Andrew Jackson and Abraham Lincoln dominated the scene for brief periods because of their powerful personalities and the historical contexts in which they were operating. But the authority which they gathered into their own hands did not stick to the office. The presidency itself suffered sharp setbacks in both authority and prestige when the strong men left; there were periods when the institution was definitely overshadowed by the Congress and, so far as many citizens were concerned, by the potent, city political machines which had a much greater impact upon the daily lives of people than the federal government.

After Jefferson, the majority of the nineteenth-century presidents are known to Americans only because of the current popularity of trivia quiz games. Yet not all were nonentities. Madison and Monroe were men of genuine profundity. Van Buren, a subtle politician, early perceived the power that could be assembled through "the machine." Polk and Tyler were both executives of force and the much-maligned Andrew Johnson possessed an extraordinary courage. All of them would occupy a much larger role in the American consciousness today had the White House of their era been closer to the center of the country's thinking. But it was a highly individualistic century in which presidents were noticed only during campaigns when they provided entertainment or during wars and social upheavals which united the citizens.

The twentieth century had hardly opened, however, when Theodore Roosevelt, "that damned cowboy," zipped into the White House. The powers that ran the nation's politics had not planned it that way. In fact, they had placed him in the vice presidency because they assumed that he would be less annoying to them in that office than in some other job where he might have real power. They did not—and could not—take into their calculations the possibility of assassination, an accidental turn which has produced a considerable amount of history. But even though Roosevelt's accession depended upon the improbable combination of a carelessly guarded president and a disgruntled office seeker with homicidal tendencies, the man himself cannot be regarded as "an accidental president." He left his stamp upon the presidency and it was never again the "weak office" it had been at times in the past.

Even with the benefit of hindsight, it is difficult to determine whether Teddy Roosevelt's impact upon the nation was due to what he did or to what he was. In terms of enduring achievement, there remains only a confused impression of wilderness conservation, action to "bust" trusts and an aura of international sabre rattling. But the wilderness was preserved only because of its inaccessibility, the "action" did not bust very many trusts and the sabre was never really unsheathed. There was always something going on. The Panama Canal became a reality (and also an enduring source of friction with our Latin American neighbors). The Great White Fleet was sent around the world despite congressional resistance. The Treaty of Portsmouth which ended the Russo-Japanese war was concluded. It is difficult, however, to find in these things any real change in the presidency other than a greater propensity to play international power games than had existed in the past.

But there can be no doubt that Theodore Roosevelt conditioned the American people to look for strength in their presidents and to regard activism as a virtue in itself. Probably, this was due more to his personality than to his actions. He was an absorbing figure who would have attracted public attention in any job. No one could live in the same nation with him and be unaware of his presence. He approached every project with a gusto and a flamboyance which was such fun to watch that few noticed, or even cared, whether the outcome was genuine achievement. His name became a household word and cartoonists of the period had to draw merely a slouch hat, pince-nez glasses and a set of teeth to produce a caricature that was both universally and instantly recognizable.

In a deeper sense, the question of whether the Teddy Roosevelt phenomenon was a matter of achievement or personality is irrelevant. The important point is that what he tried to do and what he was were both in accord with forces that were changing the manner in which Americans looked at themselves. This country no longer depended for its subsistence upon the export of raw materials to industrial nations. It had developed its own industry and its own technology. Almost imperceptibly, at least to its citizens, the United States had become an economic giant and the turn of the century had brought with it the first stirrings of a desire to move onto the scene of world power. There was a dim awareness of strength and an inarticulate urge to use that strength. The outstanding Roosevelt characteristic was his desire to employ muscle and his people responded to that desire.

The actual change, of course, did not happen overnight; it would be an oversimplification to trace the origins of American participation in the international power game to the first Roosevelt. Nevertheless, he took the first tentative steps. And after him, all the forces of history combined to drive the United States ever deeper into world politics. This factor probably accounts for the dominance of the presidency in the twentieth century.

A nation that is determined to play power politics must have a strong central government. It must have the capacity to mobilize its total resources, coordinate all of its activities, react quickly without consuming time in endless debate within divided councils. Under the American Constitution there is only one office which can supply that capacity and it is the presidency. For that reason, there has been a virtually direct correlation between the increasing participation of the United States in international activities and the increasing power and prestige of the White House.

The development of the presidency since Teddy Roosevelt has not moved in a straight line. There have been retreats from the international scene both during the term of Roosevelt's successor and during the twenties, when "the business of the nation" was "business." One of the best known of the presidents—Franklin D. Roosevelt—was actually swept into office to lick the Great Depression. But the fact remains that the least remembered and least effective presidents are those who served during periods when America was largely indifferent to the rest of the world. And there can be little doubt that Franklin D. Roosevelt will be remembered more for World War II than for the New Deal.

Since 1939, the preoccupation of presidents with international affairs has been continuous. Out of this preoccupation rather than a mere desire to grab power (which does not mean that all of them lacked the desire) the dominant position of the presidency was built.

To understand fully the nature of the modern presidency, some reflection is required on the character of international affairs for the past 35 years. The phrase can no longer be construed as diplomatic maneuvering with military forces standing in the wings to intervene in the event of a breakdown in normal relationships. Instead, it has become diplomatic maneuvering in which the disposition of military forces is a tactical device of diplomacy. The partnership of the diplomats and the generals has been recognized by the emergence of a new catch-all—National Security Policy, words which are customarily pronounced with a degree of breathless awe.

The merger was a natural outgrowth of two types of conflict that were new to American history. One was the cold war, defined as continuous and unrelenting pressure short of shooting against "enemy" communist nations. The other was "limited war" in which there was plenty of shooting but only with the goal of placing pressure upon the major "enemy" by striking at its surrogates. The objectives were quite different from those of classical warfare which was waged to subjugate a foe and had no limits short of victory. But the methods were similar, the psychology was similar and the wounded were just as wounded and the dead just as dead.

The United States has been engaged in one or the other or both continuously since a few months after World War II. For most Americans, the experience has not been particularly unpleasant until recently. The limited wars were fought at vast distances from our own shores. The cold war, at times, actually made a contribution to the prosperity of individual citizens through federal contracts that increased payrolls at manufacturing plants producing weapons and goods for economic aid overseas. Nevertheless, we were engaging in a form of war; whatever the degree of individual suffering, it necessarily called for changes in both the structure and the psychology of government.

The separate hats that presidents had worn for their diplomatic and commander-in-chief roles were discarded and replaced by a national security hat. The major foreign arm of the chief executive ceased to be the State Department and became the National Security Council. New and complex organizations—the Central Intelligence Agency and the United States Information Agency—were created to operate on a virtual parity with the historic cabinet groups. Most importantly, the psychology of warfare came to dominate all government thought.

War—cold or hot, limited or unlimited—suspends most of the standards of conduct that are regarded as proper to civilization. Victory becomes the sole criterion for policy and anything that contributes to winning—including treachery, deceit and fraud—is regarded as a virtue whatever the attitude of the people in time of peace. Only those rules of humane behavior that give neither side a military edge have any prospect for survival and even these have been largely abandoned in modern times.

Theoretically, the suspension of normal standards applies only to those who are actively waging war or supporting a war against the fatherland. But the distinction, which was never really observed with much enthusiasm, between the military foe and the home-based dissenter becomes very blurred in contemporary conflict. Whatever may be the motives of the dissenter, he or she tends to disrupt national unity and the disruption, in turn, threatens the prospect of victory. It is difficult for leaders who are directing a life-and-death struggle to contemplate such a situation in a spirit of philosophical detachment.

It is doubtful whether any of the recent presidents really wanted to transform the United States into a police state. Despite the complaints of many leftist groups, it cannot reasonably be claimed that there was large-scale suppression of dissenting opinions. In a number of instances the police overreacted to demonstrations during the Vietnamese war. Some of these instances were serious in and of themselves and involved brutality and bloodshed. Nevertheless, there was never a time when opponents of American involvement were unable to find a platform from which their voices could be heard.

What did happen, however, was the creation of a presidential environment in which the planning of national policy was conducted under the same security precautions as the planning of a military campaign. It was not possible to disclose presidential intentions to "patriotic" Americans without disclosing them to "unpatriotic" Americans. Consequently, the only "safe" course was not to disclose them at all. This resulted in the curious paradox of a shrinking circle of advisers even while presidential staffs were expanding to carry out the designs of the elite. It is doubtful whether any chief executives of any nation in history ever had so many people in their immediate vicinity and so few to whom they really listened as Lyndon B. Johnson and Richard M. Nixon.

The inevitable result was a widening gap between presidents and contemporary political forces. The White House under both Johnson and Nixon took on the aspect of a besieged fortress in which the commander trusted no one outside the walls and only a tiny handful of those who were permitted within the gates. The plumbers, the enemies' list, the "dirty tricks" specialists were not merely temporary aberrations dictated by one man. They flowed naturally from the atmosphere of a wartime command post under heavy pressure from enemy forces. Those who sent a team of burglars into the Democratic National Committee headquarters at Watergate were operating under the motives by which a regimental commander orders a patrol sent into hostile territory to gather tactical intelligence.

Secrecy and stealth were not the only manifestations of the wartime psychology. In armed conflict, efficiency is one of the most highly-prized virtues. The American political process, with its interminable debates and its inevitable compromises, is regarded, validly or invalidly, as the antithesis of efficiency. In the minds of those who are directing troops, it is a "luxury" which can be afforded when things are going well but which must be abandoned when the bullets are flying. Of course, this attitude cannot be expressed too baldly; the cold war formulators pleaded for the separation of national security policy from politics.

The closing days of the Johnson administration found both him and his more articulate assistants advocating a one-term, six-year presidency. Their rationale was that the chief executive should have ample time to work out his programs without the tensions of preparing for another election. The Nixon administration took another tack. It launched a series of governmental reorganization moves all of which tended to bring more administrative control directly into the White House where it would be less subject to the outside pressures that impinge upon the regular cabinet agencies. The motives behind these reorganizations were complex and unquestionably included a desire for greater efficiency. Nevertheless, like the six-year term, the Nixon plan rested upon an interpretation of the election process as a plebiscitary event that would give the winner a relatively free hand in running the nation's affairs until the next plebiscite.

If the external policies of the cold war presidents had met with a higher degree of success, it is entirely possible that the American political system would have evolved into a plebiscitary process. The cold war struggle had created a cult of the presidency which counted among its communicants not only normal, patriotic citizens but the bulk of the nation's intellectuals. The latter saw the White House as *their* institution—that part of the government representing modern enlightenment as opposed to the old-fashioned parochialism of the legislative branch. A significant goal of many analysts and commentators until the late sixties was to devise new governmental structures that would enhance the presidential capacity for swift and decisive action and "streamline" Congress into a body that would present fewer obstructions to "progress." Had the involvement in Southeast Asia concluded with even moderate success—or something that could be claimed as success—such plans would have been irresistible.

That mood has disappeared so thoroughly that the contemporary observer can hardly realize that it ever existed. The cult of the presidency has been shattered under the double impact of the failure in Southeast Asia and the Watergate scandal. For the first time in our history, a president has been literally driven from office before the end of his term. The White House is in the hands of a man who has achieved the position by appointment rather than by election and who is held in no awe however much he may be liked personally. The bulk of current literature on political subjects centers on the theme of weakening the presidency and strengthening the Congress.

A forecast on the future of the office can be nothing but a guess; however, it does not require a crystal ball to conclude that we have reached the end of an important era in the development of the presidency. It is extremely unlikely that the office will disappear. Possibly it may gather even more administrative authority as a reaction to the quickening pace of history. But it is doubtful whether any president will enjoy the sanctified position of his predecessors in this century and it may well be that additional powers will be accompanied by additional requirements of accountability. In this period of transition anything can happen.

Even though the future is cloudy, a period of transition is an excellent vantage point for a backward view. If we cannot see where we are going, we can look at where we have been. At the very least, a retrospective review can give us a useful insight into the trends that brought us to our present state. From our contemporary perspective of the presidency, Vietnam and Watergate loom far too large to lead us to balanced conclusions. We need a platform from which we can see the whole forest rather than just the closest trees.

This volume does not lay claim to a historical perspective. This is a collection of newspaper stories, and journalism, however important, is not history. It consists of the immediate perceptions of men and women who must deal with events as they happen. They must report their perceptions without waiting to see the results of the events and with a minimum of time and space to fit them into the context of the past. The long view is a luxury never accorded to a reporter on the scene.

But even though journalism is not history, it deals with the raw materials of which history is made. It is not the sole source of facts upon which the historian should draw, but it can present him with a unique perspective without which written history can be very misleading. Journalism records the mood of contemporary society at the time that significant events took place.

Despite its shortcomings, the press, with a high degree of fidelity, does chronicle the collective consciousness of a society as to the shape and size of the social universe. There are many reasons why the collective consciousness can be invalid in terms of objective reality. Sometimes the whole can be unaware of what is happening within its parts. This explains why a historian writing on the black revolution would find newspapers of little value for supplying facts until the 1950's. The dominant white majority simply ignored the racial minorities until that point and white journalists were no exception. However, treating blacks as though they did not exist was one of the factors that led to the ultimate explosion, and the conscientious historian would have to take note of this element.

The press has much more to offer on the presidency than absence of comment. Never in our history has either society or journalism ignored the president so long as he was doing something. Even Calvin Coolidge, the least regarded chief executive of this century, was capable of commanding national newspaper attention by posing in an Indian war bonnet. Since the administration of Franklin D. Roosevelt, no other institution in the entire world has been covered with as much persistency and as continuously as the White House. Every press secretary learns in the first few days of his tenure that the only way to clear the mansion of reporters is to throw them out and lock the doors.

To a student of the presidency, the press is a far more important element in research than it is to other scholars. The concept of "public" office takes on an extra dimension when it is applied to the White House because the ultimate power is in the hands of its occupant. That ultimate power stems from the willingness of the people to follow the president's leadership. Should that willingness end, the presidency breaks down for there is no other quarter to which the president can turn for support. Therefore, one of the most important factors in the presidential equation is the manner in which he is regarded by other Americans.

What we have in the following pages is a view of the presidents in this century as seen by their contemporaries.

This, of course, was not the intention of the journalists who wrote the stories. They were simply reporting to the public on what the presidents were doing. Precisely that quality gives these pages a higher degree of validility than would conscious effort to assess each individual president. Reporters write about the events that they consider important to their audiences. They can be wrong about individual items, but over a period of time their selection of facts will accord closely with the value judgments of the society in which they live.

Every president has many roles: administrator, policy maker, moral leader, national spokesman, diplomat, military commander, politician and symbol of the country's unity. His office is the focal point of America's life and therefore its trappings reflect the tastes, values and technology of society. Since it is also the most powerful existing magnet for men of ambition, the office is touched from time to time with scandal. All of these factors were taken into account in determining the organization of this book.

It is entirely possible that future presidents will not wear so many hats regardless of the amount of administrative authority that they exercise. Many of the roles that have been played in the past flow from the mystical overtones associated with the concept that the president has been elected "by all the people." Those who have died in office have been replaced by vice presidents who were also elected by "all the people" in theory if not in reality. In a very real sense, the presidential election was a secular form of ordination.

We are now living under a president who has not been anointed through the electoral process. He owes his position, as does his vice president, to nomination by a president and approval by the Congress. It is difficult to look upon such a man as a sanctified figure, regardless of the degree of his popularity. He is a 'hired hand' who was brought in to mind the store because the legitimate owner was incapacitated. It is a straight-out business proposition with few, if any, elements of mystique.

Of course, a fully "legitimate" president will be elected in 1976 who will theoretically have all the status of any of his predecessors. The new chief executive will be inaugurated with all the traditional pomp of the past (barring very bad weather) and will be entitled to all the ruffles and flourishes that constitute the outward symbols of a chief of state. Nevertheless, he will enter the Oval Room after two and one-half years in which the American people have lived with a leader whom they regard as just another citizen.

Two and one-half years is a long time in the modern world—sufficient time to implant new attitudes in some depth—or at least drastically change traditional attitudes. It may well be that the most significant change in the presidential office will be a new perception of the role by the people whom it serves. The public may come to regard the president as just a man paid to do a job. If so, the character of the office will undergo a profound transformation.

Whether such a change would be good or bad is a moot question. It would probably have elements of each quality—the usual outcome of altering human institutions. Certainly, it would be a healthy development to bring presidents back into the mainstream of American political life. They have been isolated far too long. The loss of the presidency as a symbol of national unity, however, would be an altogether different matter. There are very few unifying forces in our society today and the loss of any one of them is not to be contemplated with equanimity. A nation must have qualities other than good management to remain viable.

This, of course, is mere speculation. All we can know for sure is that the presidency stands at a watershed and that the future will not follow the pattern of the past. Let us, therefore, take a good look at the past through the eyes of the correspondents of *The New York Times* so we will at least know where we have been.

George E. Reedy

CHAPTER 1

Conceptions of the Presidency

What is the presidency? The constitutional definition, valid but not very revealing, merely sets forth the title and the method of selection and then enumerates, in broad terms, the areas in which the president can act and certain specific things that he cannot do.

In a sense, what the Constitution does *not* say about the presidency is fully as important as what it says. The grey areas in which the limits of authority are poorly defined or not defined at all are so numerous that each occupant of the office has the capacity to redefine the position in his own terms. This means that the Constitution is merely a starting point for an adequate understanding.

The full power of the presidency can be seen only in terms of the perceptions of each individual president and his contemporaries. The variations have been extreme—particularly in this century. Activists—particularly the two Roosevelts—constantly sought to expand the presidential role. Men like Harding and Coolidge thought that presidents should be little seen and even less heard. Dwight D. Eisenhower presided and left administration to others. Lyndon B. Johnson tried to keep his thumb on every tiny detail.

Public perceptions of the presidency have not changed as rapidly. But they have changed. Just a few years ago, the cult of the presidency reached unprecedented heights. The office was the darling of the intellectuals even though they might not approve of the specific occupant. The people at large looked to the White House for leadership whenever they were in trouble. The present mood is one of disillusionment which runs deep.

The following pages attempt to set forth the changing moods and interpretations as they were seen by presidents and their contemporaries.

GER

Theodore Roosevelt

The New York Times

The Presidency as Seen by Presidents

Compiled by SIDNEY HYMAN

The American Presidency is as much a sum of outlook and word as of law and deed. It is what all Presidents have said and felt about the place they held, and what the President of the moment may add or alter in this legacy from the past. In this sense, there is a "common law" of the Presidency, in which themes and experiences repeat themselves like figures caught in a hall of mirrors. Here are some of them:

RESPONSIBILITIES OF THE PRESIDENT

Many things which seem of little importance in themselves and at the beginning, may have great and durable consequences from their having been established at the commencement of a new general government. It will be much easier to commence the administration, upon a well-adjusted system, built on tenable grounds, than to correct errors or alter inconveniences after they shall have been confirmed by habit.—*GEORGE WASHINGTON, "Writings," May 10, 1789.*

* * *

In all great and essential measures [the President] is bound by his honor and his conscience, by

George Washington.

his oath to the Constitution, as well as his responsibility to the public opinion of the nation, to act his own mature and unbiased judgment, though unfortunately, it may be in direct contradiction to the advice of all his ministers.—*JOHN ADAMS, in "Letters to a Boston Patriot," 1809.*

* * *

A strict observance of the written laws is doubtless *one* of the high duties of a good [officer], but it is not *the highest*. The laws of necessity, of self-preservation, of saving our country when in danger, are of higher obligation. To lose our country by a scrupulous adherence to written law, would be to lose the law itself, with life, liberty, property and all those who are enjoying them with us; thus absurdly sacrificing the end to the means.—*THOMAS JEFFERSON, in a letter to John B. Colvin, Sept. 20, 1810.*

* * *

You have no oath registered in heaven to destroy the Government, while *I* have the most solemn one to "preserve, protect and defend" it.—*ABRAHAM LINCOLN, in his first inaugural address, March 4, 1861.*

* * *

Was it possible to lose the nation and yet preserve the Constitution? By general law, life and limb must be protected, yet often a limb must be amputated to save a life * * *. I felt that measures, otherwise unconstitutional, might become lawful by becoming indispensable to the preservation of the Constitution through the preservation of the nation. Right or wrong, I assumed this ground and now avow it. I could not feel that, to the best of my ability, I have ever tried to preserve the Constitution, if to save slavery or any minor matter,

John Adams.

I should permit the wreck of the government, country and Constitution together.—*ABRAHAM LINCOLN, in a letter to A. G. Hodges, April 4, 1864.*

* * *

Mistakes have been made, as all can see and I admit, but, it seems to me, oftener in the selections made of the assistants appointed to aid in carrying out the various duties of administering the government, in nearly every case selected without a personal acquaintance with the appointee, but upon recommendations of the representatives chosen directly by the people. It is impossible, where so many trusts are to be allotted, that the right parties should be chosen in every instance. History shows that no administration * * * has been free from these mistakes. But I leave comparison to history, claiming only that I have acted in every instance from a conscientious desire to do what was right, constitutional within the law, and for the very best interests of the whole people. Failures have been errors of judgment, not intent.—*U. S. GRANT, in his last Annual Message to Congress, December, 1876.*

* * *

Thomas Jefferson.

My secretaries and their subordinates were responsible to me and I accepted the responsibility for all their deeds. * * * As for getting Congress to make up my mind for me about them, the thought would have been inconceivable.—*THEODORE ROOSEVELT, in "An Autobiography."*

* * *

The Presidency is not merely an administrative office. That is the least part of it. It is more than an engineering job, efficient or inefficient. It is preeminently a place of moral leadership. All our great Presidents were leaders of thought at times when certain historic ideas in the life of the nation had to be clarified.—*FRANKLIN D. ROOSEVELT, in The New York Times, Nov. 13, 1932.*

* * *

To be President of the United States is to be lonely, very lonely at times of great decisions.—*HARRY S. TRUMAN, in "Year of Decisions."*

POWERS OF THE PRESIDENT

The most important factor in getting the right spirit in my Administration * * * was my insistence upon the theory that the executive power was limited only by specific restrictions and prohibitions appearing in the Constitution or imposed by Congress under its constitutional powers. My view was that every executive officer, and above all every executive officer in high position, was a steward of the people bound actively and affirmatively to do all he could for the people * * *. I declined to adopt the view that what was imperatively necessary for the nation could not be done by the President unless he could find some specific authorization to do it.—*THEODORE ROOSEVELT, in "An Autobiography."*

* * *

The true view of the executive function is, as I conceive it, that the President can exercise no powers which cannot be reasonably and fairly traced to some specific grant of power or justly implied

Abraham Lincoln.

or included within such express grant as necessary and proper to its exercise. Such specific grant must be either in the Constitution or in an act of Congress passed in pursuance thereof. There is no undefined residium of power which he can exercise because it seems to him to be in the public interest. —*WILLIAM HOWARD TAFT, in "Our Chief Magistrate and His Powers."*

* * *

The President is at liberty both in law and conscience to be as big a man as he can.—*WOODROW WILSON, in "Constitutional Government in the United States."*

* * *

In the event that the Congress should fail to [enact the price control legislation] I shall accept the responsibility and I will act. * * * I have given the most thoughtful consideration to meeting this issue without further reference to Congress. I have determined in this vital matter to consult with the Congress. * * * The American people can be sure that I shall not hesitate to use every power vested in me to accomplish the defeat of our enemies in any part of the world where our safety demands such defeat. When the war is won, the powers under which I act automatically revert to the people to whom they belong.—*FRANKLIN D. ROOSEVELT, Labor Day Address to Congress, Sept. 7, 1942.*

* * *

Very few are ever authorized to speak for the President. No one can make decisions for him.—*HARRY S. TRUMAN, in "Year of Decisions."*

RELATIONS WITH CONGRESS

I have yet to learn under what constitutional authority [the Senate] has a right to require of me

Theodore Roosevelt.

an account of any communications, either verbal or in writing, made to the Departments acting as a Cabinet council. As well might I be required to detail to the Senate the free and private conversations I have held with those officers on any subject relating to their duties and my own.—*ANDREW JACKSON, in a message to the Senate, December, 1833.*

* * *

After much serious reflection, I have arrived at the conclusion that no such power [to coerce the states moving toward secession] has been delegated to Congress nor to any other department of the federal government. It is manifest, upon an inspection of the Constitution, that it is not among the specific and enumerated powers granted to Congress; and it is equally apparent that its exercise is not "necessary and proper for carrying into execution" any one of those powers.—*JAMES BUCHANAN, in his Annual Message, December, 1860.*

* * *

The Executive has the authority to recommand measures to Congress. Having performed that duty, the Executive department of the Government cannot rightfully control the decision of Congress on

Woodrow Wilson.

any subject of legislation until that decision shall have been officially submitted to the President for approval.—*ZACHARY TAYLOR, in his Inaugural Address, March 4, 1849.*

* * *

A good Executive under present conditions of American life must take a very active interest in getting the right kind of legislation in addition to performing his Executive duties with an eye single to the public welfare.—*THEODORE ROOSEVELT, in "An Autobiography."*

* * *

The weakening of the legislative arm leads to encroachments by the executive upon legislative and judicial functions, and inevitably that encroachment is upon individual liberty. If we examine the fate of wrecked republics over the world we shall find first a weakening of the legislative arm.—*HERBERT HOOVER, in "The Challenge to Liberty."*

THE PRESIDENT AND THE PEOPLE

In every act of my administration I have sought the happiness of my fellow-citizens. My system for the attainment of this object has uniformly been to overlook all personal, local and partial considerations: to contemplate the United States as one great whole.—*GEORGE WASHINGTON, in a letter to the Boston Selectmen, July 28, 1795.*

* * *

If it be said that the Representatives in the popular branch of Congress are chosen directly by the people, it is answered, the people elect the President. * * * The President represents in the Executive department the whole people of the United States as each representative of the legislative department represents portions of them. —*JAMES K. POLK, in his last Annual Message to Congress, January, 1849.*

Franklin D. Roosevelt.

* * *

Your President is now the Tribune of the people, and, thank God, I am, and intend to assert the power which the people have placed in me. * * * Tyranny and despotism can be exercised by many more rigorously, more vigorously, and more severely than by one.—*ANDREW JOHNSON, in a speech on the occasion of a serenade, April 18, 1866.*

* * *

It is because in their hours of timidity the Congress becomes subservient to the importunities of organized minorities that the President comes more and more to stand as the champion of the rights of the whole country.—*CALVIN COOLIDGE, in The American Magazine, August, 1929.*

* * *

A mark of free citizens, proud and wise enough to govern themselves, is the searching scrutiny they turn upon the purposes and the performances of their own Government. It is the historic habit of a free people—it is our habit—to ask our Government at frequent intervals: Where are we going? How far have we come?—*DWIGHT D. EISENHOWER, in a Report to the Nation broadcast, Aug. 6, 1953.*

SENSE OF HISTORY

I indulge a confidence that sufficient evidence will find its way to another generation, to ensure, after we are gone, whatever of justice may be withheld whilst we are here. The political horizon is already yielding in your case at least, the surest auguries of it.—*JAMES MADISON, in a letter to ex-President Thomas Jefferson, Feb. 24, 1826.*

* * *

Gentlemen, I have been shaking hands since nine o'clock this morning [at the White House New Year's Day reception] and my right arm is almost paralyzed. If my name goes down in history, it will be for this act [the Emancipation Proclamation] and my whole soul is in it. If my hand trembles when I sign this Proclamation all who examine the document hereafter will say, "He hesitated."—*ABRAHAM LINCOLN, to his Cabinet before signing the Emancipation Proclamation, Jan. 1, 1863.*

* * *

I have often thought in reading the history of our country how much is lost to us because so few of our Presidents have told their own stories. It would have been helpful to know more of what was in their minds and what impelled them to do what they did.—*HARRY S. TRUMAN, in "Year of Decisions."*

* * *

Far from being fearful of ideas, the founders of the Republic feared only misguided efforts to suppress ideas. No less profound was their faith in man's ability to use freedom, for the achievement of his own and his country's good. * * * So convinced, they proclaimed to all the world the revolutionary doctrine of the divine rights of the common man. That doctrine has ever since been the heart of the American faith. Emphatic rejection of this faith is the cardinal characteristic of the materialistic despotisms of our times.—*DWIGHT D. EISENHOWER, in an address at the Columbia University bicentennial dinner, May 31, 1954.*

PRESIDENTIAL HUMILITY

I may have committed many errors. Whatever they may be, I fervently beseech the Almighty to avert or mitigate the evils to which they may tend. I shall also carry with me the hope that my country will never cease to view them with indulgence and that, after forty-five years of my life dedicated to its service, with an upright zeal, the faults of incompetent abilities will be consigned to oblivion as myself must soon be to the mansions of rest.—*GEORGE WASHINGTON, in his Farewell Address, Sept. 17, 1796.*

* * *

I shall often go wrong

through defect of judgment. When right, I shall often be thought wrong by those whose positions will not command a view of the ground. I ask your indulgence for my own errors, which will never be intentional, and your support against the errors of others, who may condemn what they would not if seen in all its parts.—*THOMAS JEFFERSON, in his First Inaugural Address, March 4, 1801.*

* * *

Having no pretentions to the high and commanding claims of my predecessors, whose names are so much more conspicuously identified with our Revolution, and who contributed so preeminently to promote its success, I consider myself rather as the instrument than the cause of the union which has prevailed in the late election.—*JAMES MONROE, in his Second Inaugural Address, March 4, 1821.*

* * *

Any American who had a modicum of modesty would at times be overcome by the intensity and the importance of the problems that he would meet if he were called upon to serve in the chief official position of this country.—*DWIGHT D. EISENHOWER, in an address at Charlotte, N. C., May 18, 1954.*

STRAINS AND DEMANDS OF THE PRESIDENCY

To reconcile you to your fate, I have a great mind to give you a detail of mine. A peck of troubles in a large bundle of papers, often in handwriting almost illegible, comes every day from the office of——, office of——, office of——, etc., etc., etc. Thousands of sea letters, Mediterranean passes, and commissions and patents to sign * * *.—*JOHN ADAMS, in a letter to his wife, Abigail, March 9, 1797.*

* * *

The loss of power and of popular favor I could have endured with fortitude, and relief from the slavery of [the Presidency] was more than a compensation for all the privations incident to the loss of place.—*JOHN QUINCY ADAMS, in an 1829 diary entry shortly after leaving the Presidency.*

* * *

I received the [New Year's Day] crowd in the circular parlour [of the White House] and for three hours shook hands with a dense column of human beings of all ages and sexes. * * * I could generally anticipate when I was going to have a strong grip * * *. —*JAMES K. POLK, in a diary entry, Jan. 1, 1849.*

* * *

The folly of mankind is difficult to fathom; it would seem incredible that anyone would care one way or the other about your playing golf, but * * * I have received literally hundreds of letters from the West protesting about it. * * * It is just like my tennis: I never let any friends advertise my tennis, and never let a photograph taken of me in tennis costume appear.—*THEODORE ROOSEVELT, in a letter to Republican Presidential nominee William Howard Taft, Sept. 5, 1908.*

* * *

I know that you are depending upon me to keep this nation out of war. So far I have done so and I pledge you my word that, God helping me, I will—if it is possible. But you have laid another duty upon me. You have bidden me see to it that nothing stains or impairs the honor of the United States, and that is a matter not within my control: that depends on what others do, not upon what the Government of the United States does. Therefore there may at any moment come a time when I cannot preserve both the honor and the peace of the United States. Do not exact of me an impossible and contradictory thing.—*WOODROW WILSON, in an address at Cleveland, Jan. 31, 1916.*

* * *

In the Middle Ages it was the fashion to wear hair shirts to remind one's self of trouble and sin. Many years ago I concluded that a few hair shirts were part of the mental wardrobe of every man. The President differs only from other men in that he has a more extensive wardrobe.—*HERBERT HOOVER, in a speech at the Gridiron Club in Washington, Dec. 14, 1929.*

July 8, 1956

ROOSEVELT NAMES TWO GREATEST PRESIDENTS

Sets Washington and Lincoln Above All Others.

HAD TO BE PRACTICAL MEN

Those Who Actually Do Things, Not Talk About Doing Them, Amount to Something.

PHILADELPHIA, June 19—President Roosevelt, who with Mrs. Roosevelt spent Sunday with Attorney General Knox on his farm at Valley Forge, visited the historic campground of Washington to-day. The forenoon was taken up with a long drive over the territory, visits being made to Washington's headquarters and other places.

This afternoon the President attended the patriotic services held in Washington Memorial Chapel on the campground in celebration of Evacuation Day, and addressed the meeting. In the course of his remarks he said:

"There have been other crises than those that culminated in the war for independence and the great civil war, there have been great deeds and great men at other periods of our National history, but there never has been another deed vital to the welfare of the Nation save the two—the deed of those who founded and the deed of those who saved the Republic. There never has been another man whose life has been vital to the Republic save Washington and Lincoln. I am not here to say anything about Lincoln, but I do not see how any American can think of either of them without thinking of the other, too, because they represent the same work.

"Think how fortunate we are as a Nation. Think what it means to us as a people that our young men should have as their ideals two men, not conquerors, not men who won glory by wrongdoing, not men whose lives were spent in their own advancement, but men who lived, one of whom died, that the Nation might grow steadily greater and better—the man who founded the Republic and took no glory from it himself save what was freely given him by his fellow-citizens, and that only in the shape of a chance of rendering them service, and the man who afterward saved the Republic, who saved the State without striking down liberty!

"Often in history a State has been saved and liberty struck down at the same time. Lincoln saved the Union and lifted the cause of liberty higher than before. Washington created the Republic, rose by statecraft to the highest position, and used that position only for the welfare of his fellows and for so long as his fellows wished him to keep it."

VITAL THING FOR THE NATION.

"When two lessons are both indispensable, it seems hardly worth while to dwell more on one than on the other. Yet I think that as a people we need more to learn the lesson of Valley Forge even than that of Gettysburg. I have not the slightest anxiety but that this people, if the need should come in the future, will be able to show the heroism, the supreme effort, that was shown at Gettysburg, though it may well be that it would need a similar two years of effort checkered by disaster to lead up to it.

"But the vital thing for this nation to do is steadily to cultivate the quality which Washington and those under him so pre-eminently showed during the Winter at Valley Forge—the quality of steady adherence to duty in the teeth of difficulty, in the teeth of discouragement, and even disaster; the quality that makes a man do what is straight and decent, not one day when a great crisis comes, but every day, day in and day out, until success comes at the end.

"Of course, all of us agreed that a prime National need is the need of commemorating the memories of the men who did greatly, thought highly, fought, suffered, endured, for the Nation. It is a great thing to commemorate their lives, but, after all, the worthy way to do so is to try to show by our lives that we have profited by them. If we show that the lives of the great men of the past have been to us incitements to do well in the present, then we have paid to them the only homage which is really worthy of them.

"If we treat their great deeds as matters merely for idle boasting, not as spurring us on to effort, but as excusing us from effort, then we show that we are not worthy of the sires who bore us, of the people who went before us in the history of our land.

"What we as a people need more than aught else is the steady performance of the every-day duties of life, not with hope of reward, but because they are duties.

PRACTICAL SERVICE OF IDEALS.

"I spoke of how we felt that we had in Washington and Lincoln National ideals. I contrasted their names with the names of many others in history, names which will shine as brightly, but oh, with how much less power and light.

"I think you will find that the fundamental difference between our two great National heroes and almost any other men of equal note in the world's history, is that when you think of our two men you think inevitably not of glory, but of duty, not of what the man did for himself in achieving name or fame or position, but of what he did for his fellows. They set the right ideal, and also they lived up to it in practical fashion.

"Had either of them possessed that fantastic quality of mind which sets an impossible and perhaps an undesirable ideal or which declines to do the actual work of the present because, forsooth, the implements with which it is necessary to work are not to that man's choice, his fame would have been missed, his achievement would have crumbled into dust, and he would not have left one stroke on the book which tells of effort accomplished for good of mankind.

"A man, to amount to anything, must be practical. He must actually do things, not talk about doing them, least of all cavil at how they are accomplished by those who actually go down into the arena and actually face the dust and the blood and the sweat, who actually triumph in the struggle. The man must have the force, the power, the will to accomplish results, but he must have also the lift toward lofty things which shall make him incapable of striving for aught unless that for which he strives is something noble and high—something well worth striving for.

"I congratulate you that it is your good fortune to be engaged in erecting a memorial to the great man who was equal to the great days—to the man and the men who showed by their lives that they were, indeed, doers of the word and not hearers only."

June 20, 1904

THEODORE ROOSEVELT AS I KNOW HIM

A Defense of the President, With Interesting Side-lights on the Early Career of One Who is the Object of Bitter and Contradictory Criticism in the East and Unreserved Praise in the West.

IN view of the many criticisms that have been made of the policies of President Roosevelt, which, on account of his exalted position, he is not permitted to answer, The Times sought a champion in one of Mr. Roosevelt's most intimate friends, Mr. Jacob A. Riis, who, from long personal association with and admiration for the President, is best qualified to judge the motives which actuate Mr. Roosevelt in all his policies. A list of subjects which are now being discussed both in Congress and by the press, was given to Mr. Riis, and in the following article he reviews them at length.

By JACOB A. RIIS.

IT seems strange to a man who travels much in the West, where they know and accept Theodore Roosevelt without question for what he is, a simple, straightforward, patriotic American, doing for his day and for his people the very best he can as President, to come back to New York and find him in his own city abused, cartooned, ridiculed as if he were some public enemy instead of the chosen head of the Nation. Knowing him personally as I do, and observing that the denunciation proceeds in a given case from exactly opposite poles: he is supposed to have done a thing, or not to have done it; he has unwarrantably attacked predatory wealth and thereby shaken public confidence, or he has failed to put any one into jail for owning it, and is therefore undeserving of confidence himself—it seems as if there are some people who can by no possibility be happy without having some one jammed into jail every time the clock strikes—seeing these things, I should like, as one who believes in Theodore Roosevelt without any reservation, to give the reasons for my faith. They are very simple, and I shall try to state them as plainly and as concisely as I can, without attempting any defense of him. He is not in need of it.

Jacob A. Riis.

What Aroused Roosevelt's Sympathy.

I shall have first to tell how I came to know him, since the way of it is in a sense the key to the man. It was when I had written "How the Other Half Lives" that one day a stranger came to the office and, not finding me in, left his card upon my desk. I found it there, "Theodore Roosevelt," with these words written across his name: "I have read your book and I have come to help." That was all. The book was a plea for decent homes for the people. Three-fourths of them lived in tenements, and the conditions there in those days were neither decent nor, indeed, human. He knew I had not painted them with too lurid colors, for he had had more than a glimpse of them when, as a member of the Assembly, he had championed the cigarmakers' cause against the tenement-owning manufacturers, who held their workmen in a bondage that was virtual slavery. And he had learned in that fight, as in so many another in after years, what laborious years of education, of informing the public mind and conscience, must go before the righting of such wrongs so that they shall stay righted. So he knew, and, knowing, came to help.

Ever since I have seen this motive sway all his actions. I hear people speak of his fight with the law-breaking corporations as if he hated men just because they were rich. When he was a Health Commissioner, (being President of the Police Board,) he set the machinery in motion that gave us tenement-house reform; he voted to tear down the worst old rookeries which the health officers had not dared touch before. There were tenement-owning corporations in those days that were ultra-respectable in the social scale, and very wealthy. Some of them suffered, I know, and it was a mighty good thing for the rest of us that they did. But I doubt if he as much as gave a thought to them. He was not trying to smash the landlords or take away their property. There were hideous abuses in those rookeries that meant suffering and death to the tenants, and it was their wrongs he was righting. When as Governor he was in doubt about the Factory Inspector's zeal in the matter of tenement workshops, he came down himself and went over the ground, spending the whole day in the tenements with me.

His Work as New York's Governor.

There again he ran across some eminently respectable manufacturers' trail where it was not to their credit, and they suffered in pocket too, I suppose. Yet that was not his purpose there. It was the evil they did he was trying to undo, and he did undo much of it. Some of it we struggle with yet, but are we better off, or worse, for the hand he had in tenement-house reform? The man to whom no other question is involved in tenement ownership than how high an interest it can be made to yield, will say we are worse off. The man who approved of the Chicago and Alton deal, and the kind of railroad financiering it stood for, will take exactly the same stand with reference to his attitude toward the service corporations and will charge that his purpose is to ruin them. It is the same stand, and the motive that prompts it is the same; but is the man right; is his motive right, in either case?

Politicians discuss Federal control or Government ownership as a party programme. The truth is that with Roosevelt it is not primarily Federal control per se about which he is concerned, as the ideal thing, but as a means to an end, the end being substantial justice and fair-dealing between man and man. The "programme" grew out of the effort to secure that. No one knows better than he that it is not ideal. Snags there will be in the way, disadvantages may show themselves, selfish greed will not down. But here it is; these things can happen: one is to leave the corporations unchecked. That would mean to leave the fellow who is under—in this case the whole people—in the lurch. If not that, then either State or National control. Which do we want?

The railroad themselves may be left to answer that. I am thinking of one out in Michigan of which I happen to know. It paid taxes to the State of $27,000, and in one year they raised it to $90,000. As its earnings were $1,000,000 a year, that was 9 per cent. What happened there has happened elsewhere and will happen again: the local impatience with railroad management will find ready tools of persecution in the politicians who are courting popular favor. They will frankly tell you that "we are here to sock it to the railroads; if we didn't we would be fired."

The Question of Federal Control.

There remains Federal control. Will it tend to centralize great powers that might be misused, to create public opinion in favor of Government ownership? It is at least possible. I can quite imagine President Roosevelt weighing the chances of it; for, contrary to the contention of his critics, there is no chance of any step he takes which he has not first weighed with infinitely greater care and solicitude than any and all of them; and I can give you his verdict with entire confidence, this, namely: We shall cross that bridge when we come to it. We must assume some sense and some virtue in the generation that comes after us. We cannot settle all the political and economic questions of the country forever. We can settle those that crowd to-day, so as to give the man who is down a chance to get on his feet. That is helping. Then we must await the issue.

Freeing the slaves brought us problems that are not solved yet, and will not be while we live. Is that good reason why they should not have been freed? Achieving independence saddled us as a Nation with responsibilities that sometimes have seemed dark and heavy. Should we for that cause have remained under the British yoke? Nothing in the world is perfect; no plan, no settlement of any question final. But it is in striving with the best light it has to find a way toward better things that a Nation grows; never by giving up and letting bad enough alone because so it is easiest.

What the Square Deal Means.

The corporations which Roosevelt halted had been guilty of brutal and unscrupulous use of the power their wealth gave them to crush competition. Their deliberate plan was to break every rival down. This much no one doubts. "It is inevitable," some people tell me, "it is the way of business." The same spirit puts on tenement rents "all that the traffic will bear," until the tenants rise in rebellion. The complacent view prop itself with the law of supply and demand, and, while raising the rents, because the people must have shelter, finds justification in the same economic law for paying the lowest wages the worker will endure. When he rebels and organizes his union to resist, it cries out that he is "unsettling values." If he is, are those "values" of most account to the community, or else the well-being of its toilers, who are after all, the vast majority?

I suppose "the square deal" is just a phrase to a lot of people. But Roosevelt is not among them. It is part of his moral fibre, and the biggest part of it. There came to me, the other day, a letter from a country parson in far-off Denmark. He had somewhere read a story of Roosevelt's youth, and the one thing in it that had arrested and held his attention was the account of his pursuit and capture of three thieves who, when he was ranching on the Little Missouri, stole his boat and carried it off down the river. No doubt the complacent citizen would have said "let it go," and put it down to profit and loss. It was not worth much, certainly not the toil and trouble of building another and going down in pursuit, in mid-Winter, with the river full of ice. But that is what he did. He followed the thieves three days, overtook them, and caught them.

The Story of Three Thieves in Missouri.

The easy thing then would have been to take the boat and go back. The frontier way, as he was told impatiently, was to hang the raiders off-hand and call it square. It was not Roosevelt's way. The men were thieves. They must be punished, for else nothing was safe in that wild country; but justly punished. The burden of seeing that they were so punished had fallen upon him, and it was not the square thing to the community to shift it. So he convoyed them back, through dreary days and sleepless nights on the bleak prairie, where he must needs stand guard while his prisoners slept, to the county town where there was a jail and a judge. It cost toil incredible and an outlay of money that never came back; but it was the right thing to do, and he did it.

"As I pictured to myself," wrote my correspondent, "that young man marching behind the wagon with his rifle, through snow and slush, grimly determined to see justice done, at whatever cost, the whole age-long struggle for law and order and justice, for which the Anglo-Saxon race has come to stand in the world's progress, seemed to rise up before me in that solitary, sturdy figure, and I understood that God had chosen him for a great work in his day and in his country."

The Fight Against Wealthy Criminals.

The Danish parson is not alone in that belief. While I think of it, let those who are so hot for the jail have a little of his patience. For "the man higher up" is, as we know, a slippery customer, and some corporations seem admirably contrived to keep those who use them for illegal purposes out of trouble. Saddling it upon some poor subordinate is not to Roosevelt's liking. But he got his man into jail then, and who knows but he will get him there now.

To a man so built, mentally and morally, comes the revelation of fraud and dishonesty in business of which we have all had a surfeit these days. He sees wealthy malefactors banded together, with enormous resources at their command, to make one kind of law for the rich and one for the poor. He finds them opposing with bitter vituperation every measure for honesty in business which the Administration offers, from the railroad law to the pure food law. He hears one of their hired defenders denouncing the Administration in the same breath for enforcing the law against corrupt combinations and for trying to secure National legislation to make employers liable for injuries to their workmen, difficult enough however carefully bills are drawn, for, as yet, property takes precedence of the person in the eye of the law. We have ceased to hang a starving woman for the theft of a loaf of bread but we are reluctant to fine the manufacturer who, by his neglect to provide safeguards against dangerous machinery in his shop, causes an employe to be crippled for life.

The Growth of Socialism.

All this he sees, and much more, standing in his high place where he was set to help. He sees the cloud of Socialism, which a little while ago was no bigger than a man's hand on the horizon, rise angrily over our land, and he understands that it must be so, with the people's intelligence growing all the time and those sacred "values" which must not on any account be "unsettled" represented by unwholesome aggregations of irresponsible wealth, standing in the way of fair play, of an equal chance. Standing over against poverty and actual want, which they mock with their impudent challenges. He sees the sneer of cynicism flung in the faces of those who arraign swindling in high places. He sees that the real danger to the republic, the real anarchist, is not the man who makes violent speeches from the cart-tail, but the men who looted the Alton and the Metropolitan system, and who not only go unpunished but hold power and place still in the community they dishonored. And he sets his teeth and leads on in the war which can have no other ending, despite abuse and lying and sneer to discredit it, than to bring the malefactors to their knees and give the people a square deal, every man equal before the law with his neighbor, be he rich or poor. That is the answer to those who charge him with being a Socialist in fact, just as the answer to those at the other end who charge centralization against the Government, is that the men it is fighting are the centralizers who have concentrated such vast power in their hands, that in self-defense the Government must challenge it. Roosevelt is to-day the chief bar to Socialism in our land. He is its strongest force for the preservation of the institution of private property. The utter blindness of those who cannot see it is more amazing to me than their grasping greed. If it were conceivable that Roosevelt's policies should fail, we should, I firmly believe, be quickly on the verge of a Socialistic state. It is not conceivable to me, because with my parson friend I believe that the Republic has other purposes than to make a few outrageously rich at the expense of their fellowmen, and that when that has been settled, we are to go on carrying them out. And so does he.

Danger from Consentrated Wealth.

Just now I spoke of unwholesome aggregations of wealth. I used the word on purpose because it expresses his conviction, I think, more nearly than any other. Very vast wealth does not make its possessor proportionately happier and it is of relatively less value to the community; for it is apt to set him apart, to sunder him from the State, and by its temptation to unfit him for the duties of citizenship, which the President profoundly believes are due from him in increasing ratio as he has prospered under the Government. More than that, such great accumulations tend inevitably to become a peril to the Republic in their grasping for special privilege and the corruption that follows.

Yet, while believing this, he has made no attack upon wealth as such, upon any man's right to amass as much as he can by his skill or capacity, provided only that he does it honestly. He has, indeed, urged a plan of progressive taxation akin to that adopted by most European States, because it seems to him reasonable and fair that the man who gets more from the State, doing his business under its protection, should pay more for it. As to that there may be difference of opinion, but why it should provoke any one's wrath I am unable to see. If it constitutes Socialism, then the Kaiser is a Socialistic person, which will be cheering news to some of his subjects.

Now, this is Theodore Roosevelt as I know him and understand him, and as I think he understands himself, going right on doing the work that is his to do, fighting the people's fight against evils which he firmly believes would eat out the vitals of the Republic if let alone, conscious that the people understand and are with him, content if he can leave the world even a little better off than he found it. He is not deceived; he knows that it is to be a fight to a finish, and he is willing to put in all upon it. Nor is he to be diverted by any effort to shift the issue from the ethical plane where it belongs, to lose it in economic sophistries. Shall business be done honestly? Shall justice be done between man and man? These are the questions to be answered. There is no more doubt in his mind how they will be answered, when all is said and done, than there is in mine.

Solitary Figure on the Prairie

Yet every once in a while as I watch him go, I, too, have to call up the picture of the young man on the lonely prairie shouldering his rifle in the wake of the ranchman's wagon, as a lesson in sorely needed patience. When I watch the treachery the enemy plans by day and by night, the malice and cunning with which its hirelings seek to discredit his every act, the lack of understanding here where of all places he should find friends and helpers; when I listen to the devil's advocate in all the chorus of liars sneeringly asking who shall have the last word concerning the justice or injustice, the right or the wrong of a law ardently desired by the President for the protection of the workman, that as a Nation we may line up for social justice with every civilized State abroad, either "the man who has conceived the law and has carried it for years near his burning heart, or the members of an unemotional tribunal, which, perhaps, had never heard of the Employer's Liability act until it became the subject of their arid deliberations"—when I witness these things, the solitary figure looms large. But then I take heart, for I know the answer. It is this: that to the law of the land, to the verdict of its highest tribunal, Theodore Roosevelt will bow in obedience with every lover of his country, for that way lies freedom and safety. No one who knows him has need of asking that. And yet there is still another word to be spoken.

A Supporter of the Law of the Land.

Time will speak that. There will come a day when that august tribunal shall have heard the cry of the toilers and will pass upon a law giving them other rights than that to be killed or crippled for the profit of heartless employers, and will stamp it as good, and for that day we will wait. It is because Theodore Roosevelt's whole life has been one unceasing effort by lawful and orderly means to speed that day, and so to preserve government of the people and for the people and by the people to our children, that I believe in him and will follow wherever he leads, sure that so I also serve my day best.

TRUSTS, TAFT SAYS, MUST OBEY THE LAW

Tells Illinois Leaders at Peoria That Railroads Have Been Brought Under Regulation.

NOT A PARTY EXTREMIST

President Hears Predictions That He Will Surely Be Renominated and Re-elected.

PEORIA, Ill., Sept. 22.—President Taft had a heart-to-heart talk here to-day with the leaders of the different Republican factions in Illinois, defined his status as to progressiveness, pleaded guilty to being a poor politician, acknowledged again that his ambition had lain in the direction of the office of Chief Justice, rather than the Presidency, admitted that he undoubtedly had made many mistakes, but asserted that as President he had tried to do what he thought was right. What the future held for him he did not know; he would go ahead doing the best he could.

Mr. Taft declared he was not allied with the extremists of his party, either conservatives or progressives, but had tried to take a middle ground between the two.

"But we middle-of-the-road people believe we are the real progressives," said the President, "because you do not make progress in great strides; you make it step by step."

The President was in a serious mood. He declared that while it might not be so for a time, the people in the end would distinguish between "fact and fustian" and would recognize the difference between substance in progress and platform declarations written for campaign purposes only.

The speech made by the President was the most significant and interesting of his trip thus far. He still was downcast by the defeat of the reciprocity agreement in Canada, but his only reference to that subject was made earlier in the day when he addressed the workingmen in a local manufacturing establishment where farming implements are made.

"I was sorry to hear that in Canada they do not care to have closer commercial relations with us," he said. "If reciprocity had been adopted we could have gotten our agricultural implements into Canada at a substantial decrease. But I guess we can get along."

The President's political speech followed a luncheon given in his honor by the Republican State Central Committee attended by the party leaders from all over the State, including Senator Shelby M. Cullom and Lieut. Gov. Oglesby. Gov. Deneen was unable to be present because of his broken leg. The so-called Deneen, Yates, and Independent factions were represented at the gathering at the Country Club, including one member of the Lorimer faction.

The leaders present vied with each other in pledging their support to the President and predicted that he would be renominated and re-elected. Charles H. Williamson of Quincy, a prominent member of the State Central Committee, said he had taken a poll on a train a few days ago en route from Keokuk to Quincy and that of 62 voters interviewed 58 had declared for Taft, three for Col. Roosevelt, and one for Senator La Follette. He added that he believed his poll accurately represented the views of Illinois Republicans.

Senator Cullom gave a more or less intimate talk of his association with and love for President Taft. He said that with the Chicago convention not six weeks away in 1908 Mr. Taft had told him that if Chief Justice Fuller could be induced to resign, he would prefer that honor to all others.

Lieut. Gov. Oglesby, State Senators Daly and Berry, Congressman Prince, Col. Fred H. Smith, Chairman of the local Republican Central Committee, and Representative Mesee of the Illinois Legislature were included among the speakers who preceded the President.

"If I had not been advised otherwise," said the President, with a smile, "I should think that this was a political meeting."

Mr. Taft then pleaded guilty to the indictment often laid against him that he knew nothing of politics and was a very poor politician. "But the truth is," he continued, "that my politics were limited to a very early stage of my career. Three or four years after I came to the bar I was pretty active, so that I knew something of ward politics. Since that time my fate has been such as to carry me out of politics, on to the bench, or seven thousand miles away from any American politics. But, as my dear friend Senator Cullom says, my ambition lay in an entirely different direction and was not gratified.

"I am not giving you to understand that I ran away from the nomination for the Presidency, but the fact is that it was not in the line which I had marked out, but, being nominated and getting into the fight, I did the best I could, and, being elected, I took up the discharge of the Presidency with certain tendencies, perhaps I ought to call them, that I had gathered from judicial experience.

"Of course, I made a great many mistakes. I shall continue during this term to make them. That is hardly to be avoided. But there are certain things, certain rules, that it is rather easy to follow. One is, that when you have made a promise it is your obligation to keep it.

"Now, something about the vetoes. I considered with reference to those bills that I was as much under an obligation to veto every one of them as if I had said when I was on the platform running for the Presidency that I would veto just those bills, for the reason that the whole Republican Party had taken the position that it was necessary to maintain the industries of this country by protection sufficient to give them a living method of competing with foreign manufactures, and the whole party had also said, if you could trust the resolutions of the conventions, even in Iowa and Kansas and Wisconsin, that they approved finding out the facts by a Tariff Board before we passed legislation that might strike down our industries.

"I would have vetoed those bills under any conditions, even if it would have cost me my life. I say that with all the earnestness possible, because what I did was the result of a conviction as deep seated as any principle I ever had.

"So far as the veto of the Arizona bill is concerned I just vetoed that because I could not do anything else. I wrote my heart into that veto.

"My friends, I have tried to follow what I thought to be right in the Administration of my office. There has been a division in the party, and I have been charged with not being progressive, and therefore to be condemned. What one does, this man thinks is progressive, another man thinks is retrograde. There are, however, two great schools—one which believes that the present is not perfect perhaps, but that changes from it would be dangerous. They are the strictly conservative, and perhaps are known as the reactionary. Then there is another class at the other end which is extreme in its view that the whole present condition is wrong, and there must be radical changes if we live at all.

"Now, I think—perhaps I am wrong about it—but I think I am going along in the middle of the road between those two; at least, that is what I am trying to do, and I believe the legislation of this Administration has been along that line.

"We have brought the railroads under a condition of regulation that has satisfied them that the country is bound to have their business discharged according to law and under such supervision as to insure that it will be according to law, and I have heard no complaint that the present regulations do not secure that result.

"With respect to the trusts, we are in a transition period, in this sense that the Supreme Court has decided what the law is, and now business has got to square itself with that law. We might as well make up our minds to that, gentlemen. We can protest as much as we will as to what the law ought to be, but the Supreme Court has said what the law is, and I have learned that when they have to do so they can adjust their affairs without endangering the progress to which they thought some other method absolutely indispensable.

"With respect to much of what has been discussed as to being progressive, the Federal Government has nothing to do. That is a matter of State Governments to settle, and State Governments are making different experiments, and I presume the conservative States will wait to see how these experiments work out. Occasionally, however, there crops out something extreme in the form of a judicial recall in a Constitution tendered to the Federal Government for approval. Under those conditions, when a proposition is made that seems to me to destroy all possibility of good government in the maintenance of an untrammeled judiciary, it is the function of the Executive when his judgment is invoked under the examination to say that he disapproves that feature, and that so far as he is concerned he will allow no State to come into the Union with any such radical heresy expressed in its Constitution, and with the sanction of the Federal Government upon it.

"My friends, I did not expect to make a political speech this afternoon. I want to thank the gentlemen present for their cordial expressions. What the future is I know not. I only know this—that I am going ahead to do the best I can, and I am going through this country on this trip and try to explain some of the issues which have arisen and make them clear to those people whom I can reach with my voice or through the kindly press if they report what I say—because I believe that the time has come for sober second thought.

"I have confidence that the American people can always be trusted, not only to exercise their second sober thought, but also a discriminating sense as to what is fact and what is fustian, after a time. It won't happen at once, and sometimes we have to wait for it until after we die, and that is not quite so satisfactory; but in any event, we middle-of-the-road people who are not extremists are, we believe, the real progressives, because you do not make progress by great strides—you make progress step by step.

"We can depend upon the people to recognize substance in progress rather than that which is represented by proposed legislation and platform declarations that are for the purpose, not of being put into force and into law to accomplish real reform, but for campaign uses only."

At a banquet of the Knights of Columbus to-night, President Taft took up the Philippine question. He said he might be accused of reviving a dead issue, but the issue could hardly be regarded as dead so long as the Democratic Party continued to write in its platform a declaration for the relinquishment of the islands and so long as resolutions continue to be introduced in Congress looking to the relinquishment of the islands.

Shortly before midnight the President retired aboard his train preparatory to departing later for St. Louis.

September 23, 1911

TAFT PREFERS BENCH TO THE PRESIDENCY

Chief Justice Compares Each Office and Declares White House More Trying.

LIKES DETECTIVE STORIES

Summer Home in Canada Offers Respite in Which He Reads Much and Walks Little.

By The Associated Press.

WASHINGTON, July 6. — Untroubled by the swirl of politics, William Howard Taft is rounding out his seventieth year happier in his daily work than he ever has been before, in or out of office.

As he looks back over the two-score years of public service, the only man who has been both President and Chief Justice says quite frankly that he does not consider that he was "fitted" for the political arena and that he would rather be where he is today than in the White House.

He is so well satisfied and so greatly encouraged over the recent improvement in his health that he has no intention of leaving the bench when he becomes eligible for retirement. He will be 70 years old in September and if he chose could retire on full pay in 1931, when he completes ten years' service as Chief Justice. But he prefers to remain in harness.

These disclosures were made to The Associated Press by Mr. Taft in a friendly and intimate talk just before he left Washington recently for his Summer home in Canada. He now has consented to publication of this talk, in which he touched on many personal subjects and discussed, with a knowledge no other man ever possessed, the comparative requirements of the Presidency and the Chief Justiceship.

The talk took place in the study which he fitted out for himself some years ago in his home on Wyoming Avenue. It is a third-floor room, jutting out from the main structure of the house. Formerly a sleeping porch, it has windows on three sides and provides what the Chief Justice described, with his infectious chuckle, as "a commanding view." In the centre of the room stands a large desk. Between the windows rise stacks of law books. On the fourth side is an open fireplace and above it hangs a large portrait of the Chief Justice's father, who once was Secretary of War and later Attorney General. Near by are pictures of Abraham Lincoln and of various personal friends, including Elihu Root and President Lowell of Harvard.

Refuse Roosevelt's Offer.

As he approached his comparison of the two great offices he has held Mr. Taft made a passing reference to Theodore Roosevelt. Although he has near him no memento of the years of his association with Roosevelt the Chief Justice mentioned without a ruffle in his customary good nature the man who was his stanchest political friend and then his bitter opponent. He related how Roosevelt had offered him a place on the Supreme Court bench. At that time Justice Taft was Governor General of the Philippines, and he refused the offer.

"I declined because it was not deemed wise at that time, from a Philippine standpoint, to have a change in the office of Governor," he said. "The people wanted me to stay, and I yielded, although it had always been my ambition to serve on the bench. I do not care for politics."

With a smile that rippled into a hearty laugh, he added:

"Not that I have no interest in such matters, but I am not fitted for the hustings and controversy."

He enlarged upon this theme by pointing out that with him elevation to the highest judicial office in the country had not, as with some of his predecessors, broken personal contacts with friends or with the people generally. He retains a keen interest in current events and reads much, and he does not find himself lonesome for the society of office-seekers and politicians.

"I do not mind what is sometimes called the monastic life of the bench," he continued. "I have most delightful associates in the court and very pleasant relations with members of the bar.

More Isolated as President.

"These are, it should be noted, exactly defined, but the truth is you are more isolated in the Presidency. While a President sees a great many people, he cannot avoid defending himself against too great familiarity. He has got to be reserved and careful.

"The responsibilities of the Presidency are nerve-racking. If one is constituted like an ordinary man, life in the Presidency, while not requiring the same mental and intellectual labor that attaches to the Chief Justiceship, does enormously consume nervous energy, and is more trying than work on the bench.

"The difference between the exactions of the two offices is that in work on the bench you have the assistance of your colleagues, who share in the responsibility of the conclusions; the benefit of oral arguments by counsel and of briefs submitted on both sides of the controversy.

"And you have control of your time for careful study. In the Presidency you often have to make a decision on a question on the instant or overnight, or in so short a time that the risk of mistake is great, and then you have not the benefit of argument on both sides, often no argument on either, and you cannot always consult your Cabinet.

"Of course the Presidency is the office that attracts in the sense of power one is supposed to exercise, and there are those who greatly enjoy its constant exercise. But even in the strongest it takes much out of a man, and the strain is felt long after retirement to private life.

"The character of work on the bench, its steadiness and the regularity with which you can order your life, if you do not overdo the social part, makes it consistent with long life, hard as the work is."

The Chief Justice added that he now can enjoy a "real vacation," something he could not do while President. He puts aside entirely the duties of the court during his Summer recess, and at his place on Murray Cove, Canada, has a genuine respite from work, and makes the most of it. But it is a quiet vacation, for he has been warned by his physician that he must not overtax his heart.

"I gather all the books I can before starting on my vacation," he explained, "and spend most of my time on my porch overlooking the St. Lawrence River, which is nearly thirteen miles across. Free from study and concentration I rest until late in the vacation, when I receive briefs filed during the recess to enable me to catch up a little before starting upon real work of the court when I get back."

He continued that his doctors' advice had led him to give up the golf of his Presidential days, to abandon his practice of writing his court opinions in longhand, and to have an electric elevator installed in his home to obviate the necessity of stair climbing.

"When I had warning about my heart," he said, "I concluded to have an elevator installed. The arrangement puts my office on the same floor with the rooms occupied by my secretary and my law clerk.

"I used to write my opinions out in longhand, but since my illness I find it too confining. Therefore, I dictate and correct and revamp. Writing makes an exact man, as Bacon says; makes one more concise, more economical of space; but it is not as convenient. I work over the opinions so much that, as to conciseness, it makes no difference whether I write or dictate, I change and revise so much.

Studies Every Angle of Each Cast.

"I have a law clerk who goes over the records and the briefs. He makes a statement for me of what is in each, and then with that statement before me I read the briefs and make such references to the records as seem necessary. But I always read the briefs so as to know what the claim on both sides is, and then I read the opinions of the Courts below so I become familiar with the case and know what the issues are. When these petitions for review come before us we know what the cases are about, and whether they present questions we should pass upon.

"I walk every day for about half an hour. While I used to walk a great deal I feel that I am getting enough exercise."

Asked what he selected for his vacation reading and for his moments of quiet recreation during his busy moments, he replied unhesitatingly that autobiography was his favorite literature.

"I do not care particularly about novels, except by certain authors," he said, and then as an afterthought:

"I do not mind detective stories, if I can get a good one, and have read many of them."

Now that he has accustomed himself to the regimen of diet and relaxation prescribed bv his physician, the Chief Justice expects to benefit greatly by his Summer's sojourn in Canada. But he would be less happy in his vacation respite if he did not know that after it was over he could return to carry on the work of that unparalleled public career which began forty-six years ago when he became a minor county official in Ohio.

July 7, 1927

GOV. WILSON'S VIEW OF THE PRESIDENCY

We Need Presidents Who Have National Principles, He Said Three Years Ago.

THESE UNITE US IN SYMPATHY

Country Must Apply Old Principles to New Policies and Think in Terms of the World.

At a dinner of the Friendly Sons of St. Patrick, in Delmonico's, on March 17, 1909, Gov. Woodrow Wilson spoke to the toast, "Our Country and Our Day." During that speech he frankly expressed his opinion of the Irish as a race and individually, and of the duties of the President of the United States.

Speaking of the President's office, he said:

"There is only one National voice in this country, and that is the voice of the President of the United States. A Senator of the United States complained to me, in a tone that I thought was actually peevish, a couple of years ago, that the Constitution had given to the President the right to send messages to Congress. I said:

"'Senator, I don't think that is your real difficulty. The trouble is not that the Constitution gives to the President the right to send messages to Congress. The trouble is that the Constitution could not prevent the President from publishing his messages to the country. It would not do you any harm if the messages were merely sent to you. They are sent to everybody else, and if the country happens to agree with the President it doesn't stop to hear what you have to say.'"

This brought laughter and applause, and there was a good deal more applause as Gov. Wilson went on to say:

"That is the real circumstance in this country. The President's views are printed everywhere by every paper, and there isn't a man in Congress, in either house, whose views are printed everywhere by every paper. The consequence is that the voice of the President is the only National voice in our affairs. The President can sow his opinions broadcast. No man else can sow except in his own private field.

"If you want National processes, therefore, elect Presidents who will have National thoughts and National principles, and then you will see slowly taking head under the inevitable leadership of such men those impulses, those thoughts, those convictions, those determinations, which are slowly to link together in a common understanding and a common sympathy."

Gov. Wilson declared that Nations are not conducted upon reasoned opinion, but upon the common impulses of the heart. Later on he said:

"The thing that will link all America together is the quickening of universal understanding and universal sympathy."

"We have now," he added, "to think in the terms of the world, and not in the terms of America. We have come out upon a stage of international responsibility from which we cannot retire. That responsibility is not the responsibility of showing the world the way to material success, because the world knows the way to material success without our suggestion. Germany knows some of the ways of material success, for example, a good deal better than we do. Germany does not need to be drawn into the tutelage of America to learn how to make money; but every nation of the world needs to be drawn into the tutelage of America to learn how to spend money for the liberty of mankind, and in proportion as we discover the means for translating our material force into moral force shall we recover the traditions and the glories of American history."

July 4, 1912

PRESIDENT WILSON'S INAUGURAL ADDRESS

Justice, and Only Justice, to be His Motto—Duty of Safeguarding Property and Individual Right—Seeks to Restore, Not Destroy—Not a Day of Triumph for Him, But a Day of Dedication.

WASHINGTON, March 4.—President Woodrow Wilson, after he had taken the oath of office, delivered the following inaugural address:

There has been a change of Government. It began two years ago, when the House of Representatives became Democratic by a decisive majority. It has now been completed. The Senate about to assemble will also be Democratic. The offices of President and Vice President have been put into the hands of Democrats. What does the change mean? That is the question that is uppermost in our minds to-day. That is the question I am going to try to answer, in order, if I may, to interpret the occasion.

It means much more than the mere success of a party. The success of a party means little except when the Nation is using that party for a large and definite purpose. No one can mistake the purpose for which the Nation now seeks to use the Democratic Party. It seeks to use it to interpret a change in its own plans and point of view. Some old things with which we had grown familiar, and which had begun to creep into the very habit of our thought and of our lives, have altered their aspect as we have latterly looked critically upon them, with fresh, awakened eyes; have dropped their disguises and shown themselves alien and sinister. Some new things, as we look frankly upon them, willing to comprehend their real character, have come to assume the aspect of things long believed in and familiar, stuff of our own convictions. We have been refreshed by a new insight into our own life.

We see that in many things that life is very great. It is incomparably great in its material aspects, in its body of wealth, in the diversity and sweep of its energy, in the industries which have been conceived and built up by the genius of individual men and the limitless enterprise of groups of men. It is great, also, very great, in its moral force. Nowhere else in the world have noble men and women exhibited in more striking forms the beauty and the energy of sympathy and helpfulness and counsel in their efforts to rectify wrong, alleviate suffering, and set the weak in the way of strength and hope. We have built up, moreover, a great system of government, which has stood through a long age as in many respects a model for those who seek to set liberty upon foundations that will endure against fortuitous change, against storm and accident. Our life contains every great thing, and contains it in rich abundance.

Evil Has Come With Good.

But the evil has come with the good, and much fine gold has been corroded. With riches has come inexcusable waste. We have squandered a great part of what we might have used, and have not stopped to conserve the exceeding bounty of nature, without which our genius for enterprise would have been worthless and impotent, scorning to be careful, shamefully prodigal as well as admirably efficient. We have been proud of our industrial achievements, but we have not hitherto stopped thoughtfully enough to count the human cost, the cost of lives snuffed out, of energies overtaxed and broken, the fearful physical and spiritual cost to the men and women and children upon whom the dead weight and burden of it all has fallen pitilessly the years through. The groans and agony of it all had not yet reached our ears, the solemn, moving undertone of our life, coming up out of the mines and factories and out of every home where the struggle had its intimate and familiar seat. With the great Government went many deep secret things which we too long delayed to look into and scrutinize with candid, fearless eyes. The great Government we loved has too often been made use of for private and selfish purposes, and those who used it had forgotten the people.

At last a vision has been vouchsafed us of our life as a whole. We see the bad with the good, the debased and decadent with the sound and vital. With this vision we approach new affairs. Our duty is to cleanse, to reconsider, to restore, to correct the evil without impairing the good, to purify and humanize every process of our common life without weakening or sentimentalizing it. There has been something crude and heartless and unfeeling in our haste to succeed and be great. Our thought has been "Let every man look out for himself, let every generation look out for itself," while we reared giant machinery which made it impossible that any but those who stood at the levers of control should have a chance to look out for themselves. We had not forgotten our morals. We remembered well enough that we had set up a policy which was meant to serve the humblest as well as the most powerful, with an eye single to the standards of justice and fair play, and remembered it with pride. But we were very heedless and in a hurry to be great.

We have come now to the sober second thought. The scales of heedlessness have fallen from our eyes. We have made up our minds to square every process of our National life again with the standards we so proudly set up at the beginning and have always carried at our hearts. Our work is a work of restoration.

Things Wilson Would Change.

We have itemized with some degree of particularity the things that ought to be altered, and here are some of the chief items: A tariff which cuts us off from our proper part in the commerce of the world, violates the just principles of taxation, and makes the Government a facile instrument in the hands of private interests; a banking and currency system based upon the necessity of the Government to sell its bonds fifty years ago and perfectly adapted to concentrating cash and restricting credits; an industrial system which, take it on all its sides, financial as well as administrative, holds capital in leading strings, restricts the liberties and limits the opportunities of labor, and exploits without renewing or conserving the natural resources of the country; a body of agricultural activities never yet given the efficiency of great business undertakings or served as it should be through the instrumentality of science taken directly to the farm, or afforded the facilities of credit best suited to its practical needs; water courses undeveloped, waste places unreclaimed, forests untended, fast disappearing without plan or prospect of renewal, unregarded waste heaps at every mine. We have studied us perhaps no other nation has the most effective means of production, but we have not studied cost or economy as we should either as organizers of industry, as statesmen, or as individuals.

Nor have we studied and perfected the means by which government may be put at the service of humanity, in safeguarding the health of the Nation, the health of its men and its women and its children, as well as their rights in the struggle for existence. This is no sentimental duty. The firm basis of government is justice, not pity. These are matters of justice. There can be no equality of opportunity, the first essential of justice in the body politic, if men and women and children be not shielded in their lives, their very vitality, from the consequences of great industrial and social processes which they cannot alter, control, or singly cope with. Society must see to it that it does not itself crush or weaken or damage its own constituent parts. The first duty of law is to keep sound the society it serves. Sanitary laws, pure food laws, and laws determining conditions of labor which individuals are powerless to determine for themselves are intimate parts of the very business of justice and legal efficiency.

"We Shall Restore, Not Destroy."

These are some of the things we ought to do, and not leave the others undone, the old-fashioned, never-to-be-neglected, fundamental safeguarding of property and of individual right. This is the high enterprise of the new day: to lift everything that concerns our life as a Nation to the light that shines from the hearthfire of every man's conscience and vision of the right. It is inconceivable that we should do this as partisans; it is inconceivable we should do it in ignorance of the facts as they are or in blind haste. We shall restore, not destroy. We shall deal with our economic system as it is and as it may be modified, not as it might be if we had a clean sheet of paper to write upon; and step by step we shall make it what it should be, in the spirit of those who question their own wisdom and seek counsel and knowledge; not shallow self-satisfaction or the excitement of excursions whither they cannot tell. Justice, and only justice, shall always be our motto.

And yet it will be no cool process of mere science. The Nation has been deeply stirred, stirred by a solemn passion, stirred by the knowledge of wrong, of ideals lost, of Government too often debauched and made an instrument of evil. The feelings with which we face this new age of right and opportunity sweep across our heart-strings like some air out of God's own presence, where justice and mercy are reconciled and the judge and the brother are one. We know our task to be no mere task of politics, but a task which shall search us through and through, whether we be able to understand our time and the need of our people, whether we be indeed their spokesmen and interpreters, whether we have the pure heart to comprehend and the rectified will to choose our high course of action.

This is not a day of triumph; it is a day of dedication. Here muster, not the forces of party, but the forces of humanity. Men's hearts wait upon us; men's lives hang in the balance; men's hopes call upon us to say what we will do. Who shall live up to the great trust? Who dares fail to try? I summon all honest men, all patriotic, all forward-looking men, to my side. God helping me, I will not fail them, if they will but counsel and sustain me!

MR. WILSON BARES A PRESIDENT'S WOES

In Remarkable Speech He Describes His Inner Self and Conflicting Emotions.

TRYING TO AVOID BLUNDERS

Feels Like "a Fraud" Sometimes, and Wants to "Tip the Wink" —Likes Detective Stories.

Special to The New York Times.

WASHINGTON, March 20.—President Wilson told the members of the National Press Club this afternoon how it feels to be President. It was an impromptu speech delivered in a very informal way, and was not intended for publication. But afterward the President yielded to importunities and consented to release it for newspapers. The occasion was a "housewarming" of the club's new quarters in the Riggs Buildin. President Wilson was introduced by Frank B. Lord, the President of the club.

The President put his heart into his remarks. He showed that he chafed under the restrictions that surrounded the President, and would appreciate it if he were placed in a position where he would be treated more like a human being. His constant embarrassment, he said, was to restrain the emotions that were inside of him.

According to Mr. Wilson, he never thought of himself as President of the United States, because he never had any sense of being identified with that office. He felt now, he declared, just as much outside of the Presidency as he had before he was elected to it. In a humorous way the President contradicted any impression that might exist that he was a cold, austere person.

The President wore a sack suit and stood with his hands in his pockets as he spoke. He was in a happy mood, and his remarks were constantly punctuated with laughter and applause. Mr. Wilson is a member of the Press Club, having been elected as an author long before he became President. Members of the Cabinet, Speaker Clark and many officials also were guests of the newspapermen.

"Some Kind of a Fraud."

"I was just thinking of my sense of confusion of identity, sometimes, when I read the articles about myself," Mr. Wilson said. "I have never read an article about myself in which I recognized myself, and I have come to have the impression that I must be some kind of a fraud, because I think a great many of these articles are written in absolute good faith. I tremble to think of the variety and falseness in the impression I make—and it is being borne in on me so that it may change my very disposition—that I am a cold and removed person who has a thinking machine inside which he adjusts to the circumstances, which he does not allow to be moved by any winds of affection or emotion of any kind, that turns like a cold searchlight on anything that is presented to his attention and makes it work.

"I am not aware of having any detachable apparatus inside of me. On the contrary, if I were to interpret myself, I would say that my constant embarrassment is to restrain the emotions that are inside of me. You may not believe it, but I sometimes feel like a fire from a far from extinct volcano, and if the lava does not seem to spill over it is because you are not high enough to see into the basin and see the caldron boil. Because, truly, gentlemen, in the position which I now occupy there is a sort of, I do not know how else to express it than to say, passionate sense of being connected with my fellow-men in a peculiar relationship of responsibility, not merely the responsibility of office, but God knows there are enough things in this world that need to be corrected.

"I have mixed, first and last, with all sorts and conditions of men—there are mighty few kinds of men that have to be described to me, and there are mighty few kinds of experiences that have to be described to me—and when I think of the number of men who are looking to me as the representative of a party, with the hope for all varieties of salvage from the things they are struggling in the midst of, it makes me tremble. It makes me tremble not only with a sense of my own inadequacy and weakness, but as if I were shaken by the very things that are shaking them, and if I seem circumspect, it is because I am so diligently trying not to make any colossal blunders. If you just calculate the number of blunders a fellow can make in twenty-four hours if he is not careful and if he does not listen more than he talks, you would see something of the feeling that I have.

Collects All Brains Borrowable.

"I was amused the other day at a remark that Senator Newlands made. I had read him the trust message that I was to deliver to Congress some ten days before I delivered it, and I never stop 'doctoring' things of that kind until the day I have to deliver them. When he heard it read to Congress he said: 'I think it was better than it was when you read it to me.' I said: 'Senator, there is one thing which I do not think you understand. I not only use all the brains I have, but all I can borrow, and I have borrowed a lot since I read it to you first.'

"That, I dare say, is what gives the impression of circumspectness. I am listening; I am diligently trying to collect all the brains that are borrowable in order that I will not make more blunders than it is inevitable that a man should make who has great limitations of knowledge and capacity. And the emotion of the thing is so great that I suppose I must be some kind of a mask to conceal it. I really feel sometimes as if I were masquerading when I catch a picture of myself in some printed description. In between things that I have to do as a public officer I never think of myself as the President of the United States, because I never have had any sense of being identified with that office.

"I feel like a person appointed for a certain length of time to administer that office, and I feel just as much outside of it at this moment as I did before I was elected to it. I feel just as much outside of it as I still feel outside of the Government of the United States. No man could imagine himself the Government of the United States; but he could understand that some part of his fellow-citizens had told him to go and run a certain part of it the best he knew how. That would not make him the Government itself or the thing itself. It would just make him responsible for running it the best he knew how. The machine is so much greater than himself, the office is so much greater than himself, the office is so much greater than he can ever be, and the most he can do is to look grave enough and self-possessed enough to seem to fill it.

"I can hardly refrain every now and again from tipping the public the wink, as much as to say, 'It is only "me" that is inside this thing. I know perfectly well that I will have to get out presently. I know that then I will look just my own proper size, and that for the time being the proportions are somewhat refracted and misrepresented to the eye by the large thing I am inside of, from which I am tipping you this wink.'

"For example, take matters of this sort. I will not say whether it is wise or unwise, simple or grave, but certain precedents have been established that in certain companies the President must leave the room first, and people must give way to him. They must not sit down if he is standing up. It is a very uncomfortable thing to have to think of all the other people every time I get up and sit down, and all that sort of thing. So that when I get guests in my own house and the public is shut out I adjourn being President and take leave to be a gentleman. If they draw back and insist upon my doing something first, I firmly decline.

Detective Stories as a Refuge.

"There are blessed intervals when I forget by one means or another that I am President of the United States. One means by which I forget is to get a rattling good detective story, get after some imaginary offender, and chase him all over—preferably any continent but this, because the various parts of this continent are becoming painfully suggestive to me. The Post Offices, and many other things which stir reminiscence have 'sicklied them o'er with a pale cast of thought.' There are Post Offices to which I wouldn't think of mailing a letter, which I can't think of without trembling with the knowledge of all the heartburnings of the struggle there was in connection with getting somebody installed as Postmaster.

"Now, if I were free I would come not infrequently up to these rooms. You know I never was in Washington but a very few times, and for a very few hours, until I came last year, and I never expect to see the inside of the public buildings in Washington until my term is over. The minute I turn up anywhere I am personally conducted to beat the band. The Curator and the Assistant Curators and every other blooming official turns up, and they show me so much attention that I don't see the building. I would have to say 'Stand aside and let me see what you are showing me.'

"Some day after I am through with this office I am going to come back to Washington and see it. In the meantime I am in the same category as the National Museum, the Monument, the Smithsonian Institution, or the Congressional Library, and everything that comes down here has to be shown the President. If I only knew an exhibition appearance to assume—apparently I can assume other appearances that do not show what is going on inside—I would like to have it pointed out, so that I could practice it before the looking glass and see if I could not look like the Monument. Being regarded as a national exhibit, it will be much simpler than being shaken hands with by the whole United States.

"And yet, even that is interesting to me, simply because I like human beings. It is a pretty poor crowd that does not interest you. I think they would have to be all members of that class that devotes itself to 'expense regardless of pleasure' in order to be entirely uninteresting. These look so much alike—spend their time trying to look so much alike—and so relieve themselves of all responsibility of thought—that they are very monotonous, indeed, to look at; whereas, a crowd picked up off the street is just a jolly lot—a job lot of real human beings, pulsating with life, with all kinds of passions and desires.

If He Were a Free Citizen.

"It would be a great pleasure if, unobserved and unattended, I could be knocked around as I have been accustomed to being knocked around all my life; if I could resort to any delightful quarter, to any place in Washington that I chose. I have sometimes thought of going to some costumer's—some theatrical costumer's—and buying an assortment of beards, rouge, and coloring and all the known means of disguising myself, if it were not against the law.

"You see I have a scruple as President against breaking the law and disguising one's self is against the law, but if I could disguise myself and not get caught I would go out, be a free American citizen once more and have a jolly time. I might then meet some of you gentlemen and actually tell you what I really thought."

March 21, 1914

PRESIDENCY A 24-HOUR JOB WITH NEW DEMANDS DAILY

CONGRESS A HARD MASTER

Some Recent Laws Add Many Obligations to the Office

TARIFF IMPOSED BIG TASK

Harding Often Goes to His Desk at 8 o'Clock and Golf Gave Way to Growing Load.

A LITTLE less than two years ago Judson C. Welliver, executive clerk at the White House, stepped across the corridor which separates his office from that of President Harding to place some papers on the President's desk. To his surprise, for it was but a few minutes after 8 o'clock in the morning, he found the President already seated and busily signing papers from a two-foot stack.

"Good morning, Mr. President," Mr. Welliver said. "I didn't know you had come to the office."

"Yes, I came in just now," the President replied. "I had a lot of papers to sign, and thought I might as well get them out of the way."

"Anything important?"

"Yes and no," said the President. "I am beginning to find out something about being President and the amount of time it demands. You can hardly imagine what I am doing now. This stack of papers is just so much routine. They are the wills of Indians. The President has to countersign the will of every Indian with whom the Government has dealings. If the will is not so countersigned it is null and void. And so I expect to put in the next hour or so countersigning these wills."

"But can't some one else sign them for you?" Mr. Welliver inquired.

"No; not under the law. There are only two—possibly three—persons in the United States authorized to sign the President's name. They are employes of the General Land Office and they sign the President's name, under certain safeguards and precautions, to the patents granted by that office. But there is no one else who may do so.

"I am beginning to find out," Mr. Harding went on, "that this job of being President is one that makes almost inordinate demands upon a man's time."

Since that March morning of 1921 Mr. Harding has been finding out more about the job of being President and the demands it makes upon his time. Upon the eve of his departure a few days ago for Florida Mr. Harding discussed the burdens of the Presidency with a group of friends. He was eagerly looking forward to the trip.

"I shall be mighty glad to go," the President told his friends. "Year by year, month by month, day by day Congress is adding to the work of the President."

Making His Job Harder.

But much of the work has come from Mr. Harding's own initiative and his policy of common council with associates. Turning back to outstanding events of the two years which have brought their added burdens to the man in the White House, the high points include adoption of the budget system, proposals for reorganizing the Government departments, reorganization of the Veterans' Bureau, the ship subsidy, enactment of the tariff law, the arms conference, the unemployment and agricultural conferences, the Debt Funding bill and other measures, some of which originated with the President and all of which have had his intense personal interest, frequent conferences and careful guidance.

Time was when the White House day was pretty much the same as a day anywhere else in its division of eight hours for work, eight hours for recreation and eight hours for sleep. But it is different now. The hours for recreation have been almost eliminated and the hours for sleep often are shortened.

Mr. Harding used to play golf — virtually his only recreation—almost every day, if only for a couple of hours. When work began to encroach, the President tried to shift the burden to his hours for sleep. He got up mornings long before Washington was astir, and joined other enthusiasts on the public links in Potomac Park. But that did not work, and on the advice of his physician he quit it. During the two months preceding his departure for Florida Mr. Harding managed to get a few short motor rides and about four afternoons on the golf course. That constituted virtually the full measure of his recreation.

Mr. Harding rises about 7 o'clock, breakfasts at 7:30 or 7:45, and half an hour or more before the army of Government clerks reach their desks at 9 he walks from the dining room to the executive office, seats himself at the mahogany desk, brightened by red roses, and begins his day's work. His forenoons are devoted wholly to the papers on his desk and to callers. These come in a stream greater than ever poured through the White House offices. Up to the time of Mrs. Harding's illness, the President devoted at least two hours a day to callers, all of whom he saw by appointment. Recently he has curtailed his interviews considerably. The time he otherwise would have spent with visitors has been divided between his desk and Mrs. Harding.

Interviews with the President have not been hard to get where a friendly Representative or Senator has made necessary arrangements, but they have been uniformly short. The bulk of the time spent with the visitors is on official business and with members of the Cabinet, the independent offices and the Houses of Congress.

One of the first things that Mrs. Harding did when she entered the White House was to order the big iron gates, locked for years, to be thrown open. The public trooped in by hundreds and thousands. It was her idea to bring to the White House a home atmosphere, and a part of the program with which the President agreed was the meeting of visitors every day at 1 o'clock.

That program has been carried out almost without exception, even during her illness. Every day about 1 o'clock the President receives the sightseers, honeymooners and others who call. The line sometimes is several hundred long. The visitors move quickly past the President, but not without a handshake for each one. Often the President spends the half hour just before luncheon receiving callers.

Afternoon His Play Time.

The afternoon is the time that Mr. Harding has endeavored to devote to recreation. General Sawyer, who almost literally keeps his finger on the President's pulse, has become more and more insistent on less work and more play, but until the Florida trip General Sawyer's urging has been almost in vain.

President Harding has told his close friends that he feels the people of the United States elected him President with the expectation that he would perform all of the President's duties conscientiously He considers himself as under contract with the American people carefully to examine everything that requires his attention, and devote becoming consideration to all legislation and questions of policy, domestic and foreign. He is working to fulfill that contract.

Why is it some of the work cannot be delegated? The writer asked that question of one of the President's official family.

"Because the President is responsible," was the answer. "When the nation elects a President it does not elect an Assistant President as well. It makes the President solely and wholly responsible; and President Harding believes that with that responsibility goes the duty of devoting his personal attention to everything he can connected with the Presidency."

The President believes in team work. He rarely, if ever, acts without conference and counsel with his advisers. In fact, he is one of the firmest believers in team work who ever sat in the White House.

The duties of the Presidency have been greatly increased since his inauguration. Take, for instance, the adoption of the budget system of national finance. Under the new system, inaugurated less than two years ago, the President is directly responsible to Congress for the annual preparation of estimates of national expenditures and for the nation's financial policy. The details of this work are delegated to the Director of the Bureau of the Budget, but that official has no authority or powers other than those conferred by the President.

In the preparation of the estimates and in framing the financial policy the Director of the Budget is under the necessity of making almost daily visits to the White House, and the President has to familiarize himself thoroughly with the details of all proposals and expenditures. The added burdens arising from these new duties alone are extraordinary and have consumed many hours of President Harding's time.

In addition it became necessary a few months ago to make drastic cuts in governmental expenditures to fit them within the compass of estimated revenues during the coming fiscal year. Every department and independent office had to retrench. It fell to the President to soothe away many disappointments in his Cabinet.

Work Still Piles Up.

The ship subsidy proposal was one that engaged President Harding's attention for days. During the fight in Congress over the bill President Harding at all times was in intimate touch with developments and was closeted for many hours with the leaders. These were the hours, most of them, which his physician had urged him to devote to recreation.

The tariff law adds immensely to the duties of the President by giving him the final decision as to its elasticity. It is necessary for the President to familiarize himself thoroughly with questions under discussion. He must study documents and probably invite interested visitors to discuss changes with him. As yet there has been no occasion for the President to exercise his new duties—and no time for him to do so, either—but the duties are there and the time is approaching when he will be called on to exercise them.

President Harding also is in intimate contact with the foreign affairs of the Government. In advance of every important move Secretary Hughes goes over to the White House and spends with the President all the time necessary to acquaint him with the latest developments.

By preference President Harding remains in the background where foreign affairs are concerned. An illustration of this trait was afforded the time of the arms conference, conceived by Mr. Harding, addressed by him at its convening session, but informed by Mr. Hughes of the American proposals.

In domestic affairs the President devotes the same careful consideration—and confers with his advisers—as in governmental or foreign affairs. The Coal Commission, for instance, was his idea.

Mr. Harding has been called upon to make an unusually large number of appointments. Perhaps the most exacting of these, in point of time, concerned the filling of twenty-four additional Federal judgeships authorized by Congress. Mr. Harding devoted more time to these appointments than he did to making his Cabinet—and that required many weeks. Not all the appointments have been announced.

Mrs. Harding's illness has shared the President from social demands upon his time during the last six months of his busy two years. The State dinners, the New Year's receptions and other ceremonials have gone by the board. But with Mrs. Harding's complete recovery, there is little doubt that they will be resumed.

What can be done to lighten the President's burdens? The writer took that question to one of the President's closest friends.

"Nothing can be done," was the answer. "Nothing, so long as the people hold the President alone responsible, and so long as Congress adds to his duties."

Not long ago it was intimated that it might be just as well to have little said in the newspapers of the all-too-few occasions when the President played golf. Why? Because here and there an unkindly critic had raised his voice to say that the President seemed to devote a lot of time to play.

March 11, 1923

Mr. Coolidge Looks Back Along the Road from Plymouth

In His Autobiography the Former President Strikes a Note of Practical Idealism

THE AUTOBIOGRAPHY OF CALVIN COOLIDGE. Illustrated. 248 pp. New York: Cosmopolitan Book Corporation. $3.

By HORACE GREEN

TODAY mention of Mr. Coolidge's name is likely to bring into the conversation the autobiographical articles which have appeared in a monthly magazine and are here issued consecutively, in a permanent and attractive form. Expressions of surprise are not uncommon that the former President, meticulous as to the proprieties while Chief Executive, should so shortly after retirement appear in print. Even before this era of control by publicity there have been precedents for the unburdening of the ex-Presidential mind. Under financial distress General Grant was persuaded to do likewise, though in his case they were reminiscences of the Civil War and printed a number of years after White House occupancy. Mr. Wilson's letters appeared posthumously via his official biographer; while in foreign countries such public characters as Mussolini, Lloyd George, Winston Churchill, Foch and Clemenceau have written, or are writing, their apologias.

Indeed, in a Commonwealth which turns to so little account the experiences of its former leaders, if living, it would seem fortunate that the greatest experience which can come to a citizen should be examined from the inside, used for a text and turned to the use of others.

In this particular instance observers of Calvin Coolidge's character believe that his promptness is the reverse shield of that watertight compartment mind, so mindful of the requirements for each office. It is as if during his political career - covering all his mature life--he had said: "As City Solicitor of Northampton I must not do thus and so. As Lieutenant Governor my actions are limited to such and such; as Vice President to such and such; as President to such and such." Comes March 4, 1929, and presto! the lid is off. In the face of the Coolidge legend of silence, how many have reported his volubility in conversation where political prudence was not involved? In place of his Yankee gravity in public, how often does one come into contact with his personal humor? ("I very soon learned," states the autobiography, "that making fun of people in a public way * * * does not lead to much advancement.") And which of the press correspondents assembled in that first memorable conference after Warren Harding's death, expecting a noncommittal statement, will ever forget the full detail of the new President's talk and the spontaneous applause at its conclusion?

"The Autobiography of Calvin Coolidge" is in form a chronological review of the author's life from Plymouth boyhood through the decision which carried him into retirement. Early preparation is particularly stressed, whereas controversial problems in the White House are largely neglected, and left for treatment, it is hoped, at some future period when more outspoken reference to persons and issues is possible. Even so, the chapter on national politics and the one called "On Entering and Leaving the Presidency" are pregnant with information and in many instances more notable for what they imply than what they say. Here is an illuminating passage.

> If the Vice President is a man of discretion and character, so that he can be relied upon to act as a subordinate in such position, he should be invited to sit with the Cabinet, although some of the Senators, wishing to be the only advisers of the President, do not look on that proposal with favor. He may not help much in its deliberations, but he should be in the Cabinet, because he might become President and ought to be informed on the policies of the administration. He will not learn all of them. Much went on in the departments under President Harding, as it did under me, of which the Cabinet had no knowledge. But he will hear much and learn to find out more if it ever becomes necessary. My experience in the Cabinet was of supreme value to me when I became President.

A layman is at liberty to interpret that passage in some such way as this: "If the Vice President is of the right sort he should be in the Cabinet. Mr. Harding knew that I would act as a loyal subordinate and so asked me to join. Was it or was it not fortunate that the Vice President during my term as President declined my invitation to join the Cabinet? A Vice President must see eye to eye with his chief. You see, a Cabinet officer may resign if the situation becomes embarrassing; but a Vice President may not resign. My experience in the Cabinet was of great benefit later. But it should not be assumed that I knew of, or was responsible for, anything in connection with the oil scandals, so-called. I do not say that Mr. Harding kept anything from us. Conversely, in my own administration it would not be fair to charge a particular occurrence to all Cabinet officers. They did not necessarily know what happened in other departments."

Similarly in these chapters Mr. Coolidge's ability to see through political ramifications, to reduce situations to their elements, is pithily, and sometimes humorously, revealed: as in the statement that he was not confused, as presiding officer of the Senate, by the intricate rules, for he soon found out there was but one fixed rule. This, with exceptions, was to the effect that "the Senate would do anything it wanted to do whenever it wanted to do it." And again the pronouncement that "the political mind is the product of men who have been twice spoiled. They have been spoiled with praise, and they have been spoiled with abuse." Apparently they have neglected Kipling's advice to treat those two impostors just the same. It is also in this section of the autobiography that Mr. Coolidge expresses the opinion that the social obligations of the Vice President have been grossly exaggerated in the press. He points out that the Senate, with the Vice President in the chair, is usually in session from noon until *after tea time*. The italics are ours. As for dinners, he says that they occur on an average of three times a week, and it is the privilege of the Vice President as ranking guest to arrive last and leave first. In the author's case it was usually early enough to put him home by 10 o'clock.

Direct and convincing is the former President's analysis of his actions in the much-argued Boston police strike. He explains why he did not until the last moment step outside what he conceived to be the Governor's province, and opponents will be thankful that he makes an admission of error in not calling out the State Guard as soon as the police left their posts.

To this reviewer, however, the story and philosophy of the days of preparation are the most distinctive. With what discernment does the autobiographer debunk certain Coolidge legends. There is the famous "modesty" story about the young man's neglecting, until it appeared in the papers, to tell his father that he had been awarded the $150 gold medal by the American Historical Society. Mr. Coolidge explains that the news reached him one evening and was published the next morning. Also he had "a little vanity" in hoping his father would learn of it first through the papers. And the time-honored anecdote of the domestic animal with a loud bray which some boys stabled on the second floor of the Ludlow schoolhouse. Prudence still prevents our former Chief Magistrate from discussing "his own connection," if any, with this escapade. But this writer is at liberty to state that young Mr. Coolidge was not involved. Even in those days he was too good a Republican to go near a donkey.

At the outset the boy relives Plymouth farm days, takes us to "prep" school and through Amherst College, where he pays an unusual tribute to Professor Charles E. Garman, instructor in philosophy. He tells of the epochal trip (twelve miles in a buggy) from home to the Black River Academy. That was one of the greatest events of his life. The impression it made was so deep that whenever he started a new enterprise in later life he was engulfed by the same feeling. It was so when he began a public career in Boston, when he started for Washington to become Vice President, and when, after Harding's death, he was finally called to the helm. "The packing and preparation for that trip required more time and attention than collecting my belongings in preparation for leaving the White House. I counted the hours until it was time to go. * * * I was going where I would be mostly my own master. I was casting off what I thought was the drudgery of farm life." Then he muses:

> I did not know that there were mental and moral atmospheres more monotonous and more contaminating than anything in the physical atmosphere of country life. * * * Country life does not always have breadth, but it has depth. It is neither artificial nor superficial, but is kept close to the realities.

Calvin Coolidge reappears in this book as the practical idealist. In politics, as in other forms of endeavor, he preaches that tricks do not avail; they rebound against the trickster. He has strong prejudices, as former Dean Briggs of Harvard says every strong man should have, concerning the things which are good or bad—for him. He does not underestimate his intentions, but vastly underestimates the strength of his example to the country. He sees events clearly in relation to himself and his own preferment as the product of constant work, without intuition. There may have been written, though one would be pressed to find it, a creed which brings public life closer to the average man, or high places within nearer reach of the average American boy.

November 10, 1929

Herbert Hoover's Own Story

THE MEMOIRS OF HERBERT HOOVER: The Cabinet and the Presidency, 1920-1933. Illustrated. 405 pp. New York: The Macmillan Company. $5.

By HAROLD B. HINTON

ONLY a few of our Presidents have given us the benefit of publishing their recollections after completing their terms of office. The latest addition to the ranks of Theodore Roosevelt and Calvin Coolidge is Herbert Hoover, who here presents the second volume of his memoirs.

Mr. Hoover has been planning to publish his memoirs for a quarter of a century or more. The technique he has employed (book one dealt with his Quaker career around World War I) lends an added interest to what he has to say and, at the same time, illustrates that he is not a man who lightly changes his views or his conclusions.

Much of the material was written twenty-five years or more ago. Mr. Hoover has kept it on intellectual ice all these years to see whether his thoughts and judgments, set down soon after the events that prompted them, were accurate. In most cases, he apparently thinks they were.

The present volume deals with his eight years as Secretary of Commerce under President Harding and President Coolidge, and his own four years in the White House. These were the years in which the world depression of the late Twenties and the early Thirties was developing, the seeds of World War II being sown. Mr. Hoover's almost contemporaneous texts show an awareness of what was looming, and suggest remedies he then believed, and still believes, might have solved them:

"I RETURNED in 1919 [he writes] from several years abroad (including most of the years of World War I) steeped with two ideas: first that through three hundred years America had developed something new in a way of life of a people, which transcended all others of history; and second, that out of the boiling social and economic caldron of Europe, with its hates and fears, rose miasmic infections which might greatly harm or even destroy what seemed to be to be the best hope of the world. Therefore, soon after my return I began public speaking, writing articles for magazines, and even published a small book of diagnosis and warnings.

"After some hesitation I came to believe that through public service I could contribute something to ward off the evils; something to the reconstruction of the United States from the damage of the war; something to advance the reforms which discoveries in science, invention, and new ideas had imposed. And I believed that I could contribute to strengthen the principles and ideals which had given us such an abundance."

The period was also one of gilded youth, eccentricity and get-rich-quick phenomena such as the country had not seen before and has not seen since. Mr. Hoover didn't miss all of the fun, even while worrying over such matters as conservation of national resources, labor relations and foreign loans.

TAKE radio, for an obstreperous example. From the days of the crystal set and head-phones until Congress finally passed a regulatory law in 1927, Mr. Hoover realized the new medium had to be saved from death by self-strangulation. Through national conferences, he achieved a measure of cooperation in the employment of channels and other precautions against stations interfering with each other.

These steps were not uniformly acceptable, of course, to the rugged individualists of the epoch. Among these hardies Mr. Hoover lists Aimee Semple McPherson, the evangelist, whose broadcasting station habitually wandered all over the radio spectrum. Miss McPherson sent him this terse telegram of appeal from temporal to spiritual power:

"You cannot expect the Almighty to abide by your wave-length nonsense. When I offer my prayers to Him I must fit into His wave reception."

One of the book's revelations tells how Philippine leaders who publicly clamored for independence privately told him they hoped he would veto a pending bill granting independence, and said they would claim they had been "misunderstood" if he made their true stand public.

To those who consider Mr. Hoover the arch-conservative of our time, it may be a shock to learn that he was regarded as a dangerous radical by some of the right-wing elements of his own party when President Harding appointed him to the Cabinet in 1921. He recalls speaking before the Boston Chamber of Commerce against the twelve-hour day and eighty-four-hour week (then fairly prevalent in some industries).

"The applause would not have waked a nervous baby," Mr. Hoover dryly observes.

In those days, Mr. Hoover reminisces, the Cabinet was a unified, usually friendly board of counselors for the President. The members' administrative duties, in running their own departments, gave them useful background for discussing with their chief the large questions of the day.

Whatever the topic, each member felt free to offer his views and they seem to have been granted courteous consideration by the others and by the Chief Executive. The compartmentation of duties, the frequent and open hostility between members, figured less in the White House meetings of those days than under President Roosevelt and President Truman.

HIS account of the eight years at the Department of Commerce sketch a President in the making. By the time he campaigned for the Presidency in 1928, Mr. Hoover had fairly fixed ideas of the role he would play if elected to the White House. He found few great issues on which he was opposed to Governor Alfred E. Smith, and he was glad afterward that "no word had been spoken or misrepresentation made by either of us which prevented sincere friendship the day after the election."

The prohibition issue, he writes, was introduced by Al Smith. He himself had considerable doubt that consumption of alcoholic beverages could be controlled by Federal law, but the law was on the books as a part of the Federal Constitution which he would have to swear to uphold.

He deplored the religious bigotry some of his partisans injected into the campaign against Governor Smith. In one of his seven major campaign speeches, Mr. Hoover reminded his listeners that he was a Quaker bound to stand "for religious tolerance both in act and in spirit," adding that "the glory of our American ideals is the right of every man to worship God according to the dictates of his own conscience."

The picture of the thirtieth President emerging from these memoirs is that of a simple, straightforward man with whom one can disagree and still respect; a man of instinctive honesty, dignity and lack of pretense; a man of gentle humor, not given to taking himself too seriously; and, above all, a man who would not, if he could, have been an opportunist.

Mr. Hoover's recollections should be of considerable value to historians. The next volume will be devoted principally to the Great Depression, for which some older voters still hold him personally responsible.

Any writer of the future trying to judge the confused events through which Herbert Hoover lived should take a good look at what the former President has said about them. Like many of our Presidents, he will probably continue to grow in popular stature and national esteem as the years give perspective to the turbulent scenes over which he presided.

Mr. Hinton, a TIMES *man in Washington, has covered Herbert Hoover's activities for decades.*

April 27, 1952

THE PRESIDENT HOLDS TO HIS PHILOSOPHY

On His Birthday in a Crucial Year His Deep Faith in His Social Mission Remains Unshaken

By CHARLES W. B. HURD

WASHINGTON.

THERE will be an informal supper party in the White House next Thursday, attended by a dozen or so persons who have gathered annually for more than ten years to celebrate the birthday of Franklin D. Roosevelt.

These persons, including two of the White House secretaries, others of the President's personal staff and two or three newspaper men, are those who in 1920 were with Mr. Roosevelt when he played the rôle, remembered by few, of candidate for Vice President on the Democratic ticket.

To the President a birthday is a distinct milestone in the life of an individual; thus it may be fitting at this time to observe what almost three years in the White House have done to him and for him.

Some of us who, as newspaper correspondents, have been with him daily in the White House and accompanied him on his many travels since he became President have thought on occasion that his character was being remolded by the demands of his office; but usually the apparent changes have been only the tempering and reshaping of ideas, dictated by circumstance and experience. Any changes are superficial, not deep.

* * *

THIS birthday finds Mr. Roosevelt at the lowest point of political force since he entered the White House, and facing a campaign for re-election in which the prospect of victory is made uncertain by currents and tides of feeling that the most astute cannot predict.

But optimism is the President's forte. It is an optimism based partly on his proverbial luck and partly on an innate belief, amounting practically to fatalism, that no forces can stand against the working out of his social program.

Sometimes, in the dreary Winter days, when the calling list is brief and he sets aside hours for studies of reports and correspondence, he may look from the windows of his office over the empty White House grounds and wonder how circumstances gave him the most thankless public office in the United States—an office that repaid but poorly its greatest holders, bringing unpopularity to George Washington in his lifetime, assassination to Lincoln, gibes and ridicule to Theodore Roosevelt, and the hisses of the mob to Woodrow Wilson.

However, such moods do not last long, for Franklin Roosevelt, with a vitality that has surprised his closest associates, views his occupancy of the office in the manner of an evangelist who feels himself "called" to the pulpit.

There is an anecdote based on recollection still fresh in the minds of many persons living at Campobello, N. B., from whom this writer heard it, that gives a close insight into the President's views of his destiny.

It was at Campobello, at his mother's Summer home, that he was stricken with infantile paralysis shortly after concluding the unsuccessful campaign of 1920. The attack left him pitifully weakened and without hope just when he was laying plans for a political career. When he was able to be moved he was taken from the Campobello house on a stretcher. Scores of neighbors and friends gathered to wish him well and commiserate with him. He brushed aside their condolences. As he shook hands with them he said:

"You'll see me again when I am President of the United States."

Those neighbors next saw him in the

Times Wide World.

"He Has a Belief, Amounting Practically to Fatalism, That No Forces Can Stand Against the Working Out of His Program."

early Summer of 1933, when, fresh from handling the first special Congressional session of his administration, he sailed the schooner Amberjack up the New England coast to visit again the scenes of his younger days.

Even if that story were apocryphal it still would illustrate faithfully the ingrained belief of President Roosevelt that a hand stronger than his own has shaped the course of his actions. This belief of his is not religious fanaticism and it is not blind faith that what he does must be good because he does it. But it is a conviction that is not shaken even when criticism runs highest.

Not that he is an impractical person. As a politician of the first water he is ranked beside the astute James A. Farley, Postmaster General and Democratic National Chairman. He has studied politics as carefully as he has studied sociology; he learned as a boyish member of the New York State Senate that idealists fare badly if they are not armed with the weapons of politics.

* * *

HIS keen political sense for organization was most apparent in 1932, when the Democratic National Convention of that year revealed a large body of the delegates already pledged to this man who had never held an elective office in Washington. His sense of showmanship as expressed in shirt-sleeve talks to farmers, a disarming smile and a God-given speaking voice, hoisted him into office with such overwhelming support that for a while in 1933 he was viewed generally as "all things to all people."

He would like to have again such popularity, because it would make it easier for him to carry out his social program; but he has learned by hard experience that there are limitations both to public acclaim and to the authority of his office.

Mr. Roosevelt is not anxious about his chances for re-election, for he is certain that the mass of public opinion is behind him. Despite the opposition of the great majority of the newspapers to most of his acts, and the formation of opposition groups such as the American Liberty League by men who once counted as his advisers, he pictures himself in the position in which in a recent speech he portrayed Andrew Jackson—every one was against him except the public.

He believes that the growing opposition to his policies—his spending for relief, his social program—is largely from groups which he has characterized with such names as "tories," "autocrats" and "selfish minorities." He will not believe that the newspapers in large cities and the business organizations which sound notes of warning bespeak the feeling of the majority of the people.

However, the evidence that such opposition has become a source of worry to him is easily found in his last message to Congress, a message timed — with extreme political shrewdness again—so that it would go out over the radio when the maximum number of persons would be able to tune in upon it.

* * *

QUESTIONS are often asked concerning the Rooseveltian view, as of today, of politics and social matters and life in general. His views are not easily catalogued, for he himself admits that they shift and change.

If he were asked to give a one-word description of himself, he probably would reply that he is a "conservationist," for conservation is the work in which he feels he has a positive mission, as it concerns both human beings and the natural resources on which they depend for life. His political views are not those of any party, although he always has been a titular Democrat; they are as loose and informal as the sack suits he wears on all possible occasions.

Roosevelt has upset one of the greatest traditions of his party, the doctrine of States' rights, because he believes that the development of a modern social economy requires centralized control over business and agriculture, to the point of having Congress enact two sweeping laws, the NIRA and the AAA, which were subsequently overthrown by the Supreme Court. At the same time he has attacked the Republican doctrine of the tariffs by entering into reciprocal trade treaties.

Neither major political party has a precedent for what the President considers his greatest work, the Social Security Act, setting up unemployment insurance and old-age pensions. Equally without precedent in national policy are his soil-conservation program and its accessory, the Civilian Conservation Corps.

By his personal acts in less than three years President Roosevelt has achieved the position of leader of a great number of persons who believe in him and would believe in him regardless of his party label; likewise he has won the bitter opposition not only of conservative Republicans and conservative Democrats but also of the mass of discontented who feel he has not gone far enough in his social policies.

So far as labels are concerned, he gives the impression of caring little what he is called, except that he becomes angry at occasional hints that he would be a dictator. He contends he has a public mandate for every step he has taken.

* * *

THE President believes today, as he was convinced when he was inaugurated, that certain changes are necessary in the social system and that these can be accomplished within the limits of the Constitution, even though the Supreme Court has ruled against some of the principal measures enacted under his administration.

He has stated repeatedly, not only in his public speeches but in more informal talks with intimate groups, that economic life in the United States has become too complicated and too interdependent as between one region and another to be handled by the mechanism of State control.

As the President sees it, agriculture presents a problem, both in times of surpluses and shortage, that is entwined with the business life of the country. On his charts he sees the line indicating industrial production and the one showing purchasing power following the same curves as the one reflecting farm prosperity or poverty.

Within the last month, in fighting for a program to substitute for the AAA, he has laid more and more emphasis on conservation of resources, reiterating the lessons shown by wasteful usage of once fertile land and the tillage of soil never fit for anything but pasture land.

He hammers into the ears of those with whom he talks—and he can be serious and forceful as well as smiling and dramatic—his belief that none of the immediate problems of unemployment and business depression has a fraction of the importance of this threat to the national welfare.

* * *

OF a naturally restless disposition, a man who seldom sits more than five minutes without changing his position, the President would like to reach out his long hands and grasp Time by the forelock. He would pay any price in current resources and lay even heavier burdens on the national credit if by so doing he could advance by a generation his social program.

If the means were at hand, Mr. Roosevelt would rebuild the slums of all the cities, give to every farmer a decent bit of land, banish cut-throat competition from industry, assure education for every child, and decent comfort for every aged person, lay a paved highway on every dirt road, give every one who wanted to work a job—and then guarantee all this in perpetuity.

His ideals in these matters are probably shared by most Americans. The difference of opinion between him and his opponents lies in a choice of methods. Mr. Roosevelt has suffered many disappointments, but he is not discouraged. Rather, his defeats have rekindled the ardor of his advocacy and magnified his crusading spirit. He has dropped his "fireside chats," couched in neighborly terms to explain the progress of his administration, in favor of more frequent radio speeches on definite topics, given over to forceful statements of his arguments.

* * *

ROOSEVELT today is a far wiser man than he was when he entered the White House. His office has lessons which can be learned only through experience. Also, his position has changed, in that he has been put on the defensive.

However, the defensive with Roosevelt does not consist in explanation and exposition. Having a quick temper, he is inclined to hit back as hard as he is attacked. But his temper is controlled. Peppered though some of his speeches have been with epithet and rebuke to his critics, it is well known that many of his addresses have been blue-penciled by him to a milder form than that in which they first were dictated.

The President reads half a dozen newspapers regularly and he consults scores of persons each week, but his own barometer of popular feeling remains the White House mail. That mail is not as heavy as it was three years ago, when he first invited the public to write to him, but thousands of letters arrive daily.

They come neatly typed on bond stationery, penned on indifferent paper, sometimes scrawled with a pencil in almost illegible lettering on brown wrapping. They all are opened and bound in bundles of about 100 each. Obviously the President cannot read them all, but in quiet moments he will order the mail room to send him several bundles. Seated alone at his desk, he then will cut the strings of the bundles and run through the letters.

These letters are read by few people other than the President. Their contents are withheld as matter private to the President and the authors. But if an outsider could spend a day reading them, taken as they come from the White House mail bags, he probably would find the key to the President's belief that, while business leaders, industrial spokesmen, newspapers and professional men voice their criticisms of him, the public supports him.

President Roosevelt's Wyoming Speech

Governor Miller, Governor Ammons of Colorado, and I think I can say my old friends of Cheyenne—because, as you know, since 1932 Cheyenne has been on my annual visiting list:

Some of you may wonder why I am here today. Back in January, 1937, of this year, a friend of mine came to me and said: "Why during the next four years don't you take it easy? Why don't you coast? You came up a long steep grade for the last four years and now, during the next four years, you might as well have a good time."

Well, I said to him that I was going to continue during these four years the practice of the last four. And that, incidentally, in so doing I would have a good time.

I do not want to coast, and the nation does not want me to coast with my feet up on the front wheels. I have thought it was a part of the duty of the Presidency to keep in touch, personal touch, with the nation, and so this year since January I have already made one trip through a number of the Southern States on my way back from catching some fish, and now I am going out to the Coast for the third time since I have been President, not counting campaign trips—going out to take a "look-see" to try to tie together in my mind the problems of the nation in order that I may, at first hand, know as much about the questions that affect all of the forty-eight States as possible.

Says Emergency Is Not Over

As you know the greater part of the emergency is over—not all of it, because there are still a great many difficult problems—and I want to talk to you very briefly about some of the things that the National Government has done and is doing.

For example, we during the past three or four years have spent in every part of the country a great deal of Federal money—in putting people to work. That is the primary objective. But at the same time we have tried our utmost to accomplish useful things, and there is not a State, or a very, very few communities in the whole nation, that have not been benefited by these Federal expenditures, not in a temporary way, but in a permanent way.

I was thinking this morning of the question of airports, and I do not know whether it is thoroughly realized, but you are one of the stations on one main transcontinental airline, and you know that the Federal Government has assisted in the actual building, not of several dozen new airports in the country, not several hundred but many, many thousands, with the result today that the United States is checker-boarded with airports in every State.

That is an accomplishment of the past three or four years. And in the same way not dozens or hundreds, but thousands of schools have been built or renovated with a combination of State and Federal funds.

We have to come some day to an end of the greater part of that program, and just the other day in Washington we allocated the last of the Federal money for public works projects. Those consisted of more schools, more sewer systems and more water works and things of that kind, where there was a very clear need for replacement or where the States or localities had already voted bonds.

Library Really Did Burn

I will tell you one amusing story of the allocation for school projects. Congress told me to confine them to those schools or to those places where the schools had been burned down or where new schools had to be built to replace buildings that were about to tumble down, and there came a project from one of the Southern States for the building in that community of a new school building and a new library.

The new school building was to replace one which was about to tumble down, and we granted the project, but in the case of the library, they apparently did not have a library and it was not a replacement, and with great regret we rejected the application.

The head of the school came to Washington to see me, and I told him how sorry I was, but that we could not spend Federal funds just for new buildings, no matter how much they were needed, unless they were to replace something that had been burned down.

He said: "Mr. Roosevelt, our library was burned down."

I said: "That is funny, because there is nothing said about that in the application. When was it burned down?"

And he came back and said: "Mr. President, our library was burned in 1864 by General Sherman."

And so, on this trip, I am looking at many, many types of projects. I am always keen when I come West to get more people out of the East to come West and see things with their own eyes.

The other day I read in a great newspaper of the Middle West an editorial that took as its text the fact that one of the WPA projects—a dam, I think, in Kansas—a part of it had washed out, with undoubtedly the loss of a good deal of money, and pointed out that this was the way that the Federal Government was wasting its funds.

I believe you know that engineers are human, just like I am, and that they do not make a home run every time they come to bat.

But the editorial went on, taking that as a text, and pointed out from their point of view, which I do not believe is the point of view of the nation, that in the construction of these great dams by the Federal Government we are creating millions of kilowatts of power which will never be used by the people. I think that you and I and most people realize that when you do create power the public finds some useful way to use it.

In the same way they went on to tell the people that these reclamation projects are a pure waste of money—that by building projects like Casper-Aicova or Grand Coulee we put in use unnecessary farm lands, that there was enough good farm land in the United States to take care of all the people who needed it for fifty years to come.

You and I know that is not so. You hear on this great central highway and know of a number of people, families, who have had to leave their homes and farms in the drought area, some of them from the eastern part of the State, from the Dakotas, Nebraska, Oklahoma, Texas—people who could not make a go of it on poor land, forced to leave their homes to avoid starvation—and those people have headed farther west, looking for a chance to earn their livelihood, looking for good land and not being able to find it.

Land Must Be Provided

So, in the same way, there are thousands of families in the East who are unable to make good on the land they are tilling now for very obvious reasons. It is land that ought not to be put under the plow. And so, for these families, I believe it is the duty of the Federal Government and the State Governments to provide them with land, where it is possible to do it, where they can make a living.

And so I could go on talking about WPA and PWA and soil erosion and the CCC camps. As a matter of fact, it has all served a pretty useful purpose. It is a better country for having spent for a few years more than we were taking in in taxes; and do not let anybody deceive you—the Government of the United States is not going broke.

So here I am, trying on this short trip—for it must be short—trying to get a cross-section point of view, the point of view especially of the rank and file of the American people of this Western country.

Yes, it is a part of the duty of the Presidency to represent, in so far as possible, all the people, not just Democrats, but Republicans as well, not just rich people, but poor people as well.

And I have been trying very simply to do the most good for the greatest number. Out here, in the cattle country and the sugar beet country, of course I am interested in the prosperity of the raisers of cattle and the growers of beets. Perhaps somewhere down in my heart I am a little bit more interested in the ten men who have a hundred head of cattle apiece than I am in the one man who has a thousand head of cattle, and perhaps I am a little bit more interested in the ten men who have a hundred acres of beets apiece than I am in the one who has a thousand acres of beets.

National Viewpoint Grows

It seems to me that that is one of the necessary things that go with the Presidency, and we, in the past four years, have tried, I think honestly and I think fairly successfully, to do the greatest good for the greatest number. And so, in these next few years, four years, eight years, twelve years, twenty years, I am very firmly convinced that the people of the nation have more and more a national point of view.

You people out here realize, far better than you did four years ago, that your prosperity is tied up very intimately with the prosperity of the cotton growers of the South, and with the industrial workers of the East; and in the same way, those people in the great factories of the East and Middle West and on the cotton farms of the South, and in the corn belt, and in the wheat belt, they know that their prosperity is affected by your prosperity out here. That, I believe, will be written in history as a great accomplishment of these years we are living in now—the welding together of the people of the United States.

And so, my friends, I am glad to have been able to come out here on this annual trip, and I hope and expect to come out during the next three years again.

Stimson's Biography Criticizes Roosevelt on Leadership in War

President's Failure to Rely Upon Others Cost His Life, Caused United States to Suffer Losses, Ex-Secretary of War Says

Henry L. Stimson has recorded in his official biography his belief that the United States war effort suffered losses at times as a result of the determination of President Franklin D. Roosevelt to "keep all the threads in his own hands."

At the same time, the eminent Republican, who served as Secretary of War from the summer of 1940 until the close of the conflict, pays a glowing tribute to President Roosevelt's war-time leadership in the biography, the first installment of which will appear in the January issue of The Ladies Home Journal.

Mr. Stimson also asserts that if either he or Gen. George C. Marshall had been the Commander in Chief in place of Mr. Roosevelt, the invasion of Normandy would have taken place in 1943 instead of 1944, but he acknowledges that no one can tell whether this would have ended the war sooner.

He gives the fullest and most authoritative account yet published of the long struggle between American proponents of a cross-channel invasion, led by General Marshall, and the British strategists, headed by Winston Churchill, who hoped to defeat Germany by a series of attritions in Italy, Greece and the Balkans.

Tells of Threatened Break

Mr. Stimson discloses that in July, 1942, he and General Marshall wanted to threaten the British that "we will turn our backs on them and take up the war with Japan" because of their stand against a cross-channel invasion. President Roosevelt overruled the threat, however, on the ground that it was "a little like 'taking up your dishes and going away.'"

The former Secretary of War also writes at length of the difficulties that United States military leaders encountered in dealing with Generalissimo Chiang Kai-shek of China and Gen. Charles de Gaulle. In both cases he is somewhat critical of Mr. Roosevelt's handling of the situation.

He reveals that he personally telephoned to Wendell Willkie and told him that if he publicly attacked the deal that had just been made with Admiral Darlan, he would endanger the success of the United States invasion of North Africa. Mr. Stimson says Mr. Willkie reluctantly withheld his criticism until the immediate crisis in North Africa had passed.

The biography was written in the third person by McGeorge Bundy of Harvard University, but Mr. Stimson in his foreword, makes it clear that the book is the product of their joint effort. It is entitled "On Active Service" and will be published in book form by Harper & Brothers in April.

Roosevelt Stand Criticized

Mr. Stimson's strongest criticism of Mr. Roosevelt comes in his account of the difficulties Gen. Joseph W. Stilwell had with Chiang Kai-shek, whom he described as "an ignorant, suspicious, feudal autocrat with a profound but misconceived devotion to the integrity of China and to himself as her savior."

"More than any other American Theatre Commander in the war, Stilwell required the constant and vigorous political support of his own Government, and less than any other commander did he get it," the biography says. And after the withdrawal of General Stilwell at Chiang's demand, Mr. Stimson concludes:

"This seems an illustration in specific terms of the losses incurred through Mr. Roosevelt's constant effort to keep all the threads in his own hands. One man simply could not do it all and Franklin Roosevelt killed himself trying."

Mr. Stimson also records his belief that General Eisenhower was handicapped seriously at the time of the invasion of France by the restrictions imposed upon him by President Roosevelt in dealing with General de Gaulle and his followers. The biography says that Mr. Stimson was disappointed by the extent to which personal feeling entered into the thinking of both Mr. Roosevelt and Secretary of State Cordell Hull, both of whom, he conceded, "had been sorely tried, over a long period, by the personal peculiarities of the Free French leader."

Lack of Coordination Cited

Reviewing these matters in his mind after the war, Mr. Stimson concludes that "Mr. Roosevelt's personal virtuosity in high politics carried with it certain disadvantages which might have been limited if the President had been willing to provide himself with a War Cabinet for the coordination and execution of his policies—a body which might have done in war diplomacy what the Joint Chiefs of Staff did in military strategy."

"He had served in too many Cabinets to expect that all decisions would match his advice, and it was not his disagreements with the President on details of policy that bothered him, as he looked back in 1947; it was rather that Mr. Roosevelt's policy was so often either unknown or not clear to those who had to execute it, and worse yet, in some cases it seemed contradictory," the biography asserts.

Mr. Stimson's final judgment of President Roosevelt's war leadership is summed up thus:

"Franklin Roosevelt, as a war-time international leader, proved himself as good as one man could be—but one man was not enough to keep track of so vast an undertaking."

Mr. Stimson believes, however, that Theodore Roosevelt would have provided better leadership in the pre-Pearl Harbor period in 1941 than Franklin D. Roosevelt did.

Differences In Two Men Weighed

"T. R.'s advantage would have been in his natural boldness, his firm conviction that where he led, men would follow. He would, Stimson felt sure, have been able to brush aside the contemptible little group of men who wailed of 'war-mongers' and in the blunt strokes of a poster painter he would have demonstrated the duty of Americans.

"Franklin D. Roosevelt was not made that way. With unequalled political skill he could pave the way for any given specific step, but in so doing he was likely to tie his own hands for the future, using honeyed and consoling words that would return to plague him later."

In his long and detailed account of the battle between the Americans and the British over the cross-channel invasion, **Mr. Stimson flatly denies the allegation that frequently has been made that the British opposition was based on a desire to block Soviet Russia by an invasion farther East.**

"This view seemed to Stimson wholly erroneous," the biography says. "Never in any of his long and frank discussions with the British leaders was any such argument advanced, and he saw no need whatever to assume any such grounds for the British position."

He records many instances in which he differed sharply over war policies with Mr. Churchill, but nevertheless, Mr. Stimson, according to the biography, holds the "considered opinion that with the single exception of Franklin D. Roosevelt, no many in any country had been a greater factor in the construction of the grand alliance that destroyed the Nazis."

AN INTERVIEW WITH TRUMAN: HE SEES MAN'S BETTER NATURE BRINGING PEACE TO ILL WORLD

COVERS WIDE FIELD

He Says Normal Dealing With Soviet Is Hopeless —Broken Pacts Cited

DEFICIT SPENDING DECRIED

G.O.P. Tax Slash Is Blamed— 'Red Herring' Held to Apply to Spy Hunters' Methods

By ARTHUR KROCK
Special to THE NEW YORK TIMES.

WASHINGTON, Feb. 14—In the age of atomic energy, transmuted into a weapon which can destroy great cities and the best works of civilization, and in the shadow of a hydrogen detonant which could multiply many times that agent of destruction, a serene President of the United States sits in the White House with undiminished confidence in the triumph of humanity's better nature and the progress of his own efforts to achieve abiding peace.

This President, Harry S. Truman, is a controversial figure in the world and in domestic politics. But to those who talk with him intimately about the problem of global life and death, his faith that these good things will happen, and probably in his time, shines out with a luminous and simple quality which no event or misadventure of policy can diminish.

The following is an account of the President's current views on the international and domestic issues of his time which I can vouch for as to accuracy. It may serve further to reveal to doubters and critics what manner of man he really is; and crystalize in the minds of those who instinctively supported him in the campaign of 1948 what were the personal qualities they sensed but did not always comprehend.

Undaunted by War Clouds

He sits in the center of the troubled and frightened world, not a world he ever made; but the penumbra of doubt and fear in which the American nation pursues its greatest and most perilous adventure—the mission to gain world peace and security while preserving the strength of the native experiment in democracy—stops short of him. Visitors find him undaunted and sure that, whether in his time or thereafter, a way will be discovered to preserve the world from the destruction which to many seems unavoidable, as moral force is steadily weakened by the conflict of two great rival systems and by new skills in forging weapons of destruction that make the discovery of gunpowder seem like the first ignition of the parlor match.

His reasons for this serenity and this sureness emerge from current conversations with the President on the issues of the time. For Mr. Truman is the kind of American who must be observed at first-hand, free to speak with the candor and natural piety of his make-up, to be wholly understood.

In such meetings he answers questions that bear directly on the problems before him. And these questions and his answers that follow (the latter put mostly in the indirect discourse which is due to a President for his own protection and that of the country) reveal the man and what he conceives to be his mission and his methods of accomplishing it better than the formal record can do.

Change on Soviet Explained

Q.—You recall the hopeful prospect of peace that surrounded you, and you expressed, at San Francisco in 1945 when the United Nations was organized. What has happened since to bring about deterioration to the point where a member of your Cabinet can say of it: "The cold fact is that we are still in a hot war"? When did you conclude that normal negotiation with the Kremlin was hopeless?

A.—The President said he remembered that time well, and with what good-will toward the Russian people and their rulers he went to Potsdam shortly thereafter. There he planned to offer help for reconstruction, of Russia as well as the rest of the world, on a very large scale. He remembered with pride and sympathy how Russians had smashed the German armies in the East, and he believed their assistance was necessary to win the war against Japan. But he found that all Stalin wanted to talk about was the abrupt cessation of lend-lease; hence the atmosphere was unfavorable to what Mr. Truman had in mind.

"To abolish lend-lease at the time was a mistake." But he was "new" then; the papers had been prepared for Roosevelt, and represented a Government decision. He felt there was nothing else he could do but sign. He had no staff and no Cabinet of his own. Now he has both.

The agreement the Russians made at Yalta to enter the war against Japan was the only one they ever kept out of nearly forty. He has no hope they will keep any which now it would be good policy to seek. But he remains hopeful of the outcome.

When the Russians, after the Potsdam agreements, blocked East-West trade he began to lose the last vestige of hope that what seemed so good a peace prospect at San Francisco had survived. Gen. George C. Marshall, he recalls, came back from Moscow deeply discouraged. And when Ambassador Bedell Smith reported to the President from Moscow that the Russians were carefully concealing from the people all facts about the war assistance we had given them, and what our proposals had been for joint reconstruction of the world, that last vestige disappeared.

Barred Division of Japan

It would have been the same in Japan as in Germany if the President had not demanded an American as the Allied generalissimo there at the signing of the surrender on the Missouri. Otherwise the Russians would have divided that country as they have Germany; and the situation in the Far East would have been so much worse than it is that one can take comfort from it.

The real trouble with the Russians is that they are still suffering from a complex of fear and inferiority where we are concerned. If a campaign had not been in progress in 1948 he would have sent Chief Justice Fred M. Vinson to try to straighten out Stalin and the other Russian leaders on this and on our real intentions. Maybe that will be the thing to do some time. But in nothing must we show any sign of weakness, because there is none in our attitude. To appreciate some of the importance of this read "Berlin Command" (a book by former Brig. Gen. Frank L. Howley, published by Putnam's, New York).

He is reliably informed that the Russians have 16,000,000 people in concentration camps. This is the way of the police state, which he finds utterly abhorrent.

Q.—In view of your background, training and dislike of debt, how do you reconcile these with your toleration of deficit spending and your advocacy of new spending programs? Critics of the Fair Deal program say it proposes permanently to burden the more able, diligent and successful with the cost of "insuring all others against the results of their own improvidence, ill-luck or defective behavior"; that this is very nearly the Marxian doctrine, "to each according to his need, from each according to his ability."

A.—In no sense does the President tolerate deficit spending. There wouldn't be any now if the Republicans had not cut the income taxes in the Eightieth Congress. Tax changes should not have been made piecemeal at any time, but conformed to a general and revised plan. This was equally true when he approved the repeal of the excess profits tax. He wishes he had not done this, because it was piecemeal also. But then again he was new at the job.

Aims at Expanded Economy

His object is steadily to expand the economy so as to provide jobs and careers for the million and a half young people who come annually into the stream of commerce. This cannot be done without the measures outlined in the Fair Deal. From a peak of 59.6 millions of persons employed in civilian activities last September, the number has gone down to 56 millions, with 4.8 millions unemployed. A certain amount of unemployment, say from three to five millions, is supportable. It is a good thing that job-seeking should go on at all times; this is healthy for the economic body. But the main thing is to keep the economy rising to absorb the new entrants into the stream of commerce. There are now 62 millions employed in the labor force in the United States, including the military. Ten years ago whoever had suggested that this could happen would have been written down a fool or a dreamer.

Senators George and Byrd call for a reduction of $6 billions in the budget. They know very well it can't be done. The President has cut the defense requisitions this time from $22 billions to less than $14 billions and paid for the military aid program for the North Atlantic treaty nations out of it also. He is an old hand at budget-making, and at the last session he sent a tight one to the Capitol and they sent it back with increased totals. He feels he has cut this one as much as can be done in consideration of the basic needs of the foreign program and of the dynamic domestic economy he seeks to create and maintain. This in itself will bring an end to deficit spending, which represents exactly the amount the tax cut of the Eightieth Congress cost the revenues. He hates deficit spending "as much as Harry Byrd ever could," and it is only a temporary condition, brought on by necessities which could not be removed by any genius of statecraft known or available to him.

A reduction of more than $8 billions in the defense bill, with $1 billion for the Military Assistance Program [MAP] found extra, compares rather well with the blueprint of the economizers.

He has no policy which contemplates permanently burdening the more able, diligent and successful with the cost of insuring all others against the results of their own improvidence, ill-luck or defective behavior. This charge—also that the Fair Deal approximates the Marxian doctrine—is absolutely untrue. The President's aim is to preserve life and property and expand opportunity and the standards of living. "There isn't a drop of Marxist or Socialist blood" in him.

The globe shows vast areas inhabited by hundreds of millions of people who want to improve their lot, and this can be done with our American surpluses and with a moderate amount of our assistance, financial and technical. When that is done, the chief threat of international communism will pass, and this is the primary objective of his policy.

Q.—Your views on party obligation: that all elected as Democrats must abide by platform pledges. Suppose (1) you construe a pledge in detail differently from a member of Congress; or (2) he has made a commitment to the contrary prior to the adoption of the platform. Is he recreant as a party man?

A.—The President does not expect 100 percent support from those elected to Congress on the same platform with him. He recognizes that local situations may require some members to refuse to follow a President on certain matters. As a Senator, he reserved the right of independence at times for himself. But he does believe that, after a platform has been duly adopted by a convention, all those who have participated or run on that platform should generally abide by its detailed construction by the national candidate.

Only that national candidate, the President, can translate a platform into actionable terms. There are few chairmen of Congressional committees who follow the platform and the President's construction of it more than 50 percent of the time, and this is very bad. These chairmen should be the right arm of the Administration in orderly government by party. If there is any other way to have a responsible government, he does not know what it is.

Gives His Stand on F. E. P. C.

Q.—You favor the Fair Employment Practice Commission legislation providing Federal police powers in the states to correct employment discriminations, some of which are implicit in the present condition of racial minorities. You know intimately the condition of the Negro race and the limitations of its capacity to fill certain kinds of employment. Many believe that education will be required before an FEPC could operate even on a voluntary basis. Why then is it desirable in mandatory form, requiring that the burden of proof be on the employer?

A.—The President would not support or continue to support any legislation which deprived a citizen of the right to run his own business, for which that citizen was responsible, as he thought best. The President does not agree that the Administration's FEPC legislation would have any such result. If he thought so, he would not be for it, and under him it will not be so administered.

But opportunities to get jobs for which applicants are fitted by every fair test must not be denied in this country on grounds of race, color or any similar discrimination. The value of the FEPC bill will be to give this position the dignity, strength and clarity of a national policy, not just political, but social and economic as well. For that reason he wants the bill passed, even if it were only to serve as a club in the closet.

Early "Inadequacy" Described

Q.—When you became President you expressed a sense of inadequacy which many thought was far too humble for your abilities. Now and for some time you seem to have dropped that feeling overboard, where it belongs. How did this change come about?

A.—When Mr. Truman became President he did not intend to convey the sense of inadequacy which many people thought he did. He came into office without a single member of the Cabinet who was devoted to him personally, without having been briefed on the processes or current problems of government, without knowing who the people were to whom he should apply for the counsel and facts a President must have to serve the best interests of the country. Often some member of that Cabinet tried to see him privately to complain about another one. He stopped that: first, by recounting the incident at the Cabinet meeting and asking the two or three involved to work it out; second, by getting his own Cabinet. Now he is served by the best personal staff he could find and by a loyal and able Cabinet. The problem remains how to find the very best qualified persons outside for counsel and for collecting the facts in special matters. That is an unending task, as well as a vital one. But the inadequacy of the position he was in to do that has disappeared, and that was all he meant at the time.

Q.—It is true that chairmen in Congress get these places through seniority, and it is a bad system. Have you any idea of a better one, or any other that would be operable?

A. The seniority system by which chairmen of committees in Congress are selected is a defective one because the best qualified men do not always get the jobs. But any substitute that has been proposed is unworkable, and the present system has the merit of keeping order in the legislative process. If the Administration were allowed to pick the chairmen, which is one substitute that has been proposed, the Executive would dominate Congress and this is not only undesirable but contrary to the intent of the Constitution.

Q. Will you explain your use of "red herring" and "hysteria" in the context of the spy trials and hunts since you are charged (1) with not comprehending the gravity of this situation or (2) playing for votes of groups under suspicion?

A. When Mr. Truman on several occasions spoke of "hysteria" and "red herrings" in connection with revelations about espionage, etc., he was criticizing the *methods* employed by the Un-American Activities Committee and by individuals in Congress and out of it. The objective of having only loyal citizens in Government service and in positions of importance and responsibility has been his fundamentally, too.

His loyalty board (Chairman Seth W. Richardson) has done much more effective screening of this kind without headlines and personal publicity than the Congressional spy-hunts, which have been animated chiefly by quests for headlines and personal publicity. These produced the "hysteria" he was talking about, reminding him of the public excitement in the days of the Alien and Sedition Acts, the Know-Nothing Movement, the Ku Klux Klan and the Red scares of 1920. And he has never changed his opinion that the way the Un-American Activities Committee handled the Hiss and other cases was a red herring to distract public attention from the blunders and crimes of the Eightieth Congress.

When the President was chairman of the special Senate committee during the war, he followed a method which he sought to endorse by contrast when he made the above comments about hysteria and red herrings. Whenever he found something wrong or some indication of potential wrong in the war program, he privately communicated the facts to the departments concerned, and usually it was corrected or averted without the kind of publicity that unfairly shakes public confidence, and spreads through the more than two millions in Government employ a feeling of insecurity in their jobs which hampers and damages their work.

The result was that no major scandal occurred in the war. This is the responsible method which, because it was not followed in these other matters, impelled him to say what he did. The Government service is 99 per cent plus loyal and secure.

If the facts about a Government employe show the contrary, out the man will go at no expense to public stability—though, it is true, without a headline for a politician who has that chiefly in his mind.

* * *

Such are the President's statements of his views.

Those who have the privilege, necessarily a limited one, of searching in this way the mind and purpose of Harry S. Truman usually come away with faith in his honesty and courage. They usually come away also with the conviction that, whether or not he has the greatness which the times require—a question that must be left to the verdict of history—he means to preserve the basic system by which this nation attained its greatness, and to achieve and maintain that peace which has been its highest aspiration since 1783.

President Gives His Reasons For Not Seeking Re-election

In Extraordinary 300th Press Conference He Tells Editors Office Is a Continuous One With Nobody Indispensable in It

By ANTHONY LEVIERO
Special to The New York Times

WASHINGTON, April 17—President Truman said today that the Presidency was the greatest office in the history of the world, a continuing office, and no man should consider himself the indispensable occupant of it. That was why he had decided not to seek it again, he explained.

Mr. Truman became philosophical on the Presidency during his 300th news conference, which was a rather special one. In addition to the correspondents who regularly cover this "greatest show in Washington," the mass interview was attended by members of the American Society of Newspaper Editors, who are meeting here.

Thus Mr. Truman had 520 editors and reporters throwing questions at him on numerous topics for thirty minutes and he answered almost all of them. The "no comments" were at a minimum for this conference, which was held in the auditorium of the Natural History Building of the Smithsonian Institution.

Alexander F. Jones, president of the A. S. N. E., and editor of The Syracuse Herald-Journal, started the conference, one of the longest on record, by asking:

"I wonder if you would care to comment on your political philosophy in retiring, irrespective of any personal considerations?"

The President expressed the opinion that maybe a million people in this country could have done a better job as President than he had. But he was the one who held the job and had to carry the responsibilities, he declared. He quoted the epitaph of Jack Williams, buried in Tombstone, Ariz., to say, "He done his damnedest."

Mr. Truman said he would have occupied the Presidency practically eight years by next Jan. 20 and felt that was enough for any man to demonstrate whether he could do well for the welfare of the nation.

"The Presidency itself is a continuing office—the greatest office in the history of the world—and that office ought to be continuing as far as individuals are concerned," said Mr. Truman.

"And another thing in connection with it—when a man has been in this very responsible position for eight years, which I will practically have been by the 20th of January, 1953, he has, or should have by that time, made all the contribution he possibly can to the welfare of the nation. He has either done it well or not well. I have tried my best to give the nation everything I have in me.

"There are a great many people —I suppose a million in the country—who could have done the job better than I did it, but I had the job and I had to do it."

"I always quote an epitaph which is on a tombstone in the cemetery at Tombstone, Ariz. It says:

"Here lies Jack Williams. He did his damndest."

Mr. Truman said he thought that was the greatest epitaph a man could have.

While he favored the two-term tenure for Presidents, however, Mr. Truman expressed the view that it was different with political parties.

An editor asked whether Mr. Truman believed a party should be limited to twenty years of control of the Administration. That has been the span of the Democratic party under Presidents Roosevelt and Truman.

Mr. Truman said he thought there should be no such limit if the party worked for the good of the greatest number of people of the country.

While Mr. Truman in his political campaigns has often attacked former President Herbert Hoover, he said today that upon leaving the highest office he hoped he could make a contribution to the welfare of the country as Mr. Hoover had done. He referred to Mr. Hoover's chairmanship of the Commission for the Reorganization of the Government. Mr. Truman has adopted many of its recommendations and Congress has enacted them.

Every man who has been President accumulates knowledge that ought to be available for the welfare of the country and he would do anything asked of him in retirement, said the President.

Mr. Truman said it would please him to serve in the Senate again, but he could not in good ethics make a race for it for two reasons. In the first place, he would not want to use the influence of his high office to make the race.

Secondly, he would not run for the Senate in later years, after he was in retirement because that would pit him against the present incumbent, a Democrat, Thomas C. Hennings Jr., of Missouri. A Republican, Senator James P. Kem, is up for re-election this year.

An editor recalled that Mr. Truman felt that his greatest contribution as President had been to prevent World War III. He wished to know what Mr. Truman considered as his greatest achievement in the domestic field.

Mr. Truman replied that in this field the achievement was as great as in foreign affairs.

He said that his Administration had been able to maintain full employment and had assured a fair distribution of incomes so that farmers were in better shape, and so was labor and industry.

Asked if this prosperity would continue in the absence of the defense program, the President said it would if his Point Four program to aid underdeveloped countries could be pushed to raise standards of living in those countries by 2 per cent. That would keep the production machinery of the United States going for twenty-five years, he declared.

Then Mr. Truman defined a role for the individual citizen in these times.

The average person, said Mr. Truman, should inform himself fully on just what the United Nations stands for and what it was doing for the peace of the world. Then the citizen should do everything possible in every community to fulfill his responsibilities, he declared.

Every citizen, he continued, should become a first-class politician, because politics was Government, and newspaper men were doing themselves and the country no good by disparaging politicans. He was a politician, said Mr. Truman, and he was proud of it.

April 18, 1952

Does the President Have Too Much Power?

That is the question inherent in the debate that now goes on in Washington.

By HENRY STEELE COMMAGER

IT is a familiar experience to miss the forest for the trees. There is reason to suppose that the American people are now going through this experience. So intense is our interest in the day-by-day controversies that blaze in our newspapers and clamor on the air that we are scarcely aware of the larger issues involved in those controversies. To the journalist what is important in Washington may be the R. F. C. investigation one day, the Wherry resolution another, price controls a third, and the latest McCarthy burlesque act a fourth. The future historian of the Truman Administration, however, may well single out the attack upon the Executive power as the most significant of all post-war developments in the domestic field.

The Twenty-second Amendment is a case in point. That amendment introduced a far-reaching change in our constitutional system, but perhaps the most remarkable thing about it was that it took the country so completely by surprise. No one, apparently, knew what was happening, least of all the people who woke up one morning to discover that they had struck a blow at democracy — and themselves — by denying the next generation the right to do what they themselves had done in 1940 and 1944.

The ratification of the two-term amendment is one of three major assaults upon the Executive power that have come to a head in this last year. The other two are the attempt to limit the power of the President as Commander in Chief of the armed forces of the nation, and the attempt to hamstring Presidential control of foreign relations. Each of these is dangerous. Taken together they constitute an invasion of the Executive power which, if persisted in, may result in the substitution for our Presidential system of a hybrid of the parliamentary and the Presidential systems.

That this result would be neither unanticipated nor unwelcome in certain circles is clear from Representative Coudert's resolution calling for a constitutional amendment which would require the President to resign in the face of a vote of no-confidence. Whatever may be the relative merits of the Presidential and the parliamentary systems — a question which we need not consider here — no one familiar with our Constitution or our history can suppose that the one can be grafted onto the other without changes that would be fateful and might be fatal.

THIS is not the first time that the Presidential system has been threatened by Congressional usurpation. This happened once before, in the Presidency of the luckless Andrew Johnson; then, too, the assault came from the Republican party — a party which has for the most part favored a strong Executive. That earlier attack, like the present one, was inspired not by a theoretical preference for the parliamentary over the Presidential system, but by hostility to a particular President and considerations of partisan advantage. Historical analogies are always a bit dangerous, but it is relevant to note that that earlier attack upon the Executive power misfired, and that the policies which it was designed to facilitate—Radical Reconstruction—likewise misfired. Historical prophesies, too, are a bit dangerous, but it is fairly safe to predict that eighty years from now the present attack upon the Presidential power will seem as misguided and pernicious as the Congressional attack upon Johnson seems to us today.

THERE is another feature of this attack, too, that must command our attention and excite our concern. That is its doctrinaire character. It proceeds not out of real but out of imagined dangers. It is rooted not in experience but in fears. For the limitation on the Executive power—with a corresponding expansion of the legislative power —finds no justification in our history. To the generation of Thomas Jefferson and Thomas Paine history taught that Executive power was always dangerous, but the history of democracy teaches a different moral. Call the roll of the "strong" Presidents—those who have used the Executive power boldly—Washington, Jefferson, Jackson, Polk, Lincoln, Theodore Roosevelt, Wilson, Franklin Roosevelt. None of these Presidents threatened democracy or impaired the constitutional system. It is, on the contrary, the "weak" Presidents—men like Fillmore and Buchanan — and Harding — who bring democracy into disrepute and expose the Constitution to grave perils.

There is, in fact, no basis in our own history for the distrust of the Executive authority. Nor is there any sound basis for the fear, the meddling, or the limitations that are explicit in the three current assaults upon the Executive power. Certainly there has been no correlation between length of Presidential service and danger to democracy or to the Constitution. The American people have on the whole acted wisely in re-electing Presidents; they have never re-elected a dangerous man and only once—in 1872—a weak man. And the only referendum that the American people ever held on a third term was an overwhelming endorsement of that innovation—an endorsement confirmed—four years later.

IN this constitutional crisis it is important that we recur to basic principles of our constitutional order, and to our experience with these principles over a period of a century and a half. These are actually two sides of the same shield, for our Constitution consists not only of the document drafted in 1787 but of the additions to it over 150 years of practice.

Let us look first to the principle involved in the Twenty-second Amendment. Why does this amendment violate sound constitutional principles? It violates sound principles because it writes into the Constitution a quantitative rather than a qualitative limit on popular authority. It writes into the Constitution a limitation not on authority itself but on the degree of authority already granted. It limits not the arena in which democracy may function but the way in which democracy functions in that arena.

This takes, perhaps, a bit of explanation. The wise men who drew up our Constitutions, state and Federal, feared government. They feared, especially, that government might invade areas in which government had no standing and no right. There were certain things, so this generation held, that no government could do. Government could not "deprive men of life, liberty or happiness" without due process of law; it could not impair the right of men to worship as they pleased, or the right of free speech or free press, of petition or of assembly. All these powers were beyond the authority of government altogether, and the Constitution framers saw to it that they were removed from governmental authority either by omitting them from the Constitution proper or by writing safeguards into bills of rights.

BUT where government did have authority, properly and logically, it had sufficient authority to do the job. Where power was granted, it was granted in all fullness. Thus the power to wage war is the power to wage war successfully. The power to regulate commerce among the states is the power to regulate the whole of such commerce—and the word "regulate" is broadly interpreted. The power to tax knows no limitations other than those written into the Constitution, and any effort to limit that power quantitatively is unsound in principle. In short, the Constitution acknowledges qualitative limitations on the powers of government, but few quantitative ones except those of a purely mechanical nature.

Now apply this principle to the election of a President. Once grant that the American

Fitzpatrick in The St. Louis Post-Dispatch

"The Endless Feud."

Presidential Power

HENRY STEELE COMMAGER, Professor of History at Columbia University, is the author of "The American Mind" and other works.

people (through the rubber-stamp Electoral College) have the authority to elect a President, it follows that they have authority to elect him as often as they choose. Granted they may make a mistake—but they may make a mistake in their original choice, for that matter, and presumably they have a better chance of avoiding a mistake the second time than the first, the third time than the second. If the Constitution is to be designed to prevent people from making mistakes, it might as logically start with Congress, for on any fair comparison Americans have made more mistakes with their Congressmen than with their Presidents.

Let us look to the second major assault upon the Executive power—the attempt to limit the power of the President as Commander in Chief of the armed forces. Specifically this assault has centered upon the right of the President to commit American forces to danger points outside the boundaries of the United States without prior Congressional authorization.

I HAVE recently discussed the strictly constitutional issues involved in this controversy in THE TIMES Magazine and made clear that the overwhelming weight of authority supports Presidential discretion in this field. Congress can, to be sure, limit Presidential power here by the simple expedient of refusing appropriations. But no comfort is to be drawn from that argument. For that matter, Congress could, in effect, abolish the Presidency and the Supreme Court by refusing to vote the necessary appropriations; no one would defend the constitutionality of such conduct.

But the issue is, of course, more than one of constitutionality; it is one of power. We must beware the common fallacy that because a thing is constitutional it is necessarily sound; we must guard against the comparable fallacy that if anyone can raise any hypothetical constitutional objection to a policy it is necessarily unsound. Preoccupation with the abstract constitutional issue and with the particular issue of sending a certain number of divisions to Western Europe has served to confuse the principle involved in the question.

THAT principle is one of Presidential power and Presidential duty. The President is Commander in Chief of the Army and the Navy, and he is under oath to "preserve, protect and defend" the Constitution—and by implication the nation. It should be clear that these general powers and obligations apply with equal force to the disposition of all the armed forces of the nation. If he does not have authority to send land forces to points of danger, neither does he have authority to send the Navy or the Air Force to points of danger outside the boundaries of the nation, for his constitutional authority in the one arena is precisely the same as in the others.

Those who deny the President the right to send land forces to such places as are essential to the defense of the nation, by logical implication deny his power to order the Navy to the waters around Formosa or the Air Force to air stations in the Mediterranean and the Middle East.

There are some further considerations that have not received sufficient attention in this discussion—a discussion which has centered overmuch on the constitutional question. There is, for example, the consideration that insistence upon specific authorization from Congress may serve to deprive the Executive of effective bargaining power in negotiations with the Kremlin, or of influence in negotiation with our associates. There is the consideration that if Congress ties the President's hands in the matter it in effect invites aggression whenever it is not available to untie them. A generation ago this consideration would not have been alarming, for in an emergency Congress can convene speedily and act with dispatch. But modern blitz warfare does not wait upon Congressional reconvenings.

Theory may mislead us; experience must be our guide. Has the Presidential power in this arena served us well or ill? Have Presidents, in fact, been more war-minded than Congresses, or have they been more mistaken in their understanding of international crises? What shall we say of Jefferson's undeclared war on the Barbary pirates; of Lincoln's personal conduct of the war for the Union from April to July, 1861; of Theodore Roosevelt's intervention in the Venezuela crisis and in the Caribbean; of Wilson's determination to arm American merchantmen? Were the Presidents wrong, in these and other ventures, and was Congress in the right? But these questions may be academic. Clearly it is not the remote past that concerns Congress now, but the immediate past.

THOUGH Truman is the ostensible object of attack, Franklin Roosevelt is the real object of attack. It is his foreign policy that is under fire; it is his decision to trade destroyers for island bases, to land troops in Iceland and Greenland, to order the Navy to shoot on sight—that is the issue in the minds of most of those Congressmen who are pressing for limitations on the Presidential power. Who, now, looking back upon those critical months of 1940 and 1941, would repudiate the Presidential decisions — who but unregenerate isolationists of The Chicago Tribune school?

THE personal and almost petty form of the third attack upon the Executive power should not conceal from us the significance of the issues involved. This is, of course, the Republican demand that "Acheson must go." It is not a little curious that those most vociferous in their hostility to communism should thus center their attack upon the man who has done more than any other to stop communism, but it is not the merits of the debate that concern us but the principles.

On the one hand are long-established traditions of Presidential control over the Cabinet and of the President as the sole organ of the Government in the conduct of foreign relations; on the other hand, is the oft-refuted notion that Congress may dictate membership in the President's Cabinet, and the new and original notion that a minority party should control the Government.

It is difficult to know whether to be more astonished at the effrontery of Congressional claims or at their folly. It is, to be sure, the effrontery that is most ostentatious, for the Republican party, defeated in every Presidential election for twenty years, and in every Congressional election but one, is acting as if it actually won the election of 1950! But it is the folly that is most serious. For if successful, in their attack upon the Secretary of State the Republicans may do irreparable harm to the Presidential system. They may succeed in destroying Presidential control over his Cabinet and Presidential control over foreign relations.

LET us look briefly at what is involved here. The Cabinet is a product of our unwritten Constitution—and a very important part. It is made up, traditionally, of heads of departments; these are selected, in the first instance, by the President, report to him, and are subject to dismissal by him. He may consult with them—but is not legally bound to do so. He may prefer to consult with others—a Kitchen Cabinet or a Brain Trust—and is not answerable to Congress for this preference. The relationship between the President and his Cabinet is, in other words, personal and intimate. Whatever the precise nature of that relationship, the nice balance of personality and power, one thing is clear: the President must be in control.

THIS has been the theory of our Government since the second Washington Administration and during most of that time it has been the practice as well. Now and then strong Cabinets—or individual Cabinet members—have tried to dominate weak Presidents. Sometimes — as in Lincoln's case—they have tried to dominate strong Presidents, and come a cropper. Students will recall how Andrew Jackson asserted his command over the Secretary of the Treasury, how the luckless Tyler defied Webster and his colleagues, how Woodrow Wilson fired Lansing because he thought that Secretary had usurped Executive power.

If the principle of Presidential control of the Cabinet is sound generally—as it is—that principle is crucial where the Department of State is concerned. For the President is the sole organ of the Government in the conduct of our foreign relations. This was made clear at the beginning of our history when Washington announced the neutrality proclamation on his own; it has been confirmed by a century and a half of subsequent experience. If there is, then, one part of the Cabinet where Presidential control must be complete it is the State Department. Adams recognized this when he dismissed Pickering for disloyalty; Lincoln recognized this when he put Seward firmly in his place; Wilson recognized it when he forced the resignation of Bryan and dismissed Lansing.

The claim now advanced by certain Senators that they can force the President to oust Secretary Acheson—and by implication dictate Presidential appointment of his successor—is a claim which, if sustained, would reverse 150 years of practice and precedent and make all but impossible the effective conduct of our foreign relations. It is a claim without precedent in history, without basis in law, and without foundation in logic. Like the insistence upon limiting popular will in Presidential elections and upon qualifying the power of the President in the realm of national defense, it is a product neither of necessity, of reason nor of statesmanship, but of partisanship, confusion and folly.

WHAT is at stake in all this is nothing less than the

integrity of our constitutional system. Those who are now so assiduously engaged in undermining that system are not aware of what they are doing. They would doubtless claim the most exalted motives—and we must give them the benefit of the doubt on this.

To a public rightly disturbed by revelations of confusion, incompetence and chicanery in the Executive departments, they appear engaged in a laudable effort to check the unwise exercise of Presidential power.

But more is at stake here than appears on the surface. What the critics and enemies of Presidential power are doing is clear enough. They are engaged in substituting for the Presidential system a bastard product of Presidential and parliamentary, with the disadvantages of neither. If they succeed they will impair and may destroy the constitutional fabric of the Republic.

April 1, 1951

EISENHOWER LIMNS HIS GUIDING CODE

Staff Work, Decentralization, Responsibility Stressed in Single Conference

By JOSEPH A. LOFTUS
Special to The New York Times.

WASHINGTON, Jan. 12—In a single news conference, President Eisenhower underscored today the principles that guide his Administration.

In half a dozen answers to questions on diverse subjects, he gave the country a comprehensive view of his concepts of Government and the standards of public servants under such general headings as:

The staff work principle—responsibility, integrity, duty and decentralization.

His faith in the staff work principle has been revealed many times in his public support of associates who have been under criticism, but never more forcefully than in the case of Wolf Ladejinsky today.

Here was a case in which one agency, the Department of Agriculture, decided for security reasons not to retain an expert, but another agency, the Foreign Operations Administration, decided he was not a risk and hired him.

Ladejinsky Discussed

The President himself made no judgment of the individual in this case. What was important to him was the right of two subordinates to disagree, and his own principle of backing up both of them.

He was not going to try to say what animated either side. The President said: Honest men have reached different answers. More probing questions, he added, should be addressed to those responsible for the decisions.

The President does not have time to deal immediately with every issue, he pointed out; he has to place his faith in men.

Ethics, perhaps even morals, entered into the President's answer to the question whether he would inquire into the "philosophy" of the new chairman of the Civil Aeronautics Board before appointing him, to see if he favored new competitors in commercial aviation.

He would certainly inquire into the man's general philosophy about the relationship of government and free enterprise but—and here he became grimly emphatic for the only time in the meeting— he would never really insult any individual by trying to ask him about his answers in advance to specific questions of every kind, whether he favored a route here or a route there.

General Eisenhower's belief in bringing government closer to the people — decentralization — came out as he answered a question about Nnagara power—should it be a public or private enterprise?

He thought first that was a question for the State of New York. Informed that the Federal Government must issue a license for such a project, and asked whether he had a preference, the President said he didn't think it made any difference whether he had or not. He saill would rather have the state make the decision, but there was to be a Federal decision it should be made without injecting White House influence.

January 13, 1955

President's Liking For Office Growing

By JAMES RESTON
Special to The New York Times

WASHINGTON, May 31 — President Eisenhower spoke about the office of the Presidency today in more laudatory terms than at any time since he entered the White House.

In fact, he not only had a few good words to say for the Presidency as a "very fascinating experience," but he also handed down a significant personal opinion about the Vice Presidency—namely, that a Presidential nominee should get an "acceptable" Vice Presidential running mate or immediately resign.

Summarizing his political experience three years after he returned from Paris to seek the Republican Presidential nomination, the President told reporters at his seventieth news conference that he "still didn't like politics"—in the derogatory sense of that term—but that working with and influencing people in the cause of world peace was "a fascinating business."

"It is the kind of thing," he added, working up enthusiasm for the subject, "that would engage the interest, intense interest, of any man alive.

'Intriguing and Fatiguing'

He continued:

"There are in this office thousands of unique opportunities to meet especially interesting people because the Government here in Washington has become the center of so many things that, again, you have a very fascinating experience in meeting scientists, people that are leaders in culture, in health, in governmental action, and from all over the world.

"There are many things about the office and the work, the work with your associates that are, well, let's say, at least intriguing, even if at times they are very fatiguing. But they are—it is a wonderful experience."

For a man who is supposed to be fretting under the burdens of the office and longing for retirement at his farm in Gettysburg this was an unusual statement.

In the weekly efforts of the reporters to get some kind of indication of how the President was regarding his job, General Eisenhower has carefully avoided being either too enthusiastic or too critical of his duties, but on the whole he has tended to dwell on the burdens rather than on the satisfactions of his office. Today he was more on the enthusiastic side.

Moreover, his remarks about the Vice Presidency took on more than usual interest as a result of the maneuvering that is now going on within Republican ranks for the Vice Presidential nomination in 1956.

Knowland Support Noted

For example, there has been some talk here about the conservative wing's backing Senator William F. Knowland of California for the Vice Presidential nomination.

Mr. Knowland is the Republican leader in the Senate, but he has broken with the President on the Bricker amendment, on several important foreign policy questions, and on the issue of censuring Senator Joseph R. McCarthy of Wisconsin.

This was the background against which the President was asked for his views on the Vice Presidency this morning. It was particularly interesting because the President recalled that he had refused to hand-pick his running mate in Chicago in 1952 but had written five or six name on a piece of paper and had said that any one of them would be acceptable to him. The President declined an opportunity to answer who, in addition to Mr. Nixon, had been on that list, but it is known that Mr. Knowland was one of them.

The President said he didn't know enough about the political scene, when he was nominated in 1952, to pick a candidate. Accordingly, he explained, this was when he had written down the five or six names. When he was asked for his philosophy about picking Vice Presidential nominees now, however, he made it clear to the reporters that he had some definite views on the subject. He said:

"It seems obvious to me that unless the * * * [Vice Presidential nominee] were acceptable to the Presidential nominee, the Presidential nominee should immediately step aside, because we have a government in this day and time when teamwork is so important, where abrupt changes could make so much difference.

"If a President later is suddenly disabled or killed or dies, it would be fatal, in my opinion, if you had a tense period on, not only to introduce now a man of an entirely different philosophy of government, but he, in turn, would necessarily then get an entirely new Cabinet.

"I think you would have chaos for a while. So I believe that * * * if there isn't some kind of general closeness of feeling between these two, it is an impossible situation * * *."

Though the President did not allude to it, the situation in 1841, when William Henry Harrison died and was succeeded by John Tyler illustrates his point. Harrison, a Whig, was the first President to die in office. Tyler, his Vice Presidential running mate, was an aristocratic Democrat, not a Whig, and he was immediately in trouble with Henry Clay and the other leaders of the party.

Indeed, feelings ran so high that the Whigs tried to deny the powers of the Presidency to Tyler on the ground that he was merely a Vice President acting for the dead Harrison. This for a time produced the kind of "impossible situation" to which General Eisenhower referred this morning.

Six Have Died in Office

Since Harrison, six other Presidents have died in office. In other words, seven of the thirty-three Presidents since the beginning of the Republic, or more than one-fifth, have succeeded to the Presidency because of the death of the incumbent.

This is a subject that has interested General Eisenhower ever since he took office. Born Oct. 14, 1890, he is conscious of the fact that, if he runs and is re-elected, he would be, at the end of his second term, the oldest President in the history of the country. Therefore, he has insisted on playing up the role of the Vice Presidency.

"I personally believe," he told the reporters this morning, "the Vice President of the United States should never be a nonentity. I believe he should have a very useful job. And I think that ours [Mr. Nixon] has. Ours has worked as hard as any man I know in this whole Executive Department."

Reporters at the conference drew two inferences from the day's exchanges:

1. The President has taken note of the criticisms within his party that he has been sounding too negative about a second term.
2. If he runs again, he is not going to write "five or six names" on a piece of paper next time a Vice Presidential nomination comes up, but is going to name his own candidate, one "acceptable" to him, and probably not the Republican leader in the Senate.

June 1, 1955

Eisenhower Revisited— A Political Genius? A Brilliant Man?

By RICHARD H. ROVERE

IT has been slightly more than a decade since Robert Frost greeted the dawn of a "next Augustan age . . . of poetry and power" and Dwight D. Eisenhower, ex-President, left Washington for Gettysburg—still an immensely popular figure who, had the law permitted and the spirit and the flesh been willing, could easily have been the man taking the oath of office on January 20, 1961, thus deferring the Augustan age for at least four more years. Eisenhower was held in high esteem for the rest of his life, but throughout most of the sixties those amateurs who sit in more or less professional judgment on Presidents—other politicians, historians, journalists—came more and more into agreement that his eight years in the White House had been a period of meager accomplishment and lackadaisical leadership. The greatest failure, the consensus seemed to be, was one of anticipation. What a prescient statesman could have foreseen in the fifties, the argument runs, was that the ship of state was headed for a sea of troubles, and this the 34th President conspicuously failed to perceive. He lacked foresight and imagination and thus bore considerable responsibility for the difficulties of the three men who succeeded him in the sixties.

RICHARD H. ROVERE is the author of the "Letter From Washington" column in The New Yorker.

Many of those who judged him most harshly until only a few years ago are now having second and third thoughts about the man and his Presidency — thoughts that should ring most agreeably in the ears of those whose faith had never never wavered. Such nay-sayers on the left as Murray Kempton and I. F. Stone are finding virtues in him they failed to detect while he served, and others are making claims for him that not even his partisans made when he sought office or held it. Garry Wills, the eminent Nixonologist, advises us in "Nixon Agonistes" that Eisenhower was "a political genius." Walter Cronkite, who first knew Eisenhower in France during the war and saw him often in subsequent years, recently said that he never thought highly of Eisenhower "either as a general or a President" but that in the post-White House years he discovered that Eisenhower was in actuality a "brilliant" man — indeed, "more brilliant than many brilliant men I have met."

A political genius? A brilliant man? Who ever said or thought that about Eisenhower in his own time? Certainly not Eisenhower himself. It was not that he was lacking in vanity; he had his share, but there is no evidence that he ever thought of himself as possessing a great talent for politics or a towering intellect, and the aspect of his "genius" that Wills calls "realism" would have deterred him from this kind of self-appraisal. He was, and we can be sure that he knew he was, no slouch politically (had he been below average in this respect, he would not have risen in the Army), and he was certainly not lacking in intelligence. But his real strengths lay elsewhere, and the Wills and Cronkite superlatives seem, one has to say, silly.

In the case of Garry Wills, the judgment supports a theory. Wills maintains that Eisenhower all along saw Richard Nixon in the light in which Wills today sees him. In Cronkite's case, the delayed but nonetheless dazzling illumination appeared in the course of many meetings he had with Eisenhower while taping some television interviews in the mid-sixties. He asserts his discovery of the ex-President's "brilliance" but does not tell us how it was made manifest.

For my part, I think the revisionist phenomenon as a whole can be rather easily accounted for — though I do not wish to suggest that new judgments are erroneous simply because they are new or, at least as I see it, obvious in their origins. Seen from 1971, the most important single thing about Dwight D. Eisenhower was that, through luck or good management or some combination of both, *we did not go to war while he was President*. To be sure, we came close on occasion, and his Secretary of State practiced a brand of cold-war diplomacy in which what was called "brinkmanship" at the time—risking war, including nuclear war — was an indispensable strategy. It can also be argued that Dulles's and Eisenhower's Indochina policy made Kennedy's and Johnson's and Nixon's all but inevitable and that, had Eisenhower held office for a third term, he would have found himself at war in Vietnam. The contrary can also be argued, but it does not matter; we were at war when he came to office, and six months later we were out of it, and we did not enter another war during his tenure. Eight years of Eisenhower: seven and a half years of peace. Ten years of Kennedy, Johnson, Nixon: almost ten solid years of war.

WHAT else is there to celebrate about the Eisenhower years? I can think of a few things, but they are of far less consequence and, moreover, they are not blessings of the sort that can be appreciated only in hindsight — unless one chooses to include among them such engineering projects as the St. Lawrence Seaway and the interstate highway system. Though I have myself altered some of my views about Eisenhower over the years, I have felt since 1958 or thereabouts that the country benefited from his first term but would have been better off if he had not had a second. I think I can defend this view in 1971. By 1953 we had made our point in Korea — the expulsion of the invading armies — and it was time for a settlement. It required a Republican President (not necessarily Eisenhower, though of course it helped that he was a successful military man) to end that war on terms short of the "victory" for which Gen. Douglas MacArthur said there was "no substitute." As Harry Truman was to say, he or any other Democrat would have been "lynched" for agreeing to the settlement Eisenhower so cheerfully accepted. It also required a Republican in the White House (though, again, not necessarily Eisenhower) to bring about the downfall of Senator Joe McCarthy.

Eisenhower, to be sure, never took the initiative against McCarthy. He declined to "get into the gutter" with the demagogue, and he tolerated, for a while, a certain amount of high-level appeasement. But the fact remains that 15 months after Eisenhower took office McCarthy was done for. With an active, militant President, the job might have been done somewhat sooner and with less loss of dignity all around. However, a Republican President did not have to be an activist to draw McCarthy's fire. Though nominally a Republican, McCarthy was bound by the nature of his mission in American political life to attack *any* administration, and when in time he attacked his own party's stewardship of affairs, resistance was bound to be offered. It tends now to be forgotten that McCarthy scored most of his triumphs when the Democrats controlled both the White House and Congress, and he would probably have been more difficult to deal with had they remained in control. It has always seemed to me that the election of Adlai Stevenson in 1952, however desirable it might have been in certain respects, would have prolonged both the Korean war and McCarthyism, and I have reason to think that, in later years, Stevenson believed this, too. The country was bitterly divided in 1952, and 20 years of Democratic governance was one of the causes of disunity.

Putting Eisenhower in the White House seemed a way of promoting national unity, which, though hardly the highest of political values, is not one to be disregarded. But by 1956 Eisenhower had achieved just about all that it was in his power to achieve. The war was over, McCarthy was a spent force and the President had, at the Geneva Summit Conference of 1955, helped negotiate a limited but nonetheless helpful *détente* in the cold war.

The second term was anticlimax almost all the way. It was also rather melancholy and at times squalid. The President was not a well man. The Democrats, growing in power in the Congress and knowing that no one would ever again ride Eisenhower's coattails, were openly seeking to embarrass him and passing bills he felt he had to veto. In midterm, he lost the two men he had relied on most heavily. John Foster Dulles left office and soon died, and Sherman Adams, who was general manager at the White House, had to retire because of a clear conflict of interest. Eisenhower began on his own to practice some of Dulles's peripatetic diplomacy, but it didn't work. In 1960, he started for another summit meeting, in Paris, but Nikita Khrushchev refused to make the final ascent because of the unpleasantness over the U-2 affair. Eisenhower set out for Japan, but for security reasons (rioting anti-American students, etc.) was advised to turn around and go home.

THERE is more to being a President than entering or ending wars — and more than instituting or failing to institute political and social change. Style and character are important and closely related aspects of leadership. Eisenhower came to us as a hero — not in the old sense of a man who had displayed great valor but in the newer sense of having been an organizer of victory. His style, though, was anything but heroic. It was in part fatherly, in larger part avuncular. He was not an exhorter — except now and then in campaigns — and as a counselor his performance was as a rule inadequate. He had difficulties with language, particularly when he extemporized. Readers of press-conference texts found his syntax all but impenetrable and often concluded that his thinking was as muddled as the verbatim transcripts. Actually, he was seldom as unclear as he appeared to be when encountered in cold type. Those who listened and watched as he talked were rarely in doubt as to what he was saying. Inflection and expression conveyed much of what seemed missing or mixed up in print. But he was never, to put it mildly, eloquent, never a forceful persuader. He never influenced, or sought to influence, American thought.

Eulogizing Eisenhower in April, 1969, President Nixon said of his late mentor: "For more than a quarter of a century, he spoke with a moral authority seldom equaled in American public life." Nixon did not explain how, when or where the impact of this "moral authority" was felt. Eisenhower was an upright man, a believer in the Protestant ethic he seemed to embody. But the man he twice defeated was no less honorable, and Stevenson had a moral vision that seemed somewhat broader, deeper and less simplistic than Eisenhower's. Do any survivors recall the Eisenhower years as a period notable for elevated standards of morality in public life or elsewhere? In our public life, there were two issues full of "moral" content — McCarthyism and race. On neither did the President personally exercise any of the kind of authority Nixon attributed to him. He was not a McCarthyite or a racist, but he conspicuously failed to engage his personal prestige or that of his office in the struggles against demagogy and racial injustice.

A President can also provide leadership by improving the quality of public life — the quality of the people he appoints and associates himself with, the quality of the acts he and they perform, the quality of the ideas his administration espouses. If in the future, the brief Presidency of Eisenhower's successor is well regarded, it will be largely because of his quest for "excellence." Kennedy brought many first-rate people to Washington, and if one of the lessons they taught us is that first-rate people can sometimes mess things up as badly as third-raters or fourth-raters, it is nevertheless true that some of them performed brilliantly and should continue to serve the Republic for some years to come. No such praise, so far as I am aware, accrues to Eisenhower—except in the case of one institution, the Supreme Court.

He appointed a Chief Justice and four Associate Justices, and all but one of the five (Charles Whittaker, who sat only briefly) served with high distinction. In this respect, Eisenhower's record may be as good as any in history. There was about it, though, a kind of inadvertent quality — as if some architect had achieved splendor while seeking only mediocrity. The President was surprised and in some cases hugely disappointed by the performance of the institution he had created.

In the executive branch, mediocrity was the rule. The one Cabinet member of stature was John Foster Dulles, an imposing man in many ways but also a stiff, self-righteous Calvinist who intensified the cold war as an ideological conflict and sometimes seemed bent on making it a theological one as well — making, as he put it, "the moral force of Christendom . . . felt in the conduct of nations." Nevertheless, Dulles was a man of some intellectual prowess, and nothing of the sort could be said for anyone else in the upper echelons. Eisenhower's measure of expertise in any field was that of the Bitch Goddess: success, usually financial success. Especially in the early days, it was a businessman's administration—to a degree that bred misgivings even in the mind of the first Senator Robert Taft of Ohio, who made no bones about being a spokesman for business but said, when he heard of the first appointments, "I don't know of any reasons why success in business should mean success in public service. . . . Anyone who thinks he can just transfer business methods to government is going to have to learn that it isn't so." Eisenhower's appointments were uninspired and uninspiring; one cannot think of any major office holder whose example might have led any young man or young woman to feel that public life might be a high calling. On the White House staff, there were from time to time highly gifted younger men—Maxwell Rabb, Emmet Hughes, Malcolm Moos — but for the most part they lacked power and visibility, though Moos exerted an influence of a kind when he wrote the line about the "military-industrial complex" into Eisenhower's farewell address.

STILL and all, who in 1971 wouldn't exchange a trainload of mediocrities, incompetents and even pickpockets for a speedy end to the war in Vietnam and to the rancor and discord it has created? There may be some survivors of the better-dead-than-Red set, but even a number of these, one suspects, no longer see the conflict in Vietnam as one that compels a choice between extinction and the surrender of American independence. There was peace under Eisenhower, and the question of historical interest to those of us who survived the ensuing decade is whether this indisputable fact is to be ascribed to his stewardship or to luck or to some combination of both. I lean toward the combination theory, with perhaps a heavier emphasis on luck than others might care to make.

The opportunities for military involvement during his tenure were fully as numerous as those of the Kennedy, Johnson and Nixon years. In Asia, there were Korea, the Formosa Strait and Indochina;

in Europe, Germany and Hungary; in the Middle East, Suez and Lebanon, and in our own hemisphere, Cuba. In some of these troubled areas, intervention was seriously contemplated; in others, it seemed out of the question from the start. In the Suez crisis of 1956, our policy from the onset was to stay out militarily; we made our disapproval so clear to the British and the French that we were not consulted in the planning stages. Nor was there ever much likelihood of our doing anything about Hungary, which erupted just after Suez in the closing days of the Presidential campaign; the Dulles line on Eastern Europe was always that we stood ready to help in the task of "liberation," but it was never much more than a line, and in moments of crisis behind the Iron Curtain — except when there was trouble in Berlin — we looked the other way. In 1958 in Lebanon, we did, at the request of its beleaguered President, land combat-ready Marine and Army units, but there was no combat and the troops spent their time girl-watching on the beaches they had stormed.

But elsewhere the risks were large. Even before his inauguration, Eisenhower went to Korea in search of peace, and in a matter of months a welcome (though far from satisfactory) settlement was made. Politically, in this country, the credit was all his, and if the whole truth is ever known— it will probably never be — it might turn out that he deserves it all. From what is currently known, his principal strategy seems to have been nuclear blackmail — a threat conveyed to our adversaries that if they dragged their feet much longer in the truce talks while pressing on with the war, this country would not consider itself bound to a reliance on conventional weapons. (Eisenhower was never opposed to the use of atomic weapons on moral grounds. He regarded them simply as explosives, suitable for some demolition jobs and not for others. His later assertions about general war's being "unthinkable" in the atomic age were based not on a moral judgment but a military one. He saw no point in a war no one would survive. But tactical "nukes" were another matter.) Maybe that did it, and maybe not. The truth could only come from the other side, and about all we now have on any other factor is Khrushchev's memory of Chou En-lai later explaining that the Chinese losses in Korea had become militarily insupportable. In any case, with all due respect for and gratitude to Eisenhower, one is compelled to wonder what would have happened — what *could* have happened — if the Communists had said that they weren't afraid of our bombs and intended to carry on with the war. Did he have a fallback position? If so, was it credible? Or did he, as seems so out of character, stake everything on a wildly dangerous threat of holocaust? These are questions that await answers that may never come. We know only that the war was terminated the following summer.

IN Formosa we have what is perhaps the clearest case of prudent management during the Eisenhower Presidency. The danger was that we would be suckered into at least an air and sea war against Communist China, which was, as it still is, insisting on the rightness of its claim to sovereignty over Formosa and all the islands between it and the mainland. Eisenhower was, in 1954 and 1955, under enormous pressure from his own military and diplomatic advisers, among them Dulles, from Congressional Republicans and from many prominent Americans who had supported his

'52 GOING ON '60

This photograph, made in Mr. Eisenhower's White House office the month before John F. Kennedy's inauguration, symbolizes one of the dramatic transitions in U. S. history.

candidacy (Henry Luce, for example) to give Chiang Kai-shek every form of assistance he asked for and to help in the defense of every rock in the Formosa Strait — not only to help keep the Generalissimo in his fortress but to aid in preparations for a return to the mainland by the Nationalist armies that had been driven out half a decade earlier. Eisenhower quite clearly had no taste for the entire enterprise. He knew that Chiang alone could never dislodge the Communists, no matter how much matériel we gave him, and he knew, too, that Mao Tse-tung's forces, no matter how many shells they lobbed at the close-in islands, were unequipped for an amphibious invasion of Formosa. So he jollied Chiang with hardware and money and high-level visitors, meanwhile protecting himself with a Congressional resolution and a treaty that pledged direct military assistance to Chiang only if we — not he — determined that Peking's maneuvers in the Formosa Strait were unmistakably preparatory to an assault on Formosa itself.

Had Admiral Radford, then Chairman of the Joint Chiefs, been in control, he might have made that fateful determination a dozen times over. Eisenhower read the cables and studied the maps and found no occasion for invoking those parts of the agreements that could have led to war. His methods were in certain ways dubious — there were questions about the constitutionality of the treaty and the resolution — but at least in the perspective of the present he found a way of averting a war that could have been far costlier than the one we have been in for most of the last decade. There can be little doubt that this was his will and his doing, for, as far as Communist China was concerned, he was the only "dove" in his administration.

Indochina — as always, it is the most complicated of matters. Eisenhower did not get involved militarily, but he may, by his patronage of his Secretary of State and by other words and acts, have made subsequent intervention all but unavoidable. It was Eisenhower who articulated the "domino theory" for Southeast Asia, and we know from his memoirs that on several occasions he seriously considered intervention and was deterred not primarily by political or moral considerations but by military and, to some extent, diplomatic ones. An obvious restraint was our lack of troops and weapons suitable for fighting the kind of war he quite correctly judged it to be. He gave thought to the use of nuclear weapons, and two carriers whose planes had nuclear bombs were in the Tonkin Gulf. But, as Earl Ravenal writes in Foreign Affairs, he "could not identify an appropriate enemy or target to fit the massive nuclear response [and] narrowly declined to intervene."

He considered using ground troops to aid the French but stipulated that under no circumstances would he go it alone—that is, without Asian and European allies. Dulles looked for suitable allies but found none. Had Eisenhower found either the appropriate targets for nuclear retaliation or willing partners in intervention, he might still have come up with an excuse for staying out, for nonintervention seemed almost always his preference; his distaste for war was general and a consistent factor in his reasoning. But it was indisputably under Eisenhower that we made heavy commitments to the powers that were and were to be in Saigon, and it was with Eisenhower's blessing that Dulles set up the Southeast Asia Treaty Organization, at once a political joke and a political disaster.

DURING his time, Eisenhower was not called upon to make good on any of Dulles's commitments in the region. I think it quite conceivable, however, that had he held office in the early sixties he might have found himself a prisoner of his own past and of then-current events and have followed pretty much the course of his successors. One advantage he had over his successors, though, was confidence in his own military judgment, and this might have saved him, us and the Vietnamese from the horrors that were soon to come.

Eisenhower's two terms fell between the two great Berlin crises—the one brought on by the blockade of the Western Sector in 1948 and the one brought on by the Berlin Wall 10 years ago. There was continuous tension over Germany throughout the fifties, but the dangers of war lessened as NATO, whose supreme command he had left to seek the Presidency, grew in strength and as circumspection seemed increasingly to prevail in the Kremlin. These were the early days of the world of two nuclear superpowers, and the "balance of terror" would probably have held under any leadership save that of a madman. Though in Europe Dulles made a good many enemies for himself and for his Government, his European diplomacy was always more traditional and more prudent, as witness the Austrian treaty, than his diplomacy elsewhere in the world, and it would, I think, be rather difficult to fault Eisenhower for his handling of American policy in Germany.

In his memoirs, Eisenhower wrote of the Bay of Pigs as a "fiasco" for which "indecision and untimely counterorders" were "apparently responsible." He did not elaborate. But whatever he meant by Kennedy's "indecision," the original conclusion that we should sponsor an invasion came out of the Eisenhower, not the Kennedy, Administration. As he acknowledged, his military and intelligence people had, with his encouragement, armed and trained the forces in exile and, as we learned in the aftermath, completion of the scheme was urged on the new President by such holdovers as Allen Dulles of the C. I. A. and Gen. Lyman Lemnitzer, Chairman of the Joint Chiefs of Staff. Kennedy took responsibility for the bad show of which Eisenhower was the original producer. Eisenhower was lucky enough to be out of office when the rehearsals were over and the performers were ready for the opening. We can only conjecture as to whether he would have called off the whole business or gone about it in some other way. But he surely bears some responsibility for the policy and for the crucial failure of intelligence which led the executors of the policy to believe that the Cuban people would welcome the invaders as liberators and would take up arms to join them.

I HAVE been somewhat surprised in thinking and writing about the Eisenhower years a decade later to discover that we know a good deal less about the Eisenhower Administration than about most recent ones. The historians haven't got around to it yet, and the few memoirists it produced haven't revealed very much except about themselves. Eisenhower's two large volumes were put together mainly with scissors and paste. Richard Nixon's "Six Crises" is all about Richard Nixon. Sherman Adams's "First-Hand Report" is not first-hand at all but second- and third-hand — dealing extensively with large events, such as Indochina and Formosa, about which he knew little and, despite his closeness to the President, was seldom if ever consulted. Robert Murphy's "Diplomat Among Warriors" is a stiff-necked but instructive work, only part of which bears on the Eisenhower period. Emmet Hughes's "Ordeal of Power" is a thoughtful, critical work, but Hughes's experience was limited to two brief tours in the White House as a speechwriter and political consultant. A few journalists — notably Robert J. Donovan in "Eisenhower: The Inside Story"—produced creditable works, more useful on the whole than the memoirs, but the literature by and large is thin.

"The President of the United States," Alfred Kazin wrote in reviewing the first volume of Eisenhower's memoirs, "had to look up the public record that most of us more or less knew in order to find out what happened during his Administration." This, I think, comes close to the heart of the matter about Eisenhower. For eight years as President, he presided in the most literal dictionary sense—he occupied the seat of authority. But he exercised authority only when there was no other choice. He headed an administration but he rarely administered. In foreign affairs, he stepped in only on certain European questions and when, as Commander in Chief, he was required to make command decisions. In domestic affairs his temperament was in line with his economics — laissez-faire. Whenever possible, he let the Government run itself —and it was possible a good part of the time.

In fairness, though, it must be recalled that Eisenhower never offered himself as an activist. He never pledged innovation or any sort of basic reform. One cannot quite contend that he was the product of a political "draft," but, at least as much as any chief executive in this century, he had the office thrust upon him. His style was well known to those who engineered his nomination and to those who elected and reelected him. Whatever else may be said in dispraise, he did not betray his trust. He construed it rather narrowly, but in doing so he embodied a long tradition and a specifically Republican tradition.

His command decisions seem, in retrospect, to have been generally wise. He was clear about the hazards of intervention in Asia. However, he deputized Dulles to contract military alliances all over the place — confident, perhaps, that in crises he could prevail as he had in Korea. He deputized much to the other Dulles, Allen, too—and it was under him that the C.I.A. became a force in world affairs and undertook such missions as the overturn of Governments in Iran and Guatemala. Eisenhower was anything but an empire builder — he was by almost any definition an anti-imperialist—but it was while he presided that this country began, if not to acquire new holdings overseas, to use its power in an imperial manner far beyond the Americas.

Domestically, he and we marked time. In the first few years, this was more or less defensible. The country might not have sustained him if he had tried to remake it. Once the Korean war was over and McCarthy's fangs had been drawn, complacency was the dominant American mood, and very few Americans were aware of the large structural faults in many of our institutions. In 1954, the Supreme Court ruled that if we were to be true to ourselves and our pretensions, racism had to be deinstitutionalized, but this was about the only blow to complacency until, in the second term, sputnik went aloft and made some Americans wonder about our educational system. With hindsight, we can see that practically all the problems that bedeviled us in the sixties had been worsening in the fifties. It can be said, to be sure, that nearly all of them predated the fifties by decades, even centuries, and that Eisenhower was no more to blame in such matters than most of his predecessors. And this is only just. He was not a cause of any of our present domestic disorders. Neither, though, did he perceive them or heed the prophets of his time—and there were several —who did perceive them.

WHAT Eisenhower clearly lacked—and this was due as much to the education and experience that had been his lot as a servant of his country as to any deficiency of mind or spirit—was the kind of knowledge of the American condition he might have gained if his background had been in politics rather than in the military. He went through most of the fifties and on into the sixties with an image of this country formed in Kansas *circa* 1910. Nowhere is this so dismayingly clear as in the closing words of the second volume of his memoirs, which was published in a dreadful year for this country, 1965—after his successor had met violent death in Dallas, at a time when violence increasingly characterized our race relations, when the generation gap was widening alongside the credibility gap, when our sons were marching by the tens of thousands into the Vietnam quagmire. In that year, he could bring himself to this apostrophe:

"I have unshakable faith that the ideals and the way of life that Western civilization has cherished . . . will flourish everywhere to the infinite benefit of mankind . . . At home . . . our level of education constantly rises . . . Opportunity for the properly ambitious boy or girl increases daily. Prospects for the good life were never better, provided only that each continues to feel that he, himself, must earn and deserve these advantages.

"Imbued with sense and spirit we will select future leaders [who will] keep a firm, sure hand on the rudder of this splendid ship of state, guiding her through future generations to the great destiny for which she was created."

A good man? Of course. A "brilliant" man? Hardly. "A political genius"? If so, the evidence remains concealed. A good President? Better than average, perhaps, and very useful in his early years. But by and large not what the times required. ■

February 7, 1971

OUT OF A GREAT OFFICE, GREATNESS

Two New Studies Illuminate the Role And Powers of Our Chief Executives

THE PRESIDENCY TODAY. By Edward S. Corwin and Louis W. Koenig. 138 pp. New York: New York University Press. $3.

THE AMERICAN PRESIDENCY. By Clinton Rossiter. 172 pp. New York: Harcourt, Brace & Co. $2.95.

By ROBERT K. CARR

THE Presidency is America's most precious political heritage. Our climb to greatness as a nation has again and again depended in most crucial fashion upon the strength and character of this greatest of political offices and upon the wisdom, vitality and courage of the men who have occupied it. Thus Washington almost single-handedly brought the young nation through a trying-out period that was by no means destined from the start to end in success. It was Jefferson as President who determined upon the acquisition of the Louisiana Territory, thereby paving the way for the emergence of the United States as a great power.

It was President Jackson who set in motion the forces that have so largely shaped the character of American democracy. It was President Lincoln who made the far-from-inevitable decision that force of arms should be used to protect the Union against dissolution. In our own century, it was President Wilson who first insisted that the time had come to recognize the great role America must play in world affairs. And it was those two resolute and resilient occupants of the White House, T. R. and F. D. R., who saw clearly the necessity of bringing into being a welfare state capable of providing social and economic justice and incidentally of preserving the free-enterprise system.

COULD Congress have found within itself, without benefit of Presidential leadership, the necessary wisdom and will to action to have made these same positive decisions at the same crucial moments along the way? Was the taking of any one of these momentous steps materially aided by a vital decision of the Supreme Court? The answer to both questions is so surely in the negative as to underscore the fact that the development of America is more closely intertwined with the history of the Presidency than it is with that of any other agency of Government. The Presidency is, in Clinton Rossiter's words, "the most thoroughly American of institutions." It is primarily through this office that our ablest and most energetic statesmen have found it possible to help build a great nation.

Why, then, have so many Americans of our own times become so afraid of a strong Presidency? Why do they strive so unceasingly to deprive the President of vital power and prestige through constitutional amendment? Why do so many seem almost thankful that the accidental forces of politics, personality and one man's faltering heart threaten to convert the Presidency into an office whose occupants will reign but not govern?

Can we yet come through this crisis of nerve with the power and glory of the Presidency unabated? Clearly this is a moment when we desperately need from our best scholars and wisest commentators a careful and dispassionate

Mr. Carr, Professor of Law and Political Science at Dartmouth College, is the author of "Federal Protection of Civil Rights" and "The Un-American Activities Committee."

re-examination of the Presidency and of its true tradition as a great and powerful office. This need is well served in the two books here under review. Both books are modest in scope and purpose. Neither purports to present any striking new historical evidence about the Presidency. Neither attempts to develop a new thesis about the character of the office or about the role it should play in the future. But both books are the work of extremely able and intensely loyal Americans.

The two books have much in common. Each describes the almost miraculous emergence of a monolithic, powerful Presidency from the confusion of the Constitutional Convention. Each carefully traces the history of the office through the more than century and a half that have followed, describing the men who have filled it, discussing the slow evolution of the present fearfully complex office, setting forth the many and varied roles our Presidents have come to play and evaluating current reform proposals pertaining to the office.

Both books are essentially conservative. Both are basically pro-Presidency. Both are distrustful of drastic changes in the office and argue instead that it should be allowed to develop, as it has in the past, in a way that reflects the subtle and felt necessities of a slowly changing political and social order.

"The Presidency Today," by Edward S. Corwin of Princeton and Louis W. Koenig of New York University (both of whom have written elsewhere about the Presidency more profoundly and at greater length), is perhaps most useful in its examination of the sources and nature of Presidential powers. The legal bent of the authors is reflected in their careful analysis of the President's "prerogative 'powers'" (a compound of "personality, crisis and Constitution") and of his statutory or "delegated powers." While recognizing the importance of the former, the authors are anxious that Congress do its best to preserve its position as a co-equal branch of Government by providing the President with a careful statutory basis for his policies and acts, even in time of crisis.

The book also provides a brief, but valuable, restatement of the case for a new type of Cabinet that will include legislative leaders as well as heads of executive and administrative agencies. There is a similar examination of problems of Presidential election and succession.

IN spite of its limited scope and purpose, Mr. Rossiter's little volume, "The American Presidency," is quite possibly the best general book on the Presidency that has ever been written. It is certainly the most readable. It is reassuring to discover one of the ablest of our younger political scientists writing with such grace and unabashed fervor about the Presidency. But this is more than a mere piece of fine writing.

Mr. Rossiter's pages are filled with much carefully organized information about the Presidency, with many striking judgments about the events and men who have made the office great. It contains wise insights into the importance of a strong Presidency in the difficult times through which we are now passing.

There is, for example, no better treatment in print of the varied roles that a strong President plays. In addition to excellent analyses of such well-known Presidential roles as Chief Executive, chief legislator, Commander in Chief and chief diplomat, Mr. Rossiter supplies highly discerning treatments of the President as "Protector of the [domestic] Peace," "Manager of Prosperity" and "Leader of a Coalition of Free Nations."

Mr. Rossiter, who teaches at Cornell and is the author of "Seedtime of the Republic" and other books, does not share the fear of a strong Presidency that seems at times to bother Messrs. Corwin and Koenig. This is not to say that he fails to give proper stress to the many ways in which the American political system balances and restrains Presidential power. Indeed, he directs the attention of his readers to certain of these limiting factors that are often overlooked. One of these is the "natural obstinacy" a President must face in "a whole train of civil servants, most of whom were on the job long before he arrived and will be there long after he has departed." Another is the pluralistic character of American society that makes it impossible for a President to put through a major political program "without the concurrence of a clear majority of the social and economic interests with a stake in the outcome."

ALTHOUGH welcoming these restraints upon a too bold or aggressive President, in the end it is in the Presidency that Mr. Rossiter finds the clearest understanding of social problems, a high ability to act wisely and decisively and a maximum concern for safeguarding the national interest against the divisive force of pressure groups. Since Mr. Rossiter believes that the American national Government today must act both positively and democratically in attacking a host of problems—ranging all the way from providing relief to local communities in time of storm and disaster to strengthening far-distant nations and peoples in the cause of world peace — he naturally values the Presidency as our most effective political instrumentality.

It is perhaps for this reason that, although basically conservative in his own political orientation, Mr. Rossiter finds so much to praise in the records of Franklin Roosevelt and Harry Truman. Mr. Rossiter also has many kind words for the present occupant of the White House. But he is obviously more concerned about the preservation of a strong Presidency than he is about the sensibilities of one man, when he spells out the exacting character of the office in terms like these: "Not only must the President be healthy, in the sense of freedom from ailments; he must have that extra elasticity, given to few men, which makes it possible for him to thrive on the toughest diet of work and responsibility in the world."

And again: "The President cannot be a successful Chief of State if he turns all the little ceremonies and visits over to the Vice President. He cannot lead Congress if he is unwilling to spend hours listening to Congressmen. And he cannot be a vigorous Commander in Chief unless he studies the defense budget item by item. For him as for all of us there is no final escape from hard and pedestrian labor. * * * Above all, he must leave channels open to the political and social pressures that excite imagination and breed sensitivity. Unfriendly visitors, hostile newspapers and free-swinging press conferences are three such channels he must have the insight and bravery not to block off."

May 13, 1956

NIXON CRITICIZES KENNEDY'S VIEWS ABOUT PRESIDENCY

Says Senator Is Confusing 'Table Pounding' With Strong Leadership

EISENHOWER DEFENDED

By RUSSELL BAKER

Special to The New York Times.

MIAMI BEACH, Jan. 16— Vice President Nixon opened his 1960 campaign against the Democrats today by challenging Senator John F. Kennedy's concept of what a strong President should be.

Mr. Kennedy, he suggested, seemed to confuse Presidential "table pounding" with strong leadership.

By characterizing President Eisenhower as a weak leader, he continued, the Massachusetts Democrat indicated that he was more concerned with the manner of exercising power than with getting results.

Senator Kennedy, the front-runner for the Democratic nomination, outlined his concept of a strong President in a speech Wednesday before the National Press Club in Washington.

Rated Eisenhower Weak

He listed Theodore Roosevelt and Abraham Lincoln as strong Republican Presidents but likened General Eisenhower's conduct of the office to Calvin Coolidge's.

Mr. Nixon, in Florida for his first speaking appearance since announcing his own candidacy, defended President Eisenhower's record and set forth his own list of qualities the next President should have.

These, he said, are a thorough grasp of domestic and international problems, the ability to rally support for his policies and the strength to resist the temptation to purely flamboyant action in times of great crisis.

Mr. Nixon spoke in answer to a news conference question for comment on Senator Kennedy's speech.

Nixon Voices 'Respect'

He said he had "real respect" for Mr. Kennedy's analyses of today's problems and regarded him as a "very serious student of public affairs."

But, he went on, his own studies led him to differ with the Kennedy concept of what made a President strong or weak.

"The problem of leadership cannot be described in terms of rigid, black and white categories," he said.

What determines whether a President was strong or weak, he said, were the results he obtained and not the way in which he got them.

"I would disagree with him whole-heartedly that Mr. Eisenhower was not a strong President," Mr. Nixon said. Mr. Kennedy had included Harry S. Truman on his list of strong executives and Mr. Nixon did not entirely disagree.

"Truman was in some respects a strong President," he

said. He cited the Truman decisions to intervene in the Korean War and to drop the atomic bomb on Japan in 1945 as examples of strong leadership.

But, he went on, some Presidents achieved results by "table pounding" while others worked more quietly by "persuasion."

"Truman," he said, "was somewhat of a table pounder. He got some results that way. Mr. Eisenhower is a persuader. He's gotten results too."

Democrats who charge the President with weak leadership object to the way he handled the Suez crisis in 1956, the Iraq-Lebanon crisis of 1958 and the tension over Quemoy and Matsu, Mr. Nixon said.

Yet in each case, the President's response had dispelled the crisis without involving the United States in wars, he said.

Too often, he said, people who clamored for more "leadership" were actually looking for somebody to go out and charge—"lead the people up to the mountain top."

The electorate, he suggested, should be on guard against such men.

Nixon Points to History

"The American people and the free world need in the United States Presidency a man who has judgment, a man who in a crisis will be cool, a man who won't go off half cocked and give an appearance of leadership when, actually, his speaking out might be disastrous to the whole world," he said.

"History will record that Mr. Truman was a strong leader in some respects. I also believe that history will record, despite what Mr. Kennedy says, that Mr. Eisenhower was a strong leader."

The Vice President opened this brief political tour through Florida with an hour and a half question and answer session last night at the University of Florida in Gainesville.

He arrived here shortly after midnight amid the cheers of several hundred partisans assembled at Miami International Airport by the Republican State Committee.

The committee also arranged a mass reception for him this afternoon at the Miami Beach Civic Auditorium. Their objective was maximum political exposure and a heartening of the party faithful by personal contact with Mr. Nixon.

At the reception about 5,000 persons came to grasp his hand and to exchange a few words of small talk. The reception ran through the afternoon and into the evening.

Tonight Mr. and Mrs. Nixon were guests at a private dinner in the Miami Beach home of John S. Knight, publisher of the Knight newspapers.

The dinner had a bipartisan accent. Other guests included Senator George A. Smathers of Florida, probable favorite son candidate for the Democratic nomination, and Senator Stuart Symington of Missouri, an undeclared contender for the same honors. Mr. Symington was here today doing spade work in other sections of Miami to bolster his own candidacy.

January 17, 1959

KENNEDY PLEDGES FIRM PRESIDENCY

Attacks Eisenhower Concept of the Office—Reports on 1950 Interfaith Incident

By JOHN D. MORRIS
Special to The New York Times.

WASHINGTON, Jan. 14—Senator John F. Kennedy proclaimed his intention today of exercising "the fullest powers" of the office if he were elected President.

In a luncheon speech before the National Press Club, the Massachusetts Democrat sharply contrasted his own concept of the role of a President with the one that he attributed to President Eisenhower.

He promised to conduct himself, if elected, in the tradition of such "strong" Presidents as Lincoln, Jackson, the two Roosevelts and Harry S. Truman.

During a question period that followed his speech, Senator Kennedy acknowledged that he had complied with the advice of Roman Catholic authorities in canceling an engagement to participate in an interfaith ceremony at Philadelphia in 1950.

He explained in his answer and in a latter statement, that he had been invited not as a public official but as "the spokesman for the Catholic faith." He could not attend in that capacity, he said, because the ceremony was in connection with a memorial to be located in the sanctuary of "a church of a different faith." For that reason it was not endorsed by the Catholic Archdiocese of Philadelphia.

"Therefore," Mr. Kennedy said, "I felt I had no credentials to attend in the capacity in which I had been asked."

In his speech to an overflow audience, Senator Kennedy said the next President "must above all be the Chief Executive in every sense of the word."

"He must be prepared to exercise the fullest powers of his office—all that are specified and some that are not," the Senator said. "He must master complex problems as well as receive one-page memoranda. He must originate action as well as study groups."

It was Mr. Kennedy's first major speech since announcing his candidacy for the Democratic Presidential nomination. It was at the same time a definitive statement of his views on the Presidency as an institution and an attack on President Eisenhower's conception and conduct of the office.

The address was sprinkled with historical references, the effect of which was to classify President Eisenhower with such "weak" Presidents as Buchanan, Taft and Harding.

"In the decade that lies ahead—in the challenging, revolutionary Sixties—the American Presidency will demand more than ringing manifestoes from the rear of the battle," Senator Kennedy said.

"It will demand that the President place himself in the very thick of the fight, that he care passionately about the fate of the people he leads, that he be willing to serve them at the risk of incurring their momentary displeasure."

In the question-and-answer period, Mr. Kennedy expressed the belief that the vast Presidential powers embraced the ability "to place us in a war * * * without the consent of Congress." He said this was demonstrated in 1950, when Harry S. Truman, as President, committed the United States to fight in Korea.

Won't Take 2d Place

He was also asked whether he would accept the Vice-Presidential nomination if satisfied that his religion played no part in his rejection for first place on the ticket.

"No," he said, "I am not going to accept the Vice-Presidency under any conditions. And I say secondly that I am confident that my religion will not play any decisive part in whether I am nominated. To be frank, I have thought that the issue is overrated."

He drew laughter by adding:

"I will say that anyone who says he is going to run for President and makes a decision even in their own minds that they are going to settle for second prize, then that's what they are going to get."

The Senator, his words flowing so fast that listeners were hard put to get them down, answered a sheaf of other questions, mainly on politics and national issues.

He declined to say whether he would enter the Wisconsin Presidential primary despite a recommendation against it by his brother, Robert F. Kennedy. He suggested that he and Senator Hubert H. Humphrey of Minnesota might arrange for the Minnesotan to enter the New Hampshire primary and for him to contest Mr. Humphrey in Wisconsin.

"Meanwhile," he added, "I am going to advise and consent with my brother Robert."

Senator Kennedy said he was "entertaining" the idea of entering the California primary against Gov. Edmund G. Brown, a favorite-son candidate.

The interfaith incident of 1950, about which Senator Kennedy was asked, was described by the Rev. Dr. Daniel A. Poling in his recent autobiography, "Mine Eyes Have Seen." The episode was reprinted last month in The Christian Herald, a Protestant publication of which Dr. Poling is editor.

Dr. Poling reported that Mr. Kennedy, then a member of the House of Representatives, had agreed to speak at a dinner at the Bellevue Stratford Hotel in Philadelphia celebrating the end of a fund drive to build the Chapel of the Four Chaplains.

The chapel, erected on the grounds of Temple University, memorializes Catholic, Protestant and Jewish Chaplains who went down with the Army transport Dorchester in World War II. Dr. Poling said Mr. Kennedy had withdrawn from the ceremony because the late William Cardinal Dougherty had requested him to do so.

Dr. Poling said today that Mr. Kennedy had declared his support of the doctrine of the separation of church and state. Dr. Poling added:

"Today, though I respectfully read what Senator Kennedy has to say, one thing in his record is unmistakably clear. The church did claim and exercise authority over him while he was in high public office."

Pierre Salinger, a press aid of the Senator, reported that Mr. Kennedy said he had not talked to Cardinal Dougherty about the invitation before declining, as had been reported in some quarters.

At the luncheon today, W. H. Lawrence, president of the press club, asked Senator Kennedy this question:

"Senator, I have perhaps a half-dozen questions dealing with the general subject of a Philadelphia interdenominational religious service to dedicate a chapel up there, and putting them all together, in brief it is this: Did you or did you not refuse to participate in such a ceremony and did you or did you not take this action on the advice of a Cardinal?"

The Senator replied:

"The answer to both questions is—the first question is yes. The answer to the second question is on the interested advice of the leading church groups, which I assume to be the Cardinal [William Cardinal Dougherty of Philadelphia] the answer to the second question is yes.

"I will say that the problem really was that the chapel was located in the sacristy of the Baptist Church there, which is against the rules, customs, procedures of the Catholic Church. When I accepted the invitation I was invited to speak as the representative, according to Dr. Poling's words in his recent article, of the Catholic faith. I was not invited as a public officer. I was not invited as a member of Congress. I was coming there—perhaps it was unwise to accept the invitation in that form but anyway I accepted it in 1950.

"Now without really knowing much about it, my impression had been that it was a memorial to four chaplains. Shortly before I was due to go, I was informed by a clergyman whom I knew, who came from Philadelphia, that the clergy was very upset because I came from a family which had some prominence as a Catholic—that I was representing the church. This was not in accordance with church procedures. I explained this to Dr. Poling. I said I would be delighted to come at any time there was a memorial but it is difficult for me to come without any credentials in the area in which he hoped I would.

"It was an embarrassing incident and I regretted it. It is to be regretted that Dr. Poling nine years later should choose to revive it and draw the conclusion he did. I think the conclusion was a wholly inaccurate one. I have been in Congress for fourteen years and my record in regard to these matters I think a conclusion can be drawn from. But in this case, however, the conclusion he drew was inaccurate. The facts that he described were accurate."

Senator Kennedy later issued a statement "with respect to the invitation tendered to me by the Rev. Daniel Poling."

In the statement Mr. Kennedy said:

"I was invited by the Rev. Dr. Poling to come to attend a dinner in connection with a financial drive to build the Chapel of Four Chaplains. I was happy to accept. A few days before the event, I learned, as Dr. Poling described it in his book, that I was to be 'the spokesman for the Catholic faith.' I was not being invited as a former member of the armed services or as a member of Congress, or as an individual, but as the official representative of a religious organization. I further learned that the memorial was to be located in the sanctuary of a church of a different faith. This is against the precepts of the Catholic Church.

"Because of this fact, the Archdiocese of Philadelphia was unable to support the drive. Therefore, I felt I had no credentials to attend in the capacity in which I had been asked. As the Rev. Dr. Poling noted in his book, a number of Catholics attended the dinner and participated in the drive as individuals, which was quite different. I informed the Rev. Dr. Poling of my difficulty and told him I would have been delighted to have taken part in any joint memorial to which I was invited as a public officer.

"My record on the question of the relationship between Church and state has been written in the past fourteen years in Congress and I believe that my support for the constitutional provision of separation of church and state is well known."

January 15, 1960

Politicians Preferred

PRESIDENTIAL POWER. The Politics of Leadership. By Richard E. Neustadt. 224 pp. New York: John Wiley & Sons. $5.95.

THE ULTIMATE DECISION. The President as Commander in Chief. Edited with an introduction by Ernest R. May. 290 pp. New York: George Braziller. $6.

By TOM WICKER

ONE of the least encouraging spectacles of the recent campaign was that of the President and Vice President of the United States appealing to the voters to elect the "best man" without regard to something they called "politics" and apparently considered distasteful. In so far as this was a stratagem planned by Richard Nixon to beguile registered Democrats into voting for the outnumbered Republicans, it was understandable. However, President Eisenhower's vaunted sincerity as well as the record of his two terms raise the question whether he realizes even yet that a democracy is governed by politics—that more than any office in the world the Presidency demands and rewards political mastery.

In its finest moments, the White House has been occupied by men of political genius—Lincoln, Wilson, Franklin Roosevelt. General Eisenhower has helped to prove that it is no place for a political amateur. Yet, the notion persists that the "best man" is one who is somehow "above politics"—and a perusal of a list of those who have supported General Eisenhower in his two campaigns shows that this persistence is not just among unsophisticated voters.

THESE two books leave no such illusion. Richard Neustadt, in fact, assaults it directly. "The Presidency is a place for men of politics," he concludes. "But by no means is it a place for every politician. * * * If we want Presidents alive and fully useful, we shall have to pick them from among experienced politicians of extraordinary temperament."

In the Neustadt view, it is a matter of political experience and perception to detect and develop the sources of power and to guard its resources. It is a matter of temperament to risk it willingly, to exercise it forcefully for an end—or to dissipate it for nothing.

A subtle blend of both produces Presidential expertness—the ability to function effectively as a national policymaker, leader and administrator. As Harry Truman thought of the problems that would face his successor in 1953, he tapped his desk and said: "He'll sit here and he'll say, 'Do this! Do that!' and nothing will happen. Poor Ike—it won't be a bit like the Army."

How a President makes things happen is what concerns Mr. Neustadt in "Presidential Power." His book is based largely on examples from the Eisenhower and Truman Administrations, and it minutely analyzes the play of influences and events upon three incidents—Truman's dismissal of MacArthur, his seizure of the steel mills and Eisenhower's dispatch of Federal troops to Little Rock.

The author, who served on Mr. Truman's White House staff and is an adviser to President-elect Kennedy, obviously admires Mr. Truman's firmness and courage and gives him high marks for Presidential ability, too. Of General Eisenhower, he agrees with Speaker Sam Rayburn's dictum in 1952: "No, won't do. Good man. Wrong profession."

"The Ultimate Decision," edited by Ernest R. May of Harvard, is concerned not with the Presidency in general but with our war Presidents and how they performed in the special function of Commander in Chief. It is notable here, too, that politician-Presidents—Polk, Lincoln, Wilson, F. D. R., Truman—came off better.

NO President, for instance, ever displayed greater political skill than Mr. Lincoln in mobilizing the interest groups of the country behind the Union war effort and in keeping Republicans and Democrats in some kind of harness. Extending the arts of patronage to military appointments, reports T. Harry Williams in an essay taken from "Lincoln and His Generals," may have "saddled the Army with some prize incompetents" but it also resulted in "good investments in national cohesion."

Mr. May, contributing essays on McKinley in the Spanish-American War and Eisenhower in the recurrent crises of the Cold War, considers both to have been uncertain Commanders in Chief. Marcus Cunliffe, though kinder to Madison than most historians, leaves almost intact the Virginian's reputation for ineptitude in the War of 1812.

Leonard D. White on Polk, William R. Emerson on F. D. Roosevelt and Wilber W. Hoare on Truman contribute generally admiring but unworshipful estimates of their subjects. The volume's most striking analysis is Mr. May's discussion of Woodrow Wilson. The World War I leader is seen as a commander who refused to act as one, in order to avoid post-war political commitments and entanglements.

"When the armistice was negotiated," Mr. May writes, "[Wilson] could and did demand acceptance of his principles, his conditions for peace, not only by the enemy but by the Allies as well. He evaded duty as Commander in Chief in order to do his larger duty as President of the United States."

Mr. May concludes that all our war Presidents, even Madison and McKinley, "whether wisely or stupidly, rightly or wrongly * * * waged war as politicians—with a sense of responsibility to public opinion as well as to national interest abstractly conceived."

For the future, "the increasing complexity of the Commander in Chief's tasks may, in fact, make it all the more important that his choices be those of a politician rather than those of a technician." Amen to that.

December 18, 1960

When Presidents Take Pen in Hand

Whether they are statesmanlike or 'saucy,' deal in principles or personalities, books by Chief Executives reveal the man.

By ANDREW HACKER

GENERAL EISENHOWER'S announcement that he intends to write the memoirs of his eight years in the White House should have come as no surprise. For every President in this century who has left office alive or in good health has succumbed to the temptations of authorship. The exceptions were William McKinley, Warren G. Harding and Franklin D. Roosevelt, all of whom died while President, and Woodrow Wilson, who was tragically ill until his death in 1924. But we do have books—autobiographies, memoirs, lectures — by Theodore Roosevelt, William Howard Taft, Calvin Coolidge, Herbert Hoover and Harry S. Truman. If for no other reason than the perpetuation of what is fast becoming a political tradition, it is welcome news that Dwight D. Eisenhower will make his addition to this growing shelf.

Most of our Presidents have been practicing politicians for the greater part of their adult lives. In consequence, they have had little time for book-writing and meager opportunity to reflect, in this manner, on the larger implications of political life. Even prior to 1900, when a career in politics was less demanding, there were few instances of serious Presidential authorship.

Jefferson, Madison, and the two Adamses wrote numerous essays and articles, but it is stretching a point to consider more than one or two of these "books" in the conventional sense. The same must be said for James K. Polk's "Diaries" and Grover Cleveland's lectures on "Presidential Problems." Ulysses S. Grant penned his "Memoirs" while at death's door, not because he felt any literary urge but because their sale would insure a measure of security to his family.

ANDREW HACKER *is an assistant professor in the Department of Government at Cornell.*

PERSONAL MEMOIRS

U. S. GRANT

Theodore Roosevelt

AN AUTOBIOGRAPHY

In this century the picture is a brighter one for the compilers of Presidential bibliography. Theodore Roosevelt and Eisenhower wrote books on non-political subjects before entering the White House, and Wilson and Kennedy authored noteworthy political texts prior to becoming President. But if a generalization of any sort is in order in this instance, it is that the typical Chief Executive has postponed embarking on the author's craft until the leisurely days of retirement.

AS might be expected, the books produced by our author-Presidents reflect the personalities of the men who wrote them. Theodore Roosevelt's "Autobiography" is ebullient and his chapters on the Presidential years leave no doubt that he had a grand time in office. Coolidge's "Autobiography" on the other hand, is terse in style, reserved in manner, and uncommunicative on political information.

On the whole, however, the Presidential books tend to take one of two forms. The first sort is statesmanlike in tone rather than political, it is respectable if not sententious, it dwells on principles instead of personalities. Under this heading come the slim volumes of Taft and Coolidge and the multi-volumed memoirs of Hoover. Interestingly enough, these three men all took a conservative view of the Executive office and a restrained outlook on Presidential power.

In a series of lectures entitled "The Presidency: Its Duties, Its Powers, Its Opportunities, Its Limitations," which were given at the University of Virginia in 1916, Taft said: "The truth is that, great as his powers are, when a President comes to exercise them he is much more concerned with the limitations upon them, to see that he does not exceed them, than he is affected, like little Jack Horner, by personal gratification over the big things he can do." Which is, of course, to say that Taft's own conception of the Presidency was a limited one. It was by choice that he never exercised the great power inherent in the office. He defined his role, to use the phrase of the political scientist Richard E. Neustadt, as that of a clerkship.

COOLIDGE echoed this sentiment. His sojourn in the White House may have been the culmination of a political career, but it is difficult to find any "politics" in his reminiscences. Neither legislation nor executive decisions nor personalities are mentioned. But his reflections in his autobiography—in the chapter, "Presidential Duties"—are, nevertheless, revealing of the man. Among other things, we are told:

"One of the doormen at the White House was an excellent barber, but I always preferred to shave myself with old-fashioned razors, which I knew how to keep in good condition. It was my intention to take a short walk before breakfast, which Mrs. Coolidge and I ate together in our rooms. For me there was fruit and about one-half cup of coffee, with a home-made cereal made from boiling together two parts of unground wheat with one part of rye. To this was added a roll and a strip of bacon, which went mostly to our dogs."

Hoover's "Memoirs," written two decades after he left the White House, also echoed Taft's conception of a limited Presidency: "I had little taste for forcing Congressional action or engaging in battles of criticism," he wrote. Indeed, it was his view, as President, that "the independence of the legislative arm must be respected and strengthened."

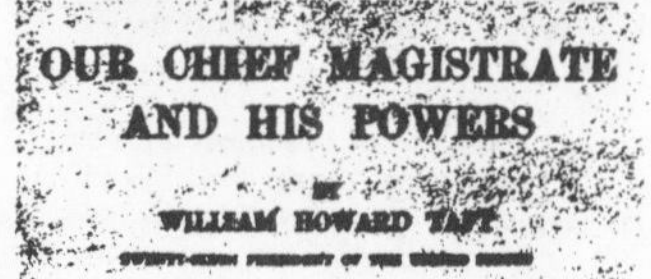

OUR CHIEF MAGISTRATE AND HIS POWERS

BY WILLIAM HOWARD TAFT

THE MEMOIRS *OF* Herbert Hoover

Contrary to the impression given by unfriendly critics, Hoover did know that there was an economic depression. While his memoirs offer no searching analysis as to what might have caused that severe downturn, its existence is acknowledged and the inauguration of public-works projects to alleviate the distress is recorded: "I recommended the San Francisco Bridge as the type of public improvement which should be undertaken; I used it as an example of constructive remedy for unemployment." But he seems to have been less concerned with relating how many people were put to work for how long and more interested in assuring the reader that the tolls charged on the Golden Gate Bridge eventually repaid the initial Reconstruction Finance Corporation loan—with interest.

HOOVER, too, forbears from bringing in the interplay of personalities and the clash of political interests. His recording of history is dignified but not intimate, and it leans on documents already in the public domain rather than on personal impressions.

There is reason to believe that Dwight D. Eisenhower's memoirs will be much like Hoover's. Eisenhower is already the author of "Crusade in Europe" which, since its publication in 1948, has sold over a million copies in the United States and a quarter of a million abroad. In this sober account of the invasion and its aftermath, the magnitude of the events described tends to overshadow the role of the author. When his Presidential memoirs are published, it is safe to assume that they will run to at least two volumes and will probably reproduce generously from his official messages and public pronouncements. There is the suspicion, in short, that it will be a conservative record of a conservative Administration.

While he was in the White House, President

Eisenhower refused to discuss personalities and it is doubtful if he will do so in his published memoirs. This is not to predict a disappointing book. For his were the years of crisis in Korea, French Indochina and the Formosa Strait. They were the years of Joseph McCarthy, Sherman Adams and Little Rock. Whatever Eisenhower has to say about these matters will be of interest and importance. For he was at the center of the scene and he alone was charged with chief responsibility.

BUT at least one warning is in order: it is altogether possible that Eisenhower will refrain from speaking his full mind on the major problems of his Administration. And there will always be the accusation made by some that he, like Hoover, was not fully aware of the implications of the events swirling about his head. But even if this is so, it is itself a significant historical fact. And the silences or omissions in Presidential memoirs can be just as memorable as the explicit references.

Theodore Roosevelt's "Autobiography" and Truman's "Memoirs" stand in contrast to the other Presidential books. Both are saucy and highly personal. Roosevelt and Truman talk less of "the Presidency" in magisterial tones and more of what they did as individuals. At the same time, both men looked on the Executive office as one invested with elastic powers and neither apologizes for taking such an expansive view.

Roosevelt wrote: "My view was that every executive office, and above all every executive officer in high position, was a steward of the people bound actively and affirmatively to do all he could for the people, and not to content himself with the negative merit of keeping his talents undamaged in a napkin." And there then follows an account of how he exercised this power in the anthracite coal strike of 1902.

And Truman: "I believe that the power of the President should be used in the interest of the people, and in order to do that the President must use whatever power the Constitution does not expressly deny him." And then there follows a depiction of how he used this power to seize the steel mills in 1952. These are forthright sentiments — accompanied by forthright action — and they reflect the men who uttered them.

SOME commentators have suggested that both these Presidents were better talkers than performers. Roosevelt discoursed grandly on using a big stick and subduing the trusts, but his legislative record was a meager one. Truman initiated elaborate Presidential commissions on civil rights and health insurance, but he was unable to persuade Congress to act in these vital areas. Yet for Truman, at least, there is a significant record of Executive accomplishment: the atomic bomb, the Berlin blockade, Korea, the steel seizure and the Marshall Plan. But most of these measures were carried out independently of legislative consent and they threw some doubt on the view that the test of Presidential power lies in how far its holder can bludgeon the Congress into supporting his program.

The books of these two activist Presidents make delightful bedtime reading. In the chapters of his "Autobiography" dealing with the Presidency, Roosevelt named names, especially

Harry S. Truman

VOLUME ONE YEAR OF DECISIONS

those of Congressmen who seemed to him to stand in his way. Senators Aldrich and Hale and Speaker Cannon —all fellow Republicans—are characterized as so many roadblocks. "I was forced to abandon the effort to persuade them to come my way, and then I achieved results only by appealing over the heads of the Senate and House leaders to the people, who were the masters of both of us."

HE is especially outspoken in his assessment of Taft, his hand-picked successor for the Presidency, who is criticized for holding the "narrowly legalistic view that the President is the servant of the Congress."

By far the most prolific of Presidential authors, Roosevelt produced, in all, twenty-four volumes, including, besides his famous account of "The Winning of the West," a naval history of the War of 1812, journals of big-game hunting in Africa and Brazil, and biographies of Oliver Cromwell, Thomas Hart Benton and Gouverneur Morris.

Roosevelt's chapters on his White House years are refreshingly egotistical; the same may be said for Truman's "Memoirs" as a whole. Not only does he take personal responsibility for his acts, but he takes personal credit for the origination of ideas. The Marshall Plan is recorded as his brain child and so is the controversial civil-rights plank in the 1948 campaign platform. The choice of John Sparkman as Stevenson's running mate in 1952 is made out to be a Truman decision as well.

The point, of course, is that policy decisions such as these are hammered out in conferences and the origination of ideas must not be confused with the authority of the chairman.

At the same time, Truman reproduces his personal correspondence—letters sent and letters received—and this stands in stark contrast to Hoover's reliance on public papers. He recounts his interviews with domestic subordinates and foreign coequals and is generous in quoting what actually went on in the interchanges. Not simply Harry Truman himself but Stalin and Churchill, Henry A. Wallace and Douglas MacArthur come vividly to life.

The conclusion must be that Truman's "Memoirs" are a model which Eisenhower would do well to emulate. They have few pretentious passages on the "philosophy" of the Fair Deal and no arid recitals on the "nature" of the Chief Executive's office, but are frank and informal.

BUT can the memory of a memoir-writer be trusted? The answer is that even if the writer surrounds himself with all the available records he is bound to suffer from certain mental blocs, to fall victim to periods of self-deception. Everyone who has been close to the White House can cite an instance of such Presidential lapses. For example: Francis Biddle had been Franklin D. Roosevelt's Attorney General and, as is customary, he submitted his resignation to Truman when the latter succeeded to office. Truman's account is short and simple: "I asked Biddle whom he would recommend to take his place, and he suggested Tom Clark."

Now, to those familiar with the Biddle-Clark relationship in the Department of Justice, the idea that Biddle would suggest Clark as his successor is nothing short of fantastic. At all events, Biddle has said that he was never asked or consulted on who was to succeed him; Truman simply confronted him with Clark as an accomplished fact.

The only point to be made here is that even a President's memory can be vague and that even Presidential memoirs can be fallible. Fortunately we have sufficient additional sources by which to check doubtful or conflicting statements. And, it may be added, without doubts or conflicting statements, there would be nothing for the historians to do.

TRUMAN and Eisenhower live in an age of recording instruments, filing cabinets, and multiple copies. The White House and its inhabitants keep elaborate records that are as carefully filed as they are voluminous. By custom the White House papers belong to the President himself, and he may take them back to Independence or Gettysburg at the end of his term. All future memoirists may rely on extensive research in original documents, both official and unofficial; not only state papers, but informal memoranda and personal correspondence may be drawn upon.

There has been no serious objection to this carting away and subsequent use of private papers. It is true that the Secretary of Agriculture, for example, is supposed to leave his papers behind because they are not his property but that of the Department of Agriculture. Even Henry Morgenthau, who made extra copies of his correspondence at his own expense, was asked to return them to Washington when it was learned that he had them in his private possession.

A PRESIDENT is given a free hand in this sphere, and the policy is a good one. The only danger is that a memoir-writer may choose to overlook certain documents which do not display him in the best of lights. However, so long as the entire files are eventually released to a library open to scholars and the public, these momentary acts of vanity can be tolerated.

As has been noted, Wilson and Kennedy both made substantial marks for themselves as writers prior to coming to the White House; one as a Professor of jurisprudence and political economy at Princeton and the other as a Pulitzer Prize-winning biographer. The first question that arises is how

DWIGHT D. EISENHOWER

Crusade in Europe

much these pre-Presidential books reveal about the political roles their authors were later to play.

Wilson's famous "Congressional Government" was written while he was a 28-year-old graduate student at Johns Hopkins. In its first fifteen years it ran into fifteen printings and it was regarded by many as the definitive textbook on the functioning of American government. The chief theme was that Congress "has virtually taken into its own hands all the substantial powers of government," that it is the lot of the President to "wear a clean and irreproachable insignificance."

The President's seal.

This view of legislative supremacy has plagued all Presidents who have sought to take an activist role, and Wilson himself was later to regret and repent his youthful analysis. He revised his opinions substantially in his "Constitutional Government," published four years before he entered the White House, and this lesser-known book of his might well have been taken as a guide to the way he would comport himself as President.

"He is the representative of no constituency, but of the whole people," Wilson wrote of the Chief Executive. "When he speaks in his true character, he speaks for no special interest. If he rightly interpret the national thought and boldly insist upon it, he is irresistible * * *." These were the words of an academic; and who can tell in advance if he was the man who could bring them to life when power was in his hands?

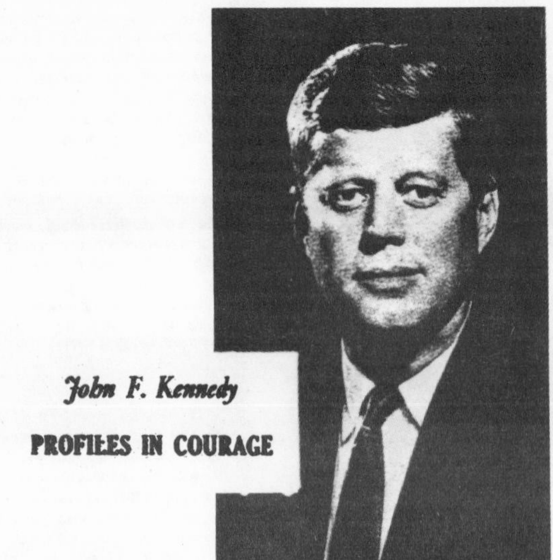

AND what of John Fitzgerald Kennedy? Like Wilson, his first book was the product of his student days. "Why England Slept," written while he was a Harvard senior, has some important reflections on the conflict between democracy and dictatorship, on the relationship between leadership and public opinion in a free society.

"We must be prepared to recognize democracy's weaknesses and capitalism's weaknesses in competition with a totalitarian form of government," wrote this young man who, just a short time before had become old enough to vote. And the chief weakness is the apathy of the ordinary citizen, the man in the street who is unwilling or unable to recognize the threat of external aggressors. The villains of the young Kennedy's book are not Stanley Baldwin or Neville Chamberlain, but the tens of millions of somnolent Britons who refused to take Hitler seriously.

The dilemma of whether it is the political leaders or "the people" who are to be held chiefly responsible for the course of a nation's policy is an old and vexing one. One senses that the future President had hopes that an aroused and enlightened citizenry of a democracy might show their leaders the way.

SOME of this faith is missing from "Profiles in Courage," written a decade and a half later when Kennedy was a Senator from Massachusetts. Here the emphasis is on highly individualistic Senators of the past, men like Daniel Webster and Thomas Hart Benton, George Norris and Robert A. Taft. These legislators, liberals and conservatives alike, are depicted as rising above the passions and interests of their local constituents. While Kennedy does not berate the average voter for his short-sightedness, he honors those leaders who pursue national principle rather than parochial popularity.

What "Profiles in Courage" tells us is that Senator Kennedy admired courage. It is interesting to note that virtually all of the heroes of his book paid the price of individuality: they rose no higher than the Senate and some of them lost what office they had.

In this, John Kennedy has been different. He has aspired to the Presidency and this must inevitably mean that courage must be tempered with compromise. There is little doubt that he knows that the Presidency of the United States can only be achieved at a cost. But he clearly assigns high values to courage, vigor, and political leadership. If he remains the man who wrote "Why England Slept" and "Profiles in Courage," then he may have some surprises in store for us.

August 27, 1961

Master of 'The Art of the Possible'

By RUSSELL BAKER

WASHINGTON.

FEW men in American history have come to the Presidency so well prepared for the task as Lyndon Baines Johnson. A leader by temperament, he has worked intimately with Presidents and statesmen for 25 years. For half a decade, in the Eisenhower era, he wielded power second in dimension only to the President's own. He has been called by one of his critics a man "of great and proven political genius," and few of his bitterest old enemies—and they are many—would dispute the judgment.

To the Presidency he brings a fierce personal pride that may be the equal to President de Gaulle's, an energy that is utterly cyclonic, a Rooseveltian zest in crisis and, at the moment of decision, an iron will. None of the seven other Vice Presidents in history who have preceded him to the highest office, upon the death of Presidents, had been so thoroughly educated in the work to be continued.

Much has been made in the past week of the contrasts between President Kennedy and President Johnson—the cool, intellectual Eastern millionaire and the flamboyant, emotional Southwesterner who started as a country school teacher in the hard-scramble Texas hills and had to come up struggling and clawing. "My daddy used to wake me up at dawn, he often reminisced, saying, 'Hurry up, boy, all the other boys in the county are already two hours ahead of you.'"

THE obvious contrasts in style, however, have tended to obscure the essential similarity between the two. In their approach to government, both were pragmatists acting with a highly developed sense of the limitations of power.

"Pragmatist" is not the kind of word that Lyndon Johnson is at ease with; he prefers to say that government is "the art of the possible." But whatever the terminology, in this he and Mr. Kennedy were of the same spirit. And so, despite the dashing style that characterized Mr. Kennedy's leadership, it soon became apparent that the Kennedy Administration would not be fundamentally different in philosophy from what might have been had Mr. Johnson won their 1960 fight.

Indeed, in his handling of domestic affairs, Mr. Kennedy seemed only to be carrying out lessons he might have learned from the back row of the Senate, when Mr. Johnson, as Senate leader, was expounding "the art of the possible."

The differences in style, of course, are not to be minimized, for style in an office as personal as the Presidency becomes substance and content. Mr. Kennedy's seemed to flow from his cerebral approach to government and his controlled intellectual responses to its trials. President Johnson, by contrast, is an instinctual man whose politics were inherited, whose philosophy grew out of experience and whose actions have usually hinged as much on his reflexive assessment of the country's mood as on detached mathematical calculation.

"This Senate," he once told an interviewer during his leadership days, "is like a dangerous animal that you're trying to make work for you. Push him a little bit, and he'll go. Push him a little bit harder, and he may go or he may balk and turn on you. You've got to sense just how much he'll take and what kind of mood he's in each day, and if you lose your feel for him he's going to turn around and go wild."

What, then, are the assets that President Johnson brings to the White House? His energy, his long experience in Congressional affairs, his unsurpassed political intuition, his relatively intimate knowledge of what has gone across Mr. Kennedy's desk these past 34 months, a Presidential temperament, an experience of decision-making and of large responsibility.

THERE is more. He will start with an immense reserve of Congressional respect and goodwill. The Southern committee chairmen who paralyzed the Kennedy program this year are old friends who are likely to feel an emotional commitment to his success such as they never felt to President Kennedy's.

Many of them must feel that he is their creation.

RUSSELL BAKER is a reporter and columnist in The New York Times Washington bureau.

They brought him to the leadership in 1953 and cooperated with him for eight years to make his leadership a triumph. Moreover, as a Southerner, he is one of them. A successful Johnson Presidency could conceivably end the galling century-old Presidential bar against the South. And finally, they respect him as a peer.

"You've got to remember," one Southern Senator confided just prior to Mr. Kennedy's Inauguration, "that a lot of us up here still look on Jack as a junior Senator who used to sit in the back row."

IN addition, he brings a commitment to the concept of the "strong" Presidency. His political idols—besides John Garner and the late Sam Rayburn, who taught him the trade—are Franklin Roosevelt and Harry Truman. He believes that they showed how to lead. He is fond of telling how Gen. Lucius Clay, after making a lonely plea for the idea of supplying Berlin by air when the 1948 blockade began, started out of Mr. Truman's office convinced that he had lost the argument. As Mr. Johnson tells the story, the general paused at the door and caught the President's eye, and Mr. Truman said, "Clay, you'll get your planes."

Few things exasperated him more during the late nineteen-fifties than demands from his party that he use the Senate to lead the country beyond President Eisenhower's vision of where it could go. "That's like putting me in the cabin of a four-engine jetliner and locking me out of the cockpit and telling me to fly it to Los Angeles," he once complained. "There's only one man who can lead. That's the President."

And, finally, among his assets are his intuitive feel for the mood of the country and his skill at sensing the consensus and developing the accommodation necessary to realize it. The litany of his Senate leadership was the plea from Isaiah to "come let us reason together."

THE history of his Senate career suggests that he will seek to grasp the dominant mood of the country on the great issues before it, isolate the fringes and strike hard, ruthlessly if necessary, to enforce his decisions.

Personally, the new President is a tower of paradoxes, a man of chameleon moods and inexpressible complexities. He is easy to caricature but impossible to paint, and most of the popular notions about him are either distorted or misleading. He can be imperial and humble, impetuous and patient as a statue, vain and radiant with human warmth, sentimental to the point of tears and hard as granite, garrulous and infuriatingly close-lipped, exasperatingly coy to his closest associates and incredibly confidential to a stranger he is meeting for the first time.

HIS demands on his staff and his treatment of them is frequently demonic, yet his kindnesses to them are incessant, and their devotion to him borders on the religious. For his friends, he is capable of the most considerate kindness. A few years ago, a friend who had just written a book and been asked to sit in a local bookshop to autograph copies was startled to see a large part of the Senate walk in for autographs.

As someone later explained, "Lyndon heard his friend was scared to death that nobody would show up, so he sent the Senate down to guarantee a good turnout."

As a public speaker, he lacks the magic that moves crowds. His accent is Southern, his voice hoarse and high-pitched. As a Senator, he rarely spoke at length in the formal style. But, like so many successful politicians without great platform style, he can be mesmeric and irresistible in the small group. He seems to require close personal contact to project his personality. He has said of himself, "I have to press palms and feel the flesh."

In the intimacy of the Senate chamber, his personality was at its most effective. A rangy, broad-shouldered giant with a cowpuncher's lope and hands always in motion, he seemed constitutionally incapable of repose.

He roamed the Senate floor constantly, pumping a hand here, clapping a back there, seizing this lapel, whispering to that Senator, leading this man back to the cloakroom, conferring with a secretary, pausing now and then to delight some vaporous orator with the announcement that he would be proud to tell his grandchildren he had served in the Senate with this paragon of statesmanship.

WATCHING him go after a vote was one of the rare delights of the Senate. It was a form of hypnosis by movement, which seemed to leave the victim pliantly comatose. He might saunter up to his man and begin by seizing his lapels. Then the big hands would start flashing around the fellow's ears and the leader would lean into him, nose to nose, talking constantly, pounding fist into palm, kneading the victim's lapels, bobbing and weaving, withdrawing abruptly, then thrusting his face just as abruptly against the gentleman's own, forcing him to retreat in mental disarray.

Immensely sensitive to the slightest affront to his dignity and capable of tigerish rebuttal, he is nevertheless able to joke about himself. When first elected to the Senate, for example, his majority was a fantastically skimpy 87 votes, whence the early nickname "Landslide Lyndon." In a proper mood, however, he will tell the story of "Little Juan," who, found crying on a curbstone and asked why, explained, "Because my father didn't come to see me."

"But your father has been dead six years," the story goes. And Juan replied, "Yes, but last Tuesday he came back to vote for Lyndon Johnson and he didn't come to see me."

Lyndon Johnson, the political man, was born into the impoverished rural Southwestern society that bred so much bitterness for the big-city machines and so much reflexive loyalty to the Democratic party. His childhood memories are of hard work, hard times and poor people, and inevitably, with the coming of the New Deal, Mr. Johnson gave his heart to Franklin Roosevelt.

As he matured in the Senate leadership during the nineteen-fifties, however, his early liberal background proved useless for promoting his ambitions to the Presidency. Mr. Johnson's regional political liabilities—the need to protect the oil and gas industry, the less than total commitment to civil-rights legislation, the Southern accent and all the rest—brought him the implacable opposition of the Northern liberals, and his 1956 campaign for the nomination was dismissed as "a Southern candidacy."

DURING the four years that followed, he struggled to free himself of the "Southern" label. He put through the Civil Rights Act of 1957, the first since Reconstruction, and the subsequent Civil Rights Act of 1960 in an effort to reduce Northern hostility. In passing, it must be said that he is without racist feelings and seems to regard the plight of the Negro with the same instinctive pity he still holds for the "little man" of his early New-Deal days.

He tried, too, to change his public image by presenting himself as a Westerner and sitting in at meetings of the Senate's Democratic Western bloc. It was not enough, of course, and despite a good deal of personal sympathy from some of the powerful Northern chieftains, he received little delegate support outside the South when he challenged Mr. Kennedy in 1960.

It is being freely predicted that the young intellectuals who have made the Washington atmosphere so yeasty under the Kennedys are not long for the new Administration. This may be so, but the implication that Mr. Johnson is anti-intellectual would be erroneous. As Senate leader, his operating method was to surround himself with "idea men" who drew up programs for him to enact. Mr. Johnson's concept of the leader's responsibility was that he should concentrate his powers on bringing ideas to realization.

The type of men on whom he relied were people like Dean Acheson, the ultimate Ivy League intellectual - activist, and Gerald Siegel, the brilliant young Harvard Law man, who was brought from Cambridge to hammer out the Civil Rights Act of 1957.

Others who typify the kind of men whom President Johnson respects are David Lawrence, the former Governor of Pennsylvania and a veteran machine politician; Carl Rowan, the Pulitzer Prize reporter who served President Kennedy at the State Department and as Ambassador to Finland, and Senator Hubert H. Humphrey, the assistant Senate leader, who is Mr. Johnson's idea of what the effective liberal should be.

It is useless, of course, to attempt to tell a Presidential fortune from the history of the man's previous performance. It it trite, but nonetheless true, to say that the White House works an unpredictable alchemy upon the men who occupy it. All that can be said of Lyndon Johnson, as he takes up his duties, is that he looks far more promising than any Vice President who has ever succeeded to power under similar circumstances before him.

His personality and career seem to indicate the chemistry that makes good Presidents. But how he will change—and change he almost certainly will—no one can foresee.

PRESIDENT TELLS STORY ON HIMSELF

At House Lunch He Recalls Rayburn's Power to Deflate

Special to The New York Times

WASHINGTON, Dec. 4 — President Johnson told a story today and applied it to himself.

He slipped out of the White House to lunch with his former Democratic Congressional colleagues from Texas in the Capitol. There he told his story.

His political mentor, the late Speaker Sam Rayburn of Texas, he said, went to the White House to swear in Harry S. Truman after the death of President Roosevelt.

Mr. Rayburn, he said, told Mr. Truman:

"You know there will be some people around you who will try to build a wall around you. They have never been so close to the seat of power and they'll want this position for themselves.

"Now some farmers from Missouri will want to see you and they'll come to Washington, but someone in the White House will say you can't see them right away and make an appointment for later.

"But the farmers can't afford to stay around for four days and they know they have to catch that 5 o'clock train back to Missouri. So they do.

"Now there will be a lot of self-serving people, special interests, who are around here and can't afford to wait for an appointment. Then when they're summoned, they'll come sliding in here on their vests and tell you over and over that the President is a smart man, smarter than anyone else.

"Now Harry, you and I know he ain't."

Amid laughter and applause, Mr. Johnson added:

"And you all know he ain't."

Advised Not to Attend

The President said he had been advised by White House aides not to attend the luncheon, a regular Wednesday meeting, which he had attended for years as a Representative, Senator and as Vice President.

"But I'm not going to be shut behind the wall," he went on. "And I know that there is no man in the Texas delegation who would hesitate to tell me when I'm wrong about something."

He apparently had decided to attend on the spur of the moment, or had suddenly remembered it was the meeting day. He had invited two newsmen friends to luncheon at the White House and took them along to the Capitol for roast beef.

His two-car entourage drove up to Capitol Hill with a motorcycle escort, lights and sirens on. Capitol guards, hastily alerted, stood at the entrance to the private dining room to reinforce the Secret Service. The room is opposite the entrance to the main House restaurant on the first or street floor of the House side.

The story the President told had often been recounted by Mr. Rayburn in various versions. The Speaker once recalled he had told it to President Eisenhower, Mr. Truman's successor.

He said General Eisenhower had laughed, "and I said, 'You better not laugh, the story applies to you, too.'"

It was recalled that Mr. Truman, on his first day in the Presidency, April 13, 1945, went to Capitol Hill for lunch.

He called Leslie L. Biffle, then secretary to the Senate, and asked him to arrange a luncheon in the secretary's office with Congressional leaders. It was attended by thirteen Senators and four Representatives.

Most Texas Democrats were surprised by Mr. Johnson's visit. One said "he just called up before he left the White House and asked if we could make room for him."

As the President left, he put down three $1 bills to pay, he said, for himself and his two companions, Philip Potter and Gerald E. Griffin of The Baltimore Sun.

December 5, 1963

PRESIDENT FAVORS A STUDY OF OFFICE

Tells Scholars He Sees Need for Modern Re-evaluation

By JACK RAYMOND
Special to The New York Times

WASHINGTON, April 30 — President Johnson said today that the believes "there is a genuine need to re-study, reevalute, reassess" the office of the Presidency in modern times.

"The nation has been blessed with strong and popular and successful Presidents," he said. "But [in] the emphasis upon individuals, perhaps some of our understanding of the office itself has gone neglected.

"If the President is to serve the people in these times as they want to be served, we need the fuller appreciation of the concepts and the powers and the limitations of the office."

Mr. Johnson discussed the Presidential office during a ceremony at the White House commemorating the 175th anniversary of the inauguration of George Washington.

A group of scholars on the Presidency, including writers on the office as an institution and authors of Presidential biographies, joined in the ceremony in the Fish Room.

Urges a New Study

The President read a proclamation calling for a "new study" of the origins and history of the office "and new efforts to understand its functions and potentials within our democratic society."

He and the group then lunched together and discussed in private the problems of the office.

Before he read the proclamation, however, the President regaled his visitors and the press with reminiscences and jokes all focused on his serious observation, as follows:

"This office is a difficult office, and any who occupy it must be a humble man before the task that he faces. This office is also a great institution of freedom. No man could be more aware than I of how the office towers above the man who occupies it and gives to him strength that is much greater than his own.

"I would hope that during the ensuing year, irrespective of political campaigns, we might make a constructive effort to focus more of our study and more of our discussion and more of our talent upon understanding this office and adding to the strength of this office."

He appealed to the scholars with him to use their influence throughout the country for a widespread discussion of the Presidential office.

Will Wait A Bit

Then, in an apparent jest based on the idea that it would be better to wait until he had been elected President in his own right, he added:

"I won't go into that now, because I am saving those views either for next year or perhaps for my own memoirs."

Saying it was a "proud day for the republic," the President introduced his guests as follows:

Richard E. Neustadt, author of "Presidential Power;" Sidney Hyman, "The American President," and Clinton Rossiter, "The American Presidency."

All of them, he said, have written outstanding works on the Presidency.

"We have also some distinguished authors of presidential biographies," the President went on "Mrs. Catherine Drinker Bowen, author of a notable work on John Adams; Mrs. Margaret Leech Pulitzer, who wrote, 'In The Days of McKinley,' which is the name of her book, not a report on the period of her writing; Roy Nichols, who has written many books on Presidents between Jackson and Lincoln.

Hails Writer on Lincoln

"David Donald, noted for his writings about Lincoln; Samuel Flagg Bemis, the Pulitzer Prize winner for his work on John Quincy Adams; George Dangerfield, author of a valuable study, 'The Era of Good Tidings;' and James MacGregor Burns, known to us for his work on President Kennedy; Arthur Walworth, noted for his Wilson biography.

Prof. Eric F. Goldman of Princeton University, the President's special consultant on new ideas, also was present. The President publicly thanked Professor Goldman for having invited the group to the White House for the anniversary commemoration.

Jokingly, the President compared the role of the press and his own office quoting from Oscar Wilde:

"In America the President reigns four years and journalism governs forever and ever."

"I wanted to be a teacher, and was until the pay scale pushed me into the line of work that I am now in," Mr. Johnson went on.

At times, especially after reading the newspapers, the President went on, laughing and turning to the press group, he had strong urges to be a writer.

"In fact," he said, "if I may turn the tables, I sometimes think some of my friends in the press need some new writers."

May 1, 1964

The Twilight of the Presidency

By George E. Reedy.
205 pp. An NAL Book. New York and Cleveland: The World Publishing Company. $6.95.

The President Steps Down

A Personal Memoir of the Transfer of Power.
By George Christian.
282 pp. New York: The Macmillan Company. $6.95.

Was the trouble with Johnson the trouble with the job?

By MAX FRANKEL

Why did Lyndon Johnson, an obviously shrewd politician, end up a political failure? We have to thank George Reedy, who worked with him as press secretary and special assistant before the heady climb and hapless fall, for posing the question as a vital issue of American government and no longer just a biographical curiosity.

Many, of course, deny the premise or the need for historical generalization. The Kennedy people doubted that Lyndon Johnson ever possessed much political skill; a legislative manipulator, they scoffed, who fell into the White House and then lucked into Goldwater. The McCarthy people blamed Vietnam, plain and simple. The old Johnson circle of Texas and Capitol Hill saw tragedy in a betrayal of his heritage and common sense, in his deadly embrace of the civil-rights and labor crowds up North. The Johnson loyalists who went down with the ship accepted their captain's judgment that he knowingly chose the unpolitical course because it was right, and that his heroism passed unnoticed because he lacked style, spoke in a Southern drawl and incurred the opposition of an ignorant and biased communications industry.

Reedy's alarming answer, however, in one of the most thoughtful and stimulating essays on American government, is that the imperial fortress we call the White House is bound to deny the occupant all contact with reality, to encourage his most immature impulses, to deprive him of all normal sense of life in America and to cheat him even of the chance to learn from his mistakes.

We designed the office, Reedy says, when we thought the nation needed stability more than flexibility, endowed it with monarchical powers, and then, in misguided deference to its burdens, sealed off the throne room from real contact with rival power, including the will of the people. "It is only an inference, but an inescapable one," he concludes, "that the White House is an institution which dulls the sensitivity of political men and ultimately reduces them to bungling amateurs in their basic craft—the art of politics."

Reedy exempts Franklin Roosevelt because he seemed somehow capable of learning from error and keeping his court in such a turmoil of rivalries that information from afar could still seep through to his intuitions. I suspect that he exempts Roosevelt also because that is his private way of telling Lyndon Johnson that he failed to measure up to his idol and failed to grasp his methods. Indeed, some might say that Reedy's whole thesis is a coy copout, a puffed up generalization to make more gentle his indictments of the man he long served as aide in the Senate and press secretary and adviser at the White House. But I accept the thesis as a fair and frightening portrayal of the whole institution of the Presidency.

Eisenhower, too, reigned over American society, sadly ignorant of our social tensions. Kennedy's regal popularity did not make him any less the king, sliding toward war in Asia to protect his hold on the scepter and mistakenly engaging Khrushchev in a game of imperial chess around the globe. And Richard Nixon, for all his everyman pretensions, has not convincingly refuted the Reedy thesis. His policies in Asia reflect not what the people so clearly want but only what he thinks they might tolerate. His response to public outcry over Cambodia and Kent produced not an earnest study of the passions now loose in this land but only a rush to put out the public-relations fire.

"There is a deep-seated human tendency to confuse unhappy news with unhappy events and to assume that if the news can be altered, so can the events," Reedy writes. "The reality is that a President has no press problems (except for a few minor administrative technicalities), but he does have political problems, all of which are reflected in their most acute form by the press. . . . But no President can find it within his ego to concede that he has failed in any degree with the public. It is far more satisfying to blame his failures on the press because his problems then can be attributed to a conspiracy."

Where Prince Spiro treads, can King Richard be far behind?

The signs of opposition in press and television evoke constant shock, Reedy writes, because White House staff maneuvers almost always shield the throne, because the Cabinet is both impotent and imploring, because even dissenting Senators address the sovereign in deferential, almost apologetic tones and because the party machine is airily left to rust between quadrennial rides to the polls.

Reedy shows that decisions are therefore reached in an unreal chamber wherein the king loses all sense of other men's passions, problems and egos, and forgets even what it is like to call a plumber, service a car, shop for groceries or get yelled at by someone angry. In this sanctified environment, secrecy itself becomes a national necessity and the more important a problem, the fewer the number of minds at work on it. But Reedy does not know what to do. He ends up deeply pessimistic and religiously convinced that our sin of deifying mortals makes retribution certain.

By comparison, George Christian, the most successful and least communicative of Mr. Johnson's four press secretaries, has composed a cheerful and chatty memoir devoted largely to the last months of the reign. It depicts the President struggling to cling to his waning powers, hungering for a final gesture of peace at the summit or with an arms agreement, while he watches Ho Chi Minh winning their battle of perseverance, Nguyen Van Thieu maneuvering with his political rivals, Hubert Humphrey straying off the reservation, Richard Nixon claiming influence even before it is his due and once-obedient Cabinet ministers running off with policy in unauthorized directions.

Christian does not directly address the riddle of the larger failures, except perhaps when he suggests that the misjudgment on Vietnam dealt not with the enemy or the terrain but the staying power of the American people. To him, the main problem was not that Johnson failed to hear, but that he failed to persuade. But more than he may realize, even this loyal witness supports the deepest of Reedy's misgivings.

"Perhaps God saves the Republic from dictators by giving all of its leaders an Achilles heel," Christian concluded. "A combination of the Johnson drive and ability with the Kennedy charm and youth appeal would have been devastating."

And how. ■

Mr. Frankel is chief of The Times Washington Bureau.

NIXON PROMISES TO HEED DISSENT IN MAKING POLICY

Says He'd Look for Officials of Widely Diverse Views, Including Democrats

CONCEPT OF PRESIDENCY

Candidate Asserts a Leader Must Direct and Inspire, Not Administer 'Trivia'

By E. W. KENWORTHY

Richard M. Nixon said yesterday that his administration would listen to the voice of responsible dissent and would draw officials from "the broadest possible base" in order to insure "a true ferment of ideas."

In a nationwide radio address carried by the Columbia Broadcasting System and the National Broadcasting Company, the Republican Presidential nominee said that he wanted his administration to include Democrats and independents, career civil servants and men from the academic community, business and the professions.

Of dissent during any debate on American commitments abroad, Mr. Nixon said:

"If we expect a decent hearing from those who now take to the streets in protest, we must recognize that neither the Department of State nor of Defense has a monopoly on all wisdom. We should bring dissenters into policy discussions . . . not only because the critics have a right to be heard, but also because they often have something worth hearing."

Decries Isolation

Of the diversity of talents and views he wants in his administration, Mr. Nixon said:

"The President cannot isolate himself from the great intellectual ferments of his time. On the contrary, he must consciously and deliberately place himself at their center."

In what seemed patently a thrust at President Johnson and his philosophy and practice of consensus in decision-making, Mr. Nixon declared:

"The lamps of enlightenment are lit by the spark of controversy; their flame can be snuffed out by the blanket of consensus."

Therefore, Mr. Nixon said, his administration would seek for diversity in its officialdom in order "to invite an interplay of the best minds in America."

Concept Akin to McCarthy's

Mr. Nixon made these statements in the course of a speech setting forth his conception of the Presidency — a conception that turned out to be at variance with the President's and also akin in many ways to that of Senator Eugene J. McCarthy, as the Minnesota Senator outlined it in his unsuccessful campaign for the Democratic nomination.

Mr. Nixon chose the radio for his message instead of television, as he has done on several occasions when dealing with substantive ideas rather than campaign appeals, for a number of reasons.

Perhaps the most important is his belief, based on the advice of experts in the field, that the ear is more attentive when not distracted by the eye.

Radio also enables him to read his speech, which he does not like to do before a live audience because he feels it looks contrived, and it demonstrably reaches a wide audience and is far cheaper than television.

Last night's 15-minute broadcast, reported to have cost no more than $3,000, was carried on more than 400 radio stations—between 200 and 220 on C.B.S. and 214 on N.B.C.

Mr. Nixon said that a President today "must have an activist view of his office," and he pledged that his administration would be "deeply involved in the entire sweep of America's public concern."

At the same time, he emphasized that his idea of "activist" was quite different from that of President Johnson.

Mr. Nixon said that the President "should not delude himself into thinking that he can do everything himself, or even make all the decisions himself."

He should not permit his time to be "drained away in trivia" nor the functions of his office to "become cluttered," Mr. Nixon said.

Nature of the Office

To do so, Mr. Nixon asserted—and here he and Senator McCarthy were at one — was to misconceive the nature of the office, which was not administrative but really inspirational and directive.

The President, Mr. Nixon said, must be an activist in the sense that he "must articulate the nation's values, define its goals and marshal its will."

This is so, he said, because one of the President's resources is "the moral authority of his office."

"It's time we restored that authority," Mr. Nixon declared, "and time we used it once again, to its fullest potential — to rally the people, to define those moral imperatives which are the cement of a civilized society, to point the ways in which the energies of the people can be enlisted to serve the ideals of the people."

Mr. Nixon's ideas on a Cabinet also seemed to approximate those of Senator McCarthy, who said during his campaign that members of the Cabinet should have "a constituency of their own" so that their views would carry more weight in the inner councils of the administration. Mr. McCarthy also advocated that Cabinet officials be allowed more authority within the general policy of the administration.

Yesterday, Mr. Nixon said that Cabinet members — and he wanted them to include young men—should be "men of stature" in their own right and not derive that stature "merely by virtue of appointment."

In this way, he said, they would not only "command the public's respect" but also the President's attention "by the power of their intellect and the force of their ideas."

Again, in a palpable blow at Mr. Johnson, he said:

"Such men are not attracted to an administration in which all credit is gathered to the White House and blame parceled out to scapegoats, or in which high officials are asked to dance like puppets on a Presidential string."

"I believe," he continued, "in a system in which the appropriate Cabinet officer gets credit for what goes right, and the President takes the blame for what goes wrong."

Finally, Mr. Nixon said that if it is the President's duty "to bring his own best judgment to bear on the best ideas his administration can muster," it is also his duty to explain cogently and candidly the reasons for his decisions and what those decisions portend for the future.

"Only through an open, candid dialogue with the people can a President maintain his trust and his leadership," Mr. Nixon said.

In a personal note at the end, Mr. Nixon said he had conducted his campaign for the nomination "in a way that would make it possible to unite the party," and now he intended to conduct the election campaign "in a way that will make it possible to unite the nation."

He said he wanted the Presdency to be a force "for making the nation" because "we have had enough of discord and division, and what we need now is a time of healing, of renewal and of realistic hope."

His first hope, he said, is set on peace, because "history can bestow no honor greater than the title of peacemaker."

Yesterday, Mr. Nixon delivered his unvarying campaign speech to an enthusiastic crowd of several thousand in Springfield, Mo., and to several hundred in Peora, Ill., where there was a hard rain an hour before his arrival. Last night he spoke to a private fund-raising dinner here in New York.

Mr. Nixon's speech at the dinner in the American Hotel was carried on closed-circuit television to a series of $1,000-a-plate dinners in 19 other cities across the country.

Mr. Nixon's director of campaign communications, Herbert G. Klein, said the dinners were attended by 5,000 persons, for a contribution of $5-million.

September 20, 1968

Nixon Asserts He Is a Progressive—'T.R., Not F.D.R.'

Special to The New York Times

WASHINGTON, March 7 — President Nixon, who has refused to grant interviews to individual American reporters, spent part of a morning early last month with Peregrine Worshthorne, a British columnist for The London Sunday Telegraph.

From the interview, Mr. Worsthorne produced two copyrighted pieces, which appeared in his paper Feb. 15 and Feb. 21. The interviews contained little that Mr. Nixon had not already said publicly before.

To many observers here, the most revealing aspect of the Worsthorne interview—part of which was reprinted in yesterday's Washington Post—was not the interview itself but rather a memorandum that Mr. Nixon dictated to a secretary the day after he had seen the British journalist.

The memorandum was an attempt to answer in greater detail a question raised by Mr. Worsthorne the day before. Mr. Worsthorne had asked the President whether he might not have turned out to be a New Dealer if he had begun his political career in the nineteen-thirties instead of the nineteen-forties.

In the memorandum, sent to Mr. Worsthorne through Patrick J. Buchanan, a Presidential assistant, Mr. Nixon described himself as a "progressive in my political thinking in the T.R. [Teddy Roosevelt] sense, but definitely not New Deal in the F.D.R. [Franklin D. Roosevelt] sense." He suggested that he would have found the New Deal philosophy at odds with his own philosophy of individualism.

"This attitude was influenced in great part by the fact that I could not go along with the stand-pat attitude in view of the massive unemployment which I saw on all sides around me, and the fact that I did not embrace the New Deal philosophy at that time as I indicated to him [Worsthorne] was due to a strong streak of individualism which probably was more than anything else rooted in my family background," the President said in the memo.

"Not only at home but in church and school we had drilled into us the idea that we should if at all possible take care of ourselves and not expect others to take care of us."

Mr. Nixon recalled at some length, for example, his parents' refusal to put his older brother Harold in a public tuberculosis sanitarium near Los Angeles although the costs of private care had forced the Nixon family into debt.

"They adamantly refused to do so and borrowed money in order to keep him in a private sanitarium during the most critical last days of his illness," Mr. Nixon recalled in the memo. "Both my mother and father were almost fierce in their adherence to what is now deprecatingly referred to as Puritan ethics.

"Not only were they deeply religious, but they carried their principles over into their lives in other respects and particularly in an insistence that to 'accept help from the government' no matter how difficult our own circumstances were, was simply wrong from a moral standpoint.

"They did not object to others receiving such help, but they felt strongly that those who were able to take care of themselves ought to make an all-out effort to do so."

March 8, 1971

Nixon Tells of His Work: A Life Without Relaxing

By SAUL PETT

The Associated Press

WASHINGTON, Jan. 13—"It's important to live like a Spartan," President Nixon was saying, "to have moderate eating and drinking habits."

"That's not to say I don't enjoy a good time," he went on. "But the worst thing you can do is to relax, to let up."

The President described his view of his job and of himself in an interview Dec. 20 in his Oval office. He continued:

"One must have physical and mental discipline here. This office as presently furnished probably would drive President Johnson up the wall. He liked things going on. He kept three TV sets here. I have none here or in my bedroom.

"I find to handle crises the most important qualities one needs are balance, objectivity, an ability to act coolly."

The President's mood seemed to be one of confidence and, as his points developed, rising stimulation, perhaps even exhilaration.

He spoke of some of the "tough decisions" he has made, mentioning the movement into Cambodia and the decision last May 8 to bomb North Vietnam and mine Haiphong Harbor on the eve of his trip to Moscow.

"People," he said, "probably think the President was jumping up and down, barking orders, at those times. Actually, I have a reputation for being the coolest person in the room. In a way I am. I have trained myself to be that. The great decisions in this office require calm.

"I could go up the wall watching TV commentators. I don't. I get my news from the news summary the staff prepares every day and it's great; it gives all sides.

"I never watch TV commentators or the news shows when they are about me. That's because I don't want decisions influenced by personal emotional reactions."

"The major weakness of inexperienced people," the President said, "is that they take things personally, especially in politics, and that can destroy you.

"Years ago when I was a young Congressman, things got under my skin. Herblock the cartoonist got to me. But now when I walk into this office I am cool and calm. I read the news summary and get both sides. That's important because there are so many emotional issues these days, such as the war and busing and welfare.

"But I never allow myself to get emotional. Now, there are Congressmen and Senators who cut me up—[J. W.] Fulbright, for example. But when he come here, we're the best of friends, at least I feel I am.

"Now, it's not true that I don't feel emotional or pay attention to what others feel. But the most important thing I can do is make decisions for the long run.

"Vietnam, for example. Now, we're having a difficult time. Things don't seem as bright as they did. So, we've had to continue the May 8 policy [to bomb the North]."

The President continued his discussion of crisis handling, a subject he has found compelling for years.

"I'll probably do better in the next four years, having gone through a few crises in the White House, having weathered them and learned how to handle them coolly and not subjectively.

"I probably am more objective—I don't mean this as self-serving—than most leaders. When you're too subjective, you tend to make mistakes."

He was asked if it was "possible to relax at all in this job after four years?"

The President thought a moment, and then said:

"In speeches or press conferences or interviews you have to be up and sharp. You can't be relaxed. The Redskins were relaxed in their last game of the regular season and they were flat and they got clobbered.

"You must be up for the great events. Up but not uptight.

"Having done it so often, I perhaps have a finer honed sense of this. But you can overdo it, overtrain and leave your fight in the dressing room."

He cited as an example a law school exam for which he had overstudied at Duke University, one he apparently did not score well in. But then, if you are relaxed at a news conference, he said, "you can muff one."

Mr. Nixon returned to his larger theme.

"When I came into office, I'd been through enough—those shattering defeats in 1960 and 1962, and then those eight years in the wilderness, the way De Gaulle and Churchill were.

"The result was I was able to confront tough problems without flapping. I don't flap easily. An individual tends to go to pieces when he's inexperienced.

"Now, there are just not many kinds of tough problems I haven't had to face one way or another. In that respect, the fact that my political career required a comeback may have been a blessing."

The President was asked if he felt a sense of relief at being free from re-election pressures. He replied:

"Well, campaigning is a great experience, win or lose. People should not be afraid to step up to it. You know, there are people in the House and the Administration who are 40 or 45 who should run for higher posts, but they get too cautious, they want to stick to the safe jobs. You can't be afraid to take chances in politics. But not foolish chances.

"This game affects the life of the nation and the world. For that reason, an individual, whether he's a President or a member of Congress or the Senate or the Cabinet, must always play the game of politics and statesmanship right up to the hilt.

* * * * *

January 14, 1973

CHAPTER 2

The Executive Branch of Government

Organization. The Constitution places all executive power—and therefore all executive organizations—in the hands of the president. It is something of a paradox that twentieth-century presidents have been forced to spend so much of their time seeking to gain control over the executive branch of government. The paradox lessens when we contrast the enduring quality of the executive agencies with the fleeting character of each presidential administration.

There was no such contrast in the early days of our republic. An incoming president had the capacity to eradicate every trace of his predecessor by firing all his predecessor's appointees. In isolated instances, such large-scale housecleaning led to arguments with the Congress or with the judiciary. But such cases, however important in terms of setting legal precedents, did not alter the characteristic of the executive branch to hold presidential power closely.

The advent of mass government brought an end to this situation. Some agencies, notably Agriculture, Labor and Commerce, were created to perform services directly for American citizens. Others, such as Defense and its predecessors, were given authority to grant enormous commercial contracts that could bring prosperity to large areas of the nation. Such agencies tended to develop constituencies and Congressional relationships independent to a degree from the president's sources of support. Furthermore, the extension of the Civil Service concept reduced the number of employees that a president and his assistants could fire. When Richard M. Nixon entered upon his first term, the White House discovered that it had the legal authority to replace only 6,000 people out of a Federal establishment that numbered about 3,000,000.

The executive agencies do not have the capacity to defy a president openly, and he can still get done what he wants done provided he is willing to follow through personally on his orders. But this is an exhausting process and there is plenty of room for bureaucratic foot-dragging, which sometimes is useful. White House staffs have a tendency to generate enthusiasm for poorly considered projects simply because the people who inhabit the mansion have little previous experience with government. The departments are possessed of institutional memories and frequently they block White House initiatives that should never have been launched. Nevertheless, it is a frustrating environment for a chief executive who has only eight years at the most to put his stamp upon history.

The Presidents' Men. The continuing frustration of presidents with the executive agencies has led to an increasing reliance upon personal aides. Until the 1930s, this meant close, personal friends—such as Colonel House in the Wilson administration. Franklin Delano Roosevelt

Woodrow Wilson

The New York Times

changed the atmosphere by institutionalizing the White House staff into a group of men and women with tremendous power but no permanent constituency other than the president himself.

Roosevelt started with a ''brain trust,'' a group of distinguished intellectuals whose job was to advise him on the best methods of pulling the country out of the Great Depression. He soon discovered that it was not a satisfactory situation from his standpoint. The ''brain trust'' consisted of men who had reputations of their own and were quite willing to air their differences with ''the Chief.'' Some of them, such as Raymond Moley, became his bitterest opponents. Eventually, Roosevelt asked and received authority from Congress to bring into the White House a corps of special assistants whom he described as men who would have ''a passion for anonymity.'' In practice, this meant young, energetic, ambitious, able men who were given an extraordinary chance for success early in life with the sole condition that they devote all their zeal to his administration. There were not many of them at first, but they set the pattern for the modern White House.

The White House staff today has grown to proportions where it constitutes a new branch of government. No one can give an exact figure (except possibly the Secret Service), as many of its members are actually on the payrolls of regular government agencies. But it may be in the neighborhood of 6,000—all devoted to the service of the president. It includes such officers as the Director of the National Security Council, who if he cares to exercise his power can have a greater voice in foreign affairs than the secretaries of State and Defense. It includes the Domestic Council which is the economic arm of the president. Most important, it includes the men and women who see the president on a daily basis, transmit his orders and bring him information on the outside world. Each individual has clout at the very highest level—and can be fired at any moment of presidential displeasure.

The resemblances between this staff and a monarchical court are many. As the system developed the staff aides ceased to be advisers and instead became doers, engaged in a wild scramble to satisfy the source of their status. Court intrigue became commonplace and the result was a high degree of presidential isolation from political realities. The president himself became the only object of loyalty; when Chuck Colson said he would walk over his grandmother's grave for Mr. Nixon he was merely expressing the psychology of the presidential assistant.

GER

COMMERCE DEPARTMENT BILL PASSES SENATE

Measure Adding to Cabinet Goes to President To-day.

Appointment of Private Secretary Cortelyou to the New Portfolio Regarded as Certain—Uses of the New Office.

Special to The New York Times.

WASHINGTON, Feb. 11.—In the brief space of a minute and a half the conference report on the Department of Commerce bill was called up in the Senate during Senator Depew's speech against the Statehood bill and agreed to without a word of debate or dissent. The House having taken similar action yesterday, this consummated the passage of the bill, and to-morrow, with the customary signatures of the Speaker and the President of the Senate, the bill will go to the President for his examination and approval.

Thus the newest of the executive departments has been born, and with it has come upon the statute books in the shape of what has been known during the past few days as the Nelson amendment the principle that the Federal Government shall exercise Constitutional powers to control and restrain combinations in trade that are to the prejudice of public policy and individual rights.

The new department will be in existence the moment the President signs the bill. It is a curious fact that although applications have been rushing in for minor positions in the new department, there has been little or no talk about the Secretaryship. This is because it has been taken for granted that George B. Cortelyou of New York, the Secretary to the President, would be appointed to that place. The only other man whose name has been connected with the appointment except in the most irresponsible gossip has been Representative Lucius N. Littauer of New York.

Mr. Cortelyou will undoubtedly be appointed, and this will give New York two of the places in the Cabinet. It is not customary to have more than one man from a State in the Cabinet, but President Roosevelt has already demonstrated his disregard for that tradition. He has given portfolios to two Iowa men, Secretary of the Treasury Shaw and Secretary of Agriculture Wilson. In addition he offered a Cabinet place to Gov. Crane of Massachusetts, although Secretary Long was from that State.

The appointment of Mr. Cortelyou will be a distinctly non-political one. He has never been a politician, was originally a Democrat, and has never formally announced his secession from that party, though he has for years been looked upon as a Republican. He accompanied the President to Long Island last Fall and voted in a precinct near Oyster Bay. His extraordinary efficiency as Secretary to the President has given that office a higher standing and dignity than it has ever had before, and has raised it above a clerical position to an executive one.

Mr. Cortelyou probably owes his advancement to the high position of Cabinet Minister primarily to his mastery of shorthand. It is also worthy of mention that the principles of civil service reform are in great measure responsible for his success.

After teaching for several years in New York he entered the Government service as a stenographer in 1889, and was detailed as private secretary, first to the Post Office Inspector in charge at New York, then to the Surveyor of the Port, and later to the Fourth Assistant Postmaster General here in Washington.

In November, 1895, he was chosen as stenographer to President Cleveland. The following year he was made executive clerk, and in July, 1898, he became assistant secretary to President McKinley. With the retirement of the late John Addison Porter the following April he was designated as secretary to the President.

Mr. Cortelyou was at President McKinley's side when he was shot at Buffalo, and through the terrible ordeal of the wounded President's struggle for life and his tragic death he was on duty night and day, demonstrating magnificently his strength of character under stress and strain.

* * * * *

February 12, 1903

LABOR PORTFOLIO CREATED.

Senate Now Passes Bill Adding Another Member to the Cabinet.

Special to The New York Times.

WASHINGTON, Feb. 26. — After last night's bitter filibuster the Senate passed the bill this morning creating a new Department of Labor without a roll call and practically without debate. The efforts of its opponents under the active leadership of Senator Simon Guggenheim of Colorado to amend the bill out of all resemblance to its original purpose were abandoned this morning. The measure adopted is so similar to that already passed by the House that it is practically certain there will be ten members in President Wilson's Cabinet.

Senator William E. Borah handled the bill in the Senate, and it is understood that he used plain language to the opponents of the measure. At any rate, when he asked for consideration of the measure, which seemed last night to have been indefinitely postponed by a short filibuster, he got it without difficulty. The only practical amendments adopted were one including the Children's Bureau in the new department, and another dividing the Bureau of Immigration and Naturalization into two bureaus.

A formal amendment adopted out of courtesy to the office of President eliminated the express provision that the Secretary of Labor should sit in the Cabinet. It was explained that the Cabinet is extra-constitutional, and that the President may call to its councils whomsoever he pleases. It is understood, of course, that the new Secretary will be a Cabinet officer, but technically his seat will depend upon the President's invitation.

February 27, 1913

PRESIDENT VETOES BUDGET BILL AS UNCONSTITUTIONAL

Objects to Section Empowering Congress to Remove Controller General and Assistant.

IN SYMPATHY WITH MEASURE

But Declares Provision Usurps Executive's Function to Remove Officials He Appoints.

HOUSE FAILS TO OVERRIDE

Lacks Nine Votes of Necessary Two-Thirds—Friends of Bill to Urge Correction.

WASHINGTON, June 4.—The bill to establish a national budget system was vetoed tonight by President Wilson. The measure was held by the President to be unconstitutional because it took from the Chief Executive the power to remove the Controller General and the Assistant Controller General, officers who would be appointed by him with the advice and consent of the Senate.

The President said he returned the measure without his approval "with the greatest regret," because he was "in entire sympathy" with its objects. He added that he returned it at the "earliest possible moment, with the hope that the Congress may find time before adjournment to remedy this defect."

An unsuccessful attempt was made in the House to pass the measure over his veto. The vote was 268 to 103, or nine less than the required two-thirds majority. Thirty-five Democrats joined with the Republicans in voting to pass the measure.

The vote came at midnight, and when the motion to override was defeated leaders were undecided what would be their next move. Supporters of the measure were expected, however, to urge that it be amended to meet the President's objections and repassed tomorrow.

President Wilson in his veto message said:

"I would gladly approve it [the bill] but for the fact that I regard one of the provisions contained in Section 303 as unconstitutional. This is the provision to the effect that the Controller General and the Assistant Controller General, who are to be appointed by the President with the advice and consent of the Senate, may be removed at any time by a concurrent resolution of Congress after notice and hearing, when in their judgment the Controller General or Assistant Controller General is incapacitated or inefficient, or has been guilty of neglect of duty, or of malfeasance of office, or of any felony or conduct involving moral turpitude, and for no other cause, except either by impeachment or a concurrent resolution of Congress. It has, I think, always been the accepted construction of the Constitution that the power to appoint officers of this kind carries with it, as an incident, the power to remove.

"I am convinced that the Congress is without constitutional powers to limit the appointing power and its incident power of removal, derived from the Constitution.

"The section referred to not only forbids the Executive to remove these officers, but undertakes to empower the Congress, by a concurrent resolution, to remove an officer appointed by the President with the advice and consent of the Senate.

"I can find in the Constitution no warrant for the exercise of this power by the Congress. There is certainly no expressed authority conferred, and I am unable to see that authority for the exercise of this power is implied in any expressed grant of power. On the contrary, I think its exercise is clearly negatived by Section 2 of Article XI. That section, after providing that certain enumerated officers, and all officers whose appointments are not otherwise provided for, shall be appointed by the President, with the advice and consent of the Senate, provides that Congress may by law vest the appointment of such inferior officers as they think proper in the President alone, in the courts of law, or in the heads of departments.

"It would have been within the constitutional power of the Congress, in creating these offices, to have vested the power of appointment in the President alone, in the President with the advice and consent of the Senate, or even in the head of a department. Regarding as I do the power of removal from office as an essential incident to the appointing power, I cannot escape the conclusion that the vesting of this power of removal in the Congress is unconstitutional and therefore I am unable to approve the bill.

"I am returning the bill at the earliest possible moment with the hope that the Congress may find time before adjournment to remedy this defect."

June 5, 1920

HARDING SIGNS BUDGET BILL

President is Expected to Appoint Director Within Two Weeks.

WASHINGTON, June 10.—The bill establishing a budget system of Government expenditures was signed today by President Harding.

In order to put the new system quickly into effect the President expects to appoint a Director of Budget as provided for in the bill some time within the next two weeks. It is understood that a number of available men have been under consideration, and that the field has been narrowed to three or four men.

June 11, 1921

ROOSEVELT BUREAUS TOP THE HOOVER COMMISSIONS

Master Chart of the Federal Government Shows Agencies of Action Displacing Fact-Finders.

COORDINATOR FINDS SNAGS

Attempt of the Secretary of the President's Executive Council to Link Groups Is Futile.

By ARTHUR KROCK.

WASHINGTON, March 24.—This week the United States Information Service, a creation of the National Emergency Council, distributed a master chart of the Federal Government. Any one who looks upon this formidable diagram will find a more graphic explanation than any other published form can provide of why coordination of his far-flung activities is one of the President's greatest problems.

No more striking illustration could be given of how things have changed in this country since Democratic orators were attacking President Hoover for appointing so many commissions. That criticism began with the first year of the Hoover administration; it was reflected in the platform on which Franklin D. Roosevelt was nominated and it became fervid during the campaign of 1932.

The master chart reveals a multiple government in which Mr. Hoover's special groups are exceeded in number, and with this important added fact—Mr. Roosevelt's agencies are administrating, functioning Federal boards; Mr. Hoover's commissions were only "fact-finders." Mr. Roosevelt's agencies spend, save, reward, punish, make regulations that have the force of laws and are specifically immune from the operation of certain statutes suspended by the recovery bills. Some of them, like the Federal Surplus Relief Corporation, by incorporating in Delaware, have sought to take the same advantage of the easy laws of that State that the government criticizes in private business.

What is disclosed by the master chart is not new. But the diagram method is highly clarifying.

A Coordinating Body.

The National Emergency Council, which set up the official information service that produced the chart as its first important work, is that coordinating body directed by Frank C. Walker of Montana and New York. He is also the secretary of the President's Executive Council. When his directorship was created, it was accompanied by a warrant of such powerful authority that in this correspondence it was then suggested Mr. Walker would rank second only to the President. These powers, however, he has never exercised. He has been busy trying to coordinate the government's attack on its problems.

Coordination has by no means been achieved. A survey of the chart does not make this seem strange, or justify criticism of Mr. Walker that he has not achieved it. Rather it gives rise to the belief that complete coordination of this vast front is not within human power. When one thinks of the thousands of people, toiling daily for long hours, nearly every one intent on the problem of recovery, who make up these agencies, the belief grows stronger. Many among the thousands are individually devoted to an idea or a set of ideas in conflict with one another. Some are stubborn or ill-tempered and drive ahead for a plan which they have been asked to coordinate with another. Some are sly and deliberately slip sand into the machinery, justifying this by their belief their own engines are better.

Some Self-Coordinators.

A few, I presume, are disloyal or dishonest, and coordinating them in such a long battle line is asking for a miracle. Dr. Wirt's account this week of a score of "brain-trusters," plotting to check recovery in order to set up a new form of government, using the President for "the Kerensky of the revolution" and having a Stalin ready to produce, struck me as high-grade kidding of somebody by somebody. But no doubt there are a few key-men who are coordinating with themselves only.

Recently have come more examples of the difficulty of maintaining a united front. It was not smooth work for Chairman Jones of the Reconstruction Finance Corporation and Governor Black of the Federal Reserve Board to collide in mid-air over the Capitol dome with two plans for direct loans to industry. The President had previously endorsed the intermediate bank plan of Mr. Black. But the coordinators got busy, and two days later it was explained that the administration also favored Mr. Jones's bill to the extent that the RFC should be placed in a position to make such loans as commercial and intermediate banks were unable to make.

It was not smooth work for the Secretary of the Treasury, Mr. Morgenthau, to have publicly decried a pro-silver move when, as the next few hours revealed, the Speaker and the House were determined to make one, and did so. The Treasury also produced confusion when Tom K. Smith, the Secretary's banking adviser, implied before a House committee that the department did not favor the revised Rayburn-Fletcher Stock Exchange regulations. Next day the proposals had received the public approval of the Federal Reserve Board, and Mr. Smith was back explaining that the Treasury was not in any sense opposed to any section of the bill. Along the line the coordination had somewhere been poor.

But Mr. Walker is a diligent man, and he, with the aid of his chart, may be able to put the government agencies more closely in step. He makes no effort to get publicity; he is quiet, sincerely modest and able. Having not much liking for social distractions, Mr. Walker puts in most of his time here working, and doubtless time will reveal the fruit of this effort in closer coordination.

Details of the Chart.

The chart shows the two upper strata of the government as always before: The constitution on top, from which everything is derived; below it the executive, the legislative and the judicial. Under the legislative, which occupies the left-hand half of the chart, the first change appears in the new importance of the Bureau of the Budget, which is attached to the horizontal line from which also dangle the Cabinet squares. Then below are to be found the astonishing list of government agencies under Mr. Roosevelt. Those which are entirely new since March, 1932, follow:

The Export-Import Banks (2) of Washington. The Farm Credit Administration. The Federal Home Loan Bank Board. The Federal Deposit Insurance Corporation. The Commodity Credit Corporation. The Federal Farm Mortgage Corporation. The Home Owners' Loan Corporation. (All of these designed to maintain credit and renew trade.)

The Federal Subsistence Homesteads Corporation. The Petroleum Administrative Board. The Agricultural Adjustment Administration. (The first and third of these are socially directed.)

The National Recovery Administration. The National Labor Board. The National Recovery Review Board. The Federal Emergency Relief Administration. The Federal Coordinator of Transportation. The Federal Surplus Relief Corporation. (This is a mixed labor-industrial and social service group.)

Emergency Conservation Works. Federal Civil Works Administration. Federal Emergency Administration of Public Works. Public Works Housing Emergency Corporation. Tennessee Valley Authority. Federal Alcohol Control Administration. Central Statistical Board. Electric Home and Farm Authority. Tennessee Valley Associated Cooperatives, Inc. (Here is a group to coordinate!)

In all this list, Mr. Hoover would not recognize any. But on the chart he would find the Reconstruction Finance Corporation, a thing he made his own. When he surveys the chart, as undoubtedly he will, the retired engineer of Palo Alto may raise his eyebrows at two new and strange boxes hanging below the one labeled "The President" and in the same ranking line with a box marked "The Cabinet." These new boxes are inscribed: "The Executive Council" and "The National Emergency Council."

It is this last one to which the job of coordination has been assigned, with the important aid of the Central Statistical Board. Mr. Walker's chart is a mute, though unintentional appeal for public clemency.

March 25, 1934

PRESIDENT ASKS 105 BUREAUS BE PUT INTO 12 DEPARTMENTS, CREATING 2 CABINET POSTS

CAPITOL STARTLED

Message Puts Five-Point Reorganization Plan Up to Congress.

FOR A WELFARE SECRETARY

Public Works Would Be Second New Department—Interior Would Be 'Conservation.'

A CAREER CIVIL SERVICE

Controller General Is Slated to Go—Committee Urges Six New White House Aides.

By TURNER CATLEDGE
Special to THE NEW YORK TIMES.

WASHINGTON, Jan. 12.—A five-point program of governmental reorganization, designed to restore to the President authority commensurate with his responsibilities, and involving fundamental changes in the executive branch from top to bottom, was flashed upon a startled Congress today by President Roosevelt.

Congressional reaction to the plan was uncertain tonight. All that could be said with any degree of finality was that, as a group of individuals, the Senate and House was in a state of amazement over the daring and revolutionary nature of the proposals.

Though presented by the President under five general headings, themselves paraphrases of recommendations of his Committee on Administrative Management, the program would involve twelve major changes.

President's Proposed Changes

The twelve changes proposed were as follows:

Creation of six assistants to the President to keep him in easier touch with the operations of the various departments.

Establishment of two new Cabinet posts, a Department of Social Welfare and a Department of Public Works, and redesignation of the Department of the Interior as the Department of Conservation.

Distribution by the President of all existing bureaus among the twelve Cabinet offices, including the two new ones.

Abolition of all existing independent agencies as such, and the parceling of them among the regular departments for purposes of management with only their quasi-judicial functions (such as those of the I. C. C.) remaining independent.

Abolition of the office of Controller General, as well as all authority of Congress to "pre-audit" the expenditure of appropriations by the executive branch.

Establishment of a system of "post-audit" of executive expenditures, with a report to Congress.

Sweeping Civil Service Plan

Abolition of the Civil Service Commission and the creation of an office of Civil Service Administrator as a managerial arm of the President.

Creation of a non-salaried citizen board as a "watch-dog" of the merit system.

Extension of the merit system throughout the Federal establishment, and increases in pay virtually from top to bottom.

Establishment of the Director of the Budget as practical "office manager" of the government under the President, dealing with all matters relating to the budget and managerial efficiency, and even to information and legislative program.

Creation of a planning board as a management arm of the Chief Executive to assist him in long-range programs for the promotion of the welfare of the country.

Continuing authority to the President to shuffle and reshuffle the various executive bureaus and agencies among the twelve departments or three managerial arms—Budget Bureau, Civil Service Administrator and planning board—to obtain the maximum efficiency of administration.

Predicated primarily upon efficient management rather than economy, the program as presented by the President in a special message would group all existing governmental bureaus and agencies, numbering 105, into the twelve major departments and three management units—all to be brought more directly under the control of the Executive and watched by him through the eyes of his six new assistants. The assistants would be selected in addition to the White House secretariat.

The anticipated economy would range between 1½ per cent and one-half of 1 per cent of the present Federal budget, according to official calculations.

The President asked of Congress fullest cooperation in helping put the program into force, saying that it was vitally involved in the battle to preserve "that freedom of self-government which our forefathers fought to establish and hand down to us."

Although obviously disturbed over the probable long-drawn-out battle that might be necessary to fill this request of the President, Congressional leaders went about the task of providing for consideration.

Immediately after the message was read in the House, Representative Buchanan of Texas, chairman of the Appropriations Committee, obtained the consent of Chairman O'Connor of the Rules Committee for a hearing tomorrow on two resolutions creating committees to pass on legislation.

Senator Byrd, explaining that he was acting as spokesman for the committee named by the Senate in the last session of Congress to study government reorganization, said the committee will meet at 10 o'clock Monday morning when the President's suggestions undoubtedly will be considered.

No Additional Power, He Says

The President insisted in his message that he was not asking for additional power. He was only seeking to retrieve the power of administration which the people had given 150 years ago when they ratified the Constitution. As a means to that end he asked Congress to cut away such restraints as it had imposed upon the Executive from time to time by creation of independent agencies, especially the Controller General, who lately had attempted, he said, to exercise authority over the fiscal policies of the Executive Department.

"What I am placing before you is not the request for more power," the President said, "but for the tools of management and the authority to distribute the work so that the President can effectively discharge those powers which the Constitution now places upon him. Unless you are prepared to abandon this important part of the Constitution, we must equip the Presidency with authority commensurate with his responsibilities under the Constitution."

The opportunity and need had indeed met in this instance, he said. The country is "out of the trough" of the depression, and "the time has come to set our house in order," and, according to the committee's analysis as accepted by him, the "house" is indeed in a state of disorder.

A "Chaos of Establishments"

Mr. Roosevelt recited the conclusions of the committee that no enterprise can operate effectively if set up as in the case of the Federal Government today. With more than 100 separate departments, boards, commissions, corporations, authorities and agencies to carry on the work, neither the President nor Congress can exercise effective supervision over "such a chaos of establishments." Nor, he added, can overlapping, duplication and contradictory policies be avoided.

He confessed that the committee had not spared him in its indictment of the managerial service of the government when it said that the President cannot adequately handle his responsibilities under present conditions.

"With my predecessors who have said the same thing over and over again, I plead guilty," said Mr. Roosevelt.

Attention was directed to the committee's attack on the Controller General for his failure to give Congress a complete audit each year and for his "unconsitutional assumption of executive power."

Mr. Roosevelt cited, too, the committee's criticism of boards and commissions in administration, and its condemnation of the careless use of "corporations." It was to meet this situation, he said, that he offered the five-point program, entailing: (1) Expansion of the White House staff; (2) strengthening and development of the managerial agencies of the government; (3) extension and reorganization of the merit system in government employment; (4) overhauling of independent establishments and creation of two new departments, and (5) establishment of true accountability of the Executive to Congress.

Prompt Action Is Pledged

From his experience as a legislator, as a subordinate in an executive department, as Governor of a State and as President, he endorsed this program and pledged himself to deal energetically and promptly with the executive responsibilities imposed by it "when you shall have made this possible by the necessary legislation."

The latter condition set official Washington to speculating tonight. Of all the things that President Roosevelt has asked Congress to do since he came into office, including the cuts in veterans' benefits and reduction in Federal salaries in 1933, the plan as submitted today was deemed the most disagreeable.

Inherent was the proposition that Congress should turn over to the President many of the powers it has given to its specially created independent commissions and boards, and that it should impose upon individual members of the Senate and Congress restraints against much of their present participation in the affairs of the Executive departments.

It is purposed, for instance, that, with notable exceptions, the whole matter of personnel shall be turned over to an officer directly responsible to the President, and under a merit system to be watched closely by a citizen board.

This means, first, that individual Senators and Representatives would be choked off from patronage, and that the Senate would have neither the responsibility nor the power to ratify many of the minor appointive offices, such as United States marshals, postmasters, collectors of internal revenue &c., as has been the custom for so many years. Authority for appointment of the latter would be turned over completely to department heads and administrative merit and competence would be the sole standard for selection.

Test of Democracy Is Seen

The basis for the whole program recommended by the President was the report of his Committee on Administrative Management, consisting of Louis Brownlow of Chicago; Luther Gulick of New York, and Charles E. Merriam of Chicago, all experts in governmental management. Joseph P. Harris of the Committee on Public Administration of the Social Science Research Council acted as chief of staff for the group.

The committee went into considerable detail as to the various changes and innovations and supported each recommendation with extensive argument. Like the President, it insisted that the fundamental reorganization recommended in the report was vital to the purpose of making democracy workable in a day when it is doubted and attacked.

The committee confined itself to general recommendations, however, leaving legislative specifications to be worked out by the President and Congress in keeping with the political requirement for their enactment.

In setting up a standard for the proposed assistants to the President, the committee said they should be men capable of discharging their functions with restraint, "possessed of high competence, great physical vigor and a passion for anonymity." They should be installed in the White House itself and be directly accessible to the President.

Linked to Executive Office

The committee also proposed that the new Civil Service Administration, the Bureau of the Budget and the National Resources Board—the planning board—should be a part of the Executive Office.

As to the merit system, the committee specified that it should be extended "upward" to include all permanent positions except those of high executive and policy-making character; "downward" to include skilled workmen and laborers in regular government service; and "outward" to include all permanent and continuing positions not now under civil service.

It was in this connection that the committee recommended abolition of the present Civil Service Commission and the substitution of a Civil Service Administration, under a single executive, and a non-salaried Civil Service Board to keep a watchful eye on the merit system.

Higher Pay for Merit Is Urged

It was also in relation to the subject of personnel that the committee proposed increases in government salaries, with pay of Cabinet secretaries, under secretaries and assistant secretaries fixed respectively at $20,000, $15,000 and $12,000, instead of the present scale of $15,000, $10,000 and $8,000.

The committee's argument was that salaries in the higher grades must be raised or they will defeat the development of a career service. Government employes, it said, "should not be given salaries for responsible work so low that they are tempted to cater to special interests which held out hopes of remunerative private employment."

Under the committee's recommendation the Director of the Bureau of the Budget would be raised from the position of a glorified bookkeeper, charged largely with preparing budgetary estimates for submission to Congress, to a virtual office manager for the whole Federal establishment. He would have general responsibility for the budget as at present, but he would also have more to do with research and managerial planning.

New Job for Budget Director

One of the new functions which the report would have placed upon the Budget Director would be supervision of a division of information to act as a central clearing house for corelation and coordination of the administrative policies of the several departmental informational services "and to perform related duties."

Newspaper correspondents arched their eyebrows at this, first because the White House heatedly denied a recent dispatch to The New York Times, stating that a central information bureau was being pressed as part of the reorganization plan, and also because they feared that the words "perform other related duties," might be translated into a central press bureau, advocacy of which was also denied by the White House.

All through the report the committee insisted that the President should be accountable to Congress for expenditures of money, but that the accountability should be after the expenditure and not before. This was the basic reason for recommending abolition of the office of Controller General. Instead there would be created an Auditor General to make a post-audit of the executive branch's stewardship, but the current responsibility for auditing of expenditures and making them comply with law should be lodged in the Treasury and the Attorney General.

Independent Agencies Criticized

The plan for taking the independent offices, agencies, commissions, authorities, &c., into the regular departments, is the part of the reorganization that is expected to create the greatest sustained discussion in Congress. The committee blamed these, and the various governmental corporations, more than anything else for the muddled condition of the administrative arm.

"They are in reality miniature independent governments set up to deal with the railroad problem, the banking problem or the radio problem," said the report. "They constitute a headless 'fourth branch' of the government, a haphazard deposit of irresponsible agencies and uncoordinated powers."

These agencies do violence to the basic theory of the American Constitution, the report said, because they are responsible to nobody. "The Congress has found no effective way of supervising them, they cannot be controlled by the President, and they are answerable to the courts only in respect to the legality of their activities."

Where these agencies, authorities, corporations, &c., would fall into the general scheme of reorganization, would, in the program outlined today, be left largely to the President. Congress's responsibility would be largely to define where their administrative functions ended and their judicial functions began. They would no longer be independent as governmental units, however.

A basic point of the program is that the Cabinet officers, the policy-making heads of each of the twelve major departments, would be relieved of most of these routine duties, and would, in fact, constitute a "council of State." Contacts of their departments with the President, so far as managerial and administrative matters are concerned, would be maintained more on a "functional" basis than is possible through the regular cabinet organization, with the six assistants to the President as the main points of contact.

By proposing that authority be granted him personally to distribute and redistribute the various bureaus and agencies among the twelve major departments, the President is believed to have removed one source of opposition to the reorganization program.

By not mentioning any specific bureau in the bill carrying out the program, he will not stir up its Congressional friends or even its personnel.

The President's committee is thought to have provided other trading points that might give the program a better day in Congress, among them the proposal to make minor executive appointments the responsibility of Cabinet heads instead of the President. Senators undoubtedly will resist any attempt thus to circumscribe their authority to ratify executive appointments.

HOUSE KILLS REORGANIZATION BILL, 204 TO 196; VOTE CALLED LACK OF CONFIDENCE IN PRESIDENT; NEW PUBLIC WORKS DRIVE IN RECOVERY PROGRAM

BILL RECOMMITTED

Rayburn and Bankhead Fail to Stem Tide, Even With Patronage Bids

O'CONNOR CLINCHES VOTE

108 Democrats Join With Solid Republican Phalanx of 88 in Dooming Measure

By CHARLES W. HURD
Special to THE NEW YORK TIMES.

WASHINGTON, April 8.—A tense House of Representatives tonight killed the Reorganization Bill by voting, 204 to 196, to recommit the measure to its special Committee on Reorganization.

It took this action in the face of warnings by Administration leaders that such a result would be interpreted as "a vote of lack of confidence" in President Roosevelt and in the face of offers alike of political compromise and patronage as unprecedented in the Roosevelt administration as was the importance of this defeat.

Those voting to recommit the bill included 108 Democrats, 88 Republicans, 6 Progressives and 2 Farmer-Laborites.

The bill was so amended and emasculated in all important particulars that it hardly counted in the issue; it was much milder than other measures similar to its essential sections which were passed by the House in the special session last Winter.

President Central Issue

The only issue was the question of whether the country wished the Congress to vest greater authority in the President than he has now—an issue which has aroused probably more controversy than even the Supreme Court Bill fight last year, and the vote showed that a large section of the Democratic membership agreed with the Republicans that the public answer was in the negative.

Seldom has the House cast such a close vote on any question. The leaders of various groups themselves were so uncertain about the final result that they declined to make predictions half an hour before the balloting started at 6:30 P. M.

At that hour Speaker Bankhead and Representative Rayburn, the majority leader, who had mustered every available vote by prevailing on friendly members to cancel out-of-town engagements or make special trips to Washington, thought they possibly held control, but were not certain.

Chairman O'Connor of the Rules Committee, organizer and leader of the dissident Democrats, was hopeful for ultimate defeat of the bill, but thought that the opponents would gain their ends through a disagreement by conferees over the bill passed by the Senate and that about to be voted upon by the House.

The House members were silent while the tellers took almost five minutes to cast up the tally after the roll was called and while Speaker Bankhead stood immobile on the dais waiting for them to pass to him the slip of paper containing the figures.

When he did announce the result, the membership was so filled with suppressed excitement that several seconds passed before the victors collected their energies to give the usual cheer. But when the cheering did break out it lasted for several minutes, and hundreds in the galleries joined in the applause.

O'Connor Clinches Victory

Representative O'Connor quickly made certain that the bill would be completely buried and not subjected to a possible motion to reconsider, by pressing that motion immediately, coupled with a motion to table the motion to reconsider. His followers chorused "aye," thereby foreclosing the House from bringing up the bill again, and incidentally, killing just as dead the Reorganization Bill over which the Senate had labored for weeks.

The bill was no more than a shadow of the reorganization authority requested by President Roosevelt last year, and it was amended so that it represented only a strongly diluted semblance of the Senate's bill. In this case, the Senate had voted to give the President more than the House, which usually plays the role of Administration follower.

In addition the leaders had accepted this afternoon an amendment which, in effect, would have restored the old practice of giving Representatives control over the highly important patronage list of first, second and third class postmasters. This amendment, reported to have been approved at the last minute by the White House, in effect repealed President Roosevelt's executive order specifying that the top-ranking man receive appointment to each vacancy, and authorized selection to be made from a list of three approved applicants.

By long-established practice prior to Mr. Roosevelt's reform, Representatives were permitted to designate which of the three approved men should receive an appointment. This was one of the largest concessions the Administration could have given to the House, shorn as it has been of much of its major and minor patronage alike in the past five years.

Other Vital Points Rewritten

In addition the Reorganization Committee, which already had accepted amendments restricting greatly the proposed authority of the President, today rewrote the sections dealing with the Controller General and the Civil Service in a manner which answered many criticisms based on assumed Presidential control of these agencies.

But all of this action was insufficient. It had no more force, in fact, than the personal efforts of some of President Roosevelt's most active lieutenants, who went to the Capitol to assist the Administration leadership.

Among these were Postmaster General Farley, Jesse H. Jones, chairman of the Reconstruction Finance Corporation, and Charles O. West, former Representative and now Under-Secretary of the Interior, who acts as President Roosevelt's principal liaison agent with Congress.

Almost every member on the floor thought that passage of the bill was assured in mid-afternoon when Representative Fuller of Arkansas introduced, as the last amendment to the bill, a measure by Representative Faddis of Pennsylvania restoring the old method of selecting postmasters. This bill, too, had once been passed by the House and sent to the Senate, where it now lies in committee.

"My amendment is exactly what the law is now and what it has been, except for an executive order issued by the President," Mr. Fuller said.

Ramspeck Shouts Charge

Most members were unaware of the purport of the amendment until Representative Ramspeck of Georgia jumped to his feet, obtained recognition and shouted:

"You can't buy my vote with this bill."

He told the House that if it "swallowed this bait" as payment for passage of the Reorganization Bill it probably would be the first thing to be stricken out by conferees.

After the House had voted about a score of amendments approved by the committee, there was perhaps an hour of jockeying with minor discussions until, at 5:45 P. M., Representative Rayburn took the floor to give a five-minute speech summarizing the issue. He addressed the House as a committee of the whole, over which Representative McCormack of Massachusetts presided.

The question at issue, said Mr. Rayburn, was whether the House, sitting as a committee, should vote to report this measure to the House sitting in formal session for third reading, a vote on recommittal and, if that failed, a final vote on passage.

"I do not think that the most intense opponent of this bill can say time has not been granted to members for debate or that there has not been opportunity to offer amendments," he said.

Storm a Mystery to Rayburn

Mr. Rayburn reminded the House that it had passed stronger reorganization measures in 1932 and 1933 and acted last year "upon a bill which is the heart of this one," all these actions being taken "without a storm being raised."

But a "rumble" arose a month or six weeks ago, he went on, and "the rumble has grown into a storm which I must confess I do not yet understand."

"Whether you like Roosevelt or not," he exhorted the members, "he is the President of the United States and will be for two years and eight months more. Do not vote lack of confidence in him, for such a vote would add tremendously to doubt and lack of confidence in the country."

The question was whether "we as citizens can afford to throw disturbance into the minds of citizens."

"We ought not to send out to Americans the message," he said, "that tonight Democrats voting with Republicans have voted and said in effect that our President is no longer the leader of his country."

O'Connor Replies to Rayburn

Representative O'Connor replied that the issue was entirely different from what Mr. Rayburn had pictured it.

"I don't believe the issue of supporting the President enters into this," he said.

The Fuller amendment, he said, was an empty gesture, and announced that a motion to recommit the bill would be offered as soon as the House had made the third reading.

"A motion to recommit is not as serious as you have been told," he argued. "It simply means the question will be given further study. We have had this problem of possible reorganization with us for 150 years, ever since there has been a government. Many suggestions have been made. A few more years devoted to study of it won't hurt anything."

Pounding the table, he reiterated the contention that while the country did not mind such legislation a few months ago, sentiment had changed and "it is offensive to people now."

"I have never seen anything that threatened to destroy our party as much as this bill," Mr. O'Connor exclaimed, "and when it destroys our party it will destroy the party members with it.

"I love the President myself, and almost all the members of the Democratic party in this chamber love the President, but this issue is above party. it is above any individual. I am appealing now for the interests of my party.

"If this bill is not recommitted for further study, it will be disastrous to my party and to my country, and I love my country above my party."

Applause from both sides of the House followed Mr. O'Connor's brief talk.

Speaker Bankhead told the House that "this issue has been magnified far beyond what it deserves" and that, "stripped of its window dressing," the bill was "just a sensible proposal any great private institution would have put into operation long ago."

"A vote to recommit this bill," he said, "would be a repudiation out of the whole cloth of public confidence in the Democratic party."

"If you recommit the bill," he told the membership, "there will be a lethal blow to it. You will say 'The House of Representatives by Democratic votes repudiates the President of the United States.'"

When the Speaker, who used much less than his allotted time, walked to a seat there was a rising ovation, in which almost every Democrat joined.

The House Committee of the Whole voted to resolve itself in the House for a third reading of the bill, and Speaker Bankhead took the chair.

The clerk read the title of the bill. Representative Boileau of Wisconsin demanded a separate vote on the postmasters' amendment, which was carried by a standing vote, 165 to 106.

Representative Cochran, sponsor of the Reorganization Bill, shouted for the "previous question," a direct vote on the bill, but Representative Taber of New York, ranking minority member of the Reorganization Committee, won recognition to move that the bill be recommitted. Speaker Bankhead put the question and the clerk began to call the roll.

As the great majority of members were in their seats, the roll-call was completed in about twenty minutes, instead of the customary forty.

While the tellers rechecked their figures, there was a long pause and cries for a recapitulation. Speaker Bankhead stood imperturbably waiting until the totals were given to him. He stated then that the vote was not close enough to warrant a recapitulation and then announced the result.

Speaker Bankhead ordered the Clerk to read, just prior to adjournment, a message sent to the House by President Roosevelt vetoing a minor piece of legislation. But few members heard it. They were streaming out through the doors to the corridors en route home.

April 9, 1938

Messner in The Rochester Times-Union and Elderman in The Washington Post

The House didn't like the accessories.

April 10, 1938

OUR FOURTH BRANCH OF GOVERNMENT

The administrative agencies, rapidly growing in number, are ruling over more and more of our national life

By DELBERT CLARK

WASHINGTON.

ON July 1, as a result of President Roosevelt's two reorganization plans, there will become effective a broad revision of the administrative structure of the Federal Government, involving the creation of some new agencies, the consolidation of numerous old ones and the abolition of one or two.

But although this will to a considerable extent simplify the mechanism of government it will in no wise answer the fundamental question of the independent administrative agency, which in recent years has come to be one of the most urgent mechanical problems of government in the United States. The President is permitted, under the Reorganization Act, to transfer agencies, consolidate them, even abolish them, on paper, but he may not abolish functions or in any way alter the organic acts under which the many administrative agencies operate.

The sprawling independent agencies have to a degree invaded the law-making field assigned to Congress by the Constitution makers of 1787, the interpretative field assigned to the judiciary and the enforcement field assigned to the Executive. In many respects they are a fourth branch of government. They have caused some observers to fear that eventually, unless checked, they will come to control most of the daily activities of American life.

THEY say how much railroad fare we shall pay; how much it shall cost us to ship freight; how a banker may conduct his business; the conditions under which we may receive commercial shipments from abroad; in case of dispute, how much income tax we have to pay.

They lay down the basis upon which electric utilities operate, they regulate the ethics of competition between merchants and strive to protect the interest of the consumer. They dispense largesse to war veterans and help us build houses, subject to supervision as to location and design.

They regulate relations between employers and organized employes, lend money to financial and business interests, take mortgages on private homes, help farmers buy washing machines, and supply the power to run the washing machines. They lend money to farmers, subsidize education, dispense unemployment relief by the billions.

They insure our bank deposits, prescribe Marquis of Queensberry rules for our stock markets, regulate telephone, telegraph and radio, disburse old-age pensions and unemployment insurance, tell the ship master and the air transport pilot how he must operate, and do many other things.

THEY came slowly into the American scene, but, once established, they have flourished like the wicked or the green bay tree.

The first of the independent administrative agencies was not created until this nation was 100 years old. By that time the steamboat, the railroad, the cotton gin, the power loom and a hundred other mechanical devices had helped to revolutionize our mode of living and perplex our economists and our sociologists, but virtually nothing had been done by our semi-archaic country to make these inventions fit snugly into the American scheme.

If a law needed to be passed, it was left for the President to enforce, through his Cabinet officials. Only once, toward the end of that first century—in 1883—had Congress set up an agency independent of the Federal departments; this was the Civil Service Commission, and its powers were strictly special and limited.

The first really independent administrative agency, the Interstate Commerce Commission, was set up at the century mark in 1887, long after the railroads it was supposed to regulate had penetrated every section of the country. And it was not until a quarter century later that the next one arrived.

But, beginning with the first Wilson Administration, the number has risen rapidly. Congress, when Wilson was President, recognized the importance of new economic problems by creating such organisms as the Federal Trade Commission, the Federal Power Commission and the Federal Tariff Commission. Other agencies followed.

Since Franklin D. Roosevelt has been President there have been created the Tennessee Valley Authority, the Securities and Exchange Commission, the National Labor Relations Board, the Social Security Board, the United States Maritime Commission and the Civil Aeronautics Authority. Not only have new agencies been formed but also old ones have been endowed with new and important powers, so that it may be said that our government, as it enters one field after another, is undergoing a profound change.

THE independent administrative agencies have a status that is not easily defined. Each is created by Congress to administer a specific law or body of laws which the Congress for one reason or another—many times because of an innate jealousy of the executive branch—does not desire to entrust to an executive department. The agency is in theory responsible only to Congress. It is an executive arm of the legislative branch and to this extent may be regarded as a rival of the executive branch itself.

Generally, the agency is endowed with limited judicial powers and, by reason of this, infringes continually upon the province of the Federal courts.

At the same time, either because Congress cannot anticipate the nature of the agency's problems or is too indolent to mark out the task specifically, the agency is instructed not only to administer a given law but also to promulgate regulations within its framework for its better administration. Through these regulations the agency is enabled, and in fact required, to amend, in effect, the law that brought it into being. Thus it legislates, often in a highly important way.

TO make the picture even more complicated, the membership of the agency is selected by the President, and it can be assumed that no President will appoint a man who he thinks is unsympathetic to his own views. Thus the agency's membership owe a dual allegiance. While they carry out the will of Congress (and their own), because they are designated

by the Executive, they carry out his will as well (or instead).

Obviously, the framers of the Constitution never envisaged such a delegation of power by the Legislature, or, particularly, such a remarkable amalgam of three major functions of government—legislative, executive and judicial—in one small body of men as is represented in the independent administrative agencies. And the arrangement is satisfactory to none of the three major branches.

Thus some time ago President Roosevelt instructed the Attorney General to make a special study of the agencies, with particular reference to charges that they have at times overreached their legal authority. The courts have held, now and again, that the agencies have overstepped the bounds of their judicial authority. And Congressmen themselves for long have wondered whether they should not modify the powers given to some of these commissions, so as to make them more truly responsible to the Legislature which created them.

Fitzpatrick in The St. Louis Post-Dispatch

A critic looks at the Federal agencies —"About time they were reorganized."

The complaints against the agencies intensifies, naturally, in direct ratio to the controversial character of the laws they administer. The hoary Interstate Commerce Commission is firmly established; there is no argument about the necessity for the regulation of railroads and commercial motor carriers.

THERE is little, if any, quarrel over the purpose of the Federal Trade Commission, the Federal Reserve Board or the United States Tariff Commission. But the Communications Commission, the Power Commission, the National Labor Relations Board, the Securities and Exchange Commission have continually to battle against unfriendly forces.

The arguments, when analyzed, often appear to simmer down to the question, not of the actual authority conferred, but of the manner in which it is administered, and various recent suggestions would never have arisen had it not been for the somewhat incautious exercise of power.

The National Labor Relations Board has come in for especially bitter criticism, perhaps largely because of the fact that it was set up as a sort of public defender for organized labor as against the opposition of employers, whereas most of its sister agencies adjust disputes or control relations between economic equals. The board now stands out as Example No. 1 of an agency with discretionary powers so great as to be able virtually to alter at will the character of the act under which it operates.

Congress, in the law, stated its desire to promote collective bargaining and listed certain "unfair practices" to which employers might not resort in frustrating unionization. Then it gave power to the board to investigate complaints brought by employes and to issue decisions, subject to enforcement by the courts. The board was left to promulgate a body of by-laws, or regulations, which, as definitions of policy or guides to administration, have the force of law.

THE board gets a complaint of suspects an abuse. It sets staff investigators to work developing the facts; when these are in, it issues a formal complaint against the supposed offender; later, either through a trial examiner, who is a salaried board employe, or en banc, the commission hears the evidence and gives its decision.

This same method of investigation is used by the Interstate Commerce Commission and the Federal Trade Commission, but seldom, in proportion to the number of cases heard, does either have to go into court to defend itself. The Labor Board, on the other hand, has, in a number of cases, found the courts reluctant to enforce its orders; and the Supreme Court held not long ago that in some of its decisions the board had either exceeded its power or drawn conclusions unwarranted by the evidence submitted.

Further, the Labor Board is the only one of the agencies mentioned by whose regulations only one party to a dispute has the right of petition. There is nothing in the organic act which stops an employer from petitioning the board for a collective bargaining election among employes or for redress of grievances against a union. But the board, foreseeing circumvention of the law if such petitions were permitted, has forbidden them by regulation.

Again, the law does not specify the procedure by which a particular union is to be legally designated as the collective bargaining agent for a group of employes; so the board, by regulation, has set up a number of alternative procedures to this end.

Such points as these, the result of rules promulgated in the absence of specific statements in the law, are the source of a very large part of the acrimonious atmosphere in which the board lives and has it being.

THE question automatically arises, once the situation has been stated: What is to be done about the independent agencies? There is no good reason to believe that the Federal Government is going to take a back track and suddenly cease doing for the people all the things it has begun to do. The functions that were most inveighed against at their inception are now generally accepted, fifteen or twenty years later, as useful and necessary.

No one who is aware of national problems will argue, for instance, that the Federal Trade Commission, the Securities and Exchange Commission, the Maritime Commission, the Civil Aeronautics Authority, the Communications Commission and the Interstate Commerce Commission could be abolished without serious harm to the national economy. Their functions and those of many other independent agencies must be carried on.

Unfortunately, there appears to exist a profound paradox in the reasoning of some who feel that these agencies should somehow be coordinated and their powers redefined. These persons start by saying that the agencies by their very nature and prerogatives go far beyond the spirit of the Constitution, that they are in fact a strange governmental hybrid, or tribrid, and that something ought to be done.

THE first answer that suggests itself, and which suggested itself to President Roosevelt, was that all, or virtually all, of the independent administrative agencies should be absorbed into the executive departments. But to this suggestion the objection was raised that it would give too much power to the President.

Obviously, Congress cannot have its cake and eat it. If Congress desires to enact a law for all the people, it must provide for the enforcement of that law. If it does not want too much discretion vested in the Executive, it can continue to set up independent agencies with judicial powers; otherwise it can entrust law enforcement in the Executive as in the past, without recourse to a separate agency responsible to Congress. But it certainly cannot do both.

The usual reason assigned for the creation of these agencies is that they are endowed with judicial powers which should not be given to a Cabinet officer or his subordinates. But there are semi-legislative and semi-judicial powers already vested in Cabinet officers, and so the question is one of degree only.

If Congress does not desire to have these agencies absorbed into the regular departments, where they could be very readily absorbed, it has but one valid alternative solution of the problem. That is to re-examine all of the organic laws under which such bodies operate, and so revise and tighten them as to make it impossible for an agency to get into dangerous territory. This is the one thing Congress has never been willing to do on a broad scale. Congress usually has been too anxious to get its work done and go home, with no particular reference to the manner in which the work is done.

June 25, 1939

ROOSEVELT UNIFIES WHITE HOUSE TASKS

As Step for Any Emergency He Orders Reorganization of the Executive Department

By FELIX BELAIR JR.

Special to THE NEW YORK TIMES.

HYDE PARK, N. Y., Sept. 9.—President Roosevelt ordered today an immediate reorganization of the White House executive offices as one step toward preparing the Federal Government for prompt emergency action "in order that the nation may not again be caught unaware" in a period of international crisis and to facilitate as well the normal operations of the government.

As a surprising development of the new order from the President, White House sources invited the interpretation that, for the future, "those creatures of the imagination" popularly referred to as "the brains trust" were "out the window."

In an executive order carrying into effect on Monday the overhauling of the executive offices of the President as authorized by Congress under Government Reorganization Plan No. 1, Mr. Roosevelt followed up the military and naval expansions which he ordered yesterday by directing the establishment within the White House, in the event of a national emergency or the threat of one, of "such office for emergency management as the President shall determine."

With this first official intimation that the President was planning the creation of a "war council" if and when the need should arise came an explanatory White House statement suggesting that Mr. Roosevelt did not regard the present situation as sufficiently grave to warrant a proclamation of a national emergency.

Emergency Needs Emphasized

The statement, given out by the President's secretary, Stephen T. Early, said:

"In the time of national emergency, domestic or foreign, the job of the President is even more difficult. In such periods it has always been found necessary to establish administrative machinery in addition to that required for the normal work of the government.

"Set up in a time of stress, these special facilities sometimes have worked to cross purposes both within themselves and with the regular departments and agencies. In order that the nation may not again be caught unaware, adequate resources for management should be provided in advance of such periods of emergency.

"Although these management facilities need be brought into action only when an emergency or serious threat of emergency exists, they must function in an integral relationship to the regular management arms of the President."

Unified Control Is Established

Intended primarily to translate Presidential decisions into quick administrative action, the Executive order brings under direct White House control the Bureau of the Budget, the National Resources Planning Board, and two new management adjuncts—a liaison office for personnel management and an office of government reports.

The President on several occasions has expressed the view that the world's democracies must prove themselves the equal of the totalitarian States in deciding issues promptly and in acting without delay if democratic self-government is to meet present-day problems. Hence his move today was regarded in White House circles as notice that America was prepared to meet the challenge of totalitarian efficiency within the limits of democratic self-rule.

Throughout the executive order of the President ran the thought that the Federal bureaucracy in general must be speeded up. One of the functions newly imposed on the National Resources Planning Board was to discover "the emergency necessities of the nation." Similarly, the Budget Bureau was directed by the order "to aid the President to bring about more efficient and economical conduct of government service," while the duties of the liaison officer for personnel were set forth as helping the President to maintain "closer contact with all agencies dealing with personnel matters."

To Watch Public Complaints

Among the duties of the newly created Office of Government Reports is the task of keeping the President "currently informed of the opinions, desires and complaints of citizens and groups of citizens and of State and local governments with respect to the work of Federal agencies."

It was in citing one part of the executive order detailing the functions of the two Presidential secretaries in their relations with members of Congress, the press, radio and the general public that White House sources invited mention of the "imaginary" brains trust.

Mr. Early stated after referring to the section of the order outlining his own duties and those of General Edwin M. Watson, that there had been many stories in the past which, rightly or wrongly, had created a few imaginary persons supposedly having influence with the President and being charged with responsible duties by him.

Asked whether he was referring specifically to Thomas G. Corcoran and Benjamin C. Cohen, Mr. Early said that his auditors well knew whom he had in mind. Having denied that such a thing as a "brains trust" had any factual basis today, Mr. Early pointed out, that the President yesterday had proclaimed a limited national emergency in which it would be well to evaluate Administration advisers according to the duties entrusted to them.

The government reorganization law under which the President acted today was sponsored by the Administration several years ago in an effort to promote economy and efficiency throughout the executive branch. The entire proposal was once defeated by Congress after repeated charges that Mr. Roosevelt would make himself a dictator. This the President denied in an anonymous open letter addressed only to "Dear John" from the little White House at Warm Springs, Ga., last November, in which the President said that he had neither the inclination nor the qualifications of a dictator.

President Gets a Good Sleep

The President was in periodic telephone communication today with the State Department and officials of other Washington agencies watching developments on the European front. He had discarded the usual means of commercial calls, and was using direct private wires to Washington.

Last night, for the first time since the crisis started, he had a good sleep. He was not awakened until 9 o'clock this morning—several hours later than he had been permitted to sleep in Washington because of constant messages from abroad.

This morning the President inspected the site of the memorial library which he has donated to the nation and which is to stand on the north field of his estate. He was accompanied by John McShain, the contractor, and W. J. Moore, the superintendent. After studying plans and discussing general problems, the group toured the countryside by car, inspecting buildings made of the same native fieldstone as is to be used in the construction of the library.

In the afternoon Mr. Roosevelt went to his Dutchess Hill cottage and watched the installation of porch and living room furniture which he had brought with him on his private train. He had no appointments for the day and will have none tomorrow. He will leave for Washington tomorrow afternoon.

September 10, 1939

Truman Asks Full Power To Reorganize Agencies

President, in Message, Says No Unit Should Be Exempt if Efficiency Dictates a Change —Congress' Rights Preserved

By BERTRAM D. HULEN

Special to THE NEW YORK TIMES.

WASHINGTON, May 24—President Truman asked Congress in a special message today to enact legislation "without delay" to give the Chief Executive permanent authority to reorganize the executive branch of the Government. No agency should be made exempt, he declared.

The request was based on the need of dealing efficiently with war-time organizations and also with the permanent agencies. It asked for authority to deal with them in the future as circumstances warranted. It did not designate any specific agencies as headed for consolidation or for dissolution.

Mr. Truman contended that it was "imperative that these matters be dealt with continuously if the Government structure is to be reasonably wieldy and manageable and be responsive to proper direction by the Congress and the President on behalf of the people of the country."

"The legislation," he suggested, "should be sufficiently broad and flexible to permit of any form of organizational adjustment, large or small, for which necessity may arise."

The President said the legislation should be on a permanent basis and generally similar to the Reorganization Act of 1939 under which the late President Roosevelt operated until it expired and was succeeded in 1941 by the First War Powers Act. The 1939 act provided for improvements in the organization of the executive branch and in executive agencies through Presidential initiative, and for the grouping, coordination, consolidation and abolition of agencies.

Mr. Truman also suggested that Part 2 of Title 1 of the 1939 act should be utilized intact. This protects Congress in the disapproval of any executive orders, through the passage within sixty days of a concurrent resolution which is not subject to Presidential veto.

The message was favorably received by many in Congress where it was regarded as the beginning of a return of separate agencies to the executive departments. President Truman's announcement yesterday of his intention to place the War Food Administration in the Agriculture Department was in line with such a program.

Members of Congress were particularly impressed with that part of the message calling for no exemption of Government agencies. The late President Roosevelt asked for the same thing in the 1939 act but Congress made exemptions because of its fondness for a number of agencies.

Byrd Expresses His Views

Views were divided today on the efficacy of this feature of the program. Senator Harry F. Byrd, Democrat, of Virginia, who is chairman of the Joint Economy Committee of Congress, said:

"I think the scope of the legislation should be as broad as is wise in affecting all the agencies of Government, excepting that there are certain agencies such as the General Accounting Office and others performing semi-judicial functions that perhaps should be exempted, as was done in the Reorganization Act of 1939."

Congress had not decided today what to do with the message or when to take it up for action, although members generally conceded that a contraction would have to be made in the Government after the war.

The matter was referred by the Senate to its Judiciary Committee, but a move developed to assign it to Senator Byrd's Economy Committee which has long been studying the subject.

The need for prompt action, however, was stressed by the President. He stated that the First War Powers Act, which gave the President power to readjust the executive organization for war purposes, would expire automatically six months after the termination of the war and that steps taken under it would then revert to the pre-existing status.

"Such automatic reversion is not workable," he declared.

Moreover, he asserted, it would result in the re-establishment of some agencies that should not be re-established.

"I believe it is realized by everyone," he said, "that the problems I have mentioned will not be met satisfactorily unless the Congress provides for them along the general lines indicated in this message."

He went on to make the point that Congress "cannot deal effectively with numerous organizational problems on an individual item basis."

Experience showed, he said, that if substantial progress were to be made, it must be through action started or taken by the President. Congress, he warned, could not consistently criticize the executive branch for deficiencies and at the same time deny the President the means of removing the causes of criticism.

Senator Byrd's committee has been working on a reorganization plan which will be given to the President and Congress soon. It would outline in definite terms agencies which should be abolished or consolidated, the Senator said, and contain an estimate of the reduction in number of employes which could be made.

"At the conclusion of the war," he stated, "we will be faced with a colossal task in demobilizing the 3,000,000 Civil Service employes. Likewise, there are many duplications of effort and conflicting authorities existing among the nearly 1,200 main Government departments and bureaus.

Thousands of Offices Cited

"Any effective reorganization must include the thousands of branch offices that have been established throughout the country, in many instances side by side, performing work of a similar character."

At the same time the joint committee filed a protest against war agencies increasing the number of employes. Senator Byrd told the Senate that these showed a net increase of 1,556 employes during March and April. He singled out OPA, which added 1,359 employes in the two months and the WMC, which had an increase of 523.

Plans under study by the joint committee call for a reduction of 1,141 principal component parts of the executive branch of the Government to a minimum and for the cutting of the 3,000,000 employes here and in the field at least to the pre-war figure of around 1,000,000.

When Franklin D. Roosevelt entered the White House in 1933 the number of employes had been cut to 528,000 from 975,000 at the end of the first World War.

The 1,141 component parts include thirteen in the executive office of the President, 499 in the ten Federal departments, 364 in twenty-three emergency boards, and 265 in twenty-six independent establishments, boards, commissions, corporations and the like.

May 25, 1945

POWERS OF PRESIDENCY STIR CAPITAL DEBATE

Question Is Sharply Raised in Plans To Reorganize Federal Agencies And in Truman's Labor Bill

LEGAL AND POLITICAL ASPECTS

By ARTHUR KROCK

WASHINGTON, Feb. 5—An ancient issue that grows out of the American system of tripartite government was strongly revived this week in statements made by President Truman at a press conference and in an opinion given to the Senate Labor and Welfare Committee by Attorney General Tom C. Clark. The issue concerns the powers of the Presidency, both stated and implicit, and the degree to which they can be extended without unbalancing the system in which Congress is a coordinate branch of the government.

Mr. Truman raised his part of the issue by saying he wanted no Federal agencies or commissions excluded from the grant of power he is seeking from Congress to reorganize the executive arm of the Government. His present limited authority over the quasi-judicial groups would thus be vastly increased—over the Interstate Commerce Commission, the Securities and Exchange Commission and others.

A fact well established by public experience is that when the President is given the control over any agency or commission that the Hoover Commission recommended Mr. Truman be given over them all, its independent judgment will be guided to the extent he desires. Administration policies affecting the areas of decision would necessarily become fixed boundaries for officers who can be removed if they do not conform. This is a consequence which even the Presidential power of appointment to the quasi-judicial groups does not now assure, and to prevent it Congress carefully provided that many such officers cannot be removed by the President except for inefficiency, neglect or malfeasance, on which charges they may have a hearing, and that some may only be removed by Congressional resolution.

Court Test

President Franklin D. Roosevelt brought about a court test of one of these statutory restrictions on removal in October, 1933, by dismissing Commissioner Humphrey of the Federal Trade Commission. Twice he asked Humphrey to resign, and gave this reason:

You will, I know, realize that I do not feel that your mind and my mind go along together on either the policies or the administering of the Federal Trade Commission, and, frankly, I think it is best for the people of this country that I should have a full confidence.

Mr. Roosevelt based this exercise of executive power to remove on a sweeping though divided Supreme Court decision of 1926 that a former President, Chief Justice Taft, delivered for the court. The Chief Justice, upholding the power of the President to remove a first-class postmaster, one Myers, though his fixed term of four years had not expired, added that Congress could not in any way limit this power "so far as executive officers of the United States appointed by him" were concerned. He found this endowment in Article II of the Constitution, and Mr. Roosevelt concluded it was broad enough for the removal of Humphrey for the reason he gave.

Boundaries Limited

But the Supreme Court unanimously sustained Humphrey's claim that he had been illegally removed and set out to narrow the boundaries of the Taft decision. "The Federal Trade Commission," said Justice Sutherland for the court, "is an administrative body created by Congress to carry into effect legislative policies embodied in the statute. * * * Its duties are performed without executive leave, and in the contemplation of the statute must be free from executive control. * * * The authority of Congress, in creating quasi-legislative or quasi-judicial agencies, to require them to act in discharge of their duties independently of executive control, cannot be well doubted. * * * It is quite evident that one who holds his office only during the pleasure of another cannot be depended upon to maintain an attitude of independence against the other's will."

This finding has never been reversed. But if Congress, reserving, however, a veto power over proposed reorganizations, gives to the President permanently the powers over the whole executive branch that the Hoover Commission recommends, it will cease to have any practical effect. That is the issue Mr. Truman raised.

Court Injunctions

The Attorney General's contribution — endorsed by Mr. Truman also — was a statement to the Senate committee that, under Article II of the Constitution, the President has implicit power to take all necessary steps to prevent or dissolve conditions or situations that threaten the national welfare, nation-wide strikes by labor unions being the type of emergencies under discussion. He said the President does not need the specific authority to seek court injunctions terminating such strikes which the Taft-Hartley Act confers and which is erased in the Administration's substitute for that legislation. And he cited the litigation by the Government in 1947 by which John L. Lewis and his union were heavily fined and Mr. Lewis was forced by the courts to order his miners back to work in mines then under Government operation. At his press conference the next day Mr. Truman cited measures taken in emergencies by previous occupants of the White House.

Points Raised in Dissent

Immediate dissent to the Attorney General's thesis was expressed not only by Republicans on the committee and outside it but by lawyers familiar with the subject. They made these point

(1) Nothing in the Constitution can logically be read to give such implicit power to the President.

(2) The Federal Government is one of limited powers, fixed in the Constitution and the statutes.

(3) The power of the Government to seize struck industries, which enabled it to go to court successfully against Mr. Lewis in 1947, has lapsed except with respect to railroads. Nothing in the Administration labor bill restores it.

(4) If no authority to seek injunctions to protect the national welfare is written into any statute, the legal record is overwhelmingly against the exercise of this power by any implication.

(5) This is especially true in peacetime, and even in the war period of 1943—though Presidential powers were greatly extended by Congress—President Roosevelt felt he had no legal means to require Mr. Lewis to obey an order of the National War Labor Board to sign a wage agreement.

The Secretary of Labor, Maurice Tobin, had preceded Mr. Clark by saying public opinon would operate sufficiently in the event of national emergencies to produce the necessary remedies. And others expressed the view that the Federal courts as now constituted could be relied on to support Mr. Clark's thesis if a situation becomes dangerous enough. But on this issue over Presidential power there was no more legal agreement than there is political agreement that quasi-judicial agencies should be placed completely within it.

These issues, briefly sketched here, are examined in detail in the new book by Prof. E. S. Corwin of Princeton: "The President—Office and Powers," New York University Press.

"APRON STRINGS"

Alexander in The Philadelphia Evening Bulletin

COMMUNIQUE ON UNIFICATION: MAJOR GAINS BUT NOT VICTORY

Despite Advances, Important Rivalries and Problems Remain in the Way of the Ultimate Goal

By HANSON W. BALDWIN

When President Truman signed the bill embodying the revisions of the National Security Act of 1947 last week and appointed General Omar N. Bradley the first official chairman of the Joint Chiefs of Staff, the armed services opened a new chapter.

It is a chapter in which some new faces are appearing in the top-rank hierarchy of the military establishment. Gen. J. Lawton Collins, General Bradley's leading corps commander in France and Germany during the war, was tabbed by the President to become Army chief of staff as successor to General Bradley. General Collins, a forceful leader and able field commander, is also the author of the famous "Collins plan" for unification, bitterly opposed by the Navy, a plan which would have merged the three services in one department and would have provided a single Chief of Staff.

The term of Admiral Louis E. Denfeld, Chief of Naval Operations, was also extended for two years by the President, thus establishing the top team in the Joint Chiefs of Staff as General Bradley, Admiral Denfeld, General Collins and Gen. Hoyt S. Vandenberg, Chief of Staff of the Air Force.

Rivalries Continue

The new chapter, it is hoped, will be brighter than the bitter ones now closed, but the surface indications of a new-found unity are somewhat belied by rumblings which indicate that the same basic strategic differences and the same struggle for power and money and position will be the problem of the future as it has been of the past.

The Congressional investigation of the B-36, which started last week, focuses squarely upon these differences, and Navy bitterness and resentment, which has been much accentuated since Secretary of Defense Louis Johnson took office, was intensified by advance predictions that the 1951 fiscal year defense budget would cut the naval and Marine air arm approximately in half. There is no change, therefore, in the armed services' weather prediction—surface tranquility, perhaps, but storms brewing.

More Integrated System

The new unification law does provide, however, the organizational mechanism for a more efficient and better integrated defense establishment. It moves a step closer to what many feel should be the ultimate, though remote, ideal—a single service and a single uniform.

The new law makes the Secretary of Defense the "top man" in the military hierarchy to a greater extent than he was before. For the Secretary of Defense is given a Deputy Secretary (title changed from Under Secretary), who is superior to the service secretaries; three Assistant Secretaries (these positions did not previously exist) and the executive departments of the Army, Navy and Air Force are down-graded to military departments with the Department of Defense (formerly called the "National Military Establishment") now an executive department in its own right.

Moreover, the Secretaries of Army, Navy and Air Force, who were formerly members of the highly important advisory National Security Council, which is instrumental in the coordination of military and foreign policy, are now excluded from this body; the Secretary of Defense speaks for them all.

Limitations on Power

The specific limitations put upon the power of the Secretary of Defense—he must report semi-annually to Congress; he must allow access of the service secretaries and individual members of the Joint Chiefs of Staff to Congress to present views contrary to his own; he cannot change the combatant functions of the services—are less impressive than the unspecified but implicit increase in his powers.

In a sense this power is further increased by the provision creating a chairman of the Joint Chiefs of Staff, who has no vote, but takes precedence over all other officers of the armed forces, and who presides at JCS meetings, provides agenda and "informs" the Secretary.

The limitations on the power of the new chairman are definite; since he has no vote and no command authority he cannot decide split votes or debated issues. The Joint Chiefs of Staff—not the chairman—are explicitly named as the principal military advisers to the President and the Secretary of Defense. Despite these legal restrictions, the prestige that goes with the top rank and highest uniformed job in the services will undoubtedly tend to make General Bradley individually, rather than the Joint Chiefs collectively, more and more the "principal military adviser." In the discussions of the Joint Chiefs the chairman's role may be chiefly that of a catalyst, to bring about by his personality and logic a meeting of divergent minds.

This position of chairman, now legalized, has been filled, strictly unofficially and without legal authority, by General of the Army Dwight D. Eisenhower, who is now succeeded by his principal World War II field commander, General Bradley.

JCS Staff Enlarged

The creation of the office of chairman of the JCS, and a little noted provision, the increase of the Joint Staff of the JCS from a limit of 100 officers to an authorized 210 officers, is viewed by some as still another step toward the long-desired Army concept of unification—a concept bitterly opposed by the Navy—of a single chief of staff over all the armed forces, aided by a greater general staff.

This concept, however, is still some distance off; the new law preserves the separate individuality of the three military departments and provides for their separate administration, and each of the services retains its own secretary, under-secretary and two assistant secretaries.

One of the most important and least controversial of the new law's provisions modernizes the budget and fiscal structures of the services and sets up a "performance budget," thus establishing for the first time comparable budgetary forms and practices for the armed forces. A controller, to be one of the new Assistant Secretaries of Defense is provided for and each service department will also establish a controller.

Whether this revised law will be more successful than the original unification act in promoting service unity is questionable. Unification is not an end in itself; the aim—greater combat efficiency and more economy—is even more the product of personalities, of education, and of some resolution of the strategic differences between the services than it is of organization or blueprint.

Economy—or rather less expense—it seemed clear last week, was on the way, but mainly by edict rather than integration, unification or administrative reorganization. The President's ceiling for the national defense budget of the 1951 fiscal year starting next July 1 apparently has been set at about $13 billions, according to advanced reports—$1 to $2 billions less than this year. The preliminary slicing of the pie among the three services indicates that the Navy is going to come out on the short end, with the Army taking a slight cut but with the Air Force holding even.

The Navy's argument — implict also in the B-36 hearings before Congress—is that our increasing dependence upon the long-range strategic bomber and the atomic bomb and the increasing weakening of the surface forces may promote more economy in the form of a reduced national defense budget but will certainly not produce combat efficiency, or greater security.

The Navy's Question

The Navy poses this question: Does the lang-range bomber carrying the atomic bomb justify the high priority given it in defense dollars and in strategic plans?

This major strategical question, and many other important problems face the new Department of Defense and its ancillary agencies as the "cold war" continues. The new chapter in our defense history now opening focuses a greater amount of authority in the office of the Secretary of Defense, and provides the mechanism for a sounder organizational and budgetary system. But men, not blueprints, make organizations work, and the new defense "team" still has to be proved.

THE NEW SET-UP OF THE NATIONAL SECURITY ORGANIZATION

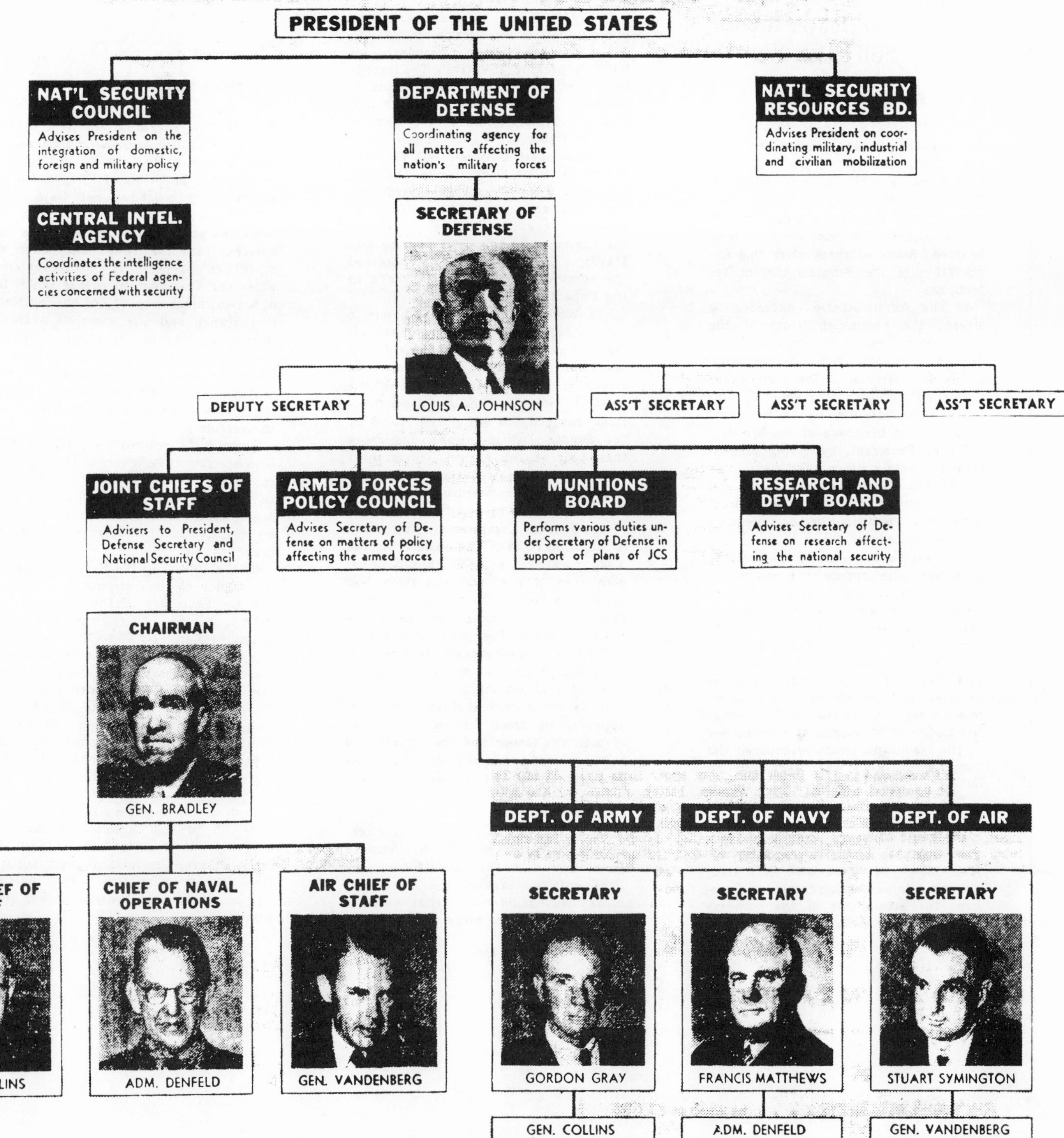

Photos from Harris & Ewing, Associated Press and The New York Times

The Office of the Secretary of Defense is structurally strengthened by the addition of a Deputy Secretary and three Assistant Secretaries. Another important change is the establishment of the post of Chairman of the Joint Chiefs of Staff, to which General Omar N. Bradley was appointed by President Truman last week. Besides their duties within the Defense Department the Joint Chiefs are advisers to the President, the Secretary of Defense and the National Security Board on matters of security.

August 14, 1949

In The Nation

Net Score on Hoover Reports Still Good

By ARTHUR KROCK

WASHINGTON, May 18—Though the Senate has disapproved the first five of the twenty-one plans to reorganize the executive branch which the President submitted in March, and prospects for six more are dim, friends of the general enterprise are not downhearted. Some of them offer this explanation of the Senate's current rejections:

1. The Administration exceeded or altered the recommendations of the commission headed by former President Hoover, sometimes fundamentally, as in the instance of the plan to return the functions of the general counsel of the National Labor Relations Board to the members of the board.

2. The President, by giving precedence to certain plans that were open to charges of partisan animation, and by the timing of those he submitted, materially changed the commission's plan of procedure.

3. These tactics enabled members of Congress who oppose the entire reorganization concept because they want to protect certain Government personnel to cite bases of opposition more acceptable to the large public which the Citizens' Committee, the Junior Chamber of Commerce, etc., have assembled in favor of the Hoover Commission reports. In the words of Senator Lodge of Massachusetts, co-author of the resolution which established the commission, "they gave everybody an out."

But Mr. Lodge is only one of those who believe that what has already been made effective in the commission program justifies its creation and its cost. And many of these also feel that, though Administration tactics will prevent the attainment of the economy that otherwise was possible, the net score will be considerable when all the plans have been acted on.

The History So Far

In 1949, when the reorganization plans submitted were much more faithful to the commission's proposals, all but one became effective. The exception established a new Department of Welfare. The remaining six shifted two employment units to the Department of Labor; added to the powers of the Postmaster General; put the National Security Council and the National Security Resources Board into the President's executive office; increased the administrative powers of the chairmen of the Civil Service and Maritime Commissions and transferred the administration of public roads to the Department of Commerce.

The 1950 submissions, twenty-one in number, of which the Senate has already rejected five, to date have drawn seventeen resolutions to disapprove eleven of them. By the terms of the General Reorganization Act a constitutional majority of either the House or the Senate (which means one more than half of the entire membership) is sufficient to reject a plan. This arrangement was opposed by the Administration and by many of the members of the Hoover Commission. But, while it might have been responsible for the disapproval of a good, non-political plan even if the Administration had been more faithful to the commission's blueprints, the arrangement is in the public interest. The political pressure a President can successfully exert on the House is fortified by the restrictive rules of that branch.

If, as the Administration urged, disapproval by constitutional majorities of both the House and the Senate had been required to kill any plan the President submitted, the legislative branch would have been too greatly subordinated in business where its responsibility is at least as great as the Executive's. Already, by the veto powers granted him in the Constitution, the President can prevent the enactment of any legislation except that which is supported by two-thirds majorities of the House and the Senate. And these must be assembled and held together for the act of overriding a veto.

Too Much Power

To have made it possible for the President to reorganize any part of the executive branch and the independent, semi-judicial agencies and commissions unless both branches of Congress disapproved by constitutional majorities would have given him a new affirmative power as great as the negative one he derives from the veto. And, once a statute is enacted, this veto power enables the President to defeat the will of a two-thirds majority of one legislative branch and one short of a two-thirds majority of the other if these favor repeal of the statute. He can disapprove the repeal, and it can be effected only by two-thirds majorities in both the House and the Senate on a motion to override.

These facts induced many legislators who are sincere believers in the Hoover commission's work to deny the Executive request that, to disapprove a reorganization plan, it must be rejected by constitutional majorities of both branches.

Of the 1950 crop the Senate followed the advice of the banking community and the Secretary of the Treasury in voting, 65 to 13, against the new Treasury plan. By 66 to 13 it defeated reorganization of the Interstate Commerce Commission that would have taken away its independence of the Executive. It voted 50 to 23 against the Federal Communications Commission plan, and 63 to 12 against the most controversial proposal—that which affected the National Labor Relations Board.

But, if the American Legion's overture of protest against legislation carrying out Reports 2, 9, 14 and 15 of the Hoover Commission is an indication of how noisy this actual battle will be, we haven't heard any real uproar yet.

May 19, 1950

Our Super-Government—Can We Control It?

An examination, in light of the Hoover reports, of 'the most complicated enterprise on earth.'

By JAMES MacGREGOR BURNS

DURING a campaign talk in 1920 Warren G. Harding said airily that "government is a simple thing." A year in the White House was enough to change his mind. "I can't make a damn thing out of this tax problem," he exploded to a secretary one day. "I listen to one side and they seem right—and then—God! I talk to the other side and they seem just as right, and here I am where I started. God, what a job!"

Stronger Presidents than Harding have had trouble managing "the toughest job on earth." Much of the difficulty has stemmed from the creaking machinery, the fuzzy organization and the sheer bulk of the executive branch of the National Government. For decades our Chief Executives have been trying to overhaul and modernize the administrative apparatus, which Franklin D. Roosevelt once termed a "higgledy-piggledy patchwork of duplicate responsibilities and overlapping powers." Since McKinley's time distinguished committees have been appointed, elaborate studies made, reforms recommended. But our administrative structure has remained sadly out-of-date; the Chief Executive's job has become more grueling than ever.

GUIDED by an ex-President who had wrestled with the problem in his own day, the latest excursion into the Dark Continent of the national bureaucracy is now coming to an end. The reports of the Hoover Commission on Organization of the Executive Branch indicate that our Federal Government has become the most colossal and complicated enterprise on earth. It employs over two million persons. It spends over forty billions a year—more than the total income of all Americans hardly a generation ago. It employs over half the types of skills found in all private enterprise. It owns one-fifth of the area of the United States.

The Government is big because its jobs are big. The Treasury Department handles almost fifty million individual income tax returns every year, the Postoffice Department almost forty billion pieces of mail. The Veterans Administration manages about forty billion dollars of insurance policies. Sometimes work failures come in proportion to work accomplished. A medium-sized agency confessed to the Hoover Commission last year that it had on hand a backlog of over a quarter-million cubic feet of wartime records that had not yet been processed.

Many Americans eye this burgeoning giant with suspicion, if not with open repugnance. Some of them look eagerly to the day when large parts of it can be dismantled. But the extraordinary fact seems to be that the commission on organization headed by Herbert Hoover himself and sprinkled with conservative business men and Congressmen—has supplied the most convincing evidence we have yet had that our super-Government is here to stay.

IN setting up the commission Congress emphasized an interest not only in economy and efficiency but also in "abolishing services, activities and functions not necessary to the efficient conduct of government." Here was a mandate to the commission to track down the hundreds of worthless bureaus that—according to popular notion—make up a large part of the National Government. But the commission took no such tack. Its efficiency experts found waste, duplication of effort, lack of order, poor control. It has urged the consolidation of activities and the adoption of sweeping reforms. But after sixteen months of exhaustive investigation the commission has not recommended the abolition of any significant function. Indeed, the commission has urged the expansion of a number of Government services.

How can this result be explained? The answer is that the commission and its staff carefully studied the facts of governmental life instead of contenting themselves with generalities about "bureaucracy rampant." They discovered—if they did not already know—that government is not a single entity that can be easily deflated like a balloon. It is a collection of hundreds of separate agencies, rendering a tremendous variety of services to "clients" who depend heavily on those services. It is a collection of human beings with many tasks: a hoof-and-mouth disease inspector in Texas; an economist in Washington; a weather forecaster in New York; a veterans' counselor in Seattle; an expert on Korean affairs in the Pentagon, and thousands of others.

VERY few of these functions compete with private enterprise; on the contrary, almost all of them are responses to needs that only government can meet. It has long been agreed that our Government should deliver the mail, wage war, regulate interstate commerce, take the census, and the like; few seriously argue that such tasks could or should be turned over to private individuals.

Our super-Government, in short, has become a fixed part of the "American way of life." It has become a vital instrument for social progress. But its very size and importance make it a costly and dangerous instrument if not properly managed. It is precisely on this point that the Hoover Commission, while recognizing that big government is here to stay, has raised storm warnings.

The American people directly hire and fire only one person—the President—out of the two million in the Executive branch. The Chief Executive must serve as a firm link between the people and their bureaucracy. His office is the funnel through which their needs and urges are translated into administrative action. Everything depends on the responsiveness of the bureaucracy to the President's—and hence to the people's—direction.

THAT is where the trouble lies. By far the most significant finding of the Hoover Commission is that the Chief Executive does not have full control of his own establishment. Authority is scattered about; lines of control are tangled and broken. Broad policy does not flow from the White House to the agencies as clearly as it should, but is confused and dissipated.

For one thing, the agencies are not set up in well-defined, cohesive groupings. President Truman has shown visitors a huge chart on his office wall picturing well over 100 officials required by law to report to the Chief Executive alone, and has complained that "I cannot even see all these men, let alone actually study what they are doing." Even if the President were able to ignore his legislative, political and ceremonial duties and concentrate wholly on administration—which he cannot do—he would have only a few minutes a week to meet with these officials.

WITH an adequate staff the Chief Executive might give a measure of direction and coordination to this labyrinth of departments and commissions. But he is lacking some of the indispensable tools of good management. Control of personnel is not fully in his hands, and he lacks the means to check on the performance of the agencies. The President cannot choose his own staff as freely as he would like. Nor can he rely on his Cabinet for disinterested advice, because the members are concerned mainly with their departmental duties and often represent warring factions in the party. A dozen years ago President Roosevelt's Committee on Administrative Management summed up the situation simply: "The President needs help." The need is even greater today

The strong chain of command that should tie the bureaucracy to the President and thus to the people is broken at other points. Subordinate officials have been given power by law to act independently of the Chief Executive. For example, the Secretary of the Interior can control the sale of helium to foreign nations, and the Army Chief of Engineers can prepare river development plans without referring to superior authority. Independent boards make vitally important decisions that are beyond Presidential reach. The Maritime Commission's control

---

JAMES MacGREGOR BURNS, Assistant Professor of Political Science at Williams College, served on the Hoover Commission staff. His book, "Congress on Trial," comes out in July.

of shipping can sharply affect our foreign relations. Yet the President must negotiate with the Maritime Commissioners almost as with foreign plenipotentiaries.

THE chain of command is also weakened at the departmental level. Often the departments are mere "holding companies" for semi-independent bureaus that go their own way. Such a situation breeds administrative slackness and aloofness, and what Pendleton Herring called "quiet sabotage by unsympathetic technicians and genteel blackmail by high policy officials." Delay and fumbling are hard enough to curb under any conditions. Harry Hopkins complained during the war, according to Robert E. Sherwood, that after important decisions had been reached by Mr. Roosevelt and Mr. Churchill and by the generals and admirals, months-long delays would occur—"and then you start investigating and it takes you weeks to find out that the orders have been deliberately stalled on the desk of some lieutenant commander or lieutenant colonel down on Constitution Avenue."

If failures of top control are serious in the civilian agencies, they are positively dangerous in the military. Traditionally, Americans have had a healthy fear of military cliques and of the "man on horseback." Knowing something about military oppression, the framers of the Constitution carefully put the Army and Navy under civilian control. The safeguards they provided are all the more important under conditions of modern war, whether of the atomic, bacteriological, or "push-button" variety. The fact that the per capita cost of defense is now $100 annually has given taxpayers a tremendous stake in the efficiency of the military as well as its responsibility.

ON this score, too, the Hoover Commission has uttered an urgent warning. It reports that centralized civilian control "scarcely exists." It has found a weak link in the chain of command between the Secretary of Defense and the service departments – the Army, Navy and Air Force. The basic trouble here arises from the manner in which the new military establishment was tacked together as a federation of competing services rather than as a unified, integrated system with clear control in the hands of the President and the Secretary of Defense. The Joint Chiefs of Staff—composed of military chiefs—are virtually a law unto themselves.

To clear up the disorganization and irresponsibility in both the civilian and military parts of the Executive branch, the Hoover Commission has proposed some old-fashioned remedies. Among these are intelligent grouping of agencies in major departments, centralization of authority in the President, clear lines of command and accountability, and adequate staff services. These suggestions are, indeed, so obvious that the question arises: Why is it that after a decade or two of big government we are still trying to apply first principles to the running of our administrative machinery?

IF our Chief Executives had had the power to manage the Executive branch as they wished, they long ago would have applied these first principles in an effort to lighten their own heavy burdens. But the Constitution, while vesting the "executive power" in the President, does not give him exclusive authority over his own branch of government. Under our system of checks and balances Congress has considerable control of administration, just as the President in turn takes part in lawmaking through his veto and other powers.

Congress determines whether a new function of government will be placed firmly under the President or will be somewhat independent of him. It can give the President a good deal of leeway in setting up agencies, or it can specify provisions that bind the President at every turn. Congress, in short, has the power to organize the Executive branch—and to reorganize it. Even more important, the Senate and House of Representatives hold the "power of the purse" through their appropriations committees.

ALONG with these constitutional powers are others that have grown up by custom and usage. The House and Senate have expanded their investigating power into strong tools for influencing administrators. Sometimes the probes are full-dress committee inquiries conducted amid exploding flash bulbs; sometimes they are quiet "fishing expeditions" by one or two Congressmen with special interests. In any event, they help to make the harassed administrator watchful of his Congressional relationships. Finally, Congress has considerable weight in the selection of officials. Under the Constitution the Senate must confirm major appointments; moreover, the President, by the unwritten rule of "Senatorial courtesy," must clear thousands of selections with interested Congressmen.

Inevitably Congress has come to wield day-to-day influence over large parts of the Executive branch. Inevitably, too, the bureaucrat has come to look not simply to the White House for orders and support, but also to Capitol Hill. Administrators are quick to see that Presidents may come and go, political parties may rise and fall, but the committee chieftains in Congress seem to go on forever.

WHAT is the result? Not only is control of the bureaucracy divided between President and Congress. In Congress it is further divided among Senate, House, legislative blocs, committees, subcommittees and individual members. As a result of this fragmentation of power in Congress one finds lines of authority running horizontally from committee or Congressman to department or bureau chief, so that authority is shifted from the President and dispersed throughout the bureaucracy.

Under such conditions any hope of pinning responsibility for mistakes or achievements on the proper officials often becomes forlorn indeed. The source of administrative direction often seems to be far underground, lost in a maze of subterranean channels among President, administrators, Congressional blocs and committees. "There is no danger in power," Woodrow Wilson said, "if only it be not irresponsible. If it be divided, dealt out in shares to many, it is obscured; and if it be obscured, it is made irresponsible."

The Hoover Commission wants to pin on the President as much executive responsibility as the Constitution will allow, and thus to make him strictly accountable to Congress *as a whole* and to the people. Its pleas for a stronger chain of command from the President downward stem from its conviction that singleness of control is the essence of both responsibility and efficiency.

UNHAPPY experience indicates, however, that any move to reorganize the Executive branch will run head-on into the opposition of the groups that profit from the present state of affairs. Every major function of government is carried on amid intense pressures from the interests affected. Agency heads are often caught squarely in the storm center of labor politics, farm politics, transportation politics, medical politics, as the case may be. They cultivate close ties with interests they promote or regulate. Sometimes they find it hard to mediate between the national welfare and the interest of a particular group.

Congress as a whole genuinely favors responsibility and efficiency in government. But individual Congressmen and blocs in each chamber are likely to demand that their own agencies be left out of any plan for firmer control by the President. They prefer the agencies to be more vulnerable to Congressional control, to be more responsive to the affected interests. The Congressmen cannot be blamed for holding such views, for they too are under pressure from the groups dominant in their states and districts. The Hoover Commission had only to suggest the shift of some public works functions from the Corps of Engineers to the Interior Department for a storm of protests to descend on Capitol Hill.

A SIZABLE group of Congressmen opposed to reorganization can log-roll the proposals to death. The process is much like the traditional handling of tariff bills, when Congressmen forgot their free-trade principles in their zeal for protection for the "folks back home" and busily swapped concessions with one another. The only remedy for such log-rolling is to delegate extensive power to the President to draw up proposals. In 1912 Congress granted President Taft power to make reorganization changes without referring back to the Legislative branch.

More recently Congress has been niggardly in giving the President reorganization powers. Changes proposed by Presidents Coolidge and Hoover failed in the face of stout resistance. In 1937, after hearing the advice of his Committee on Administrative Management, President Roosevelt asked Congress for broad reorganization authority. Along with specific changes he proposed that the President have the power to draw up reform proposals; these would become law unless disapproved by both Senate and House within sixty days.

THIS proposal provoked a great hue and cry from groups that feared the effect of the plans on their favorite agencies. Although Taft had received far greater reorganization power, the President's bill was soon dubbed the "dictator bill." The violent fight over the Supreme Court reform proposal had just taken place, and many Americans swallowed the charge that the reorganization bill was but another move toward executive tyranny. Deluged by telegrams, the House killed the bill. In 1939 a far weaker act was passed, later to be renewed in about the same form until 1948.

President Truman recently asked Congress to re-enact and broaden the power to initiate reorganization plans. The Hoover Commission heartily supports this request. It has warned, moreover, against putting limitations on the President's power, for "once the limiting and exempting process is begun," the commission says, "it will end the possibility of achieving really substantial results." No safeguard is necessary other than the right of Congress to veto Presidential reorganization plans as a whole.

THE renewal of the Reorganization Act—and the form in which it is renewed—will be one of the important issues facing Americans during the immediate years ahead. Already a sharp battle seems to be shaping up. Last January Congressional leaders told President Truman flatly that no reorganization bill could pass unless several independent commissions were exempted. More "grasshopper bites," as Chairman Hoover called them, were taken out of the bill before it passed the House. Recently Congressmen have complained of lobbying against proposed reforms by pressure groups and even by agency heads.

Much will depend on the ability of Americans to understand that granting the President more power over the Executive branch is a move not toward dictatorship but toward more responsible government. Years ago Lincoln stressed the need of maintaining a Government strong enough to fulfill its obligations but not too strong for the liberties of the people. A Chief Executive accountable to people and Congress and firmly in control of the bureaucracy is a first step in meeting that need. For in the age of super-government, nothing can last very long without skillful and responsible management—not even our own democracy.

April 24, 1949

HOUSE KILLS PLAN FOR CABINET OFFICE OF PUBLIC WELFARE

Socialized Medicine Stressed by Foes of New Department —Vote Is 249 to 71

EWING IS MAJOR TARGET

Senate Group Backs Plan to Put Federal Budget on a 'Performance' Basis

By CLAYTON KNOWLES
Special to THE NEW YORK TIMES.

WASHINGTON, July 10 — President Truman's second bid to give departmental status to the Federal Security Agency was rejected, 249 to 71, by the House today.

The outcome of the vote was influenced by a belief, strongly expressed in debate, that the case for compulsory health insurance would be advanced if the agency, which operates the Public Health Service, received a voice in the Government at the Cabinet level.

The drive against the reorganization plan was spearheaded by Republicans. However, 106 Democrats joined 143 Republicans to doom the proposal to create a Department of Health, Education and Security. Among the Democrats were a number of normally stanch Administration supporters as well as eleven committee chairmen.

Seventy Democrats and one Republican, Representative Jacob K. Javits of New York, supported the plan.

Ewing Heavily Attacked

By its action, the House exercised the right of veto, reserved for either it or the Senate under the Reorganization Act of 1949. The vote of a constitutional majority in either chamber is needed to kill a plan. This requires 218 votes in the House and forty-nine in the Senate.

A year ago, the Senate killed a similar plan that would have transformed the Federal Security Agency into a Department of Welfare. The opposition at the time was on identical grounds, and then, as today, Oscar R. Ewing, the Federal Security Administrator, was repeatedly attacked. He is an outspoken advocate of compulsory health insurance.

Envisaging Mr. Ewing as the probable secretary of the new department, Representative Clare E. Hoffman, Republican of Michigan, said that medical doctors would fall "under the orders of a master politician."

"If we were so unfortunate as to get Dr. Ewing," he asserted, "we might be getting medicine from a veterinarian."

Mr. Ewing is not a doctor, but the Michigan member, seeking to drive home the danger of political influence in the field of medicine, overstated a case that others had presented for the effect it would have. Mr. Hoffman sponsored the resolution of disapproval.

G. O. P. 'Smokescreen' Seen

In vain, Representative John W. McCormack of Massachusetts, the Democratic leader, and other Administration stalwarts argued that health insurance was not involved in the plan. They asserted that it was an extraneous issue and a "smokescreen" put out to "befog the situation."

Health insurance, they said, could not be put into effect without substantive legislation, acted on independently by Conrgess. The only purpose of the plan, they insisted, would be to give health, education and security, affecting all of the population, representation in the Cabinet.

However, Republicans, who freely quoted the American Medical Association's opposition arguments to the plan, derided these assertions. The Republican point of view was perhaps best expressed by Representative Charles A. Halleck of Indiana, who said:

"Your vote on this plan will put you definitely on one side or the other of this great issue of socialized medicine."

The Republicans also argued that the President's plan did not conform to the recommendations of the Commission on Organization of the Executive Branch of the Government, an official nonpartisan agency headed by former President Herbert Hoover that studied Federal operations for two years.

Representative Clarence J. Brown, Republican of Ohio, a member of that commission, recalled that while there had been a recommendation that the Federal Security Agency be made a department, it was conditioned on another recommendation that the Public Health Service be transferred to a new United Medical Administration.

Representative Chet Holifield, Democrat of California, replied that this separation would require legislation, and that adoption of the plan would, in no wise, prevent passage of such a bill.

The possibility that Mr. Ewing might be selected as Democratic candidate for Governor in New York was brought into the debate by Representative A. L. Miller, Republican of Nebraska. He expressed hope that this might come to pass "to get him out of our hair."

"Don't wish that on us," Representative Kenneth B. Keating, Republican of New York, said.

The House vote today just about completed action on the twenty-seven reorganization plans the President has submitted to Congress this year. The Security Department proposal was the seventh plan to go to defeat. All previous vetoes had occurred in the Senate.

Only one plan remains to be cleared. It provides for reorganization of the Treasury Department. An earlier plan to the same general effect was defeated because it put the Controller of the Currency under direct rule of the Secretary of the Treasury. In resubmitting the plan, President Truman exempted this office, thereby removing the only basis of opposition. The reorganization, seemingly now assured, will become effective July 31.

But the Senate Expenditures Committee reported today by unanimous vote a bill instituting the bulk of budgetary and accounting reforms sought by the Hoover Commission. This bill, on which hearings will start in the House tomorrow, is slated to be acted on at this session of the Congress. The Citizens Committee for the Hoover Report considers action in this field of major importance in effectuating Federal reorganization.

"Performance Budget" Set

The committee, meeting in the morning, also reported favorably by a 6-to-3 vote a resolution to disapprove elevating the Federal Security Agency to departmental rank. In view of the House action, the Senate will not need to consider the resolution.

The reform bill approved by the committee proposes to introduce the "performance budget" into departmental fiscal operations. Under it, emphasis would be put on the work or service intended, rather than on individual items of personal or contractual service, supplies, materials and equipment. It is designed to show the relationship between the volume of work to be done and the money it will cost, something now difficult to ascertain.

To a degree, the bill also fosters business-type budgets for Government-owned corporations which are, in effect, businesses.

Accounting, now done by the Controller General's office, would be assumed by the individual departments under standards set by the Controller General and maintained by the Secretary of the Treasury. Auditing, as now is the case, would be done by the Controller General.

While substantially following Hoover Commission recommendations, the bill differs in one major aspect. The commission had recommended that standards for accounting in the departments be set by a new officer, an accountant general serving under the Secretary of the Treasury. Enforcement of these standards also would have been under him.

The Senate Committee and its staff that worked on the problem for a year switched this provision because of a belief that the Controller General must remain the Congressional watchdog on Federal spending. Unless he sets the methods of accounting, it was argued, he cannot properly audit the accounts.

Before the committee voted on the bill, it was approved in executive session by John W Snyder, Secretary of the Treasury; Frederick J. Lawton, Director of the Budget; Lindsay Warren, Controller General, and with some qualifications, by Robert L. McCormick, research director of the Citizens Committee for the Hoover Report.

July 11, 1950

TRUMAN REBUFFED ON MERGER POWERS

Congress Refuses to Let Him Reshuffle Agencies—Votes Pact-Reopening Authority

By JOHN D. MORRIS

Special to THE NEW YORK TIMES.

WASHINGTON, Jan. 2—Congress gave President Truman emergency procurement powers today, but set aside a companion request for wide authority to reorganize Federal agencies and create new ones.

Mr. Truman, in a special message Dec. 18, had asked for approval of both during the session that ended today. He said that they were needed immediately for the mobilization effort.

Voice votes in the House and Senate today granted him half of what he had asked as Congressional action was completed on a bill whereby the Executive Branch will be able to modify contracts already entered into. Because of rising costs of materials, adjustments in many fixed-price contracts were held necessary to speed defense procurement.

The rebuff to the President on his request for emorgency reorganizational powers was attributed largely to concern that he might use them to establish a Department of Welfare or take other action opposed by Congress.

Truman Assurance Ignored

This was despite Mr. Truman's assurances, in his Dec. 18 message, that he would not use the authority to make permanent changes, limiting any action to temporary reorganizations aimed at furthering the defense program.

He also specifically mentioned the possibility that the powers would be needed to carry out organizational arrangements now under study by Charles E. Wilson, director of defense mobilization.

The rejected recommendation will be taken up again in the Eight-second Congress, which convenes tomorrow, but early action is not considered likely.

The emergency powers bill was first stripped of reorganizational authority in the Senate, and House leaders acceded after failing before the Christmas recess to bring to the floor a measure embodying both requests.

The House accordingly passed the Senate bill today with an amendment to give the General Accounting Office authority to inspect the books of companies whose contracts with the Government are adjusted under its terms. The Senate promptly accepted the revision and sent the measure to the White House.

"Bailing Out" Opposed

Specifically, the bill reactivates part of the War Powers Act of 1941, which was in effect throughout World War II. By his recent declaration of a national emergency, Mr. Truman obtained authority to let contracts by negotiation. There was doubt, however, whether he could adjust contracts after they had been let.

The Army alone holds forty-nine contracts with companies that now find themselves unable to meet the original prices because of rising costs.

Representative Emanuel Celler, Democrat of New York, floor manager of the bill, told the House that many of them consequently would be unable to fill their orders unless the contracts were adjusted. Some faced bankruptcy. Letting new contracts would consume time and impede the defense program, he said.

Representative Robert F. Rich, Republican of Pennsylvania, protested that "you are just bailing out a bunch of business men dumb enough not to cover themselves with necessary manufacturing materials before contracting with the Government."

On passage of the bill, Mr. Rich was the only member heard to vote "No."

January 3, 1951

HUGE WASTE CITED IN U. S. JOB TACTICS

Civil Service League Lists Red Tape, Duplication and High Cost of Economy

A report on "The Government's Wasted Manpower," made public yesterday by the National Civil Service League, 120 East Twenty-ninth Street, documents charges that millions of dollars are wasted in Federal personnel operations through "red tape, duplication of effort and paper shuffling."

The report, prepared by Melvin Purvis, former agent of the Federal Bureau of Investigation and now chief counsel for the Senate Subcommittee on Federal Manpower Policies, is termed "the climax to a series of probes that began with the Hoover Report and one which may well hold the key to significant and constructive changes in the Federal personnel picture."

The report specifies the following items:

¶At a cost of more than $2,500,000, the Defense Department is sending eighty-seven Army, Navy and Marine officers to civilian law schools, although these branches already have on active duty 3,420 officers with law degrees who are not being used in legal work.

¶The Government method of recruiting employes is wasteful. The report cites an instance in which four recruiting teams looking for typists and stenographers visited Uniontown, Pa., a city of 20,000, within sixty days.

Maze of Regulations Noted

¶The maze and bulk of the Government's administative regulations have helped defeat effective utilization of personnel. It is pointed out that every major agency has its own administrative instructions for implementing manpower and personnel policies.

¶Fifty to 60 per cent of the top jobs in certain new defense agencies are being filled by persons brought in directly by their supervisors, thus limiting job competition for these important posts.

¶Civil Service Commission standards and examinations are too broad and unselective, eligible registers are not current, and the rule of three (limiting the choice to one of the top three names on an eligible roster) is too severe a restriction on appointing officers.

¶The best available supervisory personnel is not being obtained because, the report says, too much emphasis is being placed on technical ability and too little on leadership qualities.

High Cost of Economy Cited

¶The cost to the Government in cutting employes from its payroll is far too high. Many man-hours are lost in shifting persons from job to job to provide for the lost personnel. "In one case, approximately six times as many people as were separated were moved," the report says. Through confusion there is a consequent loss of efficiency and morale. Asserting that it will cost the Government $50,000,000 to remove 25,000 persons from the payroll, the report says that this figure can be cut in half.

The study has been published in the current issue of Good Government, the league's bi-monthly magazine. As to the lawyer-officers not assigned to legal duties, it says:

"Officials of the Office of Judge Advocate General of the Navy have stated it costs $15,000 a year to maintain an officer in law school, and it has been necessary to call Reserve officers to active duty to replace officers who are going to law school.

"Even if conservatively estimated on the basis of $10,000 per officer, the cost of sending eighty-seven officers to school is $870,000 a year," and over a normal three-year course would cost the Government $2,610,000."

May 15, 1952

EISENHOWER OFFERS PLAN TO GIVE F.S.A. STATUS IN CABINET

Proposal Is Basically the Same as Submitted by Truman but Approval Is Indicated

CONGRESS SETS HEARINGS

Mrs. Hobby Slated to Be Chief, With Agency Still Stressing Security and Health

By ANTHONY LEVIERO

Special to THE NEW YORK TIMES.

WASHINGTON, March 12—President Eisenhower submitted to Congress today a reorganization plan to convert the Federal Security Agency into a Department of Health, Education and Welfare.

Approval of the plan would make Mrs. Oveta Culp Hobby, Federal Security Administrator, the tenth member of the Cabinet with the title of Secretary of Health, Education and Welfare. It also would sweep out of office hold-over officials of the Truman Administration, notably Arthur J. Altmeyer, the controversial Commissioner of Social Security, who is an advocate of national health insurance.

The plan submitted today was basically the same offered in 1950 by President Truman. The Truman plan was defeated, but President Eisenhower's proposal today found a new climate on Capitol Hill and speedy action and approval were indicated.

The basic pattern of F. S. A., which will be retained in the new department, consists of three major services—Social Security Administration, Public Health Service and Office of Education. There exist several subordinate staff offices for administration purposes that may or may not be altered by the new Secretary.

Hoffman Proposes Speed-Up

This was the first reorganization plan submitted by the President under the authority recently granted by Congress. Such plans go into effect sixty days after submission unless the House of Representatives or the Senate disapproves by a constitutional majority, meaning 218 votes in the House or forty-nine in the Senate.

A speed-up of the reorganization procedure was proposed, however, by Representative Clare E. Hoffman, Republican of Michigan, who introduced a bill to put the plan into effect ten days after approval by the House and Senate. He is chairman of the House Governmental Affairs Committee, and his bill was scheduled to go before the Rules Committee on Monday or Tuesday. Representative Leslie C. Arends, Republican of Illinois, assistant House leader, announced the House would take up the bill on Wednesday.

In the Senate the reorganization plan was promptly scheduled for hearings on Monday by Senator Joseph R. McCarthy, Republican of Wisconsin, the chairman of the Senate Government Operations Committee. He designated Senator Margaret Chase Smith, Republican of Maine, as chairman of a subcommittee to conduct the hearings.

Senator McCarthy reflected the concern of some members of Congress who were not sure a reorganization plan was adequate to remake the big independent security agency and give it cabinet status. They had raised the question whether regular legislation might not be required.

While suggesting legislation rather than a plan was needed "to get rid of deadwood and debris" in F. S. A., Senator McCarthy said he approved of the plan on the whole.

With these strong moves toward early action, and Democrats indicating support, the plan seemed destined to succeed. Based entirely on the present structure of F. S. A., the plan proposed neither to take out nor add any units, an action that might have aroused special advocates of pet agencies.

Mrs. Hobby to Get Post

The plan would make these changes:

¶The head of the new department would be a Secretary of Cabinet rank, and the White House has indicated that Mrs. Hobby, the first chief of the Women's Army Corps and former executive vice president and publisher of The Houston (Texas) Post, will get the position.

¶These new policy-making positions would be created: Under Secretary of Health, Education and Welfare, and two Assistant Secretaries of Health, Education and Welfare.

¶The position of "special assistant to the Secretary (Health and Medical Affairs)" would be created and would require Senate confirmation, like the Secretary, Under Secretary and Assistant Secretaries.

¶There would be a Commissioner of Social Security, as there was now, but he would require confirmation by the Senate in order to hold office. This would mean Commissioner Altmeyer would be forced out because of his support of national health insurance.

He gained Civil Service status in 1949, when, in a reorganization of F. S. A., all top jobs except those of Commissioner of Education and the Surgeon General were put under Civil Service. Mr. Altmeyer has indicated to friends that he planned to retire when he reached 62 years of age on May 8.

¶The new Secretary would be authorized to centralize all functions that were common to the various agencies of the department, such as "procurement, budgeting, accounting, personnel, library, legal and other services," and to transfer personnel, property records and funds to improve administration.

¶Present top officials of the F. S. A. would be authorized to hold the new positions for not more than sixty days, until the changes could be implemented.

Eisenhower Cites Need

In a message to Congress, President Eisenhower said the need for the reorganization had "long been recognized." He referred to past efforts to achieve this goal, mentioning only the Republican efforts, beginning with President Harding in 1923. He also noted that in 1949 the Commission on Organization of the Executive Branch, headed by former President Hoover, had proposed the same essential plan, too.

President Eisenhower, like President Truman, ignored, however, one of the principal recommendations of the Hoover Commission. Thus the basic pattern of their plans remained similar. What they both ignored was the recommendation that the Public Health Service be taken out of the Federal Security Agency and placed, along with three other major medical activities of the Government, into a United Medical Administration, which would be an independent agency.

The other activities that the Hoover Commission had proposed to put in the united agency were the General and Station Hospitals of the armed forces within the continental limits, except those at outlying posts; the entire hospital functions of the Veterans Administration; and the non-military hospitals of the Canal Zone.

With Mr. Ewing out of the way, however, Congress was not expected to revive the issue over a united Medical Administration.

President Eisenhower said in his message today that the Surgeon General, the Commissioner of Education and the Commissioner of Social Security "will all have direct access to the Secretary." He introduced, however, a new official between the Surgeon General and the Secretary with the proposed "Special Assistant to the Secretary (Health and Medical Affairs)."

This special assistant would be a leader in the nongovernmental medical field, who "shall review the health and medical programs of the department" and advise the Secretary on the improvement of such programs and on legislation.

Indicative of the relative rank of the new Special assistant was the specification that he should receive the salary given to assistant secretaries of executive departments, which is $15,000 a year. The Commissioner of Education receives $14,800, and the Surgeon General, who rates equally with the Surgeon General of the armed forces, receives base pay and allowances of $14,186.16, although he receives an additional $1,200 extra pay yearly now accorded to physicians and dentists by the uniformed services. The salaries of the latter two officials would remain unchanged.

The salaries for the other top officials will conform to those of equal rank in the established departments. Mrs. Hobby, who now receives $17,500, would receive $22,500; the Under Secretary would receive $17,500; and the Assistant Secretaries, $15,000.

March 13, 1953

The Super-Cabinet For Our Security

By CABELL PHILLIPS

WASHINGTON.

WHEN Vice President Nixon stood up before the television cameras a few weeks ago to reassure the nation about—among other things—the "New Look" in our foreign policy, he offered as a sort of guarantee of its merit the fact that it had originated in the National Security Council. The same device has been employed by other high Administration spokesmen in the past, with the result that "Passed by the N. S. C." is beginning to acquire, in the field of our larger national and international affairs, some of the magic that a hallmark has on gold or silver.

If the analogy seems somewhat far-fetched it is only for the purpose of emphasizing the enormous new importance that has been conferred upon this obscure agency of government by the Eisenhower Administration. No well-informed person will brand this move categorically as an unwise decision or a dangerous delegation of power. The consensus is, indeed, that the N. S. C., or some near equivalent, is a necessity in these times of perilous uncertainty. But there are many who, while granting all of the foregoing, still are concerned to know just what the vast implications of this development are.

For, almost without notice, and certainly without debate, the Security Council has become a super-Cabinet, a sort of Supreme High Command, where the most momentous policies of government are formulated in secret by a handful of men responsible to no one but the President himself. Thus, the new doctrine of "instant retaliation," which was about as formidable a departure in foreign policy as we have taken in a decade, was quietly evolved behind the closed doors of the N. S. C. and only revealed to the nation as a *fait accompli* by the Secretary of State in a speech last January.

This is a very "New Look," indeed, for our traditional processes of government. Does it mean that the old familiar idea that a democracy's business should be conducted in a goldfish bowl is being abandoned? Are Congress, the Cabinet and even the public to be bypassed in the policy-making function? Is there danger of delegating too much power to too few men?

THE answer to these rather ominous questions is, fortunately, "No; not at present, anyway." But no such assurances can be given about the future, for the *possibility* of such evils cannot lightly be brushed aside. It seems useful, therefore, to take a hard look at this rising power focus in our Government to see what it is, what it does and who makes it go.

CABELL PHILLIPS is the Washington representative of The Times Sunday Department.

A good place to start is with the first official caller at the White House each Wednesday morning. At a few minutes before 8, just as the Secret Service detail is changing shifts and sleepy-eyed aides are getting their feet under their desks, Robert Cutler shows up with a fat tan briefcase under his arm. Mr. Cutler is the Special Assistant to the President for National Security Affairs. An intense, sharp-featured and taciturn Bostonian, he knows more of what the President needs to know than any man in Washington, and he is never kept waiting.

There is a crisp and friendly greeting—"Mr. President," "Bobby"—but no dallying over amenities, for these two fast friends, with a vast mutual respect, have to get down to cases on the most vital problems of government and the "cold war." If Mr. Cutler had to carry his briefcase more than the forty paces across West Executive Avenue that separate his office from the White House, he probably would have to be accompanied fore and aft by a detachment of Marines. In it are documents as highly classified as the formula for the hydrogen bomb, and of possibly even greater concern to the agents of the Soviet Union. They are the policy papers and the working papers of the Security Council itself. He lays them out on the President's desk, and for the next half to three-quarters of an hour they discuss what is in them. The President is unlikely to be surprised by anything he discovers at these sessions, for he keeps abreast on a day-to-day basis. But the Wednesday conference with Mr. Cutler is his final updating and briefing preliminary to the regular meeting of the full Security Council at 10 o'clock the next morning, which, in a literal sense, is "decision day."

"THE President prefers to get his information orally rather than through reading a lot of documents," Mr. Cutler says. "He is amazingly perceptive and has an excellent memory for facts and details. It takes me half the preceding day to get ready to answer all the questions he will ask. If there is an especially complex issue in the bunch, he will hold that out to study during the evening.

"Anyway, when he sits down at the council table the next morning he knows as much about these problems as anyone else there, and usually more."

THIS interest of the President's emphasizes one campaign promise that political opponents cannot accuse him of falling down on; that is his vow to strengthen the N. S. C.—to make it a more efficient, more sensitive instrument in the development of national policy. There can be no questioning that Mr. Eisenhower has infused it with new power and vigor, or that he leans on it more heavily and with greater confidence than did his predecessor. The fact that he asked Congress last year to appropriate $220,000 for it as against Mr. Truman's outgoing request of $160,000 suggests, but does not tell the full story.

The Council was created under the National Security Act of 1947, the same act that consolidated our separate military services under the Department of Defense. The N. S. C., however, was not designed to be an appendage of the Defense Department or of anything else. It is the keystone of our whole defense system. It is a planning and advisory agency which stands at the very pinnacle of government, and of which the President himself is the active chairman. Its function is to maintain a continuing evaluation of our position and commitments in the world at large measured against our political, economic and military capacities.

The specific job of the Council is to work out for the President broad, basic policies for the national security as it may be affected by the realities of the present or by the probabilities of the future. It does *not* concern itself (except incidentally) with the tactics of meeting those situations, but rather with the fundamental and long-range strategy to be employed. And it is not expected to dissipate its efforts on purely domestic affairs. Its preoccupation is with the seismic tremors from around the globe which threaten to shake our security at home.

NOT all policies formulated in the N. S. C. are of the same magnitude as the "instant retaliation" doctrine, but they are of the same general order—continental defense strategy for the United States, which has involved the "New Look" in our armed services; closing the defensive ring around the southern boundaries of the Soviet Union, which has involved the decision to ignore India's protests and to proceed with a military pact with Pakistan; policies with respect to our position in Southeast Asia, Indonesia, the Arab countries of the Middle East; policies for Europe and Latin America; our standing and interests in the world petroleum picture, and so on.

How and by whom are these momentous decisions made?

Sitting on the Council with the President as statutory members are the Vice President, Mr. Nixon; the Secretary of State, Mr. Dulles; the Secretary of Defense, Mr. Wilson; the Director of Foreign Operations, Mr. Stassen, and the

Director of Defense Mobilization, Mr. Flemming. In unofficial but regular attendance at all Council meetings are the Secretary of the Treasury, the Director of the Budget, the Chairman of the Joint Chiefs of Staff, the Director of Central Intelligence and the Special Assistant to the President for Cold War Planning.

THIS is not a varsity and second-string grouping. The intention from the outset has been to keep the Council itself a compact and efficient body. While the statutory members are the only ones who, so to speak, cast a vote, the advisory members share in the deliberations of the group on virtually a basis of equality. Mr. Cutler, too, though not a statutory member of the Council, is a regular attendant at its meetings.

The Council's sessions on Thursday mornings have the highest priority of any conference in the Government; only the most extraordinary and pressing reasons can excuse an absence. They are held around the long octagonal table in the Cabinet room and usually last for three hours. The President himself presides.

The first order of business is a fifteen-minute summary of the most important intelligence from around the world, which is supplied by C. I. A. Director Allen Dulles. Thereafter Mr. Cutler brings up, item by item, the matters on that day's agenda. Generally, the President asks for comments around the table, starting with Vice President Nixon. But it frequently happens that this orderly routine gets sidetracked by the heat and intensity of the discussion, in which Mr. Eisenhower himself takes a lively part. Ultimately, however, all get a chance to be heard, and the buck comes to rest, inevitably, before the President's chair.

"He doesn't temporize or search his soul in indecision," one who has sat through many of these meetings said recently. "When he has heard all the arguments, and feels that he has all the information, he makes up his mind then and there. And when he initials a paper the next day, down there in the lower right-hand corner, it becomes official policy of the United States Government."

The Council is a deliberative body. Immediately below it is the Planning Board, which is a sort of working-level carbon copy of the parent body. Mr. Cutler is its active chairman and it has five regular members from State, Treasury, Defense, Foreign Operations and Defense Mobilization, each of whom has the rank of Assistant Secretary or its equivalent.

The Planning Board meets three times weekly, and sessions often run for half a day. Like the Council, it also has a standing group of non-member advisers who meet with it regularly, representing the C. I. A., the Joint Chiefs of Staff, the Bureau of the Budget and the Operations Coordinating Board. Each member has three or four persons assigned especially to him for work with the Planning Board.

ROBERT CUTLER, Special Assistant to the President for National Security.

These, together with a group of board associates, comprise the operating staff.

Finally, there is a small secretarial and housekeeping staff under the Executive Secretary, James S. Lay Jr., to keep operations smoothly afloat. The whole N. S. C. organization, from the President down to the last clerk-typist, numbers somewhat less than a hundred. The rationale for this compact organizational structure is that it can focus, as sharply and intensely as a magnifying glass, all the knowledge, experience and brain power of government upon the solution of a given problem of national security.

AN axiom of the N. S. C. is that it works only on those problems on which a policy decision by the President is required. They can originate almost anywhere—with the President himself, within the Council or the Planning Board, upon the application of some other department of government, or—and this governs in most instances—in the succession of world events. When the council decides that a certain problem needs study, Mr. Cutler takes over.

The first step in the process is to put the problem before the Planning Board and to block out a *modus operandi*. What sort of questions does the problem raise, and what method of attack will be most likely to produce the answer? When this has been settled, the work is parceled out to representatives of the various agencies which are likely to have something to contribute.

Robert Amory Jr., the adviser from C. I. A., gets his people to work digging out all the intelligence reports that have a bearing on the subject. If some new information is needed, or new evaluations have to be made, this mission gets top priority over anything else the C. I. A. may be engaged on at the moment.

THE board member for State is Robert R. Bowie, who is also the director of the State Department policy planning staff. He assigns a crew to assemble everything available on the diplomatic aspects of the problem. And, similarly, the members from the Department of Defense, the Treasury, the Foreign Operations Administration, the Bureau of the Budget and the Office of Defense Manpower all go to work in their respective agencies pulling together all the facts and estimates and judgments about the question at hand.

Mr. Cutler represents the catalytic agent which, through many hours-long sessions of the Planning Board, resolves this mass of data into usable form. As it takes shape, it is organized into five parts, four of which are as brief as clarity will permit.

The first is a statement of general considerations—basic elements which underlie the issue. Next is a statement of objectives—ends that should be sought in view of the existence of the problem. Third is recommended courses of action. Fourth is an estimate of whatever financial burdens may be involved. Finally, there is the documentation, the thickest section of the paper.

This is a "working paper." It often requires three or four revisions before being circulated to members of the board and Council. If the President approves, the first three sections are adopted as a formal policy statement. Bound in prosaic paper covers bearing the legend, "National Security Council, Policy On ———," it then becomes a part of the body of official policy of the United States Government.

A PRINCIPAL weakness of the Council in the past has been the absence of any mechanism to see that policies adopted at the top were properly carried out in the echelons below. To correct this, President Eisenhower set up last September the Operations Coordinating

Board mentioned above, which, like C. I. A., is an official appendage of the Council. It has the duty not only of carrying through N. S. C. policies, but also of seeing that there is a proper meshing of all security and foreign policies of the Government and that they are adequately presented to the world in our information and propaganda programs.

The standing of O. C. B. is comparable to that of the Planning Board. Its members, in other words, pack enough influence within their respective agencies to gain top priority for the jobs assigned to them under N. S. C. The chairman is Gen. Walter Bedell Smith, Under Secretary of State. Sitting with him are Robert M. Kyes, Deputy Secretary of Defense; Mr. Stassen, Director of Foreign Operations; Allen Dulles, director of C. I. A., and the President's assistant for "cold war" planning. The executive secretary is Elmer Staats, formerly Deputy Director of the Budget.

SO much for the machinery of the Council and the compact group of men who run it. What about the questions that have been raised concerning the role it is playing?

One is: What does it do to the standing of the Cabinet?

The answer is that the N. S. C. is undoubtedly a super-Cabinet—not only a smaller and more select body, but one equipped far more effectively than the regular Cabinet to marshal all the forces of the Government behind a given objective. It also is a more disciplined body in terms of meeting the President's policy aims and needs. Cabinets, with their greater diversity of interests and personal ambitions, often lack cohesiveness and harmony, to say nothing of group efficiency.

"War cabinets" are not, of course, uncommon in times of emergency—smaller and more effective groups of advisers and administrators to whom

the President can turn for expeditious action. The N. S. C. is, in a sense, a peacetime "war cabinet." And it would seem inevitable that, although it is supposed to confine itself to security matters only, more and more of the pressing day-to-day problems of government will be routed to it for solution rather than to the more cumbersome regular body.

This may make for efficiency, but, the critics agree, it also seems to threaten one of the more delicate checks and balances that distinguish our system. Though the Cabinet has no status under either the Constitution or statutory law, it has, almost from the beginning, brought a measure of widely representative opinion to the President's council table.

ANOTHER question raised is whether the N. S. C. is not an incipient oligarchy, which might, in some future crisis, take over the reins of government. This question arises from two circumstances: (1) the Council is the repository of the most vital and confidential information about our Government and about whatever crisis might embroil it; and (2) it is a non-elective group (and therefore supposedly deficient in its sense of public accountability) which is accustomed to working in secrecy.

No one is losing much sleep over this prospect. Not through any smug conviction that "it can't happen here"—indeed, the Security Council would be a first-rate weapon in the hands of an unscrupulous demagogue—but for the reason that no responsible person thinks it will.

Finally, there is the broader question of the wisdom of the Executive making policies of paramount importance—policies that are binding upon the total resources of the nation—in secret and without the benefit of public discussion or consultation with Congress.

Here it is argued: first, the President has always been responsible for policy-making and the N. S. C. is simply a modern and efficient device created by Congress to help him make policy wisely. Second, any N. S. C. policy can be blocked by the massing of public opinion or by the refusal of Congress to provide the necessary funds. Some contend, however, that the effect in such cases is a little like locking the barn door after the horse is stolen. Our intentions have been disclosed, and they cannot be called back. Moreover, the resulting confusion often creates almost as many difficulties as allowing an unwise policy to go into effect. As a case in point, the ex post

facto explanations by the President and Mr. Dulles over what "instant retaliation" means have done little to clear up the international controversy over the question.

Mr. Cutler takes such criticisms of the Council hard. He feels—and it can be assumed that he reflects the viewpoint of Mr. Eisenhower in this—that such a body is, first of all, a necessary adjunct of the Presidency today. The weight of decision is too great, and the complexity of problems too overwhelming, for any man to shoulder them alone. If there were no National Security Council today, he says, something very much like it would have to be created to prevent the nation from wallowing in confusion and indecision. And that would be true regardless of who was President.

Secondly, so long as we have such an instrument at hand, Mr. Cutler contends, it would be reckless not to employ it at its maximum efficiency. At the President's direction, he has therefore overhauled the Council from top to bottom, streamlined and speeded up its workings and, he candidly believes, greatly improved its end-product.

SUCH an operation, he says, cannot be conducted in a fishbowl any more than delicate diplomacy can be negotiated under floodlights. The subjects with which the Council deals are too explosively involved with the objectives, the prejudices, and often the very existence of other Governments—or even our own—and to reveal our hand by repeatedly exposing all our policies to public gaze would, in many cases, be comparable to a military commander telegraphing his plan of battle to the enemy.

At all events the National Security Council is now firmly imbedded in the fabric of government and seems destined to stay there. Succeeding Presidents may esteem it greater or less than does Mr. Eisenhower, and may alter its functions and status accordingly. But none in the foreseeable future of an unstable world will dare wholly to abandon it.

THE EXECUTIVE BRANCH OF THE GOVERNMENT—A CHART OF THE PRESIDENT'S VAST RESPONSIBILITIES

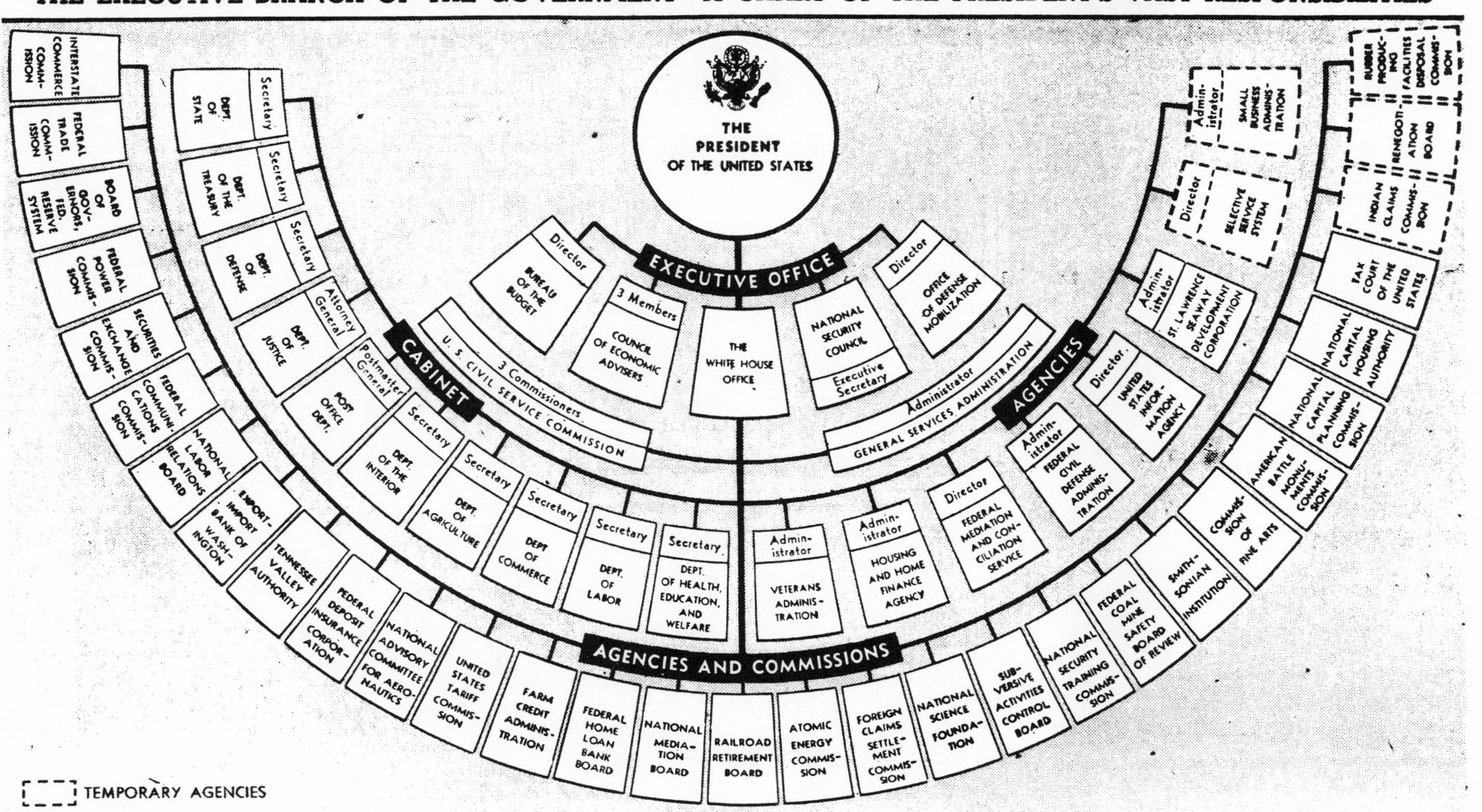

This chart indicates the multiplicity of functions and agencies that fan out from the President. President Eisenhower has set up the machinery of the Executive Branch so that almost all decisions and operations have been channeled through the White House Office, headed by Assistant to the President Sherman Adams.

PRESIDENT ENDS 41 COMMITTEES

Continues Move to Transfer Burden of Decision From Groups to Individuals

Special to The New York Times.

WASHINGTON, April 8—President Kennedy abolished forty-one Government committees today in his continuing effort to simplify the Executive Branch and place responsibility for decisions on individuals rather than on groups.

The President also signed a bill that will permit him to reorganize Government agencies, subject only to the specific disapproval of Congress rather than to Congressional permission.

The new law, reviving the Reorganization Act of 1949, "should result in promoting improvements in Government organizations and it should make possible more economical operation," Mr. Kennedy said.

The President, who spent most of the morning conferring with Prime Minister Macmillan, also worked on domestic affairs before flying to his rented estate in Virginia by helicopter for the week-end.

Address Planned

The White House did not indicate when he would return but it is known that the President plans to address military leaders of the North Atlantic Treaty Organization and throw out the first ball for the season's opening baseball game here Monday.

President Kennedy received a visit today from Helen Keller, the noted blind and deaf woman who was scheduled to receive the annual humanitarian award of the District Lions Club tonight.

Miss Keller, who will be 81 on June 27, was accompanied by her secretary, Mrs. Evelyn Seide, officials of the American Foundation for the Blind and representatives of the Lions Club.

Miss Keller "spoke" to the President through Mrs. Seide, using a manual alphabet. She thanked Mr. Kennedy for becoming an honorary president of the Foundation for the Blind, and she asked him to send a kiss to his 3-year-old daughter, Caroline.

Early Meeting Recalled

The President said he was sorry that Mrs. Kennedy and his daughter were not present to meet Miss Keller. They had left yesterday for Glen Ora, the Virginia estate.

Miss Keller observed that she had been meeting Presidents since Grover Cleveland, and the President pointed out that he was using a desk that had been presented to President Cleveland by Queen Victoria.

Mr. Kennedy's action in terminating forty-one interdepartmental committees followed up an earlier one abolishing seventeen. The White House described it as part of a "continuing effort to abolish nonessential governmental agencies and place responsibility in specific individuals to the maximum extent possible."

"Any work which must be continued after these groups are abolished has been assigned to the department heads that have provided chairmen of the special committees," the White House added.

April 9, 1961

JOHNSON DECISION ON HOUSING NEARS

New Department in Cabinet Needs Officials and Duties

By BEN A. FRANKLIN

Special to The New York Times

WASHINGTON, Jan. 1 — After four months of delay, President Johnson is finally approaching one of his most crucial and politically sensitive decisions to keep the Great Society from bogging down in the Great Bureaucracy.

A Presidential announcement is expected next week, just before Congress reconvenes on Jan. 10, on the new Department of Housing and Urban Development.

The 11th Cabinet department, approved by Congress last August, is expected to become the key operating agency of Mr. Johnson's ambitious "hopes of the American city." The President, more than most people, is acutely aware that the cities, with their multiplying problems, are where more than 70 per cent of the population live.

Mr. Johnson must choose not only the seven top Cabinet and sub-Cabinet leaders of the new department — appointments he has repeatedly postponed since last September—but also a new definition of the scope of the Federal role in reforming the urban environment.

New Legislation Seen

The departmental reorganization is likely to require legislation. Thus, the main thrust of the President's proposals to reform the new department before it really begins may be withheld for a special message to Congress early in the year.

But the President probably cannot put off the politically delicate and administratively portentous selection of a Secretary of Housing and Urban Development.

Under the timetable written into the legislation, the department has been in suspended animation since Nov. 9, when Mr. Johnson allowed it to come into being "in name only." He instructed its predecessor, the Housing and Home Finance Agency, to remain alive—operating as if it were the department—though the Congressional mandate declared that the agency "shall lapse" Nov. 9.

This was done under a Justice Department memorandum that cited a definition of "lapse" in Webster's New International Dictionary, Second Edition, as meaning "to pass gradually." The result of this "gradualism" in the agency has been declining morale, mounting confusion and a spate of legal questions about the authority of its officials.

Robert C. Weaver, the administrator of the agency and a candidate for the new secretaryship, has been labeled the "nontitular head of a nondepartment."

The fact that the department, known as H. U. D. or Hud, is still without leaders and still requires administrative pruning five months after its creation by Congress and two months after its nominal beginning is considered certain to spur partisan election year criticism in Congress.

'Bungling in Secrecy'

Some Republicans have already accused the Administration of "bungling in secrecy" in its attempt to redraw H. U. D.'s organization. Others have charged that the H. U. D. legislation was "forced through Congress without adequate debate."

The Republican criticism of "secrecy" was an allusion to the special urban study group Mr. Johnson assigned in November to review the new department's organization, powers and duties, and thus to prevent the Housing and Home Finance Agency from acquiring departmental status without significant reform.

Critics of the agency, an 18-year-old conglomeration of autonomous New Deal and Fair Deal housing bureaus, have charged for years that it was among the most impenetrable of bureaucratic thickets and that its alliances were primarily with the housing and banking industries rather than with urban communities.

Even Mr. Weaver has called his agency "an administrative monstrosity."

The President's eight - man panel, headed by Dr. Robert C. Wood of the Massachusetts Institute of Technology, completed its recommendations in almost air-tight secrecy. The meetings here were held under such elaborate security precautions that even the meeting place, a room in the United States Maritime Commission, was unknown to most interested Government and industry officials.

Some Democrats Annoyed

They were thus prevented from campaigning for or against proposals. The secrecy, however, invited Republican criticism and even the annoyance of some Democrats.

Dr. Wood submitted his committee's findings to the White House last week. The recommendations, reported to have included some "wild proposals," have remained secret. One proposal, however, was reported to call for the moving of one of the principal operating arms of the anti-poverty campaign, the Community Action program, from the Office of Economic Opportunity to the new department.

The President's public dreams for a better urban society have been generous. In his special message to Congress on the cities last March, he called for urban housing construction during the balance of this century that would equal "all that we have built since the first colonists landed on these shores."

"It is as if we had less than 40 years to rebuild the entire urban United States," he said.

He said that "much of our hope for American progress will

depend on the effectiveness with which the critical Federal programs are carried forward" by the Department of Housing and Urban Development.

Some changes reported to have been suggested by the study group would probably be **so unpopular with the large circle of pressure groups surrounding the new department that they would most likely be toned down or abandoned.**

There apparently is no way the President can muffle the political consequences of his selection of a Secretary of Housing and Urban Development and a contingent of under secretaries and assistant secretaries.

Mr. Weaver, President Kennedy's choice for the post, not only is a respected housing economist, but also the highest ranking Negro in the Federal Government. However, he has been criticized for weak administration, for poor relations with Congress, and for having candidly declared himself eager to head the new department.

If Mr. Johnson does not nominate him—many observers, reportedly Mr. Weaver among them, would now be surprized if he does—Negro citizens would regard it "as a rejection of them" by the Johnson Administration, according to Roy Wilkins, head of the National Association for the Avancement of Colored People.

Another Negro leader, Whitney M. Young Jr., served on the study group and has been reported on the President's list. Mr. Young, executive director of the National Urban League, has publicly backed the appointment of Mr. Weaver.

Speculation on the President's choice, particularly in the housing and banking trade journals, has been so rampant that last week the magazine, Architectural Forum, reported that the leading candidate was "Mayor Beauregard O'Malley" of the nonexistent city of "Middletown, W. Va."

January 2, 1966

PRESIDENT SIGNS BILL SETTING UP TRANSPORT UNIT

Defers Naming Secretary of 12th Cabinet Department but Wants 'Strong Man'

SEES WEAKNESS IN BILL

Johnson Hopes New Agency Will Eventually Acquire Maritime Jurisdiction

By ROBERT E. BEDINGFIELD
Special to The New York Times

WASHINGTON, Oct. 15.—President Johnson signed today a bill creating the country's 12th Cabinet unit, a Department of Transportation.

The President did not name a Secretary of Transportation but told several hundred guests in the East Room of the White House what kind of a person he wanted for the post.

He said:

"Because the job is great, I intend to appoint a strong man to fill it. The new Secretary will be my principal adviser and strong right arm on all transportation matters."

The President had been reported to be planning to name Joseph A. Califano Jr. for the job. Industry executives who attended the bill-signing ceremony shortly after 1 P.M. said they did not believe Mr. Califano's appointment had been "foreclosed." Mr. Califano is a special assistant to the President.

Mr. Johnson appeared enthusiastic as he talked to the Government officials, representatives of the transportation industry, members of Congress and about 30 Mayors whom he had invited to the White House.

He acknowledged that the bill he received from Congress Thursday establishing the Transportation Department had some deficiencies, particularly in that the new agency did not include the Maritime Administration.

The President expressed the hope that "as experience is gained in the new department" Congress would re-examine its decision to leave functions of the Maritime Administration outside the Transportation Secretary's jurisdiction.

Since early March, when the President formally asked for the new Cabinet office in a special transportation message to Congress, the proposal has been under attack from various maritime groups, especially the maritime unions. Key backers of the plan for transferring the Maritime Administration to the new Transportation Department finally gave up their fight this week rather than risk losing the bill entirely.

In an interview after the President has handed out pens used in signing the Department of Transportation Act, Mr. Califano said of reports that he might be named:

"There is nothing to it. The boss called it to my attention this morning when I came in. I hadn't seen or read it."

Mr. Califano was alluding to an article on Page 1 of The New York Times today.

Mr. Johnson stressed that transportation was the nation's biggest industry, involving one of every five dollars in the economy. He described the nation's transportation system as the "greatest in the world," but declared:

"We must face facts. It is no longer adequate."

The President predicted that during the next two decades, the demand for transportation in the United States would double. He said it would be a mammoth task to untangle, coordinate and build the national transportation system that was required.

I.C.C. Undisturbed

The new department will bring together 31 agencies and bureaus dealing with transportation. It does not, however, disturb the Interstate Commerce Commission's regulatory authority over all forms of surface transportation, nor the Civil Aeronautics Board's regulatory powers over the aviation industry. Much of the department's activities will be devoted to dealing with how the nation's transportation resources should be invested.

The Secretary of Transportation will have the responsibility for developing a national transportation policy. He will be expected to advocate policy guidelines to the independent regulatory agencies, while making recommendations to the President and Congress on all phases of domestic and international transportation.

Among the agencies transferred to the new department are the following:

¶The Federal Aviation Agency, in its entirety, with all its functions.

¶The Bureau of Public Roads, which has been part of the Department of Commerce. The Federal-aid highway program now is a responsibility of the Secretary of Transportation.

¶The Office of the Under Secretary of Commerce for Transportation and all transportation functions vested in the Secretary of Commerce. These include the so-called Northeast Corridor project, which provides for research, development and a demonstration starting next year of the feasibility of high speed trains between Washington, New York and Boston.

¶The Coast Guard, which has been part of the Treasury Department. The Coast Guard, as in the past, would revert to naval jurisdiction in wartime.

¶The Great Lakes Pilotage Administration, which has been part of the Department of Commerce. This agency, under the Great Lakes Pilotage Act of 1960, provides for the establishment of an effective system of regulated pilotage on the Great Lakes.

¶The Alaska Railroad. The operation of this 870-mile carrier, which extends from Seward to Fairbanks, has been under the direction and supervision of the Secretary of the Interior since it was opened in 1923.

¶The St. Lawrence Seaway Development Corporation, which has been a responsibility of the Secretary of Commerce.

Among the new department's other responsibilities are the safety functions of the Civil Aeronautics Board, including the responsibility for investigating and determining probable causes of aircraft accidents.

The department will also absorb the functions of the Interstate Commerce Commission relating to safety laws affecting railroads and motor carriers. It will also have the responsibility for fixing standard time zones and daylight savings time.

The new department has, in all, 25 positions to be filled by Presidential appointment. Among those positions, in addition to that of the Secretary and Under Secretary, are the five members of the National Transportation Safety Board. Their job is to determine the cause of transportation accidents and to review on appeal the suspension, amendment, modification, revocation or denial of a license issued by the Secretary or by an administrator.

There are six administrators in the new department. With the exception of the Federal railroad administrator, the administrators of the F.A.A., highway and St. Lawrence Seaway administrations are taking over agencies that already exist.

The one responsibility in the law that the Federal railroad administrator will carry out is that pertaining to the functions, powers and duties of the Secretary relating to railroad and pipeline safety.

October 16, 1966

Nixon's Reorganization Plan Follows Historic Advice

By JACK ROSENTHAL

Special to The New York Times

WASHINGTON, June 11 — For 33 years, commissions, White House advisers and students of the Presidency have insisted, with increasing urgency, that the President of the United States does not have enough power.

For all the talk of his being the most powerful man in the free world, they say, the President's capacity to act in domestic affairs has not nearly kept pace with the explosive growth in the size and complexity of domestic problems.

After Dwight D. Eisenhower was elected President in 1952, President Truman remarked:

"He'll sit right here and he'll say, 'Do this, do that,' and nothing will happen. Poor Ike. It won't be a bit like the Army. He'll find it very frustrating."

President Nixon acted yesterday on the advice of those who say his power is too limited. He appointed Secretary of Labor George P. Shultz, one of his most valued associates, as director of a powerful new Office of Management and Budget, a position that some knowledgeable observers believe could soon be virtually that of an assistant President.

Domestic Council

At the same time, the President designated John D. Erlichman, his chief domestic affairs aide, as director of a new Domestic Council.

The two new bodies were recommended to the President in secret proposals from his Advisory Council on Executive Reorganization, headed by Roy L. Ash, the California industrialist.

The Ash Council's specific recommendations are still not known. Their confidentiality was illustrated last Aug. 20, when the President asked Mr. Ash to brief him orally so no memorandums would be left around the White House.

But it is plain that the central thrust of the recommendations parallels that of President Johnson's equally secret reorganization commission.

The time is long gone, the Ash group said in effect, when problems could be matched to a traditional Cabinet department. Issues such as pollution involve numerous agencies, which means that some higher authority must pull all the pieces together.

Mr. Ash is reported to have put the issue to the President in the form of four tasks: What do you want to do, how to do it, doing it and how well did it work?

The Ash group proposed that the Domestic Council deal with the first question: the area of policies and priorities. How to do it and doing it, particularly in interagency concerns such as pollution or urban affairs, would be done by the new management and budget agency.

In regard to the fourth task, the Ash group is reported to have been particularly critical. It said the Executive Office of the President had been handicapped by the absence of serious evaluation and recommended such a function for the new management agency.

President Nixon's willingness to act on this advice has won him praise from both parties. Last month, Joseph A. Califano Jr., chief domestic aide to President Johnson, testified in behalf of the basic Nixon reorganization plan.

"The pluses so far outweigh any minor deficiencies that the plan should be approved," he said.

Ben W. Heineman, a Chicago corporation head, who directed President Johnson's secret reorganization study, said todav: "This is very much what the executive department needs."

The White House has yet to disclose many details about how the two new bodies will work—particularly how they will relate to each other. A number of questions are being asked by students of governmental organization.

"I think George Shultz is first-rate," said a member of the Heineman study commission, asking anonymity, "but there really is a question about power here. Presidents are elected and Cabinet members are confirmed by the Senate. But is it wise to put so much power in the hands of a super-Cabinet member who is neither elected by the public, confirmed by Congress, nor accountable to either?"

Another question involves potential rivalry between the two new bodies.

Collision Predicted

In the absence of information about how Mr. Shultz and Mr. Ehrlichman will relate to each other — "Those who can't stand ambiguity can't be creative here," Mr. Shultz said yesterday — executive office insiders predicted a collision between the two men.

"We hear Ehrlichman is going to have a staff of either 50 or 90 or 100. Why will there be two new bodies, each with big staffs?" one asked. "We'll have to see what happens the first time Ehrlichman tells Shultz, 'The President says he wants you to . . .' "

Yet another question was raised today by Richard E. Neustadt, a Harvard professor who is a renowned student of the Presidency.

"The Domestic Council is obviously too unwieldy to do much except soothe the Cabinet," he said. "Otherwise it is only a screen for the new staff. And yet there's something screwy about the staff."

The Heineman Commission, he noted, proposed a managerial staff headed by a director of the Executive Office of the President. Another policy development staff in the Budget Bureau was proposed.

The current plan "appears to do it upside down," Mr. Neustadt said.

Roy L. Ash, head of a commission that recommended that President Nixon establish two new organizations.

"The managerial, coordinating staff will be in the Management and Budget Office. The planning staff is to be under Ehrlichman in the White House. And that doesn't seem to make much sense," he said.

Others discounted the prospect of conflict between the two new offices.

"Why should there be any?" asked a Budget Bureau aide, citing cordial relationships between White House staff members and the Budget Bureau in the past, notably between Mr. Califano and Charles Schultze, budget director in the Johnson Administration.

"Most probably," he said, "the relationships cannot be defined yet and will have to work themselves out in time."

In general, the Ash panel's recommendations accord with the views of study groups dating back to the Brownlow Commission of 1937-39, which proposed moving the Budget Bureau out of the Treasury Department and into the Executive Office of the President, to give the President enhanced managerial ability.

In 1946, the Office of War Mobilization and Reconversion advised President Truman to establish a permanent interagency management staff in the White House, but he demurred in the face of a Republican Congress.

Under the Eisenhower Administration, an advisory commission was established to find ways to lighten the burden on an ailing President. This body, composed of Nelson A. Rockefeller, Milton S. Eisenhower, and Arthur S. Flemming, concluded that managerial problems were rapidly becoming too severe for any President. It also proposed an executive management body.

The 12-member Heineman Commission, which sent its report to President Johnson June 15, 1967, said there should be six supersecretaries for such interagency categories as human resources and natural resources. It also proposed expansion of field operations, with high-ranking regional Federal executives reporting directly to the supersecretaries.

The proposals were so volatile, Mr. Califano said today, that action was deferred until after the 1968 election.

June 12, 1970

Rising Presidential Staff Outlays Hint Nixon Power Consolidation

Special to The New York Times

WASHINGTON, Jan. 29—The budget for the fiscal year 1972, released today, lends statistical support to the judgment of most observers here that President Nixon has consolidated within his own executive office more power than any of his predecessors.

His executive staff, the budget indicates, is without question the largest in history. Meanwhile, estimated expenditures for the policymaking and personal machinery surrounding the President will rise by more than $5-million in the next fiscal year.

Expenditures for the executive office of the President, which includes everything from his $200,000 salary to the costs of operating policy-making units such as the National Security Council, totaled $36.3-million in the fiscal year 1970 and jumped to $49.8-million the following year.

A major reason for the increase was Mr. Nixon's decision to start counting as White House positions a large number of Government jobs whose occupants had worked for President Johnson while remaining on other agency payrolls. This was also a major reason for the sharp jump in personnel attached to the President's immediate personal staff—from 250 in the fiscal year 1970 to 533 the following year.

For the fiscal year 1972, the President's immediate staff—his speechwriters, press officers, political aides, secretaries, administrative personnel, and the like—will grow by only seven persons, to 540 permanent positions. Over-all expenditures for the executive office of the President however, will rise from a level of $49.8-million in the fiscal year 1971 to an estimated total of $55.2-million.

This is largely attributable to the following factors: the growth of the new Domestic Council under John D. Ehrlichman, to serve the President on domestic policy and programs; the creation of a new Council on Environmental Quality, to advise Mr. Nixon on conservation issues; and the growth of the old Budget Bureau, now known as the Office of Management and Budget.

January 3, 1971

THE PRESIDENT.

The people of the United States will regret that the President has not directed Secretary TAFT, giving over his journey to the Philippines, to remain at his Cabinet post. Mr. ROOSEVELT has need of the sage counsel and the help of Secretary TAFT, and of other and further aid at this time when duties and responsibilities of unusual weight and moment devolve upon him. The retirement of Mr. ROOT and Mr. KNOX deprived the President of the services of two of his most trusted Cabinet advisers. The death of Mr. HAY removes another, and one to whom not only the President but the country turned with confidence in times of doubt and perplexity when there was need of wisdom's light to reveal the true path. Attorney General MOODY being pretty fully occupied with the business of the Law Department, there remains in the circle of the President's advisers no man of first-rate capacity whose opinions he can consult or whose aid invoke in larger matters of the public business. Secretary TAFT is not only a man of first-rate capacity, but one of untiring industry as well. He is capable not only of giving counsel to the President but of sharing his labors, relieving him of many tasks which Mr. ROOSEVELT would probably be disinclined to intrust to any other hand than that of his Secretary of War. The trip to the Philippines is not vital. Mr. TAFT is already informed, very well informed, as to conditions in those possessions of the United States. If Congress needs more information it can be obtained by the members of the Lower House who set out with the Secretary's party.

Few of our Presidents have assumed heavier burdens than Mr. ROOSEVELT, and fewer still have been compelled to rely to the same extent upon their own strength and unguided judgment. Mr. HAY'S marvelous efficiency in the dispatch of the highest order of international business would have stood the President in good stead during the coming months, but that was not to be. The further negotiations necessary to bring about the meeting of the Japanese and Russian plenipotentiaries, and the ceremonies incident to the beginning and progress of the conference will make demands upon the energies and the time of the President. In Santo Domingo and in Venezuela unsettled questions are pending which may at any moment require the serious and vigilant attention of the President, or of some trusted adviser capable of right action and sound decisions gravely involving the National interests.

Upon the Isthmus of Panama there have arisen conditions upon which it is not necessary here to dwell, that must give the President great uneasiness. His responsibility for the successful prosecution of the canal work is so great as to be almost undivided. It was he that chose the Panama route under the act of Congress which made the Nicaragua route an alternative, it was his decision and his act that precipitated the uprising in Panama. The payment of $40,000,000 to the Frenchmen for their rights and of $10,000,000 to Panama was in accordance with his determination. The Commission is of his appointment and acts in accordance with his will. Thus far things have gone so badly on the Isthmus that if an immediate and radical change is not made the Government will be involved in a scandal and the public disapproval will be manifested. The affairs of the canal will for months demand an exertion of the best powers of Mr. ROOSEVELT'S mind. He cannot afford to neglect them.

There are, besides, questions of public revenues brought into some urgency by the deficit for the fiscal year just closed, questions of new laws affecting corporations which, we suppose, the President has not altogether dismissed from his mind, and the new problems affecting our interest that will arise out of the Russo-Japanese settlement.

The country will feel like congratulating the President upon his retirement to his Summer home, where in healthful conditions he will be able in some measure to enjoy his well-earned rest. It is to be hoped that his rest will not be broken by the importunities of politicians or the impertinencies of unsummoned visitors. The labor of public addresses, too, let us hope, has been cut off. Mr. ROOSEVELT puts so much of himself into his speeches, and they have been so frequent that the draft upon his energies has of late been heavy. In view of the demands made upon him by his great office, it would be a matter of public concern should he continue to lay waste his powers in discoursing to his fellow-citizens upon subjects which neither the Constitution nor custom and prescription require him to deliver. Even his rugged strength must have its limits.

July 2, 1905

KITCHEN CABINETS.

There is no kitchen Cabinet. There are no backstairs advisers.—The World.

When did Colonel HOUSE resign?—The Sun.

When Colonel HOUSE calls on the President he always goes in the front door.—The World.

Order, gentlemen, order; let there be no violence. What is a kitchen Cabinet? How many Presidents of the United States have been subjected to sinister influences? How many of them have had visitors who did not come in through the front door? GARFIELD had General SWAIM and Colonel ROCKWELL, but they were in evidence not only at the front door, but on the steps, and all the world knew of their relations with the President—relations in no way discreditable. CLEVELAND'S chum was E. C. BENEDICT, but Mr. CLEVELAND went cruising on Mr. BENEDICT'S yacht in sight of all the world, ROBLEY D. EVANS being frequently in the party. ABNER MCKINLEY seldom went to the White House, and his brother's kitchen Cabinet consisted almost solely of MARK HANNA, who was a Senator and was entitled to give the President his advice. Mr. ROOSEVELT'S kitchen Cabinet consisted almost entirely of public officials, such as his Secretary of the Interior, and if there were exceptions they were such honorable and distinguished men as Dr. ALBERT SHAW and President BUTLER of Columbia University. Mr. TAFT was perhaps occasionally the victim of bad advice, but it always came from men entitled to advise him, such as Secretary BALLINGER, and if CHARLES P. TAFT exercised any influence over him it never became apparent. HARRISON and ARTHUR had no kitchen Cabinets of any kind.

As for Colonel HOUSE, his relations with the present President are simply those of friendship, and there is nothing to criticise in the fact that the President chooses to ask for his judgment in matters wherein Colonel HOUSE is an authority. Our Presidents are not and never have been the kind of men to be amenable to "backstairs influence," if that phrase is used in any unpleasant sense.

March 8, 1915

INTRIGUE, UNTRUTH, AND FRIENDS ALOOF MAKE HARDING SAD

He Reveals Worries of His Position in a Little Speech to Fellow-Masons.

CABINET SEEMS A TANGLE

Special to The New York Times.

MARION, Ohio, Jan. 6.—Senator Harding's tentative Cabinet slate is becoming blurred, and those close to him believe that the eraser may be used unsparingly and new names substituted.

The present state of mind of the President-elect and his worries over Cabinet and Federal appointments was illuminated by his speech at the Columbus Masonic Temple last night, when, during his initiation into the higher degrees of Masonry, he received the gift of a ring from Marion friends who accompanied him to Columbus.

"I wonder if you know just the feelings of a man who has been called to the greatest office in the world?" he said.

"There is an aloofness of his friends, and this is one of the sad things. And in me there is a deepening sense of responsibility.

"I have found already that intrigue and untruth must be guarded against. One must ever be on his guard. This everlasting standing on one's guard spoils a man. I wish for an atmosphere of truth and sincerity in our Government, and I have no higher ambition to establish during my Administration than an autocracy of service."

The first sign that the President-elect was wavering about putting political managers in the Cabinet was seen today when he told a group of former National Guard officers that he sought as head of the War Department a civilian interested and acquainted with military affairs. This, despite the fact that A. T. Hert of Kentucky has been mentioned as a strong candidate for Secretary of War.

Hays and Daugherty Opposed.

There is every indication that opposition is being aroused against the candidacies of Harry M. Daugherty and Wil. H. Hays, who have been mentioned for Attorney General and Postmaster General respectively. Ex-Senator Beveridge of Indiana, who took luncheon with Senator Harding after a long conference with him, is understood to have spoken against the selection of Hays. It can be stated positively that Mr. Beveridge came to Marion with no thought of seeking Cabinet or diplomatic appointment. On the other hand, he would neither confirm nor deny reports that he intended running against Senator New two years hence.

Reports from Indiana say that Hays is sympathetic to New's desire for a renomination. Mr. Hays, if he became Postmaster General, would have much power as a dispenser of patronage, and this is believed to be one reason for Mr. Beveridge's opposition to Hays being chosen to the Cabinet. With the backing of patronage New would have considerable advantage at the start over Beveridge.

But opposition to political managers is only one of Senator Harding's troubles in Cabinet making. It is understood that no reply has been received from Charles E. Hughes as to whether he would be receptive to an invitation to become Secretary of State.

In the cases of Hughes and Charles G. Dawes no final invitations have been delivered, it is said by those close to Harding. Mr. Hughes's silence, in view of the new storm over appointments of political managers, is disconcerting to the President-elect, who wished to announce his Secretaries of State and Treasury before the rest of the Cabinet. Senator Harding's approach to Mr. Dawes is understood to be less positive even than his indefinite invitation to Mr. Hughes in that Mr. Dawes was asked whether he would be available if the President-elect should decide upon him for Secretary of the Treasury.

Hoover Also Is Attacked.

The President-elect continues to receive conflicting advice relative to the Departments of Interior, Agriculture and Labor. Herbert Hoover, who has been regarded by some of Harding's friends as ranking with Hughes as a Cabinet certainty, is opposed by Gifford Pinchot. Today John E. Ballaine of Seattle, who has long been concerned with Alaskan development, urged upon Senator Harding the appointment of a secretary familiar with irrigation, reclamation and Alaskan problems.

Senator Sherman of Illinois, who will retire on March 4, had a long conference with Senator Harding today. He said afterward:

"I find that Senator Harding has in mind the wish to establish an association of nations, quite independent of the establishment which was sought to be created at Versailles. I believe that Senator Harding is proceeding along the right lines, and that there is an excellent prospect that he will work out the program to which he is now devoting himself."

The five National Guard officers who talked with Senator Harding today were Henry J. Reilly of Chicago, Colonel of the 149th Field Artillery: Forty-second Division; Tom S. Hammond, Lieutenant Colonel of the same command: Horatio B. Backett, Colonel of the 124th Field Artillery: Noble B. Judah Jr., Lieutenant Colonel on staff of Rainbow Division, and Karl Klumm of Kansas City, Colonel of the 129th Field Artillery. They told him that they realized that universal, military training could not be put into effect at present, owing to public opinion. Senator Harding agreed, and said that he advocated the largest possible plan of national defense, commensurate with public opinion and a policy of economy.

To them he suggested as the type of a man whom he wanted for Secretary of War some one like Senator James W. Wadsworth Jr. of New York. The President-elect added that he used Wadsworth's name by way of illustration and that his name was not under consideration for the post.

January 7, 1921

SECRETARY FALL'S SOLILOQUY ON QUITTING HARDING CABINET

I HAVE been in public life now for a good many years. It has been a mixture of roses and thorns So I must say that I feel justified in expressing a grateful sense of satisfaction when I contemplate my approaching political demise. I hope this confession will not be wrongly interpreted. I have spent a considerable part of my life in one sort or another of political service, and have no disposition to pretend that I have not enjoyed it.

I have no wish to pose as a disillusioned zealot who at the end would sit in sackcloth and ashes and bewail the vanity of a public career. To the contrary, I am convinced of the genuine attractions which are offered by the public service to the man or woman who is willing to take its career on the terms our present-day political life makes possible.

The aspirant for a public career must recognize the possibilities of a judgment of "thumbs down," and if he is not prepared to take it philosophically, he will do well to reorientiate his aspirations. For a politician voluntarily to resign is a sufficiently rare circumstance to confer a certain individuality; and without urging any other claim to distinction, I do insist upon this one. If the procedure of resigning does not become too common—and of that I have little fear—it may ultimately win recognition as a means to introduce real distinction in a good many careers otherwise egregiously lacking in colorful originality. Should this prescription seem harsh, at least do me the justice to remember that I am taking my own dose.

A Thundering Row the Outcome.

From that viewpoint of philosophical detachment which can only be occupied by one in my present relations, I may be pardoned if I indulge a few animadversions on public life and careers. Whether in our own country or in others, there never has been a time when the public expected so much of its public servants as it does today. As a class, public men are not of a particularly bad sort. They really want to do about what the people want them to do; their difficulty, in times like these, is to find out what their public wants. It is no reflection on the community's intelligence to say that it insists on having a lot of things done, but doesn't know what they are. I undertake to say that there is no political community in the world today that has as a whole crystallized anything like an adequate notion of what it wants done for itself by its legislators and administrators. There is mighty little of direction and guidance for the public man in the knowledge that his constituency expects him to "do something about things."

In the long run, legislators and administrators do not get much further than to formulate into working policies and programs the purposes at the bottom of the community mind. If the community doesn't know pretty well what it wants, and especially if it is in a frame of mind to be dissatisfied with whatever it gets, it can be reasonably sure of not getting much. Now, that is just about the state of the public mind today in most communities that enjoy the privilege of choosing their lawmakers and administrators. I say this without purpose of reflecting on the intelligence or sincerity of the voters.

I don't care what particular group in the community might be called in to prescribe for the present illness of the body politic throughout the Western world; whether you send for the diplomats, or the college professors, or the lawyers, or the trade unionists, the butchers, the bakers, the doctors of medicine or the doctors of divinity, the politicians who have jobs or those who, having none, are classified by other folks as "lame ducks" and by themselves as statesmen—no matter which group or stratum of the community you send for, you will find when it attempts to agree what sort of medicine society requires at this time, it will be pretty likely to talk a long time and then break up in a thundering row.

There never was a time when the critic on the outside looking in found more to criticise than he can find in these days. There never was a time when conversation was easier or construction harder. If any man doubts this, just let him take a year or two of leave from his regular job and frame up his own scheme to rehabilitate the world, to balance its budgets, reduce its taxation where it ought to be reduced and increase it where it ought to be increased, to demobilize its armies, scrap its navies, restore the gold standard, doctor up the international exchanges, put an end to the menace of militarism without enthroning the piffle of pacifism, insure the co-operation of nations and the peace of continents without detracting from the sovereign independence of any State.

Draw up your own program for setting everything right everywhere. When you have finished it, which you may possibly be able to do within the period of your natural life, then call in ten of your sanest, most intelligent, most reasonable friends, and get them to accept it.

I undertake to say that before your conferences have brought agreement on the first clause, the press agent will long since have stereotyped his announcement that "The conversations will be continued." When finally you and your ten friends have agreed, survey the difficulities you have encountered, multiply them by all the possibilities of trouble that confront Congresses and Parliaments and Reichstags, and Leagues of Nations and Associations of Powers, and Limited Alliances, and see how good a calculation you can make as to the time that is likely to be required to "get the world straightened out."

For myself, I feel pretty sure that at the end of the calculation, you will decide that it might be better, instead of insisting upon complete and all embracing counsels of perfection, to start with a few plain simple and obvious formulas for accomplishing some very commonplace improvements. I knew one man who told me he had spent six months trying to frame up a way to rehabilitate international finance, and had wound up with the firm resolution to use five gallons less gas a week. I am not at all sure but that he had the right idea.

I have said that a public man is likely to be appreciated just about as much as he deserves. Perhaps I ought to qualify that rather brief statement and emphasize as earnestly as possible the fact that the general rule as to public judgment of public service can only apply when the public itself is thoroughly and fully informed as to the acts and intentions of such public servants. I would say that the tendency today is not only to criticise a public servant for any act of omission, or of commission, but to charge him personally with being actuated by ulterior motives or motives of personal or purely selfish interest.

The Secretary's Illustrations.

Very recently I had called to my attention the fact that within the City of New York one of the great civic organizations, supposed to be devoted to the full discussion and consideration of both sides of great public questions, has, through its regular channels, forwarded to a department of this Government resolutions condemning certain proposed legislation supposed to be approved by the department (as it is the duty of the department either to approve or to disapprove such pending measures), and endorsing by a unanimous vote of all the members and invited guests present to the number of one thousand, another pending bill upon the same subject.

No discussion was had from the standpoint of any one who approved the pending legislation which was denounced, nor was any one invited to discuss the matter upon the other side, but, under the hysteria of the moment, through a sentimental appeal and vociferous charges against public officials, resolutions were adopted.

I myself dictated, signed and mailed letters to many members of the Executive Committee of this organization, which had always had my respect both because of its membership and because of its announced objects—men whose names are household words in the United States; prominent lawyers, financiers and business men noted for charity and public spirit, and, without exception, have received replies to the effect that neither of those addressed was present at the meeting referred to; that neither had heard anything of the matter until receipt of my letter; that neither had read any portion of either bill denounced or approved.

One of the writers, a man for whom I have always had respect, in very frankly making these admissions, stated that he had not known that this organization ever took such action without full discussion of both sides of any proposition presented and until after full consideration of the subject by the members of the organization.

In this state of the public mind the public itself cannot be informed as to the acts of a public man thus denounced and the public mind cannot crystallize into judgment upon such man unless information is conveyed to it thereafter. History has shown that such information is often never acquired, or, if so, after the object of this public attack has not only gone out of the public service, but has departed from life.

It is the duty of every American to take part as an American citizen in public affairs; it is his duty to give some attention and to seek to inform himself upon public questions, even upon such questions as may not apparently touch him individually. It is his duty to cast his vote for or against a measure if submitted for such vote, or for or against candidates for each office at every election, municipal, State or national.

How many conscientiously discharge this duty?

Is it not within knowledge that upon occasions some high-minded official, acting as his conscience dictated, has in some action received the lip-approval of a vast number of citizens who supposed themselves to be the representatives of the intelligent and particularly of the business interests of the country, and yet felt the effects of such action at the polls when those who shouted the loudest in approval taking advantage of the fact that election was a quasi-holiday, donned their golf clothes and repaired to the links, while those who disapproved such action hurried to the polls to vote against the policies advocated by such public official and carried with them every friend and voter whom they could secure, from the opening of the voting booth in the morning until its close in the evening?

No Detached Problems.

The problems of public life are nowadays more complex, more difficult to chart, than they have ever been, in my sincere judgment. There are, we may fairly say, no local and detached problems. Everything is related to everything else, everywhere. A few years ago the burden of government's cost was so slight that most people had only the vaguest notion that they actually helped pay for government; now it is so heavy, in every country, that the most casual of business operations must be considered in the light of present and prospective policies in finance and taxation. Time was when, if Europe didn't raise all it wanted to eat, it came with the money and bought from us. Now, Europe is in greater need than ever, but it can't buy; it hasn't the means, and the American producer suffers accordingly. During the war, we all convinced ourselves that the world would never again be as it was before; and I guess we were right to that extent. But more than four years have passed since the war's end, and we haven't yet a notion what sort of world we are going to have.

One of our troubles, as it strikes me, is that too many among us were carried away with the notion that a new order of things was going to be precipitated, with the return of peace, like manna from heaven. Somehow it was imagined that institutions that have been countless thousands of years evolving themselves, would be shoved aside and something ideal and Utopian substituted. There was a widespread readiness for such a program—but nobody had the program. For myself, I just naturally don't believe any such program ever will or ever can be devised. Mankind will go on slowly and rather painfully, picking its way step by step. It will make mistakes and suffer some backsets, but on the whole it will move forward more easily and uniformly, its periods of stagnation or of retrogression will be shorter than in other times; for among men there is now a measure of social understanding, a clearer apprehension of economic problems, a better grasp of underlying principles in human organization.

I am one of those who regard as mostly bosh the fears that we may confront a long epoch of misfortune for mankind, a return of something like the Dark Ages. For myself, I don't hope for millennium, nor fear a collapse of civilization, in any future that is going to concern us who are now here. Beyond that I do decidedly think that if a lot of the millennialists and the collapsionists would forget it all, go to work at something useful, and quit bothering the rest of us with their hopes and fears, they would be rendering a big service.

We may wish sometimes for a return to the "good old times" of free competition, of laissez faire, of unrestricted and unregulated freedom in business; but we know perfectly well that we will never live in those times again. Things are too complex and too rapidly changing to make it safe to do away with our safeguards.

An Extravagant Generation.

It is constantly stated—and I am sure rightfully so—that the vital need of business is new capital. Plants must be expanded and improved, in keeping with the growth of cities and country, and to do this requires, in terms of money, more than ever before. The difficulty is that everything needs more capital. Government needs more taxes, the steam railroads must have more capital, billions of it; everything needs it. There is more money than there ever was, and there are yet huge reserves seeking investment.

It strikes me as just possible that we don't recognize the true relationship between money and capital. Capital has been described as stored-up labor employed for production of new wealth. Money is a very different thing, as one may note by the most casual study of, say, Russia and Germany. They have oceans of money, such as it is; but of capital useful for production of new wealth they are woefully short. Money may be produced by fiat, or by the lucky discovery of new gold mines; but these processes don't add greatly to the real wealth of the world. Nothing but work will do that; and we need more than financial formulas or economic theories to get the world back to work. Even then, its work will be largely wasted if we go on spending it for wars and the material with which to make wars.

We are an extravagant generation; extravagant with human life and labor, as well as with nature's bounties. We need to stop, turn about, and take a good, square, honest look at ourselves. If we will do that, I think it will go far to convince us that neither the panaceas of the millennialists nor the chaos which the collapsionists seem to hope for will help us out of our scrape. There is nothing for it but to get back at work, use common sense, spend less than we produce, pay our debts, and recognize every man's right to a square deal and a just share of what he produces.

THE "CABINET" MR. ROOSEVELT ALREADY HAS

The Group of Advisers Who Assist Him in Plotting His Course on Political Seas

By JAMES KIERAN.

POLITICAL campaigns, as Philip Guedalla said of historians, repeat themselves. The same smiling candidates, the same red-fire parades of crowds, the same pledges, the same pomp and circumstance of official appearance.

But behind the histrionics that naturally accompany a successful campaign for the Presidency of the United States are the actions and relations of a trusted group of men who disobey the ordinary rules of imitation. These are the "no" men and, as it is recognized that good political leadership, like charity, begins in the home, theirs is an important function.

Franklin Delano Roosevelt goes to the White House next March with a unique gallery of associates who have labored as prompters far from the footlights. One or two of them have been pushed downstage for a bow now and then. But their real work has been in the informal talk at a picnic, in the heated exchanges of a council of war, in the idle argumentation over a small dinner.

These little groups that surround a political leader have been called "kitchen Cabinets," "turkey Cabinets," "brains trusts" and all kinds of other names. But it is agreed that they occupy an effective place in the determination of the course followed by the men they serve.

A Variegated Group.

Governor Roosevelt, as much as any other leader in recent history, has assembled a strangely variegated group of intimates with whom he bandies ideas to obtain the distillate for public expression.

There is Louis McHenry Howe, a newspaper man known as the "headman"; there is James A. Farley, the Democratic national chairman; there is Henry Morgenthau Jr., farmer conservation commissioner; there is Samuel I. Rosenman, legislative expert and political buffer, who formed the "brains trust"; and there is Raymond Moley, the "brains trust" head, professor at Columbia, expert on public law, tireless worker and chief aide of the Governor on the final draft of public statements.

There are the other members of the "trust" A. A. Berle, another Columbia professor, and R. G. Tugwell, still another "man from Columbia." There is General Hugh Johnson. He is what is called the "man" of Bernard Mannes Baruch, financier, on whom Governor Roosevelt has relied for considerable guidance in past months.

There is Edward J. Flynn, Secretary of State in New York and leader of the Bronx—a man who loves everything except politics but is recognized as an expert in the field.

There is Joseph P. Kennedy, fiery Boston and New York financier, who fights so hard in conferences for his proposals and his convictions that he sometimes arouses temporary enmity within the group.

There is Senator James F. Byrnes of South Carolina, ironically enough, the successor of Cole Blease. Alert, unpretentious, but wary in the ways of Washington, he is generally understood to have been chosen as the liaison man between Mr. Roosevelt and Congress.

There is Senator Key Pittman of Nevada, slow-talking, anecdotal, but wise in political affairs from many years of service, an "inner circle" associate of the Governor on his swing through the West.

There is D. Basil O'Connor, the Governor's law partner—a man who openly declares he wants none of politics but who, as the "Doc," cuts through the verbiage of advice to give the Governor his forceful opinion about required strategy.

Experts in Many Branches.

There are many experts in various branches summoned either by the Governor or by his informal aides to express their opinions or present data. To the Roosevelt household come, too, many industrial leaders with whom the President-elect talks informally.

But in naming the members of the "inner Cabinet" one must not forget the President-elect's wife, Eleanor Roosevelt. She, as much because of her own forthrightness of opinion as because of her position in the family, is a powerful force.

When Franklin D. Roosevelt was unexpectedly nominated for the Governorship for the first time, it was popularly said that the really dominant power in the Roosevelt family was "Mrs. R.," as she is known among the intimates. That was because she had remained in active politics while her husband was recovering his health.

But when Mr. Roosevelt donned the mantle of official position, once more it was quickly demonstrated that he was master of his own destinies. Mrs. Roosevelt, out of her own long experience in public, offered advice but never dictation. She was able to speak her mind freely and with effect to her husband. Mrs. Roosevelt has the reputation of never interfering, but when she is asked for her opinion she minces no words in stating her view.

Colonel Howe to Remain.

One man certain to remain as the bright star in the galaxy of Roosevelt aides is Colonel Howe—he really is a Colonel by commission of Governor Laffoon of Kentucky—who has worked in close association with the President-elect since the days when the youthful Roosevelt first went to Capitol Hill in Albany.

To the frequently asked question—"Who is going to be the Colonel House of the Roosevelt administration?"—the obvious answer is that it will be Colonel Edward M. House himself, as indicated by the telephonic conversation the President-elect held with the veteran of the Wilson régime before he replied to President Hoover on the invitation for the war debt conference. But closer to the new President than Colonel House ever was able to penetrate to the wartime President will be Colonel Howe. He worked with Mr. Roosevelt in the Navy Department; was his personal representative in the Vice Presidential campaign of 1920; and, so the story goes, stood firmly for a political career for his friend when Mr. Roosevelt was battling his way back to health after the attack of infantile paralysis, and even during Mr. Roosevelt's illness began laying plans for the capture of the Presidency.

In 1930 Jim Farley joined the select group. M. William Bray, now Lieutenant Governor-elect, was State chairman, but had fallen into disfavor for one reason or another. Mr. Farley was secretary of the State committee.

After Mr. Roosevelt was renominated for the Governorship Mr. Farley was chosen State chairman at the Governor's suggestion. Mr. Farley was thenceforth prominent in the drive to name Mr. Roosevelt for President. As delegate garnerer for the New York Governor, he traveled many miles. He slapped many backs. He does not do it as a politician. He is that way.

An Adviser on Farm Questions.

Henry Morgenthau Jr. came into contact with the President-elect when Mr. Roosevelt was re-entering public life. In Mr. Roosevelt's campaigns for Governor, as in his campaign for the Presidency, Commissioner Morgenthau has been a constant source of advice and information on farm problems. Last Spring he made a wide tour of the agricultural belt of the mid-West to bring back his findings to the Governor.

Supreme Court Justice Rosenman was in the legislative bill drafting department when he was selected to go with the Gubernatorial candidate on his first campaign in 1928. He won Mr. Roosevelt's friendship, was named counsel and became a close adviser. When a New York City justice died, Tammany fought for the place; it did not want the Governor's counsel named, but Governor Roosevelt named him. More recently, when it was time to nominate for the unexpired term for Supreme Court Justice, Samuel I. Rosenman was rejected by the Democratic organization in favor of Samuel H. Hofstadter, a Republican.

Meanwhile, Mr. Rosenman had inaugurated the "brains trust" led by Professor Moley. As far back as last May the little corps which arranged data for the Governor came into being. It gradually assumed more importance. How much of the original body will continue is, of course, conjecture. On men like Bernard M. Baruch, Owen D. Young and Colonel House, Mr. Roosevelt relies greatly; but of those in the personal gallery who have worked for months, some of them for years, in direct touch with him, some, at least, will carry on in Washington.

ROOSEVELT FEELS LOSS OF ADVISER

Gap Left by Howe's Death to Be Filled, as During His Illness, by a Group.

NO SUCCESSOR IN SIGHT

By CHARLES W. B. HURD

WASHINGTON, April 25.—The death of Louis McHenry Howe, chief secretary to the President and his political mentor for more than twenty-five years, created a vacancy in the intimate staff assisting Mr. Roosevelt which cannot possibly be filled in the same manner as before.

This is due to the fact that, although Mr. Howe's rôle as steward of the President's political ambitions and public acts was often exaggerated, his intimate knowledge of the President's mind was combined with political acumen and training that made him the only individual who could fill his post in relation to Franklin D. Roosevelt as he did.

Some other person in time may be appointed a member of the White House secretariat, but the circumstances of the new appointee's position, in relation both to the President and to the other secretaries, cannot be the same.

Three Secretaries Permitted

Under a law passed at the request of former President Hoover, the President may have three secretaries, each of equal rank and each drawing a salary of $10,000 per year. Common practice has created definite divisions in the work done by these secretaries: one serves as a political agent and adviser, one handling personal contact work at the White House and the arrangement of the President's personal appointments, and one combines the duties of correspondence with that of handling news inquiries.

Mr. Hoover laid out this pattern of work for his official secretaries and President Roosevelt perpetuated it.

On the day that Mr. Roosevelt was inaugurated, March 4, 1933, he signed secretarial commissions for three men, each of whom had been associated with him at least thirteen years prior to that time.

He named Mr. Howe as Secretary to the President, and gave commissions as assistant secretaries to Stephen T. Early and Marvin H. McIntyre. These two gladly acquiesced in the suggestion that they be subordinate to Mr. Howe out of respect for his seniority. However, they were granted salaries equal to his, and other prerogatives such as the use of White House limousines.

Howe's Unique Position

Mr. Howe literally moved into the White House, being assigned a suite there to live in. He continued to exercise all the advisory functions, as well as wide political contact he had started in behalf of "the Chief" back in 1910.

After Mr. Howe's illness became serious, Mr. Roosevelt found himself turning to a group of men for the same advice and assistance he had relied upon his secretary to give him. Secretary Hull has grown constantly in intimacy with the President, being called upon as a man of mature conservatism to analyze many problems besetting the administration. Postmaster General Farley, of course, has continued to be the practical political agent of the administration and the buffer for many criticisms leveled against

ROOSEVELT ADVISERS

Times Wide World.

Three close to the President—Secretary Cordell Hull, Postmaster General Farley and Charles West.

it. Added to this list also is the name of Joseph P. Kennedy, former chairman of the Securities and Exchange Commission, who, whether in office or not, has a rich, ripe vocabulary that on more than one occasion has been uttered into the Presidential ear.

Changes Made Necessary

Advice and political management, however, had been only two of the things supplied by Mr. Howe, and the President saw soon after the secretary became inactive that he needed to do considerable rearranging in the routine of his immediate assistants. Some one must handle the large bulk of correspondence that once went across Mr. Howe's desk, and still another was needed who could go to the Capitol or take up a telephone and "talk turkey" with administration leaders on Capitol Hill.

The correspondence problem was handled simply by shifting the bulk of it to Mr. Early and giving the latter a special assistant, William Hassett, a former newspaper man, to handle the principal routine of Mr. Early's former primary responsibility.

Then the President drafted Charles West, a young former Representative from Ohio and a Democrat with many friends in the Senate and House, to do what is commonly known as "leg-work" in connection with pet administration legislation. Mr. West did his work well, so well that he was rewarded with the specially created post of Under-Secretary of the Interior, a position that carries much prestige, pays him a salary comparable with a White House secretaryship and leaves him free at all times to act as liaison man between the White House and Congress.

If no personal attachment existed between Mr. Roosevelt and his two assistant secretaries, it is not improbable that Under-Secretary West might have been assigned to the office formerly used by Mr. Howe. That assignment, however, would hardly be possible under the circumstances.

April 26, 1936

BRAIN TRUSTERS MAKE WAY FOR EXECUTIVES

President's Aides Work Quietly Behind Scenes

Academic Advisers Now Out of Politics

By DELBERT CLARK

WASHINGTON.

If there is one change that stands out in the political Washington of 1937 as compared with that of 1933 it is the almost complete disappearance of what an inspired reporter four years ago embalmed in history as the Brain Trust. Soon after President Roosevelt began his first term there was milling around the capital city an oddly assorted group of young men, most of them with an academic background, who fairly merited this title.

Today they are not milling around Washington. Most of them are not in Washington. Not only have new personalities replaced them. The Brain Trust as an institution has altered almost out of recognition as the administration's problems have taken new forms.

Four years ago a dire crisis confronted the country. The times called for venturesome planning and quick execution, and the men to do these things were precisely the young men from the universities, trained in economic theory but usually indifferent to politics. As the crisis wore itself out the need for speed was lessened, but reform was in the air simultaneously with recovery. The men who planned the liquidation of the immediate crisis were equally well equipped, broadly speaking, to draft far-reaching changes in our social and economic structure. This they did.

But as recovery progressed and the reform program assumed legislative shape there was less and less need for a cohesive group of philosophers and program-makers. The need was for administrators, and very few of the original Brain Trust group displayed marked ability in this field. So they drifted away and the offices that knew them know them no more. It cannot honestly be said that at any particular point in his administration President Roosevelt lost confidence in them. Loyalty to those whom he has trusted and who have never consciously let him down has been one of his most spectacular traits. He has refused to dismiss men while they were under fire. He has tried to let them go with flying colors.

It should not be inferred that because there is no longer a Brain Trust as such, there is no heavy thinking going on in Washington. There is, but with this difference:

The one and only Brain Trust, which carried over from the campaign of 1932 into tangible government jobs quite by accident, was composed principally of idea merchants. They were like the old professor of philosophy who was mistaken in a Pullman smoker for a salesman, and when asked what his "line" was replied: "Notions."

The neo-Brain Trust of the New Deal is just as full of ideas, and just as colorful ideas, as that group which preceded it, but its members are in the President's entourage not primarily because they are idea men but because they know how to get a job done and are open-minded enough to know how to proceed when there is no precedent to lean on. Such men are Harry L. Hopkins, Harold L. Ickes, Henry A. Wallace, Cordell Hull and Jesse H. Jones, all administrators, but all wise councilors and men of imagination in their fields.

And yet it cannot truthfully be said that here is a sort of substitute Brain Trust, for the President reaches far afield for ideas and advice, and many individuals whose names would mean little or nothing in the country at large have had their brief, private moments of glory when Mr. Roosevelt has delved down into the recesses of his memory and brought them to the White House for a conference on a subject on which they were experts. Others, previously unknown to the President, have been invited to speak their minds after some one has told him that they had something original to contribute.

Thus the President is constantly being sold ideas — mentation did not depart with Raymond Moley and Rexford Tugwell—and the ideas he declines to buy, by the same token, are legion. Yet he hears all, and as often as not the full-blown plan which emerges is really and peculiarly his own. It has come to be the fashion to speculate on who gave the President this idea and who was behind that. Probably what happened was more on this order: A problem, perhaps only half realized, presented itself. At various times and without prearrangement Mr. Wallace, Mr. Hopkins and Mr. Ickes called to take about it. Each had an idea, each a sovereign remedy for the national ailment of the moment. Mr. Roosevelt heard them all and stored what they said in his memory. The problem grew with the comprehension bred of free, informal discussion. Chats or telephone calls went out to these men and others, asking for factual memoranda with recommendations. None knew of the part the others were playing. When all the data and all the recommendations were in, Mr. Roosevelt compared them carefully, noting points of agreement and disagreement, and sat down to think. The problem stayed with him, waking and sleeping, at luncheon and in the receiving line at a formal reception, until he had worked out, from the material and diverse opinions before him, what was essentially his own answer. This might be a composite of all the others, or part of them, or something entirely independent and a surprise to all his advisers.

Associated Press.

Tom Corcoran (seated) and Ben Cohen, once dubbed "the Jolly Hot Dogs," are two surviving members of the corps of experts recruited early in the New Deal.

THUS it can be seen that Mr. Roosevelt is president and chairman of the board of his own Brain Trust, that he too has ideas, and that the ultimate decision is always his, and his alone. But it will be a decision reached with the aid of many willing advisers and idea men, in and out of the government—present administrators, former administrators, and men who never in their lives held or expect to hold a Federal job.

It is possible to trace Mr. Roosevelt's theory of unemployment relief to Mr. Hopkins, lean, restless, imaginative former social worker, hard-boiled and sentimental at once, beloved by all who know him well, burning himself out on the altar of humane service. But the theory is not Mr. Hopkins's alone—Mr. Hopkins only furnished the technical background and the experience.

The "peace-at-a-fair-price" foreign policy displays the philosophy of both Secretary Hull and Secretary Wallace: Hull the dignified, sedate man of one fixed purpose, the lean Tennessee sharpshooter, the uncanny politician; Wallace the intense, slightly puritanical young man from the prairies, obsessed with the farmer's problem and, by direct connection, with the problem of rational world trade.

Others in this loose aggregation of advisers are more catholic in their usefulness to Mr. Roosevelt—they advise him as he seeks their advice on a multitude of questions—with the possible exception of Secretary Ickes, the tall-building-and-big-dam crusader, who thinks only of permanent public works programs, low-cost housing and hydroelectric power.

Members of the original Brain Trust—Raymond Moley and Rexford Tugwell in a conference with the late Secretary Woodin and the President.

Ex-Brain-truster Rexford G. Tugwell, called "the complete philosopher in action."

Associated Press.

EXPANDING our definition of the Brain Trust to include these men, some who were not popularly associated with it, and some who held subordinate positions, we find a few other survivors.

"As recovery progressed there was less need for philosophers and program-makers. The need was for administrators."

Technically James M. Landis, Professor of Law at Harvard and chairman of the SEC, met the qualification, though he never ran around much with the group. He turned out to be a first-class administrator, young, intense, full of humor, sociable in his habits, able to win the liking and respect of the very men he was employed to regulate. He won over the honest but worried financiers from profound distrust to almost pathetic faith in his integrity and ability. Landis is leaving government employ, not because he was an administrative failure but because his sucess in Washington confirmed Harvard's good opinion of him. He is to be dean of the Harvard Law School.

Among the less spectacular members of the earlier group who are still hereabouts are Ben Cohen, now general counsel of the National Power Policy Committee of the PWA, and Tom Corcoran, once a storm center of policies and politics but now working quietly as counsel for the RFC. Once cruelly dubbed "the Jolly Hot Dogs," they now make it a point to preserve impressive anonymity. There are also H. R. Tolley, scholarly AAA Administrator, who will never spread his personality over a front page if he can help it; Mordecai Ezekiel, brilliant but retiring economist of the Department of Agriculture; Isadore Lubin, formerly of the University of Michigan, then of the Brookings Institution, and now for several years Commissioner of Labor Statistics, and Leo Pasvolsky, late of the Brookings Institution, and now a special assistant to the Secretary of State. Add a scattering of professors and ex-professors in various non-policy-making agencies, or agencies which definitely call for the academic mind, and you have what might be called a Brain Trust—but not a Brain Trust in the original sense in which that phrase was used.

The very term "Brain Trust" implied an intellectual coalition, a group acting if not always as a unit then under a highly centralized leadership; a close corporation organized for constructive thought, for national planning. Four years ago the core of this group kept bachelor quarters together or met frequently at lunch or dinner and threshed out questions of common interest. Not so now. There is only a diffusion of trained intellects, from the college cloisters or the mentally more aristocratic law offices, who do various individual jobs within the government. These more and more resemble the scientific and economic specialists who, year in and year out, under changing administrations, do the solid work of bureaus and departments.

They take a back seat as far as publicity is concerned, and most of them are glad to do so. The Brain Trusters who courted publicity and who did not understand the ingrained distrust of the old-line politician for the scholar have disappeared. The survivors are satisfied to do their thinking behind closed doors.

THEIR places in the public eye have been, to a great extent, taken by a new breed of government workers who are excellent administrators in their special fields but who cannot be thought of as being in any sense members of an unofficial Cabinet.

M. L. Wilson, who succeeded Mr. Tugwell as Under-Secretary of Agriculture, has learned about farming and farmers through thirty years as farmer, county agent, research and university teaching. He is scientific and practical at the same time. When he talks to a gathering of farmers they know that he knows what he is talking about. His present job is a "natural" for him. A shrewd idealist, he knows it fore and aft.

John Collier, for more than a decade the executive secretary and mainspring of the Indian Defense Association, was a severe critic of the former Indian Bureau administrations. He had definite ideas for maintaining the tribal life and independence of the Indian, and was "agin" the white land-grabber and exploiter. The President gave him a chance to work out his ideas. But Collier, like Wilson, is mainly preoccupied with his specific task—he is not part of a "brains pool."

Policy-maker—Secretary Hull's philosophy is reflected in the "peace-at-a-fair-price" idea.

Edward F. (Eddie) McGrady is the one genuine labor leader who has ever come within striking distance of the Cabinet. Back in the Summer of 1933, when the NRA was being fought through the Senate, it was McGrady, then legislative representative of the A. F. of L., who manipulated votes to save it. He was Senator Pat Harrison's shock troop, and his work of persuasion was singularly effective. When the NRA was set up McGrady became friend and confidant of General Johnson, but, luckier than the general, found himself with a permanent job as Assistant Secretary of Labor. McGrady would have little opportunity to sit in at meetings of the Brain Trust, if one still existed. He is so constantly on the move adjusting labor difficulties that so far as Washington is concerned he is little more than a voice, a gust of wind and a glimpse of vanishing coat-tail.

So much has been said about Jesse Jones, shrewd chairman of the RFC, that he has become almost a legend. When the New Deal was really new and the President's advisers were being denounced as "impractical theorists" the administration's supporters could point to Houston's pride.

"All that may be as you say," they would remark smugly, "but look at Jesse Jones! If there ever was a hard-headed business man he is one, and he's a New Dealer."

Jones has had a dual function—to disburse government money in the form of loans where it would be of the most help to industry, and to keep a return flow, with interest, moving steadily into the Treasury. This he has done, and he anticipated with considerable plausibility the day when the RFC will be liquidated, if not with a profit, then with a perfect balance, except for the outright gifts to relief that were made for a time.

He is renowned as a hard bargainer, who always sees that the government gets everything it can out of a deal. He would like to be head of all the government's financial agencies, if such a post ever were created. His friends, though not too seriously, have even higher aspirations for him. On Christmas, each year, as they receive with his compliments cases of selected pink grapefruit from Texas, they chant: "Jesse Jones for President."

More recently Roswell Magill, Professor of Law at Columbia University, has taken a year's leave of absence from his teaching job to serve as Under-Secretary of the Treasury.

AS to the future, the chances of survival for those who have replaced the old Brain Trust or who have emerged from it into new rôles may be measured by what happened to the original members. Mr. Moley, alone of all the pioneers of 1933, made the mistake of trying to match political wits with his immediate superior, and presently found himself giving advice in the pages of a magazine rather than directing foreign policy from the inside.

Mr. Tugwell made no such error. He seemed never to have any greater ambition than to do the best job he could, in untried fields and with untried methods. He was, like Woodrow Wilson, the complete philosopher in action, and a philosopher with the courage to act can be one of three things: a colossal failure, a brilliant success, or an extremely dangerous man—perhaps a little of all three.

He was, at any rate, not constructed for the rough give-and-take of politics; he could get on with Jim Farley, but he did not resemble him. To those who really knew him he could be charming; to those whom he didn't know or didn't care for he could be arrogant and irritating. He never quite grasped the fundamentals of amiable relations with the public through the press. He got on better with farmers than with Congressmen. These characteristics, together with a certain pontifical manner on occasion, resulted in his being personally credited with virtually every fault of the New Deal and certainly with every one of its more daring experiments. They led people to stick the contemptuous epithet "Tugwelltown" on his suburban housing ventures, and invariably to label him "Doctor" or "Professor."

MR. TUGWELL might have

Times Wide World and Harris & Ewing.

Members of today's advisory board—Secretary Wallace, Jesse Jones, Harry Hopkins and Secretary Ickes are not primarily idea men but administrators.

lingered in Washington if he had been a gifted administrator. But his Resettlement Administration took a long time to get on its feet, like a gargantuan but somewhat rachitic child. A year ago it could not have been inventoried and transferred without the mislaying of half a dozen or so miscellaneous divisions. By the close of 1936 RA had been whirled into a semblance of form, and with a few judicious press releases on its achievements, an incredibly gaudy report and a farewell dinner given by the newly organized Friends of Tugwell at $2.50 a plate a national cycle completed itself. Tugwell thus marched out with the honors of war. He went into the molasses business, not for the amusement of hostile paragraphers but because two of his former Brain Trust buddies, Charles William Taussig, who crossed the Washington stage briefly in 1933, and Adolf Augustus Berle Jr., happened to be connected with the "long-sweetenin'" industry.

Mr. Berle was one of the most fortunate or most discreet of the original group. He left, to become City Chamberlain of New York, before the Presidential honeymoon was over. He had no administrative position in Washington, and played his cards so consistently and quietly that he is still understood to be on call whenever the President desires his advice.

As one looks back over the four years it is thus apparent that the Brain Trust belonged to a phase of the Roosevelt crusade which is now past. You have to hunt for the Brain Trust in the files, and ultimately you will have to hunt for it in the pages of history. It had its day. It said with Whitman:

Come, I will make the continent indissoluble,
I will make the most splendid race the sun ever shone upon.

It made some progress toward this objective, but just now the spotlight rests on those who, like Jesse Jones, take the continent for granted and, like him, reduce all propositions to the question, "How much money on the cracker barrel?"

March 7, 1937

The Men Around the President

They range from personal cronies to official advisers—but there is an important difference in the nature of the roles they play.

By CABELL PHILLIPS

WASHINGTON.

INFLUENCE is Washington's most treasured commodity. The next dearest is knowing, and having access to, people who have it. Politicians, bureaucrats, lobbyists, newspaper men and the inevitable "five percenters" spend their professional lifetimes cultivating influence or the influential, and their usefulness on the Washington scene is measured in precise—and rewarding—ratio to the success of that quest.

The inevitable focus of the influence seekers is the White House. For some the claim of "a contact at the White House" can be traded for cash or other tangible emolument. For others such an entree may mean the furtherance of major political plans, the advancement of an idea or a national policy, or it may mean a source of accurate and important information on world affairs. Whatever the use to which it is put—venal or selfish or in the public interest—propinquity to that mythical White House "inner circle" is a distinction that is avidly sought in Washington.

THE recent involvement of Maj. Gen. Harry H. Vaughan, the President's military aide, in the Senate investigation of "five prcenters" has vividly dramatized this professional preoccupation of Washington with influence. It has raised again the perennial argument over "government by crony," what it is and how much of it exists in the Fair Deal. And it has focused the spotlight of public curiosity on the men around President Truman, upon whom the tides of influence seekers break with relentless persistency.

Just what do we mean when we speak of the White House "inner circle"? And having defined it, who are the men who really belong in it?

A President's need for help in the discharge of his enormous duties falls into four broad categories. First, he has to have around him people with sound knowledge and active imaginations to aid him in the creation and development of broad policies. Second, he has to have completely loyal and competent lieutenants for the execution not only of these policies but to help him carry out the day-to-day chores of his office. Third, he has to have effective and dependable liaison officers with the legislative branch of the Government. And, fourth, he has to have men who are his eyes and ears in the arena of partisan politics.

These are the official and, generally speaking, visible members of any White House "inner circle." But there is a fifth group, not always official and not always visible to the public eye, who stand in a close, intimate relationship to a President. They are his personal friends, people with whom he likes to relax on a week-end of fishing or an evening of poker and forget the cares of office. They may be, and often are, drawn from the official echelons already mentioned. But there are also usually a few outsiders.

Bearing in mind that there are constantly shifting tides of preferment and favoritism in any group of such critical importance, and that there is a considerable amount of overlapping, let's see just who the people are that fit the various segments of the "inner circle" of the Fair Deal in this late summer of 1949.

Policy Advisers and Idea Men

THIS is an extremely fluid group. At times it may embrace the whole Cabinet, Congressional leaders and Democratic party leaders, or individuals from any one of these groups may exert a dominating influence with the President on some given problem. But to reduce the number to that select few who appear, week in and week out, to carry a fairly constant load or responsibility for the President in determining broad and creative policy, we get a list approximately like this:

Clark M. Clifford, counsel to the President. His office is in the White House and he sees the President frequently each day. He is generally regarded as the principal articulator of the Fair Deal and is the chief author of most of the important Presidential speeches and papers. He is also the main pipeline through which ideas generated in the labyrinth of Government departments reach the President's attention. He is an able and aggressive salesman, particularly for those measures that appeal to his progressive and liberal instincts. His is the most potent influence in the White House today.

Dean Acheson, Secretary of State. For the last decade any Secretary of State could always be counted high among the policy advisers of the President. It is abundantly true with regard to Dean Acheson, whose precise and cultivated mind the President respects enormously. The range of Acheson's influence is, naturally enough, limited to our role in the world at large, but this is a limitation of barely discernible outlines today.

Edwin G. Nourse, Leon Keyserling and John D. Clark, the council of economic advisers. Virtually every domestic and foreign program involves an impact at some point on the American economic system. To assess these probable effects, and to devise new policies affecting the economic system, the President turns always to his council of economic advisers. Their counsel is supreme in nearly all such matters. However, the President tends to regard the three-man council as an entity and seldom consults them individually. It is evident, however, that the New Deal-minded Keyserling has been somewhat more successful in getting his particular slant on economic questions accepted at the White House than have his more conservative fellows. This is possibly explained by the natural rapport which exists between him and Clifford.

Secretary of Agriculture Charles Brannan. To pick one member of the Cabinet as belonging to this elite group and to exclude the others, is to invite bitter controversy. But in view of the prominence which farm legislation has taken in the whole structure of the Fair Deal, Brannan must be accorded this special distinction. His controversial 'Brannan Plan," or some closely related version of it, continues to be one of the principal objectives of the Truman Administration.

Admiral Sydney W. Souers, executive secretary of the National Security Council. Properly speaking, Admiral Souers is not in a policy-making capacity. He is titularly only the administrative officer of a strategy board composed of the President, the Secretary of Defense, the Secretaries of the three armed services and the chairman of the National Security Resources Board. But in reality he is the President's chief informant on all matters, at home and overseas, bearing directly on the national security. He consults with the President daily and alone, immediately after the morning staff conference, and fills the gap left by the retirement of Admiral William D. Leahy, Chief of Staff to the Commander in Chief. He is, moreover, an old and admiring friend of the President's. Unquestionably, a great deal of policy bearing on national defense and our relations with other nations of the world evolves from the daily briefings which Admiral Souers supplies.

BUT the most fertile source of Government policy is not in the White House at all. The seedbed where ideas are conceived and slowly germinate is in the lower echelons of the executive departments—among the under and assistant secretaries, the bureau and division chiefs, etc. A great many of these are brilliant and dedicated young men who have chosen government as a career, and who pursue it with an avidity of which their Cabinet-officer bosses are often incapable. They are largely unknown to the general public, for when one of their projects matures to the point where it is publicly unveiled it usually has some Cabinet member's name attached to it.

There is, indeed, an informal "Little Cabinet Club" which meets for dinner once a month, as one member explained it to me, "just to kick some of these ideas around and to get some steam behind them." Typical of the sort of men involved are Oscar Chapman and Gerard Davidson, Under-Secretary and Assistant Secretary, respectively, of the Department of Interior; Edward H. Foley Jr., Under Secretary of Treasury; James E. Webb and John E. Peurifoy, of the State Department. There are about thirty in this group altogether, and it is a safe bet that some of them have had an important part in shaping every important White House decision on policy of the last twelve months.

Executive Aides

THE President's executive aides are the men who help him get things done. They may consult with him on policy, or undertake long studies and recommendations upon which policy is based. But essentially they are the President's legmen and chore boys, the extra heads and eyes and hands of the world's busiest executive.

The Hoover Commission, as well as previous investigators of the same type, recommend an expanded staff of helpers for the President. Presumably this may be achieved in the next piece of reorganization legislation. At present there are three secretaries, four administrative assistants and five other officers who may be properly identified as the personal staff of the President. Five of these, by their contacts with the President, seem to qualify for the "inner circle." They are:

John R. Steelman, the first man in history to bear the title of Assistant to the President. A durable and indomitably cheerful Arkansan with many years' experience in the Government, he is the President's chief liaison officer with the infinitely ramified executive establishment.

Matthew W. Connally, appointment secretary. He screens the hundreds of weekly requests from big and little men to take up a part of the President's time.

Charles Ross, the long-suffering and abuse-absorbing press secretary.

Frank Pace Jr., recently elevated to the position of Director of the Bureau of the Budget. He has the dual job of preparing and monitoring the annual budget and is also the President's chief deputy for administrative management of the Federal bureaucracy.

UNDER varying circumstances members of the Cabinet move in and out of this inner circle. Usually their functions are so closely related to their individual departments, however, that it would be unrealistic to number them among an "inner circle." The case of Louis Johnson, Secretary of Defense, is somewhat different.

The problems and operations of his department are the most pervasive and the most expensive of any branch of the Government. The policies governing it were laid down before he took office. The job of putting those policies into effect makes him, more than any other man of Cabinet rank, a principal executive aide to the President.

Legislative Liaison

GETTING his legislative program through Congress is probably the most relentless preoccupation of any President. This has certainly been true of President Truman, as much with the Democratic Eighty-first as with the Republican Eightieth Congress. He is one of the few Presidents of this century who have faithfully maintained frequent and regular conferences with their legislative leaders.

The "Big Four," who meet with the President in his oval office each Monday morning, is composed of Vice President Alben W. Barkley and Majority Leader Scott Lucas of the Senate and Speaker Sam Rayburn and Majority Leader John W. McCormack of the House. In these conferences, of course, major legislative strategy is planned.

But in addition to the "Big Four" there are others who belong to this particular branch of the White House "inner circle." Leslie Biffle, secretary of the Senate, is an old and intimate friend of the President's with an intuitive sense for Senate moods and tempers. He is a "dopester" and strategist on whom the President relies heavily. Matt Connally, the appointment secretary, doubles also as a most effective liaison man with Congress and performs many confidential missions on The Hill for his boss. Charles S. Murphy, one of the President's executive assistants, is the principal analyst of bills which the President is either to sign or veto. Upon his interpretation of the confused gobbledegook in which legislation is written often depends some of the President's most farreaching decisions.

Political Contacts

THERE is a tendency in the tradition of American public life to make out that politics doesn't exist. Politicians themselves have been guilty of dressing it in the most repugnant connotations. But among the major responsibilities of a President is the successful leadership of his party. This is a bifurcated operation: Its most obvious aspect is in the President's relations with his party leaders in Congress; less obvious (in recognition, no doubt of the old taboo) is his relation with the party leaders themselves.

The inner circle of President Truman's political aides is headed, naturally enough, by William M. Boyle, the former Kansas City police chief who has worked his way spectacularly to the top in party councils during the last two years. He recently succeeded Senator J. Howard McGrath of Rhode Island, as chairman of the Democratic National Committee. McGrath, however, does not drop out of the political picture. As Attorney General, which he has just become, he will be the largest dispenser of Federal patronage in the Cabinet. His position in the inner circle is thus secure.

Oscar Chapman, Under Secretary of Interior, is one of the quietest and most effective political technicians in Washington, and one of the most highly regarded at the White House. Advance man for the Western campaign tour last year, he is credited with a large share of the Democrats' victory in those states. Oscar Ewing, Federal Security Administrator and a high official off and on for many years in the Democratic National Committee, is another close political confidant of the President. And the versatile Matt Connally has lately extended his operations in this direction too, with measurable results.

* * *

HERE, then, is a reasonably accurate and comprehensive roster of the White House "inner circle" that has shaped and directed so much of what is called the Fair Deal. There are nineteen individuals and one three-man board included. Of the number, four are from the President's home state, Missouri — Clifford, Souers, Ross and Boyle. Of these four, three are friends from his pre-Washington days — Souers, Ross and Boyle. Of the nineteen, only eleven knew him during his Senatorial days. The remaining eight of this highly select "inner circle" got to know their chief only after he became President—or, as in the case of Secretary Brannan, after he had designated them for the positions they now hold.

Some will be surprised to find the names of Secretary Snyder and General Vaughan missing from this list of the elite. The simple fact is that they do not belong to the "inner circle." The two men are, perhaps, the closest and most intimate friends the President has in Washington—cronies in the truest sense of the word. The basis of those friendships is as different as the two men are personally disparate. But neither is close to Harry Truman, the President, in the sense that the others in this roster are.

Secretary Snyder is, of course, an important wheel in the governmental machine. But today he exercises little influence upon the President's thinking or actions. He disapproves most of the Fair Deal; the President disapproves—and overrules—most of Snyder's conservatism. The two have worked out an acceptable compromise on that level and each retains the respect, the admiration and the affection of the other.

GENERAL VAUGHAN has never, so far as it can be learned, attempted to influence policy decisions at the White House, and probably would have been reproved if he had done so. He is a congenial, stimulating friend to the President, and a faithful legman for a variety of chores. And apparently a mutually acceptable compromise has been worked out on that basis too.

When the President goes on one of his frequent week-end cruises down the Potomac on the Williamsburg he goes for one or two purposes—to get important work done away from the heat and pressures of Washington, or to forget all about Washington.

When it is a working mission the list of guests for the cruise is dutifully announced—a few members of Congress, a Cabinet officer or two, several of the White House staff and a full complement of secretaries and stenographers. When it is a non-working mission—and there have been three or four this summer—there is an impregnable silence. It is a non-official junket for Citizen Truman and his friends.

And therein lies the key to that sinister specter of "government by crony." For on most of these secret cruises there will be found such Machiavellian influences as Chief Justice Fred M. Vinson, Secretary Snyder, the former Attorney General and new justice of the Supreme Court, Tom Clark; Clark Clifford, Matt Connally, General Vaughan, and the redoubtable George Allen. Plus, of course, whoever of the other faithful happens to be available at the time.

These are the President's cronies, along with whatever other positions of trust and confidence they may hold. On the whole they do not present a particularly ominous aspect.

September 11, 1949

WHITE HOUSE ROUTINES ADJUSTED TO NEW TENANT

President Eisenhower and His Staff Apply Their System to the Tasks

By ANTHONY LEVIERO

Special to THE NEW YORK TIMES.

WASHINGTON, Jan. 24—Gen. Dwight D. Eisenhower was at last installed in his highest command post this week and in no time at all was acting like a President of the United States.

Some of his first callers were just cowboys who wanted a handshake. Some were his friends. A couple were Governors lobbying with the President—urging him to get the Federal Government out of fields of taxation that belong to the states. He conferred with Cabinet members and his staff on the toughest problems of the nation. He amiably helped pose some of his appointees in front of newspaper cameras.

A President has to see a lot of people, a cross-section of America, and "Ike," the man who was liked, was doing that. A President has to receive pressure groups, and President Eisenhower was doing that in listening to Governors Thornton of Colorado and Kohler of Wisconsin.

President Yields

A President, unlike a general, cannot order something and invariably expect to get what he wants, and President Eisenhower experienced this in two important respects. His Secretary of Defense-designate, Charles E. Wilson, had to accommodate himself to the law and to the will of Congress. And the President himself had to give up his plan to nominate former Gov. Val Peterson of Nebraska as Ambassador to India in the face of objections from the Senators from Nebraska.

A President belongs to the people, and no matter how irksome he may regard the dogging of his footsteps by reporters and photographers, he has to show himself. President Eisenhower met the requirements for "the first picture at your desk," "the first picture with your staff," "the first picture with your Cabinet," "a picture of you saying good-by to your son."

To be sure, things were being done somewhat differently. But it would be wrong to say that things were being done a soldier's way. In the techniques of office and staff procedures, the observer could find no more difference than one would normally expect to find between one man's approach and the next man's.

To be sure there was a Republican air about the place. Only a week ago virtually all the callers were Democrats. Now they were virtually all Republicans, the prominent exception being that Democrat in the Eisenhower Cabinet, Martin P. Durkin, Secretary of Labor. The pressures being applied were Republican, but that was to be expected.

In some ways, however, the air began to clear when the Eisenhower Administration-to-be moved out of the Hotel Commodore in New York and acquired authority by moving to the positions of power in Washington. Pre-eminent was the announcement that White House news conferences would be continued on a regular basis and probably widened in scope.

The public discussion of this threatened curtailment of White House press coverage, which Washington correspondents viewed as hurtful to the new President, evidently resulted in a thorough examination of the problem with a result that pleased the working press.

In his Army role Eisenhower, of course, had considerable experience with the press all during the war and saw often and vividly the importance of public opinion. And in this first week the new President, as he faced the cameras and as he spoke through his press secretary, must have been struck not only with the importance but the sheer necessity of making himself understood by the vastly interested American public.

There has been a good deal of speculation in recent weeks over the type of staff organization that would surround the President. The appointment of Sherman Adams, former Governor of New Hampshire, as the Assistant to the President, with the authority of a chief of staff, caused some misgiving. It was feared that if all the other staff members reported to Mr. Adams and only saw the President sparingly, the effect would be to isolate the General too much from the broad range of advisers that a President needs.

Systems Compared

Here is how the system worked this week, with some comparisons with the Truman operation.

On Wednesday, the first full day in the White House, the entire staff met with the President and had a general meeting which of necessity was devoted mainly to a discussion of their physical surroundings and facilities and how they would operate.

On Thursday morning the staff, desiring to discuss their own inter-office procedures and plans, did not meet with the President but with Mr. Adams. They decided that it was not necessary for the entire staff to see the President every morning. The plan worked out was that they would meet each morning with Mr. Adams and then those members who had problems requiring Presidential advice or decision would go in to a meeting with President Eisenhower.

The armed forces aides were not present at these first meetings and it was not known whether they would attend those of the future.

The pattern indicated in these first meetings — and it was one that was deemed alterable as experience was gained—thus resembled the military chief of staff system. Mr. Adams, like a commander's chief of staff, could decide whether a problem should be resolved within the staff or should be discussed with the President. It was apparent, however, that the system was not being applied as rigidly as it would be in a military set-up.

Good Staff Work

Members of the staff make no bones of the fact that the President has always relied on staff work, and said they believe that a good staff, working smoothly, can do a great deal of work without running continually to the President for advice or decisions. They have been working together since the election, have learned each other's ways and are confident they will do a good job, though they realize they have a lot to learn in the new and real problems that will pour in on them at the fountainhead of government.

The President himself has appeared relaxed and amiable. Unlike a general accustomed to barking out the surnames of his subordinates, General Eisenhower is on a first name or nickname basis with his principal staff members.

Here is the way it was under President Truman:

There was no single member with authority over all other members of the staff. The main function of Dr. John R. Steelman, the assistant to the President (staying on for a few weeks to help the new team), was to follow through on Presidential directives and see that they were carried out properly. He also functioned as a negotiator in labor disputes.

On the other hand, Charles S. Murphy, special counsel, worked out policy questions and supervised and participated in the writing of speeches and documents in which these policies were enunciated. This function of reducing the President's philosophy and programs to writing was given high importance in the Truman Kitchen Cabinet.

Under Mr. Truman, policy-making and the expression of it were regarded as inextricable and most of the administrative assistants participated in writing speeches or statements in close collaboration with the President himself. It was not deemed a task for mere ghost writers who had little contact with the President.

Speech Writers

On the Eisenhower staff, Emmet Hughes, an administrative assistant, is the principal speech-writer. Another writer is Gabriel Hauge, who specializes in domestic and foreign economics. A typical operation would be for Mr. Hauge to write the domestic side of a message, while Mr. Hughes would do the foreign. Then Mr. Hughes would weave it all together in one speech.

During the week Mr. Hughes had at least two sessions with the President on the forthcoming State of the Union message, and in one of these sessions other collaborators were Senator H. Alexander Smith of New Jersey and Secretary of Labor Martin P. Durkin, presumably on labor legislation. This was novel. No Senator had directly worked on a draft of a Presidential speech in the Truman Administration, so far as any observers knew.

Mr. Truman held a daily morning conference wide open to all members of his staff, including the armed forces aides There specific problems as well as the news of the world were discussed, with the advantage that every member knew the views expressed by the President that day. If a problem requiring action arose, it was assigned to some member whose work load permitted him to assume it. On the Eisenhower staff the duties of individual members are more closely defined.

Whatever the merits of the two systems, the nation's business was going forward and the head man was operating like a chief executive.

January 25, 1953

The Eisenhower 'Inner Circle'

By CABELL PHILLIPS

WASHINGTON.

AMONG the popular notions about the Presidency to which Dwight Eisenhower does not subscribe is that the occupant of the White House, like some tragic hero out of Sophocles, is the prisoner of his palace, self-condemned to solitude and the lonely penance of daily balancing the fate of mankind in his own trembling hands.

Thomas Jefferson helped to create the notion when he described the President's job as "a splendid misery." Nearly every successor in office has found occasion to bemoan both the isolation and the awesome indivisible responsibility that are a President's inescapable lot.

There is, of course, a great deal to all this: the Presidency is unquestionably a most formidable job, and Presidents are, of necessity, largely cut off from the normal intimacies of human intercourse. One thinks of the troubled Lincoln pacing the midnight shadows of Lafayette Square in lonely agony of spirit. Or of the blithely gregarious Truman, whose innocent stroll across the White House lawn to peer through the fence at a sand-lot baseball game snarled Washington rush-hour traffic and sent his Secret Service bodyguards into a dither.

Mr. Eisenhower probably is no less conscious of his responsibilities than others who have held the office before him, but it is manifest that he suffers a good deal less from loneliness, either of the person or of the spirit. He is the most recreation-minded President of modern times, and it has been illness far more than duty that has cut into his indulgence in such favored pursuits as golf, fishing and bridge. He has a wide circle of friends who beat a steady but discreet path to the White House "back door," to the family farm at Gettysburg and to such favored vacation spots as Augusta when the President is in residence there. He and Mrs. Eisenhower have always liked company—lots of it, in gay, heterogeneous informality. The White House barrier has naturally cut down some on the quantity and drastically regulated the quality of the company they keep today. But their family and private social life is as full as that of most lesser citizens.

SIMILARLY, in the discharge of the ordinary duties of office, and in the graver processes of serious policy making, Mr. Eisenhower is buttressed in depth by an intricate staff system and by scores of advisers of both official and unofficial caliber. No President before him has created such an elaborate executive and administrative apparatus for getting the work of the Presidency done, nor relied so heavily upon it. And not many, certainly, have assembled such an impressive battery of anonymous confidants to counsel them in private. Mr. Eisenhower's genius both as a military commander and an executive lies not in his capacity as an innovator but in his ability to synthesize a course of action out of the views and judgments of other people.

"The President likes to have every aspect of a problem laid before him, the dissents as well as the concurrences," one of his intimates said the other day. "Then he will pick and choose until he finds what he believes the right thing to do.

"Don't forget that this man grew up under the intellectual discipline of the Army. The staff system is a natural part of his mental equipment—and, by the way, he was one of the best staff men, either as chief or subordinate, the Army ever had.

"He doesn't go in for long, rambling philosophic discussions of a problem he's working on. He assumes that the people who are working with him have done that. But he will 'kick it around,' so to speak, at dinner or on the golf course or almost anywhere else with someone whose judgment on the matter he respects."

Identifying and assessing "the men around the President" is always an intriguing enterprise in Washington. In many Administrations it has been fairly easy, for so-called "palace guards" have usually stood out in bold—and often boastful—relief. It is less easy in the case of President Eisenhower for the reasons, first, that there are few obvious favorites whose rank and influence above their fellows are beyond dispute—there is no Harry Hopkins or Colonel House in his Administration—and, second, that the unofficial group seems to find the rule of

CABELL PHILLIPS is the Washington representative of The Times Sunday Department.

anonymity wholly congenial. A few who chose to be indiscreet were quietly but firmly dropped from grace.

THIS élite and amorphous group—which some of its members refer to offhandedly as "the White House crowd," and those on the outside more reverentially call "the inner circle"—consists at any given time of about fifty men. Neither the total nor the individual memberships are static: they vary with the President's mood and the needs of the hour. About half are full-time servants of the Government—members of the Cabinet, the diplomatic corps, the Armed Services or the White House staff. The others are private citizens who, with only a few conspicuous exceptions, are titans of big industry, big banking and big law. Their relationship to the President falls into one or more of three categories — aide, adviser, recreational companion—but the lines are blurred and frequently crossed, particularly in the last two classes.

The man upon whom President Eisenhower depends above all others, either within or without his Administration, is Sherman Adams, whose official title, the Assistant to the President, is just about the most precise and meaningful in Washington. This wiry, incisive, tough-minded Yankee (he is a former Governor and Congressman of New Hampshire) is the White House Chief of Staff and the screen through which virtually every problem or question or supplication must filter before it reaches the President's desk. He sits *ex officio* at every meeting of the Cabinet and the National Security Council, the two top policy-making bodies in the Administration; coordinates the multifarious operations of the Executive Office of the President; directs liaison between the White House and Congress, and is in personal touch with the President half a dozen times or more each day. "Clear it with Sherm" is as inviolable a rule of the road in official Washington as "Stop for the red light."

WITHIN the staff which Mr. Adams commands are half a dozen others whose relationships to the President are almost as close, if not so all-embracing. James C. Hagerty, press secretary, is the principal spokesman for the President to the outside world and a principal channel by which the news of the world reaches the President. Bernard M. Shanley, the appointment secretary, is the traffic manager in charge of the President's time and the censor, so to speak, over which persons and issues he will hear. Maj. Gen. Wilton B. (Jerry) Persons, an old Army friend of many years' standing, is deputy to Mr. Adams and directly in charge of Congressional liaison. Gerald D. Morgan, special counsel, is "the White House lawyer" responsible for reading—or inserting—the legal fine print with respect to just about everything done in the President's name.

A unique position in the White House hierarchy, and one not classifiable according to the ordinary rules, is held by Vice President Richard M. Nixon. The esteem and the affection which the President holds for his young stand-in has been repeatedly demonstrated—so also his determination to make him an active and responsible partner in the management of the Executive enterprise. He is a statutory member of the N. S. C.; he sits regularly with the Cabinet; he is the principal legislative strategist for the White House; he is the Administration's and the Republican party's chief political "front." His executive duties are to be broadened even further during the second term, making him in fact, if not in name, truly a deputy President.

THE standing of Cabinet members in nearness to the President tends to shift with events; when matters involving their departments are dominant in the news, they move in close; at other times, they recede into the wings.

This does not hold, however, for John Foster Dulles, Secretary of State, and George M. Humphrey, Secretary of the Treasury. Day in and day out they are in closer touch with the President than any one not on the regular White House staff. Not infrequently the ivory telephones in their homes—with direct connections to the White House switchboard—will ring after dinner and the President will suggest, half apologetically, that he would like to see "Foster" or "George," as the case may be, for an hour or so—"if you can spare the time."

Mr. Humphrey is unquestionably the "strong man" of the Cabinet — poised, incisive, articulate, knowledgeable over a wide range of public affairs. The President admires his practical wisdom and enjoys his buoyant company (a quail shoot at the Secretary's Georgia plantation is an annual event); his counsel is sought on all sorts of problems, foreign as well as domestic.

MR. EISENHOWER'S attitude toward Foster Dulles is that toward a respected mentor. He has said that the Secretary's life-long concern for international affairs makes him "the best Secretary of State I have ever known."

There is some reason to think that a little of the shine may have worn off this image in recent months; that the President's eagerness to bring in Massachusetts' former Governor, Christian Herter, as Under Secretary was evidence that he wanted a reliable backstop for the peripatetic Mr. Dulles and the *ad hoc* brand of diplomacy which he practices. Whether this is true or not, there is no public evidence of any lessening of the Secretary's standing at the White House nor of the total confidence which the President reposes in him as the chief architect and administrator of American foreign policy.

Somewhere between the staff and the Cabinet in the rather fuzzy table of organization of the Presidential Office there is a box labeled "Special Assistants to the President." The half a dozen functionaries so represented are watchdogs for the President over certain specialized and crucial areas of Presidential responsibility—atomic energy, foreign economic programs, cold-war activities and, among several others, national security affairs. This last has a very special significance in that it deals exclusively with the secret inner workings of the National Security Council, and its Special Assistant, Robert Cutler, has a very special relationship to the President.

Mr. Cutler, a precise Boston banker (he calls it "fiduciary") whose well-furbished mind has the meticulousness of an I.B.M. machine, has just returned to Washington to pick up the job which he held with distinction during the first two years of the first Eisenhower Administration. He was, in fact, summoned, for the President is known to feel that the N. S. C. has never been in more competent hands than Cutler's and that in the enveloping crisis of the Middle East the Council and its director are more than ever essential to the preservation of our international security. Mr. Cutler is not only an occasional bridge partner of the President, he is in a very real sense his personally designated foreman of the most important policy factory in the Government.

IN the gallery of unofficial advisers to the President, three men stand out with distinctive clarity.

One is Milton Eisenhower, the younger brother of the President. From the days of their childhood in Abilene a peculiarly close bond has existed between these two. Ike was the husky defender, the man of action; Milton, "the brains of the family" and the man of ideas. Neither has ever let the other down, and the stresses of the last four years have brought them closer together than ever. Milton has been his brother's most intimate confidante and an almost weekly visitor to the White House. Last year he resigned the presidency of Pennsylvania State University to become president of Johns Hopkins at Baltimore, primarily, it is said, to be in easier reach of Washington.

Another is Gen. Alfred M. Gruenther, who, though several years younger than the President, grew up like him through the commissioned grades of the Army. The careers of the older and younger man, in fact, show some singular parallels. Neither has personally led troops in combat, yet each is renowned as a great commander and as a soldier-diplomat. When Eisenhower became Commander of the Allied Forces in World War II, he picked Gruenther as his Deputy Chief of Staff. When Eisenhower was named Supreme Commander of the North Atlantic Treaty forces, he took Gruenther to Paris as his right-hand man. When Eisenhower resigned from NATO to run for the Presidency, Gruenther was his choice as a successor. And a few months ago, when Gruenther retired from the Army, it was his friend and mentor, Ike, who persuaded him to accept the presidency of the Red Cross rather than any of the more munificent offers which poured in on him from private industry.

General Gruenther's new office looks across the Ellipse to the "back door" of the White House. This propinquity is both real and symbolic, for there probably is no man whose all-around ability the President more greatly respects, nor one whom he more desperately strives to clobber at the bridge table. If and when John Foster Dulles is to be replaced at the State Department, Al Gruenther's name will be high on the list of possible successors.

THE third figure in this select galaxy is an even older side-kick of the President's Army days, Gen. Walter Bedell Smith, and one who followed him into the civilian service of the Government as, finally, Under Secretary of State. "Beetle" Smith retired from active Government service in 1954, but he remains "on call" by the President, and the desk in his business office in Washington has a telltale ivory telephone.

Less conspicuous among Mr. Eisenhower's unofficial advisers and occasional companions is a group loosely defined as "the Wall Street crowd." These are the big corporation executives and investment bankers whom the President has come to know since he entered politics.

BY and large, these are men with a keen, well-informed interest in world affairs, a generally enlightened political outlook, who bear little resemblance to the cartoonist's familiar stereotype of the Wall Streeter. Among them are many of the unseen powers of the internationalist Eastern wing of the G. O. P. who backed Mr. Eisenhower's initial campaign for the Presidency and who continue today to exert a subtle but powerful influence on the political philosophy of the President and the party. "Eisenhower Republicanism" had at least a part of its maturation in the canyons of lower Manhattan as well as in the oval study of the White House.

There is no such thing as a reliable roster of "the Wall Street crowd" but a few of its more obvious members are easily spotted. Among them are Gen. Lucius Clay, a career soldier and an occasional civilian official in the Government, now chairman of the Continental Can Company and director of a dozen large corporations; John J. McCloy, also a one-time public servant, board chairman of the Chase Manhattan Bank and member of various boards; Ralph Cordiner, president of General Electric; Lewis Douglas, former Congressman and Ambassador, chairman of the Mutual Life Insurance Company of New York; W. Alton Jones, chairman of the Cities Service Company and an officer of numerous other oil enterprises; William E. Robinson, former publisher and public-relations executive and now president of the Coca-Cola Company; Clifford Roberts, investment banker and reputedly the man who parlayed the President's royalties from "Crusade in Europe" into a tidy small fortune (he is also president of the Augusta National Golf Club); Sidney Weinberg, frequent servant of government, an original sparkplug of Citizens for Eisenhower, a partner in Goldman, Sachs & Co.; Eugene Holman, board chairman of the Standard Oil Company (N. J.), and Benjamin Fairless, chairman of the board of the United States Steel Corporation.

These are the wealthy and successful men of large affairs toward whom the President, with an ingenuous admiration, has become socially and intellectually oriented in the last few years. With some his relationship is purely social—they are golfing or hunting or occasional dinner companions. With others it is more strictly "business"—he seeks their private views on legislation, programs of Government, the state of the nation and of the world. But most often, the relationships are both social and business, blending congenially one into the other.

MANY in this circle are tapped from time to time to do a prestige job for the Government—to head up various commissions or to sit on the Business Advisory Council. The new Ambassador to Britain, John Hay Whitney, is a member in good standing of "the Wall Street crowd"; Mr. Fairless currently is shepherding an expedition of foreign-aid observers around the world. From time to time one or another may be asked to come to Washington for a personal conference or a small, private dinner at the White House. Or again, when they are in the capital, they will just "drop in"—via one of several private entrances which are off-bounds to the ubiquitous corps of White House reporters. Others give the President their views on affairs of the day in long letters, and receive his in return.

It would be hard to overestimate the influence of this group on Mr. Eisenhower's thinking or in shaping the frame of reference against which he weighs a great many of the issues and problems which confront him as President.

* * *

EACH President has organized the Presidency to conform to his own peculiar whims and talents. Mr. Hoover made of it a hair shirt. Mr. Roosevelt, at least in his earlier years, endowed it with a sort of chaotic exuberance. In Mr. Truman's time it had something of the quality of a state of siege, defensive and suspicious.

Mr. Eisenhower's concept is that of an efficient and all-comprehending machine which embraces features both of the military staff and the corporate board of directors. He has brought this concept to a high state of operational perfection and relies upon it with confidence. So much so, indeed, that the job—"splendid misery" or not—never seems to get him down.

February 3, 1957

U.S. FOREIGN POLICY MACHINERY ONCE AGAIN UNDER SCRUTINY

Professionals Cite Latin-American Relations as One of Several Cases in Which Rusk Is By-Passed by White House Advisers

By E. W. KENWORTHY
Special to The New York Times.

WASHINGTON, May 27—There is a gnawing unease here about the conduct of foreign affairs. The Administration, which came to power so confidently four months ago, seems now, after Cuba and Laos, rather disheveled. It appears fluttery, if not jittery. In its apparent nervousness, it seems sometimes to be substituting words for reflection, activity for considered action.

These impressions may be unfair, but they are widely held and particularly on Capitol Hill. If President Kennedy seeks a cause for the deep concern, he might see a clue in an essay by Dean Acheson on the relations of the President and the Secretary of State. Mr. Truman's First Minister wrote:

"It is highly desirable that from first to last both parties to the relationship understand which is the President. * * * The other obligation * * * is recognizing who is Secretary of State. A President may, and will, listen to whom he wishes. But his relationship with the Secretary of State will not prosper if the latter is not accepted as his principal adviser and executive agent in foreign affairs, and the trusted confidant of all his thoughts and plans relating to them. We can all recall times when this has not been true. Such times have always called for make-shift arrangements, the cost of which has often been considerable."

Associated Press
Dean Rusk, Secretary of State.

McGeorge Bundy, Assistant to the President for National Security Affairs.

Array of Advisers

There is a growing feeling here that the President's troubles derive in part from the fact that—at least on some issues and in some areas—he has not made Secretary of State Rusk his principal adviser on policy and action, but has been guided by his White House staff.

The difficulty described by Mr. Acheson has been compounded, in the opinion of many observers here, by the fact that President Kennedy does not have a single confidant—as Wilson did in Colonel House and Roosevelt in Harry Hopkins—but an array of advisers. McGeorge Bundy, Walt W. Rostow. Arthur Schlesinger Jr., Richard N. Goodwin, Ralph A. Dungan—all have a hand in foreign policy.

This multiplicity of White House advisers was seen from the outset as a potential source of confusion in policy and untidy administration. The contention was, however, that the President wished them at hand simply to widen his alternatives, to make certain that he had all points of view laid before him. It was not their function, it was said, to make policy and certainly not to dominate it.

Evidence

What evidence is there, then, that these advisers are usurping the traditional function of the Secretary of State, that they are standing between Mr. Rusk and the President?

The evidence is mixed. Officials in some State Department bureaus concede the line of authority between Mr. Rusk and the White House is not always so clear or firm as they would like. But they have no large complaint, and they believe "the situation will shake down."

On the question of the Vienna meeting between the President and Premier Khrushchev, the evidence is fuzzy. The official line is that this is not truly a summit conference, in the accepted sense of the word, since there will be no agenda and no negotiations. It will merely be an informal meeting for an "exchange of views."

There is some reason for believing that this is a rationalization designed to paper over differences of views about the uses, the value and dangers in summitry. Charles Bohlen, former Ambassador to Moscow, has long maintained that if you are to deal with the Soviet Union, "you must talk to Mr. Khrushchev." This view has found strong support from the President's advisers in the White House.

However, in a Foreign Affairs article last spring, Mr. Rusk argued against the practice of summitry. Why, he asked, should the Soviet Union be allowed "to set the style of international negotiations." Many observers here doubt whether he really finds his reasons no longer applicable and the risks removed simply because the two leaders will not formally negotiate. There is no such thing as an informal meeting between the President of the United States and a Soviet Premier.

The Cuban Case

On the issue of the Cuban prisoners-for-tractors exchange, the evidence is quite clear. Mr. Goodwin, with the support of Mr. Schlesinger, conceived the idea of inducing Mrs. Eleanor Roosevelt, Walter Reuther and Milton Eisenhower to sponsor a campaign for private contributions to pay Dr. Castro's ransom price. Mr. Goodwin sold the idea to the President. According to State Department sources, the State Department was not consulted on this decision.

Indeed, it is in the area of Latin American affairs—admittedly one of the most sensitive and crucial — that the White House advisers have assumed the most authority and created the greatest confusion.

Adolf A. Berle is the President's Coordinator of Inter-American Affairs and heads a Presidential task force. Although his office is in the State Department, he reports chiefly to the White House, where Mr. Goodwin and Mr. Schlesinger are also handling Latin-American policy. Neither of these two has had any experience in the area.

Many officials and Senators agree that the situation in the Bureau of Inter-American Affairs is chaotic, the morale low. Latin American ambassadors complain that they do not know whether to carry their problems to Mr. Berle and Mr. Goodwin — the two apparent loci of power—or to officers in the State Department, who may have no power to advise or act.

There is no Assistant Secretary for Latin American Affairs, and the President's search for a man to fill the post has so far been fruitless. Some senators have said bluntly that no first-rate candidate would take the job until Mr. Berle goes.

Last week Senator Wayne Morse, chairman of the Senate Subcommittee on Inter-American Affairs, said "The Administration ought to get this regularized. We need a clear line of command from the President to the Secretary of State to the Assistant Secretary for Inter-American Affairs."

Congress Slighted

One of the consequences of division of authority between the State Department and the President's aides—and this may cost the Administration dearly—is the frequent failure of communications with Capitol Hill. The chairmen and ranking minority members of the Senate Foreign Relations and the House Foreign Affairs committees, and the various subcommittees, are accustomed to being consulted while policy is being formulated. They do not like to get their first information from White House news releases delivered after reporters have received them.

Senator George D. Aiken, Republican ef Vermont and ranking minority member of the Inter-American Affairs subcommittee, said this week that never in his twenty years in the Senate had there been so little consultation as now.

In the aforementioned essay, Mr. Acheson expressed his conviction that in the conduct of foreign affairs, the President's best guide is "a belief that the man [chosen as Secretary of State] can help him more than others in dealing with the problems he sees ahead."

A growing number of experienced diplomats and members of Congress here believe that President Kennedy will eventually come to this conviction about Mr. Rusk, and that when he does the direction of foreign policy will take on a much-wanted firmness.

May 28, 1961

President Forbids Staff To Interfere in Agencies

By JOSEPH A. LOFTUS
Special to The New York Times.

WASHINGTON, June 25—President Kennedy has ruled out any interference by his White House staff in the operations of departments and agencies. White House aides said this was not a new decision but was emphasized now because of newspaper reports that divided authority had hobbled operation of the State Department's Inter-American Division.

For several months there was no Assistant Secretary of State for Inter-American Affairs. In this little power vacuum some of the President's staff reportedly made their presence felt. The career men did not like this. At the White House it is felt that such friction as may have occurred has been exaggerated by the press.

The President admittedly is not deeply interested in organization-chart thinking, but persons close to him say, nevertheless, that his sense of organization line is good.

Sheer Volume Is Factor

Communication between department heads and the President, because of the sheer volume, has to be routed largely, but by no means entirely, through White House staff members and advisers.

McGeorge Bundy, the President's most seasoned staff man, handles for the President the most sensitive areas of Government: the State Department, Defense Department and the Central Intelligence Agency.

Having been associated with two independent Secretaries of State, Henry L. Stimson and Dean Acheson, after they had left office, Mr. Bundy is aware that his function is to expedite the flow of information in both directions, and out not to interpose his own policy ideas. A strong Secretary of State would not long tolerate such interference.

If President Kennedy recalls Gen. Maxwell D. Taylor and installs him in the White House, it is expected that the former Chief of Staff will give of President an additional point of view and not substitute his own for the Joint Chiefs of Staff or the Secretary of Defense.

President Kennedy has held only seven Cabinet meetings since he took office. Some Cabinet members would like to feel a little closer to the President and hear more about the rationale leading to Presidential decisions.

The President's aversion to formal meetings is no rejection of his incumbent secretaries. He is simply not attuned to group thinking, and sensitive observers say that he has found no gentlemanly way of insisting in such meetings on the conciseness his temperament demands. The man in trouble with President Kennedy is the man who has not learned the art of brevity, they say.

The President's temperament also does not permit him to hold regular staff meetings. He prefers to pick up a telephone, or walk to a man's desk and ask him to do something, as the problem arises or the spirit moves him.

The President's aides characterize his approach as informal. The organization man has another word for it. He would find Mr. Kennedy's method chaotic, as Mr. Kennedy finds the chart-bound method suffocating.

The President meets frequently with Mr. Bundy and Mr. Bundy holds staff meetings. But Mr. Bundy is not chief of staff in the sense that Sherman Adams under President Eisenhower directed the White House staff and screened everything that reached the President.

Mr. Kennedy has direct contact with Theodore C. Sorensen on every item that is to leave the White House as a public paper of the President, with Frederick G. Dutton on communications involving the Agriculture and Labor departments, with Ralph A. Dungan on foreign aid, with Lawrence F. O'Brien on Congressional relations and with many others.

This method calls for a lot of cross-checking among staff members to keep things tidy, but they say they like it.

This close relationship with the President implies no authority on the staff man's part to run any agency of Government. A White House staff is necessary because of the size and complexity of Government.

Somebody—to illustrate at the ground level—has to open the mail. The White House averages 40,000 pieces of mail a week. A lot of this should have been addressed to some department in the first place. But until somebody opens and reads it, the mail cannot be channeled to the proper department.

The flow of information and documents in Mr. Bundy's area is enormous. They come from the agencies, from leaders across the world, from personal friends and from the public at large. Mr. Bundy has to do some screening, of course, but if he screened out information the President wanted, or loaded him with secondary data, he would be in trouble.

He has to go to Kenneth O'Donnell, who is paid to be miserly with the President's time, and declare whether he needs five minutes or an hour. Usually he will get as much time as he asks for, but his judgment had better be good.

In the President's folder will be many more items than the President will have time to read in full. He will brief the President on them and the President will have the choice of reaching for a particular paper he wants to ponder fully.

Thus the staff men, and the advisers are a line of communication with the President, but not an exclusive line. They are not part of the Presidency. There is no palace guard, or kitchen cabinet, so far.

The great danger to be avoided, said President Washington in the first days of the republic, was "seclusion from information, by too much reserve and too great a withdrawal."

This is what President Kennedy wants because he is the man who has to make the decisions and answer for them.

June 26, 1961

CABINET HOLDING INFORMAL TALKS

Sessions Without Kennedy Help Members in Work

By JOSEPH A. LOFTUS

Special to The New York Times.

WASHINGTON, July 24 — President Kennedy's Cabinet, which is seldom summoned to official meetings, has decided to hold unofficial gatherings.

Two of these have now taken place, the latest last Wednesday in the dining room of the Secretary of State. The plan is to meet every second Wednesday, with each member taking a turn as host.

So far, these meetings have been get-acquainted affairs. They reflect the need of most Cabinet members to know one another better, to share information and problems and to achieve a greater degree of identity and institutionalization than Mr. Kennedy accords the Cabinet as a Cabinet.

The meetings have been held, of course, with the knowledge of the President. Attorney General Robert F. Kennedy, the President's brother, missed the last meeting but sent his deputy, Byron R. White. Robert S. McNamara, Secretary of Defense, and J. Edward Day, Postmaster General, also were otherwise occupied.

The President clarified his relationship with the Cabinet in a broadcast three months ago. He said he considered it important, but he thought meetings were a waste of time. He sees little logic, for example, in having the Secretary of State listen to the problems of the Postmaster General.

The President, however, is in frequent touch with Cabinet members individually, or in small groups.

Cabinet meetings had been scheduled for every second Thursday at the White House, but the schedule had been loosely observed. Mr. Kennedy has called the Cabinet into session eight times, an average of less than one every three weeks. The last meeting was held July 7.

Reports Are Chief Business

Cabinet meetings are described as pleasant affairs, lasting sixty to eighty minutes. The President customarily is the last to enter the room, an oblong chamber that looks out on a lovely rose garden. The members rise for a few moments and pleasantries are exchanged.

The President, his back to the rose garden, sits in the middle of one of the long sides of the table. Usually the meetings are reporting sessions. That is, an agenda of one to three items, distributed in advance, means that one to three members will report on some problem in their jurisdiction. Budget Director David E. Bell may discuss budgetary procedures and problems; Dr. Walter W. Heller, chairman of the Council of Economic Advisers, may discuss the economic outlook.

Occasionally the agenda is discarded. This occurred when the President briefed his Cabinet on the Cuban invasion. On another occasion Secretary of State Dean Rusk briefed the Cabinet on foreign affairs.

There is no time for the President to call on everybody in turn. Those who feel impelled to speak seek recognition and usually proceed. New issues are rarely raised by a member and, of course, no votes are taken. The President terminates meetings as his work schedule and disposition dictate.

Dislikes Long Speeches

To the extent that there is a Cabinet secretary, Frederick G. Dutton, special assistant to the President, serves in that position.

Some believe that Prof. Richard E. Neustadt of Columbia University, and his book "Presidential Power," influenced Mr. Kennedy to take this view of the Cabinet meeting. Mr. Kennedy, however, is temperamentally predisposed to operate as he does, according to other opinions. For example, he can not sit still for long speeches and, for him, a speech with one unnecessary sentence is long. Although he likes the clash of ideas, apparently he does not believe the ideas will flow freely across a crowded room.

Mr. Kennedy's approach to Cabinet meetings is a sharp break with the formal, almost ritualistic methods of former President Dwight D. Eisenhower. It is difficult to demonstrate, however, that one approach is better than another.

July 25, 1961

Our Head Budgeteer: A Close-in View

It reveals how much more than a mere 'bookkeeper' Bell of the Budget Bureau is.

By SIDNEY HYMAN

WASHINGTON.

IN his daily routine, David Bell, President Kennedy's Budget Director, lives intimately with the prime sources of power in this city. Half his working time is spent at the White House in direct contact with the President or with key White House aides. The remainder Mr. Bell spends in other action stations where the President's purpose can be served—in his own office across the street from the White House, in the company of Cabinet and agency chiefs, and in the company of Congressional committees.

Yet in a town that has a single-minded interest in the facts of power, the details of Mr. Bell's place in the Administration and the role of the Budget Bureau itself, remain strangely vague. Most people seem to think that Bell and his Bureau are an alias for J. Edgar Hoover and the F. B. I.—or bookkeepers with green eye-shades who merely run fleshless fingers down a column of figures to make the pennies come out even. Bell and his staff are aware of these views but waste no time in trying to correct them. Living as they do by the Budget Bureau's code of "passionate anonymity," they stand aloof from Washington's ceaseless fights for personal and agency publicity.

STILL, Bell and his Bureau do deserve a close-in view to pinpoint their exact role and influence in the Kennedy Administration—and where they have moved beyond the boundaries within which previous Budget Directors and the Bureau itself generally worked. The close-in view is particularly timely right now when a new fiscal year is under way, and the Budget Bureau is in the first stages of work on the vast project that will be unveiled next January as the first authentic Kennedy budget.

The Budget Bureau Bell heads is not only the largest of several staff agencies in the Executive Office of the President, but its 275 professional members (out of 437 members in all) comprise the élite corps of the career Civil Service. Indeed, the long-time professionals in the Bureau—men like Deputy Director Elmer Staats and Executive Assistant Director William Carey—know more than any group of men in the nation about how to make the inner wheels of the U. S. Government go round. They have done this in peace or war, boom or bust, under successive Presidents of different parties, in every part of the executive machine at home and abroad.

Yet, neither the Budget Bureau nor Director Bell manages any programs directly, after the manner of Cabinet officers and their departments. As "the President's men," solely and exclusively, they form the principal institutional instrument through which the President can coordinate his many constitutional duties and, at the same time, obtain coldly objective judgments about how best to discharge those duties.

THE President, to be sure, has many sources of help. Yet the other staff agencies in the Office of the President—for example, the Council of Economic Advisers and the National Security Council—are necessarily too specialized to provide help on an across-the-board basis. The individuals on the White House staff itself, however gifted personally, stand alone without support of special staffs of their own. As for Cabinet officers, no matter how loyal they are to the President, they tend to plead the special cases worked up by their departmental staffs. Thus the help the President needs but cannot find elsewhere in his entourage, the Budget Bureau and its Director are meant to provide.

This function of the Bureau gives the Budget Director an impressive voice in policy decisions—but only if he has the confidence of the President. If that confidence is missing, as was the case during a certain period in the Eisenhower Presidency, both the Director of the Budget and the Bureau itself are declassed to the role of outsider. If that confidence is present, then the Budget Director, and through him, the professionals in the Bureau, are upgraded to insiders' roles in a great sweep of policy decisions. Budget Director Bell is very much an insider, a felt presence at meetings where broad issues of policy or of management are defined and resolved.

PREPARATION of the master budget document for a fiscal year is, of course, the most important of the Bureau's functions. Bell has already met with President Kennedy, Secretary of the Treasury Douglas Dillon, the Council of Economic Advisers and others, to consider estimated revenues for fiscal 1963 as against prospective claims on those revenues. Moreover, following these consultations, he has worked with the President and other key White House members in devising the general guidelines that have already gone forth to all agencies to help them in the preparation of next year's programs and budget requests. And again, specialists in the Budget Bureau have begun to hold hearings on agency requests for funds, with the object of making their own tentative recommendations.

The difficulty of preparing the master budget document cannot be overstated. Competing national and international requirements must be tested against each other and against the resources available to the total budget. Marginal choices must be identified. Judgments about them must be formulated, though the criteria are often uncertain. For example, will a marginal outlay for military forces as against a marginal outlay for basic scientific research—or for higher education—do more or less to strengthen the nation's security? Thousands of questions of this kind must be faced and answered before the President can submit to the Congress a coherent budget.

YET as matters now stand, many other things add to the difficulties budget makers face. They are plagued by uncertainties about how the economy will behave, and thus about the size of the revenues they can work with. They are plagued even more by the fact that national security requirements, which now run to at least one half of the total budget, are in constant flux—because of rapid changes in weapon technology and sudden shifts in the international climate and in the temper of our allies.

In the final analysis, President Kennedy himself must resolve these imponderables. Yet, in his role as a scout for the President, Budget Director Bell will have to deal with the same imponderables in his own way at the stage of budget making known as "the Director's review." This is when he receives all the reports and recommendations from the hearing and examining officers of the Budget Bureau, formulates his own position on agency requests, and isolates the issues they pose for the President. Then, in a further step taken in close contact with the White House, he will try to win the assent of the agency chiefs to his views, resolve their conflicts short of a direct appeal to the President, or convoy them to the White House for the President's personal decision.

IN addition to this work, the Budget Bureau and its Director perform a wide range of other chores for the President. As a conduit for the expert knowledge present in the Bureau, Bell has helped the White House teams of Theodore Sorenson, Myer Feldman, McGeorge Bundy and Walt Rostow draft virtually all the major messages and legislative proposals the President has thus far sent to the Congress.

Moreover, in line with the Bureau's work of reviewing all legislative proposals originating within the Congress that are sent to the Executive Department for comment, Bell's views have left their mark on the more important of the replies sent back to the Congress.

Nor is this all. Since the Bureau is also the President's "business agent," Bell monitors the spending of authorized funds, their rate of flow, the effects they produce, and he evaluates agency requests for appropriations beyond those approved in the master budget document. And again, since the Bureau is the President's "efficiency engineer," its Director is thrust into the very center of all work entailing the reorganization of existing agencies or the creation of new ones.

In recent months, for example, Bell was deeply involved in reorganizing the administration of the foreign aid program, in launching the Peace Corps, in placing the new Area Redevelopment Program under the Department of Commerce, in preparing reorganization plans for the regulatory agencies, and in drafting the proposal to create a new Cabinet Department of Urban Affairs and Housing. In addition, he has worked on the internal reorganization of great executive departments like State. The object has been to simplify the way decisions are reached, to clarify lines of power and responsibility, and to mesh the gears of the department with these of other departments so that any many-sided program will be better served by all concerned with it.

It should be emphasized again that the original impulse and final decision on all these matters lay with President Kennedy. And the measure of Bell's influence on the President's final decision was not in any way exceptional for a Budget Director. What was true about him would be true of any other Budget Director who enjoyed the confidence of the President. Still, the precise nature of the influence a director actually wields depends on the nature of the President under whom he serves—and Kennedy is not Eisenhower.

In the case of the Eisenhower Administration, Budget Directors who dealt with the substantive merits of any proposal could base their own positions on President Eisenhower's desire to hold the line against any expansion of Federal activities and to limit Government spending to a fixed budgetary ceiling. The different approach of the Kennedy Administration had its origin in November of last

year when Bell met the President-elect for the first time and was offered the post of Budget Director. Bell then expressed the view that the Budget Bureau, in its proper concern for efficiency and economy, had tended to forget that true economy and efficiency meant the balanced and effective use of available resources over a cycle of years to meet current and prospective national needs.

IF the President-elect agreed with this concept of budgeting, Bell would want to bring an economist of high professional repute to a top place in the Bureau a place provided for by law but generally filled in the Eisenhower days by certified public accountants. With the support of a leading economist, the Budget Bureau could do two things. It could get more deeply into the substantive content of various programs instead of concentrating merely on their costs. It could also become an effective partner with the Council of Economic Advisers, the Treasury Department and others in the formulation of economic and fiscal policy.

The President-elect swiftly agreed to all this, and the sequel has been a quiet revolution that started when Bell obtained the services of Robert Turner, who had served briefly as a White House economic adviser in the Truman Administration. Since then, the Budget Director has been able to make his own influence felt in such matters as tax policy, hard-core unemployment, revenue outlook based on long-range employment prospects, the future implications of Federal programs now in operation or being proposed. The object has been to make budget and economic policies fall in line with each other.

A NUMBER of institutional innovations have gone hand-in-hand with all this. Formerly few Government agencies had any genuine planning staffs, though planning and budgeting are indivisible. Now the drive is on to create such planning staffs in all Government agencies to work with their counterparts in the Budget Bureau.

Moreover, the Budget Bureau is working closely with the Defense Department in pioneering what are known as "program packages." The traditional method was to group defense expenditures by services (Army, Navy, Air Force) or expenditure category (personnel, procurement, research and development). Under the new budget concept of "program packages," expenditures for strategic (nuclear) warfare are now grouped in one place, while expenditures for conventional war are grouped together in a second place.

This should provide the President and his defense chiefs with a more accurate comparative analysis of alternative possibilities and a more realistic understanding of what is proposed to be done.

In much the same way, the budgeting of foreign aid military and economic—is now being grouped into separate "country programs." This permits the budget makers to consider in relation to each other the various alternative military and economic measures of assistance to a given country—and further, to relate the assistance properly to the recipient country's own efforts, to America's political objective in the country, to our diplomatic effort there, and so on.

On top of all this Bell has been pioneering a difficult two-stage innovation in drawing up the national budget. In the first stage, expenditures, new obligational authorities and revenues will be projected forward from 1962 to 1966. The object will be to help the President focus his attention on the major factors that will control the level and trend of the budget over the next five years. Within the context of this long view, the second stage will deal with the specific needs of the budget for fiscal 1963.

• • •

BELL, in many ways, is naturally cut out to be an intimate of President Kennedy —something the best of Budget Directors must be to the Presidents they serve. At 42, he is tall, lean, cheery, unpretentious and approachable in outward manner, laconic in speech, succinct in thought. He is also self-driven, rigorously disciplined and a prodigious work horse. In a day-and-night schedule of work since his appointment was announced on Dec. 3, he has had only a few Sundays of rest. If his work schedule makes it hard on the professionals in the Bureau who have wives and children at home and lawns to cut, the Bureau's morale has nevertheless skyrocketed since his arrival.

Or perhaps it would be more precise to say "his return." Bell, an honor graduate of Pomona College and Harvard—where he was trained in economics—began his government career in 1942 as a Budget Bureau staff member.

Following a wartime interlude as a Marine Corps officer, he returned to the Bureau in 1945 and from then until 1953 moved back and forth between it and the White House, where he was one of President Truman's bright young assistants. (Two of his White House associates at the time, Clark Clifford and Richard Neustadt, were chiefly responsible for bringing him to the attention of Sargent Shriver who brought him to the attention of President-elect Kennedy.)

In 1953, Bell returned to Harvard for another year of graduate study in economics. There followed three years in Pakistan where he was the Karachi head of a group of specialists recruited from Harvard's Littauer School of Public Administration, and financed by the Ford Foundation, to help draw up Pakistan's first five-year plan. As the plan covered both the private and public sectors of the country's economy, it provided Bell with an intensive education in the question of how one applies scarce resources toward national objectives.

IN September of 1957, he returned to Harvard as a lecturer on economics and as a research associate in the Littauer School. With his appointment as secretary of that graduate school in July, 1959, he was content to settle down to a career divided between teaching and work on economic and social plans for under-developed nations. But then, a few weeks after the 1960 election, in the midst of arranging for a trip around the world due to start on Christmas Eve, there came a rapid series of events that culminated in President-elect Kennedy's announcement that Bell would be his Budget Director.

To the professionals in the Bureau it was the happiest of announcements, for they had maintained friendship with Bell since his first employment there. To Bell, too, the appointment had the character of a happy homecoming.

SINCE then, his growing stature in the eyes of the leaders of the Kennedy Administration from the President on down has led to an enlargement of the standing the Bureau's professionals enjoy throughout the Administration. Thus two senior staff members have been kidnapped and made Assistant Secretaries in the Department of Defense. A dozen or more other Bureau staff members have been detailed, at the request of Cabinet and agency heads, to assist them personally in getting a grip on their new jobs.

Indeed, the new concern is whether the Budget Bureau will be overtaxed with requests for help. As things now stand, the professionals "on loan" elsewhere leave gaping holes in the ranks of the professionals who remain at their desks in the Bureau. Moreover, this imposes a new strain on Director Bell, since, contrary to what he told President-elect Kennedy at the time of his appointment—that he could not be of much use to Mr. Kennedy "on the Hill," since he had no personal standing there—he is regularly being called on to testify before Congressional committees. And that means more staff work for a staff that is already shorthanded.

So far, however, the Bureau, under Bell's guidance, has been equal to the tribute paid it by President Kennedy on June 9, when he saluted the Bureau on the occasion of its fortieth birthday.

"The objectivity and the deep knowledge of the process of government of the Bureau's staff," he said, "have made it a highly valued part of the President's Executive Office. One President is said to have called the Bureau 'his good right arm.' I should like to second that motion. The work of the President would be very difficult indeed without the staff support of the Budget Bureau."

Robert Kennedy Begins One-Month Goodwill Trip Around World

Associated Press Wirephoto

Attorney General Robert F. Kennedy speaking yesterday before he and Mrs. Kennedy left Friendship International Airport. Flanking the Kennedys are Ambassadors Zairin Zain, left, of Indonesia and Koichiro Asakai of Japan.

By ANTHONY LEWIS

Special to The New York Times.

WASHINGTON, Feb. 1—Attorney General Robert F. Kennedy took off today on a goodwill trip around the world. He is scheduled to be gone about a month, returning at the end of February. He will spend a week each in Japan and Indonesia and make shorter visits to Hong Kong, Iran, Italy, West Germany, the Netherlands and probably some other countries. It will be a relatively informal tour, with the emphasis on meeting young people. Mr. Kennedy's wife, Ethel, will be with him. Also in the party are Mrs. Donald Wilson, wife of the deputy director of the United States Information Agency, a family friend; John Seigenthaler, the Attorney General's administrative assistant; Brandon Grove, a State Department guide, and four reporters and a photographer.

According to diplomatic reports, the host countries regard this visit as the most important and they could receive from any American other than the President. Mr. Kennedy had to decline strongly pressed invitations for other stops because his trip had already grown to a most unusual length.

The trip symbolized the extraordinary role played by Robert Kennedy in this Administration.

"The second most powerful man in Government." That is the estimate of the Attorney General given by insiders with reason to know.

Far more than any previous Attorney General, he is involved in affairs outside the problems of law enforcement—foreign policy, intelligence, even the farm program. No Cabinet officer is unfamiliar with the sound of his voice on the telephone.

Entertained Adzhubeis

No one thought it unnatural when he and Mrs. Kennedy entertained Premier Khrushchev's son-in-law, Aleksei I. Adzhubei, at lunch yesterday. It will be no great surprise if the now-disavowed approach made to him to visit the Soviet Union leads eventually to such a visit.

The reasons for his unusual position are evident.

He is the President's brother. He is a trusted confidant, a position that does not automatically follow from his relationship to a President who confides in few men. He is the political expert who helped make his brother President.

The exact nature of his activities and influence is less easy to pin down. So much depends on his intimate relationship with the President that an aide says:

"Probably no one but the two men really knows what Robert's role is."

But there are clues.

Trujillo Incident Recalled

When Generalissimo Rafael Leonidas Trujillo Molina, the dictator of the Dominican Republic, was assassinated last May, the President was in Paris. Members of a special task force that met at the State Department that night found the Attorney General there, participating actively and sitting in, as one member put it, for his brother.

During the preparation of the new farm program, a regional expert on one crop was telephoned by the Attorney General and asked to come to Washington for a talk. Mr. Kennedy explained:

"You know my brother is very busy with international problems. We try to help all we can on the domestic side."

The President turned to his brother publicity in a most difficult hour—to head an inquiry into the Central Intelligence Agency after the abortive Cuban invasion last April. The President seeks his brother's counsel privately on numberless problems.

"Call Bobby, get together with him and come back with an idea on this." A White House aide says that is a familiar order from the President.

Advises on Appointments

Robert Kennedy plays an important part in advising on appointments, some believe with more influence in that area than on policy. He was influential, for example, in the choice of John A. McCone to head the Central Intelligence Agency. There are unconfirmed reports that he played a part in the dropping of Gen. C. P. Cabell as the C. I. A.'s deputy director.

He is useful in estimating political responses to ideas, notably on Capitol Hill. He maintains the relationships he built up with members of Congress in both parties while he was counsel to the Senate committee. When a Democratic Governor comes to Washington, he usually heads for the Attorney General's office.

From what is known about the Attorney General's activities, it is clear that he does not have operational responsibilities outside the Justice Department. He is no Sherman Adams—a general administrative arm of the President.

Rather, his importance lies in his influence on the President and in his usefulness as a stimulant to other men.

From the President's point of view, it is said, candor is probably the most important factor in the relationship. There is no one from whom he can get advice so frank and so free of inhibition or fear.

Robert Kennedy does not have to worry about pleasing the President when he puts forward an idea. Nor does the President have to be delicate in saying no. An observer comments: "Robert doesn't lose any face — or any sleep—if his ideas are rejected."

Indeed, officials who have dealt with them say they see no evidence that the President gives his brother's opinion special weight just because they are brothers.

A notable example was a National Security Council meeting at which the question of aid to the Volta Dam project in Ghana was discussed. Robert Kennedy sat behind his brother.

The President went around the table, heard the comments and remarked that the consensus was in favor of advancing the aid. Then he added:

"The Attorney General has not spoken, but I can feel the hot breath of his disapproval on the back of my neck."

Robert Kennedy spoke against aiding the dam, emphasizing what he termed the bad influence of Ghana's President Kwame Nkrumah on the rest of Africa. The President then made the decision to aid the project.

In addition to candor, the Attorney General brings to the relationship with his brother a special ability to size up problems swiftly, even when he is not familiar with them, and to propose a concrete course of action.

Those who have dealt with the Attorney General on affairs outside his immediate area, such as foreign policy, remark on the same characteristics. They say that even when he has not been briefed and is not well informed he always knows the President's objective and quickly grasps the problem.

In this respect, for all their differences in personality, he may be something like Harry Hopkins, Franklin D. Roosevelt's assistant, whom Winston Churchill dubbed "Lord Root of the Matter." And he may be playing a similar sort of role for the President.

The freshness of his approach may stimulate those over-educated on a problem. He played a large part in the reappraisal of policy toward Cuba after the invasion fiasco, and one official remarks on the way he then "questioned assumptions."

Informality is, of course, a trademark of Robert Kennedy. A typical photograph shows him grilling hamburgers on the office fireplace for a group of children. The same informal air characterizes his dealings with Secretary of State Dean Rusk, or any Government official.

For example, he is in the habit of picking up the telephone when he has an idea instead of waiting to draft a memorandum. Once those on the receiving end get used to the technique, they seem to enjoy its artlessness and enthusiasm.

The Attorney General may see something in the morning paper about a fellow Cabinet member's political problem. He is likely to telephone and say something like "stick it out," or "go ahead, you can pull it off."

This telephone habit may create an impression that he spends more time on matters outside the Justice Department than he really does, an aide of his pointed out.

The aide estimates that the Attorney General spends 80 per cent of his working hours on Justice Department business, 5 per cent on meetings with members of the press (an extremely large proportion), 5 per cent on political activities and meeting visitors and, finally, 10 per cent on foreign policy and other government affairs outside the Justice Department.

There is much less resentment of the Attorney General's special role than might be expected among other Government officials. One hears grumbling about "Little Brother" at lower levels but virtually none higher up or among men who have actually dealt with him.

Among the reasons may be the very informality with which he plays the part, plus the realization that he has no Svengali-like control over the President's views.

But officials emphasize another reason for the lack of resentment. This is the apparently unanimous feeling that personal ambition plays no part in his activities—that he is motivated instead by an overwhelming desire to help his brother and to make the Kennedy Administration a success.

"That is one of the most engaging things about him," one official remarks. "He is really quite a selfless guy."

"I'm not saying he will go to the pasture after his brother has served eight years," the official says. "But ambition is not what's motivating him now. He is serving the President."

Inevitably, questions have arisen about Robert Kennedy's future. Will he want to move officially into some foreign affairs role? Will he run for President himself some day? The answer from those who know him best is that the questions are simply premature — he is not thinking about them now.

Recently the President read somewhere that his brother had been called "the second most important man in the Western world." He told the Attorney General wryly:

"You have nowhere to go but down."

February 2, 196

The Transition Over, the White House Staff Is Strictly Johnson in Outlook

By CHARLES MOHR

Special to The New York Times

WASHINGTON, June 12—President Johnson has completed the transition from an inherited White House staff to one that is intensely his own.

During the political campaign year of 1964, when hours were long and tempers short, the staff was both pitied and censured. Today it demonstrates self-assurance and impressive skill.

Although all members of John F. Kennedy's staff agreed at Mr. Johnson's request to stay on for a time after the President's assassination on Nov. 22, 1963, some of them never achieved, or tried to achieve, a workable rapport with the overpowering man from Texas. As a result, Mr. Johnson leaned on the handful of personal friends he had brought with him, saddling them with a bewildering variety of unfamiliar tasks.

"He didn't really have a staff," says one scarred victim of that period. "He was just experimenting. Now he has one that suits him very well indeed."

Mr. Johnson has retained three former special assistants of President Kennedy—Lawrence F. (Larry) O'Brien, McGeorge Bundy and Richard N. Goodwin. He has also retained Maj. Gen. Chester V. (Ted) Clifton as military aide.

Influence Has Risen

All these men have made the transition between masters well. If anything, the influence of Mr. Bundy and Mr. O'Brien appears to have increased under Mr. Johnson, who seems to pay them more deference than Mr. Kennedy did.

Mr. Bundy, who is special assistant for national security affairs, and Mr. O'Brien, special assistant for Congressional liaison, are among the few real specialists on the Johnson staff. Both run substantial operations of their own, with staffs that could be described as departments attached to the Presidency and almost outside the personal staff of the President.

There is no sign that Mr. Bundy, an acerbic man, wants to or will leave the White House anytime soon.

Mr. O'Brien gave his resignation some months ago but has learned that this has little meaning with Mr. Johnson. He agreed to stay on until this year's legislative program was "launched"—but a friend says that "he and the President didn't have quite the same definition of 'launched.'"

3 Texans Added

There are unconfirmed reports that Mr. O'Brien would like to become chairman of the Democratic National Committee or Postmaster General or run for Governor of Massachusetts.

So far this year, the President has added three Texans to his staff—W. Marvin Watson, E. Jake Jacobsen and Harry C. McPherson Jr. This brings his major personal staff to a total of 12, six of them

Texans. He is entitled by law to 14 special assistants, but says he doubts he needs that many.

Mr. Watson has assumed the title of appointments secretary, sits in the office adjoining Mr. Johnson's and has the job that many believe to be the most personally punishing in the White House. An almost shy man he is a former Democratic state chairman of Texas, former economics instructor at Baylor University, he last worked as executive assistant to the president of the Lone Star Steel Company.

Mr. Johnson describes Mr. Watson as "methodical and cautious, an easy man to be with all the time— Mrs. Johnson says she'd give $100,000 a year to have him run her business."

One of Mr. Watson's tasks is to help deal with politicians, politics and the Democratic National Committee.

Mr. Jacobsen, Texan by choice who was born in New Jersey, was administrative assistant to former Texas Senator and Governor Price Daniel. He came to the White House this spring from an Austin law office.

'I Just Like People'

Mr. Jacobsen, who says "I just like people," has been a favorite social companion of the President since his arrival. He is being primarily used as an assistant to Mr. O'Brien, handling liaison with Congressmen from the New England states, Pennsylvania, New York and Texas, and as an extra White House lawyer to assist Lee C. White, the special counsel.

Mr. McPherson, former Assistant Secretary of State for Educational and Cultural Affairs, has been at the White House for weeks but has not formally assumed any title.

Mr. Johnson describes him as a liberal "and adventurous man on ideas and with a strong sense of social consciousness."

Mr. McPherson played a role in helping to prepare the voting rights bill this year and is also helping draft legislation to curb the Ku Klux Klan.

He is, in effect, an understudy to the special counsel and may replace Mr. White if the latter moves on to a job as chairman of a Government agency.

Associated Press

Bill D. Moyers, 30, helps development of President Johnson's domestic program.

Moyers's Role Increased

There is general agreement that the man who has blossomed most spectacularly in his job is Bill D. Moyers, who is only 30 years old.

His main job is overseeing the development of the Johnson domestic program, working on new legislation, special messages to Congress and the like. He also sits in on all foreign affairs and national security meetings.

A Kennedy veteran says, "Moyers is every bit as good an idea man as Ted Sorensen [President Kennedy's special counsel and ghost writer] and has a greater capacity to get along with people, to enlist their confidence and admiration."

One of the President's principles is that every senior staff man report directly to him. There is no supervisory chief of staff, but Mr. Moyers does perform some direction of staff efforts.

'My Bomb Thrower'

Mr. Johnson sometimes jokingly refers to Horace Busby Jr. as "my bomb thrower," an arch reference to Mr. Busby's "radical" career as editor of the student newspaper at the University of Texas, here he campaigned for academic freedom and other causes.

Mr. Busby first worked for Mr. Johnson in 1948, but from 1951 until last year was mostly in private life as founder of a business research concern and newsletter. He is Cabinet secretary, occasional speech writer and one of Mr. Johnson's most respected advisers. His choirlike directions of Cabinet meetings has turned them into precision affairs rather than rambling sessions.

Jack Valenti, who has the most stereotyped image of any staff members, says, "Every time I see a story about myself I'm described as a fast-talking Houston ad man who wears metallic suits—but Goodwin isn't the only guy around here who has ever read a book."

Richard Goodwin is chief speech writer and might be described as an orthodox intellectual. Mr. Valenti might be described as a very smart fellow who has become valuable to the President.

All staff members are expected by Mr. Johnson to be able to do almost any chore, but Mr. Valenti is most active. He is currently helping with the immigration bill on Capitol Hill, serving as liaison with the Republican Senate leader, Everett McKinley Dirksen, arranging Mr. Johnson's calendar, relaying orders and, above all, funneling enormous amounts of information from almost anyone in town who cannot reach the President directly.

Douglass Cater, the former Washington correspondent for Reporter magazine, has charge of overseeing the White House programs in education and health and in undertaking a wide range of other tasks.

Mr. Johnson has given increased freedom to his staff except for George E. Reedy, his press secretary, whom he has not given the chance to do his job either freely or well.

Mr. Johnson's staff must operate differently than any previous staff because his own methods are different. A Kennedy veteran says that "the White House today much more resembles a great corporation and Johnson is more businesslike."

Although ideas are debated freely, Mr. Johnson works a great deal through memoranda, which he checks "approved" or "not approved" or to which he appends marginal comments.

A Budget Bureau official says that it is relatively easy to get a 24-hour decision from Mr. Johnson that might have taken two weeks from Mr. Kennedy.

Say Advice Is Frank

All the Johnson staff contends that they give the President frank, blunt advice.

"Yes men don't last long because they are of no value to him," says Mr. Valenti. "You are only valuable to him when you can increase his knowledge, so your objections have to be informed and thoughtout."

There is, however, agreement that disagreement with the President needs careful handling and ex post facto disagreement is almost forbidden.

Most sources say that Mr. Johnson does not want advocates of special interests on his staff, but there are ideological shadings. Most say that Mr. Watson, a figure in the conservative wing of the Texas Democratic party, is the most conservative member, with Mr. Jacobsen and Mr. Busby tending in the same direction. Mr. Jacobsen says that "I am fiscally conservative but not on social questions." Mr. Busby would not seem conservative in Congress or in most state capitals.

Mr. Watson concedes that he is perhaps more conservative than liberals like Mr. Moyers and Mr. Goodwin, but says it hardly matters these days. Although he has reservations about the proposed repeal of section 14(b) of the Taft-Hartley Act, which authorizes state "right-to-work" laws, Mr. Watson has been set to work to help round up votes for the project.

"Around here the only ideology that counts is the President's," says a source.

Since the election, the working hours at the White House have decreased from about 15 hours to as little as 10 a day. The President's habit of growling at men in front of others has diminished, if not entirely disappeared.

Despite his heavy demands, Mr. Johnson appears to inspire very strong loyalty. One reason is that, far more than most Presidents, he has made his assistants his close personal and social companions. He likes them, trusts them; and, partly because he is addicted to shop talk, likes to have them around for an evening drink, a late dinner or a lazy weekend.

Washington: The Johnson System

By JAMES RESTON

WASHINGTON, March 5 — The "Johnson system" of executive administration never ceases to astonish Washington. He hedges all his bets. He always moves, but he moves in irregular jig-time, two steps forward and one back. He is a cautious extremist, who wants to keep everybody off balance, so he backs into the future.

His choice of Under Secretary of State George Ball to serve as executive chairman of a new and powerful interdepartmental committee to "direct" the country's nonmilitary operations abroad is only the latest example of his one-two punch.

Mr. Ball is Mr. Johnson's loyal opposition in the State Department and both words are equally accurate. Mr. Ball has been fiercely loyal to the President, but he has fought him all the way on Vietnam.

Ball's Prophecies

Long before Mr. Johnson came to the White House, Under Secretary Ball warned President Kennedy that if he raised the American military force in Saigon from a few hundred "advisers" to 15,000 or 20,000 fighting men, he would create a wholly new political and psychological situation that could easily get out of hand. This was back at the end of 1961.

At that time, Under Secretary Ball raised the central question: are you willing to see this through to the end? Do you want to help and advise the South Vietnamese or do you want to replace them in the battle? As things have turned out Mr. Ball was modest in his estimates, though he seemed wildly radical at that time. If you go up to 15,000, he said, you will commit the prestige of the United States and you will have to commit 300,000 Americans to redeem it. Do you want to do that?

Civil Arguer

Secretary of Defense McNamara and Secretary of State Rusk accepted this at that time as a fair question. They said "yes", he said "no", and he lost. Nevertheless Mr. Ball stayed on and kept arguing, with great force but with civility and even amiable good humor, against the trend toward deeper and deeper involvement in the war.

President Johnson's reaction to this was interesting and significant. He believes more in people than in ideas, and though he has differed with Ball, he believes in him as a person. The President has the reputation of being a man who cannot tolerate opposition but in this case he invited it. He not only gave Ball more opportunity and time for opposition than President Kennedy had given him, but established Ball as the official "devil's advocate" of the Administration to make the case against the advocates of more troops, more bombing, and more risks of war with China.

The human side of this exercise is interesting. There is a long history in Washington of vicious competition between Secretaries of State and Under Secretaries of State, and between the State Department and the Defense Department, but Secretary of State Rusk and Secretary of Defense McNamara, while differing with Ball, accepted his opposition, without personal recrimination, and without trying to use their superior rank to silence him.

Accordingly, Ball had his say. He put his views into a series of sharp memoranda against the commitment of over 100,000 American troops last summer and against a renewal of the bombing of North Vietnam after the peace offensive, and in the end he lost every argument.

Ball in Charge

Nevertheless, after McGeorge Bundy left the White House to head the Ford Foundation, and the President had to choose how to reorganize the system of deciding on major questions of foreign policy, he chose Ball, with the approval of Secretary Rusk, to head the main interdepartmental committee on the direction of foreign policy.

It would have been easy for the President to get rid of the Under Secretary and give the main job of advising the President to somebody else who would preside over the heads of the State and Defense Departments, the Joint Chiefs of Staff and the Central Intelligence Agency—somebody who would have approved of the escalation, the bombing, and the search-and-destroy policy in Vietnam.

Mr. Ball was perfectly willing to resign. After his last defeat on the renewal of the bombing of North Vietnam, it is understood that he was even eager to return to his private law practice in June, and he may still do so. But President Johnson had a different view.

Dove Over Hawks

The President does not want to be left alone with the hawks. He wants "consensus" even if it leads to confusion. He does not want to choose between extremes. In fact, when he renews bombing, he wants somebody around who opposes bombing. So he created an advisory committee of hawks presided over by a dove, just as he asked Hubert Humphrey, the liberal, to oppose the liberals on Vietnam and just as he invited the conservative Bill Martin at the Federal Reserve Board to help advise on a Keynesian budget and low interest rate Martin is known to doubt.

All this, however, is typical of the "Johnson system." This is Johnson, the President, applying the techniques of Johnson, the Majority Leader, on Capitol Hill. Will they work? Can the devices of the Senate Cloak Room be applied successfully to the White House? This is the question that fascinates Washington, and nobody really knows the answer.

March 6, 196[illegible]

You Don't Know Where Johnson Ends And McNamara Begins

By NEIL SHEEHAN

WASHINGTON.

AT a White House conference last April to discuss the then impending railway strike, President Johnson asked what the exact cost to the railroad management would be if it accepted one of the complex union wage demands. A Cabinet member whose concern with labor is only peripheral made some rapid calculations in his head and gave Mr. Johnson an answer within less than five seconds. It took several experts from the Department of Labor another five minutes to work out the same calculations on paper,

NEIL SHEEHAN, who formerly reported from Vietnam, now covers the Pentagon for The Times.

but when they had finished they confirmed his answer.

"Thanks, Bob," said the President.

Robert Strange McNamara, the former Harvard Business School professor from California with the rimless glasses and the high part in his slicked-down hair, an executive of the Ford Motor Company for 14 years and its president for a brief 42 days, had supplied another of the innumerable and precise answers he has been giving two Presidents for six and a half years. The unvarying ability to come up with the options for the endless decisions an American President must make, the talent for citing statistics which, accurate or not, pass at the moment for hard facts, have helped make McNamara "the favorite son" of the Cabinet. He is, without a doubt, the first among equals.

He was the most valued member of President Kennedy's Cabinet within six weeks, even though Mr. Kennedy had not met him before appointing him Secretary of Defense. He is now the most trusted and affectionately held of Johnson's aides.

Oliphant in The Denver Post.

McNAMARA is the one Cabinet member whom Johnson has repeatedly said he could assign to any post, including that of Secretary of State, with perfect confidence. Although Johnson has no intention of replacing Dean Rusk, it is interesting that the President does not attribute to Rusk the ability to handle McNamara's job. And there is probably not a member of the Cabinet who has not grown envious long ago from hearing Johnson remark: "Why don't you fellows run your department like Bob McNamara runs his?"

His work habits have not changed since McNamara first entered the dull-gray Pentagon across the Potomac from the White House in December, 1960. He still works 12 hours a day, six days a week, but the 12 hours are no longer devoted entirely to Defense business. He is called upon for advice and assistance on taxes, aluminum price rises, labor disputes and other economic problems, the poverty program, education and whatever else happens to be troubling Johnson.

IN Robert S. McNamara there has been a unique meeting of a man and his times. In a period of vast social and technological change, with vast domestic and international problems arising from this change, Robert S. McNamara is the managerial type par excellence. He has mastered the technique of the statistical approach, the careful analysis of the available options, the ability to qualify the disparate elements of a complex situation. He also has arrived at a time when the United States is at the height of its power, with crisis after crisis flowing through the operations room of the White House. For two Presidents, eager to make today's multitude of decisions and go on to tomorrow's, McNamara has provided the ready answers.

Yet his managerial prowess alone is not what has made McNamara such an accomplished servant of princes. Other men have shown this quality and it has not brought them the power McNamara wields. He has another quality which has been equally important in his relations with two Presidents. It is his absolute loyalty to his superior.

Those who knew him in his auto-industry days say he displayed the attribute then and was ever-ready to assert the authority of the central office over Ford's complex operations. In the service of the Presidency, the trait has become more pronounced. Within the inner councils of the Administration, McNamara will argue vigorously, even doctrinairely at times, for his point. Once the decision has been made, however, he will completely submerge his own feelings and beliefs in its rigorous execution.

"Why does the President hold McNamara in such high regard?" a member of the Joint Chiefs of Staff was recently asked. "Because McNamara will be hatchet man for the President on anything the President wants," was the unhesitating reply. "If the President told McNamara to call a press conference and announce that I'd gone berserk this morning and jumped out of a window, he might argue, but he'd do it without batting an eye," the officer said, "even though he knew I'd died of a heart attack from overwork."

When the aluminum producers attempted to raise their prices in November of 1965, McNamara took up the cudgels at the President's wish and bludgeoned them back into place. When Gen. William C. Westmoreland, the United States commander in Vietnam, had to be taken down a peg because he was asking for more troops than the President could give him without the political and economic repercussions of mobilization, McNamara obliged during his latest trip to Vietnam in July.

Without ever mentioning the general by name, McNamara criticized him for poor intelligence work and bad management. There were not as many North Vietnamese and Vietcong troops in the jungle as the general's headquarters had reported, Mr. McNamara said, and there were too many American soldiers in the rear echelons who should be moved into combat units. In short, the general didn't need all the troops he had asked for and, after a dutiful display of unity in Washington, General Westmoreland finally settled for slightly more than half the troops he had requested.

What makes Mr. McNamara even more trustworthy from the President's point of view is his willingness to assume personal responsibility for a Presidential decision regardless of his own feelings. The elements of discussion within the inner council, composed of Johnson, McNamara, Rusk and Walt W. Rostow, special assistant to the President, are rarely allowed to go any further. Members of the Joint Chiefs complain that McNamara frequently does not tell them why the President made a certain decision. He simply announces after a White House meeting that "I have decided" on a particular course of action.

This is resented by the Chiefs, since it is normal military procedure to explain to one's immediate subordinates why a decision was made. The Chiefs also suspect that on some occasions the Secretary of Defense did not wholeheartedly support and may even have opposed decisions he announced as his own. "It makes it pretty hard to deal with him the next time something like that comes up," one officer said, "because you don't know where McNamara begins and Johnson ends."

McNamara also demonstrates his loyalty to the President in smaller, but perhaps equally important ways.

When Mr. Johnson was Vice President, he noticed that Mr. McNamara did not allow anyone to criticize President Kennedy in private. Mr. Johnson—as sensitive to criticism as President Kennedy was—believes the Secretary of Defense shows him the same loyalty in private.

McNamara has managed to flatter the President without giving Mr. Johnson the impression he is deliberately currying favor. The President worked extremely hard to secure passage of the consular treaty, calling important Senators to the White House and arguing his case. McNamara apparently noticed this. The morning after the treaty was passed, he telephoned Johnson, told the President he realized how much effort Johnson had devoted to the treaty and said he was "proud" to serve such a leader.

Before the Secretary of Defense goes on one of his infrequent vacations, he writes the President a note, two weeks to 10 days in advance. The note specifies exactly what time and date McNamara will be leaving, if the President has no objections, where he will be staying and the time and date of his planned return. McNamara also carefully states that he will be available to return to Washington at any time the President desires. A day or so before he leaves, McNamara telephones the President to make certain there is no objection. There never is, but Johnson is flattered by the elaborate procedure.

McNamara is always prompt for Cabinet and other White House meetings and for the post-midnight crisis gatherings. When Johnson picks up the telephone beside his desk and asks to speak to "McNamara," McNamara always comes on the line, not a secretary, as is sometimes the case when the President telephones Dean Rusk. How McNamara manages this is an electronic mystery, but he does. Since McNamara is virtually always in his office by 7:15 each morning, he is usually the first Cabinet member the President telephones every day. "He's always there," Johnson was once heard to remark. "The only difference is that on Saturday he wears a sport coat."

THE McNamara managerial skill is applied with equal vigor to both the 51-year-old Secretary's personal and public lives and this may be perhaps why he has succeeded in maintaining the pace he has set for six and a half years without a coronary, or a nervous breakdown. He and Mrs. McNamara normally get to bed by 10 P.M. each night, unless they have a social engagement. The Secretary is up at 6:15 A.M. and he has the trip to his office on the second floor of the Pentagon timed—the drive takes seven minutes from the McNamaras' large, Spanish-style home on Tracy Place in Washington's posh Kalorama section.

His time throughout the day is carefully budgeted. He does not permit small talk. His Assistant Secretaries of Defense and the Service Secretaries, a number of whom are remarkably like him in their view of the world, have learned this long ago. If they do not keep closely to the business at hand, or if they argue their point a bit too long, McNamara glances with just a hint of impatience at the clock on the wall opposite his desk. The hint is enough to bring the discussion to a close.

At the beginning of the morning his desk is often piled high with documents and reports in black and red binders. The desk is an expansive oak affair that once belonged to a man of equally assertive character, General of the Armies John (Black Jack) Pershing. Behind the desk is a large oil portrait of the first Secretary of Defense, James Forrestal, who ended his life under the strain of Government service and his own private troubles. A North Vietnamese sniper's rifle is displayed on a small table on the other side of the room, and on the wall behind it is a Vietcong propaganda poster, crudely hand-lettered in red ink with the Vietnamese words "Down With the Imperialist McNamara."

When an ordinary visitor enters, McNamara continues to read with a frown whatever document he is working on at the moment until he finishes the paragraph. Then he looks up with a smile, stands and shakes hands, relaxes back into his swivel chair—and the conversation begins. One visitor recently suggested that he leave before his allotted half-hour was finished because McNamara seemed to be unusually busy that day. "No, that's all right," the Secretary said with his unvarying politeness, "you still have 12 minutes."

As the day unfolds between appointments, he slowly works his way through the stacks of documents. By 7:30 or 8 P.M., as the Secretary leaves for home in his black Cadillac limousine, General Pershing would admire the cleanliness of the desk.

Mrs. McNamara says he leaves his work behind him. "He is not a worrier," she said. "Once he makes a decision, it is done and it no longer bothers him." At home he relaxes with a book. It may be a serious novel, nonfiction or poetry. Even when reading for pleasure, McNamara does not waste his time. Some of his recent reading has ranged from a history of the Sierra Nevada range published by the Sierra Club to Rebecca West's "The Birds Fall Down" and "Report to Greco," by Kazantzakis. His favorite poet is Yeats, but he is also fond of Frost and Yevtushenko. Now and then he plays a game of chess with his wife.

The McNamaras attend obligatory state dinners and receptions and smaller private affairs with their close friends. The Robert Kennedys and Mrs. Jacqueline Kennedy are among their closest, and they occasionally visit the President's widow in New York. Other friends are McGeorge and Mary Bundy, Orville and Jane Freeman, Nicholas and Lydia deB. Katzenbach, and Cyrus and Grace Vance. McNamara is reputedly an excellent guest. He relaxes well, is a provocative conversationalist because of his wide interests and has the grace and erudition to entertain the lady next to him at the dinner table with a recitation of Yeats. He and Mrs. McNamara were among the chosen on the guest list for Truman Capote's much-publicized party last fall. They did not attend, ostensibly because the Secretary was too busy and possibly because they felt their attendance would constitute questionable taste at a time when young men are dying in Vietnam.

But the most significant fact about the McNamara's social life is its sparseness. They guard their privacy and do not seek society. In Ann Arbor, Mich., an academic community where they lived before coming to Washington, they had virtually no social life. "We like being alone," Mrs. McNamara said.

EXHAUSTION through intense physical exercise is another way in which McNamara unwinds from the tension of his job. He and Mr. Freeman play a wild half-hour of squash two or three times a week on the Pentagon courts. At times the game becomes so furious that they both collapse on the floor and gasp for breath before continuing. After one recent match, Freeman assured his aides that the badly bruised lip they were staring at had not been inflicted by an angry farmer. The Secretary of Defense had accidentally hit him in the mouth with a squash ball. McNamara also sometimes gets in a game of tennis before work in the mornings. On vacation he seeks the same physical outlet in skiing and mountain-climbing.

Sundays are reserved, and McNamara does not work unless he is forced to because of a crisis. He spends the day reading in the sunshine of his azalea garden. To allow himself as much time as possible to relax, he has dispensed with many of the ordinary mechanics of living. Mrs. McNamara says he has bought only two new suits in six years.

In the evenings he and Mrs. McNamara, the former Margaret Craig (Margie to her friends), take a walk before dinner. Their eldest daughter, Margaret, is married and lives in New Haven. Their second daughter, Kathleen, is studying anthropology in Athens, and their son, Robert Craig, attends St. Paul's, a pedigreed boys' school in New Hampshire.

By 6:15 Monday morning the Secretary of Defense is ready to spend another week working like "a goddamn jackhammer," as one of his associates described his pace. Even the President, who is a constant worker, marvels at McNamara's capacity and attempts to persuade him to relax more, for fear he will ultimately collapse.

THE impact of McNamara's management skill upon the defense establishment has obviously been profound. The controversy surrounding his work does not obscure the reasonable certainty that much of it will endure long after he has gone.

McNamara has brought reason to bear upon the management of the armed forces and thus by proxy upon the immense and disparate industrial base which supports them. For the first time since World War II a coherent defense policy for the country has been developed and the services assigned complementary roles within it.

A red-bound looseleaf folder in the controller's office in the Pentagon encompasses much of this change. The folder is several inches thick and it is marked top secret. It contains the defense plans of the United States for the next five years. Within it more than 100,000 items are listed, with their estimated individual cost, under functional headings such as Strategic Retaliatory Forces and Continental Air Missile Defense Forces (both for nuclear war), General Purpose Forces, Airlift - Sealift Forces, Reserve and Guard Forces (for conventional war) and Research and Development. The plans will undoubtedly alter — Vietnam proves that — but the detailed projection allows a President and his Secretary of Defense to see where the country's defense establishment is going and to make their decisions accordingly.

IN the past, the individual services fought over the budget, once the Administration had set a ceiling, and then the admirals and the generals bought whatever hardware they and their staffs decided they needed after they had been allotted their share of the available funds. Under McNamara this has ended. Now each service is allowed to buy only what McNamara and his aides decide it needs to fulfill its function within defense policy as a whole. The conflict between McNamara and the military arises from this innovation, for inherent in the McNamara method is the transfer of the real decision-making power from the military heads of the services to the Secretary of Defense.

Only a man with a character as forceful as McNamara's would have had the courage to make these innovations, to do battle with the sacred dragons of Washington and to slay them without mercy. Yet it is the inevitable complications and even contradictions of such a strong personality which have made McNamara an enigma to much of Washington and the rest of the country. He often arouses as much concern for his methods as he does confidence for his achievements.

He has become a Doubting Thomas on Vietnam. The war has been the one great failure of his career thus far. The manager who excels at analyzing a problem, and then bringing to bear the resources necessary to solve it, has succeeded in making this problem only larger and more unmanageable despite the steady escalation of the resources applied. On the basis of a mistaken estimate of the effectiveness of U. S. military power on the Asian mainland, he came out in favor of the commencement of regular bombing of North Vietnam in in February of 1965 and the commitment of U. S. ground troops to the war in the South in June of that year. Over the past year, however, some of his friends say he has developed serious doubts about the usefulness of military power in bringing the war to a successful conclusion. In private, they say, he expresses misgivings and melancholy over the course of events.

Yet, while McNamara the man no longer apparently shares the unquestioning faith in the war of Dean Rusk and Rusk's fellow apostle of victory over Communism in Asia, Walt Whitman Rostow, McNamara the Secretary of Defense has not become an Administration dove. There is no sign of conflict between McNamara and his two principal colleagues. Unlike George Ball, the former Under Secretary of State, he seems, within the inner councils of the Administration, still to accept the basic tenet of policy—the establishment of a viable, pro-Western South Vietnam. His doubts appear in a growing hesitancy over the implementation of that policy. The hesitancy has been most apparent in his efforts to act as a brake on the escalation of the air war against the North, where his disillusionment has been greatest.

This hesitancy has sometimes placed McNamara second only to Ho Chi Minh as a suspicious character in the eyes of the generals, but his doubts have made him more respectable to the opponents of the war outside the Government. The anguished clergymen and liberal intellectuals who visit the Pentagon to protest the war go away feeling they have talked to a reasonable man who would like to help them if he could.

His carefully reasoned argument against another major escalation of the air war in late August before the Senate Preparedness Investigating Subcommittee increased his stature with the doves. As John Stennis of Mississippi, the subcommittee chairman, and the other Senate hawks supported the Joint Chiefs of Staff in a concerted cry for escalation, McNamara became an even more sympathetic figure—a voice of reason trying to stem the crash of the bombs.

Johnson decided against his Secretary of Defense on this occasion and escalated, but there is no reason to believe that the relationship between McNamara and the President suffered because of the incident. For domestic political reasons, Johnson appeased the hawks, as he has periodically done, and McNamara seems to have accepted this political consideration as valid.

For his part, McNamara has helped the President to hold the line against the really drastic escalation of the bombing which the generals and their political friends are seeking. For the generals want much more than a few important bridges and airfields. They want to conduct an unrelenting campaign of strategic air interdiction against North Vietnam. They want to demolish or otherwise completely neutralize all of the port facilities at Haiphong, to bomb the air defense command and control centers in the populated areas of Hanoi and Haiphong, to destroy the hydroelectric dams and locks in the Red River delta and cause widespread flooding and crop damage and to make virtually unrestricted attacks on the rail lines and highways close to the Chinese frontier. All of these objectives are still denied them.

McNamara was not, however, arguing for an end to the bombing, as the doves desire. A restricted air campaign, with periodic suspensions, has its place in his strategy. His stand against an escalation of the bombing arises as much from his present conviction that the war will be decided on the ground in the South as it does from his lack of faith in the efficacy of air power.

WHAT the doves also forget is that McNamara's managerial skills have made the war much more palatable to the public than it might otherwise have been. McNamara, in fact, removed some of the inhibitions the President might have experienced in undertaking it. He placed a 467,000-man expeditionary corps in South Vietnam for Johnson without the political repercussions of mobilization and, by frequently calculating war production needs with dangerous narrowness, has eased the inflationary impact on the American economy.

Under the pressure of war spending, some of McNamara's famed systems-analysis techniques have, in fact, amounted to just saving money. In one instance last winter, General Westmoreland requested a mechanized infantry brigade to operate on the coastal plains of Binh Dinh Province in central Vietnam. The request was returned from the office of Alain Enthoven, Assistant Secretary of Defense for Systems Analysis and one of McNamara's original whiz kids, with the question why an ordinary infantry brigade would not do as well. The Army patiently explained that the mechanized brigade was wanted for the specific mission of pursuing and killing Vietcong guerrillas in an area of flat rice lands. Ordinary infantrymen would have to walk through the paddies because they do not possess the tracked armored personnel carriers of a mechanized unit and thus would not be nearly as effective in apprehending the guerrillas, the Army pointed out. Enthoven's office continued to resist and the Army soon discovered the reason—an ordinary infantry brigade would be cheaper.

"This," said one officer, "is like deciding you want to sell used cars in Manhattan and then opening your office and lot in Brooklyn because the rents are cheaper there."

His speech in New York last fall showed how deeply McNamara is concerned with the poverty and social anguish of the urban ghettos. Yet again, however, his creation of a flexible military establishment that can respond to the varying needs of foreign policy has permitted the Administration to project American power overseas in an aggressive and imperial fashion, which is, in turn, creating dissension within the country and distracting from the effort to solve the crisis in the cities.

Similarly, at a time when the steady accrual of power by the executive branch has become worrisome to many, McNamara, for all his liberal beliefs, has helped accelerate this trend by providing the management tools the executive needs to manipulate what power it has and to acquire more.

ALTHOUGH McNamara has spoken out on a number of occasions to defend the right of public dissent over Vietnam, within the Defense Department itself he practices something akin to Lenin's concept of democratic centralism. He permits free discussion only while a decision is in the process of being made. Even then he often becomes irritated if the pros and cons of the discussion become a matter of public knowledge and debate through the press.

Once a decision has been made, however, he will tolerate no dissent. Pentagon officials are more frightened of frank discussion with journalists and outsiders than any other executive department in Washington. Many officers assume their telephones are tapped periodically, and one senior general believed McNamara had planted spies in his office to report on his private opinions of the Secretary's policies.

The so-called McNamara rule, under which journalists were accompanied to interviews by Pentagon public-information officers, or the official interviewed had to report the substance of the conversation to the public-information office "before the close of business that day," was a unique feature of the Defense Department and Communist countries. The rule was finally abolished last June 30 after the Freedom of Information Act was passed.

But the explanation McNamara gave in his memorandum announcing its abolition was as revealing of his attitude as the rule itself. "While there will always be some degree of parochialism," he said, "special pleading by special interests has largely been ended within the department." The rule, he continued, "has served its purpose and it is rescinded immediately."

In other words, officials were now so well indoctrinated that McNamara did not have to worry about subordinates expressing disturbing and possibly independent opinions to journalists. The rule has, in fact, "served its purpose" and reporters have noticed no perceptible change since its abolition. Pentagon officials are as cautious as ever and most still have a public information officer present to protect themselves.

ANOTHER study in contradiction is McNamara's unquestioned integrity as a Secretary of Defense and the frequent incredibility of his public statements. Some senior officials even wonder if he knows any longer when he is telling the truth and when he is deceiving to put a better face on his own and the Administration's policies. His concept of public information, as one general put it, "is like selling Fords. You tell 'em all the good things but none of the bad."

The deception is usually practiced by deliberate semantic evasiveness or the deletion of pertinent facts, a technique that has spread to other departments of the Government. Sometimes, however, the process is more obvious.

In testimony before the Senate Foreign Relations Committee last July 26 on the Defense Department's arms-sales program, McNamara contended that the Pentagon bore no responsibility for a $2.518-billion portion of the sales.

He referred to this portion as "commercial orders," and went on: "These are generally for cash and represent transactions directly between a foreign government and a U.S. corporation. We play no role in these."

This portion is technically commercial, because the actual sales contract is signed by the American armaments firm and the foreign company, and the arms do not first pass to United States Government ownership before they are exported. But it is common knowledge that 90 per cent of these sales are concluded by the companies at the direction of the Pentagon after the Defense Department has negotiated the sale with the foreign government concerned. Since he has been intimately involved in the arms-sales program, McNamara could not have failed to know this.

It has become clear over the years that McNamara is fascinated by ideas that affect the human race but does not have the same interest in and understanding of people themselves. This inability to posit the human and thus often the political factors in a given situation is a curious limitation in this man which even his intimates acknowledge. It may account for the political naiveté he has displayed at times and for some of his difficulties with the military.

Shortly after McNamara became Secretary of Defense in 1961, one senior member of the Joint Chiefs of Staff decided that while he was a brilliant and resourceful young man, he was acting without regard for the human element in his relations with the military. He told McNamara this and invited the Secretary to a party to get acquainted with the Chiefs on an informal basis.

McNamara duly went to the party, but he did not follow up the initiative and so his knowledge of the members of the Joint Chiefs of Staff has been limited to what has emerged from their professional relationship. Perhaps McNamara decided he did not have time to familiarize himself with the personalities of his military subordinates. He similarly does not socialize with his civilian staff. Even if he had taken the time to become acquainted with the country's military leaders, the knowledge gained might not have affected their disputes. The important thing, however, is that he did not try.

His failure to speak at the service academies and at the staff and war colleges has likewise been resented by the military.

This limitation where human factors are concerned has also affected adversely his relationship with the Europeans. The dispute with Britain in 1962 over the cancellation of the Skybolt missile project was the first prominent example. The Skybolt was an air-launched, nuclear-tipped missile with a planned range of 1,100 miles. It was to have been fired from B-52 bombers at ground targets in the Soviet Union in the event of a nuclear conflict. The United States had promised to sell the missile to Britain to use on its Vulcan bombers, and the former Conservative Prime Minister, Harold Macmillan, had, in the face of virulent criticism from the opposition Labor party, sold the scheme to the British public as a means of preserving an independent British nuclear striking force.

McNamara decided the ground-launched Minuteman missile and the submarine-launched Polaris version were sufficient to meet American strategic requirements and that the Skybolt was an expensive luxury the United States could well do without. He apparently intimated his intention to cancel Skybolt to the British but did not make himself sufficiently clear. Worse, he did not consider the political repercussions the cancellation of the project would bring in Britain.

The Kennedy Administration terminated the project and presented Prime Minister Macmillan with a *fait accompli* at the Nassau conference in December of 1962. The result was anger and resentment among the British and a political crisis in London which seriously weakened the Macmillan Government.

The pattern of the Skybolt affair was repeated in the unbending fashion with which McNamara forced the West Germans to purchase American armaments under the so-called Off-Set Agreements. West Germany signed three such agreements with the United States, the first in 1961, to purchase $4.05-billion worth of American arms to meet the foreign-exchange costs of stationing 225,000 American troops in Germany.

When the Germans began to falter in their scheduled purchases in the spring of 1966 because of economic problems, McNamara somewhat crudely threatened them with retaliation. The United States, he said, would reduce the number of its troops in Germany in proportion to the amount of arms the Germans failed to buy. In his zeal to ease the United States gold drain, he appears to have completely disregarded the serious budgetary and political complications the arms purchases were bringing the German Government, and thus contributed to the fall of former Chancellor Ludwig Erhard last fall. McNamara is still cordially disliked in Bonn, where he is viewed as a computerized cash register.

Even McNamara's intimates acknowledge that their intense loyalty to him does not arise from any qualities of charismatic leadership. Rather, their loyalty springs from their admiration for his remarkable intelligence, his great dedication to his work and the satisfaction they obtain, as managerial types of the same cloth, from aiding him in his enormous task.

It is a tribute to McNamara that he has been able to attract and to retain in Defense Department service such highly qualified civil-servant intellectuals as Paul Ignatius, the Secretary of the Navy, and David McGiffert, the Under Secretary of the Army. Under previous Secretaries of Defense such positions rotated frequently among lawyers and businessmen with political connections — and continuity and efficiency of management suffered accordingly.

McNamara's great self-confidence ("It is the only thing that exceeds his energy," one admiral said) is also a source of strength, but again a source of some of his difficulties with Congress and the military. It has become evident that occasionally this self-confidence is indistinguishable from arrogance and stubbornness.

He studies a problem with such care and listens to so many opinions before making up his mind that when he does reach a decision he apparently develops an unshakable faith in its correctness. Thus, when McNamara makes a mistake, he is prone to make a big one and to defend it relentlessly in the face of criticism.

The naval version of the F-111 multipurpose jet is probably the most outstanding example in his six years in office. McNamara concluded in 1962 that $1-billion in development and production costs could be saved if the Air Force and the Navy developed an aircraft of common design for two quite different missions. Convinced that this concept of commonality, as he called it, was feasible, he ordered the two services to undertake the project.

To meet the Air Force requirements for low-level supersonic flight, the plane gained so much weight that it is still unacceptable to the Navy, which needs a lighter aircraft for carrier operations ("unless we want to build new carriers," one officer said, "to fit the plane"). The cost of the Navy version has also more than doubled from the 1962 estimate and will soon likely triple to more than $10-million per aircraft. The Navy would have preferred to abandon the scheme and design another plane to fit its specifications, but McNamara has insisted that the Navy modify the F-111 and somehow make it acceptable for carrier operations. His insistence appears to have hardened in proportion to Congressional criticism of the project. The admirals do not dare oppose him, for they know that retaliation in the form of a shortened career would follow.

So the modification work continues and the Navy hopes that the F-111 will either undergo a transformation into a useful aircraft or just fade away some day like a bad dream. "The word," one officer said, "is don't knock the F-111 but don't buy any either."

McNAMARA'S surprising sensitivity to anything which suggests less than perfect management of the Defense Department has been another disturbing character trait. Early last year he vehemently denied press reports of serious shortages of air munitions in Vietnam, terming the reports "baloney," even though the existence of the shortages was common knowledge within the military establishment.

He has since refused to grant security clearance to two reports documenting the shortages which were drawn up by the Senate Preparedness Investigating Subcommittee. When Congressional testimony by members of the Joint Chiefs of Staff has disclosed lapses in the management of war production, McNamara has asked them to alter their testimony for the record.

"The whole business is rather silly as far as I'm concerned," one of the country's senior military officers said. "Hell, everybody knows there have been shortages. There always are when you're running a war. I'm surprised we haven't had more shortages in this one than we've had. Why spend 100 man-hours trying to build up a phony case that a shortage doesn't exist every time some reporter writes about one?"

McNamara's very brilliance has also caused him problems through no fault of his own, for it inevitably arouses jealousy. He has made it his business to know more about the defense establishment than anyone else in or out of Government, and he displays an uncanny ability to memorize facts.

At one defense budget review session during the Kennedy Administration at President Kennedy's vacation home in Palm Beach, Fla., Gen. Curtis E. LeMay, the former Chief of Staff of the Air Force, appealed to the President to restore an Air Force project that he said McNamara had deleted from the budget. McNamara answered that the general was wrong and that he had not deleted the item. While General LeMay sat in embarrassed silence as his aides began fumbling through the cumbersome budget document to find the item, McNamara gave them the number of the page.

His habit of marshaling a dazzling array of statistics to support his case in Congressional testimony has dismayed and irritated the Southern conservatives on the Armed Services Committees. Many of these men, like Representative L. Mendel Rivers, Democrat of South Carolina and chairman of the House Armed Services Committee, are anti-intellectuals and superpatriots who have vigorously resisted change and who have been particularly disturbed by McNamara's unceasing efforts to reform and modernize the Reserves and the National Guard. "They listen to him rattle off all those facts and figures which they can't comprehend and they can't answer and they say to themselves, 'You smart son of a bitch, you're too goddamn smart. I'm going to take you down a peg,'" one associate of McNamara's said. "And then when they try and they don't succeed, they get a little bit madder."

What the Secretary's colleague did not mention is that the anger is sometimes justified when the Congressmen later discover they have been hoodwinked by McNamara's tactic of supporting a weak argument with an adroit combination of statistics and sophistry.

The Secretary's unwillingness to admit to mistakes has puzzled his intimates and others in Government who know him well. Some believe it results from a hidden shyness. If Johnson needles him in Cabinet meetings, he reacts with embarrassment at first, apparently fearing that the President may mean what he says, and it is often several moments before McNamara realizes the President is only joking and laughs. Others, who like McNamara less, believe he fears that if he admits to one major mistake, he will have to concede more and that he cannot bear to do this.

Whatever may be the case, there is no sign that his will to assert himself is weakening or that he is any less convinced of the rightness of his decisions today than he was six and a half years ago. He does not allow his wife to beat him at chess and Orville Freeman admits that McNamara has a 60-40 edge over him on the squash court, which McNamara gives no indication of relinquishing. When McNamara bowls at the Presidential retreat at Camp David during weekend conferences there, a game with which he is not familiar, he may score low on the first two frames, but by the third frame he is winning.

When he does take leave, he is off to the ski slopes or slogging his way to the top of another mountain. One of the few things in life he decided he could not do successfully was to play golf, and he gave that up as soon as he found out.

HE shows a greater willingness to compromise with Congress on some of his programs, but only on the trimmings, not on the essentials. President Eisenhower and his Secretary of Defense, Neil McElroy, had planned a reorganization of the Reserves and the National Guard in the late nineteen-fifties. They retreated precipitately when an uproar sounded from the state Governors and the Congressional protectors of the prerogatives of the Reserves and the Guard. McNamara was not cowed by a repetition of the uproar, even though his reorganization plan was twice rejected by Congress. He persisted doggedly and this year achieved his basic aims.

He has also learned to accept an occasional and major political compromise in defense policy. He retreats as slowly as possible, however, giving ground with the greatest reluctance.

The Administration's decision last month to spend an estimated $5-billion over the next five years to build a so-called thin antiballistic missile defense system is perhaps the greatest such compromise of his career thus far. Since the news last fall that the Soviet Union had begun deploying an ABM defense, McNamara has fought as hard as he could to prevent the United States from following suit.

He is convinced that any such defense can be overwhelmed by offensive missiles and has expressed fears privately that once a decision has been made to build the thin system, the public pressure to steadily expand the defense and to spend $40- to $50-billion to construct the so-called thick ABM system may become irresistible. He believes that this outcome not only would be an enormous waste of resources, but also would destroy much of the progress achieved through the nuclear test ban treaty in another atomic arms race between the two principal powers.

With a Presidential election looming, Johnson could not afford to concede to the Republicans the made-to-order issue that the Soviet Union was gaining a strategic nuclear superiority over the United States, and so the decision was made to build the thin ABM defense. In his distinctly unenthusiastic speech last month announcing this, McNamara skillfully maneuvered around the real reason for the decision — the Soviet construction of an ABM defense. In a finely honed argument he contended that any ABM system was useless against the Soviet Union. The Administration was building the thin system, he said, on the "marginal grounds" that it was needed to counter a possible Chinese intercontinental ballistic missile threat in the nineteen-seventies.

The unpleasant compromise was made, but the speech gained time which the Administration is using to attempt to induce the Soviet Union to enter negotiations directed at limiting ABM defenses in both countries. The Secretary of Defense is intimately involved in this enterprise. If the negotiations prove abortive, he will undoubtedly seek some other way to attack the problem and ultimately to assert his will.

For whether right or wrong, Robert Strange McNamara is a man who needs to win.

October 22, 1967

Nixon's Way

A Passion for Order and Privacy

WASHINGTON — After four months in office, President Nixon has started running the United States Government in a style and manner that is very much his own.

"Running the Government" is, of course, a misleading term. No modern President has exercised complete executive control over the Federal bureaucracy, although Lyndon Johnson gave it a valiant, protean try. Mr. Nixon is no exception. There is no visible evidence that he takes a day-to-day interest in, say, George Romney's problems at the housing agency. Like all Presidents, he prefers to reserve his energies against the day when George Romney's problems become Presidential problems.

Even so, there is a Nixon style and a Nixon pattern to the way he conducts the public business. It is a style distinguished mainly by two charcteristics: a passion for order, and a passion for privacy. Order, to insure that the President receives a regular flow of the best advice that Government is able to give him; privacy, to insure that when he gets all these options he can retreat and, in an atmosphere of studied detachment, reach the correct decision.

Imposing Order

Like most executives, President Nixon has tried to impose order on the decision-making process through machinery. His own peculiar machinery is rather simple on paper, although in practice it is frequently cumbersome and occasionally inept.

There are three major elements to it: the National Security Council, revitalized under Henry A. Kissinger, which churns up foreign policy options for Presidential decision; the Urban Affairs Council, under Daniel Patrick Moynihan, which churns up domestic options for Presidential decision; and an administrative apparatus, headed by former Nixon campaign official H. R. Haldeman, who monitors the flow of both people and paper in and out of the President's office and who zealously budgets the President's time.

There are other groups, such as the Cabinet and his economic advisers, to whom the President turns fairly regularly for advice. And this weekend he established yet another Cabinet-level advisory group, known as the Environmental Quality Council to serve as the "focal point" of the Administration's efforts to protect the nation's natural resources.

In the first hundred days (the ratios have changed little since then), Mr. Nixon met with his National Security Council 15 times, his Urban Affairs Council nine times, the Republican Congressional leaders nine times, the joint Congressional leadership three times, and the Cabinet four times. These figures, incidentally, give a pretty fair indication of his priorities and preoccupation during the last few months. He is clearly dominated by foreign policy, and so far he prefers to talk to Republicans.

Presidential Methods

Mr. Nixon is reportedly a good moderator at these meetings. He enjoys watching Dr. Moynihan and the conservative Dr. Arthur Burns, his counselor, spar over an issue; and he does not indulge in either the long-winded harangues or the endless, heavy silences of Lyndon Johnson. He is, by all accounts, a good listener and a perceptive questioner, and when he is unsure of something raised in the meeting (e.g., whether malnutrition in fact causes brain damage in children), he will later ask Mr. Haldeman to dispatch a memo to an aide to find the answer (in this case, Dr. Moynihan, who sent a note back saying that the statistical evidence was inconclusive).

When the options are finally in, the President leaves the field of debate and retreats—sometimes to his oval office, more often to the Lincoln sitting room in the family quarters of the East Wing — to make up his mind. His aides are never sure what will emerge.

Mr. Nixon's decision to move ahead with the major assault on hunger, for instance, took most of his staff by surprise. His decision to name Warren Burger as Chief Justice was reportedly shielded from all of his closest advisers including the ubiquitous Mr. Haldeman. When the time came to make a decision on whether or not to alter the 7 per cent investment credit and the 10 per cent surtax, aides were so unsure of Mr. Nixon's mind after a 90-minute meeting on April 23 that they prepared one announcement justifying changes in the credit and surtax, and another announcement justifying no changes at all.

And just this weekend Mr Nixon retreated with a couple of thick notebooks to Key Biscayne, Fla., to examine the options on the welfare system and the supersonic transports. His associates insist they really don't know what he will do.

In short, Mr. Nixon's manner is distinguished by a kind of progressive isolation, beginning at the committee level, where the alternatives are reduced to manageable proportions, and ending with the President alone in the Lincoln sitting room. While there are obvious virtues to such a system, and obvious advantages to Presidential detachment, there are disadvantages as well.

For example, Mr. Nixon tends to concentrate on one issue at a time, and occasionally lets other issues slide. He was so preoccupied with the Burger appointment to the Supreme Court, according to aides, that he was not even aware until the next day of Senator Edward Kennedy's savage attack on his military policy in Vietnam.

Ceding Authority

Moreover, wide areas of authority are ceded to others. Mr. Haldeman, John Ehrlichman and Peter Flanigan (all friends, all close) make important decisions on who goes where in the White House hierarchy, with the result that some men who thought they were close to and respected by the President find themselves in far-off corners of the Executive Office Building or inexplicably on the skids.

Isolation also produces embarrassing episodes. Mr. Nixon has been forced to rescind unwise appointments (Willie Mae Rogers, Dr. Franklin A. Long) that a President more fully engaged in day-to-day business might never have made in the first place. Another President might have taken a more careful sounding of the political opposition on Capitol Hill to the antiballistic missile system.

But good or bad, this is the Nixon style — considerably less rigid than President Eisenhower's yet far more carefully structured than Lyndon Johnson's, and something must be right. Mr. Nixon has negotiated his first four months rather smoothly, given the narrowness of his election mandate, and beyond that he is visibly happier and more relaxed in the job than most of the men whose styles he has chosen not to emulate.

—ROBERT B. SEMPLE Jr.

June 1, 1969

Most in Capital View Mitchell As Man of Pre-eminent Power

By WARREN WEAVER Jr.

Special to The New York Times

WASHINGTON, July 27 — President and Mrs. Lyndon B. Johnson were waiting at the South Portico of the White House one morning last November to welcome the new tenants on their first visit after the Republican election victory.

A black limousine drew up. From it stepped President-elect and Mrs. Richard M. Nixon and, to the surprise of the host and hostess, a dour, dark-browed, full-faced man, hard on the heels of Mr. Nixon.

It came as no surprise, then, when the outgoing President later expressed the opinion that John Newton Mitchell, a campaign manager still a month from being named Attorney General, would be the top man of the political flock that Mr. Nixon would bring to Washington with him.

Nearly nine months have passed, and that view, expressed variously in terms of admiration, awe or naked hostility, has become widespread in the capital. Many cannot agree on what kind of man Mr. Mitchell really is, but most mark him as a figure of pre-eminent power and influence in the new Administration.

Examples of Role

It was Mr. Mitchell, more than any other single adviser, who moved the President toward the nomination of Warren E. Burger as Chief Justice of the Supreme Court. It was Mr. Mitchell who was largely responsible for including the controversial preventive detention concept in the Administration's first crime legislation.

It was the Attorney General who was charged with shaping the President's voting rights proposal to fulfill campaign promises Mr. Nixon had made in the South against regional legislation. It was Mr. Mitchell who set the Administration policy of greater willingness to wiretap—and then reduced the level of surveillance.

Few men are as broadly involved in the activities of the Administration. Presiding over the Justice Department, with its higly sensitive crime, civil rights and civil liberties problems, is only a very small part of what Mr. Mitchell does.

He sits on the Urban Affairs Council, with its multiple concerns in housing and welfare. He is a member of the National Security Council, and his foreign policy discussions with the President go far beyond internal security problems. He receives daily briefings from the Central Intelligence Agency.

Mr. Mitchell talks to the President on the phone once or twice a day on the average, sees him two or three times a week. It is difficult to gauge these things, but there is probably no top-level generalist in the Administration who is continuously closer to Mr. Nixon, except for the White House staff lieutenants like John D. Ehrlichman and H. R. Haldeman.

Most efforts to sum up the Mitchell influence so far have tended to categorize the Attorney General as a major conservative influence on the President, but this is a role that he himself rejects with some asperity.

In the Republican ideological spectrum, Mr. Mitchell puts himself somewhere in the middle, certainly not on the right. To avoid such fuzzy identification, he prefers to call himself a pragmatist, a Nixonian problem-solver unfettered by abstract philosophical considerations.

But there is a clear air of procedural and personal conservatism about the man. His aides describe him as instinctively cautious and slow-moving, rejecting precipitate change, likely to resist efforts to modify a program once it has been worked out.

As a man, he tends to be remote and rather stern in public situations. Testifying at Congressional hearings, he refuses to indulge in the sort of mutual jollying that passes for humor on Capitol Hill. One member of the House Judiciary Committee swears it took three appearances for Mr. Mitchell to smile once.

Some of the men closest to Mr. Mitchell dispute the currently popular view that he lowers the temperatures in any room he enters.

"He is really a very warm and personable fellow," one of them said. "He just isn't a bleeding heart. It's true that he tends to keep people at arm's length, but that's because he likes to play his cards close to his chest."

The Attorney General is not overjoyed that he seems to have been cast as the heavy in the unfolding Nixon drama, but he assumes philosophically that every Administration demands one.

Predictably, reaction to Mr. Mitchell at the Justice Department is mixed. Some of his top associates praise the way he operates the shop like a law firm, throwing out questions to meetings of division heads on the theory that the law is not so specalized that any one of them cannot contribute ideas.

The Attorney General has not made any sweeping personnel changes. He retained three of the eight assistant attorneys general and a number of bureau heads, including the sacrosanct J. Edgar Hoover. Aides estimate there are only about 50 new Republican faces on the staff of 1,000.

At the higher civil service levels, there is some grumbling about secrecy and a lack of communication. One lawyer complained that Administration program bills, like the preventive detention measure for the District of Columbia, were being hatched in private, rather than being fully circulated in the department.

The Mitchell personality seems to have fared better at Justice than elsewhere. One lawyer observed, "He's warm and cuddly compared to Katzenbach."

Sensitive over accusations that the Administration's voting rights and school desegregation programs have been tailored to please the South, Mr. Mitchell denies that any political considerations are weighed at the Justice Department, except perhaps where winning Congressional support may be involved.

But there is no question that the Attorney General is a political adviser to the President, and the role of politician is not one he declines. Although the 1968 Republican campaign was his first official work in the field, his highly specialized law practice actually had given him a good deal of practical background.

In denying that the Administration is developing a "Southern strategy" in office leading up to the 1972 election, the Attorney General likes to argue that there was really no such thing in 1968. All the Nixon forces did, he says, in the words of Barry Goldwater, was to "go hunting where the ducks are."

The Nixon campaign, its manager insists, was formed more by circumstance than conscious plan, with its attention focused where people would vote for a Republican candidate.

Circumstances also make it hard to divorce Mr. Mitchell from politics. A visitor leaving his office the other day found waiting in the anteroom Fred LaRue, the former Republican National Committeeman from Mississippi who played a major role in holding Nixon Southern strength at the 1968 convention.

July 28, 1969

Ehrlichman Gets Major Increase in Powers in Nixon's Shake-up of the White House Staff

By **ROBERT B. SEMPLE J.r**
Special to The New York Times

WASHINGTON, Nov. 5—As the dust settled from yesterday's staff shake-up at the White House, it seemed plain to most observers here that one man had emerged with a major increase in formal powers over the decision-making process in the domestic field: John D. Ehrlichman, the President's 44-year-old counsel.

Under the revised staff arrangement, Mr. Ehrlichman will preside over a newly created domestic affairs staff with powers and duties in the domestic field roughly comparable to those held by Henry A. Kissenger, who runs the National Security Council, in the foreign affairs field.

He and his group will serve as the focal point for domestic policymaking, encouraging the many executive agencies to come forth with ideas and then, through a system of interagency subcommittees, reconciling different points of view and shaping these ideas into actionable proposals for the President.

At the same time, the new arrangement will shift Daniel Patrick Moynihan, the urban affairs adviser, and Bryce N. Harlow, the Congressional relations adviser, to essentially advisory roles, with a broad mandate to devise a coherent long-term strategy for urban and other domestic problems.

But while both men will have direct access to the President, and thus considerable influence of their own, it is Mr. Ehrlichman to whom the President has given control over the day-to-day business of devising specific Administration answers to the problems of the cities, the schools and the environment.

Accordingly, it seemed equally plain to observers here that Mr. Nixon had done the one thing his associates said a year ago he would not do, create a successor to Joseph A. Califano Jr.

Mr. Califano was the young and exceptionally powerful aide who presided over the domestic machinery in Lyndon B. Johnson's White House and with whom most bureaucrats in the executive agencies were forced to deal if they wished to obtain the President's ear.

In the Nixon White House, Mr. Ehrlichman is clearly the man with whom the bureaucrats must henceforth reckon.

This appears to represent a switch in the President's thinking. Mr. Nixon said at the start that he wanted "all of the options . . . all of the alternatives" in every area of policy to reach him undiluted by intermediate selection and judgment.

But he soon learned — as other Presidents before him had learned—that someone has to goad the agencies into action, make judgments about the options that emerge and develop formal proposals for Presidential decision.

Mr. Ehrlichman pointed out yesterday that his chief still believed that the agencies must carry the main burden of program development, but that it was impractical to allow all the options to flow into the White House in disorganized form.

The new arrangement is traceable to the long and divisive internal debate over the President's welfare proposals last summer, which found the President's closest advisers deeply at odds.

Mr. Moynihan and Secretary of Health, Education and Welfare Robert H. Finch stood on one side of the issue; Dr. Arthur F. Burns, whom the President had originally hoped would perform the evaluative and coordinative function now assigned to Mr. Erlichman, stood firmly on the other side.

The President relieved Mr. Moynihan and Dr. Burns of responsibility for staff coordination—leaving them in advocacy roles, where they were more at home anyway—and assigned it to Mr. Ehrlichman.

Mr. Ehrlichman in turn assigned one of his aides, Edward Morgan, to preside over a panel composed of experts from H.E.W., the Budget Bureau, the Labor Department and other agencies. This small group then put together the various components of the plan.

The new arrangements call for the formation of similar "project groups" to study major programs and problems. The groups will consist of key department officials and White House and Budget Bureau personnel and will be supervised by six staffers, most of whom have been working for Mr. Ehrlichman all along.

They are Mr. Morgan, who will supervise welfare and education groups; Egil Krogh Jr., Justice groups; Henry C. Cashen 2d, urban affairs and post office groups; Leonard Garment, civil rights, youth and culture groups; Peter Flanigan, an assistant to the President who will also oversee project groups in the financial field, and John C. Whittaker, former secretary to the Cabinet, who will oversee project groups in natural resources and the environment.

These groups, in turn, will draw not only on the resources of the agencies and Budget Bureau but also on a variety of lesser policymaking units within the White House, including the Urban Affairs Council which Mr. Moynihan headed; the Environmental Quality Council, and the Cabinet Committee on Economic Policy.

There was some thought that Mr. Moynihan's Urban Affairs Council, which has also had some experience with devising programs through interagency subcommittees, might be expanded to give the President a domestic equivalent of the National Security Council.

But this alternative—promoted by some members of the President's Advisory Council on Government Organization—was apparently rejected.

The staff of the council was small and its focus narrow. Its director, Mr. Moynihan, had expressed a desire to devote more of his energies to devising a long-term national urban policy and less to the day-to-day operational duties of the council.

November 6, 1969

Nixon's Presidency: Centralized Control

By JOHN HERBERS
Special to The New York Times

WASHINGTON, March 5—Frederic V. Malek is a 36-year-old self-made millionaire with boyish blue eyes, degrees from West Point and Harvard Business School and a reputation for being a super manager and an effective but restrained hatchet man in the jungles of Washington bureaucracy.

As the new deputy director of the Office of Management and Budget, Mr. Malek has set up a network of men like himself in key positions throughout the department to help President Nixon get control of the permanent government run by 2.5 million civil servants.

Mr. Malek is the prototype of the managerial and business people whom Mr. Nixon has placed in high positions, and the Malek operation is an example of the President's methods as he has gone further than any modern President in trying to shape the bureaucracy to conform to both the style and purposes of the President.

The result is a highly centralized and homogeneous leadership in the executive branch that accelerates a long trend of concentrating more authority and decision-making under the White House umbrella.

Mr. Nixon, by executive order, has put in force the main features of an Administration-wide reorganization plan that Congress had refused to pass. The Nixon order created a super Cabinet devoid of any former elected officials. He has moved into the White House authority over a variety of affairs, such as lobbying and press relations, that had rested in the departments.

Students of government agree that a wayward and stubborn bureaucracy has frustrated the goals of every President and that the President should exercise control. However, fears have been aroused that because of the manner in which the President proceeded, public access to the decision-making processes has been severely curtailed. This comes at a time when the Presidency has become the most powerful instrument of United States Government in history.

The New York Times/March 6, 1973

Thomas E. Cronin, a visiting fellow at the center for the Study of Democratic Institutions, in Santa Barbara, Calif., who has written widely on the Presidency, said in a recent interview that the White House "has become a powerful inner sanctum of government, isolated from traditional, constitutional checks and balances."

Mr. Cronin said it was now common practice for "anonymous, unelected and unratified aides" to take important actions in both foreign and domestic areas "with no semblance of public scrutiny."

There also are complaints from the President's critics that in his massive reorganization he has weakened his system of advisers and Cabinet members. Traditionally, Cabinet posts and other high offices have been held by politicians with diverse constituencies, scholars, innovators and in some instances political hacks, who represented a broad spectrum of the President's party and a sprinkling from the opposition.

In his first term, Mr. Nixon followed this pattern. But now high posts, with rare exceptions, are held by little-known Nixon loyalists who can be dismissed or transferred at will without creating a ripple in public.

Arthur M. Schlesinger Jr., the historian who was an aide to President Kennedy, wrote recently, "In his first term, President Nixon kept his Cabinet at arm's length; and in his second term he has put together what, with one or two exceptions, is the most anonymous Cabinet within memory, a Cabinet of clerks, of compliant and faceless men who stand for nothing, have no independent national position and are guaranteed not to defy Presidential whim."

Drive Called Reform

President Nixon has explained his move against the bureaucracy as a reform effort.

"Americans are fed up with wasteful, muscle-bound government in Washington and are anxious for a change that works," he said Jan. 5. He made the comment in announcing that he was issuing an executive order to place into effect his reorganization proposal that Congress had long ignored.

Even Mr. Nixon's enemies agree that a President must control the bureaucracy to some degree if he is to carry out goals promised in his campaign for election. Every President has acknowledged the frustration of doing so.

President Kennedy once became so discouraged that he told an aide not to abandon a minor project of remodeling Lafayette Park across from the White House, quipping, "Hell, this may be the only thing I'll ever get done"

No one is sure, not even Mr. Malek, how Mr. Nixon's extensive changes will work out. But the desire of Presidents to control the bureaucracy is so great that if Mr. Nixon succeeds, in the opinion of some Government experts, he may well set a precedent that will shape the future of the Presidency.

Nevertheless, the erosion of decision-making from the departments, which are relatively open, to the White House, which is inaccessible to many groups, has been increasing for some time, during the Kennedy and Johnson Administrations, but more rapidly under Mr. Nixon.

Senator's Source Shifts

Senator Ernest F. Hollings, Democrat of South Carolina, said in a 1971 speech, "It used to be that if I had a problem with food stamps, I went to see the Secretary of Agriculture, whose department had jurisdiction over the problem. Not any more, I must go to the White House. If I want the latest on textiles I won't get it from the Secretary of Commerce. I am forced to go to the White House."

This is due partly to the fact that in a more complicated society there are conflicts between the departments that have to be settled at the top. There has to be a referee between them.

But much of the reason is that the White House frequently does not trust the departments, which have constituencies of their own.

Examples of departmental loss of power abound. The Treasury Department, with a competent research staff, has for years been at the forefront of administration innovations on tax legislation. Now, sources say, the department is rarely consulted as high-level policy discussions go on in the White House.

The Office of Management and Budget, a White House agency, recently suspended housing subsidy programs without consulting the Department of Housing and Urban Development. The State Department has been even further removed from foreign policy decisions than under the Johnson and Kennedy Administrations.

As a result, the White House staff, in Mr. Nixon's words, has "grown like topsy." At least 4,000 people were employed on the President's personal staff and in the executive offices at the first of the year, and others there had been borrowed from other agencies.

Big Reduction Planned

President Nixon has said that this figure will soon be reduced to 2,000, but most of the reductions are coming from the Office of Economic Opportunity, which was put directly under the President in 1964 to receive special attention but is now being dismantled.

"Agencies that really amount to entire ministries operate out of there under names the public rarely hears, such as the Office of Telecommunications Policy, [headed by Clay T. Whitehead] which oversees the entire communications industry," an Administration official said.

The White House assistants have a strong influence not only over the executive departments but also over the supposedly independent regulatory agencies in several ways. One example is that the Office of Management and Budget can stop investigations by the agencies simply by reducing their funds.

Miles W. Kirkpatrick, former chairman of the Federal Trade Commission, said that several of his investigations had been eliminated in this way. Senator Lee Metcalf, Democrat of Montana, has introduced legislation to restore budget control to Congress.

In 1968, shortly before Mr. Nixon's election to office, he said, "I want a Government drawn from the broadest possible base—an administration made up of Republicans, Democrats and independents, and drawn from politics, from career government service, from universities, from business, from the professions—one including not only executives and administrators, but scholars and thinkers."

In his first term he complied with that philosophy, appointing a range of executives that included former Michigan Gov. George Romney, a liberal, as Housing Secretary, and former Texas Gov. John B. Connally, a conservative Democrat, as Treasury Secretary.

But some of his appointments caused him problems and frustrated his purposes. Administration sources frequently cite the example of Robert Ball, the Social Security administrator who was dismissed at the end of the first term.

"The President would make a policy and enunciate it," said a close Nixon aide, "but then Ball would go up to Congress, the doors to the committee room would close and he would say what he really thought. He was very persuasive. We couldn't have that."

Difficulty With Hickel

And there were more personal difficulties. Former Alaska Gov. Walter J. Hickel, Mr. Nixon's Secretary of Interior, who was dismissed after several disagreements with the President, wrote a book about his experiences. In his last meeting with Mr. Nixon, Mr. Hickel wrote:

"He repeatedly referred to me as an 'adversary.' Initially I considered that a compliment, because to me an adversary within an organization is a valuable asset. It was only after the President had used the term many times and with a disapproving inflection that I realized he considered an adversary an enemy. I could not understand why he would consider me an enemy."

For his second term, Mr. Nixon has cleaned house of adversaries and policy thwarters. His new high-level appointments come mostly from the business world or from lower Administration posts.

Frederic V. Malek, deputy director, Office of Management and Budget.

The most controversial is that of Roy Ash, former president of Litton Industries, who is now director of the Office of Management and Budget. Because of the enormous policy decisions in that office and the fact that Litton is a Government contractor with cost overruns, Congress is demanding through legislation likely to be enacted that the office be subject to Senate confirmation.

But this is considered largely a symbolic protest. Even if Congress should prevail by overriding the President's expected veto on the issue, the President's power is so great in the selection of assistants that he could simply give Mr. Ash another title and let him perform the same duties, according to authoritative sources outside the Administration.

Foreign policy has increasingly centered on Henry A. Kissinger, who has the title of Presidential assistant for national security affairs but is frequently called the de facto Secretary of State.

"Henry is in foreign policy, outside the President himself, of course," said an Administration official. "When Henry is off on peace negotiations or somewhere and something happens, say in Africa, the State Department just flounders around and waits until he gets in touch. Sometimes things are just put aside. Henry even handles all his own press relations and tells his assistants not to say anything.

"It is the most centralized kind of operation you could devise."

Mr. Malek's operation cuts across virtually the entire executive branch. The pattern has been for the President to pick a trusted White House staff member and appoint him to a higher position in a department or agency—John C. Whitaker as Under Secretary of Interior, for example.

There were conflicting reports on how the operation will work. Some sources said that Mr. Malek, with four or five Assistant Secretaries for management and Budget, would work directly with White House loyalists out in the departments to achieve goals and timetables to see that the President's policies were carried out.

Others, however, said it would mostly involve Mr. Malek and his assistants working with assistant secretaries for management, with full participation of the Secretaries. Nevertheless, the entire operation points to great White House participation in departmental operations, according to several sources, and this is enhanced by the fact that Mr. Malek was formerly the President's talent scout who recruited into government many of the officials involved.

In the past, department heads have frequently generated policies of their own not completely in accord with those of the President.

'Thing of the Past'

"This is a thing of the past now," said a high Nixon aide.

There are other operations of a similar nature, such as the following:

¶The lobbying operation for the executive branch is being reorganized at Mr. Nixon's direction under William E. Timmons, the President's assistant for government relations, to make all of its members more responsive to the White House. Departmental lobbyists in the past have been picked by individual Secretaries and thus have been loyal to the Secretary first and the White House second, particularly if the Secretary does not see eye to eye with the President. Hereafter all Government lobbyists will be picked by the White House team and come directly under its jurisdiction.

¶The public information offices in the executive branch are being more centralized under a White House operation now undergoing revision. It is expected that the operation will be headed by Ronald L. Ziegler, the President's press secretary, with Ken W. Clawson, deputy director of communications for the White House, holding a top position.

Already the practice is for the White House to approve the public information officers in the agencies, insisting in most cases that they be strong on Nixon salesmanship.

The growing White House responsibility has required another layer of overseers to oversee the overseers. Mr. Nixon has brought four officials into the White House as counselors, while permitting them to retain Secretary functions. They are George P. Shultz, Treasury Secretary, for economics, James T. Lynn, Housing and Urban Development Secretary, for community development: Caspar W. Weinberger, Health, Education and Welfare Secretary, for human resources. and Earl L. Butz, Agriculture Secretary, for natural resources.

Among students of government there is less concern about the concentration of power than about the processes of government becoming obscured in the executive offices of the Presidency.

"We know almost everything about Presidents," James McGregor Burns wrote recently. "But we know all too little about the vast gray executive establishment that expands, proliferates, and partly devours the decision-making apparatus of the rest of the Government, behind the pleasantly deceptive 'low profile' of the White House."

March 6, 1973

Finally, A Little Good News

By James Reston

WASHINGTON, Aug. 23—With the appointment of Henry Kissinger as Secretary of State, there is now virtually a whole new Cabinet and top White House staff moving into place here, and what is probably more important, they are bringing new attitudes to their work.

The transition from the old to the new is far from complete. It takes time to master the complexities of the great departments of Government and sort out new personalities and routines in the White House. But something interesting, and maybe even important, is happening here in the aftermath of Watergate.

It is all on the surface so far. The essential policies of the Administration are the same. The defensive and even deceptive arguments are the same. In short, the Administration is backing into the future, and clouding its movements as it goes, but it *is* moving.

The tight and secretive little power center in the White House is gradually dispersing into the departments and agencies. Gen. Alexander Haig, H. R. Haldeman's replacement, Mel Laird, John Ehrlichman's successor as the President's Assistant for Domestic Affairs and Mr. Kissinger, the President's principal adviser on security affairs, are now coming out from behind the White House screen.

After the President's first televised press conference in over a year, General Haig was available to talk to the press about the background of the President's problems. Mr. Kissinger followed with a press conference promising to open things up and be available to questioning by the Congress, the press and the critical ideas and suggestions of the public.

In these melancholy days of contention and confrontation, even if the fundamental questions of the past have not been resolved, these tentative symbols of change, and maybe even of reconciliation, may be even more important than the President's arguments that he was right all along, and if he wasn't, it was somebody else's fault, and anyway, was no worse than what other Presidents did in the past.

Everybody in Washington now, including the President, says we must "learn the lessons of Watergate," and some people have. Most of the new key Cabinet members are showing a new independence, and this is an important lesson.

Vice President Agnew is in deep trouble. He is fighting for his political life, and he is fighting on his own. He is not *asking* the President whether he can have a press conference to argue his case. He is "informing" the White House what he intends to do, and doing it in his own way.

Similarly, the new Attorney General, Elliot Richardson, is not asking the President or the Vice President whether it's all right to inform Mr. Agnew that the Vice President is under investigation for criminal activity, but telling them this is a fact and putting Mr. Agnew on notice.

This causes trouble between the Attorney General and the Vice President, who goes on public television to denounce the leaks out of the Justice Department, but at least the struggles are not being concealed or directed by a White House staff out of the President's control.

These emerging changes of attitudes, assumptions and power centers in Washington may be more important than anything else. After all, it was probably the Administration's mistrust or fear of dissent that led to the centralization of power, the secrecy, the conspiracies and the Watergate tragedies, but at least there is now a change of tactics, if not a change of heart.

The new Nixon team in Washington is now urging the President that he has more to gain by talking out than by hiding out in Camp David or Key Biscayne or San Clemente, that he gains more by facing the reporters than by evading them, and that he will be better served by trusting and liberating his Cabinet and his White House staff than by controlling and intimidating them.

He has either seen this point on his own, or had it imposed on him by his advisers and by his troubles, but in any event, he is no longer in a position to impose his will on a frightened and obedient staff.

His aides, consciously or unconsciously, now seem to be acting on the assumption that they can serve him best by insisting on the powers of their offices, by asserting their independence to tell him the truth, and by offering to leave and tell why if he doesn't like it.

Maybe nothing has changed in policy or the President's arguments about the war or Watergate, but everything has changed in the minds of most of his new aides. They are asking for more freedom. At least some of them are insisting on doing what they think is right, and he seems to have got the point.

This is an important change. The President needs his Cabinet and his staff now more than they need him, and though gradually and grudgingly, he seems to be accommodating himself, as he did to China and Russia, to a new approach to the realities.

CHAPTER 3

Congressional-Executive Relations

The greyest areas of the Constitution are those outlining the boundaries between executive and legislative power. The Founding Fathers were a remarkably sophisticated group of men who were well aware of the dangers of overprecision in a basic charter. Therefore, they contented themselves with defining the roles of the president and the Congress and granting to each some exclusive pieces of authority. Such an arrangement left plenty of room for argument and a large part of America's history has been the story of the struggle for preeminence between the White House and Capitol Hill.

Both sides have had their ups and downs in the course of the struggle. Generally speaking, the most advantageous moves on the president's side have come from the capacity for initiative inherent in a one-man operation. Congress, on the other hand, has relied largely upon its ultimate control over the pursestrings plus its ability to hold widely-publicized investigations. In an overall sense, the American people have probably been best served during those periods when the branches were roughly equal and therefore treated each other with mutual respect.

The past 40 years have been decades of crisis, highly conducive to presidential domination of the scene. People who perceive themselves as in trouble yearn for strong executive leadership; with the exception of Dwight D. Eisenhower, our recent presidents have been more than willing to oblige. Unfortunately, strong executive leadership usually does not accord with the normal processes of political persuasion, and forceful presidents easily fall into the habit of acting without much consultation. Inevitably, this results in policies—such as the effort to sustain South Vietnam—which lack viable political support.

The combination of Vietnam and Watergate was just too much; we have now reached the end of an era of presidential domination. Hopefully, we will not fall into the other extreme of congressional domination. Meanwhile, it is instructive to review those matters over which the executive and the legislative have fought in this century. Perhaps we can get some clues on what to avoid.

GER

Franklin Delano Roosevelt

The New York Times

ROOSEVELT ATTACKED BY SENATOR BACON

Georgian Says to Refuse His Bidding Means Fight for Political Existence.

HE DOMINATES CONGRESS

In House Willett Says He Has Done More to Destroy Business Than Any Man in Our History.

Special to The New York Times.

WASHINGTON, March 18.—In one of the bitterest attacks ever made in the Senate upon the President, Senator Bacon of Georgia to-day announced what he termed the usurpation of legislative power by the White House. He referred immediately to the series of conferences that preceded the drafting of the bill by which the Sherman Anti-Trust law is to be amended.

Although representatives of the executive branches of the Government were present at these conferences, he pointed out, to listen to the suggestions of the agents of special interests, no member of the Senate or the House was invited to participate.

"This usurpation of power by the White House has gone on for years," he said. "It has gone on so unblushingly and so boastingly that we have become accustomed to it."

The Senator read extracts from newspapers, detailing the conferences with the President. He showed that, aside from the Cabinet officers present, the conferrees were representatives of J. P. Morgan & Co., the big railway systems, and steel trust and the labor interests. The bill, he said, was framed by the President and his advisers, but really was dictated by the special interests.

Senator Bacon then read from another newspaper clipping to the effect that the President was about to attempt to force certain legislation through at the present session. He read a list of the bills enumerated, and insisted that it would be a physical impossibility for Congress to consider wisely such a mass of legislation before the early adjournment this year.

"Still we are to be browbeaten into rushing this through," he thundered. "That is, the Senators on that side are to be whipped into line. I saw a cartoon the other day which depicted the President, big stick in hand, putting an extinguisher over some ten or a dozen Senators. I could not recognize the Senators, for only their feet and legs were shown."

The Senator drew a parallel between this situation and that of a foreign country, which he visited last year, and said:

"The Parliament was a Parliament of puppets, completely under the domination of one man, before whose will they had to bow."

Senator Bacon contended that President Roosevelt so far dominated the Congress of the United States that to refuse his bidding meant a fight for political existence.

When he had finished the Senator paused for a moment, and then, addressing the Chair, said:

"Perhaps I should apologize for this arraignment. It may have been imprudent. In fact, I may have said more than I should have said."

Tillman and other Democratic Senators protested against the apology. Tillman was especially wroth.

"It's the truth, isn't it?" he demanded. "Then, why apologize for the truth?"

After a whispered colloquy with other members of his party, Senator Bacon practically withdrew his apology.

"I will admit it may have been imprudent," he said. "Some of my friends do not believe I should apologize to the Senate. What I have charged is true—absolutely true."

No serious attempt was made by the Republicans to defend the President. Practically all sat with the pleased "I've just-eaten-the-canary" expression.

In the House Mr. Willett of New York denounced the President. He insisted that the distressing effects of the panic of 1907 were still being felt.

Mr. Willett charged that President Roosevelt had "done more than all other Presidents and all other public men in the history of the country to shake the confidence of the people in our form of government, and has done more than any one man in our Nation's history to destroy legitimate business and shatter confidence among the people."

March 14, 1908

JUDGE CRITICISES TAFT.

Van Orsdel Objects to President Forcing Legislation on Congress.

Special to The New York Times.

WASHINGTON, March 10.—The President was criticised from an unusual source last evening when in an address to the Bachelor Club here Justice J. A. Van Orsdel of the District Court of Appeals took the President to task for forcing legislation upon Congress.

"I look with alarm on the tendency of the executive branch of the Government to dictate to the legislative branch," declared Justice Van Orsdel, warmly. "It is a new thing in this country, and I do not believe it was intended that the Executive should say to Congress: 'You pass this law or I'll call an extra session and compel you to stay here until you do pass it.'

"I, as a member of the judiciary, may have gone beyond the bounds of propriety in making this criticism, but I am sure that that theory was not the one on which our Government was founded."

March 11, 1911

GOVERNORS CLASH ON THE REFERENDUM

O'Neal of Alabama Stirs First Spring Lake Session with an Attack on Modern Prophets.

WILSON JOINS DEFENDERS

Tries Role of Peacemaker, but Brings Out Vigorous Retort from Southerner —Twenty-one Governors There.

Special to The New York Times.

SPRING LAKE, N. J., Sept. 12.—After a somewhat humdrum reading of papers for several hours the conference of Governors which began its sessions here today took on a lively aspect late this afternoon when the initiative, referendum and recall were brought into the discussion by Gov. Emmett O'Neal of Alabama, who read a paper on "Strengthening the Power of the Executive." He spoke in approval of the tendency in that direction and then denounced the opposite tendency as shown in the movement for direct legislation and the recall. Gov. Woodrow Wilson was one of those who took issue with him on that subject, and the discussion became very warm. To those who defended these new political nostrums Gov. O'Neal retorted that the recall "would concert the public officer into a spineless and servile hireling, stirred by every passing breeze of public opinion, obeying every popular impulse and yielding to every wave of popular passion or prejudice."

In his paper Gov. O'Neal had traced the power of the Executive in our Government from Colonial times to the present, and praised the modern tendency to extend it. Then he said:

"But there is another movement that seems to be gathering strength in certain sections of the Union which tends to weaken rather than strengthen Executive authority, and that is the system of the initiative, referendum, and recall. It is manifest that if the people can frame and enact laws without the aid or the intervention of the Governor or the Legislature, to that extent their control over legislation is destroyed. The Governor has no power to veto or amend a law initiated by the people and adopted by referendum. If the law is in violation of the Constitution, invades vested rights, or destroys individual liberty, the only remedy can be found in the courts; and where the system of recall of Judges prevails, overthrowing as it does the independence of the judiciary, the courts would no longer furnish a bulwark of defense against arbitrary power or the tyranny of the majority, but would degenerate into tribunals organized chiefly to register popular judgment on legal questions."

When Gov. O'Neal made this thrust everybody expected Gov. McGovern of Wisconsin, who has long been one of Senator La Follette's chief lieutenants, to come to the front for them, and they were not disappointed. It would be unfortunate, he said, for the idea to go out that the conference of Governors was opposed to the initiative, referendum, and recall for the reason that they would hamper the Governor. If the extension of the power of the Governor would facilitate his work in carrying out the will of the people, he was in favor of it, but if the object of such an extension was to permit him to defeat the popular will, he should oppose it.

"Don't attempt," he said, "to array the Governor under any conditions against enlightened public opinion."

Wilson as Peacemaker.

Gov. Wilson said an apparent difference of opinion had arisen in the conference which he believed was only apparent.

"It seems to me," he said, "that on the question of the initiative and referendum it is necessary that we carry the analysis a little further than it has been carried. A very important thing, a fundamentally important thing, is the source of the law. Some of the laws that we have are bad laws and they are bad for a reason that there is a suspicion as to their source. The people of the United States want their Governors to be leaders in matters of legislation because they have serious suspicion as to the source of the legislation, and they have a serious distrust of their Legislatures."

Gov. Wilson then cited Great Britain as an example of a country where the Executive undertakes to formulate practically all the legislation for the kingdam, and when the Legislature refuses to follow, the Executive dissolves the Legislature and goes to the people and says: "Will you send us men who will follow us or will you not?" As a consequence, he said, it is the strongest and most directly democratic Government in the world.

"Therefore," he continued, "what I would urge as against the views of Gov. O'Neal is that there is nothing inconsistent between the strengthening of the powers of the Executive and the direct power of the people."

He spoke of the caprice of the majority. "I have known of instances of the caprice of the mob," he said, "but I have never known of any instance where the vote of the pouulation was spoken of as a caprice. I have read of gentlemen speaking recently in distrust of the people and using that old, erroneous phrase, 'mob rule.'

"What is a mob? A mob is a body of people immediately associated with each other, acting under the impulse of passion, but that does not apply to a thousand men in a community in scattered portions casting their ballots.

"I don't believe there is any distrust of the fundamental principles of democracy. I believe we are all democrats if we use a small 'd.' I wish for the salvation of your souls that I could use a large 'D' also. I believe that Gov. O'Neal feels as Gov. McGovern feels, and that we are merely at odds as to the best method of giving expression with reference to that great public opinion upon which all depends."

O'Neal Vigorously Retorts.

Gov. Wilson bowed and sat down. Gov. O'Neal sprang to his feet and shouted the reiteration of his belief.

"I would rather stand with Madison and Hamilton," he said, "than to stand with some modern prophets and some of our Western statesmen."

"The whole purpose of a Constitution," he also said, "is to protect the minority and limit the power of the majority. There has never been a government by the majority without a constitutional limitation on its power that has outlived a generation. Gov. Wilson has overlooked the fact that when I spoke of the caprice of a majority I was speaking of the recall of Judges. When you establish an arbitrary recall of Judges you have instituted mob law in this country. I agree that the British system is a good one, but that is quite different from the initiative and referendum. I believe that if the Legislature will not co-operate with the Governor to carry out the people's will he should have the power to appeal to them to commission other men as legislators, but not to enact laws themselves."

"Then don't you think," asked Gov. Hoke Smith of Georgia, "that it would also be in order for the Legislature to have a chance to bring about the recall of the Governor?"

"If the Governor doesn't carry out the will of the people," replied Gov. O'Neal, "let him try for re-election and he will soon find it out."

What Colorado Did.

"The trouble is," said Gov. John F. Shafroth of Colorado, "that lobbyists swarm in the halls of legislation and the people's will is ignored. The people have voted for certain laws explicitly, and yet they have been defeated year after year in the Legislature. In my own State certain proposals were adopted unanimously by the convention of my party and were largely indoised by the other party, yet the Legislature adjourned without passing one of them.

"What would you do in such a case as that? Is it possible that the people should be helpless? I called a special session just before the time that the members were up for renomination, and they finally passed the initiative and referendum. In the election it was ratified by the voters 3½ to 1, but it had been beaten in the Legislature year after year. I don't believe the people would be willing to give me an increase in power if we as Governors stood remote from them. With the initiative and referendum the corporations will not pay money to men who can't determine legislation and who are not the final arbiters."

"I would like to ask," interjected Gov. Albert W. Gilchrist of Florida, "if it was not the caprice of a majority that foisted all of you into the executive chair?"

The question of strengthening the power of the executive was the subject of a paper by Gov. Edwin L. Norris of Montana, as well as by Gov. O'Neal. Gov Norris advocated giving the Governor power to remove peace and prosecuting officers. The people, he said, held the Governor responsible for the non-execution of laws which he was sworn to enforce, and yet the Governor lacked any power to compel an unwilling Sheriff or District Attorney to enforce them. As the people put the responsibility on the Governor he believed they would willingly give him the power. The Governor was also held responsible for the enactment of legislation that had been promised, and yet he had no power to bring it about. The Governor should have power to submit to the voters legislation he desired enacted. He should submit bills to the Legislature, and if they were not passed then they should be put before the people. He would thus have the power to carry out the pledges on which he was elected. Conversely, the Legislature should have power to submit to the voters a bill passed by it and vetoed by the Governor. In this way legislation desired by the people could not be defeated by a reactionary Governor or by an unwilling Legislature.

"Instead of needing Governors with more powers, we need Governors with more backbone," said Gov. Gilchrist.

Gov. William W. Kitchin of North Carolina seemed to envy the other Governors who complained of lack of power, and drew a pathetic picture of his own position. In his State the Governor has nothing to do with legislation, either to approve or veto it, and no power of appointment or removal, except a few boards governing State institutions.

"One of the questions Mr. Bryan has been asking," he said, "is, 'Are you in favor of the absolute separation of three functions, executive, legislative, and judicial?' If he asked anybody in North Carolina that he would get this answer: 'Yes, because that's the way we have it.' We have no Pardon Board, and the result is that the Governor is overrun with applications. When a Pardon Board is suggested they say: 'Oh, let the Governor attend to that; he has nothing else to do.'"

Gov. John Burke of North Dakota said the purpose of giving the Governor more power was not for his aggrandizement, but to give him the means of serving the people more efficiently.

Gov. Herbert S. Hadley of Missouri said the initiative and referendum would increase the power of the Governor as a leader in many cases and in others they would not. The recall would impair most seriously his function as a leader of thought and action.

Twenty-one Governors Present.

There were twenty-one Governors in attendance to-day and more are expected to-morrow. The presence of several who have been prominently mentioned as Democratic Presidential possibilities, such as Gov. Wilson of New Jersey, Gov. Harmon of Ohio, and Gov. Foss of Massachusetts, led to some pleasantries at the beginning of the conference. The Governors were welcomed by Gov. Wilson and Gov. Joseph M. Carey of Wyoming responded. He warned his fellow Governors against Jersey lightning, but said there was another kind of lightning most of them were on the lookout for.

"I understand," he said, "that there are only two Governors in attendance who are not seeking to be struck by the Presidential lightning. One is the Governor of Wyoming and the other is that Governor who was born outside the United States."

Gov McGovern, when he was introduced as Chairman of the morning session, related a story that he said had been told to him by ex-Gov. Peck of Wisconsin.

"After he had been Governor for some time," he said, "and long enough to reach the conclusion that he was a pretty good Governor, he felt that he had become a victim to the Presidential bee. His feeling was unusual but not unpleasant. One day he happened to eat a sour pickle and found that what was ailing him was only the mumps. He suggested that any others troubled as he was try a pickle."

Gov. Wilson and Mrs. Wilson gave a reception to the other Governors to-night at the State Cottage at Sea Girt. To-morrow, after a session in the morning, they are to go to Fort Hancock, where, by authority of the Secretary of War, the big guns will be fired in their honor. In the evening a business session is to be held to give the Conference of Governors, which was instituted by President Roosevelt in 1908 and met again in Louisville last year, a more detailed and comprehensive organization.

September 13, 1911

WILSON TO READ HIS MESSAGE TO CONGRESS

Breaking a Century's Precedents, He Will Go to the Capitol to Speak in Person.

AN APPEAL TO THE COUNTRY

To be Made by the President if Hostile Senators Block the Tariff Bill.

FIVE SENATORS ARE BALKING

Senate Leaders Want to Put Wool and Sugar in Separate Bill—Congress Gets Measure To-day.

Special to The New York Times.

WASHINGTON, April 6.—To test his belief that the people of the United States demand a sweeping revision of the tariff President Wilson is prepared to go to extraordinary lengths. He has indicated to some of his party friends, it was stated to-night, that if necessary he will make a direct appeal to the people against those Democratic Senators who are suspected of arranging already to fight some of the most important provisions of the general Tariff bill, which will be introduced in the House to-morrow. This appeal, which will be made in a manner never before practised by a President engaged in a contest with Congress, will be used only as a last resort, according to those who know the President's purposes.

And as if this were not enough indication of the Chief Executive's disregard for precedents that hamper accomplishment, it was made known to-night that, President Wilson would on Tuesday go to the Capitol and deliver in person before the Senate and House of Representatives assembled jointly his message outlining the business for which he has called the Congress together in extraordinary session. John Adams was the last President of the United States to take advantage of this Constitutional right, and this was 112 years ago on the eve of giving up the Presidency to Jefferson.

With reference to the possible appeal of the President to the Nation against those, who may, according to his view, be trying to prevent the carrying out of party pledges, enunciated in the Baltimore platform, friends of Mr. Wilson say that he will go to this extreme only in case of a deadlock in the Senate over the tariff. His appeal to the people will be an answer to the challenge that if the President is to dictate tariff legislation in advance of consideration by Congress, the Legislative body might as well be abolished.

The President's friends say that he is not frightened by suggestions that such a course might mean the wrecking of the Democratic Party. In fact he has stated to some of his supporters, it was said, to-night, that he is convinced that the only way to save the Democratic Party, now that it is in complete control of the Government is by redeeming the pledges, made in the Baltimore platform. He purposes to do his share toward insuring that redemption.

Has Studied Tariff Deadlocks.

The President's active participation in the drafting of the Tariff bill and his intention to appeal to the people, if the bill is deadlocked in the Senate, was decided on only after prolonged study. It is said that he reviewed with great care the history of every session of Congress at which tariff legislation was considered. He decided in his own mind what he thought were the mistakes of former Presidents in handling tariff situations in Congress, and planned how he could profit by the errors of his predecessors.

As events are likely to shape themselves, any direct appeal to the people by President Wilson will not come until late in the extra session, certainly not until the bill has passed the House, and some Democratic Senators, enough to deadlock the Senate, have shown unyielding opposition to the proposed changes.

It seems certain that the bill will pass the House substantially as presented to that body by the Ways and Means Committee, and by a decisive majority. There will be a lively protest against some provisions of the bill in the caucus of House Democrats on Tuesday. Several of the Democrats of the committee will probably refuse to abide by the decision of the committee to support the bill as it stands. But the overwhelming Democratic majority assures the passage of the bill by the House.

Message Plan Astounds Legislators.

Announcement of the President's purpose to go to the Capitol on Tuesday to deliver his message before the joint session of Congress caused profound astonishment among Senators and Representatives. There was little criticism of his plan, possibly because they were too startled by the news to give any coherent expression to their views.

Disbelief was expressed in Congressional circles when the report was first circulated that the President would read his message in person to Congress. Direct confirmation of the report was obtained by THE NEW YORK TIMES's correspondent, however, from Secretary Tumulty.

After a consultation with Mr. Wilson, Mr. Tumulty said the President had told him the report was correct. Washington and Adams had delivered their messages in person, the President said, and he thought the practice a dignified way of bringing about closer intimacy between Congress and the Executive.

Leaders of the Senate and House of Representatives are delving into old records to-night to learn the proper course to pursue in connection with the coming visit of the President. The records show that whenever President Washington wanted to deliver an address in person to Congress he would notify the House, before which he would appear, that he intended "to meet and advise" with that body on a specified date.

The leaders of Congress intend, however, to save President Wilson any diffidence he may feel about inviting himself to go in person into the halls of Congress to meet and advise the legislative branch of the Government by having both Houses adopt a resolution asking the President to read his message in person.

Plan for Joint Invitation.

Representative Underwood, the floor leader in the House, will take the initiative in this procedure after the House has organized to-morrow, presenting a concurrent resolution extending the invitation to the President. By the same resolution or a separate one the members of the Senate will be invited to appear in the hall of the House to listen to the address.

No explanation of the reason for the President's revival of the long-abandoned practice is forthcoming other than from Mr. Tumulty. He stated that the President did not intend to make a practice of appearing personally before Congress to read all his messages, but would probably confine himself to the personal delivery of his annual messages at the opening of regular sessions or his messages to extra sessions.

Should the Senate and House follow the precedent established in the days of Washington and Adams, each House will adopt a reply to President Wilson's address, and it will be delivered to him by the Speaker attended by the members of that body and by some member of the Senate selected for the purpose, attended by all his associates.

Jefferson Ended the Custom.

The custom which President Wilson will revive was the cause of great dissension in its time. President Jefferson, founder of the Democratic Party, abandoned it, as he said in a communication to the presiding officers of the two houses, out "of regard to the economy of their time, to their relief from the embarrassment of immediate answers on subjects not yet fully before them, and to the benefits thence resulting to public affairs." It was commonly understood at the time that Jefferson's abandonment of the "President's speech" was part of his plan to restoring Democratic simplicity in the Government.

The President's speech, as it obtained under Washington and Adams, was a serious affair, and in Adams's administration it caused an upheaval in the House. The custom was for the President to inform the houses that he would meet with them at a time mentioned. On such occasions, accompanied sometimes by his Secretary, and sometimes by his entire Cabinet, the President took the place of the presiding officer of the body, receiving him, and the two presiding officers sat beside him.

The inconvenience to which Jefferson referred had chiefly to do with the "answers to the speech," which both houses made after deliberation. The answers were delivered separately to the President, each house proceeding in a body to the President's residence. During the Adams Administration Matthew Lyons, a Jeffersonian Representative from Vermont, refused to march in the procession to acknowledge President Adams's speech, and the Federalists in the House assailed him with startling frankness, a resolution being offered calling for his expulsion as a "diabolical personage."

The Lyons incident is thought to have had much to do with Mr. Jefferson's decision not to follow the precedent set by Washington and Adams. In his letter to the presiding officers of Congress, announcing his intention to send a "message in writing," he added that he would follow that custom for the rest of his term. The custom has been followed by succeeding Presidents ever since.

Republicans are laughing to-night over the possibility of formal replies to the President's speech and the attendance there would be for a procession of either chamber from the Capitol to the White House to thank the President for his remarks.

The President's speech will be on the tariff and it is suggested that it will certainly be August before an "answer" can be agreed upon. The seat of government was not in Washington when "President's speeches" were in vogue. A walk to the White House from the Capitol would probably be longer than the processions demanded of Congressmen to the President's house, in what were then the small towns of Philadelphia and New York.

The strong position President Wilson has assumed in the conduct of foreign affairs has raised the interesting question whether the President will use his undoubted prerogative to discuss treaties with the Senate in its executive sessions behind closed doors.

Washington was the only President who ever did that and his experiences on two days decided him not to repeat the occasion. He simply informed the Senate on Aug. 21, 1789, that on the next day he would meet to advise with them concerning an Indian treaty. That he did, being received under the rules as the "Head of the Senate," though occupying a seat on the floor. The tradition is that he liked so little the cross-questioning to which he was subjected that when he left the chamber after the second session, he muttered to a member of his Cabinet:

"I've been to the Senate, and I'll be d—— if I ever go there again."

While no President since Adams has addressed either house, or as far as the records show, visited the floors of either house while in session, both Grant and Lincoln were familiar figures at the Capitol. Grant confined his visits to the room of Speaker Blaine, a personal friend. But Lincoln, in the stress of war legislation, occupied the President's room and conferred at close range with his friends in the Senate.

April 7, 1913

FEDERAL LEADERSHIP.

President WILSON is making a determined effort to establish an effective leadership of his party in Congress. With the means he employs or contemplates, or with the use he may make of his leadership if he secures it, we are not now concerned. But it is worth while pointing out that our legislative system has long suffered for something of the sort, has lacked responsible guidance, has become clumsy, inert, and confused, and has been exposed to serious errors in times of excitement. It is to be noted, also, that the experiment of Executive leadership has been undertaken, in differing spirit, by two of our recent Presidents.

Mr. MCKINLEY, in his first term, lived up very faithfully to the old notion of the relations of a President to his party. He tried to keep his party united, and when he could not quite do that he took what seemed to him the stronger side. But in the few months of his second term that were permitted to him his policy underwent a significant change. In his last public utterance he showed that he had done what he urged his party to do—he had turned his face toward the future. Had he lived, there is no doubt that he would have used all his powers of persuasion and his rare skill as a politician to bring his party into line with what he saw to be the steady advance of public sentiment toward the emancipation of business and industry from the outgrown restraint and interference of the tariff. The bullet of a crazy anarchist blocked that change and brought into the Executive office a man far more bent on leadership than any of his predecessors, and on leadership of a different sort from that of the patient and unselfish McKINLEY.

Mr. ROOSEVELT abandoned without hesitation the aim of commercial emancipation which Mr. McKINLEY cherished, and turned his energies toward a leadership which depended for its success mainly on its appeal to popular feeling. He did not neglect—far from it—the use of influence upon Congress, but he found that method tedious and not as pleasing to his temperament as the arousing of popular excitement centred on his own personality. The net result was the disorganization of his party in Congress and its utter demoralization in the country at large. The orderly advance which Mr. McKINLEY had undertaken to guide was turned into a wild scramble, a free fight raging around his personal banner. It is idle to speculate what may be the ultimate outcome, for Mr. ROOSEVELT is a man of large, though not varied, resource and of tireless energy; but for the present, not yet a year from the close of his whirling campaign, his following seems in the process of progressive dwindling. Certainly his experiment in Executive leadership has not left the situation in Congress improved, has contributed nothing to the orderly evolution of popular representative government. Quite the contrary.

Mr. WILSON, we think, sees the problem and has his own ideas as to how it shall be solved. Apparently his mind is fixed, though not narrowly, on the British system, so clearly described by Professor, now President, LOWELL, in which the initiation of all material legislation, as well as its guidance through the Legislature, is in the hands of the Executive. That system has very great advantages, as it has been worked out through centuries of experience. But its advantages depend largely on a permanent machinery for the preparation of bills and upon the direct presence and activity of the members of the Ministry in the two houses of Parliament. The latter we have not, and can hardly get without a radical change in the Constitution. The former we could adopt, but the task would be exceedingly difficult. Mr. WILSON, it seems, is inclined not to wait for it, but to do what he can to guide and influence Congress through consultation with committee leaders and, when occasion requires, with leaders, or would-be leaders, in the party caucus. This he supplements in a significant fashion by his policy of personal appearance in the Hall of Congress to lay before its members, not so much his specific recommendations but the general considerations on which they are based.

It is an important and intensely interesting experiment. It is too soon, of course, to predict its outcome. So far it has worked better than could have been expected. For one thing, it has made the President in some respects more conservative than strictly logical interpretation of some of his earlier utterances led the country to expect, though by no means so conservative as still earlier utterances indicated that he then was. It is to be remembered, also, that in this big game he is, in a sense, playing a lone hand. He has no single strong man in his Cabinet to aid him, and the strongest is there mainly to keep him from opposition.

August 4, 1913

HARDING DEFENDS SENATE AS SAVING OUR NATIONALITY

He Warmly Commends Its Record in Curbing Executive "Arrogation of Power."

WILL TRUST IT, IF ELECTED

Prefers the Advice of "96 Leading Men of the Republic" to That of Party Bosses.

MEETS OHIO LEGISLATORS

Candidate Also Makes Front Porch Speech to Forty Veterans of the Civil War.

Special to The New York Times.

MARION, Ohio, Aug. 19.—The safeguards of the Senate exercising its constitutional authority insure the security of America, Senator Harding said to a front porch pilgrimage of past and present members of the Ohio Legislature this afternoon.

In the longest and most vigorous utterance he has made since his acceptance speech, the Republican Presidential candidate, unmoved by Governor Cox's accusations that he was backed by a "Senate ring," launched into an exhaustive defense of the Senate, its powers, privileges and procedure. Mr. Harding was in a defiant mood and made his points with vigorous gestures.

His nearest answer to recent attacks was a reference to cartoon, editorial and platform suggestions "that in case of a Republican victory the incoming President proposes to permit the Senate to have some say in determining the policy of Government."

The Senator paused, drew himself together and then said with considerable force:

"I gladly proclaim all these suggestions to be literally correct.

"I rejoice that the United States Senate is functioning again. We need it to save America," and he promised that a Republican Administration would allow "ninety-six leading men of the Republic to have something to say about foreign relations as the Constitution contemplates."

Again, with an appearance of defiant emphasis, he said:

"I would rather have the counsel of the Senate than of all the political bosses of any party in America."

"Momentary clamor" about eliminating the Senate from responsibility, Senator Harding was inclined to ascribe either to imported ideas from the Paris Peace Conference or to a "reflex of mob mentality which has broken out in revolution in various parts of Europe."

Charges Ignorance by Critics.

Senator Harding opened his address by referring to his experiences in the Ohio Legislature. He said:

"For a vast majority of our public men the General Assembly has been the training ground for public service. Probably in no State in all the Union has the General Assembly been more jealous of its powers than has our own Ohio Legislature.

"Not a few of the most progressive and effective reforms brought about in the State of Ohio had their origin in the General Assembly, quite without recommendation or influence on the part of the Executive, and all our boasted progression has come from the hands of the General Assembly.

"Much is said from time to time concerning the progressive policies of the State of Ohio, and very frequently credit has been unduly claimed by the Executive who happened to be in power at the time the reforms were registered. As a mere matter of justice, the fact ought to be stated that most of the reforms have come through the leadership of House and Senate.

"A Republican General Assembly, with an Executive quite without sympathy with its general program, perfected the Workmen's Compensation act and gave to the workmen of the State probably the most nearly ideal law of any State in the Union.

"Some of us have been witnesses to the work of the Federal Senate during the last five years, and I confess amazement at the ignorance of some who cry out against the Senate, or the contempt of others for the Senate's very proper and constitutional part in Federal Government. In our own State it has been the practice, though not without exception, to send our most eminent men to the United States Senate. In easy memory, there were Sherman and Garfiled and Thurman and Pendleton and Hanna and Foraker.

"I am not disparaging the House of Congress. Indeed, I could entertain no such thought. There has ever been genius and statesmanship, and high ability and lofty purpose in the membership of that body, but with rare exceptions, like that of Reed and Cannon and McKinley and Giddings, the House was ever the training school for eminent activities in the Senate.

"I do not hesitate to say that the Senate saved American nationality in 1919 and 1920, when the Executive proposed to surrender it. The Senate preserved our independence of action when the Executive insisted that a foreign council should decide our future place in the activities of the world and call us to war and our destiny.

"It has become quite the fashion among unheeding partisans of Democratic faith to cry out against the Senate and the part it plays in the Federal Government. One might as well proclaim the Constitution a fraud. The Senate is in reality the security of stable, popular government. Many measures must of necessity originate in the House of Congress. Its members come from the people every two years. Sometimes the measures proposed are the ready reflex of the popular sentiment of the hour.

"I participated in a Senate session that appropriated $600,000,000 in twenty minutes for aircraft, which was turned over to an incompetent administration that sent hardly an airplane to the fighting front. The Senate has never failed the country in an hour of great importance, but it has saved to the country the inheritance for which heroes perished and for which the supreme sacrifices of the Republic were made.

"In cartoon, in solemn editorial, in many utterances on the platform, it has been suggested that in case of a Republican victory the incoming President proposed to permit the Senate to have some say in determining the policy of the Government. I gladly proclaim all these suggestions to be literally correct.

"I rejoice that the United States Senate is functioning again. We need it to save America. It submerged itself for the period of the war and surrendered to the Executive because we wanted to marshal all of our forces and resources under one supreme authority, but we are at peace today, actual peace, though not formally proclaimed, and we need the restoration of a constitutional Government quite as much as we need the restoration of the stable ways of peace.

"If a Republican Administration is chosen next November, you can be very certain that the Senate, theoretically, if not actually, composed of ninety-six leading men of the Republic, will have something to say about the foreign relations as the Constitution contemplates.

"There was exceptional wisdom in the fathers providing that the Senate must sanction by a two-thirds vote every foreign covenant. The early patriots were not content that a mere majority control, which might be wholly partisan, should give to the Executive the right to enter into treaties with foreign nations. A mere majority might surrender to the personality or to the partisan aims of an Executive who happened to be in political accord, but there could be no possibility of a hasty decision when two-thirds of the Senate must give its consent. The League covenant was written and negotiated in the mistaken belief that a majority could not even amend.

"In the two-thirds vote to ratify was the supreme wisdom of the founders, because in all the previous history of the world the conflicts between nations usually had their beginning in the ambition of the ruling head of Government.

Prefers Senate Advice to Bosses.

"Still another safeguard was provided by making it necessary for all appropriations to originate in the Lower House of Congress. I do not know that there is an instance in our history where the House has declined to appropriate money to make good a contract between our own and any foreign Government, but literally, and constitutionally, the House has the power to defeat the fulfillment of any compact which involves any expenditure. There has been no failure on the part of the House, because that body joins the Senate in the abiding policy of committing this republic to fidelity of contract. If we failed to keep any covenant we should be held in contempt throughout the world.

"This thought may well be applied to the proposal that this republic can subscribe to Article X. and enter into the League of Nations and submit to the rule of a Council of Foreign Powers, on the theory that only Congress can make the declaration of war. It is true that only Congress can make the declaration, just as it is true that only Congress can make an appropriation of money to carry out a covenant with a foreign power, but if this nation agrees to accept the decision of a foreign council, then we should be guilty of a bad faith, utterly unbecoming of this republic, if Congress did not keep the compact and provide for the warfare which the Foreign Council has ordered. I would think it much better to hold aloof from international relationship than stamp that relationship with perfidy from the very beginning. If the obligation is one of contract, we will keep it; if it is a moral obligation, we must keep it.

"I want America to understand that a Republican Administration stands unqualifiedly, avowedly and proudly for constitutional Government with the recognized and sustained powers of the legislative and judicial branches of the Government as well as that of the executive.

"I want members of the House to feel themselves a part of the Republican Administration, seeking to serve the interests of all the people of our common country. I want members of the Senate to understand, and the public to know, that the Senate has its functions to perform, in making good the plight of faith in the Republican platform and the fulfillment of promises to the American people.

"I had rather have the counsel of the Senate than all the political bosses in any part of America. Under the Constitution, the Senate must advise and consent to all important appointments made by the Executive. I don't think we have lived up to the Constitution in this matter in recent years.

"The tendency has been for the Executive to arrogate to himself all the powers of Government. Maybe it is old-fashioned to get back to the Constitution, but I can well believe it will be a wholesome change from the conditions we are experiencing at the present time.

Explains Party Sponsorship.

"I have said something heretofore about party sponsorship in government. I do not think any intelligent person can have misconstrued my meaning. When I speak of party sponsorship I mean that sponsorship which belongs to a political party for the determination of policies and the fixing of programs for the highest service to the American people. I want to have done with personal government in this country. I want to put an end to autocracy, which has been reared in the name of democracy. I want a Government of laws rather than of men.

"I want representative popular government in fact, not merely in name. I want an end to dictation in America and the resumption of the rule of dependable public opinion, uttered through the representatives of the people chosen for that explicit purpose.

"There has been a fevered tendency of humanity in recent years to completely alter everything which has gone before. We have that new cult in American politics which proclaims everything that is, is bad, and suggests that everything that is to be will be divine.

"We had a period of popular resentment of the existence of our courts and for a time there was a suggestion that we should submit their decisions to popular sanction, else they should not abide. There isn't very much choice between venomous assault on the integrity of the courts and the momentary clamor about eliminating the Senate from the responsibility in Federal Government.

"I do not know whether the idea is one imported from the Peace Council at Paris, or whether it is a reflex of the mob mentality which has broken out in revolution in various places in Europe. Our business is to hold America stable. Our task is to preserve popular, representative constitutional government in America.

"The particular task of the Republican Party is to appeal to the confidence of the people of this Republic and to assure them that if we are returned to power we mean to restore the exercise of the fullness of rights to the various branches of the Government, and not make America the pawn of an individual or the plaything of a party, or the plunder of the profiteers, who were developed under the rule of that party which now inveighs most loudly against them.

"Americans want the assurance of tranquillity and safety. They want to dwell in peace at home and know only friendly relations with all our neighbors throughout the world. They want a fair chance for every man and woman in this Republic, and they want that fair chance amid conditions which promise that men may achieve and be rewarded as they merit it. No one worth while in America wants the adoption of anything approximating the rule of ruin in Russia, or the impractical things of the well-meaning dreamer at home."

Greets Civil War Veterans.

Forty grizzled civil war veterans, each wearing a badge inscribed "Hardin County Soldiers '61 to '65" climbed the front porch to meet Senator Harding this morning.

"If I am elected President of the United States, and it is within my power, there will never be a surrender of that which you have handed down to the generation of today," Senator Harding told the veterans.

"You didn't enter the war to free the slave, although that was a becoming idea. You didn't go to war because you hated any group in the South or to establish any new conception of justice, but you entered the conflict because you found the Union was threatened; you went to save the Union and nationality.

"There has been a variety of opinions as to why your grandsons went to war. Your sons went to war with Spain for humanity. Some have said that your grandsons went to war for democracy and some that they went forth to insure that there would be no more wars in the future. If we went to war for democracy, shouldn't we have gone in when it first started? And if we went to war to insure that there would be no more wars, shouldn't we have gone in before so many millions had been sacrificed?

The simple truth is that your grandsons went to war when Congress made the declaration because our nationality and rights had been threatened. Then it was possible to call the sons of America to battle."

PRESIDENT'S OUSTER POWER WITHOUT SENATE CONSENT UPHELD BY SUPREME COURT

HISTORIC POINT SETTLED

Decision Ends Dispute Which Started in the First Congress.

BENCH DIVIDES BY 6 TO 3

Taft Gives Majority Ruling Against Oregon Postmaster Removed by Wilson.

FIRM DISSENT IS ENTERED

'Revolutionary,' Says McReynolds—Holmes and Brandeis See Executive Power Widened.

Special to The New York Times.

WASHINGTON, Oct. 25.—In a decision on a constitutional question of great moment that has been in controversy since the foundation of the Government and regarded by lawyers as one of the most important judicial interpretations in many years, the United States Supreme Court today through Chief Justice Taft upheld the President in the exclusive power to remove executive officers from their positions.

The majority decision and the dissenting opinions comprise a formidable document of more than 50,000 words, of which the prevailing opinion is stated in some 24,000 words, and the dissenting opinion of Justice McReynolds in more than 20,000. The dissenting opinions of Justices Holmes and Brandeis are considerably shorter.

The decision was returned in the famous Myers postmastership case arising in Oregon and was determined by a vote of 6 to 3. The Court ruled that the President—in this instance the late President Wilson—had authority to dismiss Myers irrespective of the act of 1876, which provided for removal of the first three classes of postmasters "by and with the advice and consent of the Senate."

The decision rendered the act of 1876 void and likewise invalidated other statutes which tended to curtail the power of the President to order removals from office.

Three members of the court-Associate Justices McReynolds, Holmes and Brandeis—dissented from the conclusions of the majority. Justice McReynolds criticized the majority opinion as "revolutionary." He declared the effect of the decision would be to vest the President with authority to make removals which formerly could be effected only for malfeasance in office.

In announcing his dissent from the bench he departed from his text to say that "we now have a foolish or unwise Controller General," and he indicated plainly that, in his opinion, that official, in the light of today's judgment, would not long remain at his post despite the language of the budget act giving him a fifteen-year tenure.

Myers Sued for Back Pay.

The Myers case came to the high court on appeal from a judgment of the Court of Claims. Frank S. Myers, Postmaster at Portland, was ordered removed by executive order dated Feb. 3, 1920. He asserted the illegality of the order, refused to submit and was summarily ejected. He sued in the Court of Claims for back salary, lost his case there and then took an appeal to the Supreme Court.

The importance attached to the issues involved was evidenced by the action of the Chief Justice in naming Senator George Wharton Pepper of Pennsylvania to make an argument as a "friend of the court." Mr. Pepper contended that removals from office could not be made without the consent of the Senate, basing his argument on constitutional and statutory grounds.

James M. Beck, then Solicitor General of the United States, upheld the executive prerogative to remove, and the Court's decision was regarded as a notable court victory for Mr. Beck.

Today's decision is not expected to affect the vast army of general employes of the United States. It is held to apply practically only to those whose nominations are transmitted to the Senate by the President.

Suggestion was made in the dissenting opinions of Justices McReynolds and Brandeis that today's decision ran counter to that of the Supreme Court in the case of Marbury vs. Madison in the early days of the Republic and in direct conflict with many laws of Congress.

In the majority opinion, which was concurred in by Associate Justices Butler, Sanford, Stone, Vandevanter and Sutherland, as well as the Chief Justice, it was held that the power of removal was inherent in the Executive and that it was necessary for effective administration of his office.

Justice McReynolds's dissent, which was almost as elaborate as the 24,000-word opinion of the majority, was one of the most vigorous in tone heard in the Supreme Court in some years.

Decision a Landmark, Says Beck.

Mr. Beck tonight declared today's decision "as a landmark in constitutional law." He said:

"I naturally am much gratified at the result. The decision of the court ends a controversy which has continued from the beginning of the Government. Almost the first question that the first Congress of the United States discussed was the question that is now decided. In the intervening 135 years the question has constantly arisen in the courts. The question was of such delicacy that courts naturally avoided a decision until it became imperatively necessary.

"It has now been decided, and the decision is in accord with that reached in the first Congress of the United States, when, by a majority in the House and a tie vote in the Senate, it was decided in favor of the Presidential prerogative. Any other decision would have disturbed the equilibrium of our Government, and would have made Congress almost omnipotent, for it is obvious, from the practical standpoint, that if the President could not remove any official of the Government without the consent of the Senate, the executive power of the President would be, in a practical sense, reduced to a shadow.

"One thing is clear, that this notable decision is likely to be a landmark in constitutional law for many years to come, and both majority and minority opinions are worthy of the best traditions of that great tribunal and of the magnitude of the question that has now been authoritatively settled."

Majority Opinion of the Court.

The majority opinion of the court read by Chief Justice Taft, in part, follows:

"A veto by the Senate—a part of the legislative branch of the Government—upon removals is a much greater limitation upon the executive branch and a much more serious blending of the legislative with the executive than a rejection of a proposed appointment. It is not to be implied. The rejection of a nominee of the President for a particular office does not greatly embarrass him in the conscientious discharge of his high duties in the selection of those who are to aid him, because the President usually has an ample field from which to select for office, according to his preference, competent and capable men.

"The Senate has full power to reject newly proposed appointees whenever the President shall remove the incumbents. Such a check enables the Senate to prevent the filling of offices with bad or incompetent men or with those against whom there is tenable objection.

"The power to prevent the removal of an officer who has served under the President is different from the authority to consent to or reject his appointment. When a nomination is made, it may be presumed that the Senate is, or may become, as well advised as to the fitness of the nominee as the President, but in the nature of things the defects in ability or intelligence or loyalty in the administration of the laws of one who has served as an officer under the President are facts as to which the President or his trusted subordinates must be better informed than the Senate, and the power to remove him may, therefore, be regarded as confined, for very sound and practical reasons, to the governmental authority which has administrative control.

"The power of removal is incident to the power of appointment, not to the power of advising and consenting to appointment, and when the grant of the executive power is enforced by the express mandate to take care that the laws be faithfully executed, it emphasizes the necessity for including within the executive power as conferred the exclusive power of removal. * * *

Cites Constitutional Provision.

"The constitutional construction that excludes Congress from legislative power to provide for the removal of superior officers finds support in the second section of Article II. By it the appointment of all officers, whether superior or inferior, by the President is declared to be subject to the advice and consent of the Senate.

"In the absence of any specific provision to the contrary the power of appointment to the executive office carries with it, as a necessary incident, the power of removal. Whether the Senate must concur in the removal is aside from the point we now are considering. That point is that by the specific constitutional provision for appointment of executive officers, with its necessary incident of removal, the power of appointment and removal is clearly provided for by the Constitution, and the legislative power of Congress in repect to both is excluded save by the specific exception as to inferior officers in the clause that follows:

" 'But the Congress may by law vest the appointment of such inferior officers as they think proper in the President alone, in the courts of law, or in the heads of departments.'

"These words, it has been held by this court, give to Congress the power to limit and regulate removal of such inferior officers by heads of departments when it exercises its constitutional power to lodge the power of appointment with them. Here then is an express provision introduced in words of exception for the exercise by Congress of legislative power in the matter of appointments and removals in the case of inferior legislative officers.

"The phrase 'But Congress may by law vest' is equivalent to 'Excepting that Congress may by law vest.' By the plainest implication it excludes Congressional dealings with appointments or removals of executive officers not falling within the exception and leaves unaffected the executive power of the President to appoint and remove them.

Contrary to Framers' Intent.

"A reference of the whole power of removal to general legislation by Congress is quite out of keeping with the plan of government devised by the framers of the Constitution. It could never have been intended to leave to Congress unlimited discretion to vary fundamentally the operation of the great independent executive branch of government and thus the most seriously to weaken it. It would be a delegation by the convention to Congress of the function of defining the primary boundaries of another of the three great divisions of government.

"The inclusion of removals of executive officers in the executive power vested in the President by Article II, according to its usual definition, and the implication of his power of removal of such officers from the provision of Section 2 expressly recognizing in him the power of their appointment, are a much more natural and appropriate source of the removing power.

"It is reasonable to suppose also that had it been intended to give to Congress power to regulate or control removals in the manner suggested, it would have been included among the specifically enumerated legislative powers in Article I, or in the specified limitations on the executive power in Article II.

"The difference between the grant of executive power under Article I to Congress, which is limited to powers therein enumerated, and the mere general grant of the executive power to the President under Article II is significant. The fact that the executive power is given in general terms strengthened by specific terms where emphasis is appropriate and limited by direct expressions where limitation is needed, and that no express limit is placed on the power of removal by the executive is a convincing indication that none was intended.

Power Over Qualifications.

"It is argued that the denial of the legislative power to regulate removals in some way involves the denial power to prescribe qualifications office, or reasonable classificatio[illegible] for promotion, and yet that has been often exercised. We see no conflict between the latter power and that of appointment and removal, provided, of course, that the qualifications do not so limit selection and so trench upon executive choice as to be in effect legislative designation.

"The duties of the heads of departments and bureaus in which the discretion of the President is exercised and which we have described are the most important in the whole field of executive action of the Government.

"There is nothing in the Constitution which permits a distinction between the removal of the head of a department or a bureau, when he discharges a political duty of the President or exercises his discretion, and the removal of executive officers engaged in the discharge of their other normal duties. The imperative reasons requiring an unrestricted power to remove the most important of his subordinates in their most important duties must, therefore, control the interpretation of the Constitution as to all appointed by him.

"But this is not to say that there are not strong reasons why the President should have a like power to remove his appointees charged with other duties than those above described.

"The ordinary duties of officers prescribed by statute come under the general administrative control of the President by virtue of the general grant to him of the executive power, and he may properly supervise and guide their construction of the statutes under which they act in order to secure that unitary and uniform legislation of the laws which Article II of the Constitution evidently contemplated in investing general executive power in the President alone.

"Laws are often passed with specific provision for the adoption of regulations by a department or bureau head to make the law workable and effective. The ability and judgment manifested by the officials thus empowered, as well as his energy and stimulation of his subordinates, are subjects which the President must consider and supervise in his administrative control.

Some Cases Quasi Judicial.

"Finding such officers to be negligent and inefficient, the President should have the power to remove them. Of course, there may be duties so peculiarly and specifically committed to the discretion of a particular officer as to raise a question whether the President may overrule or revise the officer's interpretation of his statutory duty in a particular instance. Then there may be duties of quasi-judicial character imposed on executive officers and members of executive tribunals where decisions after hearing affect interests of individuals, the discharge of which the President cannot in a particular case properly influence or control.

"But even in such a case he may consider the decision after its rendition as a reason for removing the officer, on the ground that the discretion regularly entrusted to that officer by statute has not been on the whole intelligently or wisely exercised, otherwise he does not discharge his own constitutional duty of seeing that the laws be faithfully executed.

"We have devoted much space to this discussion and decision of the question of the Presidential power of removal in the first Congress, not because a Congressional conclusion on a constitutional issue is conclusive, but, first, because of our agreement with the reasons upon which it was avowedly based; second, because this was the decision of the first Congress on a question of primary importance in the organization of the Government made within two years after the Constitutional Convention and within a much shorter time after its ratification, and third, because that Congress numbered among its leaders those who had been members of the convention.

"It must necessarily constitute a precedent upon which many future laws supplying the machinery of the new Government would be based and would promptly evoke dissent and departure in future Congresses. It would come at once before the executive branch of the Government for compliance and might well be brought before the judicial branch for a test of its validity. As we shall see, it was soon accepted as a final decision of the questions by all branches of the Government.

"It was, of course, to be expected that the decision would be received by lawyers and jurists with something of the same division of opinion as that manifested in Congress, and doubts were often expressed as to its correctness. But the acquiescence which was promptly accorded it after a few years was universally recognized.

Recalls Hamilton Case.

"A typical case of such acquiescence was that of Alexander Hamilton. In the discussion in the House of Representatives in 1789, Mr. White and others cited the opinion of Mr. Hamilton in respect to the necessity for the consent of the Senate to the removals by the President before they should be effective. * * *. Occasionally we find that Congress thought it wiser to make express what would have been understood.

"Thus in the Judiciary act of 1789, formulated by a Senate committee, of which Oliver Ellsworth was Chairman, which was presumably engaged in drafting the measure during the Congressional debate over removals, and which became the law a month later on Sept. 24, we find it provided in Section 27 (1 Stat. 87, C 20), 'That a marshal shall be appointed in and for each district for the term of four years, but shall be removable at pleasure, whose duty it shall be to attend the district and circuit courts.'

"Section 35 of the same act provided for the appointment of an attorney for the United States to prosecute crimes and conduct civil actions on behalf of the United States, but nothing was said as to his term of office or of his removal. The difference in the two cases was evidently to avoid any inference from the fixing of the term that a conflict with the legislative decision of 1789 was intended.

"In the act of May 15, 1820, Congress provided that thereafter all District Attorneys, Collectors of Customs, naval officers and surveyors of the Customs, navy agents, receivers of public moneys for land, registers of the land office, paymasters in the army, the Apothecary General, the Assistant Apothecaries General, and the Commissary General of Purchases, to be appointed under the laws of the United States, shall be appointed for the term of four years, but shall be removable from office at pleasure.

Points to Previous Decision.

"It is agreed that these express provisions for removal at pleasure indicate that without them no such power would exist in the President. We can not accede to this view. Indeed, the conclusion that they were adopted to show conformity to the legislative decision of 1789 is authoritatively settled by a specific decision of this court.

"In the Parson's case, the exact question which the court had to decide was whether under Section 769 of the revised statutes, providing that District Attorneys should be appointed fo[r a] term of four years, and their c[o]mmissions should cease and expire [at] the expiration of four years from their respective dates, the appellant, having been removed by the President from his office as District Attorney before the end of his term, could recover his salary for the remainder of the term.

"If the President had no power of removal, then he could recover.

"The court held that under that section the President did have the power of removal because of the derivation of the section from the act of 1820, above quoted. In Section 769 the specific provision of the act of 1820 that the officers should be removable from office at pleasure was omitted. This court held that the section should be construed as having been passed in the light of the acquiescence of Congress in the decision of 1789, and therefore included the power of removal by the President, even though the clause for removal was omitted.

"This reasoning was essential to the conclusion reached and makes the construction by this court of the act of 1820 authoritative.

"It is said that for forty years or more, postmasters were all by law appointed by the Postmaster General. This was because Congress under the excepting clause so provided, but thereafter Congress required certain classes of them to be, as they now are, appointed by the President with the consent of the Senate.

"This is an indication that Congress deemed appointment by the President with the consent of the Senate essential to the public welfare, and until it is willing to vest their appointment in the head of the department, they will be subject to removal by the President alone and any legislation to the contrary must fall as in conflict with the Constitution.

"Summing up, then, the facts as to acquiescence by all branches of the Government in the legislative decision of 1789 as to executive officers, whether superior or inferior, we find that from 1789 until 1863, a period of seventy-four years, there was no act of Congress, no executive act, and no decision of this court at variance with the declaration of the first Congress. But there was, as we have seen, clear affirmative recognition of it by each branch of the Government."

Says Construction Is Fixed.

In conclusion Chief Justice Taft said:

"This Court has repeatedly laid down the principle that a contemporaneous legislative exposition of the Constitution, when the founders of our Government and framers of our Constitution, were actively participating in public affairs, acquiesced in for a long term of years, fixes the construction to be given its provisions.

"We are now asked to set aside this construction thus buttressed and adopt an adverse view because the Congress of the United States did so during a heated political difference of opinion between the then President and the majority leaders of Congress over the reconstruction measures adopted as a means of restoring to their proper status the States which attempted to withdraw from the Union at the time of the Civil War.

"The extremes to which the majority in both Houses carried legislative measures in that matter are now recognized by all who calmly review the history of that episode in our Government, leading to articles of impeachment against President Johnson and his acquittal.

"Without animadverting on the character of the measures taken, we are certainly justified in saying that they should not be given the weight affecting proper constitutional construction to be accorded to that reached by the First Congress of the United States during a political calm and acquiesced in by the whole Government for three-quarters of a century, especially when the new construction contended for has never been acquiesced in by either the Executive or the Judicial Departments.

Holds Act of 1867 Invalid.

"While this court has studiously avoided deciding the issue until its was presented in such a way that it could not be avoided, in the references it has made to the history of the question, and in the presumptions it has indulged in favor of a statutory construction not inconsistent with the legislative decision of 1789, it has indicated a trend of view that we should not and can not ignore.

"When on the merits we find our conclusion strongly favoring the view which prevailed in the first Congress, we have no hesitation in holding that conclusion to be correct; and it therefore follows that the tenure of office act of 1867, in so far as it attempted to prevent the President from removing executive officers who had been appointed by him by and with the advice and consent of the Senate, was invalid and that the subsequent legislation of the same effect was equally so.

"For the reasons given we must therefore hold that the provision of the law of 1876, by which the unrestricted power of removal of first-class Postmasters is denied to the President is in violation of the Constitution and invalid. This leads to an affirmance of the judgment of the Court of Claims."

Justice McReynolds's Views.

In his dissent, Associate Justice McReynolds said in part:

"May the President oust at will all Postmasters appointed with the Senate's consent for definite terms under an act which inhibits removal without consent of that body? May he approve a statute which creates an inferior office and prescribes restrictions on removal, appoint an incumbent, and then remove without regard to the restrictions? Has he power to appoint to an inferior office for a definite term under an act which prohibits removal except as therein specified, and then arbitrarily dismiss the incumbent and deprive him of the emoluments?

"I think there is no such power. Certainly it is not given by any plain words of the Constitution; and the argument advanced to establish it seems to me forced and unsubstantial.

"A certain repugnance must attend the suggestion that the President may ignore any provision of an act of Congress under which he has proceeded. He should promote and not subvert orderly Government. The serious evils which followed the practice of dismissing civil officers as caprice or interest dictated, long permitted under Congressional enactments, are known to all. It brought the public service to a low estate and caused insistent demand for reform.

"The long struggle for Civil Service reform and the legislation designed to insure so[m]e security of official tenure ought not to be forgotten. Again and again Congress has enacted statutes prescribing restrictions on removals and by approving them many Presidents have affirmed its power therein.

"Nothing short of language clear beyond serious disputation should be held to clothe the President with authority wholly beyond Congressional control arbitrarily to dismiss every officer whom he appoints except a few Judges. There are no such words in the Constitution, and the asserted inference conflicts with the heretofore accepted theory that this Government is one of carefully enumerated powers under an intelligible charter.

"Constitutional provision should be interpreted with the expectation that Congress will discharge its duties no less faithfully than the Executive will attend to his.

Powers of the Legislature.

"The Legislature is charged with the duty of making laws for orderly administration obligatory upon all. It possesses supreme power over national affairs and may wreck as well as speed them. It holds the purse, every branch of the Government functions under statutes which embody its will; it may impeach and expel all civil officers.

"The duty is upon it 'to make all laws which shall be necessary and proper for carrying into execution' all powers of the Federal Government. We have no such thing as three totally distinct and independent departments; the others must look to the Executive for direction and support. 'In Republican government the executive authority necessarily predominates.' The Federalist XLVI, XVII.

"Perhaps the chief duty of the President is to carry into effect the will of Congress through such instrumentalities as it has chosen to provide. Arguments, therefore, upon the assumption that Congress may willfully impede executive action are not important. * * *

"For the United States it is asserted —except certain Judges—the President may remove all officers, whether executive or judicial, appointed by him with the Senate's consent; and therein he canont be limited or restricted by Congress.

"The argument runs thus—the Constitution gives the President all executive power of the National Government, except as this is checked or controlled by some other definite provision; power to remove is executive and unconfined; accordingly, the President may remove at will. Further, the President is required to take care that the laws be faithfully executed; he cannot do this unless he may remove at will all officers whom he appoints; therefore he has such authority.

"The argument assumes far too much. Generally, the actual ouster of an officer is executive action; but to prescribe the conditions under which this may be done is legislative. The act of hanging a criminal is executive; but to say when and where and how he shall be hanged is clearly legislative.

Protection of the Incumbent.

"The Legislature may create post-offices and prescribe qualifications, duties, compensations and term. And it may protect the incumbent in the enjoyment of his term unless in some way restrained therefrom. The real question, therefore, comes to this—does any constitutional provision definitely remit the otherwise plenary power of Congress over postmasters, when they are appointed by the President with consent of the Senate?

"The question is not the much mooted one whether the Senate is part of the appointing power under the Constitution and therefore must participate in removals. Here the restriction is imposed by statute alone and thereby made a condition of the tenure. I suppose that beyond doubt Congress could authorize the Postmaster General to appoint all postmasters and restrain him in respect of removals.

"Concerning the instance that power to remove is a necessary incident of the President's duty to enforce the laws it is enough now to say: the general duty to enforce all laws cannot justify infraction of some of them. Moreover, Congress, in the exercise of its unquestioned power, may deprive the President of the right either to appoint or to remove any inferior officer by vesting the authority to appoint in another.

"Yet in that event his duty touching enforcement of the laws would remain. He must utilize the force which Congress gives. He cannot, without permission, appoint the humblest clerk or expend a dollar of the public funds. * * * *

Calls Ruling Revolutionary.

"Congress has long and vigorously asserted its right to restrict removals and there has been no common executive practice based upon a contrary view. The President has often removed, and it is admitted that he may remove, with either the express or implied assent of Congress; but the present theory is that he may override the declared will of that body.

"This goes far beyond any practice heretofore approved or followed; it conflicts with the history of the Constitution, with the ordinary rules of interpretation and with the construction approved by Congress since the beginning and emphatically sanctioned by this court. To adopt it would be revolutionary.

"In any rational search for answer to the questions arising upon this record, it is important not to forget that this is a Government of limited powers definitely enumerated and granted by a written Constitution.

"That the Constitution must be interpreted by attributing to its words the meaning which they bore at the time of its adoption and in view of commonly accepted canons of construction, its history, early and long-continued practices under it, and relevant opinions of this court.

"That the Constitution contains no words which specifically grant to the President power to remove duly appointed officers. And it is definitely settled that he cannot remove those whom he has not appointed—certainly they can be removed only as Congress may permit.

"That from its first session to the last one Congress has often asserted its right to restrict the President's power to remove inferior officers, although appointed by him with consent of the Senate.

"That many Presidents have approved statutes limiting the power of the Executive to remove, and that from the beginning such limitations have been respected in practice.

"That this court, as early as 1803, in an opinion never overruled and rendered in a case where it was necessary to decide the question, positively declared that the President had no power to remove at will an inferior officer appointed with consent of the Senate to serve for a definite term fixed by an act of Congress.

Decision on Judicial Power.

"That the proceedings in the Constitutional Convention of 1787, the political history of the times, contemporaneous opinion, common canons of construction, the action of Congress from the beginning and opinions of this court, all oppose the theory that by vesting 'the executive power' in the President the Constitution gave him an illimitable right to remove inferior officers.

"That this court has emphatically disapproved the same theory concerning 'the judicial power' vested in the courts by words substantially the same as those which vest 'the executive power' in the President.

"That to declare the President vested with indefinite and illimitable executive powers would extend the field of his possible action far beyond the limits observed by his predecessors and would enlarge the powers of Congress to a degree incapable of fair appraisement.

"Considering all these things it is impossible for me to accept the view that the President may dismiss, as caprice may suggest, any inferior officer whom he has appointed with consent of the Senate, notwithstanding a positive inhibition by Congress.

"In the last analysis, that view has no substantial support, unless it be the polemic opinions expressed by Mr. Madison (and eight others) during the debate of 1789, when he was discussing questions relating to a 'superior officer' to be appointed for an indefinite term.

"Notwithstanding his justly exalted reputation as one of the creators and early expounder of the Constitution, sentiments expressed under such circumstances ought not now to outweigh the conclusion which Congress affirmed by deliberate action while he was leader in the House and has consistently maintained down to the present year, the opinion of this court solemnly announced through the great Chief Justice more than a century ago, and the canons of construction approved over and over again."

Dissent by Justice Brandeis.

Associate Justice Brandeis began his dissent by quoting Mr. Justice Story to the effect that in regard to inferior officers "the remedy for any permanent abuse is still within the power of Congress by the simple expedient of requiring the consent of the Senate to removals in such cases."

Justice Brandeis pointed out that Postmasters were inferior officers and that Congress might have vested their appointment in the head of the department.

"The sole question," he said, "is whether, in respect to inferior offices, Congress may impose upon the Senate both responsibilities, as it may deny to it participation in the exercise of either function."

He referred to the right of both appointment and removal.

"Continuously for the last fifty-eight years," Justice Brandeis said, "laws comprehensive in character, enacted from time to time with the approval of the President, have made removal from the great majority of the inferior Presidential offices dependent upon the consent of the Senate. Throughout that period these laws have been continuously applied. We are requested to disregard the authority of Marbury vs. Madison and to overturn this long-established constitutional practice."

Justice Brandeis disputed the theory of the majority of the court, that the President's power of removal "is beyond control, limitation or regulation by Congress."

"Nor has any lower Federal court ever so decided," he declared.

He said the power to remove a subordinate executive officer "is not a power inherent in a Chief Executive."

"The President's power of removal from statutory civil inferior officers, like the power of appointment to them, comes immediately from Congress.

"It is true that the exercise of the power of removal is said to be an Executive act; and that when the Senate grants or withholds consent to a removal by the President it participates in an Executive act. But the Constitution has confessedly granted to Congress the legislative power to create offices and to prescribe the tenure thereof; and it has not in terms denied to Congress the power to control removals.

"To prescribe the tenure involves prescribing the conditions under which incumbency shall cease, for the possibility of removal is a condition or qualification of the tenure."

Justice Holmes's Opinion.

In his dissenting opinion, which was brief, Associate Justice Holmes said:

"The arguments drawn from the executive power of the President and from his duty to appoint officers of the United States (when Congress does not vest the power elsewhere) to take care that the laws be faithfully executed and to commission all officers of the United States seem to me a spider's web inadequate to control the dominant facts.

"Congress alone confers on the President the power to appoint and at any time may transfer the power to other hands. With such powers over its own creation I have no more trouble in believing that Congress has power to prescribe a term of life for it free from interference than I have in accepting the undoubted power of Congress to decree its end. I have equally little trouble in accepting its power to prolong the tenure of the incumbent until Congress or the Senate shall have assented to his removal."

October 26, 1926

THE POWER OF REMOVAL.

How far-reaching will be the effect of the recent Supreme Court decision upholding the right of the President to remove executive officers without the consent of the Senate? Senator LA FOLLETTE has denounced the decision as "a "boost to autocracy and a blow to de-"mocracy." Senator JOHNSON sees a danger in its ruthless application by some future White House despot. Senator KING has already introduced a proposed constitutional amendment taking the power away from the President and vesting it in Congress. So great is the significance of the court's determination of this historic controversy, and so jealous is the Senate of any abridgment of its prestige, that it would not be surprising to see the decision debated at length.

Writing in The Political Science Quarterly, Professor HOWARD LEE MCBAIN takes the view that the decision will not seriously disturb the institutional balance. Apparently there is no practical way for Congress to restrain the Presidential power of removal without by the same stroke curtailing the Senate's prerogatives in the matter of appointments. Nor does Professor MCBAIN expect the President to change his course very radically. Has not the decision greatly enlarged his powers? In legal theory it unquestionably has done so. He can be as capricious as he chooses to be. "But "caprice seldom gets a President or any-"body else anywhere. The history of "the office shows that we may certainly "count upon normal political acumen in "the Presidency." The Senate retains its grip on appointments, and with Senatorial courtesy in full force "it is diffi-"cult to see what the President will gain "by making an opposed removal only to "submit to dictation in respect to a suc-"cessor in the office."

On more than one occasion President COOLIDGE has shown a disposition to overstep the bounds of executive responsibility, or at least to invade the neutral zone between executive and Congressional authority. He asked DAVID J. LEWIS, one of the Democratic members of the Tariff Commission, for an undated letter of resignation as the price of his renomination. When he called for BERT HANEY'S resignation from the Shipping Board Mr. HANEY refused, taking the ground that the board, when once appointed by the President, was an independent agency, responsible only to Congress. Under the new rule it may be that the President would have had the authority to remove him outright.

Assuming the removal power of the President in such cases, will he exercise it? Not if he is well advised. Any attempt to influence in this way the decisions of quasi-legislative or quasi-judicial boards is of questionable propriety, and a President can justify removals of this character to the country only in the most extreme cases. Throughout the executive departments the decision gives him a free hand, and that is in accordance both with tradition and sound administrative practice. Our Chief Executives will do well, however, not to try to stretch the removal power too far. Senator JOHNSON said, speaking of the differences of opinion sure to persist over the policy now determined, "these differ-"ences of opinion will be either mildly "academic or fanned into the flame of "bitter controversy, as the rule lies dor-"mant or the power under it may be ex-"ercised." It need not lie dormant, but it should be exercised with prudence.

January 9, 1927

HUMPHREY OUSTED FROM TRADE BOARD

Roosevelt Removes Him After Refusal to Resign—He Plans a Fight.

MATTHEWS, LANDIS NAMED

Wisconsin Hoover Backer and Harvard Man Appointed to Commission.

Special to THE NEW YORK TIMES.

WASHINGTON, Oct. 7.—President Roosevelt today took the unusual step of removing from office William E. Humphrey, a Republican member of the Federal Trade Commission. He asked Mr. Humphrey in July for his resignation, and this was refused. Mr. Humphrey's term of seven years, to which he was reappointed by President Hoover, has five years to run.

George C. Matthews of Wisconsin was appointed in his place.

The deposed commissioner said today that he would refuse to recognize the President's removal order and would continue to claim compensation until his term expires in 1937. In his correspondence with the President for the last three months he has insisted that he could be removed only for inefficiency or malfeasance under the act creating the commission.

Taking the point of view that the Federal Trade Commission is a quasi-judicial body, a creature of Congress, Mr. Humphrey has contended that he can be removed only under a course of procedure specified in the law. This procedure, he argues, the President has not followed, nor has Mr. Roosevelt indicated any charges as the basis for the removal.

In asking his resignation, Mr. Humphrey said, Mr. Roosevelt merely said that the interests of the administration would be better served by an appointee more closely in sympathy with the Roosevelt aims.

Report Matthews Backed Hoover.

The White House issued this statement:

"The President has removed Commissioner Humphrey as a member of the Federal Trade Commission.

"In his place he has appointed Mr. George C. Matthews of Wisconsin, for many years a member of the Public Utility Commission of that State. He is at the present time rate expert for the receivers of the Insull utilities. Mr. Matthews is a Republican."

It is understood that the new appointee voted for Herbert Hoover in 1932. Reports had been current here that an insurgent Republican, such as former Governor Philip La Follette, would be appointed to fill the vacancy.

The reorganization of the commission, which President Roosevelt has had in mind for some time, would appear to be completed today. In addition to the removal of Mr. Humphrey, a vacancy was created today by the expiration of the term of Raymond Stevens. This was filled by the appointment of Professor James M. Landis of the Harvard Law School.

The White House made the following announcement:

"The President announces the appointment of Professor James M. Landis of the Harvard Law School as a member of the Federal Trade Commission in the place of Raymond Stevens, whose term has expired.

"Mr. Stevens is under obligations to return to his service with the Siamese Government. He was on six months leave in this country this Summer, and at the earnest request of the President consented to serve on the Trade Commission up to the time of his return to Siam."

Work to Gain in Importance.

With these two members, the commission is now made up of Charles H. March, chairman; Garland S. Ferguson Jr., and Ewen L. Davis, a brother of Norman H. Davis, Ambassador at Large and chief American delegate to the Geneva Disarmament Conference.

The work of the Federal Trade Commission is expected to be of much greater importance than in the past, especially in view of its possible decisions in connection with unfair trade practices under the various codes.

It is regarded as likely that some sort of court action will be necessary to determine the legality of the appointment of Mr. Matthews to succeed Mr. Humphrey. With important decisions expected to be handed down by the commission, it is understood that the government would be unwilling to leave them open to challenge on the ground that the commission was illegally constituted.

Mr. Humphrey's action was in doubt today, he said. It was supposed that his first step would be to attempt to attend the regular meeting of the commission on Monday morning.

If ejected, or forcibly prevented from taking his place, he would have the basis for court action. He cannot, obviously, sue President Roosevelt directly for illegal removal.

Humphrey Sees Party Issue.

As he pointed out today, the commission makes its own rules. He could bring suit against the chairman of the commission for preventing him from attending its meetings, or he could sue the Controller General for withholding his salary.

"This question," Mr. Humphrey said, "is going to be made a party issue. I am satisfied, after talking with responsible leaders, that the Republican party will take the matter up and fight with me to the last ditch.

"The President and his political advisers are attempting to inaugurate the spoils system in a Federal agency which, under the law, is declared to be bipartisan in every way."

Letters on Resignation.

(Copyright, 1933, by The Associated Press.)

WASHINGTON, Oct. 7.—Following are excerpts from the correspondence between President Roosevelt and William E. Humphrey leading up to today's "removal" of the Trade Commission member:

Late in July Mr. Humphrey wrote the President saying he had heard his resignation would be asked for. He asked for a personal interview, and continued:

"For the greater part of forty years I have been in the public service. I am not aware of anything discreditable in my record or of any act that I would blot out. If that long service is ended by forced resignation, it would be to some extent a reflection on my career and would greatly injure me in my profession if I should again take up the practice of law."

The President replied on July 25, saying that demands on his time prevented a personal interview. He added:

"Without any reflection at all upon you personally or upon the service you have rendered in your present capacity, I find it necessary to ask for your resignation as a member of the Federal Trade Commission. I do this because I feel that the aims and purposes of the administration with respect to the work of the commission can be carried out most effectively with personnel of my own selection.

"I congratulate you upon your long and active service."

To this Mr. Humphrey replied in part:

"As you well understand, I have lost all professional and business connections after being out of practice for nine years. Naturally I should like to consult my friends as to my future actions. Some of these friends, as you probably know, live in Seattle—my home. Such matters cannot be discussed satisfactorily by correspondence.

"May I add that I do not feel that I go beyond right or courtesy when I suggest a reasonable time in which to consult my friends in regard to future actions."

Denies That He Resigned.

The President replied by telegram from Hyde Park on Aug. 4:

"I have your letter and I fully appreciate your desire to have a little time to make arrangements. Therefore I am accepting your resignation, but not to take effect until Aug. 15."

On Aug. 10 Mr. Humphrey wrote:

"In acknowledging your telegram of Aug. 4, I thank you for the courtesy and consideration shown. You say, 'I am accepting your resignation. * * *' In this you are in error, as I have not tendered my resignation as a member of the Federal Trade Commision, and cannot do so. If any document purporting to be my resignation has been presented to you, it was without my authority, consent or knowledge.

"The statute creating the Federal Trade Commission says: 'Any commissioner may be removed by the President for inefficiency, neglect of duty or malfeasance in office.' I must assume that the President and the public know the language of this statute.

"Congress intended that the Federal Trade Commission should be an independent, semi-judicial, continuing body, at all times qualified to deal fairly and intelligently with matters that come before it.

"The statute provides for rotation in office of its members. The vital purpose of these provisions was that the business of the country might at all times have, in the often quoted language of the Supreme Court, 'a tribunal appointed by law and informed by experience.' The very purpose of the statute, it seems to me, is destroyed by the power of the President to remove a member of that body because he wants in his place a member of his own selection.

"I am well aware of the decision that holds that the President has the unrestrained power to remove postmasters. There is no such decision made involving a statute similar to that creating the Federal Trade Commission."

Roosevelt Repeated Demand.

The President's next letter, dated Aug. 31, at Hyde Park, read in part:

"I am sure that I do not need to tell you that I would not wish to hurt you in any way if it can possibly be avoided, and that is why I still hope that you will be willing to let me have your resignation as a member of the Federal Trade Commission.

"You will, I know, realize that I do not feel that your mind and my mind go along together on either the policies or the administering of the Federal Trade Commission, and frankly I think it is best for the people of this country that I should have full confidence."

On Sept. 11 Mr. Humphrey wrote that he had "seen nothing" to indicate that their minds were not going along together; that for the last four years the commission had been unanimous on questions of policy; that he felt sure the President had heard misrepresentations and half-truths, put out by Mr. Humphrey's enemies, "from some sinister motive."

Mr. Humphrey wrote again on Sept. 27:

"I beg to suggest that by reason of the wide publicity given to the controversy the situation has been greatly changed. I want you to know that I did not give out a word of this publicity, and tried to prevent it. This publicity clearly shows that if I leave the commission, at once the matter will become a party issue. The comments that I have seen in the press, regardless of party affiliation, universally condemned anything that would tend toward this result.

"My resignation, after this wide publicity, would be, in my opinion, a great injury to the commission and to the public."

And finally, the President's note of today:

"I am in receipt of your letter of Sept. 27.

"Effective as of this date you are hereby removed from the office of Commissioner of the Federal Trade Commission."

October 8, 1933

WM. E. HUMPHREY DIES AT AGE OF 71

Stroke Fatal to Ex-Federal Trade Commissioner Whom Roosevelt Removed.

CENTRE OF CONTROVERSY

He Brought Suit in December Contesting Legality of the President's Action.

WASHINGTON, Feb. 14 (AP).—William E. Humphrey, former Federal Trade Commissioner who was removed by President Roosevelt, died suddenly tonight as the result of a stroke.

He was 71 years old.

He had been in frail health for several months, but at no time had his condition been regarded as alarming.

The President's action last Oct. 7 in removing Mr. Humphrey as a member of the Trade Commission stirred a controversy which still is rumbling in Congress and forms the basis of a suit filed on Dec. 28 by Mr. Humphrey in the Court of Claims here to contest Mr. Roosevelt's authority and to collect back salary.

Mr. Humphrey, who was born near Alamo, Ind., was a member of Congress from Washington from 1902 until 1917. In the latter year he sought the Republican nomination for Senator from Washington and was defeated.

After his service in Congress he practiced law here and in Seattle until 1925, when he was appointed to the Trade Commission by President Coolidge for a six-year term. He was named again in 1931 by President Hoover for another six-year term.

Asked to Resign in Fall.

Last September, however, he was asked to resign by President Roosevelt, who expressed the desire to name in his place a man whose ideas were more in keeping with Mr. Roosevelt's. A considerable exchange of correspondence between them culminated in the ousting by the Chief Executive.

Mr. Humphrey in contesting the removal asserted that Mr. Roosevelt was acting contrary to law in that no charges of malfeasance or wrongdoing in office were made.

The Senate recently confirmed Mr. Humphrey's successor, George Mathews of Wisconsin.

Born near Alamo, Ind., Mr. Humphrey spent his boyhood on a farm. He was graduated from Wabash College and began the practice of law in Crawfordsville, Ind. In 1893 he moved to Seattle and served as Corporation Counsel for that city from 1898 to 1902.

While in Congress he was particularly interested in the merchant marine and shipping matters.

Times Wide World Photo.

WILLIAM E. HUMPHREY.

The widow and a sister, Miss Edna Humphrey of Crawfordsville, Ind., survive.

Resented Dictation.

At both the beginning and the ending of his membership on the Federal Trade Commission Mr. Humphrey indicated his dislike of dictation. In the Spring of 1925, a few weeks after the Senate had confirmed his appointment, he challenged the right of the upper house of Congress to direct the commission to make investigations for the Senate's information. His bold assertion occurred in an address before the United States Chamber of Commerce and caused Senator Borah to remark: "It seems to me the best thing to do with the Federal Trade Commission is to abolish it." Senator Norris cordially agreed with this view.

Two days after his removal by President Roosevelt, Mr. Humphrey attended a meeting of the commission and remained silent throughout a two-hour session, merely presenting a letter recounting his refusal to recognize the validity of the President's action. But his former colleagues disagreed with him. His successor, Mr. Mathews, was not present at this meeting.

As the only appeal from the decision of the Court of Claims is to the United States Supreme Court, it had been believed certain that the case would be ultimately decided there. The legal questions involved were of deep interest. A decision was expected to clarify issues raised in the famous case of the Oregon postmaster, Myers, vs. the U. S., decided in 1926, after being before the Supreme Court for two years and twice argued. The very lengthy opinion, which constituted a posthumous victory for President Wilson, sustained the right of the President to remove a postmaster without the consultation of the Senate prescribed by the act of Congress.

ROOSEVELT, AS CRUSADER, SEEKS UNEQUALED POWER

President's Potential Authority Seen As Exceeding That of Washington, Jackson, Lincoln or Grant.

ALL UNDER THE CONSTITUTION

A Resume of the "Dictator" Bills That Are Pending or Have Been Enacted Since Administration Took Office.

By ARTHUR KROCK.

WASHINGTON, April 22.—A poetic statistician has estimated that, after forty-nine and one-half days in office, Franklin D. Roosevelt possesses, is seeking and has been offered more absolute power than the sum of the arbitrary authority exercised at various times in history by Generals Washington, Lee, Grant and Sherman, Presidents Jackson, Lincoln and Wilson, and all the Emperors of the Ming dynasty.

What power has been and will be granted is all technically within the framework of the Constitution. If that document has not been put on the shelf, as Alfred E. Smith recommended, it has been republished on India rubber to meet these unusual tests of its flexibility.

When the President was inaugurated the country was in the midst of a national banking holiday declared by the orders of the Governors of the several States. The first act he found necessary was to use the unrepealed powers granted to President Wilson in the World War to impose a gold embargo, close the banks for a period by national action and take other emergency steps.

To give fresh title and authority to these drastic regulations the President sought and received ratification and extension of his authority over banking and finance in the emergency banking act—the first of the so-called "dictator" bills. From that time on it has been a procession.

Extension of President's Powers.

Today, less than two months after the inauguration, a recital of the arbitrary powers which the President has received, has sought, will seek and have been proposed for him decidedly supports the estimate of the poetic statistician mentioned above.

Under the emergency banking bill the President, as completely as in war time, regulates credit, currency, gold silver and foreign exchange transactions. Through his Secretary of the Treasury he ordered the delivery at the Treasury of all gold and gold certificates, and a few days ago, under the same authority, he embargoed gold, except for purposes privileged under international law, thus officially taking the United States off the gold standard.

By the terms of the same act the President, through the Treasury, fixes restrictions on the banking business of Federal Reserve members; appoints conservators for any bank when that step is considered necessary to protect the depositors; guarantees 100 per cent liquidity to accounts opened after a certain date; passes on the reorganization of national banks; permits the purchase of preferred bank stock by the Reconstruction Finance Corporation; regulates bank loans by the Corporation, and may issue a large amount of new Federal Reserve Bank notes on collateral not heretofore allowed as a currency base.

Under the economy act the President has exercised the power to abolish the entire structure of veterans' benefits and has substituted a new pension system, in which he has fixed the rates and classifications. He was permitted to reduce all Federal salaries by as much as 15 per cent on a cost-of-living formula worked out on a broad basis. Upon him authority was conferred to eliminate, consolidate, transfer or curtail any agency of the government, any part of any agency (except major departments) and the right to impound in the Treasury all savings affected thereunder.

Authority in Pending Bills.

The President, through the Federal agricultural offices, is given in the farm relief bill, now pending, the power to reduce acreage, specify the growing of farm products on certain terms; employ the allotment, land-leasing and cotton-option plans on any of them; levy taxes on processing and require licenses for processors and distributers, with a heavy penalty check; enter into marketing agreements, despite the Clayton act; decide when the emergency has ended and proclaim it; withhold the provisions of the bill from any commodity he elects; admit processors and distributers to Reconstruction Finance Corporation loans; control the distribution of basic farm commodities in interstate and foreign commerce; buy the Farm Board's cotton and acquire full title to cotton under government loan or held as collateral for government loans, and organize a vast national, State and local "policing" bureaucracy.

The currency legislation, sent to Congress this week, empowers the President to direct credit expansion through the open-market purchase by the Federal Reserve of government paper not to exceed $3,000,000,000; to issue greenbacks up to $3,000,000,000 if the credit expansion does not work, replacing government bonds to that figure; to fix the gold content of the dollar by "sweating" it as much as 50 per cent and base it on any ratio he desires to silver and currencies anywhere; to accept a maximum of $100,000,000 in silver from any government in arrears to the United States at a price of not more than 50 cents an ounce, and to use this silver as a base for new currency.

The proposed farm mortgage refinancing plan authorizes a Federal Land Bank bond issue of $2,000,000,000, and permits the President, through his Farm Loan Commissioner, to make 5 per cent loans to farmers from R. F. C. funds to prevent foreclosures. The home-owners' loan act sets up a $2,000,000,000 executive corporation under the President for refinancing mortgages over a fifteen-year period on an adjusted basis, with broad executive discretion. It establishes a government funded $100,000,000 Federal Savings and Loan Association for financing home building in communities in which such facilities do not now exist.

Secretary Perkins's bill gives the Executive virtually complete control over industrial production, hours of labor and rate of pay of industrial workers. The Secretary of Labor could apply personal judgment on an arbitrary basis, subject only to the President's review. Criminal prosecution would be faced by violators of these executive regulations.

Other Proposed Grants.

The prospective trade and tariff powers grants would give the President the sole right to change tariff rates by executive proclamation, subject only to a two-thirds adverse vote in Congress (as in the case of all these powers); the authority to negotiate multilateral treaties for horizontal tariff reduction and currency stabilization, and to negotiate bilateral treaties to the same purpose. They would also give the President the right to raise and lower tariffs on a bargaining basis as well as on differences in production costs.

Unless the silver provision for war debt payments has averted the expected defaults of June 15, it is proposed that the President ask Congress for advance power to defer or otherwise deal with the debt payments during the recess of the national Legislature.

Mr. Roosevelt already has received, through his Federal Relief Administrator, the authority to recruit men for reforestation and other work purposes and has been authorized to use $200,000,000 for that.

The securities bill, still under consideration, gives the Federal Trade Commission, his executive agent, registration rights over all security issues in interstate commerce.

The Muscle Shoals measure, another pending instrument, gives a body under the President the authority to go into the fertilizer business and get lands for that purpose; to supervise power rates rigidly and to sell power and construct power sources.

Projected railroad legislation provides wide Federal control over holding companies, the right to unscramble railway systems and set up Federal and regional coordinators, and power to require such economies as they see fit.

These are but the broad aspects of the temporary transfer of legislative powers by Congress to the Chief Executive. A citation of the details, such as the right to cancel government contracts, to retire civil servants and officers of the armed forces, with their tremendous effects on human lives, would require space not available even in part here.

In Washington

Congress Flounders as Roosevelt Drops 'Boss' Role.

By ARTHUR KROCK.

WASHINGTON, June 7.—So far as Congress is concerned, the thoroughly engaging gentleman in the White House is being deferential these days to a degree that has Congress floundering in its effort to adjourn. This is a bewildering experience on Capitol Hill—to have no boss for the first time since March 4, 1933.

Instead of acting the part of "the tough guy" he described himself as being when he returned from Bahaman waters, the President is suave and retiring. Not for him to give orders to his "colleagues in the government." He would not think of using the word "must" to a coordinate branch. How could the newspaper men have thought up such a word? All the President wants (he says) is for Congress to make up its mind about certain measures for the passage of which he is "anxious."

This sudden change on the President's part from domination to a shrinking partnership has got the leaders guessing, including the Democratic leaders. They feel certain it is some sort of game, but a game too subtle for their minds and methods. Knowing that the President wants an early adjournment, the leaders and their more or less devoted followers do not comprehend why he has abandoned his fourteen-month course of (1) adopting a policy, (2) drafting a bill, (3) sending it up to the Capitol with a message, and (4) turning on the pressure for quick passage. They feel that he is smiling in his sleeve, but they are more than a little uncertain what the smile is about.

Word has come to the leaders that the President is "anxious" for the passage of the Wagner bill, the housing measure, the oil production control arrangement, the AAA amendments and the drought relief appropriation. He is represented as "hopeful" of the passage of the Silver Bill and the Communications Commission Bill. But the year-long insistence is gone, and it is being sadly missed by those accustomed to specific orders. That is why Congress doesn't know when it will or can adjourn, although it very much desires to get away from Washington.

Leaders Perplexed Over Course.

This week the President demonstrated that when he wants to push a Congressional matter he has not forgotten how to do it. He illustrated this by asking Senator Robinson of Arkansas to put an end to Senator Smith's lone obstruction of the confirmation of Rexford G. Tugwell as Under-Secretary of Agriculture. But he is bafflingly reticent about almost everything else.

It has been explained on the President's behalf that he is refraining from a "must" program because he fears the proponents of measures not on that docket would filibuster against it. This would account for his new manner toward Congress if it were getting his most favored measures anywhere in particular. Opposition to the Wagner bill seems to be growing on both sides of the party aisles under the laissez-faire policy. Committees show a disposition to pick the housing measure to pieces. Even in modified form the AAA amendments are not overwhelmingly popular.

No one seems to know what to do next. Probably Senator Robinson has been let in on whatever subtleties there may be in the Presidential policy. If he has, he isn't telling. The Republicans, eager to adjourn, have been unable to get the usual information about legislative plans for the next few days. Their leaders have told them that, after the passage of the Silver Bill, the Wagner proposals will be brought forward. But on the Democratic side there has been no assurance that this is so. If the Silver Bill had passed the Senate tonight it would have been difficult for the most experienced legislators to have guessed what Mr. Robinson would offer next.

House Is Ready for Quick Action.

Told to work out its own adjournment, Congress for the moment seems unable to do it. Perhaps this is what the President expected and wanted. It may give him an opportunity to step in effectively a few days from now and bring the session to an end. No one can then say he didn't give Congress every chance to work out its own plan. Those who have been attacking the body as controlled or supine will then be placed in rather a ridiculous position. The answer on the record will be that Congress is incapable of taking care of itself and must be bossed, down to particulars.

Probably by the end of the week the adjournment situation will be much clearer. The cloud of doubt hangs over the Senate wing only. The House, since the adoption of its stringent special rule of procedure, is in a position to adjourn on very short notice. On virtually all the major matters pending, the Democratic majority can hold its forces in line to pass whatever the President wants. The words "anxious" and "hopeful" as substitutes for "must" are strong enough to loose the springs of action in that branch.

Now that uncertainty over the war debts has been dissipated by the inevitable effects of the Johnson bill—a general default—the President has no "day of dread" such as he had last year at this time. Adjournment by June 20 will give him ample time to collect a degree or two, look over the stock at Hyde Park and embark on the Houston at Newport or New London for the turquoise seas. Adjournment before July 1 will obviate any necessity of submitting his choices for Stock and Securities Exchange Commissioners to confirmation risks, and make the world safe for J. M. Landis.

Congress is sweating and stewing and worrying over its own ineptitude. The President is reported gayer and more charming than ever, which is saying a lot. Prolongation of the session could, of course, produce some reckless action that might be calamitous to the country. But if this possibility is resolutely put aside, the situation has a distinctly comic aspect.

June 8, 1934

REINS OF RECOVERY LEFT IN HANDS OF ROOSEVELT

Departing Congress Commits Vast Loan of Power to President With Nation Relying on Him.

CONFIDENT OF HIS MODERATION

Executive's Sway Over Business, Industry, Labor, Banking, Investing, Currency and Relief Can Always Be Rescinded.

By ARTHUR KROCK.

WASHINGTON, June 16.—As his first Congress passes from the scene the President, armed with more power than any Executive of a great democracy ever had, is left to wage the final battles in the long war for recovery. His success is not yet assured, although he expects it. Failure would probably be marked, first by "controlled inflation" of a direct character, and then the cataclysm of an uncontrolled currency issue should failure be complete. This is unlikely.

The President and his key men appear to have every confidence that the campaign and the war will be won through moderate and constructive use of the vast powers Congress has delegated to the Executive. A section of the administration that particularly distrusts the huge spending program and is convinced that the NRA and AAA cannot be successful is not sanguine. Some of these persons are without much hope at all. But in this the most momentous period of the President's administration it should be recorded that the prevailing spirit is one of optimism ranging upward to confidence.

Congress is ending the second of its two sessions to return home for the primaries and the election. The Democratic organization is ready to exert every effort to increase the already huge majority of its partisans in the two branches. Although there is a deficit, the expectation is to use a quantity of money to present the political case of the administration to the people. An immense publicity machine goes with control of the government, and the administration has this added facility to illuminate its record. From the Republican viewpoint, the colossal sums that have been spent and are increasingly available for public distribution for recovery purposes transmute inevitably into the largest campaign fund ever known, reduced, however, by the Senate's limitation of unexpended RFC funds to $500,000,000.

Leaving Loan of Power.

Under the terms of the Norris amendment that went into effect last year the "short session" (from December to March) has been eliminated. Adjournment is sine die. Unless the President summons the Seventy-third Congress in extra session, which he can do up to election day next November, its existence is ended. The men and women who will be elected next Autumn will constitute the Seventy-fourth Congress and will resume the nation's lawmaking when it is resumed. About two-thirds of the Senate hold over. The tenure of all the rest must be submitted to the people.

The story of the Seventy-third Congress describes the broadest loan of legislative powers to an Executive that has been made except under a dictatorship. The process has been strictly within the bounds of the Constitution, for Congress can take back at any time what it has loaned.

Since Congress cannot convene itself under the Constitution, the loans the present body has made to the President cannot be called until it meets again according to law or unless it should be summoned in special session.

Powers Delegated in Wartime.

In past times of war Congress has delegated many of its powers to the Executive. But Franklin D. Roosevelt came to office in a time of peace, when the coordinate authority of the government's three branches was according to the ancient formula laid down by the fathers of the Republic.

In March, 1933, Congress held: the powers to lay and collect taxes; to borrow money; to regulate foreign and interstate commerce; to coin money and regulate its value and that of foreign coin; to combat counterfeiting; to guard the copyright of creative work; to set up inferior courts; to define and punish piracy and the like; to declare war and grant letters of marque and reprisal; to raise and support armies and a navy; to regulate calls for the militia and provide for its organization and discipline; to rule the District of Columbia and government reservations; and to make all necessary laws for the government.

That long paragraph is the briefest sort of summary of the powers vested in Congress by the Constitution and exercised by it in full when the President took office. But there is by no means general agreement concerning just what Congress has loaned to the President of its birthright and what it has retained.

Senator Borah and many Republican and Democratic conservatives contend that the national legislature has assigned nearly all of these powers. To judge by the public utterances of these critics, the only authorities it has retained are to combat counterfeiting, guard copyrights, set up inferior courts, suppress piracy, declare war and run the District of Columbia. The rest of its heritage it has turned over (and, some critics insist, in certain cases illegally) to Mr. Roosevelt, in the opinion of various expert observers.

Study Sustains Point.

A study of the acts of the Seventy-third Congress gives evidence to sustain this contention except as to the point about illegality, which is a matter for the courts. Aspects of the NRA and the AAA are certainly tantamount to Executive control of interstate and foreign commerce. The power over coinage and its value has definitely been assigned. Taxation through the Executive has been made possible by several of the recovery acts, particularly the Reciprocal Tariff Bill.

The function of making "all necessary laws" has been suspended in some instances. For the moment the President is the Executive branch and three-fourths of the legislative. But his expansion is twice limited—once by the fact, above, that Congress can deflate it; again by the fact that many of the powers have been contributed for a fixed period, since Congress could not legally assign them in perpetuity.

The exercise of these powers has put the government into the banking business, the mortgage business, the feed, dairy, cotton, wheat and cattle businesses, into railroading, and into work hitherto undertaken by private welfare organizations. The government plans to be a partner in the construction industry. It is underwriting billions in personal liabilities and guaranteeing the life of billions in private assets. It has arranged for taxing units and private corporations to scale down their debts.

Labor Conditions Supervised.

The government, under President Roosevelt, has undertaken to supervise labor disputes more closely than ever before, and it has fixed minimum wages and maximum hours-of-work for most of the population. It has largely suspended the anti-trust laws, although the President has not asked for a renewal of his dictatorial powers to license industry. Strict regulation of trading on the stock and commodity exchanges and of the issuance of securities has been provided. The government also has extended its powers over all mechanical forms of communication.

No longer is the gold clause in contracts valid in the United States, and the currency itself is irredeemable. In the Tennessee Valley the government is conducting a semi-collectivist experiment. A future currency ratio for silver has been set up "in principle." The leading-strings of Cuba have been cut and women have been granted full rights as nationals.

These are but the peaks in the record, as many as can be listed in this space. They were chosen because they illustrate the almost total, though temporary, dislocation in the American governing system since the President set out gallantly to combat the depression. He has not faltered in his effort or in his hope. And a succession of evidence, including polls, indicates that the country is overwhelmingly for him and believes he will put it once more on firm ground.

Of all the powers it leased, Congress has taken back only one—control of the pension system, which it surrendered in the Economy Act of 1933.

June 17, 1934

EXECUTIVE ORDERS INCREASE IN NUMBER

The President's Extraordinary Powers Are Reflected in His Use of Them

By OLIVER McKEE, Jr.
WASHINGTON.

INVESTED by Congress with powers far greater than those granted to any of his predecessors, President Roosevelt, in exercising the delegated authority, has made frequent use of executive orders. He did so notably in two recent orders, one for the nationalization of silver and one establishing the thirty-six hour week in the cotton garment manufacturing industry.

Up to Oct. 12, when Mr. Roosevelt ordered the new cotton work-week, he had approved 949 executive orders—more than half as many as Woodrow Wilson signed during his eight years in the White House. By the end of his four-year term, President Roosevelt seems certain to exceed the Wilson total, the largest hitherto credited to any American President.

Executive orders have the force of administrative law. Presidents have used them for many purposes. They rest either on the constitutional prerogatives of the office or on statute. Through them, a President shares in fact, if not in theory, in the legislative process. The more extensive the powers delegated to him by Congress, the more active will be the "ordinance making" function of the Chief Executive. The large number of executive orders issued since March 5, 1933, reflects the broad powers which the Seventy-third Congress gave to President Roosevelt.

Many Concern NRA.

Of the orders approved by Mr. Roosevelt, about half have to do with the NRA. The AAA, Emergency Relief, the CCC, the HOLC, and other emergency agencies account for many, and some are merely routine orders, of no general significance. Under the so-called Economy Act, the President received virtually a free hand in reorganizing government departments and bureaus, and in revising the compensation and pensions of war veterans and their dependents. The initial curtailment in veterans' payments was made through an executive order, and the same method was used later to authorize successive "humanizations" in the original reform program, which would have done injustice to many deserving veterans.

It was by an executive order that the President created a National Longshoremen's Board, to deal primarily with the strike threat on the Pacific Coast, and it was through executive orders again that he set up the National Emergency Council, the Industrial Emergency Committee, approved plans for the shelter belt in the Great Plains, restored part of the 15 per cent government pay cut, directed Postmaster General Farley to investigate air mail and ocean mail contracts made prior to June 16, 1933, abolished the Darrow Review Board, and established the Division of Territories and Island Possessions in the Department of the Interior.

During the early phases of the NRA, President Roosevelt, by executive order, approved and signed all codes of fair competition. On Dec. 30, 1933, by executive order, he delegated to Administrator Hugh S. Johnson the authority to approve all codes except those for major industries (in general, those industries normally employing in excess of 50,000 employes). Thereby the NRA burden on the White House was materially lightened.

Preparation of Orders.

Though the emergency legislation enacted by the Seventy-third Congress has provided the statutory basis for many of the most important of President Roosevelt's executive orders, in at least one instance, he has based his action on a much older statute. His proclamation ordering a bank holiday, and his executive order on gold, were based on the trading with the enemy act of Oct. 6, 1917. Until repealed or amended, a statute confers a continuing authority on future Presidents.

The preparation of executive orders is governed by rules. A draft order must first be presented to the Director of the Bureau of the Budget, and if on examination he finds that it contains no provisions that clash with the financial program of the administration, the draft is then forwarded to the Attorney General. Law experts of the Department of Justice examine the draft to find out, first, whether the proposed order is constitutional; second, whether it clashes with an existing statute, and, third, if based on statute, whether what it is proposed to do by the order falls within the intent of Congress in making that statute.

If the Attorney General approves the draft, it is forwarded to the Department of State, where it is examined as to form and style. The original and one additional

copy are transmitted to the President, provided the Department of State finds that it conforms to the prescribed specifications. NRA orders, however, are not referred to the State Department or the Department of Justice before they go to the White House.

An executive order usually originates in the department or agency chiefly affected by its contents. Any department may prepare an order for the approval of the President, provided it goes through the prescribed channels, and carries the endorsement of the Budget Director and the Attorney General. In many orders during the past year and a half, the initiative has come from President Roosevelt.

For the period between 1862 and 1900 the archives of the Department of State contain 122 executive orders. Between 1900 and March 4, 1933, 5,950 orders were added to the archives. The totals for recent Presidents follow:

Theodore Roosevelt	1,011
Taft	698
Wilson	1,767
Harding	484
Coolidge	1,248
Hoover	1,004
Franklin D. Roosevelt (up to Oct. 12, 1934)	949

The first executive order in the Department of State archives is one signed by Lincoln in 1862, establishing a provisional court in Louisiana. In freeing the slaves, Lincoln used a proclamation, which was based on his constitutional authority "as commander-in-chief of the army and navy of the United States, in time of actual armed rebellion against the authority and government of the United States, and as a fit and necessary measure for suppressing said rebellion."

October 21, 1934

ROOSEVELT CALLS ON COURTS TO HELP ADAPT CONSTITUTION TO OUR NEEDS

BASIC LAW UPHELD

Against Amendment but Asks More Liberal Interpretations.

CONGRESS HAILS MESSAGE

Cheers Greet Appeal Not to Let Democracy Be Imperiled by Denial of Essentials.

PEOPLE SPOKE, HE ASSERTS

Senator Robinson, in Address on Radio Later, Insists That Revision Is Needed.

By TURNER CATLEDGE
Special to THE NEW YORK TIMES.

WASHINGTON, Jan. 6.—Addressing a joint session of the Seventy-fifth Congress today, President Roosevelt was cheered to the rafters when in effect he challenged the judicial branch to join the legislative and executive branches of the Federal Government in the march for social progress, or risk a curb on its powers.

Mr. Roosevelt held the Constitution adequate as it stands, and that there is no vital need of an amendment to attain the objectives of a better social order.

"The judicial branch," he said, "also is asked by the people to do its part in making democracy successful."

The President delivered his message on the "state of the Union" before a thronged House chamber a few minutes after he and Vice President Garner were formally declared re-elected for another term of four years.

Within a few hours after he had returned to the White House, the Senate and House had passed its first major act, answering his first request, a law embargoing arms shipments to the warring factions in Spain.

The speed of action in the two houses was reminiscent of the first days of the first New Deal Congress in March, 1933, when, within eight hours, Congress passed and the President signed the Emergency Banking Act. But today the Senate recessed before the House passed the measure, and neglected to commission Vice President Garner to sign it during the recess. Hence the resolution may not reach the President's desk until Friday.

President's Control Obvious

From the riotous cheering provoked by his references to the court, as well as the action on the Spanish arms embargo, President Roosevelt appeared in complete control of the new Congress.

In placing himself in opposition to any immediate amendment of the Constitution the President demanded instead a more liberal interpretation by the Supreme Court of the economic and social legislation enacted by Congress, and implied that if these interpretations do not come Congress should look into its own powers to see what curbs can be put on the judicial branch.

The Supreme Court was not mentioned by name, however. Rather, Mr. Roosevelt spoke of the "judicial branch" and the "courts," but he left no room for doubt that he was hitting at the tribunal which gave the final interpretations on New Deal laws.

"Means must be found," he said, "to adapt our legal forms and our judicial interpretation to the actual present national needs of the largest progressive democracy in the modern world."

The Democrats cheered practically every remark which they could interpret as aimed at the court. One member of that party, sitting on the Republican side because he could not squeeze himself in among the thickly packed Democrats in the other half of the chamber, repeatedly yelled "Attaboy!"

Republicans Are Silent

Republicans sat close-lipped and silent. Publicly they mildly deplored what they termed an "attack" on the Supreme Court, but privately they regarded the President's entire message as a natural aftermath of the election of Nov. 3.

Senator Robinson of Arkansas, Democratic leader of the Senate, who has advocated amending the Constitution to clear up the trouble over judicial interpretations, hung on every word of the message. He was seated well down in front.

Tonight in a radio address over a national network of the National Broadcasting Company, Senator Robinson repeated his own views that "the most practical way to deal with the subject, and the safest way, is through an amendment to the Constitution."

The President expressed confidence that the legislative and executive branches would continue to cooperate to meet the demands of democracy. The judiciary only is out of step, according to his portrayal, and simple means should be employed to bring it into line.

"The vital need is not an alteration of our fundamental law," said the President, "but an increasingly enlightened view with reference to it. Difficulties have grown out of its interpretation; but rightly considered, it can be used as an instrument of progress, and not as a device for prevention of action."

This was the first remark which the Congress regarded as hitting directly at the court. A cheer went up from the Democrats. The galleries joined the demonstration with milder applause. Mrs. Roosevelt, sitting with a group of friends, smiled.

The challenge to the court followed an extended exposition of the intentions of his administration, including a virtual forecast of legislation which may run afoul of the interpretations made only recently by the Supreme Court.

New Deal Far From Its Goal

The President thought the New Deal was far from its goal of a "more abundant life" for all the people. Far-reaching problems are still before us, he said, "for which democracy must find solutions if it is to consider itself successful."

As an example he referred to adequate and sanitary housing, farm tenancy, perfection of social security and "the most far-reaching and most inclusive problem of all," unemployment, and "the lack of economic balance of which unemployment is at once the result and the symptom."

The immediate question of relief, he said, he would discuss later. The broader task of preventing unemployment "is a matter of long-range evolutionary policy."

Congressional leaders, Democratic and Republican, took the President's references to these specific problems as a definite indication that legislative requests on such lines would be coming from the White House soon, and that among them would be one for Federal action toward a systematized shortening of hours and increases in the wages of labor.

Unemployment Still a Problem

The President warned Congress not to be dazzled by the immediate appearances of prosperity. "We cannot assume that immediate commercial and industrial activity which mitigates present pressures justifies the National Government at this time in placing the unemployment problem in a filing cabinet of finished business."

He insisted that the problems still to be met, the same as those with which he has tried to deal in the last four years, are national in character. They cannot be met, he held, by either independent or simultaneous action by the forty-eight States. It was to sanction **national action that he demanded a more liberal interpretation by the** courts of the Constitution, which he said was intended by the original authors of that document.

"It was their definite intent and expectation," he said, "that a liberal interpretation in years to come would give to the Congress the same relative powers over national problems as they themselves gave to Congress over the national problems of their day."

It was not to be assumed that, with a better understanding of purpose and a more intelligent recognition of national needs, "there will be a prolonged failure to bring legislative and judicial action into closer harmony."

Democracy and Foreign Affairs

Part of the message dealt with foreign affairs, but Mr. Roosevelt's references were linked with the attitude of the courts. After reciting the peace aspirations of his administration and referring to the Inter-American Conference at Buenos Aires as promoting a better understanding among the nations of the Western Hemisphere, he said it was up to America to demonstrate to the world that democracy could function.

"It is patriotic as well as logical," he said, "for us to prove that we can meet new national needs with new laws consistent with an historic Constitutional framework clearly intended to receive liberal and narrow interpretation.

"The United States of America within itself must continue the task of making democracy succeed."

The President's demeanor, in the words of a Republican Representative, was "calm and reassuring." He raised his voice only once or twice; once when, after praising the National Recovery Act, he said the statute has been outlawed but "the problems have not."

Critics Praise Open Attack

The tenor of the message, according to Republican critics again, was somewhat different from that of a year ago when he challenged his political opponents to come out into the open and fight. They recalled **that the message today contained practically no adverse criticism of** business or of the motives of those who oppose his measures. The challenge today was to the Supreme Court and the judiciary, and while critics publicly repeated the usual remarks about an attack on this honored institution, they rather praised his coming out into the open with it.

Representative Snell of New York, Republican leader in the House, conceded that "it was a pretty good speech."

With receipt of the President's message Congress started on its legislative course. Both houses proceeded immediately to the task of passing the Spanish arms embargo, which the President mentioned only once in his address.

Minority "Cooperation" Over

Republicans warned, however, that today's record on this measure —passage within five hours—was not to be taken as a pattern for legislation during the rest of the session. Senator McNary, the Republican floor leader, told the Senate that only in the case of rarest emergencies would he and his colleagues stand aside, or "cooperate," as they did today.

In the House leaders thought they detected in today's proceedings a slight symptom of what might be in store in the way of obstruction to the administration's plans when Representative John T. Bernard, Farmer-Laborite, of Minnesota, who was born in Corsica, objected to the unanimous-consent request to consider the Spanish embargo. While Mr. Bernard's objection did not prevent disposition of the measure, due to the drastic and convenient rules of the House, it did delay action for possibly two hours.

Mr. Bernard was one of that group of Minnesota Farmer-Laborites elected last November because of the espousal of their candidacy by President Roosevelt.

January 7, 1937

COURT BILL DRIVE COLLAPSES

GARNER ASKS PEACE

Pays a Call on Wheeler, Tells Opponents to Offer Their Terms

NEW MEASURE NEXT WEEK

High Bench Change Is Dead, Other Roosevelt 'Reforms' to Be Modified

'SAVE PRESIDENT'S FACE'

Both Sides Join in This Aim and Shape Procedure Accordingly —Session to Be Cut Short

By TURNER CATLEDGE
Special to The New York Times.

WASHINGTON, July 21.—The administration drive to push through Congress President Roosevelt's plan for changing the Supreme Court appeared tonight to have completely collapsed.

Senate opponents of the judiciary reorganization program were in full control of the battle and the President's leaders, suing for peace, were trying to arrange a tactful surrender such as might at least save the non-controversial provisions for "reforms" in the lower courts, but end the bitter five-month fight over the issue and permit early adjournment of Congress.

An adjournment movement was rising as the Court Bill drive was crumbling and the administration was reported to favor it, even if certain important bills had to be jettisoned pending a possible special session in October.

Senator Barkley, elected majority leader today over Senator Harrison by one vote, announced tonight that a special meeting of the Senate Judiciary Committee had been called for tomorrow for "informal discussions of the Court Bill situation."

His announcement came at the end of a two-hour conference in the office of Vice President Garner, which was also attended by Senator Ashurst, chairman of the committee.

Garner Calls On Wheeler

Earlier Vice President Garner had visited Senator Wheeler, field marshal of the Court Bill opposition, and had told him in effect that the administration would abandon its effort to drive through the compromise measure now pending providing the addition of one justice a year to the Supreme Court to supplement members remaining on that bench past the age of 75.

The compromise was offered two weeks ago by Senator Robinson as an administration substitute for the President's original bill providing the immediate addition of five justices (six prior to the retirement of Justice Van Devanter) to replace or supplement those over 70 years of age.

The Vice President is understood to have told Mr. Wheeler in effect that opponents might write their own ticket on a separate bill salvaging the parts of the program dealing with the lower courts.

Mr. Wheeler announced immediately that the opponents would accept that responsibility and prepare a measure for submission to the administration leaders by early next week.

Demands Assurance as to House

He made it very definite, however, that the cooperation of the opposition was based on an understanding that the administration would take no advantage in later action, in Senate, House or conference, designed to incorporate provisions dealing with the personnel of the Supreme Court.

Senator Wheeler said, also, that the provisions in the pending bill dealing with the lower courts would be modified considerably in the opposition's redraft.

"Our group is willing to work out legislation for reforms in the lower courts," he said. "The difference between the opposition's position and the position of some of the President's advisers is that we are for reform, while they want control of the court.

"We want to speed up decisions in the lower courts, to correct abuses in the lower courts in connection with injunction matters, to speed up appeals to the Supreme Court on constitutional matters and to prevent racketeering in connection with lower court receivership cases.

"I am going to take up with our group a proposal to see if we can work out a proposition along these lines and submit it to the administration for consideration.

"We will definitely oppose the provision in the present bill creating a proctor for the Supreme Court because, while it might result in some good, the possibility of abuses is too great.

"We oppose the provision in the pending bill for creation of a group of roving judges. I would be willing to provide in the bill that the administration should have whatever number of judges it deems necessary. But I would not be will-

ing to base it on age or on political consideration.

"Where the Attorney General may say that there is need for new judges I favor giving him new judges regardless of whether twenty or fifty would be required.

"Any compromise settlements will provide a definite understanding that there shall be no reprisals. It also will provide that there shall be no changes made in the bill when it comes before the House."

Barkley Move Is Rebuffed

These remarks were made by the Montana Senator just after his conference with Vice President Garner.

The terms of the administration surrender on the controversial parts of the program were being evolved with President Roosevelt's full knowledge. Those participating in recent conferences said that he had given his leaders carte blanche authority to make the best deal possible.

Outwardly, however, he was still maintaining the position he has taken from the start, and reiterated in his letter to Senator Barkley Friday that the fight for the "objectives" of the Court Bill must go on.

Mr. Barkley was said to have made one last suggestion to the Opposition leaders late today: that some Supreme Court provisions be worked out, but he met instant refusal.

The feeling in the ranks of the President's followers on the Court Bill was best epitomized by Senator Minton, who made a vigorous speech in its defense early in the Senate debate. Asked to comment on the Opposition's earlier proposal to recommit the bill to the Judiciary Committee, he replied:

"They've got the votes. It's up to them."

Senator Logan, co-author with Senators Robinson, Hatch and Ashurst, of the compromise bill, indicated that he had definitely given up the fight. He said he was "sick and tired of the court issue" and "ready to let the whole matter drop."

Details of future procedure on the bill had not been determined tonight, but advocates and opponents both wanted to handle it in such manner as not to seem a gratuitous slap at the President.

The measure will be laid aside automatically tomorrow while the Senate considers a privileged matter, the President's veto on the Farm Mortgage Interest Reduction Bill, which the House has already passed over his disapproval. Debate on the veto is expected to consume all of tomorrow and perhaps part of Friday.

The Senate is likely to adjourn then until Monday, giving the opposition group time to work out its bill for lower court changes.

All these details will be discussed at the Judiciary Committee's meeting tomorrow. Some Senators thought tonight that to recommit the pending compromise would be construed as a slap at the President and that the best course would be to offer any new proposal as a substitute for the pending compromise.

Procedure Aims to "Save Face"

Others felt that by Monday the situation would have been so clarified, and the heat so subsided, as to make recommitment possible without a bad connotation being attached to the word.

High in the immediate purposes of both sides, as frankly conceded by some of his closest friends, was the desire to "save the President's face."

Vice President Garner conferred with Senator Wheeler soon after the Democratic caucus this morning. While they were talking Senators Barkley and Harrison were called to the White House, where at a luncheon conference the court bill issue and the general legislative situation were again discussed.

The belief tonight was that the President would insist on enactment of the remainder of his legislative program at this session with the understanding that if any bills caused much controversy they would be laid over for a special session in October.

Subject to these plans the President is said to have placed on the "preferred list" measures dealing with tax loophole plugging, further farm adjustments, the wages and hours bill, housing and administrative reorganization.

It was impossible for any one to predict today the length of time any of these measures might take. The court bill fight has been so bitter and so absorbing as to prevent many Senators from studying other matters. Therefore, it is not known definitely which, if any, of them have possibilities for controversy.

According to plans discussed at the White House yesterday a drive will be started next week to shove these through. The belief was that the movement to get Congress out of Washington would grow to such proportions that adjournment would come by the end of three weeks.

The aim is to close the present session as quickly as possible to end the bitterness that has grown up over the court fight; to get through the program which the President feels he has promised the people, but at the same time to guard against the possibility of a long and controversial session next year just before the Congressional election.

Opponents of the President's court program indicated tonight that they would cooperate to the fullest in disposing of the matter, provided Senator Wheeler's terms are lived up to by the administration.

Borah to Watch Substitute

Two of the leading court bill opponents, Senators O'Mahoney and Clark, expressed these views.

"If they had accepted a constitutional amendment when it was first suggested, it could have been enacted by this time," Senator O'Mahoney said.

Senator Borah served notice that the opposition would scrutinize carefully the lower court provisions to see that they did not interfere with the independence of the judiciary.

"I am sure that no compromise can be made, or even be considered, which surrenders in the slightest degree the principle of an independent judiciary," he said. "Anything which looks like political control of the courts, either the higher courts or the lower courts, is not contemplated by the opponents."

Senator Overton, a member of the committee of eight who yesterday urged Vice President Garner to tell the President frankly of the plight of the Court Bill, issued a statement this afternoon explaining his own position and, no doubt, indicating the feeling of other Senators who had previously remained uncommitted on the plan.

"Shortly after the President's message with the bill attached thereto proposing a reorganization of the Federal judiciary was sent to Congress, I concluded that the bill as proposed by the President would not be enacted into law," he said.

"I was unwilling to place myself at the very outset in open opposition to a bill so strongly sponsored by the President. I beheld the party, of which I have been a lifelong member, split in twain and its future success jeopardized.

"I suggested to a number of Senators who had not committed themselves on the proposal that we hold a conference to determine the best course to pursue. We concluded the fair and manly thing to do was to advise the Vice President of our attitude in order that he might, in turn, advise the President. This we did."

Senator Andrews, also a member of the committee of eight, issued an appeal for his own proposal for a constitutional amendment requiring retirement of Supreme Court justices at 75 and providing a justice for each of the judicial circuits, now numbering ten, in addition to a chief justice.

TRUMAN SEIZES STEEL; STRIKE OFF; HE SCORES INDUSTRY AS RECKLESS

PRESIDENT IN PLEA

Address on Air Charges Industry With Greed for High Profits

SAWYER WILL RUN MILLS

Washington Judge Signs Order Setting Hearing for Today on Legality of Action

By CHARLES E. EGAN

Special to THE NEW YORK TIMES.

WASHINGTON, April 8—President Truman tonight ordered seizure of the steel mills to avert a strike of their 600,000 workers. An order directing that the Government take over the mills was issued effective at midnight, one minute before the scheduled strike was to take place.

Under the terms of tonight's order, which the President said had been issued "in the public interest," Charles Sawyer, Secretary of Commerce, will take over the operation of the steel mills.

In moving against the giant of American industries the President was believed to have touched off one of the sharpest legal battles in a generation. The steel mill owners are insistent that the President does not have power, under the Constitution or under his emergency grants of authority, to take possession of the mills. Counsel for steel mills were prepared to challenge the President's action in a half dozen Federal district courts in the country tomorrow, according to reports.

[Federal Judge Walter M. Bastian signed an order early Wednesday in Washington calling a hearing for 11:30 A. M. on suits filed by two of the major steel companies—Republic and Youngstown Sheet and Tube—challenging the Government's seizure, The Associated Press reported.]

Steelman Sets Meeting

In compliance with the President's request, Dr. John R. Steelman, Acting Director of Defense Mobilization, telephoned representatives of the six big steel companies and Philip Murray, president of the United Steelworkers of America, C. I. O. Dr. Steelman asked the operators and Mr. Murray to come to Washington for a meeting with him at 3 P. M. tomorrow.

In addition, Dr. Steelman talked by telephone with Nathan Feinsinger, chairman of the Wage Stabilization Board, who has been in New York seeking to effect an agreement. Mr. Feinsinger will meet with Dr. Steelman at noon to give the Defense Mobilizer a complete report on the discussions that have been in progress in New York.

Also in response to the President's orders, Secretary Sawyer immediately designated the presidents of the steel companies as "operating managers" on behalf of the United States.

In a statement issued after the President's broadcast Mr. Sawyer said that he "neither requested nor wanted this job, but when our men at the front are taking orders in the face of great danger those of us farther back can do no less."

He indicated that he would not act on the wage question that brought about the strike threat until both labor and management arrived at an agreement.

The President announced his intention of seizing the mills to the public in a combined radio and television broadcast delivered over all major networks at 10:30 P. M.

The President in his speech called steel "our key industry."

"It is vital to our defense efforts," he declared. "It is vital to peace."

Mr. Truman castigated the steel industry, placing on the operators the blame for the present impasse in negotiations. Despite current profits which give them more than a comfortable return, the President said, the "companies are now saying they ought to have a price increase."

"That's about the most outrageous thing I ever heard of," he declared. "They not only want to raise their prices to cover any wage increase; they want to double their money on the deal."

He explained that he was taking the measures because they were the only way to prevent a shutdown.

"As President of the United States it is my plain duty to keep this from happening," Mr. Truman declared. He said the steel companies were "recklessly forcing a shutdown of the steel mills."

"They are trying to get special, preferred treatment, not available to any other industries," the President continued, "and they are apparently willing to stop steel production to get it."

Mr. Truman reviewed the activities of the Wage Stabilization Board in endeavoring to reach a fair settlement of wage claims of the steel workers. He said the recommendations that were made to the steel industry on March 20 provided "a fair and reasonable basis for reaching a settlement on a new management-labor contract —a settlement that is consistent with our present stabilization program."

"Steel industry profits are now running at the rate of about $2,500,000,000 a year," the President continued. "The steel companies are now making a profit of about $19.50 on every ton of steel they produce. On top of that they can get a price increase of close to $3 a ton under the Capehart Amendment to the Price Control Law. They don't need this, but we are going to have to give it to them because the Capehart Amendment requires it.

"Now add to this the $19.50 a ton they are already making and you have profits of better than $22 a ton."

Taft-Hartley Procedure

The President insisted that the settlement offered by the Wage Board was fair to both parties and to the public interest.

"What's more, I think the steel companies know it," he declared.

The President went on to explain that a big rise in steel prices would increase the prices of other things all up and down the line. Sooner or later, prices of all the products that use steel would go up—tanks and trucks and buildings, automobiles and vacuum cleaners and refrigerators right on down to canned goods and egg beaters, he said.

He conceded that many had been asking why he did not rely on procedures of the Taft-Hartley Act to deal with the emergency.

"This has not been done because the so-called emergency provisions of the Taft-Hartley Act would be of no help in meeting the situation that confronts us tonight," he declared.

"That act provides that before anything else is done the President must first set up a board of inquiry to find the facts on the dispute and report to him as to what they are. We would have to sit around for a week or two for this board to report before we could take the next step. And meanwhile the steel plants would be shut down."

Mr. Truman explained that the Taft-Hartley procedure could not prevent a steel shutdown of at least a week or two.

"The way we want to get steel production—the only way to get it in the long run—is for management and labor to sit down and settle their dispute," he said. "Sooner or later that's what will have to be done. So it might just as well be done now.

"At midnight the Government will take over the steel plants. Both management and labor will then be working for the Government. And they will have a clear duty to heat up their furnaces again and go on making steel.

"When management and labor meet down here in Washington, they will have a chance to go back to bargaining and settle their dispute. As soon as they do that, we can turn the steel plants back to their private owners with the assurance that production will continue.

"It is my earnest hope that the parties will settle without delay—tomorrow if possible. I don't want to see the Government running the steel plants a moment longer than is absolutely necessary to prevent a shutdown.

"There is no excuse for the present impasse in negotiations. Everyone concerned knows what ought to be done. A settlement should be reached between the steel companies and the union. And the companies should then apply to the Office of Price Stabilization for whatever price increase they are entitled to under the law.

"That is what is called for in the national interest.

"On behalf of the whole country, I ask the steel companies and the steelworkers' unions to compose their differences in the American spirit of fair play and obedience to the law of the land."

The Executive Order Cited

In his Executive Order the President said that to assure the continued availability of steel and steel products during the existing emergency, the Secretary of Commerce was directed:

¶To take possession of all plants, facilities, and other properties of more than eighty-eight companies.

¶To act through with the aid of public or private instrumentalities or persons as he may designate. All Federal agencies were directed to cooperate to the fullest extent possible.

¶To determine and prescribe terms and conditions of employment under which the plants of which the Government takes possession shall be operated, recognizing the rights of workers "to bargain collectively through representatives of their own choosing and to engage in concerted activities for the purpose of collective bargaining, adjustment of grievances, or other mutual aid or protection, provided that such activities do not interfere with the operation of such plants, facilities, and other properties."

¶To see that management of the plants continue their functions, including the collection and disbursement of funds in the usual and ordinary course of business in the names of their respective companies.

¶To keep existing rights and obligations of the companies in full force and effect. "There may be made, in due course, payments of dividends on stocks and of principal, interest, sinking funds; and all other distributions upon bonds, debentures, and other obligations end expenditures may be made for other ordinary corporate or business purposes.

¶To return the possession and operation of the plant to the private owner whenever the Secretary decides that the operation of a plant or other property is no longer necessary or expedient in the interest of national defense.

¶To issue such regulations and orders as deemed necessary for carrying out the purposes of the order and to delegate and authorize subdelegations of such of his functions under the order as he deems desirable.

Senators Fear Crisis

The decision that seizure of the mills was the only way out for the Government was reached at a three-hour conference of top governmental officials with Dr. Steelman this afternoon.

Dr. Steelman and Secretary Sawyer later called on the President and advised a direct explanation to the public. They are understood to have told him that the talk should include a sharp criticism of the steel mill owners for their failure to accept wage and other recommendations made last month by the Wage Stabilization Board.

The President has been charged with "playing politics" with the steel strike threat because he has not invoked the Taft-Hartley Law. In the Senate today, Senator John W. Bricker, Republican of Ohio, called on the President to use the provisions of the Taft-Hartley Act and asserted that the seizure of the mills "would be a perversion, a distortion of the law."

The Ohio Senator and Senator Harry P. Cain, Republican of Washington, voiced the belief that seizure of the plants would lead to nationalization of the steel industry.

"I believe there is a determination to break down private enterprise and move into heavy industry," Senator Bricker told the Senate. He called such a move "basic" to the plans of socialism, "which is in the minds of many of the planners and those who believe in centralized Government."

The steel deadlock developed when producers balked at accepting recommendations of the Wage Stabilization Board for a wage contract increasing the hourly wage of steel workers by 17½ cents an hour and allowing fringe benefits that would bring the total to slightly more than 26 cents an hour over a period of eighteen months. Wages in the industry now average $1.88 an hour.

Industry representatives insisted that the wage recommendations could not be accepted unless compensating increases in the price of finished steel were allowed by the Government. The industry maintained that a price advance of $12 a ton was essential while Government spokesmen maintained that an advance of $2 to $3 a ton was all the industry could expect.

April 9, 1952

SENATE BARS FUND FOR STEEL SEIZURE, DEFYING PRESIDENT

Votes 44 to 31 to Deny Use of Money in Appropriation Bill to Run the Industry

PLEA BY TRUMAN IGNORED

He Had Told Congress Refusal of Finances Might Shut Down Mills, Bring Korea Defeat

By C. P. TRUSSELL
Special to The New York Times

WASHINGTON, April 21—Despite a contention advanced today by President Truman that denial of funds required to carry out his steel industry seizure order might paralyze the Government in an emergency, the Senate voted 44 to 31 against permitting use for operation of the mills of any money in a pending $2,610,000 supplemental appropriations bill.

The effect of this vote was not expected to be "paralyzing." It was accepted widely, however, as an expression by the Senate of disapproval of the President's seizure action.

The 44-31 vote was seen in some Congressional quarters as a sign that, although today's restrictive action was held to a single appropriation, similar action might be taken as every other money measure went to the Senate floor. If these predictions were correct, the President's seizure of the steel mills could be "starved out."

Two Republicans Oppose Ban

Republicans, aided by some but not all Southern Democrats, won the fight for money restrictions today. Eleven Democrats helped thirty-three Republicans. Two Republicans joined in vain the twenty-nine Democrats who tried to stop this Republican-led move to "rebuke" or "repudiate" the President's seizure action.

A sharp fight had broken out in the Senate last week. The debate centered on constitutional lines but it was conceded, as informal discussions carried into the Capitol corridors, that the battle had a thick political aspect. The situation was said to have caused concern at the White House.

This morning Vice President Alben W. Barkley received a letter from the President. It was read to the Senate. In this communication the President:

1. Repeated what he said in his message to Congress on April 9 that he ordered the steel mills seizure "with the utmost reluctance; that the idea of Government operation * * * was thoroughly distasteful."
2. Again offered his cooperation to Congress for the development of legislative action that would meet the steel crisis.

From this point, the President appeared to be "talking back" to the Congressional situation that had developed.

Decries Course of Negation

"I do not believe," he stated, "the Congress can meet its responsibilities simply by following a course of negation. The Congress cannot perform its constitutional functions simply by paralyzing the operations of the Government in an emergency.

"The Congress can, if it wishes, reject the course of action I have followed in this matter. As I indicated in my message of April 9, I ordered Government operation of the mills only because the available alternatives [including resort to the Taft-Hartley Act, he emphasized] seemed to me to be even worse.

"The Congress may have a different judgment. If it does, however, the Congress should do more than simply tell me what I should not do. It should pass affirmative legislation to provide a constructive course of action looking toward a solution of this matter which will be in the public interest."

Mr. Truman contended that a denial of funds to carry out his seizure order would result in the shutting down of the steel mills. A shutdown such as this, for a material time, he added, would "immediately reduce the ability of our troops in Korea to defend themselves against attack."

"If the Communists stage another offensive in Korea this spring," he added, "the success or failure of that offensive may well depend on whether or not we have kept our steel mills in operation."

Mr. Truman then challenged the Congress to take constructive legislative action to handle the steel situation.

The letter to Mr. Barkley did not appear to disturb materially the voting lines that already had been drawn in the Senate. It had been predicted that the Republicans would get support from Southern Democrats. They did, but not with the strength that was forecast.

Just before the vote was taken—on the specific issue of whether supplemental funds for the Department of Commerce (now holding the steel mills) could be used to implement the seizure, Senator Richard B. Russell, Democrat of Georgia and a Presidential candidate, told the Senate that he would not vote for dealing with an Executive Order by cutting off appropriations.

He added, however, that he would support a "constructive legislative program" that would "take the steel mills from the hands of the President," and let the matter be dealt with through law and not by a simple denial of money.

Russell Unheeded by Some

Although Mr. Russell has been long the active floor leader in the civil rights fights in the Senate where the South usually wins, his decision on this issue did not bring united Southern support to him. Voting for the ban on use of funds for the steel seizure were Southern Democrats including:

Senators Harry F. Byrd and A. Willis Robertson of Virginia, James O. Eastland and John C. Stennis of Mississippi, Allen J. Ellender of Louisiana, Clyde R. Hoey of North Carolina, Spessard L. Holland and George A. Smathers of Florida, Burnet R. Maybank of South Carolina and John L. McClennan of Arkansas.

Herbert R. O'Conor of Maryland was another Democrat who voted for the amendment.

The two Republicans who broke loose from the Republican move were Senators William Langer of North Dakota and Wayne Morse of Oregon.

Meantime, Commerce Department lawyers in consultation with the Economic Stabilization Agency, were working on an order to put a wage increase into effect in the steel plants.

Pay Rise to Be Retroactive

An authoritative source said the increase would be retroactive to Jan. 1, the date a new contract would take effect if an agreement had been reached in the normal course of bargaining.

It is expected, without any official confirmation, however, that the order will give the steel workers what the Wage Stabilization Board recommended—12½ cents an hour and paid holidays and other adjustments estimated to cost 5.1 cents an hour. Other increases in July and next January would make the total 26 to 30 cents.

Officials in charge of prices said they knew of nothing to warrant speculation on a rise in steel prices other than the figure of "slightly less than $3" that the Office of Price Stabilization is prepared to authorize.

Charles Sawyer, Secretary of Commerce and nominal operator of the seized steel facilities, was reported to favor granting a price increase of at least $5 a ton to get the Government out of the steel business. But Roger L. Putnam, Economic Stabilization Administrator, said he did not have any figure from Mr. Sawyer. He said he had talked over the whole problem with the Secretary and that Mr. Sawyer also wanted some information and counsel on terms and conditions of employment, which he is authorized to determine under the seizure order of the President.

Mr. Putnam said he expected the President's Advisory Board on Mobilization Policy would make some recommendations on the subject and he wanted to see those before he took any action or spoke further.

The sixteen-member advisory board, composed of representatives of the public, business, labor and agriculture, holds a two-day meeting once a month at the White House.

At the first day's session today, the board heard Nathan P. Feinsinger, chairman of the Wage Stabilization Board; Ellis Arnall, Price Stabilization Director, and Mr. Putnam. Dr. John R. Steelman, acting Director of Defense Mobilization, presided at the meeting.

Mr. Arnall, after the White House meeting, reaffirmed his position on steel prices.

"As long as it remains in my hands there will be no price increase" beyond the figure previously announced, he said.

Tomorrow, according to schedule, the Senate is to take a vote on a proposal, also Republican-sponsored, that would deny all appropriations, current or past or future, to an implementing of any and all Presidential seizure orders, unless Congress agreed.

This proposal would require, for effectiveness, a two-thirds vote of the Senate. This was not expected tonight.

April 22, 1952

Truman Insists Courts, Congress Cannot End His Inherent Powers

By ANTHONY LEVIERO

Special to The New York Times.

WASHINGTON, May 22—President Truman repeatedly asserted today that he had inherent Constitutional powers, including seizure, and neither the Judiciary nor Congress could deprive him of them. Yet he said he would return the steel mills to their owners if the Supreme Court decided his seizure of the industry was illegal.

The President's restatement of his views on his Constitutional powers, a source of controversy ever since he seized the steel industry on April 9 in the wage-price dispute, confused reporters at his news conference. The White House declined to clarify the President's remarks afterward.

Mr. Truman also mystified his hearers by saying he did not think that his powers were the issue before the high tribunal as they would see when its decision was handed down. The President, however, declined to explain his view of the issue before the court.

Federal District Judge David A. Pine has ruled that the seizure was illegal, and Government attorneys, basing their arguments on the statement of Presidential authority in Article II of the Constitution, appealed to the Supreme Court.

Mr. Truman's words stimulated conjecture that he might have some new plan for dealing with the steel controversy if the court should rule against him.

The President said in effect that the inherent powers of the President were untouchable, except by Constitutional amendment, and added that he did not believe such an amendment would be adopted. The conclusion that could be drawn from his remarks was that the President was relying on the principle that there were three coordinate branches of the Government and that one could not trespass on the prerogatives of another.

Tonight a high Administration source said that what Mr. Truman was getting at was this:

¶The Supreme Court passes on specific cases and specific circumstances and might decide that in the steel case Mr. Truman had exceeded or misused the powers inherent in the Constitution, but the court would not question the validity of those powers or seek to limit them.

¶Mr. Truman himself was somewhat uncertain of the application of his powers in the steel case but in the face of a steel strike had to act to assure continued steel production. Meanwhile as a result of the uncertainty, he had asked Congress for legislation to deal with future national strikes in an emergency.

Mr. Truman opened his news conference by expressing gratification over the settlement of the 3-year-old railroad wage and rules dispute last night. This case also involved Government seizure and operation, but differed from the steel case in that there was authority in the Railway Labor Act for seizure of the railroads.

The President said the rail case could have been settled in exactly the same way back in 1950, but that people sometimes could not understand that it was better to abide by the law than not. He said he hoped that from now on railroad labor and management would abide by the Railway Labor Act, which had been very successful up to this time.

Seizure in the railway case was at the request of the unions, so they had no kick on that score, and management had favored it, too, Mr. Truman said. He added he would turn the railroads back to the owners just as soon as he could get the papers signed.

The discussion of inherent powers arose when Mr. Truman was asked if the Administration had considered seeking a law "that would operate so that neither side would want and neither side could use seizure." He replied that he had been trying ever since he became President to get a law making possible real negotiation between labor and management.

Says President Has Power

When asked if this would include the right of seizure, the President said it would have to include means to keep the country running, as in the railroad case or that of any industry affecting the whole economy. Seizure seemed to be the ultimate end when the parties could not get together, but he did not know whether seizure was the answer, said Mr. Truman.

"You would have that [seizure] authority in reserve or would you have the President go to Congress in each emergency?" he was asked.

Mr. Truman replied that the President had the power and they could not take it away from him.

"Who do you mean, Sir, Congress—?" a question began.

The President said yes.

"—the courts, who?" the reporter ended.

Nobody could take it away from the President, Mr. Truman continued, because he was the Chief Executive of the nation and he had to be in a position to see that the welfare of the people was met when necessary.

He said the reporters should study history, starting with Washington and Jefferson and Andrew Jackson and Abraham Lincoln. They should read Carl Sandburg's "Lincoln" if they really wanted to know what the President's constitutional powers amount to, Mr. Truman added. He also said that these powers had also been invoked by Hayes, the two Roosevelts and Wilson.

"I will ask it again, and I would want to press it a little further," said the reporter. "You say the President has this power, talking about seizure, and 'they' can't take it away—."

Nobody could take it from him, the President interposed.

"—And that means the courts—?" the reporter continued.

He could put the "they" any place he wanted to, nobody could take it away, said the President.

"Isn't that what is up before the Supreme Court now?" the questioner persisted.

Mr. Truman said no, he did not

think so, as the reporter would find when the decision came down.

Then Mr. Truman was reminded that on another occasion he had said he would abide by the decision of the Supreme Court. The President said that was correct, that was exactly what he intended to do.

Suppose the court says the President does not have seizure power? he was asked. Mr. Truman reiterated that he would turn the steel industry back to the companies and see what would happen.

House Unit Scores Powers

WASHINGTON, May 22 (AP)—A House Judiciary subcommittee recommended today that Congress declare the President had no inherent power under the Constitution to seize private property.

It also proposed that Congress take a stand that the President not be allowed to change wages, hours, prices or working conditions in any plant, mine, facility or other property he had taken over since April 1 or might take over in the future.

The declaration, designed by Representative Tom Pickett, Democrat of Texas, to meet questions raised by President Truman's seizure of the steel industry, was written into the subcommittee's draft of legislation to extend forty-nine of the President's emergency war powers until June 30, 1952.

These include such powers as authority to provide $250 uniform allowances for Reserve officers called into active service, duty-free importation of personal and household effects of service personnel, and various matters relating to claims against the Government.

The Administration had asked extension of sixty of the powers. The subcommittee voted against eleven of these. One that the group decided was no longer needed was the Government's authority to seize railroads and other transportation facilities, since the long rail-labor dispute had been settled and the railroads were to be returned to private control,

May 23, 1952

TRUMAN AND THE CONGRESS: ANOTHER 'COLD WAR'

By WILLIAM S. WHITE

Special to THE NEW YORK TIMES.

WASHINGTON, June 14—Not since the old, old days of 1945, when so many were so fond of speaking of Harry S. Truman's "humility," have his relations with Congress been anything more cordial than tentatively warm.

Most of the time—the word "humility" was discarded by the beginning of 1946, when the true glimpse was caught of what lay behind the flashing spectacles—these relations have ranged from chilly to freezing. Now, in what appears to be the late afternoon of the President's career in the White House, the temperature has gone down sharply again over the issue of the steel strike and the Taft-Hartley Act, which Mr. Truman has spent the better part of five years trying to repeal.

Between 1600 Pennsylvania Avenue and the great stone building on Capitol Hill it is very cool for June, just as the other Junes have nearly all been cool.

This, of course, is by no means a unique state of affairs, especially given the circumstance that Mr. Truman presumably is a lame duck. President. Presidents who are going out are looked on with far less respect by other politicians than Presidents who may be staying in.

Then, there is the fact that it is more or less in the American way for there to be trouble with Congress for any except the most supine executive. Those famous "checks and balances" are quite real.

Emphasis on the Checks

Still, with Harry Truman, the checks have been more in Congress' mind than the balances.

This Tuesday Mr. Truman went up to the Capitol in his black limousine and asked Congress to give him a seizure law to deal with the steel strike, since the Supreme Court had said he could not seize the plants under his own powers, as he had tried to do.

As he walked into the House chamber, where Senate and House were assembled to hear him, there was a stout wave of applause, arising in part from personal affection, in part from relief in some quarters that this might be his last appearance there and in part from the fact that he is, after all, still President of the United States.

As he left there was perfunctory handclapping, except from a few Administration Democrats who smote their palms lustily.

All in between there was silence, stony and absolute.

The Senate hurried back to its own quarters to rebuke the President in the sharpest way it knew, by repudiating his request for a new law and admonishing him to use the Taft-Hartley Act. To some this action, by the old club of which Mr. Truman himself used to be a member, might have seemed an unduly unkind act.

Challenge and Rebuff

But the President had stuck out his chin. One of his Senate friends—a man who likes him but doesn't care much for his program—summed up the case thus:

"Harry don't give a damn. No doubt he has done what he thought was right; and that's that."

Not in a long time had there been an incident so illustrative as this appearance before the joint session of Congress of the strange and mixed state of feelings between Mr. Truman and the members of Congress.

Never, not even when in the 1948 campaign he was belaboring the Eightieth Congress as "the worst" of a long list of bad ones, has there been a tithe of the personal hatred in Congress toward President Truman that was directed toward his predecessor, Franklin D. Roosevelt.

Never, however, not even after Mr. Truman had done the incredible job of winning the 1948 election with his left and right wings both gone, has there been in Congress a tenth of the fear of Mr. Truman as a politician that there was of Mr. Roosevelt at his most powerful point.

It is a good deal easier to state this case than to prove it, because the supporting facts are more subtle and subjective than palpable and objective. Perhaps the best way to put it is that Mr. Roosevelt, even in his comparatively low periods, had about him an aura of spectacular success, whereas there has been an illogical tendency to regard Mr. Truman, even in his highest periods, as just lucky.

Greatest Paradox

Then, there was Mr. Roosevelt's magic technique in calling down maledictions at the microphone—a technique that Mr. Truman's best efforts have never touched—which threw a chill into the stoutest anti-Roosevelt hearts.

The greatest paradox of all has been that Harry Truman, the supposedly parochial character who had come from an inland and highly parochial political machine, has got Congress to work generally with him on foreign programs of staggering scope, design and implications, and has been thrown back at almost every point on domestic affairs.

Sectional interests, particularly those of the right-wing Democratic South, have plagued him far more than they did Mr. Roosevelt, and have had a heavy place in his two greatest defeats—on labor and civil rights legislation. It is true in this connection that the Roosevelt civil rights program never attempted nearly so much as did the Truman program, but it is also true that Mr. Roosevelt was nearly everywhere dominant, in most of his long tenure, on national legislation and certainly in the labor field.

But where Mr. Roosevelt, the world figure, found it touch-and-go to put over such matters as lend-lease in a world already aflame, Mr. Truman, the American Legionnaire from Independence, Mo., easily was able in a country merely afraid of a fire to make the United States the military guarantor of half the earth.

The answer to it is that Congress itself became reluctantly internationalist toward the end of the Roosevelt years and committedly internationalist during the Truman years. The Southern sectionalists who so fought Mr. Truman at home, by and large fought for him in world affairs. In a sense, they were the saviors of nearly all his great world projects.

Analysis of Attitudes

Harry Truman was once a member of Congress, as Mr. Roosevelt never was, and for this reason Mr. Truman's view of Congress, and Congress' view of him, are complex.

The Senate rebuff on the steel message is subject to ready analysis; but analysis of the general attitudes of the President toward

Congress and of Congress toward the President is quite another story. As to steel, the position may be described, on the private explanations of a good many Senators and Representatives, about as follows:

(1) The majority of Mr. Truman's joint session audience, Democratic and Republican alike, had (a) voted for the Taft-Hartley Act, (b) voted to strike down Mr. Truman's veto and (c) in many cases lived since the election of 1948 in a nagging fear that vengeance might yet be the President's in that regard.

(2) The majority, apart from partisan emotions, probably had been genuinely shocked at the President's seizure of the steel mills and at his persistent refusal to use the Taft-Hartley Act in the strike.

(3) A good many members had gone to the session with some sort of hope that the President, having declared himself out of it for 1952, might take a "moderate" view, cease his strictures on the Taft-Hartley Act and, as a kind of farewell to controversy, announce that he would employ that instrument.

This latter group, which was mostly Republican, felt, irrationally or not, rather like a man who half resentfully and half hopefully accepts a dinner invitation from a late enemy, draws up his chair in anticipation of initiatives from the host toward reconciliation and finds that the host has anything but apology in mind.

These attitudes, as mixed as they are, give some clue to the long and largely incompatible association between Harry S. Truman and the Congress of the United States.

Congress' Hope

Congress, on its side, has been inclined, every now and then, to ignore the plain flashes of lightning in the sky over the White House and to insist in its thinking that somehow and for some reason Mr. Truman was going to return one of these days at least a little way toward those days of "humility" in 1945.

The President, for his part, has always mixed a personally friendly and even jovial attitude with an inflexible fighting spirit, and Congress often has confused the two. It has long been his habit, for example, to go up to the Capitol occasionally for lunch, precisely like one of the boys, whereas Mr. Roosevelt, on his rare trips, sometimes had about him the quite unconscious air of a great lady passing through a doubtful neighborhood in which the urchins had chalked rude words upon the sidewalks.

Congress, in short, has persisted, off and on, in regarding Mr. Truman as a "good fellow" who would not be too adamant in its book—no matter how much evidence there has been to the precise contrary.

Thus it has been that, over and over, men at the Capitol, remembering many amiable personal characteristics of and meetings with "Harry," have responded in pained shock and almost comical unbelief when he has hit them with another Fair Deal message.

Usually, the gist of their response has been:

"Harry can't do this to us."

"Harry" not only could and can, but infallibly he has.

Unrealistic Serenity

From April 12, 1945, the day he entered the White House, until Sept. 6, of that year, all was unrealistically serene between White House and Capitol. The President, digging into a new and burdensome job, was quietly getting the feel of things and pretty well letting Congress alone.

Those were the days of his "humility," the days when the Roosevelt men, who had not much time for him then, and the ultra anti-Democrats, who misread him, had the fixed notion that he would not go quite so far as to act as though he actually was President.

But on Sept. 6, 1945, there came the cloud in the sky that was far bigger than a man's hand: the President sent up a message demanding a few little items like full employment and a Permanent Fair Employment Practice Act.

From that cloud, although it took time, there descended the Fair Deal—complete, by January of 1946, with twenty-one items. The elections of November, 1946, in which the Democrats were turned out of control of Congress and it looked as if they were on the way out of the White House, too, brought a rise in the thermometer; the President then was not thought to be powerful enough really to attack very hard.

Slow to Alarm

The famous "whistle stop" speeches of the 1948 campaign did not, until the very end, really alarm or even anger the Republicans; still they followed the almost universal illusion that they were "in." After that election of 1948 the political weather between President and Congress was nearly always the same: bad.

There were, of course, relatively fine spells, Indian summers more or less, when, as in the case of his intervening in Korea, Mr. Truman acted with what appeared to be the almost universal support of Congress. But these never lasted long, and every moment of pleasant warmth was followed by progressively longer cold periods.

So Harry S. Truman is spending these presumably last days in the White House with only the insulation of personal fighting spirit—politics aside, nobody denies him that—to keep him warm.

Who Has the Power to Make War?

Ratifying of the Atlantic Pact revives the issue of the relative roles of Congress and President.

By EDWARD S. CORWIN

THE Atlantic Pact is now a part of official national policy, but it is not yet a part of national thinking. As was the case with the Monroe Doctrine, this new doctrine must go through a considerable period of incubation and particularized application before it is assimilated into the fabric of our national life. Witness the current discussion of arms for the European signatory nations.

At the core of the debate is this question: Does the pact infringe upon Congress' power "to declare war"? Those who assert that it does point especially to Article V, which says that if any one of the signatory nations is attacked, each of the others will assist that nation by "taking forthwith * * * such action as it deems necessary, including the use of armed force." As a practical matter, according to these critics, it will ordinarily fall to the lot of the President to take "forthwith such action."

THIS is not a new issue. The Constitutional questions it raises will in all probability be very much the same as those which were voiced thirty years ago in the second Lodge reservation to the Covenant of the League. What, therefore, does history say as to the respective powers of the President and Congress to initiate war?

A good starting point for our inquiry is provided by Madison's Notes on the Philadelphia Convention. The question under debate on Aug. 17, 1787, was whether Congress should be given power "to make war":

> Mr. Pinkney opposed the vesting this power in the Legislature. Its proceedings were too slow. It wd. meet but once a year. The Hs. of Rrps. would be too numerous for such deliberations. The Senate would be the best depositary, being more acquainted with foreign affairs, and most capable of proper resolutions. If the States are equally represented in Senate, so as to give no advantage to large States, the power will notwithstanding be safe, as the small have their all at stake in such cases as well as the large States. It would be singular for one—authority to make war, and another peace.
>
> Mr. Butler. The Objections agst the Legislature lie in a great degree agst the Senate. He was for vesting the power in the President, who will have all the requisite qualities, and will not make war but when the Nation will support it.
>
> Mr. M(adison) and Mr. Gerry moved to insert "declare," striking out "make" war; leaving to the Executive the power to repel sudden attacks.

Madison's motion carried.

In short, Congress' power "to declare war" was not intended to deny the President the power to "repel sudden attacks." On the contrary, the convention recognized that power, although it was perceived that such action by the President would be tantamount to "making" war.

Prophetic, too, was Jay's enumeration in The Federalist of the advantages the President would enjoy in seizing the initiative in the field of foreign affairs: the unity of his office, its capacity for secrecy and dispatch, and its superior sources of information. To which he might well have added the fact that whereas the Houses of Congress are frequently not in session, the President always is.

ANOTHER hint of the shape of things to come was Hamilton's casual remark in one of his Federalist letters that "the ceremony of a formal declaration of war has of late fallen into disuse." That Congressional declarations of war have more often than not been little more than a "formal ceremony," will be pointed out in a moment.

Yet Presidential dominance in the field of foreign relations was not achieved without a struggle. Early in 1793, when war broke out between France and Great Britain and President Washington issued a proclamation of "impartiality," Washington was assailed by pro-French sympathizers on the ground that no clause in the Constitution gave him power to take any such stand.

HAMILTON, writing under the pen name "Pacificus," answered this argument by contending that the very opening clause of Article II—"the executive power shall be vested in a President of the United States of America"—endowed the President with full prerogatives in matters of foreign affairs, except wherever the Constitution specifically provided otherwise.

Thereupon, under urging by Secretary of State Jefferson "to take up your pen and cut 'Pacificus' to pieces in the face of the public," Madison, writing as "Helvidius" (a Roman statesman of republican views), developed the argument that the power to declare war was intended to vest in Congress all large decisions in the field of foreign policy and especially those involving questions of war and peace.

Neither Jefferson nor Madison seems, however, to have been particularly sincere in adopting this position. The latter frankly admitted to his mentor that he had never

> undertaken a task less to his taste, and when Hamilton, in 1801, besought his Federalist friends in Congress to support Jefferson for President against Burr, he testified that Jefferson had, as Secretary of State, consistently supported strong views of executive power. Jefferson was good at covering his tracks.

In 1836, when Madison died, it fell to the lot of John Quincy Adams to pronounce the official eulogy on him. He paid warm tribute to the acuity of the "Helvidius" papers, but added that history had refuted them. In speaking thus Adams can hardly have forgotten his own part in the formulation and promulgation of the Monroe Doctrine thirteen years earlier—a claim on the part of the President, as bold as it was successful, to define the defensible American interest abroad and to put American power and prestige behind it.

TEN years later James K. Polk deliberately precipitated war with Mexico by sending American troops into a region disputed by the two countries. This was a course of action which has generally set the pattern ever since.

Of our six considerable wars, the declarations for the War of 1812 and the Spanish-American War of 1898 alone may be described as having been initiated on the floors of Congress. The remaining four, including the Mexican and

---

EDWARD S. CORWIN, Professor Emeritus of Jurisprudence at Princeton University, wrote, among other books, "The President, Office and Powers."

The New York Times.
PRESIDENT CALLS FOR WAR DECLARATION, STRONGER NAVY, NEW ARMY OF 500,000 MEN, FULL CO-OPERATION WITH GERMANY'S FOES
Text of the President's Address
ARMED AMERICAN STEAMSHIP SUNK

1917—Wilson asks Congress to declare war against Germany, April 2; it did four days later.

Civil Wars, were the direct outgrowth of Presidential policies in the shaping of which Congress enjoyed at most a distinctly secondary role. None the less, Congress has never failed to comply with a Presidential request that it declare war; it could not, war being an accomplished fact of a very compulsive kind.

And what, meantime, had happened to the power of the President to "repel sudden attacks"? It had developed into an undefined power—almost unchallenged from the first and occasionally sanctified judicially—to employ without Congressional authorization the armed forces in the protection of American rights and interests abroad whenever necessary.

In his work, "World Policing and the Constitution," James Grafton Rogers lists 149 such episodes between the undeclared war with France in 1798 and Pearl Harbor. While inviting some pruning, the list demonstrates beyond peradventure the power of the President, as Chief Executive and Commander in Chief, to judge whether a situation requires the use of available forces to support American rights abroad and to take action in accordance with that decision.

To be sure, such decisions have frequently been justified as being "acts of self-defense" rather than "acts of war," but the targets in every case were entitled to treat them as acts of war nevertheless.

AMONG latter-day examples of the President's power to "dispose" American military forces are three contributed by the two Roosevelts: Theodore Roosevelt's coup in 1903 when he "took Panama"; his exploit in 1907 in sending the fleet around the world to impress Japan, leaving it to Congress to provide the wherewithal to bring it back home; and finally, Franklin D. Roosevelt's transference in the summer of 1940 of fifty over-age destroyers to Great Britain in return for certain sites and naval bases in the west Atlantic. Here the power to dispose the forces became for the nonce the power to dispose of them.

The implied historical foundations of Senator Lodge's second reservation — wherein the United States disclaimed any mutual defense obligations without Congressional approval — were therefore spurious. But the question remains whether it is a good thing that the President has achieved so dominant a position in the realm of foreign policy and, further, whether Article V of the Atlantic Pact is not calculated to aggravate this condition of affairs.

That Presidential conduct of American foreign relations has been spiced at times with a considerable element of personal adventuring is beyond question.

Polk's Mexican policy answers to this description, even though no one today would wish to think away the magnificent empire which it achieved. Lincoln's failure to summon Congress on the fall of Fort Sumter (this suited in all essentials the designation of "a sudden attack" by a foreign foe) may likewise have proved beneficial in aiding the North to make up its mind to challenge secession; it was, however, at the expense of serious "interstitial detriments" to the Constitution which continue to be felt.

Theodore Roosevelt was unquestionably fond of playing with fire and of the "hush-hush" of secret diplomacy. Honest man that he was, Woodrow Wilson's anti-submarine policy was somewhat less than candid, and left thousands of his supporters in the 1916 election flabbergasted or thoroughly indignant when war came. On the late President Roosevelt's dependence on the counsel of those who were responsible only to himself, we have a magnificent textbook in Mr. Sher-

1941—Roosevelt addresses Congress before the formal statement of war against Japan, Dec. 8.

wood's "Roosevelt and Hopkins," a culminating chapter of which is the one dealing with the Yalta Conference.

IT is thus significant that the United Nations Participation Act of 1945 definitely bases American implementation of the United Nations Charter not on Presidential prerogative but on the national legislative power. The theory of the act is that American participation in the United Nations is a matter for Congressional collaboration. This theory the Atlantic Pact abandons in effect.

The obligations created by the pact for the United States must, we assume, be addressed to the organ of the national Government whose Constitutional powers are most nearly adequate to their discharge. This means that the obligation created by Article V will ordinarily rest with the President, just as has the discharge in the past of similar obligations in the protection of American interests abroad.

Furthermore, in the discharge of this obligation the President will ordinarily be required to use force and perform acts of war. Of course, if such acts of war are countered by the original aggressor with more aggression, then Congress will be asked by the President "to declare war" formally, a request which it will have no real option to refuse.

ON the other hand, this does not signify that Article V spells further aggrandizement of Presidential power. What distinguishes the article is the conception which it sets forth of a defensible American interest abroad; and in this respect it only records, as the Committee on Foreign Affairs has insisted,

> what is a fact, namely, that an armed attack within the meaning of the treaty would in the present-day world constitute an attack upon the entire community comprising the parties to the treaty, including the United States. Accordingly, the President and the Congress, within their sphere of assigned Constitutional responsibilities, would be expected to take all action necessary and appropriate to protect the United States against the consequence and dangers of an armed attack committed against any party to the treaty.

Thus Presidential prerogative in the realm of foreign policy remains in substance what it was before the ratification of the pact. The only difference is that the country is alerted—as it was by the Monroe Doctrine 126 years ago—to a new and enlarged conception of American interest abroad, a conception the substantial truth of which cannot be denied.

THE problem of keeping the President's role in foreign relations safely within the bounds of democratic processes is not to be solved by shutting our eyes to the facts of life, especially as they relate to the power and position of the United States in the contemporary world.

The problem, in short, is one of domestic Constitutional reform. The diplomatic powers of the President cannot be substantially curtailed; but their exercise can be subjected to the counsel and scrutiny of advisers some of whom acknowledge a primary allegiance not to the White House but to Capitol Hill. The Atlantic Pact is, in fact, the product of just that kind of joint counsel, the ready availability of which should become a fixed part of the Constitutional system.

July 31, 1949

HOUSE AND SENATE OVERRIDE VETO BY NIXON ON CURB OF WAR POWERS; BACKERS OF BILL WIN 3-YEAR FIGHT

Vote Asserts Control of Congress Over Combat Abroad

By RICHARD L. MADDEN
Special to The New York Times

WASHINGTON, Nov. 7—The House and the Senate, dealing President Nixon what appeared to be the worst legislative setback of his five years in office, today overrode his veto of a measure aimed at limiting Presidential power to commit the armed forces to hostilities abroad without Congressional approval.

The House voted first—284 to 135, or only four votes more than the required two-thirds of those present and voting—to override the veto. The Senate followed suit nearly four hours later by a vote of 75 to 18, or 13 more than the required two-thirds.

It was the first time in nine attempts this year that both houses had overridden a veto and the first time legislation has become law over the President's veto since Congress overrode a Nixon veto of a water-pollution-control measure in October, 1972.

Supporters of the measure, who had waged a three-year effort to enact it into law, said it was the first time in history that Congress had spelled out the war-making powers of Congress and the President.

The White House said in a statement that Mr. Nixon felt the Congressional action today "seriously undermines this nation's ability to act decisively and convincingly in times of international crisis." It declined, however, to say what the President planned to do as a result of the overriding of his veto.

With the veto overridden, the war-powers measure—couched in the form of a joint resolution, which in Congress has the same status as a bill—immediately became law. It contains the following provisions:

¶The President would be required to report to Congress in writing within 48 hours after the commitment of armed forces to combat abroad.

¶The combat action would have to end in 60 days unless Congress authorized the commitment, but this deadline could be extended for 30 days if the President certified it was necessary for safe withdrawal of the forces.

¶Within that 60-day or 90-day period Congress could order an immediate removal of the forces by adopting a concurrent resolution, which is not subject to a Presidential veto.

The Nixon Administration had previously been stung by the legislative branch through such actions as the Senate's rejection of two nominees for the Supreme Court, Clement F. Haynsworth Jr. and G. Harrold Carswell, and the Congressional decision to end the program to develop a United States supersonic transport.

But the votes today were regarded as a rebuke of potentially greater significance because they dealt directly with the President's interpretation of his Constitutional authority.

Beyond reflecting the low political estate to which President Nixon has fallen, the Congressional action represented the most aggressive assertion of independence and power by the legislative branch against the executive branch in many years.

Several Republicans insisted that they were not striking at Mr. Nixon because of the Watergate scandal, but up to now he had managed to rally enough Republican strength in Congress to sustain his vetoes. Voting against him today were 86 Republicans in the House and 25 in the Senate.

Earlier this year Congress forced a halt in the United States bombing in Cambodia as of Aug. 15, but until today both houses had never been able to muster a two-thirds vote to override Mr. Nixon's vetoes of measures dealing with the nation's involvement in combat abroad.

Mr. Nixon had vetoed the war-powers bill Oct. 24 on the ground that it was "clearly unconstitutional." He said then—as the White House reiterated today—that it would "seriously undermine this nation's ability to act decisively and convincingly in times of international crisis."

Before the House overrode the veto, Representative Gerald R. Ford of Michigan, the minority leader and Vice President-designate, made a strong appeal against the bill.

Mr. Ford said that the bill "has the potential for disaster" because it takes away the President's flexibility to deal with a foreign crisis.

In the Senate, Senator Thomas F. Eagleton, Democrat of Missouri, taking another tack, said that the bill was "a horrible mistake" because it gave the President "unilateral authority to commit troops anywhere in the world for 60 to 90 days."

He said that under it, Mr. Nixon could order the armed forces deployed in the Middle East immediately and be required only to inform the Congressional leaders. He shouted: "How short can memories be? My God, we just got out of a nightmare."

The principal authors of the measure, Representative Clement J. Zablocki, Democrat of Wisconsin, and Senator Jacob K. Javits, Republican of New York, argued that had the measure been law earlier, it would not have restricted Mr. Nixon's recent actions, such as the alert of the armed forces, during the Middle East war.

Immediately after the Senate vote Senator John G. Tower, Republican of Texas, said that he hoped that the constitutionality of the measure would be tested in the courts "at the very earliest opportunity." Mr. Tower, who opposed the bill, did not say how such a test might be initiated.

The vote had been expected to be close in the House, which had approved the measure on Oct. 12 by a vote of 238 to 123, just short of two-thirds.

One factor in the success of the move to override the veto was a gain of several votes from a handful of liberal Democrats who had voted against the measure previously on the grounds that it gave the President additional war powers.

Among them were Representatives Bella S. Abzug of Manhattan and Elizabeth Holtzman of Brooklyn, both Democrats, who watched the tally boards and then in the final seconds before the voting period ended inserted their cards into the electronic machine and voted to override the veto.

The Democratic side of the House broke into cheers and applause when Speaker Carl Albert, Democrat of Oklahoma, announced at 1:44 P.M. that two-thirds of those present had voted in the affirmative and that the measure hed been passed, "the President's objections to the contrary nothwithstanding."

In the House, 198 Democrats and 86 Republicans voted to override the veto, while 32 Democrats and 103 Republicans voted against overriding. In the Senate, 25 Republicans and 50 Democrats voted to override while three Democrats and 15 Republicans voted against.

Legislation to curb the President's war-making powers was first proposed in 1970 as a reaction to the long United States involvement in the Indochina conflict without a Congressional declaration of war.

The proposals languished until last year when, with the support of Senator John C. Stennis, Democrat of Missisisippi and the influential chairman of the Senate Armed Services Committee, who became one of the sponsors, a bill was approved by the Senate. But the House approved a much milder version, and the measure died in conference.

Legislation on war powers was introduced again when the new Congress convened in January. On July 18, by a vote of 244 to 170, the House passed a measure that would have set a 120-day limit on the commitment of United States troops to combat abroad without Congressional approval. Two days later, the Senate, by a vote of 70 to 18, approved its own version making the limit 30 days.

On Oct. 4 there emerged from a Senate-House conference committee the compromise with a 60-day limit that both houses subsequently adopted, that the President vetoed and that went into effect today.

November 8, 1973

THE CASE AGAINST A THIRD TERM STATED

By WILLIAM CABELL BRUCE,
U. S. Senator From Maryland.

I AM one of those who believe that the third-term tradition is based upon a sound and salutary principle of political prudence; and that it is gravely to be regretted that this principle was not, in some form or other, made a part of the Federal Constitution. We know that its omission from that instrument, as finally adopted, was earnestly deplored at the time, and notably by Jefferson, who in his autobiography makes this statement with respect to the Federal Constitution, as actually adopted:

"The absence of express declarations insuring freedom of religion, freedom of the press, freedom of the person under the uninterrupted protection of the habeas corpus, and trial by jury, in civil as well as in criminal cases, excited my jealousy; and the re-eligibility of the President for life I quite disapproved."

In the same work Jefferson, speaking of the "continuance" of the President in office, says:

"That this continuance should be restrained to seven years was the opinion of the convention at an earlier stage of its session, when it voted that term by a majority of eight against two, and by a simple majority that he should be ineligible a second time. This opinion was confirmed by the House so late as July 26, referred to the Committee of Detail, reported favorably by them, and changed to the present form by final vote on the last day but one of their session. Of this change three States expressed their disapprobation: New York by recommending an amendment that the President should not be eligible a third time, and Virginia and North Carolina that he should not be capable of serving more than eight in any term of sixteen years."

Jefferson's own view was that the President should be elected for seven years and be ineligible afterward. So general was this view, at the time of the ratification of the Federal Constitution, that the third-term tradition became, by common consent, for all practical purposes, as much a part of the Constitution as if it had been expressly made a part of it. Never has a tradition been sanctioned by a fuller measure of popular acquiscence, or dignified by more illustrious examples of individual fidelity to its mandate.

The Precedent Accepted.

That the announcement by Washington of his intent to retire from the Presidency at the end of his second term was accepted by the people as prescribing a precedent of great value to their political security is evidenced by an address to him made by the House of Representatives on Dec. 15, 1796.

"We cannot be unmindful," they said, "that your moderation and magnanimity, twice displayed by retiring from your exalted stations, afford examples no less rare and instructive than valuable to a republic."

In a letter addressed to the Legislature of Vermont, dated Dec. 10, 1807, and printed in The Philadelphia Aurora on the nineteenth day of that month, Jefferson declared that he "should unwillingly be the person who, disregarding the sound precedent set by an illustrious predecessor, should furnish the first example of prolongation beyond the second term of office."

The example set by Washington and followed by Jefferson was afterward followed by Madison, whose Administration had brought our country safe through the perils of the War of 1812; by Monroe, one of the most popular of all our Presidents; by Jackson, the most arbitrary and self-willed of all. Jackson, fearing that tradition might not always retain the force of law, even proposed a constitutional amendment which would have limited the re-eligibility of the President.

From the day until the futile effort was made in 1880 to nominate Ulysses S. Grant for a third term, the tradition maintained a firm hold upon the convictions of the American people; and there could be no better proof of this fact than the inability of even the great military prestige of Grant, backed by the leadership of such a renowned party chieftain as Roscoe Conkling, to shake that hold. Five years before the House of Representatives had, by a vote of 251 to 18, resolved as follows:

"That, in the opinion of this House, the precedent established by Washington and other Presidents of the United States, in retiring from the Presidential office after their second term, has become, by universal consent, a part of our republican system of government, and that any departure from this time-honored custom would be unwise, unpatriotic and fraught with peril to our free institutions."

Grant's Defeat.

That it was the sincere popular fears, reflected in this resolution, that produced the defeat of Grant's third-term aspirations cannot be denied. Since Grant the only President who has sought a third term was Theodore Roosevelt, and he sought it only to incur defeat.

In his autobiography Jefferson also says:

"The example of four Presidents voluntarily retiring at the end of their eighth year, and the progress of public opinion that the principle is salutary, have given it, in practice, the form of precedent and usage; insomuch that, should a President consent to be a candidate for a third election, I trust he would be rejected on this demonstration of ambitious views."

And, of course, that was exactly what did happen in 1880, when even the profound measure of gratitude due to Grant for his conspicuous part in bringing the Civil War to an end could not save him from such rejection. The rebuke administered to his "ambitious views" by a Republican Presidential Convention convincingly showed that the third-term tradition was still as firmly set as ever in its socket of precedent and usage.

What good reason, therefore, is there for believing that the great majority of the American people are not as resolutely faithful to this tradition now as they have ever been? None, so far as I can see. And what good reason is there to believe that the considerations by which it was originally inspired have now lost their force? None, I again answer, so far as I can see.

The idea of our forefathers was that if the President were re-elected for a third term the third term might ripen into a fourth term, the fourth into a fifth, and so on until the tenure became, for all practical purposes, a tenure for life; and that tenures for life easily "slide into inheritances," to use one of Jefferson's phrases in relation to the re-eligibility of the President.

The Wisdom of Rotation.

In other words, it was feared that if an ambitious and unscrupulous man were possessed of an office of such supreme importance, in both a civil and military sense, as the Presidency, free from the trammels of any constitutional provision or popular tradition prohibiting his election for a third term, he might, with the patronage and other means controlled by his powerful office, build up around himself an organization of office holders and other adherents pledged by both self-interest and cordial loyalty to do all in their power to keep him indefinitely, from term to term, in his exalted place, until the public mind gradually lost its sense of the security to liberty that is found in rotation in high executive posts and became reconciled to the thought of a President for life, or even of a President by heredity—who, of course, would be a king in everything but name.

When we remember how recently Grant died, and how few he had of the public attributes that impelled Washington and Jefferson to decline a third term, and how many (despite some admirable personal virtues) he had of the personal attributes that make such a man a serviceable instrument for the vast host of human beings who are prompt to seek, in the permanent aggrandizement of a popular hero, conspicuous honors and rewards for themselves—can we doubt that the fears of our ancestors were not unreasonable?

And how readily, but for the check of the third-term tradition, might Grant have been elected for a third term if our country had been deeply involved at the time in the perplexities and perils bred by socialistic or communistic agitation, or other agencies of social disaffection and economic revolution. We need not go as far back as the succession of events by which the great Napoleon began as First Consul of France and ended as Emperor, or the succession of events by which the lesser Napoléon began as President of the French Republic and ended likewise as Emperor.

Since the World War we have seen the Italian people, notwithstanding their devoted attachment to free institutions, brought to believe by domestic machinations, which gravely threatened their peace and happiness, that it was necesary for them to place themselves under the sway of a masterful individual, who declared in a recent address to the Italian Chamber of Deputies that the "Greater Italy which he contemplates will have no room for "a moribund democracy" but will be able, at a given moment, to mobilize 5,000,000 men, thoroughly armed, and will have aviation organized on such a scale that the wings of its airplanes will obscure the sun.

What Might Happen Here.

There is certainly no such situation in the United States at the present time to justify the belief that we may be hurried as rapidly as Italy has been along the pathway that leads to such utterances as those. We may never tread that pathway at all. But if a trying era of adversity should succeed the extraordinary era of prosperity that the United States has been recently enjoying, and if the enemies of organized society in its bosom (even now quite numerous and vociferous enough) should be greatly increased by the transition from the one era to the other, it is by no means improbable that in such a condition of things might be found a plausible excuse for a successful violation of the third-term tradition—which might gradually work in its consequences a radical change in the jealousy of executive power which has always been believed by the American people to be one of the chief muniments of their civil liberties.

Other Means Than Swords.

Nor is a military chieftain, hostile or indifferent to the principles of American civil liberty, the only instrument that might be selected at some crisis in our history to lay in a third term the foundations of a life tenure—or even of a hereditary dynasty. Unless the crisis were of such a revolutionary nature as to call for nothing less than a man of the sword the choice for a third term made by those powerful elements of our corporate life which are especially interested in the maintenance of business prosperity and the security of property might even fall upon some commonplace civilian, highly recommended to the good-will of the American people by reason of his personal respectability at the same time to win the confidence of the American plutocracy by reason of his obsequious fidelity to its material interests.

Other arguments may be advanced against the third term in addition to those derived from its tendency to promote autocracy in the Presidential office. One of the serious blemishes on American history is the extent to which the American President, during his first term, has employed the powers of his office to obtain a second term for himself—a blemish that has taken on its darkest tinge from the efforts made at times by such a President to "capture" negro delegates from the South to national conventions.

On the other hand, one of the brightest features of American history is the impulse that the American President has been induced to give to different forms of political progress, during his second term, by the fact that he was about to lay down his head on his Presidential deathbed, and was no longer solicited by the selfish hopes and fears which attend the close of a first term.

Noticeably true is this as respects the extensions of the national civil service laws that have been made by American Presidents during their second terms when actuated no longer by any motive except the desire to stand well with posterity. Franklin once said, in his humorous way, that all old women are good women; and all Presidents who have entertained no wish for a third term have, during their second terms, been good Presidents.

The Unfinished-Term Theory.

An attempt has been made to curtail the obligatory scope of the third-term tradition by drawing a distinction between a President who aspires to a third term after having been twice elected President and a President who aspires to a third term after having served one term as President by reason of the devolvement of the powers and duties of the Presidency upon him as Vice President, and having been elected to another as President. But this distinction is a wholly artificial one, for the objections to a third term do not turn upon the conditions under which a President has been twice elevated to the office of President. It is altogether immaterial to those objections whether a President who has had two terms has attained both through popular election or not.

The vice of the third term is that it encroaches upon the wholesome principle of rotation in office by opening the door to an indefinite succession of Presidential terms, likely, sooner of later, to result in a tenure of unbroken continuity perilous to the popular liberties. Not all law is founded upon written constitutions and statutes. Much of it resides in custom, usage and tradition, and no law, as a rule, is more highly entitled to respect than the latter, because it is upheld, not by legal sanctions, which may or may not be entirely in accord with existing public opinion, but by popular convictions and feelings strong enough to stand of their own vigor without the aid of such sanctions.

Such a tradition is not only the third-term tradition, which does not violate any express words of the Federal Constitution, but the party tradition also, which, in the very teeth of the provisions of the Federal Constitution relating to the Electoral College, nominates candidates for the Presidency entirely through the agency of party conventions.

The Federal Constitution should be so amended as to make the President eligible for a fixed term and afterward ineligible; and until the Federal Constitution shall have been amended in this or in some similar manner the American people should, whenever a President shall become a candidate for a third term, deem him unworthy to sit in the lofty seat ennobled by the patriotic scruples of Washington and Jefferson and safeguarded by a deep-seated popular instinct of self-preservation.

July 31, 1927

COOLIDGE OPPOSES THREE-TERM IDEA

Writes Eight Years' Adulation Is All President Can Stand Without Getting 'Swelled Head.'

In his second article written for the May issue of Hearst's International-Cosmopolitan Magazine, which will appear on the news stands today, former President Coolidge will discuss "Why I did not choose to run," Ray Long, editor of the magazine, disclosed yesterday. "The publishers of the magazine," Mr. Long said, "felt they could allow only one quotation from the article. Mr. Coolidge says:

"'They [retiring Presidents] have only the same title to nobility that belongs to all our citizens, which is the one based on achievement and character, so they need not assume superiority. It is becoming for them to engage in some dignified employment where they can be of service as others are. Our country does not believe in idleness. It honors hard work. I wanted to serve the country again as a private citizen.'"

A statement issued by Mr. Long explained that the publishers felt it would be unfair to Mr. Coolidge to permit further quotation from his article, because "his statements are so important and are so dovetailing that to permit the publication of any fragment might lead to misunderstanding."

The statement says further: "Mr. Coolidge bases his statement that no man should be President more than two terms on his belief that no human being can stand for eight years the constant adulation with which the President is surrounded without getting a swelled head."

April 5, 1929

2-TERM AMENDMENT IN FORCE AS THE 36TH STATE RATIFIES; TRUMAN EXEMPT FROM LIMIT

NEVADA, UTAH VOTE

Proposal Becomes Law Automatically as Two Legislatures Approve

POLITICAL EFFECTS WIDE

By ROBERT F. WHITNEY
Special to THE NEW YORK TIMES.

WASHINGTON, Feb. 26—The Constitution of the United States was amended tonight to forbid any President from being elected for more than two terms or from being elected more than once if he had served in excess of two years of his predecessor's term.

The amendment will not apply to President Truman. He may run again for his second elected term in the Presidential election of 1952 or in future campaigns, should his party wish to nominate him.

It was the Twenty-second Amendment to the Constitution and its ratification became complete with the approval of the Legislature of the State of Nevada providing the needed thirty-six states, or three-quarters' approval. Earlier in the day Utah's lawmakers had backed it as the thirty-fifth state.

It was eighteen years since the Constitution had been changed. Then the ratification was that of the Twenty-first Amendment repealing National Prohibition Dec. 5, 1933. The dry law repeal was initiated by President Roosevelt and completed in the first year of his first term.

Inspired by Roosevelt

It was President Roosevelt who "inspired" the Twenty-second Amendment by his election four times to the Presidency. The Eightieth Congress, in which the Republicans gained control for the first time since President Hoover's term, started the action on the opening day, the third of January, 1947.

This was the introduction of a joint resolution by Representative Joseph W. Martin Jr., of Massachusetts, then Speaker of the House of Representatives, and Senator Arthur H. Vandenberg, of Michigan, then President pro tem of the Senate, both Republicans.

The amendment was prepared by former Representative Earl C. Michener, Republican of Michigan, then chairman of the House Judiciary Committee.

It was passed in the House Feb. 6 and in the Senate March 12. The House agreed to a Senate amendment March 21. It was presented to the Secretary of State March 24.

The Twenty-second Amendment provides "no person shall be elected to the office of the President more than twice, and no person who has held the office of President, or acted as President, for more than two years of a term to which some other person was elected President shall be elected to the office of the President more than once."

Thus a Vice President or other person in the legal succession who became President on the death, resignation or impeachment of a President could be elected subsequently twice if that service were only two years but only once if it were more than two years.

Truman Is Exempt

The Amendment would not apply to the President holding office when it was first proposed to Congress (Mr. Truman).

The resolution on the proposed amendment required ratification within seven years of its introduction in Congress. The Twenty-second was well ahead of its limit —March 24, 1954. But it was a flurry of action by the states that made it law today.

Until late last month only twenty-four states had ratified. But in the last few weeks twelve "signed up" in a hurry. Before Utah and Nevada had come Indiana, Montana, Idaho, New Mexico, Wyoming, Arkansas, Georgia, Tennessee, Texas and North Carolina.

The twelve states that have not yet approved are:

Alabama, Arizona, Florida, Kentucky, Maryland, Massachusetts, Minnesota, Oklahoma, Rhode Island, South Carolina, Washington and West Virginia.

Minnesota had wished to be the thirty-sixth and clinching state but was beaten by Nevada for the distinction. By a coindident, Nevada was the thirty-sixth state admitted to the Union.

Late in January of this year, members of the Republican National Committee meeting here put impetus behind the ratification drive, which, of course, was an issue with the party.

Although Democratic opponents of the Amendment regarded it as directed against the late President Roosevelt, it had picked up important ratifications in Democratic states. North Carolina and Texas, for example.

The amendment has great political importance aside from the bare fact that it limits the Presidential tenure.

While President Truman is excepted, the fact that the country has spoken for only two terms may well have an effect on his decision whether to run in 1952.

One astute political observer suggested tonight that Mr. Truman could not ignore that the legislators of three-fourths of the states have said:

"Two terms."

The amendment, of course, would make it mandatory for the United States to change its President at required intervals no matter what peril the country was in.

This would throw overboard Lincoln's old adage, "Don't change horses in midstream." If the amendment had been in effect in 1940 when World War II started Mr. Roosevelt could not have been reelected.

The fact that he could not have been a candidate might have meant that whoever was nominated by the Democrats could not have beaten the late Wendell Willkie.

Thus not only the person in the Presidency but the party in power might be changed as the result of the operation of the amendment, not only in times of national crisis but in a calm era.

But on the reverse side, students of government believe that the amendment, by stimulating a greater competition for the nomination, might build stronger and more able candidates and perhaps result in the better definition of issues.

Another implication of the amendment would seem to be that the person of the President, as soon as he started his second or last eligible term, might lose a degree of control over his party.

A President in such circumstances would not have the strategical position of being a threat for a third term—whether he wished it or not—right up to the time when he publicly declined to run.

This control might limit the power of a President to choose, or have a weighty influence in the selection of, his party's candidate for the next election.

Just the opposite of this loss of party power and influence in naming the candidate for the next election could be a result of the amendment in the view of some observers.

For example, a President, knowing that he could not run again, might choose to use the prestige of his office to groom a successor for the nation's highest post. This, of course, has historical precedents.

The success of such a course would depend on the prestige of the President with his party as well as the prestige of the office.

JOHNSON OFFERS SPACE PROGRAM

Senator Sketches 5-Point Plan to Meet Soviet Gains —Sees Challenge to U. S.

HOUSTON, Tex., Dec. 4 (UP) —The Senate Democratic Leader, Lyndon B. Johnson, proposed tonight a five-point program to speed the United States into "the world of space."

He called for the "mobilizing" of talents and abilities of persons who had retired, the centralizing of responsibility in a single Government agency, and perhaps the creation of a space "academy."

In a speech before a testimonial dinner in his honor, the Texas Senator said "there is something much bigger in front of us than a few pieces of military hardware."

"What is really before us is something that should have a deep appeal to the American soul."

He offered the following as a program of "what must be done" in the space age that is approaching with "breath-taking speed":

"First, we must step-up the development of weapons which will assure our survival.

"Second, we must revise our methods of teaching and our curricula so that science and technology are no longer ignored.

"Third, we must mobilize our population to face the challenge —tapping the now unused reservoirs of talent and ability among people who are retired.

"Fourth, we must step up our research into the physical and biological problems of outer space—perhaps through a space academy.

"Fifth, we must lodge—either in a new or an existing agency —specific responsibility for the physical, economic and legal problems of exploring outer space."

Johnson Cites Peril

He said Americans could ignore only at great peril the fact that the Soviet Union had outstripped the United States "in a field where we thought we were supreme"—in numbers of scientists and engineers, in weapon development and in the exploration of outer space.

The challenge posed by those facts, the Senator said, will not be met "if our only reaction is to build weapons."

He said "no sane man can underrate" Russia's scientific achievements in recent years. He said, however, that he does not regard those facts as "depressing."

"I consider them a challenge —a spur to achievement," he said.

December 5, 1957

A Propaganda Victory In Satellite Conceded

WASHINGTON, Jan. 9 (AP)—President Eisenhower confessed to Congress today—or so it appeared from his carefully chosen words—that his Administration had failed to foresee the advantages to be won by launching the first man-made earth satellite.

The Soviet Union, in achieving the feat, scored a great political and propaganda victory over the United States.

In his State of the Union Message, President Eisenhower was talking about the importance of having an adequate economic assistance program.

"Admittedly," he said, "most of us did not anticipate the psychological impact upon the world of the launching of the first earth satellite.

"Let us not make the same kind of mistake in another field, by failing to anticipate the much more serious impact of the Soviet economic offensive."

January 10, 1958

Text of Johnson's Statement on Status of Nation

Special to The New York Times.

WASHINGTON, Jan. 7—Following is the text of a statement by Senator Lyndon B. Johnson, Senate majority leader and chairman of the Preparedness subcommittee, to a meeting of Democratic Senators today:

For this preparation this morning, I shall divide my own remarks in two parts.

I shall, briefly, summarize certain of the findings which have been made thus far by the Senate Armed Services Preparedness subcommittee. Other members of the subcommittee will, in greater detail, deal with specific areas of the investigations.

In all candor, however, I cannot begin these remarks with a simple recapitulation of the work we have done. Illuminating as such might be, I realize—as I know all members realize—that we have, thus far, barely begun a work that will occupy and dominate the Congresses of free men for lifetimes to come. It is, therefore, of first importance that —no matter how feeble our understanding — we strive to establish perspective.

Our security may very well depend, above all else, on how well and how quickly we grasp such perspective.

Let us begin with this fact: the ground beneath us when we last met has been, largely, swept away. How much is gone, how much remains are questions no man can answer with authority.

The peril of the hour is obvious.

Less obvious, but of far greater importance, is the fact that beyond the peril lies a potential for peace that exceeds any ever before within man's reach.

Since Aug. 30, when the first session of this Congress adjourned, the human race itself—without regard to flags or philosophy—has multiplied its capabilities to infinity.

Subjugation a Prospect

The exploitation of these capabilities by men of selfish purpose holds the awful threat of a world in subjugation.

The mastery of such capabilities by men wholly dedicated to freedom presents, instead, the prospect of a world at last liberated from tyranny, liberated in fact from the fear of war.

What this Congress does will, at best, be only a small beginning on what must ultimately be done—and will be done in decades and perhaps even centuries ahead. But, small as our effort may be in the long view of history, we can see that lack of sufficient effort on our part would be compounded throughout the ages ahead into a failure of tragic proportions.

We cannot, in the months of this session, assure the nation's superiority: the era we have entered is too young, its ultimate dimensions too far beyond our vision, for us to anticipate so fruitful a result from our labors.

We can, however, by hesitation, by dissension, by narrow partisanship do much to build an insurmountable barrier about ourselves and perpetuate our relative inferiority.

Responsible men have no choice.

We must work as though no other Congress would ever have an opportunity to meet this challenge, for, in fact, none will have an opportunity comparable.

We must, furthermore, bring to this opportunity a freshness, an originality, a diligence far exceeding our previous standards, for many of the concepts and ideas and rules which have applied to our actions in the past are no longer pertinent and applicable.

Let me expand this by dealing first with certain general facts which have been established in the short time of our hearings:

1. Our national potential exceeds our national performance.

2. Our science and technology has been, for some time, capable of many of the achievements displayed thus far by Soviet science.

3. That the Soviet achieve-

ments are tangible and visible, while ours are not, is a result of policy decisions made within the governments of the respective nations. It is not—as yet, at least—the result of any great relative superiority of one nation's science over the other's.

National Policy Differs

The heart of the matter then is the national policy of the two great world powers, for this fact stands higher than all others: we could have had what the Soviets have in the way of technical achievements if it had been the aim of our government to employ our resources and capabilities in comparable pursuit of comparable goals.

From this, we deduce these matters of importance:

First, it is obvious that the Soviet valuation on the significance of control of outer space has exceeded that of our officials.

Second, it is equally obvious that our valuation has been based on factors other than the fullest realization of our scientific capability.

In essence, the Soviet has appraised control of space as a goal of such consequence that achievement of such control has been made a first aim of national policy. We, on the other hand, have—or so the evidence suggests—regarded other goals and aims as having a higher imperative.

Which nation is correct?

If our policy is correct in the approach that has been taken, then the Soviet is ludicrously wrong, and some might dismiss the sputniks as playtoys.

If the Soviet policy is correct in its approach, however, then we face the judgment that our own position may be tragic.

At the root, this Congress must—before it does much else—decide which approach is correct. If the Soviet is wrong, the.. we would be wrong to undertake any sort of great acceleration solely to produce counterparts for the visible Soviet achievements. If the Soviet is correct, then we would again be wrong to limit our response to nothing more than a stride-for-stride matching of their progress.

From the evidence accumulated, we do know this: the evaluation of the importance of control of outer space made by us has not been based primarily on the judgment of men most qualified to make such an appraisal.

Our decisions, more often than not, have been made within the framework of the Government's annual budget. This control has, again and again, appeared and reappeared as the prime limitation upon our scientific advancement.

Against this view, we now have on the record the appraisal of leaders in the field of science, respected men of unquestioned competence, whose valuation of what control of outer space means renders irrelevant the bookkeeping concerns of fiscal officers.

The testimony of the scientists is this:

Control of space means control of the world, far more certainly, far more totally than any control that has ever or could ever be achieved by weapons, or by troops of occupation.

From space, the masters of infinity would have the power to control the earth's weather, to cause drought and flood, to change the tides and raise the levels of the sea, to divert the Gulf stream and change temperate climates to frigid.

The meaning is, to my limited view, quite clear.

We have, for many years, been preoccupied with weapons.

We are, even now, concerned with what some currently regard as the ultimate weapon. But, when we perfect such a weapon for ourselves we may still be far behind.

The urgent race we are now in—or which we must enter—is not the race to perfect long-range ballistic missiles.

There is something more important than any ultimate weapon. That is the ultimate position—the position of total control over earth lies somewhere out in space.

This is the future, the distant future, though not so distant as we may have thought. Whoever gains that ultimate position gains control, total control, over the earth, for purposes of tyranny or for the service of freedom.

Where do we now stand?

Let me summarize briefly the work of your committee.

34 Witnesses Heard

Our staff has spent more than fifty days in intensive preparation for hearings which now have filled nearly 3,000 pages of transcript. Thirty-four witnesses have been heard before the committee. In addition, the staff has conducted 150 to 200 interviews with individuals concerned with the missile and satellite programs. Searching questionnaires have been sent to industrial organizations, leading scientists and engineers, and leading educators.

An effective, comprehensive and important job has been done. Credit of the highest order is due each member of the subcommittee of both parties. Seldom have I seen men work with greater dedication; the debt due them is great. Likewise, the effectiveness and thoroughness of the committee's work is a direct result of the splendid direction afforded by our counsel, Mr. Edwin L. Weisl and his partner, Cyrus R. Vance. Mr. Weisl and Mr. Vance are distinguished New York lawyers, members of the firm of Simpson, Thacher and Bartlett, and we are fortunate in securing their services.

From this committee effort, the essential findings developed thus far are these:

The sputniks now orbiting around the earth are not military weapons, but have a military potential.

Whatever their military potential may be, the present significance of these satellites is this:

First, the Soviet ability to put satellites of this size in orbit indicates a rocket ability far beyond any capacity we have developed; and, second, the satellites have gathered for the Soviet vital information about outer space which we do not have and which is decisive for any nation seeking to enter the Space Age.

Our primary effort to put a satellite into the skies ended in humiliating failure. It is my opinion the humiliation could have been avoided; it was unfair to the dedicated scientists who are striving to do a difficult job and it reflected unnecessarily upon our scientific capabilities.

The people must have the truth, good or bad, but truth begins with perspective. It is not a proper perspective to reflect the responsibility for our lack of a satellite upon the men at work now in Florida. They are neither the source nor the cause of our failure.

Beyond the satellites, our committee has learned facts in open sessions about Soviet capabilities which are far more disturbing in relation to our present security.

First, the Soviets have almost as many army divisions as all the nations of the free world combined, and a great proportion are highly mechanized.

Second, Sovet air strength is probably close to our own.

Third, Soviet submarines now number 500, while ours total 110, and there is evidence that they have some with missile capability.

Fourth, the Soviets are building 100 submarines annually, while we are building fewer than ten.

Fifth, there is no certain evidence of a Soviet nuclear submarine. But they have launched an atomic ice-breaker, and nuclear submarines if not now in existence, will be soon.

In the field of the intercontinental and shorter range missiles, the facts again are not comforting. The capacity to launch a one-half ton satellite is interpreted by our scientists as evidence of the capacity to launch an ICBM against our cities. Other problems than the problem of propulsion are involved, however. We cannot fully appraise Soviet capacity in this regard. The safe assumption is that they have solved or will solve such problems as remain.

Research Speed-Up Urged

In part the answers that have been given to the committee are these:

1. Strengthen our strategic Air Force, about which Senator Symington will tell you more;

2. Accelerate and expand our research and development programs;

3. Speed up the development and manufacture of the intermediate and intercontinental missiles now being worked on;

4. Strengthen our educational system;

5. Provide a top level nonservice-connected military planning staff for the Secretary of Defense;

6. Establish a new, advanced weapons development agency outside of the Defense Department to reduce the lead time in the production of new weapons—which, incidentally, according to evidence presented at the hearings, is over twice as long as the lead time required by the Russians;

7. Streamline the decision-making process;

8. Accelerate the nuclear submarine program;

9. Eliminate all overtime limitations;

10. Increase cooperation with our Allies particularly in the exchange of information;

11. Build shelters and store food and machinery as a precaution against Russian attack;

12. Build as quickly as possible an early warning radar system capable of detecting missiles;

13. Increase our interchange of scientific information between the free nations; and

14. That twe must begin to do all of these things with a strong sense of immediacy and urgency.

The question in your minds, I am sure, is whether or not there has been progress in actions taken during the past few weeks. I believe it is fair to say that some progress has been made since the inquiry began.

The President has named Dr. Killian as his personal scientific adviser. Also, the President has designated the Pentagon's special assistant on missiles as a "missile director," although in candor it must be said that it is difficult to define his powers.

The Secretary of Defense has been active:

1. He has removed the overtime restrictions.

2. He has restored research and development funds.

3. He has speeded up development and production schedules for missiles.

4. He has ordered both Jupiter and Thor into production.

5. He has reinstated a previously canceled launching pad for the Titan intercontinental missile.

6. He has established a new

agency to develop advance weapons.

7. He has ordered the Army into the satellite project.

These actions—as all, I am sure, will agree—constitute only a beginning of what evetntually must be done. We can hope that the rate of acceleration will be adequate to the great challenge before us.

Our problems have been listed. The suggestions about our future course have been listed. The actions taken have been listed. All of these relate to matters which are, essentially, military in character.

Nation Must Be Strong

It is fundamental, I believe, that however urgent these military problems may be we are faced with the unchanging problem of building a strong country, not a strong military force alone.

In this perspective, we cannot ignore the problems of three to four million unemployed workers.

We cannot ignore the grave problems of our farmers.

We cannot ignore the problems of our school children.

We cannot ignore the probnem of housing.

We cannot ignore the problem of credit.

We cannot ignore the soft spots in our economy which are bringing some of our most vital industries into a difficult and troublesome climate.

We cannot ignore the growing problems of small business.

We cannot ignore the issue of conserving our natural resources.

These problems—and many more—must occupy our attention, and it becomes all the more imperative that we seek and reach answers of lasting durability for the road ahead.

One final question, the most important of all: where do we go? What should be our goal?

If, out in space, there is the ultimate position—from which total control of the earth may be exercised—then our national goal and the goal of all free men must be to win and hold that position.

Weapons Stalemate Seen

Obviously, attainment of that goal is no overnight thing. It may not come within our lifetime. Until it does, we must continue to have weapons—but we must recognize both their limits and their potentially short life.

With weapons, whatever their form, our ultimate gain is likely to be stalemate—such as we have had during the atomic age. But our position must remain flexible. We must forego a fixation on weapons as the ultimate of security. For, if we do not, we may build the Space Age's first—and last—Maginot Line.

Total security perhaps is possible now, for the first time in man's history. Total security—and, with it, total peace. This potential we must not underestimate.

Within the short weeks since Oct. 4, man has become master of horizons far beyond our imagination. We must respect this mastery, and from that respect we must, more than ever, seek to bring all men together in cooperative effort. The goals now within reach of the human race are too great to be divided as spoils, too great for the world to waste its efforts in a blind race between competitive nations. The conference table is more important now than it ever has been, and we should welcome to its chairs all men of all nations.

January 8, 1958

President Proposes 'Science for Peace'

By JOHN W. FINNEY

Special to The New York Times.

WASHINGTON, Jan. 9—An international "science for peace" program to attain "a good life for all" was suggested today by President Eisenhower.

As the first step toward such an international scientific program President Eisenhower invited the Soviet Union to join with the United States in a joint scientific attack on malaria, cancer and heart disease.

The President, in his State of the Union Message, offered his "science for peace" proposal as one of the "works of peace" that could turn the world in the direction of disarmament and peace.

The President seemed to view the program as an eventual objective, rather than a new international organization to be formed immediately. Leading up to this program, he suggested, would be a series of cooperative projects on specific scientific problems.

General Eisenhower noted, for instance, that the United States was cooperating with other nations in a five-year campaign to blot out malaria.

"We invite the Soviets to join with us in this great work of humanity," he said. "Indeed, we would be willing to pool our efforts with the Soviets in other campaigns against the diseases that are the common enemy of all mortals—such as cancer and heart disease."

"If people can get together on such projects," he asked, "is it not possible that we could then go on to a full-scale cooperative program of science for peace?"

The President was not specific about how the "science for peace" program would work. The only detail he offered was that it might provide a means of funneling into one place the results of scientific research and then making it available throughout the world.

The suggestion was reminiscent of his "atoms-for-peace" proposal of December, 1953, before the United Nations. This led to the formation last year of the International Atomic Energy Agency.

In his prepared text, General Eisenhower described the "atoms-for-peace" proposal as "a guide and inspiration" for the "science for peace" program. This reference, however, was omitted by the President in delivering the speech.

General Eisenhower also told Congress that it was "off the highest importance" that legislation be passed to permit closer scientific cooperation with allies, particularly in the development of new weapons.

It is "wasteful in the extreme," he said, for friendly allies to consume talent and money solving problems their friends have already solved—"all because of artificial barriers."

Furthermore, he said, "we cannot afford to cut ourselves off from the brilliant talents and minds of scientists in friendly countries. The task ahead will be hard enough without handcuffs of our own making."

Weapons Sharing Favored

The President apparently was referring particularly to the atomics weapons field. The Administration will request Congress to amend the Atomic Energy Law of 1954 to permit greater sharing with allies of information about the atomic weapons.

At home, the President recommended increased Government support for education and research to "create the intellectual capital we need for the years ahead."

This would include a four-year, $1,000,000,000 program to improve teaching and increase student opportunities, particularly in the sciences. In addition, General Eisenhower said, there will be "substantial increases" in funds for basic research.

General Eisenhower, cautioned, however, that "Federal action can do only a part of the job." In both education and research, he said, "redoubled exertions will be necessary on the part of all Americans if we are to rise to the demands of our times."

Idea Welcomed at U. N.

UNITED NATIONS, N. Y., Jan. 9 (UP)—President Eisenhower's call for a "science-for-peace" mobilization today struck a responsive chord at the United Nations, where the idea had been incubating for months.

January 10, 1958

Congress Holds Initiative As Easter Recess Begins

Its Record to Date Augurs Aggressive Action, Independent of Executive, on Soviet Challenge and Recession

By JOHN D. MORRIS

Special to The New York Times.

WASHINGTON, April 5— One of the most prolific sessions on Capitol Hill appears to be in the making as an aggressive and self-reliant Congress pauses for a ten-day Easter recess.

In three months of a session likely to continue for about four months longer, the Democratic-controlled Congress has steered a bold and increasingly independent course.

It has assumed to a large extent the leadership traditionally exercised by the Executive Branch. This has been particularly true in the handling of two pressing issues of the times—the Soviet challenge to United States supremacy in space-age technology and the continuing economic recession.

For the most part, it has operated with a remarkable degree of bipartisan cooperation despite the political pressures of a Congressional election year.

So successfully has it held the initiative on the two dominant questions—how to meet the Soviet military-scientific threat and how to stem the recession—that much of President Eisenhower's legislative program has been forgotten.

The tactical skills of the Democratic leaders, Lyndon B. Johnson in the Senate and Sam Rayburn in the House, are mainly responsible for the aggressive mood, fast pace and largely harmonious functioning of Congress so far. But the skills of these Texans face crucial tests in the months ahead.

The President's request for a five-year extension of his tariff-making powers under the Reciprocal Trade Agreements Act, for example, is under heavy attack from protectionists in both parties. The fate of the extension bill, now before the House Ways and Means Committee, is in doubt.

For another example, the annual drive to curtail foreign aid is again under way, and the Administration's requests for Mutual Security authorizations and appropriations face the prospects of sharp reductions.

Bipartisan Agreement

On both of these issues the Democratic leaders are in accord with the Administration's aims. But they probably will have to make concessions to opponents if acceptable legislation is to be produced.

On most other pending Administration proposals the leaders can be expected to pursue a policy of skepticism and discrimination—to challenge, criticize, reshape and substitute.

The policy is likely to be demonstrated particularly on such issues as reorganization of the Defense Department, for which President Eisenhower submitted a controversial plan just before adjournment Thursday.

It is likely to be applied also to proposed programs of Federal scholarships to improve scientific education, regulation of improper practices by labor unions, pay increases for military, civil service and postal employes and increases in postal rates.

Alaska Statehood Gains

Statehood for Alaska, as recommended by the President, is given a good chance this year. But his proposal of Statehood for Hawaii will doubtless be discarded.

Various other Administration recommendations already have been buried. These include basic revision of the immigration laws, expansion of the Federal minimum wage and Federal aid to chronically depressed areas of the country.

When Congress reconvenes April 14, the economic downturn will continue to claim its most immediate attention.

As the recess began, leaders were steering through Congress a package of anti-recession legislation devised under Senator Johnson's direction with Speaker Rayburn's full cooperation.

A $1,850,000,000 housing bill was signed by President Eisenhower in the final week. A bill for a $1,800,000,000 speed-up of Federally aided highway programs was sent to the President on the final day before the recess.

Republicans Force Delay

The third part of the package, a $1,000,000,000 program of Federal loans for community public works, is pending on the Senate floor. Senate Republicans forced postponement of action until after the recess. Their cue came from President Eisenhower, who warned against doing too much too hastily in trying to stem the recession.

Other booster-shot measures call for expansion of airport construction and irrigation and reclamation programs.

Democratic and Administration bills for supplementary payments to jobless workers who have exhausted their unemployment insurance benefits are also scheduled for early action.

So far, both Congress and the Administration have shied away from tax relief as an anti-recession measure. If the slump continues, however, Congress may try to cut taxes whether or not the Administration approves.

Gentlemen's Agreement

Meanwhile, Democratic leaders and Robert B. Anderson, Secretary of the Treasury, are abiding by a gentlemen's agreement to delay a decision at least until mid-April.

Behind the intense Congressional activity to combat the recession is Senator Johnson's remarkable talent of sensing major national issues and grasping the initiative even before the issues have fully materialized.

Thus, he was ready with Congressional resolutions calling on the Administration to speed expenditures or available public works appropriations while some others were still debating the existence of a recession.

Earlier, he demonstrated the same talent as chairman of the Senate Preparedness subcommittee with public hearings that dramatized the Soviet challenge in military missiles and space science.

The subcommittee's unanimous recommendations for strengthening the United States military position, particularly by speeding development of ballistic missiles, were embraced by the Administration. Some had been put into effect while the hearings were still under way.

Arms Spending Voted

Congress later gave quick approval to supplementary military appropriations of $1,300,000,000 proposed by the Administration. A second supplementary request for $1,500,000,000 was submitted this week. If approved, as expected, it would raise the year's projected defense appropriations to $41,900,000,000.

The session's single major clash with the Administration came over the flexible farm price-support policies of Ezra Taft Benson, Secretary of Agriculture. President Eisenhower vetoed a Democratic bill, passed with considerable Republican backing, to freeze the supports at levels no lower than those of 1957.

Leaders will decide when Congress reconvenes whether to try to override the veto. At adjournment, the required two-thirds majorities were not available in either the House or Senate. But Democratic strategists suggest that the situation may change when legislators return from their first extended consultations this year with constituents.

April 6, 1958

It Is the People Who Face the Test

They will determine whether the new President can overcome standpattism in Congress, which tends to put constituents ahead of the nation; when they give the word, it will move.

By TOM WICKER

WASHINGTON.

"BEFORE my term has ended," John Kennedy told Congress on Jan. 30, 1961, "we shall have to test anew whether a nation organized and governed such as ours can endure. The outcome is by no means certain."

Mr. Kennedy could not know then how soon his term would end. But the test he foretold, the uncertainty he foresaw, may now be upon us. That is not just because an assassin's unspeakable deed has placed the Presidential Government of the United States in the hands of Lyndon Baines Johnson of Texas.

It is because the shots fired that day in Dallas have not altered by one iota the 20th-century alienation between Mr. Johnson's office and a Congress that has steadily lost its status as a coequal branch and become more nearly an opposition.

Can Lyndon Johnson make Presidential Government work in tandem with that opposition? Can any man? Will Government and opposition grind together in inevitable deadlock, as they seemed to be doing the last months of John Kennedy's Presidency?

To our grandfathers, in what the French called *La Belle Epoque* of 50 years ago, the question might have seemed absurd. In the 19th century upon which their lives and views were built, the President and Congress were roughly compatible partners in government. Operating in constitutional equality and in a democracy that was raw, vigorous, expanding and self-assertive, their problems produced at worst alternating periods of supremacy and balance.

WHEN strong executives like Jefferson and Jackson, or national emergencies, made the Presidency paramount for a time, the natural suspicions and asserted interests of the people forced Congress swiftly to reassert itself. If lackadaisical Presidents left the field to Congress and to colliding interests and parties in the melancholy twilight of the 1850's, national interest made it necessary for Abraham Lincoln to emerge in the 1860's as the strongest, most assertive President the nation ever has had.

Overall, popular self-government through an elected Congress was not far from a fact. Landmarks of national policy—the Homestead Act, for instance, or the Sherman Antitrust Act or the Missouri Compromise—originated more often in Congress than in the White House. The great issues of that century—slavery, secession, the tariff, currency, industrial development, the westward expansion—were internal and personal. They immediately touched the people, who could respond vigorously and directly to a Congress capable of comprehending these problems.

But in the 20th century, matters largely have been taken out of the hands of the people and their Congress. Popular self-government is no longer a fact; it only remains a faith. Presidential Government has taken its place.

NO longer is this a country of isolated pockets of population, each reasonably self-sufficient, united only for external protection and internal convenience, sheltered behind its oceans. Giant industries and giant transportation have linked it into an economic whole and such giants require equitable control that only powerful national government can exert. The wealth and power of the nation, of necessity, have had to be projected into a world made small by communications, and particularly into the power vacuum left by the decline of the old European empires.

Four massive crises in this century—two world wars, the great depression, the cold war—have had to be met with national power. The colossal concerns of modern technology, from superhighways to space exploration, demand colossal government, both for financing and execution; what private interests are capable of developing, say, communications satellites or a supersonic passenger aircraft? A military establishment capable of exerting conventional and nuclear power in two hemispheres and across all oceans dwarfs the biggest of private combines.

Congress, hierarchically managed, responsible to hundreds of jealous constituencies, cumbersome in organization and procedure, heir to the conflicting claims and prejudices of numerous lesser interests, is not the body to manage such affairs. For these are matters of national power, and that is pre-eminently the President's to wield. He alone has the direct responsibility and the autonomy to view such problems in a national light. He alone has the ability to mobilize the national force, determine priorities, expend while preserving the national resources—all with a view to the national interest.

AS a result the President has become Commander in Chief, the military director of foreign policy, chief legislator, chief appropriator (the national interest he defines determines whether the budget shall be $50 billion or $90 billion; it is left to Congress only to say whether it shall be $90 billion or $89 billion), strongest influence on revenue and taxes, most effective shaper of public opinion, chief architect of the practical forms of its expression, chief administrator, even, in a sense, chief justice. For as the President devises means to act as necessity requires him to, as he shapes a public climate that affects the judicial attitude, he gives the Constitution itself much of its contemporary meaning and its *contemporary* meaning must change as the times change.

But what has this left for Congress? As the national power—the power of the Presidency—has increased, it has inevitably imposed itself upon the local powers, the local interests, the local beliefs and attitudes, of which the national legislature is made up. And as those local interests and powers have resisted the growth of national power, their opposition has become centered in Congress.

Thus the great shift in American government that came to a climax in the 20th century can be stated with some precision. The proponent forces of all major governing steps are the President and the Administration, with some impetus from the courts; the opponent force is Congress.

SINCE Congress retains its constitutional powers and has armed itself with formidable institutional weapons, over the years, the contest is by no means one-sided. In Mr. Kennedy's years Congress thwarted him often—on farm policy, aid to education and important phases of foreign aid, to mention a few. On tax reduction and civil rights, battles yet to be won or lost. Congress had become, at his death, a powerful, glacial resistance.

What basically has happened is a 20th-century magnification of the split personality of the American system, reflected in the dual roles of the American voter. He is a member of the President's national constituency, a citizen of the nation. He is also one of the people, a resident along the Wabash, or the Columbia or the Suwannee, a member of one of the 535 local constituencies of Congress. There is in him an impulse to follow the President, the leader; there is in him also an equal and sometimes opposite impulse to assert the mystic power of the people to define their own immediate interests and guide their own destinies—to resist the creeping control of their lives and affairs that they sense the national power to be assuming.

IT is easy to fix the blame for the resulting deadlock and delay upon Congress. It is speckled with men of irresponsible power, provincial ideas, baseless suspicions. Besides, the idea of national interest expressed by the President has the ring of patriotism and selflessness; the notion of local interest, so often acted upon by Congress, smacks of the pork barrel and the gravy train. So the case against Congress is being passionately made, these days, in something like the following overall terms:

Senescence: The deadly conjunction of the seniority system with the large number of one-party districts and states. Only about 125 Congressional districts are truly competitive between the parties. In 1962 only 67 new members were elected to any of the 435 seats in the House of Representatives. The retention of the same old faces, year after year, session after session, makes the seniority system a deadening institution, a guarantee that youth of the physical, mental or spiritual varieties shall not often be served.

IN 1961 President Kennedy, with his great charm, recalled amusingly his early indoctrination into the hierarchical life in Congress. At a banquet in Phoenix honoring the indomitable Senator Carl Hayden, who, at 74, was getting ready to run again Mr. Kennedy recalled his first talk with the Arizonan as follows:

"After I had been in the Senate about two months in 1953, I got up to take part in the debate as a new member. And, after speaking for a few minutes, I sat down near Senator Hayden and said, 'Senator, what's the difference between the Senate as you knew it and now?'

"And the Senator said, 'New members did not speak in those days.'

"So I went back to my seat."

Localism: The charge that members are too bound to their own localities and its needs, too intent upon taking home a Federal grant or a new space center, too callous as a result of the national interest to recognize the President's greater ability to define that interest, and the necessity for him to act upon it.

Trickery: The charge that Congressional rules of procedure (constitutionally sanctified only by the founders' laconic statement that each house may determine its own) are designed for more Machiavellian purposes than that of insuring order.

One is to permit delay of a piece of proposed legislation until it can be watered down, buried, torn to shreds or caused to lose its effectiveness. The other is to give single members, or power blocs, or coalitions of them a fighting chance to defeat it, even when there is majority sentiment for it.

* * *

THESE specific charges against Congress blend into one basic indictment that it fiddles while Rome burns, that it is not responsive to the nation's needs, that it prevents or harasses the passage of needed national legislation.

Congress undoubtedly is guilty on all counts. But the reason—perhaps as sweeping and as oversimplified as the charges—is not that Congress is a deliberate structure of ignoble Congressional potentates, but that it is a natural outgrowth of a political system that rests on states and districts and their less-than-national interests, all clamoring to be heard, protected, advanced.

FOR instance, as huge urban areas in an increasing number of states come to dominate Senatorial (statewide) elections as well as Presidential elections, the Senate, like the giant of national power, increasingly is influenced by the same urban areas and their interests; in current political jargon, the Senate becomes more "liberal." And, as the Senate moves more nearly into line with the Presidential wish and the national power, the House, its local districts less reflective of urban growth and national trends, becomes the bulwark of Congressional opposition to national power.

As if to multiply its resistance, the districts that make it up are turning more and more in upon themselves and sending the same old faces and attitudes to the House. An average of 96 new members entered it after each election from 1940 through 1948, but in 1960 and 1962 an average of only 65 new members was elected.

The night before President Kennedy died, he heard Democratic Representative Albert Thomas go to the heart of the matter. At a dinner meeting of his Texas supporters, Mr. Thomas, one of the most powerful men in the House, told them bluntly, "You are my boss." Mr. Kennedy thereupon paid homage to Mr. Thomas for his services to the nation, but Mr. Thomas had left no doubt where lay the real power over his actions and attitudes.

Representative Howard Smith of Virginia expanded on the point in a House debate in 1961:

"When I am asked to pledge aid to the passage of any resolution or bill in this House that I am conscientiously opposed to, I would not yield my conscience and my right to vote in this House to any person or any member or under any conditions. If there is any other member here who thinks he ought to *yield his conscience and the views of his constituency* to the will of somebody, then he ought to vote the other way." (Italics supplied.)

IT is not only that the typical member of Congress often feels impelled to reflect his constituency; it is more nearly that his own views, interests and prejudices are shaped largely by the nature and environment of that constituency.

Moreover, that constituency in modern times makes appalling demands upon him as its personal servant as well as its political representative. One example is the insistent demand that he produce the goods of prosperity—defense contracts, power projects, government installations. Another is the astronomical volume of correspondence that spews daily upon his desk, dealing with everything from private immigration bills to his latest remarks on farm prices. These demands derive directly from the vast power and influence of the Federal Government upon private life in America. As a result, only the most able, conscientious member can be an enlightened legislator after he has performed all his constituent services.

Thus, localism is built into Congress and is only exacerbated by the rapid growth of the giant of national power. Similarly, seniority (which, to give it its due, can produce committee chairmen of skill and effectiveness, like Wilbur Mills and J. W. Fulbright of Arkansas) has its natural cause: even if there were in Congress no hard-and-fast seniority system, senior men, as they do in every organization, would arrogate leadership and privilege to themselves. And seniority can only become a powerful factor when one-party states and districts give it to their representatives.

GRANTED that Congressional rules give great power to minorities and individuals; so does the Constitution of the United States, which is built on the principal of limited powers. The less-than-national interests of a democracy surely should have means, at least a fighting chance, to make their case against a national interest that could swallow them. And if any man or section wants its interests protected in Congress, it must acquiesce in a system that will permit, at one time or another, the protection of all members and sections. Big-city members who fume when, say, urban renewal is hamstrung, do not hesitate to fight farm subsidies, with any weapon at hand.

It is, finally, oversimplification to say that Congress preprevents — irrelevantly, because callous members want to do so—the passage of legislation demanded by the country. More often, that legislation is being demanded by the national interest, a palpably different thing.

THE case of Federal aid to education is instructive. A recent poll showed that 59 per cent of the population favored such aid, as a general proposition. When the proposition begins to be examined in Congress, however, that sufficient majority falls rapidly apart. Should the aid go to Catholic schools, too? Should it go to segregated schools? Should poor Mississippi or populous New York get more per child? Should the money go for teachers' salaries or just for buildings? Who controls it? Who, then, controls the schools?

In 1960 the House Committee on Rules killed an aid-to-education bill after differing versions of it had been passed in both House and Senate. Outrageous? Maybe—but there is no evidence that if the committee had stood aside, Southern Senators would have accepted the House version, which would have prevented aid to segregated schools; or that the House would have dropped its insistence on that provision; and if either had happened, President Eisenhower might well have vetoed the bill, anyway.

In such complex situations, Congress — malapportioned as it is, burdened with seniority, bound by procedures and provincialism—may represent the divisions and hesitations of the people rather accurately. When the national power demands an action, a strong and vocal opposition almost always arises among varied less-than-national interests of the country and it is not always the same opposition. Today's proponent of one action often is tomorrow's dedicated opponent of another; one man's obstructionism is another's fearless stand for the right as he or his constituency sees it.

CONGRESS, like the people, does learn and grow slowly. The Social Security bill was enacted in a terrific struggle in 1935, to the accompaniment of cries of Socialist doom. In 1962 a far-reaching modernization of welfare state procedures attracted almost no attention as it whizzed through both houses. When a Kennedy bill to permit voluntary limitation of feed-grain production reached Congress in 1961, it was damned as dictatorship; by 1962, when mandatory limitation was proposed, the former critics of the voluntary plan rapidly discovered its considerable merit. The thalidomide scandal revived a drug control bill that had been bogged down. Even the Southern Senators, in 1957 and 1960, found reason to compromise around the edges of the civil rights controversy; they may well do so again in early 1964. And the reluctance of Congress to act on that issue may well be reflective of the plain hesitation and fears of the people themselves.

It is true that some means ought to be found to lighten the deadening hand of seniority, and that the rules of procedure ought to be simplified. Apportionment of the House ought to be more equitable. But those are mere truths, not solutions.

FOR to "reform" the institutions of Congress, assuming that could be done, would be to change its way of functioning, ***but not the reasons it functions that way.*** If that happened, a Congress still based on states and districts and local interests, many of them one-party, would have to find means to function differently to the same end—the representation of the less-than-national interests of the country against the growth of national power.

After a jungle of outmoded committees was cleared away by the LaFollette-Monroney Act of 1946, it was not long before a jungle of subcommittees arose. If unlimited debate were destroyed at a stroke, the necessity for state and local representatives to protect their own interests and that of their constituencies by allowing others the means to protect theirs would eventually result in a new usage or rule to replace the filibuster. The revolt against the dictatorship of Speaker Cannon in 1910 produced the autocracy of the House Committee on Rules. To improve apportionment would be to send to the House a somewhat altered set of local interests, only marginally more representative of the cut and shape of the whole people—and blending them not at all into some kind of national whole.

THUS the real test that approaches, which John Kennedy foresaw, is not a test of the presidency. It is not a test of Congress. It is not Lyndon Johnson who is on trial, nor the men of the House and Senate. It is not only the Executive and the Legislative branches that are approaching deadlock.

It is the people of the United States who face the test. It is their ability to resolve, in a sprawling and immensely varied continent, in a system that was designed to limit all forms of power, the underlying clash of national interest and less-than-national interest—of national power and local resistance.

This does not mean that local interest or resistance to the national power should disappear; often that resistance is needed, and in any case local interest is inevitable. It means that if the American people are going to make their form of government work, in a land so full of conflicting interests and diverse beliefs, they will have to develop a sharper and surer sense of what is truly important in American life, of what the real national necessity is, of what is fundamental to their local interests and what is meretricious.

Certainly Presidential leadership, wise and articulate, will be vital to that task. Probably Congressional reform would lessen the conflict. But if Americans would reach the "new American greatness" Lyndon Johnson has envisioned, they will have to begin at home—right where the trouble lies.

December 8, 1963

Johnson Is Hopeful House Will Debate Rights This Month

By JACK RAYMOND

Special to The New York Times

WASHINGTON, Jan. 18 — President Johnson was reported today to be hopeful that the civil-rights bill would reach the floor of the House of Representatives by the end of the month.

The bill is now before the House Rules Committee, which must clear it for floor action. The Senate will take up the omnibus bill after the House votes on it.

President Johnson's hopes for speedy House debate were reported by four Negro leaders after a surprise hour-and-a-half meeting at the White House.

The President discussed his campaign for civil rights and against poverty with the Rev. Dr. Martin Luther King Jr., head of the Southern Christian Leadership Conference; Roy Wilkins, executive director of the National Association for the Advancement of Colored People; Whitney Young, representing the National Urban League, and James Farmer, National Director of the Congress of Racial Equality.

The Negro leaders were invited to the White House by telephone last night. They explained, after the meeting, that the President had asked them to consult with him and advise him in the future.

They stressed also that in today's meeting they had discussed chiefly the President's pending message on his plans to cope with poverty in the nation.

It was in that context that the civil rights measure came up for discussion, the Negro leaders explained, and that the President had said he shared their hopes that the House of Representatives would get a chance to debate it on the floor before February.

Mr. Wilkins cautioned against assuming that the President was attempting to exert pressure on Congress to speed the civil rights measure by issuing statements through the group that had just visited him.

Dr. King, who was first to speak for the group, said that they had had a "lengthy and fruitful discussion with the President on vital issues concerning our nation."

United Press International Telephoto

JOHNSON MEETS WITH NEGRO LEADERS: President Johnson confers at the White House with leaders of civil rights groups. With the President are, from left: Roy Wilkins, the executive secretary of the N.A.A.C.P.; James Farmer, the national director of CORE; the Rev. Dr. Martin Luther King Jr., the head of the Southern Christian Leadership Conference, and Whitney Young, the executive director of the National Urban League.

Poverty Discussed

Dr. King said that all were agreed during the White House discussion that the President's crusade against poverty was dependent upon improvements in education, both general and vocational, and that these in turn were inextricably tied to the civil rights issue.

The war against poverty, Dr. King said, "is a problem that affects the whole nation in general and the Negro in particular."

Asked whether they had discussed with President Johnson the possibility of a compromise on the civil rights bill as a means of insuring its passage, Dr. King answered emphatically that such a compromise was not discussed. He added:

"We feel that this bill should not be watered down any further. We are not prepared to compromise in any form."

The bill includes a fair employment practice commission, a ban on segregation in restaurants and other places of public accommodation, fresh steps against school segregation and a half dozen other provisions supporting equal rights.

January 19, 1964

Transcript of the President's News Conference

Special to The New York Times

WASHINGTON, Jan. 25— ***Following is the official transcript of President Johnson's news conference today in his office:***

Progress on Civil Rights

We are very happy about the progress being made in civil rights. I have said to the leadership that I thought it would be rather unbecoming to go out and talk about Lincoln when we still had the civil rights bill that Lincoln would be so interested in locked up in a committee that couldn't act on it.

Therefore, I was very hopeful that we would get civil rights out and get it voted on in the House, getting at least half of the job done so that we could take it up as soon as we finish the tax bill in the Senate. When we take it up, we expect to stay on it until they act upon it.

Considering the fact that we have been here 60 days and we had five appropriations bills out of 15 that have been signed—and we have them all signed—we have the manpower development, which is retraining, which is very important to us. We have all the education bills signed, which are in the budget already. We have the budget formulated. We have the tax bill out of the committee; now we hope we will get it through by the 11th.

We have civil rights ready to come out and we hope we will have it through the 11th. I don't think the Congress should be charged with delaying it. They have been doing a pretty good job, including the foreign aid bill, despite the fact on it—even if we did have to come back Christmas.

I mentioned the education bills. We had the agriculture appropriation dealing with the laboratories and all of them have been solved. So we are very happy about it.

We have hopes of getting medicare out. They have finished the hearings and I am going to talk to the chairman of the committee at the appropriate time and see what the problems are there, and I will express my hopes.

January 26, 1964

CIVIL RIGHTS BILL PASSED BY HOUSE IN 290-130 VOTE; HARD SENATE FIGHT SEEN

FILIBUSTER LIKELY

Sweeping Measure Is Victory for Coalition of Two Parties

By E. W. KENWORTHY
Special to The New York Times

WASHINGTON, Feb. 10—The House of Representatives passed tonight the most far-reaching civil rights bill ever considered by the Congress.

On a roll-call vote, ordered at 7:55 P. M., the bill passed by a margin of 290 to 130.

The measure will be sent to the Senate next Monday. There it will receive a first reading at once but will not be debated before the end of the month.

The sweeping legislation would strengthen voting guarantees for Negroes in the South, ban discrimination in privately owned public accommodations as well as in publicly owned facilities and prohibit discrimination by employers and by unions.

Suits Are Authorized

It would empower the Attorney General to sue for desegregation of schools and would seek to bar discrimination in Federally assisted programs.

In the Senate the measure faces strong opposition. The Senate's Southerners, armed with the filibuster, will mount a far more formidable attack on the bill than could the Southern bloc in the House and its handful of Republican allies.

In the House, debate is limited by agreement, ruling out a filibuster—extended talk for the purpose of killing a bill or forcing modification of it. The Senate has no limitation on discussion except by closure—a motion to close debate, requiring approval by two-thirds of the members present and voting.

From the moment the House debate started nine days ago, the issue in that chamber was never in doubt. The coalition of Northern Democrats and Republicans that supported it outnumbered the opponents of the bill by about 2½ to 1.

Johnson Lauds House

Voting for the bill were 152 Democrats and 138 Republicans. Voting against it were 96 Democrats and 34 Republicans.

President Johnson hailed House passage of the measure tonight. He said it marked a "historic step forward for the cause of human dignity in America."

"Now the task is for the Senate," he said in a statement. "I hope the same spirit of non-partisanship will prevail there to assure passage of this bill, guaranteeing the fundamental rights of all Americans."

The end of the House debate found the two sides in the same good temper that had marked the beginning and the discussion of more than 125 proposed amendments.

The last amendment to be disposed of was offered by Representative Joe D. Waggoner Jr., Democrat of Louisiana, who proposed that the bill not become effective until it was approved in a national referendum.

"Are you afraid to take the chance?" Mr. Waggoner challenged the coalition.

His amendment went down before a wave of noes.

Then Representative Emanuel Celler, Brooklyn Democrat, chairman of the Judiciary Committee and floor manager of the bill, moved that the Committee of the Whole House of the State of the Nation rise and resolve itself into the House.

At that point, the long battle all but over, members of both sides of the question broke into applause. Representative William C. Cramer, Republican of Florida, moved to recommit the bill to committee. The motion was defeated.

Then, after the passage of the bill by voice vote, the roll-call was requested and ordered.

The measure has 11 titles, or sections.

The House, before coming to a vote, spent a good part of this afternoon in further debate on the bill's Title VII, outlawing discrimination by employers and unions.

Dogged Fight by Southerners

Although the Southerners fought doggedly over two days to weaken the fair-employment section and to circumscribe the powers of the commission that would administer it, the bipartisan coalition fended off any substantial change.

On Saturday the Southerners were able to add sex to the list of discriminations in employment to be banned, in addition to race, religion and national origin. Officials of the Justice Department had no great objection to this, although they said it would complicate administration of the program.

On Saturday also, the House accepted an amendment permitting an employer to refuse to hire an "atheist." Justice Department officials were not much worried by this either, because they believed it could not survive a constitutional test.

The amendments to the fair-employment section approved by the House today were relatively minor.

First, the House accepted a provision that in the first year after the effective date of the ban, businesses having fewer than 100 employes would not be covered; in the second year, those with fewer than 75; in the third year, those with fewer than 50, and thereafter, those with fewer than 25.

The same limits of coverage would apply to the ban on discrimination in labor-union membership.

In the committee bill, the drop in coverage would have been from 100 employes the first year to 50 the second and 25 thereafter. The ban becomes effective one year after the bill becomes law.

The House also agreed today to an amendment allowing an employer to refuse a job to a member of the Communist party or any Communist-front organization on the Attorney General's list.

Accepted by Celler

Representative Celler accepted this because, he said, nothing in the act prevented an employer from refusing to hire a Democrat, Republican or Socialist if he wanted to.

Another amendment accepted by the House permits an employer to advertise for, and hire, an employe of a specified sex where sex would be a "bona fide occupational qualification."

The same exceptions are permitted for religion and national origin.

The House rejected Southern proposals to limit the life of the Commission on Equal Employment Opportunity to four years and to strike out a clause empowering the commission to prescribe what records must be kept.

The House required only an hour late this afternoon to debate Title VIII of the bill. This section directs the Secretary of Commerce to have the Census Bureau compile statistics on voting and registration in areas recommended by the Civil Rights Commission.

There is an implied warning in this section to Southern states that have kept Negroes from registering and voting. The statistics could be used to enforce Section II of the 14th Amendment. This says that a state's delegation in the House of Representatives shall be cut proportionately to the number of its citizens not allowed to vote. This constitutional provision has never been applied.

There were only two important amendments to this section proposed. The first, offered by Representative William M. Tuck, former Governor of Virginia, would have required that statistics be collected for the whole country.

The second would have permitted Congress, rather than the Civil Rights Commission, to say where the surveys should be made.

Both were defeated.

Southerners did not put up the extended battle that had been expected over Title IX. This would allow defendants in civil rights cases involving arrest for trespass, sit-in demonstrations or parades without permits to appeal from orders of Federal District Courts remanding the cases to the state courts from which they had been removed.

At present, such remand orders are not reviewable, and many District Court judges in the South have refused requests for removal.

An amendment to strike out the whole section was defeated overwhelmingly.

At this point, Representative Robert T. Ashmore, Democrat of South Carolina, offered as a new title in the bill a proposal originally contained in the civil rights measure sent to Congress last June by President Kennedy but removed by the Judiciary Committee.

This would establish a Community Relations Service,

headed by a director appointed by the President. The function of the service would be to help communities resolve racial disputes and difficulties attending desegregation.

Whenever possible, the service would cooperate with appropriate state and local agencies.

This proposal — designated Title X in the bill—was adopted by voice vote.

There was a sudden rash of amendments, some of them frivolous, to the final title of the bill. This provides that nothing in the measure shall be construed to impair any right of the Attorney General or of the United States to intervene in any court proceeding under existing laws.

It also provides for authorization of funds to carry out the act. Finally, it provides that if any provision of the act is held invalid the remainder is not affected.

One amendment, proposed by Representative Howard W. Smith, Democrat of Virginia, would have stated that the act was not to be interpreted as requiring any individual to perform service against his will. This was defeated on voice vote.

Representative Thomas G. Abernathy, Democrat of Mississippi, proposed an authorization of $100 million, which he said would be necessary to carry out the act. This, too, was defeated.

One amendment was adopted to reassure some Republican states' rightists. It declares that there was no intention by Congress to pre-empt state laws.

In Senate handling of the bill, this is the strategy decided upon by Administration leaders:

When the bill reaches the Senate Monday, it will be met at the door and placed before the clerk, who will give it a first reading by titles.

Bills must be read twice before being referred to a committee. But Administration leaders do not want this bill referred to the Judiciary Committee, presided over by Senator James O. Eastland, Democrat of Mississippi. Civil rights bills do not get reported out of his committee.

Therefore, after the bill is read the second time on Tuesday, the majority leader, Mike Mansfield of Montana, will object to further proceedings on the bill. This objection, under the Senate's Rule 14, should result in the bill's being placed on the calendar instead of being referred to committee.

However, at that point, Senator Richard B. Russell, Democrat of Georgia, leader of the Southern bloc, is expected to make a point of order. He will contend that Rule 14 has been superseded by Rule 25, which was adopted after the 1946 Legislative Reorganization Act.

He will argue that Rule 25 requires reference of all bills to committee.

According to the plan of the Democratic leadership, the chair will not rule on the point of order but will ask the Senate to decide the issue. Debate will ensue.

After a period, a pro-civil rights Senator will move to lay the point-of-order motion on the table—in effect, to kill it. The Senate is expected to approve the tabling motion, thus sustaining Mr. Mansfield's move to get the bill on the calendar.

A motion to call the bill off the calendar for debate will not be made until toward the end of the month, after the tax bill has been finally passed.

The motion to call up is debatable, and at that moment the filibuster is expected to begin.

February 11, 1964

JOHNSON GAINS WIDE SUPPORT IN SOUTH

President Draws Praise Throughout the Region Despite His Strong Stand on Civil Rights

By CLAUDE SITTON
Special to The New York Times

CANTON, Miss., Feb. 29—The forthcoming civil rights filibuster will raise the curtain on one of the most delicate political balancing acts ever attempted by President Johnson.

He must win Senate approval of meaningful civil rights legislation over the opposition of a small but powerful group of Southern opponents. And he must do this in such a way as to bolster his strength among liberals in the North without arousing mass enmity among conservatives in the South.

Mr. Johnson goes into the battle with a number of points in his favor, not the least of which is that, as a Texan, he is the first Southerner in a century to hold the Presidency.

Political polls and other soundings of sentiment indicate that he is highly popular among a majority of the region's whites. This popularity shows no apparent decline as the result of his outspoken advocacy of the sweeping civil rights measure passed by the House.

Reverse Trend

Further, the pro-Johnson sentiment appears to extend into those states that supported the Republican Presidential ticket in 1960—Florida, Tennessee and Virginia.

In Florida, for example, a survey of elected officials, political party leaders and the man on the street found that a majority believed Mr. Johnson could return the state to the Democratic fold and reverse a trend set by Republican victories in three consecutive Presidential elections. The survey was conducted by The Florida Times-Union, Miami Herald and St. Petersburg Times in 42 of the state's 67 counties.

Even more surprising are well-founded reports of Mr. Johnson's strength in Mississippi, whose eight unpledged electors cast their votes for Senator Harry F. Byrd of Virginia in 1960, and in Alabama, six of whose elector votes went to the Senator.

Another factor in the President's favor as he presses for enactment of the civil rights bill is the sharp difference seen by voters in his position on the issue and that of President Kennedy.

Mr. Kennedy's commitment to the cause of Negro advancement was unquestioned. Many whites in the South and the North felt he had gone too far, too fast and was responsible to some degree for the racial crisis. Thus he was on the defensive in attempting to override opposition to his program.

President Johnson does not have this handicap despite his endorsement of the Kennedy civil rights program. His commitment to civil rights is in question because he is a Southerner. As a result, he can wage a far more aggressive fight for the bill in the Senate without risking the criticism that would have met his predecessor.

Most Southerners recognize the political realities of Mr. Johnson's position and will tend to pardon his vigorous support for civil rights legislation as an act of necessity.

Moreover, there is an increasing realization throughout the South that the old social order must change, that it is only a question of time before Negro pressure breaches the barriers of segregation. Many consider the fight against the civil rights bill a holding action.

Reaction to Failure

This realization has penetrated into Mississippi. Phil Mullen, editor and publisher of The Madison County Herald, took note of it this week in discussing reaction to the failure of Southern Representatives to defeat the rights measure. "While many down this way continue to shout and to

Seibel in The Richmond Times-Dispatch

"Just wait 'til I catch you alone."

Dobbins in The Boston Traveler

"Old man river—today."

proclaim 'never' to the evolving issue in Congress, there is no question but what a civil rights measure with teeth in it will be passed before summer is in its zenith," he wrote. "Sooner or later the South will have to face reality and it is not going to be much later."

President Johnson's civil rights position has cost him little if any support among Southern Democratic leaders, nor is it likely to do so unless it leads to a mass popular disaffection. The reason is that the party chiefs and officeholders need him as much as or more than he needs them.

The surging fortunes of Republicans have struck fear in the hearts of Democrats from Virginia to Texas. They see in the Johnson candidacy an opportunity to restore the party unity necessary for combating this threat.

These leaders long ago reached the conclusion that there were no basic differences of positions of the two national parties on civil rights and that none were likely to develop. Most believe that third parties or unpledged electors are futile. Further, the national Democratic leadership has become less tolerant of such aberrations in its Southern wing and have given some indication that a continuation would endanger the seniority of Southerners in Congress.

It is highly significant that Representative Howard W. Smith, one of Virginia's leading Byrd Democrats and a key opponent of the civil rights bill, has expressed the belief that President Johnson is the favorite in his state.

Even more striking are the words of Georgia's Senator Richard B. Russell, chief of the Southern filibuster forces in the Senate. He was a very reluctant supporter of President Kennedy in 1960. But in a speech last month at Valdosta, Ga., he had this to say:

"President Johnson and I have enjoyed an intimate personal friendship stretching back over almost 30 years. I know that he is a man of unusual ability with an immense capacity for leadership. He has a fine understanding of the workings of government and an appreciation for the delicate arrangement of checks and balances that is the genius of the American constitutional system. In my opinion, Lyndon Johnson has the potential to become one of the country's great Presidents."

Even in Mississippi, center of what neo-Dixiecrat sentiment remains, many highly placed Democrats indicate that they are favorably disposed toward the President.

Nevertheless, the filibuster still presents a grave political threat to the President.

A series of civil rights demonstrations is already in progress. Seemingly endless debate on the Senate floor or the emergence of an unacceptable compromise would intensify these protests and possibly bring serious racial violence.

These developments, in turn, could generate a backlash of anti-civil rights sentiment among whites in the South and elsewhere, placing Mr. Johnson in somewhat the same position in which Mr. Kennedy found himself last year.

Perhaps the President's sole advantage in the South if this point were reached would be that summed up in a recent remark of an aide to Senator Barry Goldwater. "Johnson is going to get the benefit of the doubt from the Southern people," he said.

March 1, 1964

JOHNSON ASKS ALL TO AID RIGHTS BILL

Seeks Public Pressure After Getting a Gloomy Report

By TOM WICKER

Special to The New York Times

WASHINGTON, May 12 — President Johnson, echoing Congressional pleas, called today for heavy public pressure in support of his civil rights bill.

The President spoke out shortly after Senator Mike Mansfield of Montana, the majority leader, had told him that "progress on the bill to date is nil."

Without public pressure, Mr. Johnson said, the bill would fail and "we will have some very dark days in this country."

The civil rights bill will be defeated, Mr. Johnson said, unless the people "in righteous indignation" make known their support for it.

His statement was part of an exhortation to businessmen to support the bill and to work for equal employment opportunities for Negroes. In turn, that speech was part of a typically diversified Johnson day that kept him busy in several directions.

He signed a bill bringing the sale of pesticides under tighter regulation and commented that the measure marked his concern for "the health of every one of our fellow Americans."

Prods Business on Jobs

He conferred with members of the executive board of the National Association of Manufacturers, challenging them to help bring unemployment below 5 per cent of the working force by the speeding the economic rate.

Mr. Johnson also accepted, and obviously was pleased with, an honorary membership in the National Forensic League, an organization of about 200,000 debaters in 1,500 high schools.

In response, he said the greatest disappointment of his life was "losing the state championship of Texas the first year I coached debate" at Sam Houston High School in Houston.

But that only happened, he suggested, because his team had been assigned the affirmative on the proposition that the jury system ought to be abolished.

The judges could not be expected to approve that position, Mr. Johnson said, "although for a while they were wavering," and finally brought in a split vote against his team.

Meanwhile, it was reported that the President was planning a California speaking tour next month with stops at Los Angeles and San Francisco. The White House would not comment except to say there was no definite schedule.

Sees Democratic Leaders

The President opened his day with his customary Tuesday morning breakfast meeting with Democratic Congressional leaders. He also addressed the National Farm Editors Association, proclaimed World Trade Week and Women Voters Week and announced a quarter-million dollars more disaster relief for Indiana.

May 13, 1964

The Strategy of Closure

Bipartisan Drive, Mapped in October, Led to Victory for Civil Rights Bloc

By ANTHONY LEWIS
Special to The New York Times

WASHINGTON, June 10—The remarkable victory for the civil rights bill in the Senate today was the work of many hands over many months.

The essential groundwork for it was laid last October, when the Kennedy Administration and Republican leaders in the House agreed on a bipartisan bill and a bipartisan strategy to pass it. The Senate Republican leader, Everett McKinley Dirksen of Illinois, added an essential bit of oil to the machinery when closure lacked the last necessary handful of votes.

News Analysis

And Lyndon B. Johnson, this country's first Southern President since Reconstruction, made it all possible by his outspoken commitment to Negro rights.

Nearly everyone has by now forgotten the chaos and bitterness into which the civil rights legislation had fallen last autumn. It seemed then that only a miracle could save it from suffocation at the hands of its own supporters.

Democrats were quarreling with Republicans over political credit for the bill. In the House Judiciary Committee, a liberal bloc was pushing a subcommittee draft of the legislation so far-reaching that it affronted moderate Republicans whose votes were needed.

Compromise Worked Out

At this point Attorney General Robert F. Kennedy and Representative William M. McCulloch of Ohio, ranking Republican on the Judiciary Committee, stepped in and set the bill on the course that led to the victory this morning.

They did two things. One was to work out a compromise bill that could attract the necessary broad spectrum of support. The other was to agree on a joint strategy of sticking resolutely to this compromise and abjuring all temptations of partisanship.

Their agreement was made formal Oct. 29 in a compact between President Kennedy and the House Republican leader, Charles A. Halleck of Indiana. Vice President Johnson, as he than was, sat in on the talks leading to the compact and entirely agreed with the course chosen.

The bipartisan strategy had many critics at that time, especially among liberals. Their theory was to start with the most voluminous bill possible and let opponents whittle away at it in the House and Senate until something reasonable was left.

Amendments Proposed

Nothing succeeds like success, of course, and tonight the bipartisan approach has been proved wise. But even before now events on the House and Senate floor demonstrated how dangerous the ordinary partisan approach to legislating would have been on this bill.

In the House, dozens of amendments were considered. Without the strongest control by the bipartisan managers the whole affair would probably have collapsed. As it was, the coalition held fast even for the job discrimination section, about which Mr. Halleck was unenthusiastic and which the Attorney General doubted could pass.

In the Senate, even the bipartisan House bill was too strong for conservative Republicans. And without them, the required 67 votes were simply not there for closure. Indeed, until quite recently, President Johnson was most pessimistic about obtaining closure.

Senator Dirksen supplied the required magic, as Democratic leaders are quick to affirm. He worked out with the Justice Department amendments that did not affect the substance of the legislation but were sufficiently deferential to states' rights and gradualism to produce all but six Republican votes today.

President Johnson's role in the legislative struggle since last Nov. 22 has been a varied one. Most significant has been his repeated public advocacy of the bill. Certainly, if he had been lukewarm there could have been no vote for closure.

Presses for Legislation

In his first speech to Congress, on Nov. 27, he put civil rights at the head of his legislative list. He spoke for racial equality in Georgia as well as in Washington, and he never gave an inch in talks with his old Southern friends in the Senate.

The President has had less of a direct hand in the day-to-day parliamentary tactics than some might expect, considering his skill in this department. He evidently felt that the wiser course was to leave most of the job of dealing with Capitol Hill to the Justice Department officials most familiar with the bill.

When the bill came to the floor of the House, Mr. Johnson told the Justice Department men to go ahead and handle it as planned—and to call on him for any help they wanted. After House passage, he took the public and private position that the Senate should accept the House bill without change.

Senator Dirksen persuaded the President in private conversation that closure could not be obtained without amending the House bill. The changes were then worked out with Justice Department lawyers, again with the President's backing.

Talked for 75 Days

At least some direct lapel-pulling by President Johnson could be traced in the vote today. It is most unlikely that Senator Howard W. Cannon, Nevada Democrat, would have gone for closure without a personal appeal from the President, and he doubtless shored up other wavering Democrats.

In the end, the South managed to keep the talk going in the Senate for 75 days before the showdown came. But there is good reason to believe that the Southerners will be the big losers from this affair in several senses.

By refusing ever to admit the existence of any racial discrimination in the South, they exposed the weakness of their position. A high point came when the Attorney General asked Senator Sam J. Ervin Jr., Democrat of North Carolina, whether there might be some bias against Negroes in Mississippi—and the Senator changed the subject.

Rules Change Backed

The length of the filibuster may also bring retribution. Already there is revived support for a change in Senate Rule 22 to allow closure by three-fifths instead of two-thirds—60 instead of 67 of the 100 Senators, —a difference that would probably have ended this debate sooner.

Finally, the very stiffness of the Southern resistance dramatizes the breadth of the national consensus that overrode it. For today's 71 votes for closure surely represent the broadest kind of national commitment to equal opportunity for the Negro in voting, schools, jobs and public accommodations.

This bill, when it passes, will not be the work of nine Supreme Court justices who can be conveniently denounced. It will bear the stamp of the overwhelming majority of an elected Congress coming to the support of the Supreme Court 10 years after the school degregation decision began a new era in race relations.

June 11, 1964

The Vocabulary of Presidents

By George E. Reedy

MILWAUKEE—As in so many other things that involved the relationship of men to power, the Greeks had a word for it—*hubris.* It would be a good one to cast in six-inch letters of bronze and place on the most prominent wall of every room in the White House.

The word can be translated loosely as "too big for one's britches." But another way to describe it would be as the feeling that might overwhelm a man who has just won re-election to the Presidency by a landslide vote.

This thought is prompted by the Washington scene as it appears from the viewpoint of a city several hundred miles away. In this perspective, it does not look as though the capital is getting ready for an inauguration but as though Mr. Nixon is getting ready for fifteen rounds with Congress —a bout in which he is the challenger.

Why he should be the challenger is something of a mystery. Politically, he is the undisputed champ. He has all the advantages that come from an undisputed victory. His tactical position is superb. He has nothing to gain from further confrontations and everything to lose. It is certainly a time for magnanimity and for pouring salve on the wounds of the losers.

It is not working out that way but quite to the contrary. It is not a question of his pursuing policies that the opposition does not like. He has not only a right but an obligation to stand for his principles. In terms of statecraft, however, it is stretching both the right and the obligation when he proceeds as though all political differences have been settled, and he no longer needs to take into account the system of checks and balances.

Although I personally feel that the unrestricted bombing of North Vietnam was a tragic mistake, I do not question his authority as Commander in Chief to do so. But I believe that the interests of the nation would have been far better served had he first granted the opposition leaders a chance to have their say.

Although I personally feel that the environment is one of our most urgent problems, I do not doubt his sincerity in opposing Congressional action in that field. But to impound funds voted over his veto is certainly a challenge to the legislative branch.

There can be no doubt of his dedication to improving the efficiency of government. But to propose a reorganization plan to Congress and then act before there is a legislative response is just asking for trouble.

Perhaps Mr. Nixon and his advisers should re-examine the meaning of a landslide victory—preferably with the word *hubris* on the wall facing their desks. There have been quite a few in American history and in many cases the aftermath has been chilling. There is no need to pick up textbooks for such a study. There is ample material available in what has happened during the lifetimes of the present generation of American leaders.

It requires considerable humility for a man to realize that nothing is really decided by an election except the identity of the President for a four-year period. All of the issues remain to be settled one by one in an arena of constantly shifting political forces and constituencies.

For the time being, all of the issues appear to be riding with Mr. Nixon. As long as his spine is stiff, there is really very little that Congress can do to frustrate him, however much it may thunder. There are inherent advantages to the Presidential position which make it very difficult to block an executive in the initial stages of his Administration.

Issues have a habit of shifting without warning, however. One of the few immutable rules of politics is that no victory is final and no coalition of support is ever solid. The men and women who are being disdained today may be vitally needed tomorrow and if all bridges to them have been burned, they simply will not be there at the crucial moment.

These thoughts probably have little appeal to people who are flushed with the euphoria of a truly remarkable victory. But the word *hubris* has a special connotation. It was regarded as an evil gift from the gods to men whom they would destroy. A little study of this aspect of Greek philosophy might pay some rich dividends for both the people in the White House and the country.

George E. Reedy, former press aide to President Johnson, is dean of journalism at Marquette University.

Nixon's Presidency: Crisis for Congress

By JOHN HERBERS
Special to The New York Times

WASHINGTON, March 4 — "You just think we're dumb," Senator Clifford P. Case, Republican of New Jersey, told George P. Shultz, Secretary of the Treasury and Counselor to the President, during a recent hearing on Capitol Hill.

Senator Case was not only right about White House disdain of members of Congress, he was also understating it.

"Congress is lazy, too," said a Presidential aide, pounding his fist on his desk for emphasis during a recent interview. "They work short hours. They don't know how to consult. They say they want to consult with the President, but then they come up here and don't say anything."

"They criticize us for not advising or consulting them in military matters," he continued. "But they cannot keep a secret. If we tell them anything it is out within 30 minutes after they have gone back to the Hill."

That attitude toward Congress runs deep in the White House, and it underscores the seriousness of the constitutional struggle being waged between the executive and legislative branches of the Government as President Nixon, wielding perhaps more power than any President in history, moves into a second term with a landslide victory behind him.

At the heart of the contest is the President's recent move to reorder domestic priorities by impounding funds and liquidating some agencies despite Congressional mandates. But it also involves a general erosion of powers from the Congress to the Presidency, a process that has been under way for many years but has accelerated in the Nixon Administration.

A survey of a wide range of authorities on the Government during the last several weeks shows that, in the opinion of many, the struggle is so weighted to the side of the Presidency that if Mr. Nixon does not relax his demands—his aides insist that he will not — Congress could be left far weaker than it already had become when Mr. Nixon took office in 1969.

"We are now in the midst of a grave and domestic constitutional crisis brought on by the Administration's unilateral efforts to reorder our domestic priorities," said Senator Jacob K. Javits, Republican of New York, who actively supported Mr. Nixon's re-election. "This crisis covers every aspect of legislation pending in the Congress or which may be proposed."

Some Administration Concern

On the other hand, there is concern within the Administration that the fight will become so embittered and members of Congress so enraged that they will find ways to upset the President's goals and priorities.

"I agree 100 per cent with what the President is doing," said a high Administration official. "But I fear the spending fight with Congress may go too far."

Nevertheless, beyond the immediate issues and priorities, what is at stake is whether Congress survives as a strong and effective branch of the Government and whether more power continues to accumulate in the Presidency without accompanying restraints and means of accountability to the public, according to many students of government.

Some contend that the erosion of Congressional authority to the Presidency already has gone further under President Nixon than is generally recognized. Following are some of the developments:

¶President Nixon broadened and institutionalized the war powers of his office by conducting the war in Southeast Asia at his pleasure under precedents and practices used by former President Johnson, but without as close consultation with Congress, which under the Constitution holds the authority to declare war. He also extended the practice of using executive agreements in foreign affairs in place of treaties, which require Senate approval. Thus, "an illegal war was ended by an illegal agreement," according to a Congressional staff member referring to the recent settlement of the war in Vietnam.

¶While the nerve ends of many members of Congress were still raw from the long and bitter fight on war powers, President Nixon served notice in his recent budget message that in order to control inflation and carry out his campaign pledge not to seek a tax rise, he would not fund some programs enacted by Congress and would curtail others, with Great Society social programs enacted under Democrats in the nineteen-sixties bearing the brunt of the cuts. This went further than any other President had in moving against Congressional power to spend.

¶Although his aides strongly deny it, it is the opinion of many nonpartisan authorities on the subject that President Nixon has broadened the use of executive privilege to protect himself and members of his Administration from Congressional and public inquiry.

¶Reorganization of the executive branch by the President has curtailed Congressional access and authority in some areas of the Government. For example, by increasing the budgetary controls by the executive branch over the regulatory agencies, a power that once rested solely with Congress, the Administration forced the Federal Trade Commission, through a cut of funds, to cancel a planned investigation in hospital and medical practices, according to the testimony of the former commission chairman, Miles W. Kirkpatrick.

¶In a number of little ways, the Nixon Administration has defied Congress. When the Senate Finance Committee wanted to conduct its own study of the welfare situation, the Administration would not let the committee use its computers and would make only that information available for the computers that the Administration wanted it to have.

President Nixon, who terms himself an activist in the Presidency and views the office as the chief representative of the public, said in his Jan. 31 press conference that Congress represented special interests while the President represented all of the people.

"The Interior Committee wants to have more parks and the Agriculture Committee wants cheap R.E.A. [Rural Electrification Administration] loans and the Committee on Education and Labor wants more for education, and each of these wants we all sympathize with," he said. "But there is only one place in this Government where somebody has got to speak not for the special interests which the Congress represents but for the general interest." That place, he said, is the White House.

Little Sought From Congress

On the spending issue, President Nixon is in a unique position. He is the first President since the Federal budget became an important instrument in managing the economy—a development of the last two decades—to be caught in a position of having steadily rising Government costs collide head on with his policy for controlling inflation. That policy is to hold spending to a budget level of $268-billion for the fiscal year beginning July 1, rather than raising taxes.

The fight with Congress is essentially over which branch of the Government will decide which programs will be cut and by how much. Mr. Nixon has moved to do so by executive action while legislators contend that such power belongs to the Congress under the Constitution.

Further, according to sources both in and out of the Administration, there is not much Mr. Nixon wants from Congress this year. His program is for contracting many Government services, not expanding them.

Charles L. Schultze, who was budget director under President Johnson and is now with the Brookings Institution, pointed out in an interview that other recent Presidents all wanted something from Congress in legislation, usually quite a lot.

"In the past," said Mr. Schultze, "funds would be impounded for a time, as Mr. Nixon is doing now, but they became a matter of negotiations between the President and Congress and eventually most of them would be released."

"For at least 15 years," he continued, "Presidents have been trying to get rid of the Rural Environmental Assistance Program or have it reduced, but they always gave in to Congress in the end because there was something they wanted from Congress. Now Nixon has simply cut it off and there is no bargaining position."

A Test of Wills

The program, called REAP, which helps farmers reclaim land, has been costing more than $200-million a year. Congress, as a test of wills, is in the process of passing legislation that would force the President to spend the money, but White House sources say the President is confident that his opponents on the Hill can never muster the two-thirds vote in both houses needed to override his veto.

At the same time, the President's men are happily dismantling the Office of Economic Opportunity, the agency established by the Johnson Administration to help eradicate poverty, despite specific prohibitions in the law against doing so. White House lawyers say they are acting under other laws, delegations of power from Congress, that give the President authority to do so.

Nevertheless, Mr. Schultze and other experts agree that

what Mr. Nixon is doing is boldly extending the power of the Presidency "in degree if not in kind." Mr. Schultze pointed out that the President's actions in impounding funds as Commander in Chief of the armed forces have far more precedent than impounding funds to eliminate entire domestic programs.

Thus President Jefferson's refusal to buy gunboats and President Truman's order to impound $700-million appropriated for the Air Force, examples cited by Mr. Nixon and his assistants, are not precedents at all for what is being done now, according to Mr. Schultze.

On the use of executive privilege, a debate has raged between the White House and Congress on whether Mr. Nixon has expanded that power, which most authorities agree is needed to protect the autonomy of the Presidency but is frequently used to hide waste, corruption or other misdeeds from the legislative branch.

A recent example of its use was the refusal by Air Force Secretary Robert C. Seamans Jr. to disclose the conversations he had with members of the White House in regard to the dismissal of A. Ernest Fitzgerald, who exposed the $2-billion overrun on the C-5A transport plane.

John D. Ehrlichman, assistant to the President for domestic affairs, said in an interview with U. S. News & World Report Feb. 18 that Mr. Nixon had adopted a procedure to minimize the use of executive privilege. He said that Mr. Nixon had invoked the privilege only three times in four years, whereas President Kennedy invoked it six times in three years.

"The President has been very openhanded in providing witnesses and documents to the Congress," he said.

Clark R. Mollenhoff, a former Nixon aide who is now Washington bureau chief for The Des Moines Register, has made a detailed study of the issue over a period of years. He contends that Mr. Nixon has broadened the use of executive privilege in several respects over practices of the Kennedy and Johnson Administrations, especially extending it to officials lower down the line.

"The President now says that all actions by White House officials can be treated as confidential and not subject to the subpoena process of the Congress or the courts," Mr. Mollenhoff wrote.

"The White House game plan has been to refuse initially all requests for information that are potentially embarrassing, and to clothe all members of the White House staff with the 'executive privilege,'" he said. "If the issue becomes too hot to handle, as it did in the International Telephone and Telegraph case, the President will permit the White House officials to appear and answer questions in a manner as restricted as the practical political situation allows."

Law Is Passed Over

President Nixon has extended powers over Congress in ways that have received little attention. After Franklin D. Roosevelt devalued the dollar during the Depression, Congress passed a law in 1945 providing that only Congress could set the price of gold, the step involved in devaluation. Despite the law's explicit provisions, however, Mr. Nixon has twice devalued the dollar by executive action, and it drew no protest because of Congressional recognition that the world money markets should not be tipped off in advance, as Congressional action would have done.

This is an example of how power has steadily accumulated in the Presidency. Over the years, Congress and the President have repeatedly waged war over constitutional authority, but most of the fights in the 19th century and well into the 20th involved Presidential revolt against Congressional dominance.

Congress Struggles

James A. Garfield in 1881, in fighting that dominance by refusing the advice of friends to compromise with a Senator on the appointment of the Federal collector of the Port of New York, said:

"If it were a difference between individuals there could be some sense in such advice. But the one represents a whole independent function of the Government. The other is one-seventy-sixth of one-half of another independent branch of the Government with which compound vulgar fractions the President is asked to compromise."

Today it is Congress struggling to find ways to resist Presidential dominance.

In the past, once a President gained new powers they remained for his successors. Clinton Rossiter, the historian, wrote during the Eisenhower Administration that "strong Presidents have been followed by weak ones; in the aftermath of every 'dictator,' Congress has exulted in the 'restoration of the balance wisely ordained by the fathers.' Yet the ebbs have been more apparent than real, and each new strong President has picked up where the last one left off."

Presidential scholars, who have educated millions of Americans on the need for a strong Presidency and are now frightened by the Nixon phenomenon, still by and large advocate a strong Presidency but want to keep a vital Congress as a check on the executive office.

Henry Steel Commager, asked for an answer to the current struggle, said, "One answer would be impeachment if the Congress had any guts, but it doesn't. The simple answer is to really assert the appropriation power."

But the question is whether the country would support the Congress even in that endeavor. The Nixon White House is confident that it would not.

* * * * *

March 5, 1973

President Is More Yielding In Clashes With Congress

By JOHN HERBERS
Special to The New York Times

WASHINGTON, July 28 — While the impeachment drive against President Nixon has been attracting widespread attention, a related development has gone virtually unnoticed: That Mr. Nixon has made important concessions of authority to the Congress that must decide whether he remains in office.

This trend has been under way for several months, but there have been recent actions such as the following that go to the heart of the struggle for power between the legislative and executive branches:

¶A few days ago, Mr. Nixon quietly reversed himself and agreed to permit Kenneth Rush, his counselor for economic policy, to testify before Congressional committees. He had been strongly opposed to such a step, high Administration sources said, because he had felt that he must preserve the long-asserted Presidential prerogative that White House aides are not subject to the same Congressional scrutiny as are Cabinet officers and others whose appointments are confirmed by the Senate.

¶The effort that Mr. Nixon undertook early in 1973 to impound at will funds appropriated by Congress and to end by Executive order some programs established by Congress has now been abandoned. The President also signed legislation providing for Congressional review of impoundments that may be necessary for the economy or other reasons.

Congressional authorities have noted that the Administration is more cooperative in providing Congress with information and access to officials of the executive branch than it was.

And the President himself in the last two to three months has consulted Congressional leaders of both parties more often on the wider range of issues than was his practice. Over the last few weeks, when the President was in Washington, there was a steady stream of Senators and Representatives into the White House, and he frequently entertained members of Congress aboard the Presidential yacht Sequoia.

A little more than a year ago, Mr. Nixon was challenging Congress for power on a broad front. In addition to impoundment and restrictions on Congressional access to information and aides, he was attempting to reshape areas of the Government without Congressional authority and to effect important foreign and domestic policies without Congressional participation. Congressional leaders were fighting back.

Now, according to a number of authorities, the balance of power is close to where it was under the previous Presidents and there are no indications of further new challenges from the White House.

Throughout the last few months, Mr. Nixon has continued to exert his authority on legislation. He has continued to veto bills, even though some members of Congress say he has not been as bold in the use of the veto as he would have been had the impeachment drive not been under way.

For example, Senator James A. McClure, Republican of Idaho, said last week that he expected Mr. Nixon to sign recently enacted legislation creating a legal services corporation even though it ran counter to the Nixon policies. The White House announced Thursday that the President had signed the legal aid bill.

'Playing Both Sides'

"The President is trying to stay in office, and his staff assumes that means trying to placate everybody," Senator McClure said. "That means playing both sides. It can't be done."

The important concessions that Mr. Nixon has made, however, are in the area of Congressional authority and prerogatives that Congressional leaders over the years have jealously guarded. The use of the veto is considered in Congress to be a legitimate exercise of Presidential authority. Wiping out programs enacted by Congress is not.

Mr. Nixon's concessions on impoundings and on allowing Mr. Rush to testify were made under pressure, but it was not considered likely Mr. Nixon would have given in so easily on either had it not been for the impeachment inquiry.

A Usual Presidential Stance

Traditionally, Presidents have resisted Congressional attempts to question their top aides on policies. Mr. Nixon himself has rejected a number of requests for such testimony on the ground that it would violate the separation of powers.

Mr. Rush, however, was given unusual authority as a Presidential counselor—coordinator of economic policies throughout the administration. When George P. Shultz held that role he was, in addition to being a Presidential assistant, Secretary of the Treasury and thus subject to giving Congressional testimony.

Senator William Proxmire, Democrat of Wisconsin, threatened to hold up Senate confirmation of Alan Greenspan as chairman of the Council of Economic Advisers until the President agreed to allow Mr. Rush to submit to Congressional questioning.

Mr. Nixon was reported at the time to be strongly opposed and determined not to give in. After a few days, however, he did. Administration sources said it was felt that he could not at this time afford a struggle with Congress relating to Congressional authority.

On impoundment, the Administration had lost a series of court battles on the issue and Roy L. Ash, director of the Office of Management and Budget, said on June 29 that the economic reasons for impoundment were not as compelling as they had been.

However, last year, the Nixon White House pledged to fight the impoundment issue all the way. Much of the effort was not so much to achieve fiscal restraint, as to allocate resources according to the Administration's formula and to eliminate expenditures that it considered wasteful or ineffective. It is that battle that has now been given up.

CHAPTER **4**

Technology and the Presidency

The technology of the twentieth century has created a profound revolution in the public perceptions of the presidency. The full implications of that revolution, however, are not clear and certainly the results have not constituted unmixed blessings. The new developments in transportation and communications have increased enormously the presidential capacity to meet Americans and talk to them. At the same time, they may have increased his burdens by obliging him to travel more and limiting his communications more and more to one-way affairs.

Nineteenth-century presidents did little traveling because it was too difficult. Furthermore, poor communications between Washington and the rest of the nation meant that liaison with the seat of government was hazardous when the president was ''out of town.'' Except for an occasional vacation, this meant that the chief executive would spend most of his term in the White House.

Conditions have certainly changed. The president can now reach any part of the United States within a few hours and any part of the world within a couple of days. No matter where he is, he has virtually instant communication with the vast, governmental complex in the District of Columbia and can transact most of his business at 35,000 feet in the air. His mobility is unparalleled and recent presidents have taken full advantage of it. The presidential plane, Air Force One, has become as much a symbol of the presidency as the White House.

In many respects, this situation has made the president a much more familiar figure to the public than he has been in the past. He is quite likely to be seen in person in the course of a year by any big city resident. Those who do not see him in person are almost certain to see him not once but several times on television. Wherever he goes and whatever he does, a camera will be trained on him much of the time.

Strangely enough, the increased personal and visual contacts with the president do not seem to have made him a less remote figure. If anything, he seems to be at a greater distance than in the past. Perhaps this is an inevitable outcome of employing the mass media which have a superb ability to increase the size of an audience but which also stifle dialogue. Perhaps it is an inevitable accompaniment of jet fatigue which leaves little humanity in a man who has just finished crossing two or three time zones. It really does not matter because presidents will continue to use the instruments of modern technology. The simple fact is they give them more listeners and therefore more potential votes.

GER

Harry S Truman

The New York Times

ROOSEVELT FAVORS BILL FOR PRESIDENT'S FARES

Summons Correspondents to Approve of $25,000 Appropriation.

NOT RIGHT TO BE DEADHEAD

Desirable to Have the President Visit the People—A Bill to Provide the Money.

Special to The New York Times.

WASHINGTON, June 11.—On the President's initiative there was another "symposium" for newspaper correspondents at the White House this afternoon. The occasion was similar to the gathering six weeks ago when the President announced his decision to substitute for the Long court review amendment to the Rate bill the so-called Allison amendment providing for a broad court review.

The subject on which to-day the President desired to be understood was the item in the Sundry Civil bill providing an appropriation of $25,000 for traveling expenses for the President and his official household. The number of correspondents who were summoned was smaller than on the former occasion, a circumstance due no doubt to the fact that the President was not entirely pleased with the result of the other symposium or with its subsequent treatment in the discussion in the Senate.

The ground on which the proposed appropriation for the President's traveling expenses is based was plainly set forth to-day. It was urged that the appropriation was not a personal one. The President was too high-minded to be seeking such a thing. Essentially it was an appropriation for those parts of the country where the occasions arise requiring or justifying the presence of the President.

There could be no question of the wisdom of the occupant of the high office of President of the United States visiting in person the various parts of the country. Such journeys brought the people in sympathetic touch with their Government; made the great body of American citizens, if possible, more patriotic than they might otherwise be, and gave them a wholesome personal interest in the great issues of Government which so vitally concern them all, their homes, their lives, and the future of themselves and their children.

To expect the President to travel as a dead head violated every decent feeling of respect for the office. To expect the incumbent to respond to the many proper and necessary demands for his presence and himself pay all the heavy expenses was out of reason. It had, therefore, seemed nothing more or less than proper and just that a certain sum should be appropriated for such expenses, and the President would be pleased to have Congress take the same view of the matter.

Representative Watson of Indiana introduced a bill in the House to-day intended as a general statute, that an annual appropriation of $25,000 may be made to cover the expenses of Presidential trips.

Mr. Watson was in the chair in the House when the provision in the Sundry Civil bill making an appropriation of the amount named for this purpose was under consideration. Under the rules of the House he felt bound to, and did, rule the provision out of the bill. Should the bill he introduced to-day become law it will be in order to include the amount hereafter in the Sundry Civil bill.

The bill provides that hereafter it shall be lawful to appropriate $25,000 annually, and so much thereof as may be required shall be used by the President to pay his traveling expenses and those of friends he may invite, the amount to be accounted for by the President himself. The bill also carries a $25,000 appropriation "for the coming fiscal year."

June 12, 1906

PRESIDENT GETS $25,000 FOR TRAVEL EXPENSES

Senate Passes Bill, Which Has Already Gone Through House.

A CLASS LAW, SAY DEMOCRATS

They Declare It's for Political Junkets—All Agree President Couldn't Now Accept Railroad Favors.

WASHINGTON, June 22.—The opposition to the amendment to the Sundry Civil bill appropriating $25,000 annually for the payment of the traveling expenses of the President, which was begun by Senator McLaurin, resulted to-day in the withdrawal of the amendment by Senator Hale in charge of the bill and the subsequent passage of the independent bill providing for the same appropriation which has passed the House.

The Democrats in the debate to-day opposed the bill, alleging that it would result in the President going on political junkets and that its spirit was un-American and savored of royalty.

The bill appropriates not exceeding $25,000 per annum, such sum, when appropriated, to be expended in the discretion of the President and accounted for on his certificate solely. An appropriation of $25,000 is made for the fiscal year of 1907.

Senator McCumber, the first speaker on the amendment, contented himself with a brief reference to the record of President Roosevelt in advocacy of equal privileges to all. He reached the conclusion that the President could not be held responsible for the pending proposition.

Senator McLaurin said his opposition to the bill was due entirely to the fact that such legislation tends to build up class distinctions, which he maintained should be reprobated by all. He announced his confidence that the present Chief Executive has not sought this legislation and he had confidence that if the proposition should be presented to him independently he was satisfied that he would veto it.

The provision was opposed by Senator Bacon on Constitutional grounds. The Georgia Senator also opposed the amendment on the ground of its un-American tendency, which, he said, was in the direction of royalty. It had never been intended that especial privileges should be given to officials.

Senator Foraker said he had reached the conclusion that the appropriation would be an emolument and therefore unconstitutional. The question should be investigated by the Attorney General. If he should pronounce against the policy a separate bill could be vetoed, whereas the provision as it stood in the Sundry Civil bill could not be disposed of without vetoing the entire Sundry Civil bill.

Continuing Mr. Bacon referred to the tours of Presidents Cleveland, Harrison and McKinley.

"Does the Senator mean to say that they paid their own way?" asked Senator Lodge, and when Mr. Bacon replied in the affirmative, Mr. Lodge replied that "it is perfectly well known that they did not, but that the railroads had paid their expenses." Mr. Bacon then said that he had only meant to say that the Government had not footed the bills.

Both Senators agreed that under the prospective railroad rate law the President could not accept free transportation from the railroads.

Mr. Morgan of Alabama made a humorous speech, but which he declared to be an entirely serious treatment of the subject. He said the Senate knew nothing of what was intended to be done with the $25,000 to be appropriated. "It might be used," he said, "for the entertainment of the scions of royal blood with the President giving instructions in American hunting and sports. Or, as some have suggested, it might be for political expeditions, where the President might stock a train with spellbinders to enlighten the people of the United States on subjects they know more about than the spellbinders. In that event it would be money thrown away. There is something outside social duties intended by this appropriation. It is something political or a sort of hippodrome we are providing for."

Mr. Hale withdrew the amendment and renewed his request that the House bill making an independent appropriation of $25,000 for the President's traveling expenses be laid before the Senate. The proposition was agreed to.

The discussion then proceeded with the independent bill as its basis. Senator Carmack opposed the bill on the ground that the only purpose is to give the people a free show. The next move would be to furnish peanuts and pink lemonade. He moved to strike out the appropriation, but the motion was rejected, 17 to 36.

Senator Culberson moved to so amend the bill as to make the appropriation applicable only to travel "on official business." This was voted down, 23 to 35. On this ballot Messrs. La Follette and McCumber voted with the Democrats.

After brief remarks by Senators Spooner, Patterson, Heyburn, Dolliver, Mallory, and Dick, the bill was passed, 42 to 20, the Republicans generally voting for the bill and the Democrats against it.

The Senate also passed the Sundry Civil Appropriation bill. There was an effort to strike out of that bill the provision prohibiting canteens at soldiers' homes, but instead it was made stronger. The bill as passed carries an appropriation of about $102,400,000. The bill also retains the House provision for a lock canal at Panama.

June 23, 1906

TRUMAN TO SPEAK AT 'WHISTLE STOPS'

Tells Toledo Crowd His Quest of Presidency Will Be Most Important Since Lincoln's

Special to THE NEW YORK TIMES.

TOLEDO, Ohio, Sept. 6—President Truman told a railroad station crowd here tonight that "before this campaign is over I expect to visit every whistle stop in the United States." He said that it was to be the most important Presidential campaign since the Lincoln-Douglas debates.

A crowd of several thousand enthusiastic supporters greeted the President as his special train pulled into the railroad station just before midnight on the way to Washington from a barnstorming tour of industrial cities of Michigan. Nearly a hundred party workers, labor leaders and city officials boarded Mr. Truman's private car to be introduced by Mayor Michael V. Disalle.

Noting that Labor Day was fast drawing to a close, the President said he was only beginning "the most important labor in my life." He said he knew the meaning of a tough campaign and had himself tasted political defeat.

That was in 1940, he said, when his campaign for election to the Senate was probably the "bitterest" ever waged in Missouri. The President said his candidacy had been opposed by virtually every newspaper in the state and he had gone to bed "defeated" and got up the next day a winner by 11,000 votes.

Mr. Truman's special train was running behind schedule because of its late departure from Flint and he appeared ready to go back inside his car after a few brief remarks when a heckler in the crowd said something about labor going Republican.

"You don't know anything about that," the President shouted back and then predicted labor's overwhelming support on Nov. 2. He talked on for another ten minutes.

September 7, 1948

Nixon Schedules One-Day Forays Into States to Avoid Wasting Time

By GLADWIN HILL

Special to The New York Times.

LOS ANGELES, Aug. 7—An American political tradition, the ceremonial progress of a Presidential candidate through a state for several days at a stretch, is being abandoned by Vice President Nixon in this campaign.

Instead, he plans to cover the ground in a series of one-day forays, spaced out over a longer period. He reasons that modern communications yield the maximum impact from the first day's visit to a state. After that the publicity value slopes off rapidly.

This was one of the campaign plans the Republican nominee disclosed to reporters as he wound up his first stumping excursion this week-end. It touched Nevada, California, Hawaii and the state of Washington. Other major points of his planning are: Ten days of railroad whistle-stop touring; minimal use of paid national television programs, but much use of state and regional television single visits to small-vote states and a concentration of effort on big-vote states.

The whistle-stopping, the Vice President said, will be centered in more compact and heavily populated areas of the Middle West and East, where a whole state can be covered in a day. Out West, it may take the better part of a day just to get from one state to another by train.

Last Tuesday's one-hour stopover at Reno, Nev., on his way west, Mr. Nixon said, was typical of his personal coverage of small states. He does not plan to go back to Hawaii, where he spent two days last week. It takes virtually a whole day of flying time to get there and back.

Instead, his appearances in small-vote areas will be followed up by his running mate, Henry Cabot Lodge, and other big name stumpers for the ticket.

The state of Washington, where there was an hour-long airport rally at Seattle on his return to the mainland, the candidate plans to visit again, on his way to Alaska.

California Typical

A typical big-state operation will be California, with a second-ranking bloc of thirty-two electoral votes. Mr. Nixon will make at least one flying visit each to such centers as Los Angeles and San Francisco, and possibly some hinterland points, along with follow-up stumping by Mr. Lodge and others.

Breaking his touring into one-day forays may yield Mr. Nixon one advantage he did not dwell on. He believes that many voters make up their minds the last minute on the basis of the last person they've heard. Not committing himself to a long and involved itinerary in one state gives a candidate flexibility to jump in quickly where his missionary work is most needed.

Mr. Nixon feels that on television, as many others observed in the previous two campaigns, it is too difficult to put together a nation-wide show with enough interest and drawing power to justify the expense of $100,000 or more.

The notable exception is the projected coast-to-coast television debates between Mr. Nixon and the Democratic nominee, Senator John F. Kennedy of Massachusetts.

August 8, 1960

Display of Presidential Plane

WASHINGTON, Nov. 21 (UPI)—The Sacred Cow, the first airplane used to carry United States presidents to such famous international meeting sites as Yalta and Potsdam, will be added to the National Air Museum. It will be presented by the Air Force to the Smithsonian Institution's museum on Dec. 4.

November 22, 1961

The President

A Master Politician Touches All Bases

Lyndon Johnson in orbit is the ultimate in American tourism: a frantic airborne dash from Premier to Pope, cathedral to combat, winter to summer to winter again—not so much for the experience of the thing as just to capture it on film and live off it for a year at home—in this case the fateful year of 1968.

In 120 hours last week, the President flew to remote Australia to honor the memory of a loyal collaborator in Vietnam, Prime Minister Harold Holt (incidentally provoking another gathering of all the allied leaders in Vietnam and many other dignitaries, with each of whom he duly met); then 4,600 miles over to the war zone to embrace his troops and airmen in Thailand and Vietnam; then to Rome to proffer the other palm to Pope Paul VI at the Vatican, and finally homeward to spend a family Christmas in the White House. About 27,600 miles in five days and nights, with the President's time divided almost equally aloft and aground.

Rallies and Exhortations

There were symbolic and rhetorical invocations to the community of Pacific nations in rain-drenched Honolulu, in South Seas ceremonials in Samoa. There were midnight rallies with fliers to the glories of aviation and passionate exhortations of the troops in South Vietnam, and finally, of course, the plans for peace and invocations of the Christmas spirit at the Holy See.

Frenzied is hardly the word to apply to such a race across four continents, even without the customary long scenes arranged in honor of more comfortably scheduled foreign dignitaries and haunted by fears for the safety of the President.

Except in Australia, the journey was unannounced and the war protestors, who were airily dismissed by the President as the bearers of placards and posters, were carefully deprived of any opportunity to harass the Presidential procession.

But for almost everyone else at home and abroad there was a special place or recognition in this Johnsonian extravaganza.

It began with a careful pitch to the American voter on the television screen, a Christmastime interlude in which Mr. Johnson used new words for familiar peace terms for the Vietnamese Communists, an offer that still insisted on their military surrender in exchange for the rights of citizenship in South Vietnam's constitutional scheme.

The President's TV appearance came just a few days after the end of a Congressional session that saw many of Mr. Johnson's programs blocked. In a performance that many thought was reminiscent of the radio "fireside chats" of President Franklin D. Roosevelt, Mr. Johnson ranged over a variety of foreign and domestic questions in an informal discussion with correspondents of the three TV networks.

Some confusion ensued about the President's comments on Vietnam. But even before the issue could be bounced from Washington to Saigon and back again, there were Presidents Johnson and Nguyen Van Thieu face to face in Canberra proclaiming their harmony—publicly at least—and paying their respects to the Australians who had rallied in support for their cause on the periphery of the Pacific Ocean.

The Australians appeared to be deeply grateful for the President's gesture in turning the memorial service for Mr. Holt into an international event of the first order. More even than in his scheduled journey there a year ago, Mr. Johnson successfully dramatized his theme that the United States is a Pacific power.

And too, the active theater of war turned the President from distant visions of peace to emphatic and tactical vows of resolve. This Christmas has brought no worldwide peace offensives and no demonstrative bombing pause. And the reason, the President explained in the most martial possible settings, was because his cause was just and his course was set.

Second Visit

The President dropped in on the troops in Vietnam—his second such visit in 14 months—for an hour and 45 minutes. Addressing 2,450 men assembled at the big base at Camranh Bay, he said, "I wish I had things in as good shape in the United States as you have here." He said the Vietcong and North Vietnamese were not yet beaten, but he added:

"We are not going to yield. We are not going to shimmy. We are going to wind up with a peace with honor which all Americans seek. Then we will come home and spend a happy Christmas again with our loved ones."

That the occasion also held enormous political advantage did not diminish the President's genuine sense of appreciation for the "gallant" men he visited and their leaders, whom he decorated. But once again he allowed no room to come between his military policies and his military leaders, nor did he leave such itinerant rivals as Gov. George Romney much room for profitable adventure in either Vietnam or the Vatican.

For the Christmastide pilgrimage to Rome brought the President full circle. At suborbital speeds he had literally touched all international bases. Even though this left him little time to relish or learn from the experience, it gave him another dozen potent postures for the electoral journey ahead.

Those who would belittle or even condemn the haste, the extravagance or the corn of some of Mr. Johnson's performance, had best begin therefore with the new signs last week that he remains one of the most formidable political showmen in American history.

At the same time, there were those who felt the President would need all his showmanship in the election year ahead. He faces another tough session of Congress next month against rallying Republican opposition. And he is encountering more and more opposition within his own Democratic party.

The President himself acknowledged this opposition during his TV interview last week. Referring to Senators Eugene McCarthy and Robert Kennedy as the "Kennedy-McCarthy movement," he said, "I do know the interest of both of them in the Presidency and the ambition of both of them. I see that reflected from time to time."

Nixon: Many Motives Behind All Those Trips

SAN CLEMENTE, Calif. — When Richard Nixon arrived at El Toro Marine Air Base near here a few weeks ago, reporters were astounded to hear him lecture his Senate critics on the virtues of sampling the public pulse. "I think that sometimes the Senate would do better to do what the House does, to get out throughout the country and see what the country is thinking. . . . There is sort of an intellectual incest [in Washington] which really reduces the level of the dialogue, and you have to go to the country now and then to get a real feeling of what people are thinking."

What bemused the assembled writers was the fact that these unchallengable assertions were coming from a man who had been accused of isolating himself from some of the crucial intellectual currents of his time, and whose sampling of the public pulse, that day, had consisted of a speech to 15,000 true-blue members of the Junior Chamber of Commerce in St. Louis and a few chats with servicemen at scattered military bases.

The President's aides continue to insist that both he and the public are served by his travels outside Washington, and they were still talking this way when Mr. Nixon's "Discover America" caravan rolled out of Washington late last week for yet another jet-powered garden tour of the grass roots of the nation. On Friday, he and assorted White House officials sped to Fargo, N. D., for a session with Plains States governors; then to Salt Lake City for a chat with Mormon leaders; then on to San Clemente and the Western White House, the auxiliary nesting place of Mr. Nixon's portable Presidency.

The President's peripatetic ways have become more pronounced in recent weeks, but the two-fold rationale advanced by his associates when he first started traveling last year remains the same. First, they say, these trips give him a good reading of the public temperament. Meanwhile, the people themselves get to see government in action on a first-hand basis, an argument that has also been used to justify the creation of the Western White House itself.

"Government is not an exclusively Eastern institution," Herb Klein, the President's director of communications, once told a reporter. "The San Clemente operation gives Westerners a symbolic share in the business of government, pulling West closer to East and unifying the nation."

Some Skepticism

All this is now part of the litany of the White House, and while nobody in his right mind faults the President for traveling or for roosting in such a lovely place as San Clemente, there are a few skeptical souls who wonder whether the official litany is (A) nothing short of ridiculous and (B) really necessary to justify what should by all rights be an incontestable Presidential prerogative.

It is not, for example, unfair to ask whether it is possible to grasp what "the country" is thinking when the country, insofar as the President has seen it in the past six months, has consisted of the cream of Philadelphia society gathered for a tribute to Eugene Ormandy; 10 city mayors gathered for a symbolic Urban Affairs Council meeting in Indianapolis; the employes of the Hanover sewage treatment facility near Chicago; 50,000 folks gathered for the Billy Graham Crusade in Knoxville; 15,000 Jaycees in St. Louis; the members of the Appalachian Regional Commission in Louisville; and the crowd packed into Cincinnati's Riverfront Stadium for baseball's All-Star Game.

One could not find in any of these peaceful, deferential, and sober assemblies much evidence of the blacks, the poor, the students or, for that matter, the wealthy and the powerful.

A Few Handshakes

When pressed, White House aides will concede that the President really doesn't do much talking to the "folks" and the security situation and the demands of his schedule in fact make it impossible for him to do more than shake a few hands. They contend with some justification that the conferences with the mayors and governors are useful exercises.

What they will not concede, however, is that there is anything even remotely political about the President's travels, not to mention the places he travels to. Yet there are many who believe that what he is really trying to do is consolidate his grip on "Middle America," and when one examines his recent itinerary this is hardly an unreasonable conclusion.

With the exception of the Ormandy concert in Philadelphia, an unscheduled New York City dinner to mollify disgruntled French President Pompidou, and a quick trip to Houston to decorate the Apollo 13 ground crew, all the places he has seen since January were winners for Mr. Nixon in 1968: Indiana, Tennessee, Missouri, Kentucky, Ohio, North Dakota, Utah and, of course, California, where he clearly hopes to reestablish his identity as a Californian — a sometime thing in the past—and improve on the slim margin by which he carried the state two years ago.

Mr. Nixon himself revealed more than his aides are willing to admit in a wholly honest admission of political motives during his arrival remarks in Louisville week before last: "I remember my many visits all over this state," he said. "I am also well aware of the many warm receptions we have received, and although this is not a political visit, every time I have been on the ticket Kentucky has come through for us and I have appreciated that."

There have been other indications that Mr. Nixon is not merely flying around the country for his health or intellectual enrichment; and, given the political quotient of his itinerary, there has been occasional grumbling about costs. It is not cheap to ferry about half the Cabinet in a Boeing-707, and it is an admitted fact that the Western White House alone costs taxpayers about $250,000 in fixed installation expenses, and well over $100,000 in annual operational costs.

Presidential Right

The irony, of course, is that the grumbling would be less intense if the White House did not claim so much for its voyages or tell so little about their true purposes. There are many good and simple things accomplished when the President hits the road. People appreciate the fact that the Government is coming to them, even if it is only a small slice of the Government and their exposure to it fleeting indeed. The President can unlimber his rhetorical muscles—to wit, his plea in St. Louis for national reconciliation. He learns something, and he usually gets a well-earned rest.

Beyond this, the President was quite right when he observed that Washington breeds a kind of "intellectual incest" worth escaping from. But the point is that the means of escape are not provided by the canned and docile audiences of servicemen and Nixon voters which are routinely served up to him. The President escapes and educates himself through the simple physical fact of getting away from it all.

One example will suffice. Herb Klein once argued to a reporter—his claims were corroborated by subsequent inquiry—that the President really got excited about the pollution issue during a San Clemente trip last August when he and Bebe Rebozo, his longtime friend, took a leisurely, unplanned automobile ride down the California coast and suddenly discovered the terrible ecological damage that human beings had done to their environment since Dick Nixon was a boy in Yorba Linda.

A revelation of this sort is what getting out of Washington is all about—more important to the nation and probably to the President himself than all the rhetoric about unifying the nation with a portable Presidency, which his aides eagerly claim, and the political benefits of his travels, which they do not acknowledge.

—ROBERT B. SEMPLE Jr.

July 26, 1970

WILSON TESTS RADIO PHONE

Directs While on White House Portico.

WASHINGTON, Nov. 22.—Through a radio telephone installed on the south portico of the White House, President Wilson today directed the manoeuvres of half a dozen army airplanes flying over the Potomac River, several miles away. Mrs. Wilson and George Creel, Chairman of the Committee on Public Information, were the spectators, with a group of army officers, who conducted the installation of the aerial connected with a small field switchboard at which the President stood.

The planes in formation nose-dived several times and swung around a circle 1,500 to 2,000 feet above the ground. They were scarcely visible.

Several telephone receivers were connected to the switchboard and Mrs. Wilson and other members of the party were enabled to listen to the command as well as watch the execution. A single plane carrying a flight commander rose in the air first and flew up and down, dived and looped in accordance with the order telephoned from the ground. Then following directions the flight commander flew back to Belling Field and in response to orders called upon his squadron to manoeuvre.

The telephone as used today was adjusted for three to five or six miles. It is similar to the instruments used by American aviators in France, the secret of which was disclosed after the armistice was signed.

November 23, 1918

Radio Set in Harding's Pullman To Broadcast Speeches on Tour

Special to The New York Times.

WILMINGTON, Del., June 1.—For the use of President Harding on his Western trip the Pullman Car Company is fitting out a special car at the plant in this city. It is a car with an observation end and is being equipped for the special accommodation of the Presidential party. One feature will be a radio broadcasting set, which will be located at the observation end and be so arranged that while the President speaks from the platform the speech will be broadcast to all parts of the country. The radio will be one of the most powerful sets ever placed on a car.

This is the first time that a car of this type has been equipped with wireless.

June 2, 1923

CORDIAL TO HARDING, COLD TO SPEECHES

Middle West Likes the Man, but His Set Addresses Arouse No Enthusiasm.

RADIO IS BLAMED BY SOME

President Has Had to Speak Into Amplifiers and Could Not Warm to Audiences.

Special to The New York Times.

DENVER, Col., June 24.—When President Harding's special train arrived in Denver this morning for a stop-over more than a day he had completed two-thirds of his transcontinental journey on his way to Alaska, and was glad of the Sunday rest, although the four days' trip from Washington had been enjoyable for the most part.

These four days had, however, been marked by terrific heat in all the places visited. Yesterday at Hutchinson, Kan., the President felt the effects of a blistering and enervating sun. The program of the day was strenuous, and Mr. Harding was extremely tired when he went to bed on his train last night. But his powers of recuperation are excellent and he was in good shape this morning. He is still suffering slightly from toxic poisoning of the lips due to sunburn, but is able to enunciate now without great difficulty.

Before leaving Washington Wednesday and in several of his speeches on his westward way President Harding has insisted that his tour has no political purpose. Its main object, he has explained, is to give him an opportunity, which he has been seeking for more than two years, to get first hand information as to Alaskan conditions. The development of the Territory has been retarded and in some respects appears to be retrograding. Whether this is due in any part to the fact that the governmental affairs of Alaska are administered by more than thirty bureaus in Washington the President is anxious to ascertain. There are many problems associated with Alaska, and the President is bent on obtaining an intimate understanding of them with a view to recommending legislation to Congress which will embody a constructive Alaskan policy.

It is impossible, however, to dissociate a tour of the continent by a President of the United States from political significance. The President has recognized this in some measure and has sought in addressing the crowds which have gathered to see him between Washington and Denver to discuss public questions and national or local conditions in a way that would not make him liable to the criticism that he was endeavoring to build up political capital. For the most part his addresses have been devoted to an accounting of the stewardship of the Administration.

Taken altogether, the speeches already delivered with those which are to come compose a series of informative essays with certain constructive suggestions for the betterment of national conditions. One of those on the President's train has described them as composing a book of current history.

Lack Display of Oratory.

Written in that vein, these Presidential addresses necessarily, perhaps purposely, lack those elements which tend to a display of oratory. In their delivery President Harding has avoided any effort to arouse his hearers to enthusiastic fervor. Although having, in the quiet manner of the President's delivery, no incentive to enthuse, the crowds have shown a keen interest in the President's words and have received him with marked courtesy.

According to those who have followed the President's speechmaknig closely, occasional temptation to break away from the tone of plain, matter-of-fact recital in which the addresses are delivered has come the President's way. It is apparent that in failing to yield to temptation he is dominated by the restraining influence of the radio-telephone amplifiers, into which he has talked in making all his set addresses. The arrangements for broadcasting his words have been perfect, so much so that persons on the outskirts of the crowds, beyond the limit of the carrying capacity of the President's vocal power, have been able to hear every word he said. But to accomplish this he is obliged to stand directly in front of the enunciator, without the opportunity of walking up and down the platform as an aid to oratorical display.

On several occasions, when earnestness in his subject carried him away from the printed text before him, he has stepped back from the enunciator and obviously prepared to get out in the open, with the desire to bring his audience nearer to him. But in each case he has recovered himself, and with self-abnegation has delivered himself again to the mastery of the instrument in front of him. He has acknowledged that he has been impressed by the wonder of the radio amplifier, which enables his words to be carried to the ears of interested people listening at receivers hundreds of miles away, but this acknowledgment does not modify the evidence that the mechanical contrivance worries him and that he is tempted at times to revert to the old style of direct oratory, more stimulating to both orator and audience.

Impresses at Close Range.

The obviousness of this state of affairs is emphasized by the success of the President in impressing people when he comes in close contact with them. His extemporaneous speeches to comparatively small groups, where he has the opportunity to talk in his natural voice without the aid of the amplifiers, have aroused more enthusiasm and show of friendly feeling than his formal addresses to large audiences. At Hutchinson he scored every time he had the chance of talking intimately with contingents of farmers and their families and people of that agricultural community.

The President scores in personal contact. He seems to have the ability to charm in intimate associations. It has been said that in order to appraise Mr. Harding as a public man an abstract view is necessary. This assertion carries with it the contention that personal contact with him destroys for the time being any disposition to be critical of his public purposes and acts.

In dealing with people of a section devoted to agriculture, as he did yesterday in Kansas, he was "just folks," and the people liked his ways.

In contrast with this ability of the President to make friends is the manner in which his formal addresses were received by large audiences on his present tour.

In St. Louis there was a great outpouring of people to see the President's progress through more than five miles of city streets. There was every evidence of respect for him, but the enthusiasm was confined to sporadic groups. He got a rousing welcome, however, from 5,000 Rotarians whom he addressed in the Coliseum. That speech was extemporaneous and gave the President the chance to talk with some of his oratorical fervor. When in the same place that night he read his prepared address on the World Court to an audience estimated at 12,000 to 15,000 he was not encouraged by the demeanor of his hearers.

The unresponsive attitude of this principal St. Louis audience may have been due to the rather general opposition said to exist in the Missouri metropolis to anything pertaining to the League of Nations, but in Kansas City, at the western end of the State, his reception was extremely hearty. The impression was created by the demonstration he received there on his arrival and on the following day in Kansas that there is a greater liking for the personality of Mr. Harding west of the Missouri River than there is east of it. When he entered Convention Hall in Kansas City on Friday night to read his address on the transportation problem he got a greeting from a tremendous throng that must have been inspiring to him.

The heat was oppressive, but this did not cause any stinting of the enthusiasm which was begun when the tall figure of the President was seen making its way down the platform. A little later when he was formally presented the audience broke loose again. Omitting an attempt to appraise the political significance of this demonstration, it was apparent that Mr. Harding was at least personally popular in Kansas City.

The address itself, however, did not arouse the audience to any enthusiastic outburst. There was hearty applause over his assertions that he was opposed to anti-strike legislation because he did not believe any man should be compelled to work against his will, and an equally enthusiastic outburst when he asserted that the railroads were entitled to the same consideration as any other industrial enterprise, but, in the language of the streets, he did not get a hand when he announced that he would recommend to Congress the enactment of legislation requiring the railroads to be organized into regional groups.

This policy is not popular in Kansas City, which fears that its present great terminal supremacy will be transferred to Chicago under the regional system. But the impression was created that much of the audience's quiet demeanor was due to its inability to become aroused over words delivered without oratorical effort into the mouthpiece of a mechanical amplifier.

Many of those who heard the President deliver his addresses in St. Louis and Kansas City granted him the compliment of having courage. He selected St. Louis for his plea in behalf of American participation in the World Court because he believed that St. Louis was the seat of opposition to that policy. His espousal of the regional grouping of railroads was announced in Kansas City because of the opposition to it in that place. The acknowledgment that considerable courage was necessary in both instances increased respect for Mr. Harding personally, if it did not help his political fortunes.

Interested in Local Affairs.

Political observers in Missouri and Kansas gave the impression, in discussing Mr. Harding's visit to those States, that it is difficult at this time to arouse people over things political. They are more interested in their own local affairs. Their interest has particular reference to such things as taxation and freight rates in their bearing on their own well-being. This is peculiarly the case in the middle and far West. The issue of the World Court is looked upon in most communities as an abstract thing that has not the power to grip the imagination.

As far as feeling toward President Harding is concerned there are indications, the observers say, that there has been a rebound from the unpopularity which his administration suffered after it had been in office about a year. While many farmers complain that they are not making any profits on their crops, there are evidences of prosperity in other lines. From this has come a partial revival of the kindly feeling for the Administration which prevailed for a while after Mr. Harding's inauguration. Personally, the President has the good-will of many who are dissatisfied with conditions which they attribute to the manner in which the Government at Washington is conducted. This good-will is not politically helpful, however, according to the observers, but an improvement in business may easily translate it into support for the party.

One phase of the President's experience on this tour was evident at Hutchinson Saturday. His prepared address, delivered to a large audience at the State fair grounds, was devoted to a review of the legislation enacted by Congress for the benefit of the agricultural interests. Most or much of this legislation is popular with the farmers, and the President's explanation of what had been done to aid such communities as the Hutchinson wheat belt might be expected to make a hit with an audience of the character Mr. Harding addressed at Hutchinson. Yet the President was seldom interrupted by applause as he gave an accounting of what his Administration and the Republican Congress had done to overcome conditions of which the farmer complained.

But when he was thrown in contact with groups of the population of the wheat belt it was evident that he made a distinct impression helpful to him politically. Whether it was the restrictive influence of the amplifier or some other reason that prevented his more important utterances from creating any visible impression is impossible to say.

Cordial to Mrs. Harding.

Mrs. Harding is standing the rigors of the tour better than was expected in view of her rather strenuous exertions. She appears on the rear platform of the Presidential train at every stop and on the platforms from which the President has spoken at public meetings. The interest of the people in Mrs. Harding is apparent everywhere. This is particularly so with women. At nearly every formal meeting addressed by the President the opening prayer has contained mention of Mrs. Harding's illness with an offering of thanks for her recovery. Of course the prayers are never interrupted by any demonstration, but when the presiding officers have mentioned Mrs. Harding in their introductory remarks the audiences have responded in a way highly complimentary to her.

The President has been impressed by the cordiality manifested toward him. He has noted in particular that at places where railroad workers have gathered to see or hear him there is a manifest disposition to be friendly; but here and there railroad men have not joined in any demonstrations of approval and there have been occasional manifestations of grouchiness among them, due, according to the interpretation of some in the President's party, to resentment at the Administration's action in applying for an injunction against the railroad shopmen who went out on strike in 1922. These manifestations have been few and far between, however, and it is known that the President is pleased with the disposition shown toward him by gatherings of railroad men.

June 25, 1923

SAYS REPUBLICANS LEAD WITH RADIO

Eastern Director Explains How the Campaign Is Carried On Under Business Methods.

CARAVAN A NOVEL FEATURE

Every Line of Activity Directed by Department Head—2,000,000 Buttons Sent Out.

Some details of how a political campaign today is organized and carried on by modern business methods were explained yesterday by Frederick C. Hicks, Eastern director of the Republican National Committee.

"Politics can never be an exact science," he said, "but there is nothing which tends to place it upon a higher plane than the efforts of men of executive ability to carry on its activities upon a strictly business basis.

"A little data concerning our activities at the Eastern headquarters of the Republican campaign, at 2 West Forty-sixth Street, may be of interest. They may not be sensational, but they do prove that the modern requirement for standardization of effort and large quantity production in any line of activity affecting the public at large, can be satisfied only by an extensive and highly specialized central office, and an efficiently organized distributing station.

"The States comprising the Eastern department of the Republican campaign include roughly, all the Seaboard States east of Ohio. The department functions through a large number of bureaus, some of them with sub-divisions. The Publicity Bureau, for instance, has facilities for putting out general political news, what is technically called 'spot' news, out-of-town news, and also maintains a research department.

"Like all Gaul, of which Caesar wrote, the Department of Coolidge and Dawes Clubs is divided into three parts. There is the General Bureau, the Women's Clubs Bureau and the College Clubs Bureau. The other departments can be tabulated about as follows: Speakers, Foreign Language, Colored, Congressional and Senatorial, Women's, Contributors, Legal, Shipping, Mail, Supply, Treasurer's, Auditor's, Vice President's, Director's and Radio.

"The radio is, in many ways, the outstanding novelty of this campaign. Four years ago the speeches produced by a heated Presidential contest were not refrigerated by being thrown into the ether. In the present contest the radio has been progressively effective in putting Republican oratory upon a high plane. It seems to be a psychological fact that speakers, standing before a disc, and realizing that they are addressing hundreds of thousands of invisible auditors, are conscious of the importance of delivering messages free from boastful predictions and demagogic utterances. It is for this reason, I am sure, that the Coolidge and Dawes radio speakers have been so much more effective on the air than their opponents on the platform. Our speakers are carrying on a clean campaign, without making personal attacks, or indulging in false accusations and insinuations. Radio oratory adapts itself to debate rather than to detraction. For this reason the Republicans have used the air this Fall to much better effect than their rivals.

"Another novel and highly successful feature of the activities of the Eastern Department has been the cross-continent tour of the Coolidge and Dawes Lincoln caravan. Starting from Plymouth, Vt., Calvin Coolidge's birthplace, on Sept. 9, it has crossed seventeen States, and is now in California. It goes from there to Oregon, and will end its pilgrimage at Bellingham, Ore. It has held over 300 meetings, and it is said that more than 100,000 automobiles and 1,000,000 people will have taken part in this cross-country processional before it ends its long journey on Puget Sound.

"In the matter of distributing campaign material, there has been sent out from these headquarters alone over 2,000,000 buttons, 1,300,000 copies of the Republican platform, an equal number of President Coolidge's speech of acceptance, and hundreds of thousands of other pamphlets."

October 26, 1924

22,800,000 LISTENED TO COOLIDGE ON RADIO

Thousands of persons in New York gathered before loud speakers in their homes, and crowds in the streets during the lunch hour collected in front of radio and music stores to hear the inaugural ceremonies as broadcast by stations WJZ and WEAF. The atmosphere was ideal for transmission and reception.

Station WJZ was linked by land wires with WRC, Washington; WGY, Schenectady, and WBZ, Springfield. It was estimated by an official of the Aeolian Hall Station that the total audience of the four stations was approximately 4,800,000.

Station WEAF, 195 Broadway, was connected by telephone wires with the microphone in Washington to which twenty-one other stations scattered across the country were connected. The audience of the transcontinental chain of broadcasters was calculated to be approximately 18,000,000.

The announcers came on the air shortly before noon and described the sidelights and occasionally the microphone near the Marine Band was switched into the circuit. Just a few minutes before the flourish of trumpets announced the arrival of President Coolidge, some one in the audience yelled, "Who's at bat? Who's at bat?" and it was clearly heard over the radio.

WJZ's operators apparently had difficulty in shifting from the announcer's microphone to the one in front of Chief Justice Taft, because several seconds were lost in switching and the first few words of the oath were not picked up.

Soon after the broadcasting was finished reports started to reach the studio of WEAF telling how the ceremonies were received by listeners in different sections. The first report from New England came from WDBH at Worcester, "Everything very good," and following this San Francisco flashed "Radio people thoroughly satisfied." The only trouble along the line was reported by Atlanta, Ga., where the wire between Atlanta and Washington became noisy.

March 5, 1925

RADIO RECEIVED $435,984.

Official figures show that of the $2,016,872 spent by the Republican National Committee on publicity and advertising in electing Mr. Hoover, that radio received the largest share of the fund, $435,984.

February 17, 1929

One Source of Satisfaction.

To the Editor of The New York Times:

I am so happy this morning that I cannot resist expressing my joy in the result. I can now approach the radio when an occasion arrives for the President of the United States to go on the air. For seven years, during Coolidge's incumbency, I tuned in with fear and trembling to hear what he had to say—no thrill from voice or speech or personality. Then came Hoover and a continuation of the same automatonlike delivery.

I for one will be glad to listen to a man who can open his mouth and tell his message in pleasing, free and easy language. T. J. POWERS.

New York, Nov. 9, 1932.

November 11, 1932

A NEW MARK IN RADIO

Mr. Roosevelt's Talk Sets All-Time 'High' —Greatest Network Carried the Speech

By T. R. KENNEDY Jr.

BROADCASTING is celebrating its first anniversary of operating in the interest of national defense. Enlisted "100 per cent" behind the rearmament program of Uncle Sam, the microphone is now tackling the biggest job in all its twenty-odd years of history.

How substantially it can aid was never more strikingly demonstrated than when President Roosevelt made use of it in his fireside chat last week to announce an unlimited national emergency. Mr. Roosevelt's words circled the globe. More stations, more watts and more listeners were represented on the sending and receiving ends of the vast ethereal system that carried his words than on any previous occasion in the history of broadcasting.

A "popularity poll," or survey, made of Mr. Roosevelt's address ranked the program an all-time "radio high," with a rating of 70—eleven points higher than for any other program ever measured. It is estimated that 65,650,000 people in 20,510,000 American homes heard the talk—70 per cent of the total home audience in the United States.

The second highest radio listener poll rating also is held by Mr. Roosevelt. It was made for his fireside chat of last Dec. 29, when, over a large network, he spoke on national security. A nation-wide poll of listeners taken on that occasion indicated 59 per cent of the listeners of the country, or 50,000,000 people, heard him. Radio men say that the large indicated growth of the audience is a direct measure of the growth of interest in national defense.

The record-breaking fireside chats have been approached in general listener interest by only one other broadcast, according to C. E. Hooper, Inc., New York research firm, which conducted listener polls on the programs for the Columbia Broadcasting System. That was the second Louis-Schmeling fight at Yankee Stadium in 1938, which got a rating of 57.2 per cent.

Mr. Roosevelt's famous speech at Charlottesville, Va., last June, got a rating of about 45 per cent. When the Duke of Windsor, on Dec. 11, 1936, broadcast his final message to the British Empire the talk received a similar audience rating in this country. America's top ranking radio comedians currently are basking in the glory of 30 to 35 per cent ratings.

* * *

SOME idea of the vast broadcast system over which President Roosevelt's words were heard directly in English can be had from the fact that in the Western Hemisphere alone more than 750 stations were linked together by wires or radio beams for the occasion. The basic NBC system comprised 275 stations, the CBS network added 126, WOR-Mutual 178 and Canada, Mexico, Cuba, Alaska, Hawaii and various Latin-American republics 180.

To that impressive list of American broadcasters were added at least eleven international shortwave stations heard regularly throughout the world in many languages. Intercepting the American waves, the full force of the powerful British Empire Radio Service joined the ethereal chorus to spray President Roosevelt's words farther afield over Germany, France, Italy, Russia, Spain, Australia, New Zealand and the Far East in thirty-two languages.

Reports gathered by wire and radio from foreign countries following Mr. Roosevelt's epochal broadcast indicate that to America's 65,000,000-odd listeners must be added at least another 20,000,000 in Canada, Latin-American nations and the British Isles. Thus, 85,000,000 or more people heard Mr. Roosevelt's voice, if the figures of the radio research experts are correct.

But that is not all. People in many other lands heard the program too, whether directly by radio or later by translations carried over domestic stations. Japan, it is reported, received the talk as clearly as did the British. The Japanese picked up beams hurled westward across the Pacific by Uncle Sam's big ethereal guns. Australia and New Zealand had the choice of several Presidential programs—one directly from the western shores of the United States, and at least two flashed eastward across the Atlantic to London, then relayed onward by the British stations.

* * *

IF every broadcasting station in the United States carried the talk—and most of them did carry it in one form or another—electrical power was used up at the rate of 3,300,000 watts—enough to light the electric reading lamps in 3,500 average American homes. If to that figure power used by broadcasting stations in Canada, Mexico, the British Isles and other lands is added the grand total of watts rises to 6,000,000.

Broadcasting engineers have discovered methods of greatly multiplying the effect on the air of international short-wave transmitters—the long-range guns of radio that hurl electrical bullets around the world. They do this by building aerials that direct the radio energy into narrow beams. These beams may be directed from one country to another as easily as the rays of a powerful searchlight are pointed toward a high-flying airplane. Engineers have found that by properly employing such directive aerials they can increase the "effect" of their stations from twenty to twenty-five times, and the result, in the parlance of engineers, is called "effective" power.

All of the magical devices of the modern radio engineer were put to work in the United States and England in an unprecedented way when President Roosevelt went on the air. Perhaps never before had all such forces been aligned as a single battery to carry the words of one speaker; for the first time, the voice of one man criss-crossed through space on short-wave beams at the staggering total of nearly 20,000,000 "effective" watts of radio driving power.

Just before the President began to speak at 10:30 o'clock last Tuesday night, here in New York the pointers of electric meters in power houses and substations began jumping skyward as hundreds and thousands of sets were turned on. The electric current demand rose 123,000 kilowatts or 13.6 per cent above normal at 11 o'clock, a New York Edison representative said. Promptly at 11:15 o'clock, when President Roosevelt's talk ended, the demand dropped to normal.

June 1, 1941

Radio and Television Cover the Election

By JACK GOULD

IN the coverage of the election results on Tuesday night and early Wednesday morning, radio had much the best of it over television, the video art fumbling rather badly in its first full-dress effort to cover the outcome of a Presidential campaign.

The main reason for television's inadequacy no doubt was due to the fact that counting ballots is hardly a function which lends itself to much visual excitement. But even so, there was nothing like the proper preparation which would have made the video version more viewable.

Probably the most distracting factor was the large charts on the boards used to tabulate the national returns. They were almost impossible to read over any period of time with comfort, it being much easier just to listen to the sound channel. Simplification of the tables, with the use of larger and more clearly pronounced figures, will be a "must" for the next election.

Of the coverage by the individual stations, the job turned in by NBC and Life Magazine was almost incredibly pretentious and self-conscious. The presence of both NBC and Life representatives on the screen when one man would have been ample often was just a case of muscle-bound overproduction and the terrific build-up attendant to almost every interview seldom was justified by the results. Life and NBC would be well advised in the future just to go ahead and cover the news and not intrude in the picture so much themselves.

Scooped

For sheer clarity, Ernest K. Lindley, in charge of the Newsweek-DuMont coverage, was one of the best, but otherwise his magazine's staff, too, seemed excessively concerned with the mechanics of covering their assignment. CBS turned in a professional news job, though it was far from inspired visually, while ABC was guilty of altogther too much "experting." WPIX gave a fairly satisfactory account of itself.

But the greatest surprise was that the whole television industry muffed completely its one big chance for an intensely interesting visual story: coverage of Governor Dewey's press conference after he had conceded defeat. Whatever the alibis, the television boys were caught napping.

On the radio, the Mutual Broadcasting System under Abe Schechter turned in the most alert and varied job. Comparatively early in the evening the majority of the MBS commentators were not afraid to say flatly that unexpected news obviously was in the making. Similarly, Mr. Schechter's coverage was not confined to studio headquarters but moved early and frequently out into the field.

NBC seemed a little too disinclined to believe what the figures were saying during the night, their implications in the earlier hours that Dewey would come through safely hardly being models of impartiality. ABC was seriously handicapped by the antics of Drew Pearson and Walter Winchell. CBS, as usual, in the main did a straight forward job.

On the local front, the WNYC service was once again of a high order and, if a word for a member of THE NEW YORK TIMES family may be excused, W. H. Lawrence's commentary on WQXR was admirable in its objectivity.

But of the many, many people heard on the radio on election night, there were two who sounded as though it could hardly come to end soon enough. They were Dr. Gallup and Mr. Roper.

November 7, 1948

TRUMAN, 32D PRESIDENT, IS INAUGURATED

By ANTHONY LEVIERO
Special to THE NEW YORK TIMES.

WASHINGTON, Jan. 20—Harry S. Truman denounced communism as a false doctrine and outlined a four-point program for American world leadership, and peace, as he assumed the Presidency in his own right in the most impressive inaugural of American history.

Thus with a positive statement of American aspirations, the thirty-second President of the United States concluded the traditional ceremony on Capitol Hill which reached a tremendous global audience on the radio waves.

He took the oath of office before a throng of more than 100,000 of his fellow countrymen at 12:29 P. M., a few minutes after Senator Alben W. Barkley of Kentucky took a similar oath and became the Vice President.

Unlike many of his predecessors, whose inaugural addresses were in the nature of philosophical discourses, the plain-spoken Missourian delivered a major policy statement. It was replete, like virtually all his speeches, with concrete statements and proposals.

Calls for Just Settlement

Mr. Truman drew a sharp, straight line between democracy and communism, without the slightest trace of the softening toward Russia which some observers had been suspecting recently.

The Chief Executive asserted that democracy was a vitalizing force, sustaining the initiative which was in our hands, and that we would not be moved from our faith by the Soviet political philosophy.

President Truman explained he was not making his strongly contrasting definitions of democracy and totalitarianism merely to be argumentative. He saw communism as a threat to world recovery and lasting peace, he said, and he was offering what he proclaimed to be a constructive program for all nations.

He did not leave Russia and her satellites out of his hopes. Although he mentioned none of them by name, as he neared the end of his address he expressed a belief that the countries under Communistic regimes would "abandon their delusions and join with the free nations of the world in a just settlement of international differences."

Would Share Progress

The heart of his aims Mr. Truman set forth in one, two, three, four fashion. First he reiterated unwavering support of the United Nations and here he made a friendly gesture to such nations that are aborning, as Israel, Korea and Indonesia. He said they would strengthen the United Nations as they themselves became strong with the nourishment of democratic principles.

As his second point, Mr. Truman reiterated this country's determination to work for world recovery by giving full measure to the European Recovery Program and promoting trade for all the world's markets.

On the North Atlantic Security Plan, which is now crystallizing, Mr. Truman focused his third point. He said, "We will strengthen freedom-loving nations against the dangers of aggression," but only within the recognized framework of the United Nations Charter and in the pattern of the Western Hemisphere arrangement.

In his fourth point Mr. Truman proposed a wholly new program, still to be expounded in detail, for sharing American scientific and industrial progress with the rest of the world. He made the proffer on a global scale, but it was understood that it was intended primarily for the colonial areas of Africa and Asia.

The great crowd liked what the President said, and applause was perhaps strongest when Mr. Truman stated, in connection with the North Atlantic Security Plan, that if we make it sufficiently plain that we would meet a threat with overwhelming force, "the armed attack might never occur."

Sensing that clapping with hands gloved against the cold did not carry well, the crowd began pounding their approval with their feet on the plank flooring of their seats. Thereafter for about a dozen times the dulled handclapping was almost drowned by the rumble from the raw lumber.

The ceremony of the Presidential oath, scheduled for noon, was delayed twenty-nine minutes, apparently because in the rotunda of the Capitol there were so many amenities to be exchanged among a great assemblage of statesmen and diplomats.

The signal that the ceremony would soon begin came when the Marine Band at 12:14 P. M. played "Hail to the Chief." Chief Justice Fred M. Vinson, in judicial robe and skull cap, first came into view on the inaugural stand in front of the Capitol. Soon Mr. Truman and Mr. Barkley were seen.

Associate Justice Stanley Reed, clad like Justice Vinson, swore in Senator Barkley at 12:23 and six minutes later Mr. Truman took the oath from Chief Justice Vinson.

More than 100,000 persons, it was estimated, were in the plaza and in the visible environs, and as each of the nation's leaders was confirmed in office he was warmly applauded.

Procession 7½ Miles Long

About 100,000,000 more people listened in on the ceremony on the radio throughout the nation, it was estimated, and the Voice of America beamed it to many more millions abroad in many tongues. For the first time television was at hand for the national ceremony and through this medium, it was said, 10,000,000 more were added.

It seemed plausible therefore that today's ceremony was presented to more people than all, combined, who could have attended the previous forty inaugurals.

Perhaps a million people could have been counted, too, in the close-packed ranks along Pennsylvania Avenue later as the former farm boy and the Kentuckian who came from a log cabin rode triumphantly from the Capitol to the White House reviewing stand.

Apart from the solemnities of ceremony and the serious speech, the great spectacle took on a tone of national joy and carnival. The parade route was one-and-a-quarter miles long and over it moved a procession seven and a half miles long.

Up front was the Missourian from a town called Independence and way back at the end was a steam circus calliope. Between them was the flavor, the glamour, the humor, the shadings of dialect and dress of the nation. In essence it was the American spirit and it moved forward buoyantly to the music of many bands.

Governor Thurmond Pays Respects

The basic unity of it all was attested when Gov. J. Strom Thurmond of South Carolina, leader of the State's Rights movement that had bitterly divided the Democratic party, passed by in review before the confirmed leaders.

The crowning touch of simplicity came just at 3 P. M., when Mr. Truman and Mr. Barkley arrived at the reviewing stand. They were top-hatted and frock-coated according to custom, but the day was cold. Somebody placed a stack of sandwiches and cardboard containers of coffee before them.

At the moment the cadets of West Point, smart in their gray capes and in the rhythm of their march, were passing in review. Mr. Truman and Mr. Barkley faced each other, touched their cups together and drank their coffee, in a silent toast. Then they munched sandwiches as the cadets were marching by.

For a brilliant occasion Mr. Truman had a cold but brilliant day. Only a few weak streaks of clouds were in the northern sky as the oaths were administered. The temperature ranged between thirty and the low forties. There was a wind with a sharp edge that chilled the crowds and kept the flag on the portico of the Capitol rippling continuously.

The action was not all in splendid floats, and prancing, barelegged drum majorettes, and parading politicians and fraternal organizations, however.

The speech of the President, with its overtones of concern for the common welfare and world peace, was strongly accented by the military power of the nation.

Military Power Accented

Of the atomic bomb there was only a simple reminder, but stressed as Mr. Truman voiced it, in his statement that this country had made every effort "to secure agreement on effective control of our most powerful weapon * * *"

Overhead, though, roared one of the greatest air armadas that has ever coursed over the capital—about 700 planes, led by five of the B-36 monsters capable of intercontinental action.

For the ambassadors and attachés of many nations, in their bright uniforms and silk hats on the inaugural stand, as well as for everybody else, they came in impressive and precise patterns over the trees screening the Library of Congress and passed over the Capitol Dome. The giant bombers were followed by flashing jets and by lumbering transports like those that are feeding Berlin.

The precision of the air squadrons was matched on the ground by the military and naval cadets, the soldiers and sailors, the cadets from the private military schools.

Equally eloquent was another kind of strength—the people who did, and the people who did not, vote for Truman packed literally every inch along the avenue except at the few cross streets kept open for traffic. They had come from every part of the nation. The 40,000 seats were filled and every inch of standing room was packed with old and young, white and black, from the curb to building fronts. Hundreds of simple periscopes were thrust above the heads of those in front by those at the rear for a glimpse of the carnival-like procession.

* * * * *

January 21, 1949

Veteran of '89 Inaugural Sees This One on Video

By The Associated Press.

PHILADELPHIA, Jan. 20—Luther Parsons stood in the rain on March 4, 1889, to watch the inauguration of President Benjamin Harrison.

Today, at the age of 91 Mr. Parsons saw another inauguration. He sat in a warm downtown Philadelphia department store while he and some 1,500 persons watched the television broadcast of the inauguration of President Harry S. Truman.

"A much more comfortable way," Mr. Parsons commented, recalling the sea of umbrellas that crowded Pennsylvania Avenue in Washington sixty years ago.

January 21, 1949

Newest TV Show Stars President; It's a Homey Chat and It Goes Well

By JOSEPH A. LOFTUS

Special to THE NEW YORK TIMES.

WASHINGTON, June 3—President Eisenhower starred tonight in the newest television panel show with a homey, chatty approach to some of the Government's most complex problems.

For a half hour, the President shared the camera with George Humphrey, Secretary of the Treasury; Ezra Taft Benson, Secretary of Agriculture; Herbert Brownell Jr., Attorney General, and Oveta Culp Hobby, Secretary of Health, Education and Welfare.

The technical objective apparently was to achieve a measure of spontaneity, for there were no scripts or cue cards in sight. At times, however, everybody in the cast seemed to be depending on a little of each.

Mr. Brownell won the honors for the most relaxed member of the "cast," although neither the President nor his other Cabinet members appeared to be in any great difficulty.

The President wore a dark suit, which probably was blue, and a shirt that showed up as white. Technicians recommended color for black-and-white cameras, and Mrs. Hobby observed the advice scrupulously.

What appeared as white to the amateur viewer was mostly blue. She wore a pale blue blouse with scalloped collar and a red and blue ribbon tie. Her hat was a very pale blue with white embroidery. Even her shoes, which none of the television audience saw, were dark blue. Mrs. Hobby's jewelry included dark pearl earrings and a pearl pendant lapel pin.

The details of Mrs. Hobby's attire were made known in advance.

The men, too, strove for satorial perfection, but the colors they wore were anybody's guess. Their neckties were uniformly dark and their heads mostly shiny.

The President spoke from a seated position. He leaned forward to his desk at all times and never allowed himself the luxury of using the back of his chair.

In most of his remarks, the President sought a friendly, conversational approach to his audience, but his frequent, self-conscious changes of position did not indicate living-room relaxation.

For a first appearance in an informal type "show," however, there was general agreement that the President did well.

The script, however, was another matter. Several times there seemed to be clear breaks in the continuity, giving the effect of one speaker just waiting for the other to finish so he could start his part of the program.

There was a round of introductions before any of the Cabinet members spoke.

June 4, 1953

TV Debate Switched Few Votes, Nation-Wide Survey Shows

BOTH CANDIDATES RETAIN BACKERS

Most Viewers Call Kennedy the 'Winner'—Many Say Nixon Looked Unwell

Following is a special election campaign report by The New York Times.

Neither Vice President Nixon nor Senator John F. Kennedy seems to have captured any appreciable number of voters from the other as a result of their face-to-face debate on television Monday night.

A sampling of public opinion throughout the country yesterday by The New York Times brought the clear indication that members of the television audience still held to their previous convictions.

Those who had been for Senator Kennedy before the debate were still for him, and the Vice President's adherents were also standing fast.

More than 360 persons—including Republican and Democratic voters, local leaders of both parties and uncommitted "men in the street"—were interviewed in thirty widely scattered cities.

One Switch Disclosed

Of all these, only one said his allegiance had been changed through watching the debate. He was a janitor in Topeka, Kan., a regular Republican who was won over by the Democratic candidate's performance.

Only two of the undecided voters said the television show had made up their minds.

One was a Wisconsin farmer who supported President Eisenhower in the last two elections but was undecided about this election. After watching the two candidates on television, he decided to vote for the Democrat.

The other was an investigator for the District Attorney in Denver, who was also persuaded by Senator Kennedy.

Kennedy Called Winner

Although each candidate held the loyalty of his adherents, a majority of those canvassed indicated that Senator Kennedy had turned in a better performance. These included Republicans and a few of that party's leaders.

The Democratic leaders who were questioned were unanimous in their enthusiasm for their standard-bearer as a television star. A telegram to Senator Kennedy by Michael H. Prendergast, Democratic chairman of New York State, was typical. It said, in part:

"Congratulations upon a magnificent presentation of the views of the Democratic party. We are more certain than ever that the people will show their appreciation of your courageous and sound position."

Many Republicans said the same of the Vice President. But the significant difference was that more than a few Republicans were willing to settle for a "draw" or a "stand-off."

Hope to Win Next One

Some conceded that Senator Kennedy had come off better, contenting themselves with the hope that Mr. Nixon would win the next debate.

For example, Patrick J. Hillings, Republican chairman of Los Angeles County, said:

"The general reaction from our party's leaders is surprise at Kennedy's able performance. We had a feeling that perhaps the Vice President was not as aggressive in carrying the case to him. When Nixon can discuss foreign policy, it will put Kennedy more on the defensive."

Among individual voters, Walter R. Charles Jr., a salesman in Richmond, Va., and a Republican still for Mr. Nixon, said "Kennedy sold himself and got the better of it by a slim margin."

"He was definite, sure of himself and sharper," he said.

Nashville Reactions

In Nashville, Tenn., seven of eight voters who gave opinions on the debate thought Senator Kennedy had won the debate. This majority included Louis R. Farber, a sales manager who still intends to vote for Mr. Nixon, and Mrs. Charles H. Lehning, a housewife and a Republican, who said: "Kennedy got the best of it; he came right back with his answers."

Republicans who commented concentrated on what they thought was the principal weakness in Senator Kennedy's argument—that he could finance a greater social welfare program without raising taxes or unbalancing the budget.

State Senator John H. Cooke, Republican chairman of Erie County (Buffalo), N. Y., said:

"The Vice President certainly presented a much more sensible program. Despite Kennedy's insistence to the contrary, his programs would lead to higher taxes, deficit financing, or both."

School View Questioned

This view was shared by many rank-and-filers. Mrs. William Corwin, a housewife of Fargo, N. D., noted that Senator Kennedy had left unspecified who would pay for his projected program of aid to education, medical care for the aged and other benefits.

On the question of Federal aid to education, only one person interviewed commented on the agreement of both candidates that there was danger of Federal control of education in Federal monetary aid.

He was a school teacher in St. Paul, Minn., who said:

"Both were wrong. My school district pays me, but doesn't dictate what I teach. The Federal Government would not either."

In a comparison of the "image" of the two candidates, there was frequent mention of how drawn and weary the Vice President had looked. Some viewers said Mr. Nixon appeared to be ill. He was recently in hospital for treatment of an infected knee.

William T. Thurman, Democratic chairman of Utah, was one of several Salt Lake City

United Press International Telephoto

CONVINCING? The Donald Phelans of Farmingdale, L. I., were among thousands of American families across nation who heard Vice President Nixon debate Senator Kennedy. Sample survey, however, indicated few had been convinced to change allegiance.

residents who noted this. "Nixon did not look well, seemed much thinner after his illness," Mr. Thurman declared.

In Boston, a highly placed Republican said the Vice President's "grimness was shocking" and that he was evidently not yet physically fit for all-out campaigning.

Although there was widespread interest in the debate, many in the vast audience were disappointed in the mildness of the exchanges. It was estimated that nearly 30,000,000 homes tuned in.

Some viewers said the program had not been a debate at all, merely a discussion by two candidates who had agreed as often as they had disagreed.

'Sparring Match'

"This was a preliminary sparring match; there was not enough meat in the thing," was the opinion of James W. Knight, Democratic chairman in Bexar County, Texas.

"Neither got off the ground," Mr. Knight said." They didn't have much effect on the voters. They ought to come out swinging in the future."

In Hartford a storekeeper and Republican, George R. Cohen said the same thing in other words:

"I didn't think it was much of a debate; too much like Alphonse and Gaston."

In Kedron Park, a suburb of Philadelphia, Thomas L. Pepper Jr., a management consultant, reported:

"I fell asleep while I was looking at it. It turned out to be not a hot debate like in the old times but a question and answer period."

Polling organizations estimated that this first television debate between Presidential rivals had been seen in 29,400,000 of the more than 45,000,000 homes equipped with television in this country.

This figure, projected, indicated that more than 73,500,000 persons had watched the show.

In the Times survey, about two-thirds of all those questioned had seen it.

City-by-City Reports

Following are detailed reports from some of the cities surveyed:

PHILADELPHIA

Of a score of persons questioned about 90 per cent had heard the debate. Democrats were pleased with Senator Kennedy and were sure he had gotten the better of it. Republicans generally called it "a draw," "a stand-off," "about even."

A couple of Republicans said Vice President Nixon had made good counterattacks on the Senator, but the Democrats asserted that Mr. Kennedy had been more positive in his approach.

There was general disapproval of the way in which the debate had been conducted. Some of the criticisms were that it had been a stiff, bleak set-up.

DOVER, DEL.

Seven men and five women who had heard the debate were interviewed. Three women—a housewife, a sales clerk and a teacher—said they thought Senator Kennedy had had the edge over Mr. Nixon. Four men—a banker, a merchant, a state employe and a clerk—thought Mr. Nixon had presented better arguments. A publisher and a laborer, both men, favored Mr. Kennedy.

RICHMOND, VA.

A salesman backing Mr. Nixon said Mr. Kennedy had been better "by a slim margin." He said:

"Both were perfect gentlemen. A good combination would be one for President, the other or Vice President."

Of twenty persons polled, ten had watched television, two had listened on radio and eight had ignored the program. Generally, voters thought their own candidate had done better; most considered the debate close.

BATON ROUGE, LA.

The consensus among a dozen voters, including Republicans and supporters of Vice President Nixon, was that Senator Kennedy had come out ahead. All agreed that the program had been a true debate. Most expressed surprise that the questions had been so difficult.

NASHVILLE

Of eight voters who had watched the program, seven gave the edge to Senator Kennedy. None said Vice President Nixon had bested Mr. Kennedy. A magazine circulation agent who is a Democrat said: "They were two nice boys who showed that neither would give any ground to Khrushchev. I think they came out pretty even."

TALLAHASSEE, FLA.

The debate did not appear to have changed many convictions, but twelve voters who answered questions agreed that it had been well-handled and informative. Five said they were for Senator Kennedy, four for Vice President Nixon and three undecided.

A Roman Catholic housewife, a Democrat, said:

"I don't care what Kennedy says or does. I'm for him 100 per cent." A Baptist housewife, also a Democrat, said:

"I just can't bring myself to vote for a Catholic. I have too many doubts about the influence his church would have."

CHICAGO

Reactions to the debate were mild among about a dozen persons interviewed. No switches in voting sentiment were recorded.

There wsa also some disappointment about the Vice President's performance. He was called nervous and insecure, and one woman said he had looked ill. Senator Kennedy was called effective, nerveless and sure of himself, and the projector of a "mature image."

SPRINGFIELD, Ill.

Six men and six women were interviewed. Three of the men and two of the women had watched the debate.

A woman secretary declared that Mr. Nixon had come off better. "He's been in there," she said. "He knows what's going on. Kennedy looks more like a labor leader."

A business executive said:

"Kennedy handled himself exceptionally well. He didn't hesitate and made an all-around good impression. Nixon looked sick and worried."

MADISON, WIS.

Of a dozen persons questioned, one—a farmer—said the debate had convinced him to vote for Senator Kennedy. He said he had voted for President Eisenhower in 1956.

Most of those polled said they thought both candidates had conducted themselves well, but there was a general impression that the Senator's presentation had been superior. Even some Republicans said Mr. Kennedy had appeared to be more calm, confident and articulate.

DES MOINES

A telephone company supervisor supporting Vice President Nixon was not impressed by the debate. He said the result was a "toss-up" and noted:

"I had the feeling both men were going over plowed ground. In comparing what they said tonight with their earlier speeches I found very little new."

A Democratic city employe said "Nixon got in some good points — but not enough to change my mind about voting for Kennedy."

KANSAS CITY

A restaurateur who is a Democrat said the debate had cut into his Monday night business. He preferred Senator Kennedy.

A housewife, an independent voter, said she was for Mr. Kennedy on the basis of the debate and said the questions asked of the candidates had been good.

Ten of thirteetn persons questioned had seen the program. For the most part they agreed it would have been more dramatic had Senator Kennedy and the Vice President questioned each other.

TOPEKA, KAN.

Five of nine Republicans interviewed thought Mr. Nixon had won. The four others said it had been inconclusive.

One Republican said he had been "shocked at Nixon's appearance—he looked so tired and worn."

Two of three Democrats questioned said Senator Kennedy had won, and the third said he thought it had been a draw. All the Democrats said they would vote for Mr. Kennedy. One of the Republicans—a Negro janitor—said Senator Kennedy had won him over.

DENVER

A Republican lawyer called the program "not a real debate."

Of fourteen voters canvassed, twelve had heard the debate. Six said Senator Kennedy had won, two preferred Vice President Nixon and four termed it a draw.

A woman clerk, a Republican, favored Mr. Nixon. "He talked specifically about where the money would come from, while Kennedy had much the same ideas, but didn't know how the programs would be financed," she said.

A male press agent said:

"Kennedy answered questions more honestly and directly. I had the feeling Nixon was hedging on some of his answers. Nixon used the old numbers game—statistics that didn't tell the whole story."

SALT LAKE CITY

Television officials, party leaders and the main in the street generally agreed that the debate had gone off well and should be followed by more. As a rule, the reactions were along party lines. One housewife said she was "not too impressed with either man—before or after the debate."

AUSTIN, TEX.

Of twenty voters interviewed, eight had not heard the debate. One, an insurance salesman who had been working, asked: "Who was on the program?"

Most of the twelve others seemed to be Nixon voters, but the reaction among women was that Senator Kennedy had come off better. A woman Republican party worker said the Vice President had looked "too grim" and that he had been "trying to be too liberal."

SAN FRANCISCO

A Republican housewife who supported Adlai E. Stevenson four years ago said that as a result of the debate she would find it "less distasteful now to vote for Nixon," whom she said she did not like.

She was one of eight persons questioned who had seen the debate. Two Democrats and one Republican gave the advantage to Mr. Kennedy. Three Republicans, a Democrat and an independent voter, said Vice President Nixon had done better.

LOS ANGELES

Among a score of voters interviewed, representing both parties and varied economic levels, there was little feeling that either of the candidates had gained a big edge. What differences of opinion emerged were along party lines.

Nearly everyone said Mr. Kennedy's physical appearance had been better; most said Mr. Nixon had looked haggard, tired and nervous. One Republican attributed the Vice President's appearance to television make-up man and camera men with Democratic leanings.

In The Nation

New Item in the Campaign for Presidency Exhibit

By ARTHUR KROCK

WASHINGTON, Nov. 7—Ever since the first Presidential election in our history successful candidates for the office have been identified to the voters by some slogan, or the drawing of an inanimate object (or both), associated with their careers. The slogan for George Washington was "The Father of His Country," and the object is a rowboat in which he is pictured standing at its bow in a rough and snowy crossing of the Delaware.

In the campaign of 1960 no descriptive phrases used about the candidates has sufficiently impressed itself on the public to gain a place in the American political dictionary. But there is an object which is definitely the symbol of this campaign. It is built in a number of sizes and colors, and its novelty as the symbol of a Presidential contest is made greater by the fact that it is an article of home furniture. Also novel is the fact that, while this object is constructed of materials in themselves inanimate—wood, glass and a variety of metals—it comes alive with the turn of a switch.

The item, of course, is the television set. Through the new magic of electronics it has familiarized the voters with the candidates as no previous methods of communication ever could, and in three dimensions: physical, vocal, and the emanation from these of mentality and personality. If the 1960 campaign were to be symbolized in one cartoon, the drawing would be of a television set in full blast.

Whether the next President will owe his choice to sound-equipped moving pictures will remain a question to which the answer can only be speculative. But for those who will assume this to be true, then his record in office will be a future guide to the soundness of the medium. This is probably the most comforting conclusion to be drawn from the dominance of TV in 1960, and the same prospect hereafter, in taking the candidates to the voters.

Since there are aspects of this new campaign auxiliary which distort, far more than slogans, sobriquets and symbols ever did or could, the test of Presidential capacity, a list of some of the latter may interest readers awaiting the complete results of the first television election. It took a long time for most of these tags, including the elephant and the donkey (or the post-bellum Southern alternates of the log cabin and the crowing rooster), to enter the public consciousness. And during the years that the press and the channels of distribution were growing to national scope, this public consciousness grew only in the same proportion.

A Museum of Politics

Nevertheless, the nicknames and the symbols eventually traveled from the populous areas to the sparsely settled frontiers and to the headwaters of the creeks in the wilderness. Among these "Old Rotundity" was John Adams, a pen marked "Declaration of Independence" typified Jefferson, "Father of the Constitution" was another name for Madison, and when people spoke of "The Era of Good Feeling" the face of Monroe appeared before the mind's eye.

"Old Hickory" evoked the image of Jackson and "Little Van" of his successor. A drawing of a log cabin and a coonskin cap was the same thing as writing "William Henry Harrison." Tyler was "His Accidency." Taylor was "Old Rough and Ready," Buchanan was "Old Buck," and a gangling youth splitting a rail in a cabin woodlot was Lincoln. Grant had a dozen sobriquets, and the "U. S." of his first initials were spelled out as "Unconditional Surrender." Hayes suffered under the bitter title of "His Fraudulency." Cleveland, having been a county sheriff, was pictured as "The Buffalo Hangman." The cartoonists drew an insignificant Benjamin Harrison peeping out of "Grandfather's Hat." McKinley was equated with "A Full Dinner Pail." T. Roosevelt was "The Hero of San Juan Hill" or "The Man on Horseback," according to the bias of the source. And in later campaigns there followed "The Schoolmaster in Politics" (Wilson), "Silent Cal" (Coolidge), "That Man in the White House" (F. D. Roosevelt, and "High Tax Harry" (Truman) until "Ike" became the world-wide name for Eisenhower.

The color all these gave to politics has been absent from this campaign by television. But, on the credit side, also absent are the old scurrilities because of the legal restraints imposed by Government licensing standards, and because of the tactical restraints imposed by TV's penetration into the home.

November 8, 1960

Nixon Appears on Television for 4 Hours Answering Questions Telephoned to Him

HE TERMS PEACE FOREMOST ISSUE

Subject Matter Ranges From Castro to Family Problems —Party Label Decried

DETROIT, Nov. 7 — Vice President Nixon appeared on a four-hour "Telethon" program today. The feat was unparalleled in Presidential campaigning.

Capping his campaign in all fifty states of the nation the Republican Presidential nominee appeared relaxed as he sat in a studio of WXYZ-TV here and answered questions telephoned from all sections of the country.

The subject-matter ranged from how to handle Cuba's Premier Fidel Castro to who made the decision that Mrs. Nixon should travel with her husband during the campaign.

Immediately after the Vice President left the air Senator John F. Kennedy, in hastily purchased time, appeared on the same network from Manchester, N. H., to challenge his rival's statements and to answer other questions phoned in to him.

His appearance was then countered by the Republicans, who pressed former Gov. Thomas E. Dewey into service from New York to answer the Democratic nominee's attacks on the Vice President.

Mr. Nixon told his television audience that everywhere he had traveled in the long campaign from Maine to Hawaii he had found the people concerned about the issue of keeping the peace, and extending freedom without war.

"If there's one thing I can emphasize above everything else," Mr. Nixon said, "it is that this is such an important election, since we are selecting not only the President of the United States but the leader of the free world, that it is vital, absolutely vital that we put America first rather than party first, that we put America first above every other consideration and that you, the voters of this country, think not in terms of, for example the party label I wear and you wear.

"If you are a Republican and

I'm a republican, that isn't enough reason to vote for me, and the same is true of my opponent; if you are a Democrat and he is Democrat, that isn't enough reason to vote for him. What we need is the best man that either party can produce in these times."

The program was carried over the American Broadcasting Company network.

According to telephone company officials, the response "swamped" the 100 telephone lines set up into the studio.

At one point during the program, an announcer declared in a burst of enthusiasm that "the response has been simply appalling."

The leading issue raised by the questioners dealt with "keeping the peace," according to a program announcer. The other principal questions were said to have dealt with "combating communism," personal life, and "human needs and welfare."

The program was not exclusively a question-and-answer period between the Presidential candidate and the voters.

Some of the questions were answered by Henry Cabot Lodge, the Vice-Presidential candidate, from Boston. The program was interrupted from time to time for films showing the careers of Mr. Nixon and Mr. Lodge, for parts of a speech by President Eisenhower endorsing the ticket and for statements by movie and television stars, in a studio in New York, praising the Republican ticket.

The program was put on, the Vice President said, to allow the American people for the first time in the history of American politics to question directly a candidate for the Presidency.

The telephones installed in the studio were manned by about 200 Republican women volunteer workers from the Detroit area.

The calls, totaling more than 7,000, were paid for by the sponsors.

The questions screened by a panel, consisting of Dr. James Pollock of the University of Michigan, Prof. Tibor Payzs of the University of Detroit and Dr. James Miller, director of the Mental Health Research Institute at the University of Michigan.

They said that they processed the questions for good taste, intelligibility, and to avoid duplication.

Masters of ceremonies, who appeared with the Vice President and asked the questions, were Robert Young, Lloyd Noland and John Payne, actors.

At the beginning of the program the announcer said that voters could ask "any question under the sun." They very nearly did that.

The questions included one about the admission of Communist China to the United Nations (Mr. Nixon was opposed under "present circumstances" but did not preclude the possibility that eventually China might qualify) to whether the Vice President was a "strict father" (he said he was not and that he "spoils" his children).

The two Nixon daughters, Julie and Patricia, joined the campaign today, appearing with their father on a motorcade through downtown Detroit and at a rally in the Ford Auditorium.

They also made a brief appearance with their mother and Mr. Nixon on the telethon. Mr. Young asked the girls about their aims in life.

Patricia said that she would like to be a teacher and Julie that she once wanted to be an actress but wasn't so sure now. She emphasized, though, that she wanted to go to college.

At the beginning of the program, Mr. Nixon, who flew to Detroit overnight from Alaska, showed some irritation with photographers, who were busily snapping pictures just before he went on the air.

Later he told those assisting in processing questions that he wanted a full hour of questions without a break.

"Can everything but the question," he said.

But the telethon breaks continued, with switches to Mr. Lodge, film clips, interviews with movie stars supporting him, including Ginger Rogers, and even an occasional advertisement, including one for cranberry sauce.

For the most part, the questions produced no new positions by the Vice President but did give him an opportunity to restate positions taken throughout the campaign.

One of the rare moments of political spark during the program was generated when the Vice President was asked how it was that he found time to appear alone on a four-hour television program but could not find time to appear on a fifth televised debate with Senator Kennedy.

In reply the Vice President blamed the Kennedy camp for the collapse of negotiations for a fifth debate. He said that Senator Kennedy had undertaken a "calculated program" to break up the fifth debate because he did not want to appear on a nationally televised program with his running mate, Senator Lyndon B. Johnson of Texas.

The Vice President also took the occasion to get in a jab for what he described as the apparent reluctance of Senator Kennedy to have Senator Johnson appear with him in northern states. He emphasized that he was willing to have Senator Lodge appear any time any place with him in the United States.

At another point Mr. Nixon declined to comment on Senator Kennedy's tactics in the long campaign but said that Senator Johnson had been forced to take a back seat because Senator Kennedy had put him there. But he is not a back-seat driver, Mr. Nixon said, adding that the situation had become "quite embarrassing" to both of them.

Then the Vice President went on to say that he felt Senator Kennedy had distorted the record but that the Democratic nominee also felt that he, Mr. Nixon, had done the same.

"The voters will have to decide," Mr. Nixon said.

Another questioner inquired why the Vice President objected to Senator Kennedy's criticism of United States prestige and strength, since in 1942 Mr. Nixon was charging that the nation's military position had deteriorated.

"Then it was true," Mr. Nixon said. "Now it isn't."

Answer by Kennedy

Senator Kennedy interrupted a campaign swing through New Hampshire to go to a Manchester television station to answer the Vice President's telethon statements and to answer telephone questions.

He scoffed at Mr. Nixon's suggestion that the Democratic program would endanger the economy and call for an increase in taxes. He also pledged strong efforts to maintain the peace in his half-hour appearance.

In response to a question read to him on the program dealing with his position on the separation of church and state, the Senator, a Roman Catholic, pledged that he would "not let the Pope or anyone else in my church" influence him as President.

"If the Pope, or anyone else should attempt to bring improper influence, then I should tell that person that it was improper," he said. He added that he could be impeached if he permitted such interference in the conduct of his office.

Questions on the program were read to him by his three sisters, Mrs. Peter Lawford, Mrs. Stephen Smith and Mrs. R. Sargent Shriver Jr.

In caustic tones Mr. Dewey, who appeared on the same network, but from New York City, derided Senator Kennedy's assertion that he would be a full-time President.

The former New York Governor charged that Mr. Kennedy had not even been a full-time Senator. He said that Senator Kennedy, as chairman of a subcommittee on Africa, had never called a meeting of that body and had missed most of the meetings of other committees of which he was a member.

Questions Called 'Rigged'

DETROIT, Nov. 7 (AP)—Michigan's Democratic state chairman, Neil Staebler, charged tonight that Vice President Nixon's telethon had been rigged."

Mr. Staebler said "our switchboard at Democratic headquarters was flooded all afternoon with calls from people who were told that their questions could not be accepted."

He said, "This means only friendly questions were filtered through the screen of public relations monitors and passed on to Mr. Nixon to answer."

How a President Helps Form Public Opinion

By DOUGLASS CATER

ONE sobering realization that has come to John F. Kennedy, as it does to all new Presidents, is that he must ever be speaking *to* as well as *for* a nation. Getting elected is only the bare beginning of this communication process. The success of his Presidency depends on the care with which he continues to cultivate that sovereign known as public opinion.

The constitutional causes for this are not hard to seek out. Lord Bryce once observed that "in weakening each single authority in the government by dividing powers and functions among each of them, [the framers of the Constitution] were throwing upon the nation at large, that is, upon unorganized public opinion, more work than it had ever discharged in England * * *." The President is only one bidder among many seeking the favorable attention of the public to get his job done.

But a new President soon learns, if he doesn't already know, that public opinion in America is not a monolithic thing spreading out from Washington. There are publics and publics to which he must appeal. They group and regroup in ever varying combinations, coalescing on special occasions to sustain or frustrate his purpose. A President can never be entirely certain of public opinion's depth and duration.

Polls provide a clue. In Franklin D. Roosevelt's time, when pollstering first became a discipline, the jargon about "image" and "trend analysis" came to the White House. No President has neglected it since.

But polls are at best crude indices, rarely revealing which publics want what and how intensely they want it. The President must have an intuitive feel for these things. He must be sensitive, first of all, to Congress, his co-equal, according to the Constitution, and his most vociferous court of public opinion. He must be alert to the opinion of the vast executive bureaucracy, spread out beneath him, which has its own pipelines to the public. He must make distinctions between the informed, the less informed and the uninformed opinions of the general public. He must take account of the organized publics which have come to claim an ever more assertive role in the affairs of government.

FINALLY, a President today cannot neglect his new, non-voting public dwelling outside the territorial limits of the United States. He plays front and center on a world stage. What is thought and said among our ancient allies of Europe, the newly emerging countries of Asia and Africa and even within the closed communications system of the Soviet Union has a lot to do with his success or failure.

Prof. Richard Neustadt of Columbia, a leading Kennedy adviser whose brilliant study "Presidential Power" has become a textbook for the new Administration, divides public opinion into two major categories, each of which is important to the President. His *professional reputation* is built on what in spirit, if not geography, is labeled the Washington Community. It consists of all those politicians, press, lobbyists, diplomats who "are compelled to watch the President for reasons not of pleasure but vocation." His *public prestige*, on the other hand, is based on the opinion of the broader, less knowledgeable but no less important community-at-large.

The judgments of the two groups can be quite independent of one another. Truman often won grudging admiration even when he sank to low levels in public popularity. Eisenhower, on the other hand, was frequently criticized by the professionals; yet he left office still outstandingly popular with the general public. Neither is a desirable condition of Presidential life. Ideally, Mr. Kennedy must seek the favor of both these publics if he is not to suffer an erosion of his Presidential powers.

HOW does a President communicate to the public in order to get support for the things he thinks are important? In the first glow of his election triumph it might seem to a President that he has all the publicity advantages. "We will merchandise the hell out of the Eisenhower program," one White House aide was widely quoted in 1953. He was relying on the undoubted fact that everything a President says or does is news.

But the incumbent soon finds there are severe limits set upon his capacity to communicate. As President Franklin Roosevelt, surely one of the masters of the art, once wrote to an old associate:

"* * * The public psychology and, for that matter, individual psychology, cannot, because of human weakness, be attuned for long periods of time to a constant repetition of the highest note in the scale.* * * Whereas in this country there is a free and sensational press, people tire of seeing the same name, day after day, in the important headlines of the papers and the same voice, night after night, over the radio. * * * If I had tried [in 1935] to keep up the pace of 1933 and 1934, the inevitable histrionics of the new actors, Long and Coughlin and Johnson, would have turned the eyes of the audience away from the main drama itself. * * *"

Bryce wrote nearly three-quarters of a century ago,

DOUGLASS CATER covers the White House as Washington editor of The Reporter magazine. He wrote "The Fourth Branch of Government," an analysis of the capital's press corps.

"To catch and to hold the attention of the people is the chief difficulty as well as the first duty of an American reformer." President Kennedy must be even more conscious of the duty and the difficulty amid modern-day distractions. He is not helped by the fact that what he must try to explain is both more complex and less intimately related to the life of the citizen than in Roosevelt's time when both depression and war presented fairly clear-cut conditions of life. Gold flow, balanced military forces, even the cold war itself, represent much more difficult concepts.

THIS presents a task which the development of mass communications, paradoxically, has not made much easier. During Truman's first three post-war years in office, Neustadt points out, there were eight occasions when he pre-empted all radio networks during an evening hour to take important policy issues to the country. Yet only once did his Hooper rating rise above 50 per cent of the potential listeners. It was the time he removed price controls on meat. The others followed a generally descending scale to a low rating of 30.7 per cent when Truman tried to explain why he had vetoed Taft-Hartley.

More than uninterested, the public may not be amused to have so many programs sacrificed to the President. During his second term, Eisenhower took notice of this and ceased to pre-empt all the networks for his evening addresses. It meant that the viewer had a choice between the President and, say, Huckleberry Hound.

Certainly television offers a great potential for the President who finds a way to use it. But it also has its drawbacks. It demands entertainment for the eye as well as a quickened tempo for the ear. It puts a premium on spontaneity and change of pace. Ideally, to suit its mercurial demands, the affairs of state should be presented in the mode of a Jack Paar Show.

THESE are facts of life which a President may lament but not ignore. Actually, there is no reason to suppose that President Kennedy is unaware of or unprepared for this particular new frontier. He brings to it considerable assets. Certainly more than our last two Presidents he is capable of performing extemporaneously and switching swiftly from topic to topic. During the campaign, the television inquisition on his Catholicism by the Houston ministers showed that he could comport himself well in a situation of high drama. In the great debates, he never faltered for loss of a word or misspoke himself.

These attributes undoubtedly helped shape Kennedy's decision to pioneer the "live" televised press conference. It was the final step in the development of this Presidential institution, first innovated by Woodrow Wilson as a cozy gathering at which a President could converse with Washington correspondents in an informal way.

UNDER Truman the conference lost a great deal of its informality when it moved out of the President's own office and the tape recorders were introduced. Under Eisenhower, the cameras also came in. But they made their impressions on film. Technically, press secretary Hagerty could always edit them before they were shown to the public, though in later years he never did.

Now every safe-guard has been stripped away as the President stands before the public. The Kennedy conference takes place in the vast modernity of the new State Department auditorium. Network representatives monitor the proceedings from glass-front booths high above the crowd of regular reporters. Two shot-gun microphones pick out the inquiring reporter and transmit his questions to the listening audience with an audibility not enjoyed by his colleagues in the room. Zoomar lenses bring the faces of President and press close up.

Judging by his performances so far, Kennedy has displayed clear mastery of this art form. Unlike Eisenhower, he has saved for the conference news of real importance and has related it in an interesting, informative way. He gives his answers tersely and syntactically. He appears well briefed on the details of what is going on. He remembers precisely which one among his newly selected associates he has instructed to do what. To borrow a campaign slogan, he creates the impression of a President who has got the Executive, if not the country, "moving forward again."

Kennedy professes unconcern about the dangers in a television conference that is transmitted instantly and is unexpurgated. "It seems to me that [the interests of our country] are as well protected under this sytem as they were under the system followed by President Eisenhower," he remarked at the first one. "And this system has the advantage of providing more direct communication."

FOR some observers, both systems have lost certain advantages that the press conference once had. Bringing in all the recording and transmitting apparatus has removed much of the free give-and-take. There is no longer any opportunity for background answers by which a President could offer explanations without being quoted. Unless he finds other ways of communing with the press, it precludes Kennedy from the kind of freedom in discussing troublesome issues that Roosevelt used to have. The dialogue must be conducted with the stiff awareness that the whole nation may be listening in.

Perhaps more important for the President, however, is whether the nation really is listening. Kennedy's first conferences drew pretty good ratings; an estimated 65 million viewers in 21.5 million homes saw the third of the live ones. But if Eisenhower's experience means anything, there will be a sharp drop-off in the future. In his last years in office, the networks often carried only the briefest fragments on the evening news roundups.

The sad fact of the matter is that, unlike the emotion-ridden ministerial meeting in Houston, the press conference is lacking in dramatic appeal. Reporters, whatever their other virtues, are not usually very good actors. The President, no matter how cogent his answers, finds it difficult to achieve any feats of exhortation.

Undoubtedly, President Kennedy and his aides are exploring other ways to communicate. The decision to alternate between live and traditional conferences shows a mood to vary the formula before it wears thin. Kennedy is acutely aware of the danger of overexposure.

THERE is talk around the White House of trying occasional programs on the order of N. B. C.'s "White Paper" in which the President, not Chet Huntley, would be the moderator. One aide has expressed a desire to have Kennedy and his Secretary of State, Dean Rusk, engage in a televised conversation of the kind that takes place at a regular White House meeting between the two, only denuded of security information. It was a method of informal discourse tried once or twice by Eisenhower and his Cabinet members with a notable lack of success. But Kennedy's associates are convinced he can bring it off.

* * *

THERE are an old-fashioned few in Washington who are convinced that there is still a place for rhetoric in a President's vocabulary when he prepares to talk to his publics. It may take more drudgery in preparation and the immediate audience may not always seem worth the effort. But if it is good rhetoric, with disciplined ideas for content, it has a percolative effect that lasts beyond the moment of delivery and goes beyond the listening and viewing audience. It extends the exhortative power of a President beyond his term of office and even his lifetime. It makes the arguments of Lincoln as valid today as when they were first made.

Hopefully, there was evidence in Kennedy's Inaugural Address as well as in his first State of the Union message that he intends to make certain that the poetic powers of the Presidency are rekindled. The tremendous impact especially of the Inaugural ought to reassure the new President that he can get through to the people when he says it well enough.

One further means at his disposal Kennedy obviously does not intend to neglect. By countless instances of Presidential act and gesture, he can also say things. The telephone call to Mrs. Martin Luther King while he was still a candidate, the helicopter flight to be on hand for the return of the RB-47 fliers, the swift working out of a way to permit U. S. personnel overseas to keep their families with them—these are eloquent symbols of his purpose. In an age of instant and prodigious communication it is perhaps ironic that such sign language is still a President's best way of talking with his publics.

Mrs. Kennedy TV Hostess to Nation

Tells of Restoration of Interior of the White House

By JACK GOULD

Millions of television viewers went through the White House last night with Mrs. John F. Kennedy leading the way.

With verve and pleasure, the President's wife undertook to explain the restoration she has made in the interior of the Executive Mansion. She was to prove a virtuoso among guides.

In the hour-long program, recorded on tape last month, Mrs. Kennedy was a historian savoring the small facts and human story behind the evolution of White House décor. She was an art critic of subtlety and standard. She was an antiquarian relishing pursuit of the elusive treasure. She was a poised TV narrator.

Mrs. Kennedy, wearing a wool suit of simple line and three strings of pearls, animatedly strolled through rooms on the ground, first and second floors in what was described as the most extensive public view of the White House ever shown.

The hour was rich in detail and diversity. The viewer saw the magnificence of the State Dining Room, a battered old Lincoln chair plucked from a warehouse, many of the antiques and paintings recently donated to the White House in response to Mrs. Kennedy's pleas, the rich warmth of the Red Room and the unfinished Monroe Room that is to shield the President's visitors from the perils of a passing baby carriage.

But the First Lady's vivacious scholarship was fully as vital as the visual pageantry. With her soft and measured voice, she ranged in comment from warm appreciation of past First Ladies and Presidents to delicate but telling dismissal of the second-rate in the arts. Her effortless familiarity with dates and names attested to homework done for the occasion.

Carried on Two Networks

Mrs. Kennedy's companion on the tour was Charles Collingwood, a reporter for the Columbia Broadcasting System's news department, which conceived and produced the program. C. B. S. also made the presentation available to the National Broadcasting Company. Both networks carried the program simultaneously on a sustaining basis from 10 to 11 o'clock.

C. B. S. will repeat the program March 25.

After Mrs. Kennedy completed the tour, the President appeared briefly to second his wife's efforts to impart a sense of living history to the White House.

An awareness of history can be a source of strength in meeting the problems of the future, he said.

The President reported that more than 1,300,000 persons passed through the White House last year. Mrs. Kennedy's audience last night was expected to exceed that number by many-fold, but estimates of the program's rating were not expected to be available until today.

Competes With 'Naked City'

Mrs. Kennedy's competition in the ratings last night came from "Naked City," a police adventure series presented by the American Broadcasting Company. A. B. C. said that it could not afford to share in the total production cost of Mrs. Kennedy's program, estimated at more than $100,000, because of unforeseen expense in covering the delayed orbital flight of Lieut. Col. John H. Glenn Jr.

Mrs. Kennedy and her associates and a special C. B. S. staff, headed by Perry Wolff, the program's producer, and Franklin Schaffner, director, made careful preparations for the first televised tour of the White House since President Harry S. Truman inaugurated the format May 4, 1952.

Agreement on a final outline enabled Mrs. Kennedy to go through most of the program in a single day, Jan. 15, without retakes. Close-up shots of specific antiques were taken initially and were subsequently integrated into Mrs. Kennedy's running commentary, an editing procedure designed to spare the President's wife unnecessary delay. The President chose to record his part of the program a second time.

The program started with Mrs. Kennedy's own off-screen narration of the history of the White House. Then she and Mr. Collingwood met in the curator's office on the ground floor.

Visits Original Kitchen

Next was the Diplomatic Reception Room, and then came the original White House kitchen, later used by Franklin D. Roosevelt as a broadcast room. The kitchen is now Mrs. Kennedy's upholstery repair shop.

Mrs. Kennedy went up to the first floor and in succession through the East Room, the the State Dining Room, where the table was fully set; the Red Room, Blue Room and Green Room. Then the First Lady went up the second floor, rarely visited by the public, and viewers were taken into the Lincoln and Monroe Rooms.

Mrs. Kennedy, whose restoration efforts have drawn Washington's bipartisan approval, had special praise for the past contributions of Theodore Roosevelt and James Monroe. Similarly, in admiring Gilbert Stuart's portrait of Washington, she deplored the fact that so many pictures of later Presidents had been done by inferior artists.

With delightful understatement, she recalled that Grant's renovation of the East Room had been called a unique mixture of two styles: ancient Greek and "Mississippi River Boat."

In terms of television viewing, "A Tour of the White House with Mrs. John F. Kennedy" will undoubtedly stand as a distinctive contribution of the electronic era: an unusual feminine personality imparting her own kind of excitement to national history and national taste.

Richard S. Salant, president of C. B. S. News, said last night that arrangements for the program had not included any conditions for a contribution to the Fine Arts Commission, which is assisting Mrs. Kennedy's restoration efforts.

"There is absolutely no truth to such a report," Mr. Salant said. "There was no suggestion from the White House for a quid pro quo. There has been no discussion of it."

May Make Contribution

C. B. S. might wish to make a contribution on its own initiative at a later date, Mr. Salant said.

If it were decided to aid the White House restoration efforts, he said, it has been suggested that any other network carrying Mrs. Kennedy's program might wish to join in. A. B. C., which did not carry the program, disapproved of the proposal, Mr. Salant said.

In Washington, however, it was understood that the White House had misgivings over the idea over any network contributions to aid Mrs. Kennedy's project.

Through the Federal Communications Commission, the Government exercises a degree of regulation over chain broadcasting and also licenses individual stations owned by the networks.

February 15, 1962

President's TV Ordeal

Scorer Gives Johnson No Runs, Hits Or Errors, With Issues Left Stranded

By JAMES RESTON
Special to The New York Times

WASHINGTON, Feb. 29 — President Johnson achieved his major objective in his first live televised news conference today: He survived.

He approached this ordeal like a man going to the gallows. He insisted, from the first day he entered the White House, that the TV was not his medium, and he was right. But he got through today's assignment in good order: No runs, no hits, no errors—and several issues left stranded. Lyndon Johnson is a talker rather than a performer. The more natural he is, the more impressive he is, and the smaller the room the better. So he was out of his natural element today.

News Analysis

The New State Department building, where the conference was held, is as antiseptic as a hospital. When you go into it, you almost expect to hear somebody say on the loudspeaker: "Dr. Johnson wanted in surgery, please."

Sound Piped In

And the International Conference Room, where the President recited, is one of those big square half-acre, windowless I.B.M. rooms where the air, the sound and everything else comes out of a pipe.

President Johnson, who used to charge through the swinging doors of the Senate, scattering page boys in his wake, almost slipped into this operating chamber today. He was dressed in television blue—suit, shirt and striped tie—and he came prepared.

First, a sheaf of appointments: Bill Bundy, a favorite of reporters, to be Assistant Secretary of State for Far Eastern affairs; John T. McNaughton to replace Mr. Bundy as Assistant Secretary of Defense; Daniel M. Luevano to be Assistant Secretary of the Army; Mrs. Frankie Muse Freeman, a lawyer, to be on the Civil Rights Commission.

And then a surprise.

One of this country's closest held secrets has been the development of a high-flying, extremely fast successor to the famous U-2 sky spy plane.

Subjected to Pressure

When Secretary of Defense Robert S. McNamara began to be criticized as a big rocket man who hated manned aeroplanes, there was pressure to disclose the fact that this new plane, the A-11, had been tested successfully.

Such disclosure was opposed on the ground that one day, in a crisis, the country might use such a plane to the surprise of any enemy, so why tell the world about it? Why, indeed? But the President announced it, anyway, explanation undisclosed.

All this he read out in a drone, as if he were determined to be slow and casual about the whole affair. Besides, as every President knows, the more you talk in these journalistic inquisitions, the fewer questions you have to answer. He took his time.

It was the same with his answers to questions. When a man's name was mentioned, he gave you the fellow's biography. The President is a cautious man with a sure instinct for danger: He didn't exactly filibuster at the conference, but he managed to give a maximum of background and a minimum of news.

Technique Displayed

Nevertheless, the conference indicated a number of things, including just how far a politican will go to keep the television networks happy. It also demonstrated the Johnson political technique.

This is, primarily, to minimize or evade trouble. One reporter mentioned those two terrible words, "Bobby Baker." Mr. Johnson quickly tossed Bobby to the Senators, remembering to express confidence that they, in some mysterious fashion, would take "proper action."

Another reporter mentioned all the speculation about carrying the war to North Vietnam, which the Administration itself had inspired. Mr. Johnson thought speculation was "a great disservice" and pessimism even worse.

Panama? All he wanted was to be fair. Southeast Asia? All we wanted was peace. The outlook for the future?

"I am an optimist . . . I am encouraged and I'm not pessimistic."

Would he debate with his oppponent in the Presidential election, and was it true that he had speculated on Richard Nixon as his opponent?

No, said he, he hadn't speculated on whether he'd run for President or even who he'd run against "if I do run." This he said without even a flicker or a smile.

What did he mean by saying last week that the Communists were playing a "dangerous game" in Vietnam, and what had he intended by that phrase?

He intended, by saying it was a dangerous game, to imply that it was a dangerous game. "That's what I said, and that's what I meant."

He was patient, courteous, cautious and verbose, and though he concentrated most of the time on what everybody knew, he made a better impression on the reporters in the room than he apparently did on those who saw him on television.

Nevertheless, he is now over an ordeal he dreaded, and can now return to his small spontaneous conferences, where he is usually more effective.

Washington:
The Power of the Presidency and Television

By JAMES RESTON

WASHINGTON, Jan. 27 — President Nixon has clearly decided to use the power of the Presidency, plus the power of network television, to combat his opponents in the Democrat-controlled Congress and presumably to establish a Republican Congress in November.

This is quite a combination and quite a gamble. Thoughtful observers here have wondered, ever since the inception of nation-wide television, what would happen if a determined President, who had both the will and the ability to use the networks effectively, really set out to exploit television for his political advantage.

President Eisenhower had the personality, the popularity, and the ability to use television in this way, but not the will. President Kennedy had the ability and the will to use it, but for some unexplained reason, was afraid of what he called over-exposure. President Johnson had the will, but neither the personality nor the ability to use it effectively. But President Nixon, by going to the networks to veto the money bill for health, education and welfare, has indicated both a determination and an ability to use it to appeal to the people over the head of the Congress to achieve his political objectives.

The possibilities and implications of this are worth a little reflection. The President has available in the White House a television studio hooked into the networks. This is necessary for great occasions of state or for emergencies, but it is also available to him whenever he has a major controversy with the Congress: for example, when he wants to explain his veto of the H.E.W. bill to the American people. After all, it would be rather awkward, even for Frank Stanton at C.B.S., to say no.

This, of course, is precisely what the President did in his H.E.W. controversy. He vetoed the bill on television with a flourish. He did not deliver a balanced Presidential presentation of the problem, but a one-sided, self-serving and even self-righteous argument for his veto. It was very effective and very misleading, and it raises questions far more important than the H.E.W. bill.

The Doctrine of 'Fairness'

What about the doctrine of "fairness," which Vice President Agnew was so concerned about not so long ago? How can Senators who oppose the President get "equal time" when they are talking to a half-empty chamber, while the President is arguing his case, from the majesty of the White House, before an audience of millions?

Beyond this, there is a more immediate problem. This is that the President is now by-passing or reaching beyond the Congress to the people, and this is his gamble. He is just going into his second year in the Presidency. He has indicated the outlines of his policy—welfare, taxes, crime, conservation, and all the rest—but his major proposals have not been voted into law.

The Power of Congress

They have to go through the Congress. The Congress is controlled by the Democrats. The Democrats are divided, with a cooperative saint as their leader in the Senate, and a weak and tired octogenarian, or thereabouts, as their leader in the House, and a liberal Senator from a conservative state as chairman of the Democratic National Committee.

In short, the Democrats are in deep trouble. But nothing will unify them more, or arouse their partisan dander, than a President who tries to ride over their majority by partisan television appeals to the people. This is a provocation to a partisan battle at a time when the country needs a little time and unity to put through many of the sensible programs the President has suggested.

The Partisan Furies

After the President's televised veto message, the partisan furies are rising. After proclaiming in his State of the Union Message that "what this nation needs is an example . . . of spiritual and moral leadership . . . which would inspire young Americans with a sense of excitement. . ." Mr. Nixon, who has been talking about an era of quiet understanding at home, and of negotiation rather than confrontation abroad, has now gone to the television with a narrow political argument which is building up a real confrontation in a Democratic Congress, whose support he needs for the programs he says are essential to the nation.

It is very odd: a noble generous State of the Union Message one day, and a narrow party speech on television a few days later. All this is a fairly good illustration of why there is so much distrust and cynicism in the country, particularly among the young, about American politics and politicians.

The impact of the tube in politics

Presidential Television

A Twentieth Century Fund Report. By Newton N. Minow, John Bartlow Martin and Lee M. Mitchell. 232 pp. New York: Basic Books. $8.95.

By GEORGE E. REEDY

In the long view of history, the impact of television upon our society may well turn out to be more profound than the atomic bomb, the discovery of antibiotics or the exploration of outer space. We are literally bathed in the new medium. It has altered our perceptions of the universe. It has shrunk time and distance and changed our concepts of community.

Yet, despite a flood of analyses on the relationship of electronics communications to our society, the literature remains curiously unsatisfying. Words have been counted ad nauseum; audiences have been probed by scientific pollsters; psychologists have conducted careful experiments with controlled groups. It is still impossible to find any consensus on what "the tube" is doing to us. We know "it" is tremendous, but we really don't know what "it" is.

Messrs. Minow, Martin and Mitchell address themselves to one aspect of this problem in "Presidential Television," a Twentieth Century Fund report. As men superbly qualified in the legal problems of the media, they have produced a coherent, readable account of the increasing fascination of Presidents, Congress and politicians generally with television. They have also reduced to understandable language the incredible complications of the "fairness doctrine" and the failure of the Federal Communications Commission to produce standards that insure "balance" in the presentation of political issues.

George E. Reedy, press secretary to Lyndon Johnson, is dean and Nieman professor at the college of journalism, Marquette University.

The statistics are awe-inspiring. In the 1970 non-Presidential elections, candidates spent $58-million on broadcasting. From April through June, 1971, members of the House of Representatives made more than 1,683 hours of radio recordings, 172 hours of videotape and 12 hours of film in their special recording facility. When Lyndon B. Johnson announced that he would not be a candidate for re-election to the Presidency in 1968, he faced an audience of 75,000,000 people.

The figures, however, are merely a backdrop for the major thesis of the authors—that Presidential command over television time has altered the balance of political forces in the United States. The fact of Presidential command is well documented. No White House request has ever been declined by the networks. (The authors might be interested to know that even a request is not necessary. Mere notification that the President is willing to appear can be sufficient.) Congress has moved sessions from the traditional noon hour to late evening so Presidential addresses could be carried in prime time. Political opposition has very little opportunity under the best of circumstances to present a sharply focused reply to Executive appearances.

The clarity and precision with which the authors marshal their facts qualifies their work as a basic, although not necessarily definitive, book. Certainly, it will be very useful as a text (at least I intend to use it) in communications schools throughout the country. But some disturbing questions arise out of their conviction that the balance of political forces has been changed. They accept too easily the assumption that command of the frequencies and command of political forces go together. And they bolster the assumption with evidence that is far from conclusive.

"Hi, there . . ."

For example, they cite poll rises of 4 per cent in public support of a Kennedy tax proposal, 30 per cent for Johnson's Vietnam policies and 18 per cent for President Nixon's Southeast Asia stand after Presidential television addresses. Although I have not looked them up, I do not doubt the figures in the slightest. The only problem is that political issues are not settled by the polls. I do not recall any great success for the Kennedy tax proposal or for the Johnson Vietnam policies. As for President Nixon, it seems to me that he quieted the public on Southeast Asia *not* by television speeches but by withdrawing ground troops and reducing casualties.

There is also a tendency on the part of the authors to assume that when two events are related, the first in point of time *caused* the second. For example, in their account of Nixon's 1952 "Checkers" speech explaining the hitherto secret fund from wealthy California contributors he had enjoyed as a member of Congress, the authors write: "The public was carried away by the sentimental and patriotic passages of the speech and by Nixon's attacks on the Truman Administration and on the Democratic ticket. And newspaper editorials were drowned out by the emotional impact of television."

Maybe so! But as a minor participant in that campaign, I had a strong feeling that the public, even before the speech, *wanted* to believe that Mr. Nixon was innocent because they did not want to admit the slightest blemish on their hero, Dwight D. Eisenhower. It could well be that any explanation would have satisfied the public and that the only service television performed was to speed the explanation to the American people.

These are not isolated instances. The authors cite radio broadcasts made by Rep. William Lemke, of North Dakota, in the thirties and claim "These efforts resulted in House passage of his bankruptcy legislation." Heavy weight is given to television for the censure of the late Joseph R. McCarthy and, paradoxically, both the opposition to and the support for the Vietnamese war. The writing team could have used one more member—one steeped in the intricate complexities of the forces that move people politically.

The need for political expertise becomes apparent in the proposals to right the imbalance created by Presidential domination of the channels. A key suggestion would be to grant the national committee of an opposition party the right of "automatic response" to any Presidential address made during the 10 months preceding a Presidential election or the 90 days preceding a Congressional election in non-Presidential years. As one who has been involved in the preconvention jockeying for a Presidential hopeful, I am ready to predict flatly that few candidates will ever permit such power to be lodged in "their" national committee. Candidates do not trust committees that much.

A second key proposal would provide for periodic prime-time telecasts of important House and Senate sessions. It is dif-

ficult to conceive of a program that would be more dreary. With a few exceptions that cannot be foreseen or scheduled, legislative debate is always dreary to the casual observer who cannot relate it to the clash of political forces that is going on behind the scenes. The camera lens is necessarily a casual observer that can neither comprehend nor communicate these clashes. A third proposal to insure all "significant" Presidential candidates free television time probably has merit but is standard.

In summary, "Presidential Television" is a sound, basic history of the development of political use of the electronics medium. But it falls far short of demonstrating just how television has changed the political forces in our society as distinguished from changing the tactics of our politicians. ■

November 25, 1973

TV and Impeachment

Hearings Found to Give House an Image Of an Institution Worthy of Respect

By R. W. APPLE Jr.
Special to The New York Times

WASHINGTON, July 31—Some months ago, Thomas P. O'Neill, the genial Bostonian who serves as the Democratic leader in the House of Representatives, was reflecting on the way his elevation to the leadership had changed people's perceptions of him. "I used to be an Irish hack," he said. "Now I have become a statesman."

News Analysis

Something of the same thing has happened in the last week to the House Judiciary Committee as a result of its deliberations on the impeachment of President Nixon, and by extension to the House as a whole. Suddenly, the House is seen and sees itself as an institution worthy of respect. For the moment, at least, there would seem to be few takers for the derisive judgment of Representative Big Tim Sullivan of New York, who said upon his retirement in 1906, "Congressmen? In Washington they hitch horses to them."

The consensus in Washington is that the committee's six days of nationally televised meetings were marked by a dignity commensurate with the occasion. To be sure, there were some pomposity and some posturing and some pettiness (members on both sides were irked by an attack on Albert E. Jenner Jr., the associate special counsel, for his views on prostitution).

Competence and Eloquence

But for all that, what struck most of those who watched the hearings close up, including reporters accustomed to dismissing the House as 435 orators in search of an idea, was the competence of lawyers like Wiggins of California and Jordan of Texas; the eloquence of Mann of South Carolina and Sandman of New Jersey; the evident emotion felt by Railsback of Illinois and Waldie of California.

The onlookers were impressed as well with the patience and evenhandedness of the committee's chairman, Peter W. Rodino Jr., Democrat of New Jersey. He proved to the satisfaction of many that the Truman tradition was not dead in America, that a relatively obscure, somewhat scorned backbencher could rise to even the most intimidating occasion.

"They didn't look like renegades," said a man with close connections to the White House, "and we'd been led to believe that they would."

Nor did the committee give the impression of ritual partisanship. Only eight Democrats voted for all five proposed articles of impeachment; only 10 Republicans voted against all five. By far the largest group, 20 members — 13 Democrats and 7 Republicans—voted for some and against some.

Representative William S. Cohen of Maine, a handsome 33-year-old Republican, was commenting at a break in one of the sessions last week. The impeachment deliberations, he said, were giving the country a chance to see what he had concluded shortly after arriving here—that the House was full of talent that got lost "because of the sheer numbers."

Relevance and Decorum

Television clearly had much to do with the tone of the debate. There were complaints about the lights, and Hungate of Missouri finally took to wearing sunglasses. There were complaints last night from the Republicans that the Democrats had deliberately delayed discussion of the tax article so it would be seen during prime time.

But the presence of the cameras held the members to a reasonable standard of relevance and decorum and guaranteed that all would be in their seats. It also gave those who feared that they were voting against the grain of their constituents a better chance to explain themselves than could a whole year of speeches, newsletters and news conferences.

If television is permitted to cover future Congressional debates on momentous questions, it could work a profound change in Congressional politics — in some ways as profound as its impact on Presidential politics since 1960. Through a means the Founding Fathers never dreamed of, the Representative could truly become the Federal office-holder closest to the people.

With the assistance of television, the committee did much to ruin the climate for the kind of counterattacks on which the White House has relied almost since the advent of the Watergate scandals more than two years ago.

It becomes more difficult, for example to describe the case as the illegitimate product of the news media when detailed accusations are issuing from the mouths of those who have studied the case for weeks.

It becomes difficult to persuade the country that a committee looks like a kangaroo court when the most impassioned defenders of the President lard their speeches with compliments for the fairness of the chairman and the procedures that he devised.

And it becomes more difficult to picture the "prosecution" as a partisan lynch mob, out of touch with middle America, when, on the first two articles of impeachment there is a coalition of Republicans and Democrats of urban, suburban and rural antecedents; of ideologies rated from zero (Mann of South Carolina) to 100 (Drinan of Massachusetts) by Americans for Democratic Action; of legislators from Tuscaloosa and Bangor, Roanoke and Akron, Moline and Flatbush and Harlem.

It is for that reason, perhaps, that White House spokesmen have abandoned their caustic critiques and begun speaking of the fairness with which they hope Congress will attend to its "Constitutional responsibilities."

August 1, 1974

CHAPTER 5

Party Politics in the Nominating Conventions

Presidential enthusiasm for party politics has diminished noticeably in recent years. It is now commonplace for campaigns to be handled by special committees with titles that give no indication of partisan affiliation and which are tied directly to the president as a national rather than a political leader. The regular Democratic and Republican national committees cease to play any considerable role once the nominating process has been concluded.

It was not always so. Until the administration of Dwight D. Eisenhower, candidates were meticulous in expressing their partisan identities. This was probably in deference to the various state and city machines around the country that could really produce votes in significant quantities. They were important to victory and therefore the entire political party was a major election factor. Despite heavy liberal pressure, even Franklin Delano Roosevelt was reluctant to repudiate ''Boss'' Hague in Jersey City, ''Boss'' Kelly in Chicago and ''Boss'' Pendergast in Kansas City.

The decline in party prestige was a function of the decline in ''Boss'' prestige. By the mid-fifties, very few bosses were doing any real bossing and today there is only one with substantial power—Richard J. Daley, of Chicago. The surest way to victory has become a drive to draw votes from both Democrats and Republicans, as well as the ever-growing segment of Independents. Such a strategy is incompatible with the old free-wheeling partisanship.

It would be premature, however, to interpret this trend to a nonpartisan election strategy as signifying the end of the traditional political parties. They have declined in prestige but still remain useful instruments for making coalition nominations—a vital necessity in a presidential structure which provides no machinery for coalition government. We cannot coalesce one man but we can set up arenas in which contending ideological factions can arrive at rough compromises in selecting the candidates.

The Democratic and Republican parties have provided us with those arenas every four years. It would be difficult to regard their conventions as contributing to the intellectual life of the nation. But government is more than an intellectual response to social problems. It works only when a successful effort has been made to find some level upon which competing ideologies can work together. The conventions are quite well adapted to testing and measuring the raw passions behind those competing ideologies. They provide the face-to-face confrontations which enable men and women to learn where they will stand and where they will compromise.

The pages that follow will make much more sense if read in that context.

GER

Dwight D. Eisenhower

The New York Times

TAFT FIRES ON HIS OPPONENTS

Refers to Them as Extremists Who Would Bring Conditions of French Revolution.

NOT PROGRESSIVES AT ALL

But Political Emotionalists or Neurotics—His Party Has Kept the Faith.

RINGING CAMPAIGN SPEECH

The Party Goes Before the People on Its Record of Things Done—Reiterates His Tariff Views and Policies.

In a ringing speech last night President Taft replied to all who are opposing his election under the guise of progressives, whether Republican or Democratic. He mentioned no names and made no accusations of disloyalty, but as he cast scorn on the doctrine of the recall of the judiciary his audience thought of Oyster Bay and cheered loudly. He was speaking before the Republican Club at its Lincoln dinner in the Waldorf, after a visit to Newark. He went on to the dinners of the Dry Goods Association and the Graduates' Club, but the speech which ex-Senator Chauncey M. Depew declared afterward would be taken as the "textbook of the campaign" was delivered to the representatives of his own party.

At the very beginning of the evening the significance of the occasion was noted. Otto T. Bannard, President of the Republican Club, drew an analogy between Mr. Taft and Lincoln. As the great war President at the end of his first term saw doubts in his own supporters as to the wisdom of his renomination, but was saved by the appeal of his honesty to the common sense of the Nation, so Mr. Taft was the inspiration and blessing of the Republican Party.

The President made a direct appeal to the common sense of the Nation. He declared that the extremists were not progressives and they would bring us into a condition that would find no parallel except in the French Revolution or of that anarchy which once characterized the South American republics. He spoke of the security of the Constitution and the necessity of its observance to give equal opportunity to all men. He scorned the catch pharse that we should prefer "the man above the dollar."

Then he settled down to a review of the things that he had accomplished during his Administration He dwelt on the necessity of tariff revision according to actual information. He spoke of his desire to make as little disturbances in business as possible in effecting tariff changes by schedules and he denounced the habit of making general denunciations without suggesting any affirmative policy.

Democrats Habitually Wrong.

The Democrats, he asserted, in their attempt to do away with five regiments of the best cavalry in the world and their determination to refuse the two battleships on this year's programme, were carrying out their habitual policy of doing the wrong thing at the wrong time, and now, under present conditions, such action was least defensible.

"The Republican Party," he said in conclusion, "is the truly progressive party. It realizes responsibility in action with constitutional limitations. If we appeal for a vote of confidence on what we have done in the last ten years, especially in the last three years, why should we doubt the result? We know what we propose to do. We offer a definite programme. We need not fear those who only speak of the principles of Jefferson and Jackson and do not tell us what they are. We need not fear those who speak of unrest and do not tell us of what it consists.

"We know what we have done and that makes us confident."

As he sat down the audience rose and shouted its applause. The ladies in the boxes joined in the ovation and the orchestra played "The Star-Spangled Banner." For two or three minutes the cheering was kept up and it was realized that the President had at last struck with more than his usual force at those who were trying to undermine his candidacy.

While the dinner was in progress several telegrams were received by Mr. Taft informing him that he had been indorsed in different parts of the country. From Colorado came the word that the Republican State Central Committee at Denver had yesterday declared for his renomination by a vote of 105 to 10. The Alaskan Republicans at Nome had done the same thing, and the Eighth District of Virginia had been instructed to support him.

The news was circulated among the 750 members of the Republican Club and their guests who filled the banquet hall of the Waldorf to overflowing.

Lincoln Also Beset.

President Taft entered the dining hall after the guests had reached their tables. He was on the arm of Mr. Bannard, and was greeted by all present standing and cheering loudly. In introducing him Mr. Bannard's allusion to the difficulties that beset Abraham Lincoln when he faced a convention for the second time was quickly taken up and applied to the guest of the evening. He said in part:

"Toward the end of Lincoln's first term as President his political fortunes seemed to hang in the balance, and now, almost half a century later, it is difficult for us to realize that when he was nominated for a second term in June, 1864, in Baltimore, there was a wave of discontent in many of the States, and doubts freely expressed as to whether he could be elected.

"Noisy demands were made that his candidacy be withdrawn until Lincoln hmiself was haunted by dark forebodings of political defeat. But the sober sense of the plain people told them that power was safe in his hands, and above all that he was honest, and from the beginning of September enthusiasm grew, and long before the day of the election the Nation had made its decision, and from the East and from the West could be heard the glorious song, 'We are coming, Father Abraham, 300,000 strong.' And they did.

"We are grateful for the presence of the head of our party, the highest officer of this great Nation, the twenty-sixth President of the United States, 'Honest Bill' Taft."

The President's Speech.

President Taft said:

"This is Lincoln's Birthday. We are met to celebrate it. We cannot claim Lincoln as belonging exclusively to us Republicans or treat his name as a mere party symbol. He belongs to the country and to the world as one of its great characters. But the fact is that during his whole career, and especially during that part of it in which he disclosed those traits that made him great, and that have rendered his memory sacred, the principles that he followed and that he was able to vindicate and put far on the way of becoming the foundation stones of the Republic were the principles of the Republican Party; and the reason why the Republican Party may not now claim him exclusively as one of its great leaders and its great saint is not because the party stands for something different from what it stood for when Lincoln was at its head, but it is that, being a party of progress, it has achieved and made of permanent acceptance by the whole people the things for which it fought and in which it followed Lincoln's leadership.

"Men praise Lincoln to-day and attack the Republican Party, altogether forgetful of the fact that in Lincoln's life the man and the party were so closely united in aim and accomplishment that the history of one is the history of the other. The truth is that the history of the last fifty years, with one or two exceptions, has been the history of the Republican Party. The progress that has been made has been made by the Republican Party in the legislative and executive power intrusted to it by the people at large.

Pulling Down the Pillars.

"There are those who look upon the present situation as one full of evil and corruption and as a tyranny of concentrated wealth, and who, in apparent despair at any ordinary remedy, are seeking to pull down those things which have been regarded as the pillars of the temple of freedom and representative government and to reconstruct our whole society on some new principle, not definitely formulated, and with no intelligent or intelligible forecast of the exact constitutional and statutory results to be attained.

"With the effort to make the selection of candidates, the enactment of legislation, and the decision of courts to depend on the momentary passions of a people necessarily indifferently informed as to the issued presented, and without the opportunity for time and study and that deliberation that gives security and common sense to the government of the people, such extremists would hurry us into a condition which would find no parallel except in the French Revolution or in that bubbling anarchy that once characterized the South American Republics. Such extremists are not progressives—they are political emotionalists or neurotics, who have lost that sense of proportion, that clear and candid consideration of their own weakness as a whole, and that clear perception of the necessity for checks upon hasty popular action which made our people who fought the Revolution and who drafted the Federal Constitution the greatest self-governing people that the world ever knew.

Equality of Opportunity.

"The Constitution was framed to give to all men equality of right before the law, and the equality of opportunity that such equality of right before the law was intended to secure. A review of the history of this country, with the mutations in the personal fortunes of the individuals that have gone to make up the people, will show that never in the history of the world has there been such equality of opportunity as in these United States, and it has been secured by upholding as sacred the rights of individual liberty and the right of private property in the guarantees of the Federal and State Constitutions.

"It has been said, and it is a common platform expression, that it is well to prefer the man above the dollar, as if the preservation of property rights has some other purpose than the assistance to and the uplifting of human rights. Private property was not established in order to gratify love of some material wealth or capital. It was established as an instrumentality in the progress of civilization and the uplifting of man, and it is equality of opportunity that private property promotes by assuring to man the result of his own labor, thrift, and self-restraint. When, therefore, the demagogue mounts the platform and announces that he prefers the man above the dollar, he ought to be interrogated as to what he means thereby—whether he is in favor of abolishing the right of the institution of private property and of taking away from the poor man the opportunity to become wealthy by the use of the abilities that God has given him, the cultivation of the virtues with which practice of self-restraint and the exercise of moral courage will fortify him.

Correcting Corporation Abuses.

"Now I am far from saying that the development of business, the discovery of new and effective methods of using capital, have not produced problems which call for additional action by the Government to prevent the abuses of the concentration of wealth and the combination of capital. Moreover, in order to tempt investment, we have doubtless in times past permitted the State to pledge to individuals privilege more permanent and of wider scope than the public demanded, and we have permitted the establishment of corporations and the acquisition of power through the corrupting use of money in politics, so as at times to give to a few dangerous control in legislation and government; but during the past ten years much progress against such abuses has been made in this regard. Statutes have been passed—notably the anti-trust statute and the inter-State commerce law and its amendments—to restrain a misuse of the privileges conferred by charter, and, if need be, there is nothing in the future of the country to prevent and everything in the principles and history of the Republican Party to forecast progress in this direction. Indeed, the only progress that has been made has been by the legislation and execution of those whom the Republican Party has put in power. In so far, therefore, as progressive policy in politics means the close regulation of State-given privilege, so far as to secure its use for the benefit of the public, and to restrain its abuse for the undue profit of the grantee of the privilege, the Republican Party is entitled to be called truly progressive."

The President explained that it was Republican statesmen who had drafted and passed the anti-trust law, and when the inter-State commerce law was a dead enactment, he said, the Republicans passed the Rebate bill, and finally the party brought the railroads under control.

"Now, I admit," said he, "that we have progressed in our ideas since the last century in the general view that the Government is more responsible for the comfort, safety, and protection of the individual than it was thought to be under the laissez faire Jeffersonian doctrine of government. We have come to recognize that the common law as it affected the relation of the employer and the employe was a law framed under the influence of the employer, and that the principles that obtained in that law, said to be based upon public policy, could not be justified by any proper modern view."

From this President Taft passed to a discussion of the courts.

Fashion to Attack Courts.

"It has come to be the fashion to attack courts," said he, "on the ground that they are not sufficiently progressive in their sympathies and are too much bound by the letter of the law, and do not yield in their construction of statutes to the popular view of what the law ought to be rather than what it actually is in written or customary form.

"The suggestion is made by which Judges are to be subject to the discipline of popular elections whenever the conclusions they reach do not suit the people, or their decisions are to be submitted for confirmation or rejection by a vote of the people. Such propositions undermine existing Governments and are directed toward depriving the judiciary of the independence without which they must be an instrument of either one man or majority tyranny. The Republican Party, I am very certain, as a National party, respecting as it does the Constitution of the United States, the care with which the judicial clauses of the fundamental instrument were drawn to secure the independence of the judiciary, will never consent to an abatement of that independence in the slightest degree, and will stand with its face like flint against any constitutional change in it to take away from the high priests who administer justice the independence that they must enjoy of influence of powerful individuals or of powerful majorities."

The Republican Party was not blind to the defects in the administration of justice, and there was great room for improvement, "but this is far, very far, from a change in the structure of our courts, by which the ratio decidend of judgments is to be changed from that of law and eternal and uniform justice to that of the voice of the majority in individual instances."

His Tariff Policy.

"The Republican Party is not a hidebound tariff party," he said. "It has changed its position from that Chinese wall and the imposition of customs duty sufficient to make the tariff as high as possible on everything that needs to be protected. It has come to a much more reasonable view, to wit, that the tariff rates on merchandise imported ought not to exceed those which will furnish living protection to the industries of this country with which such imported merchandise will come into competition. The Republican Party has come to recognize that high tariff duties encourage combinations of capital by suppressing competition to take advantage, in the domestic prices charged, of the excessive rates of duty, and that that is a much safer system which limits the duties to the measure of the difference between the cost of production here and the cost of production abroad than to the wholesale system of imposing high rates in order to secure protection at the expense of everything else.

"So far as is consistent with the maintenance of the industries in this country under living conditions of reasonable profit, the Republican Party is in favor of a revision and reduction of rates on imported merchandise. The only position it insists on is that the facts in respect to the amount of protection needed by established industries in this country shall be ascertained after a full and complete report by an impartial tribunal upon the facts governing the production of such merchandise abroad and in this country. In other words, gentlemen, the Republican Party has taken its position and must maintain its position in favor of as little disturbance of the business of the country as possible in respect to tariff changes by requiring that those changes shall only take place schedule by schedule, and then only after a full ascertainment of the facts by a non-partisan tariff board or commission, which shall enable Congress and the public at large to know what must be the necessary effect of the proposed legislation. This I consider a progressive policy.

Hits the Democratic House.

The President said that while the Republicans believed in peace they were not blinded to dangers, and were in favor of a suitable army to protect American interests in many parts of the globe. We were just now completing the Panama Canal, and in protecting it and Hawaii 3,000 or 4,000 more soldiers were needed, yet it is proposed by our Democratic friends in Congress to reduce that army by eliminating one-third of our cavalry. They would cut out some of the best cavalry in the world, five regiments which are needed for a nucleus of a larger army should we ever be suddenly called into war. For the same reason they propose to depart from the time-honored practice of adding to our navy each year two battleships by cutting them off altogether this year. In considering our many responsibilities in different parts of the world, I think this is a great mistake. Certainly the diminution in the additions to the fleet ought not to be contemplated until the Panama Canal is completed. In other words, our Democratic friends are doing the very thing that they are always reputed to do; they are doing the wrong thing at the right time. With unfailing accuracy they have selected as their policy that which is least defensible under existing conditions.

"I have not enumerated, and could not, because time would not permit, the many measures for which the Republican Party is responsible. The postal savings banks, the parcels post, the corporation tax, the maximum and minimum clause of the tariff, free trade with the Philippines, the successful administration of Colonial Governments, the negotiation of the Japanese and other treaties, the satisfactory solution of the question of immigration—all have claimed the attention of the party.

"I have said this much to show that the Republican Party since its beginning, more than fifty years ago, has always been a progressive party, and it has always recognized its responsibility by action.

"Its construction of the powers of the General Government is a more liberal one than that of its old-time opponent, the Democratic Party. It may be counted upon to respond much more promptly to modern needs in this regard than its old-time opponent. If we have a record in the last ten years, and especially in the last three years, of responding to popular needs by legislation specifically adopted to afford the proper remedies, why should we not be sure of winning a vote of confidence from the people.

The Defeat of 1910.

"It is true we were beaten in 1910, but that was by a defection of Republicans through what I must think was a misunderstanding, but not by a change from Republicans to the Democratic Party. Their defection reduced the vote of the Republicans, but did not increase the vote of the Democrats, showing that what they were waiting for was to give the Republican Party what they considered a 'locus poenitentiae,' and an opportunity of still proving the genuineness of its promises in the platform of 1908. That we have done so in the last two sessions of Congress, and that we are procuring definite results I think every one who has followed the course of National events will realize. We know what we propose to do; we offer a definite programme, show definite results, and we believe that those results are what the people wish. We do not hesitate to ask for their support. The arguments of most Democrats in favor of a return to their party have a general likeness. We have first a general denunciation of conditions, said to be due to the Republican Party, which every man would deprecate, but the existence of which and the Republican Party's responsibility for which depend chiefly upon the authority of the speaker alone. Then the statement of general good results that must be accomplished by following the principles of the Democratic Party and of Jackson and Jefferson, without specification as to what they are, and, finally, a pressure for an invitation to that party to assume power. There is nothing definite in what is said; nothing definite promised, only general denunciation and general promise.

"They speak of a spirit of unrest everywhere; they don't describe what that unrest depends upon, and if they do they don't tell how it is to be remedied or what legislation will accomplish it.

"We are going to have a four months' campaign, from the middle of June until the first of November. In that time the people will have the right and opportunity to ask of each party what it proposes to do, and it will not be sufficient to answer that they propose generally to introduce good legislation and execute it. The question is what legislation they will enact, how are they going to formulate it, and how execute it. Four months will test the substance of the criticisms, and of the proffers of new policies which are to be offered by either party, and it is because of my confidence that the Republican Party can point to definite deeds already accomplished, to laws already on the statute books and being enforced and carried to a useful purpose, and to proposed statutes, with a clear description of the terms and effect of such statutes, that I confidently rely upon an ultimate verdict by the people in favor of the old Republican Party, the party of Lincoln and Grant, the most progressive party in the history of this country or any other country, the party of achievement, and not of broken promises; the party of liberal, effective government in which far-sighted economy is the watchword, without that spasmodic penuriousness which ignores great National needs on the score of political emergency, the party that stands by the fundamental principles of free and well-ordered government, preserving the rights and equality of opportunity of the individual, and not interfering with the only steady, practical progress that is possible."

February 13, 1912

ROOSEVELT SAYS HE WILL ACCEPT THE NOMINATION

Puts Himself in the Race to Stay Until the Convention Expresses Its Preference.

WANTS PEOPLE TO SPEAK

Believes That Where Possible They Should Instruct Delegates at the Primaries.

ANSWERS THE GOVERNORS.

Long-Awaited "Yes" Brings Prediction of His Defeat from Press of the Country.

DENOUNCED IN HIS PARTY

Republican Newspapers and Leaders Criticise and Few Praise Him.

TAFT MEN ARE CONFIDENT

Believe the Colonel's Columbus Speech Was Fatal—Koenig Says New York Will Be For Taft.

Col. Theodore Roosevelt's announcement of his willingness to accept the Republican nomination for President, printed above, was handed out at The Outlook office last evening by Secretary Frank Harper, in the absence of the Colonel, who is in Boston. The Roosevelt letter was in answer to the following:

Chicago, Feb. 10, 1912.

We, the undersigned Republican Governors, assembled for the purpose of considering what will best insure the continuation of the Republican Party as a useful agency of good government, declare it our belief, after a careful investigation of the facts, that a large majority of the Republican voters of the country favor your nomination, and a large majority of the people favor your election as the next President of the United States.

We believe that your candidacy will insure success in the next campaign. We believe that you represent as no other man represents those principles and policies upon which we must appeal for a majority of the votes of the American people, and which, in our opinion, are necessary for the happiness and prosperity of the country.

We believe that, in view of this public demand, you should soon declare whether, if the nomination for the Presidency comes to you unsolicited and unsought, you will accept it.

In submitting this request we are not considering your personal interests. We do not regard it as proper to consider either the interests or the preference of any man as regards the nomination for the Presidency. We are expressing our sincere belief and best judgment as to what is demanded of you in the interests of the people as a whole. And we feel that you would be unresponsive to a plain public duty if you should decline to accept the nomination coming as the voluntary expression of the wishes of a majority of the Republican voters of the United States through the action of their delegates in the next National Convention. Yours truly,

WILLIAM E. GLASSCOCK,
CHESTER H. ALDRICH,
ROBERT P. BASS,
JOSEPH M. CAREY,
CHASE S. OSBORN,
W. R. STUBBS,
HERBERT S. HADLEY.

The Hon. Theodore Roosevelt, New York City, N. Y.

ROOSEVELT CONSENTS.

New York, Feb. 24, 1912.

Gentlemen: I deeply appreciate your letter, and I realize to the full the heavy responsibility it puts upon me, expressing as it does the carefully considered convictions of the men elected by popular vote to stand as the heads of government in their several States.

I absolutely agree with you that this matter is not one to be decided with any reference to the personal preferences or interests of any man, but purely from the standpoint of the interests of the people as a whole.

I will accept the nomination for President if it is tendered to me, and I will adhere to this decision until the convention has expressed its preference.

One of the chief principles for which I have stood, and for which I now stand, and which I have always endeavored and always shall endeavor to reduce to action, is the genuine rule of the people, and therefore I hope that so far as possible the people may be given the chance, through direct primaries, to express their preference as to who shall be the nominee of the Republican Presidential Convention.

Very truly yours,
THEODORE ROOSEVELT.

The Hon. WILLIAM E. GLASSCOCK, Governor of the State of West Virginia, Charleston, West Va.
The Hon. CHESTER H. ALDRICH, Governor of the State of Nebraska, Lincoln, Neb.
The Hon. ROBERT P. BASS, Governor of the State of New Hampshire, Concord, N. H.
The Hon. JOSEPH M. CAREY, Governor of the State of Wyoming, Cheyenne, Wyo.
The Hon. CHASE S. OSBORN, Governor of the State of Michigan, Lansing, Mich.
The Hon. W. R. STUBBS, Governor of the State of Kansas, Topeka, Kan.
The Hon. HERBERT S. HADLEY, Governor of the State of Missouri, Jefferson, Mo.

His "No Third Term" Pledge.

On Nov. 8, 1904, Col. Roosevelt made this announcement at the White House:

On the 4th of March next I shall have served three and a half years, and this three and a half years constitute my first term. The wise custom which limits the President to two terms regards the substance and not the form, and under no circumstances will I be a candidate for or accept another nomination.

On Dec. 11, 1907, he declared:

I have not changed and shall not change that decision thus announced.

In an editorial article two weeks ago The Outlook paved the way for the Colonel's present attitude by declaring that his announcement in 1904 was to be interpreted as referring to a consecutive third term. It gave this illustration:

When a man says at breakfast in the morning, "No, thank you, I will not take any more coffee," it does not mean that he will not take any more coffee to-morrow morning or next week or next month or next year.

There was not much disposition among Republican leaders last night to comment on the Roosevelt statement. In Washington the feeling, even among the progressives, was not one of great jubilation. It was said there that the Colonel's Columbus speech had driven into the Taft ranks some State leaders who had planned to line up with Roosevelt when he announced his candidacy.

President Taft was quoted yesterday as being confident of the result, and his supporters saw no serious menace to his chances in the Roosevelt announcement.

In the press comment obtained last night by THE TIMES, the preponderance of opinion was that Col. Roosevelt was doomed to defeat.

ROOSEVELT GETS CHICAGO CHEERS; TAFT WINS 62 MORE DELEGATES

Contests All Decided, President's Managers Claim Victory.

566 ON FIRST BALLOT

Rivals Dispute These Figures, Claiming Doubtful Delegates in Many States.

"THEFT," SAYS COLONEL

Spends Night Hours Fixing Plans to Open a Whirlwind Campaign To-day.

SEEK FOR WAVERING ONES

Roosevelt to Make a Personal Plea to Each of Them for Support.

NO FIGURES FOR COLONEL

His Managers Decline to Issue Detailed Claims—Roosevelt Won't Say He'll Attend Convention.

Special to The New York Times.

CHICAGO, June 15.—Col. Roosevelt came to the convention city this afternoon, roared forth to a cheering crowd his defiance of the National Republican Committee and of everybody else who would "dare to thwart the will of the people" by refusing him the nomination for the Presidency, and then started to summon his leaders to him and tell them what they must do to prevent the control of the convention by "the thieves, robbers, and highbinders" who would "steal the people's liberties."

The quoted words are his, as used in his public utterances here to-day, and each time that the Colonel uses them he gathers new frenzy. He is in conference now, which will last most of the night, with "My seven Governors," "Boss" Flinn of Pennsylvania, Ormsby McHarg, his Southern negro delegate missionary; George W. Perkins, and others, trying to figure out ways and means to overcome the Taft forces.

The Taft leaders are going ahead in their efforts to hold their delegates and gain new ones as though the spectacular advent of Roosevelt was simply a big side show to the convention, for they say that they have him beaten. While they are looking to him and his followers to make the convention proceedings the most disorderly in the history of the Republican Party, they say they have the votes to renominate the President, and they give the figures, which the Roosevelt leaders do not.

Lowest Estimate 556 Votes.

The contests before the National Committee to-day resulted in Col. Roosevelt getting 6 votes, giving him a total of 18 out of 238 contests. Taft had 62 delegates seated, of whom 26 had been conceded to him, making his net gain for the day 36 votes. This should give Taft 566 delegates on the first ballot, or 26 more than is necessary for a nomination. However, a more conservative estimate gives him only 556 on the first ballot.

This does not mean that the renomination of Taft is an assured fact. It is simply a presentation of the figures as they can be obtained from the best sources possible. What the 1,078 delegates to this tempest-torn convention will do before they get through is open to all sorts of conjecture.

It can fairly be said, though, that the thunderbolt which Col. Roosevelt attempted to hurl into the convention crowd this afternoon quickly passed over, and by 10 o'clock to-night the crowds had cooled down and were waiting for him to give them something else to howl about.

A Fight from the Start.

Precedent promises to be thrown to the winds in this convention. It is seriously stated to-night that the Roosevelt leaders, believing that they will go down to defeat if the roll call of the convention as it has been made up by the National Committee is allowed to stand, intend to try to upset it at the very outset of the proceedings instead of waiting to present their claims to the Committee on Credentials.

This would mean that as soon as the temporary roll was read some Roosevelt man would move to correct it by substituting the names of Roosevelt claimants who have been cast out by the National Committee for Taft delegates who have been seated by the same body. It would be an entirely revolutionary move in convention proceedings. But it would serve to turn the convention into a rough house at the very start which might serve the purpose of an angry minority who openly advocate a bolt if they cannot win.

Coup Planned by Taft Men?

Equally revolutionary is a plan which it is stated that the Taft leaders have in mind. Taft will have a majority on the temporary roll call as prepared by the National Committee. What the Taft leaders want to be assured of is that they have a majority that will control the convention for them in its three vital functions—the naming of the temporary and permanent Chairmen, the naming of the Committee on Credentials, and the naming of the Committee on Resolutions.

Unless so assured, it is said, the Taft leaders plan to keep the National Committee in continuous session, and, if necessary, increase the Taft vote in the convention by referring back to the National Committee contests which have been decided in Roosevelt's favor for revision.

This seems like a wild plan, but the Republican Party here now is groping in a political wilderness.

A National Convention is always an inspiring spectacle, and its proceedings are calculated, as a rule, to arouse a feeling of patriotic pride in every believer in a republican form of Government. There is one shadow over this gathering, however, that the men who are not rank factionalists do not like to discuss. That is the belief that they have down deep in their hearts that the nominee for President may owe his selection to the votes of Southern negro delegates.

Both factions are charging that bribery is going on. It will take a roll call to prove it circumstantially. If the negro delegates are not found voting as they were pledged or instructed to vote there is going to be an awful howl and a solidification of the solid South for the Democratic candidate that will make campaigning for Taft or Roosevelt there a waste of time.

The Roosevelt hopes of victory seem to hinge largely upon winning away enough Taft negro delegates to make up their deficit. For this purpose they claim at least thirty of the men on the first ballot. But there will be only fifty-seven negroes in all in the convention, and most of these, by actual count, are ironbound for the President.

The Taft manager in charge of negro delegates concedes at most only eight Taft men to the Colonel, with the qualification that probably the number will not exceed three or four. Their personal standing at home, they say, will make a violation of their instructions impossible.

Colonel Hopes to Run Against Bryan.

Col. Roosevelt, according to his intimate friends, is obsessed with the idea that if he captures the nomination here the Democratic Convention at Baltimore will be compelled to nominate William Jennings Bryan against him. He thoroughly believes that the whole country is inflamed with what he calls the progressive spirit, and cannot conceive that the Democratic Party might oppose him with a conservative like Gov. Wilson of New Jersey or Gov. Harmon of Ohio.

Col. Roosevelt definitely declined to-night the suggestion that he stand as a candidate for the position of Temporary Chairman of the convention. This proposal has been discussed more or less during the past few days. It was made to the Colonel to-night by Alexander P. Moore of Pittsburgh.

Senator Elihu Root will arrive here to-morrow. By to-morrow evening it is expected the building of the Taft platform will be begun. The platform will be a conservative document, denouncing the radical doctrines of Col. Roosevelt, recommending progress along conservative lines, and upholding the Administration of President Taft and recommending his re-election because he has shown his veneration of the Constitution and representative government.

New York Resolution for Taft.

Seventy-seven of the ninety members of the New York State delegation met to-night and sixty-nine of them voted for a resolution supporting the candidacy of Taft and opposing that of Roosevelt. Timothy L. Woodruff was one of three who did not vote. The five who voted against it were those well known to be against the President.

After the conference of the New York State delegation to-night Chairman Barnes stated that the New York vote now stands Taft 76, Roosevelt 9; against Roosevelt, but not yet for Taft, 3; doubtful 2.

The idea of a Roosevelt-La Follette combination to defeat Senator Root for Temporary Chairman by the election of Mr. La Follette's man, Gov. McGovern of Wisconsin, got a little more impetus to-day. Mr. McGovern announced his candidacy. The Roosevelt people are in somewhat of a dilemma over the scheme because the La Follette men still maintain their air of haughty indifference toward the whole proposition, while it has been discovered that the ten Cummins votes cannot be swung for it.

La Follette's thirty-six votes will be cast solidly for McGovern, and the Badgers say they do not care whether the Roosevelt men vote that way or not. The Roosevelt votes in Illinois and probably in New York and Ohio will go for Root, so that the whole La Follette and Cummins strength would have to be cast for McGovern to put him through. To-day, however, the Cummins men were loudly announcing that they did not want McGovern and did want Borah. Borah was the original Roosevelt choice for the place. Cummins himself is nearer to the Borah type of progressive than to the La Follette-McGovern stripe, and his followers intend to make that fact manifest when the vote comes. They have not yet gone so far as to say that if McGovern and Root are the opposing candidates they will put up Borah anyhow, but the gossip in the Cummins headquarters was truculent enough to justify that impression.

June 16, 1912

BOLT STARTS IN CREDENTIALS COMMITTEE AND ROOSEVELT MEN ALL WALK OUT; PLAN NOW IS FOR A THIRD PARTY

Hot-headed Roosevelt Men Force Action Ahead of Schedule.

IN ROW OVER CONTEST

Quit Room Once, Ordered Back, and Then All But One Quit for Good.

COLONEL'S PARTY PLANS

Full Ticket in Every State Which He Believes He Can Control.

TO SPLIT THE SOLID SOUTH

Also Confident of Winning the West, Pennsylvania, and West Virginia.

HADLEY FOR RUNNING MATE

Wants the Missouri Governor Because He Is a Fighting Man—May Be at Convention To-day.

CHICAGO, June 19.—After bolting once from the Credentials Committee "under the orders of Col. Roosevelt," and being called back by Roosevelt managers to the committee room, all of the Roosevelt members of the Credentials Committee except R. R. McCormick of Chicago left again at 11:45 o'clock to-night, declaring they were out for good.

The cause of the bolt was the refusal of the committee to give a full hearing on all contest cases. After the Roosevelt men had left, the committee took up the cases, but had not proceeded far when a motion to adjourn until 9 o'clock to-morrow morning was proposed and carried.

Senator Dixon, the Roosevelt campaign manager, who had been hurriedly summoned after the first bolt, left with the Roosevelt men.

"These men are tired and will go home and go to bed," he said. "I think the other fellows are wasting time to stay here to-night."

Francis H. Heney and Hugh T. Halbert of Minnesota, who had led the bolt, were the only ones who would talk at length on the situation.

"Is this a bolt?" Mr. Heney was asked.

"You can call it what you want to," he said. "These are the facts: Every Roosevelt man with the exception of McCormick has walked out because he was convinced from the rules which were proposed that there was no intention of giving a valid hearing.

"The cases that were heard before the National Committee were a farce, and this is a worse one. The line-up was perfectly plain, 32 to 19."

Mr. Halbert declared the break came because the committee limited time and excluded evidence.

"We claimed and insisted that the Credentials Committee should hear all evidence, as a court of original jurisdiction, and that the National Convention, not the Credentials Committee, should be the court of last resort."

Before adjourning the committee adopted the amended rules by a vote of 36 to 4.

Chairman Devine said the adjournment was taken because most of the contesting had left the Coliseum.

How the Bolt Started.

Th Roosevelt men broke out of the committee room at 10:30 o'clock to-night, after attempting to break open the doors and bring all newspaper men into the room.

The doors of the committee room were suddenly thrown open by J. J. Sullivan of Ohio, who rushed out with the cry: "All Roosevelt men walk out."

He was followed by Hugh T. Halbert of Minnesota, Francis H. Heney of California, Georgt L. Record of New Jersey, and other Roosevelt men.

As they pushed open the swinging doors after Sullivan, they cried out to the newspaper men:

"All newspaper men come inside and see what they are trying to do to us."

Col. Shay, assistant sergeant at arms, shouted to the doorkeeper to admit no one. The Roosevelt forces shouted again for every one to come in. Mr. Thayer called for policemen, who pushed their way through, and kept the crowd from coming in.

The Roosevelt men poured from the room, declaring they were acting under orders from Col. Roosevelt.

"Everybody go to the Florentine Room at the Congress," shouted one man.

They rushed out, followed by the crowd, and in the street outside of the Coliseum they were overtaken by Secretary Hayward.

Roosevelt's Orders, They Say.

"Why did you act that way?" he demanded of Heney. "Why didn't you wait until some rules had been passed?"

"We are acting under the direct orders of Col. Roosevelt," retorted Heney.

"We are obeying a better General than you," shouted George Record of New Jersey. "He told us to leave that room and we did it."

Hugh T. Halbert declared the break came as the result of the refusal of the majority in the committee to open all evidence in the cases. Mr. Halbert presented resolutions asking that the temporary roll of the convention be considered as only prima facie evidence of the right of delegates to sit, and that all evidence, testimony, and the like be gone into.

He declared the committee refused to do this, and attempted to "gag" the minority by making rules that would have left the action of the National Committe as practically decisive in all the contests.

Mr. Heney later came back to the lobby and urged the Roosevelt contestants to go to the Florentine Room of the Congress, where the Roosevelt headquarters are located, and be heard by the members of the Credentials Committee representing Roosevelt.

Believing they had acted too hastily some of the Roosevelt men, including Mr. Halbert, returned to the committee room after a short conference in the street. While Mr. Record and Mr. Heney declared they were acting under Mr. Roosevelt's direct orders, others believed they should have remained until definite action was taken by the committee upon the time for argument, and the character of evidence to be considered.

R. R. McCormick of Chicago also remained in the committee room. Mr. Halbert declared they would stay until they had obtained a vote on his resolution for consideration of all evidence in the contest cases, and would then again leave.

James R. Garfield of Ohio, former Secretary of the Interior, came to the door and attempted to enter the room. It was understood he had some message from Col. Roosevelt. The police and doorkeepers thrust him back, although one of the committeemen attempted to pull him in.

With the aid of Ormsby McHarg, he was ushered into a committee waiting room through a side door. Later the full bolt was ordered.

The rules which brought on the fight were presented by James A. Hemenway of Indiana. They provided:

"That no contest cases should be considered except those appealed from the decisions of the National Committee.

"That none should be taken up where the decision of the National Committee had been unanimous.

"That cases should be consolidated where such action had been taken at the previous hearing.

"That the contestants who were not seated (usually the Roosevelt men) should open the arguments.

"That ten minutes be allowed for State cases and five for district cases for counsel on each side.

"That no evidence be considered that was not considered at the previous hearing."

The last two provisions brought on the fight, Hugh T. Halbert of Minnesota and other Roosevelt men claiming the committee should open all evidence in all cases.

After the return of the Roosevelt members an amendment was introduced making the limit of time on State cases thirty minutes for each side and for district cases fifteen minutes.

On the roll call adopting the rules R. R. McCormick of Illinois, C. St. Clair of Idaho, W. S. Lauder of North Dakota, and John M. Early of Tennessee voted "No."

The Roosevelt men who were shown by this roll call to be absent were: F. J. Heney of California, Ralph Harris, Kansas; Lex N. Mitchell, Pennsylvania; Jesse H. Libby Maine; Edward G. Carrington, Jr., Maryland; Hugh T. Halbert, Minnesota; H. E. Sackett, Nebraska; C. H. Cowles, North Carolina; J. J. Sullivan, Ohio; Don L. Norton, Oklahoma; A. V. Swift, Oregon, and S. X. Way, South Dakota.

Jesse A. Tolerton of Missouri, who was one of those who made the first rush to the door during the first bolt, declared that he had never intended to leave the meeting, but had rushed outside to bring in the newspaper men.

"Missouri is not bolting," he said, "but will vote for Roosevelt in the convention."

R. R. McCormick, when he came out of the room, said he was "with the Roosevelt men in spirit, but perhaps not to the extent of leaving the hall."

"They were forced out of the committee," he said. "Rules were adopted that were outrageous."

After adjournment Chairman Devine declared that the committee would take up the contests to-morrow morning, and finish them as rapidly as possible, in their regular order.

Before the Row.

The Credentials Committee organized immediately after the adjournment of the convention, and in the first test the Taft forces elected Thomas H. Devine Chairman over the Roosevelt candidate, W. T. Lauder of North Dakota, by a vote of 30 to 18, four members being absent or not voting.

The Taft forces expected the vote on the majority of the contest cases to be 33 to 19, basing their prediction on the attitude of the respective delegations on the convention roll calls of the last two days.

Immediately after the election of Mr. Devine a recess was taken until 9:30 P. M. Soon after the night session opened the row started.

June 20, 1912

TAFT RENOMINATED BY THE REPUBLICAN CONVENTION

Sherman Again Chosen Running Mate of the President.

VOTE FOR TAFT WAS 561

107 for Roosevelt, but 344 Obeyed Him and Refused to Vote.

DELEGATES COME TO BLOWS

Convention on the Verge of Riots Several Times While the Balloting Was On.

ROOSEVELT SENDS DEFIANCE

Through Allen of Kansas the Colonel Repeats His Cry of Fraud and Theft.

WOMAN LEADS TAFT CHEERS

Widow of Gen. Logan Starts Demonstration as Harding of Ohio Ends Nominating Speech.

Special to The New York Times.

CHICAGO, June 22.—Amid scenes of turbulence and disorder, which at times bordered upon a riot, the Republican National Convention wound up its labors late to-night by nominating William Howard Taft of Ohio for President and James Schoolcraft Sherman of New York for Vice President.

President Taft was renominated at 9:28 o'clock by the narrow majority of 21 votes. The total vote cast for him was 561. Vice President Sherman did much better. His vote was announced as 597.

The vote on the Presidential candidates was:

Taft	561
Roosevelt	107
Cummins	17
La Follette	41
Hughes	2
Not voting	344
Absent	6
Total	1,078

President Taft's and Senator La Follette's names were the only ones formally presented to the convention. The votes for the others were cast by delegates who insisted on following their instructions and two who favored Justice Hughes.

While this nomination was made Col. Roosevelt had declared himself a candidate for President, and announced the organization of a third party to meet in convention in August. The Grand Old Party is for the moment smashed to pieces.

Before it proceeded to its final business Col. Roosevelt informed the convention through Henry J. Allen of Kansas that his delegates would not vote on any proposition that came before it. The reason given was that robbery and fraud controlled the convention and that it was not a Republican convention any more, but an illegal and unofficial body. These unpalatable things were said to the convention in so many words. It howled and protested, but not for long, and the amazing thing about it was that such statements could be made without evoking more of a fight.

Listen to Bitter Attack.

There has always been a tradition that no matter how bitter your feelings may be against the man who is opposing your candidate you must preserve the fiction of its all being a friendly disagreement, your real antagonism being to the party which is to nominate the opposing candidate. To-day that fiction wa entirely disregarded. Taft was renominated in the face of a plain declaration to the convention by some of its own members that it was fraudulent and crooked, and that its ticket would be defeated at the polls.

Any other convention would have roared such a speaker off the platform in a tempest of indignation. This one kept silent during most of these assaults and merely barked sullenly at the worst of them.

By the Colonel's orders the Roosevelt men sat mute during the session and refused to vote on any proposition. His name was not presented to the convention. Both the Colonel and Allen explained that this was because, having exhausted every means of protest and finding that they were the victims of plain, ordinary burglary and highway robbery, they refused any longer to take part in or sanction by their participation the proceedings of such an assemblage.

Allen, speaking for the Colonel, and the Colonel, speaking for himself through a printed statement, read by Allen, declared that this was not a convention at all; that it was made up by the seating of men who had no right to sit in it, and that to countenance such performances by taking part in the deliberation of such a body was impossible. Therefore the Colonel ordered his followers not to vote either on the rules, the platform, the nominations, or anything else that might come before this illegal and piratical body. When Allen said these things, with the announcement that he was saying them for Col. Roosevelt, the crowd in the hall—William J. Bryan being one of them—joined heartily in the applause that the Roosevelt men set up.

Disorder at the End.

This convention will go down in political history as one of the most momentous in the annals of the Republican Party. It will surely be remembered as one of the longest drawn out, for it has been in progress for almost a week. The scenes that attended the closing session to-night will render it conspicuous as one of the most rowdy and disorderly of party gatherings.

The representatives of the sedate Commonwealth of Massachusetts in the convention were the central figures in one of the most turbulent scenes to-night. Half of the delegation, who were for Col. Roosevelt in pursuance of a pact, declined to vote at all. In doing this they followed the other States called earlier on the roll. When Senator Root proceeded to force a vote from unwilling Bay State delegates by calling the alternate where a delegate did not vote, half of the Massachusetts men stood up in a body and shook their fists at the Chairman.

Again and again scenes of that nature were enacted which delayed the convention's labors hours beyond the time when it should have finished.

Roosevelt Men Jeer Taft's Name.

A convention wherein the name of its candidate is received with jeers, hisses, and taunts when he is proposed for nomination cannot be said to start out on its campaign under the happiest auspices. That was happened to Mr. Taft to-night, not only when Warren G. Harding of Ohio presented his name, but every time that name was mentioned.

A convention which knows perfectly well that at the moment it is making its nomination the defeated candidate is busy arranging for a third party cannot be said to be beginning its campaign under cheerful auguries.

Col. Roosevelt was declaring himself a candidate for a third party nomination to be made, he said, in August, and the delegates were aware of that fact.

Renominated for President by the Republican Convention in Chicago.

What makes it worse is that there is no certainty about the attitude of Senator La Follette. A few nights ago his friends and managers were announcing positively that under no circumstances would La Follette bolt. Yet when the conservative Taft platform was read to the convention to-night by ex-Vice President Fairbanks and adopted by the usual vote, Walter L. Houser, La Follette's manager, arose on the floor and announced that the Senator would not be bound by a platform which did not stand for progressive principles. What this means cannot yet be definitely ascertained. Houser refuses to explain. It seems to mean that La Follette will stand by the candidate in a sort of half-way fashion, while at the same time denouncing the platform.

The Silent Protest.

The silent protest ordered by the Colonel was not as silent as it should have been. Some of his followers refused to go with him. After the Colonel discovered that he could not get up a respectable bolt he evolved the idea of having his men sit silent in the convention, and refuse to vote on any proposition that came before it. He got out his orders in a printed pamphlet, and had it distributed to the delegates.

Then he designated Henry J. Allen of Kansas to get up in the convention and read the pamphlet. The Roosevelt men heard their master's voice as uttered through the Allen megaphone, but not all of them obeyed it.

Only five of the Roosevelt men from New York stood out. Illinois, which is a strong Roosevelt State, voted on the platform. Missouri and Idaho, the States for which Gov. Hadley and Senator Borah are responsible to Roosevelt, voted. On most questions, however, the Roosevelt States obeyed the Colonel's orders and refrained from casting a vote. It was the West Point "silence" administered by a great party to its President and its Presidential candidate.

The work went on throughout the day. On the part of the Roosevelt men there ceased to be any protests; the fight was all gone from them.

State after State was taken up in the fight over credentials, which was not really a fight any more, and in each case the Taft men voted to sustain anything that the committee might report. The Roosevelt men mechanically and wearily voted the other way. The convention buzzed and hummed with conversation, and during most of the time the votes were inaudible.

The Committee on Rules and that on Permanent Organization made their reports, the latter retaining Senator Root in the Chairmanship, and by prearrangement Col. Roosevelt's order to his followers to keep still during the rest of the convention was then read to a convention which already had it in pamphlet form. It was irregular and unparliamentary to the last degree, but the Taft men, knowing that it would make not the slightest difference, had consented to have Allen read it, and Chairman Root ordered the reading. He asked unanimous consent, but that was a mere form, for if the unanimous consent had been refused he would have had Allen read it just the same.

June 23, 1912

WILSON BACKS UP BRYAN'S PROTEST

Parker Issue Makes Sharp Line-up Between Party Factions.

EXPECT JUDGE'S DEFEAT

Bryanites Say Majority of the National Committee Oppose Him for Chairman.

DENY PARKER IS RYAN MAN

Bryan Said to Have Welcomed Injection of Judge to Project His Own Nomination.

ALL EYES ON NEBRASKAN

Some Leaders Fear Situation Will Develop Similar to That at Chicago.

FOR A LABOR TARIFF PLANK

Redfield Would Feature the Tariff's Human Side as Being a Burden to Modest Homes.

Special to The New York Times.

BALTIMORE, June 22.—This convention is going to develop into a straight line-up between the Progressive and the conservative wings of the Democratic Party. The correspondent of THE NEW YORK TIMES who writes this, having arrived to-day from the Republican National Convention at Chicago, during the sessions of which he had the pleasure of sitting next to William Jennings Bryan, can see nothing so important as this in the situation here to-night, particularly in view of this answer sent by Gov. Wilson of New Jersey to Mr. Bryan's message asking him to stand out against Alton B. Parker as Temporary Chairman of this convention on the ground that the Temporary Chairman should be a Progressive:

"You are quite right. Before hearing of your message I clearly stated my position. The Baltimore convention is to be a convention of Progressives, of men who are Progressives in principle and by conviction. It must, if it is not to be put in a wrong light before the convention, express its convictions in its organization and in its choice of men who are to speak for it.

"You are to be a member of this convention, and are entirely within your rights in doing everything within your power to bring that result about. No one will doubt where my sympathies lie, and you will, I am sure, find my friends in the convention acting upon clear conviction and always in the interest of the people's cause. I am happy in the confidence that they need no suggestion from me."

There is to be seen a community of interest between Gov. Wilson, an avowed candidate claiming about 300 pledged votes in this convention, and Mr. Bryan, who is not an avowed candidate, but who certainly has the candidate habit, which will be watched closely.

Charles F. Murphy of New York is watching it. Roger Sullivan of Illinois is watching it. Tom Taggart is watching it, and the leaders of the Clark, Gaynor, Marshall, Harmon, and Underwood booms are watching it. You can't blame them, for while Mr. Bryan has always expressed his liking for Gov. Wilson as a candidate their union on an issue that will unquestionably be decisive is one to make the managers of Presidential aspirants sit up and take notice.

Says Bryan Isn't in the Race.

Everybody is, of course, asking whether Bryan is going to stay out of the race for the Presidential nomination, as he has repeatedly said he would. Dr. P. L. Hall of Nebraska, who has been a Bryan man ever since Bryan went to congress in 1890, and who usually knows just what plans the Peerless Leader has in mind, was told this afternoon that the word was being passed around here that Bryan's declaration of his opposition to Judge Parker as Temporary Chairman was very ill-timed.

"Why, how can that be?" said Dr. Hall. "This is a convention dominated by the progressive element. Bryan is progressive. Parker is not. Why, then, should Bryan be criticised for opposing Parker to be Temporary Chairman?"

"But," was suggested, "it is being said that Bryan is really promoting his own candidacy and that the purpose of bringing on this fight against Parker is to get the centre of the stage, so that he can have an issue on which to appeal to the delegates and turn them toward him from candidates who think they have them lined up for themselves. They say he has been a candidate all along."

"I have a letter here that should settle all that talk," said Dr. Hall, reaching into his coat pocket. "It is from Bryan. Came since I arrived here. It was very frank and straightforward."

But Dr. Hall did not have the letter. He said it was in his room, and that its substance was that Bryan was not a candidate for the nomination, and did not want to be nominated. Bryan said further in the letter, Dr. Hall stated, that he would not allow his name to be used, as he was sure he could do more for the Democratic Party by promoting harmony and the adoption of a real Democratic platform if he was not to run upon it.

That was important news indeed, and Dr. Hall was urged to go to his room and get the letter. Its publication, he was told, would be a real service to the Democratic Party at this time. Dr. Hall seemed to agree with this, and started for his room to give the letter out for publication. But Dr. Hall never got back with that letter, so the public for the present must be satisfied with his verbal summary of it.

The reason that Dr. Hall changed his mind about giving the letter out was that he was waylaid by some Bryan men, who pleaded that its publication would be doing Mr. Bryan a great injustice. Dr. Hall finally agreed to wait until to-morrow and let Mr. Bryan speak for himself.

Gov. Wilson certainly played a master stroke by replying to Mr. Bryan's request to stand out against Alton B. Parker as Temporary Chairman as promptly and as flatly as he did. The other candidates either could not or did not reply as definitely, and that is the reason why Gov. Wilson is being advertised throughout the land, and particularly to all the State delegations traveling in this direction, as standing shoulder to shoulder with Mr. Bryan for a Progressive ticket and a Progressive platform, while the position of the other candidates is negative.

Parker Row Up To-morrow.

The row over the selection of Alton B. Parker will be settled on Monday if Mr. Parker's name is not withdrawn in the meantime. There was a good deal of talk all day about Mr. Bryan having already beaten the Parker plan, but this talk was confined to the Bryan men. The face of the situation makes it appear that Judge Parker will be set aside by the National Committee. Both sides of the controversy were busy for many hours to-day lining up their forces. After this work had been completed, the statement was made that Judge Parker would lack enough votes to seat him in the temporary chair. Plenty of figures were forthcoming to prove this assertion. All of these figures are based on past performances. The men who were known to have been friends and supporters of the Nebraska leader were placed on his side of the score, and all of the others were set down on the Parker side. The result showed thirty-two National Committeemen in opposition to Parker and twenty in favor of him.

After these figures had been given out by the Bryan men there was a rumor that a meeting of the sub-committee had been called for to-night for the purpose of selecting a less objectionable man for the Chairmanship. Charles F. Murphy was asked about Parker, and he said: "We will stick to Parker to the last."

Later came a story saying that Parker had sent word to his friends here that in view of the opposition to his selection he desired to have his name withdrawn as a candidate for the place, but this report could not be verified. If it should happen that the Bryan matter is disposed of by Parker's withdrawal either by his own action or by the action of the sub-committee the Bryan men say they will be sorry.

Instructed Against Parker.

The Kansas delegation held a meeting this evening and instructed National Committeeman Sapp not to vote for Parker for Temporary Chairman at the meeting of the National Committee on Monday. The delegation is instructed for Clark and backers of the other candidates hailed their action as a verification of their predictions that the Clark strength can't be delivered to the support of the New York man, as the leaders have been trying to arrange.

By injecting Parker into the situation the issue between the Bryan Progressives and the conservatives, say the Bryan men, has been made sharp and clear. Reports from the headquarters of the Nebraska man indicated that the selection of Parker tickled Bryan more than any political happening since he was last nominated for the Presidency. It is said for him that the selection of Parker was instigated by the financial interests, that Parker is the counsel for all of the interests that put Root in the Presidential chair at the Chicago Convention, and that to permit him to preside will place the Democratic Party on the same level as the Republican Party, and might lead to the defeat of the Democratic candidate.

Anyway, it is certain that the Bryan men have gone into the fight to beat Parker with the highest spirits. It is a fight that has made many of them hopeful of the nomination of the candidate that will represent everything that Bryan stands for now, but not any of the things that be stood for in his three campaigns.

The Bryan men always make this clear. They want everybody to understand that the Bryan of 1912 is a made-over Bryan and that he has been through the fire and been purged of all the heresies that brought him three defeats. His friends say that as Bryan stands for progress he must himself have advanced. Whatever platform is adopted by this convention will suit Bryan, it is said, so long as it advocates progress.

While the enthusiasm for Bryan is brisk enough in many quarters, there is no little talk of his nomination. One of his closest friends said: "His nomination is possible, but not probable."

A glance at the National Committeemen who, it is said, will resist the selection of Parker as Temporary Chairman would indicate that Bryan's strength was sufficient to control the convention absolutely and all of the preliminaries. But this is not so. Some of the committeemen who will vote with him on the Parker proposal would be against him if he were a candidate.

Baltimore does not seem like a convention city to-night, but rather like a town that was celebrating old home week. The streets are ablaze with electric lights, the buildings are decked with flags, and there is a band playing in the public square. All the boys and girls in town are thronging as though the occasion was Mardi Gras at Coney Island, but there are none of the excited assemblages of men shouting for their favorites, such as were seen in Chicago the week past. It is just as well that there are not. Those rushing crowds will come to-morrow and Monday, and the Lord only knows what they will do with themselves, for this city is absolutely lacking in places in which crowds can assemble and keep moving.

The New York State Progressives opened headquarters here to-night, with Gov. Wilson's name over their door. State Senator J. Franklin Roosevelt, who led the fight against Tammany Hall in the last election of a United States Senator, said to-night that between twenty and twenty-five of the New York delegates were for Wilson, but as long as the leaders held them to the unit rule they would feel bound to vote with the majority.

"Wilson delegates are scattered all over the State," he said. "But the unit rule is a good old Democratic doctrine, especially revered in the Empire State, and we have no hope that it will be abrogated at this convention."

Anti-Parker Committeemen.

The reason of this is said to be the antagonism of many of the delegates in the West and South to Parker and the men who are charged with being behind the movement to set him in a conspicuous position before the Democratic Party. A glance at the National Committee, who, it is said, will vote against Parker, shows the names of a number who are deeply interested in other candidates. Here is the list of the committeemen who are said to be willing to vote against Parker for Temporary Chairman:

Hall of Nebraska, Woodson of Kentucky, Michelson of Arizona, Cummings of Connecticut, Saulsbury of Delaware, Jennings of Florida, Wade of Iowa, Sapp of Kansas, Ewing of Louisiana, Jones of Maine, Lynch of Minnesota, Williams of Mississippi, Goltra of Missouri, Kremer of Montana, Reed of New Hampshire, Jones of New Mexico, Hudspeth of New Jersey, Daniels of North Carolina, Collins of North Dakota, Garber of Ohio, Brady of Oklahoma, Miller of Oregon, Tillman of South Carolina, Mountcastle of Tennessee, Nebeker of Utah, McGraw of West Virginia, Davies of Wisconsin, Osborne of Wyoming, Daly of Alaska, Newman of the District of Columbia, Waller of Hawaii, and Field of Porto Rico.

All of these men are of the opinion that Bryan is objecting to Parker largely for the reason of drawing the lines between his ancient friends and his ancient enemies, and, while many of them think it is a picayune thing to quarrel over, they appreciate Bryan's point of view and say that as the Nebraskan would insist upon having a division anyway, it is better to have it at the outset of the convention than to risk a bitter fight later on.

They say that the Temporary Chairman of a Democratic convention is a very small job, for it is rarely that the Temporary Chairman is ever continued as the Permanent Chairman, and that the only thing sought for in a Temporary Chairman is a well-known man who can make a good speech. These qualifications, they say, Parker has in a very high degree. But there are other men, they say, who are equally gifted and who would not give Bryan any excuse for opening the convention with a row.

Some of the Tammany men were asking how Bryan stood in regard to Senator O'Gorman, but nobody could answer this question with any certainty that it would be the right answer. Gov. Plaisted of Maine was proposed as a compromise for Temporary Chairman, but the suggestion did not meet with a very enthusiastic reception.

The conservatives are putting on their armor to fight Bryan and the men who will stand with him in the effort to oust Parker. They are of the opinion that if they can beat Bryan in this preliminary skirmish that he will be out of the way in all the subsequent proceedings, and that if he bests them the loss will not amount to much, and they will then know better how to confront him in any fight he may make to inject some of his radical ideas into the platform.

Thomas Taggart of Indiana is one of this sort. He says that there could be no line between progressives and conservatives in a true Democracy, and declared that Parker is no more reactionary to-day than he was when he was Bryan's campaign manager and championed him on the stump. Both sides are making efforts to drag into the whirl the champions of the various candidates. This has frightened the candidates, and the champions of these men are trying to adjust the quarrel, or at the worst to have it strictly confined to the extremists on both sides.

Think They Can Beat Bryan.

Despite the showing among the members of the National Committee; the conservatives believe they can whip Bryan. The Clark men are being coddled by the Bryanites. The Parker men are looking toward the Harmon forces for a good word, and are trying to show them that the hope of their candidate lies in keeping on good terms with the conservatives. The Underwoods are also receiving a good deal of attention, but the one thing that creates a feeling of shyness among the candidates is a lack of knowledge as to just how Bryan stands toward the nomination. They would not like to discover that after they had given Bryan a hand to beat his enemies they had made him strong and influential to dictate the candidate or to snatch the nomination for himself.

"If Bryan wins he will be the biggest man in the convention," the conservatives say.

"Well," the progressives retort, "he will be the biggest man in the convention, anyway."

If Bryan should declare himself out of the race for the nomination and stand for a good, strong, old-fashioned Democratic platform, his friends believe that he would be able to get anything he wants into the platform.

"But where does Bryan stand on the initiative, the referendum, and the recall?" the conservatives ask. The Bryan men say that Bryan will tell them when he arrives here. If there is any reason why it should be answered at this time, when the only question to be settled now is the filling of the Temporary Chair. Ollie James of Kentucky would like to be Temporary Chairman, it is said, and it is also said that his selection would be satisfactory to Bryan, but James will not be chosen. At least this is the general opinion.

The situation here between the two wings of the Democracy is very much the same as the situation in Chicago between the two wings of the Republican Party. It is admitted here that if a conservative is nominated to enter the contest with President Taft that a new progressive party might be formed, andthat both of the old parties might be beaten. Such an outcome of the convention is feared by some of the more thoughtful of the Democrats. Some of these men say that this would be the most gigantic blunder the Democrats could make, when it looks as if a Democratic victory was assured and the ability of the Democrats to blunder is well known. The Bryan men say that all they are striving for is to help the party to avoid blundering. The success of Parker, they say, would at once destroy the confidence of the Democrats in the West and South in the ability of the convention to nominate a man who was not controlled by Wall Street, and that the candidate would begin his fight with a heavy handicap.

There is already much talk of Parker's legal connections. Josephus Daniels of North Carolina, a member of the National Committee, made this statement:

"I believe a mistake was made in the selection of Judge Parker. No Democrat is more misunderstood than he. No one doubts his great ability. I told my colleagues on the sub-committee that some other Democrat should be named for Temporary Chairman. My view was that the selection of Judge Parker would give Roosevelt a chance to make statements which would hurt the party. What I feared was that Roosevelt would go up and down the country and proclaim that he represented the party of progress in America; that Ryan and the special interests of New York had sent Root to Chicago for the Temporary Chairmanship of the Republicans, and Judge Parker, another Ryan attorney, had made the keynote speech in Baltimore.

Ryan Not Behind Parker.

"Of course, I know that Parker is not the voice of Ryan. He is big enough to separate his attorneyship from his political views, but in view of the determination of the American people that neither Ryan nor any other man connected with trusts or public service corporations shall control the party's views I urged the selection of a man who had no personal employment that would result in the injection of the Ryan matter."

Mr. Daniels said that the trouble had been created by the New York organization. He said that a fight should be avoided if possible.

This is about the character of all the talk in opposition to Parker, except that much of it was more virulent and bitter. Nobody believed that the Temporary Chairman had anything to do with making the keynote speech. All of the National Committeemen laughed at the thought. They say that the keynote is the platform, and that in no event would a Temporary Chairman utter it. If he did, they say, he would prove himself a totally unfit Chairman.

In the midst of all this discussion about the Temporary Chairmanship there was some talk about candidates. But this talk was largely scattering, for the reason that only a few of the men in charge of individual booms have yet arrived. Jacob A. Cantor was busy all day getting the city in good shape to welcome the special train that will bring nearly 200 of the Gaynor boomers here on Monday. The activity in the Gaynor headquarters is interesting because none of the men interested in it are ready to admit that the Mayor is really a candidate. Champ Clark is in the lead for the nomination, if any dependence can be placed on noise and bands and buttons and active workers. A close second to him in outbursts of enthusiasm is Woodrow Wilson, and then come the others in a gradually thinning line until Gov. Marshall of Indiana is reached. The Marshall men are putting in some good work. They are distributing typewritten biographies of the Governor and they hand these out and say:

"The Indiana delegation will stand by Marshall to the bitter end."

Everybody agrees that the platform should declare for a downward revision of the tariff, a drastic application of the Anti-Trust law, election of Senators by the people, and an income tax. Many of the more radical delegates say that the platform will also contain a clause for the initiative, the referendum and the recall. The conservatives declare that if it does a bitter fight will be precipitated and that under no circumstances will the conservatives or the middle-of-the road men stand for it.

The first claim of delegates won away by one candidate from another was made to-night at the Harmon headquarters. The men referred to are W. J. Brennan, delegate at large from Pennsylvania, and Joseph Joyce and John O'Toole, delegates from the same State. The preference vote in Pennsylvania was for Wilson, and it has been understood that all the Pennsylvania delegates would vote for Wilson. All three men are members of the Order of Eagles, the head of which is Frank E. Hering, an ardent Harmon supporter.

"What is good enough for Hering is good enough for me," is the declaration attributed to Mr. Brennan, and the others are said to have chimed with a "Here, too."

The Order of Eagles has a membership of 400,000, and the Harmon forces intimate that the friendship existing among the fraternity will have a far-reaching effect on the attitude of the delegates who are members, of whom there are at least a score. The Harmon men have been counting on this influence to bring votes to them on account of the active part Mr. Hering has taken in the Harmon campaign, and say the defection of the three Pennsylvanians confirms their predictions.

When the matter was brought to the attention of the Wilson men they did not deny that the delegates had switched, but remarked that this was the only way in which Harmon could gain delegates, as he had been before the voters in the primaries and had obtained only six votes in them.

The Harmon people were also pointing with pride to-night to the fact that Senator Thomas A. Dean of Fremont, Ohio, who has just arrived here and who is a strong Progressive, is with Harmon heart and soul, in spite of the conservatism attributed to him by his opponents. Senator Dean is the father of the bill in the Ohio Legislature for the direct election of United States Senators.

June 23, 1912

CLARK'S THE NOISIEST OF ALL THE BOOMS

Delegates Whooping It Up for Him and His Managers Claim 612 on the First Ballot.

WILSON MEN CALMLY SURE

Relying on Bryan to Pull Their Candidate Through—Underwood, Harmon, and Gaynor Shouters Active.

Special to The New York Times.

BALTIMORE, Md., June 24.—The activities of the boomers of the various candidates for the Presidential nomination were overshadowed, and to some extent handicapped to-day, by the acuteness of the struggle over the Temporary Chairmanship and the shifting phases of the situation during the day, with the talk alternating between a compromise and a terrific contest between the Progressives and the reactionaries.

This kept the managers guessing, as their plans of campaign hung largely on the outcome of the vote in the National Committee and the final line-up in the convention between Bryan and Parker. This was especially true of the Clark boom, which is essentially an effort to walk off with the nomination by bridging the difference between the two elements in the party. That sort of campaign requires adroit manipulation and the Clark boom has some past masters in the art, headed by ex-Senator Dubois of Idaho, ex-Senator Pettigrew of South Dakota, and Senator Stone of Missouri. But, with its own councils divided, though tending more and more to the Parker side, and with the result of the chairmanship contest in the greatest doubt, the Clark people had to move warily and avoid laying out any very definite programme for nominating their candidate.

The Clark boom, which continues to be the biggest and loudest in town so far as general claims and the talk of delegates is concerned, is the best-equipped of all in the matter of organization, with campaign committees, Executive Committee, Steering Committee, Congressional Committee, and a Special Committee on the Chairmanship. While newly arrived delegates stood in the hall and sang the "Houn' Dog" song and coddled a live speciment of the real Ozark hound, these various committeees were hard at work trying to figure out how, by supporting Parker, they could get enough votes to give them at least a majority on the first or second ballot.

Clark Men for Parker.

The Parkerites apparently converted ex-Senator Dubois, who had been against throwing the Clark strength to the New York man and who trotted out Ollie James, the new Senator from Kentucky, as a candidate when the question came up in the sub-committee. Dubois was said to have reached the conclusion that Parker could be put through the National Committee and through the convention if practically all the Clark strength could be delivered to him. One plan for bringing this about, despite the large Bryan element among the Clark delegates, was to have the delegations vote to support the recommendation of the National Committee, whatever it might be, in the interest of harmony and party regularity. This was done in the case of Washington and a number of other instructed Clark delegations. The theory was that the Clark delegates, many of whom will go to Harmon if a point is reached where they can legitimately take the position that Clark cannot be nominated, would vote for the Speaker on the first ballot certainly and on the second, probably, even if the Clark members of the National Committee should vote for Parker. It was argued that if enough delegations could be tied up to supporting the action of the National Committee, so that it would be possible to elect Parker in the convention, the doubts of some of the wavering National Committeemen would be resolved and enough votes would be lined up to put Parker through the National Committee.

The effect of all this would be, the Clark managers figured out, that they would get the support of the New York, Indiana, and other conservative delegations without the loss of the Bryan men among the delegations on the first two ballots, and it is practically admitted that Clark must win on one or the other or see his forces dispersed among the other candidates. If the 512 delegates now claimed as sure for Clark should vote for him on the first ballot, the addition of New York and Indiana alone would give him a total of 632, a substantial majority of the 1,094 delegates in the convention, and the Clark men figure that once they have a majority the two-thirds vote requisite for nomination would come to them. If they get a majority a great effort will be made to have delegations who voted for other candidates switch to the Speaker before the vote is announced and thus nominate him on the first ballot.

Fear Defections from Clark.

The Clark people are wide awake to the probability of defections right after the start, although they talk confidently of holding their delegates in line indefinitely. The sixteen Maryland delegates, it was said to-day on good authority, will stick to Clark for only one ballot and will then swing to either Harmon or Underwood. The thirty-six delegates from Massachusetts are also lightly attached, and after the first vote most of them are likely to go to Wilson. The Illinois delegation of fifty-eight, most of whom are instructed for Clark, are largely under the domination of Roger C. Sullivan, who is not a Clark man, but may become one if an alliance to make Parker Temporary Chairman and to nominate Clark by conservative votes should be effected. Otherwise the Illinois votes will go elsewhere. There is much Wilson sentiment among them, and the Harmon men claim some of them for their man as second choice.

Clark headquarters were filled with boomers from many States, and they tried to create the impression that the demand for the Speaker was well-nigh universal. Theodore A. Bell, who was Temporary Chairman of the Denver Convention, went down to the station and met a delegation from his State, California, and they marched to their quarters, headed by a band. Among the alternates from the State are three women, Mrs. Emma V. Loy of Los Angeles, Mrs. Robert F. Garner of San Bernardino, and Mrs. J. Henry Stewart of Los Angeles. Mrs. Loy said the women of Southern California were strong for Clark. William Mulvaney and Congressman Pepper spoke up for Iowa.

Col. Hoffman said his fellow-Oklahomans were for Clark as first and second choice. Gov. McCreary of Kentucky declared his delegation would vote for Clark till he was nominated. Frank Lucey said Illinois, whence he hails, and the Middle West generally was solid for the Speaker. L. T. Irwin of Fairfax, Alaska, said a majority of the delegates from that far Territory were for Clark. There is a contesting delegation from Alaska, however, as well as from most of the Territories. Judge P. H. O'Brien, a delegate at large from Michigan, said Clark had a strong following among the twenty-two delegates who arrived to-day out of the State's thirty, but that Wilson and Harmon each claim ten from Michigan.

Whoop It Up for Clark.

Arhtur F. Mullin of Omaha, who was Clark's campaign manager in Nebraska which instructed for the Speaker, talked of his popularity in that State. Ex-Gov. Lon B. Stephens of Missouri predicted that if nominated Clark would carry Missouri by 40,000. Will H. Merritt of Washington said Clark would carry that State by 25,000. Henry G. Dooley of Porto Rico said the six delegates would cast a solid vote, probably for Clark, but here again it must be noted that there is a contesting delegation. Kentucky was represented in the talk by W. Vernon Richardson of Danville.

Mark Ways spoke up for Maryland, and H. C. Little of the Arizona delegates said his colleagues and himself would stick to Clark to the last. The Mississippi delegation is instructed for Underwood, but Governor-elect Vardaman was quoted at Clark headquarters as warmly praising the Missouri candidate. Senator Johnson of Maine, whose delegates are uninstructed, was cited as a strong admirer of the Speaker, and it was intimated that the Maine men would go to him. The Clark people even intimated that there was much sentiment for him in Buffalo, although it is well known that the New York delegates are bound by the unit rule and Clark's Buffalo admirers would have to convert a majority of the ninety delegates from that State before they could cast their own votes for Clark.

To reinforce this talk, the Clark men have arranged for a parade to-morrow, which, they say, will include 10,000 marchers. At the head of each division will be 25 boys, each carrying a banner with the name of a State instructed for Clark. Kansas City, they say, will have 225 men in line, Pittsburgh 200, St. Louis 250, and Washington (D. C.) 500.

A somewhat discordant note was struck by Mrs. Hutton of Washington, one of two women delegates in the convention. She visited Clark headquarters with a view to finding Mrs. Pilzer, a delegate from Colorado, who is Speaker Clark's sister-in-law. Mrs. Hutton lamented that instructions compelled her to vote for Clark at least once, and declared that Bryan should be nominated and nobody but Bryan.

"He will surely be nominated," she said. "I don't think so, I know it. It is the only thing to head off socialism, and will only head it off for a few years. It is a groundhog case this year, and Bryan is the only Democrat we are sure of electing."

Wilson Men Serene.

The Wilson men wore an air of serenity to-day, although they were not claiming everything in sight like the Clark boomers. They believe that the convention is Progressive; that Clark has put himself out of the running by the dickering of his managers with Charles F. Murphy, Roger C. Sullivan, Thomas Taggart, and other conservatives, and that Bryan will be in control and will get behind Wilson. The situation is entirely simple from their point of view and they do not go into claims of picking off a delegate or two here and there. They believe that the issue will turn on the question of progressiveness and conservatism, and that the delegates will come to the front all right once the Bryan element takes control.

W. F. McCombs, the general manager for Wilson, was at first opposed to the Wilson men taking any part in the fight over the Temporary Chairmanship, but Wilson's telegram to Bryan taking sides squarely with him against Parker and the conservatives caused practically all the Wilson men to fall right into line, and the Wilson boom took a perceptible spurt. The advantage gained at that time will be held, according to the views of all the Wilson managers, and they await with confidence the outcome of the struggle over the Chairmanship.

One of the striking features of the undercurrent for Wilson is his strength in the New York delegation. Senator O'Gorman is more than favorable to him, J. Sergeant Cram is quoted as for him, and William G. McAdoo is one of his most enthusiastic supporters. President McAneny of Manhattan, who is not a delegate, tells everybody he is for Wilson, and that if he or some other Progressive is not nominated Roosevelt will sweep the country.

Mr. McAneny, who has talked with many of the New York delegates, said to-day that twenty of the ninety were for the New Jersey man.

The unit rule, of course, is a big element here. Many of the Pennsylvania and Texas delegates, most of whom are instructed for Wilson, are here, and they are whooping it up for him tirelessly at the Stafford Hotel, where their headquarters are, although admitting that two or three of the Pennsylvanians will vote for Harmon. The Chairman of the Kansas delegation, Benjamin J. Sheridan, said that, although they were instructed for Clark, Wilson was the second choice of most of them.

* * * * *

June 25, 1912

CONVENTION BEATS BRYAN, 579 TO 510; PARKER, CHAIRMAN, URGES HARMONY

Nebraskan Fails to Stir the Delegates as of Old.

HIS PARTY GRIP BROKEN

Little Fear Now of a Stampede to Make Him the Candidate.

CLARK MEN ARE JUBILANT

Believe Aid They Gave Murphy Must Be Repaid with the Nomination.

NEW YORK LEADER SILENT

Fears Effect of Hearst Stamp in State Campaign—May Switch at Any Moment.

WILSON MEN UNDISMAYED

Count on Getting Many Clark Deserters After the First Ballot—Gaynor Boom Grows.

DISORDER IN CONVENTION

Police Called in Once—Night Session Held to Hear Parker's Speech.

Special to The New York Times.

BALTIMORE, June 25.—William Jennings Bryan made a personal appeal to the Democratic National Convention at its first session to-day to make him its Temporary Chairman instead of Judge Alton B. Parker of New York, whom he designated as the candidate of the "predatory Wall Street interests." It was the last card that Bryan had to play, and he lost by a vote of 579 to 510.

To-night he and his followers, sobered by the blow, are wondering what they can do next to save the Progressive Democratic spirit from being entirely eliminated from the results of the convention.

Bryan made an heroic effort to "come back," but he had not the force to do it, nor did he have an audience that he could reach. The delegates that represented the majority were of the sort that Charles F. Murphy and others call "hand-picked." The spectators were not of the partisan sort, but rather a disinterested crowd, largely composed of women and children, who had obtained their seats through the courtesy of local contributors to the convention fund.

The convention itself was utterly unlike the session of any National Convention in twenty years. It was without snap and ginger, without inspiration, seemingly without a man or a cause to cheer for—just a large assemblage of people watching the business-like operation of the machine which had been organized to put the Peerless Leader out of business so far as the control of the Democratic Party was concerned.

Even with this Bryan might have been able to do something had he been the Bryan who carried the Chicago Convention in 1896 off its feet with his great "Cross of Gold" speech; but he was not that Bryan. He had not a battle cry as he had then with which to arouse the delegates and make them forget the ties that bound them to other leaders, and his declaration that "The Democratic song of triumph should on this eve of possible party victory be sung by one who had been steadfast in the fight for the Progressive spirit" did not ring clear. This speech, which he intended to be a war hymn, had the sad cadence of a swan song, so much so that even those who were rejoicing in Bryan's defeat could not help but sympathize with him.

Bryan Passive, Not a Bolter.

From every indication to-night the vanquished Commoner will remain comparatively passive in the convention from now on, even though, as a delegate at large from Nebraska and a member of the Committee on Resolutions, he must be more than a mere on-looker. He does not harbor any plans for a bolt.

In defeat, the Nebraskan was far from a lonesome figure. The hearty regard in which he is held by the Progressive Democrats was amply testified to by the vote and by the great throng that lavished sympathy on him in his hour of defeat. To all such callers Mr. Bryan showed a smiling, happy face. His friends said that they felt convinced that both the platform and the nominees of the convention would be such that Mr. Bryan could give them his support.

Nor was there the slightest disposition in the camp of those who accomplished Mr. Bryan's downfall, and whom he designated in the convention as the "Wall Street interests," to gloat over his downfall, or if there was such a disposition it was suppressed. It would have been bad policy, and besides, they were too busy trying to bring about a combination of delegates that would result in the nomination of a ticket to their liking.

In their case is [illegible] the cry to-night that Champ Clark will surely win now; but he is not the man they want, and he is not the man they will help to win if they can find a way to beat him. They don't like the Hearst stamp on the Clark candidacy. Murphy, particularly, believes it would hurt him in his New York State fight this Fall.

This disposition of the victors of to-day not to arouse the ire of the vanquished by trampling upon them was shown strongly to-night, when Judge Parker urged the Committee on Resolutions to make Col. Bryan its Chairman, which request will undoubtedly be complied with, but the fact that Bryan would preside over the deliberations of the platform constructors does not mean that he would prevail there, as his friends would be in a minority.

Clark Men Claim Victory.

The question arises of how the various candidates for the Presidential nomination stand in the light of to-day's votes in the convention. The analysis of the vote which elected Parker Temporary Chairman to-day justifies the remark that it was a "cross between the Houn' Dawg and the Tammany Tiger" that produced the result. The question is what the result of such a union can be. The Clark men say that the elimination of Bryan leaves only Clark, but less interested observers say that Tammany has simply "taken the B off Bryan and left Ryan," and that Mr. Clark and some others who are looking to Tammany for support will find it out to their sorrow.

The Clark men claim all the tactical advantage of the Parker victory, saying that it was made possible by their votes, although half the Clark delegates could not be delivered by the managers and voted for Bryan. The Clark men expect to gather in the support of the Murphy-Sullivan-Taggart combination, with the uninstructed delegates from the North and East and those nominally for Gov. Marshall of Indiana and Gov. Baldwin of Connecticut as favorite sons. They say the narrow margin by which Parker won makes it clear that Conservatives must help nominate Clark or Bryan would regain control. They hope to nominate Clark on the first ballot, as they will have trouble in a number of the delegations instructed for Clark after that, such as those from West Virginia and Louisiana, where there is much Wilson sentiment.

Hope in the Other Camps.

The Wilson men say their candidate has lost no ground through the outcome of the Chairmanship contest, that many of the delegates feel that they have done quite enough for the Conservatives, and that the elimination of Bryan as a candidate, which they say has been accomplished, leaves Wilson the only Progressive in the field. The ambiguous position of the Clark forces on both sides of the fence, they say, will lead to a concentration of the Progressive vote on their candidate, which, with the thirty or forty Wilson men who voted for Parker, will give them a majority and lead to their getting the necessary two-thirds.

Underwood and Harmon have dropped into the background as a result of today's developments, and there was talk to-night of Harmon withdrawing. Neither seemed to fit into a situation with Clark and Tammany Hall on one side and the Wilson-Bryan forces on the other. The Underwood people are still hopeful, however, of a shift that will bring their man to the front.

Senator Cantor and the other Gaynor boomers are burrowing beneath the surface for second choice Gaynor sentiment, and say they are finding plenty of it, but it is admitted only a deadlock will make the Mayor a formidable factor.

An Analysis of the Vote.

The Clark interests may be overplaying the obligation that they think they have put the anti-Progressive leaders under by delivering votes to them to-day for the election of Judge Parker. It will be observed from a study of the tabulated vote that Parker received the votes of practically all the instructed delegations to the convention except those pledged to Gov. Wilson and to Speaker Clark. Of the Wilson vote Parker got little and of the Clark vote he only got about one-half.

Idaho, Kansas, and Montana, Nebraska, Oklahoma, Washington, and Wyoming, cast practically their entire votes on the Bryan side. Iowa, Massachusetts, New Hampshire, New Mexico, and West Virginia split nearly even, and in Kentucky, California, and Clark's own State of Missouri Bryan got approximately a third of the delegates.

As indicative of the uncertainty of the whole situation it can be stated that Murphy has issued a positive order to the New York State delegates not to adorn themselves with the buttons or badges of any candidate and not to join in the shouting for any one of them. He will tell them when he is ready to have them show his hand.

Vice Presidential talk is idle at this time. That must be determined after the Presidential candidate has been agreed upon by those who can control. The conservative or progressive character of the head of the ticket must determine the sort of a running mate he shall have. The section of the country from which the Presidential nominee comes must determine the section from which the man for the second place must come.

Names that are suggested in connection with the Vice Presidency are those of Senator O'Gorman of New York, Congressman William Sulzer of New York, and Gov. Dix of New York. Gov. Marshall of Indiana and Gov. Burke of North Dakota are urged in case the Presidential nomination goes to the East. The only active candidates are Congressman Redfield of Brooklyn and Mayor Preston of Baltimore.

Others who have received some attention are Gov. Foss of Massachusetts, Francis Burton Harrison of New York, ex-Gov. William L. Douglas of Massachusetts, ex-Gov. J. A. Montague of Virginia, Clark Howell of Georgia, Josephus Daniels of North Carolina, ex-Gov. Folk of Missouri, Senator Culberson of Texas, Gov. Baldwin of Connecticut, and Mayor Gaynor.

The Platform Makers.

To-night for the first time the leaders turned their attention to the platform instead of to the more exciting question of organization. The pronounced feature of the platform situation remains what it was before, and that is a determination on all sides to have a moderately Progressive platform, with planks so chosen as to cause the least possible break in harmony. The only prospect for trouble lies in the wishes of William Jennings Bryan to take a seat in the Committee on Resolutions, but his most radical planks this time are one for an income tax and one for a Presidential primary law. The wording of either of these may cause trouble, and the primary proposal may be rejected altogether, but the trouble is of a kind that, while it may lead to warm sessions of the committee, can hardly cause a serious split in the party. Even Mr. Bryan has no idea of inserting any reference to the initiative, referendum, and recall in the National platform, and Gov. Wilson is of the same mind.

The next important tussle before a committee of the convention promises like the one ended to-day, to go against the Wilson-Bryan forces. It will come before the Committee on Rules, and will hinge around an effort to modify the unit rule in a way to permit district delegates, though in the minority in their own States, to vote according to the instructions of their district instead of according to the instructions of the State Convention. Such a change would allow Gov. Wilson to claim 20 votes in Ohio, 2 in Illinois, and 2 in Wisconsin, but all the other candidates except Gov. Burke, North Dakota's favorite son, is against him, and they poll at least 35 out of the 53 votes on the committee.

June 26, 1912

CONVENTION SMASHES THE UNIT RULE; GREAT DEMONSTRATION FOR WILSON

Delegates Cheer 31 Minutes for the New Jersey Governor.

GAINS VOTES IN OHIO

Convention's Decision May Also Cause Split in Other Bound Delegations.

NOMINATIONS DUE TO-DAY

No Choice on the First Ballot Is Likely—Murphy May Cause Deadlock.

CLARK MEN STILL HOPEFUL

Believe Deal with Murphy and Taggart Will Give Them Victory on Second Ballot.

PLATFORM TO BE FINAL TASK

Bryan's Proposal on That Point Accepted—Harmony Pleas in the Day Session.

Special to The New York Times.

BALTIMORE, Md., June 26.—Following a remarkable outburst of enthusiasm for Gov. Wilson in the Democratic convention to-night, the delegates voted, 565½ to 491 1-3 against the unit rule. This was a victory for the Wilson supporters, and led to another demonstration for the New Jersey Governor.

The Committee on Rules reported in substance that the instructed delegation from any State should be bound by its instructions so long as the majority of the delegation decided to stand by the candidate for whom they were instructed. A minority report was presented by the Wilson-Bryan members of the committee, which provided that the delegation from any particular State should not be so bound, but that the individual members of any delegation could be released from instructions as soon as they individually saw fit to change their votes after the first ballot.

The effect of this can directly be seen in the State of Ohio, where the majority of the delegates are Harmon men and are seeking to bind a Wilson minority of about nineteen delegates under the unit rule. This will mean a loss of nineteen votes for Harmon in his own State and a probable gain of nineteen for Wilson.

In view of this it was stated to-night on excellent authority that the Harmon men in the Ohio delegation are to confer with a view of advising the Governor not to permit his name to go before the convention.

When Mr. Bryan reached his hotel tonight after the spectacular scene in the convention he was caught by a crowd of enthusiasts who almost carried him to the elevator, cheering and yelling like madmen. In his room, Mr. Bryan would only say for publication:

"I am very much gratified at the result of the vote in the convention."

To his friends he explained the situation by saying: "The election of Parker to make the keynote speech in the convention has been resented by nine-tenths of the Democrats in the country, and they have been letting the delegates know how they feel."

A nomination does not seem to be possible on the first ballot, as the delegations are divided to-night. Unless a deal is made by the Murphy-Sullivan-Taggart combination with some of the leading candidates before the roll call the result, as closely as it can be estimated to-night, reducing the claims of all candidates to bedrock, will be about as follows:

Clark	464
Wilson	340
Underwood	108
Harmon	48
Marshall	30
Baldwin	14

This makes a total of 1,004 votes out of the 1,094 delegates in the convention. The difference of 90 votes represents the exact strength of the New York State delegation. Charles F. Murphy controls the 90 votes, and, with the largest force of Wall Street lawyers ever seen in one city behind him, it does not seem likely that he will throw that vote where it is not likely to do him the most good.

But the power of Murphy to make or break the chance of any candidate for the Presidential nomination does not rest alone in those 90 united-by-the-unit-rule delegates from New York State. It is an open secret here that standing with Murphy is Taggart of Indiana, with 80 delegates, Sullivan of Illinois with 58 delegates, Smith of New Jersey with 4 delegates, Col. Guffey of Pennsylvania with possibly 20 delegates, Thomas F. Ryan of Virginia with 14 delegates, and National Committeeman McGraw of West Virginia with 9 delegates.

Here, then, is an element of 225 votes in the convention which cannot be placed as a certain factor. They may control the result. They may not. But they are banded together for that purpose.

The one vote in the convention that stands out, clean cut, not to be dealt with except on the basis of the candidate's nomination, is the vote for Gov. Wilson. His 340 men are all for him and for nobody else. Under the decision of the convention to-night they may number 359, gaining 19 in Ohio. They will stand together, and if after the first ballot there is a desertion of other candidates by instructed delegates they hope that the tide will turn in their direction. The friends of Bryan, they believe, will turn to Wilson sooner than to any other candidate. It is to be remembered that Bryan had 510 votes in his fight against Parker for Temporary Chairman.

Champ Clark has a bigger vote than Wilson in sight. His boom is the "big noise" of the show at present, and, on the assumption that the Murphy-Taggart-Sullivan combine is going to give him votes in return for the votes the Clark men gave them in the Parker fight, he seems to have the best chance. But there seems to be a weakening in the Clark line to-night, and a suspicion that they sold their votes for Parker, without the usual Missouri guarantee. To-morrow will tell the tale, but even if Murphy delivers, Clark's nomination is an uncertainty on the first ballot and would have to be cinched by deliveries from other members of the combine.

The weak showing that is being made by the Gaynor boom here should not be taken as any measure of the strength which the Mayor of New York City would develop as a candidate if his own State delegation had given the slightest evidence of being behind him. The fact of the matter is that Mr. Murphy to-day told some of his few confidants that he was not for Gaynor, and they spread the word among the Tammany shouters to keep quiet about candidates until Murphy makes his wishes known.

That the Bryan spirit in the party is not dead, but only sleeping, has been made evident to-day by every move made by those who would only be too glad to sit as a Coroner's jury on the cause of the Commoner. They made a concession to him, for the sake of harmony, by offering him the Chairmanship of the Committee on Resolutions, but he declined it and put up his good friend John W. Kern there. They agreed to make his old friend Senator-elect Ollie James of Kentucky Permanent Chairman. They also conceded his demand that the usual procedure of making the platform and then naming the candidates to stand upon it should be reversed. At this convention the candidates will be named first and the platform made to suit them.

Bryan's purpose in all this is evident. He wants to be free to do as he pleases after this convention gets through its work. Not that he has any idea of bolting, but he is mapping out his course so that he can disclaim responsibility for the result, and maintain that he did his best to avert it if the people of the country reject it. Up to this point nobody can accuse him of refusing to play his hand out when he has apparently lost the game, but he has not committed himself so that he cannot call for a new deal of the cards in any other game in which he chooses to sit.

Talking of Bryan Again.

In view of the general tendency of the day's developments in the direction of the Progressive element of the party there is a disposition around the hotels at midnight to suggest that matters may so shape themselves as to bring Bryan himself before the convention as a candidate for the nomination.

Bryan could not allow himself to be put in that position without opening himself to the charge of placing his personal ambition above party success. He would split the party in two. His declaration that he was not a candidate, made long ago, followed by his declaration during the dark hour of yesterday that he was only fighting to keep the Democratic ship on an even keel, fighting to make this convention, its candidates, and its platform such as he believed the majority of the Democrats of the country demand, would seem to make it incumbent upon him to pick another standard bearer than himself for the fight.

All that he has said about Woodrow Wilson and all that Woodrow Wilson and Wilson's supporters have done to uphold Bryan's hands in the progressive fight would seem to make it certain that Bryan to-morrow will do everything he can to put Wilson at the head of the ticket.

How the Vote May Shift.

With a nomination on the first ballot seemingly impossible, although a deal may be made at any hour before morning that will settle the matter, the question arises as to the subsequent line-up. Whether the delegates instructed for Clark would fall away from him heavily after the first ballot and to whom they would go are the uncertain factors. How many of the instructed delegates for other candidates than Clark and Wilson would turn toward either of them after the first ballot is also a matter of pure guess work at this time.

Then, like a shadow over the whole situation, is the question of where the 225 votes of the Murphy-Taggart-Sullivan combine are going to land. They might be used as the neucleus of a movement for Harmon, Underwood, Marshall, Gaynor, Baldwin, or Foss.

The whole battery of brains behind what Bryan calls the "predatory interests," but what might better be called the anti-progressives, would like to bring out of this muddle a conservative ticket, and to-night they are talking of Underwood for President and Congressman Redfield of Brooklyn for Vice President. They also put out a feeler for Gov. Marshall of Indiana to-day, but it did not arouse much enthusiasm. Underwood's candidacy did receive one rousing cheer in the convention hall.

Wilson developed strength in the convention to-night, and Harmon lost votes by the change in the application of the unit rule, the details of which are told in the story of the convention proceedings.

There were two sessions of the convention, one this afternoon and one to-night. The first was devoted entirely to stump speeches, the tone of which was almost entirely progressive. The night session cleared the way for to-morrows nomination speeches.

The convention had been until to-night remarkably devoid of the scenes of wild enthusiasm and excitement that usually mark National Conventions. This does not mean that there is not enthusiasm here, but it has not been prolonged and boisterous, as usual, which is due in part to the fact that it is insufferably hot, and the real battle is not being fought on the convention floor, but in the rooms of the leaders of the different factions. Tomorrow the fight will be in the open, and the convention crowd will have a chance to break loose.

June 27, 1912

WOODROW WILSON IS NOMINATED FOR PRESIDENT

Convention Deadlock Is Broken on Forty-sixth Ballot at 3:30 P. M.

ACTION MADE UNANIMOUS

After 990 Votes Had Been Cast for the New Jersey Governor and 84 for Clark.

ILLINOIS STARTS THE SLIDE

Then Underwood Is Withdrawn as a Candidate and Clark Delegates Are Released.

CHEERS BY TIRED DELEGATES

Demonstration in Honor of the Nominee Hearty but Not of Long Duration.

Special to The New York Times.

BALTIMORE, July 2.—Woodrow Wilson was nominated for President on the forty-sixth ballot this afternoon at 3:30 o'clock. The vote was never announced, for it was made unanimous before the clerk could finish counting it up, but on the last roll call Wilson had received 990 votes to 84 for Champ Clark and 12 for Judson Harmon.

The first ballot of the convention was taken in the early hours of Saturday morning, after an all-night session, and the convention had remained deadlocked through Saturday and Monday.

The final ballot was preceded by a sort of love feast in which the spokesmen for the other candidates pledged their hearty and enthusiastic support to Wilson, despite the fact that he had not been nominated. New York went so far as to propose, through Representative Fitzgerald, that the forty-sixth ballot be dispensed with and that Wilson be nominated by acclamation.

The only reason why this was not done was that the supporters of Clark desired to place themselves on record once more—for the purpose of demonstrating their love for "Old Champ Clark," as their spokesmen all called him.

It was 12:05 when Chairman James ascended the platform and called the convention to order in the broken and husky tones which are all that remain of the voice that a week ago sounded like a forest storm.

He immediately called for the forty-third ballot. Mr. James was weary and worn, and although he kept himself under admirable control and won the respect of everybody for his patience and firmness in dealing with the hard task before him, he had none of that patience for the people who clogged the aisles and made the voices of the clerks inaudible.

Trouble Restoring Order.

"Please cease conversation or get out," he shouted at them, "to some place where you can talk without disturbing the convention."

Forty times during the day he had to suspend the proceedings to order the police to clear the aisles. Those wonderful Baltimore policemen only grinned sheepishly each time, and now and then one would timidly lay his hand on the shoulder of some disturber and then take it off again when he saw the disturber paid no attention to him.

This forty-sixth ballot was to be the ballot whereon Illinois was to start an expected stampede. Everybody was waiting for the vote of that State. It was, indeed, the vote of Illinois which made Wilson's nomination sure, but the other candidates managed to hold on for two more ballots, the forty-fourth and forty-fifth.

On the forty-third ballot the first change was in Arizona, where Clark lost a vote to W. J. Bryan. Connecticut followed by taking two votes from the Clark column and turning them over to Wilson, amid a "rebel yell" from the irrepressible Texans.

Idaho gave Wilson one additional vote and then Roger Sullivan arose in the Illinois delegates. Every face was turned expectantly toward him.

"Eighteen for Clark, forty for Wilson," announced Sullivan briskly. The stampede had begun. The Texans arose and cheered Illinois, facing the delegation and waving their hats at it. Many of the Wilson men cheered Sullivan individually. Under the unit rule the whole of Illinois, 58 votes, had to be counted for Wilson.

But the Clark and Underwood men hung on grimly, and it was soon evident that whatever might be the ultimate effect of Sullivan's announcement, it would not succeed in bringing about a nomination on this ballot, nor, perhaps for several more. The avalanche was starting slowly.

Iowa gave Wilson a gain of 1½, Louisiana 2, Michigan 8, North Carolina 2, and then there came a gain of real importance. Virginia cast her entire 24 votes for Wilson. Up to that time she had been casting 12 of them for Clark.

"Hurrah for Virginia," shouted a delegate from Texas, and the Old Dominion got nearly as big a welcome into the Wilson camp as had Illinois. So did West Virginia when she followed her older sister and Illinois into the Wilson ranks.

West Virginia Helps Wilson.

West Virginia had been particularly active and prominent on the Clark side from the beginning of the convention, so that her surrender was specially welcome. Through ex-Governor McCorkle she had done a lot of talking, and it had all been done on the Murphy side. The delegation had always been divided, but as the majority was against Wilson her votes had to be cast under the unit rule. Now they were cast the other way under the same rule, and she contributed 16 toward starting the landslide.

While this was going on Senator-elect Vardaman of Mississippi was over in the Alabama delegation urging upon Senator Bankhead that the time to withdraw Underwood had come. Mississippi wanted to join the procession, but could not do so as long as Underwood was a candidate. Bankhead and his fellow-Alabamans insisted on sticking it out a little longer.

Wisconsin gave Wilson a gain of 1, Alaska 1, and Hawaii 1. The District of Columbia, in announcing her vote, said she was casting 1/2 for "Dear Old Champ Clark." Maryland had asked to be passed when her turn came for the reason that the Wilson men in her delegation were making a dead-lift effort to bring over the others and vote Maryland solid. They failed, however, and Wilson gained only half a vote in that State.

Wilson went up to 602 on this ballot. Clark was down to 329 and Underwood to 98½. Harmon had 28, Foss 27, Kern 1, and Bryan 1.

On the forty-fourth ballot the Arizona man who had voted for Bryan went over to Wilson. Colorado gave Wilson ten out of her twelve, which was a gain of nine for him. He gained two in Indiana, one from Clark and one from Kern, and this gave him Indiana's solid vote of 30.

But it was evident that there was no chance of nomination on this ballot. No big delegations were going to swing. He kept on picking up delegates here and there, but his gains were not sufficient to promise anything definite. Wilson gained a vote in Louisiana, one and a half in Maryland, two in Pennsylvania, and four in Wisconsin. Utah's eight went over in a body.

Trouble Over the Proxies.

A poll of Washington developed that some of the votes were being cast by men who were not delegates, but held proxies, the delegates having gone back home to save the remnant of their bank rolls Chairman James promptly ruled that no man but a delegate or alternate could vote.

"But the State of Washington has no alternates," cried one of the proxies, "and these delegates have gone home."

"The fact that Washington has no alternates is her misfortune," replied Chairman James calmly.

"I object to the ruling of the chair," shouted one of the Washington men, "as being part of the fraud that has been practiced."

This did not ruffle Mr. James, who looked at him with patient placidity and replied: "The gentleman has the privilege of appealing from the decision of the chair."

The man was misguided enough to take this hint, and his appeal was laid on the table with a mighty shout of "aye" from the whole convention. A call for the noes brought only a feeble and lonely cry from the Washington men themselves.

The forty-fourth ballot resulted as follows: Wilson, 629; Clark, 306; Underwood, 99; Harmon, 27; Foss, 27.

While the forty-fifth ballot was proceeding there were signs of great activity in the New York delegation. All the leaders were busy conferring over the question, "Shall we do it now?" It was finally decided to wait until Alabama broke, and Murphy again cast New York's 90 votes for Clark.

The changes on this ballot were so unimportant as not to be worth chronicling. Mississippi asked to be passed, while Vardaman made another effort to get Alabama in line, but, though Senator Bankhead was now ready to withdraw Underwood, he wanted the record to stand as it was made on this ballot.

Those who were expecting the final break thought it would come from New York, not from Alabama, because of their knowledge of the close relations between Murphy, Sullivan and Taggart. Sullivan and Taggart had already thrown Illinois and Indiana to Wilson, and it seemed likely that the third of the three musketeers would come next. Murphy, however, still stood out, and it was Bankhead who was destined to put an end to the deadlock and bring about a nomination. Yet so general was the belief that Murphy was to start it that when he arose this time there was a breathless hush over the whole convention, hitherto so noisy, and every eye was fixed on him.

On this, the last real ballot, Wilson received 633, Clark 306, Underwood 97, Foss 27 and Harmon 25. It was commented on as a sinister omen for Clark that for the last two ballots he had been sticking at 306, the number which stood out to the last for Grant in the deadlocked Republican convention of 1880.

Underwood Quits the Race.

Chairman James now ordered the forty-sixth ballot, and the clerk was preparing to call the roll when Senator Bankhead appeared on the platform and spoke to Chairman James. The Chairman announced that the Senator wished unanimous consent to make a statement, and his manner as he pleaded for silence and attention indicated that the statement was to be one of the utmost importance. No one had any doubt what it was to be, and the convention listened in eager silence. Senator Bankhead said:

> Mr. Underwood entered this contest hoping that he might secure the nomination from this convention, but I desire to say for him that his first and greatest hope was that through this movement he might be able to eliminate and eradicate for all time every remaining vestige of factional feeling in this country.
>
> Mr. Underwood to-day would willingly, anxiously forego this nomination if he has succeeded and if the country has concluded that the Mason and Dixon line has been tramped out and this is once more a united country. We have demonstrated here, my friends, in my judgment, that no longer sectional feeling exists. The liberal support Mr. Underwood has had from the East satisfies us that if an opportunity were offered to nominate this splendid man and Democrat they are ready and would hasten to his aid. Mr. Underwood did not enter this contest to defeat any man's nomination. He will not be a party to the defeat of any candidate before this convention. His only hope was that the great record that he has made as the leader of the Democracy—his hope was that what he had accomplished for the Democracy of this country—his belief was that under his leadership these things which had been achieved which would secure the election of a Democrat in the next November election. He has always said: "I take no personal part in this campaign; I have not the time."
>
> He said: "I have a full man's work marked out for me in Washington, and my first duty is to make it possible to elect a Democrat, whoever the nominee may be." Upon that high ground he stands to-day; upon that high ground he will stand to-morrow and all other days. He has no concern, my friends, about his own nomination or election beyond that which naturally comes to every man who feels he is thoroughly equipped and qualified for that high office. But I think the time has come when it is demonstrated that he cannot be nominated in this convention; and he cannot be used to defeat the nomination of any other candidate.
>
> **Desires Party Success.**
>
> He and his friends everywhere stand ready to give the nominee of this convention their hearty support. He has stood upon every platform that has been written since 1896. He will stand upon any platform that this convention may write. I would not undertake, knowing him as I do, to say that all of its planks—and I don't know what they are—would meet his judgment, but he is a Democrat and stands for the success of his party.

At this point in Senator Bankhead's eulogy of his candidate some impressionable enthusiast called out, "Make him Vice President." Senator Bankhead raised his fists above his head and shook them savagely at the author of this handsome suggestion, and roared in a voice which rang and echoed through every corner of the great hall: "No; Vice President, no."

Senator Bankhead's face was flushed and his eyes sparkled with anger as he continued, shaking his fists and his voice was ringing. No member of the Democratic Party would dare, he said, with heavy emphasis on the word "dare," "to suggest the taking of that man from his present post to fill any other except the highest in the land."

"Vice President," he cried, with a scornful sneer. "Anybody can sit in the Vice President's chair."

The convention laughed at this unexpected tribute to the supposedly second office in the land, but Senator Bankhead was dead in earnest.

"Anybody," he went on, "can sit in that chair, where all he has to do is to say, 'the Senator from New York moves that the Senate do now adjourn.' Anybody can say that. The man who has made it possible for the Democratic Party to win in this contest will stay where he is."

Here there were interruptions, but Senator Bankhead broke them up by shouting, "My voice is not strong, but my standing capacity is as good as ever, and I can stand as long as you can holler."

He then went on to announce Mr. Underwood's withdrawal from the race and his release of the Underwood delegates from their obligation to vote for him, saying:

> This great Democrat, the Democracy's best asset: this great Democrat who has made it possible for the Democratic Party to win in the next contest will stay where he is and perform the duties that he has been performing without complaint. To take that man from the field of usefulness and con-

struction which he now occupies would be a crime, unless he can be promoted to the Presidential chair, the only promotion that you could give him. I hope no gentleman here will suggest his name for Vice President. He has repeatedly said, "No," and he is a man who stands by his word.

Now, one word and I am through. Mr. Underwood directs me as the humble instrument by which his campaign has been conducted, to withdraw his name from before this convention. He directs me further to thank most sincerely those devoted friends who have stood by him so loyally through the tedious hours of this convention. They can never be blotted from his memory. He further directs me to say to the members of this convention that no feeling of resentment or animosity exists in his heart toward any member of it.

I withdraw his name from before the convention and he authorizes me to release from their obligation all the friends who have been elected for and instructed to vote for him, which they have so loyally done as long as his name is before the convention. His friends are at liberty to vote for whom they please.

During the cheering which followed the announcement Senator Stone of Missouri, the Clark manager, ascended the platform steps and told Chairman James that he, too, wanted to make a statement.

Stone Releases Clark Delegates.

"Speaking for Mr. Clark," he said, "I release all who are under any obligation to vote for him. I would not have a delegation here under the sense of obligation to him. I would have them vote as they now think best.

"So far as the Missouri delegation is concerned, under the peculiar circumstances that have surrounded this convention and its proceedings, we shall vote for Speaker Clark until the last ballot. If the verdict shall be against him I need not go to the trouble of telling this convention and the American Democracy that 'old Champ Clark' and his friends will stand by the candidate who is nominated."

Senator Stone's implications seemed to be that the personal nature of the controversy between Bryan and Clark made it impossible for Clark's own State to consent to any compromise until some other man had actually been nominated.

Next came Mayor Fitzgerald of Boston to withdraw Gov. Foss's name. "It is Gov. Foss's idea," he said, "that he should not oppose the will of the great majority in this convention, and in behalf of the Massachusetts delegation I withdraw the name of Eugene Noble Foss and say that Woodrow Wilson is our candidate."

But all these speeches were now to be put in the shade by Murphy. There was a general rush to take some action or make some speech which would bring about a harmonious atmosphere, and send the victors and vanquished away from the convention with a desire to pull together in the campaign. Each was trying to outdo the other. Murphy was the victor in this friendly game, and he now played an ace.

New York Goes to Wilson.

Representative Fitzgerald of Brooklyn appeared on the platform and the moment he did so there was an excited yell, which instantly changed into an excited silence.

"The desire of every Democrat in the convention," cried Mr. Fitzgerald, "is to leave this hall harmonious and united and victory assured. Whatever personal differences of opinion there may have been about candidates, every loyal Democrat should be willing to subordinate his personal desires for the success of the Democratic Party.

"In order that this convention may adjourn without bitterness, without bad feeling, without rancor that may affect the success of the candidates of this convention; in order to demonstrate that no matter how hard we may strive for the mastery of our honest opinions, I now as a member of the New York delegation, anxious that the electoral vote of New York shall be in the Democratic column—I move that the roll call be dispensed with and that this convention unanimously nominate for President of the United States, that splendid Democrat of New Jersey, Woodrow Wilson."

Mr. Wilson's name was lost in the cyclone of cheers that swept over the hall. It did not last long, but in volume it was tremendous. However, New York's plan was blocked by Missouri, though she did it in a good-tempered way which did not disturb the harmonious feeling that had descended over the convention.

"Without the slightest desire," said Senator Reed, "to indicate any feeling or resentment, I make objection to this motion, because Missouri wants to be recorded on this ballot for 'old Champ Clark.'"

Mr. Reed was so earnest in his disclaimer of ill-feeling that, although the motion was unpopular, no display of antagonism was made.

It was felt that Missouri should have the privilege she wanted of dying in the last ditch, and that there was nothing unreasonable or unjust in her position, despite the fact that it would delay the convention uselessly for the sake of taking an unnecessary ballot. Congressman Palmer, the Wilson manager, was hissed by his own followers for objection to a Missouri man's making a speech, and he saw at once that he had made a mistake and withdrew the objection.

Then the roll was called, and Alabama's 24 votes for Wilson brought out a burst of "yee-O!" When California was reached Theodore A. Bell asked permission to explain his vote, and the only thing of the day that marred the harmony developed. Mr. Bell was ill-advised in trying to talk. The convention had steadily refused to let him talk ever since he went over from Bryan to Murphy, and the man who presided over the convention of 1908 has been unable to get a hearing in the convention of 1912.

The same thing happened that has happened every time Bell has risen to speak. He stood up for some minutes, amid a steady din of groans and hoots, and finally Chairman James was able to stop the disorder only by directing that California be passed for the present.

The disorder ceased as if by magic, and everybody was good natured again. Each got a cheer, and when Vardaman announced the vote of his State there was a call for three cheers for Mississippi. He had worked hard to bring about the break, and the delegates all knew it.

When the four "Jim Smith" delegates from New Jersey voted for Clark, thus preventing Wilson's own State from giving him its unanimous vote, there were hisses.

All Wanted to Hear Murphy.

When Charles F. Murphy arose for New York the desire to hear him was so great that people all over the hall cried, "Sh, sh," in order to bring about absolute stillness. Mr. Murphy looked startled, thinking at first that he was being hissed, and then he recognized that it was a tribute and not a taunt. When he called out, "New York casts 90 votes for Woodrow Wilson," he got the biggest cheer of the roll call. The Texas delegates saluted New York, waving their hats and cheering.

When Ohio was reached Judge Edward Moore, by unanimous consent, was allowed to make a statement, and he delivered a eulogy of Gov. Harmon, which sounded more like a nominating speech than what it was expected to be, a speech of withdrawal. But it was neither. Ohio simply wanted to be passed. When Texas was reached, her Chairman called out:

"Texas will announce her vote through one of her fairest flowers, Miss Mary Frances Hall, the mascot of the delegation."

Miss Mary Frances Hall is a pretty girl of 13 years. In her mascot capacity she had been very busy and very happy all day, leading the cheering whenever anything happened. A brawny Texan held her up in his arms, and, waving a flag with a delighted smile, she screamed:

"Forty votes for Woodrow Wilson."

At the end of the roll California was again called, and the misguided Mr. Bell again got up on a chair to make a statement, amid cries of "No, No," and "Put him out." After a while Mr. Bell went upon the platform, where the shout of disapproval became a roar. He was saved at last by the intervention of Chairman James, for whom this convention had come to entertain a real affection. Enforcing silence with difficulty the Chairman said with great earnestness:

"I hope this convention will be in order. The gentleman from California is a distinguished Democrat. He has fought the battles of our party in the past, and we should give him a hearing."

Mr. Bell said that as soon as he returned to California he would begin work for Woodrow Wilson, and at the end of the roll would move to make the nomination unanimous, but that he felt it his duty to vote for Clark. Missouri gave California a cheer.

Ohio was the last State to vote. She gave Wilson 33, Harmon 12, and Clark 1.

The vote Speaker Clark got on the last ballot was made up as follows: Twenty-four of the 26 in California, 5 of the 12 in Florida, 2 of the 20 in Louisiana, the 36 of Missouri, the 6 of Nevada, 4 of the 28 in New Jersey, 1 of the 48 in Ohio, and the 6 in the District of Columbia.

Nomination Made Unanimous.

The vote, however, was never announced. Before the clerk could finish adding it up Senator Stone, Clark's manager, appeared on the platform and moved to make the nomination of Woodrow Wilson unanimous. It was carried with a shout of delight, and Chairman James declared Woodrow Wilson of New Jersey the nominee of the Democratic Party for President of the United States. It was exactly 3:30 o'clock in the afternoon.

There were a few minutes of yelling, and then, on motion of Congressman Palmer of Pennsylvania, the convention adjourned, to meet at 9 o'clock to-night.

July 3, 1912

ROOSEVELT NAMED BY RUMP CONVENTION

Special to The New York Times.

CHICAGO, June 22.—Col. Roosevelt has at last openly broken off all connection with the Republican Party as represented in the National Convention.

He was nominated for President on an independent ticket to-night in the dying hours of the Republican National Convention in which he had met a defeat.

The followers of Col. Roosevelt gathered in Orchestra Hall, less than a mile from the Coliseum, and pledged their support to the former President. In accepting the nomination, Col. Roosevelt appealed to the people of all sections, regardless of party affiliations, to stand with the founders of the new party, one of whose cardinal principles, he said, was to be "Thou Shalt Not Steal."

The informal nomination of Col. Roosevelt was said to be chiefly for the purpose of effecting a temporary organization. Beginning to-morrow, when a call is to be issued for a State convention in Illinois, the work of organization will be pushed forward rapidly, State by State. At a later time, probably early in August, it is intended that a National convention shall be held.

Col. Roosevelt, in accepting the nomination to-night, said he did so on the understanding that he would willingly step aside if it should be the desire of the new party when organized to select another standard bearer.

* * * * *

June 23, 1912

HAIL NEW PARTY IN FERVENT SONG

"Battle Hymn of the Republic" Sways 1,000 Delegates to the Roosevelt Convention.

NO LEVITY, LITTLE CHEERING

Beveridge, in Opening Speech, Skillfully Plays on Fanaticism of His Audience.

JOHNSON ON THE TICKET

Slated to Run with Roosevelt—Negro Issue Still a Disturbing Factor.

Special to The New York Times.

CHICAGO, Ill., Aug. 5.—About one thousand serious, earnest, almost fanatical men and women met in the Coliseum today at noon to create a new party. Every one of them believed that he or she was a crusader. There was no levity, and there was a solemn gravity that was striking and impressive.

To-day's work was all preliminary. To-morrow Col. Roosevelt will make his declaration of faith. On Wednesday a platform will be adopted and Col. Roosevelt will be nominated for President. Gov. Johnson of California will probably be named for Vice President.

Let no one mistake the Progressive Party. Theodore Roosevelt may or may not be bitten by personal ambition, but the men who are following him believe sincerely that they are followers of the Lord enlisted for the battle of Armageddon. They may be absolutely wrong about it, but about the strength of their conviction there cannot remain a doubt in the mind of anybody who saw the strange, moving, and compelling spectacle in the Coliseum to-day.

It was not a convention at all. It was an assemblage of religious enthusiasts. It was such a convention as Peter the Hermit held. It was a Methodist camp meeting done over into political terms. From Jane Addams of Hull House fame, sitting in the first rank below the platform, to Judge Ben Lindsey of Denver, sitting half way down the hall, there was an expression on every face of fanatical and religious enthusiasm. Perhaps such men as William Flinn of Pennsylvania may have had a more worldly expression on their faces, but they were lost in the crowd of visionaries who listened to their Chairman, ex-Senator Beveridge, and believed—obviously and certainly believed—that they were enlisted in a contest with the Powers of Darkness.

Mr. Beveridge's speech was a great one in its apepal to the kind of sentiment that he knew to be prevalent in the convention. It was the best speech he ever delivered in his life. He knew the Lutheran and Garrisonian strain in his audience, and he skillfully bent his speech to that element. He is a phrasemaker equal to Col. Ingersoll. He has developed tremendously in the last few years. The sophomoric element has disappeared, and he is as polished and complete an orator as Martin Littleton.

Women Eager and Earnest.

The men and women before him listened with rapt faces. Some of them had their jaws set, and seemed to be biting their lips. Here and there men were seen wiping tears from their eyes. There was little cheering; the men and women were too earnest for it. They sat there, bent forward in their places, many of them with their hands to their ears, anxious to catch every word. When they did cheer it was always for some sentiment in which Beveridge expressed the aspiration of the new party for a better day for humanity. To his talk about details they remained callous.

The women were vastly in evidence. Most of them were old or middle-aged; the gay, half-serious, and brightly dressed crowd that represents woman suffrage in New York was largely absent. Every woman there was one whose name compelled respect. Miss Addams sat in the first row, and for an hour before the convention came to order she held a regular levee. There was not a moment when a procession was not passing in front of her, partly of women and partly of men. Everybody who came stopped to speak to her, and usually lingered for many minutes. Every one who stopped spoke to her with an earnest face and manner Miss Addams herself acted like a religious devotee. Once, when Mr. Beveridge committed the new party to woman suffrage she smiled and her eyes flashed. But mostly she sat with the same intent and almost reverent look on her face that the shouting Methodists and Presbyterians behind her wore.

The band played such airs as "My Country 'Tis of Thee" and "The Battle Hymn of the Republic," Julia Ward Howe's famous hymn, and when the men and women delegates got up and joined in such songs they did it almost with frenzy. Everybody there, except possibly such calculating and sedate persons as William Flinn, unmistakably regarded himself as a soldier of the Lord.

No Ward Heelers There.

And here was another thing. It was a good-looking convention. Wherever you looked you saw clean-cut looking young fellows or old men who evidently stayed home at night and read the Bible. It looked less like the average Republican or Democratic Convention than anything you ever saw. The tough type was not there, that was all. It was like a convention of Sunday School Superintendents.

When the Rev. T. F. Dornblazer, Lutheran pastor, delivered the opening prayer, he was interrupted continuously with shouts of "Amen." Mr. Beveridge wound up his speech with a quotation from Julia Ward Howe.

"Mine eyes have seen the coming of the glory of the Lord."

And the whole convention burst out spontaneously in song. They sang every verse of Mrs. Howe's majestic hymn, except one, and nobody had to tell them the words:

Mines eyes have seen the glory of the coming of the Lord;
He is tramping out the vintage where the grapes of wrath are stored;
He hath loosed the fateful lightning of His terrible swift sword:
His truth is marching on.

I have seen Him in the watchfires of a hundred circling camps;
They have builded Him an altar in the evening dews and damps;
I can read His righteous sentence by the dim and flaring lamps.
His day is marching on.

I have read a fiery gospel writ in burnished rows of steel;
"As ye deal with My contemners so with you My grace shall deal;
Let the Hero, born of woman, crush the serpent with his heel,
Since God is marching on."

He has sounded forth the trumpet that shall never call retreat;
He is sifting out the hearts of men before His judgment seat:
Oh! be swift my soul to answer Him! be jubilant my feet!
Our God is marching on.

Different in "Purple Row."

Yes, it was a convention that was "different." The convention was to have met at noon, but it was an hour later before it began business. The delegations cheered each other as they came in, in a friendly and hospitable spirit, and when the band began playing "The Battle Hymn of the Republic," the Indiana delegation climbed its chairs and led the singing. The galleries were very sparsely filled, but this was not a gallery convention; it was a delegates' convention. The hall was the same as that in which Taft was nominated a few weeks ago, and the arrangements were so much the same that it seemed as if one convention might have adjourned over night and left the hall to the other. About the only difference was that the Texas delegation was to the left instead of the right of the hall, as it had been when the Republicans met.

"Purple row," where in June the millionaires' wives sat, presented a strangely different appearance. It was filled with women in shirtwaists and young girls, who occupied the same seats in which the "millionairesses" sat six weeks ago. The "millionairesses" used to sit with frozen faces, and the only time they woke to enthusiasm was when Assistant Chief of Police Schuettler issued orders to keep a Roosevelt woman enthusiast in her seat by force.

But the women there to-day did not cheer loosely, were intent and earnest, with a good deal of the attitude that Miss Addams assumed, and leaned forward and listened to the speeches with intent and rapt faces. Probably not one of them ever saw as much money in her life as one woman in "purple row" spends in a day. It was a different type, on the whole, a type that it was pleasanter to look at.

* * * * *

August 6, 1912

ROOSEVELT NAMED SHOWS EMOTION

"Of Course, I Accept," He Tells Progressives Who Give Him Third Term Nomination.

JOHNSON FOR SECOND PLACE

Dramatic Scene as Candidates Join Delegates in Singing of the Battle Hymn.

TAKE UP ROLE OF CRUSADERS

Colonel, Much Affected, and Happy, Plans to Open a Vigorous Campaign.

Special to The New York Times.

CHICAGO, Ill., Aug. 7.—Col. Theodore Roosevelt has attained the goal of his ambition. Before the first National Convention of his new party passed into history to-night it handed him on a silver platter the honor that Washington and Jefferson modestly declined and Ulysses S. Grant, though crowned with a hero's laurels, sought in vain. He was nominated as a third-term candidate for President of the United States.

Hiram W. Johnson, the militant and Progressive Governor of California, who was a Republican until the Republican Convention, six weeks ago, refused Col. Roosevelt the coveted glory of a third term, was chosen as his running mate. Both nominations were made by acclamation under a suspension of the convention rules and amid scenes which fluctuated strangely between the solemn and impressive and the merely spectacular and melodramatic.

The closing scenes of the first National Convention of the Progressive Party were unlike the scenes that have marked the closing of any National Convention within the memory of living politicians of any party. Amid an ovation that was as striking and sincere as it was impressive the two candidates were brought out on the platform to face the delegates and to deliver in their hearing, and with crowded galleries looking on, their pledges to fight manfully for the principles and policies of this new party for which it is claimed that it will usher in a new dispensation in politics and in public life. Both nominees, but the Colonel especially, seemed deeply affected as they stood face to face with the men and women who are to shape the destinies of the new party and who had selected them as their standard bearers to do "battle for the Lord."

Tremor in Colonel's Voice.

There was a suspicious tremor in the Colonel's voice as he acknowledged, the nomination. Nor was it strange that he and his running fate should display such evidence of feeling. Wave upon wave of emotion swept over the audience as men and women joined in singing the stirring patriotic and partly religious airs which the band played. It was more like a Methodist consecration meeting than a political gathering.

It was after the Colonel's platform, embodying the vast scheme for "social and industrial justice," that he has advocated in recent public utterances, had been adopted, and after a dozen men had made nominating and seconding speeches of varying length for Gov. Johnson, that Senator Albert J. Beveridge of Indiana, Permanent Chairman of the convention, declared that Col. Roosevelt and Gov. Johnson had been duly nominated for President and Vice President, respectively.

It was nearly 7 o'clock, and the delegates and spectators had been through a long and wearing day of speeches and routine business, but there was no sign of apathy in the tremendous cheer that broke when it was proclaimed from the platform that the most important business of the convention had been completed and that the hat of the new party was in the ring.

The two nominees at that time were behind the convention scenes waiting for their cue. The two Committees of Notification, made up each of one or more members from every State delegation, had assembled on the rostrum and formed in a semi-circle very much like the chorus in an opera the moment before the hero makes his entry.

Into this semi-circle the Colonel and Gov. Johnson were conducted. Slowly they were led to the little inclosure in front of a sounding board under a brightly gleaming electric lamp. The Colonel was on the right, his running mate on the left. Between stood Chairman Beveridge.

Mrs. Roosevelt Waves Bandanna.

The convention stood up and cheered and cheered, but for the first few seconds the Colonel seemed oblivious of what was going on in the hall and in the galleries. He shot a rapid glance toward what in other conventions has been known as "Purple Row." In the first row of seats in that section a woman dressed in black stood up and waved a red bandanna, the favored emblem of the Bull Moosers, in the most frantic fashion. The woman was beaming, and the Colonel's lips parted in a smile as he saw the happy expression on her face. The woman was Mrs. Roosevelt, who for seven years was mistress of the White House and leading lady of the land, but who seemed to thrill with the scene before her as though it had been the Colonel's first experience at being nominated for President.

After a while the Colonel's glance shifted to the audience. Delegates stood on their feet and cheered. The hired band had gone to supper, but there was a volunteer band on the platform. It began to play, but the music was drowned in the thunder of acclaim that rolled up from the hall and down from the galleries where men and women waved flags and bandanas.

The cheering had been in progress for something like five minutes, with Gov. Johnson bowing, but with a face that was strangely solemn and with the Colonel's expression more sober than that of a man who merely experiences the pleasure of being the object of acclaim.

While the demonstration was in progress several Coliseum stage hands could be seen climbing to a little platform high under the arched ceiling of the huge auditorium. For a few minutes they busied themselves with ropes and pullies. Under their combined efforts a huge white canvas was released and unrolled. It was the first campaign banner of the Progressive Party, and the convention crowd rose to cheer the latest party slogan that appeared on it. Here is the legend:

ROOSEVELT AND JOHNSON.
NEW YORK AND CALIFORNIA.

HANDS ACROSS THE CONTINENT.

For there is neither East nor West,
Border, nor breed, nor birth,
When two strong men stand face to face,
Though they come from the ends of the earth.
—Kipling.

When the demonstration had been in progress about ten minutes it subsided somewhat. Then the band on the platform struck up "The Battle Hymn of the Republic." The compelling strains of that melody have stirred this very strange convention into fervent singing a dozen times since the convention first met. It had not lost its charm. Men and women sprang to their feet and sang, with shining eyes, the first two stanzas of the hymn. Col. Roosevelt and Gov. Johnson joined in the singing. The spell of the solemn words seemed to hold the audience even after the music died away. Chairman Beveridge had no use for his gavel. He placed his hand on the Colonel's shoulder and drew him gently a little closer to the audience.

"There is no need of introducing Col. Roosevelt," he said, a little huskily amid the hush "He is going to be our victorious Captain for the common good and the next President of the United States."

The Colonel's Speech.

There was some applause at this, but the audience seemed more anxious to hear what the Colonel had to say than to show the Colonel what they thought of him. The very first sentence the Colonel uttered showed that he was as deeply moved as was the audience. His voice trembled and he seemed to forget all the little tricks which he ordinarily brings into play to help out his oratory. He stood looking straight ahead and his face wore a very sober expression.

"I come forward to thank you from the bottom of my heart for the great honor you have conferred on me and to say that of course I accept," said Col. Roosevelt.

"I have been President of the United States. I have seen much of the world and know much of life, but I hold it to be by far the greatest honor and the greatest opportunity that ever has come to me to have been called upon by you to be for the time being the leader of this great movement in the interest of the American people."

For a moment the Colonel, who is such a ready speaker, faltered and seemed to search for thoughts and words with which to express them. The audience sat silent and waited for him to resume.

"Of Course I Accept"—Roosevelt.

Col. Roosevelt in his speech of acceptance said:

"Mr. Chairman and men and women who in this convention represent the high and honest purpose of the people of all of our country, I come forward to thank you from my heart for the honor you have conferred upon me and to say that of course I accept. I have been President and I measure my words when I say I have seen and know much of life, I hold it by far the greatest honor and the greatest opportunity that has ever come to me to be selected by you to the leadership for the time being of this great movement in the interests of the American people.

"And, friends, I wish now to say how deeply sensitive I am to the way in which the nomination has come to me and to tell those who proposed and seconded my nomination that I appreciate to the full the significance of having such men and such women put me in nomination, and I wish to thank the convention for having given me the running mate it has given.

Praise for Gov. Johnson.

"I have a peculiar feeling toward Gov. Johnson. Nearly two years ago, after the elections of 1910, when what I had striven to accomplish in New York had come to nothing, and when my friends, the enemy, exulted—possibly prematurely—over what had befallen me, Gov. Johnson, in the flush of his own triumph, having just won out, wrote me a letter which I shall hand on to my children and children's children because of what the letter contained, and because of the man who wrote it, a letter of trust and belief, a letter of ardent championship from the soldier who was at the moment victorious, toward his comrade who at the moment had been struck down.

In Gov. Johnson we have a man whose every word is made good by the deeds he has done. The man who at the head of a great State has practically applied in that State, for the benefit of the people of that State, the principles which we intend to apply throughout the Union as a whole. We have nominated the only type of man who ever ought to be nominated for the Vice Presidency, we have nominated a man fit at the moment to be President of the United States.

"Friends, I have come here merely to thank you from the bottom of my heart for the honor you have conferred upon me and to say that I appreciate it exactly as I know you meant it. For the greatest chance, the greatest gift that can be given to any man is the opportunity, if he has the stuff in him, to do something that counts in the interests of the common good.

Promises No Cause for Regret.

"I appreciate to the full the burden of responsibility, the burden of obligation that you have put upon me. I appreciate to the full that the trust you impose upon me can be met by me only in one way, and that is by so carrying myself that you shall have no cause to regret or to feel shame for the action you have taken this afternoon.

"And friends, with all my heart and soul, with every particle of high purpose that there is in me, I pledge you my word to do everything I can to put every particle of courage, of common sense, and of strength that I have at your disposal, and to endeavor so far as strength is given me to live up to the obligations which you have put upon me, and endeavor to carry out in the interests of our whole people the policies to which you have to-day solemnly dedicated yourselves to the millions of men and women from whom you speak. I thank you." •

Gov. Johnson's Acceptance.

There was a prolonged demonstration as Col. Roosevelt concluded. It was renewed when Gov. Johnson was introduced. He said:

"It is with the utmost solemnity, the deepest obligation that I come to tell you that I have enlisted for the war. I enlisted long ago, and I enlisted in that fight that is your fight now, the fight of all the Nation, thank God, at last. Humanity's fight politically all over the land.

"Enlisting as I have in that contest for humanity that desired governmentally to make men better rather than to make men richer, there is no question of course that of necessity I must accept any place where I may be drafted, and that I accept such a place as you have accorded me in the Nation's history to-day, (because again you are making history in this land,) that I accept it with grateful heart and with the utmost singlesness of purpose to carry out as well as I may the little that may be my part to do.

* * * * *

August 8, 1912

Harmony Committees In Today's Conferences

Special to The New York Times.

CHICAGO, Ill., June 7.—As a result of conferences tonight between Republican and Progressive leaders, the following was agreed upon as the personnel of the joint harmony committee:

For the Republican—Senator Boies Penrose of Pennsylvania, Senator H. C. Lodge of Massachusetts, Senator William E. Borah of Idaho, ex-Senator W. Murray Crane of Massachusetts, and Samuel A. Perkins, delegate from Washington.

For the Progressives—George W. Perkins of New York, Victor Murdock of Kansas, William Hamlin Childs of New York, William Allen White of Kansas, and as the fifth man, either E. A. Van Valkenburg of Philadelphia or Walter Brown of Ohio.

June 8, 1916

HUGHES ACCEPTS REPUBLICAN NOMINATION FOR PRESIDENT

LANDSLIDE FOR HUGHES

949½ Votes on Day's Sole Ballot—Fairbanks His Running Mate.

EXPECT COLONEL'S SUPPORT

Fuller Statement from Hughes Alone Deemed Necessary—May Mean End of Moose.

T. R. FORESAW THE RESULT

Quick Acceptance by Hughes in Line with Tacit Agreement—Conventions Adjourned.

Special to The New York Times.

CHICAGO, June 10.—Charles E. Hughes and Theodore Roosevelt, both of New York, were nominated for President by the Republican and Progressive conventions at 12:49 and 12:47 o'clock today, respectively, the Roosevelt nomination beating the Hughes nomination by exactly two minutes. Charles Warren Fairbanks of Indiana was nominated for Vice President on the Republican ticket and John M. Parker of Louisiana on the Progressive. The Hughes nomination was made on the third ballot of the convention, the Roosevelt nomination by acclamation.

Colonel Roosevelt sent a tentative declination of the nomination, with the understanding that it was to stand if Hughes turned out to be sound on the issues of Americanism and preparedness, and that if Hughes turned out to be pacifistic, pussy-footed, or pro-German he would accept and make the race as the Progressive candidate.

FOR PRESIDENT,
CHARLES EVANS HUGHES

Justice Hughes broke all records by accepting the nomination by telegraph, without waiting for a formal notification by the regularly appointed committee, and declared his position not only on the issues regarded by Colonel Roosevelt as the test issues, but also on the other principal questions raised by the Republican platform. For a long time a third telegram, this one from Mr. Fairbanks declining the Vice Presidential nomination, was anticipated, because he already had sent a private one to that effect, but, instead, he accepted over the telephone. The Republicans went home stolidly and apathetically, the Progressives gloomily.

The Conference Committee scheme failed because the Republicans would name no candidate. At the last minute, after every effort to induce them to do so had proved ineffective, Colonel Roosevelt himself proposed union on Senator Henry Cabot Lodge of Massachusetts. The two Conference Committees so reported, but the Progressive Convention laid the telegram on the table and the Republicans paid no attention to it.

Hughes Statement Criticised.

Nevertheless, union against Wilson, though it was not handsomely accomplished, and though technically it was not accomplished at all, is regarded here as practically in effect. It is not yet complete because Justice Hughes has not yet shown how far he is in agreement with the Roosevelt position. His telegram of acceptance does declare emphatically that he stands for the protection of American rights and would have passed as a complete indorsement of the Roosevelt position if he had not specifically emphasized the Mexican question.

That emphasis raises in the Progressive mind the question why he should pick out only one phase of the Wilson foreign policy and not couple it with greater infractions of American rights from other countries, as in the case of the Lusitania. He follows closely the lines of the Republican platform, but the Progressives will want more; they will want a declaration as clear and specific as those which Colonel Roosevelt has been making.

The general tone of the Hughes telegram, however, is such as to warrant the expectation that when he speaks more in detail he will not refer solely to the Mexican question and that his expressed intention to safeguard American rights "on land or sea" will be explained so fully that no one will have any excuse for coupling it with similar utterances by, for instance, President Wilson or Secretary Lansing, and maintaining that there is no difference between the candidates. The Progressives do expect that that will come to pass, and in that case Colonel Roosevelt's tentative declination will stand.

A Rump Ticket Probable.

If it does stand, there will be union on Hughes so far as practical effectiveness goes. The Roosevelt men in the Republican Party will not bolt, and the Roosevelt men among the Progressives will vote for Hughes. There may even then be a bolting ticket, and very likely there will be, but it will be a rump ticket. When Henry George withdrew from the United Labor Party, (which he had built up and which he carried near to victory in 1886,) and supported Cleveland as representing the nearest available approach to the principles of that party, the irreconcilables kept the United Labor Party together.

Since they could not nominate George they nominated a Chicago man unknown to fame as Robert C. Cowdrey for President. But as the campaign went on all the George men gravitated into one or the other of the big political camps, and without their leader the party petered out. The United Labor Party's vote, which had been appallingly large two years before, and big enough to hold the balance of power in many places one year before, followed. George, and Cowdrey's vote was too small to count. It did not affect the election in the least degree.

If Hughes's principles turn out to be identical with Roosevelt's and if Roosevelt's declination continues to stand, the general expectation here is that that chapter in history will be duplicated. It is even possible that no Progressive ticket will be put into the field. That matter is in the hands of the Progressive National Committee, which could nominate Hughes or could name somebody like Victor Murdock and repeat the Cowdrey chapter.

Moose Divided as to T. R.

As for Roosevelt himself, there is a wide difference of opinion among Progressives tonight. Some are denouncing him as a quitter and saying that he has betrayed them, others are enthusiastically applauding his position and declaring that he has played a patriotic and statesmanlike part in subordinating his own grudges for the good of the country in a time of crisis.

Among the Republicans there is distinctly a better feeling toward him than when the convention met. There is still harsh talk about the bolter of 1912, but his attempts to bring about a union against Wilson have moderated some of the bitterness of it. For the last day or two the charge that he is insincere and self-seeking in his efforts to promote harmony have practically disappeared, and his good faith has not been argued about.

Tentative as it was, the Colonel's declination is taken as final, because it is expected everywhere that Justice Hughes will remove the only obstacle. He has gone much further already in that direction than was expected. The telegram which he sent was, of course, not the accidental product of a sudden inspiration. It was known to the leaders that he would send such a telegram, with the definite purpose of satisfying Roosevelt's followers, and they communicated that information to the Colonel. They received in return the information that if Hughes proved to be "all right" on Americanism and preparedness the Colonel would not run; otherwise he would.

These exchanges constituted the real harmony agreement, and the Conference Committee made no great effort to reach one, because it knew of them. The Republican members made known to the Progressives early in the sessions of the committee that they could not carry out the Colonel's idea of eliminating one candidate after another and settling down on a dark horse like Lodge because they could not deliver the convention. They could not do anything with the favorite sons, who clung to their crass idea that they stood a chance to win in the shuffle, except by taking a vote in the convention that would bring conviction to these darkened minds: and the moment they took a vote Hughes would be nominated, and Roosevelt promised that if Hughes did and was "all right," he would not run against him.

That was the real harmony agreement: but for show-window purposes the formal conferences were kept up. The Colonel has given no promise to support Hughes by taking an active part in the campaign; he has promised only that he would not oppose him if he took the right position.

Appeals to the Conventions.

At last, when the Conference Committee was ending its sessions, he decided to try one last attempt at nominating a dark horse. The Republican conferees had assured his conferees that the leaders could do nothing, that the convention alone would decide on the candidate. He therefore appealed directly to the convention; in fact, to both conventions. He urged each party, for the sake of the country, to lay aside its own candidate, one of whom was himself, and to unite on Lodge. But the Progressive convention, to which this appeal was first read would have none of it. It listened in silence until the name of Lodge was read, when there were shouts "No," "No." There was no disrespect, no anger, simply an irrevocable determination to have but one candidate. The temper of the convention was so unmistakable that it was Mr. Perkins himself who moved to lay the suggestion on the table, which was done without a dissenting voice.

When Senator Smoot later reported the Colonel's suggestion to the Republican Convention he was able to add that the Progressives had laid it on the table. This, of course, left the Republican Convention with nothing to do about it. It made no great difference. If the Progressives had accepted the Colonel's suggestion there would have been a fight in the Republican Convention, and the Hughes victory, perhaps, would have been delayed for a ballot or two, but the result would have been the same; the suggestion came too late.

It would have been a practicable scheme if it had been a different kind of convention, but the plans of the bosses had worked out too well. Ever since 1912 the work of picking out these delegates had been going on. It was determined to fill the convention of 1916 with solid men who could not be stampeded, and who had no liking for Roosevelt. It was done so well that it not only could not be stampeded, it could not be moved or argued with. It would no more listen to the leaders than it would listen to Roosevelt. It was a convention of hard-headed reactionaries, who saw no more reason why they should take advice from Penrose than from Hiram Johnson.

Penrose Clear-Visioned.

Penrose himself saw this and acted with discretion and common sense. He is the only one of the Old Guard who comes out of this convention with much credit. From the first he has been open-minded, intent only on doing the right thing for party victory, and he has shown a perception of the real situation which most of the others have not shared. It has been really amazing to see the perverse blindness of men who are accounted able politicians, and their inability to understand things as plain as the noses on their faces.

Fairbanks, for instance, really believed as late as the assembling of the convention this morning that he was going to be nominated, and last night he would not consent to letting his men join the others in throwing the booms into the Hughes melting pot. The other candidates were abandoned between midnight and dawn by a series of conferences. Sherman, Burton, and others released their men in those hours; even La Follette abandoned his usual tactics and released his.

But Fairbanks would not let his go, and insisted on an appeal to Roosevelt over the telephone to support him. Roosevelt flatly refused. It was a tragedy to Fairbanks, but it was merely the result of taking too lightly Roosevelt's public announcement, "I will support no man who pussyfoots on this issue." Later, when Fairbanks heard that he was going to be nominated for Vice President he sent a telegram which was taken to indicate that he would decline the nomination, or at least that there was danger he would. It was a private telegram and did not become known to the delegates, and they nominated him.

Justice Hughes carried out his part of the agreement by instantly resigning and sending the telegram which had been promised. The Colonel had no inkling of its contents except the assurance that it would satisfy him. These assurances were so confident that the Colonel expected it to be of a stronger character than it has proved to be. He did not expect that Justice Hughes would talk about defending American rights and then single out Mexico for special mention and thereby call attention to his silence about Germany, which would otherwise have passed unremarked.

No Attempt at Deception.

Nevertheless, the telegram is sufficiently strong to necessitate no modification of the Colonel's declination. He was led, however, to believe that the telegram would take ground as strong as the ground he has taken himself. No implication is intended that the Colonel was deceived or misled, or that Justice Hughes does not honestly believe his telegram is everything that was to be expected. The Republican members of the Conference Committee so understood it and undoubtedly so understand it now, and gave their assurance to the Progressive members in entire good faith.

It was the Colonel's counterpromise not to run that made them so well satisfied with themselves and the situation when they told the newspaper men that nothing had been arrived at in the way of an agreement between the two conventions, and yet that progress was being made and harmony would result.

There is reason to believe that one member of the Conference Committee, Senator Borah, communicated the Justice's promise to the Colonel two days before the committee was appointed, communicated it over Mr. Perkins's telephone, and received in return the Colonel's promise that if the agreement was carried out he would not run against Hughes.

The telegram itself is an unprecedented thing. No Presidential candidate is supposed to know that he has been nominated until the notification committee has waited upon him and given him the information, bringing with it proper credentials to show that it is officially appointed and is likely not to be playing any practical joke on him. Then he makes a speech accepting the nomination and tells the committee that later on, when he has recovered from his surprise and can collect his thoughts, he will comunicate his views at length, that the party may find out whether it has nominated the right man. Then he writes a letter of acceptance, and it is found that by a strange coincidence his views are the same as those set forth in the platfom, so that evidently the convention has made no mistake in his nomination.

An Unromantic Convention.

This time the candidate is notified by a private telegram sent by the Chairman, and replies in a telegram addressed to the convention. The reason the convention did not hear it read is because it wanted to go home. A really enthusiastic convention would have been glad to wait, but this let-her-go, phlegmatic, heavy-footed convention had no romance in its nature. Chairman Harding was so well aware that a motion to take a recess would be unwelcome that he did not call for one, though he gave the convention a hint on which it could have acted if it had wanted to. But it sat, as usual, unresponsively in its place, and did not even cheer the announcement that its candidate had accepted, except by a few individual and momentary cries, light in calibre, and sudden in their ending. The Progressives would have taken a recess for a day if necessary to get such a message from their leader.

In the Progressive Convention today Victor Murdock predicted the nomination of a Prohibition-Pacifist ticket consisting of Bryan and Ford. Senator William Alden Smith and others are apprehensive of a pacifist bolt, but no signs of it are evident here.

The balloting in the Republican Convention was without life or enthusiasm. The fact that the favorite sons, except Fairbanks, had decided overnight to cash in was all over town before the convention met. Nothing remained except to meet, ratify the decision, and go home.

The Progressives supplied plenty of life, but when the news came that the Colonel had declined the nomination the life went out of them. They felt extremely sore, some of them at the Colonel, and all of them at the Republicans. They felt and said that they had made all the overtures for harmony and that the Republicans had ignored them.

John M. Parker, their Vice Presidential candidate-to-be, said the Progressives had proposed union in the statement issued by their National Committee last January; the Republicans had never taken the least notice of it, and since the conventions the Progressives had continued to be the only ones who offered anything.

"Not once," he said, "have the men from the Coliseum offered the olive branch."

Moose Win by Two Minutes.

Perkins made a gallant, uphill fight, even then, urging the Progressives to hold back the nomination of Roosevelt until the Republicans had taken another ballot, so as to see if the Colonel's proposal of Lodge had any effect. But they would not, they were too much afraid that the Republicans would name Hughes before they named Roosevelt and deprive them of the right to say that they had acted independently. As it was, they only beat the Republicans to a nomination by two minutes, though Bainbridge Colby cut his nominating speech down to a minute and a half, and no ballot was taken.

The Republican convention was in a class all by itself. One more such convention would work a revolution in the nominating machinery. It was a convention which had no enthusiasm, no life, but went to work at everything in a dogged and practical way. The reason why its bogus pretenses of enthusiasm, its imitations of the usual convention trills, have been so comical or so disgusting is not because such things are necessarily funny in themselves, but because they were in such direct contrast to the spirit of the convention.

Certain financial and business results are reached by Charlie Chaplin when he stumbles over a gutter or kicks a policeman. It is quite proper in his case, and nobody thinks the less of him. Suppose, however, that the Trustees of the Equitable Life Assurance Society, also aiming at certain financial and business results, should think it necessary to imitate his methods in opening a meeting of their board. It would be displeasing and incongruous and would not advance the objects they had in view.

There are certain campaign methods, once quite proper, that have gone out of date. Men no longer put on uniforms and march in torchlight parades as they did in Garfield's time, and they no longer drink and hold barbecues as they did in Henry Clay's, and they no longer open barrels of hard cider and march behind imitation log cabins as they did in William Henry Harrison's.

It is a prediction freely made around Chicago tonight that the roaring, shouting conventions will follow these political toys into the discard and that future conventions will be business-like, mechanical affairs, with no more cheering and standard waving and stampeding than there would be in a bank. It is, however, equally possible that the strange spectacle seen this week will go into history as altogether solitary, that it will have no successor, as it most certainly has had no predecessors.

June 11, 1916

MOOSE INDORSES, HUGHES ACCEPTS AND THANKS T. R.

National Committee Quarrels for Hours Before Putting O. K. on the Nominee.

THE FINAL BALLOT 32 TO 6

Nine Refuse to Take Part in Action That Is Called Death-blow to Progressive Party.

ATTACKS WILSON'S POLICIES

Candidate Sends Message to Chicago and a Letter to Oyster Bay Asking Early Meeting.

The Progressive National Committee at a meeting in Chicago yesterday voted to adopt a recommendation from Theodore Roosevelt that the Progressive Party indorse Charles E. Hughes for President.

The resolution indorsing Hughes was adopted after six hours of wrangling, in which the members present divided, roughly, 32 in favor of supporting the Republican nominee and 15 in favor of putting a third ticket in the field.

A motion to substitute Victor Murdock of Kansas as the Progressive nominee for President, in place of Roosevelt, was defeated, 31 to 15. The vote to indorse Hughes was 32 to 6, with 9 members not voting.

The action taken was regarded as marking the death of the Progressive Party. Most of the fifteen dissenters are expected to support Wilson.

The committee based its action on a letter received from Colonel Roosevelt declining the Progressive nomination and recommending that the Progressives indorse Hughes. The letter contained a bitter attack on President Wilson and declared that the public interest demanded that the Progressives combine with the Republicans to defeat him.

Hughes and T. R. Join Forces.

Mr. Hughes and Colonel Roosevelt joined forces openly yesterday in an effort to overthrow the Wilson Administration. From now on they will work together, without concealment of the fact, and they will meet soon to discuss campaign plans.

The Mexican situation, which has caused Mr. Wilson to call out the militia; the sinking by German submarines of the Lusitania and other ships bearing American passengers, and "100 per cent. Americanism," as advocated by Roosevelt, will be made the big issues, according to a statement by Mr. Hughes. It was predicted freely last night that the nominee and Colonel Roosevelt would both take the stump for a vigorous campaign and fight shoulder to shoulder.

Colonel Roosevelt made his position known in a long statement he sent to the National Committee of the Progressive Party, in session at Chicago during the afternoon. He called on all Progressives to support Hughes, and the committee, as a result, indorsed the Republican nominee.

Mr. Hughes, on receiving this word, sent a special messenger to Oyster Bay with a letter to Colonel Roosevelt, indorsing the principles enunciated by the Colonel in his pre-convention campaign. In the letter he also took the first step toward a complete reconciliation by closing with the words, "I hope I may have the pleasure of seeing you at an early day."

Letter to Colonel Roosevelt.

The letter to Colonel Roosevelt read:

Hotel Astor,
New York City, June 26, 1916.

My dear Colonel Roosevelt:

I warmly appreciate the cordial letter of indorsement which you have sent to the Progressive Committee. No one is more sensible than I of the lasting indebtedness of the nation to you for the quickening of the national spirit, for the demand for an out-and-out—100 per cent.—Americanism, and for the insistence upon the immediate necessity of a thoroughgoing preparedness, spiritual, military, and economic.

I am in this campaign because of my conviction that we must not only frame but execute a broad constructive program, and that for this purpose we must have a united party, a party inspired by its great traditions and reconsecrated to its loftiest ideals. I know that you have been guided in this emergency by the sole desire to be of the largest service to the United States. You have sounded forth the trumpet that shall never call retreat. And I want you to feel that I wish to have all the aid that you are able and willing to give. I want the most effective co-operation with all those who have been fighting by your side. Let us work together for our national security and for the peace of righteousness and justice.

I inclose a copy of my telegram to the committee, in which I have set forth my attitude. I shall later undertake a full discussion of the issues of the campaign.

Hoping that I may have the pleasure of seeing you at an early day, I am, my dear Colonel Roosevelt, with cordial regards.

Faithfully yours,
CHARLES E. HUGHES.

Colonel Theodore Roosevelt, Oyster Bay, Long Island, N. Y.

The telegram to the Progressive National Committee, to which Mr. Hughes devoted much thought, while the committee was holding a stormy session in Chicago, was looked upon by many as a notice to Old Guard leaders that Mr. Hughes would work with them only on the same basis that he would work with the Progressives and Roosevelt Republicans. He received a full report of the committee's action by wire at the Hotel Astor, and released the telegram upon hearing of his indorsement, although the committee had adjourned without indorsing his running mate, Mr. Fairbanks. Here is the telegram:

Telegram to Committee.

Hotel Astor,
New York City, June 26, 1916.

O. K. Davis, Secretary Progressive National Committee, Blackstone Hotel, Chicago, Ill.:

I welcome the support of Progressives. We make common cause in the interest of national honor, of national security, of national efficiency. We unite in the demand for an undivided and unwavering loyalty to our country, for a whole-hearted patriotic devotion overriding all racial differences. We want a revival of the American spirit—a nation restored. We insist upon prompt and adequate provision for the common defense; upon the steadfast maintenance of all the rights of our citizens, and upon the integrity of international law.

The most serious difficulties the present Administration has encountered have been due to its own weakness and incertitude. I am profoundly convinced that by prompt and decisive action, which existing conditions manifestly called for, the Lusitania tragedy would have been prevented. We strongly denounce the use of our soil as a base for alien intrigues, for conspiracies and the fomenting of disorders in the interest of any foreign nation, but the responsibility lies at the door of the Administration. The moment notice is admitted responsibility is affixed. For that sort of thing could not continue if the Administration took proper measures to stop it. That responsibility the Administration cannot evade by condemning others.

It was officially stated by the Secretary of State in the Mexican note of June 20, 1916, that "for three years the Mexican republic has been torn with civil strife; the lives of Americans and other aliens have been sacrificed; vast properties developed by American capital and enterprise have been destroyed or rendered non-productive; bandits have been permitted to roam at will through territory contiguous to the United States and to seize, without punishment or without effective attempt at punishment, the property of Americans, while the lives of citizens of the United States who ventured to remain in Mexican territory or to return there to protect their interests have been taken, in some cases barbarously taken, and the murderers have neither been apprehended nor brought to justice."

"Unpardonable Neglect."

What an indictment by the Administration of its Mexican policy! And still we are unprepared. That unpreparedness in the midst of perils, and after the experiences of three years, is a demonstration of an unpardonable neglect for which the Administration is responsible.

The Government now has and must have most emphatically the unstinted and patriotic support of every citizen in the existing exigency. But unquestioning, loyal and patriotic support of the Government is one thing; approval of the fatuous course which the Administration has followed is quite another. I cannot in this message adequately review that course; that I shall do later.

No intelligent man is deceived by the temporary prosperity due to abnormal conditions and no one can fail to appreciate the gravity of the problems with which we shall be faced when the war ends. We are alive to the imperative necessity of assuring the bases of honest business. I am in deep sympathy with the effort to improve the conditions of labor; to prevent exploitation; to safeguard the future of the nation by protecting our women and children. I believe in workmen's compensation laws; in wise conservation of our national resources so that they may be protected, developed, and used to the utmost public advantage. But underlying every endeavor to promote social justice is the indispensable condition that there shall be a stable foundation for honorable enterprise. American industry must have proper protection if labor is to be safeguarded.

We must rescue our instrumentalities of interstate and foreign commerce, our transportation facilities, from uncertainty and confusion. We must show that we know how to protect the public without destroying or crippling our productive energies.

"Our Common Cause."

To what agency shall we look for the essential constructive program on which our security and prosperity must depend? It is vain to expect it from the Democratic Party. That party has not the national outlook. Both its traditions and dominating influences are fatal handicaps. I have no sectional word to utter. We are to elect a President of the whole country, not of a part. The South, as well as the North, East, and West, will be the gainers from our endeavors. But it is sober truth as I see it that as we go forward we must make the Republican Party the instrument of our advance. We want deeds, not words; far-reaching national policies. The Progressives have insisted on responsible, not invisible, government; on efficient administration. I yield to no one in that demand. I am eager to call the best ability of the country to our aid. For the conduct of the great departments the Executive is directly responsible and there is no excuse whatever for the toleration of incompetence in order to satisfy partisan obligations.

I am deeply appreciative of your indorsement. I find no difference in platform or in aim which precludes the most hearty co-operation and the most complete unity. It is within the party that the liberalizing spirit you invoke can have the widest and most effective influence. I solicit your earnest effort for the common cause.

CHARLES E. HUGHES.

Colonel Ready for Meeting.

The Hughes letter did not reach Oyster Bay until late last night, and it was impossible then to obtain any comment from Colonel Roosevelt. It was known on excellent authority, however, that Colonel Roosevelt was willing to meet Mr. Hughes on a common basis of promoting the doctrines to which they both have subscribed, and that the only thing which has stood in the way of such a meeting was the fact that no invitation had come from the nominee. It is generally believed that they will meet within a week or ten days, either in this city or at Mr. Hughes's Summer home at Bridgehampton, L. I. No definite information on the place or date of a proposed meeting could be obtained here, however.

The open announcement of the combination between Hughes and Roosevelt and the cordiality of the letter sent by Hughes to the man whom they fought so bitterly in 1912, when he split the Republican Party, and against whom most of them were solidly aligned in the recent Republican Convention, was received by most of the Old Guard leaders without extended comment.

When Mr. Hughes made public his statement at the Astor last night he had gathered about him, as far as could be learned, only a few of his close advisers, such as Public Service Commissioner Whitney and Major Crossett, who helped him open his campaign headquarters when he made his hurried trip here from Washington after his nomination before the Old Guard faction could get here from Chicago to forestall him.

There were other important developments about the Hughes headquarters yesterday. It was reported, for one thing, that the selection of a national Chairman would be made within a day or two, and that William R. Willcox, former Chairman of the Public Service Commission, was leading in the race.

Joseph B. Kealing, former National Committeeman from Indiana, has been selected tentatively as a Vice Chairman for the Middle West, with headquarters in Chicago; and Ralph E. Williams, National Committeeman from Oregon, as Vice Chairman in charge of headquarters in San Francisco.

Hughes Silent on Chairmanship.

Kealing and Williams, especially Kealing, have been pretty closely affiliated with the Old Guard interests, but there is no such tag on Willcox, who would have direct charge of the campaign, if the slate talked about yesterday should go through. There was some talk of National Committeeman Charles B. Warren of Detroit as Vice Chairman of the Middle West, instead of Kealing, but Mr. Williams, on behalf of Mr. Warren, gave out a statement last night in which he said that the Detroit man was in no sense a candidate for the national chairmanship. This was taken by some as an indication that Warren was not even in the race for Vice Chairman and that Kealing's selection for the Middle West post was practically assured.

Mr. Hughes refused to make any comment on this topic, but there was a feeling that the final announcement might be made some time today before Mr. Hughes left at 4 o'clock for his Summer home at Bridgehampton, L. I., to remain over the Fourth of July.

Mr. Hughes had a conference with W. Murray Crane, Chairman of the steering committee, when he got to town yesterday morning, but neither would talk about what took place. Another visitor was Nelson O'Shaughnessy, former Chargé d'Affaires in Mexico City. He said he did not discuss Mexican matters with Mr. Hughes, but to correspondents he said he considered it unfortunate that the country had got into the Mexican trouble in "such a bad way."

James R. Goodrich, Republican candidate for Governor of Indiana, and National Committeeman Williams of Oregon were among others to confer with Mr. Hughes.

June 27, 1916

* * * * * *

DEMOCRATS AT MIDNIGHT RENOMINATE WILSON

WESCOTT NOMINATES WILSON

New Jersey Judge Performs Same Service As He Did at Baltimore.

MEXICAN POLICY CHEERED

Mention of Wilson's Name Sets Convention Cheering and Tumult Lasts 45 Minutes.

Special to The New York Times.

ST. LOUIS, Friday, June 16.—After a demonstration of approval of President Wilson late in the night which lasted forty-five minutes the Democratic National Convention renominated President Wilson and Vice President Marshall by acclamation. Mr. Wilson was renominated at 11:53 and Mr. Marshall at 11:55.

President Wilson was placed in nomination by Judge John W. Wescott of New Jersey.

The program called for a seconding speech from every delegation in the case of President Wilson, but after ex-Governor Harmon of Ohio and Governor Stuart of Virginia had made seconding speeches the delegates called vociferously for a vote and the nomination followed immediately.

Robert E. Burke of Illinois refused his consent to the unanimous nomination of the President amid a storm of hisses. No further attention was paid to him, and Chairman Ollie James declared the motion to nominate by acclamation carried.

Senator Kern of Indiana immediately nominated Mr. Marshall for Vice President without making a speech, and on motion the nomination was made by acclamation. The Friday hoodoo was escaped by four minutes.

At 11:59 the Notification Committees had been authorized and Chairmen Glynn and James had been appointed to the respective chairmanships of them.

Platform Report Delayed.

The routine motions of thanks and routine announcements of committee meetings, which are usually made at the end of a convention, were made, and then nothing remained but the platform. Chairman James's call for it brought no response, and a committee consisting of Senators Hughes, Vardaman, and Taggart was appointed to wait on the Resolutions Committee and find out what was the matter.

This was at 12:07 A. M. The convention waited impatiently for the committee to return. Many of the delegates had their hats on and were moving restlessly about the hall, while the galleries were shouting for Senator James Hamilton Lewis to make a speech.

Senators Hughes and Taggart returned at 12:20 and informed Chairman James that the Resolutions Committee had agreed on a report and was whipping it into shape, but would not be ready for two hours. There was nothing to do but while away the time with speechmaking for those two hours, and Representative Thomas J. Heflin of Alabama started it.

At 12:32 Senator Hughes informed the convention that the committee was not able to say when it would be ready with its report and a recess was taken until 11 o'clock today.

Nominating speeches were to have begun at the opening of the night session, but before getting to work William J. Bryan was invited to address the convention as an honored guest. He was greeted with great enthusiasm. The compliment conveyed in the invitation gained weight from the fact that no other man outside the convention had been either invited or permitted to address it.

It was at 10:14 P. M. that nominations for President were called for. Alabama yielded to New Jersey, and Judge Wescott, who placed Woodrow Wilson in nomination at Baltimore four years ago took the platform. Applause greeted his remarks on the policy toward Mexico. The crowd was attentive and quiet. It voiced approval of America's maintenance of international law. Some of the crowd, however, were eager for the nomination.

"Name him! Name him!" came cries from the galleries. Judge Wescott hurried his speech a little. He made such good time that he got into the peroration of his speech at 10:42 o'clock.

"The prophecy is fulfilled," said Judge Wescott; "the right has prevailed. Undisturbed by vituperation, the schoolmaster, the statesman, the financier, the emancipator, the pacificator, the moral leader of democracy has prevailed. The nation is at work, the nation is at peace. It is accomplishing the destiny of democracy.

Mr. Wescott said that four years ago the nation was not at work and men were idle. He struck a responsive chord when he referred to Mexico.

"Help Mexico!" he shouted, "or over the graves of the dead will be sown the dragon's teeth of our own destruction."

The speaker went on to speak of the European war.

"Who now can close his eyes to the destiny of democracy to bring the warring nations together in lasting peace?" he asked. "The American standard of peace and justice floats in the air. Out of the ruins of the present contest will arise a temple of justice."

As the President's sponsor proceeded the murmur of those talking and whispering grew until in some parts of the balconies spectators audibly demanded better order. The heat had a visible effect on the speaker, whose face dripped beads of perspiration.

Demonstration for Wilson.

As Judge Wescott closed with a mention of the name "Woodrow Wilson" the crowd broke into a great demonstration. Moving picture flashlights blazed and flags were paraded in front of the stand. The band played "The Star-Spangled Banner," while a huge banner bearing the President's likeness was unfurled from the roof of the hall.

The delegates began a parade bearing State stanchions. The crowds on the floor and balconies rose to their feet. Many delegates stood on their chairs.

"Dixie" and other melodies by the band evoked fresh bursts of cheering.

Chairman James yielded the chair during the demonstration to Representative Heflen of Alabama. Women delegates were among the paraders in the aisles. Senators and Representatives helped carry banners. Senator Hughes personally bore the New Jersey flag.

Sergeant at Arms Martin stirred up the enthusiasm by waving the Texas Lone Star flag, handed over the heads of the crowd from the Chairman's rostrum. Other State flags were taken to the platform.

The crowd joining in singing a medley, including "How Dry I Am," "Old Black Joe," "The Red, White and Blue," and other songs.

Renewed After Thirty Minutes.

After the demonstration had been under way thirty minutes New York and some other delegates resumed their seats. Waving a cane over the rail at the Chairman's desk Senator Hughes renewed the clamor by leading three cheers for the President.

The band exhausted the list of popular national airs, then it turned to "Tipperary," and the crowd joined in the chorus. Then the musicians went back to American airs. Some of the delegates stopped demonstrating long enough to drain pop bottles and then went back at it again.

The band was so vigorous keeping up the din that the musicians went short of breath, so they lay back and let the bass drummer perform alone for a while. He belabored his drum industriously until the bandsmen got their second wind, and then they went back to "Tipperary."

There was absolutely no attempt to control the crowd in the Coliseum while the demonstration was going on. Men and women wearing various kinds of badges to which they were not entitled overran the platform and the press sections at will. The passages to the telegraph rooms were so packed with persons who had no business in the vicinity that only those who had their telegraph instruments on the platform could send the news of the convention to the outside world. The police made no effort to control the situation.

The crowd roared when several woman suffrage workers with golden umbrellas and yellow sweaters who mounted the platform and held a suffrage umbrella over the head of Representative Heflin of Alabama, one of the most vigorous "antis" in Congress. He apparently enjoyed the situation.

The New York delegates, who had been seated, were again forced to arise by insistent clamor from nearby delegations. The band, its repertoire taxed, finally turned to such ancient ballads as "On the Banks of the Wabash" and "Turkey in the Straw."

Occasionally the demonstration would die to a droning noise, then some incident would stir a livelier note. One of these came when three woman delegates started a parade with a banner inscribed: "Wilson, Peace, and Prosperity." The hall was too congested for a swift-moving procession. The flags and banners were wormed in and out among the delegates, who were hardly more than swaying back and forth.

When Mr. Martin, the Sergeant at Arms, began to wave the big Lone Star flag of Texas from the platform, he started a flag rally there and soon numerous flags were being waved by willing hands.

The Georgia delegates paraded with a big banner on which was printed "Georgia, Woodrow Wilson, Dixie's gift to the Nation."

When the crowd began singing the first air taken up was the song the Pennsylvanians had been forbidden to sing—"Hail! Hail! the Gang's All Here." Southern songs were taken up later. Those who didn't know the words whistled the tune.

At 11:30 all but a few delegates had taken their seats, apparently ready to go on, and at 11:33 Chairman James sounded the first gavel rap. The demonstration had lasted forty-five minutes.

Only Two Seconding Speeches.

The roll call of States was resumed and Arizona yielded to Ohio. Ex-Governor Judson Harmon of Ohio made the first seconding speech in behalf of President Wilson.

Ex-Governor Harmon, who was considered a strong Presidential possibility himself four years ago, was greeted with applause. He has grown thinner in the last two years, and his voice is not so commanding as it once was. Persons ten feet from him could not hear what he was saying, and the galleries began to get noisy. But every once in awhile he mentioned the name of President Wilson loud enough to be heard and the crowd gave him a cheer. It was a short speech, and he soon sat down.

Again Secretary Smith started to call the roll. He reached Arkansas. The Chairman of the delegation yielded at once to Virginia, "that State which is the mother of Presidents," and Governor Stuart took the platform.

Governor Stuart, a bulky man with a deep voice, spoke of the President keeping the country out of war, and was applauded as he sat down and the crowd began to yell for a vote.

Senator Hughes moved that the rules be suspended, and that the vote be taken by acclamation. Chairman James repeated the motion. Robert E. Burke, a delegate at large from Illinois, jumped up and asked for a roll call. There were objections from all over the hall. Chairman James put the Hughes motion. There was a shout of "AYE!" The Chairman then called for the "nays." A few were heard here and there.

Chairman James then announced the renomination of President Wilson by acclamation. A mighty yell of approval went up. The Chairman next announced that nominations for Vice President were in order.

The nomination of Vice President Marshall was put through in three minutes, a record. Senator Kern of Indiana was recognized to put Mr. Marshall in nomination. The Senator discarded his prepared speech and merely said: "I nominate Thomas R. Marshall of Indiana to be Vice President."

The rules already had been suspended to permit a vote of acclamation, and Chairman James at once put the question. There was a call for Roger Sullivan of Illinois, but no one formally proposed his name, and the nomination was voted unanimously. Applause for both nominees was short.

A resolution was at once adopted appointing ex-Governor Glynn Chairman of the committee to notify President Wilson of the convention's action. Senator James was named Chairman of a similar committee to notify Vice President Marshall.

There was great confusion throughout the convention hall at this time, due to persons in the galleries leaving. Many of the delegates were on their feet anxious to follow the exodus of the sightseers.

The convention now had nothing else to do until the platform committee should return its report. The confusion continued without any effort on the part of the Chair to stop it. One of the clerks finally got order and announced that the new National Committee would meet this afternoon at the Jefferson Hotel.

Somebody saw James Hamilton Lewis on the platform and a cry for the Illinois Senator went up all over the hall. Delegates remembered the witty speech he made at the convention four years ago in Baltimore. The demand became insistent and it took concrete shape in the suggestion of a delegate from Ohio that the Senator be allowed to address the convention. Chairman James put the motion to the convention, and there was a shout of approval. Some voices were heard, however, opposing the idea, and Mr Lewis declined to speak. He took the platform only long enough to say the hour was late and business must be performed.

Representative Heflin of Alabama, a silver-tongued orator, next was called. He said the solid South was still solid and that the status of the Union was firm.

While Mr. Heflin was talking, Senator Hughes of New Jersey and Senator Taggart, who with Senator Vardaman of Mississippi had been appointed to visit the Committee of Resolutions, reported that the platform would not be ready for two hours. Cries for an adjournment were at once raised.

A motion for a recess until 9 A. M. was rejected. A vote then was taken on a recess to 11 A. M., and this prevailed. Recess was taken at 12:33 A. M.

June 16, 1916

OLD GUARD USING HARDING TO HELP KNOCK OUT WOOD

Sudden Revival of Senator's Campaign Is Attributed to the "Elder Statesmen's" Plan.

TO HOLD OHIO DELEGATES

Party Chiefs Believe He Can Prevent Them from Turning to Wood.

WON'T GO TO CONVENTION

General Vetoes Proposal and Says He Will Leave Chicago When Delegates Meet.

Special to The New York Times.

CHICAGO, June 1.—The "elder statesmen" in the Republican Party who are determined at all hazards to defeat Major Gen. Leonard Wood as a candidate for the Presidential nomination, just now are using Senator Warren G. Harding of Ohio as their principal stalking horse to attain that end.

While there is not believed to be any serious intention by any among the leaders who will play an important part in the National Convention, which will open here a week from today, to contend for the nomination of Senator Harding, his boom, which has been regarded as all but dead ever since the preferential primaries in Ohio, took on new life today under circumstances clearly indicating that it had been the subject of expert treatment and artificial stimulation.

The importance of Senator Harding in the game the Old Guard Republican bosses are playing lies in his ability to hold together the delegates from his own State as long as he remains in the fight, thus preventing them from going over in a body to General Wood, who received the next highest number of votes in the Ohio primaries.

The leaders opposed to the nomination of General Wood are keenly alive to the fact that, with the vanishing of minor booms, the General would be likely to gain an ascendency in the early ballots in the convention that might prove perilous to their plans. Their strategy contemplates an inconsequential test of strength preliminary to a general process of elimination on the first three or four ballots, then a long recess, during which the "elder statesmen" may repair to the secret council chamber and select a candidate for the convention, while approximately 1,000 delegates sent to Chicago on business of the utmost importance to their constituents and the country at large are marking time.

Declares Harding Will Stick.

Until today Harding headquarters in "Presidential Row" at the Congress Hotel has presented a picture of unrelieved lonesomeness, which may account for the many rumors that Senator Harding was preparing to withdraw as a candidate before the convention and seek re-election to the United States Senate. His term expires this year.

With signs of renewed activity at his campaign headquarters today came a statement from Harry M. Daugherty, his campaign manager, who had just returned from a conference with the Senator at Columbus, Ohio, that the Senator would stick and was preparing to make an aggressive fight for the Presidential nomination. It was also announced that Senator Harding would be here in person in a day or two to direct his pre-convention fight.

Incidentally, word came from Columbus that matters had been so arranged that if Senator Harding should be candidate for re-election he may delay filing his papers until June 11. By that date the convention will have been in session three full days, the early balloting undoubtedly will be out of the way, the process of hand picking a candidate for the convention to name, if the bosses should be lucky enough to carry their program into effect, undoubtedly will have begun, and Senator Harding will have served the sole purpose for which the elder statesmen want him, since his nomination appears to be out of question.

In the Wood campaign headquarters they are well aware of the plotting and planning that is going on with a view to placing obstacles in the way of General Wood. The General has put in a busy day at the hotel, greeting incoming delegates and conferring with Senator George Moses of New Hampshire, his Washington manager, and Colonel William Cooper Procter, head of the Leonard Wood League.

Former Chairman Frank H. Hitchcock of the Republican National Committee has been conspicuously absent from the conferences, spending his time at the Coliseum, where the National Committee has continued its hearings of contests.

Wood in Command.

To all practical purposes, General Wood has taken supreme command of the forces fighting for his nomination, and unless there is a change in the plans he will continue in command until the convention meets. He announced today that he would spend the greater part of every day from now on at his campaign headquarters.

General Wood has vetoed the plan to seek a seat for him in the convention, pressed upon the General by some of his enthusiastic friends. The General announced today that the moment the opening gavel falls in the national convention a week from today he will leave Chicago, not to return until the convention has adjourned. The fight on the floor of the convention has been fully planned by the General in conference with his advisers today, but he said tonight he was not prepared to make any announcement of what they were.

Despite repeated denials by General Wood, the rumors of friction between Mr. Hitchcock and Colonel Procter are persisting. It was very evident, too, that the former Chairman of the Republican National Committee, was doing nothing to check these rumors or offset any effect they might have on the Wood boom.

"These rumors," said the General this evening, "are absolutely without foundation. They are enemy propaganda, designed to destroy the morale of our forces. Apparently, however, they have not had that effect. Colonel Procter has talked to Mr. Hitchcock at the Coliseum today."

Hitchcock and Procter Meet.

The meeting between Colonel Procter and Mr. Hitchcock occurred in the room at the Coliseum Annex where the hearing of contests is being conducted by the National Committee. Colonel Procter went to the Coliseum after a talk with General Wood and some of his campaign workers, including Senator Moses. The meeting lasted less than five minutes and what little talking there was was done by Colonel Procter.

There was a host of curious onlookers when the two met. The room was filled with committee members, delegates to the convention and others who had heard the rumors of existing friction and watched the meeting with interest. Colonel Procter stood for a long while back in the committee room before he advanced toward Mr. Hitchcock, who, whether he noticed him or not, did not stir from his seat and gave no sign of recognition.

Finally Colonel Procter walked up to the former Republican National Chairman, placed a hand on his shoulder and greeted him. Mr. Hitchcock looked up with a wan smile, greeted the Colonel, but not warmly, and the two sat down. For five minutes, perhaps, they remained together, Colonel Procter talking earnestly in a low tone of voice. Most of the time Mr. Hitchcock appeared to have little to say.

After they met, Mr. Hitchcock, in reply to questions, said he had not talked with General Wood and had not been invited to attend the conferences held at his campaign headquarters.

"I am here in my capacity as a former chairman of the Republican National Committee to study the evidence presented in these contests," he said.

Procter Says Nothing.

Colonel Procter, who has denied repeatedly that to his knowledge there was any friction, made no statement as he returned to the Congress Hotel, where General Wood still remained at his headquarters.

It was learned this evening that Col. Procter had been sent as an emissary to invite John T. King, Republican National Committeeman from Connecticut, and until the coming of Col. Procter, General Wood's campaign manager, to call upon the General. Mr. King, who came here with a proxy from Senator Penrose to sit as his representative on the sub-committee hearing contests, declined the invitation.

Senator Moses, of New Hampshire, who arrived here with General Wood, said tonight that the sentiment for Wood shown throughout the country made him the logical candidate for the convention to name.

"General Wood will have votes from more than thirty States," said the Senator. "He will have a majority of the votes from more than fifteen States and will have all the votes from more than a dozen States. His aggregate of votes on the first ballot will be at least twice as many as those given to any other candidate, and we can readily see accessions to his strength which point to his nomination on an early ballot.

"By every test, whether in primary, convention, a straw vote or a nation-wide poll, he has shown that his popular strength is widespread and deep-rooted. Every day's development, whether at home or abroad, points to him as the man who especially fits the hour. The United States, Mexico and the world at large all furnish evidence of the necessity of a man like General Wood at the head of the Republic for the next four years."

No Second Place for Johnson.

At the headquarters of Senator Hiram W. Johnson, in the Auditorium Hotel, a report that the Senator would be willing to take second place on the ticket if a candidate agreeable to him was named for first place was emphatically denied.

"The Senator is a candidate for the nomination for President and will take nothing less than first place on the ticket," said a statement issued by his campaign managers. "And Senator Johnson will win the nomination not on the first ballot but on the fifth or sixth, after the delegates have thoroughly realized that he is the candidate who surely can bring victory to the party."

There was less activity today at the headquarters of Governor Lowden of Illinois regarded in Old Guard circles as the leading candidate for the Presidential nomination at this time, possibly because Governor Lowden caught a cold while reviewing a Memorial Day parade yesterday and as a result has been confined to his bed.

It was said today that Governor Lowden was practically assured of the united support of the Illinois delegation, with the possible exception of one of the delegates—Edgar J. Cook—who in all probability will vote for Senator Johnson on the first ballot and continue to support the Californian to the end.

This statement was made by a Republican closely allied with Mayor William Hale Thompson, who controls the delegates from the ten Congressional districts in Chicago.

From the fact that close friends of Mayor Thompson expect him to be returned as Republican National Committeeman without serious contest by the delegates controlled by the leaders who have been training with the Governor's friends, it is assumed that a deal or modus vivendi has been patched up between the erstwhile bitterly antagonistic leaders of the rival factions in the Republican organization in Illinois.

BEECKMAN HITS SENATE OLIGARCHY

RESENTS AUTOCRATIC RULE

Rhode Island Executive Wants Others Than Senators Consulted.

OPPOSES "THE OLIGARCHY"

Expresses the Hope That No Outside Body Will Run the Convention.

HARMONY IN WOOD CAMP

Hitchcock Gets a Free Hand—Rodenberg to Name Lowden.

Special to The New York Times.

CHICAGO, June 3.—The so-called "Senate Oligarchy," which on more than one occasion in the recent past has shown its opposition to Major Gen. Wood as a candidate for the nomination for President, and which—although composed of less than a dozen members of the United States Senate—now is suspected of harboring designs to arrogate to itself dominant power in the Republican National Convention which will meet here next week, may face open revolt if it attempts to carry out that purpose.

The first note of rebellion was sounded here late this afternoon, under the most auspicious circumstances, by Governor R. Livingston Beeckman of Rhode Island, who will sit in the convention as head of the delegation from his State. Governor Beeckman, who arrived here today a little ahead of the other delegates from Rhode Island, unburdened himself in a short address to a representative gathering of newspaper correspondents from all parts of the country.

Will H. Hays, Chairman of the Republican National Committee, presented Governor Beeckman to the newspaper men and stood by, a silent listener, while he talked to them.

"I got here today," said Governor Beeckman. "I read in the newspapers in Rhode Island, and others I obtained on my way here from New York, Indiana and Illinois, that Senator So and So was to be Temporary Chairman of the Convention, and Senator So and So thinks he will become permanent chairman if he can get the support of Senator Somebody Else. I read also that Senator So and So thinks he can be Chairman of the Committee on Resolutions, if he gets the support of Senator Somebody Else. And the proxy of some other Senator Somebody Else.

Caucus Instead of Convention.

"One would think that the gathering here next week was to be a Senate caucus, instead of a Republican National Convention.

"I did not see anywhere the mention of a Republican member of the House of Representatives or any of the twenty-seven Republican Governors who will be here next week.

"I am the dean of Governors in this country. I have served three terms and have been offered a fourth nomination for the same office. I think I have the right to say that the Republican members of the House of Representatives and the twenty-seven Republican Governors should at least have been considered, if not consulted, in the preliminaries to the convention."

Governor Beeckman delivered his little talk in one of the committee rooms in the Coliseum adjoining the large room where the Republican National Committee was hearing testimony on pending contests for seats in the National Convention. Chairman Hays and some attachés of the National Committee who were in the room and overheard what the Governor said showed signs of uneasiness, but the Governor from Rhode Island did not appear to notice this.

"I am in great hopes that the convention will run the convention," he went on after a short pause. "I am in hopes that it will not be run by an outside autocratic body. I am not an autocrat. I do not believe in the substitution of autocratic for representative methods in our political actions."

Hays Hears Enough.

It was very clear at this point that Chairman Hays thought Governor Beeckman had said all the occasion demanded, and he stepped forward to "ease" him out of the room. One of the newspaper correspondents, however, intervened. He asked the Governor if he favored the nomination of General Wood.

"I am here as a delegate from Rhode Island, and our delegation was not instructed for any candidate," Governor Beeckman replied.

"I understand," he added, as he prepared to leave the room, "that there are twelve United States Senators who aspire to the Presidency at this very moment."

"Are you opposed to the nomination of a United States Senator for President?" the Governor was asked.

"Yes," he replied. "We have never nominated a United States Senator for President yet."

Governor Beeckman in response to a question said the Senators he had in mind were Lodge, of Massachusetts, Medill McCormick, of Illinois, and James E. Watson, of Indiana. Senator Lodge has already been selected to preside as temporary chairman and deliver the keynote speech. Senator McCormick is a candidate for permanent chairman, and Senator Watson wants to become head of the committee on resolutions which will present the platform.

"Have you talked about this matter with any of the other Republican Governors?" the Governor was asked.

"I only got here today. I have no doubt they would agree with me to a man," said the Governor.

Credited as Wood Supporter.

While not instructed for General Wood, Governor Beeckman, according to the Wood campaign managers, will support the General on the first ballot, as will a majority of the delegates from Rhode Island.

The bitterness against the Senate oligarchy which furnished the keynote of Governor Beeckman's talk has been strongly and generally reflected among Republicans who are here for the convention. That has been true especially during the last three or four days, since the damaging disclosures regarding the expenditure of Lowden money in Missouri were made before the Senate committee investigating campaign contributions and expenses.

The Republican Senators, who wielded great influence in the Republican National Convention four years ago and are believed aiming at fastening their grip on the party gathering next week, may be prevented from carrying out their purpose through this sentiment, due to a general recognition here among the convention functionaries that responsibility for the Senate investigation, which has brought to the surface many things that inevitably will come back to plague the party during the campaign, rests entirely with the Republican Senators. They, it has been pointed out, had it in their power to block the proposal for an investigation, regarded as having been inspired by Senator Hiram W. Johnson and to have been prompted by a desire to injure the candidacy of General Wood, in the first instance, and that of other rivals contending with Senator Johnson for the nomination. By many persons here the smoothness with which the resolution was put through is ascribed to the existence of a common purpose among members of the "Senatorial junta" in Washington.

Hitchcock to Lead Wood Forces.

With delegates to the convention due to arrive in great numbers during the next three days, the campaign managers of General Leonard Wood are said to have composed their differences and placed Frank H. Hitchcock in charge of the work of winning enough support to "put him over."

This action was taken at a luncheon held today at the Chicago Club. General Wood was at the club at least a part of the afternoon. All the men actively identified in prominent positions with his fight here on the eve of the convention sat down at the luncheon, at which harmony apparently was brought about by letting Mr. Hitchcock have his own way. Those who attended included Senator George Moses and Frank C. Knox of New Hampshire, Colonel William Cooper Procter, Lieut. Col. Theodore Roosevelt and Colonel Thomas W. Miller, who has been in charge, with Representative Norman R. Gould of General Wood's pre-convention campaign in the East.

According to a report emanating from the Wood camp, there was a very frank discussion of the differences that have led to so many reports of a serious estrangement between Mr. Hitchcock and Colonel Procter, who has backed his enthusiastic leadership in the fight for Wood with a very large contribution to his campaign fund.

When the matter had been talked over across the table it was found that the only things to which Mr. Hitchcock had taken exception were the amateurish methods employed by some of the General's friends who had been prominently identified with his campaign. Mr. Hitchcock expressed the opinion that more progress would be made during the time that remains before the convention proceeds to nominate a candidate if a little political expertness was applied in the game of getting delegates for the General.

The Senator was then invited to try his hand at it, and, it is understood, consented to take charge of this phase of the fight, that may mean so much to both the General and those who have been standing with him in his long fight.

Announcement was made tonight by Governor Lowden that his name would be presented to the convention by Congressman William Rodenberg of East St. Louis.

Reports of Desertions.

There were reports of further desertions among the Missouri delegates, nine of whom were said to have followed Edward W. Foristell of St. Louis, one of the delegates at large, out of the Lowden camp. At the Lowden headquarters in the Congress Hotel it was stated tonight that no word had been received that any delegates had deserted the Governor's banner.

Governor Lowden got into the fray today to strengthen his shattered lines and rally his forces.

There has been little visible activity at any headquarters today.

All the candidates and the leaders have been marking time for the last twenty-four hours, waiting for the delegates to get in. Only then will it become apparent whether the disclosures regarding the Missouri delegates have so seriously affected the standing of Governor Lowden with the Republican voters throughout the country as to place his nomination out of the question.

In the meantime, rival candidates are quietly laying their lines to win over delegates from the Lowden camp the moment they become footloose.

Few delegates are on hand. Of the New York delegation Tax Commissioner George Henry Payne, who is a Wood man, and John J. Lyons, one of the New York County leaders, alone have been much in evidence. The only entire delegation to arrive here today was that from the Philippine Islands, composed of two members with alternates.

At the Harding headquarters announcement was made tonight that Senator Harding, scheduled to arrive here tonight, had been detained in Washington and would not get here until Saturday.

Senator Miles Poindexter of Washington, a "dark horse" in the Presidential race, whose managers profess to be not altogether without hope, will arrive here tomorrow.

Robert Taft, son of ex-President Taft, came here today to help in the work for Herbert Hoover. Young Mr. Taft said he had found a great deal of sentiment for Hoover in Ohio, where all of the delegates, with the exception of one, might be persueded to turn to Hoover if the Harding and Wood booms should fail.

"I am for Hoover, first, last and all the time, and feel confident that he could lead the Republican Party to victory in November," said the son of the former President.

June 4, 1920

PROPHESIED HOW HARDING WOULD WIN

Daugherty, His Campaign Manager, Said Fifteen Tired Men Would Put Him Over.

SENATE "JUNTA" MADE DEAL

Attended All Conferences Behind Scenes and Blocked Move to Let Wood Bolster Forces.

Special to The New York Times.

CHICAGO, June 12.—"At the proper time after Republican National Convention meets some fifteen men, bleary eyed with loss of sleep and perspiring profusely with the excessive heat, will sit down in seclusion around a big table. I will be with them and will present the name of Senator Harding to them, and before we get through they will put him over."

This statement, substantially as written here, was made by Harry K. Daugherty, campaign manager for Senator Warren G. Harding, Ohio, shortly before the Presidential primaries were held in that State. Daugherty afterward entered the primaries as a candidate for delegate at large, pledged to support Senator Harding. He was beaten but the utterance which led the Republican voters in his own State to oppose him in view of unfolding events at the national party gathering here, appears to have been full of prophetic meaning.

The sweltering crowd which sat down in the Coliseum this morning gazed on the usual picture of a national convention bent on getting through with its business of nominating a candidate for the President of the United States and preparing to go back home. That picture may have appeared to many of the onlookers as one fraught with unusual interest and importance, but the history of this final day of Republican Convention was really made behind the scenes and very much after the fashion suggested in Daugherty's statement.

Two days ago Senator Harding's fight was looked upon as a forlorn hope by practically every trained political observer at the convention. In fact, up to the very moment the convention took its adjournment last night his prospects were not regarded as rosy. As recently as last night Senator Harding himself could not have entertained much hope of a successful issue, for at three minutes before midnight he filed with the Secretary of State at Columbus, Ohio, the necessary papers to qualify him as a candidate for re-election to his present position in the United States Senate.

Conferences Held Friday Night.

The conference at which steps were taken to break the deadlock by steering the convention toward Harding were begun soon after it finished its big day's job yesterday. During the night the conferees divided into several small groups, which kept in communication with each other by members intervisiting, in two Chicago clubs and at the Blackstone and the Congress Hotels.

While the convention was sitting today a dozen or so leaders met on the rostrum at the Coliseum after the result of each ballot had been announced to discuss strategic moves and means of bringing about a decision, as advantageous to the party as circumstances would permit. While at times in full view of the huge audience in the convention hall, the big party chieftains enjoyed as much privacy with that great crowd near, as if they had gathered in seclusion at a club or some other secret meeting place.

The high temperature and the high cost of hotel living in Chicago undoubtedly were contributory factors in the rapid decision and Senator Harding's surprising victory. Had it been possible to hold the delegates in Chicago over Sunday the result almost certainly would have been different.

The Republican members of the United States Senate who almost to a man are here at the convention, where they have become variously known as the "Senatorial Junta" and the "Senate Oligarchy," won the day for their colleague from Ohio. A United States Senator invariably was the central figure in each of the half dozen conferences held during the night, and those that hurriedly assembled in the recess of the convention today.

Wood Wanted an Adjournment.

At that final conference, after the stock of Senator Harding had been soaring during the forenoon's balloting, General Leonard Wood, still in the lead, pleaded warmly but in vain for an adjournment over Sunday, to enable him to rally his forces and make another attempt to win over converts.

Senator William E. Borah of Idaho, who attended the conference, representing Senator Johnson, Senator Henry Cabot Lodge of Massachusetts, Senator James E. Watson of Indiana, and Senator Reed Smoot of Utah, who attended also, declared that it would be impossible to hold the convention in Chicago over the week-end and that the business of nominating must be gone through with before the session scheduled for a later hour was ended.

At that time assurances had been received by the group of Senators who were working for Harding from a number of State delegations, including New York, Massachusetts and Pennsylvania, that if Senator Harding continued to gain on the first ballot after recess, the ninth, they would throw their strength to him.

The veto of a week-end adjournment spelled doom to the hopes of General Wood. His followers who had been fighting every step of their way through the convention gave up and released the pledged and instructed delegates. The only one of the candidates to refuse to release those pledged to him was Johnson.

At the time the recess was taken John T. King, former National Committeeman from Connecticut, and also former campaign managers for General Wood, had let it become known that he had received a telephone message from Senator Boies Penrose of Pennsylvania, approving the candidacy of Senator Harding.

There have been conflicting reports at the convention with regard to the condition of the stricken Republican chieftain of the Keystone State. Some said that he was too ill to take intelligent interest in what was going on at the Coliseum. It is certain that though absent Senator Penrose's influence, phantom-like, has been present at this convention to sway the decisions reached.

Borah Told First of Deal.

Senator Borah, when he came from the conference during recess, brought the first definite word that "Harding would be put over" when the convention reassembled. He said that Senator Johnson's delegates would not be released for the purpose of coming to the aid of the Senator from Ohio.

"They will have to leave of their own accord," said Borah. "They may succeed in putting Harding over for all that."

"Will Johnson accept second place on the Harding ticket?" was the next question put to Senator Borah, and suggested by a conference between the two Senators during recess.

"He will not," said the Senator from Idaho.

"Can Harding win?" Senator Borah was asked.

"I hate to put a proscription on every man who is being mentioned for the nomination," said Mr. Borah with a laugh as he moved away.

Super-strategy devised by the Old Guard, odd as this may seem, kept General Wood in the lead on several ballots today, when, it is declared, they would have been in a position to take away delegates who were still clinging to his fading fortunes.

The Old Guard leaders who led the fight realized that the strength of Governor Lowden, who was running neck and neck with General Wood at the head of the procession of candidates, was due to a great extent to opposition among the Old Guard "regulars" to the General. With the General out of the race they feared that the Lowden delegates might begin to scatter their votes in too many directions to make possible the early decision for Senator Harding, at which they were aiming by swinging Lowden delegates in a block to the Senator from Ohio.

June 13, 1920

* * * * * *

PRESIDENT SILENT AS TO CANDIDATES

Close Friends Declare He Has Never Spoken for or Against Any Aspirant.

COLBY VISITS WHITE HOUSE

Former McAdoo Supporters Not United in Efforts to Swing Nomination to Glass.

Special to The New York Times.

WASHINGTON, June 20.—Cabinet members and others of the limited number who have been in personal contact with President Wilson during the last six months have been closely questioned in an effort to ascertain whether President Wilson was favoring or in any way aiding the candidacy of Mr. McAdoo, Mr. Palmer or any one else.

These men have in private conversation reiterated to THE NEW YORK TIMES correspondent the assurance of their belief that the President was not lending his support to any candidate. They have united in the statement that the President has never spoken to them about candidates and declared their belief that he has not told any man that he favored or opposed any candidate for the nomination. So far as can be learned the President has not even discussed candidates with his own private secretary, Mr. Tumulty.

Secretary of State Bainbridge Colby, who will leave Washington tomorrow for San Francisco as a delegate from the District of Columbia, was at the White House this afternoon. It is not understood that Mr. Colby saw the President, but he was closeted some time with Secretary Tumulty, and left the White House with him.

Mr. Colby has been mentioned for permanent Chairman of the convention. The persistence of these rumors reached the point yesterday when Mr. Colby felt called upon to issue a denial that the reports had any foundation. But Mr. Colby will be one of the staunch Administration supporters in the convention and will be ready on every occasion to rally to the support of the President in any crisis that may arise.

Efforts of supporters of William Gibbs McAdoo among the delegates at San Francisco to keep his boom going are expected to flatten out before the meeting of the convention on June 28. By that time most of them probably will be convinced that Mr. McAdoo meant what he said in his letter of refusal to Assistant Secretary Shouse of the Treasury Department. If not convinced before, the McAdoo supporters will be disillusioned soon after the arrival at San Francisco of loyal McAdoo workers with a set plan to advance Senator Glass for the nomination in place of Mr. McAdoo.

While Assistant Secretary Shouse and some of his associates in the McAdoo movement are now waging a vigorous fight for the nomination of Senator Glass, not all of the higher McAdoo workers are so engaged. Raymond T. Baker, Director of the Mint, is understood to have joined the Palmer forces after receiving a private telegram from Mr. McAdoo in New York, which notified him in advance regarding the letter of withdrawal.

Whether there is any particular significance in Director Baker's action remains to be proved by developments during the coming week. Mr. Baker is a close personal friend of Joseph P. Tumulty, private secretary to the President, and has been on close terms of association with the White House. Secretary Tumulty is also a close friend and admirer of Attorney General Palmer and is believed to have been very much interested in the earlier stages of the Palmer campaign. There is nothing so far disclosed, however, to show that the President is favoring the nomination of Mr. Palmer as against other rivals in the field.

Senator Claude Swanson, one of the delegates at large from Virginia, will not attend the San Francisco convention, it was announced today. The explanation given was that serious illness of Mrs. Swanson prevented the Senator from going. Mrs. Swanson, it was stated, had been in the Mayo Sanitarium at Rochester, Minn.

Politicians here have assumed that Senator Swanson is a bit piqued over the selection of Carter Glass, his colleague, as the President's spokesman at San Francisco. He has been a consistent Administration supporter in the Senate, and at one time there was a report that he was to displace Senator Hitchcock in charge of the treaty fight. It was about that time that Mrs. Swanson became ill.

June 21, 1920

DENIES PRESIDENT IS LEADER OF PARTY

William F. McCombs Attacks Wilson's "Autocratic Assumption of Authority."

ACCEPTED BY 'DAZED NATION'

Ex-Democratic Chairman Declares League Question Is for President and Senate to Settle.

CHICAGO, June 21.—William F. McCombs, Chairman of the Democratic National Committee from 1912 to 1916 and manager of President Wilson's 1912 campaign, issued a statement here tonight, before leaving for San Francisco, attacking what he characterized as the President's autocratic assumption of authority.

President Wilson, he said, had no more right to call himself leader of the Democratic Party, "a conception theretofore never entertained by any American," than had Chief Justice White, former Speaker Champ Clark or Vice President Thomas R. Marshall.

Mr. McCombs announced that arrangements had been made to obtain for him a seat in the New York delegation if he decided to take the floor at San Francisco. The New York delegation, he predicted, would throw its support to Governor James M. Cox of Ohio after casting a complimentary vote for Governor Smith. He added that he believed a Westerner, possibly from the Pacific slope, would be nominated for Vice President.

Mr. McCombs's statement in part follows:

"They tell me that America has pledged its word to Europe and that this word must be redeemed in the process of a national campaign. In my belief America has pledged itself to nothing. One individual, speaking as such, permitted Europe to believe that he spoke for a nation, for in the last analysis he was nothing more than a self-appointed emissary. Nevertheless, America is asked to validate this signature affixed abroad, a signature which apparently was accepted in good faith by all the European peoples as absolute.

"The President negotiates a treaty, but the Senate may or may not concur by two-thirds majority. In this particular instance there has been no concurrence.

"Other nations may want a league of nations, and it may be that we do, but we do not want to commit ourselves to the League of Nations as it was brought back from Paris. It is an international issue, but it is a highly debatable question as to what importance it should have in a national campaign. Ultimately it is a question for the President and the Senate to settle."

The statement then declares for reconstruction at home, rehabilitation of railway and internal waterway transportation, and for solution of the high cost of living, wholly apart from any international affiliations.

"When the great war broke out in 1914," the statement continues, "naturally America was more or less dazed and was willing to accept any kind of leadership which might draw it through a possible difficulty. In this moment the Chief Executive again repeated that he was the leader of his party, a conception theretofore never entertained by an American. As well might the Chief Justice of the United States, Mr. White, a Democrat, have made the same proclamation. So might the Speaker of the House of Representatives, Champ Clark. So might the Vice President, Mr. Marshall, Constitutional President of the Senate. But America was concerned with great issues, and paid no attention to what appeared to be a detail.

"It was in such manner that for the first time in the history of this country autocracy came into being. It was an autocracy which was questioned, but which was accepted by virtue of necessity.

"But this unhappy hour has passed, and at San Francisco we again return to true democracy, regardless of place holders and pot hunters. We have finished with the fine phrases. This country is determined to act in accordance with its unfailing sense of justice. The indignities of autocracy will never again be accepted by this nation. This is fundamental, and no confusion will be brought about by diplomatic or financial machinations."

June 22, 1920

Text of Message Acclaiming President Wilson Adopted Unanimously by Democratic Convention

SAN FRANCISCO, June 28.—The Democratic National Convention today, on motion of Governor Gardner of Missouri, directed Chairman Cummings to send to President Wilson this message, which was adopted by unanimous vote of the convention:

> In recognition of the fact that the mantle of Jackson and Jefferson has fallen on your shoulders as the unquestioned leader of our party, the hosts of democracy, in national convention assembled, have directed me to send you the following resolution of appreciation and greeting:
>
> > The Democratic Party, assembled in national convention, extends to the President of the United States its admiring and respectful greetings.
> >
> > For seven of the most fateful years in the history of our country Woodrow Wilson has occupied and by his character, learning and power has adorned the highest office in the gift of his countrymen.
> >
> > He has initiated and secured the adoption of great progressive measures of immeasurable value and benefit to the people of the United States.
> >
> > As the Commander in Chief of the Army and Navy of the United States he has led the patriotic forces of his country through the most momentous struggle in history and, without check, reserve or retardation to an honorable part in the immortal victory for liberty and democracy won by the free nations of the world.
> >
> > We hail these achievements, Sir, and are proud that they have been accomplished under your Administration.
> >
> > We rejoice in the recovery of your health and strength after months of suffering and affliction, which you have borne with courage and without complaint.
> >
> > We deeply resent the malignant onset which you have most undeservedly been called upon to sustain from partisan foes, whose judgment is warped and whose perceptions are obscured by a party malice which constitutes a lamentable and disgraceful page in our history.
> >
> > At this moment, when the delegates to this convention from every State in the Union are about to enter upon their formal proceedings, we pause to send an expression of cheer and admiration and of congratulation.
> >
> > We rejoice and felicitate you upon your speedy recovery from your recent illness and congratulate America that, though temporarily broken in body, you have been able, with unclouded vision and undaunted courage, to press on for the great reforms which you have fathered for the preservation of peace throughout the world in the interest of humanity and the advancement of civilization. Long may you live to serve America and the world!

June 29, 1920

COX NOMINATED ON 44TH BALLOT FOR PRESIDENT

COX TOOK LEAD AT NIGHT

Passed McAdoo Early In Session on the 39th Ballot.

PALMER DELEGATES FREED

Announcement Was Made from Platform After the 38th Ballot.

BLOCKED MOVE TO ADJOURN

Cox Men Voted Down Proposal to Quit After the Forty-first Ballot Was Taken.

NIGHT SESSION
Beginning With the 37th Ballot

By Direct Leased Wire to THE NEW YORK TIMES.

CONVENTION HALL, SAN FRANCISCO, Tuesday, July 6, 1:39 A. M. (5:39 New York time).—Governor James M. Cox of Ohio was nominated for President by the Democratic National Convention at 1:39 A. M. today.

The nomination came on the forty-fourth ballot. When the night session began, the thirty-seventh and thirty-eighth ballots were taken. Attorney General Palmer then released his delegates. In the succeeding ballots Cox gained steadily, until on the forty-fourth he had secured 699 votes and it was apparent that before the ballot was completed he would obtain more than 729 votes, the two-thirds majority required to nominate.

Vice Chairman Amidon of the Democratic National Committee, manager for McAdoo, interrupted the voting and moved to make the nomination unanimous which was done amid uproarious applause.

It was 1:43 o'clock A. M. (5:43 o'clock A. M. New York time) when Cox was declared the nominee.

Thereupon the convention adjourned until noon today (Tuesday), when it will complete the work by nominating a candidate for Vice President.

Cox was nominated by acclamation before the finish of the ballot. He had 699 votes at that time and McAdoo 270 when the motion was made to declare the nomination unanimous.

SAN FRANCISCO, July 5.—The Democratic convention was called to order by Chairman Robinson for its night session at 8:44 o'clock (12:44 Tuesday morning, New York time).

The thirty-seventh and thirty-eighth ballots were taken, with no material change, and then came the sensation of the night. Charles C. Carlin, manager for Attorney General Palmer, took the platform and announced that the Palmer delegates were released. The convention quickly voted a recess of twenty minutes to allow caucuses on the new situation.

It was called to order again at 10:15 P. M.

Balloting was resumed, and at the end of the fortieth ballot it was admitted by both Cox and McAdoo leaders that no break of the deadlock could be effected tonight.

They could not reach an agreement on a proposition to vote on adjournment. It was said, however, that such a bargain would be struck after the forty-first ballot, which the Secretary was instructed to get under way at once.

But despite the announcement the Cox leaders declined at the close of the forty-first ballot to agree to an adjournment.

E. H. Moore, manager for the Ohio Governor, said he would not consent to stop balloting until the nomination of Cox. Representative Linebaugh of Oklahoma moved an adjournment to 10 A. M. He was greeted with howls of "No!" mingled with cries of "Yes!"

On a roll call the motion for adjournment was beaten.

The forty-second ballot was completed at 12:45 (4:45 A. M. New York time) and on this ballot Cox for the first time passed the 500 mark. The results were:

Cox 540½, McAdoo 427, Davis 49½, Owen 34, Glass 24, Palmer 8, Cummings 3, Clark 2, Colby 1.

Cox was only 7½ votes short of a majority.

On the forty-third ballot finished at 1:10 A. M. Tuesday (5:10 A. M. New York time) Cox gained still further. The result of this ballot was: Cox 567, McAdoo 412, Davis 57½, Owen 34, Palmer 7, Glass 5½, Cummings 2.

When the night session was opened the thirty-seventh and thirty-eighth ballots were put through rapidly. The result of the thirty-seventh ballot was: McAdoo 405, Palmer 202½, Cox 386, Davis 50½, Owen 33. The scattering votes weren egligible.

The ballot showed a gain of 6 for McAdoo, a loss of 38½ for Palmer and a gain of 9 for Cox.

An incipient demonstration for McAdoo following the announcement of the result of the thirty-stventh ballot was easily nipped, but not before a parade of McAdoo boosters had gone around the hall. The Chairman showed every disposition to let it linger but the punch was lacking. A few raps of the gavel brought enough order to allow the taking of the thirty-eighth ballot.

On the thirty-eighth ballot the first change came when California was called. Palmer gained three in that State, taking two from McAdoo and one from Cox. In Florida Palmer gained four, taking them from Cox. Illinois reduced McAdoo's strength in the State to 16, giving two to Davis, two to Palmer and 38 to Cox.

Massachusetts took one vote from Cox and gave it to Owen. Missouri took two from Palmer and divided them equally between Cox and McAdoo. Montana took two from Palmer and gave its entire strength to McAdoo.

New York underwent no change on this ballot. Pennsylvania gave McAdoo two of its votes. Rhode Island took one away from Palmer and two from McAdoo, giving them to Cox. South Dakota took one from Palmer and one from McAdoo. These also went to Cox.

Tennessee again gave its entire vote to Davis, while Virginia gave Palmer 3½ and McAdoo the same number, switching them from Glass.

There were no changes in the Territories and the tellers began to count up the vote. The result was as follows:

McAdoo, 405½; Cox, 383½; Palmer, 211; Cummings, 4; Owen, 33; Davis, 50; Glass, 1, and Clark 3.

After the thirty-eighth ballot, at 9:39 o'clock, it became known that A. Mitchell Palmer's managers were releasing the delegates pledged to Palmer. They were going about the auditorium giving the releases, and it was prophesied that the deadlock would be broken within the next few ballots, possibly on the thirty-ninth.

Chairman Robinson introduced Charles C. Carlin of Virginia, who is Palmer's campaign manager. There was a hush as Mr. Carlin went to the platform and announced that he had been requested by Mr. Palmer to make an important announcement. Mr. Carlin said.

"I am going to make an important announcement, at the end of which I shall move a recess of twenty minutes in order that you may have an opportunity to deliberate. I am requested by the Hon. A. Mitchell Palmer to express to the delegates who have so faithfully supported him his sincere gratitude and to advise this convention that Mr. Palmer is unwilling to delay the deliberations longer.

"He feels that you should have the opportunity tonight to nominate the next President of the United States, and with that object in view I am also authorized by him unreservedly, absolutely and finally to release his delegates. Mr. Chairman, I move a recess for twenty minutes."

A shout went up as delegates and spectators realized that Palmer had finally withdrawn. When the proposal was made to take a recess of 20 minutes there were shouts of "No." If Chairman Robinson put the motion, nobody heard it. The convention simply suspended business to give the leaders a chance to consult.

Such leaders as could be reached amid the confusion were of the opinion, however, that, while there would be accessions to the Cox vote, they would not be sufficient to nominate him. The prevalent view accorded with what Mr. Palmer had said in his statement to THE NEW YORK TIMES at 8 o'clock that a dark horse would be the victor in the end.

The delegates seemed to appreciate the opportunity to stretch themselves for a few minutes. Many crowded around the Pennsylvania standard and showered congratulations upon the Palmer men for deciding to "end the agony," as one Eastern delegate expressed it.

The air was more vibrant with excitement than at any time since the balloting began. Every one knew that something was about to happen, and every one was discussing what it would be. When the end of the twenty-minute recess came the delegates began to shout "time's up."

A woman delegate, evidently grievously disappointed over Palmer's withdrawal, got into a violent quarrel with several men. One of the men talked to her rather roughly and bystanders interfered. The incident was typical. The nerves of the delegates were on edge.

During the intermission the Cox and McAdoo men began to argue the merits of their respective candidates, with the

Summary of the Ballots

[Ballots 1 and 2 in the table below were cast on Friday; from 3 to 22 inclusive on Saturday, and those beginning with 23 were cast yesterday.]

Ballot.	McAdoo.	Cox.	Palmer.	Davis.	Marshall.	Cummings.	Owen.	Glass.
1st	266	134	256	32	35	25	33	26½
2d	289	159	264	31½	36	27	29	25½
3d	323½	177	251½	28½	26	26	25	27
4th	335	178	254	31	34	24	32	27
5th	357	181	244	29	29	21	34	27
6th	368½	195	265	29	13	20	36	27
7th	384	295½	267½	33	14	19	35	27
8th	380	315	262	32	12	18	36	27
9th	386	321½	257	34	7	18	37	25
10th	385	321	257	34	7	19	37	25
11th	380	332	255	33	7	19	35	25
12th	375½	404	201	31	7	8	34	25
13th	363½	428½	193½	29½	7	7	32	25
14th	355½	443½	182	33	7	7	34	25
15th	344½	468½	167	32	..	19	31	25
16th	337	454½	164½	52	..	20	34	25
17th	332	442	176	57	..	19	36	26
18th	330½	458	174½	42	..	19	38	26
19th	327½	468	179½	31	..	19	37	26
20th	340½	456½	178	36	..	10	41	26
21st	395½	426½	144	54	..	7	36	26
22d	372½	430	166½	52	..	6	35	25
23d	364½	425	181½	50½	..	5	34	25
24th	364½	429	178	54½	..	5	34	25
25th	364½	424	169	58½	..	4	34	25
26th	371	424½	167	55½	..	3	33	25
27th	371½	423½	166½	60½	1	3	34	25
28th	368½	423	165½	62½	..	4	35½	24
29th	399½	404½	166	63	..	4	33	24
30th	403½	400½	165	58	..	5	33	24
31st	415½	391½	174	57½	1	3	34	12½
32d	421	391	176	55½	..	3	34	9½
33d	421	380½	180	56	..	3	34	13
34th	420½	379½	184	54	..	3	37	7½
35th	409	376½	222	39	..	1	38½	5
36th	399	377	241	28	..	3	36	4
37th	405	386	202½	50½	..	3	33	1
38th	405½	383½	211	50	..	4	33	1
39th	440	468½	74	71½	..	2	32	..
40th	467	490	19	76	..	2	33	..
41st	460	497½	12	55½	..	2	36	24
42d	427	540½	3	49½	..	3	34	24
43d	412	567	7	57½	..	2	34	5½

hope of impressing the Palmer men as to where they should go when they broke away.

As the recess ended it was learned that Georgia would cast its whole vote for McAdoo the coming thirty-ninth ballot, while Massachusetts would give 33 to Cox, 1 to McAdoo, 1 to Colby and 1 to Owen. Thus Cox was to get 17 out of 19 Palmer votes in Massachusetts.

The Virginia delegation decided to vote 11 for Cox, 10 for McAdoo and 3 for Davis on the next ballot, while Chairman Robinson was rapping for order to begin the roll call. The roll call began at 10:17.

It was evident that McAdoo would get much support from the former Palmer followers. The Pennsylvania delegation caucused and decided to vote solidly once more for Palmer, then to split up about as follows on the fortieth ballot: Palmer 17, Cox 11, Davis 3, McAdoo 43 and two not voting.

Convention Again in Session.

At 10:15 Chairman Robinson again called the convention to order and instant quiet prevailed. His only announcement was that the Secretary would call the roll of States.

Alabama gave McAdoo eight of its votes and Davis sixteen, thus throwing the whole of the Palmer strength there to Davis, with the exception of one vote to McAdoo.

Arizona gave McAdoo four and Cox two. Arkansas gave one Palmer vote to McAdoo, making his total four from that State. The other four went to Cox, a gain of one.

California transferred two Palmer votes to McAdoo, whose total in that State was brought up to fourteen. Cox got three of the Palmer votes. Colorado threw one to Cox at McAdoo's expense, which raised his vote to seven in that State.

Connecticuit gave the Palmer votes to Cox, bringing the Ohio man's total up to ten. McAdoo gained two in Connecticut, taking them from Cummings, giving him a total of three in the State.

Delaware repeated its vote, 4 for McAdoo and 2 for Cox. There were no Palmer votes in that State.

Florida gave a Palmer ovte to Cox, making the Cox vote 9. McAdoo held the 3 Florida votes he had on the last ballot.

Georgia swung its entire vote of 28 to McAdoo. This delegation was solid for Palmer on the previous ballot. Idaho stood by McAdoo again, giving him eightvotes. The two Palmer votes in Illinois went to McAdoo, making his total 16. Cox again got 38 votes from Illinois and Davis got two, the same number as on the previous ballot.

Cox Rooster Is Brought Out.

The Cox people brought out their live rooster, which had been cooped up in a nearby corridor awaiting the proper instant for a triumphal entry. The rooster was borne in a Cox parade perched on a high pole, while the band played and the crowd cheered.

Indiana proved a keen disappointment to the McAdoo forces. The State gave McAdoo only 11 this time, a loss of 18. Cox got 19.

Iowa stood by Cox, delivering to him 26 votes. Kansas came back with 20 for McAdoo, and the McAdoo men got a chance to yell. Kentucky took three away from McAdoo. Davis got 1.

Louisiana gave Palmer one vote as a compliment, switching it from Davis. McAdoo got 7 and Cox 12, as on the previous ballot. Palmer did not have any votes in that State on the previous ballot.

The five votes that Palmer had in Maine went to McAdoo, giving him twelve from that State. There was no change in the Maryland figures, as Palmer had no votes in that State.

McAdoo got 5½, Cox 8½ and Davis 2.

Outburst Over Bay State Vote.

Then came Massachusetts, where the Cox gain started the biggest demonstration of the night and stopped the balloting for ten minutes. Cox got 33, a gain of 19, which represented the entire Palmer vote. McAdoo got only one, as on the previous ballot. Owen took one, a loss of one. This went to Colby.

In Michigan McAdoo lost 2, Cox gained 7 and Davis gained 3. This made the Davis total in Michigan four. Minnesota gave McAdoo 16, a gain of two. Cox gained 3 here.

One of the McAdoo leaders remarked during a Cox outburst: "We'll give them a real demonstration on the next ballot." He was referring to the Pennsylvania delegation's intention to give McAdoo 43 votes on the fortieth ballot. Mississippi delivered its 24 to Cox. In Missouri McAdoo received 20½ and Cox rose to 11½ from 7, taking his strength from Palmer.

Montana's 8 stayed in line for McAdoo. Nebraska gave him 7 and Owen 9, as before. Nevada stood by Cox, continuing to give him 6. New Hampshire gave McAdoo 5 and Cox 2, switching a single Palmer vote to Davis.

New Jersey delivered its 28 to Cox. New Mexico gave McAdoo 6 as usual. New York stood pat, 20 for McAdoo and 70 for Cox.

North Carolina again gave twenty-four to McAdoo. North Dakota gave its Palmer vote to McAdoo, making his total nine, and repeated its one vote for Cox. Ohio, of course, kept its forty-eight votes in the Cox column, and Oklahoma's twenty refused to budge from Owen. Oregon stood fast for McAdoo with ten votes.

Pennsylvania refused to switch, despite the announcement that Palmer had withdrawn. The State gave him 73, McAdoo 2 and Cox 1, as before. The Palmer vote was complimentary, and every leader on the floor knew what Pennsylvania had decided to do on the next, the fortieth, ballot—that is, give a majority of its votes to McAdoo.

Rhode Island gave one Palmer vote to McAdoo and two to Davis. Cox got the other seven votes in that State. He had them on the last ballot.

South Carolina, after a poll of its delegation, gave McAdoo its 18 votes again. South Dakota cut Cox down from five to three. It gave McAdoo six as compared with three on the previous ballot, one delegate not voting.

Tennessee again gave Davis its 24 votes. Texas gave McAdoo 40, as usual, and Utah followed in the McAdoo column, where it had been from the beginning.

Vermont split the Palmer votes, giving one each to McAdoo and Cox making the total of each four. McAdoo gained 3½ of the Palmer strength in Virginia, making his total in the State 10. Cox got ten from Palmer in Virginia, raising his total to 11. Davis gained two, with a total of 3, in Virginia.

Palmer had no votes in Washington and McAdoo got his 11 there. Cox got 2½, a gain of one-half, which he took from Davis. West Virginia continued to give Davis its strength of 16. Wisconsin did not change its vote, 19 going to McAdoo and 7 to Cox. Wyoming continued to give McAdoo 6. Alaska went 4 for McAdoo and 2 for Cox, no change.

The District of Columbia switched its 6 votes from Palmer to Cox.

Hawaii's vote remained 1 for McAdoo and 5 for Cox. The Philippines also kept in line, 3 for McAdoo and 2 for Cox.

Porto Rico gave all its 6 votes to McAdoo, taking 3 from Palmer and 1 from Cox. The Canal Zone no longer divided its 2 votes between Palmer and McAdoo, but gave both to McAdoo.

The result of the thirty-ninth ballot was: McAdoo, 440; Cox, 468½; Palmer, 74; Cummings, 2; Owen, 32; Davis, 71½; Clark, 2; Colby, 1.

The Secretary was ordered to call the roll for the fortieth ballot at 10:54 o'clock, but shouting by Cox followers and others stopped him for a few minutes.

Pennsylvania Gives McAdoo 42.

On the fortieth ballot McAdoo lost one to Cox in Arizona, another in Arkansas, another in Connecticut and two in Illinois, where Cox gained one vote from Davis. But McAdoo regained one in Massachusetts and another in Minnesota. New York still stood 20 for McAdoo and 70 for Cox.

Then came Pennsylvania and everybody paused to learn the disposition of the residuary Palmer votes. But Bruce Sterling, Chairman of the delegation, announced that some delegates had gone away leaving proxies, a practice which he understood was not permitted, and that he would ask that the delegation be allowed to pass and be polled at the end of the roll call.

In Virginia McAdoo lost 2 and Cox 1½ to Davis, but in Washington Cox took 3 of McAdoo's votes. There was a cheer when Wisconsin announced its 19 for McAdoo and 7 for Cox, as it had stood from the very first. Cox got 2 of McAdoo's 4 votes from Alaska. The other Territories showed no change.

Then came the poll of Pennsylvania. The reading clerks, unfamiliar with the names, read slowly and with difficulty. The first two voted for McAdoo, and there were cheers, but it turned out that somebody who was not a delegate had shouted "McAdoo" when a name was called, and when the chairman identified him he ordered a policeman to remove him from the hall.

Some of the delegates stuck to Palmer. The eighth man called, Paul A. Fagan, gave the first Pennsylvania vote to Cox. More "McAdoos" followed and there was a cheer for every name of the ex-Secretary's supporters.

The galleries and the crowd on the floor listened to the call for the most part in eager silence that contrasted strikingly with the noisy discontent of earlier periods. The most prolonged demonstration, and even that was brief, came when Vance McCormick, Democratic National Chairman in 1916, voted for McAdoo.

Pennsylvania's total vote on the fortieth ballot was McAdoo 42, Cox 12, Palmer 18, Davis 3, absent 1.

While the votes were being counted a cannon cracker went off outside and somebody yelled, "Hurray for Johnson!"

There was a wilder hurrah, however, at the announcement of the 42 votes for McAdoo. It was rumored that many of the McAdoo votes would shift on the next ballot.

The band was silent and Cone Johnson of Texas rose and shouted the inquiry:

"Does the band up there belong to the whole convention, or to some one else?"

Chairman Robinson attempted to shut off this violation of neutrality by saying that the band had been very generous in dispensing music and by way of appreciation the band and organ joined, while the crowd rose and tried to sing "The Star-Spangled Banner."

The result of the fortieth ballot was: McAdoo 467, Cox 490, Palmer 19, Davis 76, Owen 33, Cummings 2, Clark 2, Colby 1.

There was a big cheer from the Cox supporters when the announcement from the Chair showed that their candidate had received the highest number of votes yet given to anybody in the forty hard-fought ballots. The McAdoo people had nothing to say, but there were a few cheers for Davis, and at 11:35 the Secretary began the roll call for the forty-first ballot.

Cox Gains on 41st Ballot.

The beginning of the roll was delayed by Chairman Robinson's appeal: "Delegates will please take their seats." There was much moving about.

Alabama swung fifteen of its delegates from Davis to Cox and there was a roar of cheering. There was no change, however, in any other State until Illinois was reached. It shifted one from Cox to McAdoo. Indiana stood as before, with 11 for McAdoo and 19 for Cox. Cox took one from McAdoo in Kentucky. In Massachusetts Cox lost one to Owen and one to Davis. In Minnesota one vote changed from McAdoo to Cox.

New York continued to divide 20 and 70. A white haired woman announced Ohio's 48 votes for Cox and there was a weak cheer. Pennsylvania passed again, and there was much discussion in the delegation. Cox and McAdoo each gained 1 in South Dakota. Virginia swung its 24 votes back to Carter Glass, Cox losing 9½ and McAdoo 8.

Then Pennsylvania was announced as 44 for McAdoo, 14 for Cox, 14 for Palmer, 3 for Davis and one for an unidentified man named Upton. But Joseph O'Brien of Scranton challenged the accuracy of the result as announced by the Chairman of the delegation and called for a poll. The galleries groaned, but the polling of the delegation proceeded.

By this time the galleries were half empty. The San Francisco crowd had evidently despaired of a nomination tonight and much of it had gone home, but many others, determined to stick to the finish, had seized the opportunity afforded by the poll of Pennsylvania to go downstairs for a sandwich and a cup of coffee before the next rollcall started.

Members of delegations from several States conferred in groups under their standards while the balloting was on. The big leaders like Murphy, Taggart and Brennan remained in their places.

There were no outside conferences. They had decided that the only way to end the deadlock was to let the voting go on. Besides, most of the deals that were possible had been effected. The seventy New York votes controlled by Murphy had gone to Cox. The organization leaders in other big States—Illinois, Indiana and New Jersey—had done their utmost to throw the votes of their delegations to Ohio's Governor.

McAdoo supporters said at this juncture that Cox had developed his full strength. If another break came, they declared, it was likely to go to McAdoo. They believed that Bryan, if he saw Cox winning the goal, would throw his influence to McAdoo. Bryan and his following in Nebraska had been voting for Senator Owen.

The result of the Pennsylvania poll showed 3 votes fewer for Palmer and two more for McAdoo. The mysterious Mr. Upton did not appear in the total and apparently he had come in by a misunderstanding of a name. Pennsylvania stood McAdoo, 40, Cox 14, Palmer 11 and Davis 3.

The result of the forty-first ballot was: McAdoo 460, Cox 497½, Palmer 12, Davis 55½, Owen 35, Cummings 2, Clark 2, Colby 1, Glass 24.

Motion to Adjourn Is Beaten.

Cox had gained 7½ and McAdoo had lost 7. Thereupon ex-Governor Linebaugh of Oklahoma moved amid howls of "No" that the convention adjourn until 10 A. M. tomorrow.

New York demanded the ayes and noes, and as it seemed doubtful if a majority rose to vote for this proposal, the Chairman announced that the Secretary would call the roll on the motion to adjourn.

There was much buzzing on the floor as the vote was taken. The galleries were two-thirds empty by this time, but those who remained were apparently there for the night. Word came to the press seats that Senator Glass had said he did not think it would be possible to make a nomination tonight.

The first States on the roll voted heavily against the motion to adjourn. Illinois and Indiana voted solidly against it. It was understood that the Cox forces hoped to "put over" their candidate if they could hold the convention long enough, though they were still more than 230 votes short of the required two-thirds.

Charles F. X. O'Brien shouted New Jersey's twenty-eight noes and New York divided as on the vote for the nominee, the twenty McAdoo men voting to adjourn and the seventy Cox supporters against it.

The motion was beaten before the roll call was two-thirds past, and at 12:20 A. M. (4:20 New York time) those who had been keeping count settled down for another ballot. While the house was waiting for the announcement of the result various persons on the floor and in the galleries relieved their emotions by boisterous shouts, mostly for McAdoo. The searchlights were turned on, but the band remained silent.

Only 406 voted for the motion to adjourn and 637 against it.

42d Ballot After Midnight.

TUESDAY, July 6.—At 12:26 A. M. the roll call was started for the forty-second ballot. Alabama voted as on the previous ballot, but in Arizona, Cox gained half a vote from McAdoo. The first big change came when the Georgia delegation, the old Palmer group, threw its 28 votes for Cox, taking them from McAdoo.

All over the floor Cox supporters rose and shouted, hoping that the tide had turned. But many in the hall had not heard the announcement from the Georgia delegation and not until the reading clerk announced it did the real howl break out. It lasted only a moment, however, and the roll call proceeded.

Illinois voted as before and so did Indiana. In Kentucky the lone supporter of John W. Davis turned to Cox.

McAdoo gained one of Owen's two votes in Massachusetts and in Michigan Davis's four votes went to Cox. McAdoo gained one in Minnesota, a vote that had shifted back and forth between him and Cox for several ballots. Two of Montana's eight votes, hitherto cast solidly for McAdoo, broke away and went to Cox. Davis's one vote in New Hampshire went over to McAdoo. New York voted as before.

McAdoo got three of the remaining Palmer votes from Pennsylvania, Cox holding 14 of the others, Palmer 8 and Davis 3, while McAdoo's total was 49. Cox gained one from McAdoo in South Dakota. Tennessee's 24 votes stayed with Davis.

Virginia once more voted solidly for Carter Glass, and there were hisses from the galleries, where the few remaining spectators were hoping to see somebody nominated.

At last the Wisconsin delegation showed a change, for the first time in the balloting, two of the 19 McAdoo votes going to Cox.

Three of the McAdoo votes in Porto Rico went over to Cox, and the Canal Zone ended by keeping its two votes for McAdoo.

Cox had gained 37½ votes on the forty-second ballot and McAdoo had lost 28½. The result of the ballot was: Cox 540½, McAdoo 427, Palmer 18, Davis 49½, Glass 24, Clark 2, Owen 24, Cummings 3, Colby 1.

The announcement of Cox's vote, 7½ short of a majority, brought a roar of applause, but it did not last long. The night was too far gone for demonstrations.

There was much talk late tonight about intervention by President Wilson to end the deadlock. Nothing has come out to show that the President has changed the position which he made clear in a telegram to Senator Glass yesterday that he had not, and would not express preference between the candidates for the nomination.

As the situation stands no means have been found to end the deadlock and the prospect is that the convention will equal and perhaps exceed the record of the convention of 1912, when Wilson was nominated on the forty-sixth ballot.

July 6, 1920

Bryan Thinks Convention Courts Defeat at Polls; He Says That It Is Not His Kind of a Convention

Special to The New York Times.

SAN FRANCISCO, July 5.—William J. Bryan, according to friends, has come to believe that the action of the convention is not making for Democratic success at the election in November.

At the end of the day session this afternoon he was stopped by a group of admirers as he was leaving the auditorium and told that they hoped to hear a speech from him tonight.

"Oh, no!" replied Mr. Bryan. "This is not my kind of a convention. Four years from now it will be my kind of a convention."

"Can't you change it to your kind of convention?" he was asked.

"The leopard cannot change its spots," was Mr. Bryan's reply.

SAN FRANCISCO, July 5 (Associated Press).—After the twenty-fifth ballot today W. J. Bryan made this statement:

"I think what they are really looking for is some one who will be satisfactory to the three elements represented in the deadlock, some one who will respond without protest to every demand that comes from the White House, from Wall Street and from the liquor interests.

"Those are the large interests represented in the convention, and they have not yet been able to agree on a man."

Special Cable to THE NEW YORK TIMES.

LONDON, July 5.—The suggestion by William J. Bryan that the name of Justice Brandeis should be among those considered by the Democratic Convention came as a surprise to the Justice.

He was attending a meeting here preliminary to the Zionist Convention when THE NEW YORK TIMES correspondent took the dispatch announcing it to him this afternoon. He appeared much gratified and said it was the first he had heard of it. He declined to comment on it further.

July 6, 1920

Coolidge Decides on 'Hands Off' Policy As to the Choice of His Running Mate

Special to The New York Times.

WASHINGTON, June 3.—President Coolidge let it be known today that he did not intend to take any part in the choice of the Republican candidate for the Vice Presidency. No secret was made at the White House that the President had been influenced in this decision by the fact that President Roosevelt had followed the same course in 1904, when he was the overwhelming choice of his party for the Presidential nomination, as Mr. Coolidge is now.

According to the view of President Coolidge, as it was indicated today, it would be better for the delegates to the Republican Convention to make their own choice of the Vice Presidential candidate without any White House prompting.

Political advisers of the President have urged him to let the convention determine upon its Permanent Chairman and to give the members of the Platform Committee full sway in selecting their Chairman. These advisers are credited with having told the President that the wise thing to do would be to make his own choice of the Vice Presidential candidate and leave other matters of importance to the convention itself and its committees.

Apparently, however, the President has not regarded this advice as sound. He was responsible for the choice of Representative Burton of Ohio as Temporary Chairman and has put forward Charles B. Warren of Michigan, Ambassador to Mexico, for the Chairmanship of the Platform Committee.

The announcement from the White House that President Coolidge will keep hands off the Vice Presidential contest leaves the field open. A strong opinion exists here that the best choice would lie between Senator Borah and Secretary Hoover. Mr. Borah has made it known to his friends, however, that he would not accept the Vice Presidential candidacy in any circumstance, and, although a boom to nominate Mr. Hoover has been started the Secretary of Commerce has stated publicly that he does not care to be so honored.

June 4, 1924

COOLIDGE'S PLATFORM ADOPTED

PLATFORM WINS AMID CHEERS

20-Minute Demonstration, for President, Then It Goes Through.

ALL WISCONSIN PLANKS FAIL

But La Follette Spokesman Gets a Hearing After Being Jeered as an Insurgent.

DELEGATION SITS UNMOVED

Neither Hisses Nor Taunts Could Win the 28 Badger Men to Rise for Coolidge.

By ELMER DAVIS.

Special to The New York Times.

CLEVELAND, June 11.—At 10:35 tonight the Republican National Convention adopted the platform prepared by the Committee on Resolutions, indorsing the policies of President Coolidge, including the World Court nd the Mellon tax plan, and adjourned until tomorrow morning, when it will reassemble to nominate the President as candidate for another term.

The platform, presented to the convention by Charles B. Warren, Ambassador to Mexico and Chairman of the Committee on Resolutions, was carried by a vote of about 13,000 to 28. None voted against it but the La Follette delegates from Wisconsin; and 12,000 spectators in the galleries and the rear of the hall joined with the delegates in the viva voce vote for the Coolidge declaration of policy.

Just before its adoption the La Follette radical platform, presented in a minority report by Representative Henry A. Cooper of Wisconsin, which may later reappear as the platform of a new third party, had been voted down, none but the Wisconsin delegation voting for it, and everybody, delegates and spectators alike, shouting their noes.

The formal trampling on the Wisconsin program was the culmination of a day devoted chiefly to the glorification of old-fashioned Republican orthodoxy, in which Coolidge men and old-line Republicans united, as against the radical program of the Northwest.

It began in the morning session with the speech of Frank W. Mondell, Permanent Chairman of the convention, which avoided the attacks on orthodox Republican leadership in Congress such as had been made in the keynote speech of Theodore E. Burton the day before, but was full of denunciation of insurgent movements such as that of the La Follette group.

Demonstration for President.

In tonight's session, made dull and dolorous by the reading of the orthodox platform, which occupied nearly an hour, and of the Wisconsin platform, which took up half an hour more, there were interludes of excitement when the resentment of the regulars against Wisconsin insurgency broke out.

The first display of this feeling came just after Mr. Warren had begun the reading of the regular platform, when he first mentioned the name of President Coolidge. This led to a demonstration in which the delegates rose and shouted for twenty minutes—some old-timers making it a trifle more—the spectators standing and shouting too. Everybody stood and shouted for Coolidge but the form is the World Court plank. Direct and positive statements on Ku Klux Klan are avoided, and the document does not declare directly for strict enforcement of the Eighteenth Amendment. The latter issue is placed under law enforcement.

The demands of the women for an "equality plank" did not find a place in the platform. There is a plank opposing immediate independence for the Philippines. The subjects of taxation and immigration are disposed of in general terms, except that a plank dealing with taxation recommends a conference between the States and the Federal Government for an adjustment of taxation, as proposed by President Coolidge in a statement issued when the Revenue bill was signed.

The World Court Plank.

The World Court plank reads:

"The Republican Party affirms its stand for agreement among the nations to prevent war and preserve peace. As an important step in that direction we endorse the Permanent Court of International Justice and favor the adherance of the United States to this tribunal, as recommended by President Coolidge. This Government has definitely refused membership in the League of Nations and to assume any obligations under the Covenant of the League. On this we stand."

The platform may be briefly summarized as follows:

Commends the Administration of President Harding and names as a major achievement the Washington Conference on the Limitation of Armament.

Demands public economies as recommended by President Coolidge.

Recalls the reduction in expenditures, which made tax reduction possible. Favors further progressive reduction in taxes and endorses the plan of President Coolidge for a conference between the States and Federal Government for adjusting questions of taxation between the States and Federal Government.

Endorses re-creation by legislation of a non-partisan Federal commission to study the taxation of State and Federal Governments so as to permit of intelligent taxation revision.

Advocates the calling of another conference on the limitation of armament as proposed by President Coolidge. "When, through the adoption of a permanent reparations plan, the conditions in Europe will make negotiations and cooperation opportune and possible."

Favors the holding of international conferences from time to time for the advancement and codification of international law.

Refuses to consider the cancellation of the foreign war-time debt.

Reaffirms the protective tariff policy and commends the elastic feature of the present tariff law. Favors higher tariff on farm products if necessary to protect the farmers.

Relates efforts of the last Congress to aid the farmers and pledges the Administration toward "broadening our export markets. Assures the farmers that the Republican Party "will place the agricultural interests of America on a basis of economic equality with other industry to insure its prosperity and success."

Commends the Administration for its efforts to eliminate the twelve-hour seven day week in the steel industry and favors higher standards for the employment of women.

Favors lower railroad rates, consolidation of railroad properties and amendments to the law creating the Labor Board wherever experience shows it to be necessary.

Opposes nationalization of the railroads and "all attempts to put the Government into business."

The platform is silent on the bonus, but recommends that all necessary money be expended for the care of the wounded soldiers.

It suggests that industry as well as citizens be drafted in time of war.

Endorses the policy of the present Administration respecting Alaska, and favors the continuance of Alaska and Hawaii as territories.

Advocates enactment of legislation that will tend to promote commercial aviation.

Opposition is expressed to any further weakening of the army and navy and pledges the party to round out the navy to the full strength provided in the arms conference treaty.

Declaration on the Scandals.

Enactment of a Federal anti-lynching law is urged.

As to the recent Congressional investigations, the platform declares that "dishonesty and corruption are not political attributes," and that these investigations showed "instances in both parties of men in public life who are willing to sell official favor, and men out of office who are willing to buy them in some cases with money and in others with influence."

The plank relating to the investigations also demands the prompt and fearless prosecution of all wrongdoers and admits "the deep humiliation which all good citizens share." That our public life should have harbored some dishonest men, that these undesirables do not represent the standard of our national life.

The platform is silent on the Eighteenth Amendment, but contains a general law and order plank which concludes:

"The Republican Party pledges the full strength of the Government for the maintenance of these principles by the enforcement of the Constitution and of all laws."

Instead of declaring opposition to the Ku Klux Klan, the plank labeled as "Constitutional Guaranties" reads:

"The Republican party reaffirms its unyielding devotion to the Constitution, and to the guarantees of civil, political and religious liberty therein contained."

In order to place the Administration and Congress on the same basis, despite the difference of opinion between President Coolidge and Congress, the last plank urges the voters to elect not only a Republican President but a Republican Congress to sustain his policies.

In the opinion of Republicans, the platform will not cause much difference of opinion in the party except over the World Court plank and the policies advocated by the Radicals which were rejected by the platform makers.

Senators opposed to the World Court said tonight that they would not be controlled by the platform declarations or the Court, but would continue to vote their convictions in the Senate despite the Coolidge plank favoring entry by the United States into the Court with reservations.

June 12, 1924

COOLIDGE AND DAWES NOMINATED

REVOLT PUTS DAWES OVER

Old Timers Resent Butler's Domination of the Convention.

HE ASKED FIRST FOR KENYON

Regulars Named Lowden Instead and Then He Switched to Hoover.

DISAFFECTION SPREADING

Talk of Asking Coolidge to Select Another Man to Conduct Campaign.

By RICHARD V. OULAHAN.
Special to The New York Times.

CLEVELAND, June 12.—The Republican National Convention completed its work tonight and adjourned sine die after having chosen Calvin Coolidge of Massachusetts as its candidate for President and General Charles G. Dawes of Illinois as its candidate for Vice President.

Three sessions of the convention were held on the concluding day. The night session was made necessary by an extraordinary situation produced by the refusal of former Governor Frank O. Lowden of Illinois to be the party's candidate for Vice President after the convention had conferred that honor on him.

Mr. Lowden had been chosen on the second Vice Presidential ballot at the afternoon, or second session. Messages from him refusing to accept the nomination, written in advance, were produced after some of Lowden's friends had sought to prevent their being presented.

This remarkable state of affairs compelled a recess to give the party leaders an opportunity to lead the party out of the maze in which it found itself. At the night session the situation was remedied by undoing the nomination of Mr. Lowden and proceeding to ballot again for a candidate for Vice President. On the first ballot at the night session, its third ballot on a candidate for Vice President, victory went to the supporters of General Dawes.

Convention Revolts on Butler.

While only a gesture of protest was made against choosing President Coolidge to head the Republican national ticket in the campaign of 1924, the effort to nominate the candidate for Vice President put a fly in the Republican ointment and threatened to produce serious differences within the party management. Lack of harmony is already apparent among those who are charged with the conduct of the Presidential campaign this year.

The futile nomination of Mr. Lowden for Vice President was in part the outcome of an abortive, inept effort to draft Senator William E. Borah of Idaho for second place on the national ticket.

At an early hour this morning William M. Butler, political manager for President Coolidge, had made known that President Coolidge desired that Senator Borah should be the Vice Presidential nominee, and that Mr. Butler had assurances that Mr. Borah would accept. The Borah boom collapsed when Mr. Borah positively refused to accept the honor.

Mr. Butler countered on the disappearance of Mr. Borah from the Vice Presidential picture by offering Judge William S. Kenyon of Iowa. Leading men of the party who made wry faces when they were asked to support Judge Kenyon, whom they regarded as a near radical and not too loyal to the Republican cause, demanded a request direct from the White House that they put Judge Kenyon in second place on the National ticket. President Coolidge declined to comply with the request.

After that the leaders felt free to make their own choice of a Vice Presidential candidate. Out of their attitude in this connection came the nomination of former Governor Lowden and brought about the embarrassing situation with which the party was confronted when the convention assembled this evening for its third session.

The embarrassment was remedied, as far as straightening out the physical difficulties of the tangle was concerned, by the acceptance of Mr. Lowden's declination and the subsequent nomination of General Dawes.

But the Vice Presidential maze had another and more important phase than was apparent from surface indications. Mr. Lowden's nomination marked a revolt against the domination of Mr. Butler.

Accuse Butler as Dictator.

Feeling against him has been growing on the part of leading party workers, especially members of the National Committee, ever since they began gathering in Cleveland. He was charged with being dictatorial, with paying no attention to the counsel of veterans in party affairs, and generally with attempting to use his authority as President Coolidge's agent in a way detrimental to harmony among those who will bear the brunt of battle in the coming campaign. His critics accused him of attempting to be the entire party management.

Last night the revolt took form in the decision of the Indiana delegation to place the name of Senator James E. Watson of their State before the convention as a candidate for the Vice Presidential nomination. While he had been endorsed for this office by the Indiana Republican State Convention, Mr. Watson had given notice that he would not permit his name to be placed before the convention if the leaders decided upon some other man. Within the past few days, however, Mr. Watson has been smarting under the way in which he felt he was being ignored by Mr. Butler and the group of administration men who were meeting practically continuously in Secretary Week's room with the object of agreeing upon a candidate. Mr. Watson was not invited to these meetings.

Senator Watson sent out emissaries to sound State delegations to ascertain if delegates would support his candidacy for second place on the ticket as a protest against the arbitrary way Mr. Butler had been conducting things.

After the movement from Mr. Butler's quarters to nominate Judge Kenyon for Vice President had collapsed as the Borah effort had, leading men of a number of delegations from big States got together with a view to reaching an agreement among themselves as to whom to support for the Vice Presidential choice. There was an inclination on their part to concentrate on Representative Everett Sanders of Indiana. But Mr. Sanders did not appeal to many delegates, and when nominations for Vice Presidential candidates were called for at the afternoon session a host of names were brought forward.

Representative Theodore E. Burton of Ohio, who had made a very favorable impression when he delivered the "keynote" speech Tuesday, was the favorite of the New York delegation and got large support. But former Governor Lowden went to the front and on the second ballot he was chosen to be the Vice Presidential nominee.

The old timers, those who have been chafing under the rule of Mr. Butler, were delighted. They felt that they had administered a rebuke to Mr. Butler and his ways. Mr. Butler countered by insisting that the message received from Mr. Lowden saying that he would not accept the nomination be presented to the convention. A hasty conference of leading men in the convention was held on the stage. Mr. Butler's critics did not want the Lowden message read, but Mr. Butler had his way and produced the embarrassing situation which confronted the convention when it resumed for its night session.

Old Republican regulars who resent Mr. Butler's attitude are saying tonight that there is a serious revolt within the party ranks. There is talk that President Coolidge may be asked to withdraw his decision to have Mr. Butler named as Chairman of the National Committee. As matters stand there is a chance of a flare-up when the National Committee meets formally at the conclusion of the convention to elect its Chairman.

When the complication over the nomination of former Governor Lowden had been adjusted at the night session leaders of various State delegations got together and agreed to support General Dawes. To the activity of Secretary Mellon this arrangement is credited.

Mr. Butler made an eleventh hour effort to have Herbert Hoover chosen as the party's candidate for Vice President. He went from his place on the stage down on the floor and pleaded with Senator Wadsworth of New York, Senator Reed of Pennsylvania, and Senator Edge of New Jersey to swing their delegations to Mr. Hoover. None of them would make any concession to Mr. Butler. His action convinced delegates that they were right in their belief that if President Coolidge could not succeed in getting Senator Borah or Judge Kenyon to be the Vice Presidential candidate he would turn to Mr. Hoover as the most outstanding progressive and vote-getter available.

The selection of General Dawes as the Vice Presidential nominee is regarded as a compromise between the wishes of the Old Guard and the Administration element in the convention, which was not in sympathy with the effort to select as a candidate for second place any man who had shown semi-radical tendencies or was inclined to hold aloof from working with the party management.

It is understood that President Coolidge was informed over the telephone today, after Judge KKenyon had been indicated as the President's choice, that it might be impossible to swing the New York and Pennsylvania delegations to Judge Kenyon. Secretary Mellon is credited with having given this information to the President.

The Old Guard contingent, angry with Mr. Butler, is finding satisfaction in the selection of General Dawes mainly because he was not the candidate of Mr. Butler. The more moderate of President Coolidge's close supporters are pleased over General Dawes's selection because they believe he will appeal to th business element of the country and has already laid the foundation of support among the people generally by reason of his services as head of the committee of experts which drafted the plan for the adjustment of the German reparation problem.

Much talk has taken place among delegates since the convention adjourned tonight about "amateur politicians." This is aimed at Mr. Butler and may be the forerunner of an effort to induce President Coolidge to choose another campaign manager.

The nomination of the candidate for Vice President followed a period of sensation, excitement and confusion covering many hours. Early this morning, when the tired Republican leaders went to bed after a long day of conferences over the Vice Presidential situation, the contest seemed to be over. The word had been passed by Mr. Butler, recognized as the authorized mouthpiece of President Coolidge, that Senator Borah would accept the nomination. The weary ones who had been trying to avoid a deadlock in the convention accepted Mr. Butler's statement as meaning that the man in the White House, whose domination over his party was everywhere recognized, had picked Mr. Borah for his running mate and that Mr. Borah, yielding to persuasion, had abandoned his attitude of refusal.

Piecing together the shuffled parts of this Vice Presidential picture-puzzle has not been an easy process, but the completed puzzle shows Mr. Butler placing his hand on Mr. Borah's shoulder and telling a group of Cabinet officers, Senators, Representatives and leading Republican politicians that Mr. Borah would be Mr. Coolidge's side partner in the national political contest of 1924.

Until Mr. Butler made his appearance before the tired group of Vice President makers its members were still in a confused state of mind over the situation. Their deliberations of several days had not been productive of anything concrete. They had backed and filled, permitted shadows to frighten them, been actuated by hope to find it displaced by gloom. A name of some one acceptable to President Coolidge and likely to add strength to the national ticket would be suggested and received with approbation, then the pessimists would get to work. They would find bad spots in the political armor of the proposed one. Heaving heavy highs, the conferees would return to their task. Another ray of hope, then another deluge of gloom. It was a game of putting up straw men to knock them down.

The Cabinet-Congress group, as distinguished from what may be called the Coolidge personal group, consisting of Mr. Butler, Secretary Slemp and Frank W. Stearns of Boston, was measurably distant from an agreement on a Vice Presidential candidate when it decided to take a recess at 8 o'clock last night to enable its members to attend the evening session of the convention, resuming its conferences about 11 o'clock in Secretary Weeks's rooms in the Cleveland Hotel. For hours preceding that time Herbert Hoover had appeared to be the favorite in the Cabinet-Congress group. But the conferees had by no means narrowed their choice to Mr. Hoover. Hovering in the near distance were Senator Curtis of Kansas, General Harbord of Kansas and the army, and Ex-Representative Good of Iowa.

When the conferees reassembled about 11 o'clock last night after the convention adjourned a sudden change had taken place in Mr. Hoover's status. He had suffered a material lessening. Just why is not quite clear, but the best explanation obtainable indicates that the conferees concluded that Mr. Hoover did not possess those spell-binding qualities essential in a Vice Presidential candidate. There was a rise in Senator Curtis's stock. Mr. Good's chances rose and fell.

That was the situation in Secretary Weeks's smoke-filled quarters just before 1 o'clock this morning, when Mr. Butler, who had his rooms on a lower floor of the same hotel, suddenly appeared before the conferees. Among those present at that time were Secretaries Weeks and Mellon, Postmaster General New, Senator Wadsworth of New York, Senators Pepper and Reed of Pennsylvania, Charles D. Hilles, New York National Committeeman, and Senator Harreld of Oklahoma.

When Mr. Butler informed the group of Cabinet officers, legislators and others that Mr. Borah would accept the nomination the conferees felt that their work was done. President Coolidge had wanted Mr. Borah from the first, and Mr. Butler's assurance that the Idaho Senator would accept left nothing further for the conferees to do except to work to bring about the registration of the Presidential will by the convention. Meanwhile Senator Borah was at his home in Washington presumably calmly sleeping.

But his old friend, former Senator Albert J. Beveridge of Indiana, was awake, out here in Cleveland. Along about 1:30 o'clock this morning Mr. Beveridge heard that an informal announcement had been made that Mr. Borah had agreed to accept the nomination. Mr. Beveridge could not believe it. He knew that Mr. Borah had twice, in the most positive way, told him and President Coolidge that under no circumstances would he become the Vice Presidential candidate on the Republican ticket.

Mr. Beveridge, from his hotel room, arranged to have Senator Borah called on the telephone at 3:30 o'clock this morning. In some way Mr. Borah's telephone was connected up with Mr. Beveridge's telephone at 3:30 o'clock this morning. Mr. Borah declined again to serve if an effort were made to draft him for second place. Mr. Beveridge crawled back into bed. When he woke several hours later and began to think over what Senator Borah had authorized him to say to the convention to kill any attempt to nominate Borah it occurred to him that he had not a line in writing to show that he was Mr. Borah's authorized spokesman.

So Mr. Beveridge sent a telegram to Senator Borah asking him to telegraph authority to notify the convention that Mr. Borah would not consent to be the candidate. Shortly thereafter Mr. Beveridge received a telegram from Senator Borah which confirmed the telephone authorization to withdraw Mr. Borah's name if it were presented to the convention. "Please be sure to do this," the telegram said. If the convention should nominate him anyway, continued Mr. Borah, he desired Mr. Beveridge to read a message contained in the telegram, which said that Mr. Borah greatly appreciated the convention's manifestation of confidence, but that he must be permitted to serve in the way in which he could serve best. Therefore, he said, he must respectfully but positively decline the nomination for the Vice Presidency.

When the announcement was made by Mr. Butler in Secretary Weeks's room that Senator Borah would accept the nomination his auditors were astonished. One of them, Senator Pepper, had talked with Senator Borah over the telephone on Tuesday and had been convinced that Mr. Borah would not accept.

Mainly on account of that conversation, emphasized by other telephonic and telegraphic messages, Mr. Borah's name was dropped from consideration by the Cabinet group. In the light of their direct information from Senator Borah, the conferees were fairly dumfounded. Senator Reed of Pennsylvania questioned Mr. Butler as to the source of his authority that Senator Borah would accept. Two of those present in that early morning gathering said that Mr. Butler's response to Senator Reed was as follows: He could tell the conferees that Senator Borah would be acceptable to President Coolidge as the Vice Presidential candidate and he (Mr. Butler) had assurance that Senator Borah would not decline, if nominated. This assurance, he said, came to him from a second man and not directly from Senator Borah, but he was satisfied of its correctness.

For a few hours the big men of the convention were lulled in sleep by comforting dreams that the vigorous Senator from Idaho had agreed to be the Republican Party's candidate for Vice President, thus giving assurances of victory through the adherence of the dissatisfied West to the Republican Party.

Telephone conversations between Cleveland and the White House were followed by an authoritative intimation that President Coolidge would be glad to have the convention nominate Judge Kenyon. But the old time Republican leaders, the organization men who are chary of showing party favors to those whom they regard as impregnated with radicalism and lacking in a sense of party loyalty, declined to take their cue on a mere intimation from Mr. Butler. What they wanted was a direct request from President Coolidge himself that he desired them to put Judge Kenyon in second place.

Mr. Butler was informed of this attitude of the old timers. Their position was strengthened by the course of some of the President's closest associates and personal supporters, one of whom under the stress of his indignation made the assertion that if Judge Kenyon were nominated he would quit the Republican Party. It looked as if an incipient revolt was in progress against President Coolidge himself, although old guardsmen practically bound themselves to vote for Mr. Kenyon if the President made a direct request for his nomination.

President Coolidge was communicated with by telephone. He declined to designate the man for whom they should vote when nominations for Vice President came to be made.

The President's attitude made the old-timers feel that they were free to act as they pleased without giving offense to the President. Immediately they began again to discuss the situation. Out of a conference that included some of those who had been members of the group of Cabinet officers, Senators and Representatives and others who had been trying to adjust the Vice Presidential situation came what appeared to be a tentative agreement to support Representative Everett Sanders of Indiana for second place.

That was the understanding after the morning session of the convention got under way. Then there was a quick change. Some of the old-time leaders felt that it was unwise to bind themselves to a man who was little known to the country and ignore others whose party service entitled them to preference. When meetings of various State delegations were held during a recess between the morning and afternoon sessions, it was apparent that delegates had minds of their own.

Out of this state of affairs came the real revolt against the domination of Mr. Butler, the man chosen by President Coolidge to be Chairman of the Republican National Committee, an office which carries with it the management of the party's Presidential campaign.

June 13, 1924

* * ✻ ✻ * *

BITTER FIGHT LOOMS ON TWO-THIRDS RULE IN CONVENTION HERE

Kentucky Governor, a McAdoo Supporter, Comes Out For Majority Nomination.

TEXAS ALSO PLEDGED TO IT

But McAdoo Leaders Fear Initiative by Them Might Defeat Their Candidate.

CHANGE THOUGHT UNLIKELY

Strategists, However, Consider Moves to Bring Issue Before Delegates.

Governor W. J. Fields of Kentucky, who will head the McAdoo-instructed delegation from his own State, is coming to the Democratic National Convention prepared to make an aggressive fight against the two-thirds rule under which the Democrats have nominated their Presidential candidates for almost a century.

Objections to the rule have been raised frequently heretofore, but every attempt to abolish it has failed. Now, however, indications point to a real fight in the convention, or at least in the convention Committee on Rules.

The growth into its present strength of the movement to nominate by a mere majority has been generally attributed to friends of William G. McAdoo, who will enter the convention with greater delegate strength than any other candidate. However, leaders thought to be in a position to speak for Mr. McAdoo said yesterday that they did not think Mr. McAdoo's supporters would take the initiative in a fight on the two-thirds rule. But they qualified this by saying it would be necessary for Mr. McAdoo himself to confirm their impression of his attitude. Mr. McAdoo is expected here tomorrow.

Texas for Majority Rule.

Meanwhile the Texas delegation, which is for McAdoo, will come to the convention committed to a rule providing for nomination of President and Vice President by simple majorities. Thomas B. Love, Democratic National Committeeman from Texas, has been one of the principal supporters of Mr. McAdoo and was one of his spokesmen in the Democratic National Convention four years ago.

Democratic leaders generally predicted that any attempt to abrogate the two-thirds rule this year would fail. Members of the Democratic National Committee who will wield a strong influence in the convention oppose the change, almost to a man.

With a simple majority rule in force, aspirants for the Presidency would be in a far better position to insure their nomination in advance of the convention. On the other hand, with the two-thirds rule in operation, a time comes at every convention when candidates begin frantic drives for delegates, and these afford delegation leaders opportunities for driving hard bargains which they otherwise would not have.

Friends who feel that with the two-thirds rule out of the way Mr. McAdoo could be nominated on an early ballot are well aware of the strength of this opposition. They are well aware also that the opening of such a fight on their initiative might alienate elements now friendly to their candidate. The result would be a loss of delegates as well as a loss of prestige if the fight were lost, which well might mean the defeat of Mr. McAdoo.

Strategists Get Busy.

It is intimated strongly that Mr. McAdoo's friends may attempt to manoeuvre the supporters of the two-thirds rule into a position where they would be compelled themselves to initiate a fight for its retention.

In connection with this the McAdoo supporters have made exhaustive search of the records and profess to have found that there exists neither legal nor historic grounds for perpetuating the rule. They take the ground that every convention is competent to make its own rules and cannot be governed by rules adopted by conventions that preceded it. This point is certain to be raised before the Committee on Rules and possibly in convention. The contention will be made that when the convention meets there is no two-thirds rule, and hence no need for aggressive action to abrogate it, the only question being whether the convention, acting without regard to past conventions, shall decide that nominations be made by a two-thirds rule or by a simple majority.

Colonel Dixon C. Williams of Illinois, Treasurer of the McAdoo Pre-Convention Campaign Committee, said he believed the McAdoo supporters would be well content to let advocates of the two-thirds rule take the initiative in a fight to uphold it.

"The chances of Mr. McAdoo getting the nomination are improving hourly," he said. "There has been a strong drift toward him. That is true with regard to delegates. It is true also with regard to public sentiment throughout the country, especially since the Cleveland Convention.

Finds Dissatisfied Republicans.

"We are exhibitors at a railroad supplies exhibition which is going on at Atlantic City at present. While this has been in progress I have talked with many people. I find that since the Cleveland Convention many Republicans who do not like the Republican platform or candidates would be glad to vote the Democratic ticket in the event Mr. McAdoo were nominated."

Mr. McAdoo, according to Colonel Williams, has eleven Illinois delegates and many of the remaining forty-seven members would gladly turn to him the moment it appeared that he could win the nomination.

"Who is second choice of the Illinois delegates?" Colonel Williams was asked.

"There is no second choice—in my opinion it will never come to a second choice," he replied with a laugh. "I think that's the way to put it at this stage of the convention preliminaries."

June 17, 1924

FIERY SPEECH BY M'ADOO

He Says 'Invisible Government' Now Rules the Nation.

600 Supporters Applaud His Declaration of Ten "Real Issues" of the Campaign.

SEEK HEARST'S AID FOR HIM

Commissioner Wallis Gets Virtual Promise of Publisher's 'Passive Support,' at Least.

Greeted with almost religious fervor by six hundred of his supporters, William G. McAdoo attacked Wall Street and the editors of the New York newspapers in a speech to the delegates supporting him at a "get-together meeting" in the Della Robbia room of the Hotel Vanderbilt last night.

Mr. McAdoo did not refer to the Ku Klux Klan by name, but he accused his opponents of attempting to raise false race and religious issues to obscure the real issue, which he said was "the restoration of the administration of national affairs to the people from the control of a sinister, unscrupulous, invisible government, which has its seat in the citadel of privilege and finance in New York City."

He did not mention the oil investigation, but referred to the difficulty of his candidacy and his triumphs in primaries as the greatest tribute he ever had received.

Mr. McAdoo enumerated ten issues which he declared were the real issues of the 1924 campaign, the ten virtually constituting his personal platform. Among these were included the removal of the influence of the "invisible" Government, the repeal of the Fordney-McCumber Tariff bill, the protection of natural resources, the repeal of the Esch-Cummins railroad law, and the ending of the isolation of the United States and the beginning of a period of international cooperation.

This reference to what was construed as at least a partial declaration for the League of Nations brought great applause, which was intensified when Mr. McAdoo drew a parallel between the present situation and that at the 1912 Baltimore convention, and pleaded with his supporters to stand fast for "progressive democracy, just as the supporters of Woodrow Wilson did at Baltimore."

"If you stand fast in this convention they can't beat us from now to doomsday," was his prediction, which ended his speech and brought forth a redoubled volume of cheers.

The meeting started with a fervor that has not been displayed generally in any political movement since the Progressive movement of 1912. Cheers were given for Mr. McAdoo and his national campaign manager, Judge David Ladd Rockwell. Those present joined in a chant that "McAdoo'll do," and joined in the singing of half a dozen McAdoo songs.

* * * * *

June 23, 1924

MORE GAINS COUNTED BY SMITH'S BACKERS

Delegates From 21 States Tell Governor They Are For Him —Six From Colorado.

MACK WORKS ON THE SOUTH

Deal With Taggart Reported—Morgenthau Assails McAdoo as "Disinherited Heir."

Adherents of Governor Smith began an intensive campaign yesterday among delegates known to have Smith leanings to get them to favor the New York Governor in event the McAdoo forces weaken after the first test of strength in the convention. Word has gone out among the Smith workers that the McAdoo strength was showing signs of waning and that this is the psychological time to put Smith over.

"Get out and do missionary work," was the advice given the Smith men by Franklin D. Roosevelt at a meeting of the New York State Committee for the nomination of Alfred E. Smith at the Smith headquarters in the Prudence Building, Forty-third Street and Broadway. Mr. Roosevelt aroused the members of the committee to great enthusiasm when he told them the Governor's prospects never looked better.

An unmistakable feeling of confidence was apparent in the headquarters after Mr. Roosevelt had had a long conference with Tom Taggart, the Democratic "boss" of Indiana. Mr. Roosevelt said the conference was satisfactory but would not go into details.

Smith to See Taggart Later.

Governor Smith did not meet Mr. Taggart, but it was said they would confer in a short time. The fact that the Indiana delegates in caucus had voted for Senator Ralston did not lessen the belief among the Smith men that Mr. Taggart would throw Indiana's support to New York's Governor when the proper time came. A perfect working agreement among the Tammany-Taggart-Brennan forces is said to have been reached.

The fact that Edmund H. Moore, a strong Smith sympathizer, had been elected National Committeeman by the Ohio delegation also cheered the Smith people. The Ohio delegation will be for James M. Cox on the first ballot, but Moore is expected to swing the delegation to Smith when the first breakaway from favorite sons sets in. In fact, the result of the caucuses of many of the State delegations gave a favorable reaction to the Smith forces. They considered that they had got more than an even break.

Norman E. Mack, National Committeeman from New York, will be one of the Smith supporters to do missionary work among delegates who still are unconvinced of Governor Smith's availability as a Presidential candidate. Mr. Mack will confine his Smith propaganda to the Southern delegates.

Opposition in South Breaking.

"Many of the delegates," he said, "are coming to realize that Al Smith is the man to be named if we are to carry the industrial East and North, including States like Massachusetts, Connecticut, New York and New Jersey. I am also sure that much of the opposition to Smith from the South is breaking down. This is the political change that I have noticed within the last twenty-four hours."

Governor Smith and his campaign manager had an active day. They saw delegates from twenty-one States and discussed with them the Governor's availability as a candidate. The Governor passed most of the afternoon reviewing the munipical parade, and received an ovation when he left the Biltmore Hotel to go to the reviewing stand. Thousands were jammed about Madison Avenue and Forty-second Street when the Governor, accompanied by Rodman Wanamaker, Chairman of the Mayor's Reception Committee, started for the reviewing stand, escorted by a squadron of mounted police.

A great cheer broke from the crowd. The Governor smiled and bowed until he reached his car, when another great cheer sent him on his way.

Before going to the parade the Governor shook hands with many visitors, among whom was Governor Sweet of Colorado, who believes that because of a deadlock between Smith and McAdoo the nomination will go to a dark horse. Governor Sweet was accompanied by a majority of the Colorado delegates, to whom Mr. Smith made a short speech, saying he would have another talk with their Governor today.

Smith Gains in Colorado.

"We're going to talk over matters of State, and I hope after it is over everything will be all right," he said.

Both Governors joined in the laughter that followed.

Governor Sweet said he met Governor Smith at the Washington conference of Governors and was impressed when Mr. Smith had passed along a slip of paper on which was written "Zev wins."

"That is true," said Governor Smith. "I got my information about Zev from a gold-laced flunkey who was whispering it in the ear of Attorney General Daugherty."

The Colorado Governor later said his delegation, after the first ballot, would vote 4 for McAdoo, 6 for Smith and would split the rest between Davis and Underwood.

General Charles H. Cole of Massachusetts, one of the leaders of that State's delegation, told the Governor he was sure the thirty-six delegates from his State would be for Smith.

John J. Fitzgerald, former Mayor of Boston, known as "Honey Fitz," also had cheering words to the newspapermen he said:

"Democrats like Mr. Bryan, from the far West and South, should realize that Smith is the only man who can carry New York and the other industrial States in New England. Without victory in these States the party is lost. Only a small portion of the people participated in the last Massachusetts election. About one million kept away from the polls but they'll be out for Al."

Sees Connecticut Backing.

The Governor also talked with delegates from Connecticut and later said: "The people of the State are for me and that's a good reason why I should get the delegates' support."

The Governor also conferred for a short time with Charles S. Barrett, President of the Farmers' Crop Educational Union, an influential farm organization in the South. The Governor told Mr. Barrett about his interest in agricultural problems.

At his regular session with the newspaper men, Chairman Roosevelt reiterated that Governor Smith would go into the convention with at least 200 votes.

"One thing is certain," said Mr. Roosevelt, "and that is that the candidate for Vice President will not come from New York."

Mr. Roosevelt said the day's series of conferences had been "very encouraging, revealing many unexpected sources of support," for the Smith movement. It was explained, however, that while the delegates, who called, did not, in all cases, represent the full delegations from the twenty-one States they represented, they let it be known that Governor Smith had "votes in them."

The States, represented either in whole or in part, were named by Mr. Roosevelt, as follows: Tennessee, Virginia, North and South Dakota, Kentucky, Missouri, Washington, Oregon, Utah, Colorado, Nebraska, Louisiana, Florida, Mississippi, West Virginia, Maryland, Massachusetts, Connecticut, Rhode Island, New Hampshire, and Maine.

Returning to headquarters late in the afternoon, the Governor again was besieged by callers and gave his time to them until called to go to Mayor John F. Hylan's dinner tonight for New York State and other delegate guests of the city.

Among these who talked with Mr. Roosevelt was Henry Morgenthau, former Ambassador to Turkey. He said that of the prominent Democrats who were for Woodrow Wilson in 1912—men like Cleveland H. Dodge and Dr. Abram I. Elkus—not one was now in line behind William G. McAdoo.

"He may be Mr. Wilson's heir," said Mr. Morgenthau, "but he is a disinherited one, disinherited by his own party and his friends."

He predicted that if Governor Smith was nominated he would win by a large majority, and added:

"The Republican Party is disintegrating. The detached units, the radicals, are leaving the contest of this election to those conservatives who are advocates of normalcy and the condoners of dishonesty.

"It is, therefore, up to the Democratic Party to exorcise its own evil and dishonest spirits and select a real progressive, courageous Democrat as its leader in the coming struggle.

"We must not experiment with untried people. We must not take a counterfeit progressive nor a demagogue. We must select some one who has proved his capacity by administering high office to the satisfaction of all his constituents; some one who is above all suspicion; some one who has such daring feats to his credit as defying Hearst in 1922 and now is successfully preventing the capture of the Democratic nomination by McAdoo; a man who has successfully and to the entire satisfaction of his constituency filled the office of Governor of the State of New York for two terms and who has, like Governors Tilden, Cleveland, Hughes and Roosevelt, been given an opportunity for a larger sphere of usefulness. As a New Yorker, I am proud that we can offer to the country one of our own boys: Alfred E. Smith.

"Four years ago the Democratic Party suspended its activities. Fortunately, it did not go, like the Republican Party now has gone, into moral bankruptcy. Next year it will resume functioning as the Government of all people.

"How refreshing to us older citizens and how encouraging to the youth of America will it be to again have one of 'God's noblest works'—a real man—in the White House."

June 24, 1924

M'ADOO IS 'TOO OILY,' SAYS GOVERNOR NEFF

Texan Also Holds That Smith Is Too Wet—He Favors John W. Davis.

Governor Pat M. Neff of Texas, in a statement last night, declared that William Gibbs McAdoo, because of his former connection with the Doheny oil interests, his alleged improper employment by the Republic Steel Corporation and "his practice of political influence" before the Government departments in Washington was "absolutely unacceptable as a party leader to the millions of voters who constitute the virtue and backbone of the American people."

Governor Neff was designated to be a delegate-at-large from Texas, but declined to accept when the Texas convention instructed for Mr. McAdoo, explaining that to do so would be to stultify himself. The Governor is the only Southern Governor who has openly opposed the McAdoo candidacy. John W. Davis is believed to be Neff's first choice for the Presidential nomination.

The Governor is also opposed to the nomination of Governor Smith, his objection being that Governor Smith is too wet. That was the only criticism he had to utter as to the candidacy of the New York Governor. Just now the big battle, he said, was to block the nomination of Mr. McAdoo, and with that accomplished the convention could settle down and nominate the best candidate.

The statement said, in part:

"The Democratic Party meets tomorrow to name a candidate who should and who can win. The selection of either Mr. McAdoo or Governor Smith means defeat for the party. Smith is too wet, McAdoo is too oily.

"The unfortunate division of our party at this moment between these two impossible candidates has caused the delegates to overlook temporarily the strength and virtues of many abler and better fitted men, such as Davis, Copeland, Ralston, Baker and Bryan."

The statement of Governor Neff brought a hot rejoinder from Marshall Hicks of San Antonio, chairman of the Texas delegation, which has its headquarters at the Hotel McAlpin. After he had read the statement, Mr. Hicks said:

"Neff has been utterly repudiated in Texas. He abandoned the duties of his office and for two weeks canvassed the State against McAdoo and made the identical charges against McAdoo that he makes here in New York in this statement. Notwithstanding his activity, Texas Democrats overwhelmingly endorsed McAdoo. Neff's own county sent him to the State convention instructed for McAdoo.

"At the Texas State convention at Waco, over which I presided and which elected the delegates to this national convention, Governor Neff's name was put on the list of delegates at large, but it was on the distinct promise of two close personal friends of his that as soon as he was named he would decline. Those two friends notified him as soon as his name was announced and if he had not immediately declined I would have recognized at once a delegate to the State convention who would have moved to have the Governor's name stricken from the list. If Neff had not acted quickly his name would have been taken off the list by the convention."

June 24, 1924

Committee Rejects Change of Two-Thirds Rule; Plans to Have Candidates Put in Nomination Today

The official death of the plan to amend the time-honored party rule requiring a two-thirds vote to nominate Democratic candidates for President and Vice President was accomplished speedily yesterday when the convention Committee on Rules of Procedure rejected the proposal as put forward by W. L. Thornton, the Texas delegate.

Only three of the forty committeemen—those from Florida, Texas and Utah—voted in favor of the change, which has been supported by some McAdoo leaders as a means to further the ex-Secretary's nomination. There is now little likelihood of the question reaching the floor of the convention.

The Rules Committee voted to recommend that nominating speeches for candidates for President be made today without waiting until the platform is adopted. It was urged, however, that balloting for Presidential candidates should not start until the platform has been adopted. Today's session, therefore, is likely to end with the close of nominating speeches.

June 25, 1924

LAST NOMINEES ARE IN

LAST NOMINEES IN FIELD

Call of the States Ends With Sixteen Candidates Named.

MANY SECONDING SPEECHES

John W. Davis, Glass, Cox, Silzer, C. W. Bryan and Brown Added to the Long List.

WOMEN LEAD IN ORATORY

They Stir Up Weary Delegates and Start Real Demonstrations.

By ELMER DAVIS.

The Democrats are through at last with making nominations for the Presidential nomination. They devoted six hours and a quarter yesterday to that necessary but painful task, finishing up a work that had been begun on Wednesday afternoon and carried forward through most of Thursday's sessions.

According to the stenographic record, only about 40,000 or 50,000 words were spoken yesterday, but anybody who had to sit through it all would be willing to swear that there were at least 40,000,000.

The convention is supposed to resume its operations at 9:30 o'clock this morning, though it will probably start late, as usual. The adoption of the platform, probably after considerable argument, is the first thing in the order of business. Before the day is over the balloting for the Presidency may begin.

Six new Presidential candidates were placed before the convention yesterday. Ohio nominated James M. Cox; Nebraska, Governor Charles W. Bryan; New Hampshire, Governor Fred W. Brown; New Jersey, Governor George S. Silzer; Virginia, Senator Carter Glass, and West Virginia, John W. Davis.

This makes sixteen candidates presented altogether. Oscar W. Underwood, Joseph T. Robinson and William Gibbs McAdoo were nominated on Wednesday, and Alfred E. Smith, Willard Saulsbury, David Franklin Houston, Samuel M. Ralston, Jonathan M. Davis, Albert C. Ritchie and Woodbridge N. Ferris on Thursday.

If you don't see your favorite among the belauded sixteen, don't worry. A lot of other people will be voted for on the first ballot, and later. Quite possibly the eventual nominee of this convention will be somebody who has not been formally placed in nomination at all.

But the nominations were not half of it yesterday. There were also seconding speeches. Mr. McAdoo was seconded seven times, Governor Smith four times, and Senator Underwood once. This makes their total score: McAdoo 11, Smith 7 and Underwood 2, for all of them had been extensively seconded on Thursday. Messrs. Silzer, Ritchie, Davis, Glass and Brown also were seconded yesterday.

The big wind accompanying the thunderstorm of Wednesday evening had a higher velocity than the winds that blew in Madison Square Garden from 11:40 yesterday morning till nearly 6 o'clock last night, but the Democratic wind was considerably larger in volume.

Under the influence of this fearful epidemic of oratory, this Black Death of talk germs, strange, fearful and unnatural things were done. Usually a State which has nominated its candidate lets some other State second him, to show his nation-wide appeal. But if he has no nation-wide appeal, it seems he must be seconded anyway.

New Jersey not only nominated Governor Silzer but seconded him herself. So did West Virginia with John W. Davis. Virginia went even further with Carter Glass and gave him one nominating and two seconding speeches.

Pennsylvania Leads in Seconding.

Worst of all was Pennsylvania. That well-known State has no favorite son this year, and its delegation is split several ways. Every faction insisted on seconding its favorite candidate, and so Pennsylvania responded to the roll call with no less than five seconding speeches. Pennsylvania delegates talked for Messrs. Smith, Underwood, Ritchie and McAdoo. Nobody knows who the fifth Pennsylvania seconder was seconding, for he was howled down and booed off the platform before he got to the name. All the crowd learned was that he was in favor of somebody who was his own platform—a good line which was promptly taken by several subsequent seconders.

All in all, it was a terrible day, yet it had its mitigations. Here and there some flower bloomed in the dismal desert, like a window box in a tenement. The Pulitzer prize for unstinted praise must be awarded to Governor E. Lee Trinkle of Virginia, who said of Carter Glass that, "no man can point the finger of scorn at him except with pride."

Other oases in the sandy wastes were the speeches of three ladies, near the end of the session, who not only received but earned the attention and admiration of the crowd. Chief among them, most praiseworthy of all orators of this oratorical convention, was Mrs. Averill Beavers of Kennewick, Wash., who said she was for Mr. McAdoo, and, having uttered ten words, sat down.

Then there was Mrs. Kate Waller Barrett of Washington, D. C., who has a voting residence in Virginia. She seconded Carter Glass with such fire and enthusiasm that she almost warmed up somnolent delegates. And Mrs. Izetta Jewel Brown of West Virginia, seconding John W. Davis at the very end of this protracted and burdensome day, was so handsome and suave and entertaining that she got eight minutes of respectful attention, followed by authentic applause, from a crowd which would have pitched out any male orator in eight seconds.

Demonstrations in Between.

Mixed in between the speeches were demonstrations. None of the minor candidates feels called upon to let his friends demonstrate as extensively as those of Smith and McAdoo, but local pride permitted New Jersey to shout and sing and parade the hall for twenty-five minutes. Carter Glass's friends made noise for twenty minutes.

And there was a twelve-minute demonstration for Mr. Bryan. Yes, the old, original, undiluted Bryan. Be not alarmed; William Jennings Bryan isn't running this time, at least, he is not running yet. Anybody in the party is likely to be running before the balloting is over. William Jennings's brother Charley had got Nebraska's nomination, as he will get Nebraska's vote, but the demonstration was for William Jennings.

Then there was a seventeen-minute demonstration by and for Ohio. This one must be assigned geographically, for it still is open to doubt whether the incentive of the demonstrators, in so far as they had one, was James M. Cox, who had been nominated, Newton D. Baker, who had nominated him, or Woodrow Wilson, whose doctrines had been the principal theme of Mr. Baker's speech. In some respects this speech was the most interesting item of the day, not for its present interest but for its connection with the past and possible connection with the future.

In the first place, Newton D. Baker, Secretary of War in the Wilson Cabinet, is the only one of Mr. Wilson's personal aids who has yet appeared before this convention. President Wilson had great confidence in him, and was preparing with him a statement of principles (unfinished at the President's death), which rather inaccurately has been called "Wilson's Political Testament."

One of the first objects of Mr. Baker's speech was to correct the impression that Mr. Wilson's political estate had descended by a sort of entail to his son-in-law. Several speakers said yesterday, in effect, that Mr. Wilson's doctrines had not been copyrighted by Mr. McAdoo or anybody else; but Newton D. Baker said it most convincingly, and he said it in a speech, renominating James M. Cox, who dared to be for the League in 1920 and is not afraid to say he is for it still.

It was noteworthy that in a speech lasting half an hour Mr. Baker talked twenty-five minutes before he said anything at all about his candidate; twenty-five minutes about Woodrow Wilson, his doctrines and his record, and five minutes about James M. Cox, who ran on Woodrow Wilson's record in 1920.

Mr. Baker's speech, indeed, sounded rather like a keynote, so comprehensive was its treatment of all the issues likely to be argued in this campaign. He was for the League, and for it hard—as all men know, since he has been fighting for a strong pro-League plank in the Platform Committee. He also spoke out hard and straight against the Ku Klux Klan.

The heroes of the nightshirt and hood heard a lot of hard words about themselves yesterday. A woman from Pennsylvania denounced the Klan in her speech seconding Governor Smith, and a Catholic delegate from North Dakota took occasion to hop on the Klan as hard as he could while he was seconding Mr. McAdoo.

There is nothing in this convention like the aristocratic reticence of the Republicans. When the Democrats have opinions they speak right out in meeting. One could admire that if they spoke with less prolixity.

June 28, 1924

PREDICT KLAN ROW WILL INJURE PARTY

Leaders of Masked Order See Split in South, No Matter How Platform Reads.

OPPOSITION A SURPRISE

Strength of Its Enemies Here Led to a Hurry Call for Klan Reinforcements.

Klan leaders were predicting yesterday that as the result of the injection of the Klan issue into the Democratic Convention the nominees of the party, no matter who they might be, would shoulder the heaviest burden ever bequeathed to the candidates of any party.

A delegate to the convention, a man who is a member of the House of Representatives and whose election was said to be the result of Klan endorsement, even went so far as to express the opinion that the party, having challenged the Klan, should be consistent and nominate an out-and-out anti-Klan candidate for President.

"We might just as well make it a clean cut issue between the Klan and the anti-Klan," said this man, "and go to the country with a candidate who stands four square on the platform, instead of pussy-footing in an effort to win votes both ways."

This man declared himself in full sympathy with Senator Underwood's public statement that the convention, if it approved the Klan, should say so, and on the other hand, if it was against the hooded organization, it should say so just as frankly. He said it would do no good to denounce the Klan without naming it, "for the damage is done and the issue is here."

In the opinion of many of the leaders in the convention, men who are not of the Klan, the handling of the Klan issue in this convention is one of the worst bungles in the history of the party. These men insist that the wise course would have been to have passed a simple resolution, if necessary, reaffirming the Jeffersonian principles of religious freedom, and then leave the Klan to go its own way, a way which they declared was becoming more and more downhill every day.

Klansmen express the opinion that the convention has handled the problem in such fashion as will in the end bring thousands of new members into the "invisible empire" in all parts of the Union. As the situation now is, the Republican Party, they say, is certain to be chief beneficiary of the Madison Square Garden row.

The defeat in committee of the plank which mentioned the Klan by name was looked on by the White-robed Knights as a victory, but they conceded that it was not a decisive one. After all the publicity of the last few days and the big anti-Klan demonstration which followed the nomination of Senator Underwood, putting in or omitting the name of the organization, they argued, is a minor consideration.

Klan Surprised by Opposition.

An outstanding fact of the situation disclosed in the proceedings of the last two days, is that the Klan came to New York confident that it would be able to block the anti-Klan forces just as it did at Cleveland. When it found opponents in the majority it was one of the biggest political surprises in the history of the Klan. It was something the Klonclilium did not think possible.

When the Klan leaders, who had come to New York to direct the work of the organization, awoke to the fact that they were a minority they sent out hurry calls for reinforcement. One of the men summoned, according to information, was William Hanger of Fort Worth, and the chief counsel for Senator Mayfield before the Senate committee which heard the evidence produced by the anti-Klan forces in the effort to unseat the Senator.

Mr. Hanger is said to have started on the trip to New York, but deciding that he would not arrive in time to exert any influence, he returned to Fort Worth.

Just what effect the bitter anti-Klan fight in the convention will have in Texas, Oklahoma, Arkansas, Mississippi and Georgia, the Southern States in which the Klan is strongest, is a question that is causing no end of worry in the anti-Klan camps of the South.

It is frankly admitted that a situation may develop in these States which will greatly reduce, if not actually imperil, Democratic chances so far as the national ticket is concerned.

A Klan delegate, talking to a representative of THE NEW YORK TIMES, said that so far as he was concerned he did not care what action was taken by the convention. He added that he was leaving for home tomorrow, and he was leaving in a very bitter frame of mind.

All of this relates to those who are members of the Klan, and the non-Klan element which favored temporizing with the hooded men.

There is another element in the convention, namely, those delegates who demand that the issue be joined, that the Democratic Party, even though it be defeated in November, shall take a position no person can misunderstand. These men declared that an uncompromising position spells victory in November. The leaders of this group are Forney Johnston, who nominated Senator Underwood; George E. Brennan of Illinois, Edmund Moore of Ohio and other old-time leaders, as well as many of the newcomers.

June 29, 1924

BRYAN'S HOSTILITY AROUSES DAVIS MEN

West Virginians Resent His Attempt to Hold Mississippi to McAdoo.

SAY HE IS UNGRATEFUL

Recall Strong Support Given to Him by Davis's Father in Past Campaigns.

William J. Bryan aroused the intense indignation of several of the delegates from West Virginia yesterday by going to the Mississippi delegation, immediately after Mississippi had switched its 20 votes to John W. Davis, and insisting that Mr. Davis must not be nominated.

"This convention must not nominate a Wall Street man," said Mr. Bryan, according to one who was close beside him at the time. "Mr. Davis is the lawyer of J. P. Morgan."

"And who is Mr. McAdoo the lawyer for?" asked a young woman in the Mississippi delegation.

"McAdoo never got close enough to Doheny to get the friendship of Wall Street," Mr. Bryan retorted.

"I know the temper of the Northwest," Mr. Bryan went on, "and I offer as my opinion to this delegation that you are throwing Democratic chances to the wind in voting for Davis. His clients and his connections in the East make him desirable there, but he can command no following in the Northwest where the election will be decided.

"I tell you that La Follette will take more votes from Davis than he will from the Republicans," Mr. Bryan added.

* * * * *

July 2, 1924

DELEGATES FEEL NEED OF A 'BOSS'

Comment Is Growing on the Seeming Lack of Leadership in Convention.

CAMPAIGN EFFECT FEARED

Appeal Made by Virginian to End Turmoil With Selection of Glass.

There was a great deal of comment last evening, following the convention, that the Democratic Party was without leaders, that those directing the candidacies of the leading aspirants for the Presidential nomination had no real programs and were merely drifting, hoping by such a negative policy to wear down the patience of the delegates who are bound to candidates and to end in due time the chaotic situation to their own advantage.

Daily the lack of leadership is emphasized, the comment ran, in the course of the convention and the conferences held by leading candidates and their advisers. In the early days of the convention, it was asserted, this lack of cohesion came to the front in the struggle over the platform, which developed into a lively debate on the floor over the Klan and League of Nations issues. The echoes of this fight instead of dying away in the bustle attending the more important work of the convention—the nomination of standard bearers—have not lessened as an element which is holding the rival forces apart. The need, it is declared, is for a "boss," one powerful leader, able to compose the present difficulties and direct affairs.

Some of the conservative Democrats said last night that the discord and lack of leadership were factors to consider in their possible effect on the coming campaign. They felt that the party was being wrecked by personal ambitions which did not look beyond State lines. There was much comment by some upon the death of Charles F. Murphy, who, although condemned by many for years, was now greatly missed.

In the midnight conference on Wednesday, which fathered the several proposals made in the convention yesterday, those responsible for the laws admitted that nothing could be gained by the proposal to hear the candidates. They knew that the convention would not adopt such a resolution, but they persisted. One of the men responsible for the move said that it was made to "weaken McAdoo who could not afford to come before the convention and expose himself to examination."

Richmond P. Hobson addressed an open letter to the candidates and delegates yesterday, suggesting that the candidate for President, leading on the ninety-ninth ballot, be selected as the nominee and the candidate second in the balloting be the nominee for Vice President, irrespective of the two-thirds rule. This was accepted by some weary delegates as a good way to end the deadlock.

Captain Hobson's letter read:

"A Democratic convention must expect trouble when the people are in trouble. The people now are in unusual trouble, not only to mete out political justice to those guilty of mal-administration, but also to meet a "throwback" to the primal struggles that our forefathers finally composed in the Constitution of the United States. In our platform we have wisely invoked that instrument, let us be as wise in choosing our candidates. By a simple formula, that all can accept, we can turn our struggles into a union of forces able to win and to serve, at the same time setting an important precedent for the future. It is important and opportune that we live up to our platform and the Constitution and require religious test for nomination. Yet it is not logical or wise suddenly to nominate a Catholic for the Presidency.

"Let us nominate a Protestant for President and a Catholic for Vice President. It is important to recognize the honesty of purpose of "wets" who stand for the Constitution and enforcement of laws, but it is not logical or wise to nominate a "wet" for the Presidency. Let us nominate a "dry" for President and a conscientious "wet" for Vice President. It is the essence of democracy to compose differences between organized groups by working together for a common cause, each side conceding to the other what it claims for itself, honesty of purpose and the right to honest convictions. Let us bring the major groups in this convention together on the ticket.

"These factors are combined in the following formula which as good sportsmen and good Democrats all candidates and their adherents can accept, namely:

"The candidate leading on the ninety-ninth ballot shall be nominated for the Presidency; the candidate second on the ninety-ninth ballot shall be nominated for the Vice Presidency.

"Unless the deadlock breaks, this formula obviously will bring forth the ticket McAdoo and Smith. This is the true ticket under all the circumstances.

"It may be advanced that neither candidate would accept the Vice Presidency. Both candidates will do what the convention drafts them to do for the good of the party, the country and humanity.

"It may be advanced that preliminary bitterness makes it hard for the two groups to team. This is the more reason why the two groups must team. Only personal reasons can be advanced against this formula.

"At this juncture, when the country in perplexity and humanity in suffering are longing for relief, which a successful democracy alone can bring, "willing sacrifice" is the motto of leaders worthy of the party. Will the people at home promptly issue the mandate to their representatives in the convention and through them to the candidates, and thus deserve and win a memorable victory in the bonds of comradeship for service?"

Appeals for Senator Glass.

After the withdrawal of Senator Ralston, those pushing the candidacy of Senator Glass held that he was the logical compromise candidate. They asserted that he would inherit some of the McAdoo delegates and had not been offensive to the Smith faction. There was talk that the Smith following might be willing to permit the Governor to accept second place on a ticket headed by Glass. There was also a report during the recess that Ralston's boom would be revived and that Smith would be his running mate.

John Stewart Bryan of Richmond, who has been manager of the Glass boom, said in a statement that the Democratic Party would not be wrecked as the Republicans were hoping, but that the convention would end in the selection of a strong ticket.

"The Republicans," Mr. Bryan said, "are gravely mistaken if they interpret the protracted fight in the convention as presaging the wreck of the Democratic campaign. The struggle has been long and intense but it has been between individual Democrats with honest convictions, not bosses with back-room deals; and the very sharpness of the contest demonstrates the freedom, the vitality and the power of the Democratic Party. With these attributes the Democrats will be formidable challengers of the smooth, well-lubricated machinery which was so ostentatiously paraded at the Republican Convention in Cleveland. Unlike their historic opponents, the Democrats are not the unwilling victims of inherited incompetence.

"Whatever the differences of opinion may be, at least it will be admitted that both McAdoo and Smith have great personal force and are acknowledged leaders. Nor does the fact of their obvious elimination rob the Democrats of outstanding leadership.

"There are a number of Democrats fitted for the difficult duties of the Presidential office, any one of whom, if nominated, could unite the party, lead the attack on incompetency and corruption at Washington and win the victory for progressive legislation and honest Government. One of them must be chosen and we submit, as one candidate upon whom all can agree and behind whom a united and invincible party can march to victory, Carter Glass.

"Author and champion of the Federal Reserve act, Chairman of the joint Congressional committee that framed the great Federal Farm Loan act and friend and rescuer of agricultural interests.

"Opponent of tax spoliation and defender of the overburdened taxpayers.

"Supporter of all effective, constructive and liberal legislation. Consistent advocate of international cooperation through the League of Nations and the World Court.

"The friend in whose judgment and justice both labor and business have confidence.

"Uncompromising advocate of religious freedom.

"The man who has cooperated most sympathetically and aggressively with the women of the nation in their new duties and responsibilities as franchised citizens. And author of a resolution recommending equal representation for women as delegates at large in the Democratic National Congress.

"Trusted counselor, forceful fellow-laborer and affectionate friend of Woodrow Wilson.

"Sincere, simple and courageous, a profound thinker and a forceful campaigner—here is a man under whose leadership the Democratic Party can restore to the people of the United States the government of this nation."

Tennesseans.

It seemed to be the general feeling among delegates of the Tennessee delegation, who held a caucus yesterday at the Prince George Hotel, that the convention should choose a nominee or adjourn tonight, subject to call by the National Committee.

Several members of the delegation said it would be necessary for them to return home by Monday and the fear was expressed that only a shell of the delegation would remain. The matter of presenting the proposition of an early adjournment was left in the hands of Representative Finis J. Garrett.

Members of the delegation who are voting under the unit rule feel that if it becomes necessary for members of the delegation to return home, the vote of the delegation might be challenged from time to time. In this event, it was pointed out, only the votes of the majority present would be considered, and not the whole delegation.

The matter of clearing the galleries during the rest of the convention was discussed at the caucus. Mr. Garrett said that it was his belief that it would not be possible to do this, principally because that in financing the holding of the convention in New York tickets for the convention were sold, and the buyers were legally entitled to attend.

July 5, 1924

CANDIDATES' MANAGERS BEGIN PARLEYS TO END DEADLOCK; WEARY DELEGATES AFTER 77 BALLOTS CHEER TAGGART IDEA; SMITH VOTE REACHES 368, ENOUGH TO VETO RIVAL'S HOPES

PEACE MOVE IS WELCOMED

Taggart Plan Is Adopted After Several Others Are Voted Down.

COMPROMISE IS EXPECTED

But It Is Believed That It Is Possible Only by the Withdrawal of Smith and McAdoo.

ROBINSON TO THE FRONT

Glass, Underwood, Davis and Walsh Are Also Considered to Have a Chance.

By RICHARD V. OULAHAN.

Realizing at last that the deadlock in which it found itself could not be broken by continued balloting for a Presidential candidate, the Democratic National Convention adjourned yesterday afternoon until Monday morning at 11 o'clock, and under what amounted to an instruction from the convention the managers of the various aspirants for the nomination will utilize the interim in attempting to reach an understanding which will break the deadlock.

Obeying the convention's dictum, to which they had assented in advance, these managers and others went into conference yesterday afternoon with Representative Cordell Hull of Tennessee, Chairman of the Democratic National Committee, and were engaged early this morning in seeking a solution of the problem which had produced bad party feeling and threatened real peril to party prospects in the coming campaign.

None of the outstanding candidates for the nomination would acknowledge that the conference meant his elimination, but, as leading men of the convention viewed yesterday's principal development, there can be no positive outcome of the existing attempt at settlement unless William G. McAdoo of California and Governor Alfred E. Smith of New York consent to retire from the contest.

With party chiefs in session during the forty-three hours permitted for conference between the adjournment of the convention yesterday and its reassembling Monday morning, no one can predict with even an assumption of confidence the outcome of the armistice—for the period until Monday morning amounts to an armistice in the sense that it may be followed by the hoped-for peace.

Robinson's Name Becomes Prominent.

At an early hour this morning Senator Robinson of Arkansas had a superior position as a compromise candidate. He is the second choice of Brennan of Illinois and others who have been behind the movement to nominate Governor Smith. According to those in the counsels of the anti-McAdoo forces, Senator Robinson's name has been suggested to McAdoo adherents and has been received favorably.

From all accounts the proposal to select Robinson for the nomination has taken form, and the expectation seemed to exist that he, more than any other of the contenders in the Presidential contest, would be acceptable to all the warring elements of the party.

Among those who believed that Senator Robinson would be the compromise candidate, there was an evident purpose to work for his nomination with Senator David I. Walsh of Massachusetts as the candidate for Vice President. Senator Walsh is a Catholic and is in favor of the selection of Mr. Robinson as the candidate for President.

But nothing has appeared to confirm the statements of the anti-McAdooites that Robinson would be acceptable to the McAdoo workers.

This morning while the conference was on the understanding was that every possible device suggested for ending the deadlock will be considered. A proposal to rescind the rule of the convention in existence for ninety-two years, by which the votes of two-thirds of all the delegates are required to determine the choice of the candidate for President was in the minds of some of those intimately concerned in the attempt at adjustment. This proposal carried with it the repeal of the unit rule by which the entire membership of certain State delegations may be voted solidly by a majority of their number. Other proposals have also been advanced.

Changes in Candidates' Votes Between 1st and 77th Ballots

This table shows how the candidates for President stood on the first ballot taken on Monday and on the seventy-seventh ballot, the last cast yesterday, with the net change in the vote for each contender:

Candidate.	1st Ballot.	77th Ballot.	Net Ch'ge.
McAdoo	431½	513	+ 81½
Smith	241	367	+126
Cox	59	1	− 58
Harrison	43½	0	− 43½
Underwood	42½	47½	+ 5
Silzer	38	0	−38
J. W. Davis	31	76½	+ 45½
Ralston	30	6½	− 23½
Ferris	30	0	− 30
Glass	25	27	+ 2
Ritchie	22½	16½	− 6
Robinson	21	24	+ 3
J. M. Davis	20	0	− 20
C. W. Bryan	18	4	− 14
Brown	17	0	− 17
Sweet	12	0	− 12
Saulsbury	7	6	− 1
Kendrick	6	0	− 6
Thompson	1	0	− 1
Owen	0	4	+ 4
Baker	0	1	+ 1
Roosevelt	0	1	+ 1

All such methods, however, do not afford promise of acceptance by those who are attempting to find a way out of the maze in which the Democratic Party has lost itself. A very general feeling existed last night that no solution would be possible unless those representing the various personal elements provided a plan that would take the leading contenders out of the race and give the victory to a "dark horse."

Eight of the prominent Democrats whose names have figured in the balloting before the convention in Madison Square Garden since last Monday are represented in the series of armistice conferences now in session. Three of these eight are attending the conference in person. One of them is Senator Thomas J. Walsh of Montana, who was invited to be present, however, more in his capacity as the convention's presiding officer than as a full-fledged candidate, for Mr. Walsh's name was never formally entered in the contest. The others directly representing their own interests are Senator Robinson of Arkansas and Senator Harrison of Mississippi.

The interests of Mr. McAdoo are represented by the generalissimo of his forces, Judge David Ladd Rockwell of Ohio; Governor Smith's representatives are George E. Brennan of Illinois and Norman E. Mack, National Committeeman for the State of New York. The interests of Senator Underwood of Alabama are being cared for by Governor W. W. Brandon of Alabama, and T. L. Shaver of West Virginia is the spokesman for John W. Davis.

Two others represented in the conference are Senator Samuel M. Ralston of Indiana and former Governor James M. Cox of Ohio, who formally withdrew as candidates on Friday. That spokesmen for them were invited to attend the conferences was regarded as significant and accorded with the view expressed at the time the announcement was made of the retirement of Mr. Cox and Mr. Ralston that the latter, at least, might still have to be reckoned with when it came to the selection of the convention's nominee. J. Henry Goeke, a former Representative from Ohio, and George White, who managed the Democratic national campaign when Mr. Cox was the party's candidate for President four years ago, appeared for Mr. Cox, with Edmund H. Moore, National Committeeman for Ohio, as an adviser. Former Senator Thomas Taggart of Indiana represented Senator Ralston.

One feature in connection with the armistice conference was the opinion generally expressed by those concerned in the attempt at settlement, that the Democratic Party was in danger of a split. Some went so far as to predict that the outcome of the convention would be the nomination of two candidates for President—McAdoo and another, possibly—Governor Smith.

The admission of William Jennings Bryan into the conference produced some irritation. While ostensibly the representative of the interests of his brother, Governor Bryan of Nebraska, Mr Bryan's presence in the conference is resented as an attempt to dominate the gathering of those Democrats who, by reason of their propinquity to the outstanding candidates, are privileged to be parties to the effort to produce party harmony. As at San Francisco four years ago, Mr. Bryan is looked upon by many as democracy's Old Man of the sea, pressing a burden on the back of the party and unwilling to make any sacrifice that does not accord with his own interests.

Change the scene from the Blackstone Hotel in Chicago to the Waldorf-Astoria Hotel in New York; make the time July instead of June, and the session that is being held in this city early this morning resembles, except in its designedly broad and representative character, the famous conference of four years ago when a group of Republican Senators and others of note in the party, sat in a smoke-filled room, and by a process of elimination decreed that Warren G. Harding should be the party candidate for President.

The Republican Party was severely criticized for this method of choosing a Presidential candidate, the burden of the criticism being that Harding's selection was due to a senatorial oligarchy. In the gathering at the Waldorf this July morning are Senators Walsh of Montana, Robinson and Harrison, all prominent figures in the Democratic Party's affairs.

The motion which brought about the conference now in progress was made in the convention yesterday by Thomas Taggart of Indiana. It followed a morning and afternoon of further futile balloting. Several ballots had been taken without any indication that the convention was likely to reach a decision when Mr. Taggart proposed to the representatives of nearly all the leading candidates his plan of bringing them together during the week end with the object of producing a settlement.

A striking willingness to agree to what Mr. Taggart proposed was shown on the part of candidates and their managers. Mr. McAdoo and Governor Smith both endorsed the suggestion.

When Mr. Taggart was recognized by Chairman Walsh yesterday afternoon he submitted the motion that when the convention adjourned "the Chairman of the Democratic National Committee and the Chairman of this convention be requested to call a conference of the representatives of the candidates whose names are now being balloted for, who have been formally presented, for the purpose of reaching an understanding so as to hasten the conclusion of this convention."

The tired delegates rose to the proposal. The applause came as an outburst and there were cries of "good, good." When Chairman Walsh put the question there was not a dissenting vote and more applause came when the Chairman declared that the motion had been carried. The whole attitude of the delegates indicated that they were glad to adopt anything that would give them a chance to finish their business and adjourn sine die.

At the time adjournment over Sunday was taken, or immediately following the adoption of Mr. Taggart's motion, the convention had completed its seventy-seventh ballot, six ballots having been taken during the course of yesterday's session. On the first ballot yesterday Mr. McAdoo continued to lead with 528½ votes. This was the figure he reached on the seventieth ballot when the convention adjourned Friday night. Governor Smith trailed with 334½, John W. Davis of West Virginia had 67, Oscar W. Underwood of Alabama 37½ and Newton D. Baker of Ohio 56. Votes also appeared for Joseph T. Robinson of Arkansas, Carter Glass of Virginia, Albert C. Ritchie of Maryland, Willard Saulsbury of Delaware, Thomas J. Walsh of Montana, Robert L. Owen of Oklahoma, Charles W. Bryan of Nebraska, James M. Cox of Ohio and Samuel M. Ralston of Indiana. One vote was cast for I. R. Kevin of New York.

The next ballot, the seventy-second, brought no greater promise of a solution. McAdoo had 527½ and Smith 354. After touching 510 on the seventy-fourth McAdoo closed with 513. Smith's score was 367; Davis had 76½.

During yesterday's session various attempts were made in the interest of helping the convention to arrive at a decision on a candidate. A resolution of Edward M. Semans of Oklahoma providing for the elimination of the lowest candidate on each ballot until only two were left was drowned with a chorus of "nays." For Senator Gilbert M. Hitchcock of Nebraska proposed another method of elimination which would bring the number of candidates down to five. On a roll call it got 496 yeas against 589½ nays. A resolution offered by A. H. Ferguson of Oklahoma provided that if no nomination were made on the seventy-fifth ballot the convention should adjourn to meet in Kansas City July 21. Punta Gorda, Fla., was offered by ex-Governor Gilchrist of that State as a substitute for Kansas City. Mr. Ferguson's resolution was snowed under by 1009.3 to 82.7.

Ex-Governor Thomas H. Ball of Texas suggested that the lowest name be dropped from the list of candidates until only two remained, and if no nomination was made under the two-thirds rule selection should be determined by a majority. This shared the fate of the other proposals.

These efforts, together with the dreary balloting, which had become a matter of routine, produced the atmosphere favorable to Mr. Taggart's proposal. It was evident that the nerves of the convention were on the ragged edge and that any suggestion that gave promise of solution without being detrimental to the interests of any of the principal candidates was certain to be adopted.

* * * * *

July 6, 1924

Proposals by Smith and Minority Candidates, And the Counter Proposals Offered by McAdoo

Here is the text of the resolution and pledge to release delegates, signed by representatives of all the candidates for President except McAdoo:

The Resolution.

Resolved, that the time has arrived when, in the opinion of this Democratic Convention, all delegates should be and are hereby released from any pledges or instructions of any kind whatsoever, touching upon any candidacy for the nomination for President.

The Pledge.

The undersigned do hereby release all and every delegate from any pledge, instruction or obligation of any nature whatsoever, in so far as his candidacy for the Democratic nomination for the Presidency is concerned, as completely as if his name had been withdrawn from the convention.

This statement has been submitted to each candidate whose name has been placed in nomination and has been accepted by those whose names are subscribed hereto, either in person or by duly authorized representative.

GOVERNOR ALFRED E. SMITH
SENATOR O. W. UNDERWOOD
SENATOR J. T. ROBINSON
EX-SENATOR W. SAULSBURY
DAVID F. HOUSTON
GOVERNOR JONATHAN DAVIS
GOVERNOR A. E. RITCHIE
JAMES M. COX
CHARLES W. BRYAN
GOVERNOR F. H. BROWN
GOVERNOR G. S. SILZER
SENATOR CARTER GLASS
JOHN W. DAVIS
SENATOR S. M. RALSTON
SENATOR W. M. FERRIS.

The Reply By Mr. McAdoo.

This was Mr. McAdoo's reply:

Hon. Thomas J. Walsh, Permanent Chairman, Democratic National Convention; Hon. Cordell Hull, Chairman, Democratic National Committee, New York City.

Gentlemen: The agreement just submitted to me, signed by the various candidates before the convention, for releasing their delegates from any "pledge, instruction or obligation of any nature whatsoever, in so far as their candidacy for the Democratic nomination for President is concerned," does not, in my opinion, offer a solution of the unfortunate deadlock in the convention. We must, therefore, adopt a practical plan which will end the deadlock, no matter what effect it may have on any individual candidacy.

I therefore propose that, in addition to releasing all delegates as proposed in the agreement submitted, the unit rule in this convention be abrogated; that the majority rule be substituted for the two-thirds rule in nominating a candidate for President and Vice President; that each of the delegates present from each State shall be entitled to pass his pro rata of the vote of all the delegates from such States as may have delegates absent from the convention; that, after the next ballot and after each succeeding ballot of the candidates formally placed before this convention, the one receiving the lowest number of votes shall be dropped from the roll of candidates until a nomination is made.

I submit herewith a form of the proposed agreement, which I am willing to join all the other candidates in signing. Respectfully yours.

W. G. McADOO.

Agreement He Proposed.

We, the undersigned, agree that the unit rule in this convention shall be abrogated and that only a majority vote shall be required to nominate candidates for President and Vice President.

The undersigned further agree that after the next ballot, and after each succeeding ballot among the candidates formally placed before this convention, the one receiving the lowest number of votes shall be dropped until a nomination is made.

The undersigned do further agree that each of the delegates present from each State shall be entitled to cast his pro rata vote of the delegates from such States as are absent from the convention.

The undersigned do hereby release each and every delegate from any pledge, instruction or obligation of any nature whatsoever in so far as their candidacy for the Democratic nomination for President is concerned, as completely as if their names had been withdrawn from this convention.

This statement has been submitted to each candidate whose name has been placed in nomination, and has been accepted by those whose names are subscribed hereto, either in person or by duly authorized representative.

July 7, 1924

Text of McAdoo's Letter to the Convention Freeing His Delegates from All Pledges to Him

The Madison Square Hotel, July 9, 1924.

Honorable Thomas J. Walsh, Chairman, Democratic National Convention, Madison Square Garden, New York City.

Dear Senator Walsh:

I am profoundly grateful to the splendid men and women who have with such extraordinary loyalty supported me in this unprecedented struggle for a great cause.

The convention has been in session two weeks and appears to be unable to make a nomination under the two-thirds rule. This is an unfortunate situation, imperiling party success.

I feel that if I should withdraw my name from the convention I should betray the trust confided in me by the people in many States, which have sent delegates here to support me.

And yet I am unwilling to contribute to the continuation of a hopeless deadlock. Therefore I have determined to leave my friends and supporters free to take such action as in their judgment may best serve the interests of the party.

I have made this fight for the principles and ideals of progressive Democracy and righteousness and for the defeat of the reactionary and wet elements in the party which threaten to dominate it. For these principles and ideals I shall continue to fight. I hope that this convention will never yield to reaction and privilege and that the Democratic Party will always hold aloft the torch which was carried to such noble heights by Woodrow Wilson. Cordially yours,

W. G. McADOO.

July 9, 1924

LEADERS ACCLAIM CHOICE OF DAVIS; SEE PARTY UNITED

"Shows Democrats Have Feet on the Ground," Says Former Governor Cox.

DANIELS PAYS TRIBUTE

Brennan of Illinois and Moore of Ohio See Breaches Healed —Bryan Pledges Support.

The nomination of John W. Davis as Democratic candidate for President was received yesterday with general acclaim by the party leaders and Democrats of prominence. Among those commenting were the following, who said:

William Jennings Bryan (who the other day omitted from his list of candidates meeting his approval the name of John W. Davis).—"You can say that I shall support the ticket. That is all—for the present."

James M. Cox, former Governor of Ohio.—"It is an instance of the party nominating one of the most conspicuously able men of his generation, and it is an evidence of the fact that nothwithstanding the spirit of contest over controverted questions the Democratic Party, in the last analysis, had its feet on the ground. The country has always found the Democratic Party safe in an emergency.

"This is merely a matter of history repeating itself. Mr. Davis will make a profound impression on the country at the very outset of the campaign. None of the elements which make him an able man are more conspicuous than his intellectual courage and honesty."

"Biggest and Brainiest Available."

George E. Brennan, Democratic leader of Illinois—"We are more than pleased with the nomination of John W. Davis. We are delighted. The hard work of weeks has been rewarded. We now present to the voters as our candidate the biggest and brainiest man available for the honor. Behind him is arrayed the entire Democratic Party, united for the campaign as it was united in the tremendous enthusiasm that broke forth when Mr. Davis's nomination became assured. We look forward to an unbroken continuance of this good feeling among all Democrats, right up to the day of election. That can mean only one thing, the election of Mr. Davis."

Edmund H. Moore, Democratic leader of Ohio—"John W. Davis is the biggest man who has run for President, with the possible exception of Wilson, since 1876."

Josephus Daniels—"I think they nominated a man whom the whole country recognizes as a great man in learning, in character, and one who measures up to the highest of those who have held the position of President. He stands for independence and equality and illustrates how a man of ambition and poise can reach the heights. He has illustrated his ability for public service as legislator in West Virginia, in the House of Congress as Solicitor General and as an Ambassador. He is a great American."

Franklin D. Roosevelt.—"In John W. Davis the Democratic Party has found a candidate of whom it can be proud and the voters of the country a man on whom they can unite with confidence that he will make a President worthy to rank with the other great Democrats who have held that office.

"A warm personal friend of mine, I have found him to be a man of splendid intellect, clear thinking and high, progressive ideals. Mr. Davis will have my heartiest support and I intend to leave nothing undone that lies in my power to secure his eletcion."

Thomas Taggart, leader of Indiana—"Davis is a big, capable man, and I am for him. If a man has enough ability to hold the position with the big corporation that he does, he has enough ability to be President. He will win without a doubt."

David P. Houston, former Secretary of Agriculture and Secretary of the Treasury—"I am very much delighted at the news. The Democrats could not have chosen a better man, I believe, than Mr. Davis. I admire him for what he is and for what he stands. He is nobody's man but his own. He is a good lawyer and stands for the best and most fundamental things in Democracy, and that means he stands for the things that are best for the country. America, fundamentally, stands for a decent regard for the average man, as Abraham Lincoln so ably puts it. Mr. Davis differs from a lot of progressives and other forward-looking people in knowing where he is headed and how to get there."

Senator King of Utah—"Mr. Davis is a big man. He has a great intellect and is intellectually honest. We'll elect him in November."

"Nomination a Master Stroke."

Senator Pat Harrison of Mississippi, Temporary Chairman of the convention—"The nomination of John W. Davis was a master stroke; it could not be improved on and in my opinion it means victory for the party in November. We have every reason to be proud and we are."

Senator Thaddeus H. Caraway of Arkansas—"We have nominated a fine, clean man, an able man, a candidate of whom we can all be proud. Mr. Davis's nomination means that we can stand four square to the country in this campaign. I believe we are going to elect him. I certainly shall do all I can to bring it about."

Governor Trapp of Oklahoma—"After two weeks of sparring, snarling and getting nowhere the convention woke up and nominated the best man in the United States. Davis will make a great President and I believe he will be elected."

Senator Edwards of New Jersey—"In the end the convention showed a lot of horse sense and put over a man who in every sense of the word is worthy to be the President of the United States."

Representative Dominick of South Carolina—"Davis suits me and I believe he will suit the country and that he will be elected in November."

Joseph P. Tumulty, President Wilson's Secretary for eignt years—"After stress, strain and storm the Democracy of the nation has again shown its vitality and vigor by nominating John W. Davis. **Here is presented a man of distinction who will hold high the banner of our** party and lead the Democratic hosts to victory in November."

Governor Davis of Kansas—"I think we nominated a very capable man, one whose experience in domestic and foreign affairs fits him for the Presidency. I feel very happy over the conclusion of the long-drawn-out struggle. He was easily the choice of Kansas after we got away from the interpretation of our instructions. One of Mr. Davis's strongest characteristics among his close friends and acquaintances is his sincere honesty. I sincerely endorse him as one of the ablest men for the exalted position for which he was nominated."

Senator Heflin of Alabama—"In nominating John W. Davis the Democratis Party selected a great Damocrat and a great American for the Presidency."

Former Governor Gardner of Missouri—"In John W. Davis we elect one of the greatest men in America. He will make an ideal President and will carry Missouri by 50,000 votes. We are going back home now, take off our coats and go to work for his election.'

Governor Ritchie of Maryland—I think Mr. Davis is the best candidate the Democratic Party could offer.

July 10, 1924

FARM BODY REJECTS HOOVER OR COOLIDGE

Corn Belt Federation Chiefs at Des Moines Hail Lowden's Candidacy.

START TALK OF A BOLT

Special to The New York Times.

DES MOINES, Iowa, June 1.—The Executive Committee of the Corn Belt Federation today served notice on the leadership of the Republican Party that "it will not tolerate the selection of such a man as Hoover or Coolidge" at the Kansas City convention.

Should an opponent of farm aid legislation receive the nomination, the committee proclaimed, the party will be deprived of the votes of millions of "farm men and farm women who voted for Coolidge four years ago on the assumption that he was honest and sincere."

The committee met here today for the purpose of formulating the political program of its member groups, through which it asserts it represents more than 1,000,000 organized farmers from Indiana to Montana.

The course of the federation, it was decided, will be to make one more appeal to the Republican Party and, if that fails, to swing its allegiance to the Democratic Party. It expects that the Democratic Party would welcome the opportunity to cut into the hitherto "normal and voiceless" Republican farm vote of the Middle West.

Lowden Called Only Candidate.

William Hirth of Columbia, Mo., Chairman of the federation, acted as spokesman for the meeting. Mr. Hirth predicted that "unless the nominee at Kansas City is acceptable to the farmers, the convention will mark the breaking up of the old Republican Party."

Frank O. Lowden of Illinois was described as the only man considered as a possible candidate from the farmers' point of view.

In the event of the nomination of Secretary Hoover or the renomination of President Coolidge, or "such a man as the party leader, the farmers will utterly refuse to lend support," said a resolution adopted by the conference.

"No longer will the American farmer be content to be dealt with in wordy declarations of interest and sympathy," the resolution continues. "We will accept nothing less than a definite statement of policy and a Presidential nominee on whom we can depend for the carrying out of proposals giving to agriculture a position of equality with other American groups."

The resolution expressed appreciation to two Congresses for passing the McNary-Haugen bill, as well as for the manner in which Senator McNary and Representative Haugen had labored for "the farmers' cause." The committee characterized the President's last veto as "intemperate in its language" and displaying "a vindictive spirit."

The conference called on farm organizations throughout the Middle West to send official spokesmen to the Republican convention at Kansas City to complement the groups of farmers expected to descend on Kansas City in a mass protest.

June 2, 1928

PLATFORM AFFIRMS COOLIDGE POLICIES

Conservative Farm Plank and Dry Law Adherence Held to Reflect Party Tradition.

NO NEW OR DUBIOUS ISSUES

Tax, Debt, Foreign and Defense Pledges Offered as 'Program That Has Given Prosperity.'

By CHARLES R. MICHAEL.

Special to The New York Times.

KANSAS CITY, June 14.—In its platform, adopted today, the Republican Party maintains its conservative attitude upon public questions, unqualifiedly endorses the Coolidge Administration, promises continuance of its farm, taxation and foreign policies and pledges an upward revision of the tariff laws to benefit agriculture and industry.

In dealing with the Eighteenth Amendment and the farm problem, two issues that are expected to figure largely in the coming campaign, the platform declares for strict enforcement of the former and for application of sound methods to help solve the latter.

No solace was offered to he corn and wheat States by compromising on the McNary-Haugen bill with its equalization fee provision.

In standing for enforcement of the Volstead law the leaders feel that they placed the party on safe ground and perhaps eliminated prohibition as a real issue in the campaign.

Free From Doubtful ssues.

As viewed by the delegates generally, the platform charts the way for the Republican nominee for President, without offering any new or doubtful issues.

In the opinion of the majority, it is a straightforward statement of the record of the present administration, an assurance that the "program that has given prosperity" will be continued and that the campaign will not seek to compromise with the disaffected agricultural voters.

There are no planks with a progressive trend, and no advocacy of social changes—just promises that the Republican Party will endeavor to go forward on the traditions of the past with as little interference with business as possible.

Borah Fund Plank Outstanding.

Apart from the planks on farm relief and prohibition, few issues in the platform excited comment. Among the new planks, one that is of interest because of the recent vast expenditure of money, is that submitted by Senator Borah, which pledged the Republicans to file with the House and Senate a statement of expenditures and contributors every thirty days after Aug. 1. It further pledges that the party shall not create or permit to be created any deficit which shall exist at the close of the campaign.

The platform contains thirty-six planks and is over 7,000 words in length. It follows closely the planks and treatment of the 1924 platform.

Its agriculture plank promises reorganization of the marketing system on more economical lines and the creation of a farm board with power to set up farmer-owned and controlled corporations to prevent and control surpluses through orderly distribution. It merely recites what the Coolidge Administration has attempted to do for agriculture.

As to the national defense it repeats the 1924 plank declaring for the drafting of men as well as industry in war, and authorizes the President to stabilize "prices of services and essential commodities whether utilized in actual warfare or private activity."

Another plank pledges maintenance of the navy "in all types of combatant ships to the full ratio provided by the Washington Treaty."

Coolidge Policies Incorporated.

President Coolidge is commended for his fundamental policy of economy and the party pledges itself to "live up to that high standard." Secretary Andrew W. Mellon is commended for his "unrivaled and unsurpassed" administration as Secretary of the Treasury.

Promise is made that reduction of the national debt, already cut by $6,411,000,000 in the past seven years, will be continued.

Another plank recites that the Republican party will continue to oppose the cancellation of foreign debts.

All of the foreign policies are commended and the administration program in Central America, China and Mexico upheld. The Kellogg multilateral treaty to outlaw war is approved.

Conservative planks on labor uphold collective bargaining and support a feasible plan to stabilize the coal industry with "justice to the miners, consumers and operators."

Maintenance of an American-built, owned and operated marchant marine and sale of the Shipping Board fleet to private owners, with the assertion that the Government should get out of private business, form the plank on merchant marine.

June 15, 1928

COOLIDGE SENDS WORD NOT TO VOTE FOR HIM

Informs Connecticut Delegation of His Wishes in His First Direct Message.

KANSAS CITY, June 14 (AP).—President Coolidge has sent word to the Connecticut delegation, which has held out for him to the last, asking that it not cast its seventeen votes for him. The delegation will adhere to the request.

Senator Bingham, of Connecticut, announced today that the delegation had finally left Mr. Coolidge at his specific request. He said the word was sent to Connecticut through Everett Sanders, Secretary to the President, who is attending the convention.

Although the decision of Secretary Mellon and of William M. Butler, close friend of Mr. Coolidge and Chairman of the Republican National Committee, not to vote for Mr. Coolidge had been accepted by the party as expressing the determination of the President not to be a candidate in any sense, the message to Connecticut was the first direct word from Mr. Coolidge.

As a result of his action, it was the understanding of convention leaders that Mr. Coolidge did not wish to be brought before the convention in any way on the balloting tonight, and there seems to be little likelihood that any considerable number of votes would be cast for him in view of his desires.

The message to Connecticut did not state any preference on the part of the President as to a nominee. He has steadfastly declined to take sides in the party's delibartions over his successor.

It is the final answer to the question of what Mr. Coolidge meant when he declared last August that "I do not choose to run for President in 1928."

Mr. Sanders held rigidly to the silence he has held since he came from the White House to the convention. He would not discuss in any way the message delivered to the Connecticut delegation, though nct denying that the message was transmitted.

June 15, 1928

Convention's Only Ballot for President Which Made Hoover the Nominee

Total Vote...	STATE	Coolidge....	Hoover....	Lowden....	Watson....	Curtis.....	Goff........	Norris......
15	Alabama ..	..	15	..	..	..	..	..
9	Arizona ...	..	9	..	..	..	..	..
11	Arkansas ..	..	11	..	..	..	..	..
29	California .	..	29	..	..	..	..	..
15	Colorado ..	..	15	..	..	..	..	..
17	Connecticut.	..	17	..	..	..	..	..
9	Delaware ..	..	9	..	..	..	..	..
10	Florida	..	9	..	..	1	..	..
16	Georgia ...	..	15	..	..	1	..	..
11	Idaho	..	11	..	..	.	..	..
61	Illinois	13	24	16	4	..	..	..
33	Indiana	..	..	..	33	..	..	..
29	Iowa	..	7	22	..	..	..	..
23	Kansas ...	..	..	..	..	23	..	..
29	Kentucky ..	..	29	..	..	..	..	..
12	Louisiana ..	..	11	..	..	1	..	..
15	Maine	..	15	..	..	..	..	..
19	Maryland ..	..	19	..	..	..	..	..
39	Mass.	..	39	..	..	..	..	..
33	Michigan ..	..	33	..	..	..	..	..
27	Minnesota .	..	11	15	..	1	..	..
12	Mississippi.	..	12	..	..	..	..	..
39	Missouri ..	..	28	1	3	4	..	..
11	Montana ..	..	10	..	1	..	..	..
19	Nebraska ..	..	11	..	..	..	..	8
9	Nevada	..	9	..	..	..	..	..
11	New Hamp..	..	11	..	..	..	..	..
31	New Jersey	..	31	..	..	..	..	..
9	New Mexico	..	7	..	..	2	..	..
90	New York..	..	90	..	..	..	..	..
20	North Caro.	..	17	3	..	..	..	..
13	N. Dakota..	..	4	8	..	..	..	1
51	Ohio	4	36	..	..	10	..	..
20	Oklahoma ..	..	..	..	..	20	..	..
13	Oregon	..	13	..	..	..	..	..
79	Penn.	..	79	..	..	..	..	..
13	Rhode Island	..	12	..	..	1	..	..
11	S. Carolina.	..	11	..	..	..	..	..
13	S. Dakota..	..	2	9	2	..	..	..
19	Tennessee ..	..	19	..	..	..	..	..
26	Texas	..	26	..	..	..	..	..
11	Utah	..	9	..	2	..	..	..
11	Vermont ...	..	11	..	..	..	..	..
15	Virginia ...	..	15	..	..	..	..	..
17	Washington.	..	17	..	..	..	..	..
19	W. Virginia	..	1	..	..	..	18	..
26	Wisconsin .	..	9	..	..	..	..	15
9	Wyoming ..	..	9	..	..	..	..	..
2	Alaska	..	2	..	..	..	..	..
2	Dist. of Col.	..	2	..	..	..	..	..
2	Hawaii	..	2	..	..	..	..	..
2	Philippines.	..	2	..	..	..	..	..
2	Porto Rico.	..	2	..	..	..	..	..
1,089	Totals..	17	837	74	45	64	18	24

TOTAL VOTES CAST, 1,084 | NECESSARY TO A CHOICE, 543

SCATTERING VOTES—5. DAWES—Illinois, 1; Ohio, 1; Missouri, 2. Total, 4. HUGHES—Missouri, 1. NOT VOTING—Illinois, 3; Wisconsin, 2. Total, 5.

June 15, 1928

CONVENTION SPEEDS CURTIS NOMINATION

Only an Hour and Five Minutes Required to Name Kansan for Second Place.

OPPOSITION IS NEGLIGIBLE

Special to The New York Times.

KANSAS CITY, June 15.—With Senator Charles Curtis decided upon as the running mate for Herbert Hoover, the Republican National Convention met here for its final session at noon today.

Local interest in the convention had waned since Secretary Hoover was nominated last night. There were only a few spectators in the galleries when Senator Moses, the Permanent Chairman, started to call the convention to order at five minutes after noon. The delegates, however, stuck to their job and, while there were quite a number absent when the session began, they came in rapidly after it opened. The galleries filled later, and about two-thirds of the seats were occupied finally.

Senator Moses called the convention to order at 12:10. Bishop E. L. Waldorf of the Methodist Episcopal Church, Kansas City, offered prayer.

Chairman Moses opened the session by reading a telegram from Secretary Hoover in reply to one sent by Senator Moses last night informing the Secretary of Commerce of his nomination for President. Senator Moses before reading the telegram referred to Mr. Hoover as "the next President."

Hoover's Message Mildly Received.

There was surprisingly little applause for Mr. Hoover's telegram, considering that it was virtually an acceptance message from a man just made the party nominee for President. There was some applause at the nominee's declaration that he would stand on the platform adopted, more applause when he asserted that the Republican Party must find a solution of the farm problem, a little applause at the Secretary's assertion that he intended to follow the policies of Calvin Coolidge, and only a slight amount of handclapping when Senator Moses read the name of Herbert Hoover as the signer of the message.

July 16, 1928

TAMMANY TO MOVE ON HOUSTON QUIETLY

Delegation Will Avoid Any Demonstration Likely to Arouse Antagonism.

The Tammany delegation to the Democratic National Convention at Houston will travel quietly and sedately through the South and will avoid all semblance of demonstration for Governor Smith, the leaders have decided.

The Smith forces have in mind the resentment caused by the gallery demonstrations at Madison Square Garden in 1924 and wish to avoid arousing any antagonisms by overenthusiasm. The Tammany trains—there will be two of them—will carry no bands or other music and will not be decorated. At this time it is thought the delegation will not even parade through the streets of Houston, as is customarily done at conventions.

Tammany will rely upon Governor Smith's friends in other parts of the country to provide the noise which is an important part of every national convention, although, of course, the New York delegates will be allowed to join. The Smith leaders are afraid of creating an impression that the Tammany contingent is trying to stampede the convention for the New Yorker.

The Tammany trains will leave on the afternoon of June 23. One will go by the Pennsylvania Railroad and will carry 205 delegates, alternates and Smith supporters. The other will go over the New York Central lines with seventy passengers. This train will pick up the delegates up-State. Another group of Tammanyites is going to Houston by boat, necessarily leaving earlier. William F. Kenny and William H. Todd plan to travel in their private cars and will probably take small parties with them. Mayor Walker, his secretary, Charles S. Hand, and a few close friends also will go by private car.

June 8, 1928

MACK SAYS SMITH HAS VOTES TO WIN ON SECOND BALLOT

Committeeman, Reaching Houston, Counts 678 on First and 760 on the Next.

EARLIER SHIFTS DISCUSSED

But New Yorker Advised Against It at Outset—Dry Plank Seen as Chief Contest.

HEADQUARTERS IS SET UP

Van Namee Confirms That F. D. Roosevelt Will Nominate Governor—Heat Hits Arrivals.

From a Staff Correspondent of The New York Times.

HOUSTON, Texas., June 20.—Norman E. Mack, Democratic National Committeeman from New York; George Van Namee and Thomas Spellacy of Connecticut arrived here today and opened convention headquarters for Governor Smith in the Rice Hotel. They found much enthusiasm among the Democratic advance guard for Governor Smith, whose nomination on the second ballot was predicted, due to the withdrawal of Governor Ritchie of Maryland and the desire of the party leaders for harmony. The heat here today was oppressive.

"Governor Smith will be nominated on the second ballot," Mr. Mack said after he had conferred with leaders from other States, who assured him that the "favorite son" support would be diverted to Governor Smith after the first ballot, at least.

"Governor Smith will enter the convention with 678 assured delegates, and this number may be increased if certain States abandon their 'favorite sons' upon the request of the 'favorite sons' themselves," Mr. Mack continued. "Several such candidates have offered to cast their lot with Governor Smith at the outset, but it would appear to be wiser if they discharged their obligation by casting their first ballot for the pledged candidate.

Mack Analyzes Smith Strength.

"Our analysis, which is most conservative and includes only the known Smith delegates, gives Governor Smith 678 delegates on the first ballot, with assurance that Arkansas, 14 votes; Oklahoma, 20, Colorado, 12, and Ohio, 36, will be voted for Smith on the second ballot."

These changes would give Smith 26 more than the 734 votes necessary to a choice, and his leaders expect to pick up more delegates before the balloting begins because of the movement in the party, with Senator Reed excepted, to nominate by acclamation. Senator Reed, at present, stands in the way of such action.

Reports have reached Houston that former Senator Pomerene of Ohio is considering following Governor Ritchie and casting his strength to Smith on the first ballot.

As the Smith leaders analyze the situation, the chief contest will be on the platform, especially the plank dealing with prohibition. There is evidence of trouble ahead in the Resolutions Committee, of which either Senator Pittman of Nevada or Senator Glass of Virginia will be Chairman.

The problem is to make the party's position square with Governor Smith's attitude.

Smith's "Wet" Views Outlined.

The Smith leaders here today did not emphasize any possible divergence of opinion on the "wet and dry" issue. They said, however, that the plank should represent Governor Smith's views, and if it did not define them in set terms, the Governor, as the party's nominee, would have an opportunity to elaborate them in his speech of acceptance.

"I hope that the prohibition plank will square with Governor Smith's position," Mr. Mack said. "He is for State's rights, that is for the States deciding whether they shall permit the sale and manufacture of beer after Congress shall define more liberally the limit as to an intoxicant under the Eighteenth Amendment.

"The prohibition question is not going to cause the party any trouble, and the convention, in my opinion, will agree to a plank that is entirely satisfactory to the nominee and a great body of the electorate.

"Governor Smith has and always will stand for personal liberty and State's rights," Mr. Mack added. "He is opposed to prohibition. He is for temperance. The millions of dollars that are being spent by the people of the United States in foreign countries is a detriment to the business of the United States.

Pictures Loss in Prohibition.

"Take the Province of Ontario in Canada, for instance. Millions of dollars have been spent in that Province by American people, principally for liquor. The people in the States of Michigan, Ohio, Indiana, Illinois and New York spend a great part of their time and money imbibing the liquors so easily obtained in Canada in the various Provinces. It is absolutely criminal for this country to lose the tremendous amount of money to foreign nations simply because of prohibition.

"The trouble with the American people is that they do not appreciate what prohibition has meant and does mean today. If they only realized what a hardship it is to the business of this country they would not stand for it.

"Governor Smith believes that if any State desires a certain alcoholic content of beverage, that State has the right to determine that content," Mr. Mack said. "If the State desires to be dry, then it is the right of that State to be dry.

"As to the farm question and tariff revision, these are questions of the greatest moment and ones that must be carefully considered before the party declares its position. These are economic problems that mean much to the country and decision on them should be reached after the best minds in the party have consulted.

Mack for "Adequate Protection."

"It is a great mistake to say that the Democratic Party is a free trade party," he added. "It is a party that stands for an adequate protection to American industries and a tariff that will produce sufficient revenue. The Democratic Party today stands for a proper tariff, but not a robber tariff."

Mr. Mack said that he was greatly impressed with the "sensible and clear-cut" statement made Monday by Governor Ritchie, and hoped that the country would not make religion the issue, but would consider Governor Smith solely upon his record, a record of four times Governor of New York, which "made him the best equipped man in the country to be President of the United States."

George Van Namee, the New Yorker's pre-convention manager, who, with George C. Norton and Howard Cultman, will be in charge of the Smith headquarters, had an informal chat with the newspaper men. It developed subsequently that Franklin D. Roosevelt, former Assistant Secretary of War, who is scheduled to arrive Friday, had been agreed upon to nominate Governor Smith.

About 750 New Yorkers, including the leading Democratic politicians will be here for the convention. They will have no bands and the plan of the Smith leaders is to conduct a dignified campaign without making any effort to dislodge votes from the "favorite sons."

No Choice for Vice President.

"New York stands for tolerance, free speech and good will to all," said Mr. Van Namee, "and will show that attitude in this convention. We will enter the convention in that spirit and hope to leave it with good feeling and general saisfaction existing."

He said that New York had no choice for Vice President and indicated that Governor Smith would not suggest his running mate.

In the party arriving today were Mrs. Van Namee, Mrs. Mack, Mrs. Philip Metz of Buffalo, Mr. Norton and Mr. Cultman. Miss Elisabeth Marbury, New York's National Committeewoman, will arrive tomorrow and become active for Governor Smith among the women. Judge Olvany's personal party is scheduled to reach here Friday.

Mrs. Smith, wife of the Governor, will come with William Kenny and Mrs. Kenny, arriving early Sunday morning. They will have rooms in the Warwick Hotel. With Mr. Kenny also are Miss Rose Pedrick, former private secretary to Governor Smith; Major John A. Warner, Mr. and Mrs. Arthur Smith, Mr. and Mrs. Francis Quillinan, Walter Smith, Mr. and Mrs. John Glynn, Joseph J. Riordan and John Raskob.

June 21, 1928

Text of Senator Robinson's Plea for Tolerance Which Set Off Explosion on Convention Floor

Special to The New York Times.

HOUSTON, June 27.—Here is the official transcript of the sentences by which Senator Robinson altered the original conclusion of his speech as Permanent Chairman and set off the first violent burst of sentiment at the Democratic Convention this noon:

We must demonstrate willingness to enter into honorable compromises and to make personal sacrifices. In no other way can the best interests of this nation and the Democratic Party be promoted.

Jefferson gloried in the Virginia Statue of Religious Freedom. [Prolonged applause, the delegates rising.]

He rejoiced in the provision of the Constitution that declares no religious test shall ever be required as a qualification for office or trust in the United States. [Prolonged applause, the delegates rising and parading, bearing the standards of various States.]

When this convention has performed its tasks, nominated its candidates and adopted its platform, let us advance with measured tread and irresistible energy and force to the overthrow of the forces which have corrupted and which are dominating this great Government. [Applause.]

June 28, 1928

The Single Ballot Which Made Gov. Smith Democratic Party's Candidate for President

BEFORE THE SHIFTS

Total Vote	STATE	Smith	Reed	George	Hall
24	Alabama	1		8	6
6	Arizona	6			
18	Arkansas	17	1		
26	California	26			
12	Colorado	12			
14	Connecticut	14			
6	Delaware	6			
12	Florida			12	
28	Georgia			28	
8	Idaho	8			
58	Illinois	56	2		
30	Indiana				
26	Iowa	26			
20	Kansas				
26	Kentucky	26			
20	Louisiana	20			
12	Maine	12			
16	Maryland	16			
36	Mass'h'setts	36			
30	Michigan	30			
24	Minnesota	24			
20	Mississippi				
36	Missouri		36		
8	Montana	8			
16	Nebraska				
6	Nevada	6			
8	New Ha'hire	8			
28	New Jersey	28			
6	New Mexico	6			
90	New York	90			
24	No. Carolina	4⅔			19⅓
10	No. Dakota	10			
48	Ohio	1			
20	Oklahoma	10	8		2
10	Oregon	10			
76	Penn'ylvania	70½	1		2½
10	Rh'de Island	10			
18	So. Carolina				
10	So. Dakota	10			
24	Tennessee				24
40	Texas				
8	Utah	8			
8	Vermont	8			
24	Virginia	6			18
14	Washington	14			
16	W. Virginia	10½		4½	
26	Wisconsin	26			
6	Wyoming	6			
6	Alaska	6			
6	Dist. of Col.	6			
6	Hawaii	6			
6	Philippines	6			
6	Porto Rico	6			
6	Canal Zone	6			
2	Virgin Islands	2			
1100	Totals	724⅔	48	52½	71 5-6

AFTER THE SHIFTS

Total Vote	STATE	Smith	Reed	George	Hall
24	Alabama	1		8	6
6	Arizona	6			
18	Arkansas	17	1		
26	California	26			
12	Colorado	12			
14	Connecticut	14			
6	Delaware	6			
12	Florida			12	
28	Georgia			28	
8	Idaho	8			
58	Illinois	56	2		
30	Indiana	25			
26	Iowa	26			
20	Kansas	11½	4		
26	Kentucky	26			
20	Louisiana	20			
12	Maine	12			
16	Maryland	16			
36	Mass'h'setts	36			
30	Michigan	30			
24	Minnesota	24			
20	Mississippi	9½			
36	Missouri		36		
8	Montana	8			
16	Nebraska	12			2
6	Nevada	6			
8	New Ha'hire				
28	New Jersey	28			
6	New Mexico	6			
90	New York	90			
24	No. Carolina	4⅔			19⅓
10	No. Dakota	10			
48	Ohio	45			
20	Oklahoma	10	8		2
10	Oregon	10			
76	Penn'ylvania	70½	1		2½
10	Rh'de Island	10			
18	So. Carolina				
10	So. Dakota	10			
24	Tennessee	23			1
40	Texas				
8	Utah	8			
8	Vermont	8			
24	Virginia	6			18
14	Washington	14			
16	W. Virginia	10½		4½	
26	Wisconsin	26			
6	Wyoming	6			
6	Alaska	6			
6	Dist. of Col.	6			
6	Hawaii	6			
6	Philippines	6			
6	Porto Rico	6			
6	Canal Zone	6			
2	Virgin Islands	2			
1100	Totals	849⅔	52	52½	50 5-6

BEFORE

TOTAL VOTES CAST..........1,100
NECESSARY TO A CHOICE, 733 1-3.
SCATTERING VOTES, 203.

WOOLLEN—Ala., 2; Ind., 30; Total, 32. JONES—Ala., 3; Tex., 40; Total, 43. DONAHEY—Ala., 4; Pa., 1; Total, 5. AYRES—Kan., 20. HARRISON—Miss., 20. HITCHCOCK—Neb., 16. POMERENE—Ohio, 47. THOMPSON—Pa., 1; W. Va., 1; Total, 2. WATTS—So. Car., 18.

AFTER

TOTAL VOTES CAST........1,097½
NECESSARY TO A CHOICE, 731 2-3
SCATTERING VOTES, 92½.

POMERENE—Ohio, 3. JONES—Ala., 3; Texas, 40; Total, 43. HITCHCOCK—Neb., 2. AYRES—Kans., 3. WOOLLEN—Ind., 5; Ala., 2; Total, 7. DONAHEY—Ala., 4; Pa., 1; Total, 5. HARRISON—Miss., 8½. THOMPSON—Pa., 1; W. Va., 1; Total, 2. BILBOE—Miss., 1. WATTS—S. Car., 18.

NOT VOTING, 2½.
Kans., 1½; Miss., 1; Total, 2½.

June 29, 1928

GOV. SMITH DECLARES FOR CHANGE IN DRY LAW; ROBINSON IS NAMED FOR VICE PRESIDENT

DELEGATES CHEER MESSAGE

It Silences Grumblings of Wets on Platform 'Pussyfooting.'

ROBINSON WINS BY 1,035 1-6

With Victory on the First Ballot, Every State Gives Him All or Most of Its Votes.

LEADERS GO HOME PLEASED

Convention Ends Its Work Ahead of Schedule and With More Harmony Than Expected.

By W. A. WARN.

Special to The New York Times.

HOUSTON, June 29.—The Democratic National Convention at a three-hour session today wound up its work and at 1:47 P. M. adjourned after having nominated Senator Joseph T. Robinson of Arkansas for Vice President, thus completing a ticket headed by Governor Alfred E. Smith of New York as the nominee for President.

Senator Robinson, who is the first member of either of the two major parties from below the Mason and Dixon Line to get a place on a national ticket, won in a landslide. He received a total of 1,035 1-6 out of the 1,100 votes in the convention, and every State in the Union and every territory and possession was represented in the vote for him.

The demonstration which greeted the first mention of his name for the Vice Presidency lasted a little more than five minutes, and while not as noisy as some before, it was characterized by earnestness and fervor. There was a new demonstration when he was officially declared the nominee of the convention. This was briefer. No particular attempt was made to keep either alive through artificial stimulation.

The Result of the Ballot.

The vote for Vice President, as officially announced from the rostrum, stood as follows:

Senator Robinson	1,035 1-6
Maj. Gen. Henry T. Allen (Ky.)	21
Maj. Geo. L. Berry (Tenn.)	11 1-2
Gov. Dan Moody (Texas)	9 1-3
Sen. Alben W. Barkley (Ky.)	9
Sen. Fletcher (Fla.)	7
Ex-Gov. Nellie Tayloe Ross. (Wyo.)	2
Lewis G. Stevenson (Ill.)	2
Evans Woollen (Ind.)	2
Not voting	1

The vote not cast was that of an absentee member of the Florida delegation.

While the nomination of a candidate for Vice President is second in importance only to the nomination of the candidate for President, it was almost overshadowed in interest by the message received by the convention from Governor Smith in which he defined his personal stand on prohibition and prohibition enforcement, which have been burning topics before this convention. The message was read before the convention as the final session was drawing to a close amid impressive silence, followed by applause and a great burst of cheers.

In his communication Governor Smith pledged himself to full, fearless and wholehearted compliance with the official oath under which, if sworn in as Chief Executive of the nation, he would be required to defend the Constitution and all the statutory laws, as he finds them, but made it perfectly plain that he still held to a personal opinion, often publicly expressed, that "there should be fundamental changes in the present provisions for national prohibition."

Pledges Change in the Law.

He further pledged himself, if elected President, to blaze a trail toward a sane and sensible solution of the prohibition problem and a way out of conditions which he pronounced "unsatisfactory."

"Common honesty," the Governor wrote, "compels me to admit that the corruption of law enforcement officials, bootlegging and lawlessness are now prevalent throughout the country. I am satisfied that without returning to the old evils that grew from the saloon, which years ago I held and still hold ought always to be a defunct institution in this country, by the application of the Democartic principles of local self-government and States' rights we can secure equal temperance, respect for law and correction of existing evils."

The Governor further said that he stood "committed to the platform" and would welcome an opportunity to recognize and render more efficient and less costly to the taxpayer the Federal governmental machinery at Washington. He said that the platform had shattered the Republican claim that the Republican Party possessed "a monopoly on the mechanics of prosperity," praised the planks dealing with agrarian relief and labor and ended up by saying that in his speech of acceptance he would give the country his views in full upon all the issues of the campaign.

Reaction to Message Favorable.

The reaction to Governor Smith's message, so promptly forthcoming, among the party leaders and delegates in the convention, was wholly favorable. The consensus was that throughout the country it would be regarded as a guarantee that the Governor acted in absolute good faith when in his letter to the Jackson Day dinner in January he urged his party to meet all issues, including prohibition, in its national platform in a spirit of frankness. It was the general impression here after the message had been read that it would make friends for the Governor among wets and drys alike in all parts of the country.

Until the telegram from Governor Smith had been read there had been quite a little grumbling among delegates from New York, Illinois, Maryland, Rhode Island and others over the acceptance by the Governor's spokesmen on the Committee on Resolutions of a prohibition plank that was dry enough to win the approval of such pronounced drys as former Secretary of the Navy Josephus Daniels and Senator Carter Glass of Virginia, not to mention Bishop Cannon of the Methodist Episcopal Church.

Governor Smith's friends in the convention, including not a few of his Tammany confrères, who were members of the New York delegation, had expressed the opinion after the convention had adopted the platform at the night session yesterday that the prohibition plank would alienate wet supporters of the Governor on whom he would be dependent for victory because they would regard the Democratic plank as an attempt at pussy-footing and as such would resent it.

Hushed Rebellion Rumors.

The Governor's telegram hushed all rebellious murmurs. His wet critics of last night said his telegram of today would supplement the plank in a fashion that would render it satisfactory to the wets and all who favor some "sane solution" of the prohibition problem at the same time as it would make a strong appeal to the drys by its unwavering and unequivocal pledge of rigid law enforcement.

Thus, as was pointed out here tonight by a Democratic leader of great prominence, Governor Smith, meeting the issue frankly, with a few strokes of his pen had made a contribution to party harmony which the Resolutions Committee could just as well have made, provided its members had possessed the Governor's faculty for leadership and looking facts in the face.

The party leaders who gathered here a few days ago, fearful and apprehensive of what the convention would bring forth to promote party discord, having the wet and dry issue especially in view, are departing today for their homes to begin the campaign for Governor Smith's election in a jubilant frame of mind. There was not one among their number but felt that the convention had met under a lucky star. Where perils and pitfalls were lurking all along its path, the 1928 national convention, in the opinion of party leaders, was the most harmonious and successful witnessed by them in their long period of service. Its machinery moved smoothly and without a perceptible jar to the fulfillment of all its purposes.

Farm Relief Plank is Hailed.

The greatest trimph it achieved next to the nomination of a candidate who, while unacceptable only a few weeks ago to a large element within the party, was put over without serious opposition, was the adjustment of the differences over prohibition and the adoption of a farm relief plank which the party leaders believe will make a strong appeal in agricultural sections, now reported in revolt as a result of President Coolidge's veto of the McNary-Haugen bill, with its central feature the so-called equalization fee, introduced in principle though not in terms in the Democratic platform.

It is a far cry from Oliver Street on the east side of New York to the wide open spaces of the West where the corn grows, but the farm plank, in conjunction with promises made by spokesmen for the farmers in the corn belt before the Committee on Resolutions, is regarded by Democratic leaders as holding out strong hopes that the twain will meet behind the Smith-Robinson ticket.

The action of the convention today in nominating Senator Robinson for second place, according to the view held here, is bound to make a strong appeal in the corn belt.

It puts on the Democratic ticket the Democratic leader of the Senate, following the action of the Republicans at Kansas City in naming Charles Curtis, the Republican leader in the Senate, as their candidate for Vice President.

The appearance of both the Senate leaders in identical places on the rival tickets, as Democratic leaders see it, will compel a comparison by the voters of their record, with the result that Senator Robinson will be shown to have been a consistent supporter of the McNary-Haugen bill while Senator Curtis, the Republican nominee, will be shown to have been inconsistent. The latter voted for the bill in the first instance, but later voted to uphold the President's veto of it. Senator Robinson voted for the bill when it was before the Senate and voted to over-ride the veto.

Vigorous Companion in Arms.

Entirely aside from this, Senator Robinson's nomination will assure Governor Smith of a vigorous companion in arms during the campaign, and to boot a man who is known and familiar with the ways of the folks who live in the agrarian sections of the west and southwest, where the Governor will be a tenderfoot and in need of friendly introduction.

Senator Robinson, too, is a dry and Protestant, and as such will afford to the Democratic ticket a balance which, as Democratic leaders here see it, is lacking in the ticket named by their Republican opponents.

Franklin D. Roosevelt, floor leader for the Smith forces in the convention, while declining to make any comment on the Governor's telegram, said that he was well pleased with the work the Democrats had done at Sam Houston Hall.

"The result of the 1928 Democratic National Convention," he said, "leaves me a very happy Democrat, indeed. It has involved eight years of very hard work to pave the way for what has happened here by making Alfred E. Smith known to the country. But it has been well worth while, and the country will endorse my view when Governor Smith begins to function as President of the United States."

many's most distinguished son would be the next President. He would say nothing more.

Mrs. Smith, although what to her must have been the most interesting part of the convention was over with the nomination of her husband, went to Sam Houston Hall as usual this morning to lend the grace of her presence to the preceedings which culminated in the selection of his running mate. Happiness and pride were written all over her face, as, beautifully gowned in blue, she sat with members of her family in a box in the hall. After the session she yielded to the clamorous demand of half a hundred photographers to have her picture taken with Mrs. Robinson, wife of the Vice Presidential nominee.

The session of the convention today, aside from the nomination of Senator Robinson and the reading of Governor Smith's message, was devoid of outstanding features. The nomination of a Vice President, as a rule is not exciting, frequently delegates leave the hall half empty before the result of the balloting has been announced or is known. The final session of the 1928 convention, today, however, was an exception. The delegates remained in their seats and saw the finish.

Senator Robinson did not function in his capacity as Permanent Chairman. He had left Houston for some destination unknown even to the functionaries of the convention. Franklin D. Roosevelt called the convention to order and turned the gavel over to Senator Robinson's colleague, and probable successor as leader of the Senate, if Robinson should be elected, Senator Pat Harrison of Mississippi. Later Mr. Roosevelt received the honor of making the motion for the convention to adjourn without date.

Five Names Presented.

Counting the successful nominee, there were five candidates for second place on the ticket, including one woman, Mrs. Nellie Tayloe Ross, former Governor of Wyoming. The others were Major Gen. Allen and Senator Barkley of Kentucky and Senator Fletcher of Florida. The names of others who received votes on the only ballot taken had not been placed formally before the convention.

It was evident from the very beginning of the roll call that Senator Robinson would be the winner. The solid vote of such delegations as those from New York and Pennsylvania was cast for him. So it went on down the list until after the roll call had been ended he had well in excess of 900 votes. The rest was piled up by State after State changing votes cast for other candidates in favor of the man who had already carried off the prize.

The Robinson bandwagon today proved even more inviting than did the Smith bandwagon last night. Drys who could not be induced to fall in line for Governor Smith made no difficulty about casting their votes for his running mate after discharging favorite son obligations.

Tammany Leader George W. Olvany, who realized after months of careful preparations the fulfillment of Tammany's ambition to supply a national standard bearer to the party and possibly a President to the United States, was the happiest man in Houston today.

* * * * *

June 30, 1928

CHICAGOANS COUNTING ON LONG CONVENTIONS

Figure Each Day Means $500,000 —Democrats' Past Average Is 5 6-13 Days, Republicans4 3-13.

CHICAGO, June 3 (AP).—On the basis of the law of averages, the Republican National Convention would be over by the night of June 17 and the Democratic National Convention about noon July 2.

In the last fifty-two years the Democrats have averaged 5 6-13 days in session and the Republicans 4 3-13.

Speculation over the duration of the big meetings is rife in Chicago just now, as hotel owners, restaurant men and tradespeople anticipate eagerly the coming rush of convention business. What a deadlock migh mean to them can be seen in the estimate that each convention day will bring in a half million dollars.

Both tradition and present circumstances point to a brief gathering of Republicans. Their convention starts June 14, with the renomination of President Hoover a foregone conclusion. Even with a full day devoted to debate over a prohibition plank, the meeting is not expected to last more than four days. Tickets have been printed for only four days, but the fourth-day ticket entitles the holder to any and all future sessions.

The Democratic convention, with its two-thirds majority rule, holds Chicago's hopes for a financial harvest. A glance at the records gives considerable foundation for those hopes. The longest convention, of course, was the 1924 meeting in New York, when the delegates wrangled for seventeen days before they nominated John W. Davis. There have been other long Democratic conventions, notably the 1912 and 1920 meetings of nine days each.

If they hold an average convention, the Democrats would adjourn just in time to get home, or be well on the way, Sunday. Their meeting this year starts Monday, June 27. Tickets have been printed for twelve sessions, or six days, if the practice of holding two sessions a day is followed.

The following table shows the duration by days of the convention since 1880, with the nominees indicated:

Year.	Republican.	Democratic.
1928	4 (Hoover)	4 (Smith)
1924	3 (Coolidge)	17 (Davis)
1920	5 (Harding)	9 (Cox)
1916	4 (Hughes)	3 (Wilson)
1912	5 (Taft)	9 (Wilson)
1908	4 (Taft)	4 (Bryan)
1904	3 (Roosevelt)	4 (Parker)
1900	3 (McKinley)	3 (Bryan)
1896	3 (McKinley)	5 (Bryan)
1892	4 (Harrison)	3 (Cleveland)
1888	6 (Harrison)	3 (Cleveland)
1884	4 (Blaine)	4 (Cleveland)
1880	7 (Garfield)	3 (Hancock)

June 4, 1932

CHICAGO DISCUSSES CONVENTION THEMES

Officials Gathered to Arrange for the Sessions Expect Republican Battle.

ROCKEFELLER SPURS DRIVE

His Statement to Be Used in Battle for Outright Repeal Plank.

SEE A DEFEAT FOR BUTLER

Hoover Supporters Will Try to Dissuade Him From Insisting on Presenting Resolution.

By W. A. WARN.

Special to THE NEW YORK TIMES.

CHICAGO, June 7.—Interest at the Republican National Convention, due to assemble here a week from today, will centre in the controversy over a prohibition plank which now appears inevitable.

Among the small group of convention officials already on the scene there is a feeling that the announcement made in New York City yesterday by John D. Rockefeller Jr. will spur the extreme wet element among the delegates to do battle in a do-or-die spirit for a declaration in favor of outright repeal as against the resubmission plank which friends and advisers of President Hoover now apparently favor.

Needless to say, the men to whom has been entrusted by President Hoover, who it is generally agreed will be the absolute master of next week's Republican show, the management of the national conclave of their party are not viewing the prospect with any degree of equanimity.

They admit that the Rockefeller statement may attract a considerable body of new recruits to the repealist banner, but since they feel that President Hoover can never accept a repeal plank, they see only one outcome of the battle, defeat for the Butler proposal. From their viewpoint, of course, this would be a happy ending, were it not for one result of which they appear to be fearful—that their party, as a result of voting down a proposal for repeal, will be doomed to enter upon the campaign with what, at least in the large and important wet industrial States with heavy representation in the Electoral College, will prove a handicap.

Will Try to Dissuade Butler.

From what has been said here today by Republicans who will occupy positions of prominence in the convention, a supreme effort will be made to dissuade Dr. Butler from pursuing his announced purpose.

Dr. Butler has been a familiar figure at Republican National Conventions for a generation. Before personal conviction that the Eighteenth Amendment had no proper place in the Constitution prompted him to take a stand divergent from that of a majority of the party leaders, he was one of the key men at these recurring quadrennial gatherings of his party, and in those earlier years the national platforms of the Republican party showed abundant evidence of his skill as a platform builder.

That any appeal made to him on the ground of political expediency will fail is regarded as almost certain by Republicans of prominence who know Dr. Butler, nor is there any likelihood that any prohibition plank sanctioned by the powers that be at Washington will meet with his approval. A contest, as the situation is viewed here, would appear the only alternative.

James W. Wadsworth, former United States Senator, has announced that he will be here next week to second the efforts of Dr. Butler. Mr. Wadsworth, a stanch Republican, was invited to come to the convention as a delegate, but he declined on the ground that in such a position he would be bound by any decisions reached on the question of prohibition. By coming merely as a visitor or as an "outside" advocate of a repeal plank in the platform he will be under no hampering obligation to give his support to the party and its candidates in the likely event that the prohibition plank to be adopted should not meet with his approval and that of his comrades in arms for the battle for repeal.

Senator Wadsworth at present occupies the position of head of the New York division of the Association Against the Prohibition Amendment, and this group, as well as the Crusaders, the League for Modification and the Women's Organization for National Prohibition Reform, is proposing to go on the firing line for a repeal plank when the convention goes into action next week.

In advance of the convention itself both wet and dry groups will stage demonstrations here to impress delegates to the convention.

Wets to Stay on Ground.

These wet groups with a non-partisan approach where prohibition is concerned are preparing to stay on the ground through both the national conventions, and if successful at the Republican gathering next week will renew their appeal for a repeal pledge before the Democratic National Convention. Apprehension with regard to what the Democrats will do is not the least worry of the Republican leaders who have put in an early appearance for the convention of their own party.

One line of attack to be made by the extreme wets on the resubmission plank in process of being drafted at Washington was foreshadowed here today by Colonel Ira L. Reeves, director of the mid-West division of the Crusaders, an extreme wet organization. Colonel Reeves called attention to the fact that in the published accounts purporting to give the text of the Republican resubmission plank, "retention, repeal or modification" of the Eighteenth Amendment had been cited as proposals that would be submitted to State conventions.

"This does not afford the American people the opportunity they should have for a clean-cut expression on prohibition—whether they want the Eighteenth Amendment retained or repealed," Colonel Reeves said. "It offers an alternative which may have the effect of splitting the liberals into two camps. I stand for an out-and-out resubmission of the question—repeal or retention of the Eighteenth Amendment."

Prohibition the Only Snag.

Aside from the fight over prohibition the horizon promises to be harmonious. With the exception of Joseph L. France of Maryland, former United States Senator, President Hoover will have no competitor for the nomination. The candidacy of former Senator France is not looked on as serious. He has no organized strength behind him and it is doubtful whether he will have more than the thirteen votes from Oregon cast for him on the first and only ballot in the convention. The delegates under the Oregon law must vote for Mr. France, but are really at heart for President Hoover.

Some of the insurgent delegates from Wisconsin are committed to Senator Norris, but since he has announced his intention to bolt President Hoover, there is doubt whether his candidacy will receive any recognition.

Cabinet Members Among Delegates.

At least five members of President Hoover's Cabinet will have a voice and a vote in the convention in which they will sit as delegates. These are the Secretary of State, Henry L. Stimson; the Secretary of the Treasury, Ogden L. Mills; the Secretary of War, Patrick J. Hurley; the Secretary of Agriculture, Arthur M. Hyde and the Postmaster General, Walter F. Brown, the last of whom is regarded as the spokesman for President Hoover.

While there will be a liberal sprinkling of Federal officeholders among the delegates, there probably will be fewer Senators and Representatives than in any previous Republican convention, since Congress is likely to remain in session during the convention. The insurgent element, which has made trouble at earlier conventions, will be scantily represented.

Only a few of the Republican leaders who will sit in the convention are on hand. Among them are Colonel Lafayette B. Gleason, who will function as secretary; Ralph E. Williams of Oregon, vice chairman of the national committee; George de B. Keim of New Jersey, David W. Mulvane, national committeeman from Kansas, and Patrick Sullivan, national committeeman from Wyoming.

The national committee is scheduled to meet for the consideration of contests on Thursday afternoon and tomorrow, and Thursday morning will see a majority of the ninety-six committee members here. So far only six contests, an unusually small number, have been listed and most of these are local and the outgrowth of the proposal to build up white organizations to supplant those ruled by Negroes in Southern States.

There will be contests on the entire delegations from South Carolina, Louisiana, Mississippi and Georgia and on delegates from the Third Congressional District in Virginia and the First and Ninth Districts in Tennessee.

June 8, 1932

HOOVER, CURTIS RENAMED ON FIRST BALLOTS

CHEER HOOVER 27 MINUTES

Delegates Give 1,126 1-2 Votes on First Ballot, 634 1-4 to Curtis.

NEW YORK FOR HARBORD

France Ejected From Rostrum —Coolidge's Name Fails to Stir Convention.

HOOVER VICTORY COMPLETE

Administration Had 200 Votes in Reserve—Convention Ends After Nominations.

By ARTHUR KROCK.

Special to THE NEW YORK TIMES.

CHICAGO, June 16.—Under the disclosed domination of the President, the Republican national convention at its closing session today renominated Herbert Hoover and gave a grudging but safe majority to Charles Curtis of Kansas, renominated as the party candidate for Vice President.

Mr. Hoover received 1,126½ votes on the first ballot, his nomination immediately thereafter being made unanimous. Mr. Curtis, the beneficiary of a last-minute switch of Pennsylvania's 75 votes from its Republican State Chairman, General Edward Martin, to the Vice President, had a first ballot majority of 55¾, with a total of 634¼. His nomination also was made unanimous. Until Pennsylvania responded to the Administration goad, Mr. Curtis lacked 19¼ votes of the sum required for his renomination.

It has been twenty years since the obvious will of a Republican National Committee has been so completely and publicly subordinated to a President's program. In 1912, as today, both President and Vice President were renominated, the only time in its history that the Republican party has repeated its ticket.

But then Theodore Roosevelt bolted the convention and formed the Bull Moose party, badly defeating the regular Republicans under William H. Taft in the election and assuring the victory of the Democratic ticket headed by Woodrow Wilson.

No Prospect of a Bolt.

So far as the political elements of the Republican party are concerned, there were no prospects of a bolt as the result of the defeat of the repeal plank last night and the renomination of Mr. Curtis today. The only menacing element was the insurgency of the New York delegation. Today its members cast ninety-five of their ninety-seven votes for General J. G. Harbord for Vice President, ignoring the plain warning which lay in the fact that the two New Yorkers who voted for Mr. Curtis were the Secretary of State, Henry L. Stimson, and the Secretary of the Treasury, Ogden L. Mills.

Last night the New Yorkers cast seventy-six of their votes for the Bingham repeal plank. The administration, which made that struggle the test of its control, had only twenty-one. Had not Charles D. Hilles, the national committeeman, declined to aid the State chairman, W. Kingsland Macy, in his effort to supplant Representative Ruth B. Pratt as national committee woman, this steadfast friend of the President would have been defeated.

The church drys, and those who are dry before they are Republican or Democratic, will not be heard from until they meet in national conclave in August, after they have examined the prohibition plank which the Democrats will adopt in Chicago the week after next.

It may be that then, as they did against James W. Wadsworth Jr. and Charles H. Tuttle, they will put independent New York State and national tickets in the field. Should this happen, the effect of that action, joined to the demonstrated dissatisfaction with Mr. Hoover's program of New York's regular Republicans, may be as disastrous to the national Republican candidates as was Colonel Roosevelt's third-party movement twenty years ago.

For days before this convention opened, and for the first day of the session, administration leaders maintained the strategic fiction that the delegates were to "work their will" on all points. In every respect save a public statement to the contrary, this technique was officially abandoned when, the strength of the repeal sentiment being evident, the administration leaders began to pack the committees on resolutions and credentials with Federal officials.

From the Minnesota delegation the President's political secretary, Walter H. Newton, went to the committee on credentials to supervise the job of unseating the "Black and Tan" Tolbert delegates from South

AGAIN THE REPUBLICAN STANDARD BEARERS

CHARLES CURTIS.

HERBERT HOOVER.

Carolina, their claim having previously been ratified by the national committee, where the remnants of the Old Guard sought to retain control of the party machinery. To the resolutions committee from New York went Secretaries Stimson and Mills, from Missouri and Oklahoma Secretary Hyde and Secretary Hurley. The Ambassador to France, Walter E. Edge of New Jersey was also placed on this committee, as were other persons devoted to Mr. Hoover for both personal and material reasons.

The fact that Congress was in session throughout the convention kept away many of the national leaders of the party from whom recalcitrant groups in the State delegations expected aid. The absence of every Progressive Republican leader was a final blow to incipient insurgency. In all this convention of 1,154 delegates only nine from Wisconsin were anti-Hoover men. And these sat without a word today when they were castigated from the platform as traitors and Democrats by a Wisconsin Republican stalwart.

Administration Had Reserves.

In such an atmosphere it was impossible to collect votes to give the administration a real battle on anything. The Bingham repeal plank got 472 votes, but the administration could have greatly reduced that had the necessity arisen. It always had in reserve at least 200 delegates whom it permitted to vote for flat repeal for the purpose of face-saving at home.

On the Curtis renomination the test was narrower, but had New York joined the movement for Hanford MacNider, thus making him formidable, the President's manager could have brought into line delegations which were casting complimentary votes all over the map. After the administration made its first show of strength in the South Carolina case, any who doubted that Herbert Hoover was the boss and intended to prove his authority if it became necessary, doubted no longer.

For days there had been loose talk here of a stampede for repeal, for Calvin Coolidge for President, for Charles G. Dawes for Vice President. It was always pure moonshine. Today there was only a faint handclap when Illinois cast 3½ votes for Mr. Coolidge. The antis were licked and they knew it. The "magic name" had no qualities of necromancy. Presidential renominating conventions do not stampede. That was proved for all time in 1912. After the deluges of printers' ink and the headlines, the Coolidge episode today seemed actually comic.

The same thing was true of the effort of Texas today to start a rush for Vice President to Representative Bertrand H. Snell of New York, permanent chairman of the convention. National Committeeman R. B. Creager, who had invented the Dawes boom, spoke the name of Mr. Snell and waited for the effect. It did not come. Mr. Snell's request that no delegate vote for him was not necessary to assure the renomination of Mr. Curtis.

On the roll-call California, the President's State, cast her entire forty-seven for the Vice President. That was the cue for any delegation which needed one. Mississippi, which it now appears had mistakenly voted against the administration on the platform report last night through an error in signals, came back into line. The Federal machine was a juggernaut. Postmaster General Walter F. Brown had done well his preliminary work of choosing delegates.

Back on Conservative Fold.

So far as the convention could express the attitude of the Republican party, it has returned definitely and wholly to the conservative fold. The great swing was to the right. Even Wisconsin, controlled for the first time in years by stalwarts, had no minority report to offer on anything.

Ignored or forgotten was the fact that the La Follette forces lost control of the delegation because their followers, not intending to vote for Mr. Hoover's re-election, rushed into the Democratic Presidential primaries to make sure of the victory of Franklin D. Roosevelt in that State. Of the regulars' victory in Wisconsin more will be heard in November, and probably of a different tenor.

Only one incident marred the smooth operation of the administration steam-roller today. That was when former Senator Joseph Irwin France of Maryland, the only other candidate placed in nomination for the Presidency, sought to gain the platform to offer the name of Mr. Coolidge. Not being a delegate he got what is known in Broadway as "the bum's rush." A rumor spread that Mr. Snell feared the effect of the Coolidge name. Ten minutes later this was completely disproved.

Mills a Dominant Figure.

The President had many representatives here. But the most effective one was Secretary Mills. His loyalty to Mr. Hoover cost him influence in his own delegation and almost defeated Mrs. Pratt, whom he was known to favor. But on the broad convention field, Mr. Mills was dominant. It was his rugged, 6-o'clock-in-the-morning oratory which dispelled opposition in the resolutions subcommittee to the prohibition plank.

Before that, in long conferences, Mr. Mills had drafted and re-drafted the document, yielding his own opinion in many respects in the interest of a compromise which he believed would yield votes for the party ticket. It was Mr. Mills who persuaded former Governor Henry J. Allen of Kansas, representing the board of strategy of the Methodist Church, to accept the "new amendment" submission idea. In last night's debate Mr. Mills was the one pro-platform speaker who was not booed by the hostile galleries.

Mr. Mills led the administration show of friendship for Mr. Curtis when Texas began the Dawes movement. It was he who communicated to Washington his belief that the General, whom he knew did not want the nomination, should be explicit in declining it as a gesture of complete loyalty to the administration.

The subsequent statement from General Dawes revealed the weakness of the Texas effort. As soon as the General realized that his name was being used to embarass the administration program, he spoke out and the one hopeful prospect of independence faded away.

Unconsciously today Will H. Hays, former chairman of the national committee, gave a clear clue to the cut-and-dried nature of the convention's "deliberations." His motion to notify "Mr. Hoover and Mr. Curtis of their renominations" was offered before the tally clerk had announced the result of the Vice Presidential poll. And, also before the result was made known, the Hays resolution was adopted.

June 17, 1932

* * * * * *

Text of Ex-Governor Smith's Announcement Of His Willingness To Be Democratic Candidate

The text of Alfred E. Smith's statement yesterday on his Presidential candidacy follows:

Office of Alfred E. Smith
Empire State Building
New York, N. Y.

So many inquiries have come to me from friends throughout the country who worked for and believed in me as to my attitude in the present political situation that I feel that I owe it to my friends and to the millions of men and women who supported me so loyally in 1928 to make my position clear.

If the Democratic National Convention, after careful consideration, should decide it wants me to lead I will make the fight; but I will not make a pre-convention campaign to secure the support of delegates.

By action of the Democratic National Convention of 1928 I am the leader of my party in the nation. With a full sense of the responsibility thereby imposed I shall not in advance of the convention either support or oppose the candidacy of any aspirant for the nomination.

ALFRED E. SMITH.

February 8, 1932

ROOSEVELT MEN SEE STIFF FIGHT AHEAD

Prepare Campaign to Prevent Smith Bloc Big Enough to Stop a Two-thirds Vote.

THEY DOUBT HE CAN WIN

Feel Avowal Makes South and West Sure for Governor—Admit Threat in East.

From a Staff Correspondent.
Special to THE NEW YORK TIMES.

ALBANY, N. Y., Feb. 7.—Stirred by former Governor Smith's announcement, the forces backing Governor Roosevelt prepared today to gird themselves for a stiff fight for the Democratic nomination for President.

Governor Roosevelt would make no comment on the Smith declaration, asserting that he had not seen it. It was intimated also that he did not expect to make in the future any direct statement on the open rivalry with his predecessor in the Executive office.

While the Governor steered clear of any statement on what his supporters interpreted as a clear-cut avowal of Smith's candidacy, it was learned that the strategists of the Roosevelt camp were making ready to battle to the limit for their candidate.

In the eyes of the Roosevelt advisers, the Smith statement constitutes the first serious threat to the nomination of he New York Executive on an early ballot at the Chicago convention. While they still remain confident of victory for Governor Roosevelt, they acknowledge that the task has been made more difficult.

A Rallying Point.

Former Governor Smith's statement, it is pointed out, gives to the anti-Roosevelt group a definite personality around whom to rally a body of delegates large enough to block a two-thirds majority for the New York Governor. Before this declaration the opposition had been somewhat aimless in its efforts to head off Governor Roosevelt.

The Roosevelt supporters, however, do not view the Smith announcement as wholly injurious. They contend that the threat of Smith as a candidate will tend to swing to Governor Roosevelt areas in the South and West that have been doubtful.

In the densely populated districts in the industrial East, they admit, the Smith candidacy will cause them some trouble. The first real test of strength will come on March 8, in the New Hampshire primary, where both men are being entered. The Roosevelt backers have the support of the State organization and they believe that this will be of great assistance in naming a slate of delegates committed to the New York Governor.

Hope for Initial Victory.

The Roosevelt leaders hope to get off to a favorable start in New Hampshire, recognizing the prestige value of an initial victory. The states where former Governor Smith's entrance as a candidate is likely to count most are Massachusetts and Pennsylvania.

In the Keystone State, Joseph F. Guffey has declared for Governor Roosevelt, while other leaders are understood to be ready to fight for Mr. Smith. The Roosevelt plans have called for his entrance in the primaries as a candidate and the Guffey group has been claiming a large group of the State's delegates for him. With former Governor Smith in the open, however, the situation may be changed.

In Massachusetts former Governor Smith has unusual popularity with the Democratic voters. Governor Joseph B. Ely and his aides are ready to fight for him there, although Mayor James M. Curley of Boston is active for Governor Roosevelt. Recently it was indicated that Governor Roosevelt's name would be placed in the Massachusetts primary, for which the candidate must sign a formal consent. Whether former Governor Smith's statement could be interpreted to mean that he would sign such a consent will be likely to play a part in determining the policy of the Roosevelt forces for the Massachusetts battle.

New Jersey, dominated by Mayor Frank L. Hague of Jersey City, is another State where former Governor Smith is known to have a very large following, and the same is true of Rhode Island. In Illinois, or at least Chicago, wet sentiment has been seeking for some time to get a candidate like Smith to work for. Governor Roosevelt has strong backing in down-State Illinois.

The question of New York State's allegiance is a vital one. If former Governor Smith entered the primaries in New York, it is agreed, his long-standing popularity would make him a powerful candidate against Governor Roosevelt. Mr. Roosevelt has fairly united support among the up-State groups, although a few exceptions, like Albany and Oneida Counties, might be made. Then also, it is contended, Tammany Hall, under the leadership of John F. Curry, is not particularly friendly to former Governor Smith. In a showdown at a primary election to name delegates persons of both camps declare it is difficult to say just what would happen.

Through the rest of the country, the Roosevelt strategists maintain, the Smith candidacy will have only beneficial effect. Governor Roosevelt, they assert, will add to his already large total of convention votes with Smith's hat in the ring. But, with the former Governor in an open battle, they admit that they are in for a stiff contest to prevent the construction of a bloc big enough to stop a two-thirds majority for Governor Roosevelt.

The Roosevelt supporters contend that former Governor Smith can never be more than a blocking candidate, but they admit that a combination of the delegates he could gather, coupled with those committed to favorite sons, constitutes a real danger to the Roosevelt drive. Now, with former Governor Smith's position clear, they are making ready to accelerate their campaign on all fronts.

February 8, 1932

ROOSEVELT WANING, W. A. WHITE BELIEVES

'Winged' by Smith in the East, Governor Has Lost Big-City 'Tammanies,' Kansan Says.

WEST FOR 'RABBLE-ROUSER'

But, Editor Adds, While 'Voting Against,' It May Turn on Smith —Picked Compromise Nominee.

By WILLIAM ALLEN WHITE.

EMPORIA, Kan., April 28.—The Massachusetts and Pennsylvania primaries seem to indicate that Al Smith and his followers have not stopped Governor Roosevelt, but have definitely winged him. Overnight, the Roosevelt band wagon has been transformed into a vehicle which may be the Democratic water wagon, or only one of those humble fertilizer-spreaders found in the open spaces of the rural West.

Franklin Roosevelt has definitely lost the support of two important elements in the Democratic party: those who love a winner and those who follow Tammany. His strength north of Maryland and east of the Alleghanies, subtracting Pennsylvania, will be negligible.

Every other successful Democratic Presidential candidate over seventy years, Tilden, Cleveland, Wilson, has won his first nomination over the dead body of Tammany. But these Democratic giants dramatized their contest with Tammany so that the loss of their home State was an asset and not a liability.

Roosevelt's loss of New York, followed quickly by the loss of the industrial sea-bordering States, advertises to the world that Roosevelt's weakness in his dealings with Tammany has emboldened the Tammany allies to fight Roosevelt wherever they are entrenched.

Roosevelt as McAdoo's Heir.

Moreover, because Smith is leading the fight on Roosevelt, for some curious and probably grossly unfair reason Roosevelt has inherited among the religious friends of Governor Smith the odium which they attached four years ago to the managers of the Hoover campaign. Put briefly and bluntly, the anti-Catholic fight of 1928 is now seething in the Democratic party. Roosevelt is the residuary legatee of McAdoo in 1924.

The friends of Smith certainly do not hope to nominate Smith, but they do hope to control the nomination and, first of all, to see that the nominee is not Franklin Roosevelt.

Every four years the American people have to learn that the Democratic nomination is made, not by a majority of the Democratic Convention, but by two-thirds of the convention. It seems now reasonably certain that the friends of Smith will control more than one-third of the convention.

It may be assumed that unless Roosevelt gets the nomination the first day on the third ballot he is lost. He stands today where McAdoo stood in April, 1924. Roosevelt will have a majority of the convention undoubtedly, as McAdoo had it. He will get his recruits from the West and from the South, where McAdoo recruited his votes. He will have the votes of the mild wets and the compromising drys. McAdoo had them.

Roosevelt will have the agrarian vote of the West. McAdoo had it. And the primaries this week have demonstrated that Roosevelt will have the opposition of the various Tammanyists in the great cities, both in Republican territory and Democratic, with probably the opposition of the aristocratic remnant of the Old South, exactly the force that defeated McAdoo after he had assembled a majority of the convention.

Rival Leaders Contrasted.

The strength of Roosevelt is found in the fact that he is the only outstanding leader in the Democratic party who is seriously a candidate. Smith is a Warwick, a maker of kings who does not and knows that he cannot aspire seriously to the throne. He probably realizes that his nomination would spell disaster from the start.

Smith is a powerful leader in the party, a leader with courage and convictions, a leader with a certain rugged honesty that inspires confidence in his friends and respect in his adversaries. He will probably dominate the party for the next three or four conventions as Bryan, though failing as a candidate, controlled either the conventions or the hearts of the Democracy when it went to the polls.

And in the contest now looming on the political horizon the battle will be between Roosevelt leading the mild liberals of the party and Smith for the moment euchred into the position of a conservative leader.

Around Smith will rally the big Democratic chiefs of plutocracy—the Wall Street crowd, that always finances the various Tammanies in our great cities—Tammanies of both parties, Republican and Democratic. These plutocratic leaders, for all their plug-hat respectability, are fundamentally responsible for the corruption that stigmatizes civil governments in American towns that pass the million mark.

Roosevelt is not sufficiently liberal to attract and to hold Bryan's following. As a rabble-rouser he is badly infected with weasel words. He has a charming sense of balance, and when he seems to be going well as a progressive or a liberal he checks himself with a string of "althoughs," "buts," "on-the-other-hands" and "on-the-contraries" which takes the heart out of Western liberals.

The West will take Roosevelt in the Democratic Convention not because it loves Roosevelt but because it hates Tammany and distrusts the plutocratic aristocracy in the Old South. So Roosevelt's Western followers will not be a last-ditch crowd as McAdoo's was.

The agrarian West is ready for a rabble-rouser. Roosevelt does not fill the bill, but he is the only one in sight, and probably will have the Western delegations in the convention, and if he is nominated will see his high tide in July. For the West is fickle, as fickle as the wind and the clouds.

Indeed, the prosperity of the West, being in agriculture, depends entirely upon the wind and the clouds. Last year short crops and low prices depressed the West as it had not been depressed for three decades. Today it is ready to make trouble. But, given a good crop and fair prices, the West may return to Hoover in the Fall.

Just now the West would probably vote against the President because it wants to vote against somebody and it isn't particular about who shall be the object of its wrath. But, given a row in the Democratic Convention, let Smith and his Tammany plutocrats defeat Roosevelt and nominate a reactionary like Ritchie, and the protest vote of the West will be divided. They will have two men to vote against, and Hoover may win. He probably will.

But the thing that has come out of Tuesday's primary as a certainty is that Roosevelt from now on will have to fight his way for the nomination, and in the fight he carries the terrible loss of New York, Massachusetts, Connecticut, Rhode Island and probably the entire industrial East, excepting Pennsylvania.

Smith's machine-gun fire has silenced the horns on the Roosevelt band wagon.

May 1, 1932

FOES ARE SUSPICIOUS OF ROOSEVELT SHIFT

Word Goes Out to Stand Firm for the Two-thirds Rule From Start to Finish.

NEW PLAN LIKELY TO LOSE

Survey of Delegations Indicates Majority of About 55 Against Compromise Rule.

By L. C. SPEERS.

Special to THE NEW YORK TIMES.

CHICAGO, June 27.—While virtually admitting defeat in their effort to put through a rule abolishing the Jacksonian two-thirds rule, which has controlled the nominations for President and Vice President in Democrttic conventions since 1832, the Roosevelt forces embarked on another campaign tonight to put the Democratic convention under a compromise majority rule and on that they are facing as hard a fight as was the losing one Governor Roosevelt halted this afternoon.

This is admitted in all camps, those for as well as those opposing the nomination of the New York Governor. A careful check-up of the delegations tonight indicates a defeat of the new proposal by a majority approximating fifty-five votes.

Tonight every pressure the Roosevelt leaders can bring to bear is being exerted to re-form the badly shaken Roosevelt lines and muster a majority for the new proposition. At the same time the opposition is just as vigorously putting forth its every effort to hold its lines intact. It now appears that only Mississippi will come back into the Roosevelt line.

Desertions from the Roosevelt camp over the movement to abrogate the two-thirds rule were showing signs of running into a stampede when from Albany came the order today to "cease firing."

The message from the Governor, which was received with undisguised suspicion in the opposition camps, came near the close of Senator Barkley's keynote speech and at a moment when the known majority against the motion to abrogate had passed fifty and was growing every hour.

On the floor of the convention the Roosevelt leaders were going into "huddles" in last-minute efforts to re-form their lines and halt the fast-increasing opposition to the abrogation policy proclaimed by James A. Farley, the manager of the Roosevelt campaign.

It was a critical moment. The Roosevelt managers realized they were losing and that only a miracle could save them when from Albany came the message to end the fight for the adoption of a majority rule "at the opening of the permanent organization," which is another name for the opening of the convention after the permanent organization is effected.

If the friends and supporters of Governor Roosevelt anticipated a favorable reaction to the message from the camp of the opposition, they failed to get it. Instead, the opposition promptly read "jokers" into the message and the order went forward to all supporters of rival candidacies to stand firm and continue to work for retention of the rule.

Probably never before in the history of Democratic national conventions has there been so sudden and emphatic an adverse reaction to the program of a leading contender for the Presidential nomination as was witnessed overnight.

At 5 P. M. yesterday a victory for the Roosevelt forces in the battle to abrogate the two-thirds rule was conceded by many, if not most, of the opposition camps. It was known that North Carolina and Mississippi were out of bounds, but there were few, if any, signs of serious revolt in the other units of the Roosevelt column.

Later the storm broke, with the disclosure that Alabama was joining the opposition, while Iowa was ready to jump; there was also a rising tide of resentment against the rule in South Carolina, Tennessee and Kentucky.

This morning found Iowa, along with Alabama, definitely in the anti-abrogation camp while the revolt in South Carolina and Kentucky had assumed serious proportions.

The Roosevelt forces had never expected such widespread opposition, and they were taken completely aback. The telephone between the Executive Mansion in Albany and the Congress Hotel headquarters of Mr. Roosevelt was reported in almost continuous use.

Almost up to the moment the change in policy was announced, the Roosevelt leaders insisted it was a fight to a finish and that the Governor had no intention of giving in anywhere along the line. Their boast was that they had the victory won and were going through with it. All this time the unyielding statistics of the situation showed that the resolution to abrogate was hopelessly lost.

The big reception room in the Roosevelt headquarters was crowded with the Governor's supporters listening to the keynoter seven miles away, when quietly and without fuss of any kind a big batch of mimeographed sheets was placed on the "news release table." No one in the room, except the campaign managers, knew the importance of the release. A few minutes later and the news had reached the floor of the convention.

The result there was broad smiles in opposition delegations and grave looks on the faces of many in the units pledged to Mr. Roosevelt. The general line of comment in rival ranks was that the statement was not quite clear enough, that it was a veiled suggestion to lead off under the two-thirds and end under the majority rule and the resultant nomination of the Governor of New York.

Two parts of the message immediately attracted the attention of the leaders of the Reed, Garner, Ritchie and Smith forces. The first was the request of the Governor that activities to force an abrogation of the two-thirds rule cease at the opening of the permanent organization, the other the expressed hope that the committee on rules would "recommend some rule to insure against the catastrophe of a deadlock or a prolonged balloting."

Those two sections, the rival organizations contended, nullified the rest of the message. They were construed as notice to the convention that unless the Governor was quickly nominated his representatives on the floor would renew their efforts to force abrogation of the two-thirds rule. The result was immediate rejection of the message and its suggestions by leaders of the opposition.

Reed and Glass Assail Move.

"I think it is meaningless," said Senator Glass after he read the message. "They say they will not undertake to force the abrogation of the rule at the opening of the convention, which is a clear implication they will try it again later on. I cannot agree to any such thing as that."

Ex-Governor Harry F. Byrd, Virginia's candidate for the nomination, was standing beside Senator Glass as he voiced his objections to the Roosevelt pronouncement. Mr. Byrd started to say something, but Mr. Glass silenced him with the remark:

"You better keep quiet and I will do the chastising for the family."

Across the way in the headquarters of ex-Senator Reed of Missouri the rejection was as prompt and emphatic. Mr. Reed recalled Governor Roosevelt's defense of the two-thirds rule in previous conventions. He was reluctant, he added, to think that Governor Roosevelt on those occasions had made statements "which did not reveal what he really believed."

When the message was shown to Governor Smith, he was not inclined at first to comment, but later changed his mind, saying:

"I am uncompromisingly and absolutely in favor of the hundred-year-old rule of the Democratic party calling for a nomination by a two-thirds vote. Any man who cannot secure the votes of two-thirds of the delegates should not be the nominee of the convention."

Jouett Shouse's reaction to the message was expressed as follows:

"The Roosevelt forces attempted in an improper way and at an improper time to upset a century-old tradition of the Democratic party. Without defense or criticism of the two-thirds rule, if it is to be abrogated it must be done in an orderly manner, not on the very eve of the nomination, and must carry with it abolition of the unit rule. The two actions, if taken, must be synonymous to insure the opportunity for a fair nomination by a clear majority.

"It is unbelievable that this mistaken attempt should be made. It is gratifying that the response to the effort by the convention delegates was such as to cause its abandonment."

Delegations Continue to Caucus.

The story was the same everywhere within the opposition lines. To a man the leaders took the Governor's gesture of friendship and good-will with a "large grain of salt." They did not see in what he proposed much difference from the original abrogation plan of Mr. Farley. The result was no slowing up in the fight.

Meanwhile State delegations continue to caucus. The decisions reached in those held today follow:

ALABAMA, 24 Votes—Voted 16 to 6½ to uphold the two-thirds rule. Vote on permanent chairman of convention postponed until morning caucus. For committees: Resolutions, William C. Fitts; rules, Cecil H. Young; credentials, Michael M. Solley; permanent organization, A. H. Carmichael.

FLORIDA, 14 Votes—Unanimous for abrogation and Senator Walsh of Montana for permanent chairman. For committees: Resolutions, Robert H. Anderson; credentials, Frank Wideman; rules, E. Clay Lewis; permanent organization, John M. Coe.

INDIANA, 30 Votes—Unanimous for election of Mr. Shouse as permanent chairman. Delegation stands 20 to 10 against abrogation of two-thirds rule. Thomas Taggart and Mrs. Samuel B. Ralston elected members of national committee, Frank M. McHale elected chairman of delegation.

MICHIGAN, 38 Votes—Decided under unit rule for abrogation. No action taken in caucus, but delegation is expected to vote for Walsh. Horatio J. Abbott and Miss Evelyn Marshon elected members of national committee. For committees: Resolutions, William A. Comstock; credentials, Michael J. Hart; permanent organization, W. Alfred Debo; rules, James H. Baker.

SOUTH CAROLINA, 18 Votes—Decision on two-thirds rule postponed until morning caucus. Unanimous under unit rule in endorsing Senator Walsh for permanent chairman, the actual vote being 14½ to 3½. Members of working committees in the convention: Resolutions, Senator Fay Des Portes; rules, A. R. Dagnall; credentials, J. Emil Harley; permanent organization, Thomas F. Pearce.

TENNESSEE, 24 Votes—No action on two-thirds rule, but delegation was standing 17 to 7 for abrogation. A number of members were wavering toward the anti-abrogation camp. Delegation will vote for Walsh for permanent chairman.

June 28, 1932

WALSH VICTORY ENDS LONG, SHARP CLASH

Davis's Plea for Reward to Shouse Is Answered by Dill's Appeal for Montanan.

SMITH FAILS TO TAKE PART

Outcome Is in Doubt Until Roll-Call Is Half Over—Winner Is Congratulated by Rival.

By TURNER CATLEDGE.

Special to THE NEW YORK TIMES.

CHICAGO, June 28.—The fight over the permanent chairmanship of the Democratic National Convention resulted today in a complete victory for the friends of Governor Roosevelt when Senator Walsh, veteran pilot of the Madison Square Garden convention of 1924, was elected over Jouett Shouse, chairman of the party's executive committee, by a vote of 626 to 528.

Despite all the efforts of the so-called anti-Roosevelt forces, crystallized in an eloquent appeal by John W. Davis, Democratic standard bearer in 1924, the convention voted to adopt a report of its committee on permanent organization, recommending the nomination of Senator Walsh.

By its action the convention also rejected the recommendation of the subcommittee of the Democratic National Committee which arranged at a Chicago meeting in April that Mr. Shouse have the honor.

The Roosevelt forces were obviously gratified by the outcome. James A. Farley, manager for the New Yorker, made no effort to conceal his joy.

"I am satisfied with the result," he said. "Everything went off as expected. That goes for all three votes."

He was speaking also of the votes on the report of the committee on credentials, also Roosevelt victories.

* * * * *

Shouse Congratulates Walsh.

The outcome of the Walsh-Shouse test was in doubt until well over half of the roll had been called. While a number of the first States called voted against the minority report, which favored Mr. Shouse, larger groups of votes from California, Texas, Ohio, New York and New Jersey kept the balloting at the height of interest.

The uncertainty as to the outcome was augmented as well by the cheering. Mr. Shouse was backed by the loudest cheering section but much of it came from the galleries.

As Senator Barkley, temporary chairman, announced the result of the vote, he appointed Senators Dill and Bulkley and Mrs. Caroline O'Day of New York to escort the Montana Senator to the rostrum.

Dignified and calm, dressed in white trousers and blue coat, with his spectacles dangling from a black cord, Senator Walsh mounted the platform with his escort.

The first to shake his hand was Senator Wheeler, his colleague. Not far behind was Mr. Shouse who congratulated the victor.

* * * * *

June 29, 1932

Roaring Delegates in Parades Give The Galleries Their Money's Worth

Democrats, in Their "Quiet Way," Begin Task of Choosing Nominee, as Orators, Organs and Bands Vie in Spurring Demonstrations—Marchers, With Standards, Choke Aisles.

By F. RAYMOND DANIELL.

Special to THE NEW YORK TIMES.

CHICAGO, Friday, July 1.—Flags waved, bands played, whistles shrilled and the crowd roared all yesterday afternoon and last night and way into the early hours of this morning as the Democrats, in national convention assembled, began in their quiet way to get two-thirds of their number to agree upon a Presidential nominee.

While that was being done in the hotels downtown, great gusts of effulgent eloquence boomed and billowed through the spacious Stadium and out over the more spacious and probably cooler country side. Caught in its path the standards of many States were uprooted and carried away like pine trees in a simoom.

The cash customers got their money's worth of oratory and spectacles, and the candidates, no matter how slight their voting strength, had fine parades.

More than a little shoe leather was worn out, some straw hats were rendered virtually useless, and the only collar that withstood the day was the one worn by William G. McAdoo, who denies it is celluloid.

The chowder and marching clubs supporting the candidacies of Governor Roosevelt, Speaker Garner and plain Al Smith all provided colorful and diverting interludes between the nominating and seconding speeches.

There was a good deal of harmless lunacy loose in the convention hall, but that is what the spectators paid for and expected.

Delegates Ready at Cue.

John E. Mack, the Poughkeepsie lawyer of Stillman and Daddy Browning fame, put Governor Roosevelt's name before the delegates. It was he who nominated Mr. Roosevelt for State Senator, his first public office, some twenty years ago.

Mr. Mack is no spellbinder, but the New York Governor did not wait for the opening of the convention to corral the delegates for his stampede.

Not many of the delegates for Roosevelt were listening to what was said about him. They were too busy draping their standards with chromos of his seriously pleasant countenance and getting ready to swarm into the aisles at the proper cue, which in all cases is, "Gentlemen, I give you," &c.

Young James Roosevelt, the Governor's son, seized the New York standard from beside John F. Curry, leader of Tammany Hall, who showed his self-control and sales resistance by remaining seated.

The Tammany leader made no objection to lending the pine pole and its cardboard placard to young Jim, who charged down the aisles like a sophomore storming the goal posts of a rival college after his team had won.

As the tall and handsome young man, whose hair is just beginning the turn, passed the box where his younger brother, Franklin D. Roosevelt Jr., was sitting the latter scrambled over the rail into the bull ring and helped bear the guidon of the State which elected their father to the Governorship by the largest plurality in history. It was surprising that some of their fine young frenzy did not spread to the galleries.

Looking out over the floor of the convention, it seemed at first glance that a miracle had happened—that the Democrats had all agreed on Roosevelt without so much as a debate, let alone a roll-call.

That was an illusion wrought by the astute Jim Farley, the Governor's manager, who had slyly distributed fans with the candidate's picture printed on both sides. Even Alfalfa Bill Murray's loyal Oklahoma delegation was too weak to resist the temptation to use them, and the effect was startling.

It was all done with fans, however, for there were a lot of State standards held as firmly to the floor as though they were imbedded in concrete.

For the most part, though, they were hidden by the Roosevelt banners and posters, which formed a moving signboard between the press boxes and the convention floor. These showed the usual marks of genuine genius and originality.

Frank McLaughlin and Dr. E. M. Tigner of Warm Springs, Ga., carried a placard inscribed as follows:

The Ship of State is going past,
There is no captain at the mast!
Time has come your votes to cast
And put a captain at the mast!
ROOSEVELT.

Some of the old salts in the Massachusetts delegation said they had always thought a captain's place was on the bridge. The strangest of all the banners perhaps was one reading:

"New York's delegates are loyal to you and will see that you come true."

That was a surprise to everybody, including some members of the delegation, which kept quietly in its seats throughout the forty minutes of the demonstration's duration. One notable exception was Lieutenant Governor Lehman.

Georgians Hurl Serpentines.

Georgia's delegation marched by hurling paper serpentines, one of which twined itself around the broad shoulders of Jim Farley, who stood upon the platform throughout the first of the endurance contests, looking as pleased as the cat which has just swallowed a canary is supposed to look.

Camera men were scrambling simian-like about the rostrum. Mr. Farley posed sheepishly with a ten-gallon hat on his head, a stunt which once tried even the great popularity of former President Coolidge.

Then he posed with the hat waving about above his head. He posed drinking a glass of water and waving the pinetree flag of Vermont high above the heads of the surging crowd.

While the photography was going on, the crowd around Farley increased. It was well that the committee on arrangements saw to it that the rostrum was supported by steel girders.

Through the huddle of men came the sleek head of J. Bruce Kremer, national committeeman from Montana, just in time for the pictures.

There was a disturbance on the platform and out of it came another of the Roosevelt leaders, no less a person than the "Kingfish," Senator Huey Long of Louisiana.

Girls Swept Off Feet.

Down the aisles the delegates were demonstrating how completely they had been swept off their feet.

One girl was, literally. A cool fresh figure in a red dress, she rode by the speakers' stand on the shoulders of two perspiring men, whose knees sagged badly after two circuits of the floor.

"Happy Days Are Here Again," the organ thundered.

A girl in white rode piggy-back around the floor. A delegate from Nebraska played the part of the downtrodden sex in that little tableau.

Roosevelt pictures were carried in every conceivable way—pinned fore and aft on delegates who looked like sandwich men advertising sales of two-pants suits; made fast to the business end of new brooms and dangling on ribbons from the crooked ends of walking sticks, sold to the delegates by street hawkers for from two bits to a dollar.

The demonstrators were lagging when a middle-Western matron, in a burst of enthusiasm, pushed through the crowd on the rostrum and inspired the perspiring delegates to further efforts by putting her all into a rendition of "Ioway, Ioway—That's Where the Tall Corn Grows."

After that Senator Thomas Walsh, the chairman, who wears the service stripe of the famous convention of 1924, decided that fun was fun and tried to call a halt.

"If you really feel the need of exercise," roared the grim-visaged and stern old chairman, "go outside and take it."

The Rooseveltians gave way easily, for they had no mark to shoot at. Had they known what was coming later they might not have been so easily persuaded.

The convention quieted down while Senator Connally of Texas gave them John Nance Garner in a voice that could have carried over the mesas of the West as easily as it did through the amplifiers of the stadium.

1,000 in Garner Parade.

Speaker Garner's delegates are not many. Include California's 44 and the 46 from Texas and you have them all. Either the votes from those States are divided into infinitesimal fractions or there was skulduggery at the gate, for instead of 100 marchers there were more than 1,000, led by the "old gray mare band," especially imported, duty free, for the occasion.

Every one of them carried a banner with the Speaker in characteristic pose, with upraised gavel thereon. There was an enfilade of banners and placards, but only two State standards in the parade.

It had "pep," though, thanks largely to a lithesome girl who sang "I've Been Working on the Railroad" and "Dixie" while tap dancing on a chair on the platform.

She was Miss Melvena Passmore, for the Speaker to the last wave of the Lone Star flags with which she wigwagged encouragement to her friends.

Mr. McAdoo, tall and gaunt, with an angular smile upon his face, marched by with two lovely ladies upon his arm. One of them was his daughter. It was a noisy and peppy demonstration, and it might have lasted more than the thirty-two minutes it did if Senator Walsh had not called a halt. He apparently was satisfied with the 1924 convention for the record it hung up for endurance.

Galleries Join Smith Acclaim.

The demonstration for former Governor Smith was the longest and noisiest of the whole session, and it was the only one in which the galleries joined, except to the extent of booing some of the speakers who arose to second the nomination of Governor Roosevelt.

Smith banners popped up in the balconies as the spectators waved handkerchiefs and flags and showered confetti. A roar with greater volume than a steamship whistle rose from 20,000 throats.

A stout and vigorous lady in the balcony right above the rostrum took a straw hat from the head of the portly gentleman next to her and bashed the top right out with her good right fist, clamping what was left down upon her head like a halo.

The man did not seem to mind, for he took the flat piece of straw that was his share and sailed it out over the floor.

A convivial-minded quartet took possession of the platform and sang those old favorites of the saloon which must never return—"Sweet Adeline" and "How Dry I Am."

More talent climbed up with them and went through ritualistic gestures with glasses and a brown jug.

With a flag waving above the entire cast, it looked like the final ensemble of a burlesque show.

Smith Fans March in Waltz Time.

How much of the zeal of the demonstrators was due to the personality of the "Happy Warrior" and how much to the appealing eloquence of Governor Joseph B. Ely of Massachusetts, who made his nominating speech, was hard to tell. The Governor proved that he could jerk tears as well as any sob sister.

The balconies were clapping hands in time with the music which, after Governor Ely's address was, properly, chiefly in three-quarter time.

Smith fans march to waltz time as naturally as the others do to the strains of "California Here I Come." They have been practicing on the "Sidewalks of New York" for nigh on to eight years.

Massachusetts had led the way, followed closely by New Jersey and Rhode Island to mention only a few of the States.

The standard of New York, which had been borne in the Roosevelt parade, was paraded again for Mr. Smith, but Mr. Curry, Mayor Walker and John H. McCooey observed strict neutrality. They have made a record for fence-sitting unequalled by any one but "Shipwreck" Kelly.

The demonstration started at twenty-two minutes of 5 and was still going strong an hour later. Screams of protest and rebellion from the galleries and the floor followed Chairman Walsh's order that it end.

Encouraged by the noise they had made, the anti-Roosevelt group then voted for a recess to give the leaders in the hotel rooms a chance to catch their breath.

Doves Freed in Byrd "Show."

The managers of the Roosevelt, Smith and Garner forces took a lesson in showmanship from Colonel Henry Breckenridge, campaign manager for Virginia's favorite son, former Governor Harry Flood Byrd.

The moment the dynamic Senator Glass concluded his nominating speech, the Richmond Light Infantry Blues marched onto the floor in their colorful uniforms, topped off with plumed kepis.

Miss Marguerite Penfield, a charming débutante of Winchester, climbed upon a table on the rostrum waving the blue banner of the Old Dominion and at that moment from the speakers' platform a covey of white doves was released to flutter affrightedly among the blazing floodlights and the bunting-draped rafters.

It was the restrained sort of demonstration fit for a gentleman from Virginia. The band marched around the aisle several times; it big bass drum, too big for the drummer to manage alone, was supported by a darky as bent as Old Black Joe himself.

On the platform, Governor John Garland Pollard and Rear Admiral Richard E. Byrd waved pleasantly at the convention crowd.

Traylorites Hit the Trail.

The Traylorites hit the trail for him when the Byrd stampeders had been corralled by the chairman. Mr. Traylor presumably had friends in the Texas and Mississippi delegations, as their standards were on the march for him.

Each marcher bore a placard with a uniform slogan, "Traylor for President." He is president now—of the First National Bank.

With the temperature somewhere in the tropical register, the organist essayed "In the Good Old Summer Time," and the demonstrators gave up.

March Forty Minutes for Ritchie.

At midnight the name of Albert Cabell Ritchie, Governor of Maryland, was presented to the convention, and for the next forty minutes the flag of Lord Baltimore waved above the coatless delegates from all corners of the floor. Mrs. W. W. Lenahan was choir leader.

A black-haired Lorelei in a flaming red dress, she stood upon the speakers' promontory as near the chandelier as she could climb, flaunting the colors of the Baltimore oriole and luring the passing guidons of the States. In her bouquet of standards were included those of Virginia, New Jersey, Mississippi, Illinois, Pennsylvania and many others.

Senator Huey P. Long, a Roosevelt leader, joined the parade when the lady blew him a kiss, but it was only in fun. There still remained many more "men of destiny" to be described in glowing terms, but Democrats are as prodigal with time as the galleries are with cheers and boos.

* * * * *

ROOSEVELT NOMINATED ON FOURTH BALLOT

ROOSEVELT VOTE IS 945

Smith His Nearest Rival, With 190 1-2 as Four States Stick to End.

McADOO, BREAKS DEADLOCK

Casts California's 44 Amid Wild Demonstration After Garner Releases Texans.

RITCHIE MEN FALL IN LINE

Tammany Holds Aloof—Cermak Forced to Appeal to the Booing Galleries.

By ARTHUR KROCK.

Special to THE NEW YORK TIMES.

CHICAGO, July 1.—California and Texas, which came to Chicago pledged to Speaker John N. Garner, broke the deadlock on the Presidential nomination in the Democratic National Convention on the fourth ballot tonight by casting their ninety votes for Governor Franklin D. Roosevelt of New York.

This started a bandwagon rush, in which only New York—the nominee's home State—Massachusetts, Rhode Island, New Jersey and Connecticut declined to join, and Mr. Roosevelt was selected by a vote of 945, the convention's two-thirds requirement being 769 1-3. His nearest rival, Alfred E. Smith, received 190½ votes, the four States named sticking to him to the last.

Roosevelt to Fly to Chicago.

Governor Roosevelt, as soon as he heard of his success, sent a message which the permanent chairman, Senator Thomas J. Walsh of Montana read to the convention. The Governor announced that he will be here tomorrow, coming by airplane from Albany, to address the convention and to receive his formal notification, thus avoiding the expense of a more formal and distant ceremony.

The national committee will also be reorganized under the eye of the nominee tomorrow with his convention manager, James A. Farley of New York, as chairman. A great occasion, led by Senator Walsh, with bands and speeches, is to be made of the notification ceremonies.

Senator Walsh, the permanent chairman, sent the following telegram to Governor Roosevelt:

"The convention extends its greetings and assurance of fealty to our nominee and welcomes the news that he will be here with us tomorrow."

William G. McAdoo, former Secretary of the Treasury, was the voice of Mr. Roosevelt's destiny. When the name of California was called by the reading clerk he took the platform to explain the change of the vote in the Western States. The news of the impending action had spread throughout the delegates.

But the galleries had not heard about it, and, when they sensed what was happening, the boos and yells with which they expressed their anger over the defeat of Alfred E. Smith required the efforts of Mayor Anthony J. Cermak of Chicago, whose presence was demanded by Permanent Chairman Thomas J. Walsh, to restore a measure of quiet.

McAdoo Speaks for West.

Mr. McAdoo said that California had not come to Chicago to deadlock the convention, that Democracy had suffered enough, as in 1924 when he himself had almost polled a majority, by such methods. He said that the opinion of the West, in which Speaker Garner joined, was that Democrats should fight Republicans and not one another.

He did not say what has been known here for several days, that William Randolph Hearst, who has great influence in the California delegation and who "discovered" the qualification of Mr. Garner as a candidate, pressed the shift to Mr. Roosevelt because he feared that a deadlock might produce Newton D. Baker or another candidate with whose international policies he is not in agreement. Mr. Hearst also is a believer in majority rule and the Texas-California contingent was responding to his ideas on that subject.

Throughout a feverish day in which, after a whole day and night of sessions, Governor Roosevelt had polled on three ballots 682 of the 769½ he needed, his leaders and their opponents were engaged in efforts to accomplish their ends. For a time it was said that Tammany was ready to cast its vote for Mr. Roosevelt if his lines held for another ballot. At the same time Mr. Smith, John W. Davis, James M. Cox and other national Democratic leaders were bending every effort to win over Roosevelt delegations, convinced that his loosely assembled strength would wilt under adversity.

But California and Texas declined to give Tammany the credit for the nomination of a Presidential candidate. They caucused at 6 o'clock after Texas delegates had besieged Speaker Garner's campaign manager, Representative Samuel W. Reyburn, for release.

Garner to Accept Vice Presidency.

The Speaker, when he heard what was going on, capitulated. While the fourth ballot was in progress Senator Corell Hull of Tennessee said that Speaker Garner had accepted a tender of the Vice Presidential nomination and would be chosen by the convention at its final session tomorrow.

Almost as soon as Mr. McAdoo began to speak standards of States went up in tiers and the space above the delegates was soon a forest of guidons. The organ pealed and the band played.

While Mr. McAdoo was waiting for the enthusiasm to subside, James A. Farley, the successful manager of the Roosevelt campaign, rushed to the platform to slap the California rescuer on the back.

When the celebration had been going on for about ten minutes the only State standards not to be observed in the air were those of Maryland, Rhode Island, Ohio, New Jersey, the Philippines, Massachusetts and Connecticut, practically all Smith States.

Demonstration Stops McAdoo.

At the start of his speech Mr. McAdoo said:

"We think that a contest too prolonged would bring schisms in the party which could not be cured before election. In a case which requires a surgical operation a life may be lost by delay.

"We believe that California should take a stand to end this contest, should take a stand regardless of her own interest.

"Our belief in Democracy is so strong that we feel, when a candidate comes to a convention as the choice of the popular will and has behind him almost 700 votes—"

Then the demonstration broke loose.

The galleries, disappointed over the defeat of Al Smith, refused for several minutes to let the proceedings continue. They booed and shrieked.

"I appeal to the Mayor of the city of Chicago," shouted Senator Walsh, "for the power to control this convention."

Mayor Cermak came to the stand and demanded order of the unruly crowd.

"Let me appeal to my friends in the galleries," he said. "The Democratic National Committee were kind enough to come to our city. You are their guests. Please act like guests. Please, I appeal to you, allow this great gathering to go back home with nothing but pleasant memories of our city. Please," he said.

McAdoo Rebukes Galleries.

This got applause, but the booing began immediately again.

"Judge in the future," called Mr. McAdoo, "whether or not this is the kind of hospitality Chicago accords to its guests. I intend to say what I have to say here without regard to what the galleries or any one else thinks."

"When any man is within reach of the two-thirds he is entitled to the nomination," continued Mr. McAdoo, "and California proposes to do her share to see that the popular will is respected. We came here for the great Texan, John N. Garner, for whom we feel love and affection and respect. But he hasn't as many votes as Mr. Roosevelt and he is in accord with the position I take here tonight. The great State of Texas and the great State of California are acting in accord with what we believe best for America and for the Democratic party. I would like to see Democrats fight Republicans, and not Democrats, unlike 1924.

"Our decision represents the will of these delegates. And so, my friends, California casts forty-four votes for Franklin D. Roosevelt."

Cheers from the convention and moans from the galleries greeted this crucial announcement.

When Illinois was called, Mayor Cermak asked leave to explain the vote first. He announced the release of his delegates by Melvin A. Traylor and said that, with Indiana's 30, Illinois would cast her 58 votes for Roosevelt, 88 votes in all.

Thomas Taggart Jr., speaking for Indiana, confirmed Mayor Cermak's statement and cast the Hoosier State on the bandwagon.

Iowa, which had been chafing at her bonds, cast her 26 votes for Roosevelt on this occasion without a demurrer.

The development as to the Pacific and Southwestern States came as a result of the unwillingness of William G. McAdoo and William Randolph Hearst either to permit Tammany to get the credit for the Presidential nomination, or by further resistance to Mr. Roosevelt, to risk the nomination of Newton D. Baker, whose international policies are disapproved by Mr. Hearst.

Conferences in rooms of the hotels on the Lake Michigan waterfront between the managers of the various candidates and leaders of the State delegations kept many of the most important figures in the convention downtown, and there were few of them present when Senator Walsh called the convention to order at 10:55, Eastern Standard Time, and introduced the Rev. Dr. John Thompson, pastor of the First Methodist Episcopal Church, to deliver the invocation.

With the prospect of a nomination for President in sight, the galleries had filled by the time the convention opened. Most of the missing party leaders, hurrying from their conference rooms by taxicab and automobile, arrived just before or during Dr. Thompson's prayer and went to their seats at once to get ready for the fourth ballot, which seemed likely to be decisive.

When California was reached on the fourth ballot William G. McAdoo addressed the chair.

Leaders Resume Their Labors.

Before noon the sleepless leaders of the factions resumed their labors. Mr. Farley and his aides tried to patch up cracks in their delegations from Iowa, Minnesota, Michigan and Mississippi and prevent further fissures, and their rivals strove to make additional breaches in the Roosevelt defenses.

There was agreement that if the Governor's lines held firm, or comparatively firm, he would probably be nominated on the fourth or fifth ballot. The report was generally accepted that Tammany stood ready to contribute the remainder of the two-thirds.

With this prospect, the managers of most of the rival candidates and a group of national party leaders worked feverishly all day to prove to Tammany that defections in the Roosevelt lines demonstrated that his support could not stand the analysis of protracted balloting, that his group was fused synthetically out of local organization necessities and had no common bond of devotion to the Governor himself.

National Leaders on Firing Line.

Laboring on the battlefront were James M. Cox, Alfred E. Smith and John W. Davis, former Presidential candidates, each of whom cherished a lingering hope that this year's standard might again be entrusted to him.

Mayor Frank Hague of Jersey City, floor leader of the "Stop Roosevelt" brigade, who has burned his bridges behind him; Governor Joseph B. Ely of Massachusetts, who put an inferential slur against Mr. Roosevelt in his speech nominating Mr. Smith yesterday; Carter Glass of Virginia; the national chairman, John J. Raskob, and others of country-wide fame joined these in the savage struggle to add the name of Mr. Roosevelt to those of Martin Van Buren and Champ Clark as the only Democrats since the party was organized who gained a convention majority but to whom the Presidential nomination was denied.

Neither Van Buren nor Clark, by the way, had a majority as large as the 682 polled by Mr. Roosevelt on the third and final ballot of the preceding session.

Accessions and Defections.

These party chieftains were encouraged by their belief that three ballots without two-thirds was the uttermost resistance degree of the Roosevelt line. That has been said many times since it became certain that the Governor would have a majority, and tonight it was put to the test.

The hope that Alabama, where, Mr. Farley said, "special interests" have been especially busy, would be among the first delegations to break from New York's Governor was quashed late in the afternoon by former Governor W. W. Brandon, chairman of the delegation.

He said that the nation's Democrats "will not submit to the dictation of a few cities like Jersey City, Tammany New York and Boston"; that his entire delegation agreed to that and that Alabama would vote for Mr. Roosevelt until he was nominated.

But news trickling in from Mississippi, Iowa, Michigan and Minnesota of increasing anti-Roosevelt strength was considered an offset to Governor Brandon's declaration and the delegates of those four States were watched intently as the fourth ballot was taken.

Look to Six States for Aid.

For their part, the Roosevelt leaders concentrated on Indiana, Illinois, Pennsylvania, New York, Texas and California. They looked to these as the sister of Bluebeard's wife looked to the highroad for the help which alone could avert tragedy. There may not have been definite terms proffered, but the rumors flew fast that Vice Presidential nominations and other forms of preferment in return for aid in time of trouble were at least suggested in conferences.

The large majority polled by Governor Roosevelt on the first three ballots put him in the position of being certain of the nomination if one large State or two medium-sized ones should turn to him before his lines broke. Therefore it did not require any specific offers to impress State leaders with the fact that his captains this afternoon were more able to insure delivery on promises than those of any other candidate.

Texas and California Caucus.

Texas and California seethed with mixed emotions over the repeated reports that in exchange for the Vice Presidential nomination for Speaker John N. Garn r they would move over to the Roosevelt reservation tonight. Delegates from these States opposed both to the repudiation and its possible materialization demanded a caucus. Others pressed for release.

For some days the Roosevelt leaders have been expecting more than suggestive aid from William Randolph Hearst, who had much to do with the Garner victory in California and who "discovered" the Speaker as a Presidential candidate.

Late this afternoon they were told that Mr. Hearst had decided not to plump for the Governor, believing that, in the event of Mr. Roosevelt's defeat, "the worst he could get would be Governor Ritchie of Maryland." Accordingly, the Roosevelt strategists sent word that the defeat of the Governor would be more likely to bring about the nomination of Newton D. Baker, anathema to Mr. Hearst because of his views on international affairs.

Move for Baker.

In the balloting which ended at 9:30 this morning Mr. Baker got votes on all three tests. The emergence of his name was swiftly followed by the unmasking of a headquarters for the former Secretary of War on C floor of the Congress Hotel. One of his former aides, who has thus far con-

The Democratic Nominee

© New York Times Studio Photo.

FRANKLIN DELANO ROOSEVELT.

fined his activities to sending out complimentary pamphlets about Mr. Baker, received newspaper men, exchanged views and prepared to be the representative of an active candidate.

Among the States which, during the day, was credited with having pro-Baker sentiment was Mississippi. This delegation presents one of the most peculiar aspects of the Roosevelt line-up. Several times it has wavered and it has been held only by strong efforts by Governor S. M. Conner and Senators Pat Harrison and Hubert Stephens. It is still a mystery why Mississippi has been so lightly infused with the pro-Roosevelt sentiment of all its Southern neighbors.

The most talked of delegation this afternoon was, of course, New York. The thrill of its dramatic poll lingered with the members of the convention. Later it was explained that this was "strategy" to enable Mayor James J. Walker to make a public demonstration of his indifference to what Governor Roosevelt does with the Seabury charges by coming in late and, with the eyes and ears of the convention strained in his direction, casting his vote for Mr. Smith.

To inquirers it was pointed out that there is really no love lost among the Mayor, John F. Curry and John H. McCooey on the one hand and Mr. Smith on the other. So when the balloting was resumed tonight New York continued to hold the real centre of the titanic picture.

Hague Tactics a Surprise Today.

But no surprise of the early morning hours today was greater than when Mayor Hague suddenly joined the efforts of the Roosevelt leaders to force a ballot before recess. Through fourteen hours of oratory and parades the anti-Roosevelt leaders had been doing everything possible to wear out the delegates and to force an adjournment.

About 2 o'clock they satisfied themselves that their barrier would hold for several ballots at least. Convinced that to demonstrate this was the one hope to keep the nomination away from Governor Roosevelt, Mr. Hague voted his State solidly against the adjournment demanded by Senator Tom Connally of Texas. If human nature could have borne the strain, Mr. Hague would have kept the convention in session all day today.

The nomination of Mr. Roosevelt on the fourth ballot and the agreement to select Mr. Garner ends one of the tensest convention periods in the party's history, considering its brevity. As the Roosevelt forces more and more established their control over the convention's machinery the bitterness of Mr. Smith, Mayor Hague and others grew.

Twice Roosevelt Nears Defeat.

Mr. Smith frantically besought delegates to deny the palm to his successor at Albany and the man who twice placed him in nomination for the Presidency. Mr. Cox rushed to Chicago for secret conferences and Mr. Davis took the platform to help elect Jouett Shouse, executive chairman of the national committee, permanent chairman of the convention over Senator Thomas J. Walsh of Montana. It was conceded that if the Roosevelt forces lost this test the nomination probably was lost with it. So Mr. Davis did all he could.

A week ago tonight, and once again on Sunday night, the Farley management almost lost control of the convention and the chances of their candidate for the nomination by losing control of their own associates. Prompted by Senator Huey P. Long of Louisiana, Senator B. K. Wheeler of Montana and others, a Roosevelt conference precipitately decided to press upon the convention a proposal to nominate by a simple majority instead of by the century-old two-thirds rule.

Their adversaries were quick to seize the advantage, and for three days, while Mr. Roosevelt was represented as entirely in sympathy with the project, his forces were hammered as faith-breakers and the candidate as a welsher in the middle of the game. When a check-up showed that the new rule would be beaten, Mr. Roosevelt ordered that the plan be abandoned, but reserved the right to reinvoke it should a deadlock ensue.

That very night in the rules committee Richard P. Metcalf of Nebraska, a Roosevelt delegate, caused the passage of an arrangement to apply the simple majority rule after six ballots without result. This was done without consultation with either Mr. Farley or the Governor, as the previous action had been taken without consultation with Mr. Roosevelt. During the night, after many telephone talks with Albany, Mr. Farley arranged that this rule too should be abandoned and told the rules committee that Mr. Roosevelt's managers were "000 per cent for the two-thirds rule."

After this crisis passed there were some doubts and dangers. Mississippi, Michigan, Minnesota and Alabama sprouted seeds of revolt, and, had not herculean efforts been applied, one or all of these might have broken after the first ballot. But they were persuaded to wait around awhile for the bandwagon, and they did not have to wait long.

The nomination on the fourth ballot dispelled a theory that had been generally accepted as to Mr. Roosevelt's staying powers in the convention. Few believed that if two-thirds did not come on a second ballot, a third would show anything but recession of his strength. Perhaps if the convention had adjourned after the second ballot early this morning, as Mr. Farley wanted it to do, an effective barrier might have been raised, although the attitude of California and Texas, as revealed tonight, would have made that difficult.

At any rate, the Hague leadership insisted on a third ballot, giving the wavering Roosevelt delegates no opportunity to test the advisability of breaking from their ties. This blunder may have had a great effect on the events of today.

It was sudden change of tactics, for all through Wednesday afternoon and night and Thursday's early hours the Hague leadership had been delaying proceedings in every possible way in an effort to avert a vote for which the Roosevelt leaders were pressing. They prolonged and added to the oratory, they artificially stimulated the parades until it was 4:27 A. M., before the roll-call of the States began.

But by that time Mr. Hague had decided to insist upon balloting. He was sure that the Garner delegates and the other "Favorite Son" groups would permanently make part of his anti-Roosevelt bloc. In this he proved badly mistaken.

Mr. McAdoo found the opportunity for which he had been waiting since 1924. Tonight he was the hero of the convention and its central figure. What Bryan did for Wilson in 1912, Wilson's son-in-law did for Roosevelt tonight, and both moves were to prevent Tammany and the East from choosing or blocking the choice of the Democratic nominee for President of the United States.

LANDON PATH EASED BY RORABACK'S AID

Connecticut Leader's Move to Back Kansan on the First Ballot Surprises Hilles.

FIGHT COALITION TICKET

Committeemen at Cleveland Fear Party Would Lose Local Prestige With Democrat Running.

By CHARLES R. MICHAEL
Special to THE NEW YORK TIMES.

CLEVELAND, June 2.—Governor Landon's path to the Republican nomination for President was made easier today by the announcement of J. Henry Roraback, Connecticut Republican leader, that his State would cast its nineteen votes for the Kansan on the first ballot.

Arriving to attend the meeting of the convention committee on arrangements, Mr. Roraback found the opposition to Landon lessening among the eastern conservative leaders.

He predicted that Mr. Landon would be nominated and expressed hope that Representative James Wadsworth of New York would be his running mate.

Mr. Roraback's desertion of the group of uninstructed delegate States leaves Charles D. Hilles of New York and David A. Reed of Pennsylvania still holding out for a fuller consideration of Landon desirability. Both are reported weakening in the determination to await the second ballot before making a final choice.

The collapse of the triumvirate not only brings Governor Landon closer to the nomination but also lessens the tension in his camp over the apprehension that Herbert Hoover might stampede the convention and cause a deadlock.

Cheered by New Gains

Some wavering southern delegates and eastern conservatives are expected to be influenced by Mr. Roraback's action, the most important pro-Landon pre-convention move.

Assured of the support of New England States, except Maine and New Hampshire, the Landon managers were taking great comfort from reported underground developments. These include, they say, Massachusetts preparing to cast its full vote for Landon on the first ballot; Pennsylvania sweeping to him after twenty-four votes are given to Senator Borah, and a probability that Michigan may start the band wagon movement on the first ballot if conferences now in progress succeed.

A proposal is now being made to the Michigan leaders that Senator Vandenberg release the delegation of thirty-eight for Landon and he become his running mate.

Mr. Hilles declined to discuss the effect of the Roraback turn to Governor Landon. He was admittedly very much surprised that his old colleagues in the national committee, with whom he has stood in many political battles, should break ranks so early.

Reports here are that Landon sentiment is increasing in the New York delegation and that forty-two of the ninety delegates are counted as for Landon on the first ballot.

Mr. Hilles was also reticent on the reiterated proposal that the convention nominate a coalition ticket, with the Vice President an anti-New Deal Democrat.

Hamilton Seeks Early Victory

"The New York delegation will decide its position on the coalition ticket and its decision on the candidate when it meets here next week," Mr. Hilles said.

The Landon forces have in their camp some of the old "war horses" of the party. Two former national chairmen, John T. Adams and Claudius Huston, are actively engaged in lining up delegates for the Kansan.

The most active Hoover lieutenant associated with the Landon group is Ray Benjamin of California, who said today that, despite claims of divided opposition, "Landon will be nominated on an early ballot; it may be the first."

That is the goal John Hamilton, the Landon manager, has set for his fight. He is busily rounding up delegates who promised to be for Governor Landon on the second ballot and is urging them to show their colors at the outset.

If he could get Massachusetts and Michigan to join with Connecticut on the first ballot, Mr. Landon would apparently win the race in the opening stretch.

Ninety-two delegates in the convention are ready to vote for Mr. Hoover if the convention should become deadlocked, a manager for one of the avowed candidates said. Some in the Hoover faction have planned to force a deadlock after the former President addresses the convention.

Revival of the discussion of a coalition ticket proposal advanced two years ago by Senator Vandenberg and former Senator Reed of Pennsylvania met with little favor among the national committeemen. Most committeemen said privately that such a suggestion was not feasible and would destroy local prestige.

"I favor a coalition Cabinet, but not a coalition ticket," former Senator George H. Moses, one of the Knox managers, said.

Carl Bachmann, directing Mr. Borah's campaign, said:

"There cannot be a coalition ticket if the Republican party hopes to win. Let the anti-New Deal Democrats join us as the Independent Republicans joined the Democrats in 1932. I am against the proposal."

June 3, 1936

LANDON'S FOES JOIN IN STRATEGIC MOVE

Hope to Recess the Convention After Blocking Nomination for Several Ballots.

HIS POWER IS CHALLENGED

'Certain' First-Ballot Votes Are Put at 350 in Check-Up—Favorite Sons Boomed.

By JAMES A. HAGERTY
Special to THE NEW YORK TIMES.

CLEVELAND, June 7.—After almost abandoning hope of blocking the nomination of Governor Landon for President, supporters of rival candidates became active today and started a campaign to canvass arriving delegates with a view to preventing his being chosen on the first ballot.

It is the hope of the campaign managers for Senator Borah, Colonel Frank Knox, Senator Vandenberg, Senator Dickinson and others whose names will go before the convention to prevent Mr. Landon's nomination even on the second or third ballots after which a motion would be made to recess the convention.

Those opposed to Governor Landon believe that his defeat is certain if he fails to win the nomination at the session at which the balloting begins.

No formal coalition of the anti-Landon candidates has been formed, but a certain understanding to work to block the Landon nomination has been reached by the managers of their campaigns.

This understanding provides that representatives of each shall confer with delegates on their arrival and urge them to give careful consideration to each of the candidates and try to nominate the man who seems to them to be the best qualified and to have the best chance of election.

Every effort will be made to convince a majority of the delegates that the nomination is foreclosed to Mr. Landon, and that the claim of his managers for a first ballot nomination is without foundation.

A check by supporters of Colonel Knox is said to have indicated that Governor Landon has only about 350 certain first ballot votes, as compared with the more than 400 claimed by the Landon forces. It is a matter of record that about 800 of the 1,003 delegates are legally unpledged, although many of the 800 are known to favor the Kansas Governor.

Landon opponents in their talks with delegates will stress the inadvisability of nominating a man whose views on vital issues are, they declare, unknown.

An attempt will be made to create a demand that the Kansas Governor be asked in advance of the nomination to state his views on a money plank, social security and the advisability of a constitutional amendment to remedy the situation caused by the Supreme Court's invalidation of New York State's minimum wage law.

The opposition to Landon will declare that the election cannot be won by compromising with the New Deal and call for condemnation of Roosevelt policies.

Another argument to be made to the delegates will concern the political inexpediency of nominating a candidate for President whom Senator Borah will not support. This contention bore fruit today when two North Dakota delegates called on a prominent party leader and informed him that they doubted Mr. Landon or any other candidate could carry that State if Senator Borah was inactive in the campaign. A similar expression from a party leader in Montana was reported.

Hoover Help Is Expected

Help in the block-Landon movement is expected from the devoted followers of Herbert Hoover, who may muster seventy to seventy-five votes in the convention. Some of these delegates are reported ready to vote for Mr. Hoover as a complimentary gesture, whether or not his name is formally presented.

Mr. Hoover in addressing the convention Wednesday night is expected to give something of a description of the type of man whom the convention ought to nominate. It is believed that the picture will not fit Governor Landon.

An effort will also be made to stimulate the entrance of new "favorite son" candidates and to keep in the race "favorite sons" who have already entered. An attempt will be made, it is said, to enter Henry Anderson of Virginia, former Special Assistant Attorney General, in the hope of holding for him the votes of that State.

In addition, the anti-Landon leaders will try to start a backfire against John D. M. Hamilton, the Landon manager, who is being charged with steam-roller tactics in trying to put through the nomination on the first ballot by misleading the delegates by extravagant claims.

The delegates will be urged to make the convention a deliberative body, both on platform and candidates, and not to permit Mr. Hamilton to force platform and candidates upon the convention without opportunity for every delegate to vote for the candidates and platform planks of their preference.

Landon Men Seek Alliance

Several developments during the day led the members of the anti-Landon group to believe that Mr. Hamilton and other Landon supporters were not so certain of the nomination of the Kansas Governor as they have tried to make it appear.

The first was an overture from the Landon camp to the supporters of Colonel Knox for a possible alliance. This had no result. While no offer of the Vice Presidential nomination was made, Colonel Knox's friends were reported to have made it clear that the publisher was a candidate for the Presidential nomination only.

The other development concerned a proposal to give a substantial number of New York votes on the first ballot to Frank E. Gannett, the Rochester newspaper publisher. The proposal, a complimentary gesture, originated with Thomas D. Broderick, Monroe County chairman, and received support from delegates in other New York cities in which there are Gannett newspapers.

Mr. Hamilton, when informed of the proposal, is said to have objected on the ground that it was important to get as large a vote for Landon from New York as possible for its effect on States coming later in the roll call; this was interpreted as meaning Ohio and Pennsylvania in particular.

This reported objection of Mr. Hamilton was interpreted as indicating that he was by no means as certain of Governor Landon's nomination as newspaper reports had made it appear. New Yorkers here said it was exceedingly unlikely that Mr. Gannett would receive as many as the forty votes.

Mr. Broderick, who arrived today, admitted that there was a proposal for some of the New York delegates to vote for Mr. Gannett, but said he could not discuss the matter before the meeting of the New York delegation tomorrow night.

Senator Dickinson on his arrival ended rumors that the Iowa delegation would go to Governor Landon. He reiterated that his name would go before the convention, that he would join no combination to block anybody and that he sought to retain friends and not make enemies.

Senator Dickinson will be placed in nomination by Robert W. Colflesh of Des Moines, who was a candidate for Governor two years ago.

June 8, 1936

HOOVER ACCLAIMED IN DAY OF OVATIONS

Great Demonstration at Convention Follows Welcome at Railroad Station.

DISCUSSED AS NOMINEE

California Delegation, Stirred by Speech, Studies Advisability of Offering His Name.

By TURNER CATLEDGE

Special to THE NEW YORK TIMES.

CLEVELAND, June 10.—Former President Hoover arrived here today to become the center of a series of rousing demonstrations leading up to his speech tonight before the Republican convention. As a result his political stock again was put on a rising market.

Following his attack on the New Deal and, for him, the virtually unprecedented demonstration which came after he called his party members to a "Holy crusade for freedom," the California delegation went into session to discuss, among other things, the possibility of placing Mr. Hoover's name before the convention for the Presidential nomination.

Whether his home-State representatives or any other delegation nominate him or not, the opinion here was that his speech tonight, and the day of adulation preceding it, had put the former President in the position of an elder statesman whose advice and assistance will be sought and used during the coming campaign.

From the time he arrived here this morning from Chicago until he departed tonight for New York, Mr. Hoover was the center of attention.

Landon Supporters on the Alert

His presence was watched closely by those interested in the candidacy of Governor Landon of Kansas to see whether Mr. Hoover would give any encouragement to the groups which previously had been unable to get together to prevent the Kansan's nomination.

Mr. Hoover avoided private conversations during the day with any of the leading candidates. He and his spokesmen sought in every way to dispel the idea that he had come to Cleveland to rally the anti-Landon forces, as many had thought he would. He insisted on confining to his speech what he had to say, leaving interpretations to the delegates.

Tonight, after the speech and the tumultuous reception given him, many party leaders closely watched for the results of the session of the California delegates. The delegation adjourned late tonight, however, without taking any action relative to Mr. Hoover, but planned to meet again tomorrow.

An ovation that continued for fifteen minutes and was stopped only upon a personal appeal from Mr. Hoover himself, greeted him upon his arrival at the convention hall tonight.

As soon as Chairman Snell announced to the assemblage that Mr. Hoover was about to be conducted to the platform, the crowd of 15,000 persons literally jumped to its feet with a burst of cheering. The band in the rear of the hall took up the familiar Hoover campaign song:

"California, Here I Come."

Chairman Snell tried to quiet the crowd but could not be heard. The former President stood out on the platform, making no attempt for the moment to stop a demonstration far greater than that accorded him in the same hall when he appeared here in October, 1932, as a candidate for re-election.

Texas Delegates Ring Cowbells

As Mr. Snell waved and pounded for silence, the Texas delegation began ringing its cowbells. The Virginia and Tennessee contingents started a parade. Other State standards were raised high in the air.

Delegates all over the great hall tore up programs or other paper matter in their hands and threw it into the air.

Mr. Snell finally appealed to Mr. Hoover. The former President walked to the lectern and held up his hand for silence, but the crowd would not stop even then for several minutes. It did not understand that radio time was flying fast.

A crowd estimated at 8,000 greeted him when he arrived in the city on a morning train from Chicago. From that moment until he left his hotel this evening for the convention hall he was besieged by hundreds of delegates and spectators, most seeking to learn, hours in advance of his address, what stand he proposed to take.

Despite his own protestations that he was not a candidate for the nomination, the ex-President's well-wishers hoped during the day for a drive that would stampede the convention into naming him as its choice.

Soon after he arrived supporters in his own delegation from California raised the new slogan: "Hoover or his choice," but Mr. Hoover himself gave no sanction to the plan to put the nomination at his disposal.

The former President was evidently suprised by the reception he got when he arrived. His train stopped on the level beneath the main floor of the station, where he received the official welcome of the city from Mayor Harold H. Burton and was greeted by Chairman Fletcher of the Republican National Committee, who pinned a gold convention admission badge on Mr. Hoover's lapel.

Among the welcomers were former Secretary Hurley, former Postmaster General Brown and others of Mr. Hoover's former political and governmental associates.

Mr. Hoover evidently thought this was all there was to the greeting. But when he reached the upper concourse he found thousands of people jammed there to see him. Persons on every side grabbed for his hand, necessitating a quick call for a police escort to see him through the lobby of the station.

In front of the station, Mr. Hoover found other thousands to greet him. On his way through the building some one yelled "Hooray for Hoover," and several hundred joined in a demonstration, waving their hats, whistling and shouting.

The former President smiled broadly. In front of the station he obliged photographers by posing for his picture, and went through a few handshakes for the benefit of the newsreels. Then he was escorted by police through the crowd to his near-by hotel.

As he walked through the lobby he received another demonstration. He was taken to his rooms on a rear elevator.

Mr. Hoover did not remain in his room long. His spokesmen stated early that he would hold open door all day, except during the time he worked on his speech. It was not long before Mr. Hoover had taken up a stand in a convention room on the parlor floor, and within a few minutes persons were flocking through the corridors to see him.

Brief Meeting With Vandenberg

Among Mr. Hoover's first callers was Senator Vandenberg. Their meeting was short, and took place in the presence of fully 200 persons.

"Chief, how are you?" said Senator Vandenberg as he shook his former leader's hand. "I am glad to see you. You're looking fine."

Mr. Hoover responded with only a few words, which, according to Mr. Hoover's spokesmen, comprised the only conversation between him and Mr. Vandenberg.

The talk with former Senator Moses, one of the managers for Colonel Knox, was equally short. In fact, Mr. Moses simply joined the line of people who were pushing forward to shake the former President's hand.

The anti-Landonites among the regular delegates and spectators, hopeful that Mr. Hoover might say something to aid their fight, gravitated toward his room when he was not in the public parlor. Private conversations could be heard among these groups concerning developments and combinations which they believed Mr. Hoover could effect against the Kansas Governor if he would do so.

Several persons tried to talk with Mr. Hoover about the party outlook, particularly about his own chances to stampede the convention, but he would not listen. He would merely smile and turn to the next person in line, seeming to enjoy being the "mystery man" of the convention for the time being until he dispelled the suspense with his own words at the meeting tonight.

Mr. Hoover did not give out advance copies of his speech, partly, it was understood, because he wanted to work on the text still further but also partly because he did not want its contents to be noised about beforehand.

Appears a Different Hoover

Delegates and observers commented that it was a different Hoover who arrived in Cleveland today—different from the man who came here in 1932 to speak in the same hall in defense of his record in the White House.

He was a tired man then, worn by the manifold problems created by the depression. His welcomers, too, were different in attitude on that former occasion. Many thousands greeted him at the station and at the hall then, just as they did today, but they were grim and solemn, unnatural under the stress of the economic conditions then obtaining. In those days one could count a half dozen breadlines near the station and convention hall.

The Hoover who appeared here today had the attitude of a buoyant leader, taking this opportunity to re-enter the national arena. He was more of the warrior on the attack and he seemed to enjoy it.

Mr. Hoover left for New York late tonight. He will hold business conferences there.

June 11, 1936

REPUBLICANS NAME LANDON UNANIMOUSLY; HE ACCEPTS PLATFORM, ADDING OWN IDEAS

LANDON SENDS TELEGRAM

To Back Constitutional Amendment if States' Wage Laws Fail.

FOR GOLD AT PROPER TIME

In His Message to Convention He Specifies Exceptions in Accepting the Platform.

BORAH WINS HIS PLANKS

Vandenberg Is Expected to Be Vice Presidential Choice at Final Session Today.

By ARTHUR KROCK

Special to THE NEW YORK TIMES.

CLEVELAND, Ohio, June 11.—An unbossed Republican National Convention, yet working like a machine, at 11:41 o'clock tonight unanimously nominated Alfred M. Landon of Kansas for President, adopted unanimously a platform embracing certain social welfare ideas of the New Deal (which otherwise is excoriated) and seated party control in a group of young Kansas politicians and editors who entered the national political field less than two years ago.

At a final session tomorrow Arthur H. Vandenberg of Michigan is expected to accept the Vice Presidential nomination.

Eighteen Borah delegates from Wisconsin and the Senator's campaign manager (Delegate Carl G. Bachmann of West Virginia) voted for Mr. Borah on the first ballot, which prevented a nomination by acclamation under the rules. But Wisconsin then moved to make the nomination unanimous, and it was done.

Hamilton Reads Message

Two dramatic events colored the night session. Before John D. M. Hamilton, the chief of staff of the nominee, presented his name to the convention, he read at Mr. Landon's request a telegram from the Governor "interpreting" three planks of the platform and stating reservations. These planks, relating to currency, civil service and State control of wages and hours, had been revised by the resolutions committee from the text submitted by the Governor as a part of the week-long effort to placate Senator Borah and win his support in the campaign.

Governor Landon "interpreted" a "sound currency" to mean a currency eventually convertible into gold, insisted that the civil service should extend as far as the government's under-secretariat and pledged himself to support a constitutional amendment to permit the States to regulate wages and hours if the statutory method were not effective. He said "in good conscience" he must make these intentions known in advance.

The other element of drama was when all the other Presidential candidates but Senator Borah, who had already left for Washington, took the platform and seconded the nomination of Mr. Landon. Mr. Borah is only fairly well-pleased with the platform, and he expects to survey Mr. Landon's speeches and the personnel of his campaign cabinet for a couple of months before deciding whether to support the candidacy. Herbert Hoover, the other eminent Republican whose opposition was feared by the Landon group, phoned here today that he was satisfied with the platform.

Senator Vandenberg was among those seconding the nomination. Colonel Knox, L. J. Dickinson, Robert A. Taft and Harry Nice, the other aspirants, followed.

Harmony the Landon Goal

Harmony among all Republicans and the support of anti-New Deal Democrats have all along been stated as the twin goals of the Landon managers, and, except for Mr. Borah, the harmony seems to have been effected.

The end of the session, amid a series of ecstatic demonstrations for Mr. Landon and Mr. Vandenberg, came after a day of anxious concern to the Kansas syndicate which, at midnight last night believed that all its worries were over. Mr. Landon's differences with the resolutions subcommittee, and with Mr. Borah, and the latter's objections to revision of planks he had been asked to submit, caused the snarl.

But by 7 o'clock tonight, except for the open reservations of Mr. Landon and the unknown future course of Mr. Borah, troubles were over. The squalls had been weathered and the covered wagon was safe.

Day of Compromises

After subcommittee sessions which endured almost all of the night and day, the platform finally emerged at 7 o'clock and its text revealed that Senator Borah had won his battles on the foreign affairs and monopolies planks and had lost only one sentence in the currency pronouncement. This sentence—"We oppose further devaluation of the dollar"—had been forced in from Topeka by Governor Landon, who also wanted a pledge to return to the convertibility of currency into gold as soon as possible, but did not obtain it.

Mr. Borah, whose support in the campaign is considered vital by the

Landon managers, demanded proscription of the World Court along with the League of Nations and got it. He will now presumably decide in due course whether, as he has further made precedent to his support, "the candidate fits the platform."

Party Pledges Are Set Forth

The platform begins with a mixture of paraphrase of the Declaration of Independence to fit modern conditions and original arraignments of the New Deal. All Americans are asked to join with the Republican party in defeating the President for re-election. The Supreme Court is defended as the sure protector of human rights and the party pledges itself to maintain its independence from the Executive. Free enterprise, free production, no hindrance to business, decreased cost of living are guaranteed under Republican rule.

The needy are assured by the platform of the necessities of life, with relief administered by non-political, local agencies, no politics, grants-in-aid to the States by the Federal Government on a fair ratio, public works separated from relief and approved on a strict basis of merit.

Social security is promised to the people on a pay-as-you-go principle, the money to be raised by a direct tax, widely distributed as grants to States, and all persons over 65 given the minimum sum they require to keep them from want.

Collective bargaining is pledged to labor, and through the statutes, rather than through a constitutional amendment; ways are to be found to give to the States powers over wages and hours. Governor Landon and Mr. Hoover wanted a constitutional amendment pledge at this point, but Mr. Borah opposed. The President in his speech at Little Rock yesterday said the country's only need was a broader view of the Constitution.

The farm plank is difficult to distinguish from the administration's soil-conservation plan, which it hails as of Republican origin. Subsidies, scientific and experimental aid and the retirement of submarginal lands are promised the farmer. He is also offered a tariff ban on imports that conflict with his own wares. Further, the platform proposes the repeal of the reciprocal treaty system and the substitution of the flexible tariff of Mr. Hoover's day.

Present and additional laws, civil and criminal, are invoked against all forms of monopolies. Such regulatory agencies as the SEC and the Federal Trade Commission are to be placed under court review if the Republicans win and keep these platform promises, and interstate utilities are to be strictly regulated.

The platform offers to place the whole government employe group under civil service; to stop Federal spending at once, and to balance the budget through economy instead of through taxation. After that the whole tax system is to be coordinated and, generally, levies are to be spread more equitably.

Isolation Plank Adopted

A foreign policy is outlined which will forever keep the United States out of the League and the World Court and any foreign entanglements, while supporting always the principle of international arbitration. The Borah flavor at this point is highly pervasive, even to a pledge to try to collect the war-debts which William Allen White says is one "will-o'-the-wisp" that got into the platform over his futile protest.

No discrimination against women in industry, solicitude for colored citizens, provisions for flood control, and a final paragraph binding the candidate of this convention to stand by every word in the document complete the pledges.

Mr. Borah never had so much effect on a Republican platform before in his long and controversial life.

Having assured Governor Landon's nomination through the public polls of New York and Pennsylvania; having lived safely through the demonstration for Herbert Hoover, and having battled on through negotiations with Senator Borah, the managerial syndicate found itself during the day involved with its own candidate, the Governor of Kansas, over some planks, and with Senator Borah, and ex-Senators Reed, Bingham and Moses over others.

The East, as represented by the ex-Senators, was insisting on a softer money plank than was favored by Governor Landon and his chief monetary advisers—Ogden L. Mills, Eugene Meyer and Dr. Benjamin Anderson of New York City.

Mr. Hoover, before he left town last night, had ranged himself with the Kansas-New York gold bloc. Mr. Borah was in opposing alliance with the Pennsylvania-Connecticut-New Hampshire monetary liberals, and was concerned over deletions he heard had been made in his planks on monopolies and foreign affairs. There were side arguments over social security, utilities, relief and a constitutional amendment to extend the power of States over wages in which various interests, including Governor Landon, were participating—he by long-distance telephone, they by personal appearances before the committee on resolutions.

A stranger situation never had existed in a Republican convention, with the Westerner, soon to be nominated, insisting on a more progressive platform socially and a more conservative platform fiscally than representatives of the Eastern States.

But there was evidently more in it than met the eye, because the Kansas control group was obviously delighted with the response from distant areas where news of the struggle had penetrated, and expressed confidence that the platform would "suit everybody." Meanwhile, the country was having a forceful view of the Governor of Kansas it had not had before.

Mr. Hoover sent from New York a telegram giving his views on the monetary plank. This was not released by the chairman of the California delegation, to whom it was sent, but it was said that all the features in which the former President is interested were included. Mr. Hoover also phoned to make sure of that.

Borah Waits and Erupts

While some of the Landonites were working hard on the platform, interviewing at regular intervals Senator Borah, who alternately waited and erupted upstairs in his room at the Hotel Cleveland, and telephoning to Topeka, others were exerting relentless pressure on Senator Vandenberg to accept the nomination for Vice President.

Thus the convention picture clouded and cleared as the baffling day wore on, with the sunny wearers of the sunflowers, the young amateurs and professionals who have been handed what many Eastern Republicans consider a doubtful chance, confident that another twenty-four hours would see a triumphant conclusion. The convention met and recessed twice while awaiting the result of the debates and the strategies.

In the conclusion, Senator Borah is to be found with his fingers crossed, according to the best available reports about his latest intentions. He said he came to Cleveland for two purposes: To put certain things in the platform and keep others out, and then to determine whether the "candidate will fit the platform."

Borah Still to Map Course

It might be considered that he is in a position to decide whether his platform efforts have been sufficiently satisfactory to preclude his departure from the party fold at once. But it was confidently stated on his behalf tonight that he will have to make observations of Governor Landon for several months before he will be sure whether "the candidate fits the platform." After completing his work at this session of Congress, the Senator will return to his re-election campaign in Idaho. After listening to Mr. Landon's speech of acceptance and taking note of his campaign counselors and speeches, Mr. Borah will come to a final determination.

This, if Senator Borah holds to the program as outlined, is the net result of the superhuman efforts made by the Landon managers to get his active support this year. He has been the central figure of the convention, waited on, sought after and granted more concessions than even he could have expected.

Whether or not it was a part of the Landon drama, the Governor's subcommittee last night even yielded Mr. Landon's views on the

© New York Times Studio Photo.

NOMINATED FOR PRESIDENT

Alfred Mossman Landon

gold standard and the World Court to Mr. Borah until they were called to account from Topeka. Whatever was the strategy of this, the Senator has been courted by the Landon group as no convention managers have ever courted him before. It leaves him with his fingers crossed, but the Kansans are full of hope.

Opposition, even nominal, to the selection of Mr. Landon began to melt away yesterday afternoon with the news from the Pennsylvania and New York delegations. But by midnight the thaw had started with a rush. Senator Vandenberg released his delegates, and other candidates followed suit, or were obliged to do so. By 3 A. M. the only question left was on the Vice Presidential nomination, with the Landon group renewing their pressure on Senator Vandenberg.

June 12, 1936

KNOX NOMINATED FOR VICE PRESIDENT

Vandenberg Rejects Bid of Landon Forces and Edge and Nice Quit.

IT'S A BULL MOOSE TICKET

Both Nominees Bolted in 1912, and Both Are From Midwest, Riding Into Party Control.

HARMONY AIM TO THE FORE

By ARTHUR KROCK

Special to THE NEW YORK TIMES.

CLEVELAND, June 12.—Colonel Frank Knox of Chicago appealed to the delegates to the Republican National Convention as the strongest possible nominee for Vice President, after Senator Arthur H. Vandenberg of Michigan formally notified them today that he would not accept the second place on the ticket headed by Governor Alfred M. Landon of Kansas. Therefore, in the same free-will spirit which has characterized this remarkable gathering, the delegates unanimously nominated Colonel Knox and adjourned soon after 1 o'clock this afternoon.

The sentiment for Colonel Knox over ex-Senator Edge of New Jersey, Governor Nice of Maryland and others was made so plain by the seconding speeches for the Illinois publisher that the others, following last night's example, withdrew on the platform, and this time even Wisconsin went along on the first ballot.

When it was over the Republicans had chosen as candidates for President and Vice President of the United States two former Bull Moosers, who bolted the party in 1912; two veterans of the World War; two men from the Mississippi River basin, where party control is now lodged.

That control was sealed, in an organization sense, this afternoon by the unanimous election of John D. M. Hamilton, Governor Landon's pre-convention campaign manager, as chairman of the Republican National Committee to succeed Henry P. Fletcher of Pennsylvania.

Although the West is in the saddle, it is riding lightly, as the process of the Vice Presidential nomination today once more revealed. Governor Landon and his young group of Kansas University classmates, Kansas politicians and Kaw Valley editors very much wanted Senator Vandenberg for second place. They carefully devised a plan to draft him today, feeling sure that he would be obliged to accept.

But Mr. Vandenberg would only consider a draft by acclamation, and did not desire even that. By the time this viewpoint was finally made known to the Landon leaders, Pennsylvania had grown tired of waiting for them to get in touch with the Senator and at 9:30 o'clock this morning pledged itself to Colonel Knox with whom Mr. Vandenberg is understood to have conferred early this morning.

Acclamation being then impossible, the Senator drafted a letter to the convention, once more taking himself out of consideration. The Kansans still insist they could have obtained acclamation if they had been able to reach the Senator by telephone last night. Yet this correspondent had a phone conversation with him as late as 1:30, an hour when the Landonites say they were informed his telephone was shut off.

Pursuing his week-long practice of attempting no dictation, Mr. Hamilton let nature take its course and Colonel Knox got every vote. With Mr. Vandenberg out of the way his only strong opposition came from his fellow-publisher, Colonel Robert R. McCormick of Chicago. The other Chicago newspaper factor in the convention—William Randolph Hearst—several months ago had publicly listed Colonel Knox among persons acceptable to him for national honors.

In addition to his personal unwillingness to run for Vice President, Mr. Vandenberg had another and very practical reason. Maine votes on its State ticket in September, and politicians all over the country issue claims based on the trend shown in the elections in that month. Mr. Vandenberg was largely responsible for the defeat of an appropriation to complete the Passamaquoddy tide-harnessing project, and he feared this might be successfully used by the Democrats against Republican State candidates and thus dampen the enthusiasm of Republican workers throughout the country a month and a half before the end of the national campaign.

The ticket of Landon and Knox is expected by the Republican leaders, young and old, to make a strong appeal to women and to the 5,000,000 of new voters who will come to the polls in November.

The platform was sufficiently influenced by the welfare legislation of the New Deal, they believe, to attract liberals and progressives who have applauded this part of the President's record, and sufficiently denunciatory of the rest of the New Deal to get the support of conservatives.

The harmony achieved this week in Republican ranks, which was one of the first objectives of the Kansas syndicate that promoted the Landon campaign, is set down as another great November asset. Only Senator William E. Borah withholds his assent, and the Landonites still hope they can win his friendly neutrality, at least.

To the last, the new group of Western leaders preserved the "folksy" atmosphere which they had taken such pains to provide for the convention. One of the last incidents of today was the delivery of a message to the delegates from Governor Landon, asking any who wished to "drop in" on him at Topeka on their way home. Ex-Senator Allen of Kansas, who extended the invitation, was the very embodiment of Western hospitality as he spoke.

The convention itself preserved to the end the flavor of an informal religious meeting, and continued to prefer "Onward Christian Soldiers" and "The Battle Hymn of the Republic" to "Oh Susanna," in the spirit of the Bull Moose convention of 1912. Many of the delegates have been convinced that theirs is a crusade for freedom against enemies of the American system. They are further convinced that the East has been made subject to the West and that the influence of "Wall Street" has disappeared from the party councils.

This belief is another testimony to the smooth work of the Kansas syndicate. The fact that much of Governor Landon's pre-convention strength and useful packets of cash were contributed by that very Wall Street has not come to the surface in Cleveland, although it is well known in New York. Once assured that Mr. Landon was "sound," the Eastern financial districts rallied to him strongly last Winter, and the results were apparent in the New York delegation.

Being very practical men, the Landon managers lost no time, however, in approaching the New York leaders today and exchanging counsel on how to carry the President's State against him in November. The entente cordiale of many months ago, erected through Ogden L. Mills, Eugene Meyer, Benjamin Anderson, Winthrop Aldrich and others, is going full blast. New York is to be a battleground, and, if the combined leaders can contrive it, a successful one. They are agreed that on New York the result of the election may depend.

The New Yorkers of the financial sector were, of course, particularly pleased with Governor Landon's telegram about the gold standard, which carried out an understanding of his views which was given authoritatively to Wall Street several months ago. Advocates of the "soft money" platform plank, which was written with an eye on the sterling bloc, are fewer in the New York deelgation than in one or two others in the East. These represent largely the industrial, as contrasted with the financial, East.

Looking back over the events of this interesting week, the conclusion is inescapable that the outward machinery of the Republican party is now in hands as clever and capable as any that have directed it in its history. Dating from the time of the arrival of the delegates in Cleveland, and putting to one side considerable of the wise handling of Mr. Landon before that, Mr. Hamilton, Roy O. Roberts and their fellow-strategists made no major mistakes in pursuing their objectives—harmony, smooth convention procedure, and every appearance of free-will choice.

While they failed in gaining the immediate allegiance of Mr. Borah after a series of fulsome courtships and huge concessions, and may never gain it, they kept him from opposing the Governor's nomination. Mr. Hoover they gratified with an invitation to speak, a royal overture and a smashing ovation, as well-managed as a Fifth Avenue parade.

They changed their Kansas-born platform in particulars on which the East was insistent—and then presented the convention with Mr. Landon's telegram of reservations after it was too late to make any difference in the result. They arranged for the withdrawal of the other candidates and the unanimous first ballot. They did not succeed in drafting Senator Vandenberg. But, on the whole, it was a brilliant job.

Now all they have to do is to defeat the President for re-election.

* * * * * *

June 13, 1936

LOYALTY TO PRESIDENT INTENSIFIED BY REVOLTS

CONVENTION OPENS TODAY

Delegates Unshaken by Smith or the Coughlin-Lemke Opposition.

ALL LOOKING TO NEW YORK

Tammany Arrives, Led by Dooling, as Interest Centers on Leaders' Disputes Here.

By ARTHUR KROCK

Special to The New York Times.

PHILADELPHIA, June 22.—In a spirit of loyalty to the President and his administration, obviously intensified by the open hostility of radical independents and conservative Democrats, the Democratic National Convention will assemble in its first session tomorrow noon in the Municipal Auditorium. After a brief period in which the temporary organization will be effected, the assembly will recess until evening for the speech of the keynoter, Senator Alben W. Barkley of Kentucky.

As the delegations began to arrive today it was quickly evident that complete control by the President, directed on the ground by Chairman Farley, always a certainty, will be certified with enthusiasm by Democrats of all the species represented here to assure the country that the recent volleys from the Left and the Right have only solidified the party.

Yet among this augmented loyalty the note of practical politics can be discerned. One remarkable development of today was the beginning of a movement to pass a resolution calling on Governor Lehman of New York to stand for re-election in the name of party loyalty.

Although New York is a single State, and this is a national convention, the Democratic politicians concede the possibility that New York's electoral decision may measure the difference between the success and failure of the President at the polls. To offset any effects in the East of the telegram addressed to the convention yesterday by Alfred E. Smith and others, and any consequences in the Middle West of the Lemke-Coughlin third-party effort, the drafting of Mr. Lehman is being agitated. Other State leaders contend that the Governor cannot stand against the request of his party in national convention assembled.

The outcome of the movement was uncertain tonight, but if the resolution should be offered, it will be overwhelmingly adopted. And, if that happens, it will constitute a precedent for national conventions.

New York State, with its forty-five electoral votes and disputing Democratic leaders, was uppermost in the minds and pageantries of the convention today. The Tammany delegation, headed by James Dooling, reached Philadelphia strong for the renomination of the President, and interested in the movement to draft Governor Lehman, but concerned over getting the chairmanship of the New York convention group. Apprehensive that the Governor is slated for this strictly ornamental honor, Tammany men were grumbling, but the murmurs were not loud enough to disturb the harmony of the scene.

A short-lived flurry was created tonight by the report that Senator Glass of Virginia, advocate of sound money and author of the 1932 currency plank, had declined to serve as a member of the Committee on Resolutions. Investigation developed the fact, however, that Virginia—with the warm urging of Mr. Farley—will draft the Senator to be a member of the platform body and that he will accept.

Mr. Glass, while disapproving many New Deal projects, has assured his Virginia constituents, from whom he seeks re-election this year, that he will support the President. It was understood that, his age and health being additional factors, he does not wish to undergo the labor of service on the subcommittee.

An inharmonious note was sounded, however, by the warring delegations from Minnesota, a State where the Democrats face a troublous election day because of the threat of the Lemke movement to absorb the Farmer-Labor supporters of the New Deal, and their own factional difficulties.

The national committee heard the contending factions and voted to seat both, with a half a vote per delegate. This was satisfactory to National Committeeman Joseph Wolf, but the group headed by Representative Ryan and State Chairman Moonan boiled over with instant wrath and talked of carrying the question to the committee on credentials and bolting the convention if the Wolf delegates are admitted on any basis.

As the day wore on, the temperatures of the Ryan-Moonan faction showed obvious signs of going down, and the party strategists hoped for a complete acceptance of the peace plan, since it includes the appointment of Mr. Farley as arbiter of the dispute over who shall be national committeeman to succeed Mr. Wolf.

Two minor contests, from Puerto Rico and the Canal Zone, were disposed of without walkout threats.

Enough Southern delegates arrived during the day to demonstrate that there will be open opposition in that section to the abrogation of the two-thirds rule, now just a hundred years old. Andrew Jackson imposed it on his party for factional reasons, and it was maintained in ante-bellum times to prevent the nomination of an anti-slavery candidate for the Presidency.

But Senator Clark of Missouri, who will be chairman of the rules committee, said today that more than 800 of the 1,500 delegates are pledged to abrogate, and he believes the unit rule should also be abolished.

Texas will vote against ending the two-thirds provision. There will be opposition from Maryland, and Senator Byrd of Virginia has been sighted on his way from Washington with blood in his eye. But Josephus Daniels, Senator Bailey of North Carolina and other Southerners are with the administration in this effort, and the strong probability is that President Roosevelt and Vice President Garner will be the first Democratic candidates to be nominated by a majority since 1836.

In hotel rooms and corridors discussion of the platform continued with growing intensity. According to those who have seen the draft prepared by Senator Wagner, chairman of the resolutions committee-to-be, the document heavily emphasizes the Senator's pet projects of social and industrial welfare, omits mention of the possible necessity for constitutional amendments and is pretty vague as to a currency program.

The effort being made here is directed toward the farm, labor and money planks. One proposal is that the constitutional question be linked with the labor declaration, leaving the door open to future amendment of the organic law if statutes "within the meaning" of the Constitution cannot be worked out for the general welfare and the protection of exposed groups.

Since it was the nullification by the Supreme Court of New York's Minimum Wage Act for Women that has played a large part in bringing the amendment question before this year's conventions, Governor Lehman will confer with Senator Wagner on the whole subject.

The Governor and the Senator have thus far agreed that, since the New York law was carefully drawn, an amendment seems to be the only remedy for the situation so long as the present Supreme Court majority remains on the bench. But it has also been definitely understood that the President wants emphasis on cure by statute, with an amendment as a last resort. After the Wagner-Lehman conference more on this subject will be available.

It was reported today that the administration has conceded specific mention of farm relief devices to the group headed by Secretary of Agriculture Wallace, which feels that to be necessary to hold the Middle West.

No bitter dispute over money is expected, although there may be a stand, for the record, on gold which will get a minority vote in the committee on resolutions.

The convention strategists, the practical politicians, who are not particularly interested in platforms, were pondering entirely another question today. It is whether the telegram from Mr. Smith and his four putative fellow-bolters shall be read to the convention.

Pennsylvania Democrats, pointing to the large Democratic vote in Philadelphia last year, urge that the message be read and promise that the city galleries will be as certain to register disapproval as the delegates. Mr. Farley has been hesitating to take the chance of having a burst of wild pro-Smith cheering go on the air from Philadelphia's Municipal Auditorium when housing the Roosevelt convention.

The suggestion of the Pennsylvanians was to have the telegram read after the permanent chairman, Senator Robinson of Arkansas, finishes his speech Wednesday night. Probably the President will be called upon to settle this argument, as all others.

Otherwise, the Smith-Colby-Reed-Ely-Cohalan telegram can be set down as a one-day sensation, and not so much of that because Sunday was the day it was released and few delegates were in Philadelphia. Tammany leaders would not discuss it today, but they did not seem particularly interested, and one of them said: "It's just a repetition of his Liberty League speech. The League cuts no ice in New York, and Al not much more." He wanted his remark kept strictly off the record.

Other delegates expressed resentment over the message; its statements, its tone, its dispatch at a time when the signers knew it could have only destructive effect, and the omission of the name of Woodrow Wilson from the list of party heroes of the past. But it is a fact that, to judge from snatches of conversation in the elevators and corridors, the convention crowd was giving little thought to the telegram.

June 23, 1936

CONVENTION ABROGATES CENTURY-OLD TWO-THIRDS RULE

SOUTH BOWS TO CHANGE

Appeased by Promise to Reapportion as Two-thirds Rule Ends.

FIGHT ON FLOOR AVOIDED

Committee Instructs Party Heads to Work Out New Representation Basis.

ON DEMOCRATIC VOTE CAST

Southerners Will Be Relatively Stronger Than Delegates of Less 'Regular' States.

By CHARLES R. MICHAEL
Special to THE NEW YORK TIMES.

PHILADELPHIA, June 25.—The century-old two-thirds rule, born in a tragic day of American history, when Jackson was President, died today in the progressive Roosevelt era. The convention tonight adopted the report of the rules committee, which recommended its abrogation and the substitution of the majority rule for the nomination of President and Vice President.

After long consideration of this troublesome issue, the rules committee, supported by administration influences, not only succeeded in overpowering the Southern opposition to a change in the rules, but avoided a fight on the floor by unanimously adopting a resolution sponsored by Senator Tydings of Maryland, which instructed the Democratic National Committee to work out a new basis of representation in the national conventions based upon the Democratic vote cast in the respective States.

The national committee was instructed to improve the system for the selection of delegates and report to the 1940 convention. The present basis of apportioning delegates will be maintained until after the next convention.

Opponents of abrogation, led by Representative Eugene E. Cox of Georgia and Beeman Strong of Texas, announced themselves entirely satisfied with this action, which they said would maintain the prestige of the Solid South and encourage the building up of the party in other sections of the country. Sectionalism is removed by the abolition of the two-thirds rule and the proposed plan of representation in the convention based upon Democratic strength in each State.

Text of Resolution

The resolution which effected a peaceful solution and satisfied those opposing repeal reads:

"Be it resolved that the Democratic National Committee is hereby instructed to formulate and recommend to the next national convention a plan for improving the system by which delegates and alternates to Democratic National Conventions are apportioned, and be it further resolved that in formulating this plan the national committee shall take into account the Democratic strength within each State, the District of Columbia, Territories, &c., in making said apportionments."

Harmony prevailed in the committee although the Southerners fought vigorously for the retention of the two-thirds rule. They had come to the convention convinced that the rule would be abolished, however, and were prepared to accept defeat in good grace, if the apportionment of delegates was made on the basis of Democratic votes and not on population.

The leaders are hopeful that the national committee will carry out the spirit of the resolution and work out an apportionment system somewhat similar to that of the Republican party where States obtain larger representation for increasing the Republican vote.

It was apparent from the outset that proponents of abolition of the two-thirds rule were in control of the situation as the proposal for repeal was supported by President Roosevelt and Chairman Farley of the national committee. The 1932 convention had recommended ending the rule.

Since that convention Senator Bennett Clark, whose father, the late Champ Clark, lost the nomination in 1912 because of the two-thirds rule, was active in stimulating the movement for abolition of the two-thirds rule, which was brought into existence by Andrew Jackson to prevent the nomination of Calhoun as Vice President and the selection of Van Buren as his successor as President.

For more than fifty years the rule has bothered the Democratic party, but agitation for dropping it was led by a small band of Northern Democrats who were outvoted by the delegates of the Solid South. The latter contended that the rule was necessary to protect their interests and prevent the nomination of candidates objectionable to that section of the country which fifty years ago was about all that the Democratic party commanded.

With Roosevelt sweeping the country in 1932, making the Democratic party a militant organization in all sections to such an extent that only six States remained Republican, the argument of the South was wiped out. The result of the election strengthened the position of Northern and Western Democrats who had fought for years to obtain the majority rule in making the party nominations.

In the committee today the strength of the repealists was almost three to one, the vote being 36 to 13.

The following States voted for retention of the rule: Alabama, Colorado, Georgia, Indiana, Massachusetts, Mississippi, New Hampshire, New Mexico, New York, South Carolina, Tennessee, Texas and Virginia.

The States voting for repeal were: Arizona, Arkansas, California, Connecticut, Delaware, Idaho, Illinois, Kentucky, Louisiana, Maine, Maryland, Michigan, Minnesota, Missouri, Nebraska, New Jersey, North Carolina, North Dakota, Ohio, Oklahoma, Oregon, Pennsylvania, Rhode Island, South Dakota, Utah, Vermont, Washington, West Virginia, Wisconsin, Wyoming, Alaska and the District of Columbia, Hawaii, Philippine Islands, Puerto Rico and Virgin Islands.

The rules committee resumed its sessions this morning with the Southerners fighting for a compromise after they found that the committee was decisively opposed to retention of the rule. Then they sought to protect solid Democratic States from being overpowered in future conventions by larger States which seldom cast a Democratic electoral vote.

Recommendations for definite apportionment were offered to effect this, but each was held not germane to the question by Chairman Clark.

Both Senator Clark and Senator Tydings, while favoring a new system of apportionment, insisted that the plans offered were unworkable, were hastily conceived and would not accomplish the purposes of their supporters.

After a long debate the Southern members agreed to the Tydings compromise. This was worked out by a subcommittee consisting of Senators Clark and Tydings, Beeman Strong of Texas, W. W. Durbin of Ohio, Senator Chavez of New Mexico and Representative O'Connor of New York.

The report of the subcommittee was unanimously adopted and the minority leaders said that they would not submit a minority report to the convention, thus assuring harmonious and speedy action in the adoption of the committee's recommendation for the nomination of President and Vice President under a majority rule.

In the two hours discussion this morning, virtually the same arguments advanced yesterday were offered by both sides. Senator Chavez pleaded for protection of the smaller States and declared that abolition of the rule without a new basis for apportionment would punish new Democratic States and put a premium on larger States that are not always Democratic.

W. W. Durbin of Ohio agreed that with the majority rule in effect a new basis of representation should be found. The present basis is two members for each Senator and Representative.

Representative Rankin of Mississippi jumped into the breach by offering a substitute for the repeal motion giving each State six delegates and two additional delegates for each Democratic member of the State and Senate. He said that the wiping out of the two-thirds rule would punish the small agricultural States and give control of the Democratic party to the larger States, which frequently do not furnish any Democratic electoral votes.

Called Change Fair

"The Republican party is much fairer under its system which gives a bonus for increased Republican votes," he said. "We must give the Democratic States a larger representation in the convention than the Republican States. Unless we do this the Democratic States will be penalized and suffer unjustly."

R. W. Robbins of Arkansas said that he was unable to go along with the Southern States and that he favored a majority rule as the only way of building up the party north of the Mason-Dixon Line.

Senator Clark declared that there was no ulterior purpose in the move to change the rule. The rule will be effective, he said, if the convention adopts it and can be changed by the next convention if it is not satisfactory.

"We can change this rule now without rancor and charges that the rule was changed while the game was in progress," he said. "There is no contest for President and the candidacies of no one would be affected by changing the rule now. If we go on a majority rule, we will be adopting the principles of Jefferson. The Democratic convention is the only place in our whole political system where a majority system is not conclusive."

W. W. Hastings, of Oklahoma, offered a motion that if the majority rule was substituted for the two-thirds rule, the representation from the States should be in proportion to the Democratic vote cast at the preceding Presidential election and that the apportionment of the territories should be the same as at present constituted.

Senator Connally supported the Hastings resolution, as did Freeman Strong. Harvey S. Fields, of Louisiana, joined the repealists and argued in favor of the new rule which he said would nationalize the Democratic party.

On motion of Leo P. Fox of Wisconsin, author of the motion to repeal, Chairman Clark ruled the Hastings proposal out of order. This confused the Southerners until Senator Clark later ruled that he would entertain a motion for a new apportionment of delegates.

Senator Tydings said that he was in entire sympathy with the position of the Southern States but was opposed to the committee adopting immature recommendations which in the end might be impractical and award more delegates to large States without consideration of their Democratic strength.

He suggested that a subcommittee be named to shape up a workable recommendation. This was done with the approval of the full committee.

T. A. Walters of Idaho, favoring repeal, said that his State was more "Borahcratic" than Democratic, but was rapidly emerging from that condition and would become thoroughly Democratic in the November election. His remarks caused the only laugh of the session.

In the opinion of Democratic leaders the rule which was buried today is undemocratic and dangerous. They held that this convention had the first real opportunity to end it without injury to any group of States or Presidential candidates.

Democratic leaders in the past fifty years have admitted it to be a bad practice, but they have been unable heretofore to command enough strength for its repeal because such action would affect the chances of candidates for the party nomination.

In 1932 Roosevelt forces had enough votes to repeal the rule, but Secretary Hull, who was on the Roosevelt advisory board, objected to this manoeuvre, which was also disapproved by Mr. Roosevelt. At that time Mr. Roosevelt indicated that he would support repeal at a subsequent convention.

June 26, 193

SALVOS OF CHEERS GREET PRESIDENT

Serried Banks of Humanity on Field Hang on the Words of His Acceptance Speech.

APPLAUD MANDATE CALL

Garner Ceremony Speeded to Bring Roosevelt Before Party as Standard-Bearer Again.

By TURNER CATLEDGE
Special to THE NEW YORK TIMES.

FRANKLIN FIELD, PHILADELPHIA, June 27.—Probably the most impressive setting for a notification ceremony in the history of the United States was that witnessed here tonight when President Roosevelt and Vice President Garner were notified by the officials and delegates of the recently adjourned Democratic National Convention that they had been called to carry the party's standard again in the campaign of 1936.

More than 100,000 persons (some put it at 110,000), the largest crowd ever gathered in Franklin Field, exploded into one great cheer when at 9:37 there came the announcement over the loudspeaker system that "your President has arrived." They refrained from the convention practice of marching only because Philadelphia safety officials had requested that they keep their seats.

The light in the demonstration meter to the left of the speakers' stand had reached 100 before the President arrived on the platform. When he walked into the presence of the immense throng on the arm of his son James, the cheers increased in volume.

The President and Vice President Garner walked to the front of the stand and lifted up clasped hands, the symbol of their joint leadership in the campaign to keep the New Deal in power in Washington.

Cheering Melts Into Anthem

Chairman Farley asked for silence. The crowd did not seem to notice him.

The great banks of humanity, describing a horseshoe around the delegates and alternates seated on the field proper, waved hats and umbrellas which they had used earlier when rain threatened to stop the outdoor ceremony.

They tore up paper cards and convention literature and sent the fragments scattering over the field like so much snow.

The cheering was halted only when Lily Pons of the Metropolitan Opera took up the strains of "The Star-Spangled Banner."

As the strains of the anthem ceased, Mr. Farley congratulated Philadelphia and the people from the other parts of the country for the impressive gathering. He then called upon the Right Rev. Bishop Tate of the Protestant Episcopal Church, who offered the invocation.

The delivery of the prayer brought silence again.

President Swiftly Presented

Mr. Farley introduced Senator Harrison of Mississippi to act for Senator Barkley of Kentucky in notifying Mr. Garner. Mr. Barkley, temporary chairman of the convention, had sailed earlier in the day for a vacation in Europe.

The speech was short. Immediately after Senator Harrison had finished Mr. Garner walked to the lectern. The crowd was the quietest it had been up to that time. He assured them that his speech would be as brief as it was sincere, and with that he proceeded to accept the nomination.

As the Vice President spoke, Mr. Farley and Colonel Edwin A. Halsey, secretary of the Senate and sergeant-at-arms of the convention, stood beside him.

Mr. Farley looked over his shoulder apparently to see when he would end his short speech. He wanted to proceed as fast as possible with the ceremony.

He next introduced Senator Robinson, permanent chairman of the convention, who proceeded immediately to notify the President. He cut his speech, copies of which had been distributed earlier in the day, to a brief few sentences, so that exactly at 10 o'clock he introduced the President.

Senator Robinson said:

"Mr. President, it should be matter of gratification and pardonable pride for you to know that you have just been nominated unanimously by the 1,100 delegates to the Democratic National Convention. Ladies and gentlemen, the President of the United States!"

The President began his speech immediately, cutting off any attempt at a demonstration.

Carries Audience With Him

The crowd cheered loudly the President's remark that "Philadelphia is a good city in which to write American history."

He talked to the great crowd almost as if he were addressing a gathering in a small room. Despite the expanse of the field, the whole group seemed near to him.

He spoke without raising his voice to oratorical volume; it was carried to the farthest recesses of the field by a well-working loudspeaker system.

It was easy, too, for most of the crowd to see him. The exception to this were the delegates and alternates sitting in the rows near the front, whose view was cut off by a large detail of police that had been sent to the field to maintain order and make other persons keep their seats.

A larger cheer rose when he said that the election of 1932 was a mandate of the people to put an end to economic despotism and economic tyranny and that under the mandate these things were being ended.

Another followed when he said:

"If the average citizen is guaranteed equal opportunity in the polling place he must have equal opportunity in the market place."

Final Dramatic Scene

The President did not finish the last paragraph of his speech before the crowd went into an uncontrollable cheer. As he started the first sentence, he said:

"I accept the commission you have tendered me." He was able to go no further on account of the roar that rose from the field and stadium.

He held his clasped hands above his head and smiled first to one side then to the other. As he stood there his mother and wife walked to his side. They were joined by his sons James, Franklin Jr. and John, and by his daughter and son-in-law, Mr. and Mrs. John Bottiger, and his daughter-in-law, Mrs. James Roosevelt.

He beckoned Mr. Garner to join the family gathering and the red-faced Texan, beaming broadly, responded. Mr. Farley also joined the group, as did Senator Robinson. The crowd continued to cheer.

The President raised his hand again. He called across to the band leader to play "Auld Lang Syne" and he stood solemnly for a moment, then waved good-bye all around the field and turned to go.

This was ten minutes after the demonstration started. At 10:37 he walked off the platform on the arm of his son, James.

Encircles Field in His Car

The crowd kept cheering. As his car rolled toward the southwest gate, the roar increased from that section of the stands. The band struck up the Democratic marching song, "Happy Days Are Here Again."

Governor Earle of Pennsylvania did a solo dance about the platform.

Instead of going out of the gate, the President's car took him about the track of the field, following closely behind a motor cycle police escort. He left the stadium by the northwest gate at 10:46, with showers of torn paper still falling in the field.

As the proceedings of the evening came to a close, an announcer chimed in over the loud-speaker with a "bit of homely advice."

"Let's have no accidents on the way home," he warned the 100,000-odd people. "Tonight is Saturday night and we have plenty of time to get home."

Clouds Threaten Early Comers

The stands in Franklin Field began to fill about 5 o'clock in the afternoon, five hours before President Roosevelt and Vice President Garner were scheduled to appear. The weather was threatening.

The seats and ground were damp from a two-hour drizzle which had stopped just about the time the crowd began to gather. Clouds were hanging low over the center of the city, but word had gone out that the ceremonies were to be held out of doors, "rain, sleet or snow."

The convention had been transferred to the field in a body. The center part of the arena, where football teams had raced and bucked up and down the field only a few months ago, was set about with seats for the various State delegations. Down in front, just as in the convention hall, were the big-hatted Texans.

The stand where the notification was to take place was a square rostrum in the extreme west end of the field. It was decorated with flags and bunting and topped by a superstructure fifteen or more feet high.

As the clouds continued threatening, workmen began installing tarpaulin that might be stretched over the speakers should the rain resume. Along each side, and not under the tarpaulin, were seats for distinguished guests.

Moist Throng in Gala Mood

Just after 6 o'clock a sixty-piece band, directed by Lieutenant Joseph Frankel, began a concert of patriotic music. By that time people were pouring into the field and grand stand.

Despite the gloom and the fatigue of the delegates, alternates and spectators, the crowd was in a gala mood and accepted every opportunity to applaud. These came as the various colorful personalities of the convention entered the field.

At 6:40 the rain started again. Umbrellas were raised by individuals throughout the stands and on the field. The clouds looked as if they meant to pour a deluge in upon the assemblage.

At 6:50 a deluge poured down. Still most of the spectators and delegates held their seats. Members of the band ran to the canopied Presidential platform with their instruments. The crowd roared, whistled and yelled.

The downpour was short, lasting only long enough to make every one not under cover uncomfortable and wet. After this the skies to the west began to brighten.

Just as the shower subsided, another gate was thrown open and more people poured into the field. Thousands in the stands cheered the courage and fortitude of the newcomers.

A broadside sheet captioned, "A Message From Organized Labor to the People of Pennsylvania," was distributed at Franklin Field before the beginning of the notification ceremonies.

Recounting what President Roosevelt had done for labor and the unemployed, the message urged his re-election on the ground that the workers were faced with no choice in the coming election and that it was "either Roosevelt or reaction."

Hush While Lily Pons Sings

With the crowd silent beyond belief, the program opened with Lily Pons of the Metropolitan Opera Company singing "Lo, the Gentle Lark," accompanied by the Philadelphia Symphony Orchestra. She declined an encore and the orchestra followed with "The Stars and Stripes Forever," "Rumba" and "Pomp and Circumstance."

Long before the President arrived, the distinguished guests and delegates had taken their seats. On the speaker's rostrum were several members of the Cabinet and other high officials of the Federal Government and the States.

A cheer went up from the crowd when Mrs. James Roosevelt, mother of the President, arrived and was escorted to a seat.

An announcement came over the loud-speaker at 9:28 that the President had arrived at the Baltimore & Ohio station a minute earlier. The scene at the station was brought to the vast amphitheatre by radio.

A second later, a big half moon appeared in the sky to the south and several political correspondents demanded the "pay off" on their earlier bets that Roosevelt luck would prevail against the rain.

DRIVE PUTS WILLKIE UP FOR PRESIDENT

'Declarations' Circulated Here, in Washington and Elsewhere Among Probable Signers

A move to organize popular support for the nomination for President of Wendell L. Willkie, public utilities official and critic of many New Deal policies, became known yesterday by the circulation of material, here, in Washington and elsewhere, favoring his candidacy.

Oren Root Jr. of 455 East Fifty-seventh Street, a grandnephew of Elihu Root, said last night that he had mailed "declarations" to a list of persons throughout the country, seeking signatures in support of the nomination of Mr. Willkie. These "declarations" are not petitions, Mr. Root said, but are forms designed to permit citizens to register support for Mr. Willkie.

The idea, Mr. Root said, was his own, and he had financed the printing and mailing of the first declarations because he believed that "there is a tremendous demand among thinking people for the nomination and election of Mr. Willkie as President." He hoped, he said, that the persons to whom he had sent declarations would interest enough others in the movement to make it national in scope.

Besides a statement favoring the nomination of Mr. Willkie and a space for signatures, the declarations carried the address of the Pandick Press, Inc., 22 Thames Street, New York City, printers of the blanks, and a statement that additional copies could be purchased by persons desiring to promote the movement. The price, Mr. Root said, $1 for 100, probably will be reduced if the demand is sufficient.

The first declarations were mailed Tuesday night, he said, with instructions to return them to his New York address. If the movement grows, he said, it will be necessary to establish headquarters.

The number of blanks sent out, he said, was in "the low thousands." He had received a gratifying response within the first twenty-four hours, Mr. Root added, but did not give figures. A copy was mailed to Mr. Willkie, but no reply has been received, Mr. Root continued. He explained that Mr. Willkie had not been consulted before the move was started.

Mr. Root, an attorney, is connected with the firm of Davis, Park, Wardwell, Gardiner & Reed of 15 Broad Street. In politics he is a Republican, being a member of the New York County Committee. His declarations, however, did not mention either political party. His father, Oren Root, retired, is a former president of the Hudson & Manhattan Railroad Company. The father at one time was connected with utilities companies.

Mr. Root said he was not acquainted with Mr. Willkie.

April 11, 1940

WAR'S TURN UPSETS REPUBLICANS' RACE

Dewey Drive Appears Slowed as Party Chiefs Reappraise Chances in New Situation

CONTEST NOW 'WIDE OPEN'

By TURNER CATLEDGE

WASHINGTON, May 25—The race for the Republican Presidential nomination is currently undergoing a recheck throughout the country as a consequence of the vicious turn of the war in Europe and the inevitable influence of that development upon the United States.

If what this correspondent heard from objective observers and political leaders—many of them delegates to the forthcoming convention—on a recent trip to eleven Mid-western States, accountable for 302 delegates to the convention, and in Pennsylvania is true, and is symptomatic of the political situation in the country as a whole, the following seems to be a Republican outlook as of this date:

(1) The race for the Republican nomination is still wide open.

(2) Thomas E. Dewey of New York, concededly the strongest "popular choice" aspirant of a month ago, is slowing down to a more even pace with others of the "big three" Republican candidates.

(3) The rigid stand of Senator Arthur H. Vandenberg of Michigan for complete "insulation" of the United States from the European war is of questionable political value to him under present circumstances.

Taft and Willkie Gain

(4) The chances of Senator Robert A. Taft of Ohio are improving in relation to both Messers. Dewey and Vandenberg.

(5) The stock of Wendell L. Willkie as a Presidential possibility is rising precipitately in certain quarters, although the great question remains as to whether he can translate this reaction into convention delegates this late in the race.

(6) The possibility of a "dark horse" nomination does not seem to increase in the ratio that the apparent closeness of the contest would warrant. The possibilty is ever present, however, and the names of Joseph W. Martin Jr., minority leader of the House, and Governor Bricker of Ohio, are heard most frequently in this connection.

(7) Other candidacies, such as those of Senator Styles Bridges of New Hampshire and Frank Gannett of New York, do not seem to be taking hold.

(8) The Republican pre-convention campaign as a whole has been slowed by a feeling of "oh, what's the use, Roosevelt will be re-elected anyway if the war keeps up like it's going now."

Quest for a Candidate

The Republicans started out early this year in quest of a man who could turn the evident reactions against New Deal domestic policies into a Republican victory in November. The urge to win came strongest from the boys around the State Capitols and County Court Houses, from former minor officials who want to get back in office and power. In short, the Republicans were looking not necessarily for a good President; they were looking for a winning candidate.

Six weeks ago Mr. Dewey began to appear as that man. He not only exhibited strength in relation to other Republican candidates, but also an amazing pulling power in the class of voters the Republicans must attract back to their fold if they hope to win.

The old-line Republicans never liked Mr. Dewey from the start. They were wary of his youth and inexperience in larger governmental affairs. They disliked his generally independent attitude, and they feared the consequences of a campaign in which he might be pitted against such a political master as President Roosevelt.

Reappraisal of Dewey

While many of these leaders, notably in States like Nebraska and Illinois, had to embrace the New Yorker's candidacy because of the results of primary elections, they maintained considerable reserve as to his merits. The new war developments have underscored the question emanating from his lack of age and experience. He and his chances of winning are undergoing a review and the results, as quite generally expressed, seem to be that

"TIME OUT FOR STATESMANSHIP"

Thomas in The Detroit News

stock of certain other candidates is improving at his expense.

The member of the "big three" who appears to be profiting most right now is Senator Taft. The Ohio candidate pitched his campaign from the outset on appeals directly to the party leaders and he has just completed a tour in which he talked to hundreds of them in the Middle West.

His principal appeal, under current circumstances, seems to be his cool, stable approach to the problems of the day; his slow, almost plodding methods at a time when excitement is common and his general attitude of realism toward the situation in Europe.

Mr. Vandenberg's managers attemped to pick up his candidacy again on the basis of his "insulationist" speech at the Michigan State Republican convention at Grand Rapids a week ago Thursday. If they succeeded in any marked degree, it was not noticeable in the Midwest. Throughout that section one finds a grim, unemotional feeling that the United States should do more to help the Allies—"something short of war." Mr. Taft went counter to this view when he called for strictest neutrality, financial as well as military, in his speech at St. Louis Monday night.

The speeches most quoted in the West right now are those being delivered by Mr. Willkie. The utilities executive will likely have some votes on the first ballot at Philadelphia, but the possibility of his hurdling over a deadlock among the "big three" to the nomination is considered quite remote at this time.

Some Hoover Sentiment

Representative Martin has important backing both in the West and South. One of his closest political friends is Alfred M. Landon of Kansas, Republican nominee in 1936. Mr. Landon today is in a position where he may turn the majority of the delegates in six or seven States in the West.

Support for Herbert Hoover is to be found in various places. One runs across quite a bit of Hoover sentiment in Missouri, due, it is said, to the influence of former Secretary of Agriculture Arthur M. Hyde.

Governor Bricker is strictly in the "dark horse" class, but his name is heard more frequently than any other when conversation turns to the possibility of a deadlock among the "big three" at Philadelphia.

All calculations in the Republican race must be made virtually on a day-to-day basis. It can only be stated that Mr. Dewey was considered the leading candidate, the man to "stop" before the German invasion of the Low Countries, and that he is thought now by many people to have slowed up in his drive for the nomination. He may be compelled to fight a defensive battle from now on.

May 26, 1940

WILLKIE IS CALLED THE 'MAN TO BEAT'

Republican Leaders Try to Explain Rapidly Growing Sentiment for Indianan

DEWEY FORCES CONFIDENT

Sprague Predicts Sure Victory at Philadelphia—Vandenberg Headquarters Opened

Special to THE NEW YORK TIMES.

PHILADELPHIA, Pa., June 18—As in a wartime "blackout" started by air raid sirens supporters of most of the Republican Presidential condidates groped in some perplexity today as they sought to explain the rapidly growing sentiment in behalf of Wendell L. Willkie and to arrive at a general conclusion that he was "the man to beat" at the convention next week.

Representative Halleck of Indiana, Mr. Willkie's only spokesman in the vanguard of delegates and campaign managers, was somewhat baffled by the wide sweep of the Willkie talk, but he was about the only one of the official or semi-official campaign chiefs on the ground who was thoroughly enjoying himself.

J. Russel Sprague of New York, campaign manager for District Attorney Dewey, reached Philadelphia too late in the day to get at first hand an idea of the number of times the question, "What are you going to do about Willkie?" was being asked.

He asserted, however, that the Dewey forces were not participating and will not participate in any movement against any other candidate.

This reply was made to a query about the possibility of a coalition by Mr. Dewey and Senator Taft to "stop Willkie" as suggested among the delegates yesterday.

Sprague Sure of Dewey

"We are here to nominate Dewey and we're going to do it," Mr. Sprague declared. "As for the details of how we are going to do it, we will meet them as they come. But you can say that we are no part and parcel of any 'stop movement' of any kind."

To this Mrs. Ruth Hanna McCormick Simms, co-manager of the Dewey campaign, added:

"Mr. Sprague and I have one-track minds. Our purpose is to nominate Mr. Dewey."

Arriving with Mr. Sprague to help direct the Dewey drive here until a ticket is chosen were Edmund F. Jaeckle, New York State chairman; John Crews, Kings County Republican leader, and Kingsland Macy, chairman of the Suffolk County committee and a member of the credentials committee of the convention.

At the Taft headquarters at the Benjamin Franklin Hotel it was admitted that the situation had looked "confused" last week-end with the Willkie movement gaining momentum, but David S. Ingalls, the Senator's manager, declared that much of this confusion had been dissipated with the arrival of early delegates and first-hand data on "certain States" where strong pro-Willkie sentiment had been reported.

From forty to fifty delegates called at the Taft headquarters during the day, among them Jay Williams, manager of the Hanford MacNider campaign, whose visit was described as a "social call."

"Very encouraging" reports had been received, Mr. Ingalls said, on the Taft "secondary strength." For example, one delegate predicted that in the Minnesota delegation Senator Taft would receive four votes on the first ballot, eight on the second, sixteen on the third.

The Willkie boom appeared to be having some effect on Pennsylvania leaders. They refused to admit that there was any thought of throwing this State's seventy-two votes to the Indianan after giving Governor James "native son" support on the first ballot, but some of the leaders said privately that the nomination lay "between James and Willkie."

Strong support for Mr. Willkie as second choice among Pennsylvania delegates was made evident in a telephone survey, although James F. Torrance, Republican State Chairman, on arriving said the State was "for Governor James first, last and always."

The Evening Public Ledger came out editorially for Mr. Willkie, asserting that he had "all those qualities which meet the specifications of what the American people are looking for as their leader.

"If the Republican party wants a dynamic human being as President, Wendell Willkie looks as if he would fit the bill," it said.

Arthur H. Vandenberg Jr., the Michigan Senator's son, opened headquarters for his father's campaign at the Hotel Adelphia, saying the Senator would "probably have votes from more States than any other candidate."

"As I size up the situation," he said, "they are candidates who are not going to be stampeded. I consider the line-up to be a completely dependable backlog."

C. Nelson Sparks, campaign manager for Frank Gannett, the New York publisher, announced receipt of a telegraphic endorsement from Edward H. Alexander of Jacksonville, Ill., chairman of the board of governors of the Young Men's Republican Clubs of that State and a delegate to the convention.

Richard J. Lyons, Illinois delegate at large, who sought the Republican nomination for Governor, also paid high tribute to Mr. Gannett, and said that the Republican party, if it hoped to win, "ought to take a definite stand as the anti-war party of the United States."

June 19, 1940

Willkie Was Democrat Until '39, Foes Reveal

Delegates to the Republican National Convention have received by mail, from an undisclosed source, photostatic copies of vital statistics concerning Wendell L. Willkie, as reported by Who's Who in America. The photostats show that Mr. Willkie, contender for the Republican Presidential nomination, was listed as a Democrat in the volumes for 1934-35, 1936-37 and 1938-39.

A check yesterday with the official list of registered voters, published by the New York City Board of Elections, showed that Mr. Willkie had enrolled as a Democrat from 1010 Fifth Avenue, in the Fifteenth Assembly District, up to and including 1938, and that he had enrolled as a Republican for the first time in 1939.

The opposition to Mr. Willkie is expected to use his recent conversion to the Republican party as an argument against his nomination at the convention. The listing "Democrat" was circled in pencil on the photostats sent to the delegates.

June 19, 1940

Summary of the Ballots

Following are the total votes received by candidates in the balloting at the Republican convention last night:

Candidate.	First Ballot.	Second Ballot.	Third Ballot.	Fourth Ballot.	Fifth Ballot.	*Sixth Ballot.
Dewey	360	338	315	250	57	8
Taft	129	203	212	254	377	312
Willkie	105	171	259	306	429	659
Vandenberg	76	73	72	61	42	0
James	74	66	59	56	59	1
Martin	44	26	0	0	0	1
MacNider	34	34	28	26	4	3
Gannett	33	30	11	4	1	1
Bridges	28	9	1	1	0	0
Capper	18	18	0	0	0	0
Hoover	17	21	32	31	20	9
McNary	13	10	10	8	9	0
Bushfield	9	0	0	0	0	0
La Guardia	0	1	0	0	0	0

*Unofficial.

June 28, 1940

WILLKIE CREDITED FOR OWN VICTORY

Convincing Delegates of His Meeting Challenge of Day Said to Have Defeated Foes

By ARTHUR KROCK

Special to THE NEW YORK TIMES.

MUNICIPAL AUDITORIUM, Philadelphia, Friday, June 28—The nomination of Wendell L. Willkie was a political revolution, but peaceful by contrast with others which have shaken the rest of the world. In normal times it could not possibly have happened.

The professional politicians, unaware that changed times and the impact of thunderous events have cracked the system which they long have practiced, sought to prevent the miracle by the usual methods.

These included an appeal to partisanship, because Mr. Willkie has so recently become a Republican; an attempt to match the personality of Thomas E. Dewey against him; an effort to overcome the tide with Senator Robert A. Taft, bred in the tradition and the son of a Republican President and Chief Justice, and finally one of those old-fashioned combinations which often have been successfully employed to "stop" a political intruder.

None of it worked because, as they compared the candidates put before them, remembered the exigencies of the country and bethought themselves of the probability that their nominee must face President Roosevelt in the campaign, the delegates resolved to do what they really wanted to do, and what public opinion seemed overwhelmingly to favor.

The spade work was done without a professional organization. Mr. Willkie himself, with pen and tongue, made a personal campaign the like of which has never been seen in this country.

It was done without the expenditure of any large sum of money for the usual purposes, the candidate having refused to accept the usual contributions, though the sources were accustomed to financial calls to accomplish the nomination of a candidate for President.

When Mr. Willkie came to Philadelphia last Saturday he still lacked this professional organization. But as soon as he realized that he was to be opposed in the old-fashioned way he set to work to form one.

Recruits From New Era

His first important recruit on the ground was Governor Raymond Baldwin of Connecticut, and he was swiftly followed by other Republicans who have discarded old methods and old shibboleths and reclaimed Republican States which had thrice endorsed the New Deal. A typical example of these recruits is Governor Harold Stassen of Minnesota.

Up to the time he was persuaded that he could no longer rely on his one-man campaign with tongue and pen, Mr. Willkie had been relying for political assistance almost wholly on Representative Charles A. Halleck of Indiana.

But Mr. Halleck was a member of the Resolutions Committee and had been appointed to present Mr. Willkie to the convention. It was soon obvious that he could not also do all the organizing on the ground and act as floor leader in addition to these heavy exactions.

Yet not until yesterday did the combination of hasty and largely inexperienced volunteers who made up the Willkie organization take on the form of a convention management.

As soon as it did, however, it seemed by another miracle to discover ways to throw the growing tide of public opinion against the professional stone wall that had been erected against Mr. Willkie.

Countering Tactics of Foes

First, members of Congress from the West were induced to hold a meeting and declare that they would not run if Mr. Willkie were nominated because their States were opposed to the Hull reciprocal trade program which in principle he favors.

This was soon countered by the recruiting of Governor Carr of Colorado and other Western Republicans and State delegations in this region were early supporters of Mr. Willkie in the balloting.

Then by whispers among the delegates the candidate's business connections, his affiliation with the utilities and the presence here of many successful business men in his behalf, were employed to persuade the delegates that he could not be elected.

Finally, when Mr. Willkie disposed of the challenge of Mr. Dewey, the politicians sought to combine against him and drew on the Southern delegations from States which rarely cast an electoral vote for the Republican ticket.

Boss-led groups from Pennsylvania and Illinois were mustered in the old partisan professional way to "stop Willkie."

Everything failed because the delegates simply would not stand for it. And yet they have always stood for it in Republican conventions before.

They refused to believe that Mr. Willkie was an interventionist, or that the country would think so, recalling his frequent counsel against entering the European war and concluding that he was the kind of man who would be taken to mean what he says.

When that barrier was swept aside, which the anti-Willkie strategists in the Platform Committee had been unable to erect against him, the last obstacle was removed.

How the Boom Began

It was Feb. 23, 1939, when the first serious mention of Mr. Willkie's qualifications as a Presidential candidate was made in this newspaper. It appeared in the "In the Nation" column on the editorial page, and followed his successful challenge of the President and the New Deal on the business policies of the Administration.

This was pointed by the course of the Tennessee Valley Authority in areas which were served by Mr. Willkie's Commonwealth and Southern Corporation.

He got a great many letters endorsing the suggestion. But nothing happened until further controversies with the Administration induced him to engage in much speaking before business groups and a great deal of political writing in the newspapers and magazines.

Then he got many more letters, and began to say, when questioned, that of course he would like to be President but that he could not take the suggestion seriously.

A short time later General Hugh S. Johnson proposed Mr. Willkie as the Republican nominee to a luncheon meeting of business men in New York City. This seemed to set fire to the smoldering idea, and thousands of letters and telegrams poured in on the astonished utilities executive. He decided to try out American politics in his own way.

THE REPUBLICAN NOMINEE
Wendell Lewis Willkie

He accepted numerous engagements to speak and to write, a striking example of the latter activity having been an article in the magazine Fortune. In this Mr. Willkie composed an address on behalf of "We the People," which set forth his political creed.

First Sponsors in the Field

That publication impelled Oren Root Jr., a New York lawyer, to start a publicity organization for him without Mr. Willkie's sanction and without any important contributions.

Later Russell Davenport, editor of Fortune, resigned his post to work independently for Mr. Willkie as another volunteer. Petitions sent out generally were soon signed by thousands of citizens, and the strangest political boom in American history was under way.

Meanwhile, Mr. Willkie went about, speaking his mind freely and writing what he thought in defiance of all the regulations and superstitions accepted by candidates.

He appeared as a guest on the "Information Please" program, impressing a wide radio audience with his fund of general information, his wit and a charm that projects itself as well over the radio as to persons with whom he comes into physical contact. He wrote book reviews on historical works.

Finally, Mr. Halleck in Indiana decided to try to get some delegates. He was encouraged in a district or two, but when Mr. Willkie came to Philadelphia he could count on few more than fifty.

Three days later his managers were trying to find ways to induce more than a hundred to withhold their votes until the drive against Mr. Dewey had been tried out. The restraint was only half way effective, and five ballots later Mr. Willkie was unanimously nominated.

It is typical of him that he said only a week ago in Washington that he had been told he would be nominated on the sixth ballot and he supposed his advisers knew what they were talking about. They did know.

Eager to Battle Roosevelt

There is no doubt that Mr. Willkie will take the fight to the foe in a slashing way. He has met Mr. Roosevelt in contest before and he is eager to engage the President in the supreme political field.

"I want to meet the champ, not Tony Galento," Mr. Willkie has said on several occasions when urging that the President run for a third term against him.

His nomination was achieved without any professional political obligations. Many volunteers worked hard for him here, particularly Mr. Halleck who, with Mr. Davenport, decided to take the challenge of partisanship and utility connections right to the convention floor and ask the delegates if they agreed with such objections.

It was a daring speech and unusual. But like the similar tactics of Mr. Willkie it triumphed.

Alfred M. Landon, who had hesitated to believe that a man of Mr. Willkie's background could defeat the Ne wDeal, finally came to his aid last night at an important moment.

The other itular leader of the party, Herbert Hoover, lent him no aid of any kind. But, as he owes no important political debts, he holds no grudges either.

So it is fair to assume that Mr. Willkie will have a harmonious party behind him in the forthcoming campaign.

June 28, 1940

* * * * * *

FARLEY STAYS MUM ON 3D TERM ISSUE

But Washington Hears President's Silence Has Made Their Break Complete

WASHINGTON, July 3 (UP)—President Roosevelt's failure to take even his closest friends and party leaders into his confidence on third-term plans was reported tonight to have severed virtually the last tie between the Chief Executive and Postmaster General James A. Farley, manager of the 1932-1936 Democratic campaigns and Chairman of the National Democratic Committee.

No public break between the pair is expected. But Mr. Farley has made it plain to friends in Congress that he would not return to Washington after the convention unless called by the President.

He is said to have stayed behind after last Friday's Cabinet meeting to discuss the convention, the platform and other party matters with Mr. Roosevelt. It was reported that the President personally had edited some lists of committeemen suggested by Mr. Farley.

Roosevelt-Farley relations bogged down over the third-term issue a year ago. At that time Mr. Farley went to the President for a heart-to-heart talk on the subject. Opponent of a third term, Mr. Farley later told friends that he had received assurance from Mr. Roosevelt that he would not run again.

Afterward, the "draft Roosevelt" movement swung into high gear and the President made no attempt to discourage third-term delegates in the primaries. Mr. Farley tossed his hat into the Presidential ring in the Massachusetts primary and announced that his name would be placed before the convention with no "if's and but's."

Friends say that he still is determined to have his name put before the convention. Whether he would manage a third campaign for the President is a subject of speculation. One group regards him as a sufficiently good soldier to drop his aversion to the third term in the interest of the party. Others say he feels so deeply on the subject that, while he would not do anything to hinder Mr. Roosevelt's third-term candidacy, neither would he promote it.

July 4, 1940

CONVENTION KEYED TO SEE 'ANYTHING'

Delegates Prepared Even for Nation's First Rejection of Major Nomination

By HENRY N. DORRIS
Special to THE NEW YORK TIMES.

CHICAGO, July 13—At least two-thirds of the State and territorial delegations to the Democratic National Convention were in Chicago tonight, sure of only one thing—that President Roosevelt would be renominated.

The undercurrent of sentiment among most of the chairmen of delegations was that the stage was set for anything, and many believed that the "anything" might happen.

This belief led to bets. One of these was at even money that Mr. Roosevelt would be the first person in United States history to decline a Presidential nomination.

There was a manner about the delegates which said better than words that they were here waiting for the time when the "word" was given from Washington what to do.

The Illinois delegation was reported to have hung about its headquarters throughout the morning on a report that a telegram might be on the way from the White House. It did not arrive. The throngs in hotel lobbies continued to propound "what's going to happen."

Booms for Second Place

The Southern delegations, nearly all of which were here, "visited" about during the day light-heartedly campaigning for two of their number, Senator Byrnes of South Carolina and Speaker William B. Bankhead of Alabama—for the Vice Presidency.

Edward H. Crump, the "boss" of Memphis, who probably will be the Tennessee delegation chairman, went the rounds verbally jousting with this chairman or that and declining to offer predictions until he had the "word."

Most of the Indiana delegates were on hand when Paul V. McNutt met scores of newspaper men at a press conference this morning at his ornate headquarters. The Indianians went forth to battle for the Vice-Presidential nomination for Mr. McNutt, proclaiming him a "perfect offset" to keep their State's electoral votes from going to another Hoosier, Wendell L. Willkie, the Republican nominee.

The Texans, led by Sam W. Rayburn, House majority leader, went about talking Garner.

The Hawaiian delegation, leading the vanguard of groups from the territorial possessions, were adorned with the customary lei.

July 14, 1940

Third-Term Statement

Special to THE NEW YORK TIMES.

CHICAGO, July 16—At the close of his formal speech as permanent chairman tonight Senator Barkley said:

And now, my friends, I have an additional statement to make on behalf of the President of the United States.

I and other close friends of the President have long known that he had no wish to be a candidate again. We knew, too, that in no way whatsoever has he exerted any influence in the selection of delegates or upon the opinions of the delegates to this convention.

Tonight, at the specific request and authorization of the President, I am making this simple fact clear to this convention.

The President has never had and has not today any desire or purpose to continue in the office of the President, to be a candidate for that office, or to be nominated by the convention for that office.

He wishes in all earnestness and sincerity to make it clear that all the delegates to this convention are free to vote for any candidate.

That is the message which I bring to you tonight from the President of the United States by authority of his word.

July 17, 1940

ROOSEVELT RENOMINATED ON FIRST BALLOT

RIVALS' POLL IS 150

Third-Term Tradition Is Upset—Garner, Tydings Stay to End

By TURNER CATLEDGE
Special to THE NEW YORK TIMES.

CHICAGO, Thursday, July 18—President Roosevelt was renominated early this morning for a third term for President of the United States by the Democratic National Convention.

The President's renomination, which climaxed a "draft" movement carried out in contravention of one of the oldest and best established traditions in American politics, came theoretically by "acclamation," but the move to nominate unanimously or by acclamation came in a dramatic surrender by Postmaster General James A. Farley and others who had stood with him against a third-term nomination.

Mr. Farley, Vice President Garner and Senator Millard E. Tydings of Maryland all had been placed in nomination in pursuance of the third-term protest. Before the move to nominate by acclamation was made by Mr. Farley more than 150 of the convention delegates had cast votes against Mr. Roosevelt, distributing them among the three named above and Secretary Cordell Hull. Governor Cooper of Tennessee explained to the convention that Mr. Hull was not and had never been a candidate.

How the Ballot Stood

The total vote before it was made unanimous was Roosevelt 946 13/30, Farley 72 27/30, Garner 61, Tydings 9½ and Hull 5 2/3.

There was but little demonstration when the convention made its momentous decision. The first thing that happened was a song led by Phil Regan, "When Irish Eyes Are Smiling," the convention's song to Mr. Farley.

Mr. Roosevelt's nomination was clinched when New York voted, giving 64½ votes for him, 25 for Farley, 1 for Secretary Hull, with 3½ missing. New York's sixty-four votes put the President over the 548 votes needed for renomination. There was no notice given by the delegates of this momentous hour. It was shortly before 1 A. M.

Senator Barkley, Permanent Chairman of the Convention, ap-

DEMONSTRATION THAT FOLLOWED RENOMINATION OF PRESIDENT LAST NIGHT

Parade in Municipal Stadium, Chicago, as Mr. Roosevelt's name was placed before the convention by Senator Lister Hill

Wired Photo—Times Wide World

pointed a committee composed of Senators Byrnes of South Carolina, Charles F. Sawyer of Ohio and Mayor Edward F. Kelly of Chicago to notify the President of his renomination.

The convention adjourned shortly before 2 A. M. until 2 o'clock in the afternoon, when it will meet to name a candidate for Vice President.

Acceptance Held Certain

The President is counted as certain to accept the nomination, despite a statement made to the convention in his behalf that he did not desire to run again. His acceptance is expected to come in a radio message to the convention before it adjourns.

He also will be expected now to indicate his choice for Vice President from among a growing list of potential candidates. He may also take occasion in replying to the Convention "draft" to express his ideas on a platform adopted by the party and which, it is understood, did not satisfy him completely by the language of its statement against intervention by the United States in foreign wars.

The Roosevelt "draft" had been indicated from a time long before the delegates assembled in Chicago, and it moved relentlessly to its successful conclusion under the management of inner circle New Dealers, assisted by Senator James F. Byrnes of South Carolina as floor leader.

Just before the roll-call of States started for the nomination, the convention howled down a proposal of Representative Elmer J. Ryan of Minnesota to restate the party's stand against a third term.

The crowd that witnessed Mr. Roosevelt's renomination was one of the largest ever to gather in the great Chicago Stadium. Delegates and alternates and spectators jammed every available inch of the floor and galleries. Outside, long lines of disappointed visitors, many of them ticket holders, were unable to push inside but stood by to hear the result.

The first part of the convention's sixth session was taken up with reading of the platform. It was presented by Senator Wagner of New York as the unanimous finding of the resolutions committee and accepted by the Convention by overwhelming vote. Mr. Ryan's abortive attempt to have the anti-third term plank inserted was the only effort made for amendment or addition.

Glass Minces No Words

Postmaster General Farley's name was presented when the name of Arkansas was reached, but his backers had no thought except to make the record for him. Arkansas yielded to Senator Glass of Virginia, who came here for the sole purpose of putting Mr. Farley in nomination.

Senator Glass tore the covers off the third-term issue when he put Mr. Farley in nomination. Complimenting the Postmaster General for never having forsaken the Democratic party, he likened him to Thomas Jefferson who, three days before his death, Mr. Glass said, urged that no man should ever be elected President for a third term.

The doughty Virginian, well past his eightieth year, braved the boos of Roosevelt supporters and spectators in the galleries to repeat that Mr. Farley had never forsaken the principles of his party. He had come from a sickbed, he said, to place the Postmaster General's name before the convention.

The mention of Mr. Farley's name was greeted by cheering from many delegations. Delegations from Montana, Massachusetts and Maryland started a parade, which was joined by Arizona, Nebraska and part of the New York delegation.

Mr. Glass stopped the paraders to say a final word. While he was sitting on the platform, he said, he had received two anonymous communications protesting Mr. Farley's nomination because he was a Catholic.

"They made me more determined than ever," he shouted as loudly as his voice would permit, "to put this great man in nomination." He recalled that Thomas Jefferson had counted his stand in behalf of religious freedom among his greatest achievements.

As the roll-call proceeded, Mr. Roosevelt's nomination was seconded by Arizona, California and others. Governor Olson of California made a short seconding speech, saying the Democracy of the West was joining with the Democracy of the East in renominating Franklin D. Roosevelt.

Mr. Hill first mentioned the name of Speaker Bankhead, but he soon turned to the subject of Mr. Roosevelt, saying the party had a man "who had come back from a living death to serve his country."

He then moved on to the name of Mr. Roosevelt, at which the convention broke into a demonstration that dwarfed anything and everything that had gone before.

Delegates Swarm Into Aisles

As Mr. Hill mentioned the President's name, winding up in a grand crescendo of old-time Southern oratory, the organ burst into "The Song of Franklin D. Roosevelt Jones," the California delegation swarmed out into the aisles, the Iowa contingent joined, waving bunches of corn leaves; Illinois followed with a portrait of Mr. Roosevelt high in the air. Then Vermont, Kansas, Hawaii, Maine, and in an instant the aisles were a mass of marching delegates with standards waving in the air. Virginia delegates kept their places, so did Texas, Oklahoma, most of New York and Maine.

Mr. Roosevelt's nomination was seconded by Connecticut through Senator Francis T. Maloney, and by New York, through Governor Lehman.

Governor Lehman recalled that he had gone into office as Lieutenant Governor of New York when Mr. Roosevelt was elevated to the Governorship twelve years ago. Eight years ago, he went on, he had voted for Mr. Roosevelt for President. In 1936 he seconded his nomination for President at Philadelphia.

"And now, it is my pleasure and my great privilege to second his renomination for President," he said.

Senator Tydings was put in nomination when Maryland was called. His nominator was State Senator Edward J. Colgan of Baltimore.

Vice President Garner was put in nomination by Wright Morrow of his home State of Texas. With his name in, the nominations were complete.

The anti-third-term block was broken a short time before the night session when Senator Wheeler of Montana withdrew from the race for the nomination and released his delegates. Senator Wheeler said he had obtained everything he wanted in the foreign policy plank of the platform and saw no need to proceed further with his fight to keep the "war label" off the Democratic party. Mr. Wheeler's few delegates were expected to go almost solidly into the Roosevelt draft columns.

The platform was ready for the delegates when they crowded into the great arena. It was topped by a plank pledging the party to stand against participation in foreign wars, against sending army, naval or air forces to fight in lands "outside the Americas," but expressing sympathy for and a determination to extend all material aid possible within American laws and defense interests to peace-loving peoples attacked by "ruthless dictators."

In international as well as domestic affairs the platform, in the main, was a ringing endorsement of the Administration of President Roosevelt and in its preamble carried a greeting "to our President and great leader."

* * * * *

July 18, 1940

DELEGATES BALKED AT WALLACE CHOICE

Grumbles Were Heard That He Would Not Help the Ticket With the Farmer Vote

SOME RIVALS ANNOYED

Supporters of Several Were With Difficulty Dissuaded From Fighting on Floor

By HENRY N. DORRIS
Special to THE NEW YORK TIMES.

CHICAGO, July 18—The name of Secretary Wallace went before the Democratic National Convention tonight as the hand-picked candidate of President Roosevelt for his running mate, a selection which was disapproved privately by many delegates who asserted that he would add no strength to the ticket.

Mr. Wallace's selection was broached by the score of candidates early in the morning, after a night in which many of them had continued their campaigns for delegates on the assumption that the race for the Vice-Presidential nomination would be left "wide open."

Openly showing chagrin at the turn of affairs, candidate after candidate withdrew. Some of them said privately that it was a mistake to believe that Mr. Wallace would hold the Middle West farmers against the combined appeal of Wendell L. Willkie and Senator McNary.

Senator Barkley, permanent chairman, adjourned the afternoon session without permitting nominations for Vice President. It was said later that the administration's chief lieutenant, Harry L. Hopkins, Secretary of Commerce, had not been able to "count noses" for Mr. Wallace and that it was deemed better to play for time until the word could be passed that other candidates were no longer in the field.

Delegates Grumble at Ruling

The delegates at the afternoon session left no doubt that they did not like Mr. Wallace. When Mr. Barkley adjourned the convention by pounding the gavel, there was a loud chorus of "noes" from those who felt the question should not be left to the night session.

Filing out of the stadium, the delegates audibly wondered how the scuttling of the candidacies of such men as Speaker William B. Bankhead, Representative Sam W. Rayburn, Paul V. McNutt, Federal Security Administrator; Governor Lloyd C. Stark of Missouri, Jesse H. Jones, Federal Loan Administrator, and others had been accomplished.

Early this morning, a group of convention leaders, including Mayor Edward J. Kelly of Chicago, called the White House to learn the President's wishes concerning his running mate.

The name of Senator James F. Byrnes of South Carolina was said to have been discussed. Mr. Byrnes for weeks has been mentioned as an acceptable running-mate, although he refused to let his own delegation present his name to the convention.

Senator Byrnes Considered

Mr. Roosevelt was represented as saying that he regarded Mr. Byrnes as "a safe man" in whom to leave the reins of government, should anything happen to him. The President was said to have added that two objections had been raised regarding Mr. Byrnes's candidacy.

First, it was said, Mr. Byrnes was considered unacceptable in certain quarters because of his stand on the racial question, since he had opposed anti-lynching legislation, and, second, because Mr. Byrnes was christened a Catholic, although he later became a Protestant.

The President was said to have been asked who was acceptable to him, and he replied that he felt Mr. Wallace would make a suitable running-mate.

The President was reported to have called certain leaders later in the day to re-emphasize that selection.

Until this later call, the Vice Presidential candidates declined to accept the word of New Deal supporters that Mr. Wallace had the endorsement of the White House.

It was when Secretary Hopkins began to call the candidates to express his regret at the necessity of informing them that the road to the Vice Presidential nomination was a one-lane, one-way highway, that it began to dawn on the candidates that their work of many weeks had gone up in smoke. One by one, they withdrew from the race.

They were confronted with but one alternative, either to accept the inevitable or to fight. Many of their delegates preferred the latter course, but leaders cautioned against this because they felt that it would be detrimental to the ticket for the convention to choose its nominee in the face of the expressed Presidential wish.

Mr. Rayburn then stated that he would not permit his name to go before the convention.

Others followed and it was reported late in the day that Mr. Rayburn and Mr. McNutt would second the nomination of Mr. Wallace.

Many delegates, some of them from mid-western States, asserted privately that they did not believe that Mr. Wallace could help the ticket among the farmers. They expressed the belief that a man who held a wide appeal, especially to World War veterans, labor and other groups, would have been preferable.

July 19, 1940

WILLKIE ENDS CANDIDACY AFTER WISCONSIN DEFEAT; SEES WEST ISOLATIONIST

SAYS HE WAS TEST

America First Man Led Delegate Vote, He Tells Omaha Audience

PLANS PLATFORM FIGHT

'It Is Obvious Now I Cannot Be Nominated,' He States—Asks Friends to Cease Work

By JAMES A. HAGERTY
Special to THE NEW YORK TIMES.

OMAHA, Neb., April 5—As a result of his overwhelming defeat in the Wisconsin Republican primary, Wendell L. Willkie announced tonight his withdrawal as a candidate for the Republican nomination for President, and asked his friends throughout the country to cease their activities for him and not to present his name to the National Convention. He declared he would continue to fight for the principles and policies he had been advocating.

Mr. Willkie made the announcement at the end of his prepared speech at the Omaha Municipal Auditorium on "What Is America's Foreign Policy?" He asserted that the United States either had no foreign policy or a dangerously personal one known to President Roosevelt alone, and declared that the President had not dealt squarely with the rest of the world and had not dealt squarely with the American people in the political conduct of the war.

Nebraska Campaign Dropped

The result in Wisconsin, where the entire slate of candidates for delegates to the Republican National Convention pledged to Gov. Thomas E. Dewey of New York was elected and the Willkie-pledged candidates ran behind those pledged to Lieut. Comdr. Harold E. Stassen, former Governor of Minnesota, and Gen. Douglas MacArthur, was a great disappointment to Mr. Willkie, as he had chosen Wisconsin for a test of the attitude of that section of the country toward international co-operation to prevent the recurrence of war.

The announcement, of course, put an end to Mr. Willkie's Nebraska campaign, where he was opposed to Lieut. Comdr. Stassen in the preference primary of April 11.

Mr. Willkie accepted the Wisconsin verdict as indicating that isolationism is still strong in the Middle West and said he was doubly disappointed because Fred R. Zimmerman, Wisconsin Secretary of State, former Governor and a Dewey-pledged candidate, who, he said, had been active in such organizations as America First, led in the vote.

[Mr. Zimmerman denied last night he ever was connected with any organization such as the America First.]

Mr. Willkie is understood to feel that the Wisconsin result makes the nomination of Governor Dewey almost inevitable, perhaps on the first ballot.

TEXT OF ANNOUNCEMENT

Announcement of his withdrawal was made by Mr. Willkie to the Omaha crowd as he closed his address. The text of the announcement was as follows:

It has been my conviction that no Republican could be nominated for President unless he received at the convention the votes of some of the major Midwestern States. For it is in this section of the country that the Republican party has had its greatest resurgence.

Therefore, I quite deliberately entered the Wisconsin primary to test whether the Republican voters of that State would support me and in the advocacy of every sacrifice and cost necessary to winning and shortening the war and in the advocacy of tangible, effective economic and political cooperation among the nations of the world for the preservation of the peace and the rebuilding of humanity.

The result of the primary is naturally disappointing and doubly so since the delegate who led at the polls is known as one active in organizations such as America First, opposed to the beliefs which I entertain.

As I have said many times, this country desperately needs new leadership. It is obvious now that I cannot be nominated. I therefore am asking my friends to desist from any activity toward that end and not to present my name at the convention.

I earnestly hope that the Republican convention will nominate a candidate and write a platform which really represents the views which I have advocated and which I believe are shared by millions of Americans. I shall continue to work for these principles and policies for which I have fought during the last five years.

Mr. Willkie's announcement of his withdrawal was very dramatic. The audience listened in silence and with complete attention, and rose and applauded him as he finished. Many went to the stage to shake hands with him.

[Mr. Willkie, according to The United Press, prefaced the text of his prepared address with these remarks: "I wish I could speak to you from my heart tonight. I cannot, because there are too many factors that prevent it. If I spoke of what's on my mind I would make too great a castigation of American politics."]

In his speech on foreign policy Mr. Willkie declared that the failure of the Roosevelt Administration to deal squarely had caused distrust both at home and abroad. He urged the Administration to abandon what he termed secret power politics and diplomacy behind closed doors, condemned the Administration's recognition of "Fascist turncoats" and declared that, if the United States by its foreign policy denied anywhere the aspirations of those who wanted to be free it would be laying the foundation for a third world war.

Calls for United Nations Council

Specifically, Mr. Willkie declared that the failure of the Administration to use the prestige and power of this country to set up a United Nations council had produced friction with Great Britain, Russia and China.

Military expedience had been used, he asserted, as a cloak to cover up "deals' in North Africa and Italy, and that our dealings with Darlan, Peyrouton, Badoglio and the King of Italy and the Administration's treatment of the French National Liberation Committee had caused Italians and Frenchmen to become bewildered, angry and to wonder where the United States stood.

Discussing what he said was the Administration's policy of withholding information from the American people because of its belief that they cannot be trusted to back policies that are good for them, Mr. Willkie declared that, if any one could state with certainty our policy toward the Argentine, Spain, Finland, Tito, Badoglio and the King of Italy he was a better man than he. He added that if any one could define our policy toward the great French people he must have found out through an ouija board.

"If the war is to be won quickly and American lives saved, we need a better foreign policy," Mr. Willkie said. "If our losses and sacrifices in this war are to be justified, we need a better foreign policy."

He charged that the Administration had discouraged efforts of the press to inform the people about the international situation and had bargained for votes on the fallacious theory that Americans vote not as Americans but as pressure groups defending the interests of cliques in countries which their ancestors left many years ago. This method, he said, was promoting confusion, cynicism and distrust.

Says He Fights for Principle

In his comment today on his defeat in Wisconsin Mr. Willkie said:

"I went down just the way I'd like to go down, fighting for a principle."

While he attributed his defeat to the strength of isolationism in Wisconsin, at least one other major cause contributed. That was a belief on the part of many Republicans that he is not really a Republican, a belief which on the surface seems to be even stronger in Nebraska than in Wisconsin.

Though the blow must have been a crushing one to Mr. Willkie, he bore it with composure. Although he did not make formal announcement of his candidacy until Feb. 14 at Portland, Ore., he had been active in the groundwork for it for the last three years.

In a luncheon speech at Fremont Mr. Willkie, without commenting directly on the Wisconsin result, expressed disappointment at the apparent lack of understanding of the international situation shown by Republican voters in both Wisconsin and Nebraska.

Remarks on Republican Party

"I had been encouraged to believe that the Republican party could live up to the standards of its founders, but am discouraged to believe that it may be the party of negation," he said. "It is apparent that the average citizen fails to realize the far-reaching effect upon him of what is going on in the rest of the world or to realize that a war anywhere has its effect upon him.

"I had been hopeful that the Middle West, in which so many moral causes have been started, would again find the leadership that is needed. The question is whether the Republican party will be the party of negation, cynicism and power-seeking or will it tell the people what is happening and what will happen to them if it does not furnish the leadership needed in this hour of crisis.

"I want the Republican party to be the leader, not the follower, in cooperating with other nations so that the fires of war can be restrained. When I think of what I have seen around the world and think of crowds that cheer wildly for petty criticism to please minor groups, I feel a bit heartbroken because I know how much my party could do and how much my country needs it. I would like to see the Republican party dedicate itself to the grand days of its birth and be the agency to arouse men.

"Perhaps the conscience of America is dulled. Perhaps the people are not willing to bear the sacrifices, and I feel a sense of sickening because I know how much my party could do to make it worthy of its traditions."

Before reaching Fremont Mr. Willkie addressed an open-air meeting at West Point.

He and Mrs. Willkie, with other members of the party, will leave for New York early tomorrow morning.

April 6, 1944

REPUBLICAN STRATEGY BUILT ON GOV. DEWEY

To Win the Election, Party Leaders Plan to Follow Recent Trends

By TURNER CATLEDGE

CHICAGO, June 24—The desire to win, the hope to win, the determination to win—above all, to win—are the motivations behind everything happening on and behind the scenes in the preliminary stages of the Republican National Convention of 1944.

Party leaders arriving early for the Chicago sessions seem intent on the one proposition that nothing to be done here in the next few days shall discount in any way the chances for success which became apparent to them in the State and Congressional elections of 1942—that everything done must take advantage of the trend which developed them and carried on through the off-year contests in 1943.

Can Clarify Results

Full acceptance of these considerations should go a long way toward simplifying for the American and international publics whatever takes place in the next few days by way of candidates and policy declarations, upon which the party will choose to go before the electorate in the election campaign, beginning immediately and continuing until the first Tuesday after the first Monday of November.

It is by virtue of such a psychology, which started showing itself long before delegates began gathering here, that Gov. Thomas E. Dewey of New York stands out unmistakably as the leading contestant for the Republican nomination for President.

Mr. Dewey's hold on the convention delegates, which appears at this writing to indicate his selection on or very near the first ballot, does not necessarily reflect his personal standing among the leaders of the Republican party, nor necessarily among the rank and file. Remarks are often heard to the effect that if the party kingmakers were sure of success, Mr. Dewey would be passed over for a more "regular" partisan, such as Gov. John W. Bricker of Ohio, or even more probably Senator Robert A. Taft of the same State.

Vote-Getting Power

But the New York Governor is regarded as having demonstrated an uncanny vote-pulling power in the primaries of 1940 and 1944, and especially in the New York State elections of 1942 and 1943, and by such token he has moved up to the top of the heap—to a position which no one seems able at this writing to challenge. And in these developments Mr. Dewey impressed the leaders and their followers with his potential for carrying New York State, the most coveted block of electoral votes in any national contest.

To win New York State is perhaps highest among the particular objectives of the party leaders arriving early for the convention.

The attractiveness of Mr. Dewey has increased steadily in the light of this objective, particularly as New York observers have told delegates that Republican chances of winning the Empire State may be favorable in November. These chances, the observers have said, will improve greatly if President Roosevelt insists upon and gains the renomination of Henry A. Wallace as the Democratic Vice Presidential candidate.

But Mr. Dewey's possibilities are not confined to New York, in the minds of leaders and delegates. Many of them have brought to Chicago stories of what happened in their primaries and conventions by way of pointing up the New Yorker's pull among the voting public.

"Favorite Sons"

A week ago the forces of Governor Bricker were encouraged to hope that the nomination at next week's convention might be staved off for several ballots by complimentary votes to several "favorite sons." They took at its face value the unhappiness many party leaders had expressed over the appearance of Mr. Dewey's great lead. Meanwhile the backers of former Gov. Harold E. Stassen of Minnesota cherished the hope that a deadlock might develop between these two leading contestants and their man might come out of a dark corner and grab the prize.

These thoughts did not, however, grow farther than the "hope" stage during the week and the chances of a "hoss race," while never completely dissipated until the balloting is over, waned perceptibly.

If by early next week the "draft Dewey" forces—he has never confessed that he is a candidate—establish their claim on the nomination beyond question, they may also take over the main job of writing the party platform. The New York Governor is understood to have been consulted already on the foreign-policy plan, which undoubtedly will be the most important declaration to be considered.

It may, indeed, require the strong hand of a potential nominee to prevent a first-class controversy over the platform. While the will and the determination to win next November influences the writing of party policy even as much as it does the selection of candidates, the formula for a winning platform does not seem as simple as the formula for a vote-getting nominee.

Divided Over Policy

There is no denying that a sharp division exists in the GOP ranks over the question of foreign affairs. The bedrock core of isolationism or nationalism is still there, to an extent that no one can estimate until the leaders get down to the "smoke-filled room" business of framing language stating the party's position.

On the other hand, there is a newly enlivened group of internationalists that persists despite the plight of its former mouthpiece, Wendell L. Willkie. The attitude of that wing was expressed forcefully this week by Governor Sumner Sewell of Maine, who challenged the party to substitute courage for timidity and take a stand in behalf of the widest possible international collaboration to insure peace and to spread the benefits of freedom throughout the world.

The more politically minded in the party will try in every way to evolve a compromise that may cover all groups, however extreme, and place them in line with the general scheme "to win." Evidence of that intention was seen late in the week in a model foreign-policy plank being circulated in the names of Senators Warren Austin and Arthur H. Vandenberg, and said to have the approval of Mr. Dewey. It proposed post-war world collaboration but contained also a definite disclaimer of a "world state."

Effect Unknown

How all this will affect the campaign remains to be seen. Party platforms are, in themselves, seldom controlling or even important. The candidate almost always sets the pace. He makes the issues.

Unless the attitudes are changed materially by the nominees, however, the effort to win will be directed largely toward tying together the many elements of dissent to the New Deal, large and small. Until now, at least, there has not emerged any more positive program.

June 25, 1944

DEWEY AND BRICKER NAMED ON 1ST BALLOT

DEWEY AT STADIUM

Says Plank on Foreign Policy Represents Big Area of Agreement

ASKS AID OF YOUTH

Military Phase of War Will Not Be Part of Campaign, He Vows

By TURNER CATLEDGE
Special to THE NEW YORK TIMES.

CHICAGO, June 28—Thomas E. Dewey, Michigan-born, racket-breaking Governor of New York, was overwhelmingly chosen by the Republican convention today as its Presidential candidate to meet the fourth term bid of President Franklin D. Roosevelt, who is expected to be nominated by the Democrats in this same hall three weeks from today.

The New York Governor, who until today had maintained publicly that he was not a candidate, flew from Albany with Mrs. Dewey to accept the nomination and to meet the Vice Presidential nominee, Gov. John W. Bricker of Ohio, who was named unanimously a few hours earlier.

In the final night session, which was the most crowded and most enthusiastic of the whole convention, Mr. Dewey pledged his utmost efforts to lead the party back to power in Washington and to new conquests in the States and Congress in the November election.

Answering the challenge of former President Hoover, who last night called for a new generation to take over the helm of the Republican party, Mr. Dewey exhorted his followers to a finish fight to drive out "the "tired and quarrelsome" Administration which has ruled in Washington for eleven years.

Says War Command Will Stand

Taking a leaf out of the book of President Roosevelt, who flew to Chicago twelve years ago to accept his first nomination, Mr. Dewey responded with the same fighting type of speech.

He brought his audience up in cheers time after time as he delivered thrusts at the New Deal, but especially where he declared that "the military conduct of the war is outside this campaign."

"It is and must remain completely out of politics," he said. General Marshall and Admiral King are doing a superb job. Let me make it crystal clear that a change in Administration next January cannot and will not involve any change in the military conduct of the war."

The change in Administration, he confidently predicted, would bring "an end to one-man government in Washington."

After Jan. 20, Inauguration Day, he said, the Government would have a Cabinet of the "ablest men and women to be found in America" who would receive full delegation of the powers of their office.

He made an appeal time after time to youth—youth to win the war, youth to keep the peace.

No organization of peace can last if it is slipped through by "stealth or trickery," he said. Making and keeping the peace was "not a task for men who specialize in dividing our people."

"It is no task to be entrusted to stubborn men, grown old and tired and quarrelsome in office," he said. "We learned that in 1919."

America's duty to win the peace was parallel with its duty to win the war, he said. Recently there had been a growing area of agreement among the American people on foreign policy. Only a few, "a very few," maintained that America could remain aloof any longer, he said, and only a few believed it would be practical for America and her allies to renounce all sovereignty and join a "super state."

He would not deny those two extremes the right of opinion, he said, but he stood firmly in the great wide area of agreement.

"That agreement," he said, "was clearly expressed in the Republican Mackinac declaration and was adopted in the foreign policy plank of this convention."

One Delegate Holds Out

Mr. Dewey's nomination was by a count of 1,056 votes to 1. The single opposition ballot was cast for General Douglas MacArthur, hero of the Southwest Pacific, by Grant A. Ritter of Beloit, Wis., who held out to the end against the Dewey avalanche.

The nomination was accomplished with a mild show of enthusiasm, made the milder, no doubt, by the sweltering heat which reached a new high in oppressiveness during the roll-call. The parade for the nominee, when his name was presented, lasted about ten minutes, and was joined by fewer than those who later participated in a demonstration for Governor Bricker.

The Dewey managers maintained the appearance of a "draft" until near the end. For, until he signified his willingness to accept to a convention committee assigned to call him on the telephone, Mr. Dewey had stood on earlier assertions that he was not a candidate and that he intended to serve out his present term as Governor of New York, which runs until Dec. 31, 1946.

All of the 1,057 eligible delegates present at the twenty-third Republican convention voted for Governor Bricker. Two others, allocated to the Philippine Islands, were qualified to sit but did not appear.

The swing to Governor Bricker for the Vice Presidency started late last night after Gov. Earl Warren of California, the previous odds-on choice, had refused to accept the nomination, and after Mr. Bricker had decided that his bid for the first honor was hopelessly lost to Governor Dewey.

Governor Warren refused because, he said, he had made certain "commitments" as Governor of California which he intended to keep. The language he used in turning back the pressure of his friends cast immediate attention on assertions Mr. Dewey had made

Thomas E. Dewey
For President

when besought to run for the Presidency about his intentions to remain on the job at Albany.

The Dewey-Bricker ticket was hailed by the Republicans as one of the best combinations the convention could have put together, although there was considerable disappointment that Governor Warren would not accept and give an East Coast-West Coast tie up which, some party leaders believed, would be more damaging to the Democrats. The Middle West is considered much safer ground by the Republicans than either coast, and the electoral votes of New York and California are therefore highly coveted.

Dewey "Gladly Accepts" Bricker

Governor Dewey was said to have "gladly" accepted Mr. Bricker as a running mate, although his managers had tried, up to the last minute, to persuade Mr. Warren to run. In fact, they had considered no other name until the Californian gave his final frowning headshake last night.

Governor Bricker's backers tried to keep up hope, and until 2 A. M., had maintained determination to put his name before the convention as the Presidential nominee. Friends of former Governor Harold E. Stassen of Minnesota had the same intention as to their man.

But the one thing that motivated this convention as much as anything else was that there should be no fights, no recrimination, no last-minute deadlocks. So when it became apparent that trouble might develop over the Vice Presidency, the Bricker forces decided not to protest. Their decision was made the easier, of course, by the hopelessness of their position otherwise.

Mr. Dewey went over as the Presidential nominee before Ohio was reached on the roll call. Governor Bricker had withdrawn in the meantime, however, and made a seconding speech for Mr. Dewey which brought the day's, and possibly the convention's, greatest demonstration.

The nomination was actually accomplished about 12:15 P. M., when New Hampshire's eleven votes pushed the Dewey column over the 529 needed by a margin of six votes. Until that point the roll call had been responded to by one State after another voting its solid delegation for Dewey. It proceeded thus until Wisconsin was reached and the delegation leader announced the single MacArthur vote.

After the roll call, Wisconsin asked for recognition. Delegates and spectators expected that the State would withdraw its MacArthur vote and make the Dewey nomination unanimous. Such was not to happen, however. The delegation's leader merely announced that the four Stassen delegates had gone over to Dewey and added:

"That's all, Mr. Chairman."

The virtual unanimity of Mr. Dewey's vote was assured when Governor Bricker went to the rostrum and announced withdrawal of his candidacy.

The Ohio Governor told the crowd that what he had campaigned for most of all, in his criss-cross visits about the country, was for a Republican victory. He was more interested in that and in a repeal of the philosophy of the New Deal, he said, than in being President of the United States. Since it was obvious that a majority of the delegates wanted to nominate Governor Dewey, he could, and would, do no less than join in the general acclaim.

A demonstration broke out in the Ohio delegation, and was joined by numerous delegates in the hall and by spectators in the galleries. It was punctuated by demands that Mr. Bricker stay in the race for President. The shouting and parading continued for fifteen minutes, topping by five minutes the cheering for Governor Dewey when his name was first presented.

The New York Governor was placed in nomination by Gov. Dwight Grisfold of Nebraska, who hailed him as "youth's spokesman for the future," to supplant the Democratic party's "spokesman for the past." Placards with huge blue and black letters, "Dewey Will Win" and "Dewey the People's Choice," appeared in all parts of the hall when his name was first mentioned.

Various seconding speeches followed.

Among the speakers was Senator Joseph Ball of Minnesota, who had intended up to the time of Mr. Warren's withdrawal, to present the name of Lieutenant Commander Stassen.

Representative Everett M. Dirksen of Illinois, who had been a candidate for vice president, said during his speech that a combination of Dewey and Bricker would be "a winning ticket for next November."

Gov. Leverett Saltonstall of Massachusetts; Representative Leonard Hall of New York; Mrs. Rose Mayes of Idaho, and former Municipal Judge Patrick P. Prescott of Chicago also seconded the nomination.

"Today we bring Sir Galahad in quest of the Holy Grail, the knight in shining armor who will burst the biggest gang that has ever infested the United States," shouted Judge Prescott. "New York now gives Thomas E. Dewey to the limitless ages."

June 29, 1944

2 WILLKIE MEN GET REPUBLICAN POSTS

Weeks and Cake Are Among 15 Named by Brownell for Executive Committee

Herbert Brownell Jr., Republican national chairman, announced yesterday his appointments to the new executive committee of the Republican National Committee. The selections have the approval of Governor Dewey, the party's candidate for President, and Gov. John W. Bricker, the Vice Presidential nominee, and are representative of all shades of Republican opinion, according to Mr. Brownell.

Among the fifteen chosen by Mr. Brownell under authority of a resolution adopted at the post-convention session of the national committee are Ralph H. Cake of Oregon, who managed Wendell L. Willkie's unsuccessful pre-convention campaign for the Republican nomination, and Sinclair Weeks of Massachusetts, former Republican treasurer and close friend of Mr. Willkie.

Others appointed were:

Mrs. Robert F. Archibald Jr. of Colorado, Clarence J. Brown of Ohio, Mrs. Chris Carlson of Minnesota, Col. R. B. Creager of Texas, Harry Darby of Kansas, Mrs. W. F. Few of North Carolina, Harvey Jewett Jr. of South Dakota, Barak T. Mattingly of Missouri, Carroll Reece of Tennessee, Mrs. Reeve Schley of New Jersey, Mrs. Worthington Scranton of Pennsylvania, J. Russel Sprague of New York and Mrs. Jessie Williamson of California.

In announcing the appointments, Mr. Brownell said: "The membership of this committee reflects the unity and harmony with which the Republican party launches its campaign to elect Thomas E. Dewey as President and John W. Bricker as Vice President."

Besides those appointed yesterday, the executive committee consists of Mr. Brownell and the other officers of the national committee who were elected after the recent convention.

Mr. Brownell declined to identify the viewpoints represented by individual members of the committee when asked specifically which of them spoke for the Republicans who accept the leadership of Col. Robert R. McCormick, publisher of The Chicago Tribune.

He noted that many of the executive committee members are newcomers to the Republican National Committee. Those who will be serving on the executive committee for the first time are Mrs. Archibald, Mr. Brown, Mr. Darby, Mrs. Few, Mr. Mattingly, Mrs. Schley and Mrs. Williamson.

On the assumption that the designation of Mr. Cake and Mr. Weeks represented an attempt to obtain Mr. Willkie's support for the ticket, Mr. Brownell was asked if he had consulted with the 1940 nominee. In reply he said he had not consulted with any party leaders yet, but expected "to see all leaders in the course of the campaign."

Mr. Brownell said that he had discussed his selections with both Governor Dewey and Governor Bricker before deciding to make them public. "They enthusiastically approved," he reported.

"All the members of the committee," he volunteered, "are Republicans enthusiastic for the election of our ticket."

The chairman said he planned to be in constant touch by telephone and correspondence with the members of the committee, who, he noted, are represenetative of all sections of the country.

Whether Mr. Willkie can be induced to declare for Governor Dewey through the retention of two of his supporters on the executive committee seemed dubious last night in view of the election of Werner W. Schroeder of Chicago as vice-chairman of the National Committee last week. Two years ago, Mr. Willkie blocked Mr. Schroeder's election as national chairman on the allegation that Mr. Schroeder represented the isolationist viewpoint of The Chicago Tribune, which he believes the party should repudiate unequivocally.

It was also noted that neither Mr. Cake nor Mr. Weeks was a newcomer to the executive committee; Mr. Weeks was a member of the last one by virtue of his former position as national treasurer, and Mr. Cake by appointment under the previous regime.

Recurrent reports that Mr. Willkie might be named as Republican candidate for United States Senator from New York to oppose Senator Robert F. Wagner, were received with scorn by those familiar with Mr. Willkie's views. These reports first gained circulation after Mr. Willkie's retirement from the race for the Presidential nomination but have never received any recognition from him.

They cropped up again after the circulation of reports that a reconciliation between the Governor and Mr. Willkie had been effected by Representative Claire Boothe Luce of Connecticut.

"I have not seen Representative Luce in several months nor have I had any political or other discussions with her of any kind." Mr. Willkie said.

July 6, 1944

PRESIDENT HINTS OF STAY IN OFFICE

He Might Meet Churchill Late Next Spring as He Doesn't Like Atlantic in Winter

By TURNER CATLEDGE
Special to THE NEW YORK TIMES.

WASHINGTON, May 26—A press conference remark by President Roosevelt that he might meet Prime Minister Churchill in an inter-Allied War Conference late next spring, was seized upon here this afternoon as the clearest public indication which the President has given to date that he expects to run for and be elected to a fourth term.

He said that he hoped to see the Prime Minister at some time in the future, either this summer, this fall or late spring. His entire assertion was made with airy good humor, which indicated his awareness of the speculation he was setting off, for indeed it set political Washington, already nervous over the imponderables, guessing as to what the President might have up his political sleeve.

Questions as to his intentions, regarding both international conferences and a fourth-term bid, were brought up at the press conference and prompted the same sort of indefinite, good-humored response.

Time Will Tell, He Replies

The matter of a fourth-term candidacy came first. A correspondent reminded him that more than enough delegates had been pledged to him in State conventions and primaries to assure his nomination.

"I'm not asking you to tell us what your decision is," the correspondent continued. "I am asking whether you have made a decision?" The President's first response was a deep, rolling laugh. He remarked that he had thought the question of his intentions had been put in every conceivable form, but confessed that this was a new one.

He continued to laugh and rephrase this reply as correspondents insisted upon an answer. He did not show the irritation he had shown four years ago when newspaper men asked questions about his third-term intentions. He finally ended the discussion with the remark that time would tell.

Coming at him from another angle, a correspondent recalled that the newly formed Liberal party had nominated him for re-election and asked if he had been notified, and if he had accepted. The President again laughed and replied that the only notification he had received was through the newspapers.

Politically, the most significant thing seen in his suggestions about a meeting with Mr. Churchill was that he looked as far ahead as next spring, to a time evidently beyond the date of the inauguration of the next President. When asked why he had left winter out of the possible seasons in which he might meet the British Prime Minister, the reply was that he did not like the stormy weather on the North Atlantic in winter.

"Do they expect to meet in Paris next time?" a correspondent whispered.

"No, Berlin," a confrere suggested.

So far as a future Roosevelt-Churchill meeting is concerned, it was the understanding from their first war conference that they would meet personally from time to time, at intervals as near every three months as practicable.

Without referring to this tentative schedule, some observers professed to believe that Mr. Roosevelt had something in mind that might take the spotlight off of the Republican convention next month, or at least give a new cast to the campaign next fall.

As Mr. Roosevelt continued to parry — some correspondents thought weakly—questions as to his fourth-term candidacy, political observers continued to consider it a foregone certainty.

Holding this view of Mr. Roosevelt's nomination and acceptance, the CIO Political Action Committee, formed primarily to campaign for his re-election, began plans for a national conference in Washington in mid-June to chart its program. CIO spokesmen said that more than 300 delegates would attend the meeting which, they emphasized, would be held on the eve of the first, or Republican, convention.

Meanwhile, reports persisted among Republicans of a budding "stop Dewey" movement arising out of factions not entirely satisfied with his candidacy. Non-Dewey leaders surveyed the field of 442 publicly committed delegates in search of support for other candidates, especially for Gov. John W. Bricker of Ohio, who appears to be the logical focal point for those opposed to the New York Governor.

So far, the "stop Dewey" movement seems to be more a matter of conversation than of substance and, like it or not, most politically minded persons in Washington continued to regard nomination of the New York Governor as highly likely, if not virtually certain.

May 27, 1944

WALLACE LOOMS LARGE IN PRE-CONVENTION TALK

Party Leaders Weigh Possibilities of Supplanting Him on Ticket

By TURNER CATLEDGE

WASHINGTON, May 27 — The Democratic quest for a Vice Presidential candidate to team with Franklin D. Roosevelt in his expected fourth-term bid in November, is compelling wider and wider notice in the political community as time for candidate selection draws inevitably nearer.

As matters stand today, this problem of the Democrats is the principal prospect out of a very few possibilities, for lifting either of the forthcoming party conventions out of what promise otherwise to be very humdrum affairs.

It can be recalled that it was only the contest over the Vice Presidential berth that prevented the Democratic meeting from fading into utter dullness in 1940. The chief reason that prompted the set-to at that time has survived these four years, and is the one behind the intra-party stirrings today. It is the simple fact that many of the most influential Democratic leaders do not want Henry A. Wallace.

How Far to Go?

But how far these leaders are prepared to go in preventing his selection is the question that must needs make any observer cautious in predicting what may happen at the Democratic meeting.

If the choice of a Vice Presidential candidate were left strictly to the convention, there would be little doubt today as to Mr. Wallace's fate. He would be dropped without ceremony. Mr. Wallace and his type of New Dealer have never been popular with the kind of men who ordinarily control Democratic conventions.

But there has been no definite indication yet that the choice is going to be left to the "duly constituted" nominators. An amusing episode which occurred at the 1940 convention illustrates the point. After Mr. Wallace, then Secretary of Agriculture, had been nominated in a rousing, noisy, protesting meeting, and his nomination had been made formally unanimous, Bascom N. Timmons, Washington correspondent for several Texas papers, walked up to congratulate him. The convention had been so irritated, however, during the steam-rolling tactics employed to select Mr. Wallace, that a delegate somewhat in his cups gained the floor and placed Mr. Timmons in nomination. Mr Timmons got one vote on each roll-call until the bitter end.

Two Men—Two Votes

"Mr. Secretary," Mr. Timmons said to the successful Vice Presidential nominee, "I want to congratulate you with all my heart. You and I came to this convention even. I had one vote, and you had one. My vote was John E. Flannagan of Wisconsin and yours was Franklin D. Roosevelt of New York."

Those who insist upon a substitute for Mr. Wallace this time have no illusions about the possible task before them, despite their certainty of what the convention would do if left to itself. They realize that he was the President's choice in the first place, and that Mr. Roosevelt can have his way this time, even more perhaps than in 1940. They are fully aware, also, that Mr. Wallace has his heart and head set on running again, and they suspect him of using every occasion to push his suit upon the President.

Moreover, from the reactions they have been able to get from Mr. Roosevelt on the subject, these Democratic leaders are anything but certain that the President will not make another demand for Mr. Wallace's nomination.

Other Candidates Proposed

The most the anti-Wallace Democrats have done to date is to try to compile a list of candidates from which the President might select, or permit the whole list to be presented to the convention. On that list are such names as Speaker Sam Rayburn, Senators Alben W. Barkley of Kentucky, Harry F. Byrd of Virginia, Scott Lucas of Illinois, and Harry Truman of Missouri. Secretary Cordell Hull and the Under-Secretary of State, Edward R. Stettinius Jr.; former Justice James F. Byrnes, former Postmaster General James A. Farley, Gov. Robert Kerr of Oklahoma, and Gov. J. Melville Broughton of North Carolina.

Mr. Wallace's opponents have been tempted with the idea that the President might conceivably ask Gen. George C. Marshall, Chief of Staff of the Army, to accept the nomination and thus help him form an "all-out-for-war" ticket.

The list-makers have suggested furthermore that, if the President

Bob Leavitt from Pix

Henry A. Wallace.

must have an outstanding New Dealer, he indicate some one of the stripe of Associate Justice Robert H. Jackson or William O. Douglas—one with more political appeal and more capable of being built up politically than Mr. Wallace. They have also given some consideration to John G. Winant, Ambassador to Great Britain, but apparently ruled him out because of his Republican connections.

"Stop Wallace" Proposals

The stop-Wallace leaders have also proposed that if the convention has free choice in the selection of the Vice Presidential candidate, they will see to it that Mr. Wallace's name is included, and even put first on the list. They would even consent that the President say openly he favored Mr. Wallace, provided Mr. Roosevelt would not lay down a "take-him-or-don't-take-me" ultimatum. They would not advise this course, however, because of their belief that under such circumstances Mr. Wallace would surely be turned down and the President and the ticket accordingly deeply embarrassed.

Deep down in the Wallace opposition is a contest for control of the Democratic party organization. Renomination of the Iowan would be an undeniable signal that Franklin D. Roosevelt still hopes to throw the party to its liberal wing, as revived, enlarged and, to a great extent, created during his incumbency, when he steps down from the Presidential chair.

Also beneath the surface is the apprehension that whoever is named the Democratic Vice Presidential candidate this year may conceivably be President. The Republicans have already indicated that they will capitalize on that apprehension during the campaign. The current search for a Vice Presidential candidate in the Democratic party is, frankly, more of a stop-Wallace movement than it is a "start" movement for anyone else. If the political leaders finally center on some one name, it will be more because of the feeling that they can succeed in substituting this particular one in the President's favor than anything else.

Meanwhile, some of the more realistic party spokesmen are beginning to realize that Mr. Wallace has certain strength which cannot be ignored under the particular conditions of the times. They know, for instance, that he has become the symbol of the ultra-New Dealers and CIO labor in their resistance to the recent so-called "rightist" tendencies within the party and the Administration.

Under more ordinary circumstances the Wallace-stoppers could ignore this showing of liberal enthusiasm for him and the demands that some labor leaders have made upon the President for his renomination. They could say—and possibly can say now—that the President would gather in this vote, no matter who his running mate. This time, however, the CIO is already putting into the field, through its Political Action Committee, a force which observers are beginning to regard as one of the most potentially important for the coming campaign.

May 28, 1944

President Laughs Again When Asked 'the' Question

Special to The New York Times.

WASHINGTON, June 27—President Roosevelt laughed off the fourth term question again today.

A reporter asked at his news conference if there was anything he could say today on the Democratic candidate for President.

The President threw his head back and laughed, then turned to the questioner and said, "So they saddled that one on you today."

It had been some time since "The" question had been asked. Some correspondents, knowing the President's way of sometimes blanketing Republican convention news with major news of his own, had thought that the eve of Governor Dewey's nomination might strike him as an opportune time to make his announcement.

But Mr. Roosevelt apparently thought otherwise.

June 28, 1944

The President's Letter

By The Associated Press.

WASHINGTON, July 11—The text of President Roosevelt's letter to Chairman Hannegan, saying he will accept a nomination by the Democratic National Convention is as follows:

Dear Mr. Hannegan:

You have written me that in accordance with the records a majority of the delegates have been directed to vote for my renomination for the office of President, and I feel that I owe to you, in candor, a simple statement of my position.

If the convention should carry this out, and nominate me for the Presidency, I shall accept. If the people elect me, I will serve.

Every one of our sons serving in this war has officers from whom he takes his orders. Such officers have superior officers. The President is the Commander in Chief and he, too, has his superior officer—the people of the United States.

I would accept and serve, but I would not run, in the usual partisan, political sense. But if the people command me to continue in this office and in this war I have as little right to withdraw as the soldier has to leave his post in the line.

At the same time, I think I have a right to say to you and to the delegates to the coming convention something which is personal—purely personal.

For myself, do not want to run. By next spring, I shall have been President and Commander in Chief of the armed forces for twelve years—three times elected by the people of this country under the American constitutional system.

From the personal point of view, I believe that our economic system is on a sounder, more human basis than it was at the time of my first inauguration.

It is perhaps unnecessary to say that I have thought only of the good of the American people. My principal objective, as you know, has been the protection of the rights and privileges and fortunes of what has been so well called the average of American citizens.

After many years of public service, therefore, my personal thoughts have turned to the day when I could return to civil life. All that is within me cries out to go back to my home on the Hudson River, to avoid public responsibilities, and to avoid also the publicity which in our democracy follows every step of the nation's Chief Executive.

Such would be my choice. But we of this generation chance to live in a day and hour when our nation has been attacked, and when its future existence and the future existence of our chosen method of government are at stake.

To win this war wholeheartedly, unequivocally and as quickly as we can is our task of the first importance. To win this war in such a way that there be no further world wars in the foreseeable future is our second objective. To provide occupations, and to provide a decent standard of living for our men in the armed forces after the war, and for all Americans, are the final objectives.

Therefore, reluctantly, but as a good soldier, I repeat that I will accept and serve in this office, if I am so ordered by the Commander in Chief of us all—the sovereign people of the United States.

Very sincerely yours,
FRANKLIN D. ROOSEVELT.

Mr. Hannegan's Letter

The letter written to Mr. Roosevelt by Mr. Hannegan read:

July 10, 1944.

Dear Mr. President:

As chairman of the Democratic National Committee, it is my duty on behalf of the committee to present for its consideration a temporary roll of the delegates for the national convention, which will convene in Chicago on July 19, 1944.

The national committee has received from the State officals of the Democratic party certification on the action of the State conventions, and the primaries in those States which select delegates in that manner.

Based upon these officials' certifications to the national committee, I desire to report to you that more than a clear majority of the delegates to the national convention are legally bound by the action of their constituents to cast their ballots for your nomination as President of the United States. This action in the several States is a reflection of the wishes of the vast majority of the American people that you continue as President in this crucial period in the nation's history.

I feel, therefore, Mr. President, that it is my duty as chairman of the Democratic National Committee to report to you the fact that the national convention will, during its deliberations in Chicago, tender to you the nomination of the party as it is the solemn belief of the rank and file of Democrats, as well as many other Americans, that the nation and the world need the continuation of your leadership.

In view of the foregoing, I would respectfully request that you send to the convention or otherwise convey to the people of the United States an expression that you will again respond to the call of the party and the people. I am confident that the people recognize the tremendous burdens of your office, but I am equally confident that they are determined that you must continue until the war is won and a firm basis for abiding peace among men is established.

Respectfully,
ROBERT E. HANNEGAN.

July 12, 1944

THE DEMOCRATIC PARTY ENTERS A NEW PHASE

Truman's Nomination Marks Attempt To Hold Together the Dissidents For the Campaign's Duration

'MAJOR NEW DEAL SURRENDER'

By ARTHUR KROCK

CHICAGO, July 22—In its national convention of 1944, just concluded here, the Democratic party—as realigned by President Roosevelt—entered upon a new phase which many believe to be the final one under its present leadership. The new phase was an attempt, through the nomination for Vice President of Senator Harry S. Truman of Missouri over Henry A. Wallace, and by the adoption of a platform which in many respects turned its back on the early New Deal, to hold in a common front for the campaign's duration the dissident groups that came into violent conflict during the convention.

On the surface the effort was successful, although it was achieved at the expense (1) of Mr. Wallace's ambition to succeed himself, (2) of the attempt of the CIO to exercise a full affirmative as well as negative power over all the proceedings of the convention and (3) of the hopes of Negro organizations that what the New Deal had so lavishly encouraged would be reflected in the Democratic platform the President dictated, line by line.

It was successful because the warnings of old-line Democrats to Mr. Roosevelt that he would risk his election by dictating to the convention the nomination of Mr. Wallace as his running mate persuaded him to make a series of substitute endorsements that put the Vice President at the mercy of his party opponents. These, by scattering their opposition on the first ballot and thus preventing Mr. Wallace from getting a majority, were able thereby to effect a winning combination with Senator Truman, who was apparently the only rival of the Vice President acceptable to the old-liners and to the CIO who could possibly defeat Mr. Wallace for renomination.

Pressure by Labor Group.

The labor pressure group assembled here under the banner of the CIO, carried by Philip Murray, president, and Sidney Hillman, chairman of its Political Action Committee, was thus enabled to prevent the nomination for Vice President of a candidate of whom it disapproved, while at the same time the party group opposed to the CIO's domination was permitted to have its first choice among the competitors of Mr. Wallace. Mr. Truman's nomination was the ultimate outcome.

The CIO, which in most other respects had a greater influence on the Democratic convention than the Democratic National Committee or any other leadership except the President's, by this compromise was kept in active sponsorship of the ticket and in political harness — except for the regular organization in Texas—with the Southerners who came to Chicago determined to reassert their position in the party. That fact was of real significance.

The Virginia Democratic organization, led by Senator Harry F. Byrd, who objects to a fourth term for the President as he did a third and is the Congressional spearhead of Democratic and coalition opposition to the domestic policies of the President and the New Deal, was put in a position where it was obliged to make common cause against Mr. Wallace with the big city bosses, or permit him to be renominated. The results were important.

Like most other Southern Democratic groups, the Virginians are unwilling to foster, follow or create an independent movement calculated to give their State electors to the Republicans in the November elections.

Eager to Compromise

Therefore they seized upon the chance offered to them by the President's agreement not to dictate Mr. Wallace's renomination, to unite upon a running mate who, in event of his succession to the Presidency, would be more of their political mind than responsive to the new elements in the party of which they strongly disapprove.

In view of their local situations, there was nothing else for them to do. Accordingly, most of them are expected to carry their States for the party ticket in November and, in Congress and outside, to make a determined effort after the election to restore the Democratic party to its traditional leadership.

If the President is re-elected with a Republican Congress, or one—the more general expectation—that will be controlled by an anti-New Deal and Republican fusion—this move of restoration can be expected to be made gradually. If the President is defeated, the combination that defeated Mr. Wallace after Mr. Roosevelt made it clear he would not interpose to prevent it, will be certain to take immediate steps to control the party as of yore.

Weakness Revealed

The weakness which, despite the war that made the President the inevitable nominee for a fourth term, was revealed here by concessions in the platform and the permitted sacrifice of Mr. Wallace, compelled the first major surrender of the New Deal. If the political reasoning of the groups that sponsored the Vice President, particularly the CIO, had been accepted by Mr. Roosevelt, the Negro leaders would not now be denouncing the platform for failing even to endorse the Fair Employment Practices Commission by name, as the Republicans did, an omission which was deliberately made to forestall if possible the electoral loss of certain Southern States. And if this reasoning had been accepted, the President, who really preferred to run again with Mr. Wallace, would have dictated his renomination as patently as he did the platform.

If the President had believed his political strength as Commander in Chief in wartime was as sure to win him re-election as it was renomination, the decisions of this convention would have been different. No attempt would have been made, as it was unsuccessfully, to compromise the basic issue between the regular and the contesting delegations from Texas, and Mr. Wallace would not have been the sacrifice to expediency he has become.

Sacrifice to Expediency

But National Chairman Robert E. Hannegan and several of the big city bosses on whom Mr. Roosevelt has relied for the assurances of victory on three successive elections, have for some time brought him reports that his campaign strength is not great enough to carry Mr. Wallace and to write into the platform the specific measures favored by his Vice President, by the "old" New Dealers and by the CIO. The President was brought to believe this after a period of doubt and dispute, and he sought instead to find compromises by which the now warring groups he assembled in 1932 could be held together for one more successful campaign for him and his party.

Texas was the one situation in the party which could not be compromised, and the electors of Texas may bring about the Republican victory which the compromises and sacrifices were desperately invoked to prevent. But whether or not that happens, the Democratic party as now constituted is clearly on the verge of violent change. For the CIO veto power which was exercised here so openly will not be accepted by the party leaders most likely to succeed the President.

GOP CONVENES ON VICTORY NOTE

RIVALS ARE LOCKED

Streets Resound to Din of Paraders as Crowds Cheer in Sessions

KEYNOTER HITS NEW DEAL

Dewey Forces Scoff at Proposal by McCormick for a Taft-Stassen Ticket

By WILLIAM S. WHITE
Special to THE NEW YORK TIMES.

PHILADELPHIA, June 21—The twenty-fourth Republican National Convention opened today with the delegates convinced that now the party was in successful pursuit of the Presidency of the United States.

The unchanging theme was attack on the Democratic administrations of the last sixteen years, those of Franklin D. Roosevelt no less than that of Harry S. Truman.

Tonight the strongest of these attacks, that of the keynoter, Gov. Dwight H. Green of Illinois, brought intermittent bursts of applause in the steamy Convention Hall. Again, as it had been this morning, the delegates were not in an especially noisy mood. Rather they seemed satisfied to ratify what was being said over the amplifiers.

Confidence moved like waves over the vast, perspiring amphitheatre. In the intermittent blasts of bands and the occasional peals of a pipe organ, the Republicans were gathered to try to break half a generation of democratic control of the White House.

Taft-Stassen Slate Urged

Outside the Municipal Auditorium, with its banks of 16,500 seats, its shifting spotlights and endless din, the forces of two of the leading Presidential contenders, Senator Robert A. Taft of Ohio and Gov. Thomas E. Dewey of New York, were fighting to improve their positions. Mr. Dewey, by all the common reckonings, held the more favorable one, but a contest of unusual determination seemed under way.

In the afternoon, Col. Robert R. McCormick, publisher of the Chicago Tribune and a powerful factor in the orthodox Republicanism of the Middle West, came out for a ticket headed by Mr. Taft with Harold E. Stassen, the former Minnesota Governor, in second place.

Senator Taft was non-committal on this suggestion, but he said that "any ticket with Taft at the head would not be beatable."

Herbert Brownell, one of the Dewey managers, told reporters that "I'm glad that the Chicago Tribune ticket is out in the open at last." He asserted that "all the facts" demonstrated that Mr. Dewey would be nominated and elected, then said that his candidate would make "no deals."

Position Unaltered, Stassen Says

As for Mr. Stassen, it was plain that he was keenly interested in "stopping Dewey." Reporters, nevertheless, were given to understand unmistakably that Mr. Stassen would not agree to such an arrangement as proposed by Mr. McCormick.

"There's nothing to it. There'll never be anything of the kind," said Gov. Luther Youngdahl of Minnesota, a member of the Stassen convention general staff.

The McCormick statement drew added interest because of his recent dinner engagement with Mr. Stassen. Informed opinion was that Mr. Stassen in no event, even if he chose, could "deliver" to Senator Taft the greater part of the strength that has been marshaled behind the Minnesotan.

Late in the day Mr. Stassen said that he had read the McCormick statement "with interest," but added that his position was unchanged, and that he expected to drive on to final victory for the first place on the ticket.

Colonel McCormick's statement was regarded not only as a development directly in the stop-Dewey drive but also a demonstration against a possibility of a draft movement for Senator Arthur H. Vandenberg of Michigan.

"I am for Taft," Mr. McCormick said, "and I have no second choice. Vandenberg can't even carry Michigan. He only got back to the Senate by making a deal with Roosevelt, backing the Roosevelt foreign policy, in return for which a stooge was put up against him who really campaigned for Vandenberg, and the logical candidate, who stepped out of the way for the stooge, was rewarded for his treachery to the Democratic party by being appointed Governor of Austria.

[Murray D. Van Wagoner, former Governor of Michigan, is military governor of Bavaria. There is not now nor never has been any such functionary as an American governor of Austria.]

"Dewey ran 250,000 votes behind the ticket in Illinois and dragged a great many state and country candidates down with him. He wouldn't do any better this year. I don't think he can carry more than twelve states again this year.

"Stassen is strong with the young people, but mature people think he lacks maturity. In 1900, McKinley was nominated for his prestige and Theodore Roosevelt for his personal popularity. Therefore, it seems reasonable to nominate Taft and Stassen for the same reasons."

The McCormick statement and the reactions to it illustrated the hard, skilled and quietly dramatic maneuvering that was going on here to bring advantage to one candidate or another in a multi-sided struggle more nearly balanced than in many years.

The big enigma in the situation, Senator Arthur H. Vandenberg of Michigan, arrived tonight. He said simply that his position was unchanged. This meant that Mr. Vandenberg, the Republican foreign policy leader, would submit to a genuine draft.

Coincident with his arrival, it was learned that on several occasions he had remarked that a man could not vote in Congress to draft men for military service and not himself be willing to respond to a call for high political service.

Mr. Vandenberg's qualified availability stirred no new excitement in Philadelphia, where another significant development was the second successive preliminary victory won by Mr. Dewey over Senator Taft.

The Credentials Committee sustained the National Committee in giving the Dewey forces control of the Georgia delegations. The unsuccessful appeal of Taft supporters against the National Committee was specifically on a motion to unseat the sixteen Dewey delegates from Georgia.

Other Southern delegations were having troubles. The control of the Mississippi delegation was hanging in suspense in Federal Court.

Alabama, first on the roster of the states, refused by a 7-7 vote to yield its favored place on the first roll-call to New York so that Mr. Dewey's name could be the first put in nomination.

A majority of the Alabama delegation, nine, still stood for Governor Dewey, but personal disagreements within it would not permit the state to give way when the nominating began. Arizona was understood to be ready, if requested, to make the gesture.

The first session of the convention, which began at 11:27 A. M. and ended just before 1 P. M., was brisk and busy. Modern as was the scene under the heat of the kleig lights, the atmosphere was heavy with tradition. The Republicans had returned to the city where first they had met, ninety-two years ago, as a national party, to nominate Fremont for the Presidency.

The two major speeches today, by Carroll Reece, Republican national chairman, and Governor Green left no doubt that the line of the Republican party this year was to be unending frontal assault.

Mr. Green denounced "the new deal party" as one of a "fantastic partnership of reaction and radicalism" and said that it had long harbored "crackpots" unfit for responsible office.

Recalling the Republican capture of Congress in 1946, Governor Green praised its record, alike on domestic and foreign affairs, as one that had redeemed the promises made two years ago.

The Republican Congress, he asserted, freed the national economy from "regimentation"; it had balanced the budget, and it had corrected a "chaotic" condition in labor-management relations.

As to affairs abroad, he said that this country was "losing the peace" through a "confused and incompetent foreign policy," and that "new deal diplomacy" by appeasement of the Soviet Union had thrown away a great victory at arms.

"Real bipartisanship," he added, "shares the making of decisions as well as the meeting of the consequences. The New Deal's idea of bipartisanship is that one party launches the ship and the other salvages the wreck. It is high time to make this fact clear. On the rare occasions when Republicans have been consulted, blunder and disaster have been avoided."

As to the future, Governor Green pledged for the Republicans a "very definite program for an American foreign policy."

"That program," he asserted, "was created at the Mackinac (Mich.) conference in 1943 and confirmed in our platform of 1944. It is a simple and clear pledge to work for a lasting peace based on justice and freedom and to preserve the strength of America.

"We adopted the Atlantic Charter—that abandoned waif, forsaken during the New Deal's tryst with communism."

The Republican party in Congress, Mr. Green said, had "supported its own principle of international cooperation in full measure" and had helped create and support the United Nations. The Republicans had voted funds for foreign relief and recovery, he added, because they "wanted to check the spread of communism and to aid freedom in Europe."

* * * * *

June 22, 1948

COMPROMISE TALK TURNS TO WARREN

Growing Coalition of Dewey and Conservatives Inclines Liberals to Californian

By JAMES RESTON
Special to THE NEW YORK TIMES.

PHILADELPHIA, June 23—Gov. Earl Warren of California is beginning to figure more prominently in the calculations of the politicians along the smoky-room circuit.

For the moment, these harassed and weary gentlemen are engaged in the task of stopping Gov. Thomas E. Dewey of New York. This is the first job and it has brought together some curious bedfellows. But occasionally they have time to wonder what they will do if they do stop him., and at this point Mr. Warren begins to come into the conversation.

Between now and the third ballot tomorrow the strategy of the Stassen - Duff - Taft - Vandenberg forces is to hold the line, keep their own and the favorite-son blocs intact, and thus avoid any move that would throw more delegates to Governor Dewey.

Then, and presumably before then, they will confer on where to go from there. Harold Stassen is certain to try to lead the coalition toward Senator Vandenberg, and in this move every effort will be made by the Michigan delegation to induce Governor Warren to go along.

Taft Promise to Bricker Reported

The barrier on this road, however, is the complicated position of Senator Taft. He can control his delegation for himself, but he cannot transfer his strength to Mr. Vandenberg. The reasons for this, according to the Taft forces, are as follows:

Even if Mr. Taft favored the candidacy of Mr. Vandenberg, which he does not, he could not get the support of Senator John Bricker, who is, in some ways, even stronger with the Ohio political organization than Mr. Taft.

Mr. Taft has promised, it is said, to do what he can to bring Mr. Bricker back into the picture, perhaps as a compromise or as a Vice Presidential candidate, if he can, and Mr. Bricker is believed to be more interested in promoting the political future and beliefs of Mr. Bricker than the political future and policies of Mr. Vandenberg.

There are two other reasons why the Taft strength is not likely to be transferred to Mr. Vandenberg: first, if Mr. Taft tried to transfer it, Illinois would desert him at once for Mr. Dewey, whom Colonel Robert McCormick of The Chicago Tribune opposes somewhat less than he opposes Mr. Vandenberg, and second, much of Mr. Taft's southern delegate strength would follow. Such a development, as Mr. Taft made clear today, would nominate not Mr. Vandenberg but Mr. Dewey.

Similar considerations prevent Mr. Stassen from throwing his strength to Mr. Taft. The former Minnesota Governor does not have "machine strength" in the sense that Mr. Taft does. His support comes largely from people who believe he is the leader of the young and liberal wings of the party. He can, therefore, cooperate with Mr. Taft to stop Mr. Dewey, but he is not interested in putting Mr. Taft's policies into power, and his delegates would not follow him if he were.

The Stassen forces, therefore, must either find a coalition minus the Taft forces that will nominate Mr. Vandenberg or they must combine with Mr. Taft on some other figure, and of the available candidates Mr. Warren is the one now being mentioned by responsible observers here as a possible compromise.

Mr. Warren is on the "liberal" side of the party, but he has not been so scarred in the battle as Senator Vandenberg. He has opposed policies favored by Mr. Taft, but he has not inspired Mr. Bricker's opposition, and this is an important consideration in the transfer of Ohio's power.

Even the Vandenberg supporters see some advantage in giving Mr. Warren a run. Announcement of Taft-Stassen support for Governor Warren would certainly introduce a dramatic new element into the battle. It would divert attention from the Dewey blitz, and while it might not develop enough strength to win the nomination for the Californian, it might deadlock the convention, which would favor Senator Vandenberg.

Talk of Vice Presidency

The developing coalition between Mr. Dewey and the most conservative elements in the party is encouraging the liberal elements to get together in opposition. The town was full of rumors tonight that Charles Halleck of Indiana, who has collaborated with the Taber forces in the House of Representatives during the past session, might be rewarded with the Vice Presidency for his efforts to produce a Dewey victory.

This has put considerable meaning into the efforts of those who are seeking to liberalize the party and they do not see much progress in a House run by Speaker Martin of Massachusetts and a Senate run by Mr. Halleck and Mr. Taft.

With this prospect in mind, efforts were made today to induce Mr. Vandenberg to change his position. A speech from the floor by a prominent figure, denouncing the Dewey tactics and the nomination of a conservative Vice President might, it was felt, scatter the opposition, as Bryan scattered it at the Democratic convention of 1912.

Vandenberg Acts Quickly

Mr. Vandenberg, Mr. Stassen, and even Gen. Dwight D. Eisenhower were all being mentioned this afternoon for this task, but Mr. Vandenberg was not interested and the Eisenhower idea had its opponents, including, evidently, the general himself.

For a time today, in fact, Mr. Vandenberg took quick action to repress the enthusiasm of his own Governor, Kim Sigler of Michigan. Mr. Sigler had told the press that he would nominate Mr. Vandenberg with the latter's consent, but the Senator immediately rebuked him and emphasized once more that he was not going to "connive" at being nominated.

The trend, for the moment, therefore, is still running to Dewey with the opposition combining only for the limited objective of stopping him. If that can be done—and it is certainly not likely at the moment—every possible combination will be tried, and in almost all of them Mr. Warren and his delegation are increasingly important.

The trouble with the stop-Dewey coalition, of course, is that its members have little in common except the objective of stopping Governor Dewey.

If Mr. Taft can hold his Southern delegates, the movement to block Mr. Dewey may have some chance, but if he cannot, the nomination of Mr. Dewey will be almost certain. That is why Governor Duff and others have been boosting Mr. Taft tonight—in the hope of inducing Mr. Taft's delegates to stick.

June 24, 1948

DEWEY UNANIMOUS REPUBLICAN CHOICE

OPPOSITION FALLS

Taft and Stassen Join in Urging Selection of New Yorker

GOP PRECEDENT SET

Dewey Is First Defeated Candidate to Be Chosen Again

By WILLIAM S. WHITE
Special to THE NEW YORK TIMES.

PHILADELPHIA, June 24—Thomas E. Dewey was nominated tonight by the Republicans for the Presidency of the United States.

His selection, on the third ballot of the twenty-fourth Republican National Convention, was unanimous after his forces had smashed an opposing coalition.

When two ballots had shown that the Governor of New York was not to be stopped, his erstwhile antagonists renounced their rivalries with him and pledged all their power to his success in November.

Mr. Dewey came at once to the convention hall and, before the hot and shouting delegates, accepted his nomination in a placating spirit toward his former opponents.

"In all humility," he said, "I pray God that I may deserve this opportunity to serve our country."

"Lasting Peace" Put First

Above all its efforts, he declared, the Republican party and the country must seek for the world "a just and lasting peace."

The convention will select tomorrow a Vice Presidential nominee in what is described in the most authoritative quarters as a "wide open field."

Mr. Dewey said pointedly that he was "unfettered by a single obligation or promise to any living person." It was understood that the Dewey group wanted to consider overnight the available men for second place on the ticket.

Governor Dewey is the only Republican in the party's history to be nominated for President after having been once defeated. He lost in 1944 to Franklin D. Roosevelt.

On the first ballot today the Governor got 434 votes to 224 for Senator Robert A. Taft of Ohio, his strongest opponent.

On the second ballot, he climbed to 515 votes, as compared with 274 for Mr. Taft.

The results of the three ballots for the major leaders were as follows:

First—Dewey, 434; Taft, 224; Harld E. Stassen, 157; Senator Arthur H. Vandenberg of Michigan, 62.

Second—Dewey, 515; Taft, 274; Stassen, 149; Vandenberg, 62.

Third—Dewey, all 1,094 votes.

When the second roll-call ended associates of Senator Taft, Mr. Stassen and other anti-Dewey aspirants brought about a three-hour recess to resurvey their position.

When the convention returned to work, word swept the arena that Gov. Earl Warren of California, a "favorite son" candidate, had released the fifty-three delegates of that state. It was obvious that the California delegation, or a great part of it, was getting ready to go over to Mr. Dewey.

At this point, Senator John W. Bricker of Ohio went before the microphones to announce the withdrawal of his old friend, Senator Taft.

He read on behalf of Mr. Taft a statement that it was plain that a majority was prepared to turn to Mr. Dewey on the third ballot. Senator Taft therefore not only released his forces, but asked them to vote for Mr. Dewey and himself pledged every support to the New Yorker, now and in the campaign.

Mr. Taft's gesture was followed by Senator William F. Knowland of California in behalf of Governor Warren. Then Mr. Stassen went to the rostrum, smiling determinedly, to declare that he too was dropping out and to recommend Mr. Dewey.

Mr. Stassen said that with the "permission" of his supporters, he would like to second Mr. Dewey's nomination. At this there were some cries of "No!" in the hall.

Second Ballot Victory Balked

Senator Vandenberg was withdrawn by his principal backer, Gov. Kim Sigler of Michigan.

Senator Raymond Baldwin of Connecticut, another "favorite son," proposed that a roll call be dispensed with, and that was seconded by Harlan Kelley of Wisconsin, a backer of General MacArthur. The convention chairman, Speaker Joseph W. Martin Jr., ruled, however, that a ballot was necessary. It was then taken as a matter of form.

Governor Dewey might have been nominated on the second ballot had not Senator Baldwin found it impossible immediately to obtain a release from 'limited commitments to the stop-Dewey group by which he was to hold the Connecticut delegation for two ballots.

The first powerful factor in breaking the earlier coalition against Mr. Dewey was Senator Edward Martin of Pennsylvania, who caused a majority of that delegation two days ago to go over to the New Yorker.

With this great lift, the Dewey campaign began to roll powerfully and irresistibly as it turned out.

Convention Recess Forced

The anti-Dewey coalition forced a recess of nearly three hours at 4:55 P. M. in the hope that in the interim they could arrest the Dewey movement.

The Dewey forces, it appeared from all that was said in recent days, would have preferred to hold the convention in session until the nominee was chosen. Presumably they feared a defeat on a collateral issue that might have been used by the opposition to argue that they had shown weakness.

This critical day in the convention opened on the note that for three days had persisted: More gains for Governor Dewey—in the real or the psychological sense.

One of the earliest of these was the withdrawal of Senator Leverett Saltonstall as the "favorite son" of Massachusetts, the consequence of which was soon to be reflected in the seventeen Massachusetts votes Mr. Dewey got on the first ballot.

Almost at the hour of Senator Saltonstall's decision, Mr. Stassen was doggedly carrying on his "stop-Dewey" campaign downtown. Cryptically, he promised "developments" in the afternoon.

The convention itself first got under way in the hottest day that Philadelphia had seen since the Republicans gathered here.

On the first roll-call the Dewey candidacy went almost exactly as had been forecast by disinterested observers, and there was not a single genuine break in the lines.

All was tense as the second roll-call proceeded for the Dewey campaigners had not really expected anything like a first-ballot nomination, but had held cautious hope for a second.

This time Mr. Dewey went out almost at once to pick up gains far down the line of states. Iowa gave the New Yorker thirteen votes, or ten more than on the first roll call. He gained in Kansas, Kentucky, Maryland, Massachusetts, Missouri, Montana and Nebraska.

Then twenty-four of New Jersey's thirty-three votes, which on the first ballot had been thrown in for the "favorite son," Gov. Alfred Driscoll, went to Mr. Dewey. New York, as on the first ballot, gave him ninety-six votes of its ninety-seven, and Delegate Peter Wynne sat grinning as he again cast the single New York ballot for Senator Taft.

Now and again, as the balloting continued in a war of nerves among the partisans a delegate would demand that his state be polled, to learn whether its announced vote was correct. Sometimes the intention was to give publicity to delegates who had resisted the majority's will.

One such polling of a state, that of Ohio, reflected the rivalry and determination that were at work at the convention.

"No turncoat; still with Taft!" shouted one delegate as the Ohio list was called on the second ballot.

"Staying with Stassen—the people's candidate!" said a second.

"I do not apologize," shouted a third, in retort to the first, "for voting for Governor Dewey!"

June 25, 1948

Dewey's Strategy Team Acclaimed As Smooth, Efficient Organization

Brownell, Sprague, Jaeckle Directed Group in Consultation With Governor—Lockwood, Hagerty Handled 'Intelligence' Work

Special to THE NEW YORK TIMES.

PHILADELPHIA, June 25—On the "first team" that won Gov. Thomas E. Dewey the Republican nomination for President are fifteen "regulars" and a somewhat larger number of "second stringers" who are called on for occasional or special services. Political observers here rate it as one of the most efficient, smooth and well organized teams they have seen in action.

The direction of the team was in the hands of Herbert Brownell Jr., who started in politics with Mr. Dewey in Greenwich Village twenty years ago; J. Russel Sprague, ebullient national committeeman for New York, and Edwin F. Jaeckle, veteran Erie County chairman. No major strategy decisions were made without consulting all three.

Advising them and the Governor himself were John Foster Dulles, generally regarded as certain to become Secretary of State if Mr. Dewey is elected; Roger W. Straus, wealthy industrialist and philanthropist; Elliott V. Bell, New York State Superintendent of Banks and former editorial writer on THE NEW YORK TIMES; and John E. Burton, State Budget Director.

The Dulles-Straus-Bell-Burton group was consulted on all matters involving governmental policy, but not always on purely political decisions, such as the timing of announcements of new accretions of strength.

Paul E. Lockwood, the Governor's secretary, headed the intelligence and operating sections of the team. Working with him were James C. Hagerty, the Governor's executive assistant; Hamilton V. Gaddis, Hempstead, L. I., town clerk; Hickman Powell, free lance writer and former newspaperman and, occasionally, Harold Keller, State Commerce Commissioner.

Mrs. Weis Heads Women Section

Special appeals to women delegates and voters were directed by Mrs. Charles W. Weis Jr., Mr. Sprague's associate on the national committee from New York, and Miss Jane Todd, vice chairman of the Republican State Committee; with substantial help on occasion from Mrs. Rebecca McNab of Schenectady.

The financing aspect of the primary and convention campaigns was in the hands of Harold E. Tablot. This former international polo player is a director of the Chrysler Corporation and a pioneer financier in the aviation industry. He is a native of Dayton, Ohio, presently living in New York.

Representative Leonard W. Hall, chairman of the National Republican Congressional Campaign Committee, served as the liaison between the inner circle of the team and members of the House of Representatives. His influence was particularly valuable in winning acceptance of Mr. Dewey. Senator Irving M. Ives performed a similar function among the Senators.

What other delegates described as the "psychological warfare" phase of the campaign for the nomination was generally in the hands of Messrs. Brownell, Lockwood and Hagerty. They were the experts on the timing of announcements, but the substance of the statements represented chiefly the work of Messrs. Sprague, Jaeckle, Brownell and Governor Dewey himself.

Glen R. Bedenkapp, Republican State Chairman; William F. Bleakley, chairman of the New York delegation to the convention; R. Burdell Bixby, the Governor's assistant secretary; Alger B. Chapman, president of the State Tax Commission; William T. Pheiffer, former New York City member of Congress; Thomas A. Stephens, former assistant to Newbold Morris as president of the New York City Council, and others figured in execution of policies and programs determined at the top levels.

Veteran Support Sought

Business, social and political connections of members of the team and their friends were used extensively to obtain personal contact with delegates. Once that was established, the delegates were brought to the Dewey headquarters for personal conversations with top members of the team. If, after this, they seemed likely first or second choice prospects, they were taken to Mr. Dewey's suite for a talk with the candidate, usually as a member of some group.

Several members of the team have good relations with war veterans organizations. They found that Mr. Dewey's support of universal military training and the speech he made at the New York convention of the American Legion last year were particularly effective in enlisting the support of delegates who are war veterans. It was also effective in getting members of veteran organizations favorable to Mr. Dewey to telephone wavering or prospective delegates while they were attending convention sessions or waiting for sessions at their hotels.

The reaction of veterans to Mr. Dewey's policies was only one of many devices used to recruit and hold support. Every other one that had possibilities for success was also employed.

June 26, 1948

WARREN SELECTED BY PARTY LEADERS

He Gets Nod From Dewey After Night-Long Canvass of Possible Choices

By C. P. TRUSSELL

Special to THE NEW YORK TIMES.

PHILADELPHIA, June 25—Gov. Earl Warren of California was chosen for nomination as Vice President before the Republican national convention was called to order today. While delegations milled around the steaming auditorium, and the galleries waited impatiently an hour and a half for something to happen, it was happening, far from their view, at a conference of leaders.

When Joseph W. Martin Jr., Speaker of the House and permanent convention chairman, sounded his opening gavel it was all over except the acclamation. Obstacles, particularly the convention votes behind the House majority leader, Charles A. Halleck of Indiana, which had indicated his probable nomination, were blasted out of the way at the meetings which persisted throughout the night and until nearly noon.

Mr. Halleck was told that he was not the choice. When the nominating roll was called, Mr. Halleck prevented his name from being entered.

"I'm a realist," he said later.

Governor Warren was decided on as "the man" acceptable to the party factions represented at the closed-door conferences after he had paid a protracted before-dawn visit to Gov. Thomas E. Dewey of New York, who was nominated unanimously last night to head the party ticket.

Although Mr. Warren had been the most adamant of those refusing the second place nomination, even up to last midnight, Governor Dewey said today that when, at 4:30 A. M. he asked the Californian to see him, he knew he would be willing to accept the nomination.

Harold E. Stassen, former Governor of Minnesota, had been represented by a spokesman at 1 A. M. as saying he would submit to "a real draft by the convention," but did not expect one, since Mr. Dewey apparently "had someone else in mind."

Later this morning Governor Dewey called Mr. Stassen on the telephone. In answer to questions concerning the Vice Presidency, Mr. Stassen was quoted as saying:

"I will not put my name in nomination for the Vice Presidency. If the convention drafts me I will accept."

Many Names Considered

Governor Dewey was reported then to have requested Mr. Stassen to prevent his name from going before the convention, a request which Mr. Stassen rejected.

Arizona, as the nominating roll was called, reserved the right to put Mr. Stassen's name up, but when New York presented the name of Governor Warren the convention received its signal, and Arizona withdrew.

Although Mr. Stassen did not prevent his name from being introduced into the nominating proceedings, he did stop a fight, it developed later. Wisconsin's delegation was ready to battle it out for the Minnesotan. Senator Joseph R. McCarthy, chairman of the Wisconsin delegation, sent word of this plan to Mr. Stassen.

Senator McCarthy received the following answer:

"Do not fight Warren under any circumstances."

Thus the party choice, backed up by the convention's acclamation, had been made. It came from long lists of aspirants and faint possibilities. All night long, Governor Dewey emphasized to the news conference today, "dozens" of men had been consulted. "Many," he said, were willing to accept.

During the night-long interviews and manpower canvasses, Mr. Dewey said, he remained a questioner and listener, giving no expressions of his own. He was asked whether he would have accepted Mr. Halleck, whose foreign policy record in Congress had been under attack, or Senator John W. Bricker of Ohio, another who had figured in the speculation.

Mr. Dewey said that he would have accepted whomever the convention nominated.

In this instance, however, those unacceptable to the nominee were eliminated in advance, even though the convention delegates, hot, bothered and inactive, had to wait until almost the last detail of the convention unity was attended to, which appeared to stun delegates as much as the puzzled galleries.

At 11:15 A. M., forty-five minutes past the scheduled convening time of the nominating session, Mr. Halleck left Governor Dewey's suite after a second meeting in the early morning.

"I have no comment to make," Mr. Halleck told reporters. "They'll have to announce it."

June 26, 1948

* * * * * * *

FEW OBSERVERS NOW DOUBT THAT PRESIDENT WILL RUN

His Western Tour Is Believed to Have Been A Profitable Venture for His Party

By CLAYTON KNOWLES

Special to THE NEW YORK TIMES.

WASHINGTON, June 19—President Truman gambled in a big way as he headed West a-politicking with the Republican Congress just entering its adjournment drive. But the gamble has seemingly paid dividends, both for the Democratic party and for the President himself.

There is widespread agreement on this point. The most prevalent view is that the President, hammering away unrelentingly at the record of Congress, has whipped up flagging Democratic interest in the 1948 campaign that so soon will be in full swing. He set up the target and showed his party how effective the ammunition at hand could be.

The very howls of indignation and outrage that came from the Republican leaders of what Mr. Truman called one of the worst Congresses in history bore testimony to the fact that he had drawn blood. Frantic late-hour gestures toward action on domestic problems the President said had been ignored gave further proof that Congress was not really oblivious to his barbs.

Gains for the Party

Yet the suspicion lingered that the gains the President was making were largely party gains. Few doubted that he had prodded Congress more effectively than he could have if he remained at the White House. He was carrying his story to the people. But all along the line stories cropped up of injured feelings among Democratic organization workers.

Unifying Influence

The potshots which the President took at the Republican Congress constituted only one happy result of the trip as far as he was concerned. On several occasions, he sniped very accurately and tellingly at Henry A. Wallace and his third-party movement. The crowds he drew on the West Coast, particularly in California, indicated that his presence served to unify the party, even if only for the time being.

The trip also served to divert attention from the Southern revolt. The President seemed to be at pains on the trip not to bring up voluntarily the civil-rights issue with which he succeeded four months ago in affronting many in the South.

And, back at the Capital, Administration forces apparently had passed along the word that they would be willing to accept the party's 1944 position on civil rights as the plank on the subject in the 1948 platform.

But there were elements in the party still hopeful that someone else could be nominated, even a Mr. Truman came home with the bacon. The more outspoken among the Southern rebels, groups still unhappy about the way Administration policy shifted on Palestine and other dissidents within the party bravely hoped that that "somebody" might be Gen. Dwight D. Eisenhower.

To most observers, Mr. Truman appeared certain to be the party's candidate in the 1948 campaign. So firmly is the Democratic National Committee convinced of what will happen that it has put $125,000 on the line for campaign literature—and all of it deals with Mr. Truman and his record. Hard-headed politicians cannot afford to spend money like that unless they are sure.

June 20, 1948

19 PARTY LEADERS MAKE CAUCUS CALL TO BLOCK TRUMAN

Wires Ask 1,592 Democrats to Meet Before Convention and Pick 'Strongest' Candidate

O'DWYER ONE OF SIGNERS

'Knock-Down' Fight Foreseen at Philadelphia—More Praise Is Given Eisenhower

By JAMES A. HAGERTY

The movement to draft Gen. Dwight D. Eisenhower for the Democratic nomination for President went into high gear yesterday when nineteen party leaders, including Mayor William O'Dwyer, sent telegrams to the 1,592 delegates to the Democratic National Convention, inviting them to attend a caucus to be held in Philadelphia on July 10. This will be two days before the opening of the convention and its stated purpose will be to pick the ablest and strongest man available for the Presidential nomination.

The idea of these telegrams, which are intended to block the nomination of President Truman, came from James Roosevelt, son of the late President, who is State Chairman and National Committeeman from California. He sent a copy on Friday to Mayor O'Dwyer for the latter's signature. The caucus will be held in the Philadelphia headquarters of the Illinois delegation.

The sending of these telegrams virtually insures "a knock-down and drag-out fight" for the Presidential nomination at Philadelphia next week if President Truman sticks, as seems certain, to his determination to seek the nomination for his present post.

Alabama Ready to Yield on Roll

With Georgia and Virginia having instructed their delegations with fifty-four votes to support General Eisenhower, it was made known yesterday that Alabama, with a majority of its delegates opposed to President Truman, would yield on the roll call to any state wishing to place General Eisenhower in nomination.

The Associated Press reported in a dispatch from Denver that Barney L. Whatley, Democratic National Committeeman, had said that Eisenhower supporters were trying to swing the first six states in the alphabetical roll-call to the Eisenhower group in the hope of starting a stampede. Colorado is one of the first six states. Its twelve delegates are instructed to vote for President Truman, Mr. Whatley said, adding that the delegation is bound to the President until caucuses at Philadelphia.

A dispatch to THE TIMES from Houston stated that the Texas delegation, with fifty votes, would support General Eisenhower, and that Gov. Beauford Jester, chairman of the delegation, and Wright Morrow, National Committeeman-elect, believed that General Eisenhower could be nominated.

The twenty-two votes of Arkansas and the twenty votes of South Carolina are virtually assured for General Eisenhower by the presence of the Governors of those states in the list of signers of the telegram.

This gives General Eisenhower 148 votes from the South, without counting a majority from Alabama and what he is likely to get in New York, Pennsylvania, Minnesota, Illinois and other northern states.

No Candidate Is Mentioned

No candidate is mentioned in the telegrams sent to the delegates but the fact that a majority of the signers have General Eisenhower in mind is indicated by the following paragraph:

"It is our belief that no man in these critical days can refuse the call to duty and leadership implicit in the nomination and virtual election to the Presidency of the United States."

Should General Eisenhower make himself unavailable for the nomination or decline it, if nominated, the group of signers is understood to be ready to shift to Supreme Court Justice William O. Douglas, the candidate understood to be preferred by Mayor O'Dwyer.

General Eisenhower could not be reached for comment but from his office at Columbia University came a reiteration of the statement that the General stood on his letter of January 23, in which he removed himself as a possibility for the Republican Presidential nomination.

Telegram As Sent to Delegates

The telegram, a copy of which was sent to every delegate, follows:

"We, the undersigned delegates, join together in our desire to hold a caucus in Philadelphia Saturday, July 10, at headquarters of the Illinois delegation, John Bartram Hotel, 8:00 P. M., to achieve an open and free Democratic convention.

"We do this from the realization that the crisis in the world today makes it obligatory that we seek for the leader of our party the ablest and strongest man available. We know that in so doing we are fulfilling the wishes of the huge majority of Americans who want the Democratic party to select a candidate of such stature that the prosperity of our nation and a lasting peace for the world will become secure."

Then follows the paragraph previously quoted that no man could refuse the Presidential nomination. Then the telegram continues:

"It is our duty to build a platform and conduct a convention which will justify our draft of such a candidate. Until this is accomplished, we have no right to ask any prior pledges from any Americans. We therefore invite and urge you and all others who are of like mind to meet with us in Philadelphia."

Signers of the Telegrams

Signers of the telegrams in addition to Mr. Roosevelt and Mayor O'Dwyer are Senator Lister Hill, of Alabama, Dr. R. R. Robbins and Mrs. Jack Garnes, members of the National Committee from Arkansas; I. G. Beall, treasurer of the Arizona State Committee; Governor Ben T. Laney, of Arkansas; Chester Bowles, of Connecticut; Col. Jacob M. Arvey, of Illinois; Joseph E. Casey, of Massachusetts; Cy Bevan, Michigan National Committeeman; Mayor Hubert Humphreys, of Minneapolis; William Ritchie, Nebraska State Chairman, Governor J. Strom Thurmond, of South Carolina; Governor Beauford H. Jester, of Texas; Clinton D. Vernon, Utah State Chairman; Carl V. Rice, Kansas National Committeeman; Governor William M. Tuck, of Virginia, and Robert Tehan, Wisconsin National Committeeman.

The sending of the telegrams, which marked James Roosevelt as a leader of the "block Truman" movement, is now known to have been the result of an undercover campaign which has been in progress for many weeks.

Although by California law the fifty-four-vote delegation from that state is bound to vote for President Truman as the unopposed winner of the preferential primary until personally released by him, dispatches from California indicate that many California delegates do not intend to do so.

For several weeks, Democrats from California and other states have been through the country contacting delegates to get them to switch from President Truman to General Eisenhower. These emissaries believe that they have had considerable success and that there is a chance of getting a majority for the General on the first ballot, unless he takes himself out of the running finally before the balloting.

Two delegates from Pennsylvania announced their support of General Eisenhower, according to the Associated Press. They are R. R. Edwards, Muncy banker, and former Representative John K. Sheridan, of Philadelphia.

On the other hand, Philip Matthews, Democratic State Chairman, declared that the Pennsylvania delegation, with seventy-four votes, would not be "stampeded for Eisenhower," and added that both the delegation and the state organization had endorsed President Truman.

In New York Frank J. Sampson, leader of Tammany, conferred yesterday with Mayor O'Dwyer at City Hall for an hour and a half and later had dinner with the Mayor at Luchow's restaurant. It was said that Mr. Sampson was in complete agreement with the Mayor on opposition to the nomination of President Truman and that it was probable that Mr. O'Dwyer would lead the fight for the nomination of Justice Douglas on the floor of the convention. Both Mr. Sampson and the Mayor are delegates-at-large.

Arvey Will See O'Dwyer

Mr. Arvey, chairman of the Cook County Democratic Committee, said in Chicago that he was "going to do a little talking" with Mayor O'Dwyer next week about their joint effort to prevent President Truman's nomination. Mr. Arvey said there would be no effort to control the Illinois delegation and that its members could vote as they individually pleased. He added that the delegation would not be badly split on the Eisenhower candidacy.

David Lawrence, National Committeeman of Pennsylvania, questioned about the Eisenhower candidacy, said that the general could "sweep the country."

William H. Kelly of Newark, New Jersey delegate-at-large, said he would vote for General Eisenhower on the first ballot and declared that President Truman had lost the confidence not only of the party's leadership but that of "independents from coast to coast." Frank Hague, New Jersey National Committeeman, was non-committal on the draft-Eisenhower movement.

In Washington, Senator Joseph C. O'Mahoney, of Wyoming, after a White House conference, expressed confidence in the President's nomination.

Joseph Nachman, Philadelphia blouse manufacturer, who opened Eisenhower-for-President headquarters in that city last week at 1413-1419 Walnut Street, directly opposite the Bellevue-Stratford Hotel, where the Democratic National Committee will have its headquarters, has offered the space to the Eisenhower supporters for convention headquarters.

Mr. Nachman said that this offer had been accepted by several of the Southern Governors who have joined the Eisenhower movement.

July 4, 1948

TRUMAN FORCES IN COMMAND

CAUCUS CANCELED

President's Foes Drop It as James Roosevelt Joins Truman Ranks

SOUTHERN HOSTILITY EBBS

Attention Turns to Rights Plank—Gloom Dominates Convention Atmosphere

By JAMES A. HAGERTY
Special to THE NEW YORK TIMES.

PHILADELPHIA, July 10 — With the collapse of the opposition to the nomination of President Truman because of the refusal of Gen. Dwight D. Eisenhower to run if nominated and the statement of Supreme Court Justice William O. Douglas that he was not a candidate for the Presidential nomination, the Truman forces today took complete command of the situation. They prepared to dictate the platform to be adopted next week by the Democratic National Convention and to name the candidate for Vice President.

Arriving delegates found an atmosphere of gloom and despondency and encountered a spirit of defeatism among the party leaders already here that amounted to confession that President Truman seemed to have little chance of election.

In a last-ditch strategy move, a group opposed to the nomination of President Truman, including Senator Claude Pepper of Florida, Leon Henderson, chairman of the Americans for Democratic Action, and William Ritchie, Nebraska state chairman, decided tonight to press for restoration of the two-thirds rule for the first three ballots, after which nomination of a Presidential candidate would be made by a majority vote of the convention.

This was on the theory that if an early nomination of Mr. Truman could be prevented the convention ultimately would nominate some other candidate. This proposal, which would seem to have little chance of adoption, would first be made to the rules committee of the convention.

James Roosevelt Gives Up

James Roosevelt, who arrived in the morning with the California delegation, announced that the anti-Truman caucus, which he, Jacob M. Arvey, Chicago leader, and Mayor William O'Dwyer of New York city had called for tonight, had been abandoned.

The caucus was to have been held in the Illinois headquarters in the John Bartram Hotel. Mr. Roosevelt joined Mr. Arvey and Mayor O'Dwyer and said he would vote for the nomination of Mr. Truman.

Mr. Roosevelt's belated decision to support the President did not save him from criticism at the caucus of the California delegation, which tabled a resolution calling for his resignation as national committeeman by a vote of 40 to 7. The 54-vote delegation, originally pledged to the President and now containing a majority for him, decided to wait developments, and a motion to instruct the delegates for the President was withdrawn.

The Douglas for President boom, sponsored by Mr. Henderson, as ADA chairman, and the Democrats for Douglas, of which Maurice P. Davidson of New York City is the head, made no progress, both because of the disinclination of Justice Douglas to be a candidate against the President and the refusal of Southern delegates to support a man whose position on civil rights is more objectionable to them than that of the President.

Justice Douglas, however, became the first choice of the Democratic high command for Vice President presumably with the approval of President Truman, on the theory that he would add strength to the Democratic national ticket by attracting liberals and the large number of young men and women who will vote in November for the first time.

Justice Douglas, according to a dispatch from La Grande, Ore., said that he was not a candidate on the national ticket and would not resign from the Supreme Court to be a candidate for either office. This created doubt that he would take the nomination for Vice President but did not remove him entirely from consideration.

Uncertainty of Justice Douglas' willingness to accept the Vice-Presidential nomination put Senator Alben W. Barkley of Kentucky in the position of leading candidate at the moment for running mate to President Truman. Those supporting Senator Barkley contended that if the national ticket should be defeated, Senator Barkley would be an ideal man to lead in organizing the Democratic party for the next Presidential election in 1952. They also asserted that nomination of the Kentucky Senator would help to placate disaffected elements in the South. Leslie L. Biffle, director of the Senate Minority Policy Committee, Sergeant at Arms of the convention and personal friend of Mr. Truman, said that Senator Barkley was his (Biffle's) personal choice for the nomination.

Objection has arisen to the nomination of Senator Joseph C. O'Mahoney of Wyoming, for whom headquarters have been opened on the mezzanine floor of the Bellevue-Stratford Hotel. The objection is not to Senator O'Mahoney personally but to belief that defeat of the national ticket might be attributed in part to his candidacy, if he should be nominated for Vice President.

Leslie L. Biffle, director of the Senate minority policy committee and sergeant-at-arms of the convention, said that Senator Barkley was his personal choice for the nomination.

The opposition of the Southern delegates to President Truman seemed to have been lessened considerably. Senator Olin D. Johnson of South Carolina failed to carry out his announced intention of introducing a resolution at the meeting of the National Committee calling upon President Truman to withdraw as a candidate. When called upon by Senator J. Howard McGrath, chairman of the committee, Senator Johnston said he had no resolution to introduce "at this time."

This was a major defeat for the anti-Truman Southern group, most of the members of which seem ready to abandon their efforts to block the nomination of the President if they get a civil rights plank in the platform that is satisfactory to them.

That efforts to get such a plank are in progress became evident when Senator McGrath at his press conference said that he favored adoption of the 1944 civil rights plank which merely declared that "we believe that racial and religious minorities have the right to live, develop and vote equally with all citizens and share the rights that are guaranteed by our Constitution," and added that "Congress should exert its full constitutional powers to protect those rights."

Asked if he favored adoption of a states' rights plank, which the Southern delegates demand, Senator McGrath replied:

"If it did not nullify the civil rights plank, I would have no objection to it."

In his press conference, attended by more than 300 reporters, Senator McGrath repeated that President Truman had not indicated to him any preference for a running mate. He said that several weeks before the convention he had received a message from Justice Douglas saying that he was not a candidate for the Vice Presidential nomination and asking him to use his influence to prevent his name being presented for that nomination.

"Do you regard Justice Douglas as eliminated as a candidate for Vice President?" he was asked.

"No, I do not," Senator McGrath replied. "I will not ask him to be a candidate but will not seek to prevent anyone else from asking him. I will not go beyond that."

Senator McGrath added that he did not think that Justice Douglas would be nominated as the candidate for Vice President unless it was known in advance that he would accept the nomination.

"I don't believe that anyone in the convention will repeat the mistake that was made about General Eisenhower and put Justice Douglas in nomination unless he knows that he is willing to accept," he said.

"Is there a chance that the convention will end on Wednesday?" Senator McGrath was asked.

"That is quite within the range of possibility, but we plan a four-day convention," he said. "It will depend upon the time needed for adoption of the platform and the number of candidates for Vice President placed in nomination."

Asked about the possibility of President Truman coming to Philadelphia to accept the nomination Senator McGrath said that it had not been decided whether President Truman would deliver his acceptance speech before the convention or revert to the old Democratic custom of accepting the nomination at his home town.

"I think at the moment the President's preference is for going home," Senator McGrath said.

The National Chairman said that President Truman would not be influenced in the least in making his decision by fear that delegates opposed to his nomination might walk out of the convention if he accepted the nomination here.

Complete dominance of the convention by supporters of the President does not mean that his nomination will be unanimous or that no one will be placed in nomination against him. Some of the Southern states are almost certain to place "favorite sons" in nomination for the purpose of obtaining a record vote in accordance with their instructions.

July 11, 1948

TRUMAN, BARKLEY NAMED BY DEMOCRATS; SOUTH LOSES ON CIVIL RIGHTS, 35 WALK OUT

VICTORY SWEEPING

President Wins, 947½ to 263, Over Russell on the First Ballot

BARKLEY ACCLAIMED

Nominees Go Before Convention to Make Acceptance Talks

By W. H. LAWRENCE
Special to The New York Times.

PHILADELPHIA, Thursday, July 15—President Harry S. Truman won nomination for a full term in the Democratic National Convention early today and promptly made the Republican record in Congress the 1948 key issue by calling a special session of Congress to meet July 26 to challenge the GOP to keep its platform pledges.

The President, selected by well over two-thirds of the Democratic delegates, although the Solid South dissented and thirty-five delegates from Mississippi and Alabama walked out, was in a fighting mood as he went before the convention with his running mate, Senator Alben W. Barkley, who was chosen by acclamation.

Confidently predicting his and Senator Barkley's election because "the country cannot afford another Republican Congress," the President said that the special session would be asked to act on legislation of various types.

Cites Republican Platform

He would call on it, he declared, to act to halt rising prices, meet the housing crisis, provide aid to education, enact a national health program, approve civil rights legislation, raise minimum wages, increase social security benefits, finance expanded public power projects and revise the present "anti-Semitic, anti-Catholic" displaced persons law.

The Republicans said they were for all these things in their 1948 platform, the President stated, and, if they really meant it, all could be enacted into law in a fifteen-day session.

President Truman set the convention on fire with his acceptance speech, which came at the end of a long, tiring, tumultuous session in which the north-south party split was deepened appreciably, although only a handful of southern delegates bolted.

The Southerners who remained were almost as angry as those in the "walk" about the convention's strong civil rights pledge and its overwhelming refusal to include a state's rights plank in the platform.

Senator Barkley promised to follow the President's leadership, agreed to carry out the platform and pledged himself to carry the story of Democratic accomplishments to every precinct to insure victory in November.

The acceptance speeches completed, the convention adjourned at 2:30 A. M.

Truman Margin of Victory

President Truman's margin over his chief rival, Senator Richard B. Russell of Georgia, was 947½ to 263, while Paul V. McNutt received half a vote in the final tabulation.

Senator Russell got almost the solid Southern vote remaining in the convention after the bolt by delegates from Alabama and Mississippi.

As soon as Mr. Truman was nominated, at 12:42 A. M., the convention moved ahead to the nomination of his Vice-Presidential running mate.

There was an attempt to present Senator Russell again for the Vice Precidency, but he stopped it and there was no opposition to Senator Barkley's selection.

The President, who came here by train from Washington, was waiting in a rear room of the convention hall to make a joint appearance with Senator Barkley to accept the nominations.

To the strains of "Hail to the Chief" President Truman entered the hall at 1:45 A. M. accompanied by Senator Barkley to accept his nomination before a wildly cheering crowd.

The wound to the South embodied in the strong civil rights program imposed on the party leadership by a combination of New Dealers and Northern city bosses went very deep indeed. It was a wound far deeper than had indication in the dramatic, but comparatively unimportant, demonstration by half the Alabama delegation and all of the Mississippi delegation.

For the first time in many years the Presidential nominee's selection was not made unanimous. There was not even a motion to make it unanimous, because the South, fighting mad, would have resisted it to the end. Those Southern delegations which stayed in the hall decided that "regularity" was most important, but there was no certainty that they would give all-out support to the ticket in November.

For the President, after he had been placed in nomination by Gov. Phil Donnelly of Missouri, there was a thirty-nine minute demonstration. When the roll call began his lead mounted steadily and he passed the majority required for nomination when New York cast 93 of its votes for him. New York later changed its vote to cast all 98 for him.

The name of Mr. McNutt, former Indiana Governor, who was War Manpower Commissioner, was placed in nomination for President by Byrd Sims of Florida, in a surprise move. Mr. Sims, opposed to the present party leadership and pledged to Mississippi's Governor, Fielding L. Wright, before Governor Wright bolted the convention, said that he acted without Mr. McNutt's knowledge or consent.

Ohio offered as its "favorite son" William A. Julian, Treasurer of the United States, but it was simply a courtesy gesture. Mr. Julian withdrew at once and asked the Ohio delegation to vote for Mr. Truman.

Party leaders, acting on behalf of the President, had sought to mollify the South by restricting the civil rights platform pledge to a generality, but the delegates, sparked by ex-New Dealers who had the support of big city machine bosses, insisted and won a floor fight for a plank with real teeth in it. Their margin was narrow—651½ to 582½—but earlier they had overwhelmingly rejected Southern demands for a states' rights plank by a vote of 925 to 309.

The platform was so strong that Governor Ben Laney of Arkansas, who had planned to have his name presented as a candidate for President, said he could not accept the platform. He and his Arkansas delegation did not leave the convention, however.

Senator Alben W. Barkley of Kentucky was slated to be the Vice Presidential nominee. He was the overwhelming favorite among delegates and the White House capitulated to their demonstrated attitude after trying and failing to persuade Supreme Court Justice William O. Douglas to take a place on the ticket.

Senator Barkley also was to deliver his acceptance speech before the convention.

The Southern walkout was dramatic, coming as it did just as Sam Rayburn of Texas, permanent chairman, ordered the roll-call of states for the Presidential nomination, but it lacked the numbers and spirit that Southern politicians had predicted.

Loud boos followed the mass walkout by all of the Mississippi delegates and alternates, and half the Alabama group. And they had the bad luck, too, to walk from this steamy, hot convention into a pouring rainstorm.

Cheers bounced against the rafters as Chairman Rayburn, a Texas "regular," recognized the rest of the Alabama delegation, headed by Senator Lister Hill, who promptly yielded to Georgia so that Senator Russell could be placed in nomination.

The Southern delegates let go in a noisy demonstration to the martial tunes of "Dixie," after Charles J. Bloch of Georgia, nominating Senator Russell, delivered a solemn warning that "the South is no longer going to be the whipping boy of the Democratic party."

His group, he declared, were not "fools" enough to walk out, but he warned that Southern voters might desert the Democratic party and asserted that the party could not win a Presidential election without Southern support.

Then it was the turn of the Truman boosters, some of them genuinely enthusiastic but more of them lukewarm to the President and accepting him only because their efforts to draft Gen. Dwight D. Eisenhower were stopped by the general's flat refusal to accept the nomination under any circumstances.

Gov. Phil M. Donnelly of Missouri offered the President's name in the first speech to the convention in which the emphasis had been laid upon Mr. Truman's accomplishments in office.

All other speakers had talked more about the late President Roosevelt, with only passing reference to the present President.

It was understood that some White House advisers tried to have more attention paid to the late President in Governor Donnelly's speech, too, but that the Missouri chief executive refused to deliver his speech except in its original form.

When he closed, a well-planned demonstration for the President began, in which most states except the South took part.

ADA Spearheads Fight

New Dealers, organized under the auspices of the Americans for Democratic Action, led the fight to expand the civil rights pledge and got the votes to put it over from Northern big city machines which realize they must hold the Negro vote if their state and local tickets are not to go down in defeat in the prospective Republican landslide this November.

What the convention did was to make specific the directive to Congress to carry out President Truman's civil rights program—but the manner in which it was done could not have failed to displease the President because it created additional hostility in the South, increased the sentiment for a convention bolt and thus defeated the harmony moves which the Administration had initiated in recent days.

The President's lieutenants here had sought a milder, more generalized declaration.

Specifically, the convention directed Democrats in Congress to guarantee "these basic and fundamental rights: (1) the right of of full and equal political participation, (2) the right to equal opportunity of employment, (3) the right of security of person, (4) and the right of equal treatment in the service and defense of our nation."

In the fifty-eight-minute debate covering the civil rights and states' rights minority reports, the issue of race relations, as such, was never tackled.

Southern orators warned that a failure to reaffirm the constitutional rights of the states was essential to Southern confidence in and support of the party.

The Northern bloc, through Mayor Hubert Humphrey of Minneapolis as its principal spokesman, said that the country was 172 years behind the times in meeting the issue of equality. Mayor Humphrey won loud cheers and a scattering of boos for his praise of President Truman's "courage in issuing a new emancipation proclamation" and his assertion that "it is time for the Democratic party to get out of the shadow of states' rights and walk forthrightly in the bright sunshine of human rights."

Lacking either band or organ music, which were kept silent by the control of Southerners in authority on the main platform, delegates led by the ADA group nevertheless staged a long demonstration for Mayor Humphrey when he closed his speech and kept it going for nearly ten minutes.

The delegates, who had sweltered listlessly through two and one-half days of campaign oratory while waiting for the real business of the convention, adoption of the platform and nomination of candidates, were spoiling for a fight when the preliminaries for the day finally were completed.

The galleries, crowded for the first time, were in general agreement with Northern demands for stronger civil rights measures and joined in cheering the demonstrations on the floor.

The debate was less torrid than might have been expected and nobody waved the flag of "white supremacy," although Southerners warned earnestly that if the states' rights amendment were rejected "you are voting down the Constitution of the United States."

Topics of The Times

Picking Up the Tab

Big business will be picking up part of the tab next month when the Democratic party meets in Chicago to select its ticket for the Presidential race that ends on Election Day. Seventy-five nationally known companies are taking part in an exhibition titled, "The American Showcase," showing the delegates the latest in household equipment, candies, drinks, jewelry, books, television sets and a host of other items. The idea behind the display is simple: The delegates, believed to be leaders in fashion as well as politics, are expected by the participating companies to bring back their messages to their communities once the business of the day has been taken care of and they have left Chicago. In other words, the convention hall becomes a new medium for advertisers.

Mounting Costs of Campaigning

But there is more to it than simply this. For the mounting cost of political campaigning has come to be an increasing problem of government, and this may lead the way to a solution. Every four years convention bureaus for cities across the country vie for the privilege of playing host to the delegates. Often they make substantial contributions to the cost of running a convention. There is more than civic pride in this: delegates generally leave behind them a substantial trail in coin of the realm at hotels, restaurants, department stores, even in bars and night clubs. One of the problems of the 1956 convention in Chicago was the matter of rent for the meeting hall, since Chicago, unlike many of the bidding cities, could offer no free municipal auditorium. The concerns taking space at "The American Showcase" are helping to pay for the use of the International Amphitheatre.

Meeting of the Citizenry

Development of the political convention starts early in our history, as far back as 1640, in the local meetings of the citizenry gathered to pick candidates for local office. But nominating conventions on a national basis waited until 1831, when the National Republicans gathered in Baltimore to pick Henry Clay as the opponent of the Democratic incumbent, Andrew Jackson. Jackson was continued in office, and the National Republican party thereupon passed into oblivion. The organized political caucus was the dominant political factor of the day, and alliances dictated all nominations for elective office. Yet despite this lack of fundamental democracy, there was little indignation on the part of the populace. The right to vote was restricted to the small minority of freeholders, and the rest of the people seemed little concerned.

Modern Communications Methods

With modern communications methods, though, interest began to perk up. The Democratic convention in Baltimore in 1844, which picked James Polk, was the first to be covered by telegraph. Symbolically, this was the first national convention to choose a "dark horse" after the first political "stampede." The Republican convention of 1860, which nominated Abraham Lincoln, was the first to bring telegraph wires and instruments directly into a convention hall, and it was also the first to admit the general public. Radio entered the political nominating arena with the nomination of Coolidge and Dawes on June 10, 1924, Graham McNamee doing the commentary on a fifteen-station hook-up ranging from Boston to Kansas City. Television cameras had their first look-in at the Republican convention in Philadelphia in 1940, which chose Wendell Willkie. Since that day, with the great growth of television, the nominating conventions have become events brought into the nation's living room. It is hardly surprising, then, that big business, which pays the bills of commercial television, should do the same at least for one of the 1956 conventions.

July 8, 1956

Merely a Convention

Analysis of Trend to Hold Big Political Meetings Chiefly for Sake of Pageantry

By GLADWIN HILL

Special to The New York Times.

SAN FRANCISCO, Aug. 23—If this convention had been realistic—an unlikely adjective for it—it would have observed an affectionate moment of silence in memory of a great institution: the American political convention.

The week's proceedings underscored the fact that that quaint antiquity is all but extinct.

The political convention has evolved down the decades into almost a piece of sheer pageantry, a symbol of facts and events remote from the scene.

It is fashionable to blame television for hamming up the proceedings. But television is only a Johnny-come-lately factor in the evolution. The real catalysts are the changing world, the ebullience of human nature and the sometimes bewildering flexibility of democratic processes.

The political convention was conceived as a parliamentary proceeding, theoretically as businesslike as a directors' meeting. Its purpose was to adopt a platform, name candidates and set up an organization to carry on until the next convention.

But these sober aims historically were quickly overshadowed by the golden pretext afforded for (A) a get-together and (B) oratory.

Titans like William Jennings Bryan emerged from the convention showcase.

Amplified Clambake

The clambake character of conventions soon pushed the critical negotiations off the convention floor and into the smoke-filled room. The public address system equalized oratory at a level of mediocrity.

Mass communication media, such as newspapers and radio, outmoded the convention floor as a forum for the exchange of ideas. All relevant ideas, and a lot of irrelevant ones, were exhaustively explored months before, over distances of thousands of miles.

This made the parliamentary mechanics of conventions, designed to facilitate the exchange of ideas, obsolete and boring. Now speeches generally can't be spontaneous. To fit the exigencies of the mass media they have to be written and mimeographed days in advance.

Hence they usually have no relationship to one another in content—except common clichés. But their delivery is part of the stage-play necessary to prolong conventions to lengths befitting the occasion, and to extend the conventioneers' visits to worthwhile lengths. What business was done at the Republican gathering in four days could have been transacted in one.

Entertainment had to be injected to keep conventions alive. Finally came television, with its demands that not only the entertainment, but also all the convention proceedings possible, be couched in terms of visual luster.

Even parliamentary procedure has been relegated largely to smoke-filled rooms. The chairman "hears" key motions so much by prearrangement that he often has to jog the movers into moving. When something spontaneous occurs, like yesterday's nomination of "Joe Smith," it momentarily throws the convention into confusion.

These converging trends came closest to perfection in the prefabricated pageantry in this year's "phantom" Republican convention.

Voting Aye for Platform

Few of the 1,323 delegates could have recited a line of the party platform they endorsed by a perfunctory unanimous vote without—in contrast to the Democrats' more traditional proceeding at Chicago—its even being read to the convention.

The platform was "dramatized" by having a parade of Cabinet members supposedly commentate on pertinent sections—although their speeches were largely puffs for the Administration's past activities.

The crowning touch in this year's extension from parliamentarianism into pageantry was the introduction of ringers.

Under the suspension-of-rules device originally designed to admit occasional distinguished outsiders to the rostrum, a brigade of outsiders, disavowing even party membership, let alone convention credentials, took part in the convention's business. Ostensibly seconders of the nominations, they actually were deliverers of additional Administration commercials with the new look of nonpartisanism.

The waning spontaneity of "demonstrations"—now largely regulated by musical impetus—was further diluted this year by the introduction of accessories to keep the TV audiences from turning off their sets.

Granted this year's political situation was unusually pat. More competitive years will bring more action. But the evolution of conventions is heading toward the day when even the vestigial drama like this year's Kefauver-Kennedy photo-finish in Chicago may be decided in a more "orderly" way.

The "order" promulgated by Gen. Henry M. Robert, the parliamentarian, is giving way in both parties to the "order" of Madison Avenue and Radio City "efficiency." Traditionalists may deplore it. But they seem to be in a minority. And this is a democracy.

August 24, 1956

Topics

The Presidential Primaries The Presidential primaries are an interesting example of a reform movement which, having failed to meet the full expectations of its advocates, yet retains enough validity and support to continue in existence in an important secondary role. Despite the high hopes which the Progressives held fifty years ago for the direct Presidential primary, it has notably failed to dislodge the national party convention as the fundamental mechanism for the choosing of Presidential candidates. On the other hand, the direct primary is assuredly not dead, or even moribund. Fifteen states, plus the District of Columbia, will hold Presidential primaries this year, and a bill repeatedly introduced into Congress by Senators Smathers and Douglas would elevate the Presidential primary to somewhere near the eminence and authority envisaged in 1908 by Jonathan Bourne, editor of The Oregon Daily Journal.

The Early Start The direct primary is believed to have been first used in rudimentary form by the Democratic party of Crawford County, Pa., in 1842. It spread slowly in the next half century, but began to win wide favor in the radical, Populist climate of the Eighteen Eighties and Nineties, when political machinations, bossism, and the moneyed Eastern interests were all lumped together as objects of intense distrust by the Western and Southern agrarians. "Pitchfork" Ben Tillman began to replace South Carolina's convention system with the primary system in 1891. In 1903, under the leadership of Gov. Robert M. La Follette, Wisconsin passed the first state-wide primary law for all state candidates, and followed that up two years later with a law providing for the popular election of all delegates to national political conventions.

Wilson and T. R. Other states enthusiastically followed Wisconsin's lead. Reform and the Progressive spirit were in the air. Theodore Roosevelt and Woodrow Wilson both came out for direct Presidential primaries. By 1912, fifteen states had adopted Presidential primary laws of various sorts. When the Republican convention of that year failed to nominate T. R., despite the fact that he had won all but one of the primary contests, a wave of indignation against the "boss-ridden" convention system swept the nation. By 1916, twenty-four states had enacted Presidential primary laws.

The Tide Turns However, since that high tide of fervor, the direct Presidential primary has settled into a niche somewhat lower than that hoped for it by its enthusiasts. Political scientists have come to see more good in the convention system than was conceded in the flush of the Progressive era, and it is widely felt that a binding, nation-wide Presidential primary might be a poor substitute for the national convention, where the practical politics of the situation are now so expertly balanced against the popular will.

Many Different Ways The fifteen states which use the Presidential primary do so in various ways. In some, the voters can express their Presidential preference, while in others they cannot. Some are binding on the delegates, others leave the delegates uninstructed. Some give the various candidates the option of "entering," whereas others may list any prominent person who is not willing to swear that he is not a candidate. They are spaced out in a whimsical manner, beginning on March 8 in New Hampshire, and ending on June 7 in South Dakota.

A Supporting Role According to the late Charles Merriam, the primary is a club that the people can hold over the heads of the politicians. "The possibility of such a revolution always has a restraining influence on the powers that be, and tends to hold them back from the extremes of arbitrary conduct," he noted in his "The American Party System." For the foreseeable future it seems that the Presidential primaries will continue to play a supporting role in the complicated process by which citizens of this country choose their national leaders.

March 13, 1960

Political Get-Together

THE POLITICS OF NATIONAL PARTY CONVENTIONS. By Paul T. David, Ralph M. Goldman and Richard C. Bain. 592 pp. Washington, D. C.: The Brookings Institution. $10.

By LEO EGAN

THE quadrennial national political convention is a uniquely American institution. For a variety of reasons the major party conventions are nearly as great a stabilizing force in American politics as the Constitution itself. Actuallly, the Constitution, because of its authors' distrust of "factionalism," made no provision for party conventions. The first convention did not meet until 1830, more than forty years after the Constitution went into effect.

The historic evolution of the Presidential nominating convention, its present functions, the manner in which it operates and the influences that operate upon delegates, party leaders and the candidates themselves are all explored thoroughly in this study. Its authors are Paul T. David and Richard C. Bain, senior members of the Brookings Institution staff, and Ralph M. Goldman, now of the faculty of Michigan State University.

Political parties in the United States, as the authors point out, differ from their European counterparts in that they are really not national parties at all but federations of autonomous state parties. While this is not a new discovery, the authors emphasize that its acceptance is essential to an understanding of the powers, limitations and functions of conventions.

Basically conventions are found to serve three main functions: (1) to reach a consensus on policies to which the party Presidential candidates (but not necessarily the Congressional candidates) will be committed and to select the candidates for President and Vice President; (2) to serve as the governing board of the party itself and to establish the framework for the party organization; (3) to provide a forum for the opening rallies of the campaign.

IN examining the ways in which conventions have performed all three functions, the study has gone deeply into such subjects as how delegates are chosen, the formation of alliances, the composition of sectional and other internal differences, and the influence of preferential primaries.

Those who believe that nominating conventions should be replaced by some national primary system receive no encouragement here. Granting that few conventions ever live up to their potentialities, the authors believe that "the continuing contributions made by the conventions to the survival and stability of the American political order are unique, indispensable and, granted our form of constitution, probably irreplaceable."

Mr. Egan is a veteran Times political reporter.

March 13, 1960

EISENHOWER ASKS CONVENTION CURB

Says Nation Was 'Horrified' at 'Confusion' in 1964—Urges Strong Chairman

By DAVID S. BRODER
Special to The New York Times

WASHINGTON, June 28 — Former President Dwight D. Eisenhower said today that the American people were "horrified" by the conventions that pick their Presidential candidates.

He urged the Republican National Committee to take the lead in changing the television viewer's "picture of confusion, noise, impossible deportment and indifference to what is being discussed on the platform."

The general said "a strong, permanent chairman, with dictatorial powers," was needed to impose discipline on the nominating sessions. He should be backed, the general continued, by tough sergeants-at-arms, preferably 6 feet 4 inches tall and drawn from the ranks of the Marines, the Army or the police.

Would Limit Delegates

The former President, whose attack on "sensation-seeking columnists and commentators" provoked one of the noisiest outbursts at last year's convention, said any demonstration "over five minutes is a spurious demonstration of unwarranted enthusiasm" and should be gaveled down.

He also proposed that reporters and cameramen be completely barred from the convention floor during business sessions.

The number of delegates, he said, should be limited to twice the number of electoral votes—or a maximum of 1,070. The Republicans had 1,308 delegates in San Francisco last July.

General Eisenhower said he was disturbed by two incidents at that convention involving a "hoodlum harassing" the wife of a speaker and someone molesting his niece, who was a convention page.

He refused to identify the speaker or his wife. The niece, committee aides said, was apparently a daughter of Col. and Mrs. George Gordon Moore Jr. Mrs. Moore is Mrs. Eisenhower's sister. General Eisenhower said the girl came to him in tears after the incident.

The general made it plain he thought reform of convention procedures was a problem for both parties. The Republicans, he suggested, could gain goodwill for themselves by leading the effort.

After his speech, Ray C. Bliss, the Republican National Chairman, said he would appoint a committee to study the feasibility of the general's suggestions.

Miller Cites Cooperation

William E. Miller, who arranged the last convention as national chairman, said he thought any reform depended on cooperation by both parties to limit delegate numbers and restrict press and television access to the convention floor. With such cooperation, Mr. Miller said, conventions could be cut from four days to two and their decorum improved.

The Eisenhower speech was the only public event in an outwardly harmonious meeting of the national committee, the first since Mr. Bliss's election last January. He took over his post formally from Dean Burch on April 1.

Mr. Bliss announced the unanimous election of three new vice-chairmen to serve on the 27-member Republican Coordinating Committee, the top party policy advisory body.

They are J. Drake Edens Jr. of South Carolina, Mrs. J. Willard Marriott of the District of Columbia and Donald R. Ross of Nebraska. The choice of Mr. Edens, who as chairman of the South Carolina delegation cast the votes that made Barry Goldwater the 1964 Presidential nominee, satisfied a demand from Southern members for a voice on the coordinating committee.

Mr. Ross was a leader in the move to bring in Mr. Bliss to replace Mr. Burch, Mr. Goldwater's choice as national chairman, and Mr. Edens and Mrs. Marriott supported that effort.

In a companion move today, New York and Michigan regained the places on the executive committee of the national committee that they had lost when Mr. Burch took over last July. George L. Hinman of New York and John B. Martin of Michigan were elected to the committee. The third vacancy on the 15-member group was filled by James C. Wood of Arizona.

The effect of the changes was to assure the new chairman strong support from his executive committee on future steps to rebuild the party.

Both Mr. Bliss and General Eisenhower referred in their speeches today to the danger of splinter organizations siphoning off funds needed by the party organization.

Mr. Bliss, whose condemnation of one such group, Mr. Goldwater's Free Society Association, had in turn been criticized by many conservatives, sought today to clarify his stand. He insisted that his opposition was not based on the conservative ideology the Goldwater group intends to promulgate but on the practical problem of finance.

The party treasurer, J. William Middendorf 2d, reported that the national committee had been kept solvent through the first half of 1965 chiefly by $10 contributions from nearly 100,000 donors. Contributions totaled just under $1 million for the first six months, against expenditures of $1.1 million, he said. The cash balance, less obligations, is approximately $180,000.

At today's meeting, Mr. Bliss also announced the appointment of three men to the committee's research division. Dr. Arthur L. Eterson, political scientist at Ohio Wesleyan University, was named research director, and Robert McCormick, a former Hoover Commission aide, and George Norris, former counsel to the Congressional Joint Atomic Energy Committee, his assistants.

June 29, 1965

DEMOCRATS PRESS FOR PARTY REFORM

Report by McGovern Panel Views Popular Control as Key to Political Survival

By R. W. APPLE Jr.
Special to The New York Times

WASHINGTON, April 28 — A Democratic party reform commission warned today in its final report that the only alternative to broader citizen participation in politics was "the antipolitics of the street."

"We believe that popular control of the Democratic party is necessary for its survival," said the report, which was written by a 28-member panel headed by Senator George S. McGovern of South Dakota. "The commission has concluded that there is a genuinely broadly based commitment to reform within the party."

Speaking at a Capitol Hill news conference, Senator McGovern predicted that the commission's guidelines for the selection of delegates to the party's convention in 1972 would be followed by state Democratic organizations.

"I suspect there'll be some struggles, he added. "Certain party leaders in some states have been critical, but they are a tiny minority. I expect that we will get a broad compliance."

But other sources in the Democratic party indicated that the guidelines would not go into effect without a fight, possibly a long and bitter one.

Former Vice President Hubert H. Humphrey is one of those who is believed to oppose some of the McGovern commission's decisions. In an interview several weeks ago, he referred to the commission's proposals as "recommendations" and said they would have to be ratified by the Democratic National Committee before taking effect.

In a foreword to the final report, he again used the word "recommendations," although he praised the commission's work.

Senator McGovern and his staff have always contended that the guidelines are rules, not recommendations, and that they must be followed by the state parties. They argue that their authority derives from the 1968 convention, not the national committee.

Credential Power

The Senator reiterated these arguments today and said he was hopeful that, at the next convention, credentials committee would agree in advance to unseat any delegation not chosen in accord with the guidelines. The commission has no other enforcement powers, he conceded.

"As a matter of practical politics," Senator McGovern said, "we will be in a stronger position to accomplish our goals if the guidelines are endorsed by the national committee next month."

The 63-page report will go before the party's executive committee at a meeting on May 22 with a recommendation from Lawrence F. O'Brien, the national chairman. Mr. O'Brien has made ambivalent comments recently when asked whether the national committee could modify the report.

As previously reported, the commission decided that future convention delgations should include women, young people and representatives of minorities "in reasonable relationships" to their proportion in the state's population. It ruled out proxy voting, exorbitant delegate fees, delegate selection systems with no rules and selection of delegates too far in advance of conventions.

"In 1968," the report said, "meaningful participation of Democratic voters in the party's nominating process was often difficult or costly, sometimes completely illusory, and, in not a few instances, impossible."

The delegates' election process was a major target of attack by the supporters of Senator Eugene J. McCarthy of Minnesota in 1968, and Senator McGovern asserted that "the anger of 1968 will be compounded in 1972 if these reforms are not carried out."

According to the Senators, 40 state reform commissions have already begun work.

April 29, 1970

CHAPTER 6

Federalism

There is probably no other issue which Americans have debated for a longer period of time than the proper division of power between the federal and local governments. And there has probably been no other issue in which observable reality has been affected so little by the debate. Regardless of what men have said or intended, the long-range trend in this country has been toward greater concentration of authority in Washington, D.C.

The Constitution itself was an instrument designed to erect a stronger federal structure than had existed under the Articles of Confederation. The Founding Fathers tried to frame the document as a compromise between the Federalists and the anti-Federalists. They were sufficiently successful to secure its adoption but not to put an end to the debate. The argument early took on the pattern which has persisted throughout our history. The anti-Federalists frequently scored in debating points; the Federalists invariably scored when the time came for action.

In the years covered by this volume, the debate has reached greater proportions. All four administrations of Franklin D. Roosevelt were characterized by ceaseless Republican attacks against "encroachments" of the federal bureaucracy on the rights of the states. Apparently, the American people were indifferent to such attacks as they kept reelecting Roosevelt while he kept on expanding presidential authority. And when the Republicans finally recaptured the White House under Dwight D. Eisenhower, they did nothing to reverse the trend—although they did slow its pace.

The debate has been complicated by the suspicion on both sides that the opposition was concealing its true motives. The twentieth-century antifederalists regarded the New Deal as a thinly disguised socialist plot. The modern federalists looked upon "states rights" as a coded phrase designed to cover opposition to civil rights and any progressive legislation. Such suspicions lent a tone of passionate fury to the arguments that frequently seemed to be out of proportion to the merits.

Our last two elected presidents apparently saw some merit to the antifederalist contentions. Lyndon B. Johnson frequently discussed what he called "creative federalism" which he never defined with precision although it seemed to have some relationship to regional groupings. Richard M. Nixon advanced what he called a "new federalism" which, in practice, meant parceling out federal tax money to the states with few or no strings. Whether either concept will have a substantial impact upon the future remains to be seen.

It will be understandable if the reader of the following articles feels that he or she is going in circles. The cure is to retain a grip on reality by looking at what our leaders have done as well as what they have said.

GER

John F. Kennedy

The New York Times

PERIL OF THE NATION AS MR. CANNON SEES IT

Says States Fail to Exercise Fully Their Governing Powers.

If It Continues Federal Government Will Be a Vast Bureaucracy, Inefficient If Not Corrupt.

Special to The New York Times.

PHILADELPHIA, Feb. 17.—Joseph C. Cannon, Speaker of the House of Representatives of the United States, in speaking before the Union League Club in this city to-night, said he thought the unfaithful public servant should be eliminated at the ballot box, and that when there were real evils the party should eliminate them. He declared that the States in controversy with the railroads have the power to handle the situation and must help themselves.

The Speaker was introduced by President Stuart of the club and said in part:

"In my judgment the greatest danger to the Republic comes from the citizen who refuses or neglects to participate in governing in local, State, and National affairs, and seeks protection from the Government to which he does not contribute according to his ability or means.

"In my judgment, the danger now to us is not the weakening of the Federal Government, but rather the failure of the forty-five sovereign States to exercise, respectively, their function, their jurisdiction, touching all matters not granted to the Federal Government. This danger does not come from the desire of the Federal Government to grasp power not conferred by the Constitution, but rather from the desire of the citizens of the respective States to cast upon the Federal Government the responsibility and duty that they should perform.

"If the Federal Government continues to centralize we will soon find that we will have a vast bureaucratic Government, which will prove inefficient if not corrupt.

"The Governor of one of the States has within a few days written to a Senator in Congress that his State is powerless to compel the railways within its borders to extend to its citizens facilities by proper connection, switching, and the furnishing of cars to enable its people to have equal and fair treatment under similar conditions with other citizens—and that this condition comes from inability to enforce law in existence and to enact additional necessary legislation, and in effect appealing for relief to the Federal Government.

"There is no adequate remedy for this condition except by the people of that State, clothed with plenary power, through the enforcement of the law and the enactment of additional legislation, if necessary, to exercise the functions of the Government. If I were asked what I'd do in this case, I'd say:

"'The gods help those who help themselves. You're up against it.'

"The Federal Government has no power to intervene, except by virtue of its power to regulate commerce among the States, and the people of the State would not be relieved as to traffic within the State."

February 18, 1906

ROOSEVELT SAYS NATION MUST CURB PLUTOCRACY

States Cannot, and Corporation Control Menaces Civilization.

FEDERAL POWER IS GROWING

Praises Pennsylvania Legislative Reforms at the Dedication of the New $13,000,000 Capitol.

HARRISBURG, Penn., Oct. 4.—Pennsylvania's new Capitol, which cost $4,500,000 to build and $9,000,000 to furnish, was dedicated to-day. President Roosevelt delivered an address in which he discussed problems that confront the American people and Government, and emphasized that the several States, individually, must act to end certain evils which neither private effort nor National Government action can curb.

The President's arrival in Harrisburg and his going to the Executive Mansion, and from there to the Capitol, were signals for loud cheers by the crowds in the streets. At the Capitol Gov. Pennypacker and Mayor Gross of Harrisburg gave the President gold medals as gifts of the State and city respectively.

When the President ascended the platform in front of the Capitol he was surrounded by men representing all branches of the State Government and specially invited guests, while the plaza in front was crowded with people. Before the exercises were started rain began falling and thousands stood in the downpour until the President had finished his address. Then a parade, including one brigade of the Pennsylvania National Guard, cadets from the Carlisle Indian School and soldiers' orphans' schools, passed in review. Gov. Pennypacker then took the President through the Capitol and entertained him at luncheon at the Executive Mansion. There were forty guests at this luncheon.

THE PRESIDENT'S SPEECH.

The President, in his speech, followed the printed copy. It was in the reformed spelling, and read as follows:

"It is a very real pleasure for me to attend these ceremonies at the capital of your great State. In every crisis of our Government the attitude of Pennsylvania has been of crucial importance, as the affectionate nickname of 'Keystone State' signifies. Pennsylvania has always lookt warily before she leapt, and it was well that she should do so. But having finally made up her mind, in each great crisis of our National history, her weight has been cast unhesitatingly upon the right side, and has been found irresistible. This was true alike at the time of the Declaration of Independence, at the time of the adoption of the Constitution, and during the terrible years when the issue was the preservation of the Union.

"Pennsylvania's soil is historic. It was within Pennsylvania's borders that the contest opened which was to decide whether the valiant soldiers of France would be able to bar this continent against the domination of the people of the English-speaking colonies. It was on Pennsylvania's soil that the Declaration of Independence was signed and the Constitutional Convention held. It was in Pennsylvania that Washington wintered at Valley Forge, and by keeping his army together during that Winter definitely turned the scales in our favor in the contest for independence. It was again on Pennsylvania's soil, at Gettysburg, that the tide turned in the civil war.

"In the composition of her people, moreover, Pennsylvania has epitomized the composition of our Union; for here many Old World races have mingled their blood to make that new type, the American. Finally, in all branches of the public service, in peace and in war, the native or adopted citizens of Pennsylvania have attained the highest eminence.

To Grapple with Present Problems.

"I do not, however, come here to-day to speak only of the past, and still less to appeal merely to State pride. We can show that the past is with us a living force only by the way in which we handle ourselves in the present, and each of us can best show his devotion to his own State by making evident his paramount devotion to that Union which includes all the States. The study of the great deeds of the past is of chief avail in so far as it incites us to grapple resolutely and effectively with the problems of the present.

"We are not now menaced by foreign war. Our Union is firmly established. But each generation has its special and serious difficulties; and we of this generation haye to struggle with evils springing from the very material success of which we are so proud, from the very growth and prosperity of which, with justice, we boast. The extraordinary industrial changes of the last half century have produced a totally new set of conditions, under which new evils flourish; and for these new evils new remedies must be devised.

"Some of these evils can be grappled with by private effort only; for we never can afford to forget that in the last analysis the chief factor in personal success, and indeed in National greatness, must be the sturdy, self-reliant character of the individual citizen. But many of these evils are of such a nature that no private effort can avail against them. These evils, therefore, must be grappled with by governmental action. In some cases this governmental action must be exercised by the several States individually. In yet others it has become increasingly evident that no efficient State action is possible, and that we need, thru Executive action, thru legislation, and thru judicial interpretation and construction of law, to increase the power of the Federal Government.

Criticism of Astute Lawyers.

"If we fail thus to increase it, we show our impotence and leave ourselves at the mercy of those ingenious legal advisers of the holders of vast corporate wealth, who, in the performance of what they regard as their duty, and to serve the ends of their clients, invoke the law at one time for the confounding of their rivals, and at another time strive for the nullification of the law, in order that they themselves may be left free to work their unbridled will on these same rivals, or on those who labor for them, or on the general public.

"In the exercise of their profession and in the service of their clients these astute lawyers strive to prevent the passage of efficient laws and strive to secure judicial determinations of those that pass which shall emasculate them. They do not invoke the Constitution in order to compel the due observance of law alike by rich and poor, by great and small; on the contrary, they are ceaselessly on the watch to cry out that the Constitution is violated whenever any effort is made to invoke the aid of the National Government, whether for the efficient regulation of railroads, for the efficient supervision of great corporations, or for efficiently securing obedience to such a law as the National eight-hour law and similar so-called 'labor statutes.'

"The doctrine they preach would make the Constitution merely the shield of incompetence and the excuse for governmental paralysis; they treat it as a justification for refusing to attempt the remedy of evil instead of as the source of vital power necessary for the existence of a mighty and ever-growing Nation.

Praises Pennsylvania Reforms.

"Strong Nationalist tho I am, and firm tho my belief is that there must be a wide extension of the power of the National Government to deal with questions of this kind, I freely admit that as regards many matters of first-rate importance we must rely purely upon the States for the betterment of present conditions. The several States must do their duty or our citizenship can never be put on a proper plane. Therefore I most heartily congratulate the people of the State of Pennsylvania on what its Legislature, upon what its Government, has accomplished during this present year. It is a remarkable record of achievement.

"Thru your Legislature you have abolished passes; you have placed the offices of the Secretary of the Commonwealth and the Insurance Commissioner upon an honorable and honest basis of salary only by abolishing the fee system; you have past a law compelling the officers and employes of great cities to attend to the duties for which they are paid by all the taxpayers and to refrain from using the power conferred by their offices to influence political campaigns; you have prohibited the solicitation or receiving of political assessments by city employes; you have by law protected the State Treasury from depredation and conserved the public moneys for use only in the public interest; you have by a law for the protection of the elective franchise made tampering with the ballot boxes and the casting of illegal votes so difficult as in all probability to be unprofitable; you have provided a primary election law which guarantees to the voters free expression in the selection of candidates for office; you have by law regulated and improved the civil service systems of your greatest cities; and, finally, you have past a law containing a provision which I most earnestly hope will in substance be embodied likewise in a law by the Congress at the coming session—a provision prohibiting the officers of any corporation from making a contribution of the money of that corporation to any candidate or any political committee for the payment of any election expenses whatever.

Asks for a Child Labor Law.

"It is surely not too much to say that this body of substantive legislation marks an epoch in the history of the practical betterment of political conditions, not merely for your State, but for all our States. I do not recall any other State Legislature which, in a similar length of time, has to its credit such a body of admirable legislation.

"Let me, however, most earnestly urge that your Legislature continue this record of public service by enacting one or two additional laws. One subject which every good citizen should have at heart above almost all others is the matter of child labor. Everywhere the great growth of modern industrialism has been accompanied by abuses in connection with the employment of labor which have necessitated a complete change in the attitude of the State toward labor.

"This is above all true in connection with the employment of child labor. In Pennsylvania you have made a beginning, but only a beginning, in proper legislation and administration on this subject; the law must, if necessary, be strengthened, and it must be rigorously enforced. The National Government can do but little in the matter of child labor, tho I earnestly hope that that little will be permitted to be done by Congress. The great bulk of the work, however, must be left to the State Legislatures; and if our State Legislatures would act as drastically, and yet as wisely, on this subject of child labor as Pennsylvania has acted within the present year as regards the subjects I have enumerated above, the gain would be literally incalculable; and one of the most vital needs of modern American life would at last be adequately met.

Lauds the Late Justice Wilson.

"So much for the State. Now for the Nation; and here I cannot do better than base my theory of governmental action upon the words and deeds of one of Pennsylvania's greatest sons, Justice James Wilson. Wilson's career has been singularly overlooked for many years, but I believe that more and more it is now being adequately appreciated, and I congratulate your State upon the fact that Wilson's body is to be taken away from where it now rests and brought back to lie, as it should, in Pennsylvania soil.

"He was a signer of the Declaration of Independence. He was one of the men who saw that the Revolution, in which he had served as a soldier, would be utterly fruitless unless it was followed by a close and permanent union of the States; and in the Constitutional Convention, and in securing the adoption of the Constitution and expounding what it meant, he rendered services even greater than he rendered as a member of the Continental Congress, which dclared our independence; for it was the success of the makers and preservers of the Union which justified our independence.

"He believed in the people with the faith of Abraham Lincoln, and coupled with his faith in the people he had what most of the men who in his generation believed in the people did not have—that is, the courage to recognize the fact that faith in the people amounted to nothing unless the representatives of the people assembled together in the National Government were given full and complete power to work on behalf of the people. He developed even before Marshall the doctrine (absolutely essential not merely to the efficiency but to the existence of this Nation) that an inherent power rested in the Nation, outside of the enumerated powers conferred upon it by the Constitution, in all cases where the object involved was beyond the power of the several States and was a power ordinarily exercised by sovereign nations.

Warrant for National Action.

"In a remarkable letter in which he advocated setting forth in early and clear fashion the powers of the National Government, he laid down the proposition that it should be made clear that there were neither vacancies nor interferences between the limits of State and National jurisdiction, and that both jurisdictions together composed only one uniform and comprehensive system of government and laws; that is, whenever the States cannot act, because the need to be met is not one of merely a single locality, then the National Government, representing all the people, should have complete power to act. It was in the spirit of Wilson that Washington, and Washington's lieutenant, Hamilton, acted, and it was in the same spirit that Marshall construed the law.

"It is only by acting in this spirit that the National Judges, legislators, and executives can give a satisfactory solution of the great question of the present day—the question of providing on behalf of the sovereign people the means which will enable the people in effective form to assert their sovereignty over the immense corporations of the day. Certain judicial decisions have done just what Wilson feared; they have, as a matter of fact, left vacancies, left blanks between the limits of possible State jurisdiction and the limits of actual National jurisdiction over the control of the great business corporations.

"It is the narrow construction of the powers of the National Government which in our democracy has proved the chief means of limiting the National power to cut out abuses, and which is now the chief bulwark of those great moneyed interests which oppose and dread any attempt to place them under efficient governmental control.

"Many legislative actions and many judicial decisions which I am confident time will show to have been erroneous and a damage to the country would have been avoided if our legislators and jurists had approached the matter of enacting and construing the laws of the land in the spirit of your great Pennsylvanian, Justice Wilson—in the spirit of Marshall and of Washington. Such decisions put us at a great disadvantage in the battle for industrial order as against the present industrial chaos. If we interpret the Constitution in narrow instead of broad fashion, if we forsake the principles of Washington, Marshall, Wilson, and Hamilton, we as a people will render ourselves impotent to deal with any abuses which may be committed by the men who have accumulated the enormous fortunes of to-day, and who use these fortunes in still vaster corporate form in business.

"The legislative or judicial actions and decisions of which I complain, be it remembered, do not really leave to the States power to deal with corporate wealth in business. Actual experience has shown that the States are wholly powerless to deal with this subject; and any action or decision that deprives the Nation of the power to deal with it, simply results in leaving the corporations absolutely free to work without any effective supervision whatever, and such a course is fraught with untold danger to the future of our whole system of government, and, indeed, to our whole civilization.

"All honest men must abhor and reprobate any effort to excite hostility to men of wealth as such. We should do all we can to encourage thrift and business energy, to put a premium upon the conduct of the man who honestly earns his livelihood and more than his livelihood, and who honestly uses the money he has earned. But it is our clear duty to see, in the interest of the people, that there is adequate supervision and control over the business use of the swollen fortunes of to-day, and also wisely to determine the conditions upon which these fortunes are to be transmitted and the percentage that they shall pay to the Government, whose protecting arm alone enables them to exist. Only the Nation can do this work. To relegate it to the States is a farce, and is simply another way of saying that it shall not be done at all.

Power Over Corporate Wealth.

"Under a wise and farseeing interpretation of the inter-State commerce clause of the Constitution, I maintain that the National Government should have complete power to deal with all of this wealth which in any way goes into the commerce between the States—and practically all of it that is employed in the great corporations does thus go in.

"The National legislators should most scrupulously avoid any demagogic legislation about the business use of this wealth, and should realize that it would be better to have no legislation at all than legislation couched either in a vindictive spirit of hatred toward men of wealth or else drawn with the recklessness of impracticable visionaries. But, on the other hand, it shall and must ultimately be understood that the United States Government, on behalf of the people of the United States, has and is to exercise the power of supervision and control over the business use of this wealth—in the first place, over all the work of the common carriers of the Nation, and in the next place over the work of all the great corporations which directly or indirectly do any inter-State business whatever—and this includes almost all of the great corporations.

"During the last few years the National Government has taken very long strides in the direction of exercising and securing this adequate control over the great corporations, and it was under the leadership of one of the most honored public men in our country, one of Pennsylvania's most eminent sons—the present Senator, and then Attorney General, Knox—that the new departure was begun. Events have moved fast during the last five years, and it is curious to look back at the extreme bitterness which not merely the spokesmen and representatives of organized wealth, but many most excellent conservative people then felt as to the action of Mr. Knox and of the Administration.

Government Ownership Evil.

"Many of the greatest financiers of this country were certain that Mr. Knox's Northern Securities suit, if won, would plunge us into the worst panic we had ever seen. They denounced as incitement to anarchy, as an apology for Socialism, the advocacy of policies that either have now become law or are in fair way of becoming law, and yet these same policies, so far from representing either anarchy or socialism, were in reality the antidotes to anarchy, the antidotes to socialism.

"To exercise a constantly increasing and constantly more efficient supervision and control over the great common carriers of the country prevents all necessity for seriously considering such a project as the Government ownership of railroads—a policy which would be evil in its results from every standpoint.

"A similar extension of the National power to oversee and secure correct behavior in the management of all great corporations engaged in inter-State business will in similar fashion render far more stable the present system by doing away with those grave abuses which are not only evil in themselves, but are also evil because they furnish an excuse for agitators to inflame well-meaning people against all forms of property, and to commit the country to schemes of wild, would-be remedy which would work infinitely more harm than the disease itself.

"The Government ought not to conduct the business of the country, but it ought to regulate it so that it shall be conducted in the interest of the public.

Will Not Halt His Work.

"Perhaps the best justification of the course which in the National Government we have been pursuing in the past few years, and which we intend steadily and progressively to pursue in the future, is that it is condemned with almost equal rancor alike by the reactionaries—the Bourbons—on one side, and by the wild apostles of unrest on the other. The reactionary is bitterly angry because we have deprived him of that portion of his power which he misuses to the public hurt; the agitator is angered for various reasons, including among others the fact that by remedying the abuses we have deprived him of the fulcrum of real grievance, which alone renders the lever of irrational agitation formidable.

"We have actually accomplished much. But we have not accomplished all, nor anything like all, that we feel must be accomplished. We shall not halt; we shall steadily follow the path we have marked out, executing the laws we have succeeded in putting upon the statute books with absolute impartiality as between man and man, and unresting in our endeavor to strengthen and supplement these by further laws which shall enable us in more efficient and more summary fashion to achieve the ends we have in view.

What Has Been Done.

"During the last few years Congress has had to deal with such vitally important questions as providing for the building of the Panama Canal, inaugurating the vast system of National irrigation in the States of the Great Plains and the Rocky Mountains, providing for a Pacific cable, and so forth. Yet in addition to these tasks, some of which are of stupendous importance, Congress has taken giant strides along the path of Government regulation and control of corporations; the inter-State commerce law has been made effective in radical and far-reaching fashion, rebates have been stopt, a pure food law has been past, proper supervision of the meat packing business provided, and the Bureau of Corporations established—a bureau which has already done great good, and which can and should be given a constantly increasing functional power.

"The work of legislation has been no more important than the work done by the Department of Justice in executing the laws, not only against corporations and individuals who have broken the anti-trust or inter-State commerce law, but against those who have been engaged in land frauds. Scores of suits, civil and criminal, have been successfully undertaken against offenders of all kinds—many of them against the most formidable and wealthy combinations in the land; in some the combinations have been dissolved, in some heavy fines have been imposed, in several cases the chief offenders have been imprisoned.

Not a Civilization of Plutocracy.

"It behooves us Americans to look ahead and plan out the right kind of a civilization, as that which we intend to develop from these wonderful new conditions of vast industrial growth. It must not be, it shall not be, the civilization of a mere plutocracy, a banking-house, Wall-Street-syndicate civilization; nor yet can there be submission to class hatred, to rancor, brutality, and mob violence, for that would mean the end of all civilization.

"Increased powers are susceptible of abuse as well as use; never before have the opportunities for selfishness been so great, nor the results of selfishness so appalling; for in communities where everything is organized on a merely selfish commercial basis such selfishness, if unchecked, may transform the great forces of the new epoch into powers of destruction hitherto unequaled.

"We need to check the forces of greed, to insure just treatment alike of capital and of labor, and of the general public, to prevent any man, rich or poor, from doing or receiving wrong, whether this wrong be one of cunning or of violence. Much can be done by wise legislation and by resolute enforcement of the law. But still more must be done by steady training of the individual citizen, in conscience and character, until he grows to abhor corruption and greed and tyranny and brutality and to prize justice and fair dealing.

"The men who are to do the work of the new epoch must be trained so as to have a steady self-respect, a power of sturdy insistence on their own rights, and with it a proud and generous recognition of their duties, a sense of honorable obligation to their fellows, which will bind them, as by bands of steel, to refrain in their daily work at home or in their business from doing aught to any man which cannot be blazoned under the noonday sun."

October 5, 1906

WOODROW WILSON ATTACKS PATERNALISM

Government Can't Do Everything, He Tells Southern Society.

ALSO ASSAILS THE TARIFF

Princeton's President Not for an Income Tax, Either—A Time for Sobriety in Judgment.

Woodrow Wilson, President of Princeton University, came out against the income tax and in favor of proper application of present laws, rather than the passage of new laws, at the twenty-first annual banquet of the Southern Society, held in the grand ballroom of the Waldorf-Astoria last night. Dr. Wilson blamed the tariff for the evils of great riches, and stated his belief that there was enough red blood in the body politic to overcome any disease. He did not make clear his position on the State's rights question, but he did say that he thought every loyal citizen should regard this country singly and as a whole.

All but one of the speakers at the banquet mentioned Secretary Root's recent speech. Augustus Thomas advised the South to contend for State's rights and William A. Barber disagreed with Mr. Root on very many points. Gen. Horace Porter refrained from any mention of politics, making a witty speech that was heartily applauded.

It was the occasion of the coming of age of the Southern Society, and was a brilliant affair. The room was decorated with fir trees and smilax, and the boxes were filled with women, who sat through the dinner in order to hear the speeches. Marion J. Verdery presided, as President of the society, and those at the guest table, in addition to the speakers, were Albert P. Massey, S. M. Gardenhire, Dr. F. J. Bowles, Edward F. Darrell, R. F. Munro, Dr. W. M. Polk, Berkeley Mostyn, J. Hampden Robb, Joseph I. Clarke, Thomas Ewing, Howard R. Bayne, Edward Owen, and Bedell Parker.

Mr. Verdery at the opening of the speechmaking spoke for purer politics and upright, honest, business methods. Then he paid this tribute to Samuel Spencer, the late President of the Southern Railroad, who was killed in a wreck on Thanksgiving Day:

"Would you have an individual example altogether worthy of emulation? Look! In the firmament of financial and industrial activities there is a dark spot. It is a deep, unfathomable mystery. Right there, until a few days ago, there shone a brilliant star. It went out in the sudden shock of terrific tragedy. The whole South sorrows over the calamity. He was one of us, and in loving tribute to his honored memory I beseech you let us all, in so far as in us lies, strive to live like him."

After Gen. Porter had entertained the diners with war recollections, Mr. Verdery introduced Dr. Wilson, who got a Princeton College yell from one corner of the room. Dr. Wilson said that America was growing anxiously thoughtful about herself, and took as the topic of his remarks "Patriotism," quoting Tennyson's lines:

> A nation still, the rulers and the ruled;
> Some sense of duty,
> Something of a faith;
> Some reverence of the laws ourselves have made,
> Some patient force to change them when we will,
> Some civic manhood form against the crowd.

"Patriotism, properly considered," said Dr. Wilson, "is not a mere sentiment; it is a principle of action, or, rather, is a fine energy of character and of conscience operating beyond the narrow circle of self-interest. Every man should be careful to have an available surplus of energy over and above what he spends upon himself and his own interests, to spend for the advancement of his neighbors, of his people, of his nation.

"Each line affords a text for the matter I speak of. It requires constant effort of the imagination and constant studious attention to the variety of conditions which diversify the life of the country from over to ocean, and an ever persistent catholicity of sympathy and of judgment to think of this country as every citizen should, as a single whole, a thing to be served not merely in its parts and in its separate interests, as the States are intended to serve it, but also in its entirety as the Federal Government is intended to serve it, keeping all interests harmonious, all powers co-operative—as a nation compact of rulers and of ruled, moving together under those who make the laws and by reason of the virtue of those who obey them.

"And yet only upon such a conception can an intelligent sense of duty be based. Genuine patriotism cannot be based upon a sense of private advantage or upon any calculation of interest. It can be based only upon a sense of duty. And duty must conceive its object, the country, the Nation we would serve. It was in America that patriotism first conceived this large way of thought and action for the ordinary citizen and put him in the way of statesmanlike thinking.

"I like to recall that passage of de Tocqueville's in which he marvels with eloquent praise at the variety of information and excellence of discretion which our polity did not hesitate to demand of its people, its common people. It is in this rather than in anything we have invented by way of governmental form that we have become distinguished among the nations, by what we expect of ourselves and of each other. I believe that there is enough red blood in the body politic to overcome any disease. Every loyal citizen should look upon this country singly and as a whole.

"America has fallen to the commonplace level of all the other nations which have preceded her, if she has not something of that faith that makes of her public idealists and of her citizens men to whom principles seem a sustaining motive of action. When she ceases to believe that all men shall have equal opportunity she goes back upon the principle on which the Nation was founded.

"'Some reverence for laws ourselves have made.' We have reverence enough for the laws if it be an evidence of reverence that we think that making law consists of legislation. I don't know that this country needs any more laws. I think we have laws enough. What this country needs is a more searching process in the application of the laws and less regard for persons in that application."

"How'll we get it?" some one in the hall cried out.

"Oh, we'll get it all right. It is proposed now that taxes shall be punitive; that men shall be punished for getting rich by a Government which has given them extraordinary facilities for getting rich. A Government which has a discriminating tariff cannot in conscience punish a man for getting rich. [Applause.] In my opinion there is only one sort of taxation that is just, and that is taxation that does not discriminate. I know of only one legitimate object of taxation, and that is to pay the expenses of the Government.

"Revenue ought always to be obtained from such sources that taxation will assist rather than check or discourage industry and enterprise. It is, in part, by the examples of Governments in such matters that individuals have used the revenue-getting powers of corporations to penalize rivals. The Government sets the example both of fosterage and of destruction.

"The right objects of law are to facilitate the life of society and to keep the conditions of profitable action upon a footing of equity, fair dealing, and equal advantage. Governments should supply an equilibrium, not a disturbing force.

"To keep such conceptions at the front in public policy is not easy in a striving and restless age. It requires not a little civic manhood, 'firm against the crowd,' to resist the admission that the Government should do everything, acting as general providence for its people, but the time has come for such sober counsel as will relieve Government of the business or providence and restore it to its normal duties of justice and of impartial regulation, a mastery over what is evil, a fosterage of what is good, but not a management of affairs of society.

"Patriotism is a mere sentiment and is blind alike to its opportunity and to its duty if it does not seek to perceive and to act upon large principles."

Augustus Thomas, who followed Dr. Wilson, made a humorous speech, touching lightly on the simplified spelling question, deploring greatly the spelling of "passed" "past," as in the President's message. Then he took up the Root speech and said in part:

"My conception of a Government is one where there are three co-ordinate branches, and not one where two of those branches may be coerced by an aspiring Executive."

Mentioning the State rights question he said:

"My topic to-night is 'The South as a Custodian.' I hope that before the additional powers are given to the Federal Government the South will fall back on a friendly contention for State rights. Such a contention will take long of accomplishment, and it will require great patience, but truth is always triumphant."

The next speaker was William A. Barber. He said in part:

"Only two nights ago, on an occasion like this, the distinguished Secretary of State, speaking in this banquet hall, gave his hearers enough constitutional law to give some people indigestion. His views are always interesting, but especially so when he speaks as the tribune of a Cabinet of which he is so important a part.

"If it be true, as there is a growing impression, that the Executive reaches out to control the courts, and, perhaps, get the new construction of the Constitution that is wanted, we invoke the warning of Chief Justice Marshall that the very safety of the Republic requires the legislative, executive, and judicial powers to remain forever separate and distinct.

"In our schools we may see a few syllables reformed out of our spelling, but we will not see State lines reformed out of our geography.

The Schools Versus the Shotguns.

"And, too, some of us believe that the fixing of qualifications for admission to the public schools is among the powers reserved to the States, and that the old Constitution will not admit the army and navy of the United States to the deliberations of our School Boards.

"And, again, not only because we believe that such matters are reserved to the States, but because we are a peaceable people, preferring the reader to the rifle and the spelling book to the shotgun, we respectfully oppose the strenuous suggestion that the power of Congress be used to add shooting galleries to our public schools."

December 15, 1906

WILSON ON STATE RIGHTS.

Governor Says States Are Full Partners with Federal Government.

LINCOLN, Neb., May 26.—Gov. Woodrow Wilson of New Jersey addressed the Commercial Club of this city at its annual dinner to-night. He said in part:

"When we discuss the powers of the States in our day we are not reviving the old academic question of 'State rights.'

"Almost of a sudden, it would seem, the States have stepped forward and reasserted themselves as full partners with the Federal Government in the inspiriting programme of progressive reform.

"The Federal Government can in the nature of the case go no further than the broad outlines of regulation, the establishment of those conditions of law which will fit the country as a whole, which will prevent the collision, the undesirable rivalry, and opposition of its several parts. It can only sketch in broad outline the economic and political regulation which is necessary for the life of the country. The States must fill in the detail.

"For the daily convenience and freedom of our people the control of trolley lines of gas companies, of electric light and power companies, is even more important than the control of great railways. The way in which these local public service corporations are managed has a vast deal to do not only with the convenience and comfort of our several communities but with their development, with their actual existence, with the whole question of the congestion of population and the maintenance of wholesome and sanitary and convenient conditions. Their control is necessarily a question for the States."

May 27, 1911

PRESIDENT STRESSES SELF-HELP TO SOLVE NATION'S PROBLEMS

Calls on States and Citizens Not to Carry Responsibilities to Washington.

CITES LINCOLN ON THE LAW

He Recalls on Radio From the Martyr's Old Study, Latter's Anti-Nullification Stand.

BIRTHDAY OBSERVED HERE

City-Wide Ceremonies Mark Day—Schools, Banks, Stock Exchange and Stores Close.

Special to The New York Times.

WASHINGTON, Feb. 12.—In a Lincoln Day address, broadcast by radio over the country tonight from Lincoln's old study at the White House, President Hoover hailed the nation's fulfillment of the emancipator's prophecy of its progress and at the same time solemnly reminded the America of today that it faced some of the same great problems that confronted Lincoln, a "builder in an epoch of destruction."

Turning to Lincoln's social and political ideals, Mr. Hoover applied them to two present-day problems arising from the trend to centralize governmeent and the economic depression.

Pointing out that "under Federal control the various conditions of life in our country are forced into standard molds," he said:

"Where people divest themselves of local government responsibilities they at once lay the foundation for the destruction of their liberties.

"The true growth of the nation is the growth of character in its citizens. The spread of government destroys initiative and thus destroys character.

"Carried to its logical extreme, all this shouldering of community and individual and community responsibility upon the government can lead but to the superstate where every man becomes the servant of the State and real liberty is lost. Such was not the government that Lincoln sought to build."

Resisting Centralization.

To resist this drift to centralized government and at the same time meet a multitude of problems, including the "critical test" of the economic depression, the President advocated strengthening in the nation "a sense and an organization of self-help to solve as many problems as possible outside of government."

Declaring the depression due "to lack of caution in business and to the impact of forces from an outside world, one half of which is involved in social and political revolution," the President told of his insistence upon organization through industry, local government and charity so that individuals and communities should "meet this crisis by their own initiative, by the assumption of their own responsibilities."

"The Federal Government," he added, "has sought to do its part by example in the expansion in employment by affording credit to drought sufferers for rehabilitation, and by cooperation with the community, and thus to avoid the opiates of government charity and the stifling of our national spirit of mutual self-help."

Recalling the stand that Lincoln took on issues persisting to this day, Mr. Hoover said:

"You will find him pounding at the public mind against nullification and for adherence to constitutional processes of government. No stronger statement has ever been made than that of Lincoln upon obedience to law as the very foundation of our Republic."

Whether the President had prohibition in mind was not disclosed in the course of his speech, but from this declaration he went directly into the fundamental question of the relations of Federal and State governments as a survival of the States' rights issue in the Civil War, now "less pregnant with disaster."

"Our concept of Federal, State and local responsibilities is possible of no unchangeable definitions and it must shift with the moving forces in the nation," he said, "but the time has come when we must have more national consideration and decision of the part which each shall assume in these responsibilities.

"The Federal Government has assumed many new responsibilities since Lincoln's time, and will probably assume more in the future when the States and local communities cannot alone cure abuse or bear the entire cost of national programs, but there is an essential principle that should be maintained in these matters.

"I am convinced that where Federal action is essential, then in most cases it should limit its responsibilities to supplement the States and local communities, and that it should not assume the major rôle or the entire responsibility in replacement of the State or local government. To do otherwise threatens the whole foundations of local government, which is the very basis of self-government."

Pointing also to Lincoln's advocacy of the protective tariff and Federal aid in waterway development, Mr. Hoover characterized Lincoln as a believer in party government, as one who "gloried" in the Republican party and bequeathed to it his tradition.

Speaking of this party, Mr. Hoover again struck the note of obedience to law, saying:

"It was and is a party of responsibility; it was and is a party of the Constitution."

Were Lincoln alive today, the President declared, he would find "a Union more solidly knit and more resolute in its common purpose than ever before in its history," a South recovered from war wounds, a South which inspired by splendid leadership has achieved a brilliant renaissance of industry and culture.

Political Significance Denied.

There was some speculation in Washington tonight as to possible political significance of the President's speech. This was largely due to a statement issued earlier in the day over the signature of Robert H. Lucas, executive director of the Republican National Committee, reminding Republicans that party rallies were to be held in various parts of the country just before and during the speech.

The statement explained that the nation-wide program was in accordance with a plan worked out in December. Whether the President approved it was not disclosed. At the White House, however, it was intimated that the speech was not political but was addressed to all the people regardless of party affiliations. It was added that the speech was not intended as an "opening gun" for the 1932 campaign.

Curtis Scores Detractors.

A Lincoln Day celebration held at the Mayflower Hotel today under the auspices of the Lincoln Memorial University was addressed by Vice President Curtis, Secretaries Wilbur and Doak, Brig. Gen. Frank T. Hines, Dr. John Wesley Hill, chancellor of the university, and others.

Mr. Curtis said that the American people of today "love and revere the memory of Lincoln, and deservedly so" and added:

"This feeling should be preserved, not destroyed. I thoroughly disapprove the tendency of modern biographers whose aim seems to be, as stated by Dr. William Lyon Phelps, 'to ruin the memories of their victims.' These men may get on the front page for a day, but they will not last long and their efforts will not succeed."

Secretary Doak said that "as the son of a Confederate soldier I yield to no man in reverent homage to the memory of this great man, whose place in the hearts of the people has so expanded with passing years and whose memory is most reverenced by every patriotic American."

A radiogram from President Masaryk of Czechoslovakia was read, as follows:

"A university in the name of Lincoln must be a teacher, nay, a prophet of democracy. Democracy is not only to take care of one's self but also to think of others and work for them. Democracy is the exact and practical fulfillment of Jesus' second command.

"Lincoln's life and death is a proof of what I always tried to express. And so I wish all success to Lincoln Memorial University, to its professors, and girls and boys. I have always loved Lincoln and learned from him. He is one of the eternal lights of freedom in darkness of egotism, sentimentality and political superstitions."

February 13, 1931

Truman for 'Small' Business, Backs 'Small' Colleges, Too

By FELIX BELAIR Jr.
Special to THE NEW YORK TIMES.

CHESTERTOWN, Md., June 1—President Truman declared his antipathy today to bigness, whether in communities or educational, business and financial institutions and said that the Government of the United States was the greatest ever conceived by man, because it provided a diffusion of powers which made it impossible for any one individual or group to gain complete control.

Because he was addressing the graduating class of the small and ancient Washington College here, the President laid special emphasis on the merits of smallness among educational institutions which he said would contribute more, in the long run, to the welfare of this generation than any other factor in the nation at this time.

Continuing, Mr. Truman said:

"I have said time and again that I would much rather see a thousand insurance companies with $4,000,000 in assets than one insurance company with $4,000,000,000. I would rather see a hundred steel companies than one United States Steel Corporation. I would rather see a thousand banks than one National City Bank."

A Matter of Comparisons Only

As a typical example of the bigness in insurance companies, to which he said he would prefer many smaller ones the President named the Metropolitan Life Insurance Company. In each instance, the President named the steel corporation, the bank and the insurance company as illustrative only of bigness. And if bigness was sometimes accompanied by greater financial strength and managerial efficiency, the President appeared to think the circumstances had no place in his address today.

In a mellow, nostalgic mood in the midst of small town surroundings, Mr. Truman was making no Rooseveltian attack on concentrated economics in the hands of big business corporations. Rather, he was complimenting Chestertown and its citizens on what he had seen on the short drive to the center of the town, the location of the Washington College campus, and where it was founded in 1782 with the First President as one of the trustees.

Mr. Truman wanted it understood that he was strictly in favor of small communities, small schools and small businesses just as he would rather be a big fish in a little pond than a little fish in a big pond. In the little corporation or business, the President point out, two or three men had the chance of being "big shots" in their own communities instead of their being just one big shot.

"Small Town" Roster Praised

So impressed was the President with the small town qualities of this Eastern Shore community, he said, that as the names of the graduates were being read off, he thought for a moment he was back in his home town of Independence, Mo., which he described as another "small town," although he asked not to be quoted as saying so back in Independence.

Although the President's principal reason for making the eighty-mile journey into Maryland was to receive an honorary LL. D. degree, the occasion also marked his first venture, in a small way, into State politics outside of Missouri.

From the very first stop, Annapolis, where he was met by Gov. Herbert R. O'Conor and Senator George L. Radcliffe, contestants in the current Democratic Senatorial primary, the President was not for a moment out of sight of either of them.

It was at the behest of Senator Radcliffe that the President agreed to make the trip and, although Governor O'Conor usually was accorded the seat of honor next to Mr. Truman throughout the day, local opinion was that the Senator had gained more ground politically than had the Governor as a result of the Presidential visit.

Eastern Shore folk do not welcome Federal intervention in their political contests, and showed it by re-electing Senator Tydings to the Senate in 1938 over the efforts of President Roosevelt, who toured the whole section on behalf of Representative Lewis as a part of his party "purge" campaign that year.

Apparently remembering this, President Truman was careful in his campus remarks and elsewhere during the day to steer entirely clear of political suggestions, except when a national or Federal question was involved. One such incident occurred when the President was met at Annapolis by Governor O'Conor and Senator Radcliffe.

The latter said apologetically that he had been up past midnight engaged in helping to pass the President's emergency anti-strike legislation. Mr. Truman smiled benignly, but could not pass up the opportunity to remind the Senator that his measure had been considerably "emasculated" from the form in which he had presented it to the Senate.

June 2, 1946

GOVERNORS STATE VIEWS ON RIGHTS

Martin Tells Oklahoma City Parley Local Governments Face Ruin by Federal Taxing

MEADOWS ASKS LIBERTIES

Says Centralization Is Not Necessarily Bad — Gates Bids Washington Cut Role

By JAMES A. HAGERTY
Special to THE NEW YORK TIMES.

OKLAHOMA CITY, Okla., May 27—Differences in points of view developed today among speakers at the Governors Conference which opened today in the Oklahoma State Capitol.

Gov. Edward Martin of Pennsylvania, a Republican, in his opening address as chairman of the conference called for decentralization of government now centralized in Washington, warned of the danger of ultimate destruction of local governments by the taxing power of higher governments and criticized those who went "tin cup in hand" to the Federal Government for "handouts."

Gov. Clarence W. Meadows, Democrat, of West Virginia, in his speech at the State dinner, declared that the liberties of men were not necessarily curtailed by the expanding activities of government and that absence of regulation by government did not necessarily mean freedom. Governor Meadows said that those who held contrary views derived them from the eighteenth-century "laissez faire" theory of government and that so-called invasions of personal liberties or States' rights had come when the States had been powerless or failed to act when action was demanded by the people.

Gates Asks State Functions

Gov. Ralph F. Gates, Republican, of Indiana, offered a resolution urging the Federal Government to return to the States all functions of Government that were not of a national character, that each State assume responsibility for meeting State-wide problems without seeking appropriation of Federal funds, and that the States urge all local governments to adopt a similar policy so that "the spirit of independence, self-reliance and self-sufficiency be restored to the American people and the blighting effect of an unbalanced budget be more immediately removed from the economy of the nation."

The resolution was referred to the committee on resolutions, of which Governor Herbert B. Maw, Democrat, of Utah, is chairman. A unanimous vote of the members of the committee on resolutions is required for submission of a resolution to the conference.

The conference opened in the Assembly chamber of the State Capitol with an attendance of twenty-two Governors, a much smaller number than would have been present had it not been for transportation difficulties caused by the railroad strike.

This was noted by Governor Robert S. Kerr of Oklahoma, in his address of welcome, when he said:

"Within the last few days we have seen the demonstration that a free people can meet the highest challenge and emerge triumphant from the severest test."

Conservation of natural resources was the chief subject discussed at the opening sesssion, with Governor Earl Snell of Oregon presiding. Discussing conservation of soil, Governor Edward J. Thye of Minnesota asserted that prevention of soil impoverishment was a problem that must be solved jointly by the Federal and State Governments and the individual farmer.

Gov. Andrew Schoeppel of Kansas declared that limitation of production of oil by the method of proration, as was done during the war, was necessary to conserve the country's oil supply, heavily drained by the demands of war and with reserves estimated at about twenty-two billion barrels.

Work Together, Truman Urges

OKLAHOMA CITY, May 27 (AP)—President Truman, who had planned to address the Governors in person until the rail and coal situation forced him to remain in Washington, sent a telegram to the conference, saying

"My message to you is an appeal to all to work together to maintain the authority of Government, national, State and local."

The telegram was addressed to the host Governor, Robert S. Kerr.

May 28, 1946

U. S. ON 'LAST MILE' TO 'COLLECTIVISM,' HOOVER DECLARES

In Address on 75th Birthday, Former President Attacks Spending by Government

'DRIVING DOWN BACK ROAD'

Average Citizen to Work Week Every Month to Pay Taxes, He Says at Stanford

By LAWRENCE E. DAVIES
Special to THE NEW YORK TIMES.

PALO ALTO, Calif., Aug. 10—Herbert Hoover warned the nation today, on the seventy-fifth anniversary of his birth, that because of pressure groups and spendthrift policies the United States was "blissfully" driving at top speed down the "back road" to collectivism. "We are on the last mile—you must give it thought," he said.

The only living former President inveighed against resorting to more Government borrowing to avoid "disasters" and advocated instead the reduction of "spending and waste" and the deferment of "some desirable things for a while."

If present spending plans were carried through, he said, the average working citizen would labor a week in every month to pay taxes, with "necessary national defense and the cold war" costing twenty-four days' work a year for the average employed individual.

Conceding that there had been no "great socialization of property" in the United States, Mr. Hoover asserted that none the less the nation was approaching collectivism "through governmental collection and spending of the savings of the people."

Truman Sends Message

As the climax of a day during which he received messages of congratulations from President Truman and a host of other notables, Mr. Hoover spoke before about 10,000 persons gathered in the Laurence Frost Memorial Amphitheatre on the campus of Stanford University, his alma mater. His words were broadcast over four major networks.

There was drama in the occasion, even though it was more like a great, friendly family party than anything else. The crowd sang "Happy Birthday" as Mr. Hoover was escorted to the grassy stage and he smiled broadly and waved. He seemed surprised as the thousands rose in greeting when he was introduced and he bashfully begged them, with a gesture, to be seated.

Introduced by Dr. Wallace Sterling, president of Stanford University, as a member of Stanford's first full-fledged class, that of 1895, Mr. Hoover cautioned that "the geometrical increase of spending" by government, local, state and Federal was "dynamite."

He blamed both private and Government pressure groups for much of what he termed, "confiscation of the work of the people."

Compares Debt Costs

Government, omitting the debt service, was costing the average family $1,300 annually today compared with less than $200 twenty years ago and would amount to $1,900 a year, including debt service, if projects now being seriously considered were enacted, he said.

He suggested that his hearers "think over" such figures as these:

That there is a Government employe for every eight of the working population; that one person out of every seven in the total population receives Government monies and that if those of age all are married they make up about half of the voters in the 1948 Presidential election; that if the Federal Government's estimate of a desirable standard of living is accepted, then 75 to 85 per cent of all the savings of the people will be absorbed by Government spending of an actual and seriously considered nature.

Mr. Hoover asserted increasing Government debts constituted "the road to inflation" and warned that attempting to solve problems by spending always meant "power, more power, more centralization in the hands of the state." The real test of America's thinking, he declared, was "not so much the next election as it is the next generation."

He referred to the "few hundred thousand Communists and their fellow travelers" in the country as a "nuisance" that required "attention," but voiced concern over a "considerable group of fuzzy-minded people who are engineering a compromise with all these European infections."

"The steady lowering of the standard of living by this compromised collectivism under the title of 'austerity' in England ought to be a sufficient spectacle for the American people," Mr. Hoover said. "They have aimed at the abundant life and wound up with a ration."

The ex-President deplored a situation in which, he said, our representatives, "who have to run for election can be defeated by pressure groups." He added:

"And in any event, our officials are forced to think in terms of pressure groups and not in the terms of the need of the whole people."

Referring by implication to criticism of his Commission on Organization of the Executive Branch of the Government, Mr. Hoover said that within the Federal Government there were "pressure groups building their own empires."

His birthday message to the country, he said, was this:

"The Founding Fathers dedicated the structure of our Government 'to secure the blessings of liberty to ourselves and our posterity.' We of this generation inherited this precious blessing. Yet as spendthrifts we are on our way to rob posterity of its inheritance."

It was not too late, however, he added, to summon "self-restraint, integrity, conscience and courage" to cope with the situation.

More than 1,200 persons had joined in contributing upward of $155,000 as a birthday fund presented to Mr. Hoover during the ceremony by Fred A. Wickett of Palo Alto for use by the Hoover Institute and Library on War, Revolution and Peace.

Mr. Hoover himself cited the library's millions of documents furnished by hundreds of persons and sixty governments as a source that would "teach the stern lessons of how nations may avoid war and revolution." It had received gifts exceeding $3,400,000.

In preparing to honor their most distinguished alumnus, Stanford researchers discovered that Mr. Hoover had received honorary degrees from fifty American colleges and universities and twenty-four foreign institutions besides twenty-three others voted to him which he never had been able to receive.

The late afternoon ceremony in the outdoor amphitheatre, with Gov. Earl Warren, high Army and Navy officers and other notables on the platform, was followed by a dinner given for Mr. Hoover by his family and close friends. It was held in the Lou Henry Hoover House, named for the late Mrs. Hoover and presented to Stanford for occupancy by its president.

Hoover family members here for the celebration were the former President's son and daughter-in-law, Mr. and Mrs. Herbert Hoover Jr.; their daughter Joan, and their son and daughter-in-law, Mr. and Mrs. Herbert Hoover 3d; Mr. Hoover's younger son and his wife, Mr. and Mrs. Allan Hoover, and their children, Allan Jr., 10; Andrew, 8; and Lou Henry Hoover, 6.

August 11, 1949

EISENHOWER URGES 'MIDDLE ROAD' WAY

Tells Bar Association Future Lies Between Concentrated Wealth, Unbridled Statism

By WILLIAM M. BLAIR
Special to THE NEW YORK TIMES

ST. LOUIS, Sept. 5—America's future in the industrialized economy of the twentieth century "lies down the middle of the road between concentrated wealth on one flank, and the unbridled power of statism on the other," Gen. Dwight D. Eisenhower said today.

Fundamental principles of American life "still dictate progress down the center, even though there the contest is hottest, the progress is sometimes discouragingly slow," he told members of the American Bar Association at the opening of their seventy-second annual convention this Labor Day.

After noting an "ever-expanding Federal Government" and saying that while Americans expected governmental action to prevent or correct abuses from the unregulated practice of a private economy, he asserted:

"We will not accord to the central government unlimited authority any more than we will bow our necks to the dictates of the uninhibited seekers after personal power in finance, labor, or any other field."

Three Fundamental Ideas

Agreement on three fundamental American principles, he said, "provides the setting within which can always be composed any acute difference."

These were, he said, "that individual freedom is our most precious possession," that all freedoms, personal, economic, social and political, were tied together in a single bundle, and that freedom to compete makes the American system the most productive on earth.

General Eisenhower's audience interrupted him nine times with applause and gave him three standing ovations. He drew heavy applause when he stated that the country's present high standard of living was "not the result of political legerdemain or crackpot fantasies of reward without effort, harvests without planting."

The issue of freedom and civil rights opened the five-day meeting. Frank E. Holman of Seattle, president of the American Bar Association, called for a check of a trend toward statism.

He noted an "attitude of acquiescence in the trend toward welfare government on the part of many leaders who actually themselves do not believe in it."

The leaders of the two major political parties, educators, and others, he said, were misreading the sentiment of a majority of Americans. There was a real hunger, he said, "for a leadership that is willing to battle for the preservation of constitutional government as against a drift toward more and more paternalism."

A majority report of a special ABA committee on the Bill of Rights questioned whether the "marked solicitude" of the courts for "unrestricted freedom of the individual has overshadowed proper concern for the civil rights in the citizens as a whole."

Coddling of Reds Is Feared

The report, to be laid before the house of delegates, cited as "a classic example of this great indulgence to the individual" the treatment of individual Communists.

"The individual Communist is prone to invoke every protection under the Bill of Rights and, having been accorded that protection, to flout not only the letter but the essential spirit behind the Bill of Rights.

"Having once attained power through the democratic process, they [Communists] then proceeded to destroy the civil rights of all citizens. They deny the very freedoms through which they rose to power, and, in this way, make the Bill of Rights the instrument of its own destruction."

The report gave as illustrations of the conflict the case of Gerhard Eisler, "who invoked every protection" of the Bill of Rights, jumped bail and fled to Europe, the trial of eleven Communists in New York, and the Terminello case in Chicago.

It posed for decision several questions of "serious import," including, "Is not the survival of our system of law and the instrumentalities, to enforce civil rights being endangered and are not these things vastly more important than the unrestrained rights of any individual to abuse and flout the Bill of Rights."

The special committee recommended a resolution approving pending Congressional legislation (H.R. 4703) which it said would "close serious gaps in our laws that permit citizens and aliens alike to disseminate information to the nation's detriment without fear of prosecution in court."

It excepted one provision which would delegate authority to the Secretary of Defense to promulgate security regulations, the violation of which would constitute a criminal offense. The committee doubted the validity and advisability of such a provision.

There were two dissents to the report of the sixteen-man committee, headed by Robert R. Milam of Jacksonville, Fla. They were made by Bruno V. Bitker of Milwaukee and Charles P. Curtis of Boston.

Mr. Bitker said the position of the United States grew stronger before the world "as we liberally interpret the basic principles enunciated in the Declaration of Independence and the Constitution."

Mr. Curtis said that until a "maze of hysteria" cleared away "the assertion and protection of individual rights are even more than unusually important." He added he was more concerned over "the precedence of the state ove the individual."

September 6, 1949

'Creeping Socialism' Scored

CUSTER STATE PARK, S. D., June 11 (AP)—President Eisenhower said tonight there had been a "creeping socialism" in the United States and that "if this group takes over again, we very gravely run the risk, we've had our last chance."

The President made the statement in a brief, informal talk to about 500 South Dakota Republican leaders at the Calvin Coolidge Inn.

He told the group he did not like to be an alarmist, "but in the last twenty years creeping socialism has been striking in the United States."

The President added it was not always the fault of "a few long-haired academic men in Washington." Some people, he said, "have not been quick enough to resent socialism if we thought it would benefit us."

June 12, 1953

EISENHOWER VOWS ALL FEDERAL HELP FOR PROSPERITY

Bars Idea of 'Boom-and-Bust America' and Warns of 'the Peddlers of Gloom'

FORESEES A GOOD YEAR

Reviews Record of Regime in Address to the Nation—Emphasizes 'Help' Theme

By JAMES RESTON

Special to THE NEW YORK TIMES.

WASHINGTON, Jan. 4—President Eisenhower sought tonight to calm fears of an economic recession by looking forward to "a new year more fruitful to the security of the nation and the welfare of its people."

In a speech reminiscent of Franklin D. Roosevelt's "the only thing we have to fear is fear itself" theme of his first Inaugural Address in 1933, the President said:

"This Administration believes that we must not and need not tolerate a boom-and-bust America."

President Eisenhower told a nation-wide television and radio audience that he hoped to decentralize the services of the Federal Government as much as possible, but he rejected Democratic charges that the Republican party was loath to use the power of the Federal Government to correct economic ills.

Promises Action

"I * * * give you," he said, "this assurance:

"Every legitimate means available to the Federal Government that can be used to sustain that prosperity is being used and will continue to be used as necessary."

The President answered some of his critics and perhaps Adlai E. Stevenson, his Democratic rival in 1952, when he said that faith in America could not be shaken by "self-appointed peddlers of gloom and doom."

Mr. Stevenson in a recent speech at Philadelphia said that the four freedoms were being replaced by the four fears: fear of depression, fear of communism, fear of ourselves and fear of freedom itself.

The "four freedoms" were first enunciated by President Roosevelt in his 1941 State of the Union Message as freedom of expression, freedom of worship, freedom from want and freedom from fear.

The President held an unusual joint session of his Cabinet and Republican Congressional leaders at the White House this morning. Later in the day he conferred with Robert Montgomery, screen star and television producer, on the technical aspects of tonight's broadcast.

Tomorrow the President will discuss the foreign and military aspects of his policy with Democratic Congressional leaders before delivering his State of the Union Message on Thursday.

Cites Administration Aid

The emphasis of the President's fifteen-minute report to the people—the first in a series designed to win public support for the Republican program—was on the responsibility and determination of the Government to deal with the adjustments of the national economy.

Though he warned that his program would not "deal in pie-in-the-sky promises to all, or bribes to a few, nor threats to any," he said time and again that the welfare of the people was a concern of the Federal Government.

His short speech was studded with words such as "welfare," Government "service" to the people; "sound planning" and "aggressive enterprise."

"I know," he said, "that you have unbounded confidence in the future of America. You need only the assurance that Government will neither handcuff your enterprise nor withdraw into a smug bureaucratic indifference to the welfare of American citizens, particularly those who, through no fault of their own, are in a period of adversity."

The President declared "'help' is the key word of this Administration" and by help "we mean service—service that is effective, service that is prompt, service that is single-mindedly devoted to solving the problem."

The President indicated that adjustments in the economy were at hand, but expressed confidence in the nation's ability to remain prosperous.

"We believe," he said, "that America's prosperity does not and need not depend upon war or the preparations for war. We know that this great country can make the adjustments necessary to meet changing circumstances without encouraging disaster and without bringing about the economic chaos for which the Communists hope. Our system is the greatest wealth-producer in the world—in terms of the life and well-being of every citizen."

The emphasis on the domestic economy rather than the threat of Communist aggression and conspiracy—which has been the main theme of most Presidential speeches in the last year—reflected considerable public discussion recently about a decline in business, in farm prices and in employment.

Douglas Sees Recession Now

Senator Paul H. Doulas, Democrat of Illinois, has been outspoken on this subject. He stated last week that the nation already was in a recession—most other economists call it a period of "downward adjustment"—and pointed to these figures in support of his assertion:

¶Currently weekly figures on automobile production were off 12 per cent from a year ago.

¶Steel production was running at only 67 per cent of capacity.

¶Mail order sales were down 16 per cent from last year.

¶Car loadings were off 12 per cent.

¶Unemployment was rising, particularly in industries such as farm machinery, heavily supported by farmers whose income was well below 1952.

In the light of this trend, there has been considerable discussion here about the possibility that the Administration's planned cut in Government spending—the next budget is expected to be down $5,000,000,000—would add to the downward swing.

President Eisenhower purposely avoided dealing in specifics tonight. He left that to the other White House messages to come. Instead, he seemed to be trying this evening to establish a climate of confidence and to be challenging the Democratic theme that the Republicans were so opposed to Government intervention in domestic economic matters that they might not deal quickly enough or effectively with any economic decline.

The President emphasized that "the Federal Government should be prepared at all times—ready at a moment's notice—to use every proper means to sustain basic prosperity of our people."

President Eisenhower defined his program in these terms:

"It is a program inspired by zeal for the common good, dedicated to the welfare of every American family—whatever its means of livelihood may be, or its social position, or its ancestral strain, or its religious affiliation. I am confident it will meet with your approval."

Here is the way President Eisenhower summarized the record of his administration's first year:

¶"The fighting and the casualties in Korea mercifully have come to an end. We can therefore take more satisfaction in other blessings of our daily life.

¶"Our own defenses and those of the free world have been strengthened against Communist aggression.

¶"The highest security standards are being insisted upon for those employed in Government service.

¶"Requests for new appropriations have been reduced by $13,000,000,000 dollars.

¶"Tax reductions which go into effect this month have been made financially feasible by substantial reductions in Government expenditures.

¶"Strangling controls on our economy have been promptly removed.

¶"The fantastic paradox of farm prices on a toboggan slide, while living costs have soared skyward has ceased.

¶"The cheapening by inflation of every dollar you earn, every savings account and insurance policy you own, and every pension payment you receive has been halted.

¶"The proper working relationship between the Executive and Legislative Branches of the Federal Government has been made effective.

¶"Emergency immigration legislation has been enacted.

¶"A strong and consistent policy has been developed toward gaining and retaining the initiative in foreign affairs.

¶"A plan to harness atomic energy to the peaceful service of mankind, and to help end the climate of suspicion and fear that excites nations to war, has been proposed to the world."

The President read his speech from a machine on which the words are written in large letters on a moving tape.

The general tendency here tonight was to wait for the specific program before entering into any detailed criticism of the theme developed by the President.

The Republicans came out of the White House today praising the "dynamic" and "progressive" aspects of the program. The Democrats, however, want to see what the program is before characterizing it in this manner.

'61 CONGRESS SPLIT ON FEDERAL ROLE

Parties Still Divided Over U. S. Duties, Study Shows

By Congressional Quarterly.

WASHINGTON, Oct. 17—The question of how great or small a role the Federal Government should play in American life continues to drive a deep wedge between the Democratic and Republican parties.

In its study of voting by Congressmen this year on questions of Federal Government responsibilities, Congressional Quarterly found that Democrats supported a larger Federal role five times as often as Republicans. Conversely, Republicans supported a smaller Federal role slightly less than four times as often as Democrats.

To provide a measure for attitudes on the Federal role, the Quarterly examined all 320 roll-call votes in 1961 and selected ten from the House and the Senate as key tests.

The test votes touched on most of the major controversies over domestic policy that have seen Democrats pitted against Republicans.

Among the tests were roll-calls in the Senate and House concerning Federal aid to education and depressed areas, public versus private power, housing and minimum-wage coverage. Other votes involved the issue of Federal-state relations in civil rights, temporary unemployment compensation, Mexican farm labor, election reform, water pollution, the interstate water resources compact and juvenile delinquency.

Democrats Score 76 Per Cent

By adding up the scores of individual Senators and Representatives, the survey found the average Democrat in 1961 **supported a larger Federal role (or opposed a smaller one) 76 per cent of the time and the average Republican 15 per cent of the time.**

The average Republican supported a smaller Federal role (or opposed a larger one) 83 per cent of the time and the average Democrat 22 per cent of the time.

More significant still were the scores of individual members, showing the balance of attitudes on the Federal role within each party in each chamber.

In the Senate, for example, seventeen Northern Democrats supported a larger Federal role or opposed a smaller one on all of the ten test votes.

Altogether, forty-three of the Senate's sixty-four Democrats supported a larger Federal role or opposed a smaller one on at least seven of the ten roll-calls. Seven Democrats, all from the South, opposed a larger role or supported a smaller one on all of the votes.

Javits First For G. O. P.

Conversely, only one Republican—Jacob K. Javits of New York—supported a larger Federal role on all of the test votes, and one—Clifford P. Case of New Jersey—supported a larger role on nine of the roll-calls. Altogether, only seven of the thirty-four supported the larger Federal role on seven or more of the votes. Eleven Republican Senators opposed a larger Federal role on all ten votes.

Among the Senate leaders Hubert H. Humphrey of Minnesota, the Democratic whip, scored 100 per cent in favor of a larger Federal role or opposed to a smaller one, while the majority leader, Mike Mansfield of Montana, scored 70 per cent.

The Republican whip, Thomas H. Kuchel of California, was 70 per cent in favor of a larger Federal role, while the party's Senate leader, Everett McKinley Dirksen of Illinois, scored only 10 per cent. The conservatives' spokesman, Barry Goldwater, Arizona Republican, had **no votes in favor of a larger Federal role.**

Among House notables, the Democratic leader, John W. McCormack of Massachusetts, scored 100 per cent and the Republican leader, Charles A. Halleck of Indiana, never voted in favor of a larger Federal role.

October 22, 1961

Transcript

Following is the text of President Kennedy's news conference yesterday afternoon in Washington, as recorded by The New York Times:

* * * * *

4 Q.—Some of the critics of your urban affairs plan charge that it's an invasion of states and local rights. Would you comment on that, and would you also comment on it in a larger frame? For instance, what do you think of the argument that big government, so called, might not need to be so big if state and local governments were more efficient in fulfilling their duties?

A.—With regard to the specific question on the—I don't believe that such a Cabinet position would interfere with the states. In my opinion, it would supplement their efforts. There is a responsibility which the states have for various, and each city has, for certain important functions in the life of every citizen, but the Federal Government also has one.

There is a Department of Agriculture, which has contact with each individual farmer in the United States. That does not interfere with the county responsibility or the state responsibility.

Now in the urban message I sent up yesterday I pointed out that in our ten leading cities, citizens pay 35 per cent of the income taxes paid in the United States. They have many serious problems which are increasing in time, particularly as our population increases by 3,000,000 a year.

I believe that these problems are entitled to a place at the Cabinet table.

Now, I'm interested in charges about big government, and I read these features, and then I receive a wire asking for the Federal Government to take over the operations of the New Haven Railroad. And we send a wire back to the states after having put $35,000,000 into maintaining that railroad, what action are the states prepared to take?

My experience usually is that these matters are put to the Federal Government by the request of cities, or states, or individual groups and it's not a question of the Federal Government anxious to extend its role but rather that there is a need and no one responds to it and the national Government therefore meet its responsibility.

And I believe that with two-thirds of our people in the cities of the United States they should be up alongside of the others in the Cabinet so that we can deal more effectively with these programs.

* * * * *

February 1, 1962

Text of Declaration of Principle and Policy Issued by G. O. P. in Congress

Special to The New York Times.

WASHINGTON, June 7—Following is the text of "A Declaration of Republican Principle and Policy" issued today by the 1962 Joint Committee on Republican Principles:

I. Basic Beliefs of Republicans

Republican philosophy is rooted in the traditions of this land of ours—in the Declaration of Independence that made this country free, in the Constitution that has kept it free, and in the free men and women who have made it the greatest nation on earth.

Republican philosophy rests on the doctrines that the individual has a God-given dignity and that government exists to serve him.

We Republicans hold these five principles as basic beliefs:

INDIVIDUAL LIBERTY

We believe in the individual's right and capacity to govern himself—to set his own goals—to make his way to them without the restraints of dictatorship or paternalism.

LIMITED GOVERNMENT

We believe that the basic function of government is to maintain an environment in which the individual can freely develop powers of mind, heart and body with which his Creator endowed him. We believe that government should do for the people only the things they cannot do for themselves.

DIFFUSION OF POWER

We believe that the Federal Government should act only when the people are not adequately served by state or local governments. We believe in separation of the powers of government. We believe in a system of checks and balances to prevent a monopoly of power in any branch of government.

GOVERNMENT WITH A HEART

We believe that government must act to help establish conditions of equal opportunity for all people and to help assure that no one is denied the requisites for a life of dignity.

GOVERNMENT WITH A HEAD

We believe that government must prudently weigh needs against resources, put first things first, rigorously tailor means to ends, and understand the difference between words and deeds. The future will be built by those who work for it—not by those who only promise it.

II. The Great Issue of 1962

The vote cast by the American citizen in the election of 1962 should be his response to the question: Which party acts more effectively to preserve and enlarge human freedom?

The current Administration has shown little understanding of, or concern for, institutions that buttress freedom at home—separation of powers, checks and balances, state and local responsibility, and a free competitive economy.

It has demonstrated neither the wit nor the will to meet effectively the assault of international communism on freedom.

We Republicans cannot witness the erosion of freedom without warning or protest. We propose a new direction for public policy in order to advance the cause of freedom at home and throughout the world.

III. Freedom at Home

In domestic policy, the most urgent national goal is steady economic progress with more and better products, more and better jobs, and a constantly improving standard of living for all.

Only with a vigorous economy can the cold war be won, education improved, slums eliminated, medical care expanded, and other urgent national goals achieved.

Only a free competitive economy will have the needed vigor.

Government should encourage economic growth, particularly by fostering an environment in which Americans can earn, spend and save with confidence. It should not compete, nor fix wages or prices, nor substitute its decision for free bargaining in the market place.

The level of persistent unemployment which has existed under the present Administration cannot be tolerated. We believe in meeting unemployment with real jobs from the released energy of private initiative. Government should help to develop skills that fit workers for new jobs in a swiftly changing economy.

A thorough overhaul of the tax system to encourage production, build jobs, and promote savings and investment is overdue.

The economic responsibility of Government requires a halt to the upward spiral of Federal spending, especially for non-defense purposes. Waste must be eliminated, and all proposals for expenditure must be subjected to the most rigid test of necessity.

Representative Melvin R. Laird of Wisconsin, head of the group that issued the Republican party statement.

This responsibility requires more than lip service to a balanced budget and reduction of the Federal debt.

This responsibility requires a stable dollar, which is not likely to result if control of the Federal Reserve System rests in the White House.

Government should exercise impartiality and forbearance when the immediate economic interests of management and labor come into conflict.

Must Not Be Partisan

Above all, government must not become the partisan of any private economic interest. We want government to be pro-business and pro-labor. An anti-business or anti-labor orientation inevitably involves government in every conflict between management and labor and can only enfeeble a free-enterprise economy.

The productive capacity of American agriculture is a blessing. The present farm problem in large part was created by government. We reject the Administration's proposal which gives the farmer only a choice between regimentation and ruin. We advocate a shift in resources, encouraged by a massive voluntary long-term land retirement program, increased emphasis on new uses for farm products, and improved marketing and distribution practices.

Problems of surp[illegible] must be met by maintaining strategic food reserves, by expansion of programs to feed the needy at home and abroad, and by adjusting price supports to permit the development and growth of markets and to remove incentives for overproduction. The ever-increasing maze of red-tape fences across the farms of this land must be torn down.

Government must encourage, not inhibit, the ingenuity and enterprise that produce scientific and technological progress.

The Administration's lack of sympathy toward a free competitive economy has been made plain by many of its principal advisers. They have expressed the pessimistic theory that the economy can attain a satisfactory rate of growth and avoid mass unemployment only through heavy-handed direction and control by government. They have argued that government must protect individuals from foolish spending by taking their money and spending it for them.

The incompetence of the New Frontier in economic policy is manifest. It has destroyed confidence. It has given the nation a multi-billion-dollar increase in Federal spending and is on the way to its third unbalanced budget. Under it the nation has had the highest annual unemployment, the greatest number of business failures since the Great Depression, and the slowest recovery from recession in the post-war period.

The oft-heard campaign cry "Get America moving again" has become a hollow echo.

THE ECONOMY

Republicans understand the workings of a free competitive economy. The present Administration does not.

We hold that American labor, business, industry, science and agriculture get the jobs done, pay the wages, and create the rising standard of living.

We advocate decentralization in scientific effort. We favor continuation of a patent system that encourages risk-taking and creativity. In fields such as space exploration and atomic power (which should be swiftly developed), the preponderant role that government must at present assume should not shut out increased participation by private enterprise in the future.

GOVERNMENT WITH A HEART—AND A HEAD

The Republican party, which came into being to reassert the rights and dignity of the individual, strongly supports measures necessary to fulfill the promises of the Constitution. It made solid progress in the field of human rights during its administration and specified its objectives in its 1960 patform.

The right to vote is denied by fraud in the casting or counting of ballots as surely as by exclusion from the polls. Republicans urge vigorous investigation of fraud at the polls and recommend corrective action.

As in civil rights, so in immigration policy, Republicans take their pledges seriously. The failure of the present Administration even to request immigration legislation exposes their 1960 platform promises as a hoax.

Republicans seek to preserve the system that has provided the highest quality of hospital and medical care available anywhere on earth. We reject attempts to run a legislative bulldozer through the structure of voluntary health insurance and private medicine.

Effective tax relief for medical and hospital insurance should be given to all. We support government action to increase the coverage of voluntary insurance plans and to help older citizens having difficulty meeting the costs of adequate coverage.

Under a system of local responsibility for education, American schools — public and private — have given the nation a higher percentage of well-educated citizens than are found in any other nation of the world.

Every American youth should have the opportunity to receive an education commensurate with his ability. Selective Federal assistance is needed. Federal direction must never be substituted for local or private control of our schools.

Tax relief should be given to those who fear the burden of financing education for themselves or others.

Public assistance programs should put a floor over the pit of poverty, never a ceiling on personal achievement. They should strive to equip individuals to become self-supporting. The qualified recipient, as well as the taxpayer, must be protected from the misuse of welfare funds.

FEDERAL-STATE RELATIONS

The Federal system of the United States was designed to prevent excessive centralization of political power and to defend individual liberty at home. Without sacrificing effieiency, it gives to the nation flexibility and durability.

The national Government should be ready to cooperate with states and localities, not elbow them aside or smother them with direction and control.

Neglect at any level of government is likely to result in the weakening of a Federal system. For example, state and local governments must deal with the urgent problems of urbanized areas, or run the risk of Federal control in these areas. Failure to eliminate the inequities in representation in state legislatures gives an impetus to further centralization of power in the Federal Government and ultimately in the Federal Executive.

June 8, 1962

Nixon's Essay for Bar Called 'Finest in 28 Years'

He Expounded U.S. System in Reply to Query

By PETER KIHSS

Former Vice President Richard M. Nixon found himself required—like any other lawyer—to explain "what do you believe the principles underlying the form of government of the United States to be," before he could win admission to the New York bar.

Mr. Nixon's 500-word reply described the principles as the decentralization and separation of powers and the balancing of freedom with order. He contrasted the America system with Britain's Parliamentary supremacy and France's primary power for the Executive. The American ideal, he said, is individual enterprise.

With his bar admission Thursday, Mr. Nixon is expected shortly to become one of four senior partners in a reorganization and renaming of the firm of Mudge, Stern, Baldwin & Todd.

His name is expected to be put first. In the same way, former Thomas E. Dewey headed the renamed firm of Dewey, Ballantine, Bushby, Palmer & Wood. Mr. Dewey, also a former Republican Presidential candidate, went back to private law practice here in 1955.

Joseph V. Kline, a member of his firm, formally proposed Mr. Nixon's admission to the bar here, and the Appellate Division approved the action Thursday.

Ordinarily, admission papers are sealed by the court for the applicant's protection. In Mr. Nixon's case, Lowell C. Wadmond, chairman of the court's committee on character and fitness, told the court that the former Vice President's statement was "the finest" he had seen in 28 years on the committee.

The text, obtained after Mr. Wadmond reported clearance from Presiding Justice Bernard Botein, was as follows:

The principles underlying the Government of the United States are decentralization of power, separation of power and maintaining a balance between freedom and order.

Above all else, the framers of the Constitution were fearful of the concentration of power in either individuals or government. The genius of their solution in this respect is that they were able to maintain a very definite but delicate balance between the Federal government and the State government, on the one hand, and between the executive, legislative and judicial branches of the Federal government, on the other hand.

By contrast, in the British system, the Parliament is supreme. In the present French system the primary power resides in the executive, and in some older civilizations the judges were predominant. Throughout American history there have been times when one or the other branches of government would seem to have gained a dominant position, but the pendulum has always swung back and the balance over the long haul maintained.

The concept of decentralization of power is maintained by what we call the Federal system. But the principle is much broader in practice. Putting it most simply, **the American ideal is that private or individual enterprise should be allowed and enouraged to undertake all functions which it is capable to perform. Only when private enterprise cannot or will not do what needs to be done should government step in.** When government action is required, it should be undertaken if possible by that unit of government closest to the people. For example, the progression should be from local, to state, to Federal Government in that order. In other words, the Federal Government should step in only when the function to be performed is too big for the state or local government to undertake.

The New York Times

Richard M. Nixon leaving Appellate Division after admission to the bar here.

The result of these somewhat complex constitutional formulas is greater protection and respect for the rights of the individual citizen. These rights are guaranteed by the Constitution not only by the first ten amendments, which specifically refer to them, but even more by the system itself, which is the most effective safeguard against arbitrary power ever devised by man.

Yet the genius of the founding fathers is further demonstrated by the fact that while freedom for the individual was their primary objective they recognized that uncontrolled freedom for some would lead to the anarchy which would destroy freedom for all. Maintaining the delicate balance between freedom and order is, in my view, the greatest achievement of the American Constitutional system. Inability to maintain that balance is the basic reason for the failure of regimes in Latin America, Africa and Asia which have tried to copy our system. They invariably go to one extreme or the other—too much emphasis on the freedom of men to do anything they please or too much emphasis on controlling the excesses of freedom. Each of these approaches leads inevitably to dictatorship either of the right or of the left, a tragedy which America will be able to avoid by continued dedication to the fundamental principles of our Constitution.

December 7, 1963

Is Washington Too Powerful?

Yes: 'There must always exist fundamental areas of political administration best left to state and local authority.'

By RUSSELL KIRK

THE United States, as Orestes Brownson wrote a century ago, is a republic in which "territorial democracy" prevails. The American allocation of powers between the general government and the states has given to modern politics the term "federalism"; and foreign observers from Tocqueville onward have seen in the American federal structure a policy friendlier to order, justice and freedom than any other political contrivance.

In theory and, to no small extent, in practice, the American system remains federal today. But pressures to supplant effective federalism by a centralized "plebiscitary democracy" are strong. When the farmers of the most remote county are supervised by Washington-appointed officials; when hot lunches in schools are subsidized and regulated by central authority; when Federal courts sit in judgment on the boundaries of state legislative districts --then the process of centralization already is well advanced.

Nowadays one not infrequently encounters, in the universities and in powerful Washington lobbies, gentlemen who would like to sweep away the whole concept of state and local powers—to abolish Brownson's "territorial democracy" and the virtues of local government admired by Tocqueville. A centralized domination, with states and localities reduced to mere administrative units, would be more efficient, they argue. Take, as an example, this passage from Dr. Henry S. Kariel's book "The Decline of American Pluralism": "To put it bluntly, government must be centralized to carry out the tasks of public regulation. Virtually all our problems today are national problems, and they must be dealt with nationally."

RUSSELL KIRK, professor of political science at Long Island University, is the author of several books, including "Confessions of a Bohemian Tory" and "The Conservative Mind."

BUT, in the phrase of Lord Falkland, "When it is not necessary to change, it is necessary not to change." A heavy burden of proof lies upon these centralizing innovators. The primary duties of the general government — the administration at Washington —are the defense of the country and the conduct of foreign affairs, together with the issuance of money, the adjudication of disputes between states and the various other functions specified in the Constitution. No sensible person desires to diminish these powers. But this division of political authority leaves to the states and their agencies the great bulk of the civil functions of the political order.

IF the Government at Washington essays to perform or even to supervise the routine operation of government as it directly affects the mass of people, then it must perform its new undertakings badly; and what is equally lamentable, it must neglect its primary functions in trying to be omniscient and omnipresent.

To say that widespread difficulties like educational reform and welfare-roll mendicancy are national problems is a truism. But it does not follow that all "national problems" can be dissipated through the mechanism of the centralized state.

The decline of private morality, for instance, is a national problem; yet we would be imprudent, and perhaps tyrannical, if we directed a Washington bureaucracy to embark upon the regulation of morality. Such reform must be left to churches and other voluntary groups, to civil improvement and to the family and the individual; the failure of the Volstead experiment should suggest the folly of socializing and centralizing "problems" that are amenable only to voluntary and local treatment.

Thus there always must exist fundamental areas of political administration best left to state and local authority (and aspects of life naturally beyond politics). The regular police functions would suffer if centralized: for though an élite organization like the F.B.I. works well in its present limited role, and though initially it might do good work in a larger sphere because a new broom sweeps clean, nevertheless, in the long run, a central secret police not only would be highly dangerous to freedom but would grow more corrupt and less responsive to demands for reform precisely because its center would be far removed from the protestors.

THE ordinary administration of civil and criminal justice, the provision of public sanitation, roads, protection against fire and all such workaday but indispensable aspects of government are more efficiently and justly performed by state administrations and their subordinate divisions. This is true especially of public schools.

To cite a writer whom no one will suspect of political obscurantism — Mrs. Agnes Meyer of The Washington Post family — "If we deprive the state and local school boards of their autonomy we undermine our whole democratic structure, since local control of education is the strongest bulwark we have left against the growing tendency in our country toward overcentralization of power in the Federal Government, in our military hierarchy, and in our industrial bureaucracy."

Even were it feasible to reduce state and local authorities to mere subordinates of central political planning, the consequences to the central government itself might be disastrous. For one thing, this nation—like most of the modern world—already is perplexed by a degree of centralization in various fields which defeats its own object. The man-killing job of the Presidency may be sufficient illustration.

Professor Wilhelm Roepke, in his book, "A Humane Economy," puts this matter succinctly: "Our world suffers from the fatal disease of concentration, and those—the politicians, leading personalities of the economy, chief editors and others—in whose hands the threads converge, have a task which simply exceeds human nature. The constant strain is propagated through all other levels, down to the harassed foreman and his like. It is the curse of our age. It is a curse twice over because these men, who can do their duty only at the peril of angina pectoris, lack the time for calm reflection or the quiet reading of a book."

The issue: One great Federal government and less important state governments,

FOR another thing, these United States, accustomed to territorial democracy, know no class of leaders and administrators competent to undertake sweeping consolidated direction. An English civil servant once told a member of the House of Commons that the British nation would be far more efficiently governed if only Parliament were swept away and the civil service put in total charge of affairs. "No doubt," replied the M.P., "and within a fortnight, you would all be hanging from lampposts."

Walter Bagehot wrote of England as a deferential nation. But in modern America we defer to no institutional class of leaders. Rightly or wrongly, we would not long take orders from a new élite of planners, consisting—in the ironic phrases of George Orwell—"for the most part of bureaucrats, scientists, technicians, trade-union organizers, publicity experts, sociologists, teachers, journalists and professional politicians . . . whose origins lay in the salaried middle class" and who "had been shaped and brought together by the barren world of monopoly industry and centralized government."

In this country, public protest against such an order probably would take the form of a wave of lawbreaking and evasion far surpassing even the disorder of Prohibition times.

Third (to offer only three objections to the centralizers' doctrines), thoroughgoing cen-

Drawing by Tom Little.

or vice versa?

tralization would destroy real democracy and true community. In proportion as the big decisions are made by remote administrators, the citizens and the local community grow feeble of will and talent. This process continues until the central authority itself withers for lack of healthy roots. In the end, the cynical possessors of power must say, with Septimius Severus, "Pay the soldiers: the rest do not matter."

"Centralized democracy" is only a mockery: it can be nothing better than "plebiscitary democracy" or "guided democracy," the nominal electorate reduced to ratifying the acts of a central administration it cannot control or effectively criticize, since a counterbalance to the force and propaganda of the regime exists nowhere. And obdurate minorities receive short shrift under such a domination — which at very best is Tocqueville's "democratic despotism."

In fine, I confess myself lost in wonder at the naiveté of the doctrinaire who maintains that the cure for all our social ills lies in consolidation of power.

Is our present general government so admirably managed that it can lightheartedly assume a great variety of new responsibilities? Take the State Department, bungling and indecisive, probably overstaffed by one-third, and oppressed by deadwood in personnel, as competent critics like Mr. George Kennan have pointed out. Well, if the Federal Government cannot manage even its primary duty of foreign relations satisfactorily, how can we expect Washington to relieve us of the conduct of urban affairs, the administration of public schools and the improvement of medicine?

OR look at the Post Office: Is this the model for effective central design? Consider the agricultural program of the Federal Government, riding in every direction at once, simultaneously taking millions of acres out of cultivation and creating new arable lands in the West, immensely wasteful. Do we find here that admirable, omniscient, beneficent, impartial authority which is to lead us to the centralists' Terrestrial Paradise?

Our emphasis, I maintain, ought to be upon the retention or restoration of vigor in state and local authorities. There exists no peril that we will fall into anarchy in America. The drift of our time, rather, is toward the triumph of the total centralized state, with correspondent atrophy of local and private vitality, and the extinction of territorial democracy.

Too Powerful? No

No: 'The Government is as centralized as it is today for the simple reason that it has to be to keep society functioning.'

By ERIC F. GOLDMAN

IN the endless argument about centralization, the nub of the matter is usually overlooked. The pyramiding of power in Washington did not come about because any significant group liked centralization for its own sake. The Government is as centralized as it is today for the simple, pragmatic reason that it has to be to keep society functioning the way most Americans want it to function.

To begin with, it has had to be centralized to some extent to keep the society functioning at all. An industrialized nation is, perforce, an interdependent nation. As the United States underwent industrialization in the 19th century, Americans tried all kinds of techniques to link the segments of their society. They went along with free enterprise, or what was called free enterprise, and enterprisers careened off in a thoroughly disruptive fashion. They tried state legislation and the legislatures proved incapable of coping with the units of economic power that sprawled across the country. Practical men facing a practical situation, Americans increasingly turned to the national government to handle national problems.

As long ago as 1887 the Interstate Commerce Commission began using the centralizing power to provide transportation which met the fundamental need of the whole society. Some of the most intrusive legislation of later days has a similar function. Oil is, of course, basic to modern life. Beginning with the nineteen-thirties, a petroleum planning mechanism in Washington has been adjusting supply to demand, thus keeping the industry profitable enough for men to carry it on and conserving a vital resource.

ERIC F. GOLDMAN, Princeton professor and author, was recently named an aide to President Johnson, charged with "channeling the nation's best thinking to the White House."

FURTHER centralization has been made necessary by the cold war. So total a national effort, carried on under the imperative of nuclear power, can be directed only from Washington. A century from now, the 1946 legislation giving sweeping control over nuclear power to a Federal Atomic Energy Commission may well seem the most radically centralizing legislation in the history of the country. Yet in the circumstances of cold war any other procedure appeared unthinkable to most Americans.

And the United States has not sought merely to protect itself from external enemies and to keep its economic system working. The most deeply felt part of the American tradition has been a conception of the United States as a land in which ordinary men have reasonably wide opportunities to achieve a comfortable way of living and to "get ahead." Putting this idea into practice inevitably whirled centralization forward.

There is a frequent warping in the whole argument over the pyramiding of power. The controversy usually takes the form: Should the Federal Government intervene in the economic area? In actual practice during much of American history, the question has been quite different: Just how is the Government going to interfere and for whose benefit?

AS industrialization speeded up during the later 19th century, Washington was intervening in important ways. It not only erected high tariffs but lavished direct and indirect subsidies on the key industry of the day, the railroads. Conservative America hardly objected. It did not even call such moves intervention, it praised them as *"laissez-faire."* We were well under way toward that characteristic American reaction: If you want the Federal Government to do something, the action is required by justice and the good of the Republic. If the other fellow wants Washington to intervene, he is an enemy of liberty.

By the early 20th century, industrialization had produced a situation in which a relatively small business class had an enormously disproportionate share of wealth and power in the nation. Opportunity for the lower-income citizen was not only being squeezed; it was being squeezed in conspicuous, endlessly goading ways.

One of the few propositions that history demonstrates beyond cavil is that if ordinary men have the vote, sooner or later they are going to use it to benefit themselves. Americans used it to protect and advance their opportunities. The antitrust legislation of pre-World War I days, the Wagner Labor Act, social security and rural electrification during the New Deal, the extensions of social security under Truman and Eisenhower, the proposed aid-to-education of the Kennedy and Johnson Administrations—all are products of this same drive and all flow ineluctably from the American tradition armed with universal suffrage.

SO far I have spoken largely of the centralization that comes through Federal legislation and that concerns economic life. But there are other varieties, equally important and quite as inevitable.

Twentieth-century America, much more than the older society, is a collection of blocs —business, labor, agriculture, regional and ethnic units, the American Medical Association, the American what-have-you. Each of these groupings has its own special interests, its own blind spots. Some powerful instrument is needed to assert effectively the public interest.

Congress is in a poor position to act upon this larger consideration. The usual Representative or Senator does too well what he is supposed to do, represent his constituents, and he often represents their avarice and their prejudices quite as vigorously as their concern for the general community. Modern America has been moving to take care of this situation by going along with the assumption of more sweeping powers by its two genuinely national institutions, the Presidency and the Supreme Court.

AFTER World War II, most informed Americans became convinced that the national interest required desegregation in the schools, both to improve the health of the society and to protect its reputation abroad. The realities being what they were the desegregation could be advanced only by the use of massive centralized power.

The most widely denounced Executive action of recent times, President Kennedy's crackdown on the steel companies, finds full justification in the same doctrine of national interest, whatever the validity of the criticism of details of his action. Inflation threatened the national pocketbook and the national foreign policy. No other instrument of Government could or would act; the President moved.

Ah, says the opponent of centralized power, but you are gliding over the heart of the matter. The American in 1900 may not have had Social Security or Federal troops asserting his equality. But he was a free man and freedom is the great desideratum. Of course, the American of 1900 was free in one sense; so is a pauper sleeping on a park bench. To give freedom genuine meaning in an industrialized society, it is necessary to put bone and sinew into the term.

Freedom must mean the condition in which a human being has a reasonable chance to be a human being--a chance to free himself from grinding concern over the next meal, a sense of dignity in the present and of confidence about the future. In this sense, centralization, far from being an enemy of liberty, has proved a potent friend.

Many American opponents of centralization have an in-between argument. They recognize that freedom has this broader meaning. They contend that liberty in all senses will be better served if local governments, particularly the state governments, are assigned more of the functions now performed in Washington.

IN 1962, the Times's James Reston, generalizing about Governors in the United States, could only sigh: "The state capitals are over their heads in problems and up to their knees in midgets." Prof. Andrew Hacker of Cornell has published in this magazine a dispassionate description of the present-day state legislatures. For the most part, he pointed out, they are made up of part-time, parochial politicians, notoriously susceptible to lobbyists and bogged down in debates over how to label eggs or whether beauty-shop attendants need high-school diplomas.

The state governments are so incompetent to satisfy the necessities of today that men who rely on them end up in caricaturing themselves. "The Conscience of a Conservative," the book by Senator Barry Goldwater which has become something of a bible among enemies of centralized power, opposes segregation in the schools. Desegregation, the Senator wrote with his own italics, *"is both wise and just."*

But Senator Goldwater is equally vigorous in denouncing the Supreme Court decision on segregation and all other "engines of national power." The states themselves—including Mississippi—are to bring about this wise and just change. "Freedom" and "states' rights" must prevail, Senator Goldwater cries with passion. The reader comes away from the passage shaking his head. The Senator is passionately against polluted water—and passionately against the use of chlorine.

FERVOR about "liberty," fervor about "the states"—the curious thing about many opponents of centralization is how much emotion they can work up over an issue that is essentially a workaday problem of adjusting means to ends and that was irrevocably decided decades ago when America chose to become an industrial nation.

Today, most friends of centralization are no crusaders about the subject. They, too, have their nostalgia for an older America of free-striding individualists. They often welcome criticism of a proposed extension of Federal power because they know full well that centralization can too easily breed more centralization. They long for the revitalization of local and state governments. They are only too aware that the genius of modern democracy is in the wary manipulation of the ever-present tension between liberty, however defined, and opportunity.

BUT that cry of outrage, that fire and fury from the opposition—one wonders. Could it be that many enemies of centralization flail and thrash so much because, in their heart of hearts, they know they are rationalizing, because they know that when they talk of glorious liberty for everyone they are really concerned with protecting the money and status of a particular group? Could it be that they argue with such passion because, like all proponents of a lost cause, they become the more fervid as their doctrine becomes the more irrelevant?

Campaign Issue

Big Government a Central Problem, But Neither Candidate Faces It Fully

By TOM WICKER
Special to The New York Times

WASHINGTON, Oct. 24 — "When I speak of big government," Barry Goldwater told a Pennsylvania Republican audience last week, "I speak of centralized government, that is, government with all the power in Washington, D.C., with all the power in the hands of the executive branch of government and, ladies and gentlemen, this has historically been the biggest enemy of freedom in the world. "Governments and freedom do not fall from outside pressure. Governments and freedom—particularly freedom—fall when government gets too big in the sense of power, when the power of government leaves your hands and leaves the hands of your local governments, your county governments and your state governments and travel all the way to central government, then your freedoms follow right along afterwards.

News Analysis

"Government is the thing you and I must worry about."

Not long before, President Johnson addressed himself to the same subject matter in Butte, Mont.

"One candidate," he said, "is roaming around this country saying what a terrible thing the government is. He seems to be running against the office of President instead of for the office of President.

Not a 'Foreign Power'

"Somebody better tell him that most Americans are not ready to trade the American eagle in for a plucked banty rooster. He better know that most people just don't believe the United States Government is a foreign power or an enemy."

These quotations pose the issue of "big government" as it exists between Mr. Goldwater and Mr. Johnson and illustrate the level at which it is being discussed. Mr. Goldwater has made his charge—perhaps the strongest tenet of his political philosophy — and Mr. Johnson has stoutly repudiated it. But thoughtful students of government lament that neither has discussed the fundamental issue involved.

Mr. Goldwater has not even cited compelling instances of freedoms lost, or explained coherently how, say, the Federally aided airports at which his campaign plane lands, have sapped away the public liberties.

Mr. Johnson has plentifully supplied illustrations of the good things Washington's politicians have sprinkled throughout the land, but he has not really explained the underlying causes for the vast mushrooming of the Federal Government in the twentieth century, nor discussed the impact on the individual.

The conflict of local self-government and strong central government, of course, has marked the American democracy from its beginning, reflecting the inevitable clash of national interest with local interest, of national necessity with individual freedom, of political reality with political myth. Not often have Presidential candidates so well symbolized the opposing positions as do Mr. Goldwater and Mr. Johnson, and never has the issue been more directly involved in a national election.

Unanswered Questions

But the Republican candidate has not articulated his ideas clearly. He has not explained, for instance, how he would maintain and finance the strong military establishment and the bold foreign policy he advocates without a strong Federal Government, taxing heavily.

In Philadelphia, he lambasted the executive branch and the courts as usurpers of power but promised to use his own executive power to pack the judiciary with judges sympathetic to his views. In the next paragraph, he charged Mr. Johnson with seeking a rubber-stamp Congress. The difference between a rubber-stamp Congress and a rubber-stamp judiciary was not made clear; nor was the difference in using executive power to create one but not the other.

Mr. Goldwater has made responsible suggestions, however —for instance, calling for "a critical re-examination of Federal, state and local tax revenues to find feasible and equitable methods of efficiently redistributing them to keep local monies closer to local projects." Since the states are running out of tax sources, and since the demand for state services is constantly increasing, this is an area in which a "critical re-examination" long has been needed.

But more often, Mr. Goldwater has resorted to this kind of hyperbole:

"Choose the way of this present Administration and you will have chosen the way of the regimented society, with a number for every man, woman and child; a pigeonhole for every problem, and a bureaucrat for every decision."

Mr. Johnson has adopted two lines of reply. First, he points artfully to the benefits the Federal Government can bestow, such as Social Security, public works projects, grant programs, welfare payments, and the like.

Then he offers such resounding reassurances as the following:

"Let us not call forth phantom fears about what the future holds. One of those fears is that the Federal government has become a major menace to individual liberty. This is not so. Far from crushing the individual, government at its best liberates him from the enslaving forces of his environment."

And again: "We live by the belief that this Federal Government exists not to grow larger, but to encourage and permit the people to grow larger than any or all of their governments."

Mr. Johnson has made a reasonably good case that big government is necessary and in many cases fruitful. History, if it does not prove Mr. Goldwater's high-pitched thesis that powerful government inevitably kills freedom, does suggest that it can threaten individual rights and harass individual citizens; every befuddled taxpayer confronted with a bureaucratic edict from the Internal Revenue Service knows that.

But if these things are so, the real question is not whether big government is good or bad; it is, in fact, here to stay and it does circumscribe liberty at least to some extent. The real question is about the relationship of the individual to such a government and to the mass, industrialized, computer-directed, automated, heavily taxed, and impersonal society it represents.

This campaign of clichés has not yet come to grips with that most fundamental of twentieth-century issues.

October 25, 1964

States and U. S.

Roles Are Changing

By TOM WICKER

WASHINGTON, Aug. 7 — The 50 states of the Union have become the red-headed stepchildren of the Federal system in this century, not so much because the Government in Washington usurped their powers but because the states lost the political and financial ability to meet modern conditions. Since voters understandably demand at least a minimum response from politicians to the needs of the day, the Federal Government has moved into neglected areas of state responsibility, not always wisely but on a broad scale.

Now there are hopeful signs that some moribund state governments may be revived, if not to their nineteenth century eminence, at least to active participation in the endless process of making the continent a fit place to live and make a living.

Tax-Sharing Plan

The Dirksen amendment, for instance, has been defeated, probably for good. If it was not quite so iniquitous or ill-advised as some of its opponents declared, still its demise will assure that the reapportioning of legislatures in many states will reflect the urban and industrial conditions and needs of those states.

In addition, there is growing interest at both the state and Federal levels in some form of tax-sharing between Washington and the state governments. The effect would be to give a sizable boost to state financial resources, at a time when state expenditures, while growing rapidly, have been outdistanced by the demand for state services, and when both state taxation and state debt have been stretched to their practical limits.

Another and more immediate development is the local action approach in the Johnson legislative achievements. The poverty and the education aid programs, in particular, not only provide states and localities with money, as Federal grant programs long have done; they also are designed to parcel out the planning and administrative functions usually lodged in Washington, and to restore the sense of participation and self-control that critics long have insisted were being destroyed by "centralized government."

Community action in the poverty program, it is true, has become entangled in politics and in race and class quarrels, particularly in big, unwieldy cities like Chicago, New York and Los Angeles. The resulting controversies have caused some to despair of, and others to deride, the whole idea.

But Sargent Shriver, the energetic spellbinder who heads the poverty program, can point to about 400 going community action programs in smaller and more homogeneous localities. In many of these, the citizenry first had to overcome its astonishment at being asked to take responsibility for meeting its own problems, and then had to set about learning to define the problems as well as the remedies. But in areas with a strong sense of community, and with established "power structures"—for instance, Atlanta and Fulton County, Ga.—community action is working.

There are all sorts of examples, major and minor. In West Virginia, all 55 counties participated this summer in Project Headstart, designed to help disadvantaged young children prepare to enter school. In order to get this project going, each county had to organize its officials and its social services, and the hope is that groups brought together for this specific purpose will stay in business for other and broader activities.

Just under way, with a $7 million grant from the poverty program, is something called Star, Inc., organized by the Roman Catholic Diocese of Natchez and Jackson, Miss. Bringing together Catholics, Baptists, Methodists, businessmen and civil rights groups, this interfaith, integrated organization — endorsed by Governor Paul Johnson—is seeking out 25,000 underprivileged Mississippi families for assistance in health, education, job training, family care and other services.

Again, the poverty program has made $5 million available to state governors—who control the money without the interference either of legislatures or Federal officials—for setting up state poverty programs. Some governors can and probably will divert their shares into enhancing their political organizations—but already officials here can point to active and effective programs established by such governors as Richard Hughes in New Jersey, George Romney in Michigan, Orval Faubus in Arkansas, Edmund G. Brown in California and Hulett Smith in West Virginia.

Toward Self-Help

And in 140 of the 182 poorest counties in the nation—each with per capita income under $750 annually—the beginnings of a permanent self-help organization have been set up in the machinery required for Project Headstart.

These and other efforts will encounter plenty of local inertia and local politics. Some governors complained that the states are being bypassed in favor of Federal-local programs. And skeptics argue that even if the action is local and state, the money is still Federal, and thus nothing but a new form of dependence on Washington is being developed.

But the essential fact is that state and local governments and private citizens are being brought back into action to meet social and economic problems. The greatest industrialized nation in history is far past the time when it can leave these problems entirely to the lower levels of government, much less to private agencies; but it also is past the point where it is either sensible or safe to hand the whole job to the Washington bureaucracy.

August 8, 1965

NEW GROUPS MESH STATES WITH U.S.

Regional Commissions Ease Administrative Burdens

By BEN A. FRANKLIN

Special to The New York Times

WASHINGTON, Jan. 21—The regional commission, a system of governmental cooperation widely praised as an answer to many of the administrative problems states face in dealing with Federal agencies, is quietly elevating the power and prestige of many of the nation's Governors.

Politically, it may satisfy some of the Governors' growing number of grievances against Washington. And some students of government believe the new form of Federal-state coexistence is a model for the future and may be the system that eventually replaces 35 years of New Deal Federal paternalism.

Next Wednesday, the concept of Federal-state collaboration that President Johnson has called "creative federalism" will be extended to six more states, raising the number of Governors who have received new powers from Washington recently to 24.

In addition, seven more states are on the threshold of adopting the new system. The application of the system in all of them now is to regional collaboration in tackling the economic revival of areas of persistent poverty. But the new administrative concept could be applied to almost all Federal, state and local government relationships.

At 11 A.M. Wednesday, in the office of Secretary of Commerce John T. Connor, John J. Linnehan of Haverhill, Mass., is to be sworn in as Federal co-chairman of a new Federal-state compact, the New England Regional Commission.

Mr. Linnehan is a 34-year-old former funeral director who has made a second career here as a Congressional liaison man both for Government agencies and trade organizations.

He will share his authority on the Governors in directing—rationalizing," in the jargon—the broad array of Federal funds flowing to their states, and to cities and counties within them.

Like his three recently established colleagues here—the Federal co-chairmen of the Appalachian Regional Commission, the Upper Great Lakes Regional Commission and the Ozarks Regional Commission—Mr. Linnehan will be paid $27,500 a year by the United States Government to work directly with and as a co-equal of the Governors.

He will have veto power over them in directing—"rationalizing," in the jargon—the broad array of Federal funds flowing to their states, and to cities and counties within them.

Governors' Veto Power

But far more important to the Governors in beginning to balance the equation of power between Washington and the states, the Governors will have veto power over him, and also, in effect, over much of the competitive, largely unplanned scramble by local units of government for Federal grants and projects. Both the states and the Federal Government must agree that a proposed expenditure is right before it can be made.

The Governors thus gain a crucial extension of their influence in the Federal grant-making process. If the application for Federal funds of a community seems neither sensible nor competitively justified against the needs and promise of other communities of his state, a Governor, through his commission, can act to stop it and divert it according to an over-all state and regional plan.

The regional, interstate and inter-county implications of the new compacts are regarded as particularly important in bringing Federal money to bear on such problems as transportation and air and water pollution.

Within each state, the Governor's new role in relations with Washington obviously has political implications, too. Weak states administrations conceivably may be made stronger.

Number Is Increasing

When it comes into being Wednesday, the New England Regional Commission — a compact of the United States with Connecticut, Maine, Massachusetts, New Hampshire, Rhode Island and Vermont — will be the latest in a growing number of area development organizations created under the Public Works and Economic Development Act of 1965, all of them on the pattern of the better-known, 12-state Appalachian Regional Commission.

The Appalachian compact, the first of these administrative groupings, has earned President Johnson's special praise as a showcase of "creative federalism." Mr. Johnson asked Congress for a two-year renewal of the Appalachian Regional Commission yesterday.

The Ozarks Regional Commission, concentrating on 125 contiguous rural counties in Arkansas, Missouri and Oklahoma, and the Upper Great Lakes Regional Commission, embracing 119 counties in northern Michigan, Minnesota and Wisconsin, were established last September.

Staffing Expected Soon

The Coastal Plains Regional Commission, covering 159 counties of eastern North and South Carolina and Georgia, and the Four Corners Regional Commission, covering 92 Rocky Mountain counties of Arizona, Colorado, New Mexico and Utah, exist so far only on paper.

But they are expected to be staffed in the next few months and other commissions may follow. Under the law, the creation of new regional commissions needs only the approval of the Secretary of Commerce.

The commissions were proposed by the Johnson Administration and authorized by Congress in 1965 in part as a logrolling gesture to the non-Appalachian states—to win support for the costly Appalachian recovery effort.

They are under the Economic Development Administration of the Commerce Department and they themselves do not have—as the Appalachian Regional Commission does—any "project funds."

They control no money to pay for construction or to make loans. Their funds are restricted to planning for and directing help to the states, and to obtaining the maximum money available under existing Federal programs.

January 25, 1967

STATES CRITICIZED ON HELP TO CITIES

By ROBERT B. SEMPLE Jr.
Special to The New York Times

WASHINGTON, March 28—A Federal advisory commission said today that state governments "are on the verge of losing control" over the mounting problems of central city decay and the rapid growth of metropolitan areas.

"If they lose this control," the report declared, "they lose the major responsibility for domestic government in the United States and in turn surrender a vital role in the American Federal system."

The warning was contained in the eighth annual report of the Advisory Commission on Intergovernmental Relations, given to President Johnson and Congress. The commission is a 26-member bipartisan body established by Congress to provide regular assessments of the working of the Federal system.

The panel's chairman is Farris Bryant, director of the Federal Office of Emergency Planning, former Florida Governor. Its members include private citizens, members of Congress and state legislatures, Federal officials, Governors, Mayors and county officials.

The report said one of the most encouraging developments in 1966 was the widespread recognition at most levels of government of the crisis in the nation's cities and metropolitan areas. But it said that, with few exceptions, the dimensions of this problem had either eluded the state governments or been ignored by them.

Although the "tremendous task of financing, servicing and governing metropolitan America clearly poses the greatest challenge to federalism since the civil war," the commission said, widespread participation by the states in the functions of urban government "continued to be the exception rather than the rule."

The report pointed out that only 11 states had established offices of urban affairs. Only eight are assisting in the construction of local sewage treatment plants, despite "critical" problems of water pollution caused by rapidly growing metropolitan areas. And, the report said, only a half-dozen are participating in urban renewal, public housing and mass transportation programs.

"One of the crucial questions regarding the crisis in the cities—indeed of American federalism—is whether the states will sign off to the national Government the responsibility for financing major urban services in the United States," it said.

Many students of state and local government believe the states have reached a critical point in their relations with the Federal Government. They believe that unless the states modernize their machinery for dealing with their troubled cities and funnel proportionately greater amounts of state revenues to urban areas, the Federal Government will be compelled to assert an increasingly larger role in urban affairs, eventually bypassing the states.

Indeed, many Mayors are arguing that the states long ago abdicated their responsibilities. These Mayors are now openly pressing for a more direct relationship between the Federal Government and City Hall.

At a recent meeting here, the National League of Cities, a Mayors' organization, formally recommended that any tax-sharing plans adopted by Congress should require that the bulk of excess Federal revenues be returned directly to the cities. The Governors, meanwhile, are supporting tax-sharing proposals designed to return money to the states.

The Federal commission did not, however, place all the blame for the states' inability to cope with urban and suburban problems on the Governors or the state legislatures.

It said the Supreme Court's legislative reapportionment decision of 1964 in Baker v. Carr had generated efforts in a number of states "for the overhaul of state government and its role in domestic affairs." The real problem, the commission indicated, was the failure of new legislatures to persuade the voters to endorse constitutional revisions and new taxes.

Despite a 12.5 per cent increase in total state tax collections since 1965—from $26.1-billion to $29.4-billion—pressures for "tax relief" from voters remained "intense" while demands for new services mounted, the commission said.

Moreover, the commission said, the problems of the states were aggravated, ironically, by the beneficent 89th Congress. Great Society legislation in 1965 and 1966 brought to more than 400 the number of Federal grant-in-aid programs, administered by 21 departments and agencies and 150 bureaus and divisions.

The commission said the mushrooming growth in Federal programs not only placed vast new administration burdens on state governments but also increased their financial obligations, inasmuch as most of these programs require sizable matching contributions from state or local governments.

On the positive side, the commission noted that near the end of last year Congress passed two programs—the Demonstration Cities and Metropolitan Development Act of 1966 and the comprehensive health planning and public health services amendments of 1966—which, in effect, gave states and localities unrestricted "block" funds to use as they wished, without the restrictions of grant-in aid programs.

March 29, 1967

Federal-State

Lots of Trouble in the Partnership

President Johnson's discussion with the New England Governors in a gloomy corner of an airport in Windsor Locks, Conn., last week was, in a sense, an echo of an earlier and somewhat more elaborate confrontation with a different set of Governors last December.

The practical issue at hand was the same: How could Federal-state relations be improved to the point where the Great Society could work smoothly (which would be a boon to Mr. Johnson) and not embarrass the Governors by exposing their administrative incapacity to run the Great Society (which would be a boon to the Governors).

A Delicate Balance

And the theoretical issue that lurked in the background of the December get-together also remained the same: how to preserve the Federal system—that is, the delicate balance between Federal, state and local governments that was so terribly threatened by the rush of Great Society legislation passed by the 89th Congress.

Last week's meeting was a bit more amicable. In December, the Governors were rebellious. In Windsor Locks, their anxiety, now, was touched by sympathy and appreciation for what Mr. Johnson had tried to do.

The difference in tone is easy to explain. In the five months since the Governors complained that the Great Society was outrunning the capabilities of the states to deal with it, the President had not only recognized the problem but tried to deal with its major components.

What are the major components of the awful problem of smoothing relations between the various segments of American government?

There are three major difficulties—the three aggravating "C's" of the Federal system: complexity, communication and control.

To take complexity first, it is necessary to remember that, according to a special analysis prepared by the Bureau of the Budget, there are 162 "major" assistance programs to the states which are financed in part by the Federal Government. A great many of these were enacted in the last 24 months.

Mr. Johnson has responded to this impossibly confusing state of affairs by trying to consolidate these programs, as, for example, in his Partnership for Health Program, which brings several different health aid schemes under the control of regional planning authorities.

Simultaneously, the Administration has taken steps to improve communication between the Capital and the statehouses.

The Office of Education, for example, has rarely consulted with local and state school officials on the distribution of $4-billion in education funds. But, beyond that, the Department of Health, Education and Welfare and the Department of Housing and Urban Development, in recent months have established special bureaus of intergovernmental relations to work with the Governors and their aides; H.U.D. has held long conferences in Virginia with selected Governors to solicit complaints and exchange information; and the President himself has appointed aides to act as diplomats between the states and Washington.

Yet while the conversation has improved (and there has in fact been substantially better coordination in the last five months), the atmosphere still remains poisoned by the issue of control.

This issue involves money, not words.

More and more, Governors and Mayors have been wondering whether more good could not be accomplished if the Federal Government would only forget all those 200 grant-in-aid programs—and the restrictions tied to them—and turn over Federal tax revenues to the people who are presumed to know most about local problems — the administrators at the local level.

This is the purpose of the so-called Quie amendment, which would take several hundred million dollars in Federal money now earmarked for specific purposes—including aid to school districts with heavy concentrations of the poor—and turn it over to the Governors to dispose of as they wish.

The Administration opposes the proposal, and so do the Mayors. "Tax sharing is the most dangerous idea in America today," the Mayor of Boston, John F. Collins, has said, and his sentiments represent accurately the feelings of the Mayors on the whole question of turning over large blocs of funds to the states. Mr. Collins's statement, and similar pronouncements of his colleagues, reflect the belief that states cannot be trusted to respond to urban needs.

Competing Claims

So far, Mr. Johnson has not resolved these competing claims. He has not given the Governors the freedom from Federal restrictions that they think they need. Meanwhile, he has not freed the cities from the states (although the model cities program—which provides what amount to bloc grants to qualified localities—is a step in the direction of greater freedom). All he has done is defend the status quo—the present system of Federal grant-in-aid programs—while making serious and, in many cases, successful efforts to make the system more humane, manageable and efficient. But the whip hand, despite all his efforts, still lies with Congress.

The answer is still a long way off. It is not an easy matter to reconcile the historic prejudices of a Congress that wishes to tailor tax revenues to its purposes and the equally strong claims of the Governors who wish to use the public monies for what they feel are the major problems at home.

May 21, 1967

Handbook for States Men

STORM OVER THE STATES. *By Terry Sanford. 218 pp. New York: McGraw-Hill Book Company. $5.95.*

By NELSON A. ROCKEFELLER

A NOTED political pragmatist, Terry Sanford was Governor of North Carolina from 1961 to 1965. Since then, with an able staff and the support of the Ford Foundation and the Carnegie Corporation, he has been drawing on his experience and dedicating his energy to the vital task of strengthening state government in America.

One result has been the Education Commission of the States, designed to deal with the concern of James B. Conant and many others that education in America is, in Governor Sanford's, words, "too important to be left to the haphazard chance of unconnected local and state efforts and too complex to be left to a single guiding national hand."

Governor Sanford was a prime mover in the organizing efforts and conferences during the past two years that produced the Commission and a Compact for Education among the states. Forty states are now exchanging ideas through the Commission, sharing their experience and debating educational goals, and the political and professional forces in education across the nation are being brought together to discuss what they can do in partnership for the advancement of education.

A second result of Governor Sanford's activities is a unique "Institute for State Programming in the Seventies." This is a new, state-created source of advice and guidance to governors, legislators and administrators who want to provide themselves with the best information and thinking in the various areas of state responsibility. The Institute's first project is to develop guidelines for long-range planning by the individual states.

This book is a third result of Governor Sanford's activities since leaving office—and important as the Education Commission and the Institute for State Programming may be, his book may in the long run prove the most significant of all.

The two premises of the book are, one, that our Federal system of government must deal more competently with the multiplying human problems of our present and our future and, two, that the present trend toward increasingly all-powerful, central government must be halted. But, as Governor Sanford points out, "we need first to change the climate" before we can achieve the essential reforms. This book should certainly help to do that.

For decades commentators have been proclaiming the death of the states as effective instruments for dealing with the problems of an urban, technological and rapidly changing society. Governor Sanford tackles this charge with vigor and conviction, arguing effectively that "the states are here to stay." "The genuine question," he says, "the one we can do something about, the one worth our attention, is how we might shape the states' actions, not their boundaries, for the most effective response to their citizens' needs." The author then proceeds to outline in detail the steps at local, state and national level that he considers vital to making our Federal system more effectively responsive to today's needs.

Governor Sanford's objectivity is a particularly valuable aspect of this book. He does not waste time on a search for villains or heroes; instead, he sees "a crisis of responsibility at every level of government." "As the crisis has risen," he says, "it is obvious that the states have not done enough, the cities have seemed paralyzed, and the national Government has inaugurated as many wrong approaches as right solutions. The answers, however, will not be found by assessing blame, but by drawing together all our resources."

In charting this mobilization of resources, Governor Sanford calls on the states to do far more than they have been doing to help meet urban problems. "Our problems are where the people are," he says. "States must bring money and programs to bear in the urban areas or find themselves permanently outside the Federal-local axis, as the cities, however wrongly, step up their reliance on the national Government for funds."

One measure of the tremendous state effort this urban challenge demands may be found in the recent experience of New York State, if I may cite an example with which I am familiar. When I became Governor, the state's financial aid to the City of New York was about $364-million a year. That figure has been tripled in nine years—totaling well over a billion dollars in the current fiscal year. Comparable increases in the flow of state money have also been made to the other large cities of the state.

As to programs, New York State currently is stressing 21 undertakings that reinforce its commitment to erase corrosive slum conditions. These programs vary widely: community development projects, expanded manpower training, support of small business, more help for working mothers, expansion of the state's pre-kindergarten program, additional aid for schools in slum areas, creation of additional urban college centers and so on.

Yet, even though New York State has traditionally been a national leader in the development of progressive programs, we still have not done enough—and many other states have even farther to go.

Governor Sanford calls on the state to serve as "coordinator, stimulator, representative, protector and advisor for local governments in their relationships with the national Government"—something which New York and many other states already are doing, but likewise a field in which much more can be done. And the author advises the states to remove outdated shackles on local governments—to permit a substantially greater measure of home rule—and to give local governments better financial support.

If I may again use an example with which I am familiar, New York State now returns 58 per cent of its total budget to the localities as state aid—and in the last nine years, the annual sum of state aid to all local governments and schools in the state has been increased by $1.7 billion a year.

This, too, serves to measure the magnitude of the problem the states have in meeting their own fiscal responsibilities. Only when a state is doing this, the Governor suggests, is it in a sound position to call for the three other adjustments in the Federal-state fiscal relationship that Governner Sanford and most authorities regard as equitable.

Firstly, the Federal Government should allow a substantial percentage of state income-tax payments as a credit against Federal income-tax liability. Secondly, Congress should adopt some version of the so-called Heller Plan for direct state sharing in Federal revenues. Finally, Congress should overhaul and consolidate Federal grant-in-aid programs to make them more flexible, more adaptable to local needs, and less wasteful because of duplication and overlapping.

Governor Sanford sees "the strengthening of our Federal system, and even its preservation" as quite likely the most important domestic task before the President. "We need a Presidential understanding that the Federal system is now being shaped by the winds of hazard," says the author, "that the national bureaucracy is inclined to random procedures that weaken the capacity of state government, and that only the White House can be effective in bringing order and balance to the Federal system."

HE further argues that Congress or the President should declare the strengthening of the Federal system to be a central national goal. He also urges that the President consult appropriate Governors and mayors in preparing legislation that will involve intergovernmental relationships. For all the importance of national action, Governor Sanford believes that the future of the American system "could well be determined" by gubernatorial performance. He calls for a marked strengthening of governors' powers, as well as for state constitutional, legislative, budget, organizational and planning reforms.

This book is the product of an experienced man who has done his homework and has something important to say to those willing to look beyond contemporary personalities and political maneuvers to the basic institutions of our government. One can only hope that many people will be listening. For as the author points out, the great American contribution to mankind has been the union of government and freedom—and the preservation of the Federal system that has produced that contribution must finally rest with the people.

October 15, 1967

NATION IS WARNED UNREST IN CITIES IMPERILS SYSTEM

Advisory Unit Calls Failure to Solve Issue Greatest Threat Since Civil War

AUTHORS 'PESSIMISTIC'

Report Says Abdication at Lower Levels Challenges Federal Political Setup

By BEN A. FRANKLIN
Special to The New York Times

WASHINGTON, Jan. 30 — The failure of government to prevent rioting, despair and "threatened anarchy" in the nation's large cities has brought the Federal system to the brink of its greatest crisis since the Civil War, a Government study commission declared today.

In a report its authors characterized as "pessimistic," the Advisory Commission on Intergovernmental Relations said the historic American system of plural government—local, state and national—was in danger.

The abdication or inability of the states, of city government, and of the Federal Government, singly or jointly, to hold back the deterioration of urban life, the commission said, raises the prospect of pervasive Federal dominance in the name of security.

14-Page Preamble

In a strongly worded 14-page preamble to its ninth annual report to the President and Congress, the commission warned that Federal authority over governmental responsibilities that had traditionally been those of states, counties and cities might be—might have to be—greatly expanded to maintain law and order. It said many cities were "seething" with racial and class revolt and that many were near public bankruptcy.

"The manner of meeting these challenges," the commission declared, "will largely determine the fate of the American political system; it will determine if we can maintain a form of government marked by partnership and wholesome competition among national, state and local levels, or if instead—in the face of threatened anarchy—we must sacrifice political diversity as the price of the authoritative action required for the nation's survival."

The commission is not confident the sacrifice can be avoided. Its report virtually acknowledged that some cities might already be ungovernable, at least without the extraordinary and aggressive efforts of private, nongovernment groups, such as industrial employers and corporations willing to invest in improving the urban environment in which they exist.

The report praised business groups generally for having "crossed the Rubicon" — for ending, for the most part, their rigid view that "the best government is the least government." But it said that among all the wielders of the political power who must co-operate in the cities to avoid a damaging spread of Federal "authoritative action," "progress seems discouragingly slow."

In an interview, the commission's staff director, William G. Colman, singled out the rapidly growing number of suburban voters in the country as "the leadership potential." Both Mr. Colman and the report spoke encouragingly of efforts to form urban-suburban "metro" governments.

"When the question is raised

on the survival of our cities—and some of them are on the verge of bankruptcy — the answer always comes back to the Federal Government," Mr. Colman said. "But these problems are all bound up in archaic and restrictive state constitutions and state legislatures, the very areas of government where suburban people now have or are getting control. There must be leadership from the suburban environment if we are to meet these problems without altering our system of government."

The report attributed much of the inaction on urban needs to local and state failures to end "repressive restrictions" on welfare, housing and education funds and on zoning and planning policies that have created "the 'white noose' of the suburbs" around the teeming poor of the central cities.

Asked to justify the "Civil War analogy" of the report, another commission staff official, Eugene R. Elkins, explained it by saying "then it was a matter of some states pulling out of the Union—now it's a matter of the Federal system going down the drain altogether."

January 31, 1968

'BIG GOVERNMENT' IS FEARED IN POLL

Gallup Finds 'Big Labor' 2d and 'Big Business' 3d

Special to The New York Times

PRINCETON, N. J., Aug. 17—"Big government," more than "big business" or "big labor," is seen by the public as posing the greatest threat to the nation in the future, according to the latest Gallup Poll.

This marks a sharp change from a survey conducted near the end of President Dwight D. Eisenhower's term in 1959, when "big labor," not "big government," was viewed as the greatest threat.

Although "big government" has been a favorite target of the Republican party for many years, rank-and-file Democrats are nearly as critical of growing Federal power as are Republicans.

Out of every 100 adults interviewed, 46 said big government would be the greatest threat to the country in the future, 26 said labor and 12 said business, while 16 did not express an opinion. The survey included personal interviews with 1,526 people in over 300 localities across the nation.

Shift Not Sudden

The following question was asked in a survey completed in mid-July:

"In your opinion, which of the following do you think will be the biggest threat to the country in the future—big business, big labor or big government?"

Here are the latest findings, compared with those recorded at the end of President Eisenhower's term:

	Aug., '68	Oct., '59
Big government	46%	14%
Big labor	26	41
Big business	12	15
No opinion	16	30

The sharp shift in opinion between the 1959 and 1968 surveys has not come just recently. A survey in January, 1966, revealed findings virtually the same as today's.

Politically significant is the fact that of the major political groups, those who describe themselves as independents were most inclined to say that "big government" constituted the greatest threat to the nation in the future, as seen in the following table:

	Reps.	Dems.	Inds.
Government	48%	41%	54%
Labor	32	23	23
Business	9	14	10
No opinion	11	22	13

Opinion among all major groups was clearly on the side that "big government" was the chief threat, with two exceptions—Negroes and persons whose annual family income was under $3,000 a year. Among these two latter groups, opinion was roughly divided between "big business" and "big labor."

Differences in Groups

Northern white people were somewhat less inclined to name "big government" than were Southern whites, who as a group have traditionally been strong advocates of states' rights.

Union members and nonmembers alike saw "big government" as the greatest threat. Interestingly, the views of both union and nonunion people on "big labor" were not far apart.

Among those who said big government was the nation's greatest threat was a youthful businessman from Rosemont, Pa. He commented:

"To get things done, a country needs initiative on the part of its citizens. Big government robs them of this initiative."

A 42-year-old farmer's wife from Midland, Tex., said:

"I don't like government telling me what I can and can't do, but in the last 10 years this has been going on day in and day out."

A Tampa, Fla., housewife said:

"The bigger the government gets, the more mistakes it makes."

A 47-year-old resident of Indianapolis offered a common view among those who said big labor was the greatest threat to the nation:

"Labor unions are becoming much too demanding—to the detriment of the public," he said. "The cost of living increases with each demand and each strike."

Those who pointed the finger of blame chiefly at "big business" frequently argued along these lines of a 29-year-old Baton Rouge merchant:

"The little man is being forced out by the big companies."

And a Cleveland resident said, "Big business is only interested in themselves—not in moving the country ahead."

August 18, 1968

Great Society: What It Was, Where It Is

By CLAYTON KNOWLES

Special to The New York Times

WASHINGTON, Dec. 8 — "Dick Nixon is going to be taking over a government one hell of a lot different than the one he left in January, 1961."

These words, spoken by a departing White House aide, dramatize the change in the Federal domestic role in the last five years because of Lyndon B. Johnson's Great Society program.

Joseph A. Califano Jr., President Johnson's man Friday in nurturing the Great Society, said in an interview that President-elect Richard M. Nixon would find that a tenfold growth had occurred in governmental activities designed to "make life better for all Americans."

45 Then, 435 Now

"There were about 45 domestic social programs when the Eisenhower Administration ended," Mr. Califano said. "Now there are no less than 435."

As the Johnson Presidency

Federal Domestic Role Has Increased Tenfold in the Johnson Era

nears an end, it is possible to look at the Great Society with some perspective and examine a few of its programs.

The larger government role described by Mr. Califano involves more than new laws, though they are counted in the hundreds. Much of the change stems from a new direction of old programs, imparted either by Congressional or administrative action, to meet broader objectives.

Topsy-like at times, the program has grown in many directions, though authorizations and funding were often cut well below Administration requests. A drumfire of criticism frequently attended a grudging acceptance of principle.

It was said that inflation watered down the dollar value of benefits to the poor, that waste and duplication threatened achievements, that overpromises created problems bigger than those up for solution.

Conservatives urged that the

Federal obligation be discharged through general area grants to the states for programs developed at the state level.

The enormous cost of the war in Vietnam limited the amount that could be spent on the social programs. The fact that the war was being accelerated while the Great Society program was being developed made what progress there was all the more remarkable.

Many of the new programs have virtually become household words — Medicare, model cities, the Job Corps, the war on poverty, truth in lending, Head Start and Upward Bound.

Programs Redirected

Others, such as the insured mortgage loan program of the Federal Housing Administration that spawned the nation's suburban growth, are now being redirected to the cities.

To put a price tag on the vast, somewhat amorphous Great Society is difficult, though it is clear that it represents a national commitment entailing billions of dollars.

Excluding Social Security payments, Mr. Califano estimates that the Great Society is a $25.6-billion enterprise, compared with the $9.9-billion social budget of 1960 and $12.9-billion of 1963. If Social Security costs are included, he says, $49-billion is being spent today against $22-billion eight years ago.

This turnabout in national policy on the homefront, signaled in a speech by President Johnson at University of Michigan commencement exercises on May 22, 1964, constitutes a recognition of mushrooming urban problems as an essential matter of Federal concern.

Though a descendant in many ways of the New Deal, Fair Deal and New Frontier, the Great Society established a new approach to problems that accented working relationships with the region, the state and the city more than direct Federal aid to the individual.

In five years, something of a national consensus has developed in support of comprehensive aid to cities. The recognition is now general that the cities, lacking a broad tax base other than real estate, do not have the resources to meet the many problems in a nation 70 per cent urbanized.

Even an economic conservative such as Representative Gerald R. Ford of Michigan, House Republican leader, acknowledges that huge Federal outlays are needed to meet the urban crisis. He argues only that the money go directly to the states in "broad problem area grants."

President Johnson described the Great Society as "a challenge constantly renewed" in his University of Michigan speech.

"The Great Society rests on abundance and liberty for all," he said. "It demands an end to poverty and racial injustice, to which we are totally committed in our time. But that is just a beginning.

"The Great Society is a place where every child can find knowledge to enrich his mind and enlarge his talents. It is a place where leisure is a welcomed chance to build and reflect, not a feared cause of boredom and restlessness. It is a place where the city of man serves not only the needs of the body but the desire for beauty and the hunger for enrichment.

"It is a place where man can renew contact with nature. It is a place which honors creation for its own sake and for what it adds to the understanding of the race. It is a place where men are more concerned with the quality of their goals than the quality of their goods."

Threaded through the address ran the promise of a broad attack on the problems of the poor and underprivileged — housing, education, equal rights and equal opportunity— as well as a drive for environmental improvement — conservation, beautification, clean air and clean water — that would benefit all.

The programs that emerged can be grouped under general headings despite constant interaction among elements in different categories, particularly in the cities.

The highlights of the Great Society, by general category:

CITIES

ANTIPOVERTY CAMPAIGN: Begun in 1964 with the Economic Opportunity Act and a one-year authorization of just under $1-billion, stepped up greatly in later years with the Department of Health, Education and Welfare, the Department of Labor and the Department of Housing and Urban Development, set up in 1965, increasingly involved.

TRANSPORTATION: Urban mass transportation acts of 1964 and 1966.

MODEL CITIES: Act of 1966 proposing grants to cities, supplemental to those available from other Federal sources, to fight urban problems in the most blighted areas, including housing, health, education, jobs, welfare, transportation and public facilities. Funded with $312-million in the fiscal year 1968. Its appropriation has been doubled for the coming year.

RENT SUPPLEMENTS: Started in 1966 to provide better housing for low-income families, funded far below Administration requests.

CRIME CONTROL: Safe Streets and Crime Control Act of 1968, providing block grants to improve state and city law enforcement.

CIVIL RIGHTS

SEGREGATION: Act of 1964 outlawing discrimination in hospitals, restaurants, hotels and employment; authorizing shutoff in Federal aid used in a discriminatory manner.

VOTING: Act of 1965 protecting voting rights at the national, state and local level.

HOUSING: Act of 1968 protecting civil rights workers and initiating fair housing requirements nationally.

COMMUNITY RELATIONS: Transfer of the Community Relations Service from the Commerce to the Justice Department.

CONSERVATION

WATER POLLUTION: Water Quality Act of 1965 and the Clean Water Restoration Act of 1966, under which $5.5-billion in grants have been made for water purification and sewage treatment plants.

AIR POLLUTION: Clean Air Act and Air Quality Acts of 1965 and 1967 seeking air cleansing through regional grants.

WASTE: Solid Waste Disposal Act of 1965.

ROADS: Highway Beautification Act of 1965 to cover 75 per cent of the cost of removing roadside eyesores.

RECREATION: Urban beautification under the urban renewal act, including the creation of vest pocket parks in congested areas.

PARKS: Expansion of the national park system by 2.2-million acres.

CONSUMER PROTECTION

MEAT: Meat Inspection Act of 1967, requiring states to enforce Federal standards or yield to Federal inspection.

POULTRY: Poultry Inspection Act of 1968.

FABRICS: Establishment of Product Safety Commission in 1967 to study dangerous household products and flammable fabrics amendments to

HEALTH FUNDS

Total federal funds
New funds

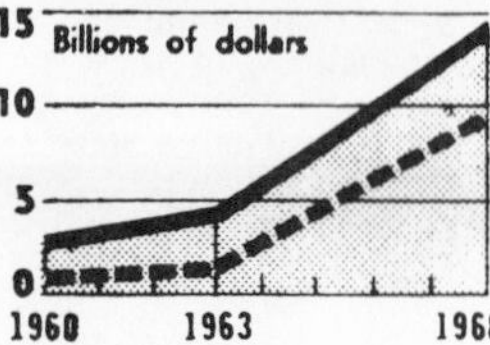

EDUCATION FUNDS

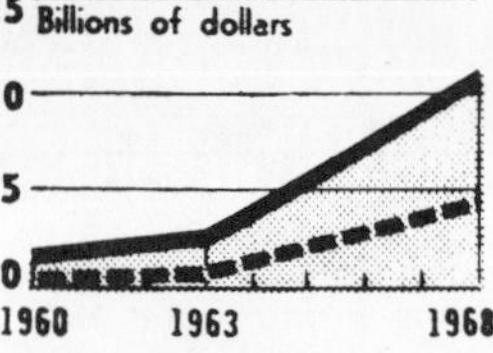

FUNDS FOR CHILDREN AND YOUTH

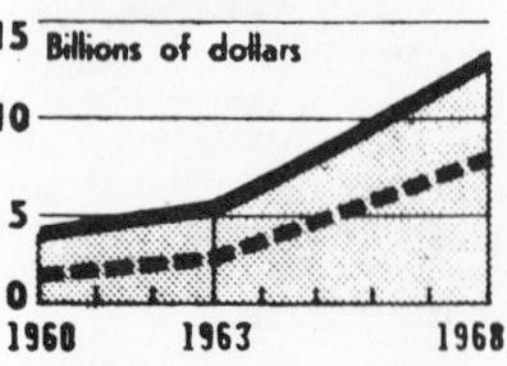

FUNDS FOR AGED

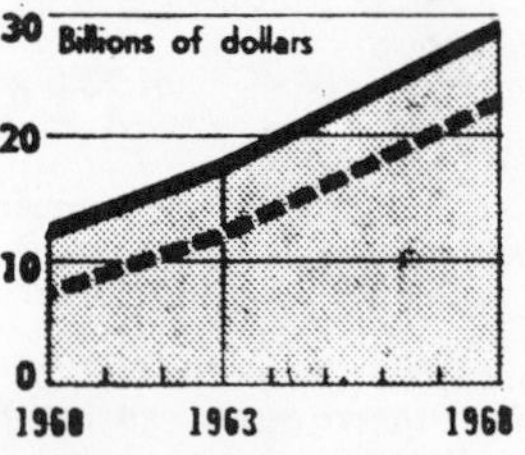

FUNDS FOR POOR

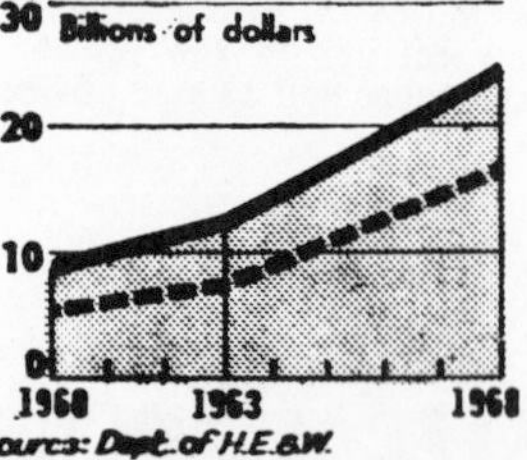

Source: Dept. of H.E.&W.

a 1953 act directing the Secretary of Commerce to fix safety standards in clothing.

FARM PRICES: Food Marketing Commission set up to study farm-to-consumer prices.

TRUTH IN LENDING: Act of 1968 requiring dollar-and-cents accounting of actual costs under "easy credit" and other financing plans.

PACKAGING: Fair Packaging and Labeling Act.

ELECTRONICS: Hazardous Radiation Act designed to reduce possible harmful effects of television and other electronic house devices.

TRAFFIC: Traffic and Highway Safety Act setting stand-

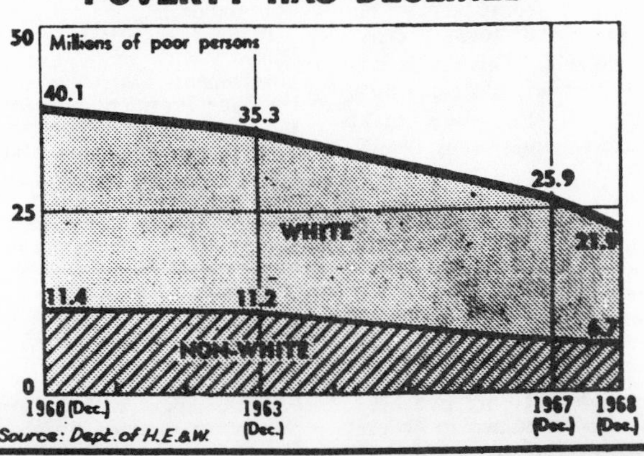

ards to be met by manufacturers for automobile safety.

EDUCATION

ELEMENTARY SCHOOLS: Elementary and Secondary Act of 1965, strengthened in 1966, providing stepped-up aid to 100 per cent in 1970 for quality education, including text books for public and private schools, with a $9.2-billion authorization for the next two years.

HIGHER EDUCATION: Act of 1965 providing liberal loans, scholarship and facility construction money.

TEACHER CORPS: Act of 1965 to train teachers.

AID TO POOR: Educational Opportunity Act of 1968 to help poor go to college.

ADULT EDUCATION: Act of 1968.

JOB OPPORTUNITY

TRAINING: Manpower Development and Training Act of 1964 to qualify persons for new and better jobs.

JOB CORPS: Economic Opportunity Act of 1964 setting up Job Corps, Neighborhood Youth Corps and new careers programs.

BUSINESS: Job Opportunities in the Business Sector, which, under the leadership of the National Alliance of Businessmen, seeks 500,000 jobs for hard-cored unemployed.

APPALACHIA: Program of 1965 seeking economic development and jobs in 11-state economically depressed area.

WAGE: Increase in minimum wage by 35 cents to $1.60.

HEALTH

MEDICARE: Set up in 1965, insurance for 20 million citizens at 65 under the Social Security system to cover hospital and doctor costs.

MEDICAID: Act of 1965, providing medical care for the needy, with 7.7 million people in 43 states now getting aid.

DOCTORS TRAINING: Health Professions Act of 1963-65 seeking to train 1,700 doctors.

NURSES TRAINING: Act of 1964, which has already provided 65,000 loans for schooling.

MENTAL HEALTH: Program of 1965-66, providing centers for treatment and training.

IMMUNIZATION: Program for preschool children against polio, diphtheria, whooping cough, tetanus and measles, under which, for example, the annual incidence of measles dropped from 450,000 in 1963 to 62,000 last year.

HEALTH CENTERS: Heart, cancer and stroke regional centers.

CHILD HEALTH: Improvement and Protection Act of 1968 for prenatal and postnatal care.

Climate Ripe

Much of all this legislation had been sought for years, and when Mr. Johnson took office after the assassination of President Kennedy, the climate was apparently ripe for breakthroughs.

President Johnson moved quickly, and kept up the pace after the landslide election in 1964 brought him large majorities in the House and Senate.

Negro rioting in the slums in 1966, capped by a Republican gain of 47 seats in the still-Democratic House, slowed the Great Society.

The election strengthened the Southern Democrat-conservative Republican coalition that had repeatedly blocked many of these projects in the past.

The Administration sought $662-million for the fiscal year 1968 ending last June 30 to fund the model cities program. It got $312-million. It sought $1-billion for 1969 and got $625-million.

However, observers considered it significant that a modest expansion of the Great Society was nevertheless made during the 90th Congress.

While noting that the Vietnam war intensified during the developing stages of the Great Society, Wilbur J. Cohen, Secretary of the Department of Health, Education and Welfare, said recently that the choice was "not between guns and butter."

"There is a third factor—quality of life," he said. "It is a decision every American must face. A third of our families have two or more cars, 15 million of us own yachts. There is a lot of money for liquor and cigarettes. We've got the money but we've got to establish our priorities."

He said that "the United States can eliminate poverty in the coming decade and go on to assure adequate income for the overwhelming majority of Americans."

The Poverty Line

Mr. Cohen noted that since 1960 the Government had "lifted 18 million out of poverty." He defined the poverty line as $3,300 annually for a city family of four. Still below the poverty level are 21.9 million Americans.

There are other Administration claims of progress, such as 10.5 million jobs created in seven and a half years, salaries and wages up 72 per cent in the period, corporate profits after taxes up 61 per cent, three record years with unemployment below 3.8 per cent, the Federal education budget up $12-million, $5.5-million spent for housing and community development.

Many impartial observers find it hard to disagree with most claims, which are accompanied with details on the job still to be done.

During the recent national campaign, Mr. Nixon did not reject any significant facet of the Great Society but at various times suggested that the drive for a better America could be achieved more effectively by other means.

He favored, for example, tax incentives to draw business more actively into the campaign against poverty and related programs.

But the country will probably have to wait until the new President's inaugural address Jan. 20 for a clearer idea of the course of the Great Society.

December 9, 1968

An Ex-Governor to Head New Agency

By WALTER RUGABER
Special to The New York Times

WASHINGTON, Feb. 14 — Vice President Agnew, overriding the objections of prominent municipal spokesmen, announced today the appointment of a former Governor to head his newly created office of Intergovernmental Affairs.

Mr. Agnew named former Gov. Nils A. Boe of South Dakota, a Republican, as director of the new agency, minutes after President Nixon, in a Cabinet Room ceremony, signed an Executive order establishing the unit.

Mr. Nixon said in a statement that by the move, the Vice President "will become more directly and vitally involved in our effort to move government closer to the people and to make it more responsive to their will.'

"Among its many fuctions," the President explained, "the office will assure state and local officials access to the highest offices of the Federal Government . . . so that Federal programs, policies, and goals will be more responsive to their views and needs."

A Staff of 12

Mr. Boe, who will lead a staff of 12 or 13 within the Vice President's office, served two two-year terms as Governor but was constitutionally prohibited from seeking reelection last year.

During a news conference at the White House, Mr. Agnew acknowledged that Mr. Boe did not come "from a state that is urban oriented." But he said the former Governor was a skillful mediator and fiscal authority.

A number of leading urban officials had urged the Vice

President not to appoint a director with a background largely in state government. They complained that the cities were already underrepresented in the administration.

The spokesmen voiced enthusiasm for the new Federal-state-local liaison and expressed no individual opposition to Mr. Boe. But they had wanted Mr. Agnew to pick at least a "neutral" director for his operation.

The most pointed objection came from Mayor Beverly Briley of Nashville, president of the National League of Cities, in a letter to Mr. Agnew about "rumors" that a former Governor would be named.

Mr. Briley registered "vigorous objection to such a move" in behalf of the league "as well as many county officials." He said in the letter, which was written on Monday, that former governors, including Mr. Agnew, were already influential in the Administration.

The Nixon Cabinet includes three former Governors and a Lieutenant Governor, the Mayor said, and the chairman and vice chairman of an advisory commision on intergovernmental relations are Governors.

"The image created by this manning of the key positions concerned with urban affairs in the Federal Government is one of a 'clique' as far as Mayors and county officials are concerned," Mr. Briley wrote.

'Could Close the Door'

"The addition of another Governor to act as a troubleshooter or mediator for local officials could close the door to effective use of your office for the purposes you intend," the Mayor warned.

The Vice President was reported to have given the city and county representatives assurances that the new office would prove itself as much a friend of local interests as state concerns.

Mr. Agnew is said to be searching for a Mayor or former Mayor to serve the agency as deputy director in a familiar effort to achieve "balance," Mayor Briley evidently had heard this rumor, too.

"The result of such a move would tend to build a state constituency behind the Governor (director)" and a local government constituency behind the Mayor (deputy director)," he said. "This would create a kind of contest which, in our opinion, would make problem-solving more difficult."

John Gunther, executive director of the United States Conference of Mayors, said his organization had expressed its concern about the lack of city representation not only in Mr. Agnew's office but also "throughout the government."

He said that only two Mayors had been named to Federal positions. They are Floyd Hyde of Fresno, Calif., Assistant Secretary of Health, Education, and Welfare for Model Cities Programs, and J. D. Braham of Seattle, Assistant Secretary of Transportation for Urban Transit Systems.

In his statement, the President said that Mr. Agnew's office, in "helping to create many centers of power in the place of one," would "facilitate an orderly transfer of appropriate functions to state and local government." Mr. Agnew did not elaborate.

In addition to serving as "my liaison" with state and local governments, Mr. Nixon said, the Vice President will inform the Council for Urban Affairs on "general governmental issues."

This aspect of the job is expected to serve as Mr. Agnew's main line to the urban policy making role. The Office of Intergovernmental Affairs itself, the Vice President said, will not be "a policy making body."

Mr. Agnew reported that his agency would take over the Federal liaison with governors previously handled by the Office of Emergency Preparedness so that state and local concerns could be melded in the same unit.

The office will not be involved in sensitive issues such as enforcement of Federal school desegregation guidelines, the Vice President said. His aides indicated that the unit did not intend to bargain away Federal interests.

February 15, 1969

PRESIDENT URGES GOVERNORS TO AID NEW FEDERALISM

Goal of 'Strategy for the 70's' Is to Gain Greater Control Over Problems

PARTNERSHIP STRESSED

Nixon to Try to Shift More Responsibility to States —Gives Peace Views

By ROBERT B. SEMPLE Jr.
Special to The New York Times

COLORADO SPRINGS, Sept. 1—President Nixon asked the nation's Governors tonight to join him in efforts to make government at all levels more responsive to national needs.

In remarks delivered at the National Governors Conference here, the President charted what he called "a new strategy for the seventies" aimed at achieving greater control over the awesome problems that afflict modern industrial society.

"The central race in the world today," he said, "is neither an arms race nor a space race. It is the race between man and change. . . . If we are to win this race, then our first need is to make government itself governable."

The essence of the new strategy, he said, is the concept of "new federalism," which he outlined in a nationwide television address on his domestic programs Aug. 8.

'A New Day Has Come'

He pledged tonight that under his concept the central Government in Washington would refrain from telling states and localities how to conduct their affairs and would seek to transfer ever-greater responsibilities to the state level.

"Washington will no longer try to go it alone," he said. "Washington will no longer dictate without consulting. A new day has come, in which we recognize that partnership is a two-way street, and if the partnership is to thrive that street has to be traveled — both ways."

As for the states themselves, he said, the concept of "new federalism" would impose upon them new obligations and new challenges.

"Continued improvement of governments at the state and local levels is essential to make these new concepts work," he insisted, adding:

"We can only toss the ball; the states and localities have to catch it and carry it."

The President professed to have found marked improvements in the quality of state governments and expressed confidence in their capacity to play a new and larger role.

He cited, however, only one "healthy indicator" of progress on the state level: the recent trend toward higher salaries for state officials. Whether he intended irony was not clear.

Mr. Nixon sought to draw a clear parallel between his domestic philosophy and his foreign policy. As power would be decentralized at home, he said, so would it be dispersed abroad.

As greater responsibilities would be thrust on the state, he declared, so too would they be thrust on America's allies.

In remarks that echoed the message of his recent global tour, Mr. Nixon forecast a new era of limited commitments and fewer expenditures abroad.

Inherited Problems

"The new strategy of the seventies also requires a strategy for peace," he said.

"This means maintaining defense forces strong enough to keep the peace, while not allowing wasteful expenditures to drain away resources we need for progress.

"It means limiting our commitments abroad to those we can prudently and realistically keep. It means helping other free nations maintain their own security, but not rushing in to do for them what they can and should do for themselves.

"It does not mean laying down our leadership. It does not mean abandoning our allies. It does mean forging a new structure of world stability in which the burdens as well as the benefits are fairly shared — a structure that does not rely on the strength of one nation, but that draws strength from all nations."

Insisting that he intended no criticism of his predecessor or of the Democratic party, Mr. Nixon nevertheless asserted that when he assumed office in January he found himself in charge of a fat and flabby Federal establishment suffering from the ills of over-centralization.

He cited a variety of inherited problems—$58-billion worth of

Federal deficits, an inflationary spiral that had raised consumer prices 18 per cent in five years and the exhaustion of tax revenue at the state and local level.

Even the Government's efforts to improve the lot of the poor, he went on, succeeded only in antagonizing them.

"Never in human history has so much been spent by so many for such a negative result," he said. "The cost of the lesson has been high, but we have learned that it is not only what we spend that matters, but how we spend it."

Washington's failure to solve social problems had, in turn, placed impossible burdens on the states, Mr. Nixon argued.

States alone have been forced to seek more than 200 tax rate increases in eight years, he said, while state and local expenditures combined have soared from $44-billion in 1958 to $108-billion 10 years later.

To increase the efficiency of Federal spending, to ease the financial burdens of states and localities, "to put the money where the problems are and to get a dollar's worth of return for a dollar spent," the President said that he had made it his first order of business to "overhaul" government and pledged to do more.

He devoted much of his address to stressing his own remedies, including the new minimum-income welfare plan, which he advertised as a boon to the states, and his revenue-sharing program, which he described as an effort to put "our money where our principles are."

The 48 Governors who have assembled here have displayed general bipartisan agreement with the President's welfare programs and his basic concept of Federal-state relations—which, in broad outline, is not remarkably different from the "creative federalism" espoused by President Johnson.

Democratic Governors have found little to criticize in the President's initiatives. They have only asked, privately, that conference statements in support of the President's programs "not be too flowery."

The President flew here aboard Air Force One this morning from his vacation retreat in San Clemente, Calif.

September 2, 1969

NIXON URGES $16-BILLION GO TO STATES AND CITIES AS REVENUE-SHARING AID

A BROAD PROGRAM

Talk on State of Union Calls for a Reversal of Flow of Power

By ROBERT B. SEMPLE Jr.
Special to The New York Times

WASHINGTON, Jan. 22—President Nixon asked Congress tonight to set a goal of giving state and local governments at least $16-billion annually in largely unrestricted funds as part of a broad program to "close the gap between promise and performance" at all levels of government.

In his second State of the Union Message, Mr. Nixon adopted as his central theme the quality of the institutions men have devised to govern them.

He asserted that local government had been weakened and the people driven to frustration and to a sense of futility by the gradual accumulation of authority in Washington, and he said that the time had come to reverse the flow of power.

Reaction Restrained

Congressional reaction to the speech was restrained, with Republicans praising the President's goals and Democrats pledging cautious cooperation.

Mr. Nixon's address to a joint session of Congress covered many areas and offered several prescriptions for change.

But crucial to his promise to return power "to the people" and create "more centers of power" was a revenue-sharing plan to provide $5-billion in new, unrestricted funds to states and cities, plus $10-billion more to be drawn from existing programs and $1-billion in new funds.

Simultaneously, he called for a vast reshuffling of the Federal bureaucracy that would reduce from 12 to eight the number of Cabinet departments and, in his words, "match our structure to our purposes."

"What this Congress can be remembered for," he declared, "is opening the way to a New American Revolution—a peaceful revolution in which power was turned back to the people—in which government at all levels was refreshed and renewed, and made truly responsive.

"This can be a revolution as profound, as far-reaching, as exciting, as that first revolution almost 200 years ago—and it can mean that just five years from now America will enter its third century as a young nation new in spirit, with all the vigor and freshness with which it began its first century."

Mr. Nixon delivered the address, which was viewed by millions of Americans over all three major television networks, in a somber, almost flat tone. He occasionally stumbled over the complex concepts.

He was interrupted by applause 11 times; he did little to solicit applause.

Before beginning his formal remarks, the President asked his audience to rise for a moment of silence in tribute to Senator Richard B. Russell, Democrat of Georgia, who died yesterday. He then warmly saluted the winners and offered condolences to the losers in the recent contests for party leadership in the House and Senate.

Although Mr. Nixon's proposals to strengthen local government with new funds and provide the Federal bureaucracy with a new form dominated the 4,500-word message, he set for himself and the 92d Congress these other major goals:

¶To complete the "unfinished business" of the 91st Congress by passing more than 35 pieces of holdover legislation, including, in particular, his plan to reform the welfare system by placing a "floor under the income of every family with children in America."

¶To achieve "full prosperity in peacetime" by approving an "expansionary budget" that would propel the economy forward without relighting "the fires of inflation."

¶To "restore and enhance our natural environment." Mr. Nixon pledged, without going into detail, to submit a "strong new set of initiatives" to combat air and water pollution, as well as a new program to expand parks and open spaces around cities.

¶To improve America's health care, especially for the poor, by providing fresh funds, increasing the number of doctors, improving the delivery of health services and encouraging better preventive medicine. In this connection, he disclosed that he would ask Congress to underwrite a special $100-million campaign to find a cure for cancer.

Sees Time for Action

The President spoke not so much of the "present" State of the Union as of his hopes for the future of the Union. While conceding that the country had suffered in recent years, he strongly argued that the moment to begin anew had come, and that it should be promptly seized.

"In these troubled years just past," he said, "America has been going through a long nightmare of war and division, of crime and inflation. Even more deeply, we have gone through a long, dark night of the American spirit. But now that night is ending. Now we must let our spirits soar again. Now we are ready for the lift of a driving dream."

The question, he said, was how best to capitalize on this spirit—how, in other words, "to set free the full genius of our people."

One answer, he said, would be to "enact a plan of revenue sharing historic in scope and bold in concept" that would provide cities and states not only with more money but also with far greater flexibility to spend it.

As sketched by the President, the $16-billion "investment" in states and cities would involve two separate kinds of revenue-sharing programs.

$5-Billion in New Funds

The first would provide $5-billion in new, unconditional, general purpose funds that states and cities would use at their own discretion and with virtually no Federal strings attached.

United Press International

President Nixon being applauded before his address by Vice President Agnew and House Speaker Carl Albert.

The second sum of money, $11-billion in all, would be channeled to states and cities with only modest restrictions but earmarked for six broad categories of use: urban development, rural development, education, transportation, job training and law enforcement. The state and local authorities, however, would be free to spend the money on projects of their own choosing within each of the six broad categories.

Could Retain Program

The $11-billion would consist of $1-billion in new funds, the President said, and $10-billion that he hoped to raise by abolishing many existing narrow-purpose programs. Informed Government officials said that nearly 100 programs were scheduled for elimination, including such well-known efforts as the Model Cities program and the programs funded by the Elementary and Secondary Education Act of 1965.

Officials stressed, however, that even if Congress agreed to abolish the Model Cities program, thereby converting funds to revenue sharing, a city could continue its existing Model Cities program, if it wished, simply by channeling the funds it receives for the broad purpose of "urban development" to its Model Cities agency.

The big difference in the new plan, they said, was that a city would now have the option of putting its urban development money to other purposes to which it might attach higher priority.

The President also stressed, as did his associate who briefed newmen in advance of the message, that the revenue-sharing proposals would "include the safeguards against discrimination that accompany all other Federal funds allotted to the states."

Stresses Two Concerns

The President said that his enthusiasm for revenue sharing, and his decision to give it a central role in his plans for 1971, arose from two concerns.

The first, he said, was his recognition that "most Americans today are simply fed up with government at all levels." "They will not—and they should not—continue to tolerate the gap between promise and performance," he said.

Secondly, he insisted, stronger local governments would provide "more centers of power" and thus broaden the opportunities for all Americans to participate actively in the decisions that affect their lives.

"As everything seems to have grown bigger and more complex in America, as the forces that shape our lives seem to have grown more distant and more impersonal, a great feeling of frustration has crept across this land," he declared, adding:

"Millions of frustrated young Americans are crying out—asking not what will government do for me, but what can I do, what can I contribute, how can I matter?

"Let us answer them. Let us say to them and let us say to all Americans: We hear you. We will give you a chance."

Would Reshape Bureaucracy

If local government must be renewed, Mr. Nixon said, so must the Federal bureaucracy be reshaped "to keep up with the times and with the needs of the people."

Mr. Nixon did not talk in detail about his new plans to overcome environmental problems, but it is known that an environmental message now scheduled for Feb. 9 will propose "a national land use policy" giving states more authority and responsibility, as well as more money, to conserve "areas of critical environmental concern."

His discussion of the economy, one of his largest single political problems, was not long, but he seemed to be preparing his audiences for a budget deficit, while urging Congress to restrain its spending impulses, and business and labor "to make their wage and price decisions in the light of the national interest."

Nixon's Presidency: A Nation Is Changed

By JOHN HERBERS
Special to The New York Times

WASHINGTON, March 6— For four years, Nixon Administration officials traveled the nation telling audiences that the Federal Government, over which they were presiding, was flawed in many ways as a means of delivering services to the public.

The standard argument, used by everyone from the President to deputy assistant secretaries, was that the Federal Government was "muscle-bound" under a "patronizing bureaucratic élite" and that local governments should be trusted and strengthened.

Now they are fulfilling their prophecy. Money and authority are flowing back to the states and the President and his men are dismantling programs built by four decades of Democratic government. Although it has just begun, this reversal of a long-term trend is one of the many ways in which the Nixon Presidency has had enormous impact on the national life.

Like all Presidents, Mr. Nixon is seeking to have an important impact on the nation. But he has undertaken to make fundamental changes in what kind of schools people attend, what kind of cities and communities they live in, what kind of news they watch on television and read in the papers, what taxes they pay and to whom, what system of justice they live under, what their employment and income opportunities will be and a host of other matters affecting their daily lives.

Mr. Nixon is making an extraordinary mark on American society, according to political leaders and students of the Presidency, by making bold use of Presidential powers and expanding in a number of ways the enormous influence that the White House brings to bear on public opinion.

With almost four years remaining in office and with a landslide victory behind him, Mr. Nixon is seeking to consolidate his gains, make new initiatives in shaping the national life and leave a legacy for his successor that would be difficult to reverse.

Some Nixon supporters expect Mr. Nixon to be so successful that the age will be named for him.

"This is going to be known as the Nixon era," said one of his aides. "I know it is."

The President's own words give an indication of his intent to be a highly active President for the rest of his Administration.

"I believe in the battle," Mr. Nixon told Saul Pett of The Asssociated Press in a recent interview, "whether it's the battle of a campaign or the battle of this office, which is a continuing batle. It's always there wherever you go. I, perhaps, carry it more than others because that's my way."

Mr. Nixon's opponents are saying that the President, in his use of his powers and in his unilateral assault on social programs, has overplayed his hand and will be rebuked, as have other recent Presidents after landslide victories — Franklin D. Roosevelt, in his attempt to enlarge the Supreme Court, and Lyndon B. Johnson, with his escalation of the Vietnam war, for example.

Rejection Foreseen

"I do not read America's mood as this President does," said Senator Edmund S. Muskie, Democrat of Maine, who sought the Presidency in 1972, in predicting that Mr. Nixon's leadership will eventually be rejected as too "negative and narrow."

But at the White House there is not much sign of concern. There, with Richard Nixon firmly in control of the nation's most powerful institution of government, which he has expanded in several respects, the skies all look blue.

To take only one aspect of the Nixon Presidency, the endeavor to dismantle assistance programs and turn more authority back to the state and local governments—New Federalism, the President calls it —is having a wide impact on education, science, agriculture, antipoverty efforts, race relations and the cities.

An example of the depth of the impact comes from William J. McGill, president of Columbia University, who said in a recent statement that there was a "major ideological component" in the action that added up to shifting public funds away from private higher educational institutions to public ones that stress vocational education.

"I believe that Columbia and other leading institutions will begin to lose substantial amounts of Federal support," he said. "Students will go into the public sector in large numbers, because all their costs will be paid there."

"Next year, instead of going to Washington looking for support, we will be going to Albany," he said, and that will mean that Federal money sent to the New York state government for education will go to state-supported colleges. "I believe it forecasts very hard days ahead for major institutions."

Some authorities, however, believe that Mr. Nixon's influence on the Supreme Court may ultimately have greater effect on the country than what he does with Federal money.

In making appointments to the Court, Mr. Nixon has taken greater precautions to see that his nominees follow his ideology than any other recent President, according to some authorities on the Court.

Presidents have frequently been surprised at how the Justices they appointed turned out. The late Felix Frankfurter, for example, was more conservative on the Court than he appeared when Franklin Roosevelt appointed him.

One way to be more certain is to elevate Justices from the lower courts. Of Mr. Nixon's six nominees to the Court, four were picked from the Federal appeals courts, where they had demonstrated the kind of "strict constructionist" rulings favored by Mr. Nixon. These were Chief Jusice Warren E. Burger, Harry A. Blackmun, Clement F. Haynsworth Jr. and G. Harrold Carswell. The latter two were rejected by the Senate.

The two other Nixon nominees were Justice William H. Rehnquist, an Assistant Attorney General with proved conservative views, and Justice Lewis F. Powell Jr., a lawyer who had written widely in support of Administration poliices, such as crime control.

With almost four years remaining in his term, it is considered almost certain that Mr. Nixon will have an ideological majority on the nine-member Court before his term is out.

Beyond appointments, Mr. Nixon has gone further than other modern Presidents in publicly attacking court rulings.

His stance against school busing—he accused the courts of "busing for the sake of busing"—seems to have brought a virtual halt to court-initiated efforts to integrate schools where new transportation is involved.

He has publicly advocated legislation to find ways to get around Supreme Court rulings against Federal aid to parochial schools.

Another institution on which Mr. Nixon is applying more than coverage pressure is the news media. He has, through Vice President Agnew and other White House officials, publicly accused the national media of bias.

His Justice Department stopped publication of the Pentagon papers for 12 days on the ground that they violated national security and has sought to force reporters to disclose confidential information in criminal cases.

His Office of Telecommunications has proposed legislation that could curtail criticism of government by making local stations responsible for news balance on network broadcasts.

The precise effect of this and other actions on the content of news is in dispute. On the one hand, Herbert G. Klein, the President's director of communications, gave the White House point of view in a "Meet the Press" television interview Jan. 7:

"I think the key thing is that while there has been a lot of rhetoric and there has been talk about intimidation, I have not met any intimidated reporters and I never want to. Secondly, the fact is that if you look at the actions, the actions of the Administration, the implementation of the Freedom of Information Act has opened more [official documents]. The actions which we are supporting in Congress, including taking a new look at [reporters'] shield laws, are ones which I think are favorable toward the media."

On the other hand, there is a strong belief in the media that the Administration's actions have made television and radio particularly cautious and timid in some respects.

For example, the number of local television and radio entries in the competition for the Robert F. Kennedy Awards, which honor reporting critical of how institutions of all kinds treat the poor and minorities, dropped sharply between 1970 and 1971. This was not true of newspapers and magazines.

One belief current among both critics and supporters of the Administration is that the White House actions have forced the media to take a healthy, critical look at content of the news.

The Nixon Presidency is having an impact, too, on non-Federal Government institutions.

When Mr. Nixon came to office in 1969, the nation's mayors were not only fearful of what he would do to the cities, but they were also hostile because they envisioned losing categorical grants, those made for specific purposes. And most were Democrats without Mr. Nixon's suburban constituency.

After four years, Mr. Nixon has made peace, even though Federal aid to large cities has dropped, if the effects of inflation are taken into account. With some exceptions, he appeased the Mayors with revenue sharing and armies of lobbyists that would descend on every national urban convention preaching the Administration policy of returning power to local officials.

"Although they are still lambasting the Administration for a shortage of funds," said a spokesman for the United States Conference of Mayors-National League of Cities, "you can bet they are all for the way Nixon is doing it, even with a little less money. Nixon has changed the whole context of the argument on national priorities. You don't hear many Mayors any more talking about helping poor minorities."

Under the categorical urban grants enacted by the Democrats, much of the aid was specifically directed to the poor, and to get the money, the Mayors emphasized the need. Under the Nixon formula, the Mayors have wide latitude in use of the funds, and the money is going largely for general purposes such as salaries of policemen and street cleaning.

Gains With Labor

In other areas, Mr. Nixon has made important gains with organized labor, once the preserve of Democrats, by making concessions and appealing to labor leaders.

He has neutralized the liberal wing of the Republican party by working for the defeat of those Republicans who publicly attacked his policies.

He is diluting the influence of Democratic lobbyist-lawyers in Washington, who have been barons of policy making, by releasing Administration officials to set up law practices as competing Republicans with better access to the executive branch. Charles W. Colson, special conusel to the President, is an example.

The list goes on.

Students of government say that much of what has happened bears on the kind of institution the Presidency has become in recent years.

For several years, some political scientists have been complaining that the Presidency has become so sanctified in the public mind that Americans equate criticism of the President with desecration of the flag.

George E. Reedy, former press secretary to President Johnson, wrote in "The Twilight of the Presidency" that the office had become the American monarchy, with all the regalia "except ermine robes, a scepter and a crown."

All recent Presidents have capitalized on the sanctity of the office to consolidate their power and put their political programs into effect. This involves conducting the outward signs of the office in the expected manner so that Americans support the style, not the substance.

In the process, political scientists say, the public does not put the President's words and actions to the same critical test that it maintains for other Governmental officials.

Thomas E. Cronin, a former White House fellow under President Johnson, who, like Mr. Reedy, found many aspects of that Administration abysmal, has written for a forthcoming book a "Script for a Cosmetic Presidency." All recent Presidents have followed it to some extent. Some of the elements are:

"Travel widely, be a statesman and run for the Nobel Peace Prize; claim to be a consensus leader when the polls are favorable and a 'Profile in Courage' leader when you drop in the polls; proclaim the open Presidency but practice White House government, decision-making centralization and Presidency by secrecy; hold numerous news conferences during your honeymoon, but afterwards appeal directly to the people by direct address; protect and strengthen the powers of the Presidency for the rewards of history; if all else fails, wage war on the press."

Most White House observers agree that Mr. Nixon has followed the script quite well.

"The most sensible resolution," Mr. Cronin concluded, "is to depersonalize and demythologize the Presidency, to understand how it works, to appreciate what it can and cannot do, and to hold Presidents critically to account."

March 7, 1973

Governors Say Power Has Now Shifted to the States

By CHRISTOPHER LYDON
Special to The New York Times

SEATTLE, June 5 — There may be comfort for President Nixon in a closing theme of the four-day National Governors Conference. It is that in the Watergate crisis the President unwittingly consolidated his decentralizing "new American revolution," and that two years of fixation on scandal in Washington have brought morale and importance back to state governments much as revenue sharing brought them money.

A novel feature of the conference has been the diminished presence of the Administration at what is commonly a show-and-tell session for the White House and the Cabinet.

President Nixon and Vice President Ford both declined invitations from Daniel J. Evans. the Republican Governor of Washington who is the conference chairman, to attend. Their representatives, Kenneth R. Cole Jr., a domestic counselor, and Caspar W. Weinberger, the Secretary of Health, Education and Welfare, were both low-voltage speakers, clearly outshone by Senator Edward M. Kennedy of Massachusetts, the most luminous of Mr. Nixon's political adversaries.

'Federal Paralysis'

The larger sense of this Governors Conference, confident to the point of cockiness, is that the states have recovered political leadership from a general collapse in Washington.

"We have a paralysis at the Federal level," Gov. William G. Milliken of Michigan, a Republican, remarked in an interview today. "I think the confusion of Washington has put a whole new emphasis on the state—on moving resources and experimentation back to the states."

Governor John J. Gilligan of Ohio, a Democrat, was characteristically blunt: "Everything is busting down in Washington," he said. "We're doing things."

The conference's time and place neatly matched a fundamental transition of power "from the city of Washington to the state of Washington," said Elliot L. Richardson, who resigned as Attorney General last fall in a dispute over the Watergate investigation. "Watergate was a watershed" in the shifting balance of power, he said.

Prof. Daniel J. Elazar of Temple University went further. In providing the "alternate circuits" of government in the Watergate era, he said, states have proved that they "can administer and manage anything. They can," he said, "innovate as well as any government. There is nothing they cannot do—including foreign policy."

In a period when decentralization is a worldwide trend and when most national governments are in crisis, Mr. Elazar declared: "Some of the strongest leaders in the world are the governors of the American states."

There are reasons beyond Watergate for the governors' heady mood. Nor do they contrast themselves only with President Nixon.

Gov. Dale Bumpers of Arkansas has been cheered as a hero by colleagues from both parties. In defeating Senator J. William Fulbright by a nearly 2-to-1 margin in the Democratic primary last week. He confirmed the contention that governors are closer to the voters than any of their representatives in Congress.

Few Serious Threats

Executive reorganizations and Federal grant regulations have professionalized most governors' staffs. Revenue sharing and numerous new state tax programs of the nineteen-sixties have greatly expanded their resources.

State spending has grown sixfold in the last 20 years,

Former Attorney General Elliot L. Richardson addressing the National Governors' Conference yesterday in Seattle. He said power was shifting from Federal to state hands.

according to the "State of the States" booklet that the conference published; state revenues have also expanded proportionally faster than Federal tax income.

Many of the governors here have budget surpluses. Of the 22 governors running for re-election this year, less than a handful appear to be seriously threatened.

A central irony of the atmosphere here is that while Presidential fever is rampant among the governors, individual governors who have confessed dreams of national office also say that Senators have a greater advantage now than ever—in national media exposure and traveling opportunities—as Presidential candidates.

But that, too, may be changing. "The trouble is," said Gov. Brendan T. Byrne of New Jersey, a Democrat, "that a dozen governors around this table this morning want to run for President. If they all run, nobody will win, but if we got together behind one governor, we might change things."

June 6, 1974

Revenue Sharing Target Of New General Scrutiny

By WILLIAM E. FARRELL
Special to The New York Times

WASHINGTON—For nearly two years, one of the smallest Federal bureaucracies in Washington has been quietly mailing out checks—reaching a total of $14.3-billion—to thousands of units of state and local government.

The Federal largesse, disbursed under terms of the General Revenue Sharing Act, has been a success among governors, mayors, county officials and others associated with state and municipal government throughout the country.

These officials, many of whom lobbied for passage of the Revenue Sharing Act, clearly like having Federal money to spend with a minimum of Federal restrictions on how they should spend it.

President Ford has just told urban leaders that he supports general revenue sharing and wants to see it renewed. The program expires at the end of 1976.

Meanwhile, some members of the House and Senate are beginning to re-evaluate the law with an eye toward possible amendments. And civic, watchdog and minority groups have become unhappy with various aspects of it.

The groups are critical of the low level of community participation in determining how the Federal dollars should be spent, they question whether anti-discrimination laws are being firmly adhered to, and they have difficulty monitoring the money once it has been mixed in with other state and municipal revenue.

Federal general revenue sharing—a pillar of the Nixon Administration's "new federalism"—was signed into law by Mr. Nixon on Oct. 20, 1972. It calls for returning a total of $30.2-billion in Federal monies to states and localities over a five-year period retroactive to Jan. 1, 1972.

The program is administered by the Office of Revenue Sharing, an arm of the Treasury Department. The revenue-sharing office employs a staff of 68 persons, a droplet in the Washington bureaucratic sea.

Recently a number of governors, mayors and county officials who have become increasingly wary of the growing—but still relatively small—group of vocal critics of revenue sharing were buoyed in their hopes for continuing the program when they visited President Ford at the White House.

Mr. Ford's message was summed up by Gov. Calvin Rampton, Democrat of Utah, who is chairman of the executive committee of the National Governors Conference.

"One of the most significant things that occurred," Governor Rampton told newsmen after the White House meeting, "was that the President assured us of his continued enthusiastic support for general revenue sharing, not only during the balance of the period for which provision is now made by law, but for an extension of the general revenue sharing and new legislation when the bill expires."

Of the $14.3-billion sent out of Washington to date a total of $2.2-billion has been funneled to the tristate area of New York, New Jersey and Connecticut. New York State has received $1.6-billion, of which $587-million went to New York City, while New Jersey received $440-million and Connecticut $179-million.

So far there has been only one Congressional evaluation conducted on the revenue sharing program, by Senator Edmund Muskie's subcommittee on intergovernmental relations, which held four days of hearings on revenue sharing in June.

Mr. Muskie, Democrat of Maine, supports the underlying concept of revenue sharing—the notion that states and localities are better able to determine their needs and priorities than a remote Federal bureaucracy working out of Washington.

But he is critical of the way the program is working in such areas as civil rights compliance and allocation of funds on the basis of need. He also fears that Mr. Nixon's assertion that revenue sharing was "new money" has been negated by the curtailment of numerous Federal categorical grant programs, particularly in the field of social welfare.

"Those who are for the program will have to carry the burden of proof" when revenue sharing comes up again in the next year or so before Congress, Mr. Muskie said in an interview.

Besides some of the citizens groups and others critical of revenue sharing to date, there is some Congressional opposition to continuing the program, the Senator said, among those members who believe state and local governments "aren't really very effective and viable."

"The points which we are looking at are civil rights and the formula for distribution of money to see if it couldn't be focused more fairly in the areas of need," Mr. Muskie said.

Asked about the degree of community participation in the use of revenue sharing funds, Mr. Muskie said, "I don't think there's much encouraging evidence on that point."

There was much rhetoric about enhanced community participation when the Revenue Sharing Act was being debated in Congress, although the act makes no specific stipulation about community participation in disposition of the funds.

At Mr. Muskie's hearings, Secretary of the Treasury William E. Simon asserted that there was "no way" the Federal funds could be more wisely spent, adding that revenue sharing curbed the era of grantsmanship in Washington in which localities with the smoothest command of the Federal labyrinth got the lion's share of the categorical funds. Mr. Simon added that revenue sharing helped restore the balance of power between the Federal Government and state and local government.

Graham Watt, the director of Office of Revenue Sharing, said that a total of 38,745 units of state, county and municipal government were recipients of revenue sharing funds, along with 178 Indian tribes and Alaskan villages.

Senator Muskie criticized the revenue-sharing office for its "most passive" role in enforcing one of the few requirements in the revenue-sharing law—an adherence to Federal antidiscrimination statutes.

Mr. Watt disagreed with this assessment but other witnesses chided the revenue-sharing office for having only two civil rights compliance field officers and for an alleged reluctance on the part of the agency to use its administrative power to defer payments to localities when civil rights questions have been raised.

At present there are civil rights complaints pending against Chicago, Montclair, N.J., and Ouachita Parish, La.

In addition, a Washington group called the Lawyers Committee for Civil Rights Under Law is attempting to get the Treasury Department to revive the funding level for Baltimore and Newark. The lawyers' group contends the two cities are being underfunded because of an undercount of blacks in the 1970 Federal census. One of the ingredients of the revenue sharing allocation formula is a locality's total population.

Mr. Muskie characterized the agency's use of its deferral power as a "very cautious, very restrained and very inhibited" exercise of its responsibility.

Mary Whitehead of the Westchester County, N. Y., League of Women Voters, one of the groups monitoring revenue sharing, told the committee that "there is a great need for stiffened accountability."

With the absence of specific Federal spending guidelines, Mrs. Whitehead said, "the national perspective is lost and human needs are not being met."

Joe Tom Easley, a member of the Southern Regional Council, which is monitoring revenue sharing in 11 Southern states, said: "We have failed to detect any special efforts whatsoever on the part of local or state governments to involve local citizens in the decision-making process on these Federal revenue-sharing funds."

Simplified Reporting Scored

Mr. Easley said that the simplified reporting procedures for informing the Federal Government on how the funds were actually used "border on farce."

June Owen of the Pasadena, Calif., Urban Coalition, another group studying revenue sharing, said that once the funds were deposited in a locality's general fund they became trackless because "all money is green."

"Finding the actual use of general revenue-sharing funds when they are handled this way through the general fund is really impossible," Mrs. Owen said.

Carl Holman, president of the National Urban Coalition, which is conducting a monitoring project of revenue sharing in 10 cities, said that the phrase "returning power to the people," which Mr. Nixon used in espousing the revenue-sharing concept, was "a mockery for the poor, minorities and working class residents of our cities."

Revenue-sharing funds earmarked for states—which receive one-third of the total, the remainder going to local governments—have only two restrictions imposed on them. They cannot be used as matching funds for other Federal grants and they cannot be used to reduce state aid to local governments.

Local governments are given generally defined priority areas by the Federal Government for using the funds. These are for capital expenditures authorized by law and for maintenance and operating expenses for public safety, environmental protection, public transportation, health, recreation, libraries, social services for the poor or aged and financial administration.

Brookings Study

One of the more detailed and long-range studies of revenue sharing is being made by the Brookings Institution with a Ford Foundation grant.

The first volume of the study is due to be published sometime this fall. But Richard P. Nathan, a senior fellow at Brookings and director of the revenue-sharing study, has prepared a preliminary paper on the study.

The institution is studying revenue sharing as it affects 65 governmental units — eight state governments, 29 cities, 21 counties, six townships and one Indian tribe.

Mr. Nathan's paper says that there is difficulty in determining how the revenue is shared under the broad categories outlined in the law because "although a given recipient government may attribute shared revenue to police protection, if it does not spend any more for police than it would have anyway then the real uses (or what we have called the net fiscal effect of revenue sharing) must be sought elsewhere."

"Although the work for our first report is not yet complete," Mr. Nathan wrote, "our data indicate that there has been a substantial substitution effect in the use of shared revenue, that is to say significant amounts of these funds have been used—not for new spending—but to cut taxes, hold down taxes, balance the budget or avoid borrowing which otherwise would have been undertaken."

This assessment "does not necessarily indict the revenue-sharing program," Mr. Nathan said. "Many of the original proponents of revenue sharing said that these funds should be used to reduce tax pressures, particularly in the field of property taxation."

But there are some in Congress and elsewhere who are beginning to talk of tighter restrictions on the use of the revenue-sharing funds and of changing the current blanket allocations of funds to all units of government, including affluent ones.

The Nation

How Much Is Government Responsible For People?

By PHILIP SHABECOFF

WASHINGTON—An old national debate is being revived over the conflict between the rights and responsibilities of individuals in the United States and the responsibility of the Government to protect the social welfare of its citizens.

The roots of the issue run all the way back to the clashes between Thomas Jefferson and Alexander Hamilton in the early days of the Republic. But the classic conservative-liberal dispute over the uses of the nation's wealth has been given new relevance by what President Ford and his advisers perceive as ominous trends in government spending, and others perceive as the social imperatives of the deepening recession.

Much of the spending involved is now paying for food stamps and medical care; some of it, in social security and veterans benefits, is the fixed and only income of the elderly. They are programs supported by a national consensus for decades, but in addressing the recession the President addressed the cost of those programs as well.

President Ford has issued in recent days a kind of manifesto about the future of the American economy. A specter is haunting the country, Mr. Ford has said in effect, a specter of total government domination of the economy at the expense of private enterprise and personal initiative, because of uncontrolled spending for social purposes by a "self-indulgent" nation.

Liberals, who have traditionally clung to the Jeffersonian principle that the common man is "the most precious portion of the State," view social spending as a necessary investment in that "precious" resource, and are for the most part particularly unmoved by the President's Doomsday warnings, especially given the outcry from a public beset by high prices and joblessness for more social services.

Mr. Ford's position is basically this: If the current growth of Federal spending on "uncontrollable" social programs goes unchecked, government will control more economic activity than the private sector within a generation. When that happens, fewer and fewer producers of goods and services will be supporting an ever-expanding group of non-producers.

The President is acting on these portents by seeking to reduce Federal spending now, especially in the area of social programs, even while he proposes reluctantly to cut taxes to stimulate the depressed economy. In the meantime, he says baleful things about the future which might suggest that the United States is in danger of going broke.

Liberal economists say the President's concerns are highly questionable, and that top priority must be given now to relieving the very real and immediate suffering caused by the economic crisis.

But the President believes that, recession notwithstanding, the problem of spiraling social spending must be checked at once. As he told Congress in his State of the Union Message: "For decades, we have been voting ever-increasing levels of Government benefits—and the bill has now come due. We have been adding so many new programs that the size and growth of the Federal budget has taken on a life of its own."

When the President talks of "bills" coming due, he really doesn't only mean next year or the year after that. He is talking about trends extending to the end of this century.

Mr. Ford's warnings are based on long-range spending projections worked out recently by Roy L. Ash, the Director of the Office of Management and Budget. The spending Mr. Ash and the President are worried about is called "transfer payments" because they transfer income, through the Government, from one sector of society to another.

These programs include some designed to help people maintain a minimum income, such as Social Security, Unemployment Insurance and welfare payments. Others are intended to assist the needy in obtaining essential goods and services. They include such things as Medicare and Medicaid, food stamps, and housing assistance.

In a speech to a business group last Thursday, Mr. Ford warned that massive Federal spending on social programs, "a trend set in motion by politicians and pundits," has been growing at an annual rate of 9 per cent in current dollars for 20 years. "The continuation of these programs at anywhere near this rate of growth, which is more than twice that of the Gross National Product, in my judgment, is very ominous," he declared.

Increasing burdens upon the Social Security system provide the President with an immediate case in point. According to the Social Security Advisory Council, a panel of private citizens which reviews the system's operations and makes recommendations to the Government, benefit payments could well begin outrunning tax receipts next year by several billion dollars. The council is proposing a series of measures to Congress to prevent serious drains on the $50-billion Social Security Trust Fund.

Only 15 years ago, social programs cost about $22-billion and accounted for slightly over 23 per cent of the Federal budget. In the current fiscal year, they will cost $138-billion and constitute 44 per cent of the budget. Social expenditures account for nearly one-third of the Gross National Product, the total of all goods and services produced.

Under Mr. Ash's projection, if all other Government costs in relation to the Gross National Product, including defense expenditures, remain constant, Federal spending would consume 60 per cent of the G.N.P. by the year 2000, unless the growth of social programs is reduced.

Why Not Trim Defense?

Administration critics suggest that necessary reductions in expenditures should come out of the defense budget, which will be over $90-billion this year.

But Mr. Ash said that the percentage of G.N.P. accounted for by defense costs has been shrinking steadily. "By reducing defense spending while allowing the transfer payments to rise by 9 per cent a year, we won't be able to afford one soldier or one rifle by 1985," Mr. Ash asserted.

Mr. Ash says that social outlays by the Federal Government have been "built up drop by drop until they have become a torrent. If we don't see it, we will be overwhelmed."

SENIOR CITIZENS
HEALTH
STROLL
MEDICARE
CLOSED

Mr. Ash asserted that the burden is upon Congress to avert such a social Armageddon. This, he explains, is why the President is asking for $17-billion in spending cuts. This is why he is asking for a deferral of national health legislation, for a ceiling of 5 per cent on increases in Social Security benefits and on raises for Federal employes; for a hike in payments for food stamps.

"We have to start pulling down that spending curve right now to make sure we are not overwhelmed by the year 2000," Mr. Ash declared.

Generally, critics view these projections as unduly alarmist, reflecting the conservative social philosophy of the President, Mr. Ash and the Administration as a whole.

To view Social Security and other social programs "as a monster out of control is nonsense," according to Alice M. Rivlin, an economist and budgetary expert at the Brookings Institution. Another Brookings expert, Edward M. Gramlich, said that the sharp rise in spending on these programs in recent years shows signs of abating, particularly at the state and local levels.

Another liberal economist said simply, "Uncle Sam is not going bankrupt." He suggests warnings are being sounded by the President and Mr. Ash because "they hate big government. It is their conservative creed." The collapse of the American economy is not at issue, he insisted.

Why then is President Ford making such dire prophecies about the trend of Federal spending? Arthur Okun, who was Chairman of the Council of Economic Advisers under President Johnson, offers one explanation. "When a conservative Republican President proposes a budget deficit of $77-billion over two years he's got to make a speech about the threat of Federal spending," he said with a smile.

Philip Shabecoff is a White House correspondent for The New York Times.

January 26, 1975

CHAPTER 7

Foreign Policies

If consistency is the hobgoblin of small minds, the international outlook of the United States in this century has been very large minded. When viewed in an overall perspective, the zigs and zags of American foreign policy have been positively bewildering. Every turn has found an appropriate president, but whether those presidents were really leading the people or merely reflecting the national mood is an open question.

The century opened with the United States flexing its muscles in a display of raw, jingoistic imperialism. The Spanish-American War had whetted the appetite for extending American control over "backward" peoples and Manifest Destiny was the watchword of the times. Of course, it was all for "good" motives—the proffering of our civilization to "little brown brothers." For some reason, the little brown brothers neither wanted nor appreciated the benefits offered them and to this day we find ourselves making red-faced apologies.

One of the episodes was marked by particular ruthlessness. It was the U.S.-inspired move that pried Panama loose from Colombia so the United States could dig the famous canal. This was the brain child of Theodore Roosevelt, a president who epitomized his whole era. He regarded Latin America as the private domain of the United States and his philosophy lived on after he retired from active politics. Even the idealistic Woodrow Wilson was perfectly willing to send marines to occupy Vera Cruz and a military force into Mexico to chase a revolutionary leader—both actions in clear contravention of international law.

To be fair, Wilson was not really an imperialist. He had his sights set on very high ideals—a world order in which nations could live in peace. But his administration provided some astonishing contrasts, from the sordid intervention in Mexico to his proclamation of a "higher neutrality" at the outbreak of World War I, his later emergence as a wartime president and his final, heart-breaking struggle for the League of Nations.

Wilsonian idealism was followed by the deepest period of isolationism in the last 75 years. As the American people turned inward, any diplomatic move whatsoever was regarded as "international meddling." In this era the popular image portrayed a diplomat as an effeminate snob clad in striped pants and sipping weak tea with his little finger extended ostentatiously. The watchword had become "no entangling alliances," which was generally interpreted as any agreement with a foreign nation.

The presidents of the twenties, Harding, Coolidge and to a lesser extent Herbert Hoover, were in step with their times. The first two were serious in their philosophy that the best government was the one that governed least and that Americans should not be bothered with

Lyndon B. Johnson

The New York Times

foreign problems. Hoover's tinge of Quaker pacifism made him receptive to agreements that would ''outlaw'' war but not to agreements that would enforce the peace. The result was a few, lofty declarations that disturbed no one.

The modern era was ushered in by Franklin D. Roosevelt and has been characterized by a ceaseless presidential search for a grand design that would bring peace and stability to the globe. In the Roosevelt administration, this meant the alliance against the Axis powers, the ''Four Freedoms'' and the United Nations. In the Truman and Eisenhower administrations, the grand design meant ''containment'' of or an effort to set boundaries to communist expansion. In the Kennedy and Johnson administrations the focus shifted from Europe to Asia but the objective remained containment.

Perhaps the major characteristic of the modern era has been the melding of diplomatic, economic and military policy into national security policy. At one time, the armed forces of the United States were regarded as instruments of last resort—tools that would come into play when diplomacy failed. Since the end of World War II, they have been regarded as instruments of diplomatic pressure. The result was two of the largest wars in which this nation has ever been engaged—Korea and Vietnam—with neither action labeled as war.

The withdrawal from ''containment'' actually began under Richard M. Nixon—a surprising chapter in the history of a man whose early ''bread-and-butter'' politics had been based on militant anticommunism. It was Nixon who brought about the thaw in the nation's attitude towards Communist China and who opened a new era of commercial dealings with the Soviet Union. It is not possible at this writing to determine the long-range effect of his moves. The Nixon administration fell under the impact of domestic scandal and we are now living under a ''caretaker.'' But it seems clear that the nation is now tired of ''grand design'' foreign policy and is in a mood to let the rest of the world alone as far as possible.

GER

THE NATION'S PROBLEMS

———————

President Says United States Must Play the Part of a Great Power.

ELLSWORTH, Me., Aug. 27.—The Presidential train arrived here at 5:45 on schedule time. The President on alighting was introduced by Senator Hale to the local reception committee, headed by Mayor Greeley, and then he was conducted to a gayly decorated platform close by. As usual applause greeted his appearance, and Senator Hale also came in for a round of cheers. In a brief speech he introduced the President. The President said:

"Mr. Senator and you, my Friends and Fellow-Citizens:

"I have thoroughly enjoyed the two days that I have spent in your beautiful State. I have enjoyed seeing the State and I have enjoyed the most meeting what really counts in any State—the men and women. [Applause.] I think that the more one studies the problems of life and of civilization, the more one realizes the infinitely greater importance of the man than of his physical surrounding. Of course, one has to have certain physical advantages in order to exercise to the best advantage one's own qualities; but it is the last that counts. There are other countries than ours just as fitted by nature to be agricultural, commercial, and industrial centres, and they fail to reach the height that ours has reached because they have not the same men to take advantage of the conditions. Now we ought not to say that in any spirit of boastfulness. We ought to say it as a reminder to us that we are not to be excused if, in the future, we do any less well than has been done in the past. There are plenty of problems ahead of us. We stand on the threshold of a new century. No one can say what trial will be before this Nation during that century, but that there must be trials we may be sure.

"No nation can face greatness without having to face trials, exactly as no man can deliberately enter upon a career which leads upward and onward without making up his mind that there will be roughness for him to surmount. Whether we will or not, we must hereafter play in the world the part of a great power. We can play that part ill, or we can play it well, but play it somehow we must. [Applause.]

"It is not open to us to dodge the difficulties. We can run away if we want to, but I do not think, gentlemen, that you are built that way. [Applause.]

"We have to face the difficulties at home and abroad, for the great problems always before any nation are the problems of keeping up its honor in international affairs and when there is armed assault from without. In international affairs, in times of peace, our honor is in our own keeping. It rests with us to keep it unstained. And all that is necessary—not that it is very easy always—is that the people should will intelligently to keep it unstained. But if there comes trouble from without it is not enought then to do well within our own borders, as you who fought in the civil war know. It was not enough in 1861 that you managed things well in Maine; you [illegible] to manage them well elsewhere, too. I earnestly hope, and I can say in all sincerity that I believe that there is but small chance of our having to face trouble abroad, but we shall avoid it, not by blindly refusing to admit that there ever might be trouble, but by safeguarding against it. And the best possible safeguard for this Nation is an adequate and highly efficient navy. I am glad to speak in the home of the Chairman of the Senate Committee of Naval Affairs.. [Applause.]

"I do not suppose it is necessary to tell any audience which has a thoroughly good common school education that you do not win victories merely on the day on which the battle is fought. You have got to prepare for them in advance. When Manila and Santiago were fought great glory came to the men aboard the ships who did the fighting, but an equal meed of praise belongs to those men who prepared in advance. Dewey's ships won their great victory under the Presidency of McKinley, but they were built under Presidents Arthur, Cleveland, and Harrison. The men and the officers aboard them were able to do what they did because through months and years of patient practice, often under officers to whom it was denied to be in actual battle, they were trained to the point of efficiency we saw.

"The men in Congress, such as my host of this evening and his fellows, who saw the need, who voted for the ships, who voted for the guns, who voted to allow money for powder which could be used to best advantage by being used up in practice—those were the men who rendered that victory possible. Now, it is the work that is being done in the navy which will render that navy fit to respond to any call that may be made upon it if, which heaven forbid, such call shall ever be made.

"So much for what is our duty in reference to matters without. Even more important is it to deal well and wisely with affairs within our own borders. No great benefit can come without bringing attendant problems of one kind or another. We are rightly proud of our great material prosperity, of the wonderful material progress that we have made. It is a great thing for this country that it should have come, but it has brought many problems in its train.

"Now, there is not any patent way of solving all those problems. There is not any pet recipe, any pet nostrum which you can take as a whole and have all the problems of the body politic solved. Fundamentally, you must approach the new problems in the spirit with which our fathers approached the problems of their day, if you are going to get a satisfactory solution. You have to do it with patience, with resolution, with courage, and, finally, with common sense.

"Take the evils that come to our mind when we speak of the trusts. The word 'trust' is used very loosely. In the ordinary significance it means simply a large corporation created in one State, probably doing business in other States, and usually with an element of monopoly pertaining to it. Now some of the evils alleged are imaginary, others are very real. Certainly the change produced along a number of lines by the increase of power of these corporations, by their increase in magnitude, is not a change that most of us welcome. There is every reason why we should resolutely declare our purpose and put into effect our purpose to take cognizance of the evils and find which of the evils are real and which are imaginary, and to find out what legislative or administrative expedients can be employed to minimize or to do away with those evils.

"But the one thing sure is that if we try to apply those expedients which in any way border upon the hysterical we are going to fail. I want to see the knife used to cut out any evil, but I want to see it used so that it will be more dangerous to the disease than to the patient. You can perfectly well reduce the prosperity of the trusts by reducing the prosperity of everybody. In 1893 no trusts flourished—nothing flourished. But we want to devise some method by which we can minimize any evil they do without interfering with the general prosperity which is a benefit to all. [Applause.]

"We wish to avoid trying any solution of the problem which would involve us all in a common disaster—a disaster that would be felt most severely by those least well off in the world's goods. On the other hand, I believe that the men of great means should understand that when we demand some method of asserting the power of the Nation over all corporations we are acting, not against their interest, but in their interest.

"When we make the law obeyed by the man of means we are not acting against him; we are acting for him. His safety lies in the law, and the worst of all possible lessons to teach would be to teach our people as a whole that the law did not reach him. It must reach him to make him obey it, exactly as it reaches him to protect him from the wrongdoing of others.

"On the one hand let men of great wealth realize that in seeking for this remedy we are both unalterably benn upon finding it, and are doing it in no spirit of hostility to them, but in a spirit to find out what is best for them and for all of us alike. That is what they must realize. And, on the other hand, let those who feel that there is something wrong and they do not quite know what, avoid above all things being led to act in a spirit of ignorant envy, of rancor, general or sectional. If we are going to solve this problem aright, it will be because we approach it with all the sanity with all the temperateness, the sound intelligence that there is at our command. But the minute that we let our eyes be dimmed by the mists of envy and hatred and rancor, we shall unfit ourselves to act either in our own interests or in the interests of our common country."

August 28, 1902

-By HY. MAYER

February 12, 1912

AMERICA'S DESTINY ON THE PACIFIC

Control of Its Waters Sure, Says Mr. Roosevelt.

But to Maintain Its Supremacy America Must Be Constantly Prepared for War.

SAN FRANCISCO, May 13.—At the Mechanics' Pavilion the President to-night made the most important speech he has delivered since he left St. Louis. His subject, "Expansion and Trade Development and Protection of the Country's Newly Acquired Possessions in the Pacific," together with the advocacy of a greater navy, was one that made his discourse of particular interest to the Californians, and he aroused his auditors to a high pitch of enthusiasm. It was a mighty gathering that listened to the President. The doors of the Pavilion were thrown open to the public at an early hour, and thousands of citizens thronged the building long before the time scheduled for the arrival of the Presidential party.

M. H. De Young, President of the Citizens' Reception Committee, opened the meeting, and Mayor Schmitz formally introduced the President to the people of San Francisco. It was some minutes before the cheering subsided and the President was able to make himself heard. He said:

"Before I saw the Pacific slope I was an expansionist, and after having seen it I fail to understand how any man confident of his country's greatness and glad that his country should challenge with proud confidence our mighty future can be anything but an expansionist. In the century that is opening the commerce and the progress of the Pacific will be factors of incalculable moment in the history of the world.

"Now, in our day, the greatest of all the oceans, of all the seas, and the last to be used on a large scale by civilized man, bids fair to become in its turn the first in point of importance. Our mighty Republic has stretched across the Pacific, and now in California, Oregon, and Washington, in Alaska, and Hawaii, and the Philippines, holds an extent of coast line which makes it of necessity a power of the first class on the Pacific. The extension in the area of our domain has been immense, the extension in the area of our influence even greater.

"America's geographical position on the Pacific is such as to insure our peaceful domination of its waters in the future if only we grasp with sufficient resolution the advantages of this position. We are taking long strides in this direction; witness the cables we are laying and the great steamship lines we are starting, steamship lines some of whose vessels are larger than any freight carriers the world has yet seen.

"We have taken the first steps toward digging an isthmian canal, to be under our own control, a canal which will make our Atlantic and Pacific Coast lines, to all intents and purposes, continuous, and will add immensely alike to our commercial and our military and naval strength. The inevitable march of events gave us the control of the Philippines at a time so opportune that it may without irreverence be held providential. Unless we show ourselves weak, unless we show ourselves degenerate sons of the sires from whose loins we sprang, we must go on with the work that we have begun.

"I earnestly hope that this work will always be peaceful in character. We infinitely desire peace, and the surest way to obtain it is to show that we are not afraid of war. We should deal in a spirit of fairness and justice with all weaker nations; we should show to the strongest that we are able to maintain our rights. Such showing cannot be made by bluster, for bluster merely invites contempt.

"Let us speak courteously, deal fairly, and keep ourselves armed and ready. If we do these things we can count on the peace that comes only to the just man armed, to the just man who neither fears nor inflicts wrong.

"We must keep on building and maintaining a thoroughly efficient navy, with plenty of the best and most formidable ships, with an ample supply of officers and men, and with these officers and men trained in the most thorough way to the best possible performance of their duty. Only thus can we assure our position in the world at large, and in particular our position here on the Pacific.

"It behooves all men of lofty soul, who are proud to belong to a mighty nation, to see to it that we fit ourselves to take and keep a great position in the world, for our proper place is with the expanding nations and the nations that dare to be great, that accept with confidence a place of leadership in the world.

"All our people should take this position, but especially you of California, for much of our expansion must go through the Golden Gate, and the States of the Pacific Slope must inevitably be those which would be most benefited by and take the lead in the growth of American influence along the coasts and islands of that mighty ocean, where East and West finally become one.

"My countrymen, I believe in you with all my heart, and I am proud that it has been granted me to be a citizen in a Nation of such glorious opportunities and with the wisdom, the hardihood, and the courage to rise to the levels of its opportunities."

DAY OF MANY FUNCTIONS.

The meeting at the Mechanics' Pavilion wound up a busy day for the President. He left the Palace Hotel at 9 o'clock this morning escorted by a squadron of cavalry. The streets were lined with people who cheered as the President's carriage passed on the way to Native Sons' Hall, where a reception in the President's honor was held. Mayor Schmitz and Secretary Loeb were seated with the Chief Executive and Rear Admiral Bickford and staff came directly behind, members of the Executive Committee following in carriages.

At the Native Sons' Building was assembled a vast throng, which as the President came in sight manifested great enthusiasm. The hall itself was crowded with members of the California Society of Pioneers, the Native Sons of the Golden West, the Native Daughters, and the Veterans of the Mexican War. Ex-Mayor James D. Phelan delivered a brief address of welcome and introduced Henry B. Russ, President of the Society of California Pioneers, who spoke briefly, as also did Gen. Stewart, President of the Society of Veterans of the Mexican War; H. R. McNoble, President of the Native Sons of the Golden West, and Miss Eliza R. Keith, in behalf of the Native Daughters.

Mr. Phelan then presented to the President a souvenir of the occasion, the work of a native sculptor, representing a bear hunt, reproduced in gold. In accepting the gift President Roosevelt responded to all of the addresses of welcome. His remarks were punctuated by laughter and applause, and at the close he was escorted to his carriage by a joint committee of the assembled orders. The Presidential party then proceeded to Van Ness Avenue, where thousands of school children had assembled. The pupils of the many schools carried banners beautifully worked in silks and other fine fabrics. Others were headed by drummer boys.

Every child had a flag, which was waved as the President passed. An incident of the ride was the presentation to the President of a photograph by a little Chinese girl, who was lifted up so that he could shake her hand.

After the review of the children, the President drove through the Presidio and had a glance at the buildings, the barracks of the different troops, and the new fortifications which stand at the entrance to the harbor and command the bay. He continued the drive along the new road, and finally reached the golf links, on which the military review was held. Gen. MacArthur was in command. Infantry, cavalry, and artillery were represented.

The President complimented Gen. MacArthur and other high officers on the excellent showing of the men and the splendid appearance of the garrison.

The Presidential party was then escorted through Golden Gate Park to the Cliff House, where luncheon was had with members of the Executive Committee, Gov. Pardee, Admiral Bickford, and other invited guests. The return was through the park. The party halted at the Baker Street entrance, where a large crowd was in waiting to watch the President turn his shovelful of earth for the McKinley monument.

Many representatives of the Spanish-American war veterans, the Grand Army, and the Pioneers were in attendance, and they were referred to in eulogistic terms by the President in his remarks.

The ceremonies were opened by Chairman A. A. Watkins, who presented to Mr. Roosevelt a souvenir shovel, made from the material of which the monument will be built. President Roosevelt said that it was appropriate that the first shovel should be turned in the presence of the old comrades of President McKinley in the time of 1861-65. He then continued:

"It is not too much to say that no man since Lincoln was as widely, universally loved in this country as was President McKinley, for it was given to him not only to rise to the most exalted station, but to typify in his character and conduct those virtues which every American citizen worthy of the name likes to regard as typically American; to typify the virtues of clean and upright living in all relations, private and public, as in the most intimate family relations, in the relations of business, in the relations with his neighbors, and, finally, in his conduct of the great affairs of State.

"And exactly as it was given to him to do his part in settling aright the greatest problem which it has ever befallen this Nation to settle since it became a Nation, the problem of the preservation of the Union and the abolition of slavery, exactly as it was his good fortune to do his part, as a man should in his youth, in settling that great problem, so it was his good fortune, when he became in fact and in name the Nation's chief, to settle the problems springing out of the Spanish war, problems less important only than those which were dealt with by the men who, under the lead of Washington, founded our Government, and the men who, upholding the statesmanship of Lincoln and following the sword of Grant, or Sherman, or Thomas, or Sheridan, saved and perpetuated the Republic.

"When in 1898 the war, which President McKinley in all honesty and in all sincerity sought to avoid, became inevitable and was pressed upon him, he met it as he and you met the crisis of 1861. He did his best to prevent the war coming. Once it became evident it had to come, he did his best to see that it was ended as quickly and as thoroughly as possible.

"It is a good lesson for nations and individuals to learn, never to hit if it can be helped, but never to hit soft, and I think that it is getting to be fairly well understood that is our foreign policy. We do not want to threaten; certainly we do not desire to wrong any man. We are going to keep out of trouble if we possibly can, but if it becomes necessary for our honor and our interest to assert a given position, we shall assert it with every intention of making the assertion good.

"In our country there is not a soldier that is not a volunteer soldier. Every officers, every enlisted man in the navy or army, is there because he volunteered to go in, and as I looked at the faces of the officers and the men under Gen. MacArthur and Admiral Glass I felt proud as Commander in Chief that they formed our navy and army, and prouder as an American citizen to see such American citizens wearing the uniform of Uncle Sam."

On behalf of soldiers of the Spanish war, Mr. King, who was a Rough Rider, presented to the President a beautiful canteen and Mr. Roosevelt made a happy response.

From the park the President was taken directly to the Palace Hotel, where he rested until evening.

May 14, 1903

PANAMA ISSUE MADE

Merely a Question of Canal or No Canal, Says the President.

Message Regarded as a Strong Statement of Administration's Position —Morgan Attacks It.

Special to The New York Times.

WASHINGTON, Jan. 4.—The message sent to Congress to-day by President Roosevelt, dealing with the Panama Canal treaty and the attitude of the Administration with regard to the revolution in Panama, was awaited with an eagerness and studied with a thoroughness seldom accorded to a Presidential utterance. Practically the entire day was devoted by the Senate to its consideration.

Following the reading of the document, the Senate indulged in an animated discussion of the message. The longest speech was delivered by Senator Morgan of Alabama, who made a violent attack upon the President's course, declaring that he believed it to be "such as to threaten the integrity of the United States," and asserting that he, for one, would not vote to ratify the wrong done by the President, who, he added, "desires this ratification to justify what he and the Panama Junta have done." Senators Stewart of Nevada and McComas of Maryland spoke in support of the Administration's course.

President Roosevelt's message conveyed additional information about the Panama revolution, and urged the ratification of the canal treaty. In plain language the President announces that whether or not the treaty is ratified Panama will not be restored to Colombia. Panama is recognized and the question of its recognition, the President declares, is not before this Government.

"The question, and the only question," says the President, "is whether or not we shall build an Isthmian canal."

It is the general belief that the President's way of putting the issue, as purely that of the Isthmian canal and not at all of the recognition of Panama, will have a decided effect on the Southern Senators. Their constituents want the canal, and the President's definition of the issue, it is thought, will make it harder than ever for them to oppose it.

A good many of the communications included in the message are apparently made public to refute arguments made against the Administration's attitude. For instance, the fact has frequently been dwelt upon that Acting Secretary Loomis notified the Consular officers on the Isthmus some hours before the revolution broke out that an uprising was reported. This has been taken to show that the Administration was in the secret. The President says that Mr. Loomis sent the telegram because an Associated Press bulletin had been shown him which stated that an outbreak had occurred.

EFFECT OF THE MESSAGE.

The effect of the message, as far as the sentiment of the majority and minority Senators could be gleaned, has been to frame and define sharply the issue in the Senate as to the ratification of the treaty and the building of the canal. Many Democratic Senators think that the minority has gone about far enough in resisting the treaty, as in the end most of the Southern Senators will have to vote for it in obedience to the wishes of their constituencies.

By some it was plainly intimated that the President had [illegible] the minority in two and separated Mr. Gorman from his recent following. The Republican Senators say unequivocally that the President has won the fight, and that there will be no difficulty now in securing the ratification of the treaty.

Senator McComas began a discussion of the Isthmian situation, characterizing the President's message as a "clearly cogent and abundantly convincing presentation of the situation."

Mr. Morgan interrupted with a question to bring out the point, as he held, that the recognition of the new republic was simply "de facto." Mr. McComas held otherwise, maintaining that the recognition was "official" and would be held so by the courts.

Mr. Culberson questioned the right of the Executive to make such recognition, but Mr. McComas maintained positively that the Executive had such authority, and he could bring to the attention of the Senate two instances in which the same power had been exercised.

"But I want to know," broke in Mr. Tillman, "whether the Senator contends that the Executive, without instruction of the Congress, can employ the army and navy to defend his executive action by warning away and preventing Colombia from asserting her supremacy, anywhere except on the Panama Railroad?"

Mr. McComas replied that the Executive not only had the right, but the exclusive right to take such action. Mr. Bacon of Georgia inquired how long the new republic would last should the sustaining power of the United States be withdrawn.

"For many years," replied Mr. McComas. He added that but for the restraining power of the United States the independence of Panama would have been established long ago.

"Will the Senator state the respective populations of Panama and Colombia?" asked Mr. Bacon.

"Panama has about 300,000 and Colombia 4,500,000," was the reply.

"And the Senator thinks the 300,000 could maintain themselves against the four and a half millions," again interjected Mr. Bacon.

Such things were frequent events in history, was the reply, and Mr. McComas mentioned the successful contest of Japan with 35,000,000 against China with 400,000,000. Mr. McComas, addressing himself to the Democratic side of the chamber, declared that some excellent men have made a political blunder and have mistaken their partisanship for a moral sense. He would not say, he added, this opposition was unpatriotic, but it was perversely and persistently wrong. The President's Panama canal record, he said, would elect him in November and result in the construction of the canal.

Mr. Stewart followed with an indorsement of the Administration on the Panama question, although, he said, he had formerly been in favor of the Nicaragua route. He declared that the object of Colombia was to delay matters until the expiration of the French canal concession and then charge the United States $10,000,000 for the concession.

SENATOR STEWART'S ATTITUDE.

"It is time," he added, "we should begin to treat them according to their true characters, as highway robbers, levying blackmail on the nations of the world. We have got the right of way now for the canal. The people want the canal, and," turning to the Democratic side of the chamber, "you had better get on to the band wagon because it is moving. The people don't care anything about that little band of robbers at Bogota, and we are going to build the canal, and I am going to try to live until the canal is constructed."

Senator Morgan then took the floor. He declared that the message of the President seemed to be an argument against the resolutions and remarks of the senior Senator from Massachusetts, (Mr. Hoar,) and of remarks of Senators on this side of the chamber. He added that he might yield in his judgment that no ship could ever pass through the Isthmus of Panama, but he could not assist in the breaking down of our fixed policy of neutrality between belligerents or in enlarging the diplomatic powers of the President by construction until they reached the whole stage of usurpation on the part of the Executive.

Mr. Morgan said that his colleagues from the South could not fail to see that the President's attitude was intended to force them to vote for the Panama route. As for himself, he was not opposing the President on slight ground, but because he believed the course of the President to be such as to "threaten the integrity of the United States."

Senator Morgan declared that, instead of the uprising being that as of one man, as declared by the President, it had been an uprising of eight men, who for months had been in conspiracy against the real people of Panama. He declared that President Roosevelt's interference in Colombia's affairs on the Isthmus was unjustified by the Constitution, and asserted that if there was to be a general policy on the part of the United States of upholding civilization, that policy must be undertaken by Congress, and "not left to blazen the lance of some individual American Sancho Panza, to be thrust into the bosom of a friendly power."

For one he would not vote to ratify the wrong done by the President, who, he added, "desires this ratification to justify what he and the Panama junta have done. And for that purpose," added Mr. Morgan, "he wants the assistance of three Democratic Senators to do what he and his party cannot do."

The speaker again referred to President McKinley's attitude toward the canal routes, and declared that "Nicaragua has a better friend in the grave of William McKinley than Panama has in the present head of the American Army and Navy," adding: "If there are Democrats who think that the best way to defeat the Republicans is to follow their lead, I must still remain an obstinate man of one idea and stand by that rather than be led or driven into commercial practices in politics or into political gambling with the laws, as pawns on the chessboard, to be moved back and forth at the will of the player with the use of the army and navy, in unlawful war, to give spectacular effect to the leader of a campaign for the Presidency."

January 5, 1904

DOMINGAN TREATY RADICALLY MODIFIED

Senate Committee Changes Many Important Provisions.

SOME TALK OF ANNEXATION

Amendment to be Offered in the Senate with This End in View—Text of President's Message.

WASHINGTON, March 8.—The wording of the Santo Domingo treaty was materially modified by the Senate Committee on Foreign Relations to-day, some of its most important provisions being entirely changed. It was agreed to take a vote on the treaty at 11:30 o'clock to-morrow morning to determine whether the report will be in favor of ratification or rejection. The belief is that it will be favorable.

The probability of the treaty being brought up in the future as a precedent was discussed freely, and it was predicted that the procedure was a forerunner of what may be expected to take place in regard to Venezuela.

It was declared, too, that this Government may have to take over the Santo Domingo country as territory of the United States. In that connection an amendment will be offered in the Senate striking out that part of the preamble whereby the United States agrees to respect the complete integrity of the Domingan Republic.

All the amendments adopted by the committee are with a general aim of making the question covered stand alone. For instance, one of the first amendments strikes out that portion of the second paragraph of the preamble which has been construed as a definition and application of the Monroe doctrine to the Santo Domingo case.

Other important amendments are as follows:

That part of the preamble which declares that the Domingan Government is in "imminent peril and urgent menace of intervention on the part of nations whose citizens have claims" is stricken out, and the preamble left to read that the proceeding is on the ground of having debts "which burden the republic."

In the first article, which describes the character of the claims this Government proposes to adjust, an amendment was adopted to include obligations "liquidated and agreed upon." This amendment is for the purpose of giving the present treaty application to the adjustments of the claims of the Santo Domingo Improvement Company.

A clause placing the employes of the United States who will be charged with carrying out the provisions of the treaty under the Dominican Government was amended so as to declare that such employes shall not be subject to the civil and criminal jurisdiction of that republic.

The article which declared that the Government of the United States at the request of the Dominican Government shall grant the latter such other assistance as the former may deem proper was amended so as to permit the Government of the United States to grant this additional assistance if it desires, but it is not bound by treaty obligation to do so.

A new article was added which provides that whatever is done under the treaty shall be binding on succeeding Governments in the Dominican Republic.

THE PRESIDENT'S MESSAGE.

The Senate made public the text of the second message of President Roosevelt on the Santo Domingo treaty. It reads:

"To the Senate:

"I wish to call the attention of the Senate at this executive session to the treaty with Santo Domingo. I feel that I ought to state to the Senate that the condition of affairs in Santo Domingo is such that it is very much for the interest of that republic that action on the treaty should be had at as early a moment as the Senate, after giving the matter full consideration, may find practicable.

"I call attention to the following facts:

"First—This treaty was entered into at the earnest request of Santo Domingo itself, and is designed to afford Santo Domingo relief and assistance. Its primary benefit will be to Santo Domingo. It offers the method most likely to secure peace and to prevent war in the island.

"Second—The benefit to the United States will consist chiefly in the tendency under the treaty to secure stability, order, and prosperity in Santo Domingo, and the removal of the apprehension lest foreign powers make aggressions on Santo Domingo in the course of collecting claims due their citizens; for it is greatly to our interest that all the islands in the Caribbean Sea should enjoy peace and prosperity and feel good will toward this country. The benefit to honest creditors will come from the fact that for the first time under this treaty a practicable method of attempting to settle the debts due them will be inaugurated.

"3. Many of the debts alleged to be due from Santo Domingo to outside creditors unquestionably on their face represent far more money than ever was actually given Santo Domingo. The proposed treaty provides for a process by which impartial experts will determine what debts are valid and what are in whole or in part invalid, and will apportion accordingly the surplus revenue available for the payment of the debts. This treaty offers the only method for preventing the collection of fraudulent debts, whether owed to Americans or to citizens of other nations.

IN INTEREST OF AMERICANS.

"4. This treaty affords the most practicable means of obtaining payment for the just claims of American citizens.

"5. If the treaty is ratified creditors belonging to other nations will have exactly as good treatment as creditors who are citizens of the United States and at the same time Santo Domingo will be protected against unjust and exorbitant claims. If it is not ratified, the chances are that American creditors will fare ill as compared with those of other nations; for foreign nations being denied the opportunity to get what is rightfully due their citizens under the proposed arrangement will be left to collect the debts due their citizens as they see fit, provided, of course, there is no permanent occupancy of Dominican territory. As in such case the United States will have nothing to say as to what debts should or should not be collected and Santo Domingo will be left without aid, assistance, or protection, it is impossible to state that the sums collected from it will not be improper in amount. In such event whatever is collected by means of forcible intervention will be applied to the creditors of foreign nations in preference to creditors who are citizens of the United States.

"6. The correspondence between the Secretary of State and the Minister of Haiti, submitted to the Senate several days ago, shows that our position is explicitly and unreservedly that under no circumstances do we intend to acquire territory in or possession of either Haiti or Santo Domingo, it being stated in these letters that even if the two republics desired to become a part of the United States, the United States would certainly refuse its assent.

"7. Santo Domingo grievously needs the aid of a powerful and friendly nation. This aid we are able, and I trust that we are willing to bestow. She has asked for this aid and the expressions of friendship repeatedly sanctioned by the people and the Government of the United States warrant herein believing that it will not be withheld in the hour of her need.

"THEODORE ROOSEVELT.

"The White House, March 6, 1905."

March 9, 1905

FLEET GOING TO JAPAN AT MIKADO'S WISH

Invitation Through Ambassador Takahira Accepted by the Cabinet.

MAY ALSO VISIT CHINA

Return to New York Delayed Until After the Close of the Roosevelt Administration.

Special to The New York Times.

WASHINGTON, March 20.—The announcement was made to-day at the Navy Department that the President had accepted the friendly invitation from Japan to have the battleship fleet visit Japanese waters on its way around the world.

The invitation was delivered to the Secretary of State by Ambassador Takahira yesterday.

The Japanese note follows:

Japanese Embassy,
Washington, March 18, 1908.

Sir: Under instruction from his Majesty's Minister for Foreign Affairs I have the honor to communicate to you that the Imperial Government, having learned of the contemplated cruise of the United States battleship fleet from San Francisco to the Philippine Islands, are sincerely anxious to be afforded an opportunity to cordially welcome that magnificent fleet and to give an enthusiastic expression to the sentiment of friendship and admiration invariably entertained by the people of Japan towards the people of the United States.

I am further instructed to inform you that the Imperial Government is firmly convinced of the reassuring effect which the visit of the American fleet to the shores of Japan will produce upon the traditional relations of good understanding and mutual sympathy which so happily exists between the two Nations, and to express to you the hope of the Imperial Government that the fleet may be instructed to call at the principal ports of Japan in its extended cruise in the Pacific.

Accept, Sir, the renewed assurance of my highest consideration.

K. TAKAHIRA.

Hon. Elihu Root, Secretary of State.

It was the subject of considerable discussion at the Cabinet meeting this morning, and the decision was in favor of acceptance.

Decided satisfaction at the receipt and acceptance of the invitation is evident in Administration circles. The visit to Japan is regarded generally as certain to "cement friendship," to use a term of diplomatic formality. And there is no question of the desirability, from the point of view of this Government, of showing to Japan an American fleet of that size and strength.

In the language of Secretary Taft, in his Concord speech, it is sometimes "necessary to fill the eye of the Oriental," and this visit of the fleet will accomplish that object.

It is recognized that there is a considerable element of risk attached to the visit. Members of the Cabinet who talked about it to-day declared their entire confidence in the ability and intention of the Japanese Government to control their people, and do not anticipate any trouble from that source. It will depend largely upon the discipline of the American bluejackets ashore whether there is any untoward development or not.

The Administration has confidence, however, in the ability of the fleet officers to maintain thorough discipline.

Ambassador Takahira was delighted with the success of his mission.

"We have not suggested the time of the visit nor the port or ports to be visited," he said. "We have been at a loss as to what action to take. We could not well invite the United States to send its fleet to us if there were no intention of the fleet being sent near us.

"The fact that we have asked for the fleet, even as Great Britain has done on behalf of Australia, and that our request has been so promptly granted, should be to quiet certain disturbing elements in Japan and the United States, and give other countries sufficient evidence that Japan and the United States are determined to maintain the sincere and friendly relations that have existed for so many years.

"You may rest assured," he said, "that the safety of the fleet and every man aboard it will be vouched for by the Japanese Government. There will be nothing to mar the exchange of courtesies."

The invitation of the Mikado has completely changed the plans of the fleet, as announced by Secretary Metcalf. It will delay the return of the vessels to New York, in all probability, until after the close of the Roosevelt administration.

It had been planned that the fleet was to leave San Francisco July 6, cruising by way of Honolulu, Samoa, Sydney, Melbourne, Manila, Colombo, Aden, the Suez Canal and Gibraltar before turning toward New York. The extension of the voyage to include visits to Japan will either necessitate an earlier departure from San Francisco or else the warships will be delayed in the arrival at New York until the middle or latter part of next March.

It is more than likely now that an invitation will be received from China for the fleet to visit some of the Chinese ports, and Great Britain will also extend an invitation for the fleet to stop in Hong Kong Roads. In case either or both invitations are received they probably will be accepted as promptly as that from Japan.

March 21, 1908

NO CONQUEST, WILSON'S PLEDGE

This Country Never "to Seek One Additional Foot of Territory" by Force.

MORALITY, NOT EXPEDIENCY

That Is Our Guide, Says the President, and Iniquity Must Not Be Condoned.

MEXICO NOT MENTIONED

But Congressman Hobson Interprets Speech as Meaning Intervention—Southerners Cheer Utterances.

Special to The New York Times.

MOBILE, Oct. 27.—"I want to take this occasion to say that the United States will never again seek one additional foot of territory by conquest," was the most striking sentence of the speech delivered here to-day by President Wilson, speaking before the Southern Commercial Congress and a great audience which included a score or more of Latin-American diplomats. Oscar W. Underwood and Josephus Daniels, respectively House leader of the Democratic Party and the Secretary of the Navy; Senators, Congressmen, and Governors of Southern States were among the other notables present.

Commenting upon this utterance of the President, Congressman Richmond Pearson Hobson said:

"I construe this to mean that we are going into Mexico, but that we will come out when order has been restored."

Senator John H. Bankhead, when asked for his opinion of the keynote feature of the speech, said:

"Everybody understands that the President is very much averse to any intervention in Mexico, such as would require the occupation of any Mexican territory. If the President should deem it necessary to send an armed force into Mexico for the purpose of restoring order and preserving life and property, he would doubtless withdraw the American forces as soon as order was restored. It is true, perhaps, that the Government of the United States would demand indemnity sufficient to pay the expenses of the expedition. That by no means implies the acquisition of territory.

"I have great confidence in the President's ability to handle the question without involving the country in a war with Mexico. I will leave it to him and the diplomatic agencies for the present, at least."

Tie of a Common Understanding.

In his address Mr. Wilson spoke of his interest in all things Southern.

"But to-day I do not need to speak of the South," he added. "She has perhaps acquired the gift of speaking for herself. I come because I want to speak of our present and prospective relations with our neighbors to the south. I deemed it a public duty, as well as a personal pleasure to be here to express for myself and for the Government I represent the welcome we all feel to those who represent the Latin-American States. The future, ladies and gentlemen, is going to be very different for this hemisphere from the past. The States lying to the south of us, which have always been our neighbors, will now be drawn closer to us by innumerable ties, and, I hope, chief of all by the tie of a common understanding of each other.

"Interest does not tie nations together. It sometimes separates them, but sympathy and understanding do unite them. And I believe that by the new route that is just about to be opened, while we physically cut two continents asunder, we spiritually unite them. It is a spiritual union which we seek. I wonder if you realize. I wonder if your imaginations have been filled with the significance of the tides of commerce?

"These great tides which have been running along parallels of latitude will now swing southward athwart parallels of latitude, and that opening gate at the Isthmus of Panama will open the world to a commerce that she has not known before—a commerce of intelligence, of thought and sympathy between north and south, and the Latin-American States which to their disadvantage have been off the main lines will now be on the main lines. I feel that these gentlemen honoring us with their presence to-day will presently find that some part at any rate of the centre of gravity of the world has shifted. Do you realize that New York, for example, will be nearer the western coast of South America than she is now to the eastern coast of South America?

"Concessions" vs. "Investments."

"There is one peculiarity about the history of the Latin-American States which I am sure they are keenly aware of. You hear of concessions to foreign capitalists in Latin America. You do not hear of concessions to foreign capitalists in the United States. They are not granted concessions. They are invited to make investments. The work is ours, though they are welcome to invest in it. We do not ask them to supply the capital and do the work. It is an invitation, not a privilege, and States that are obliged, because their territory does not lie within the main field of modern enterprise and action, to grant concessions, are in this condition, that foreign interests are apt to dominate their domestic affairs, a condition of affairs always dangerous and apt to become intolerable.

"What these States are going to seek, therefore, is an emancipation from the subordination which has been inevitable to foreign enterprise and an assertion of the splendid character which, in spite of these difficulties, they have again and again been able to demonstrate. The dignity, the courage, the self-possession, the respect of the Latin-American States, their achievements in the face of all these diverse circumstances, deserve nothing but the admiration and applause of the world. They have had harder bargains driven with them in the matter of loans than any other peoples in the world. Interest has been exacted of them that was not exacted of anybody else, because the risk was said to be greater, and then securities were taken that destroyed the risks. An admirable arrangement for those who were forcing the terms!

Emancipation of Latin-America.

"I rejoice in nothing so much as in the prospect that they will now be emancipated from these conditions, and we ought to be the first to take part in assisting in that emancipation. I think some of these gentlemen have already had occasion to bear witness that the Department of State in recent months has tried to serve them in that wise. In the future they will draw closer and closer to us because of circumstances of which I wish to speak with moderation and, I hope, without indiscretion.

"We must prove ourselves their friends and champions, upon terms of equality and honor. You cannot be friends upon any other terms than upon the terms of equality. You cannot be friends at all except upon the terms of honor, and we must show ourselves friends by comprehending their interest, whether it squares with our interest or not. It is a very perilous thing to determine the foreign policy of a nation in the terms of material interest. It not only is unfair to those with whom you are dealing, but it is degrading on the part of your own actions.

"Comprehension must be the soil in which shall grow all the fruits of friendship, because there is a reason and a compulsion lying behind all this which are dearer than anything else to the thoughtful men of America; I mean the development of constitutional liberty in the world. Human rights, national integrity, and opportunity, as against material interests—that, ladies and gentleman, is the issue which we now have to face.

No More Territory by Conquest.

"I want to take this occasion to say that the United States will never again seek one additional foot of territory by conquest. She will devote herself to showing that she knows how to make honorable and fruitful use of the territory she has. And she must regard it as one of the duties of friendship to see that from no quarter are material interests made superior to human liberty and national opportunity. I say this, not with a single thought that any one will gainsay it, but merely to fix in our consciousness what our real relationship with the rest of America is. It is the relationship of a family of mankind devoted to the development of true constitutional liberty. We know that that is the soil out of which the best enterprise springs. We know that this is a cause which we are making in common with them because we have had to make it for ourselves.

"Reference has been made here to-day to some of the national problems which confront us as a nation. What is the heart of all our national problems? It is that we have seen the hand of material interests sometimes about to close upon our dearest interests and possessions. We have seen material interests threaten constitutional freedom in America. Therefore, we will now know how to sympathize with those in America who have to contend with that, not only within their borders, but from outside their borders also. I know what the response of the thought and heart of America will be to a programme like that, because America was created to realize a programme like that.

"This is not America because it is rich. This is not America because it has set up for a great population great opportunities of material prosperity. America is a name which sounds in the ears of man everywhere as a synonym of individual opportunity, as a synonym of individual liberty. I would rather belong to a poor nation that was free than to a rich nation that had ceased to be in love with liberty. But we shall not be poor if we love liberty, because the nation that loves liberty truly sets every man free to do his best and be his best; and that means the release of all the splendid energies of a great people who think for themselves. A nation of employes cannot be free any more than a nation of employers can be.

"So, in empasizing the points which must unite us in sympathy and in spiritual interest with the Latin-American people we are only emphasizing the points of our own life, and we should prove ourselves untrue to our own traditions if we proved ourselves untrue friends to-day. Do not think, therefore, gentlemen, that questions of the day are mere questions of policy and diplomacy. They are shot through with the principles of life. We dare not turn from the principle that morality and not expediency is the thing that must guide us, and that we will never condone iniquity because it is most convenient to do so.

"So, it seems to me that this is a day of infinite hope, of confidence in a future greater than the past has been. For I am fain to believe that, in spite of all the things that we wish to correct, the nineteenth century that now lies behind us has brought us a long stage toward the time when, slowly ascending the tedious climb that leads to the final uplands, upon which we shall get the ultimate view of the beauties of mankind, we, nevertheless, have breathed a considerable part of that climb, and shall presently—it may be in a generation or two—come out upon those great heights where there shines, unobstructed, the light of the justice of God."

Secretary Daniels left the city at midnight, ordered back to Washington by the President. The seriousness of the situation in Mexico is said to be responsible for the Secretary's change of plans. Before leaving, the Secretary addressed the congress on the subject "The Panama Canal and the Navy."

Conceding the vast benefits that would accrue to commerce through the opening of the Canal, Secretary Daniels told the delegates that the event would not double the efficiency of the navy. He denied the assertions that the increased mobility of the fleets would add to that extent to the sea power of the United States. He acknowledged, however, that such mobility would render the navy much more efficient.

The so-called "Cabinet dinner" was not called off because of the absence of Secretary Daniels. It will be given tomorrow evening, the guests of honor being Senator Fletcher of Florida, President of the Southern Commercial Congress; Director Clarence J. Owens, and other distinguished visitors.

When asked about the situation in Mexico, Secretary Daniels said that the best efforts of the Administration were being directed to its peaceful settlement. Speaking in a general way he said: "One can never tell; war is a matter of psychology. Sometimes a spark may fan its flames."

Mr. Wilson spent six busy hours in Mobile. He arrived early in the morning, and was taken jointly in hand by the members of the Southern Commercial Congress and representatives of the city. He was entertained at breakfast, driven about the city by automobile, taken on a sightseeing expedition in the harbor, and started back to Washington with cheers ringing about his special train.

October 28, 1913

President Wilson Proclaims Our Strict Neutrality; Bars All Aid to Belligerents and Defines the Law

WASHINGTON, Aug. 4.—The proclamation of neutrality of the United States in the European war, issued today by President Wilson, is as follows:

BY THE PRESIDENT OF THE UNITED STATES OF AMERICA, A PROCLAMATION:

Whereas a state of war unhappily exists between Austria-Hungary and Servia and between Germany and Russia and between Germany and France;

And whereas the United States is on terms of friendship and amity with the contending powers, and with the persons inhabiting their several dominions;

And whereas there are citizens of the United States residing within the territories or dominions of each of the said belligerents and carrying on commerce, trade, or other business or pursuits therein;

And whereas there are subjects of each of the said belligerents residing within the territory or jurisdiction of the United States and carrying on commerce, trade, or other business or pursuits therein;

And whereas the laws and treaties of the United States, without interfering with the free expression of opinion and sympathy, or with the commercial manufacture or sale of arms or munitions of war, nevertheless impose upon all persons who may be within its territory and jurisdiction the duty of an impartial neutrality during the existence of the contest;

And whereas it is the duty of a neutral Government not to permit or suffer the making of its waters subservient to the purposes of war;

Now, therefore, I, Woodrow Wilson, President of the United States of America, in order to preserve the neutrality of the United States and of its citizens, and of persons within its territory and jurisdiction, and to enforce its laws and treaties, and in order that all persons, being warned of the general tenor of the laws and treaties of the United States in the behalf, and of the law of nations, may thus be prevented from any violation of the same, do hereby declare and proclaim that by certain provisions of the act approved on the 4th day of March, A. D., 1909, commonly known as the Penal Code of the United States, the following acts are forbidden to be done, under severe penalties, within the territory and jurisdiction of the United States, to wit:

"1—Accepting and exercising a commission to serve either of the said belligerents by land or by sea against the other belligerent.

"2—Enlisting or entering into the service of either of the said belligerents as a soldier, or as a marine, or seaman on board of any vessel of war, letter of marque, or privateer.

"3—Hiring or retaining another person to enlist or enter himself in the service of either of the said belligerents as a soldier, or as a marine, or seaman on board of any vessel of war, letter of marque, or privateer.

"4—Hiring another person to go beyond the limits or jurisdiction of the United States with intent to be enlisted as aforesaid.

"5—Hiring another person to go beyond the limits of the United States with intent to be entered into service as aforesaid.

"6—Retaining another person to go beyond the limits of the United States with intent to be enlisted as aforesaid.

"7—Retaining another person to go beyond the limits of the United States with intent to be entered into service as aforesaid. (But the said act is not to be construed to extend to a citizen or subject of either belligerent who, being transiently within the United States, shall, on board of any vessel of war, which at the time of its arrival within the United States was fitted and equipped as such vessel of war, enlist or enter himself or hire or retain another subject or citizen of the same belligerent, who is transiently within the United States, to enlist or enter himself to serve such belligerent on board such vessel of war, if the United States shall then be at peace with such belligerent.)

"8—Fitting out and arming, or attempting to fit out and arm, or procuring to be fitted out and armed, or knowingly being concerned in the furnishing, fitting out, or arming of any ship or vessel with intent that such ship or vessel shall be employed in the service of either of the said belligerents.

"9—Issuing or delivering a commission within the territory or jurisdiction of the United States for any ship or vessel to the intent that she may be employed as aforesaid.

"10—Increasing or augmenting, or procuring to be increased or augmented, or knowingly being concerned in increasing or augmenting the force of any ship of war, cruiser, or other armed vessel, which at the time of her arrival within the United States was a ship of war, cruiser, or armed vessel in the service of either of the said belligerents, or belonging to the subjects of either, by adding to the number of guns of such vessels, or by changing those on board of her for guns of a larger calibre, or by the addition thereto of any equipment solely applicable to war.

"11—Beginning or setting on foot or providing or preparing the means for any military expedition or enterprise to be carried on from the territory or jurisdiction of the United States against the territories or dominions of either of the said belligerents."

And I do hereby further declare and proclaim that any frequenting and use of the waters within the territorial jurisdiction of the United States by the armed vessels of a belligerent, whether public ships or privateers, for the purpose of preparing for hostile operations, or as posts of observation upon the ships of war or privateers or merchant vessels of a belligerent lying within or being about to enter the jurisdiction of the United States, must be regarded as unfriendly and offensive, and in violation of that neutrality which it is the determination of this Government to observe; and to the end that the hazard and inconvenience of such apprehended practices may be avoided, I further proclaim and declare that from and after the fifth day of August, instant, and during the continuance of the present hostilities between Austria-Hungary and Servia, and Germany and Russia, and Germany and France, no ship of war or privateer of any belligerent shall be permitted to make use of any port, harbor, roadstead, or waters subject to the jurisdiction of the United States from which a vessel from an opposing belligerent (whether the same shall be a ship of war, a privateer, or a merchant ship) shall have previously departed, until after the expiration of at least twenty-four hours from the departure of such last mentioned vessel beyond the jurisdiction of the United States.

If any ship of war or privateer or belligerent shall, after the time this notification takes effect, enter any port, harbor, roadstead or waters of the United States, such vessel shall be required to depart and to put to sea within twenty-four hours after her entrance into such port, harbor, roadstead, or waters, except in case of stress of weather or of her requiring provisions or things necessary for the subsistence of her crew, or for repairs; in any of which cases the authorities of the port or nearest port (as the case may be) shall require her to put to sea as soon as possible after the expiration of such period of twenty-four hours, without permitting her to take in supplies beyond what may be necessary for her immediate use, and no such vessel which may have been permitted to remain within the waters of the United States for the purpose of repair shall continue within such port, harbor, roadstead, or waters for a longer period than twenty-four hours after her necessary repairs shall have been completed, unless within such twenty-four hours a vessel, whether ship of war, privateer, or merchant ship of an opposing belligerent, shall have departed therefrom, in which case the time limited for the departure of such ship of war or privateer shall be extended so far as may be necessary to secure an interval of not less than twenty-four hours between such departure and that of any ship of war, privateer, or merchant ship of an opposing belligerent which may have previously quit the same port, harbor, roadstead, or waters.

No ship of war or privateer of a belligerent shall be detained in any port, harbor, roadstead, or waters of the United States more than twenty-four hours by reason of the successive departures from such port, harbor, roadstead, or waters of more than one vessel of an opposing belligerent. But if there be several vessels of opposing belligerents in the same port, harbor, roadstead, or waters, the order of their departure therefrom shall be so arranged as to afford the opportunity of leaving alternately to the vessels of the opposing belligerents, and to cause the least detention consistent with the objects of this proclamation.

No ship of war or privateer of a belligerent shall be permitted, while in any port, harbor, roadstead, or waters within the jurisdiction of the United States, to take in any supplies except provisions and such other things as may be requisite for the subsistence of her crew, and except so much coal only as may be sufficient to carry such vessel, if without any sail power, to the nearest port of her own country, or, in case the vessel is rigged to go under sail and may also be propelled by steam power, then with half the quantity of coal which she would be entitled to receive if dependent upon steam alone, and no coal shall be again supplied to any such ship of war or privateer in the same or any other port, harbor, roadstead, or waters of the United States, without special permission, until after the expiration of three months from the time when such coal may have been last supplied to her within the waters of the United States, unless such ship of war or privateer shall, since last thus supplied, have entered a port of the Government to which she belongs.

And I do further declare and proclaim that the statutes and the treaties of the United States and the law of nations alike require that no person within the territory and jurisdiction of the United States shall take part, directly or indirectly, in the said wars, but shall remain at peace with all the said belligerents, and shall maintain a strict and impartial neutrality.

And I do hereby enjoin all citizens of the United States, and all persons residing or being within the territory or jurisdiction of the United States, to observe the laws thereof, and to commit no act contrary to the provisions of the said statutes or treaties or in violation of the law of nations in that behalf.

And I do hereby warn all citizens of the United States, and all persons residing or being within its territory or jurisdiction, that, while the free and full expression of sympathies in public and private is not restricted by the laws of the United States, military forces in aid of a belligerent cannot lawfully be originated or organized within its jurisdiction, and that, while all persons may lawfully and without restriction by reason of the aforesaid state of war manufacture and sell within the United States arms and munitions of war, and other articles ordinarily known as contraband of war, yet they cannot carry such articles upon the high seas for the use or services of a belligerent, nor can they transport soldiers and officers of a belligerent, or attempt to break any blockade which may be lawfully established and maintained during the said wars without incurring the risk of hostile capture and the penalties denounced by the law of nations in that behalf.

And I do hereby give notice that all citizens of the United States, and others who may claim the protection of this Government, who may misconduct themselves in the premises will do so at their peril, and that they can in no wise obtain any protection from the Government of the United States against the consequences of their misconduct.

In witness whereof I have hereunto set my hand and caused the seal of the United States to be affixed.

Done at the City of Washington this fourth day of August, in the year of our Lord one thousand nine hundred and fourteen, and of the Independence of the United States of America the one hundred and thirty-eighth.

WOODROW WILSON.

August 5, 1914

'AMERICA FIRST,' WILSON'S SLOGAN

World Crisis Coming and We Are the Mediating Nation, He Tells Associated Press.

URGES STRICT NEUTRALITY

Not for Selfish Reasons, but to Qualify for Great Tasks Ahead.

NOYES ON UNBIASED NEWS

Explains Non-Partisan Standard of the Association—Publishers' Body Meets Today.

Strict neutrality, extreme caution in the publication of unconfirmed news, and "America first" were the keynotes of a speech by President Wilson that aroused great enthusiasm among newspaper editors and publishers from all parts of the country at the luncheon of The Associated Press at the Waldorf-Astoria yesterday.

Each telling point the President made in his speech, every word of which he seemed to weigh before uttering, was applauded by the audience of more than 300 at the tables and by a gallery of about 100 men and women.

The importance attached to his clear statement of the neutrality policy of his Administration was reflected in a request made by Melville E. Stone, Secretary and General Manager of The Associated Press, just before the Chief Magistrate was introduced, that all newspaper reports of the President's speech be based on the verbatim copy to be taken by a stenographer and supplied to all of the newspapers and news-gathering associations represented.

Frank B. Noyes of The Washington Star, President of The Associated Press, praised President Wilson's masterful maintaining of true neutrality, and said that the President had borne his great responsibility nobly. The applause that the laudatory remarks received would have done justice to a Democratic Nominating Convention. All arose and drank a toast to the President, and arose again when the orchestra struck up "The Star-Spangled Banner," and again when the President stood up to speak.

Function of The Associated Press.

In introducing President Wilson, the guest of honor, Mr. Noyes made brief reference to the scope of The Associated Press, saying he believed that it was "the greatest co-operative-non-profit making organization in the world." Its function, he said, was to furnish its members a service of world news untainted and without bias of any sort.

"To insure this," he said, "we have formed an organization that is owned and controlled by its members, and by them alone; one that is our servant and not our master. So we are here today, Democrats and Republicans; Protestants, Catholics, and Jews; Conservatives and Radicals, Wets and Drys; differing on every subject on which men differ, but all at one in demanding that, so far as is humanly possible, no trace of partisanship and no hint of propaganda shall be found in our news reports.

"Because of its traditions and its code, and perhaps also because of the never-ceasing watchfulness of 900 members, it has come to pass that few people on earth are capable of giving the management of The Associated Press any points on maintaining a strict, though benevolent, neutrality on all questions on which we can be neutral and still be what we are—loyal Americans. We know, too—none better—that the genuine neutral, the honest neutral, is always the target of every partisan, and we find some solace that this fact is now being demonstrated to the world at large.

"Today, however, we willingly lower our crest to one who has demonstrated in these agonizing times his mastership of the principles of true neutrality, and who, fully realizing the dreadful consequences of any departure from these principles, has nobly borne his terrible burden of responsibility in guarding the peace, the welfare, and the dignity of our common country.

"Our distinguished guest, who so honors us today, may surely know that in the perplexities and trials of these days, so black for humanity, he has our thorough, loyal, and affectionate support.

"God grant him success in his high aims for the peaceful progress of the people of the United States."

After the toast and cheers and hand-clapping, the Grand Ballroom became silent as the President began speaking.

THE PRESIDENT'S ADDRESS.

I am deeply gratified by the generous reception you have accorded me. It makes me look back with a touch of regret to former occasions when I have stood in this place and enjoyed a greater liberty than is granted to me today. There have been times when I stood in this spot and said what I really thought, and I pray God that those days of indulgence may be accorded me again. But I have come here today, of course, somewhat restrained by a sense of responsibility that I cannot escape. For I take The Associated Press very seriously. I know the enormous part that you play in the affairs, not only of our country, but of the world. You deal in the raw material of opinion, and, if my convictions have any validity, opinion ultimately governs the world.

It is, therefore, of very serious things that I think as I face this body of men. I do not think of you, however, as members of The Associated Press. I do not think of you as men of different parties or of different racial derivations, or of different religious denominations. I want to talk to you as to my fellow-citizens of the United States. For there are serious things, which as fellow-citizens we ought to consider. The times behind us, gentlemen, have been difficult, because whatever may be said about the present condition of the world's affairs, it is clear that they are drawing rapidly to a climax, and at the climax the test will come, not only of the nations engaged in the present colossal struggle—it will come for them, of course—but the test will come to us particularly.

Do you realize that, roughly speaking, we are the only great nation at present disengaged? I am not speaking, of course, with disparagement of the greater of those nations in Europe which are not parties to the present war, but I am thinking how their lives much more than ours touch the very heart and stuff of the business, whereas, we have rolling between us and those bitter days across the water 3,000 miles of cool and silent ocean. Our atmosphere is not yet charged with those disturbing elements which must be felt and must permeate very nation of Europe. Therefore, is it not likely that the nations of the world will some day turn to us for the cooler assessment of the elements engaged? I am not now thinking so preposterous a thought as that we should sit in judgment upon them.

Mediating Nation of the World.

No nation is fit to sit in judgment upon any other nation, but we shall some day have to assist in reconstructing the processes of peace. Our resources are untouched; we are more and more becoming by the force of circumstances the mediating nation of the world in respect of its finances. We must make up our minds what are the best things to do and what are the best ways to do them. We must put our money, our energy, our enthusiasm, our sympathy into these things, and we must have our judgments prepared and our spirit chastened against the coming of that day. So that I am not speaking in a selfish spirit when I say that our whole duty for the present, at any rate, is summed up in this motto "America first." Let us think of America before we think of Europe, in order that America may be fit to be Europe's friend when the day of tested friendship comes. The test of friendship is not now sympathy with the one side or the other, but getting ready to help both sides when the struggle is over.

The basis of neutrality, gentlemen, is not indifference; it is not self-interest. The basis of neutrality is sympathy for mankind. It is fairness, it is good will at bottom. It is impartiality of spirit and judgment. I wish that all of our fellow-citizens could realize that. There is in some quarters a disposition to create distempers in this body politic. Men are even uttering slanders against the United States, as if to excite her. Men are saying that if we should go to war upon either side there will be a divided America—an abominable libel of ignorance. America is not all of it vocal just now. It is vocal in spots. But I, for one, have a complete and abiding faith in that great silent body of Americans who are not standing up and shouting and expressing their opinions just now, but are waiting to find out and support the duty of America. I am just as sure of their solidity and of their loyalty and of their unanimity as I am that the history of this country has at every crisis and turning point illustrated this great lesson.

We are the mediating nation of the world. I do not mean that we undertake not to mind our own business and to mediate where other people are quarreling. I mean the word in a broader sense. We are compounded of the nations of the world. We mediate their blood, we mediate their traditions, we mediate their sentiments, their tastes, their passions; we are ourselves compounded of those things. We are, therefore, able to understand all nations; we are able to understand them in the compound, not separately as partisans, but unitedly, as knowing and comprehending and embodying them all. It is in that sense that I mean that America is a mediating nation. The opinion of America, the action of America, is ready to turn and free to turn in any direction.

No Racial Momentum.

Did you ever reflect upon how almost all other nations, almost every other nation, has through long centuries been headed in one direction? That is not true of the United States. The United States has no racial momentum. It has no history back of it which makes it run all its energies and all its ambitions in one particular direction; and America is particularly free in this, that she has no hampering ambitions as a world power. If we have been obliged by circumstances, or have considered ourselves to be obliged by circumstances, in the past to take territory which we otherwise would not have thought of taking, I believe I am right in saying that we have considered it our duty to administer that territory, not for ourselves, but for the people living in it, and to put this burden upon our consciences, not to think that this thing is ours for our use, but to regard ourselves as trustees of the great business for those to whom it does really belong, trustees ready to hand it over to the cestui que trust at any time, when the business seems to make that possible and feasible.

That is what I mean by saying we have no hampering ambitions. We do not want anything that does not belong to us. Isn't a nation in that position free to serve other nations, and isn't a nation like that ready to form some part of the assessing opinion of the world?

My interest in the neutrality of the United States is not the petty desire to keep out of trouble. I have never looked for it, but I have always found it. I do not want to walk around trouble. If any man wants a scrap that is an interesting scrap and worth while, I am his man. I warn him that he is not going to draw me into the scrap for his advertisement, but if he is looking for trouble that is the trouble of men in general and I can help a little, why then, I am in for it.

Self-Control and Self-Mastery.

But I am interested in neutrality because there is something so much greater to do than fight, because there is something, there is a distinction waiting for this nation that no nation has ever yet got. That is the distinction of absolute self-control and self-mastery. Whom do you admire most among your friends? The irritable man? The man out of whom you can get a 'rise' without trying? The man who will fight at the drop of the hat, whether he knows what the hat is dropped for or not?

Don't you admire and don't you fear if you have to contest with him, the self-mastered man who watches you with calm eye and comes in only when you have carried the thing so far that you must be disposed of? That is the man you respect. That is the man who you know has at bottom a much more fundamental and terrible courage than the irritable, fighting man.

Now, I covet for America this splendid courage of reserve moral force, and I wanted to point out to you gentlemen simply this: There is news and news. There is what is called news from Turtle Bay that turns out to be falsehood, at any rate in what it is said to signify, and which, if you could get the nation to believe it true, might disturb our equilibrium and our self-possession. We ought not to deal in stuff of that kind. We ought not to permit things of that sort to use up the electrical energy of the wires, because its energy is malign, its energy is not of the truth, its energy is of mischief. It is possible to sift truth.

I have known something to go out on the wires as true when there was only one man or one group of men who could have told the originators of the report whether it was true or not, and they were not asked whether it was true or not, for fear it might not be true. That sort of report ought not to go over the wires.

There is generally, if not always, somebody who knows whether that thing is so or not, and in these days, above all other days, we ought to take particular pains to resort to the one small group of men or to the one man, if there be but one, who knows whether those things are true or not.

News as Food of Opinion.

The world ought to know the truth, but the world ought not at this period of unstable equilibrium to be disturbed by rumor, ought not to be disturbed by imaginative combinations of circumstances, or, rather, by circumstances stated in combination which do not belong in combination. For we are holding—not I, but you and gentlemen engaged like you—the balances in your hand. This unstable equilibrium rests upon scales that are in your hands. For the food of opinion, as I began by saying, is the news of the day. I have known many a man to go off at a tangent on information that was not reliable. Indeed, that describes the majority of men. The world is held stable by the man who waits for the next day to find out whether the report was true or not.

We cannot afford, therefore, to let the rumors of irresponsible persons and origins get into the atmosphere of the United States. We are trustees for what, I venture to say, is the greatest heritage that any nation ever had, the love of justice and righteousness and human liberty. For, fundamentally, those are the things to which America is addicted, and to which she is devoted. There are groups of selfish men in the United States, there are coteries, where sinister things are proposed, but the great heart of the American people is just as sound and true as it ever was. And it is a single heart; it is a heart of America. It is not a heart made up of sections selected out of countries.

So that what I try to remind myself of every day when I am almost overcome by perplexities, what I try to remember, is what the people at home are thinking about. I try to put myself in the place of the man who does not know all the things that I know, and ask myself what he would like the policy of this country to be. Not the talkative man, not the partisan man, not the man that remembers first that he is a Republican or Democrat, or that his parents are Germans or English, but who remembers first that the whole destiny of modern affairs centres largely upon his being an American first of all.

If I permitted myself to be a partisan in this present struggle I would be unworthy to represent you. If I permitted myself to forget the people who are not partisans I would be unworthy to represent you. I am not saying that I am worthy to represent you, but I do claim this degree of worthiness, that, before everything else, I love America.

President Holds Reception.

President Wilson held an informal reception for the members of the organization and the guests in the gallery, after concluding his speech. He stood at the door to the ballroom and, as the persons passed out, shook the hand of each. Many of the newspaper men he knew personally, and he chatted with them briefly as they went by. Many kept the line waiting a few seconds to congratulate him on his address.

With Secretary of the Navy Josephus Daniels, who had been at home among the newspaper editors at the guest table, and Secretary Tumulty, the President took a short automobile trip up Fifth Avenue and Riverside Drive to Grant's Tomb after leaving the Waldorf, and returned to Pennsylvania Station in time to board his special car, "Superb," attached to the Sunset Limited, at 4:35 o'clock. Before the train pulled out he chatted for a few minutes with Collector Malone, who had been one of the luncheon guests and had gone to the station to see the President off.

When President Wilson reached New York at 1:09 P. M., three minutes behind train schedule, there was a crowd at the station to see him. As he left for the hotel two mounted policemen preceded his automobile, in which he was accompanied by Mr. Tumulty, Secretary Daniels, and Dr. Cary Grayson, his private physician and aid. An automobile containing secret service agents and detectives accompanied the President's car. He doffed his hat to the cheering groups along the sidewalks at the station and the hotel, and held a short conference with Mr. Stone and the Board of Directors in a private drawing room before entering the ballroom.

At his right, when the President was seated at the guest table, was Mr. Stone. Mr. Noyes was at his left. Others at the table were Secretary Daniels, Mr. Tumulty, Dr. Grayson, L. B. Palmer of the American Newspaper Publishers' Association, which will hold the opening session of its annual convention at the Waldorf this morning; W. Y. Morgan of The Hutchinson News, Colonel Charles A. Rook of The Pittsburg Dispatch, W. H. Cowles of The Spokane Spokesman-Review; W. L. McLean of The Philadelphia Bulletin; Charles W. Knapp of The St. Louis Republic; Adolph S. Ochs of THE NEW YORK TIMES; Clark Howell of The Atlanta Constitution; Daniel D. Moore of The New Orleans Times-Picayune; F. W. Lehmann of St. Louis; H. L. Bridgman of The Brooklyn Standard-Union; C. H. Clark of The Hartford Courant; Victor F. Lawson of The Chicago Daily News; General Charles H. Taylor of The Boston Globe, M. H. de Young of The San Francisco Chronicle, R. M. Johnston of The Houston Post, and A. C. Weiss of The Duluth Herald.

Vote on Proposed Amendment.

As it was impossible to complete the business of the annual meeting at the morning session, another session was held in the afternoon. This ended after a vote had been taken on a proposed amendment to the by-laws which would alter the hours during which morning and evening newspapers might publish Associated Press news, and a meeting will be held this morning, at which the result of the vote will be announced.

One of the features of the day's business was the striking out of Section 7, Article VIII. of The Associated Press by-laws, abrogating the authority of the Board of Directors to forbid members to purchase news from any other association. This was the only feature to which the United States Attorney General objected when he recently examined the methods by which the organization was conducted. The section was never enforced in any instance by the Directors. The Board of Directors struck out the section at its meeting on Dec. 10, 1914, and presented its action for ratification at yesterday's meeting. The action was upheld by unanimous vote. Section 7 read:

Sec. 7. Experience having shown that it is very difficult, if not impossible, to avoid or prevent violation of the rules prescribed by the last preceding section, or to detect or prove any such violation, if the members are permitted to purchase news from other associations, and that such purchase may be seriously prejudicial to the interest and welfare of this corporation and its members, the Board of Directors may, in their discretion, forbid the members to purchase intelligence from any other such association.

When the Board of Directors by a vote of two-thirds of all its members shall decide and notify any member that the purchase or receipt of news from any other person, firm, corporation, or association, not a member of this corporation or represented in this corporation by a member, or any other action by such member, establishes a condition that will be likely to permit the news of the corporation to be disclosed to unauthorized persons, such members shall immediately discontinue purchasing or receiving such news, or such other objectionable action. The decision of the Board of Directors as to the establishment of such condition shall be final, and the fact shall not thereafter be open to question by a member.

Frederick W. Lehman, former Solicitor General of the United States, addressed the members at the afternoon session.

"The original attitude of the law toward the press was one of repression," he said. "It was a Governor of Virginia who thanked God that they had no printing press in the Colony, and would not have for a hundred years. It was the General Court of Massachusetts which suppressed, upon its first appearance, the first newspaper attempted to be published in what is now the United States.

Two Ways of Gathering News.

"There are two possible systems of news-gathering; one to deal with it as a purely commercial enterprise for profit and the other by a co-operative institution like the Associated Press, in which any element of immediate profit to the association itself is left out of account. In a co-operative institution like the Associated Press you have not only the better restraints of men but even the baser forces work in counter-poise against each other. With a membership like yours, distributed through all the States of the Union, representing every shade of religious and political belief and every variety of commercial and industrial interest, there is but one tenure of office possible to those who manage its affairs, and that is good conduct approved by substantially all of the members of the association.

"News cannot be reprinted without every day something being said disparaging of some individual and libelous if untrue. In the fifteen years' history of the present Associated Press it has not been mulcted in damages for a single dollar, and yet it is subject to prosecution for libel for every word libelous that its report may have contained, because its transmission of its news reports to its members is just as much a publication as the printing of the same news by the newspaper afterward. And today there stands against it but a single suit for libel, and that predicated upon a report made by it of what one public man said of another public man, and not, upon the ground of misreporting what was said.

"It is objected that The Associated Press is a monopoly. If so, it has not succeeded, as monopolies usually do, in restricting output. We publish more newspapers in the United States than in all the rest of the world, but it is said that the members monopolize their news for their own columns, and do not open them to those who are not members. What is news? Roughly speaking, news is the first report of an event of public and current interest. News signifies nothing in the world except personal service. A man has as much right to say what shall be done with a 'scoop' as Caruso has to the use of his voice.

"To receive everybody who publishes a paper to membership would be to destroy the association itself, because while there is much that may go into a newspaper that may be mere routine—as market reports, still every man wishes to make his paper a distinctive publication—and if there is nothing distinctive in its general news report a newspaper will become indifferent and undertake to gain distinctive quality by something altogether aside from the budget of news furnished by The Associated Press, and it seems to me that an essential condition of maintaining a co-operative news-gathering association is that that association shall have the right to determine its own membership.

"While The Associated Press has always had a very large proportion of the leading newspapers of the country, it has never had them all. The general plan of the organization has been approved by the Attorney General, allowing the association to discriminate and to determine its own membership. But the Attorney General found that in one respect, namely, in the power given to the Board of Directors to require members to desist from purchasing news from any other agency, you had, perhaps, trenched upon the law. The effect of that opinion and your action here this morning in amending your bylaws to conform to that opinion has been to bring your profession up to the standard of your practices, and now profession and practice are in harmony with the law, and you have before you, I hope, a long and unbroken career of usefulness to the public and prosperity for yourselves."

At the election of Directors Victor F. Lawson, who is also a member of the Executive Committee; W. H. Cowles, R. M. Johnston, and Herman Ridder were re-elected. D. E. Town of The Louisville Herald was elected to take the place of the late Samuel Bowles of The Springfield Republican.

Elected to Advisory Board.

The following were elected members of the Advisory Board:

Eastern Division, comprising Maine, New Hampshire, Vermont, Massachusetts, Rhode Island, Connecticut, New York, New Jersey, Pennsylvania, Maryland, District of Columbia, Delaware, and West Virginia—John D. Plummer of The Springfield Union, D. A. Miller of The Allentown Call, James W. Greene of The Buffalo Express; I. E. Hirsch of The Pittsburg Volksblatt, Van Lear Black of The Baltimore Sun.

Southern Division, comprising Virginia, North Carolina, South Carolina, Georgia, Florida, Alabama, Tennessee, Mississippi, Louisiana, Texas, Arkansas, Oklahoma, and Kentucky—James R. Gray, Atlanta Journal; Frank P. Glass, Montgomery Advertiser; Robert Ewing, New Orleans States; H. C. Adler, Chattanooga Times; Bruce Haldeman, Louisville Courier-Journal. (All re-elected.)

Central Division, comprising Ohio, Indiana, Michigan, Illinois, Wisconsin, Missouri, Iowa, Minnesota, Kansas, Nebraska, North and South Dakota—P. E. Burton, Joplin (Mo.) News; E. P. Adler, Davenport Times; J. L. Sturtevant, Wasau (Wis.) Record-Herald, E. W. Booth, Grand Rapids Press; Thomas Rees, Illinois State Register. (Mr. Burton re-elected.)

Western Division, comprising California, Wyoming, Oregon, Colorado, Montana, Washington, Idaho, Nevada, Utah, New Mexico, and Arizona; M. H. De Young, San Francisco Chronicle; S. A. Perkins, Tacoma Ledger; A. J. Blethen, Seattle Times; A. N. McKay, Salt Lake Tribune; I. N. Stevens, Pueblo Chieftain. (All re-elected.)

The following Nominating Committee was chosen: W. J. Crawford, Memphis Commercial Appeal; G. B. Dealey, Dallas News; Frank Knox, Manchester Union; Thomas Rees, Springfield, (Ill.,) State Register; James Keeley, Chicago Herald; J. F. Conners, Oakland Tribune; S. C. Bone, Seattle Post-Intelligencer.

The members elected to the Auditing Committee were: F. I. Thompson, Mobile Register; E. B. Smith, American Record; O. D. Brandenburg, Madison Democrat; John F. Carroll, Portland, (Ore.,) Telegram.

The Directors of The Associated Press will meet to elect officers this morning and the annual meeting of the American Newspaper Publishers Association will begin at 10 o'clock in the Astor Gallery. The members of the Advertising Bureau will hold a luncheon at 12:30 o'clock.

April 21, 1915

President Says a Nation May Be So Right That It Does Not Need to Fight

From the President's speech in Philadelphia last night:

America must have this consciousness, that on all sides it touches elbows and touches heart with all the nations of mankind. The example of America must be a special example, the example of America must be the example, not merely of peace because it will not fight, but of peace because peace is the healing and elevating influence of the world; and strife is not.

There is such a thing as a man being too proud to fight; there is such a thing as a nation being so right that it does not need to convince others by force that it is right.

March 11, 1915

WILSON WOULD NOT GIVE ALL FOR PEACE

Ought to Keep Out of War, but Not by Abandoning Humanity and Justice.

HIS GRIDIRON CLUB SPEECH

Answers Clamor in Congress to Warn Americans Off Armed Ships—True Valor.

Special to The New York Times.

WASHINGTON, Feb. 27.—In a short speech delivered just before the conclusion of the Gridiron Club dinner here last night President Wilson discussed the duty of the United States in connection with the war in Europe, and inferentially answered some of his critics. He made what was taken to be a reply to the element in Congress which attempted last week to force him to modify his attitude in dealing with Germany in the armed ship issue by saying bluntly that he preferred to know what the people throughout the country were thinking rather than what was being said in Congressional cloakrooms. He made what amounted to an answer to the allegation that his course in the German submarine issue was actuated by political expediency, declaring that America should keep out of the war at the sacrifice of everything except humanity and justice.

It was a peace speech with a ring in it. It was an intimate talk, not intended for publication. One of the two rules of the Gridiron Club is that "reporters are never present" to record the speeches of guests, an inducement to freedom of language of which most of those who have addressed this organization of Washington newspaper correspondents have taken advantage. The President's speech created such an impression, however, that arrangements were made today for its publication. In giving out copies of the speech to the press tonight the White House attached to it this note:

"So many requests from those attending the dinner that the President's address be published have been received at the White House that both the President and the Gridiron Club have consented to its publication."

President Wilson was cheered wildly when he concluded his remarks at the dinner; the club members and their guests were on their feet waving napkins and cheering. So prolonged was the demonstration that twice the President felt constrained to rise and bow his acknowledgments. The greatest outburst of approval in the course of the speech came when the President declared that "America ought to keep out of the war" at the sacrifice of everything except her sense of humanity and justice, upon which the history and character of the country were founded.

The President's address follows:

Principle, Not Expediency.

I have very little to say tonight, except to express my warm appreciation of the invariable courtesy of this club, and of the reception you have so generously accorded me. I find that I am seldom tempted to say anything nowadays unless somebody starts something, and tonight nobody has started anything.

Your talk, Mr. Toastmaster, has been a great deal about candidacy for the Presidency. It is not a new feeling on my part, but one which I entertain with a greater intensity than formerly, that a man who seeks the Presidency of the United States for anything that it will bring to him is an audacious fool. The responsibilities of the office ought to sober a man even before he approaches it. One of the difficulties of the office seldom appreciated, I dare say, is that it is very difficult to think while so many people are talking, and particularly while so many people are talking in a way that obscures counsel, and is entirely off the point.

The point in national affairs, gentlemen, never lies along the lines of expediency. It always rests in the field of principle. The United States was not founded upon any principle of expediency; it was founded upon a profound principle of human liberty and of humanity, and whenever it bases its policy upon any other foundations than those it builds on the sand and not upon solid rock.

It seems to me that the most enlightening thing a man can do is suggested by something which the Vice President said tonight. He complained that he found men, who, when their attention was called to the signs of Spring, did not see the blue heaven, did not see the movement of the free clouds, did not think of the great spaces of the quiet continent, but thought only of some immediate and pressing piece of business. It seems to me that if you do not think of the things that lie beyond and away from and disconnected from this scene in which we attempt to think and conclude, you will inevitably be led astray.

I would a great deal rather know what they are talking about around quiet firesides all over the country than what they are talking about in the cloakrooms of Congress. I would a great deal rather know what the men on the trains and by the wayside and in the shops and on the farms are thinking about and yearning for than hear any of the vociferous proclamations of policy which it is so easy to hear, and so easy to read by picking up any scrap of printed paper. There is only one way to hear these things, and that is constantly to go back to the fountains of American action. Those fountains are not to be found in any recently discovered sources.

Senator Harding was saying just now that we ought to try when we are 100,000,000 strong to act in the same simplicity of principle that our forefathers acted in when we were 3,000,000 strong. I heard somebody say—I do not know the exact statistics—that the present population of the United States is 103,000,000. If there are 3,000,000 thinking the same things that that original 3,000,000 thought, the 100,000,000 will be saved for an illustrious future. They were ready to stake everything for an idea, and that idea was not expediency, but justice. And the infinite difficulty of public affairs, gentlemen, is not to discover the signs of the heavens and the direction of the wind, but to square the things you do by the not simple but complicated standards of justice. Justice has nothing to do with expediency. Justice has nothing to do with any temporary standard whatever. It is rooted and grounded in the fundamental instincts of humanity.

America ought to keep out of this war. She ought to keep out of this war at the sacrifice of everything except this single thing upon which her character and history are founded, her sense of humanity and justice. If she sacrifices that, she has ceased to be America; she has ceased to entertain and to love the traditions which have made us proud to be Americans; and when we go about seeking safety at the expense of humanity, then I for one will believe that I have always been mistaken in what I have conceived to be the spirit of American history.

You never can tell your direction except by long measurements. You cannot establish a line by two posts; you have got to have three at least, to know whether they are straight with anything, and the longer your line the more certain your measurements. There is only one way in which to determine how the future of the United States is going to be projected and that is by looking back and seeing which way the lines ran which led up to the present moment of power and of opportunity. There is no doubt about that.

There is no question what the roll of honor in America is. The roll of honor consists of the names of men who have squared their conduct by ideals of duty. There is no one else upon the roster, there is no one else whose name we care to remember when we measure things upon a national scale. And I wish that whenever an impulse of impatience comes upon us, whenever an impulse to settle a thing some short way tempts us, we might close the door and take down some old stories of what American idealists and statesmen did in the past and not let any counsel in that does not sound in the authentic voice of American tradition.

Then we shall be certain what the lines of the future are, because we shall know we are steering by the lines of the past. We shall know that no temporary convenience, no temporary expediency will lead us either to be rash or to be cowardly. I would be just as much ashamed to be rash as I would to be a coward. Valor is self-respecting. Valor is circumspect. Valor strikes only when it is right to strike. Valor withholds itself from all small implications and entanglements and waits for the great opportunity when the sword will flash as if it carried the light of heaven upon its blade.

While the President made no direct reference to the threatened outbreak in Congress last week in behalf of a resolution warning American citizens not to travel on armed belligerent merchant ships, the Gridiron company easily recognized an allusion to it in the President's speech and a defiance of the recalcitrant element on Capitol Hill when he said that he was seldom tempted to say anything nowadays "unless somebody starts something." Equal significance was attached to his declaration that he would "rather know what they are talking about around the quiet firesides all over this great country than what they are talking about in the cloak rooms of Congress."

What was construed as another allusion to the clamor of the element in Congress for warning Americans to keep off armed merchant ships was the statement that "when we go about seeking safety at the expense of humanity, then I for one will believe that I have always been mistaken in what I have conceived to be the spirit of American history."

What is believed to have been intended by the President as an explanation of his "too proud to fight" phrase, which he interpolated in a speech delivered in Philadelphia three days after the Lusitania was sunk, was contained in the concluding portion of the Gridiron speech when he made his references to valor.

Arthur Wallace Dunn, ex-President of the Gridiron Club, who wrote a recently published history of the club, said tonight that President Wilson's speech would be the first delivered at a gridiron dinner to be published with the consent of the club. The only other instance where remarks delivered by a guest at a gridiron dinner had been printed verbatim in newspapers was when Cardinal Satolli, then Papal Delegate to the United States, who was in ignorance of the rule, gave copies of his speech to the press.

PRESIDENT CALLS FOR STRONGER NAVY, NEW FULL CO-OPERATION

MUST EXERT ALL OUR POWER

To Bring a "Government That Is Running Amuck to Terms."

WANTS LIBERAL CREDITS

And Universal Service, for "the World Must Be Made Safe for Democracy."

A TUMULTUOUS GREETING

Congress Adjourns After "State of War" Resolution Is Introduced—Acts Today.

Special to The New York Times.

WASHINGTON, April 2.—At 8:35 o'clock tonight the United States virtually made its entrance into the war. At that hour President Wilson appeared before a joint session of the Senate and House and invited it to consider the fact that Germany had been making war upon us and to take action in recognition of that fact in accordance with his recommendations, which included universal military service, the raising of an army of 500,000 men, and co-operation with the Allies in all ways that will help most effectively to defeat Germany.

Resolutions recognizing and declaring the state of war were immediately introduced in the House and Senate by Representative Flood and Senator Martin, both of the President's birth-State, Virginia, and they are the strongest declarations of war that the United States has ever made in any war in which it has been engaged since it became a nation. They are the Administration resolutions drawn up after conference with the President, and in language approved and probably dictated by him, and they will come before the two Foreign Affairs Committees at meetings which will be held tomorrow morning and will be reported at the earliest practical moment.

Unreservedly With the Allies.

Before an audience that cheered him as he has never been cheered in the Capitol in his life the President cast in the lot of America unreservedly with the Allies and declared for a war that must not end until the issue between autocracy and democracy has been fought out. He recited our injuries at Germany's hands, but he did not rest our cause on those; he went on from that point to range us with the Allies as a factor in an irrepressible conflict, between the autocrat and the people. He showed that peace was impossible for the democracies of the world while this power remained on earth. "The world," he said, "must be made safe for democracy."

We had learned that the German autocracy could never be a friend of this country; she had been our enemy while nominally our friend, and even before the war of 1914 broke out. He called on us to take our stand with the democracies in this irrepressible conflict, with before our eyes "the wonderful and heartening events that have been happening in the last few weeks in Russia."

He reaffirmed his hope for peace and for freedom, and looked to the war now forced upon us to bring these about; for, he said, a world compact for peace "can never be maintained except by a concert of the democracies of the world."

The objects for which we fight, he said, are democracy, the right of those who submit to authority to have a voice in their own government, the right and liberties of small nations, the universal dominion of right, the concert of free peoples to bring peace and safety to all nations, and to make the world free. These have always been our ideals; and to accomplish them, we accept the war Germany has made upon us. In fighting it we must not only raise an army and increase the navy, but must aid the Allies in all ways, financial and other, and so order our own preparations as not to interfere with the supply of munitions they are getting from us.

Trouble-making Pacifists Barred.

The President delivered this speech before an audience that had been carefully sifted. All day Washington had been in the hands of belligerent pacifists, truculent in manner, and determined to break into the Capitol. They tried to take possession of the Capitol steps, up which the President must go when he entered, and met the same fate that Coxey's rioters fell in with twenty-three years ago at the hands of the police, who dispersed them.

A handful of them fell upon Senator Lodge and assaulted him. Others entered the Vice President's room, and were so aggressive that they were put out. But by nightfall the authorities had them eliminated, so far as any possibility of trouble was concerned, and they were not admitted to the Capitol at all.

Two troops of the Second Cavalry guarded the approaches, and admitted nobody who could not be vouched for, and the building swarmed with Secret Service men, Post Office Inspectors, and policemen on guard to see that no harm from the lovers of peace befell the President of the United States in his discharge of a constitutional duty.

He came at 8:30, guarded by another troop of cavalry. If he had come in the afternoon, as he wished to do, he would have made his entry through thousands of pacifists camped outside the building and parading its corridors and waiting for him. But at night it was easier for a camel to go through the eye of a needle than for a disturber to get within pistol shot of the Capitol, and even those who could get into the building itself could not get into the galleries without special tickets.

President Greeted with Cheers.

The House an hour before had taken a recess. When it met again it was in a scene that the hall had never presented before. Directly in front of the Speaker and facing him sat the members of the Supreme Court without their gowns. Over at one side sat the members of the Diplomatic Corps in evening dress. It was the first time any one could remember when the foreign envoys had ever sat together officially in the Hall of Representatives.

Then the doors opened, and in came the Senators, headed by Vice President Marshall, each man wearing or carrying a small American flag. There were three or four exceptions, including Senators La Follette and Vardaman, but one had to look hard to find them, and Senator Stone was no exception. It was at 8:32 that they came in, and one minute later the speaker announced:

"The President of the United States."

As he walked in and ascended the Speaker's platform he got such a reception as Congress had never given him before in any of his visits to it. The Supreme Court Justices rose from their chairs, facing the place where he stood, and led the applause, while Representatives and Senators not only cheered, but yelled. It was two minutes before he could begin his address.

When he did begin it he stood with his manuscript before him typewritten on sheets of note paper. He held it in both hands, resting his arm on the green baize covered desk, and at first

WAR DECLARATION, ARMY OF 500,000 MEN, WITH GERMANY'S FOES

he read without looking up, but after a while he would glance occasionally to the right or the left as he made a point, not as if he were trying to see the effect, but more as a sort of gesture—the only one he employed.

Congress listened intently and without any sort of interruption while he recited the German crimes against humanity, his own and his country's effort to believe that the German rulers had not wholly cut themselves off from the path which civilized nations follow, and the way in which the truth was forced upon unwilling minds. It was waiting for his conclusions, and there was no applause or demonstration of any kind for the recital.

But when he finished his story of our efforts to avoid war and came to the sentence "armed neutrality, it now appears, is impracticable because submarines are in fact outlaws when used as the German submarines are used," the close attention deepened into a breathless silence, so painfully intense that it seemed almost audible.

A Roar Answers No "Submission."

He had told Congress at the outset that the condition which now confronted us was one which he had neither the right nor the duty to cope with alone, and that he had come to ask it to make its choice of ways to deal with it; and now he said:

"There is one choice we cannot make, we are incapable of making. We will not choose the path of submission —"

There was more of the sentence, but Congress neither knew it nor would have waited to hear if it had known. At the word "submission," Chief Justice White with an expression of joy and thankfulness on his face, dropped the big soft hat he had been holding, raised his hands high in the air, and brought them together with a heartfelt bang; and House, Senate, and galleries followed him with a roar like a storm. It was a cheer so deep and so intense and so much from the heart that it sounded like a shouted prayer.

The President completed his sentence, "And suffer the most sacred rights of our people to be ignored," and Congress relapsed into its intent and watchful silence. But when he asked for the declaration of war, when he urged them to "declare the course of the Imperial German Government to be in effect nothing less than war," the scene was even more striking.

Chief Justice Leads the Cheers.

Chief Justice White had the most prominent seat on the floor; the Supreme Court sat apart from all the rest in a little island of chairs in the centre of the open space before the Speaker's desk; and, as he rose from his seat at the head of the little knot of men, he was marked out from all, as no one else was except the President himself. The Chief Justice's face wore an expression of pride and relief that was a study, and that attracted the observation of everybody; and though the cheering really needed no leader, he was its leader. At this last utterance of the President's, he compressed his lips close together as if he were trying to keep tears back, and again raised his hands as high as he could and brought his mighty palms together as if he were trying to split them.

Behind him the Senators and Representatives were cheering; and now, after a moment or two, Heflin of Alabama sprang to his feet. In a second the whole Democratic side of the House was up after him, and then Ollie James of Kentucky rose in his turn, followed immediately by the Democratic side of the Senate, and there they all stood cheering at the top of their lungs.

The same scene was repeated when the President a moment later asked Congress to recognize the state of belligerency which Germany had thus forced upon us, and to adopt measures which would bring the German Government to terms as soon as possible and end the war.

The next applause came from his statement that such a prosecution of the war would call for co-operation with the Allies, and there was more when he spoke of making them a liberal financial contribution, "so that our resources be as far as possible added to theirs." Next he took up our own preparation, independent of the Allies, and Congress applauded his proposal for strengthening the navy, for an army of "at least 500,000 men," but the applause turned to great cheering when he added, "it should be chosen, in my judgment, on the principle of universal liability to service."

After declaring that we should order our preparations so as to interfere as little as possible with the duty of supplying the Allies with munitions, which elicited more applause, the President turned to the great causes which called us into the war, and spoke no more of the injuries which Germany had inflicted upon us. It was not for revenge that we were fighting, but because we were enlisted in the battle for democracy.

"We have no quarrel with the German people," he said amid applause, and later he declared that they would be liberated, as well as the people of other lands, by the war.

When he came to this part of his address the first big cheer he got was when, painting the battle of democracy and autocracy, and the difference between the two, he said that democracies "do not fill other countries with spies or set upon a course of intrigue" and would have said more but for the cheering that split his sentence at that word.

"The Russian people have been added to the forces that are fighting for justice and for peace," he said, and they cheered again.

Not in the way of reciting injuries to which we must not submit, as he had done at the beginning, but for the purpose of illustrating the difference between self-governed peoples and those that are ruled by a few, he said, "It has filled our unsuspecting communities and even our offices of Government with spies and set criminal intrigue everywhere afoot."

The cheers which this evoked showed again that this is a particularly sore spot with Congress, though the President's object at this point was only the drawing of a contrast between the nations to which we are affiliated and those which are ruled by secret diplomacy and personal government—"a government that did as it pleased and told its people nothing."

His direct charge against the German Embassy, that these plots were directed by "official agents of the Imperial Government, accredited to the Government of the United States," brought another storm of applause.

A World "Safe for Democracy."

But these charges he made only incidentally, and for purposes of illustration. They were all designed to show that "the autocratic German Government can never be a friend," and now he said:

"The world must be made safe for democracy."

This sentence might have passed without applause, but Senator John Sharp Williams was one man who instantly seized the full and immense meaning of it. Alone he began to applaud, and he did it gravely, emphatically—and in a moment the fact that this was the keyword of our war against Germany dawned on the others, and one after another followed his lead until the whole host broke forth in a great uproar of applause.

When he touched on our relations with the German-Americans there was applause for his promises to those German-Americans who "are in fact loyal to their neighbors and the Government in the hour of test," but it was altogether overshadowed by the volume of that which broke out for the antithetical sentence. "If there should be disloyalty it will be dealt with with a stern hand and firm repression."

The President ended at 9:11, having spoken thirty-six minutes. Then the great scene which had been enacted at his entrance was repeated. The diplomats, the Supreme Court, the galleries, the House and Senate, Republicans and Democrats alike, stood in their places and the Senators waved flags they had brought in with them. Those who were wearing, not carrying flags, tore them from their lapels or their sleeves and waved with the rest, and they all cheered wildly.

Senator Robert Marion La Follette, however, stood motionless with his arms folded tight and high on his chest, so that nobody could have any excuse for mistaking his attitude; and there he stood, chewing gum with a sardonic smile.

The President walked rapidly out of the hall, and when he had gone, the Senators and the Supreme Court and the diplomats went their ways. Four minutes after his departure the Speaker called the House to order for the passage of a resolution offered by Chairman Fitzgerald of the Appropriations Committee making it possible to pass the money bills within ten days under suspension of the rules, and the first day's session of the Sixty-fifth Congress was at an end.

April 3, 1917

Text of
President's Letter Defining His Treaty Stand

Special to The New York Times.

WASHINGTON, Jan. 8.—The letter of President Wilson read at the Jackson Day dinner tonight was as follows:

THE WHITE HOUSE, WASHINGTON, January 8, 1920.

My Dear Mr. Chairman:

It is with keenest regret that I find that I am to be deprived of the pleasure and privilege of joining you and the other loyal Democrats who are to assemble tonight to celebrate Jackson Day and renew their vows of fidelity to the great principles of our party, the principles which must now fulfill the hopes not only of our own people but of the world.

The United States enjoyed the spiritual leadership of the world until the Senate of the United States failed to ratify the treaty by which the belligerent nations sought to effect the settlements for which they had fought throughout the war. It is inconceivable that at this supreme crisis and final turning point in the international relations of the whole world, when the results of the great war are by no means determined and are still questionable and dependent upon events which no man can foresee or count upon, the United States should withdraw from the concert of progressive and enlightened nations by which Germany was defeated, and all similar Governments (if the world be so unhappy as to contain any) warned of the consequences of any attempt at a like inquity, and yet that is the effect of the course which the United States has taken with regard to the Treaty of Versailles.

Germany is beaten, but we are still at war with her, and the old stag is reset for a repetition of the old plot. It is now ready for a resumption of the old offensive and defensive alliances which made settled peace impossible. It is no open again to every sort of intrigue.

The old spies are free to resume their former abominable activities. They are again at liberty to make it impossible for governments to be sure what mischief is being worked among their own people, what internal disorders are being fomented.

Without the covenant of the League of Nations there may be as many secret treaties as ever, to destroy the confidence of governments in each other, and their validity cannot be questioned.

None of the objects we professed to be fighting for has been secured, or can be made certain of, without this nation's ratification of the treaty and its entry into the covenant. This nation entered the great war to vindicate its own rights and to protect and preserve free government. It went into the war to see it through to the end, and the end has not yet come. It went into the war to make an end of militarism, to furnish guarantees to weak nations, and to make a just and lasting peace. It entered it with noble enthusiasm.

Five of the leading belligerents have accepted the treaty and formal ratifications will soon be exchanged. The question is whether this country will enter and enter whole-heartedly. If it does not do so, the United States and Germany will play a lone hand in the world.

The maintenance of the peace of the world and the effective execution of the treaty depend upon the whole-hearted participation of the United States. I am not stating it as a matter of power. The point is that the United States is the only nation which has sufficient moral force with the rest of the world to guarantee the substitution of discussion for war. If we keep out of this agreement, if we do not give our guarantees, then another attempt will be made to crush the new nations of Europe.

I do not believe that this is what the people of this country wish or will be satisfied with. Personally, I do not accept the action of the Senate of the United States as the decision of the nation.

I have asserted from the first that the overwhelming majority of the people of this country desire the ratification of the treaty, and my impression to that effect has recently been confirmed by the unmistakable evidences of public opinion given during my visit to seventeen of the States.

I have endeavored to make it plain that if the Senate wishes to say what the undoubted meaning of the League is I shall have no objection. There can be no reasonable objection to interpretations accompanying the act of ratification itself. But when the treaty is acted upon, I must know whether it means that we have ratified or rejected it.

We cannot rewrite this treaty. We must take it without changes which alter its meaning, or leave it, and then after the rest of the world has signed it, we must face the unthinkable task of making another and separate treaty with Germany.

But no mere assertions with regard to the wish and opinion of the country are credited. If there is any doubt as to what the people of the country think on this vital matter, the clear and single way out is to submit it for determination at the next election to the voters of the nation, to give the next election the form of a great and solemn referendum, a referendum as to the part the United States is to play in completing the settlements of the war and in the prevention in the future of such outrages as Germany attempted to perpetrate.

We have no more moral right to refuse now to take part in the execution and administration of these settlements than we had to refuse to take part in the fighting of the last few weeks of the war which brought victory and made it possible to dictate to Germany what the settlements should be. Our fidelity to our associates in the war is in question and the whole future of mankind. It will be heartening to the whole world to know the attitude and purpose of the people of the United States.

I spoke just now of the spiritual leadership of the United States, thinking of international affairs. But there is another spiritual leadership which is open to us and which we can assume.

The world has been made safe for democracy, but democracy has not been finally vindicated. All sorts of crimes are being committed in its name, all sorts of preposterous perversions of its doctrines and practices are being attempted.

This, in my judgment, is to be the great privilege of the democracy of the United States, to show that it can lead the way in the solution of the great social and industrial problems of our time, and lead the way to a happy, settled order of life as well as to political liberty. The program for this achievement we must attempt to formulate, and in carrying it out we shall do more than can be done in any other way to sweep out of existence the tyrannous and arbitrary forms of power which are now masquerading under the name of popular government.

Whenever we look back to Andrew Jackson we should draw fresh inspiration from his character and example. His mind grasped with such a splendid definiteness and firmness the principles of national authority and national action. He was so indomitable in his purpose to give reality to the principles of the Government, that this is a very fortunate time to recall his career and to renew our vows of faithfulness to the principles and the pure practices of Democracy.

I rejoice to join you in this renewal of faith and purpose. I hope that the whole evening may be of the happiest results as regards the fortunes of our party and the nation.

With cordial regards,
Sincerely yours,
WOODROW WILSON.

To Hon. Homer S. Cummings,
Chairman Democratic National Committee, Washington, D. C.

January 9, 1920

WILSON BY RADIO CALLS OUR ATTITUDE 'IGNOBLE, COWARDLY'

Says We Withdrew Into "Selfish Isolation" After Our Troops Won War for the Right.

SHOULD NOW RETRIEVE PAST

He Raps France and Italy for Making "Waste Paper" of the Versailles Treaty.

SPEECH HEARD BY MILLIONS

Radio Stations Give It Right of Way Throughout the Nation From Coast to Coast.

Special to The New York Times.

WASHINGTON, Nov. 10.—Speaking tonight by radio to auditors throughout the nation who may have numbered millions, former President Wilson declared that the attitude of this country since the World War had been "deeply ignoble," "cowardly and dishonorable."

He said we had withdrawn from the affairs of the world "in sullen and selfish isolation," after our soldiers won the "war for right," and that the happy memories of those "never-to-be-forgotten days in November" of 1918 were "forever marred and embittered for us" by our refusing to "bear any responsible part in the administration of peace and establishment of the rights won by the war."

To such action by us France and Italy, he added, had furnished "a sort of sinister climax," having "between them made waste paper of the Treaty of Versailles," Mr. Wilson asserted.

The former President declared that every succeeding year had demonstrated the need "for such services as we might have rendered, as demoralizing circumstances we might have controlled had gone from bad to worse."

He added that the present situation of the world afforded us an opportunity to retrieve the past, and that the "only way in which we can worthily give proof of our appreciation of the significance of Armistice Day is to put away self-interest and formulate and act upon the highest ideals and purposes of international policy."

Adds "Cowardly" as an Afterthought.

Mr. Wilson issued manuscript copies of his address after he had delivered it by radio, and it was then noticed that in speaking he had departed at several points from the text of his prepared speech.

One such interpolation in the speech as delivered was the use of the word "cowardly" in characterizing our attitude after the war.

Tonight's address was Mr. Wilson's first public speech addressed directly to the nation since his collapse during the Treaty ratification fight.

He delivered his message into the radio from the library of the second floor of his S Street residence, beginning at 8:30 o'clock. He spoke for less than ten minutes, as was originally expected, and his voice was heard distinctly and clearly for hundreds of miles.

Though his voice was husky at the opening, it grew better as he proceeded.

The air had been cleared for his words, the radio installation was ready, and the auditors throughout the country listening in were on the qui vive.

The Washington radio broadcaster briefly announced at 8:28 that Mr. Wilson would talk. Then there was a lapse of about three minutes, and Mr. Wilson began to speak.

At Mr. Wilson's home it was said that no guests were present, that Mr. and Mrs. Wilson and John Randolph Bolling, his secretary, were the only ones there. No details as to the scene were supplied, and it was inferred that Mr. Wilson would prefer no publicity on this.

Hundreds of families here heard Mr. Wilson speak over the radio, and in addition there were receiving sets installed in many public places.

Radio officials declared tonight just before the Wilson talk began that the colder air and weather conditions were favorable for good dissemination of the message. They said that the WCAP station was heard well during the past week as far as California, Wyoming, the Dakotas, Florida and Texas, and had recently been heard in England.

Promptly at 8:26 o'clock the WEAF station in New York made the announcement that Mr. Wilson was ready to speak, and then WEAF "swung off the air," the circuit was reversed and at 8:25 o'clock William T. Pierson, broadcasting manager of the WCAP station in Washington, introduced Mr. Wilson, saying:

"Mr. Woodrow Wilson, speaking from his residence in Washington, is about to say a few words regarding 'The Significance of Armistice Day.'"

Coolidge Listens in at the White House.

The utmost interest had been manifested over the event since it was announced that the great proponent of the League of Nations covenant, and the man most responsible for the armistice, would give his views on subjects suggested by the recurrence of Armistice Day and its significance. In Washington and cities where the speech was easily heard additional radio facilities were provided for the occasion.

President Coolidge tuned in over the White House radio, and the speech probably was listened to by more thousands of people than any radio transmission yet attempted.

The fact that Mr. Wilson broke his silence on international questions is accepted as indicating not only great improvement in his health but a desire on his part to be reckoned with by the Democratic Party in the formulation of its platform. Interest in the speech was great, because of the recent refusal of France to accept the Hughes proposal, and Republicans regarded it as a political document of great significance not only in the councils of the Democratic Party but in the effect it might have on the people.

Elaborate arrangements had been made under the auspices of the American Telephone and Telegraph Company of New York and the officials of the Chesapeake and Potomac Telephone Company at Washington for giving the Wilson talk the best possible facilities. The special apparatus used had a thorough test before Mr. Wilson talked, though he did not have a "preliminary try-out of his voice."

Three Big Stations Used.

Three big radio stations in the East were used. There were the WEAF station of the American Telephone and Telegraph Company, New York; the WCAP station of the Chesapeake and Potomac Telephone Company at Washington and the WJAR station at Providence, R. I.

WEAF sent on 492 meters wave length, WCAP on 496 meters, and WJAR on 360 meters. These stations have been able in combination to cover the better part of the territorial area of the United States. The WCAP station at Washington is powerful enough to reach points as far distant as Texas and along the Mississippi River. It was advised that loud speakers had been installed in auditoriums in various Texas towns for the special purpose of having audiences there listen to the Wilson speech.

To insure the best possible air conditions for the broadcasting a common understanding was reached between many of the important radio stations by which those not participating on the transmission of the Wilson speech should "get off the air" during the brief period that Mr. Wilson was talking.

Republicans and Democrats, anti-League and pro-League men, women and children had their ears to receivers or were in front of loud speakers listening to the former President's remarks.

During the day the Chesapeake and Potomac Telephone Company sent representatives to the Wilson home at 2,340 S Street Northwest with a specially equipped truck, to which was attached the equipment utilized in broadcasting the speech. The truck was stationed tonight in the driveway along the western side of the Wilson home. From the truck a trunk line ran into the library of Mr. Wilson's residence, where a microphone was in position to receive his words. Amplifiers and other delicate paraphernalia were on the truck and an ammeter before which a representative of the telephone company stood to regulate the amplification of Mr. Wilson's voice.

From this truck Mr. Wilson's message was conveyed over an underground wire to the station of the WCAP in Washington, where the talk was broadcast.

Armistice Day ceremonies at the home of Mr. Wilson tomorrow are scheduled for 3:30 o'clock P. M. Delegations will assemble at Dupont Circle at 2:30 and, headed by a band, will march to the Wilson home in S Street. The former President has promised to appear to greet the delegations.

Senator Glass of Virginia, who was a member of Mr. Wilson's Cabinet, will make an address to the former President, and it is understood that the latter will reply by a brief speech. Among the organizations which have notified the Arrangements Committee that they will participate are:

The League of Nations Non-Partisan Association of New York City, Philadelphia Women's Luncheon Club, Virginia League of Women Voters, Baltimore Women's Club, Woodrow Wilson Clubs of Princeton, Columbia and Virginia Universities; a delegation from Staunton, Va., Mr. Wilson's birthplace; a party from Raleigh, N. C., headed by former Secretary Daniels, and a party from Harrisburg, Pa., headed by Vance McCormick, former Chairman of the Democratic National Committee.

Among organizations which will have a prominent place in the parade to Mr. Wilson's home will be the Disabled American Soldiers of the World War, the American Legion, and other Veteran associations.

A number of Mr. Wilson's admirers who are unable to attend because of other engagements made for Armistice Day ceremonies, have sent messages to the committee in charge. Newton D. Baker, Secretary of War in the Wilson Administration, sent the following telegram from Cleveland:

"I cannot come for the pilgrimage, as I have to speak here on that day on the League of Nations, and that seems important, since we really change sentiment rapidly out here on that subject. 'Hail the Chief for me!' His ideals are growing into hearts once hardened and being seen by eyes once blinded. He will live, thank God, to see the harvest of his sowing, in spite of the weeds which grew so rank over the field."

Dr. Edwin A. Alderman, President of the United States Society of Virginia, sent this message:

"Nothing on earth would give me greater pleasure than to foregather with those Americans who think of Woodrow Wilson as a champion of international peace and justice. I had that opportunity and privilege last year, and I shall never forget it. This year, unhappily, I cannot come, owing to commitments that I am unable to put aside; but I shall be there in spirit to pay my tribute to the strong and gallant figure who has won so fixed a place in American history."

William C. Redfield, Secretary of Commerce in the Wilson Administration, sent the following telegram:

"Mr. Wilson is coming into his own. I hope his life may be long spared so that he may see the fruition of his great ideals. The place of leadership is always a lonely one, yet I venture to think that Mr. Wilson holds today in the hearts of our people a place of honor higher than he can realize and one that is continually expanding."

Senator William Caleb Bruce of Maryland sent the following:

"As a member of the United States Senate I shall do everything in my power to promote the early participation of the United States in the deliberations of the League of Nations and of its court, and I trust that, so far as possible, the great influence of Woodrow Wilson will continue to be exerted in behalf of this object."

HARDING DECRIES 'MEDDLING ABROAD'

Declares It Stirs Up Discord and Strife Among Adopted Americans.

BLAMES US FOR 'HYPHENISM'

Says Neglect of Foreign-Born Citizens Is Responsible for Divided Allegiance.

WARNS OF DANGERS AHEAD

Senator Tells Visitors Day May Come When a Foreign Capital Will Control America.

Special to The New York Times.

MARION, Ohio, Sept. 18.—Meddling abroad threatens not only entangling alliances, but a country divided into national groups, according to Senator Harding, speaking from his front porch today to delegations of foreign-born citizens representing thirty nationalities, who came to Marion from New York, Philadelphia, Cleveland and Chicago. Their visit was largely due to the work of Senator McCormick, who introduced them to Senator Harding, and the Foreign Language Division of the Republican National Headquarters.

One hundred and twenty-five foreign-born citizens from New York arrived this morning with Senator William M. Calder and John J. Lyons, Republican candidate for Secretary of State. Included in the delegation was James Walsh, Exalted Ruler of the New York Lodge of Elks and a member of Tammany Hall. There were several Italians, also Tammany members, who, it is said, will work for Governor Smith on the State ticket, but intend to vote for Harding.

Senator Harding warned the visitors of the dangers of "hyphenated" thinking and voting. Should voters organize in national groups, he said, the time might come when such a vote might have the balance of power and transfer control to a foreign capital.

Addresses All as "Americans."

Senator Harding said in part:

"You are, in large part, men and women of foreign birth, but I do not address you as men and women of foreign birth: I address you as Americans, and through you I would like to reach all the American people. I have no message for you which is not addressed to all the American people, and, indeed, I would consider it a breach of courtesy to you and a breach of my duty as a candidate for high office to address myself to any group or special interest or to any class or race or creed.

"Let us all pray that America shall never become divided into classes and never feel the menace of hyphenated citizenship.

"When the war clouds darkened Europe and the storm threatened our own country, we found America torn with conflicting sympathies and prejudices. They were not unnatural; indeed, they were, in many cases, very excusable, because we had not promoted the American spirit; we had not insisted upon full and unalterable consecration to our own country—our country by birth or adoption. We talked of the American melting post over the fires of freedom, but we did not apply that fierce flame of patriotic devotion needed to fuse all into the pure metal of Americanism.

"I do not blame the foreign born. Charge it to American neglect. We proclaimed our liberty, but did not emphasize the essentials to its preservation. We boasted our nationality, but we did not magnify the one great spirit essential to perfect national life.

"I like to think of an America where every citizen's pride in power and resources, in influence and progress, is founded on what can be done for our people, all our people; not what we may accomplish to the political or national advantage of this or that people in distant lands.

"It was my official duty to sit with the Senate Committee on Foreign Relations when it was hearing the American spokesmen for foreign peoples during the Peace Conference at Paris. Under the rules, we could give hearings only to Americans, though many whom we had no right to hear sought to bring their appeal to the Senate, as though it possessed some sense of justice which had no voice in Paris. We heard the impassioned appeals of Americans of foreign birth on behalf of the lands from which they came—where their kinsfolk resided. No one doubted their sincerity; no one questioned their right to be interested. But for me there was a foreboding, a growing sense of apprehension.

Sees Danger in Involvement Abroad.

"How can we have American concord; how can we expect American unity; how can we escape strife, if we in America attempt to meddle in the affairs of Europe and Asia and Africa; if we assume to settle boundaries; if we attempt to end the rivalries and jealousies of countries of the Old World strife? It it not alone the menace which lies in involvement abroad; it is the greater danger which lies in conflict among adopted Americans.

"This is the objection to the foreign policy attempted, not with the advice and consent of the Senate, but in spite of warnings, informally uttered. America wants the good will of foreign peoples, and it does not want the ill will of foreign-born who have come to dwell among us.

"Nothing helpful has come from the willful assumption to direct the affairs of Europe. No good of any kind has proceeded from such meddling in Russia. None in the case of Poland. None in the case of the Balkan States. None in the case of Fiume. On the contrary the mistaken policy of interference has broken the draw strings of good sense and spilled bad counsel and bad manners all over the world.

"That policy, my countrymen, is a bad policy. It is bad enough abroad, but it is even more menacing at home. Meddling abroad tends to make Americans forget that they are Americans. It tends to arouse the old and bitter feelings of race, or former nationality, or foreign ancestry in the hearts of those who ought never be forced to turn their hearts away from undivided loyalty and interest given to 'America first.'

"I want America on guard against that course which naturally tends to array Americans against each other. I do not know whether or not Washington foresaw this menace when he warned us against entangling alliances and meddling abroad, but I see it, and I say to you that all America must stand firm against this dangerous and destructive and un-American policy. Meddling is not only dangerous to us because it leads us into the entanglements against which Washington warned us, but it also threatens an America divided in her own household, and tends to drive into groups seeking to make themselves felt in our political life men and women whose hearts are led away from 'America First' to 'Hyphen First.'

Sounds Warning to Americans.

"For Americans who love America I sound a warning. The time might come when a group or groups of men and women of foreign birth or foreign parentage, not organized for the interest of America, but organized around a resentment against our Government interference abroad in their land of origin, might press by propaganda and political hyphenism upon our Government to serve their own interests rather than the interests of all America. It is not beyond possibility that the day might come—and may God forbid it—when an organized hyphenated vote in American politics might have the balance of voting power to elect our Government. If this were true, America would be deliveries out of the hands of her citizenship an her control might be transferred to a foreign capital abroad.

"I address this warning to you because, though it is a message to all Americans which you may spread widecast when you leave this spot, nevertheless it is of even greater importance to you, who were born on other soil, or whose parents were born upon other soil, than it is to any one else in all the world. America is peculiarly your America. Men and women of foreign blood, indeed, are America. They have come here because, under our Republic, grown upon a firm foundation, there is liberty and the light of democracy which shines in the hearts of all mankind. America is yours to preserve, not as a land of groups and classes, races and creeds, but America the one America. The United States, 'America the everlasting.'"

Senator McCormick, in presenting the delegation to the nominee, assured Senator Harding that all his hearers shared a "common repugnance for personal and arbitrary government, whether in its origin it be dynastic or elective."

"We know," he said, "that during late years there has been in high places much talk of 'common counsel,' but little of it. We know that in high places there has been much talk of 'freedom' and democracy. We know, too, that in this United States their exercise has been restricted or hampered by the interposition of the Executive.

"We know, too, Sir, that when you have assumed the Chief Magistracy of the United States, and that when those who believe with you have assumed their places in the Congress of the United States, we may count upon the sure and prompt repeal of those vast powers vested in the Executive for the prosecution of the war, and now unhappily usurped. We have learned from your own lips that we may expect the no less prompt declaration of the legal existence of that peace which for two long years has existed in fact. We hail today, in advance of their restoration, the re-establishment of the ancient rights of free election, free assembly, free press and free speech.

"We are sprung, I have said, from well-nigh all the peoples of old Europe. In our devotion to America we rejoice that under your leadership she will propose a plan for the codification of international law and for the establishment of tribunals through which justice may be done in lieu of that autocratic covenant conceived in haste and in hate, of which the end would have been the maintenance of empire by force, even though some of its proponents and supporters sought only the perpetuation of peace."

Senator Calder predicted that Senator Harding would have 100,000 to 300,000 majority in New York State. He based his prediction on the party enrollment. In Greater New York, he said, the Democratic enrollment exceeded Republican registration by 100,000, while upstate the Republican enrollment topped the Democratic registration by 400,000.

September 19, 1920

Text of the Inaugural Address Outlining Coolidge's Policies

The President, While Seeing Much to Be Thankful for, Urges the Need of Further Tax Cuts, Not to Save Money, but to Save People.

WASHINGTON, March 4.—The text of President Coolidge's inaugural address follows:

My Countrymen:

No one can contemplate current conditions without finding much that is satisfying and still more that is encouraging. Our own country is leading the world in the general readjustment to the results of the great conflict. Many of its burdens will bear heavily upon us for years, and the secondary and indirect effects we must expect to experience for some time. But we are beginning to comprehend more definitely what course should be pursued, what remedies ought to be applied, what actions should be taken for our deliverance, and are clearly manifesting a determined will faithfully and conscientiously to adopt these methods of relief.

Already we have sufficiently rearranged our domestic affairs so that confidence has returned, business has revived, and we appear to be entering an era of prosperity which is gradually reaching into every part of the nation. Realizing that we cannot live unto ourselves alone, we have contributed of our resources and our counsel to the relief of the suffering and the settlement of the disputes among the European nations. Because of what America is and what America has done, a firmer courage, a higher hope, inspires the heart of all humanity.

These results have not occurred by mere chance. They have been secured by a constant and enlightened effort marked by many sacrifices and extending over many generations. We cannot continue these brilliant successes in the future unless we continue to learn from the past. It is necessary to keep the former experiences of our country, both at home and abroad, continually before us if we are to have any science of government.

Taking the Bearings.

If we wish to erect new structures, we must have a definite knowledge of the old foundations. We must realize that human nature is about the most constant thing in the universe and that the essentials of human relationship do not change. We must frequently take our bearings from these fixed stars of our political firmament if we expect to hold a true course. If we examine carefully what we have done, we can determine the more accurately what we can do.

We stand at the opening of the one

hundred and fiftieth year since our national consciousness first asserted itself by unmistakable action with an array of force. The old sentiment of detached and dependent Colonies disappeared in the new sentiment of a united and independent nation. Men began to discard the narrow confines of a local charter for the broader opportunities of a national Constitution. Under the eternal urge of freedom we became an independent nation.

A little less than fifty years later that freedom and independence were reasserted in the face of all the world and guarded, supported and secured by the Monroe Doctrine. The narrow fringe of States along the Atlantic seaboard advanced its frontiers across the hills and plains of an intervening continent until it passed down the golden slope to the Pacific. We made freedom a birthright. We extended our domain over distant islands in order to safeguard our own interests and accepted the consequent obligations to bestow justice and liberty upon less favored peoples. In the defense of our own ideals and in the general cause of liberty we entered the great war. When victory had been fully secured, we withdrew to our own shores unrecompensed save in the consciousness of duty done.

Throughout all these experiences we have enlarged our freedom, we have strengthened our independence. We have been, and propose to be, more and more American. We believe that we can best serve our own country and most successfully discharge our obligations to humanity by continuing to be openly and candidly, intensely and scrupulously American. If we have any heritage, it has been that. If we have any destiny, we have found it in that direction.

But if we wish to continue to be distinctively American, we must continue to make that term comprehensive enough to embrace the legitimate desires of a civilized and enlightened people determined in all their relations to pursue a conscientious and religious life. We cannot permit ourselves to be narrowed and dwarfed by slogans and phrases. It is not the adjective but the substantive which is of real importance. It is not the name of the action, but the result of the action which is the chief concern.

America a Balanced Force.

It will be well not to be too much disturbed by the thought of either isolation or entanglement of pacifists and militarists. The physical configuration of the earth has separated us from all of the Old World, but the common brotherhood of man, the highest law of all our being, has united us by inseparable bonds with all humanity. Our country represents nothing but peaceful intentions toward all the earth, but it ought not to fail to maintain such a military force as comports with the dignity and security of a great people. It ought to be a balanced force, intensely modern, capable of defense by sea and land, beneath the surface and in the air. But it should be so conducted that all the world may see in it not a menace but an instrument of security and peace.

This nation believes thoroughly in an honorable peace under which the rights of its citizens are to be everywhere protected. It has never found that the necessary enjoyment of such a peace could be maintained only by a great and threatening array of arms. In common with other nations, it is now more determined than ever to promote peace through friendliness and good-will, through mutual understandings and mutual forbearance. We have never practiced the policy of competitive armaments. We have recently committed ourselves by covenants with the other great nations to a limitation of our sea power. As one result of this, our navy ranks larger, in comparison, than it ever did before.

Removing the burden of expense and jealousy which must always accrue from a keen rivalry is one of the most effective methods of diminishing that unreasonable hysteria and misunderstanding which are the most potent means of fomenting war. This policy represents a new departure in the world. It is a thought, an ideal, which has led to an entirely new line of action. It will not be easy to maintain. Some never move from their old position, some are constantly slipping back to the old ways of thought and the old action of seizing a musket and relying on force.

America has taken the lead in this new direction, and that lead America must continue to hold. If we expect others to rely on our fairness and justice, we must show that we rely on their fairness and justice.

If we are to judge by past experience, there is much to be hoped for in international relations from frequent conferences and consultations. We have before us the beneficial results of the Washington conference and the various consultations recently held upon European affairs, some of which were in response to our suggestions and in some of which we were active participants. Even the failures cannot but be accounted useful and an immeasurable advance over threatened or actual warfare. I am strongly in favor of a continuation of this policy, whenever conditions are such that there is even a promise that practical and favorable results might be secured.

In conformity with the principle that a display of reason rather than a threat of force should be the determining factor in the intercourse among nations, we have long advocated the peaceful settlement of disputes by methods of arbitration and have negotiated many treaties to secure that result. The same considerations should lead to our adherence to the Permanent Court of International Justice.

Where great principles are involved, where great movements are under way which promise much for the welfare of humanity by reason of the very fact that many other nations have given such movements their actual support, we ought not to withhold our own sanction because of any small and inessential difference, but only upon the ground of the most important and compelling fundamental reasons. We cannot barter away our independence or our sovereignty, but we ought to engage in no refinements of logic, no sophistries and no subterfuges to argue away the undoubted duty of this country by reason of the might of its numbers, the power of its resources and its position of leadership in the world, actively and comprehensively to signify its approval and to bear its full share of the responsibility of a candid and disinterested attempt at the establishment of a tribunal for the administration of even-handed justice between nation and nation. The weight of our enormous influence must be cast upon the side of a reign not of force but of law and trial, not by battle but by reason.

We have never any wish to interfere in the political conditions of any other countries. Especially are we determined not to become implicated in the political controversies of the Old World. With a great deal of hesitation, we have responded to appeals for help to maintain order, protect life and property, and establish responsible government in some of the small countries of the Western Hemisphere. Our private citizens have advanced large sums of money to assist in the necessary financing and relief of the Old World. We have not failed nor shall we fail to respond whenever necessary to mitigate human suffering and assist in the rehabilitation of distressed nations. These, too, are requirements which must be met by reason of our vast powers and the place we hold in the world.

Some of the best thought of mankind has long been seeking for a formula for permanent peace. Undoubtedly the clarification of the principles of international law would be helpful, and the efforts of scholars to prepare such a work for adoption by the various nations should have our sympathy and support. Much may be hoped for from the earnest studies of those who advocate the outlawing of aggressive war. But all these plans and preparations, these treaties and covenants, will not of themselves be adequate.

One of the greatest dangers to peace lies in the economic pressure to which people find themselves subjected. One of the most practical things to be done in the world is to seek arrangements under which such pressure may be removed, so that opportunity may be renewed and hope may be revived. There must be some assurance that effort and endeavor will be followed by success and prosperity. In the making and financing of such adjustments there is not only an opportunity but a real duty for America to respond with her counsel and her resources. Conditions must be provided under which people can make a living and work out of their difficulties.

But there is another element, more important than all, without which there cannot be the slightest hope of a permanent peace. That element lies in the heart of humanity. Unless the desire for peace be cherished there, unless this fundamental and only natural source of brotherly love be cultivated to its highest degree, all artificial efforts will be in vain. Peace will come when there is realization that only under a reign of law, based on righteousness and supported by the religious conviction of the brotherhood of man, can there be any hope of a complete and satisfying life. Parchment will fail, the sword will fail, it is only the spiritual nature of man that can be triumphant.

It seems altogether probable that we can contribute most to these important objects by maintaining our position of political detachment and independence. We are not identified with any Old World interests. This position should be made more and more clear in our relations with all foreign countries. We are at peace with all of them. Our program is never to oppress, but always to assist. But while we do justice to others, we must require that justice be done to us. With us a treaty of peace means peace, and a treaty of amity means amity.

We have made great contributions to the settlement of contentious differences in both Europe and Asia. But there is a very definite point beyond which we cannot go. We can only help those who help themselves. Mindful of these limitations, the one great duty that stands out requires us to use our enormous powers to trim the balance of the world.

While we can look with a great deal of pleasure upon what we have done abroad, we must remember that our continued success in that direction depends upon what we do at home. Since its very outset, it has been found necessary to conduct our Government by means of political parties. That system would not have survived from generation to generation if it had not been fundamentally sound and provided the best instrumentalities for the most complete expression of the popular will. It is not necessary to claim that it has always worked perfectly. It is enough to know that nothing better has been devised. No one would deny that there should be full and free expression and an opportunity for independence of action within the party.

There is no salvation in a narrow and bigoted partisanship. But if there is to be responsible party government, the party label must be something more than a mere device for securing office. Unless those who are elected under the same party designation are willing to assume sufficient responsibility and exhibit sufficient loyalty and coherence, so that they can cooperate with each other in the support of the broad general principles of the party platform, the election is merely a mockery, no decision is made at the polls and there is no representation of the popular will. Common honesty and good faith with the people who support a party at the polls require that party, when it enters office, to assume the control of that portion of the Government to which it has been elected. Any other course is bad faith and a violation of the party pledges.

When the country has bestowed its confidence upon a party by making it a majority in the Congress, it has a right to expect such unity of action as will make the party majority an effective instrument of government. This Administration has come into power with a very clear and definite mandate from the people. The expression of the popular will in favor of maintaining our constitutional guarantees was overwhelming and decisive.

There was a manifestation of such faith in the integrity of the courts that we can consider that issue rejected for some time to come. Likewise, the policy of public ownership of railroads and certain electric utilities met with unmistakable defeat. The people declared that they wanted their rights to have not a political but a judicial determination, and their independence and freedom continued and supported by having the ownership and control of their property, not in the Government, but in their own hands. As they always do when they have a fair chance, the people demonstrated that they are sound and are determined to have a sound Government.

When we turn from what was rejected to inquire what was accepted, the policy that stands out with the greatest clearness is that of economy in public expenditure with reduction and reform of taxation. The principle involved in this effort is that of conservation. The resources of this country are almost beyond computation. No mind can comprehend them. But the cost of our combined Governments is likewise almost beyond definition.

Not only those who are now making their tax returns, but those who meet the enhanced cost of existence in their monthly bills, know by hard experience what this great burden is and what it does. No matter what others may want, these people want a drastic economy. They are opposed to waste. They know that extravagance lengthens the hours and diminishes the rewards of their labor.

I favor the policy of economy, not because I wish to save money, but because I wish to save people. The men and women of this country who toil are the ones who bear the cost of the Government. Every dollar that we carelessly waste means that their life will be so much the more meagre. Every dollar that we prudently save means that their life will be so much the more abundant. Economy is idealism in its most practical form.

March 5, 1925

Text of President Hoover's Inaugural Address

* * * * *

World Peace the Basis of Prosperity

The United States fully accepts the profound truth that our own progress, prosperity and peace are interlocked with the progress, prosperity and peace of all humanity. The whole world is at peace. The dangers to a continuation of this peace today are largely the fear and suspicion which still haunt the world. No suspicion or fear can be rightly directed toward our country.

Those who have a true understanding of America know that we have no desire for territorial expansion, for economic or other domination of other peoples. Such purposes are repugnant to our ideals of human freedom. Our form of government is ill adapted to the responsibilities which inevitably follow permanent limitation of the independence of other peoples.

Superficial observers seem to find no destiny for our abounding increase in population, in wealth and power except that of imperialism. They fail to see that the American people are engrossed in the building for themselves of a new economic system, a new social system, a new political system—all of which are characterized by aspirations of freedom of opportunity and thereby are the negation of imperialism.

They fail to realize that, because of our abounding prosperity our youth are pressing more and more into our institutions of learning; that our people are seeking a larger vision through literature, science and travel; that they are moving toward stronger moral and spiritual life—that from these things our sympathies are broadening beyond the bounds of our nation and race toward their true expression in a real brotherhood of man.

They fail to see that the idealism of America will lead it to no narrow or selfish channel, but inspire it to do its full share as a nation toward the advancement of civilization. It will do that not by mere declaration but by taking a practical part in support of all useful international undertakings. We not only desire peace with the world, but to see peace maintained throughout the world. We wish to advance the reign of justice and reason toward the extinction of force.

The recent treaty for the renunciation of war as an instrument of national policy sets an advanced standard in our conception of the relations of nations. Its acceptance should pave the way to greater limitation of armament, the offer of which we sincerely extend to the world.

But its full realization also implies a greater and greater perfection in the instrumentalities for pacific settlement of controversies between nations. In the creation and use of these instrumentalities we should support every sound method of conciliation, arbitration and judicial settlement.

American statesmen were among the first to propose and they have constantly urged upon the world, the establishment of a tribunal for the settlement of controversies of a justiciable character. The Permanent Court of International Justice in its major purpose is thus peculiarly identified with American ideals and with American statesmanship. No more potent instrumentality for this purpose has been conceived and no other is practicable of establishment.

The reservations placed upon our adherence should not be misinterpreted. The United States seeks by these reservations no special privilege or advantage, but only to clarify our relation to advisory opinions and other matters which are subsidiary to the major purposes of the Court. The way should, and I believe will, be found by which we may take our proper place in a movement so fundamental to the progress of peace.

Foreign Policy One of Independence

Our people have determined that we should make no political engagements such as membership in the League of Nations, which may commit us in advance as a nation to become involved in the settlements of controversies between other countries. They adhere to the belief that the independence of America from such obligations increases its ability and availability for services in all fields of human progress.

I have lately returned from a journey among our sister republics of the Western Hemisphere. I have received unbounded hospitality and courtesy as their expression of friendliness to our country. We are held by particular bonds of sympathy and common interest with them. They are each of them building a racial character and a culture which is an impressive contribution to human progress. We wish only for the maintenance of their independence, the growth of their stability and their prosperity.

While we have had wars in the Western Hemisphere yet on the whole the record is in encouraging contrast with that of other parts of the world. Fortunately the New World is largely free from the inheritances of fear and distrust which have so troubled the Old World and we should keep it so.

It is impossible, my countrymen, to speak of peace without profound emotion. In thousands of homes in America, in millions of homes around the world, there are vacant chairs. It would be a shameful confession of our unworthiness if it should develop that we have abandoned the hope for which these men have died. Surely civilization is old enough, surely mankind is mature enough so that we ought in our lifetime to find a way to permanent peace.

Abroad, to west and east, are nations whose sons mingled their blood with the blood of our sons on the battlefields. Most of these nations have contributed to our race, to our culture, our knowledge and our progress. From one of them we derive our very language and from many of them much of the genius of our institutions. Their desire for peace is as deep and sincere as our own.

Peace can be contributed to by respect for our ability in defense. Peace can be promoted by the limitation of arms and by the creation of instrumentalities for peaceful settlement of controversies. But it will become a reality only through self-restraint and active effort in friendliness and helpfulness. I covet for this administration a record of having further contributed to advance the cause of peace.

* * * * *

BARS INTERVENTION BY MONROE DOCTRINE

State Department Adopts the Clark Interpretation Made Under Kellogg in 1928.

NOTES SENT TO DIPLOMATS

Identic Papers Were Forwarded to Our Missions in Latin America by Kellogg.

FINAL STEPS WERE DELAYED

Our Representatives Will Soon Be Told to Deliver Notes to Governments.

Special to The New York Times.

WASHINGTON, June 23.—That interpretation of the Monroe Doctrine which disclaims the right of intervention in Latin-American countries under the Roosevelt corollary and also that the doctrine, of itself, implies the right of intervention has been set forth in identic notes by the State Department and forwarded to American diplomatic missions throughout Latin America.

The interpretation is the one given by J. Reuben Clark when he was Under Secretary of State in a special study made at the direction of Frank B. Kellogg, then Secretary of State, for the Senate Foreign Relations Committee in 1928 in relation to the committee's consideration of the Kellogg anti-war treaty.

While Mr. Clark emphasized that he was expressing only a personal opinion, the act of forwarding identic notes summarizing Mr. Clark's views in the form of a definition of the doctrine as understood by the United States, makes his pronouncement that of the government.

The identic notes were transmitted by Secretary Kellogg just before he left office a year ago. They were sent to the diplomatic officers with instructions to hold them, pending further orders from the Secretary of State, but instructions to deliver the notes never have gone forward and there has been no announcement of the step.

Completion of Step Delayed.

It was learned today, however, that the Kellogg-Clark interpretation represents the view of the State Department today and of the administration. Pressure of business, particularly that of the London Naval Conference, it was indicated, has delayed completing the step taken by Mr. Kellogg but the understanding is that this will be done soon.

Mr. Clark endeavored to define the Monroe Doctrine itself, and to disassociate it from the various constructions which have been placed upon it from time to time. He was particularly careful to show that the "Roosevelt corollary," which seeks to justify intervention in the affairs of certain Caribbean countries, actually has no foundation under the doctrine as enunciated by President Monroe.

The message sent to Congress by President Roosevelt in 1904 based the American policy toward Central America and Caribbean republics on his reading of the Monroe Doctrine, and since then attempts have been made to justify intervention in Haiti, Cuba, Nicaragua, Mexico and elsewhere on that foundation.

This interpretation has roused the resentment of Latin-American countries against American policy, and has brought protests from some Americans, notably Senator Borah, who has asserted that constructions "have since been placed upon this doctrine far outside its original purpose."

Mr. Clark's Definition.

The Monroe Doctrine relates solely to relationships between European States on the one side and the American Continents on the other, Mr. Clark's memorandum holds, and does not apply to purely inter-American relations, nor does it purport to lay down any principles that are to govern the inter-relationship of the States of the Western Hemisphere as among themselves. The doctrine states a case of the United States versus Europe, not of the United States versus Latin America.

Such arrangements as the United States has made with Cuba, Santo Domingo, Haiti and Nicaragua, Mr. Clark declares, are not within the doctrine as it was originally announced. They may be accounted for as the expression of a national policy which, like the doctrine itself, originated in the needs of security or self-preservation.

Similar opinions have been expressed by Secretary Stimson in his book "American Policy in Nicaragua," written after he had brought about the armistice there in 1927 and arranged for American supervision of elections.

June 24, 1930

ROOSEVELT URGES 'CONCERTED ACTION' FOR PEACE AND ARRAIGNS WAR MAKERS; LEAGUE COMMITTEE CONDEMNS JAPAN

The President's Speech

By The Associated Press.

CHICAGO, Oct. 5.—The text of President Roosevelt's address here today was as follows:

Associated Press

The President motoring down Michigan Avenue en route to the new $11,500,000 Outer Drive Bridge development which he opened officially yesterday.

I am glad to come once again to Chicago and especially to have the opportunity of taking part in the dedication of this important project of civic betterment.

On my trip across the continent and back I have been shown many evidences of the result of common-sense cooperation between municipalities and the Federal Government, and I have been greeted by tens of thousands of Americans who have told me in every look and word that their material and spiritual well-being has made great strides forward in the past few years.

And yet, as I have seen with my own eyes the prosperous farms, the thriving factories and the busy railroads—as I have seen the happiness and security and peace which covers our wide land—almost inevitably I have been compelled to contrast our peace with very different scenes being enacted in other parts of the world.

It is because the people of the United States under modern conditions must, for the sake of their own future, give thought to the rest of the world, that I, as the responsible executive head of the nation, have chosen this great inland city and this gala occasion to speak to you on a subject of definite national importance.

The political situation in the world, which of late has been growing progressively worse, is such as to cause grave concern and anxiety to all the peoples and nations who wish to live in peace and amity with their neighbors.

Some nine years ago the hopes of mankind for a continuing era of international peace were raised to great heights when more than sixty nations solemnly pledged themselves not to resort to arms in furtherance of their national aims and policies. The high aspirations expressed in the Briand-Kellogg Peace Pact and the hopes for peace thus raised have of late given way to a haunting fear of calamity.

The present reign of terror and international lawlessness began a few years ago. It began through unjustified interference in the internal affairs of other nations or the invasion of alien territory in violations of treaties, and has now reached a stage where the very foundations of civilization are seriously threatened.

The landmarks and traditions which have marked the progress of civilization toward a condition of law, order and justice are being wiped away.

Without a declaration of war and without warning or justification of any kind, civilians, including women and children, are being ruthlessly murdered with bombs from the air.

In times of so-called peace, ships are being attacked and sunk by submarines without cause or notice. Nations are fomenting and taking sides in civil warfare in nations that have never done them any harm. Nations claiming freedom for themselves deny it to others.

No Immunity for America

Innocent peoples and nations are being cruelly sacrificed to a greed for power and supremacy which is devoid of all sense of justice and humane consideration.

To paraphrase a recent author: "Perhaps we foresee a time when men, exultant in the technique of homicide, will rage so hotly over the world that every precious thing will be in danger, every book and picture and harmony, every treasure garnered through two millenniums, the small, the delicate, the defenseless—all will be lost or wrecked or utterly destroyed."

If those things come to pass in other parts of the world, let no one imagine that America will escape, that it may expect mercy, that this Western Hemisphere will not be attacked and that it will continue tranquilly and peacefully to carry on the ethics and the arts of civilization.

If those days come, "there will be no safety by arms, no help from authority, no answer in science. The storm will rage till every flower of culture is trampled and all human beings are leveled in a vast chaos."

If those days are not to come to pass—if we are to have a world in which we can breathe freely and live in amity without fear—the peace-loving nations must make a concerted effort to uphold laws and principles on which alone peace can rest secure.

Unity of Nations for Peace

The peace-loving nations must make a concerted effort in opposition to those violations of treaties and those ignorings of humane instincts which today are creating a state of international anarchy and instability from which there is no escape through mere isolation or neutrality.

Those who cherish their freedom and recognize and respect the equal right of their neighbors to be free and live in peace must work together for the triumph of law and moral principles in order that peace, justice and confidence may prevail in the world.

There must be a return to a belief in the pledged word, in the value of a signed treaty. There must be recognition of the fact that national morality is as vital as private morality.

A Bishop wrote me the other day:

"It seems to be that something greatly needs to be said in behalf of ordinary humanity against the present practice of carrying the horrors of war to helpless civilians, especially women and children.

"It may be that such a protest might be regarded by many, who claim to be realists, as futile, but may it not be that the heart of mankind is so filled with horror at the present needless suffering that that force could be mobilized in sufficient volume to lessen such cruelty in the days ahead?

"Even though it may take twenty years, which God forbid, for civilization to make effective its corporate protest against this barbarism, surely strong voices may hasten the day."

There is a solidarity and interdependence about the modern world, both technically and morally, which makes it impossible for any nation completely to isolate itself from economic and political upheavals in the rest of the world, especially when such upheavals appear to be spreading and not declining.

There can be no stability or peace either within nations or between nations except under laws and moral standards adhered to by all. International anarchy destroys every foundation for peace. It jeopardizes either the immediate or the future security of every nation, large or small.

It is, therefore, a matter of vital interest and concern to the people of the United States that the sanctity of international treaties and the maintenance of international morality be restored.

The overwhelming majority of the peoples and nations of the world today want to live in peace. They seek the removal of barriers against trade.

They want to exert themselves in industry, in agriculture and in business, that they may increase their wealth through the production of wealth-producing goods rather than striving to produce military planes and bombs and machine guns and cannon for the destruction of human lives and useful property.

In those nations of the world which seem to be piling armament on armament for purposes of aggression, and those other nations which fear acts of aggression against them and their security, a very high proportion of the national income is being spent directly for armaments. It runs from 30 to as high as 50 per cent.

The proportion that we in the United States spend is far less—11 or 12 per cent.

How happy we are that the circumstances of the moment permit us to put our money into bridges and boulevards, dams and reforestation, the conservation of our soil and many other kinds of useful works, rather than into huge standing armies and vast supplies of implements of war.

Dealing With Lawless Tenth

I am compelled and you are compelled, nevertheless, to look ahead. The peace, the freedom and the security of 90 per cent of the population of the world is being jeopardized by the remaining 10 per cent who are threatening a breakdown of all international order and law.

Surely the 90 per cent who want to live in peace under law and in accordance with moral standards that have received almost universal acceptance through the centuries, can and must find some way to make their will prevail.

The situation is definitely of universal concern. The questions involved relate not merely to violations of specific provisions of particular treaties; they are questions of war and of peace, of international law, and especially of principles of humanity. It is true that they involve definite violations of agreements, and especially of the Covenant of the League of Nations, the Briand-Kellogg Pact and the Nine-Power Treaty. But they also involve problems of world economy, world security and world humanity.

It is true that the moral consciousness of the world must recognize the importance of removing injustices and well-founded grievances; but at the same time it must be aroused to the cardinal necessity of honoring sanctity of treaties, of respecting the rights and liberties of others and of putting an end to acts of international aggression.

It seems to be unfortunately true that the epidemic of world lawlessness is spreading.

When an epidemic of physical disease starts to spread, the community approves and joins in a quarantine of the patients in order to protect the health of the community against the spread of the disease.

Policy of Avoiding War

It is my determination to pursue a policy of peace and to adopt every practicable measure to avoid involvement in war.

It ought to be inconceivable that in this modern era, and in the face of experience, any nation could be so foolish and ruthless as to run the risk of plunging the whole world into war by invading and violating, in contravention of solemn treaties, the territory of other nations that have done them no real harm and which are too weak to protect themselves adequately. Yet the peace of the world and the welfare and security of every nation is today being threatened by that very thing.

No nation which refuses to exercise forbearance and to respect the freedom and rights of others can long remain strong and retain the confidence and respect of other nations. No nation ever loses its dignity or good standing by conciliating its differences, and by exercising great patience with, and consideration for, the rights of other nations.

War is a contagion, whether it be declared or undeclared. It can engulf states and peoples remote from the original scene of hostilities. We are determined to keep out of war, yet we cannot insure ourselves against the disastrous effects of war and the dangers of involvement. We are adopting such measures as will minimize our risk of involvement, but we cannot have complete protection in a world of disorder in which confidence and security have broken down.

If civilization is to survive, the principles of the Prince of Peace must be restored. Shattered trust between nations must be revived.

Most important of all, the will for peace on the part of peace-loving nations must express itself to the end that nations that may be tempted to violate their agreements and the rights of others will desist from such a cause. There must be positive endeavors to preserve peace.

America hates war. America hopes for peace. Therefore, America actively engages in the search for peace.

October 6, 1937

ROOSEVELT OFFERS A DEFENSE PROGRAM AGAINST RISING MENACE OF DICTATORS; THREAT OF ECONOMIC SANCTIONS SEEN

AIMS OF PRESIDENT

Arms, Plant Facilities and National Unity Urged in Message

By TURNER CATLEDGE

Special to THE NEW YORK TIMES.

WASHINGTON, Jan. 4.—In a message packed with warnings of dangers to democracy in a world harassed by the marching of dictators, President Roosevelt urged upon Congress today a three-point program of action designed to prepare America to meet threats to her institutions and discharge her responsibility of helping to protect the Western Hemisphere.

This triple-phased "adequate defense" which he proposed included armed forces and defenses strong enough to ward off sudden attack upon our shores. It involved, secondly, the immediate preparation of key facilities "to insure sustained resistance and ultimate victory." And finally—a point stressed most of all—it necessitated maintenance of a national unity which, he maintained, had been assured by the spreading of common opportunity through his economic policies of the last six years.

"Our nation's program of social and economic reform is a part of defense as basic as armaments themselves," he said.

The President intimated strongly that he would soon seek to free the Executive Department of the fetters of the Neutrality Act in directing international affairs. Other points in his address were taken to mean that he might also be considering use of economic sanctions to meet recurring threats to world peace.

The message, to be followed soon by one devoted specifically to the armed defenses, was delivered by the President in person to a joint session of the new Congress, which was host to himself and his Cabinet this afternoon in the House Chamber.

Thomsen in Diplomatic Gallery

The thousand visitors crowded into the galleries included the largest group of foreign diplomats attending such a ceremony in recent years. In a prominent place in the diplomatic gallery was Dr. Hans Thomsen, chargé d'affaires of Germany, who figured in the near break between Germany and the United States only a short time ago. Sumner Welles, Under-Secretary of State, who spoke for Secretary Hull in that famous interchange, represented the Secretary of State on the House floor today.

Diplomats or no diplomats, the President lashed out at the dictatorships which he regarded as constituting a threat to the very institution of democracy. He called upon Congress to recognize the danger and prepare this country to meet the challenge now being flung down by the dictators to the ideas of faith and humanity—those foundation stones on which governments and civilization are based.

"We are off on a race to make democracy work," he said with a tone and a manner that pumped into the microphones words carried by radio throughout the land and to the four corners of the earth.

So long as the President remained on the theme of defense of democracy his audience was with him to the man, as demonstrated repeatedly by applause and later by the comments of members of the House and Senators in approval of his general remarks.

When he started to specify, however, and especially to defend his lending-spending economic program on the basis of national defense, there developed lines of differences which finally were manifested by a good-natured exchange between him and the Republican side of the Chamber.

Insists on Continued Outlay

Further details of expenditures policy will be disclosed when the budget message is delivered to Congress tomorrow. As for today, the President practically defied Congress to curtail it, saying the legislative branch would have to take responsibility fcr any business recession that followed such a step.

He implied, too, that the reform crusade of the last few years had been completed and that henceforth recovery should be the main one of the three "R's" of the New Deal, hitherto listed as "Relief, Recovery and Reform." In his message he substituted "revision" for "reform," saying it was increasingly necessary, in the interest of national mobility, for Congress to make workable those laws which contributed to the unity and economic sufficiency of the people.

The goal for the renewed recovery drive was announced as a national income of $80,000,000,000, which, Mr. Roosevelt said, would have to be supplied in part through "government investing." The national income for this year is estimated at about $60,000,000,000.

"At that figure ($80,000,000,000) we shall have a substantial reduction of unemployment," he said, "and the Federal revenues will be sufficient to balance the current level of cash expenditures on the basis of the existing tax structure. The figure can be attained, working within the framework of our traditional profit system."

He suggested, however, the revamping of the tax relationships between Federal, State and local governments and consideration of "relatively small tax increases to adjust inequalities without interfering with the aggregate income of the American people."

All Themes Touch on Defense

Even in his discussion of the domestic situation, the idea of preparing for defense ran throughout. Congress was told that there were practical and peaceful ways in which a country could proceed to defend its interests and command for itself "a decent respect for the opinions of mankind."

"There are many methods short of war, but stronger and more effective than mere words, of bringing home to aggressor governments the aggregate sentiments of our people," he said.

These words were interpreted throughout Washington as indicating the purpose of this government to attempt to apply economic sanctions against nations with which it may be at odds, or which may be threatening the peace of the world.

Later, and by more direct reference, the President indicated his desire to be rid of the fetters of the present Neutrality Law. When we deliberately try to legislate neutrality, he said, "laws may operate unevenly and unfairly—may actually give aid to an aggressor and deny it to a victim. The instinct of self-preservation should warn us that we ought not to let that happen any more."

As he said this some Senators who engineered the present Neutrality Law through Congress looked straight ahead without joining in the mild applause which greeted the remark.

The lesson as to the ineffectiveness, or possible reverse effect of neutrality laws, was one of the lessons learned of late, the President said. But he added that this country had learned something else, namely, "the old, old lesson that probability of attack is mightily decreased by the assurance of an ever ready defense." It was at this point that he disclosed his three-point plan of rearmament, revitalization of certain industries and vigorous prosecution of the economic policies which he had followed in recent months.

He let the matter of rearmament and resuscitation of key facilities suffice with rather general reference, putting off full discussion until his supplemental defense message next week. At that time he is expected to recommend an additional authorization of $500,000,000 for aircraft for the army and navy, and possible arrangements for government aid to industries to help prepare themselves for the possibilities of war.

Six Years of Reforms Emphasized

Today he went quickly to the improvements which, he maintained, had taken place in the internal affairs of the United States and had made it more invulnerable to outside attack. He asked Congress to consider the accomplishments since 1933 against the background of events in Europe, in Africa and in Asia.

He mentioned the Administration's program for conservation of natural resources, for extending food, shelter and medical care to the population; for rehabilitating agriculture; for attempting to end the long smouldering labor difficulties in industry and for extending security to the aged and helpless. Never, he said, had there been six years of such far-flung internal preparedness in the country's history.

"And all this has been done without any dictator's power to command, without conscription of labor or confiscation of capital, without concentration camps, and without a scratch on freedom of speech, freedom of the press or the rest of the Bill of Rights," he said.

He added that the public now looked to Congress to improve the new machinery which had been permanently installed to provide for the common good. Furthermore, he asked for authority to reorganize the administrative arm of the government, so that the tools now at its command would be put to maximum effectiveness.

"We have now passed the period of internal conflict in the launching of our program of social reform," he continued. "Our full energies may now be released to invigorate the processes of recovery in order to preserve our reforms, and to give every man and woman who wants to work a real job at a living wage."

Can We Compete? He Asks

In the drive for recovery, the time element called for greater effort to attain the fullest employment of labor and capital, he said. "The first duty of statesmanship today is to bring capital and man power together," which was done in the dictatorships by main force.

"Like it or not, they have solved, for a time at least, the problem of idle men and idle capital," he added. "Can we compete with them by boldly seeking methods of putting idle men and idle capital together and, at the same time, remain within our American way of life, within the Bill of Rights, and within the bounds of what is, from our point of view, civilization itself?"

It was in this connection that he announced his national income goal of $80,000,000,000. The factors for attaining and maintaining so much are many and complicated, he said, and included a widespread understanding among business men of changes which world conditions and technological improvements have brought in the last twenty years. They included, too, the perfecting of the farm program; whole-hearted acceptance of new standards of honesty in the financial markets; reconcilement of enormous, antagonistic interests in the railroad and general transportation field; the working out of new techniques to protect the public interest and the development of a wider market for electric power.

"They include the perfecting of labor organizations and a universal, ungrudging attitude by employers toward the labor movement," the President continued, "until there is a minimum of interruption of production and employment because of disputes, and acceptance by labor of the truth that the welfare of labor itself depends on increased, balanced output of goods."

Laughs as Republicans Applaud

It was in discussion of the government spending program, which he labeled as "government investing," that the President had his tilt with the Republican side. He had begun to say that there were two ways to approach the subject.

"The first," he said, "calls for elimination of enough activities of government to bring the expenses of the government immediately into balance with income of government."

Here the Republicans broke in with wild applause. The President was forced to suspend for a moment. As the applause continued, stronger in volume, the President looked toward the source, threw back his head and laughed. His display of good nature brought silence, and he continued:

"This school of thought maintains that because our national income this year is only $60,000,000,000, ours is only a $60,000,000,000 country."

With this, the shouting of Democrats broke into the applause and the Republicans grinned. The President followed in a second with his practical dare to Congress to try to cut expenditures. If Congress decided to reduce the present functions of government, it would have to select those to curtail. He mentioned agricultural relief, veterans' pensions, flood control, highways, waterways and other public works, grants for social security and health, Civilian Conservation Corps activities, relief for the unemployed and the national defense among the activities which might have to be reduced.

As he detailed the list, Senators and members of the House began to laugh. Obviously they recognized the chops which go into the pork barrel.

Applause from both sides came a second later, however, when the President said:

"The Congress alone has the power to do all this, as it is the appropriating branch of the government."

The President said that the "common sense action of resuming government activities last Spring," had reversed a recession and started the "new rising tide of prosperity and national income which we are now just beginning to enjoy."

"It is my conviction that down in their hearts, the American public—industry, agriculture, finance — wants this Congress to do whatever needs to be done to raise our national income to $80,000,000,000 a year," he said.

ROOSEVELT LETS FRANCE BUY PLANES; SENATE INQUIRY ON POLICIES IS LIKELY

SPURS AIR WORKS

President Asks Funds to Rush First 600 of Our Own New Ships

CLARK FIGHTS PARIS SALE

Protests Cooperation—Coast Crash Stirs Senators—British Complete Purchases

Special to THE NEW YORK TIMES.

WASHINGTON, Jan. 27.—President Roosevelt announced today that he had approved the purchase in this country of an undesignated number of modern battle planes for France.

Following this announcement there were indications tonight that a searching Senate inquiry into the entire foreign policy of the Roosevelt Administration would develop. There was a strong intimation at the Capitol that the French mission had had access to military aviation secrets at the instance of the President over the heads of the Army and Navy.

Senators, disturbed recently by suspicions within the Military Affairs Committee that the present foreign policy was directed toward active participation on the side of France in any European crisis, planned to study carefully the reasons behind these developments:

1. Mr. Roosevelt's statement that the Cabinet had given the "go ahead" signal for the French contract, and his added statement that he desired the American factories to execute the order to give work to idle men.

2. Reports of a serious conflict between the President and officer heads of the army and navy over the "facilities" extended to the French, which were understood to include access to army aviation secrets, and inspection of a new Douglas light bomber that was being tested by the manufacturer for possible sale to the government.

3. A letter from the President to Speaker Bankhead asking for an immediate appropriation of $50,000,000 to build nearly 600 planes for the American Army, also for the purpose of keeping idle factories busy.

4. A closed hearing by the Senate Military Affairs Committee of Secretary Morgenthau, Secretary Woodring and General Malin Craig, Chief of Staff, on the presence of Paul Chemidlin, representative of the French Air Ministry, in the Douglas bomber when it crashed near Los Angeles Monday.

5. The announcement by Representative Vinson of Georgia, chairman of the House Naval Affairs Committee, that he had "invited" Charles Edison, Assistant Secretary of the Navy, to tell the committee next Tuesday whether or not the Administration intends to fortify the island of Guam and to what extent.

It was learned on good authority that overtures were made direct to the White House for permission for the French mission to inspect and ride in the new bomber; that General Craig as Chief of Staff resisted the request, and that the President then gave the permission through Secretary Morgenthau as Chief of Civilian Procurement. French Embassy attachés refused tonight to discuss the matter, and General Craig could not be reached at his Fort Myer quarters.

Interested in Bullitt Story

To both houses of Congress have come reports of divisions of counsel in Administration circles over fundamentals of foreign relations and the possible effect of American rearmament on international politics. Senator Clark and Senator Nye hope to get clues tomorrow from the examination of General Craig, before the Military Affairs Committee, of which both are members. General Craig did not testify today.

Mr. Chemidlin's access to a type of military airplane, not usually displayed to foreign prospective purchasers, while it interests the committee, is by no means the main issue they will try to develop. The story which several members of Congress, on both sides of the Capitol, have heard piecemeal and which they want to investigate may be summed up as follows:

Ambassador Bullitt, when he came back from France several weeks ago on leave, was impressed by the imminence of war in Europe and was desirous of getting this government to extend all the help it could to France. He is said to have approached the general staff of the army and the general board of the navy with a plan to insure rapid delivery to the French Air Ministry of the latest type American military airplanes in large numbers.

Neutrality Act a Factor

The story goes that Mr. Bullitt wanted the army and navy to order, on their own account, numbers of service-type airplanes such as could not, under the law, be sold to a foreign purchaser. When and if the crisis he feared developed, but before France was actually at war, the President was to ask Congress for authority to sell these planes to the French Government.

The Neutrality Act would prohibit sale of the planes after France was actually involved in war, and the plan was expected to work before the President was compelled to declare that a state of war existed, thus bringing the Neutrality Act into force. The professional soldiers would have none of it, and the Ambassador is supposed to have gone to the President over their heads.

Mr. Roosevelt then wrote letters to Secretary Woodring, Secretary Swanson and Secretary Morgenthau, according to the Capitol version, asking them to give every consideration to possible French needs and every courtesy to the French air mission then about to arrive in this country to buy airplanes.

Just as members of Congress were beginning to put their heads together on this story President Roosevelt sent to Speaker Bankhead his letter asking that Congress authorize and appropriate at once $50,000,000 for immediate expenditure on 565 airplanes for the Army Air Corps.

President's Talk to Correspondents

The President was asked at his press conference this morning whether the United States had "taken steps to facilitate France in buying airplanes in the United States." He replied that, as the reporter had put the question, the answer was no. Then he added, in substance:

The actual facts in the case were very simple.

The French Government had wanted to buy planes for obvious reasons. The President discussed the matter with his Cabinet, considering the matter first from the point of view of the fact that most of the airplane factories in this country were today idle, as he put it.

About six of the major companies had practically closed up and one of the largest engine companies had laid off some 1,500 men. Also, from the point of view of the projected aerial expansion program in this country, it seemed very desirable to facilitate new orders to start the plants going, especially if the orders could be placed very quickly so as to be substantially completed before the expansion program here could be authorized and placed under way.

The French Government wanted planes and no reason occurred to President Roosevelt and his Cabinet why orders for them should not be placed. In fact, as Mr. Roosevelt explained, it seemed an excellent thing that the French Government should do so.

So far as the President knew, the British Government was not in the market for more American planes at this time. As for the French purchases, they involved no financial assistance on the part of this government. Just cash on the barrel-head, as he termed it.

Plane Owned by Manufacturer

President Roosevelt was asked whether the Secretary of the Treasury had issued a special permit for the French air attaché to be aboard the bomber. The plane was being tested by the manufacturer for entry in a War Department competition on the Pacific Coast. The pilot was killed in the crash, in which Mr. Chemidlin was severely injured. Again, the President's answer was that as the question had been asked it did not accurately state the situation.

Both the Treasury and War Departments had advised the White House that there was no objection if the French bought planes from private companies, it was explained. The President also explained that the plane in which the French air attaché crashed had not yet been accepted by the United States Government.

It was a manufacturer's plane which was being flown at the time at a public municipal airport by the manufacturing company, the President said. He added that it was not yet known whether the plane in which M. Chemidlin sat as observer would be bought by this government or not, because it had not yet been placed in competition with other aircraft.

The government did not yet know what kind of planes it would purchase, President Roosevelt continued, since that decision would have to be based on competition as to type as well as price, a decision that would not be made for six weeks or two months.

When he was asked how the Treasury Department had come into the picture at all, the President said that in the first place the Treasury was interested in foreign trade as a general thing, and the plane was a potential export. In the second, Mr. Roosevelt said that in the procurement of planes and a great many other things the Treasury Procurement Division works very closely with the Army and Navy Procurement Divisions.

The Douglas plane which the manufacturer was testing had no secret devices installed at the time, but it was of advanced design, according to the understanding here. Under army regulations when a military plane is accepted from a private company it cannot be purchased by foreign governments or interests and shipped out of the country for a year, and not then except with the approval of the War Department.

While Great Britain recently had a mission in this country and placed orders for the purchase of 500 planes, no question has ever been raised concerning its procedure. It was in contact with the State Department, went to plants regularly approved by the military services, and placed orders that encountered no objection from the army and navy.

Great Britain announced at that time that she was planning no more large purchases in this country, explaining that the 500 had been bought to fill a gap while English and Canadian factories were getting into production. Most of the 500 planes have been delivered.

Some Senators indicated today that should they become convinced that unusual facilities were accorded to the French mission it might raise doubts concerning some of the purposes of this country's air rearmament program. There were hints that some of the Senators may endeavor, before the investigation is completed, to learn whether there is a possibility that in the event Great Britain and France became involved in war some of America's air fleet might be placed at the disposal of those powers. From this point of view, the inquiry offered the possibility of developing a broad consideration of foreign policy, particularly whether any informal understandings have been reached with foreign governments.

A possibility exists that at the Senate Military Affairs Committee's inquiry some members may seek to uncover what directions President Roosevelt may have issued to Secretary Morgenthau and to the Navy Department, as the Navy Department was understood to have participated in the arrangements for the visit of the French mission, although it was interested primarily in plants engaged in producing army planes. Later an army officer was assigned to the mission.

January 28, 1939

ROOSEVELT DENIES NEUTRALITY SHIFT

Does Not Consider U. S. Credit to Finland a Modification of Hands-Off Policy

BAN ON WAR AID IS HINTED

President Is Not Specific on Munitions, but He Looks for No Change in Law

Special to THE NEW YORK TIMES.

WASHINGTON, Dec. 12—President Roosevelt said today that the Administration was contemplating no relaxation of its policy against giving aid to belligerent nations and did not consider the extension of a $10,000,000 credit to Finland to aid its civilian population to be a modification of that policy.

With his explanation of Administration policy the President coupled the observation that since none of the money to be advanced through the Export-Import Bank for Finland's benefit was to be used for purchasing war materials, there was no ground for assuming that any relaxation of the Neutrality Act restrictions on dealing with belligerents was contemplated.

Although some saw in the President's remarks the implication that neither Finland nor any other victim of international aggression would be aided by the Administration in purchasing war materials in the United States, Mr. Roosevelt was not specific on the point. Such assistance would be within the letter of the Neutrality Act until the President found that the nation concerned was at war and invoked the embargo provision.

No Neutrality Changes

Mr. Roosevelt let it be known, in reply to questions, that he had no present intention of proposing modification or revision of the Neutrality Act at the next session of Congress and that, so far as the Administration was concerned, the statute seemed to be working very well.

However, the President left room for such a proposal in the future when he asked the reporters not to accuse him of inconsistency if, at some future time, he found it advisable to propose some amendments to the existing law. Meanwhile, he was content to encourage further contributions for Finnish relief, explaining that the little nation's needs would certainly increase and continue through the Winter months.

To an implied suggestion that there might be some friction between the American Red Cross and former President Hoover over the latter's independent efforts on behalf of Finnish refugees and the civilian population resident in that country, Mr. Roosevelt turned a deaf ear.

Mr. Roosevelt was asked in his capacity as president of the Red Cross, what he thought of Mr. Hoover's efforts. He replied that he thought they were fine because his predecessor had been cooperating with the Red Cross in his effort to raise funds for Finnish relief. He added, in reply to related qeustions, that he understood Mr. Hoover had been consulting with Norman H. Davis, chairman of the organization, for about two months.

Red Cross Aid Reviewed

This corporation with the Red Cross, for which the President recently asked in an effort to avoid duplication of administrative expense, had extended to all organizations receiving contributions for aid of European war victims, Mr. Roosevelt explained. Then he gave a statistical picture of Red Cross collections for such purposes and the distribution made of them to date, all of which figures had been published heretofore.

After a visit to the White House recently, Jesse Jones, Federal Loan Administrator, said he doubted whether as a matter of policy the Administration would undertake to finance shipments of supplies to belligerent nations. Although he did not specify that he had in mind belligerents within the definition of the Neutrality Act, the President's explanation today was regarded as supplying this deficiency.

Mr. Roosevelt said in reply to questions that the $10,000,000 to be made available to Finland would about exhaust the funds on hand at the Export-Import Bank. He said several months ago that he would renew his request for a $100,000,000 appropriation for the bank at the next session of Congress.

Munitions Buying Difficult

WASHINGTON, Dec. 12 (AP)—Efforts of Finnish officials to obtain American munitions quickly to help halt the Russian invasion met with difficulties today. Hjalmar Procope, the Minister, and Colonel Per Zilliacus, military attaché, conferred with war and navy officials on what they wanted to buy. Gas masks, guns, ammunition and aircraft were reported to be included.

Prospects for obtaining these in substantial quantities and without delay appeared to be slim, however, because commercial plants already are behind in their foreign orders and existing stocks are part of the regular War and Navy Department supplies.

Mr. Procope conferred with Lewis Johnson, Assistant Secretary of War, and Colonel Zilliacus with both Mr. Johnson and Charles Edison, Acting Secretary of the Navy.

Gas masks were understood to be near the top of the Finns' shopping list. Military types are made in the United States for the army at the Edgewood Arsenal, Md., and a single commercial concern, the Goodyear Tire and Rubber Company, Akron, Ohio, is turning out a comparatively few experimentally under an "educational" order for the War Department.

December 13, 1939

ROOSEVELT TRADES DESTROYERS FOR SEA BASES TELLS CONGRESS HE ACTED ON OWN AUTHORITY

LINE OF 4,500 MILES

Two Defense Outposts Are Gifts, Congress Is Told—No Rent on Rest

FOR 50 OLD VESSELS

President Holds Move Solely Protective, 'No Threat to Any Nation'

By FRANK L. KLUCKHOHN
Special to THE NEW YORK TIMES.

WASHINGTON, Sept. 3—President Roosevelt informed Congress today that he had completed an arrangement by which the United States will transfer to Great Britain fifty over-age destroyers and obtain from Britain ninety-nine-year leases for sea and air bases at eight strategic continental and island points in the Western Hemisphere.

The new American defense line thus established will stretch 4,500 miles from Newfoundland to British Guiana and include other bases on the islands of Bermuda, the Bahamas, Jamaica, St. Lucia, Trinidad and Antigua.

It is intended to make difficult, if not impossible, naval and air attacks upon the United States and much of the New World. The exact sites of the bases will be determined later by the two governments.

A solemn pledge by the British Government to the United States not to scuttle or surrender the British fleet under any conditions was revealed coincidentally by the State Department's publication of correspondence between Secretary Hull and the British Ambassador, the Marquess of Lothian.

Secretary Hull was informed that it represented the "settled policy" of His Majesty's Government not to "surrender or sink" the British fleet.

Reshaping of Naval Defense

The deal, carrying with it far-flung international as well as domestic defense implications, was hailed by President Roosevelt as the most important since the Jefferson Administration completed the Louisiana Purchase in 1803.

Informed official circles contended that it assured the British Fleet as an Atlantic sea-screen for the United States and made it possible for the American Fleet to remain in the Pacific.

Some thought it might lead to an informal defensive alliance between this country and Australia similar to the arrangement recently completed administratively with Canada, although others disagreed on this point.

President Roosevelt informed Congress that the British Government had given the right to bases in Newfoundland and Bermuda as an outright gift, "generously given and gladly received," but that "the other bases mentioned have been acquired in exchange for fifty of our over-age destroyers."

Previously, the President had insisted that the destroyer and base deals were separate.

Legal Basis for Procedure

Mr. Roosevelt explained in his message that he had acted upon a legal opinion by Attorney General Jackson which held that the Chief Executive had the right to dispose of the destroyers and complete the deal without consultation with the Senate and without its approval.

The President made clear that he would not seek the Senate's endorsement by remarking that he sent his statement merely "for the information of Congress."

Chairman Walsh of the Senate Naval Affairs Committee and several other Senators publicly condemned the proposed deal as illegal under domestic and international law when it was reported in the press some weeks ago that President Roosevelt had agreed to give Britain fifty destroyers after pleas from Prime Minister Winston Churchill.

In view of Senator Walsh's stand, some Senators privately expressed the opinion that there might be an attempt to have the Naval Affairs Committee open an investigation of the whole transaction.

After the President's message was read in the House, the Senate being in recess until tomorrow, Congressional comment flowed in a steady stream.

Republicans as a whole seemed to be against the manner of carrying out the transaction, Senator Nye of North Dakota, an outstanding isolationist, declaring that "dictatorial practices" had been followed.

Democrats appeared to be divided in their views, but a vast majority thought it a "magnificent accomplishment." Their comments ranged from that of Senator Clark of Idaho charging "an act of war" to that of Senator Thomas of Utah, a member of the Foreign Relations Committee, who asserted that "the President has been wise."

President Roosevelt, for his part, informed Congress that the arrangement was "an epochal and far-reaching act of preparation for continental defense in the face of grave danger," that it did not represent "a threat to any nation" and that it was not in any sense "inconsistent with our status of peace."

"Preparation for defense is an inalienable prerogative of a sovereign state," he stated.

"This is the most important action in the reinforcement of our national defense that has been taken since the Louisiana Purchase. Then, as now, considerations of safety from overseas attack were fundamental."

Asserting that the value of the acquired bases as "outposts of security" was "beyond calculation," he stated that our military and naval leaders held them "essential to the protection of the Panama Canal, Central America, the northern portion of South America, the Antilles, Canada, Mexico and our own Eastern and Gulf Seaboards."

"For these reasons I have taken advantage of the present opportunity to acquire them," he added.

Location of Bases Set Forth

Lord Lothian informed Secretary Hull in the exchange of letters completing the arrangement that the Newfoundland bases would be established on the exposed Avalon Peninsula and the southern coast and the Bermuda bases on the east coast of the island and the Great Bay.

The Bahamas bases would be established on the east side, the Jamaica bases on the southern coast, the St. Lucia on the west of the island, the Trinidad bases in the Gulf of Paria on the west coast, and British Guiana bases "within fifty miles of Georgetown." The location of the Antigua air and sea bases has not yet been stated.

The British Ambassador explained that the bases would be "in exchange for naval and military equipment and materials which the United States Government will transfer to His Majesty's Government."

A State Department authority subsequently said that while the destroyers represented inadequate payment for the bases, the agreement to deliver them completed the transaction. He added, however, that details with regard to other supplies would be worked out later.

The bases, Lord Lothian stated, would be "free from rental and all other charges" except for compensation by the United States to private property owners whose land holdings might be taken over.

The United States will receive "all the rights, power and authority within the bases leased" as well as territorial waters and air spaces adjacent to or in the vicinity of the bases, and apparently the British Fleet or British aircraft could use them only by special permission and under the same rules and regulations governing other United States ports and bases.

The agreement provides that any difficulties in working out this provision "shall be determined by common agreement." On this point Lord Lothian said:

"The exact location and bounds of aforesaid bases, the necessary seaward, coast and anti-aircraft defenses, the location of sufficient military garrisons, stores and other necessary auxiliary facilities shall be determined by common agreement.

"His Majesty's Government are prepared to designate immediately experts to meet with experts of the United States for these purposes."

The Navy Department announced in the afternoon the seven members of the United States delegation to take part in these negotiations. The delegations, headed by Rear Admiral John W. Greenslade of the Navy General Board, includes naval aviation and marine representation.

The State Department disclosed that American warships would soon start on a survey of the bases being acquired.

Movement of Destroyers

All of the destroyers being transferred are now in Atlantic waters. The Navy Department, through Under-Secretary James Forrestal, said that the first contingent of eight destroyers would leave Boston on Friday.

Mr. Forrestal added that the ships would be taken by American crews to Canada, where they would be turned over to British crews.

The present value of the fifty destroyers is calculated by State Department officials as about $15,000,000, as compared with the 60,000,000 francs ($11,250,000) which the Jefferson Administration paid Napoleon for the 827,987 miles of territory acquired in the Louisiana Purchase.

The Navy, however, said that as of June 30, the destroyers released to Great Britain were carried on its books as representing a current aggregate value of $85,000,000.

Jackson's Three Chief Points

In his 5,000-word legal opinion upon which the President acted, Attorney General Jackson informed the President that:

1. "The proposed arrangements may be concluded as an executive agreement, effective without awaiting referendum.

2. "That there is Presidential power to transfer title and possession of the proposed considerations upon certification of appropriate staff officers.

3. "That the dispatch of the so-called 'mosquito boats' would constitute a violation of the statute law of the United States, but with that exception there is no legal obstacle to the consummation of the transaction, in accordance, of course, with the applicable provisions of the Neutrality Act as to delivery."

The Attorney General based his opinion upon the President's right as Commander in Chief of the Army and Navy and his degree of "control" of foreign relations as far as constitutional prerogatives were concerned.

The Attorney General held that the Espionage Act of June 15, 1917, upon which opposing members of Congress base their contention that domestic law prohibited the transfer of destroyers, "is inapplicable to vessels, like over-age destroyers, which were not built, armed, equipped as, or converted into, vessels of war with the intent that they should enter the service of a belligerent."

In this respect, Mr. Jackson said, the over-age destroyers differed from "mosquito boats" now under construction, which, he had previously ruled, could not be sold legally to Great Britain.

UNITED STATES ACQUIRES DEFENSE BASTIONS

Bases at the places indicated by circled dots are being leased by Great Britain to this country for ninety-nine years. The leases for those in Newfoundland and Bermuda are in effect outright gifts; the leases for the others are in exchange for fifty over-age United States destroyers. The bases in the Caribbean area will supplement present American defense centers (black diamonds) in guarding approaches to the Panama Canal.

He held again today that the mosquito boats would come within the terms of the 1917 ban.

The State and Navy Departments immediately revealed that Admiral Harold Stark, Chief of Naval Operations, already had certified to the White House and the Justice Department that the destroyers were not essential to the defense of the United States.

Mr. Jackson, in his opinion, had stated that "the appropriate staff officers may and should certify that ships and material involved are not essential to the United States if, in their judgment, the consummation of the transaction does not impair or weaken the total defense of the United States."

An authoritative State Department source said that whether or not Congress appropriates funds for construction of the bases, the arrangement had been consummated.

Vinson for Base Building Now

In this connection Chairman Vinson of the House Naval Affairs Committee expressed the opinion that President Roosevelt could start constructing bases at once in the areas obtained from Great Britain.

"We have appropriated already $10,000,000 for auxiliary air bases, and he could use that," Mr. Vinson said. "This would provide some pretty good bases.

"Then there is the blank check for $200,000,000 which Congress gave the President for use for national defense wherever it was most neded. I believe he could use that also."

He added that he did not expect any request for more legislation at this session of Congress. In other quarters, however, a request for appropriations was considered likely.

Secretary Hull, in his letter of reply to Lord Lothian, said that should the adjustment of territory to be included in the bases not be settled by experts of the two countries, the matter "shall be settled by the Secretary of State of the United States and His Majesty's Secretary of State for Foreign Affairs."

This was taken to mean that in practice the President and the Prime Minister, who negotiated the matter directly, would iron out the difficulties.

A State Department official said today that Secretary Hull knew nothing of the proposals until the day before he departed on his recent vacation and it was common knowledge that the President himself conducted the negotiations.

September 4, 1940

The President's Message

Following is the text of President Roosevelt's war message to Congress, as recorded by THE NEW YORK TIMES *from a broadcast:*

Mr. Vice President, Mr. Speaker, members of the Senate and the House of Representatives:

Yesterday, Dec. 7, 1941—a date which will live in infamy—the United States of America was suddenly and deliberately attacked by naval and air forces of the empire of Japan.

The United States was at peace with that nation, and, at the solicitation of Japan, was still in conversation with its government and its Emperor looking toward the maintenance of peace in the Pacific.

Indeed, one hour after Japanese air squadrons had commenced bombing in the American island of Oahu the Japanese Ambassador to the United States and his colleague delivered to our Secretary of State a formal reply to a recent American message. And, while this reply stated that it seemed useless to continue the existing diplomatic negotiations, it contained no threat or hint of war or of armed attack.

Attack Deliberately Planned

It will be recorded that the distance of Hawaii from Japan makes it obvious that the attack was deliberately planned many days or even weeks ago. During the intervening time the Japanese Government has deliberately sought to deceive the United States by false statements and expressions of hope for continued peace.

The attack yesterday on the Hawaiian Islands has caused severe damage to American naval and military forces. I regret to tell you that very many American lives have been lost. In addition, American ships have been reported torpedoed on the high seas between San Francisco and Honolulu.

Yesterday the Japanese Government also launched an attack against Malaya.

Last night Japanese forces attacked Hong Kong.

Last night Japanese forces attacked Guam.

Last night Japanese forces attacked the Philippine Islands.

Last night the Japanese attacked Wake Island.

And this morning the Japanese attacked Midway Island.

Japan has therefore undertaken a surprise offensive extending throughout the Pacific area. The facts of yesterday and today speak for themselves. The people of the United States have already formed their opinions and well understand the implications to the very life and safety of our nation.

As Commander in Chief of the Army and Navy I have directed that all measures be taken for our defense, that always will our whole nation remember the character of the onslaught against us.

Victory Will Be Absolute

No matter how long it may take us to overcome this premeditated invasion, the American people, in their righteous might, will win through to absolute victory.

I believe that I interpret the will of the Congress and of the people when I assert that we will not only defend ourselves to the uttermost but will make it very certain that this form of treachery shall never again endanger us.

Hostilities exist. There is no blinking at the fact that our people, our territory and our interests are in grave danger.

With confidence in our armed forces, with the unbounding determination of our people, we will gain the inevitable triumph. So help us God.

I ask that the Congress declare that since the unprovoked and dastardly attack by Japan on Sunday, Dec. 7, 1941, a state of war has existed between the United States and the Japanese Empire.

December 9, 1941

BILL GIVES PRESIDENT UNLIMITED POWER TO LEND WAR EQUIPMENT AND RESOURCES

GOES TO CONGRESS

Measure Would Allow British Naval Repair in Our Ports

QUICK ACTION IS URGED

Aim Is 'to Do the Job Right' in Aiding Allies—Line-Up Points to Bill's Passage

By TURNER CATLEDGE
Special to THE NEW YORK TIMES.

WASHINGTON, Jan. 10—A bill to confer upon President Roosevelt practically unlimited personal power to place American war equipment, new and old, at the disposal of foreign nations in the interest of the defense of the United States was introduced in Congress today amid signs of a brewing legislative storm.

Presented as an Administration proposal by the majority leader in each house, and intended solely to implement the policy of "all out" aid to the non-Axis powers now under attack, the bill carries one of the greatest grants of authority ever extended by Congress to the President, either in peace or war.

As interpreted by authorities, including some who helped frame the measure, the President would be empowered, under its terms, to transfer the whole or any part of the Navy or Army equipment to other countries and place new defense production at their disposal—all upon such terms and under such conditions as he himself might determine. The sole limitation would be that the transfer of materials should be deemed by the President to be in the interest of American defense.

Powers Held Needed for Speed

Administration spokesmen scouted as "ridiculous" any suggestion that the President would use the bill's powers to these possible limits. The whole purpose, they said, was to do the job of aid-to-the-Allies which the country seems to be demanding and "do it right."

The President himself urged the quickest possible action on the bill, saying at his press conference that speed was the most vital element in translating the Allied-aid policy into action. He had no personal desire to have the vast powers conferred by the measure, he said, but they were needed to avoid delays.

The Capitol appeared somewhat surprised by the nature and extent of the bill, although its terms had been discounted by advance publication. Administration leaders laid plans immediately for pushing it through Congress as rapidly as possible, with hearings to start next week before the Senate and House committees dealing with foreign affairs. They want to rush it through ahead of any possible reactions which might make more bitter the fight they expect.

Stormy Debate Is Expected

The extent of opposition can hardly be gauged at this time. Enough was seen today to indicate that the measure will have a stormy legislative course whatever the result. Signs of disapproval came not alone from the "noninterventionist" group which would have fought any Allied-aid proposal, but from some others who, although they were unwilling to speak out because of the peculiar nature of the subject and the times, were nonplused at the magnitude of executive authority proposed in the bill.

Resistance to additional grants of executive powers has been mounting steadily over the last few years, but how much it has been softened under the urgency of the foreign situation with repeated underscorings by the President and other advocates of aid to the Allies is something yet to be seen.

The bill was introduced by Senator Barkley in the Senate and Representative McCormack of Massachusetts in the House. No drama attended its presentation in either body.

Shortly before introducing it the two leaders issued a joint statement explaining its terms. The major purpose was simply to translate into legislative form the policy of making this country "the arsenal of democracy," the leaders said. and to carry out President Roosevelt's pledge to send to beleaguered democracies "in ever-increasing numbers, ships, planes, tanks, guns." They explained the bill in detail, which, briefly, provides the following:

The President is empowered, "notwithstanding the provisions of any other law," when he deems it in the interest of national defense, to authorize the Secretary of War, the Secretary of the Navy, or the head of any other department or agency of the government, to manufacture in government arsenals, factories, shipyards, etc., or otherwise procure any defense article for the government of any country whose defense the President deems vital to the United States.

He is authorized to order these officials to sell, transfer, exchange, lease, lend "or otherwise dispose of" such defense article to any such government.

This means, Messrs. Barkley and McCormack explained, that the President can dispose of new material as well as equipment now in the hands of our Army and Navy, according to our own needs "as he (the President) sees them." A certificate from our Chief of Staff or the Chief of Naval Operations to the effect that transfers of materials would not impair American defense, would no longer be needed, these leaders said.

The President would be authorized to instruct his defense subordinates to test, inspect, prove, repair, outfit, recondition or otherwise place in good working order any defense article for any such government. This could mean, for example, that the British battle cruiser Renown could be repaired in the Brooklyn Navy Yard if the President considered it to be in the interest of our national defense to do so. The provision is broad enough, Messrs. Barkley and McCormack said, to permit the use of any of our military, naval, or air bases to outfit and repair the weapons of countries whose defense is deemed by the President to be vital to the defense of the United States.

Financing Terms Up to President

The President would be authorized, moreover, to communicate to foreign governments defense information, pertaining to any defense article furnished by the United States. This means that the President, in his discretion, could make available to foreign governments designs, blueprints, and other information for using particular equipment. The transfer and use of the secret American bomb-sight was said to have figured in the discussions preceding the writing of this section.

The bill leaves the matter of remuneration and financing strictly up to the President. Terms and conditions would be those the President deemed satisfactory and the benefits to the United States may be payment or repayment in kind or property or any other direct or "indirect" benefit the President elects.

Senator George of Georgia, chairman of the Foreign Relations Committee, said the bill would come before that body next Wednesday when procedure as to its consideration would be decided. He disclosed that he had asked Senator Barkley to introduce the measure because it raised the question of jurisdiction, as three committees conceivably could have handled it. It was sent to Mr. George's group, however.

An inter-committee dispute sprang up in the House over the bill after it had been referred to the Foreign Affairs Committee, headed by Representative Bloom of New York. Representative May of Kentucky, chairman of the Military Affairs Committee, insisted it should go there, and intimated he would seek to take it over.

"Are you for the bill?" Mr. May was asked.

"Yes, sir and yes, ma'am," he replied emphatically.

Nonpartisan Drafting Cited

The first adverse reaction came from the Republican side immediately upon introduction of the bill. The complaint was not lodged against the merits of the bill necessarily, but on the ground that the Administration apparently was making it a party matter. Representative Martin of Massachusetts, minority leader, demanded to know if the measure was to be considered from a partisan standpoint. Majority Leader McCormack replied that Secretaries Stimson and Knox both participated in the drafting of the bill and that they were Republicans.

The general impression in Washington tonight was that the bill would pass both Houses in substantially the form introduced, with perhaps a few and not very consequential limitations. This conclusion was based primarily upon an analysis of the practical political situation in Congress in which, to overturn the Administration, a coalition ordinarily has to develop out of a relatively solid Republican corps and dissident Democrats. The Republicans hitherto have been divided several ways on foreign issues and may be expected to be so again. Furthermore, in past anti-New Deal coalitions, much of the Democratic strength has been furnished from a conservative Southern bloc which, on the war issue, is intensely pro-Administration.

Byrnes, Harrison Praise Bill

The question likely will be fought out as much, if not more, on the issue of confidence in President Roosevelt as upon the merits or demerits of aid to the Allies.

The Democratic stalwarts who rushed to the defense of the bill today indicated that the Administration would not be lacking in skillful leadership. Senators Byrnes and Harrison, two of the most successful legislators in the Senate, each expressed wholehearted approval of the proposal and showed they would join Senator Barkley in helping to drive it through the Senate, where it is expected to encounter the most dramatic opposition on account of the liberality of the rules governing debate.

Text of President Truman's Speech on New Foreign Policy

Following is the text of President Truman's message to Congress on the Mediterranean situation, as recorded and transcribed by THE NEW YORK TIMES:

Mr. President, Mr. Speaker, members of the Congress of the United States:

The gravity of the situation which confronts the world today necessitates my appearance before a joint session of the Congress. The foreign policy and the national security of this country are involved.

One aspect of the present situation, which I wish to present to you at this time for your consideration and decision, concerns Greece and Turkey.

The United States has received from the Greek Government an urgent appeal for financial and economic assistance. Preliminary reports from the American Economic Mission now in Greece and reports from the American Ambassador in Greece corroborate the statement of the Greek Government that assistance is imperative if Greece is to survive as a free nation.

I do not believe that the American people and the Congress wish to turn a deaf ear to the appeal of the Greek Government.

Greece is not a rich country. Lack of sufficient natural resources has always forced the Greek people to work hard to make both ends meet. Since 1940, this industrious, peace loving country has suffered invasion, four years of cruel enemy occupation, and bitter internal strife.

Greece in Desperate Straits

When forces of liberation entered Greece they found that the retreating Germans had destroyed virtually all the railways, roads, port facilities, communications, and merchant marine. More than a thousand villages had been burned. Eighty-five per cent of the children were tubercular. Livestock, poultry, and draft animals had almost disappeared. Inflation had wiped out practically all savings.

As a result of these tragic conditions, a militant minority, exploiting human want and misery, was able to create political chaos which, until now, has made economic recovery impossible.

Greece is today without funds to finance the importation of those goods which are essential to bare subsistence. Under these circumstances the people of Greece cannot make progress in solving their problems of reconstruction. Greece is in desperate need of financial and economic assistance to enable it to resume purchases of food, clothing, fuel and seeds. These are indispensable for the subsistence of its people and are obtainable only from abroad. Greece must have help to import the goods necessary to restore internal order and security so essential for economic and political recovery.

The Greek Government has also asked for the assistance of experienced American administrators, economists and technicians to insure that the financial and other aid given to Greece shall be used effectively in creating a stable and self-sustaining economy and in improving its public administration.

Terrorists Threaten State

The very existence of the Greek state is today threatened by the terrorist activities of several thousand armed men, led by Communists, who defy the Government's authority at a number of points, particularly along the northern boundaries. A commission appointed by the United Nations Security Council is at present investigating disturbed conditions in Northern Greece and alleged border violations along the frontiers between Greece on the one hand and Albania, Bulgaria and Yugoslavia on the other.

Meanwhile, the Greek Government is unable to cope with the situation. The Greek Army is small and poorly equipped. It needs supplies and equipment if it is to restore the authority to the Government throughout Greek territory.

Greece must have assistance if it is to become a self-supporting and self-respecting democracy. The United States must supply this assistance. We have already extended to Greece certain types of relief and economic aid but these are inadequate. There is no other country to which democratic Greece can turn. No other nation is willing and able to provide the necessary support for a democratic Greek Government.

Britain Forced to Cease Aid

The British Government, which has been helping Greece, can give no further financial or economic aid after March 31. Great Britain finds itself under the necessity of reducing or liquidating its commitments in several parts of the world, including Greece.

We have considered how the United Nations might assist in this crisis. But the situation is an urgent one requiring immediate action, and the United Nations and its related organizations are not in a position to extend help of the kind that is required.

It is important to note that the Greek Government has asked for our aid in utilizing effectively the financial and other assistance we may give to Greece, and in improving its public administration. It is of the utmost importance that we supervise the use of any funds made available to Greece, in such a manner that each dollar spent will count toward making Greece self-supporting, and will help to build an economy in which a healthy democracy can flourish.

No government is perfect. One of the chief virtues of a democracy, however, is that its defects are always visible and under democratic processes can be pointed out and corrected. The Government of Greece is not perfect. Nevertheless, it represents 85 per cent of the members of the Greek Parliament who were chosen in an election last year. Foreign observers, including 692 Americans, considered this election to be a fair expression of the views of the Greek people.

The Greek Government has been operating in an atmosphere of chaos and extremism. It has made mistakes. The extension of aid by this country does not mean that the United States condones everything that the Greek Government has done or will do. We have condemned in the past, and we condemn now, extremist measures of the right or the left. We have in the past advised tolerance, and we advise tolerance now.

Greece's neighbor, Turkey, also deserves our attention. The future

'TO SUPPORT FREE PEOPLES WHO ARE RESISTING SUBJUGATION'

March 13, 1947

President Truman, in setting forth a new American policy, called for aid to Greece (1) and Turkey (2). He observed that if Greece fell under the domination of an armed minority the effect on Turkey would be immediate and serious and confusion might pervade the Middle East.

of Turkey as an independent and economically sound state is clearly no less important to the freedom-loving peoples of the world than the future of Greece. The circumstances in which Turkey finds itself today are considerably different from those of Greece. Turkey has been spared the disasters that have beset Greece. And during the war, the United States and Great Britain furnished Turkey with material aid. Nevertheless, Turkey now needs our support.

Since the war Turkey has sought additional financial assistance from Great Britain and the United States for the purpose of effecting that modernization necessary for the maintenance of its national integrity. That integrity is essential to the preservation of order in the Middle East.

The British Government has informed us that, owing to its own difficulties, it can no longer extend financial or economic aid to Turkey. As in the case of Greece, if Turkey is to have the assistance it needs, the United States must supply it. We are the only country able to provide that help.

I am fully aware of the broad implications involved if the United States extends assistance to Greece and Turkey, and I shall discuss these implications with you at this time.

Our Basic Foreign Policy

One of the primary objectives of the foreign policy of the United States is the creation of conditions in which we and other nations will be able to work out a way of life free from coercion. This was a fundamental issue in the war with Germany and Japan. Our victory was won over countries which sought to impose their will, and their way of life, upon other nations.

To ensure the peaceful development of nations, free from coercion, the United States has taken a leading part in establishing the United Nations. The United Nations is designed to make possible lasting freedom and independence for all its members. We shall not realize our objectives, however, unless we are willing to help free peoples to maintain their free institutions and their national integrity against aggressive movements that seek to impose on them totalitarian regimes. This is no more than a frank recognition that totalitarian regimes imposed on free peoples, by direct or indirect aggression, undermine the foundations of international peace and hence the security of the United States.

The peoples of a number of countries of the world have recently had totalitarian regimes forced upon them against their will. The Government of the United States has made frequent protests against coercion and intimidation, in violation of the Yalta Agreement, in Poland, Rumania and Bulgaria. I must also state that in a number of other countries there have been similar developments.

Choice Facing Every Nation

At the present moment in world history nearly every nation must choose between alternative ways of life. The choice is too often not a free one.

One way of life is based upon the will of the majority, and is distinguished by free institutions, representative government, free elections, guarantees of individual liberty, freedom of speech and religion, and freedom from political oppression.

The second way of life is based upon the will of a minority forcibly imposed upon the majority. It relies upon terror and oppression, a controlled press and radio, fixed elections, and the suppression of personal freedoms.

I believe that it must be the policy of the United States to support free peoples who are resisting attempted subjugation by armed minorities or by outside pressures.

I believe that we must assist free peoples to work out their own destinies in their own way.

I believe that our help should be primarily through economic and financial aid which is essential to economic stability and orderly political processes.

The world is not static, and the status quo is not sacred. But we cannot allow changes in the status quo in violation of the charter of the United Nations by such methods as coercion, or by such subterfuges as political infiltration. In helping free and independent nations to maintain their freedom, the United States will be giving effect to the principles of the charter of the United Nations.

More Than Greece at Stake

It is necessary only to glance at a map to realize that the survival and integrity of the Greek nation are of grave importance in a much wider situation. If Greece should fall under the control of an armed minority, the effect upon its neighbor, Turkey, would be immediate and serious. Confusion and disorder might well spread throughout the entire Middle East.

Moreover, the disappearance of Greece as an independent state would have a profound effect upon those countries in Europe whose peoples are struggling against great difficulties to maintain their freedoms and their independence while they repair the damages of war.

It would be an unspeakable tragedy if these countries, which have struggled so long against overwhelming odds, should lose that victory for which they sacrificed so much. Collapse of free institutions and loss of independence would be disastrous not only for them but for the world. Discouragement and possibly failure would quickly be the lot of neighboring peoples striving to maintain their freedom and independence.

Urges Resolute Action

Should we fail to aid Greece and Turkey in this fateful hour, the effect will be far reaching to the west as well as to the east. We must take immediate and resolute action.

I therefore ask the Congress to provide authority for assistance to Greece and Turkey in the amount of $400,000,000 for the period ending June 30, 1948. In requesting these funds, I have taken into consideration the maximum amount of relief assistance which would be furnished to Greece out of the $350,000,000 which I recently requested that the Congress authorize for the prevention of starvation and suffering in countries devastated by the war.

In addition to funds, I ask the Congress to authorize the detail of American civilian and military personnel to Greece and Turkey, at the request of those countries, to assist in the tasks of reconstruction, and for the purpose of supervising the use of such financial and material assistance as may be furnished. I recommend that authority also be provided for the instruction and training of selected Greek and Turkish personnel.

Finally, I ask that the Congress provide authority which will permit the speediest and most effective use, in terms of needed commodities, supplies, and equipment, of such funds as may be authorized.

May Ask for More Funds

If further funds, or further authority, should be needed for the purposes indicated in this message, I shall not hesitate to bring the situation before the Congress. On this subject the executive and legislative branches of the Government must work together.

This is a serious course upon which we embark. I would not recommend it except that the alternative is much more serious.

The United States contributed $341,000,000,000 toward winning World War II. This is an investment in world freedom and world peace.

The assistance that I am recommending for Greece and Turkey amounts to little more than 1 tenth of 1 per cent of this investment. It is only common sense that we should safeguard this investment and make sure that it was not in vain.

The seeds of totalitarian regimes are nurtured by misery and want. They spread and grow in the evil soil of poverty and strife. They reach their full growth when the hope of a people for a better life has died. We must keep that hope alive. The free peoples of the world look to us for support in maintaining their freedoms.

If we falter in our leadership, we may endanger the peace of the world—and we shall surely endanger the welfare of this nation.

Great responsibilities have been placed upon us by the swift movement of events. I am confident that the Congress will face these responsibilities squarely.

March 13, 1947

PRESIDENT ORDERS INQUIRY ON DISLOYAL JOBHOLDERS; COMMUNISTS FIRST TARGET

FBI WILL AID STUDY

In Unprecedented Step Heads of Departments Must Back 'Purge'

REVIEW BOARD IS CREATED

It Will Hear Final Appeals of All Workers or Applicants Marked For Job Elimination

By WALTER H. WAGGONER
Special to THE NEW YORK TIMES.

WASHINGTON, March 22 — President Truman, by executive decree, ordered into effect today an elaborate and unprecedented program of security and precautions against Federal employment of any person who, on "reasonable grounds," can be judged disloyal.

The Presidential Order called for an immediate investigation of the loyalty and intentions of every person entering civilian employment in any department or agency of the Executive Branch of the Government.

Present job holders who have not already been checked for loyalty will be scrutinized by the Federal Bureau of Investigation, and their fate will rest on the decision of department heads held "personally responsible" for the character of their subordinates.

Although they were not singled out in the order, Communists and Communist sympathizers would be the first targets of the President's prescribed loyalty standards, it was indicated.

There have been repeated allegations in Congress that Communists held Federal posts, and many attacks have been made on the Administration for not ridding itself of them.

Charges Made By House Group

The House Civil Service Committee charged this week that only nine persons had been discharged from Government jobs as Communists since July 1, and promised a "full-scale investigation" of additional suspected employes.

Mr. Truman called for this sweeping program on the recommendation of his six-agency Temporary Commission on Employe Loyalty, which he named by Executive Order on last Nov. 25.

The President received the Commission's thirty-eight-page report on Feb. 20. Its publication had been held up, according to Charles G. Ross, White House press secretary, so that Mr. Truman could "study it and give time for the preparation of an Executive Order which carries out and implements the recommendations of the Commission."

Introducing his order, the President stated that every Government employe "is endowed with a measure of trusteeship over the democratic processes which are the heart and sinew of the United States."

It was of vital importance that all Federal employes be of "complete and unswerving loyalty" to this country, he continued, adding that the presence of any disloyal or subversive persons "constitutes a threat to our democratic processes."

Major Provisions of Order

Other major provisions of the ruling, in summary form, are as follows:

1. A "central master index" will be compiled of the records of all persons who have undergone loyalty checks by any agency or department since Sept. 1, 1939.

2. An over-all "Loyalty Review Board" will be set up in the Civil Service Commission, consisting of three "impartial" officers or employes of the commission. The board will review cases as an authority of final appeal for employes recommended for dismissal on grounds of disloyalty.

3. One or more three-member loyalty boards will be named by the head of each department or agency to hear cases within the agency itself.

4. The Attorney General will list all "totalitarian, fascist, communist or subversive" groups and organizations, and those which have a policy of "advocating or approving the commission of acts of force or violence to deny other persons their rights" under the Constitution, or "seeking to alter the form of government of the United States by unconstitutional means."

5. Should "derogatory information" with regard to loyalty standards of any job applicant be uncovered, a "full field investigation," utilizing all the Government's resources, will be conducted.

Maximum Protection Sought

"Maximum protection must be afforded the United States against infiltration of disloyal persons into the ranks of its employes," said the President, "and equal protection from unfounded accusations of disloyalty must be afforded the loyal employes of the Government."

The President's program, although ordered into effect immediately, requires funds, which have not yet been appropriated. It is widely felt, however, that if Congress will authorize any additional expenditures, a loyalty program such as the President has set forth will be provided with funds.

In the meantime Mr. Truman instructed the Secretaries of War and Navy and of the Treasury, so far as the Treasury Department relates to the Coast Guard, to continue to enforce and maintain "the highest standards of loyalty within the armed services."

Files to be Made Available

The government's total resources will be mobilized to carry out the President's ruling. In addition, investigation of a job applicant may include reference to the files of the FBI, the Civil Service Commission, military and naval intelligence authorities, any other "appropriate government investigative or intelligence agency," the House Committee on Un-American Activities, and state and local law enforcement agencies.

Also considered as potential sources of information relating to a person's loyalty are the schools and colleges attended by the applicant, his former employers, references given on his application, and any other source not specified or excluded in the order.

Names of persons giving information about an applicant or employe under investigation may be withheld under the terms of the order. The investigating agency must, however, supply sufficient informatioin to enable the department involved to make "an adequate evaluation" of the statements.

The investigator must also advise the agency requesting the information in writing that "it is essential to the protection of the informants or to the investigation of other cases that the names of the informants not be revealed."

Condemned Activities Listed

The specific "activities and associations" condemned in the President's program are:

Sabotage, espionage, or trying or preparing for either;

Knowingly associating with spies or saboteurs;

Treason or sedition, or the advocacy of either;

Advocacy of revolution, force, or violence to change the constitutional form of the American Government;

Intentional, unauthorized disclosure to any person, "under circumstances which may indicate disloyalty to the United States," of documents or information of a confidential or nonpublic character obtained by the person making the disclosure as a result of his Government position;

Performing his duties, whatever they are, or in any way acting in a manner which better serves the interests of a foreign Government than the United States;

Membership in or affiliation with any of the groups designated by the Attorney General as "totalitarian, Fascist, Communist, or subversive."

The first step in eliminating present employes suspected of disloyalty will be the submission to the FBI of the personnel rolls of all departments or agencies covered by the order.

The FBI will then check each name against its records of persons against whom there is already a body of evidence pointing to disloyalty. Suggestions of disloyalty by any employes will be returned to the department.

Departments will make their own investigations of suspected employes or request investigation by the Civil Service Commission.

Job applicants will be investigated first by the Civil Service Commission if they are entering positions which it covers, or, if they are not, by the department or agency in which they are seeking employment.

March 23, 1947

TRUMAN ASKS $17 BILLION TO RESTORE EUROPE

PRESIDENT IS GRAVE

Warns Poverty and Fear of Tyranny Will Grip All if Europe Falls

URGES SWIFT ACTION

Asks $6,800,000,000 for 15 Months From April 1, and New ERP Agency

By FELIX BELAIR Jr.
Special to THE NEW YORK TIMES.

WASHINGTON, Dec. 19—President Truman asked Congress today to authorize a 1948-51 European Recovery Program costing $17,000,000,000 to halt the march of "selfish totalitarian aggression" and to maintain a civilization in which the American way of life is rooted.

In a message outlining the largest program of expenditure in the nation's peacetime history, the President urged haste in completing legislative action so that the program might begin on April 1. He asked that $6,800,000,000 be appropriated for use in the ensuing fifteen months. Appropriations for the three years following would be considered subsequently on an annual basis.

Justifying his program on political as well as economic grounds, the President warned that if Europe failed to recover, its people would be driven by want to surrender their rights to totalitarian control and that such a turn of events "would constitute a shattering blow to peace and stability in the world."

Holds World Freedom at Stake

"It might well compel us," he added, "to modify our own economic system and to forego, for the sake of our security, the enjoyment of many of our freedoms and privileges."

Considerably more than the future of the people of Western Europe was involved in the "grave and significant decision" he was asking Congress to make in favor of the so-called Marshall plan, the President said. It would also determine whether the free nations of the world could look forward to a peaceful and prosperous future as independent states or "whether they must live in poverty and in fear of selfish totalitarian aggression."

As President Truman described it, the substance of his proposal was that America finish the job for which he said $15,000,000,000 had been spent by us throughout the world since surrender of the Axis powers. That job would not be easy but was well within this nation's means, Mr. Truman continued, noting that it would take less than 3 per cent of the national income during the life of the program.

Predicts Further Incitements

Political as well as economic obstacles would be encountered in helping to put Western Europe and occupied Germany back on their feet and the President reminded that Communists and Communist-inspired groups were opposed to recovery on the Continent as a matter of policy.

THE PRESIDENT GREETS GEN. MARSHALL

Mr. Truman welcoming the Secretary of State at National Airport upon latter's arrival from Foreign Ministers' Conference.

The New York Times (by Tames)

"We must not be blind to the fact that the Communists have announced determined opposition to any effort to help Europe get back on its feet," the President said. "There will unquestionably be further incitements to strike, not for the purpose of redressing the legitimate grievances of particular groups, but for the purpose of bringing chaos in the hope that it will pave the way for totalitarian control."

The President said satisfaction of the import requirements of 270,000,000 Europeans would call for some self-denial on the part of Americans. It would not be possible to satisfy this demand entirely because of short supplies here and throughout the world, and the program of aid had been scaled down materially to reflect these realities and to eliminate non-essentials.

But he pointed out that a total cost of the program, amounting to about 5 per cent of the expenditure for the war effort, was "an investment toward the peace and security of the world and toward the realization of hope and confidence in a better way of life for the future." Viewed in that light, he said, the cost was small indeed.

To carry out the long-range program of loans and grants-in-aid, the President proposed a new and separate Federal agency to be called the Economic Cooperation Administration. Neither the President nor the supporting data he transmitted from a dozen Government agencies described the new organization as "independent."

State Department Powers Urged

The new agency with its single Administrator and Deputy Administrator at the top would come under the policy jurisdiction both of the State Department and the National Advisory Council. The chief foreign representative of the Economic Cooperation Administrator would take orders from his immediate chief as well as the Secretary of State.

Rejecting recommendations of the committee of private citizens headed by Secretary of Commerce W. Averell Harriman that the broadest possible powers be vested in a single Administrator, Mr. Truman said the news agency "must work with, rather than supplant, existing agencies."

"The Administrator must be subject to the direction of the Sec-

·etary of State on decisions and actions affecting our foreign policy," the President declared.

In addition, the Department of Agriculture would continue in charge of the procurement and allocation of food and the Department of Commerce in the allocation of commodities and products in short supply and administration of export controls.

It was clear from the 241-page analysis of the program transmitted by the President that while the new Administrator might propose, it would be for other agencies to dispose. The National Advisory Council would decide whether aid o a particular country should be n the form of a loan or grant .nd the State Department would letermine whether the proposed aid was in line with our foreign policy and, therefore, whether it should be forthcoming at all.

It was indicated in the supporting data that "much" of the foreign aid would be made in the form of non-repayable grants. How much was not indicated except that the yardstick of determination would be the ability of beneficiaries to repay without jeopardizing recovery progress.

The voluminous explanatory report on the program completely abandoned the original formula that the type of aid requested would largely determine whether a loan or grant would be made. This concept was that grants should be provided for food, fuel and fertilizer, since these categories would be rapidly consumed without any visible effect on recovery progress.

The $17,000,000,000 requested in the form of a Congressional authorization by the President was a rounded sum. As the supporting data explained, the actual cost of the program to the United States Treasury might go as low as $15,-111,000,000 or as high as $17,758,-000,000, depending on the behavior of prices here and in world markets during the four years.

Neither did the over-all estimate include $822,000,000 for Western Germany, to be sought in a separate appropriation for the Army Department. Moreover, the round sum asked by Mr. Truman assumed about $4,100,000,000 of financing under the plan by the World Bank, private loans, aid from other Western Hemisphere countries and credits remaining from unexpended appropriations.

Bars Gifts to Those Able to Pay

Actual management and collection of loans certified by the Economic Cooperation Administrator and approved by the National Advisory Council, would be undertaken by the Export-Import Bank, under the program.

President Truman recommended in this connection that no grants should be made to countries able to pay cash for all imports or to repay loans. At the same time, he reminded that if the participating nations of Europe became burdened with debt obligations under the European Recovery Program, participation by the World Bank and through a revival of private financing would be retarded.

The President's message and the draft legislation he submitted left the way open for European countries other than the sixteen that joined in the Committee of European Economic Cooperation at Paris to participate in the program.

The eventual entry of Spain and Czechoslovakia has been mentioned as a possibility by Administration officials. However, any new participants would first have to be accepted by the sixteen nations comprising the committee of European Economic Cooperation. After that, it would be a matter for the United States Senate through implementing bilateral treaties with each of the participants.

Self-Help Requirement Stressed

While the President went to some lengths in his message to explain this nation's interest in the European Recovery Program, he was no less insistent that the participating nations must do their part in specified ways. He said the first requirement was that each country of Western Europe and all of them collectively "should take vigorous action to help themselves."

Among action programs required of the beneficiary nations, the President mentioned financial and monetary measures to stabilize currencies, maintain proper rates of exchange and restore and maintain confidence in monetary systems. Also included was cooperation with other participants in reduction and elimination of trade barriers and toward efficient use of resources.

Recipients of grants would be required to increase their output of strategic materials in short supply in this country for purchase by the United States. This program of stockpiling here would be facilitated by a stipulation requiring the deposit in a special fund of the currency equivalent of the grant-in-aid. Strategic resources development for purchase by this Government would be among the purposes for which the fund would be available.

Officials estimate some $250,-000,000 of short materials might be acquired annually by the United States in this way.

December 20, 1947

CONGRESS VOTES A HISTORIC PROGRAM

Sixteen Nations Join The U. S. in a Great Economic Effort

By FELIX BELAIR Jr.
Special to THE NEW YORK TIMES.

WASHINGTON, April 3—The American people this week made a great monetary contribution to "contain" the sweep of Communist Russia and so help to maintain a free world. This contribution came in the form of Congressional approval of the European Recovery Program, supplemented by funds for economic and military aid to China, Greece and Turkey.

Never before in peacetime had Congress acted with such dispatch on such important legislation. But rarely if ever before had there been so clear a threat to the world's free institutions. Czechoslovakia fell. The Scandinavian peninsula was threatened. Italy's fate hung in the balance and with it control of the Mediterranean. What was to have been a measure of economic aid to Europe changed unnoticed to a "measure short of war" to counteract Russian influence.

This most ambitious program ever undertaken by any nation in peacetime takes for granted that world stability and European stability are inseparable and that free institutions and genuine independence cannot perish in Europe and flourish elsewhere.

First Year Is Crucial

Keystone of the legislation was the European Recovery Program and the $5.3 billion authorization for the first twelve months of a four-year undertaking that ultimately may entail an estimated outlay of $17 billion. Whether the full investment is to be made will depend on the degree to which the plan succeeds in its first year of operation, and by the same token, on the degree of self-help and mutual aid undertaken by the participating countries of Europe.

What the House achieved through an omnibus foreign aid bill, the Senate also approved piecemeal. Besides authorizing funds for the first twelve months of the ERP, both chambers provided $338,000,000 of economic aid to China in addition to $125,000,-000 for military assistance. To Greece and Turkey another $275,-000,000 was provided.

What follows is a discussion of the intricate problems involved in the execution of the program and an appraisal of the prospects for its success.

AMERICAN PHASE

A mass of statistics has been compiled to show the quantity and value of commodities, materials and equipment this country would supply in helping to rebuild Western European economy and productive facilities. These are valuable only as a guide indicating the points at which the American economy will feel the pinch.

Preliminary estimates by the Executive Branch indicate that of the first year's authorization, about $3.8 billion will go for so-called relief-type commodities, such as food, fuel, fiber and fertilizer. The remaining $1.5 billion would be devoted to recovery-type equipment, materials and services.

The percentage of relief-type goods is expected to decline each year and the flow of recovery items to increase. In the latter category would come farm equipment, industrial raw materials, coal mining machinery and spare parts and components of other machinery and equipment.

Probably the only adequate prospectus of United States performance is that we will be called upon to ship abroad as much food, fuel, fiber, industrial raw materials, consumers goods and capital equipment as can be withdrawn from the economy without unjustly penalizing its normal functioning or injuring American consumers.

Congress already has indicated a continuing interest in this phase of the program and readily acquiesced in the Administration's suggestion to permit purchases outside the United States for European requirements. At least $2 billion is expected to be spent in Latin America in the first twelve months.

THE MACHINERY

The legislation sets up an Economic Cooperation Administration. At its top is a single authority appointed by the President—the Economic Cooperation Admin-

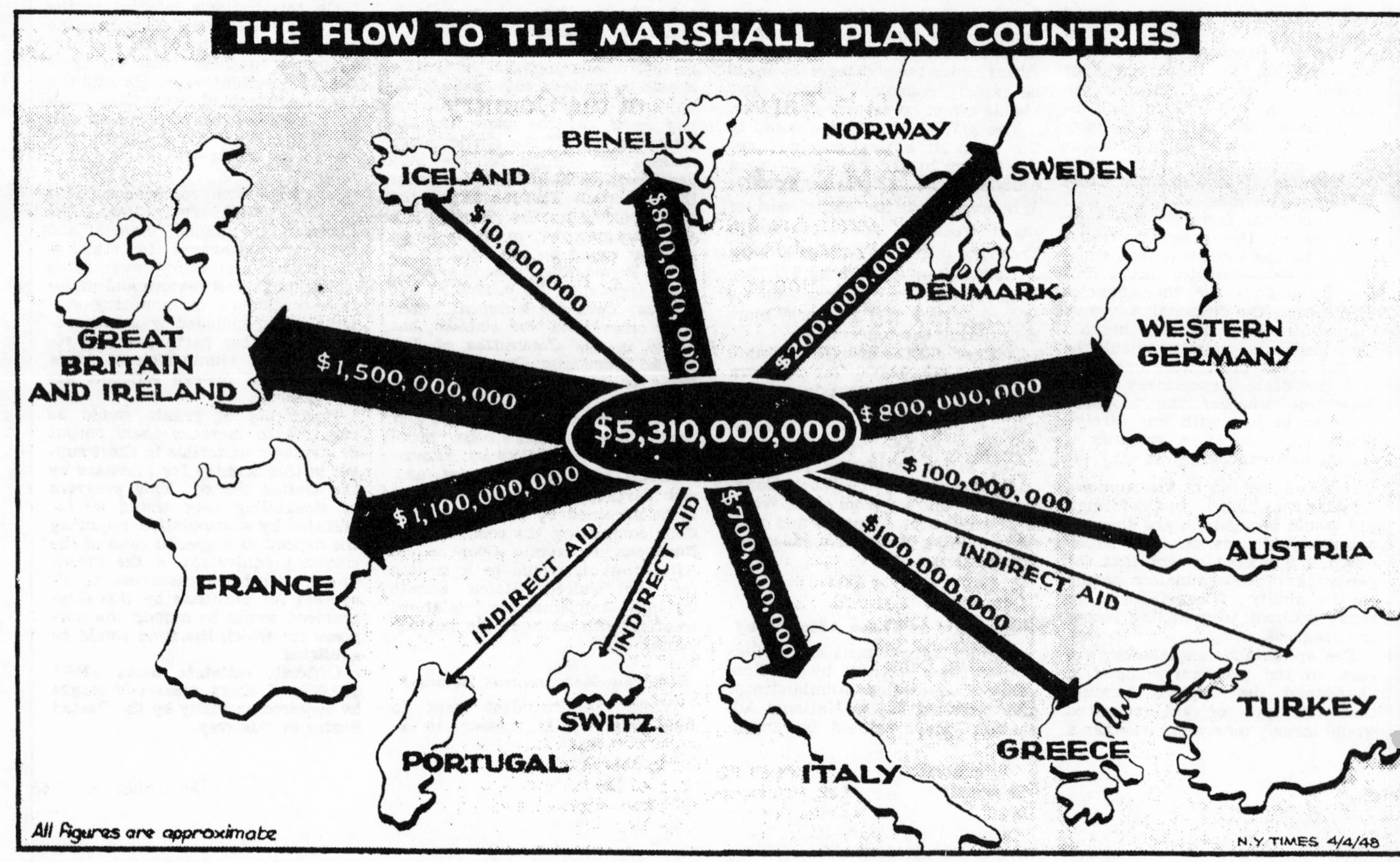

istrator—with power to make grants or loans. He must consult with the National Advisory Council, a body of top-ranking Federal officials, on matters relating to any international loans that may be made under the program.

Loans may be repaid in cash or in kind. Grants may be made if the Administrator decides a country in the plan does not have the capacity to repay a loan.

How much of the aid will be covered by "hard" loans was indicated by the House stipulation earmarking $1 billion of the first year's total for that type of advance; loans will be made through the Export-Import Bank. The stipulation sprang originally from the expectation that collectible loans of at least that amount could be made.

It is a foregone conclusion among draftsmen of the legislation that the Economic Cooperation Administrator will be no popular hero. In his own country he must shoulder whatever criticism results from sacrifices Americans are called upon to make. Abroad, he will be both judge and jury of performance toward recovery.

In judging performance of the participating countries, the views of the Secretary of State will carry great weight. For at issue will be such questions as the likelihood of Communist sabotage and the resolution with which the respective Governments meet Communist efforts to retard their own recovery.

But on the specific terms of assistance agreements between the administrator and the recipient, his findings may be reversed only by the President. If recipients fail to perform according to schedule in production, export or in dealings with other participants, he may cut them off. The same result might follow too friendly a commercial relationship with Russia or its satellites.

EUROPEAN PHASE

The recovery goals set for themselves by the sixteen nations comprising the Committee for European Economic Cooperation are no less ambitious than the American program for helping in their achievement. By the end of 1951 they propose to:

(1) Increase coal production to 584,000,000 tons yearly, an increase of 30,000,000 tons above the 1938 level.

(2) Restore pre-war bread-grain production and an intensive livestock economy.

(3) Expand electricity output by nearly 70 billion kilowatt-hours and increase generating capacity by 25,000,000 kilowatts, or two-thirds above the pre-war average.

(4) Develop oil refining capacity to two and a half times the pre-war volume.

(5) Increase crude steel production to 55,000,000 tons yearly, or 20 per cent above pre-war output.

(6) Expand inland transport to carry 25 per cent more traffic than it did before the war.

(7) Rehabilitate and restore the merchant fleets of the participating nations.

(8) Supply from European production most of the capital equipment needed for these expansions.

Goals Set Too High

No one in the Executive Branch is under any illusion as to the lack of realism in these goals. To begin with, the raw materials are not available in sufficient quantities to make them attainable. And if they were, the targets could be realized only by reducing still further the low standard of living prevailing on the western half of the Continent.

Thus, applicants for aid under the ERP will be required to revise downward their more ambitious production goals to enable greater concentration on food and coal targets and on production for export.

Nor will all "participants" in the program receive aid from this Government. Portugal and Switzerland are important participants but are scheduled to receive neither grants nor loans. Other countries will get loans only, while still others would qualify only for grants.

But the contribution of all countries will have to be substantial if they are to realize their collective pledge "to apply all necessary measures" leading to the rapid achievement of internal financial monetary and economic stability while maintaining in each country a high level of employment.

This is one of the undertakings pledged by the CEEC which will be formalized in a multilateral treaty between the United States and all participating countries. Another is "to make the fullest and most effective use of existing productive capacity and all available manpower" and "to organize together the means by which common resources can be developed in partnership."

To qualify for ERP aid each country must negotiate a separate bilateral treaty with the United States. These will be specific and intricate and governed by considerations peculiar to the individual country. But all will require undertakings to eliminate the need of abnormal outside assistance. Stabilized currencies, proper rates of exchange and restored confidence in national currencies are to be basic ingredients.

Additional demands on the participating nations were written into the legislation during the weeks of Congressional debate, among them the stipulation that such countries locate, identify and "make effective use of" assets owned by their nationals in the United States.

THE PROSPECTS

Few familiar with the intricacies of European commercial relations and industrial methods believe that the goals set for themselves by the sixteen nations can be attained as stated in the period prescribed.

Yet there is every reason to believe that substantial recovery can be attained and, given a revival of surplus exchange between Eastern and Western Europe, a significant improvement in the living standards of Europeans generally realized.

So far as a majority of Congress is concerned, the program will succeed beyond any challenge if as a result the Iron Curtain remains at its present limits or is forced back a few miles to the east at the end of the four years.

In the Executive Branch somewhat different tests of success or failure will apply. Fiscal authorities will be influenced by the billions for defense expenditures that the ERP may make unnecessary.

Test for the Future

Among those responsible for the nation's foreign policy, still another criterion would apply. A foreign-assistance program of such magnitude can never be a permanent part of our foreign policy. The test will be the extent to which the Old World and the New have been drawn together in a shrinking world and a common ground established between them in the age-old quest for the welfare, peace and security of all peoples.

The framers of our foreign policy will judge the results in the light of Soviet Russia's acceptance or final repudiation of world order based on law.

Among those responsible for the defense establishment there will be less scrutiny of the success or failure of the program. To them it has already succeeded, for it represents economic warfare that in these times must go hand in hand with any plans for the national security. Already it has drawn together a nucleus of Western powers for defense against aggression from without and, since any such aggressor would be a common foe, the result is all to the good.

Impact on U. S. Economy

No one familiar with the program is inclined to minimize the impact of the ERP on the national economy. Yet because it imposes no greater burden than the nation has borne for the past two years no one considers the obstacles insuperable. The $5.3 billion aid authorized for the first year is not much greater than has been provided in the past in various forms. The export volume involved actually is less than that of the past year, and without the ERP there would be very little commerce between the United States and the Marshall Plan countries.

One of the least discussed phases of the European Recovery Program is also one of the most important. It is the need of an American market for the expanded production of the European workshop. In the little discussion that has taken place there has been general agreement that if we are to be repaid at all it must be in the form of goods and services.

The question remaining to be decided is whether, when the time comes, we will be willing to curtail production at home and run the risk of unemployment in order to be repaid.

April 4, 1948

TRUMAN DECLARES HYSTERIA OVER REDS SWEEPS THE NATION

Situation Brought About by Spy Trials and Loyalty Inquiries Similar to Others in Past

CITES 1790S' SEDITION ACT

Excitement Will Die as It Has Before, He Holds — Judges College Stir Unwarranted

By ANTHONY LEVIERO

Special to THE NEW YORK TIMES.

WASHINGTON, June 16—This country is experiencing a wave of hysteria as a result of current spy trials and loyalty inquiries, President Truman suggested today, but he asserted emphatically that we were not going to hell.

The President likened the current situation created by the conflict with communism to the troubled atmosphere engendered in the early days of the Republic by the alien and sedition laws. He also recalled what he characterized as the crazy activities of the Ku Klux Klan after World War I, and said that every great crisis brought a period of public hysteria.

The present feeling would subside as similar situations had died out after past periods of stress, Mr. Truman contended.

The Chief Executive did express confidence, however, that the hysteria had no part of his Executive Department in its grip. He gave assurance that if this ever happened he would root it out.

The country had not gone to hell in the Washington-Adams-Jefferson era and it would not now, President Truman asserted.

The views of the Chief Executive were elicited during his weekly news conference which today took longer than usual as correspondents tried to inquire into the whole wide range of the espionage-loyalty field.

Noteworthy in the long discussion was the coolness the President indicated toward J. Edgar Hoover, who for many years has been the director of the Federal Bureau of Investigation.

For instance, when he was asked whether Mr. Hoover had his confidence, the President replied obliquely that Mr. Hoover had done a good job. He denied, however, that the FBI chief had submitted his resignation.

In summary form, some other views expressed by Mr. Truman were:

No comment to a suggestion that an inquiry on the scale of the Roberts Pearl Harbor investigation be made of the FBI and its practices.

Contempt for an investigation of school textbooks undertaken by the House Committee on Un-American Activities.

President's Views Implied

While he has withheld confidential loyalty reports from Congressional committees, Mr. Truman said he would not attempt to do this with the judiciary where, as in the Judith Coplon spy case, the requirement was a fair trial.

The President's views were mostly implied rather than explicit. That was because they were not voluntary declarative statements but answers to questions. His meaning was none the less clear. In the detailed report that follows the questions are given verbatim and in the order in which they occurred, while the President's answers are given indirectly, as required by White House rules.

The discussion was started by Frederic W. Collins of The Providence Journal with this question:

"Mr. President, my paper has suggested editorially that you appoint a special commission, something like the Roberts Pearl Harbor committee, to make a thorough inquiry into FBI practices and to make a report to you not for publication—a quiet, closed study of the FBI."

Did you ever hear of anything like that in Washington, the President answered, laughing. The allusion to the fanfare of inquiries on Capitol Hill was obvious.

"Do you think such a study might be valuable?" came back Mr. Collins.

No comment, replied Mr. Truman.

Questions on other topics followed and then came this one:

"The House Un-American Activities Committee has suggested that schools and colleges send in a list of their school books, and California University has asked for an oath from its faculty. Do you see in these developments any threat to educational freedom in this country?"

Mr. Truman said he thought the question was pretty well answered in a cartoon in the Washington Post this morning. The cartoon by Herbert L. Block ridiculed the inquiry.

"Mr. President, an awful lot of fine people are being branded as Communists, Reds, subversives and what not these days at any number of trials, hearings, the situation in the Army and things of that sort. Do you have any word of counsel you could give on this rash of branding people?"

Yes, yes, he had given it once before, said Mr. Truman. He suggested that the reporters read the history of the Alien and Sedition Acts in the Seventeen Nineties, under almost exactly the same situation. They would be surprised at how parallel the cases are when they had read how they came out.

Questions on two other topics ensued as newsmen went after their particular stories and then came this follow-up question:

"Mr. President, regarding the

alien and sedition laws, how can we apply their lesson to the problem of today?"

Just continue to read your history through the Jefferson Administration and you will find out that the hysteria subsided and that the country did not go to hell at all, and it isn't going to now, Mr. Truman replied.

[The Alien and Sedition Acts had their origins in two main causes: The possibility of war with France developed and three Alien Acts were passed by Congress to deal with naturalization, deportation, imprisonment or banishment of aliens. While they were rarely applied they scared many Frenchmen into leaving this country. The Sedition Act was inspired by the violent partisanships of the press of the times. In the face of strong public opinion, the law was used relatively few times by the Federalists against Jeffersonian Republican editors.]

"Mr. President, the first thing Jefferson did was to release eleven newspaper publishers from prison," observed a reporter.

Jefferson made a mistake on that, Mr. Truman said, but not seriously. He laughed. Then he went on to say that Jefferson not only had done that but had released a Federal judge, if he was not mistaken.

"What was that date?"

It began in John Adams' Administration and went over into Jefferson's—it was in the Seventeen Nineties, Seventeen Ninety-sevons and Seventeen Ninety-eights, he thought, said Mr. Truman.

"Do you think hysteria is causing this, and that it is fit for a country that is as strong and powerful as this country?"

Such things happened after every great crisis, after every great war, Mr. Truman replied. It had happened after the first World War, he went on, when the Ku Klux Klan went out to clean up the country. They tried to do crazy things. Out in Indiana they tried to clean up and they made a mess of things.

"Are you confident that no part of your executive branch is gripped by this hysteria?"

He was, and he would clean it out if it were, the Chief Executive said.

"In the case of Gordon Clapp [chairman of the Tennessee Valley Authority characterized as "unemployable" by the Army] you stepped in quickly to straighten that out. Do you intend to step in if an executive is involved in one of these cases?"

Certainly, he always did that, that was not new at all, said Mr. Truman.

"Did J. Edgar Hoover submit his resignation?" He had not, said Mr. Truman.

"Do you confer with Mr. Hoover from time to time?"

He makes reports from time to time and he conferred with him through the Attorney General, the President responded.

"Mr. President, there has been a lot of smoke around Mr. Hoover for the last several days; could you go further and clear that situation up?"

There was nothing for him to clear up, the President said.

"There is no idea that Mr. Hoover has any intention of resigning?"

He had never heard of it, he had just answered that, and he knew nothing about it, Mr. Truman said.

"Does Hoover have your confidence?"

Says Hoover Has Done Good Job

Hoover has done a good job, was the answer.

"You said last week that all these investigations just amounted to a lot of headline hunting."

That was all, Mr. Truman answered before the reporter finished the question with this: "Does that include Hoover?"

You could make your own assay on that situation as well as he could, the President said.

"Is your Administration giving any thought to providing protection to Executive papers?"

Every effort had been made to protect them, the President replied, but it was not the policy of the Executive to interfere with the judiciary when it is trying to give a person a fair trial.

"Would it be helpful if there were a law on the subject?"

That would relieve the executive from having to make a decision, was Mr. Truman's opinion.

"Do you think it might be a good thing to clear out of the files of the FBI all unsubstantiated allegations that persons are Reds, subversives and things like that?"

No comment, Mr. Truman said.

June 17, 1949

TRUMAN ORDERS U. S. AIR, NAVY UNITS TO FIGHT IN AID OF KOREA

President Takes Chief Role In Determining U. S. Course

Truman's Leadership for Forceful Policy to Meet Threat to World Peace Draws Together Advisers on Vital Move

By ARTHUR KROCK
Special to THE NEW YORK TIMES.

WASHINGTON, June 27—Some of those who participated in the meetings Sunday and Monday nights, at which the momentous decisions were taken to resist further Communist aggressions, beginning in the Far East, with the combat air and naval power of the United States, described the President to associates today as determined from the outset to adopt the forceful policy which was announced this morning.

As soon as the first meeting assembled, they said, Mr. Truman made it plain that these were to be the bases of his decision:

1. The situation created by Communist tactics at various points of the world, culminating in the attack of North Korea on South Korea, had been allowed to drift too long.
2. The entire Far East was deteriorating in a manner to threaten the peace of the world, a line had to be drawn at once, and the United States had to draw it.
3. National security was the primary interest, but embedded in this were world peace and the prestige and future effectiveness of the United Nations, which was the architect of the South Korean Government.
4. It was a time for courage, even boldness, and calculated risk, which other members of the United Nations would be invited to share as they saw fit.
5. It was not a time to give the slightest consideration to previous policies or to individuals associated with those policies. If, for example, the fundamental change in the Far Eastern situation created by the Communist attack from North Korea called for a revision of the Formosan policy of the Administration (not to lend it active military protection), this policy should be changed.
6. Military intervention by the United States alone conformed with the resolution adopted Sunday by the Security Council of the United Nations, particularly Article 3, which called on all member nations to "render every assistance" to enforce its cease-fire order in Korea.

Truman Gets Latest Data

Before making these premises clear, the President was given the latest intelligence reports for the purpose of deciding (1) what the situation actually was and (2) what in detail the United States Government should do about it.

First to report were the top authorities of the Department of Defense, then those of the Department of State. The Secretaries of the three armed services were heard. There was a long discussion, in which no last-ditch differences appeared, even over the renewed counsel of the Pentagon that Formosa must not be allowed to fall to the Chinese Communists. The pros and cons of that situation were thoroughly reviewed. Then Mr. Truman made his first important decision.

It was that the fleet in Philippine waters should be ordered to proceed at once to the troubled areas off the Asian mainland.

Since more than a day would be required for the fleet to reach a point of effectiveness, further major decisions were postponed for that evening.

Monday night when the conferees met they came quickly to unanimity on every point. The Navy was to be instructed to prevent the capture of Formosa and to give sea cover to the South Koreans. The Air Force was to give air cover, and a more active military policy was to be invoked with respect to Indo-China. Ground troops were not to be sent, at this juncture, anyhow. The President's communiqué, issued today to about half the length of the original draft, was to make no charge that Moscow had supplied the North Korean Communists with the added matériel required for the invasion.

Kremlin Course Left Free

This latter decision left the Kremlin free to disavow all responsibility or active interest in an expedition which was a deliberate affront to the United Nations, and its commission on the ground in Korea, and a threat to world peace. It left the Kremlin free also to accept the invitation of this Government, through Ambassador Kirk, to assist with its good offices in Korea—an invitation, it was decided, the Ambassador should be instructed to extend.

The first cause to which the harmony among the oft-differing conferees of the State and Defense Departments was today attributed by those who should know was the President's leadership and definite outline of the requirements of the situation in the light of the latest intelligence reports Sunday night. But another was the fortunate timing of the very recent visit of Secretary Louis A. Johnson and Gen. Omar N. Bradley to Japan. The conferees were thus equipped with on-the-spot reports, in addition to those forwarded by military intelligence units under Gen. Douglas MacArthur, and by John Foster Dulles, who had just left Korea. These were agreed by all to sustain the soundness of the President's position and to support the details by which he proposed to enforce it.

"He pulled all the conferees together by his show of leadership," said one today who attended the meetings, "and the undisputable facts persuaded everyone that his decisions were both inevitable and right."

The global effect of the President's decision can be summed up in this way:

Soviet agents for a long time have been asking diplomats, and urging their secret agents to furnish, the answer to this question—"How much further can we expand Cominform activities without military countermeasures from the United States?"

The President has now given the answer—"No further!"

June 28, 1950

U. S. 'NOT AT WAR,' PRESIDENT ASSERTS

Truman Allows Quotation — Calls Operation Police Action for U. N. on 'Bandits'

By ANTHONY LEVIERO
Special to THE NEW YORK TIMES.

WASHINGTON, June 29—President Truman declared today the United States was "not at war." He characterized United States combat operations in Korea as police action for the United Nations against an unlawful bandit attack on the South Korean Republic.

He expressed confidence that Republic would survive as a result of United States intervention.

The United States air and naval intervention against North Korean Communist forces was a move in favor of peace, and moreover it had the support of most members of the United Nations, Mr. Truman said.

In his weekly news conference the Chief Executive faced the correspondents for the first time since he made the momentous decisions to fight against North Korea, place a protective naval cordon around Formosa and strengthen the Philippines and anti-Communistic Indo-China.

He sharply refused to answer any question that touched on strategic plans that might be in the making. Specifically he declined to comment on questions relating to the use of United States ground troops in the conflict and to the atomic bomb.

Points to Public Support

Among the indications of the upsurge of public opinion were the more than 1,200 telegrams and letters the President has received, endorsing his position at least ten to one.

Late in the afternoon, the Chief Executive presided at an hour-long meeting of the National Security Council in which the nation's military and civil leaders studied developments in the Korean conflict and in all other sensitive areas of the world where its repercussions might be felt. None of those who attended would say a word about the course of events.

With an emphatic manner, Mr. Truman gave permission at his news conference to quote him directly on some of his observations on the war and in defense of the role in the crisis played by Secretary of State Dean Acheson. The President denied all suggestions that Mr. Acheson had been in conflict with other members of the Cabinet and had been reversed. In the circumstances he demonstrated his typical loyalty to members of his official family.

"Mr. President, everybody is asking in this country, are we or are we not at war," a reporter said.

The President replied that we were not at war. Under White House rules, the President's statements in news conferences may not be quoted without specific permission. Several other questions intervened and then Mr. Truman was asked if the phrase might be quoted.

The Chief Executive responded that he would allow the news men to use in quotes: "We are not at war."

"Since issuing your statement [on the Korea situation, Tuesday] can you give us any indication as to the effect it might have on peace?" was another question.

Actions Aimed at Peace

His idea in issuing the statement and the orders preliminary to its issuance was that they amounted to a move in favor of peace. If he had not thought so, he would not have taken these steps, the President said.

"Have you had any indications whether it is being universally accepted as that?"

Only the fact that most members of the United Nations were in full accord, replied the President. He also said he was very happy that India had decided to support the United Nations, adding he had been sure India would do that.

"Would you elaborate a little more on the reasons for this move and the peace angle on it?"

Mr. Truman recalled that the Republic of Korea was set up with the United Nations' help. It was the Government recognized by the members of the United Nations, and it was unlawfully attacked by a bunch of bandits, who were neighbors in North Korea.

The United Nations Security Council had held a meeting and passed on the situation, asking the members to go to the relief of the Korean Republic. The members of the United Nations were doing that—going to the relief of the Korean Republic to suppress a bandit raid on the Korean Republic. Mr. Truman later gave permission to quote him on the word "bandits."

"Would it be correct to call this a police action under the United Nations?"

Yes, replied Mr. Truman, that was exactly what it amounted to.

Asked whether he believed South Korea would survive as an independent republic, in view of the apparent military reverses, Mr. Truman replied that he was sure it would survive. That was what his program was for.

On Taft versus Acheson

The President was asked to comment on the demand of Senator Robert A. Taft, Republican of Ohio, for the resignation of Mr. Acheson on the ground that his policy in the Far East had been reversed.

"I think that the political statement of Mr. Taft at this time is entirely uncalled for," replied Mr. Truman, giving permission to quote this, too.

"Senator Taft also said you had reversed Secretary Acheson. Would you comment on that, too?"

"There is not a word of truth in that," said Mr. Truman. "And you can quote me on that, too."

Asked point-blank whether ground troops would be used in Korea, Mr. Truman said he could not comment.

"In that connection," was the next question, "it has been asked whether there might be any possibility of using the atomic bomb. Do you favor using it?"

Mr. Truman replied no comment to this, too.

Later a reporter brought this up, asking: "Mr. President, your 'no comment' on the atomic bomb might be subject to interpretation. Have we made any change in our disposition * * *?"

Mr. Truman sharply interrupted, **saying he would make no comment on any matter of strategy. Then he reiterated that he did not expect to comment on any matter of strategy.**

The President declined to say whether the Korean crisis would serve to expedite negotiation of a Japanese peace treaty.

June 30, 1950

EISENHOWER ASKS SOVIET DEEDS: PEACE IN ASIA AND DISARMAMENT; WOULD USE SAVINGS TO AID WORLD

5-POINT PLAN GIVEN

President Says Kremlin Must Prove Goodwill—Urges Global Fund

By W. H. LAWRENCE
Special to THE NEW YORK TIMES

WASHINGTON, April 16—Proposing a five-point disarmament program, President Eisenhower declared today that the "first great step" toward global peace must be an honorable armistice in Korea that would include "an end to the direct and indirect attacks upon the security of Indo-China and Malaya."

The President then announced that if peace could be achieved and disarmament under strict United Nations supervision approved, the United States Government was ready "to ask its people to join with all nations in devoting a substantial percent of any savings achieved by real disarmament to a fund for world aid and reconstruction."

Such an international fund would be used "to help other peoples to develop the underdeveloped areas of the world, to stimulate profitable and fair world trade, to assist all peoples to know the blessings of productive freedom," he said.

Both Parties Approve Speech

The speech received approval from both parties in Congress, many noting that the President had "seized the initiative." Republicans and Democrats felt he struck the right note in his warning to the Soviet that the free world would and could defend itself, while expressing a willingness to meet the Russians halfway toward an honorable settlement of world tensions.

General Eisenhower made his bid to regain for the United States the diplomatic "peace" initiative from the Soviet Union in a speech before a luncheon of the American Society of Newspaper Editors, which was broadcast and televised nationally by all networks and rebroadcast to the world in many languages on short wave. It was his first major policy address since Premier Georgi M. Malenkov succeeded to power in the Soviet Union on the death of Joseph Stalin.

The President declared that peace in Korea should be followed by an Austrian treaty, and by plans for closer unity of the nations of Europe including "a free and united Germany, with a government based upon free and secret elections."

Once these steps have been taken to strengthen world trust, he said, this government will welcome and enter "into the most solemn agreements" aimed at five major ends:

1. The limitation, by absolute numbers or by an agreed international ratio, of the sizes of the military and security forces of all nations.
2. A commitment by all nations to set an agreed limit upon that proportion of total production of certain strategic materials to be devoted to military purposes.
3. International control of atomic energy to promote its uses for peaceful purposes only, and to insure the prohibition of atomic weapons.
4. A limitation or prohibition of other categories of weapons of great destructiveness.
5. The enforcement of all these agreed limitations and prohibitions by adequate safeguards, including a practical system of inspection under the United Nations.

President Challenges Soviet

The President challenged the Soviet Union to reply by affirmative acts to these three direct questions:

"Is the new leadership of the Soviet Union prepared to use its decisive influence in the Communist world—including the control of the flow of arms—to bring not merely an expedient truce in Korea but genuine peace in Asia?

"Is it prepared to allow other nations, including those in Eastern Europe, the free choice of their own form of government?

"Is it prepared to act in concert with others upon a serious disarmament proposal?"

In the advance text of the President's speech, the second and third questions read:

"Is it prepared to allow other nations, including those in Eastern Europe, the free choice of their own forms of government and the right to associate freely with other nations in a world-wide community of law?

"Is it prepared to act in concert with others upon serious disarmament proposals to be made firmly effective by stringent United Nations control and inspection?"

The last parts of both questions were omitted by the President in delivery because he feared that he would be running over his allotted broadcast time.

Vacation Is Interrupted

The President interrupted his Georgia golfing vacation to fly to Washington to deliver his major foreign policy speech to the newspaper editors, and stayed on long enough to throw out the first ball at the Griffith Stadium opening game here between the Washington Senators and the New York Yankees. He watched the ball game briefly, and them flew to Charlotte, N. C., motoring from that airport to Salisbury, N. C., where he participated in ceremonies marking the 200th anniversary of Rowan County. He flew back to Augusta from the Winston Salem, N. C., airport.

Introduced to the editors by Wright Bryan, editor of the Atlanta Journal and president of the society, General Eisenhower prefaced his prepared remarks with a moving tribute to the editors of newspapers of the United States and the role they must play so that the people might know and understand facts. He recalled his own friendships with a number of them, in war and peace during both military and "electoral" campaigns.

He was solemn as he launched into his address, reading slowly and carefully, and the 1,000 editors and their guests, including most cabinet members, interrupted with applause five times.

The President said the United States welcomed "every honest act of peace" and had noted recent statements and gestures by the new Soviet leaders giving some evidence that they might recognize that the affairs of the world had reached a critical point. The Soviet Union has many opportunities beyond "mere rhetoric" to convince the free world of its sincerity of peaceful purpose, he added.

"Even a few such clear and specific acts—such as the Soviet Union's signature upon an Austrian treaty, or its release of thousands of prisoners still held from World War II—would be impressive signs of sincere intent," he declared. "They would carry a power of persuasion not to be matched by any amount of oratory.

Trust Called Basis of Peace

"This we do know: a world that begins to witness the rebirth of trust among nations can find its way to a peace that is neither partial nor punitive."

Until these assurances for peace are given through concrete acts, the free world "must, at any cost, remain armed, strong and ready for the risk of war" and maintain its unity of purpose and will "beyond the power of propaganda or pressure to break, now or ever," the President said.

General Eisenhower, who was the Supreme Allied Commander for the victorious Western Powers in World War II and in the post-war development of the North Atlantic Treaty forces, said the end of the war in 1945 had been marked by bright hopes of a "just peace" and international cooperation "to guard vigilantly against the domination ever again of any part of the world by a single, unbridled aggressive power."

"This common purpose lasted an instant—and perished," he said.

With obvious reference to the "soft line" followed by the new leaders of the Soviet Union since Stalin's death, he implied the free world must never again be taken in by "the self-deceit of easy illusion."

The new Russian leadership now has "a precious chance to turn the black tide of events" and its first concrete example must be "the conclusion of an honorable armistice in Korea," he said.

"This means the immediate cessation of hostilities and the prompt initiations of political discussions leading to the holding of free elections in a united Korea," he said.

"It should mean—no less importantly—an end to the direct and indirect attacks upon the security of Indo-China and Malaya. For any armistice in Korea that merely released aggressive armies to attack elsewhere would be a fraud.

"We seek, throughout Asia, as throughout the world, a peace that is true and total."

The President painted a somber picture of the world's future if the present trend of international events continued.

He said the worst result would be "a[illegible]ic war" and the "best" would be: "A life of perpetual fear and tension; a burden of arms draining the wealth and the labor of all peoples; a wasting of strength that defies the American system or the Soviet system or any other system to achieve true abundance and happiness for the peoples of this earth."

In terms of today's heavy preparedness effort, a modern heavy bomber costs a modern brick school in more than thirty cities, or two electric power plants, each serving a town of sixty thousand, or two fine, fully equipped hospitals, the President said. A fighter plane alone costs 500,000 bushels of wheat, and a single destroyer is paid for with "new homes that could have housed more than 8,000 people," he added.

War on Poverty Proposed

But if peace and disarmament could be achieved, the world as a whole could wage "a declared, total war, not upon any human enemy, but upon the brute forces of poverty and need," he declared.

"The peace we seek, founded upon a decent trust and cooperative effort among nations, can be fortified—not by weapons of war—but by wheat and cotton; by milk and by wool; by meat, timber and rice," the President declared.

"These are words that translate into every language on earth. These are the needs that challenge this world in arms."

April 17, 1953

EISENHOWER, OPPOSING TAFT, REJECTS GO-IT-ALONE POLICY; BARS COERCING U.N. ON CHINA

UNITY IS HELD VITAL

President Says That U.S. Must Cooperate With Allies in All Areas

By JAMES RESTON
Special to THE NEW YORK TIMES.

WASHINGTON, May 28—President Eisenhower differed publicly today with Senator Robert A. Taft of Ohio on how to negotiate peace in Korea, but there was no indication that this marked the beginning of a test of strength between the President and his Senate majority leader over the conduct of United States foreign policy.

Asked at his tenth news conference this morning whether he shared Senator Taft's view, expressed in a speech at Cincinnati Tuesday, that the United States should forget the United Nations as far as the Korean war was concerned, the President replied immediately:

"No."

Then he added that, while negotiations with our allies often were difficult and usually necessitated compromises, it was not possible to have cooperation with our allies in some spots of the globe and reject their cooperation elsewhere.

"If you are going to go-it-alone in one place," he observed solemnly, "you, of course, have to go it alone everywhere . . ." and this, he emphasized, he was not prepared to do.

Position Made Clear

Thus, the President made it clear that if he were forced to choose between breaking with his allies or breaking with the powerful senior Senator from Ohio, he would break with the Senator.

[President Eisenhower's comments eased the shock felt by Europeans at Senator Taft's speech, but officials in Paris saw the Republican party's differences on foreign affairs widening. Dr. Konrad Adenauer, West German Chancellor, described the Taft address as a warning to Europe to speed defense unification or face loss of United States aid. Moscow made no official comment, but diplomats of Allied nations there deplored Senator Taft's stand and welcomed the President's declaration.]

There was no evidence to suggest here this evening, however, that the Senator had planned to challenge the President's method of conducting the Korean negotiations, nor was there any evidence in the President's frank but conciliatory manner that General Eisenhower chose to interpret the Senator's Tuesday speech as a challenge.

The view of most observers here, including the closest associates of the Senator and the President, was that Mr. Taft merely had expressed opinions he had held for a long time, that these preferences for a nationalistic approach to many international problems differed from the President's, and that the Senator had chosen a particularly unfortunate time to emphasize the differences—just as the Korean truce talks were reaching another critical point.

Nevertheless, the President did depart from his normal custom of avoiding public controversy with Republican legislators by taking issue, not only with Mr. Taft, but with those Senators and Representatives who wanted to coerce the Allies into breaking off all commerce, strategic or non-strategic, with Communist China, and who also wanted to coerce the United Nations into refusing United Nations membership to the Peiping regime even if there was a truce in Korea.

The President left no doubt about his own views about the Chinese Communists. He said he was against allowing them in the United Nations under present circumstances. He implied, moreover, that he would continue to be opposed to their membership so long as he thought they were subservient to the Soviet Union, but he made a distinction between the policy and a policy of coercing the Allies on trade or the United Nations membership.

It would be a very grave error to allow the Peiping regime into the United Nations, he said, but it would also be a very, very drastic cure for us to threaten to withdraw financial support from the United Nations if the Peiping regime were brought into the United Nations. He added that he did not know whether he could go along with that, though he would like to think about it.

A rider to a State Department appropriation bill denying United States support to the United Nations if Communist China were granted membership was voted by the Senate Appropriations Committee yesterday.

As to trade with Communist China, the President said that no permanent policy had been established on this, but he indicated that in his judgment it would not be prudent to cut off all trade with the Communists in Europe and the Far East, lest they then be made dependent for their trade on the Soviet Union, or other nations hostile to the United States.

His Mail Not Isolationist

The President also made these points:

¶Despite all the controversy over foreign policy, his mail, which was running three to five times above the White House record, did not show any trend toward isolationism. On the contrary, he added, the mail indicated that the American people now realized that there was no safety for any free country in isolation.

¶His meeting with the Prime Minister of Britain and the Premier of France in Bermuda next month was going to be small and informal, if he had anything to say about it. He implied that if Congressmen wanted to go along, he would keep them informed of what was done, day by day, but he did not commit himself to take them into the Western Big Three talks. Nor would he commit himself to follow the Western Big Three meeting with another meeting with the Russians. If that happened it would be because of some development that justified it, he said.

¶The cuts in the defense budget had the general approval of the Joint Chiefs of Staff, all things considered; likewise, the cuts in the Air Force budget, in his opinion, did not jeopardize a "reasonable posture of defense."

¶The Allies in Korea did not question his major principle—that there should be no forcible repatration of prisoners of war—but, he added, we should certainly never adopt a solution in Korea which our own conscience told us was unfair to the South Koreans.

Reporters Cram Interview Room

All these things, however, took up very little of the thirty-five minute conference. The reporters who had covered the Eisenhower-Taft race for the Republican presidential nomination last year, and who had been watching the relationships between the two men ever since, crammed into the fourth floor Treaty Room in the old State Department building for the latest chapter in the Eisenhower-Taft story, and the President gave it to them.

He arrived in the room promptly, as usual, at 10:30, dressed in a light tan suit, tan shirt and figured tie. He was ruddy and relaxed, and he took only a few seconds on his own to say that he had heard that the Russians had changed the orders of their military command in East Germany, but that he did not really know anything about it.

Accordingly, he opened the meeting to questions, and the inevitable question was first.

"Mr. President," said Merriman Smith of the United Press, "do you share Senator Taft's view that we should forget the United Nations as far as the Korean war is concerned?"

The President said no, and then, in a statement he later permitted to be quoted direct, he added:

"I think that you will understand that if you attempt to talk about this whole business of foreign relations, one is apt to get into a lecture that runs a little long. But at the risk of being just a bit verbose, let me explain one or two things.

"I have had a great deal of experience in dealing with coalitions, in filling positions of responsibility under them. It's always difficult when if one—any one nation or any one authority—were acting singly, possibly the decision in that point would be better than to subject it to all of the trimmings and the compromises that come out of the effort to achieve some kind of unanimity of opinion.

"But you can't have cooperative action in these great developments and processes in just the spots of the globe, or in just the particular problems that you would like to select.

"If you are going to go it alone one place, you, of course, have to go it alone everywhere. If you are going to try to develop a coalition of understanding based upon decency, on ideas of justice, common concepts of governments established by the will of free men, then you have got to make compromises. You have got to find the way in between the conflicting partisan considerations that will serve the best good of all.

"Now, that is what we are up against today, because our whole policy is based on this theory: no single free nation can live alone in the world. We have to have friends. Those friends have got to be tied to you, in some form or another. We have to have that unity in basic purposes that comes from a recognition of common interests. That is what we are up against.

"Now, not being a particularly patient man, I share the irritations and the sense of frustration that comes to everybody who is working for what he believes to be a decent purpose and finds himself balked by what he thinks is the ignorance, or the errors, of someone who is otherwise his friend.

"I understand those things, but I will tell you, only patience, only determination, only optimism and only a very deep faith can carry America forward.

"Here at home we have our differences on these things, because we are 160 million people. But I earnestly believe we cannot desert the great purpose for which we are seeking—for which we are working.

"I apologize for the length of my answer. But I think that the subject deserves that much explanation."

Further Questions Asked

This did not end the questioning on the subject, however. One reporter noted that Mr. Taft had not said that he wanted to break with the United Nations now, but that he had proposed a break only if the present truce negotiations failed.

The President replied to this that he was not going to put words into Senator Taft's mouth because he had not actually read the Senator's speech in detail, but he observed that when the Senator talked about going-it-alone, he must have meant that the United States should follow its own policy, its own belief and conviction without reference to anybody else.

There must be some confusion about what the Senator really did mean, the President observed. Suppose, he said, all of us were friends and we were trying to get somebody out in the street to agree with us but could not. Did that then mean, the President inquired, that friends suddenly become enemies and break up?

Later the President likened the Grand Alliance of the United States and its Allies to a marriage or rather to a long-range partnership and drew this parallel: In a long-term partnership or an alliance, you have to take the ups and downs. You cannot say, in North Africa we all agree, in South Africa we go it alone, because it just would not work.

This alliance, he observed, was an effort to produce unity that is based on an appreciation of common values. Woodrow Wilson once used some very literary words in this regard, the President recalled: "The highest form of efficiency is the spontaneous cooperation of a free people."

This, said General Eisenhower, was what we were trying to prove. That was what we were trying to achieve and it was going to be a tough, long-term thing.

He told another questioner, that of course there had been differences of opinion on procedure in arranging the last phase of the Korean talks—differences within our own Government and within the Allied coalition. But on the main point—what Sir Winston Churchill called the "point of honor"—that no prisoner should be forced or coerced into going home against his will, there had not been any wavering anywhere.

Finally, when the President was asked whether he could read Senator Taft's speech and give a prepared statement of his views, Mr. Eisenhower replied that no, he was sorry he could not do that. He had admitted Senator Taft's right to his convictions.

What he (the President) had done in the news conference was to explain his attitude, his philosophy, and his determination to lead the Government and the people along the lines he had indicated, because, he observed, he believed in these things with all his heart. He did not believe, he concluded, that discouragement and resentment had a right to turn us from a course that is just and good. That, he said, was his comment.

The President was less definite in his comments about policy toward Communist China, though here again he took positions unlike those of some influential Republicans on the Hill.

The background of these questions was as follows:

¶In recent days, several different **moves have been made by Republican Senators to force a tougher policy on the Administration in relation to Peiping. Senator Joseph R. McCarthy, Republican of Wisconsin, for example, has been agitating for a policy that would put pressure on the Allies to cut off all trade with Communist China.**

¶Similarly, Senator William F. Knowland, Republican of California, has introduced a resolution in the Senate that favors withdrawal of the United States from the United Nations if the members of that organization vote the Chinese Communists into the world organization in place of the Chinese Nationalist Government.

¶Finally, as noted above, the Appropriations Committee voted yesterday to deny United States Government funds to the United Nations—the United States now pays more than one-third of the United Nations' bills—if Communist China was voted into the organization at any time.

Asked various questions on these and other points about Peiping, the President first of all said that, as of the present moment, nobody in this Government had proposed that Peiping be allowed in the United Nations. Believing as we do that what we call Red China is subservient to Moscow, the President said, he believed it should not be allowed United Nations membership.

Fund-Barring Called Drastic

When he was asked about the Appropriations Committee's vote against membership for the Chinese Communists, the President at first refused to answer on the ground that this was a hypothetical question. When he was told what the committee had done, he said he had not read the papers this morning, but added that he thought the committee's action sounded pretty drastic. He did not, however, commit himself further on the subject.

When a questioner asked for his position on trade with the Communists, and noted that there seemed to be some difference between the State and Defense Departments on our policy, the President said he did not think there was any deep conflict between the departments.

It had been pointed out for years, he continued, that the Communists had been helped by certain kinds of trade. But, he added, it had also been pointed out that it would be foolish for us to take the position that we were not going to trade with anybody except the people we liked.

It was at this point that he noted that if all trade were cut off between Communist China and the West, the Reds would have to trade with Moscow and thus would be thrown into the arms of the Soviet Union.

It was learned late this evening that Senator Taft read the unofficial transcript of the President's conference but sent word from his hospital in Cincinnati that he did not want to comment on it at this time.

TRUCE IS SIGNED, ENDING THE FIGHTING IN KOREA

PRESIDENT IS HAPPY

But Warns in Broadcast That Global Peace Is Yet to Be Achieved

Special to THE NEW YORK TIMES.

WASHINGTON, July 26—President Eisenhower greeted the news of the Korean armistice tonight with prayers of thanksgiving but warned the nation that the Allies had won an armistice only on a single battleground and had not achieved peace in the world.

The President spoke over radio and television networks about an hour after the official cease-fire documents had been signed.

General Eisenhower said the United States and all the free world must not relax its guard, or fail to be vigilant against "the possibility of untoward developments."

After the President had spoken, Charles E. Wilson, Secretary of Defense, issued a statement warning against any relaxation in the country's defense program because of the truce. He advised, too, that it would be a "long time" before American troops could be withdrawn from Korea "with safety."

"We must not be misled into the sar demobilization which followed World Wars I and II," he said. "Such a demobilization would inevitably again tempt an aggressor."

Dulles Sees U. N. Victory

John Foster Dulles, Secretary of State, described the armistice as a great victory for the United Nations because "for the first time in history an international organization had stood against an aggressor and has marshaled force to meet force."

President Eisenhower spoke from the White House, across Pennsylvania Avenue and about a block east from Blair House, where President Truman decided thirty-seven months ago to commit United States forces to the defense of South Korea, then being overrun by the Communist armies from the north.

REPORTS ON TRUCE: President Eisenhower making nation-wide television broadcast from the White House last night.

The President said he hoped that the coming of peace to Korea would at last convince all nations of the wisdom of composing their differences by negotiation before—rather than after "various resorts to brutal and futile battle."

He closed his brief speech by quoting from the final paragraph of Lincoln's Second Inaugural Address, which he said expressed the resolution and dedication of all Americans, now as in 1865.

These were Lincoln's words: "With malice toward none, with charity for all, with firmness in the right, as God gives us to see the right, let us strive on to finish the work we are in, * * * to do all which may achieve and cherish a just and lasting peace among ourselves and with all nations."

General Eisenhower concluded, after the Lincoln quotation, "That is our resolve and our dedication."

The President began his address with a declaration that the cost of repelling aggression had been high for the country as a whole, but "in thousands of home it has been incalculable. It has been paid in terms of tragedy."

General Eisenhower, whose son, Maj. John Eisenhower, has been on active duty in Korea since July, 1952, except for a short leave to attend his father's inauguration, went on to say he was happy that thousands of Americans now imprisoned would be returning to their homes soon. The swiftness of their return, he said, would be evidence of the good faith of the Communists.

He said the United Nations had met the challenge of aggression not with words but with deeds, and this nation was thankful for the contributions of the soldiers, sailors and airmen of sixteen Allied countries that had joined the battle on the United Nations side.

He paid a special tribute to the fighting men of the Republic of Korea, saying they had been inspired by their President, Dr Syngman Rhee, and had given on the field of battle another proof that men from the West and East could fight, work and live together side by side in pursuit of just and noble causes.

Official Word Relayed

President Eisenhower, who returned to the White House this afternoon from a conference with civilian and military defense leaders at the Quantico, Va., Marine Base, started his address at 10 P. M., twenty-two minutes after he had received official word that the truce had been signed. A message from Gen. Mark W. Clark, United Nations commander, was relayed from the Pentagon at 9:38 P. M. to inform the President of the signing.

At 9:45 the President appeared in the White House broadcast room and took his place at a big carved oak desk presented to the White House by Queen Victoria of Britain.

James C. Hagerty, White House press secretary, placed on a reading stand before him large cards with the hand-lettered text of the broadcast.

The President studied the cards for a few moments as photographers took practice shots.

Hopes Son Will Be Home

The President, wearing a brown single-breasted suit with the jacket unbuttoned, relaxed for a moment as he surveyed the thirty to forty reporters and cameramen. Someone asked him how he felt.

"The war is over," he declared with a broad smile, "and I hope my son is going to come home soon."

General Eisenhower relied considerably on the text before him during most of his talk. But when he came to the climactic quotation from Lincoln's Second Inaugural Address—"With malice toward none * * *" the President looked directly into the battery of cameras to intone the famous words of his predecessor.

Outside the White House there was little demonstration over the end of a war. Downtown Washington was quiet under a full July moon. As the President spoke, no more than a dozen persons, who appeared to be tourists, stood silently about the west gate nearest the Presidential offices.

Wilson Says Threat Lasts

Secretary Wilson said in his statement: "Words cannot express our everlasting debt of gratitude to those men who laid down their lives or suffered wounds that the assault on the free world, unleashed in June, 1950, would not pass unchallenged and unchecked."

He declared that Korea had been only a small part of the threat the free world faced from Communist imperialism and that the end of fighting would not mean the end of the threat. He warned against "any letdown in our determination to complete the build-up of our defenses and to maintain them for as long as need be."

Mr. Wilson said no important reduction in defense spending could be expected soon and assured defense industries and workers that they "need have no concern regarding an abrupt cancellation of contracts for military equipment, supplies and services."

In a statement released after the President had completed his radio and television report, Mr. Dulles noted that the North Korean Communist aggressor had been victorious at first, but now had been repulsed, and indeed was "in control of less territory than when his aggression began."

Estimates were that 2,350 square miles of North Korean territory had passed under South Korean control since 1950, while the South Korean loss of territory to the North Koreans amounted to 850 square miles.

Secretary Dulles added: "The North Korean Army is virtually extinct, the Chinese and Korean Communist Armies have sustained about two million casualties, and of the 10,000,000 people of North Korea, one out of every three has died from the war ravages and the inhuman neglects which their rulers have imposed.

Free Nations Called Safer

"These tragic results will surely be pondered by other potential nominees for aggression-by-satellite. All free nations, large and small, are safer today because the ideal of collective security has been implemented and because awful punishment has been visited upon the transgressors."

He pledged anew the intention of the United States to work for the unification of Korea by peaceful means at the forthcoming political conference.

July 27, 1953

DULLES SETS GOAL OF INSTANT REBUFF TO STOP AGGRESSOR

Aims at Prompt Retaliation at Sites of 'Own Choosing,' Not Local Defense

DEALS WITH REDS BARRED

Secretary, Honored at Dinner Here, Explains Adaptation of Military, Foreign Policy

John Foster Dulles, Secretary of State, said last night that the nation's military and foreign policy was being adapted to a basic decision: To confront any aggressor with "a great capacity to retaliate, instantly, by means and at places of our own choosing." The decision was made by the National Security Council, he said.

President Eisenhower's program seeks more effective and less costly security in cooperation with the allies of the United States "by placing more reliance on community deterrent power, and less dependence on local defensive power," Mr. Dulles said.

Speaking at a dinner given in his honor by the Council on Foreign Relations at the Hotel Pierre, Secretary Dulles promised continued efforts at negotiations with the Soviet Union on such issues as atomic energy, Germany, Austria and Korea.

But with the Berlin conference of the Big Four foreign ministers less than two weeks off, Secretary Dulles pledged there would be "no plan for a partnership division of world power with those who suppress freedom."

Dulles Hopeful on Peace

Mr. Dulles foresaw hope of peace because "there are limits to the power of any rulers indefinitely to suppress the human spirit." He reported signs that Soviet leaders were bending to their people's desire for more food, more household goods and more economic freedom.

The Secretary's speech, entitled "The Evolution of Foreign Policy," had been heralded by the State Department as a major statement. The address, which pulled together a review of the Eisenhower course, was broadcast nationally over the Du Mont television network, and rebroadcast later by the Mutual and National Broadcasting Company radio systems.

Many pre-Eisenhower foreign policies were "good," Mr. Dulles said. He cited aid to Greece and Turkey, the European Recovery Program, the Berlin airlift, United Nations resistance to attack in Korea and the building up of American and Western European armed strength.

But these were emergency actions, imposed on us by our enemies, Mr. Dulles said, and they were costly. He pictured new planning by President Eisenhower and his National Security Coun-

The New York Times

DULLES HONORED HERE: Secretary of State John Foster Dulles, center, chatting with John J. McCloy, left, chairman of the board of the Council of Foreign Relations and Averell Harriman, former Mutual Security Director, at dinner in Mr. Dulles' honor at Hotel Pierre.

cil, recognizing that there was no local defense that alone would contain the mighty land power of the Communist world,

"A potential aggressor must know that he cannot always prescribe battle conditions that suit him," Mr. Dulles said. "The way to deter aggression is for the free community to be willing and able to respond vigorously at places and with means of its own choosing."

Mr. Dulles' report tied in with President Eisenhower's notice in his State of the Union message last Thursday that atomic weapons might be used "against an aggressor if they are needed to preserve our freedom." There also had been earlier administration warnings that Communist aggression in Korea or open Chinese Communist aggression in Indo-China might evoke military reactions beyond those areas.

Out of the new planning, the Chiefs of Staff will be able to make a selection of military means instead of a "multiplication of means," Mr. Dulles said. This will make it possible "to get, and share, more security at less cost," he added.

With the Korean war ended, and armed forces no longer largely committed to the Asian mainland, a "strategic reserve" can be set up, Mr. Dulles continued.

The revised "long haul" build-up adopted for the North Atlantic Treaty Organization will avoid exhausting members' economic strength, he went on.

Secretary Dulles vowed confidence that "peace will soon have the indispensable foundation" of that European Defense Community," bringing in West Germany, and expressed hope for "a political community thereafter."

The Secretary said the new concepts of collective security would enable limiting foreign aid to "situations where it clearly contributes to military strength," such as Indo-China. With exceptions for continuing technical assistance and specific disaster relief, he forecast that economic aid would be trimmed in favor of seeking more trade and investments.

About 400 persons attended the dinner, which resumed a tradition of banquets by the Council on Foreign Relations in honor of Secretaries of State, interrupted in recent years by inability to make arrangements. John J. McCloy, the council's chairman, presided.

January 13, 1954

EISENHOWER BARS WAR INVOLVEMENT WITHOUT CONGRESS

Gives Promise When Queried on Action if Americans in Indo-China Are Killed

COUNTER TO DULLES VIEW

Statement Seen as Modifying 'Instant Retaliation' Policy Announced by Secretary

By JAMES RESTON

Special to THE NEW YORK TIMES.

WASHINGTON, March 10—President Eisenhower promised today not to involve the United States in war without a declaration of war by Congress.

Asked at his news conference what he would do if United States technicians in Indo-China were captured or killed, the President replied:

"There is going to be no involvement of America in war unless it is a result of the constitutional process that is placed upon Congress to declare it. Now, let us have that clear. And that is the answer."

By this statement, the President seemed to modify the policy of "instant retaliation" recently announced by his Secretary of State, John Foster Dulles.

On Jan. 12, 1954, Mr. Dulles announced that the President and his highest policy-making body, the National Security Council, had made a "basic decision." This, he said, was "to depend primarily upon a great capacity to retaliate, instantly, by means and at places of our choosing."

Today's statement also seemed to commit the President to the requirement of a declaration of war by Congress regardless of the unforeseen circumstances of the future and regardless of whether Congress was in session at the time of the crisis.

Five Undeclared Wars

Of ten serious and extended armed conflicts between the United States and other nations, five were conducted without Congress' declaring war at all. These were the Korean war, the United States-Mexican hostilities of 1914-17, the undeclared naval war with France, 1798-1800; the first Barbary war of 1801-05, and the second Barbary war, 1815.

The five wars specifically sanctioned by a Congressional declaration were the two World Wars, the Spanish-American War, the Mexican War, and the War of 1812. Four of the five declarations recognized the prior existence of the conflict.

Today's questions on the Administration's policy of "instant retaliation" grew out of last week-end's criticism of this policy by Adlai E. Stevenson, the Democratic Presidential nominee in the 1952 election.

Mr. Stevenson expressed some concern in Miami Beach, Fla., about the Administration's announced policy of meeting aggression with instant retaliation "by means and at places of our choosing."

"All this means, if it means anything, is that if the Communists try another Korea we will retaliate by dropping atom bombs on Moscow or Peiping or wherever we choose," Mr. Stevenson said.

The President reacted somewhat sharply to a request for comment on Mr. Stevenson's criticism of the Administration's "new look" defense program.

He said he had spent a long time in the military service and that he was as seriously concerned as any single individual alive in the security of the United States. He observed that if he had too much confidence in his judgment in this field, he was subject to criticism, but he added (with considerable bite in his voice):

"I am doing nothing in the security department that I don't believe is for the welfare and the security and the continued safety of the United States of America, and I am not going to demagogue about it."

Mr. Eisenhower responded with equal vigor when he was asked about criticism that there was less bipartisan consultation on foreign and defense policy now than during the Truman and Roosevelt Administrations.

He said that the shoe was on the other foot; that the reporter should have heard the statements made to him by Republicans that they were never consulted by the Democrats on these matters except after policy decisions had been made.

The President seemed genuinely perturbed by this question. He asserted that he was going to extraordinary lengths to bring the Democrats in on foreign and defense policy questions, and that members of his own party sometimes looked askance at him for insisting on a bipartisan approach in these fields.

Nobody here, however, expected the President to carry the principle of consultation quite so far as to imply that he would seek a declaration of war by Congress before taking any action that might lead to involvement in hostilities.

The President has broad powers over the armed services as Commander in Chief. He is also obliged under the Constitution to see that the laws of the land are "faithfully executed." These powers and obligations have been intepreted many times in the past as authorizing the President to use the armed forces of the United States to take certain actions involving risk of war, without prior consultation with Congress. Korea, of course, was the latest example.

Action Under Treaty

Moreover, the United States commitments imply the possibility of similar action. Article 5 of the North Atlantic Treaty, for example, states: "The parties [including the United States] agree that an armed attack against one or more of them in Europe or North America shall be considered an attack against them all * * *."

It goes on to say that, if such an armed attack occurs, each will assist "the party or parties so attacked by taking forthwith, individually and in concert with the other parties, such action as it deems necessary, including the use of armed force, to restore and maintain the security of the North Atlantic area."

President Truman carefully avoided any commitment that would make it mandatory to seek a declaration of war from Congress before ordering the armed forces into action under this article.

He committed himself to follow "constitutional processes," but as in the case of Korea, where he ordered the armed forces into the battle without asking Congress, he reserved the right to act on his own, believing that he had constitutional power, as Commander in Chief, to carry out the terms of treaties.

President Eisenhower did not preserve his freedom of action today, however. Nor did he limit his commitment to Indo-China. He stated flatly: "There is going to be no involvement of America in war unless it is the result of the constitutional process that is placed upon Congress to declare it."

This statement, though tossed out extemporaneously in the casual give-and-take of a news conference, attracted great attention among the North Atlantic powers.

Officials of the North Atlantic Treaty allies felt that it was open to the interpretation that, if the Soviet army began moving into Denmark, the President would feel obliged to ask Congress (which might not be in session at the time) for a declaration of war before he ordered the strategic air force into operation against the aggressor.

March 11, 1954

PRESIDENT CAUTIONS ON 'JITTERS'

EISENHOWER SPEAKS

Asks Unity—Declares Soviet Courts Ruin if It Ventures War

By ANTHONY LEVIERO

Special to The New York Times.

WASHINGTON, April 5—President Eisenhower declared tonight that communism could not prevail against the spiritual and material might of the United States.

He urged his countrymen to put an end to their internal strife, not to yield to "jitters" and to face the future resolutely.

The Soviet Union contains the seeds of its own destruction and will disintegrate if it ventures into war, the President said in a television and radio speech broadcast to the nation and the world. Therefore, he said, he does not believe Russia will precipitate a war except through some fit of madness or miscalculation.

Moreover, the United States holds the advantage of a capacity for massive retaliation with its superiority in hydrogen bombs, the President asserted. This counter-threat, he reasoned, is the greatest de[illegible]rrent to an aggressive move by Moscow.

Against this overshadowing background of a troubled world, General Eisenhower calmly discussed domestic and international problems and pleaded for unity at home. He asked the American people not to "fall prey to hysterical thinking" as a result of the controversy over Communist subversion.

Shuns 'Any Kind of Panic'

"The greater any of these apprehensions," he said, "the greater is the need that we look at them clearly, face to face, without fear, like honest straightforward Americans so we do not develop the jitters or any kind of panic."

He also argued against the abuse of power by Congressional investigating committees and spoke out against the "very grave offenses" that could be committed against the innocent by those enjoying Congressional immunity.

The President obviously was referring to the methods of Senator Joseph R. McCarthy, Republican of Wisconsin, and his Permanent Subcommittee on Investigations, now tied up in a bitter quarrel between Mr. McCarthy and the Army. But he did not name the Senator.

While speaking out against Congressional abuses, the President did not propose that Congress or the Executive Branch take any particular course in dealing with them. "In this country," he declared, "public opinion is the most powerful of all forces, and it will straighten this matter out wherever and whenever there is real violence done to our great life."

The President spoke from the White House, seemingly casual as he leaned back against his desk. Though he had no manuscript in front of him, large "cue" cards were raised for him out of range of the television camera.

The President stated the essence of the over-riding world problem this way:

"Now this transfer of power, this increase of power from a mere musket and the little cannon all the way to the hydrogen bomb in a single lifetime, is indicative of the things that have happened to us. They rather indicate how far the advances of science have outraced our social consciousness, how much more we have developed scientifically than we are capable of handling emotionally and intellectually.

"So that is one of the reasons that we have this great concern of which the hydrogen bomb is merely a dramatic symbol."

The President drew a picture of the unity of the American he said, and you have the problems of paying for a home, educating its children and paying bills. Multiply that a millionfold, he said, and you have the problems of the nation. He maintained that these problems could be resolved if the nation conquered the jitters and united to deal with the threat of subversion at home and Soviet aggression abroad.

The hydrogen bomb is not "a great threat" in itself, he declared; it is a threat only if a potential aggressor decides to use it—"it's not going to be used by our initiative."

'Let Nothing Tear Us Apart'

Against such a threat this country has to make its defenses, the President pleaded, and unity is needed, for no other nation equals the moral and material strength of this country.

"Let nothing tear us apart," he said, warning that communism was trying to set class against class, good people against good people.

The President recited the elements of what he called the weaknesses of the Soviet empire. Its reliance on satellites, its comparative economic weakness against the United States, the need of its dictators to retain power—all are weakening factors if Russia gets into a war, he said.

The men in the Kremlin realize the factors that could ruin their empire, he declared.

"As long as they know that we are in a position to act strongly and to retaliate, war is not a decision to be taken lightly," the General said. "Yet I admit, and we must all admit, that there remains a possibility they might do this in a fit of madness or through miscalculation. The atomic age, of course, as I mentioned before, the H-bomb is dangerous because those people have its secrets, posses and have exploded, as they did some months back, such a bomb.

"But we know with respect to that bomb we are not going to start a war. It is not going to be used by our initiative, and I have just talked about this sobering effect of the risks of war upon the men in the Kremlin.

"Of all those sobering effects none is greater than the retaliation that would certainly be visited upon them if they would attack any of our nations or any part of our vital interests aggressively and in order to conquer."

The President also said it would be false to minimize the danger of Communist infiltration in this country. He went on to say there were about 25,000 doctrinal Communists here and the Federal Bureau of Investigation knew pretty well who they were.

They amount to about one in every 6,000 persons, he said, "but they are dangerous." He contended, however, that "our great defense against those people is the F. B. I." He said the Federal police agency had been doing a 'magnificent job" against Communist infiltration for years, and that the Attorney General, Herbert Brownell Jr., would have more to say about this in a nation-wide broadcast on Friday night.

The President then took up "the fear that we will use intemperate investigative methods, particularly Congressional committees to combat that Communist penetration.

He asserted that the great majority of Government employes was loyal, and only a "fringe" of disloyalty had to be hunted out and that was what the F. B. I. was doing.

The President declared that one of the original functions of Congressional committees had been to protect citizens against any usurpation of power by the Executive Branch of the Government.

"Now, ladies and gentlemen," he continued, "I admit that there can be very grave offenses committed against an innocent individual if he is accused falsely by someone having immunity of Congressional membership. He can lose his job; he can have scars that will be lasting; but in the long run, you may be certain of this: America believes in and practices fair play and decency and justice."

It was at this point that the President referred to the effect of public opinion.

Before discussing this country's economic situation, the President returned to the world scene to say that no nation had ever freely adopted communism; it was imposed by a small minority using violence and slick methods. So, he said, the United States should oppose the slavery of any nation and should consider its Allies as equals rather than tools.

The President then noted the concern about economic conditions at home, but said the figure of 3,700,000 unemployed "happily shows every sign now of leveling off."

The Government is ready to act against depression "whenever necessary," he said.

April 6, 1954

EISENHOWER CALLS FOR COEXISTENCE BUT NO APPEASING

Says He 'Will Not Be a Party to Any Agreement That Makes Anybody a Slave'

INDOCHINA PACT INCLUDED

President Suggests Transfer of Anti-Communists if That Country Is Partitioned

By JAMES RESTON

Special to The New York Times.

WASHINGTON, June 30—President Eisenhower said today the hope of the world lay in peaceful coexistence with the Communists. He added, however, that he would not appease them or recognize their enslavement of peoples.

[In Ottawa Prime Minister Churchill also urged the "peaceful coexistence" of the Western and Communist worlds.]

In his first news conference since his talks with Prime Minister Churchill, the President made it clear that he would not enter into any agreements in Indochina or elsewhere that subordinated people to foreign domination against their will.

With considerable emphasis he said "I will not be a party to any agreement that makes anybody a slave; now that's all there is to it."

This statement raised considerable interest here in view of the prospect that France would negotiate an armistice in Indochina that would partition the country and leave millions of Vietnamese under the domination of the Communists.

Indochina Issue Raised

The President was asked whether his statement meant that he would have no part in a settlement based on the partition of Indochina. He replied that the United States did not yet know what the settlement in that country would be, but suggested that it might be possible to transfer populations so that those persons who did not want to live under the Communists could move to another part of the country where they would be under a government of their own choice.

President Eisenhower suggested the reporters re-read the statement of purpose issued from the White House yesterday at the conclusion of his talks with Sir Winston. He implied the principles of that document would govern what the United States would and would not do about an Indochina settlement.

The relevant part of that statement read as follows:

"As regards formerly sovereign States now in bondage, we [the United States and Britain] will not be a party to any arrangement or treaty which would confirm or prolong their unwilling subordination.

"In the case of nations now divided against their will, we shall continue to seek to achieve unity through free elections supervised by the United Nations to insure they are conducted fairly."

This policy was interpreted in official quarters in these more specific terms:

¶The United States is not going to fight to prevent the partition of Indochina, any more than it is prepared to go to war to unify Germany or Korea.

¶It is prepared to sign a declaration (preferably using the language of the United Nations Charter) binding itself not to use force to upset the settlement made in Indochina, provided that settlement is freely negotiated by the parties primarily concerned.

¶The United States will not, however, enter into any general non-aggression pact in Southeast Asia that might oblige the United States to fight against any peoples that make war to gain their freedom from Communist domination.

Anthony Eden, British Foreign Secretary, recently suggested that it might be possible to negotiate a treaty like the Locarno pact, including the United States and Britain on the one hand and the Communists on the other in which all the signatories would be obliged to go to war against anyone who broke the peace.

Pact Like Locarno Opposed

This type of pact is not acceptable to the United States Government in Southeast Asia.

For example, if Indochina is partitioned into a Communist North and a non-Communist South, it is conceivable that some time in the future a movement for unification might develop in the South and result in an attack on the Communist North by the non-Communist South.

Nobody here regards such a movement as likely—indeed the fear is that the invasion might be in the other direction—but the United States does not want to sign any treaty of the Locarno type that would oblige it to make war on anybody—including the non-Communists—who might try to break the Indochina settlement by force of arms.

When he was asked the same question put to Sir Winston Monday—what were the possibilities of peaceful co-existence?—he said that for a long, long time "everybody" in the United States had urged peaceful co-existence with the Communists, but that there had to be good faith on both sides. We must make certain that peaceful co-existence did not mean appeasement or that we were willing to see any nation subordinated against its will, he observed.

On other aspects of the Churchill visit, the President was optimistic but not very specific. He made these points:

¶The visit of the British statesmen was preceded by vast concern in this country about the United States and Britain getting together, but the visit had done much, as he put it, to get this thing back on the rails. That, he added, made things a little more hopeful.

¶Sir Winston was one of his warmest friends and he had said so many nice things about him that he did not think he could say anything more that would add to the luster of his name.

¶Middle East defense was discussed, but the problems in Egypt over the Suez Canal were for the British and the Egyptians to settle. He implied that a settlement was forthcoming but that he had received this information on a confidential basis.

¶The two leaders discussed the hydrogen bomb and talks with the Soviet leaders, but nothing specific had been decided.

¶He would be glad to see the new French Premier when the latter had time and was in a position to talk.

July 1, 1954

PRESIDENT AGREES TO SUMMIT TALK IF FOREIGN MINISTERS PAVE WAY; PUTS DUTY TO BERLIN ABOVE PEACE

CONDITIONS GIVEN

By FELIX BELAIR Jr.

Special to The New York Times.

WASHINGTON, March 16—President Eisenhower announced tonight his willingness to attend a conference of heads of government with the Soviet Union if preliminaries offered prospects of worth-while results.

At the same time, the President served notice that the United States would not "try to purchase peace by forsaking 2,000,000 free people of Berlin." He said the United States would not submit to any permanent and compulsory division of Germany or permit any nation "to dishonor its international agreements whenever it may choose."

Willingness Voiced

In a report to the nation over the major television and radio networks, the President's emphasis on these points gave them the status of conditions on which the United States would insist at any preliminary sessions looking to a summit conference next summer.

The President's willingness to attend such a meeting was expressed in these terms:

"It is my hope that * * * all of us can reach agreement with the Soviets on an early meeting at the level of foreign ministers. Assuming developments that justify a summer meeting at the summit, the United States would be ready to participate in that further effort."

Changed Tone Noted

In his appraisal of the situation confronting the United States as a result of the Soviet proposal to make West Berlin a demilitarized free city, the President was neither belligerent nor placating. He described the recent Soviet note on a foreign ministers' meeting as "a move toward negotiation on an improved basis," and added:

"We would never negotiate under a dictated time limit or agenda, or on other unreasonable terms."

The President, having thus dismissed Premier Nikita S. Khrushchev's demand for withdrawal of Western troops from West Berlin, said a reply was now going forward only in view of the "changed tone" of the recent Soviet message.

Since the President's report was entirely within the context of the Berlin crisis, he had nothing to say about the results expected from a summit meeting. He was silent on the self-enforcing provisions of a general understanding he has said must include the future of Germany as well as Berlin.

He put the United States position in these terms:

"We will not retreat one inch from our duty. We shall continue to exercise our right of peaceful passage to and from West Berlin. We will not be the first to breach the peace; it is the Soviets who threaten the use of force to interfere with such free passage.

"We are ready to participate fully in every sincere effort at negotiation that will respect the existing rights of all and their opportunity to live in peace."

By insisting on a Western withdrawal from West Berlin, the President said, the Soviet Union has presented the United States with three fundamental choices. They were:

1. To abdicate United States rights and responsibilities to help a just and peaceful solution of the German problem.
2. The resort to war, which the Russians know as well as do Americans would mean the end of civilization.
3. Negotiations. And the United States with its allies stands ready to talk with the Soviet representatives "at any time and under any circumstances which offer prospects of worthwhile results."

Brushing aside the first of the three choices, the President said that not only high principle but the freedom of 2,000,000 West Berliners was involved in the United States' insistence on standing firm in that city.

"We have no intention of forgetting our rights or of deserting a free people," the President said. "Soviet rulers should remember that free men have, before this, died for so-called 'scraps of paper' which represented duty and honor and freedom."

"As a matter of principle the United States cannot accept the right of any government to break, by itself, solemn agreements to which we, with others, are parties," the President said. "But in the Berlin situation, both free people and principle are at stake."

While conceding that the Berlin crisis could conceivably lead to war, the President insisted that nothing was to be gained by appeasement and that the prospect of war actually was minimized by firmness in the face of the Soviet threat.

"The risk of war is minimized if we stand firm," the President said. "War would become more likely if we gave way and encouraged a rule of terrorism rather than a rule of law and order. Indeed, this is the core of the peace policy which we are striving to carry out around the world. In that policy is found the world's best hope for peace."

Some modification of his stand on negotiations with the present Soviet rulers was seen in the President's willingness to meet with the Soviet Premier.

President Eisenhower has maintained that he would go anywhere and meet with anyone in the interests of peace. But after Mr. Khrushchev first indicated rejection of a foreign ministers' meeting in an election speech last month the President said he saw no purpose of a meeting with the Soviet leader at this time.

Behind the President as he made his report to the nation was a map of Central Europe showing East and West Germany and Berlin. Also shown were the air corridors and rail and highway routes from West Germany to West Berlin.

The display included a table showing the types of missiles now available to the Defense establishment together with others to be delivered this year and still others on the drawing boards.

The President was vehement in stressing the present adequacy of the nation's defenses to meet any emergency. He said the capacity of United States forces "represents an almost unimaginable destructive power" and was buttressed by a vast Early Warning System and powerful air defense forces.

Of one thing the nation could rest assured, the President reported:

"We have the courage and capacity to meet the stern realities of the present and the future."

He dismissed contentions heard in Congress that the nation's defenses were not equal to the threat posed by the Berlin crisis and that there should be an immediate increase in the armed forces.

In the course of his report the President cautioned against attempts in Congress to reduce his request for $3,930,000,000 for foreign military and economic aid under the Mutual Security Program.

These funds are vital to Western security, the President said, and added:

"Any misguided effort to reduce them below what I have recommended weakens the sentries of freedom wherever they stand."

March 17, 1959

Peace Is Theme of Toasts at Eisenhowers' White House Dinner for the Khrushchevs

PRESIDENT SEEKS COMMON PURPOSE

Premier Notes Strength of Countries—Sees Danger of 'Colossal Damage'

By BESS FURMAN
Special to The New York Times.

WASHINGTON, Sept. 15—President Eisenhower and Premier Khrushchev exchanged toasts tonight at a White House dinner attended by 100 persons.

Mr. Khrushchev, in responding to the President's champagne toast, said that a quarrel between Soviet Union and the United States could lead to "colossal damage" and a "world shambles."

Both he and the President said it was the duty of their countries to work for peace.

The President said, "We must make it our common purpose * * * that we develop for each other the maximum of fact and truth so that we may better lead—between us—this world into a better opportunity for peace and prosperity."

President Sees Obligation

The President declared that the United States and the Soviet Union "have a very special obligation to the entire world because of our strength, because of our importance in the world, it is vital that we understand each other better."

Mr. Khrushchev also noted the strength of the two countries. "If we were weak countries," he said, "then it would be another matter, because when the weak quarrel they are just scratching each other's faces and it takes just a couple of days for a cosmetician and everything comes out right again."

"But if we quarrel, then not only our countries can suffer colossal damage, but the other countries of the world will also be involved in a world shambles.

"But I am sure we can live in peace and progrress together for peace."

Guests Sing Old Favorites

The White House dinner party broke up about 11:30 P. M. Its informal nature was evidenced by the fact that the guests joined in singing old American popular songs with the orchestral entertainment that followed the meal.

A Wall Street capitalist, two Washington hostesses and a Senator and a Representative from the newest state—Hawaii—were among those present.

Associated Press Wirephoto

WHITE HOUSE FETE: President and Mrs. Eisenhower escort Premier and Mme. Khrushchev to dinner in their honor

So was J. Edgar Hoover, director of the Federal Bureau of Investigation, and Mayor Wagner of New York and Mayor Pearle de Hart of Ames, Iowa, both of whom will play host to the Soviet Premier.

The diners were served a typically American dish, roast turkey with cornbread, dressing and cranberry sauce.

In a musicale following the dinner, Fred Waring and his Pennsylvanians entertained in a program called "Best Loved American Songs."

Tonight's affair was the first big White House event at a new social season, in which many traditional receptions and dinners have been dropped.

Since so many foreign heads of state will be coming to Washington this fall, the White House has decided what entertaining is done would be combined with affairs in their honor.

Hostesses Present

Two well-known hostesses were present, Mrs. Perle Mesta, a former Minister to Luxembourg who later traveled widely in the Soviet Union, and Mrs. Herbert A. May, the former Mrs. Joseph Davies. The late Mr. Davies was United States Ambassador in Moscow. Mr. May also was present.

The symbol of the capitalistic system was G. Keith Funston, President of the New York Stock Exchange, and Mrs. Funston. The president of the United States Chamber of Commerce, Erwin D. Canham of Boston, and Mrs. Canham, also were there.

Negro leaders attending were Dr. James Birnie, a scientist and chairman of the Biology Department of Morehouse College at Atlanta, Ga., and George M. Johnson, a member of the Civil Rights Commission. Both were accompanied by their wives.

Among the Congressional guests were House Speaker Sam Rayburn; the Senate majority leader, Lyndon B. Johnson, and Mrs. Johnson; the Senate minority leader, Everett McKinley Dirksen, and Mrs. Dirksen, and the House minority leader, Charles A. Halleck, and his daughter-in-law, Mrs. Charles W. Halleck.

Hawaii was represented by Senator and Mrs. Hiram L. Fong and Representative Daniel K. Inouye.

Largest to Date

It was the largest dinner yet held in the Eisenhower Administration. The one for Queen Elizabeth numbered ninety-seven; the one honoring this country's scientists in 1957 numbered ninety-eight.

Excitement was in the autumnish air. Crowds, well-policed, gathered before 7:30 P. M. near Blair House, across from the White House, hoping for a glimpse of the arriving guests.

The Soviet Premier and his wife arrived at the White House twenty minutes before the dinner started for a family gathering.

The Khrushchev family group included his two daughters, son, and son-in-law. The Eisenhower family group included their son and daughter-in-law, Maj. and Mrs. John Eisenhower; Mrs. Eisenhower's sister, Mrs. Gordon Moore and Mr. Moore, and the President's brother, Dr. Milton S. Eisenhower.

SUMMIT CONFERENCE BREAKS UP IN DISPUTE; WEST BLAMES KHRUSHCHEV'S RIGID STAND; HE INSISTS ON EISENHOWER APOLOGY

CHARGES TRADED

Allies Leave the Door Open to New Talk—Soviet Scores U.S.

By DREW MIDDLETON
Special to The New York Times.

PARIS, May 17—The summit conference died tonight. The leaders of the West said Premier Khrushchev had killed it. The Russians blamed the United States.

President Eisenhower, Prime Minister Macmillan and President de Gaulle feel "complete disgust" at the attitude the Soviet delegation has taken here in the last two days, James C. Hagerty, White House press secretary, reported.

In a communiqué issued this evening, the three Western chiefs declared that the Soviet leader's attitude had made it impossible to begin examination of the problems that it had been agreed should be discussed.

Apology Was Demanded

Premier Khrushchev had refused to meet with the Western leaders, on the invitation of President de Gaulle, unless Presdnt Eisenhower apologized for United States espionage flights over the Soviet Union. This the President was not prepared to do.

The meeting, so long prepared and so anxiously awaited, expired in an atmosphere of gloomy foreboding. Diplomats of the three Western powers feared the world situation would deteriorate.

The Western leaders pledged their support to a settlement of all outstanding international issues by negotiation rather than by the use or threat of force. The United States, Britain and France remain ready for such negotiations "at any suitable time in the future," a communiqué said.

Soviet in Sharp Attack

A few minutes after the communiqué had been made public, a group of leading Soviet editors answered it with a sharp denunciation of the United States. The conference foundered, a Soviet statement said, because "aggressive actions" of the United States Government and the Administration's failure to accept responsibility had "torpedoed the conference which the peoples of the whole world were awaiting with such hopes."

The Western leaders will meet again tomorrow afternoon after a preliminary conference between their foreign ministers, Christian A. Herter, Selwyn Lloyd and Maurice Couve de Murville. These meetings, Western diplomats said, will review the situation arising from the breakdown.

Mr. Lloyd made a final effort to salvage the conference tonight when he conferred with the Soviet Foreign Minister, Andrei A. Gromyko. They tried without success to find some basis for getting the talks started, British sources reported, but the results were not helpful or encouraging.

Mr. Gromyko advised Mr. Lloyd to let the dust settle and try to make progress along lines previously planned after the six-to-eight-month cooling-off period proposed by Mr. Khrushchev in a blistering speech yesterday.

The Foreign Secretary concluded that the breakdown in the conference need not halt the two international meetings in Geneva, diplomats reported. These are a ten-power meeting between East and West on disarmament and a conference of the United States, Britain and the Soviet Union on a ban on tests of nuclear weapons.

There are no further contacts planned here between the British and Soviet delegation, a British spokesman said. As far as Mr. Macmillan is concerned, the conference is finished. The Prime Minister wil return to London Thursday and will make a statement to the House of Commons Friday.

Mr. Khrushchev has arranged to pay a farewell visit to General de Gaulle tomorrow morning. The Premier intends to fly to East Berlin on his way home to Moscow. His departure time has not been announced.

Observers thought he probably would discuss with the East German Government the conclusion of his long-threatened separate peace treaty. But there were no indications of immediate trouble for West Berlin as a result of the failure of the conference.

[A Soviet spokesman said Mr. Khrushchev would hold a news conference Wednesday and probably would not leave before Thursday, United Press International reported.]

President Eisenhower will remain here tomorrow. On Thursday he will fly to Lisbon to pay a scheduled visit to Portugal. After twenty-four hours he will fly to Washington.

The Soviet statement was signed by "the press group attached to the President of the Council of Ministers of the U. S. S. R." This consists of the editors who accompany Mr. Khrushchev to international meetings. The document was headed "A clumsy maneuver by the leaders of the Western powers in Paris."

Explaining the Soviet side of today's exchanges, the statement quoted a letter Mr. Khrushchev sent to General de Gaulle this evening. This restated the Soviet leader's refusal to attend a meeting at Elysée Palace unless General Eisenhower fulfilled the conditions laid down yesterday.

Reply by de Gaulle

President de Gaulle's reply said that the objective of today's meeting was to begin discussion of problems "which we agreed to consider at the summit conference and thus it should have borne the character of the first session of this conference."

This afternoon Premier Khrushchev was willing to attend a preliminary session to discuss whether "conditions had materialized" for hold the summit conference — that is, whether President Eisenhower was prepared to apologize. But the Soviet leader added that he would not confer at the summit unless the President met his terms.

President Eisenhower qualified his acceptance. A White House statement said the President assumed that if Mr. Khrushchev accepted the de Gaulle invitation, this could constitute withdrawal of "conditions" for the talks advanced by the Soviet leader yesterday.

Mr. Khrushchev, in his denunciation of the United States for the U-2 plane that was shot down May 1 and for statements interpreted as meaning that reconnaissance flights would continue, demanded three actions by the President: condemnation of the flights, that is, an apology; a prohibition on the flights, a condition met by General Eisenhower before it was stated; and punishment of those responsible for them.

The Paris conference expired only after President de Gaulle and Prime Minister Macmillan had made repeated but unavailing efforts to save it. They tried to make Mr. Khrushchev see that General Eisenhower would not go further than he did yesterday, when he announced that United States reconnaissance flights over the Soviet Union had been halted and would not resume.

Last night Mr. Macmillan emphasized to Mr. Khrushchev that the world would judge him harshly for having wrecked the conference and that, in fact, he was abandoning his role as a peacemaker.

The day's events followed an odd pattern. The West clung to the hope that Mr. Khrushchev would alter his position. The three other leaders went through the motions of assembling for the conference, although it was almost certain the Soviet Premier would not attend.

The historic day for East-West relations began at 10 A. M. when President Eisenhower and Prime Minister Macmillan met President de Gaulle in Elysée Palace. Fifteen minutes later they were joined by their foreign ministers.

The group talked informally for three-quarters of an hour. Mr. Macmillan reported his encounter with Mr. Khrushchev last night and the three leaders speculated on the Soviet Premier's next move. From reports of briefing officers on this tragically futile day the next move was always Mr. Khrushchev's.

The morning was hot and sunny. At 11 o'clock President Eisenhower and Prime Minister Macmillan went down the street to the British Embassy. There they sat under shade trees in the garden chatting and drinking coffee. Shortly afterward they left for a drive.

Mr. Khrushchev was off on a tour of his own. Accompanied by Marshal Rodion Y. Malinovsky, Defense Minister, he drove to the region east of Paris.

At 11:30 General de Gaulle issued his formal invitation to a summit conference at 3 in the afternoon.

Text of the Invitation

The invitation to President Eisenhower said:

"Having noted the declarations made during the preliminary meeting on May 16, I consider it necessary to ascertain whether it is possible for the summit conference to begin the study of the questions which we agreed should be taken up. Consequently, I propose to you that we meet today, May 17, at 3 P. M., with Prime Minister Macmillan and Premier Khrushchev to take up the study of these questions."

The United States and Britain accepted immediately. From one of Mr. Khrushchev's impromptu news conferences came a report that he was ready to attend a preliminary meeting but not a summit conference.

The rather leisurely, nineteenth century procedure of the morning gave way to more frantic activity when the three Western leaders gathered again at Elysée Palace. This was the sequence of events that killed the long-awaited conference:

2:55 P. M.—Sergei M. Kudryavtsev, minister-counselor at the Soviet Embassy, telephoned to ask, on Mr. Khrushchev's behalf, if the meeting due to begin in five minutes was to clarify the points of view expressed yesterday or was to be a summit conference.

If it was to be a preliminary discussion, the diplomat said, Mr. Khrushchev would attend. However, he added, if it was to be a summit conference, the Premier would not attend because the conditions he outlined yesterday had not been met.

3:20 P. M.—Mr. Kudryavtsev telephoned again. This time he wanted to know whether the meeting then in progress was a preliminary one and whether the conditions Mr. Khrushchev had outlined had been fulfilled.

3:25 P. M.—An official at Elysée Palace telephoned the Soviet Embassy on President de Gaulle's instructions to ask for a written reply to his written invitation.

3:30 P. M.—Another telephone call came from the Soviet Embassy. Mr. Khrushchev wanted an answer to his questions and he did not intend to answer the invitation in writing.

4 P. M.—A Soviet diplomat, again on the telephone, asked when Mr. Khrushchev would receive his answer and suggested that he would give his decision when he did.

4:15 P. M.—General de Gaulle, Mr. Macmillan and General Eisenhower—"more amused than angry," according to a British diplomat—were told that a press statement had been issued by Mr. Khrushchev answering them.

The statement said:

"I am ready to participate in anything with President de Gaulle of France, Prime Minister Macmillan of Great Britain and United States President Eisenhower to exchange views on whether conditions have materialized to start the summit conference.

"If the United States has really come to the decision to condemn the treacherous incursions of American military aircraft into the airspace of the Soviet Union, publicly express regret over these incursions, punish those who are guilty and give assurances that such incursions will not be repeated in the future, we would be ready on receipt of such assurances to participate in the summit conference."

4:45 P. M.—Elysée Palace issued a statement drafted by General de Gaulle and approved by the two other Western leaders.

The statement said:

"General de Gaulle, President of the French Republic, proposed to President Eisenhower, Premier Khrushchev and Prime Minister Macmillan to meet with him on May 17 at 3 P. M. in order to ascertain whether the summit conference could begin the examination of the questions which it had been agreed to discuss.

"President Eisenhower and Mr. Macmillan were present. The absence of Premier Khrushchev was noted.

"President de Gaulle noted that in these circumstances the planned discussions could not take place."

5 P. M.—Meeting adjourned.

Soviet officials tried to reassure the West that the death of the conference would not upset the international balance. One said that it would not interrupt the East-West conferences in Geneva dealing with a ban on tests of nuclear weapons and disarmament.

"To our mind the summit had a much broader base," he said. "The two conferences in Geneva are dealing with specific items and there is no reason why they should not continue."

Foreign Policy Is the People's Business

Only by joining informed public opinion to firm leadership, says a Senator, can we dispel the myths that befog our policies in a critical time.

By JOHN F. KENNEDY

WASHINGTON.

ACCORDING to an ancient Celtic legend, the British giant Bran, suffering from a foot wound inflicted in battle by a poisoned arrow, commanded his seven surviving comrades to cut off his head and take it to London, where it was to be buried with the eyes facing in the direction of France. No foreign foe, he said, would be able to invade the island as long as his eyes were watching. But King Arthur, ages after, dug up Bran's head because he wanted Britain to owe her power in foreign affairs and military defense to strength and courage, not to magic.

We have no buried giants' heads in the United States. But American foreign policy is surrounded by a mythology of its own. There are myths based upon the untouchability of national sovereignty; the existence of inherently good, bad or backward nations; the emphasis of governmental economy over national security; and the impairment of an aggressor's military power by refusing him our diplomatic recognition.

Many Americans persist in the myth that the scientific skill of the United States cannot be duplicated in any other country; that the democratic way of life, inasmuch as it is the best way, will inevitably be the victor in any struggle with an alien power; that the United States can never lose a war and that its shores can never be attacked. Many still hold to the belief that other allies owe homage and gratitude to the United States and to all of its views at all times. These myths are comforting to our sense of security and appealing to our sense of patriotism; and thus they continue to prevail.

SIMILAR myths prevail in other nations—in France, for example, where the ancient fear of a rearmed Germany towers disproportionately over the menace of Soviet aggression. But while we concern ourselves with the erroneous judgments of others, let us not blind ourselves to our own. My daily mail indicates that American public opinion still contains dark corners of belligerent jingoism and narrow isolationism, and that many attitudes are frequently more influenced by ethnic and cultural ties with the problem areas involved, or with ancient hostilities, than by the necessities of world security.

There are those who insist we can have both high tariffs (at least on their own products, if no others) and a market for our goods abroad, those who simultaneously request reductions in Federal taxes and indebtedness and increases in expenditures for defense and civil functions; those who reject bargaining or diplomatic pressure as a method of dealing with international disputes, while at the same time insisting that Communist aggression be halted by all available means—except the use of American boys.

There are those who believe the United States can still halt aggression by the arrival of a few American gunboats and Marines. There are those who oppose assistance to or cooperation with our allies, and at the same time resent the failure of our allies to follow blindly our leadership or contribute more to our mutual defense arrangements.

HOWEVER secure the ancient Celts may have felt in their reliance upon a buried giant's head, this discouraging prevalence of myths and misinformation causes me to urge respectfully three propositions upon our twentieth century officials and citizens.

(1) *The present crisis requires greater participation of American public opinion in the foreign policy-making process.*

It was once said that Great Britain's mastery of foreign affairs first began to deteriorate when British public opinion began to intervene with its slow-footed moralistic influences, incapable of meeting the swift fluidity and harsh practicality of *real Politik*. It is also the sophisticated view that an excess of public opinion would act as a drag on the foreign policy-making process which in ten years of dizzying reversals has made enemies of former friends and friends of former enemies. But such assertions relate to an age wholly unlike that which confronts us today.

FOR today, both war and peace are unique. In the past, public interest in American international commitments have reached their peak only in time of war, when extraordinary demands are made upon our manpower and material resources. Even then, war touched only indirectly the lives of many Americans. But the next "World War," unlike any other, will sear the lives of every American, and bring for the first time massive death and destruction within our own borders.

Moreover, what is normal in peacetime is no more relevant to a discussion of public opinion than it is to an analysis of budgets and armies; for this is a peace which resembles none previously experienced. Frequent hostilities, uneasy truces, military alliances, a world-wide struggle for the minds of men and a furious armaments race characterize the war upon which we have placed the curious epithet "cold"—a struggle which will continue in our generation to maintain the same excessive wartime demands upon our lives and pocketbooks, and maintain the same heightened public interest.

Finally, American public opinion needs enlightenment on the United States' new role as leader of the free world—a role assumed not because of the militarism or even the desires of our citizens, not because of the wishes of any nation or government, but as the result of destiny and circumstance, the sheer fact of our physical and economic strength, and our position as the only real counter to the forces of communism in the world today.

THE leadership of a loose confederacy of heterogeneous nations is not without its burdens, as Great Britain learned in the past. In recent months, some have found our pace too slow, others too fast. Many Americans understandably respond to this criticism with an attitude of irritation and withdrawal. But unless we wish to break the alliance upon which our present security ultimately depends, we must rely upon public recognition of the burdensome and unpleasant responsibilities thrust upon us.

Thus we can no longer afford to exclude the man in the street from this nation's foreign policy; for it influences him, and he in turn influences its decisions. His opinions, his votes and his efforts define the limits of our policy, provide its guideposts and authorize its implementation. In Lincoln's words, he "makes statutes possible or impossible to execute." His attitude toward the United Nations, toward the imports of friendly nations, toward the immigration of other peoples, and toward members of minority groups in his own country—all of these have an impact upon foreign policy far beyond his knowledge. Without his indispensable support and loyalty, no American foreign policy in times such as these can succeed.

OUR choice, then, is not whether public opinion should influence our foreign policy, but whether its influence is to be good or bad. The hasty withdrawal and dispersal of American troops following World War II illustrates the effect which public opinion—no matter how shortsighted and ill-informed—can have upon foreign policy. On the other hand, Ernest Griffith has pointed out that "some great upsurge of popular opinion" on international issues may be "one of those waves of intuition which are not infrequently sounder guides than the supposedly more sophisticated reasonings of the 'experts'." In any event, the public can no longer be excluded; and if its influence is to be a positive contribution, we must work to dispel the myths and mysteries we have created.

(2) *Greater participation of American public opinion in the foreign policy-making process requires firm, candid and responsible leadership.*

Public enlightenment is not only the task of the Government. The schools, churches, citizens groups, newspapers, and other mass media of communication play an increasingly significant role in molding opinion on world affairs. But it is to the Federal Government—and in the last analysis to the President, with his constitutional role of foreign policy spokesman—that we look for our initial information and guidance. Contrary to popular belief, it is the President—not the Senate—who ratifies treaties (although the consent of two-thirds of the Senate is required to give effect to such ratification). If the Government speaks with many and diverse tongues, if the President's statements lack firmness and consistency, then public opinion will flounder and drift, too.

If the public is unable to determine what our policy is in Indochina—that is, the policy of the United States, not the policy of the Vice President or the Majority Leader or the Chiefs of Staff—then whatever our policy may be, it cannot succeed. Whether or not we agreed with Franklin Roosevelt's foreign policy, he did give endless thought and effort—beginning with the famous "quarantine the aggressors" speech in 1937—to explaining our policies and molding public opinion.

CONGRESS, too, has a growing responsibility. In 1925, only one Act of Congress in twenty-five had any direct relationship to international relations, and that was generally inconsequential. Today, at least one of every six or seven enacted bills are of tremendous world-wide concern. Moreover, we do not provide the leadership needed if in talking to (or for) our constituents, we ignore the international implications of legislation normally treated as domestic issues, such as the discriminatory provisions of the McCarran Immigration Act, the extension of the three-mile limit under the off-shore oil law, the offense to Mexico in a wetback labor measure, and even the failure of Congress to act on the President's Reciprocal Trade Agreements Program.

Unfortunately, those who work intimately in the foreign or military policy field and who have access to secret information generally look with condescending disdain on those who challenge their omniscience. The average layman—or Congressman—is deemed unable to comprehend the mystic intricacies and intrigues of foreign affairs. (With all due respect to President Eisenhower, this philosophy is heightened by repeated reassurances that now our President "can read a military map.") Classified status is given to all manner of documents, including those whose publication could do no more harm than the release of the Secretary of State's laundry ticket.

BASIC decisions are only vaguely explained by the use of beguiling slogans, including most recently "the new look" and "massive retaliation." Leaders of both parties, in Congress as well as in the Executive Branch, too often take partisan delight in offering to the public easy or dramatic answers to the complex problems of the world—preventive war, withdrawal from the United Nations, the "unleashing" of Chiang Kai-shek, the renunciation of secret agreements and human slavery, or a mission to Moscow, Bermuda, Potsdam, Korea or any other place. How we "lost" China or why we are in Korea are subjects of gross oversimplification. Thus is our foreign policy mythology created, chapter by chapter.

I hope this tendency can be reversed. I hope, too, that we shall realize that public confidence is heightened, not impaired, by candid admissions of our errors. Certainly it is apparent to all that the very foundation of American assistance in Indochina rested upon a miscalculation of the military program of the French Union forces and the success of the Navarre Plan. Certainly it is apparent to all that our State Department—under both Democratic and Republican leadership—failed to recognize the nature and significance of the independence movement in Indochina, and consistently misled the American people—although not the people of Indochina—as to the degree of freedom granted by the French.

WOULD not our policies in that area have been more effective, and our citizens more willing to support effective action when the military deterioration became apparent, if our policy makers had abided by the popular and traditional opinion in this country favoring complete Vietnamese independence? On this issue, the intuitive judgment of the public was wiser than the cautious logic of our diplomats. Would it not in the long run be far wiser to confess error on these points to a knowing and mature public rather than to talk glowingly of "regaining the initiative"?

True, the line between "propagandizing the voters" and informing the public is frequently a fine one to draw, particularly in an election year. There is always a temptation to exploit public opinion for partisan purposes, and to inflame it along popular lines or brandish it as a threat, thus foreclosing some future course of action regardless of how necessary such action may subsequently be. But objective and responsible leadership, so necessary in all areas today, is particularly needed—and is now lacking—in the area of public opinion and foreign policy.

(3) *If our Government is to look to public opinion for guidance on foreign policy issues before acting irrevocably upon them, improved methods of measuring such opinion must be devised.*

Once we have recognized the necessity for dispelling the folklore of foreign policy in the hydrogen age, and have taken steps to enlighten public opinion for the positive contribution it can make, we are still faced with one of the most difficult problems of representative government. The impact of the public will—whether for good or evil—should, if it is to give constructive guidance, be determined on particular issues before irrevocable steps are taken. The public may voice its displeasure at the polls or in communications of protest, but that is too frequently too late.

In 1795, the Senate, in debating the wisdom of the Jay Treaty, was acutely aware of public feeling on the issue—if in no other way, by observing the repeated hanging in effigy of Mr. John Jay. But such demonstrations today are rare indeed, when treaties and other single acts are of significance only as they relate to numerous other items. How, in the absence of mass meetings hanging us in effigy or in person, are members of Congress and the Executive Branch to gauge opinion on foreign policy?

The State Department's Division of Public Studies compiles in its daily reports the opinions expressed in speeches, polls, editorials, columns, organization resolutions, correspondence and similar sources. A member of Congress may rely upon his mail, clippings, or his own private polls. But these are only the roughest sort of measure. They are relied upon primarily for justification of preconceived positions or as an ostentatious demonstration of concern for constituent attitudes. They are only rarely interpreted as accurate barometers of public opinion and used as guideposts on pending decisions.

PRESUMABLY the search for more scientifically accurate measures of public opinion will lead us to the overly abused (but also overly heralded) public opinion polls. In recent years, the poll has enjoyed a substantial vogue in all three branches of the Government as a means of ascertaining needs, encouraging compliance, and determining public reaction. But although the science of opinion research has made gigantic strides in recent years, most of the polling techniques employed by the Government, members of Congress and even some of the more reputable polling agencies fall far short of necessary standards of validity and reliability.

Moreover, public opinion on foreign policy issues deserves a particularly careful and sensitive barometer. Neither Congressmen nor diplomats are interested simply in mass opinion, a numerical counting of heads on a given issue at a given time. We are in the position of Judge Learned Hand, who in attempting to determine judicially the moral standards of a community questioned the value of a mere aggregate of individual opinions: "A majority of the votes of those in prisons and brothels, for instance, ought scarcely to outweigh the votes of accredited churchgoers." If public opinion is to make its potential contributions to our role in world affairs, we must require of our social scientists new and better techniques for gauging that opinion.

I WOULD say, by way of conclusion, that our foreign policy makers must, however reluctantly, give up the luxury of their exclusive control over our role in world affairs. For upon our decisions now may well rest the peace and security of the world—indeed the very continued existence of mankind. And if we cannot entrust these decisions to the people, then, as Thomas Jefferson once said, "If we think them not enlightened enough to exercise their control with a wholesome discretion, the remedy is not to take it from them but to inform their discretion by education."

August 8, 1954

The Exchange of Messages

Statement by Premier Khrushchev

By The Associated Press.

MOSCOW, April 18—Premier Khrushchev's message today to President Kennedy:

Mr. President, I address this message to you at an hour of anxiety fraught with danger to world peace. An armed aggression has begun against Cuba.

It is not a secret to anyone that the armed bands which invaded that country had been trained, equipped and armed in the United States of America. The planes which bomb Cuban cities belong to the United States of America, the bombs they drop have been made available by the American Government.

Here in the Soviet Union all this arouses a natural feeling of indignation on the part of the Soviet Government and Soviet people.

Once recently we exchanged views through our representatives. We spoke about the common desire of both sides to make joint efforts to improve relations between our countries and avert the danger of war.

Your statement of a few days ago to the effect that the United States would not take part in military operations against Cuba produced the impression that the top echelons of the United States are aware of the consequences of aggression against Cuba to world peace and to the United States itself.

How are we to understand what is really being done by the United States now that the attack on Cuba has become a fact?

Action Still Possible

It is yet not too late to prevent the irreparable. The Government of the United States still can prevent the flames of war kindled by the interventionists on Cuba from spreading into a conflagration which it will be impossible to cope with.

I earnestly appeal to you, Mr. President, to call a halt to the aggression against the Republic of Cuba. The military techniques and the world political situation now are such that any so-called "small-war" can produce a chain reaction in all parts of the world.

As to the Soviet Union, there should be no misunderstanding of our position: we shall render the Cuban people and their Government all necessary assistance in beating back the armed attack on Cuba.

We are sincerely interested in a relaxation of international tension, but if others aggravate it, we shall reply in full measure. And, in general, it is hardly possible to handle matters in such a way as to settle the situation and extinguish the conflagration in one area and kindle a new conflagration in another.

I hope that the United States Government will take into account these considerations of ours, prompted as they are by the sole concern for preventing such steps which could lead the world to a military catastrophe.

The Answer by President Kennedy

Special to The New York Times.

WASHINGTON, April 18—President Kennedy's answer to Premier Khrushchev:

Mr. Chairman:

You are under a serious misapprehension in regard to events in Cuba. For months there has been evident and growing resistance to the Castro dictatorship.

More than 100,000 refugees have recently fled from Cuba into neighboring countries. Their urgent hope is naturally to assist their fellow Cubans in their struggle for freedom. Many of these refugees fought alongside Dr. Castro against the Batista dictatorship; among them are prominent leaders of his own original movement and government.

These are unmistakable signs that Cubans found intolerable the denial of democratic liberties and the subversion of the 26 of July Movement by an alien-dominated regime. It cannot be surprising that, as resistance within Cuba grows, refugees have been using whatever means are available to return and support their countrymen in the continuing struggle for freedom. Where people are denied the right of choice, recourse to such struggle is the only means of achieving their liberties.

I have previously stated and I repeat now that the United States intends no military intervention in Cuba. In the event of any military intervention by outside force we will immediately honor our obligations under the inter-American system to protect this hemisphere against external aggression.

The Spirit of Liberty

While refraining from military intervention in Cuba, the people of the United States do not conceal their admiration for Cuban patriots who wish to see a democratic system in an independent Cuba. The United States Government can take no action to stifle the spirit of liberty.

I have taken careful note of your statement that the events in Cuba might affect peace in all parts of the world. I trust that this does not mean that the Soviet Government, using the situation in Cuba as a pretext, is planning to inflame other areas of the world. I would like to think that your Government has too great a sense of responsibility to embark upon any enterprise so dangerous to general peace.

I agree with you as to the desirability of steps to improve the international atmosphere. I continue to hope that you will cooperate in opportunities now available to this end.

A prompt cease-fire and peaceful settlement of the dangerous situation in Laos, cooperation with the United Nations in the Congo and a speedy conclusion of an acceptable treaty for the banning of nuclear tests would be constructive steps in this direction.

The regime in Cuba could make a similar contribution by permitting the Cuban people freely to determine their own future by democratic processes and freely to cooperate with their Latin-American neighbors.

I believe, Mr. Chairman, that you should recognize that free peoples in all parts of the world do not accept the claim of historical inevitability for Communist revolution.

What your Government believes is its own business; what it does in the world is the world's business. The great revolution in the history of man, past, present and future, is the revolution of those determined to be free.

April 19, 1961

KENNEDY SAYS U.S. WON'T ALLOW COMMUNISM TO TAKE OVER CUBA; DOES NOT BAR UNILATERAL MOVE

SPEECH IS STRONG

President Says Policy of Nonintervention Has Its Limits

By W. H. LAWRENCE
Special to The New York Times.

WASHINGTON, April 20 — President Kennedy said today that United States restraint was "not inexhaustible" and that it did not intend to abandon Cuba to communism.

In a speech before the American Society of Newspaper Editors that was broadcast by television and radio, he said that he would not permit the traditional inter-American policy of nonintervention to conceal or excuse a policy of inaction.

If United States intervention becomes necessary in Cuba, Mr. Kennedy said, the nation will strive for complete victory, neither expecting nor accepting the same outcome that the "small band of gallant Cuban refugees must have known they were chancing" in landing on the island.

The President spoke after the rebel beachhead had been wiped out and after he had talked secretly at the White House with Dr. José Miro Cardona, president of the Cuban Revolutionary Council, and five other council members.

Secret Trip to Washington

Late today, Pierre Salinger, White House press secretary, said the main reason the Cubans had visited the White House was to ask President Kennedy to use his influence with the Organization of American States.

He requested that it try to insure that Cubans who have been captured will not be executed and that those who have been wounded will receive adequate medical care.

United Press International Telephoto

TALKS ON CUBA: President Kennedy addressing American Society of Newspaper Editors yesterday in Washington.

The President gave assurance that he would exert his influence with the O. A. S. in the matter, Mr. Salinger said.

Dr. Miro Cardona and his associates were flown secretly to Washington yesterday from Miami, where they had been directing rebel efforts. They entered the White House by a back door. The others present were Dr. Antonio Verona, Dr. Justo Carrillo, Dr. Antonio Maceo, Manuel Ray and Carlos Hevia.

Qualified Administration sources said the aim of Mr. Kennedy's speech today was to warn the Government of Premier Fidel Castro and its Communist supporters abroad that the United States would tolerate neither a large Communist arms build-up in Cuba nor summary executions of United States citizens by the Cuban regime.

Unlike earlier pronouncements, Mr. Kennedy did not rule out the possibility that the United States—alone, if need be—would undertake armed intervention if convinced that its security interests were being endangered.

"But let the record show that our restraint is not inexhaustible," he said. "Should it ever appear that the inter-American doctrine of noninterference merely conceals or excuses a policy of non-action; if the nations of this hemisphere should fail to meet their commitments against outside Communist penetration, then I want it clearly understood that this Government will not hesitate in meeting its primary obligations, which are the security of our nation."

Time Made Indefinite

Mr. Kennedy did not imply that the time for possible unilateral action was at hand. He referred instead to the future with the phrase, "should that time ever come." A highly placed official said there was no intention at present to ask a quick judgment by the Organization of American States against the Castro regime.

The President, addressing 1,000 editors and their guests in the Statler-Hilton Hotel for barely fifteen minutes, spoke from a text completed less than an hour before.

In his remarks the President acknowledged that the news from Cuba in the last twenty-four hours had "grown worse instead of better." It was understood Dr. Miro Cardona had requested the White House conference when it became clear that the rebels' small beachhead could not hold out against the Communist-equipped Cuban forces.

Informed sources said the beachhead, established Monday, had grown to perhaps 1,200 men. Of these, a considerable number were said to have escaped with supplies and equipment to the Escambray Mountains to join guerrilla forces there.

No one could say with authority how many anti - Castro Cubans had fallen in the fighting. However, it was emphasized that the force committed never approacned the figure of 5,000 originally reported by some Cuban sources.

In his speech before the editors to whom he was introduced by Turner Catledge, president of their society and managing editor of The New York Times, Mr. Kennedy said Communist tactics in Cuba were the same as in Laos and around the world. Behind the shield of Communist armies and nuclear weapons, he explained, the forces of expanding communism use subversion, infiltration and a host of other tactics to pick off vulnerable areas one by one in situations that do not permit armed intervention by anti-Communist forces.

The President's main plea was to those Latin-American nations that have not been so concerned about the growth of communism in Cuba as has the United States.

"It is clear that this nation, in concert with all the free nations of this hemisphere, must take an ever closer and more realistic look at the menace of external Communist intervention and domination in Cuba," he said.

"The American people are not complacent about Iron Curtain tanks and planes less than ninety miles from their shore, but a nation of Cuba's size is less a threat to our survival than it is a base for subverting the survival of other free nations throughout the hemisphere. It is not our interest or our security but theirs which is now today in greater peril."

The hour is late, he added, and "we and our Latin friends will have to face the fact that we cannot postpone any longer the real issue of survival." On that issue, he declared, there can be "no middle ground."

The greatest task facing the nation and the Administration is to cope with the problems of Communist expansion not alone by arms but by subversion that could endanger the United States security without the firing of a shot, the President said.

"We intend to profit from this lesson," he declared. "We intend to re-examine and reorient our forces of all kinds, our tactics, and our institutions here in this community. We intend to intensify our efforts for a struggle in many ways more difficult than war, where disappointment often will accompany us."

"Should that time ever come," he said, "we do not intend to be lectured on 'intervention' by those whose character was stamped for all time on the bloody streets of Budapest."

That shot at the Kremlin brought a burst of applause.

On Capitol Hill the dominant reaction continued to be bipartisan support of the firm Kennedy policy. But there also were criticisms in the light of the failure of the rebel effort.

One critic was Senator Barry Goldwater of Arizona, leader of Right-wing Republicans, who said every American should be filled with "apprehension and shame" because of the abortive attempt. He blamed United States failures on "inepititude" in the State Department in recent years.

Dr. Miro Cardona and his associates talked with several Administration leaders during their brief visit. The White House would not say where they had gone from here nor how they traveled.

The Cuban situation was discussed this morning at a Cabinet meeting in the White House. Te session had been scheduled for two weeks and officials said it dealt mainly with the budget.

April 21, 1961

Washington

A Sadder and Wiser Young President

By JAMES RESTON

WASHINGTON, April 20—President Kennedy has taken the defeat in Cuba with the utmost seriousness. Behind his brave words to the editors today is a mood of self-examination and self-criticism.

In the first place, he is not looking for scapegoats. He is taking full personal responsibility for the Government's part in the adventure, and this responsibility, of course, is great.

He took the decision to continue the training of the Cuban refugees with arms provided by the Government, and for releasing the ships and gasoline to launch the attack at this time.

He did so against the advice of Secretary of State Rusk and Under Secretary of State Chester Bowles. He did so on the basis of an intelligence estimate by the Central Intelligence Agency which was convinced that Cuba was ripe for revolt.

Other intelligence estimates by the allies challenged the C. I. A.'s analysis, but Kennedy went along with the C. I. A. without arguing out the differences in the Cabinet or the National Security Council.

'The Useful Lessons'

Publicly, the President said nothing today about errors committed here. He talked about the "useful lessons" of this "sobering episode," but he is drawing more lessons than he mentioned.

One of these is that the whole system of intelligence analysis within the Government must be speedily reviewed. The Central Intelligence Agency is a vast organization with some 10,000 employes in Washington and several thousand mcre overseas or outside the Federal capital.

The question naturally arises how it could be that this apparatus, with all its access to Cuba and to friendly nations within the hemisphere, could be so sure that the Cubans would revolt, and be so wrong on the critical point of judgment.

Kennedy is not blaming Allen Dulles, the Director of the C. I. A., or Dulles' deputy, Richard M. Bissell Jr., who made the principal presentation of the intelligence estimate to Kennedy. But he does want to know where they went wrong, and they are now very much on the spot.

Reaching Decisions

The Kennedy system of reaching decisions of this nature is also very much under review. When he came into office he questioned the usefulness of the National Security Council, which is a Cabinet committee, with its own staff, charged with making recommendations to the President on foreign and defense policy questions.

His view was that these Cabinet meetings were a waste of time, so that he has virtually dispensed with them and substituted instead a series of bilateral and *ad hoc* meetings with one or two Cabinet members or members of the White House staff.

This may or may not be an improvement on the old system, but in any event, there is a feeling in some quarters here that the Cuban decision was not "staffed through" as well as it should have been before the decision was made to let it proceed. Whether this is a valid point is a matter of opinion, but the fact is that immediately after the Cuban failure the President did call a Cabinet meeting for this week and summoned the National Security Council to the White House next Saturday.

The Old Assumptions

Thus, he is ending his third month in office in anything but a dogmatic mood. Events have shaken many of the assumptions he brought into the White House both about the magnitude and complexity of his problems and the best procedures for meeting them.

His confidence in the direction of the C. I. A. has clearly been shaken, and will almost certainly be changed. His confidence in the effectiveness of the inter-American system to deal with Communist subversion in the hemisphere has also been shaken, and the Allies will be hearing more from him on this in the coming weeks.

Yet there is nothing mournful or impetuous in his reaction. He acted quickly and clearly to answer Nikita Khrushchev's note this week. He summoned the experts to the White House at 11 o'clock last night to prepare a wholly new speech on the Cuban issue for today, and was still working on it himself until a few minutes before he went on the air. In short, he is not denying his failures, but he's trying to learn from them.

April 21, 1961

U.S. AND SOVIET REACH ACCORD ON CUBA; KENNEDY ACCEPTS KHRUSHCHEV PLEDGE TO REMOVE MISSILES UNDER U.N. WATCH

CAPITAL HOPEFUL

Plans to End Blockade as Soon as Moscow Lives Up to Vow

By E. W. KENWORTHY
Special to The New York Times

WASHINGTON, Oct. 28—President Kennedy and Premier Khrushchev reached apparent agreement today on a formula to end the crisis over Cuba and to begin talks on easing tensions in other areas.

Premier Khrushchev pledged the Soviet Union to stop work on its missile sites in Cuba, to dismantle the weapons and to crate them and take them home. All this would be done under verification of United Nations representatives.

President Kennedy, for his part, pledged the lifting of the Cuban arms blockade when the United Nations had taken the "necessary measures," and that the United States would not invade Cuba.

U. S. Conditions Met

Essentially this formula meets the conditions that President Kennedy set for the beginning of talks. If it is carried out, it would achieve the objective of the President in establishing the blockade last week: the removal of the Soviet missile bases in Cuba.

While officials were gratified at the agreement reached on United States terms, there was no sense either of triumph or jubilation. The agreement, they realized, was only the beginning. The terms of it were not nailed down and Soviet negotiators were expected to arrive at the United Nations with a "bag full of fine print."

Although Mr. Khrushchev mentioned verification of the dismantling by United Nations observers in today's note, sources here do not consider it unlikely that the Russians may suggest that the observers be under the procedures of the Security Council.

This would make their findings subject to a veto by the Soviet Union as one of the 11 members of the Council.

No Big Gains Envisioned

United States officials did not expect a Cuban settlement, if it materialized, to lead to any great breakthroughs on such problems as inspection for a nuclear test ban and disarmament.

On the other hand, it was thought possible that a Cuban settlement might set a precedent for limited reciprocal concessions in some areas.

The break in the crisis came dramatically early this morning after a night of steadily mounting fears that events were running ahead of diplomatic efforts to control them.

The break came with the arrival of a letter from Premier Khrushchev in which the Soviet eader again changed his course.

Friday night Mr. Khrushchev iad sent a lengthy private letter o the President. Deep in it was he suggestion that the Soviet Jnion would remove its missiles rom Cuba under supervision ind not replace them if the Jnited States would lift the lockade and give assurances hat United States and other Western Hemisphere nations ould not invade Cuba.

The President found this proosal generally acceptable and esterday morning his aides ere preparing a private reply. hen the Moscow radio broadast the text of another letter iat was on its way.

The second letter proposed iat the Soviet Union remove its nissiles from Cuba in return for he dismantling of United tates missiles in Turkey. This as advanced as an equitable xchange.

Fearing that it would be iewed in this light by many eutral nations, the White iouse immediately postponed a eply to the first letter and issued a statement on the second.

The White House said that he "first imperative" was the emoval of the threat of Soviet nissiles. The United States ould not consider "any proosals" until work was stopped n the Cuban bases, the weapons were "rendered inoperable," nd further shipments of them ere halted.

Then White House aides urned back to drafting a reply the first letter. They hoped persuade Mr. Khrushchev to tand by his first offer.

The President accepted the rst Khrushchev proposal as he basis for beginning talks. ut he planted in it two warnngs which, the White House oped, would not be lost upon Ir. Khrushchev.

First, he said the arrangement for putting into effect the Khrushchev plan could be completed in a "a couple of days"—a warning that the United States could take action to halt the work on the missile bases if Mr. Khrushchev did not order it stopped.

Second, the President said that if the work continued or if Mr. Khrushchev linked Cuba with broader questions of European security, the Cuban crisis would be intensified.

Just before 9 o'clock this morning, the Moscow radio said there would be an important announcement on the hour. It turned out to be a reply to Mr. Kennedy's letter of the night before.

Mr. Khrushchev said that in order to "complete with greater speed the liquidation of the conflict dangerous to the cause of peace," the Soviet Government had ordered work stopped on the bases in Cuba, and the dismantling, crating and return of the missiles.

Mr. Khrushchev said he trusted that, in return, "no attack will be made on Cuba—that no invasion will take place—not only by the United States, but also by other countries of the Western Hemisphere."

Kuznetzov to Negotiate

Mr. Khrushchev said that he was sending Vassily V. Kuznetzov, a First Deputy Foreign Minister to the United Nations to conduct negotiations for the Soviet Union. He arrived in New York tonight.

Without waiting for the formal delivery of the letter, the

President issued a statement at noon, saying he welcomed Chairman Khrushchev's statesmanlike decision" an an "important and constructive contribution to peace."

Shortly before the statement was issued, the President flew by helicopter to Glen Ora, his country home in Middleburg, Va., to have lunch and he spent most of the afternoon with his wife and children.

All the communications this week between the two leaders — and there have been several more than have been made public — have been sent by the usual diplomatic route. First, they have been delivered to the Embassies, there translated, and send to the State Department or the Soviet Foreign office for delivery to Mr. Kennedy or Mr. Khrushchev.

Process Too Slow

This is a time-consuming process, and late this afternoon, the last section of Mr. Khrushchev's letter had not yet arrived at the White House when it was decided to make the President's reply public and speed it on its way.

The President said that he welcomed Mr. Khrushchev's message because "developments were approaching a point where events could have become unmanageable."

Mr. Kennedy said:

"I think that you and I, with our heavy responsibilities for the maintenance of peace, were aware that developments were approaching a point where events could have become unmanageable. So I welcome this message and consider it an important contribution to peace."

He also stated that he regarded his letter of the night before and the Premier's reply as "firm undertakings" which both governments should carry out "promptly."

The President hoped that the "necessary measures" could be taken "at once" through the United Nations so that the quarantine could be removed on shipping.

All these matters, the President said, would be reported to members oft he Organization of American States, who "share a deep interest in a genuine peace in the Caribbean area."

And the President echoed Mr. Khrushchev's hope that the two nations could now turn their attention to disarmament "as it relates to the whole world and also to critical areas."

The President by tonight had not named the negotiator for the United States, but it was reported by authoritative sources that Adlai E. Stevenson, the head of the United States delegation at the United Nations, would get the assignment. The talks are expected to begin soon, probably tomorrow.

A spokesman at the State Department said in reply to questions:

"The quarantine remains in efefct but we don't anticipate any problems of interception since there are no ships moving into the quarantine area that appear to be carrying cargoes on the contraband list."

Fears About Castro

There was also some concern that Premier Fidel Castro, out of chagrin, might cause incidents over the United States surveillance flights.

Officials here believed that Dr. Castro was making a major effort to bring in extraneous issues, such as the evacuation of the United States base at Guantanamo Bay, to salvage his prestige.

However, the United States was not prepared to deal over the base, and the feeling here was that no other matters except the President's guarantee not to invade could be discussed until the dismantling of the missiles had been verified.

Officials emphasized today, as they reflected on the events of the week, that at all times the White House was trying to keep things on the track. At no time, they insisted, was any ultimatum delivered to Mr. Khrushchev, although he was made to understand that the missiles would be destroyed unless they were removed in a short time.

October 29, 1962

KENNEDY ASSERTS NATION MUST LEAD IN PROBING SPACE

Declares U.S. Cannot Afford to Lag if It Wants to Be in Forefront of Nations

40,000 CHEER IN TEXAS

President Ends 2-Day Tour of Bases—Puts Stress on Peaceful Projects

By E. W. KENWORTHY
Special to The New York Times.

ST. LOUIS, Sept. 12—President Kennedy said today that "no nation which expects to be the leader of other nations" can afford to lag in the exploration of space.

In a speech under a broiling sun this morning at Rice University Stadium in Houston, Tex., the President declared:

"Those who came before us made certain that this country rode the first waves of the industrial revolution, the first waves of modern invention, and the first wave of nuclear power. And this generation does not intend to founder in the backwash of the coming age of space."

He paused and then departed from his prepared text: "We mean to be a part of it—we mean to lead it."

The throng of 40,000, mostly students, cheered loudly.

Visits Houston Center

This was the second day of the President's two-day tour of four space installations. Yesterday he visited the George C. Marshall Space Flight Center in Huntsville, Ala., and the Launch Operations Center at Cape Canaveral, Fla.

After the address this morning, the President rode to the temporary site of the new manned spacecraft center in Houston.

Later this afternoon he visited the McDonnell Aircraft Corporation plant in St. Louis, which is at Lambert Municipal Airport.

The McDonnell plant manufactures the Phantom II fighter-bomber used by both the Navy and Air Force. It has also made the capsules for the Mercury-Atlas man-in-space flights, and now has the contract to make the two-man capsule for Project Gemini, a forerunner of the flight to the moon.

The plant employs 21,500 workers. About 5,000 men of the first shift were gathered before the plant to welcome the President.

Introduction by Chairman

James S. McDonnell, a small peppery, "let's-get-cracking" sort of man, who is chairman of the board, began his introduction by saying:

"This is Mac calling on the team. We have with us the President of the United States."

Yesterday, in the assembly plant for the Saturn C-1 at Huntsville, President Kennedy stood by, obviously somewhat nettled, as Dr. Jeome B. Wiesner, his principal science adviser, engaged in an argument with Dr. Wernher von Braun, director of the Marshall Space Flight Center, over the best way to reach the moon.

Dr. Wiesner, according to those who overheard the discussion, disagreed with the method favored by the National Aeronautics and Space Administration and Dr. von Braun. Under this plan, a lunar "bug" with two men in it would be detached from the parent capsule while in orbit around the moon, and would descend to the lunar surface.

Rendezvous Planned

One man would remain in the parent capsule. Later, the bug would take off from the moon and rendezvous with the circling parent capsule. The bug would be abandoned before the capsule returned to earth.

Dr. Wiesner is understood to favor a method that was earlier agreed on and then discarded. Under this method, a lunar rocket would be formed by a rendezvous of parts orbiting the earth. It would blast off from that parking orbit and land on the moon. Later it would take off and return to earth again.

The President's speech this morning was devoted largely to a justification of the billions of dollars already spent and the further billions to be expended before the United States puts a man on the moon.

"But why, some say, the moon?" the President asked rhetorically. "Why choose this as our goal? And they may well ask, Why climb the highest mountain? Why thirty-five years ago fly the Atlantic?"

Again the President interpolated in his text: "Why does Rice play Texas?" The students roared.

Mr. Kennedy laid much emphasis on the intention of the United States to concentrate on peaceful, rather than military.

uses of space, if international conditions permit.

"We have vowed that we shall not see space filled with weapons of mass destruction, but with instruments of knowledge and understanding," the President said.

He declared, however, that this vow could be fulfilled only if the United States was first.

Politics of Trip

The White House has billed the President's tour as a "business trip" preliminary to the drafting of the budget for the fiscal year 1964, and White House officials have insisted that not the faintest aura of politics hangs over it.

However, if it is not so political as the President's recent visit to dam sites in the West, it at least has the political advantages that derive from large Federal expenditures in a particular state or district.

Thus, the President yesterday in Huntsville stressed what the space program there would do for the Southeast. And last night, on arriving in Houston, he stressed what the burgeoning manned spacecraft center would do for the Southwest.

Flanked this morning by Vice President Johnson and Representative Albert Thomas, Democrat, who represents a Houston district, the President reminded his audience that the manned spacecraft center "will become the heart of a large scientific and engineering community."

"During the next five years," the President said, "the National Aeronautics and Space Administration expects to double the number of scientists and engineers in this area; to increase its outlays for salaries and wages in the Houston area to $60,000,000 a year; to invest some $200,000,000 in plant and laboratory facilities and to direct or contract for new space efforts over $1,000,000,000 from this center in the city."

Vice President Johnson was quoted as saying to local reporters, soon after his arrival last night:

"I'm going to see that Houston gets its fair share of the space budget."

Commenting on the President's large and enthusiastic reception here last night as dusk was falling, Representative Thomas said:

"People like him, and he likes people, but he was surprised at his welcome here."

The Houston papers were prepared for the welcome, however. The Houston Chronicle carried a double, eight-column banner headline: "President Predicts Space Center to Boom Industrial Southwest."

September 13, 1962

Kennedy Denies Secrecy On Vietnam Is Excessive

Calls Situation Sensitive

By MAX FRANKEL

Special to The New York Times.

WASHINGTON, Feb. 14 — Responding to criticism, President Kennedy said today he was being as frank as possible about United States involvement in the war in Vietnam. He asked that such sensitive matters be left to "responsible leaders" of both parties.

The President countered charges of excessive secrecy with a statement that no American combat troops "in the generally understood sense of the word" had been sent into Vietnam. Yet he conceded, without giving statistics, that military support had been increased to match increased Communist activity.

That support, Mr. Kennedy said at his news conference, is consistent with a ten-year policy of trying to keep South Vietnam out of Communist hands. He disagreed with complaints that Congress had not been properly briefed on the situation and he expressed hope that he could maintain the present "very strong bipartisan consensus."

Uses Notes in Replying

The President came prepared with notes to answer criticism in the press and from the Republican National Committee that he was withholding information about the growing involvement of American troops in the developing warfare in South Vietnam.

Mr. Kennedy did not comment on the progress of that war—which the Administration expects to continue for years—but he displayed a new uneasiness about the situation in neighboring Laos.

The cease-fire between royal Laotian and Leftist rebel forces was "becoming increasingly frayed," the President said. He noted that renewed fighting at Nam Tha was close to the border of Communist China—it is about fifteen miles away—and by implication expressed concern about Chinese intervention.

If the cease-fire breaks down, the President added, "we would be faced with the most serious decision."

Soviet Held to Promise

It was to avoid the painful choice between surrender of Laos to the Communists and intervention by United States troops that Mr. Kennedy has tried to keep the Soviet leaders to their promise of turning Laos into a neutral and independent buffer state.

Thus far the President feels the Russians have kept their word, but he has been unable to persuade the royalist Right-wing forces in Laos to surrender power to the nominated neutralist leader, Prince Souvanna Phouma.

Progress in the negotiations among the three rival Laotian princes has been very slow over the last month, Mr. Kennedy said, noting that the dangers increased with every passing day.

Editorial questioning of the President's handling of both Laos and Vietnam has been seized upon recently by a number of Republicans and developed into major criticism.

The Republican National Committee's bulletin, Battle Line, summarized some of the charges yesterday. It said the Administration was "forcing the legitimate Government of Laos into a perilous coalition with the Reds" and promoting "the pretense that the United States is merely acting as military adviser to South Vietnam."

The people should not have to wait until the casualty lists arrive to learn of the country's commitments, Battle Line asserted. It asked whether the country was "moving toward another Korea which might embroil the entire Far East."

When asked to comment, the President was ready with a list of previous commitments to Vietnam by the Administrations of Presidents Truman and Eisenhower. As the war increased over the last two years, the United States increased its support in South Vietnam for the Government of President Ngo Dinh Diem, especially so in recent months, Mr. Kennedy said.

Repeating earlier statements on the extent of the United States build-up, the President said:

"We are supplying logistic assistance, transportation assistance, training, and we have a number of Americans who are taking part in that effort."

Recent reports from Saigon have said that as many as 4,000 United States troops were now serving with the South Vietnam forces, but the President did not go beyond "some."

No Americans are combat troops, Mr. Kennedy explained, "although the training missions that we have there have been instructed that if they are fired upon they are, of course, to fire back, to protect themselves."

Casualty List Supplied

A list of American casualties in South Vietnam in recent months, supplied later by the Pentagon, showed no fatalities in any such exchange of fire. The Defense Department listed thirteen deaths and one missing.

Two members of the Air Force were killed in the crash of a C-123 plane on a practice run Feb. 2. Six airmen and two members of the Army were killed in the crash of a C-47 last Sunday. An Army driver was killed when his truck struck a mine and two soldiers were killed by a grenade hurled into their barracks.

The President said he had fully briefed Congressional leaders on the Vietnam situation at a White House review of foreign affairs in early January. Further information had been given Congressional committees by Secretary of State Dean Rusk and Robert S. McNamara, Secretary of Defense.

February 15, 1962

KENNEDY ASKS BREAK IN COLD WAR

'PEACE STRATEGY'

President Asserts East and West Must Alter Their Basic Attitude

By TAD SZULC
Special to The New York Times

WASHINGTON, June 10 — President Kennedy proposed a "strategy of peace" today to lead the United States and the Soviet Union out of the "vicious and dangerous cycle" of the cold war.

As a first step, the President announced that high-ranking representatives of the United States, Britain and the Soviet Union would meet in Moscow soon in a renewed effort to agree on a treaty banning nuclear weapons tests.

He announced also that the United States, "to make clear our good faith and solemn conviction on the matter," would refrain from tests in the atmosphere so long as others did likewise.

Study of Attitudes Urged

The President's speech at the commencement exercises at American University here was dedicated to the theme that the time had come for a break in the cold war and that both the United States and the Soviet Union should re-examine their basic attitude toward each other.

The Moscow conference is expected to open in the middle of July. Britain will be represented by Viscount Hailsham, the Minister of Science, and the United States' chief delegate may be John J. McCloy, former adviser on disarmament to Mr. Kennedy. The Soviet Union has not indicated who might be its representative.

The Western strategy for the talks is expected to be set when President Kennedy visits Prime Minister Macmillan in London on June 30.

Mr. Kennedy announced the decisions on nuclear testing after telling his audience of about 10,000 that a test ban was a major subject of East-West negotiations where "the end is in sight" but "where a fresh start is badly needed."

Hope Tempered With Caution

"Chairman Khrushchev, Prime Minister Macmillan and I have agreed that high-level discussions will shortly begin in Moscow, looking toward early agreement on a comprehensive test-ban treaty," he said. "Our hopes must be tempered with the caution of history — but with our hopes go the hopes of all mankind."

Promising that the United States "will not be the first to resume" testing in the atmosphere, the President emphasized that "such a declaration is no substitute for a formal binding treaty — but I hope it will help us achieve one."

"Nor would such a treaty be a substitute for disarmament," he added, "but I hope it will help us achieve it."

Applause broke out from the crowd at the outdoor exercises when the President announced the Moscow meeting and when he pledged the United States to refrain from atmospheric testing.

Applauded on Civil Rights

The President was also applauded when he said that "this generation of Americans" has had more than enough of war and hate and when he defended the civil rights of all Americans. He received a standing ovation at the end of his 28-minute address.

In the Senate, which must approve any test-ban treaty, the reaction to the President's speech was mixed.

The Democratic Senators expressed approval of his policy to press for a test ban agreement, but some Republicans voiced fears that it meant simply more concessions to the Soviet Union. However, Mr. Kennedy won the support of a number of Republicans who joined with the majority last month in supporting a test-ban resolution.

In dealing with the broader aspects of the cold war, the President found that the United States and the Soviet Union had certain things in common. He said the two countries would be primary targets if total war should break out.

Both, he said "have a mutually deep interest in a just and genuine peace and in halting the arms race."

The White House had in advance described the speech as one of the most important statements by President Kennedy on foreign affairs.

While it repeated the exhortations for peace contained in his inaugural address and in his speech at the United Nations in September, 1961, it carried a new tone of conciliation toward the Soviet Union and a call to both nations to take another look at each other.

Mr. Kennedy expressed regret that the Soviet Union makes the "wholly baseless and incredible claims" that the United States is preparing for a war, but he said that this was "a warning to the American people not to fall into the same trap" of seeing only a "distorted and desperate view of the other side."

The President stressed that a "mutual abhorrence of war" was the strongest common trait of the United States and the Soviet Union.

"Almost unique among the major world powers, we have never been at war with each other," Mr. Kennedy said.

Describing peace as "a way of solving problems," the President asserted that the people of the United States could help the Soviet leaders to adopt "more enlightened attitudes" by "re-examining our own attitude."

"We must conduct our affairs in such a way that it becomes in the Communists' interest to agree on a genuine peace," he said.

"The United States, as the world knows, will never start a war," the President said. "We do not want a war. We do not now expect a war. This generation of Americans has already had enough—more than enough—of war and hate and oppression."

"We shall do our part to build a world of peace where the weak are safe and the strong are just." he said. "We are not helpless before that task or hopeless of its success. Confident and unafraid, we labor on — not towards a strategy of annihilation but towards a strategy of peace."

The phrase, "strategy of peace," was used by the President as the title of his book published in 1960.

The speech represented an important foreign policy pronouncement prior to the President's trip to Western Europe and to the Soviet-Chinese ideological confrontation in Moscow, opening July 5.

The President flew all night from Hawaii in order to deliver the speech and to receive an honorary degree from American University.

His Air Force jet transport landed at Andrews Air Force Base near Washington at 8:51 A.M. after a nine-hour non-stop flight from Honolulu. He went to the White House by helicopter and, after a brief rest, drove to the university campus.

President Kennedy received the university's highest honorary degree, the doctor of civil laws. The same degree was granted to Bishop Fred P. Corson of Philadelphia, president of the World Methodist Council, and to Bishop Angus Dun, retired Bishop of the Protestant Episcopal diocese of Washington.

Honorary degrees of doctor of laws were conferred upon: Dr. Lowell Ensor, president of Western Maryland College, Westminister, Md.; Judge Luther A. Smith, sovereign grand commander, Scottish Rite, southern jurisdiction, and Byron R. White, Associate Justice of the Supreme Court.

June 11, 1963

Kennedy Calls War Effort Key to Policy on Vietnam

Warns the Diem Regime U.S. Will Oppose All Divisive Actions

By TAD SZULC
Special to The New York Times

WASHINGTON, Sept. 12 President Kennedy placed the Saigon Government on notice today that the United States was not in Vietnam "to see a war lost."

In a series of carefully phrased answers at his news conference, the President made it clear that the United States would continue to press the South Vietnamese regime to adopt internal policies likely to bring victory over the Communist guerrillas.

But the President said that no "useful purpose" would be served by discussing publicly now the steps the Administration planned to take in the complex Vietnamese crisis.

He refused to be drawn into a discussion of whether Ngo Dinh Nhu, the brother of President Ngo Dinh Diem, should be removed from a position of power as one of the changes to restore popular backing for the regime.

The Administration considers Ngo Dinh Nhu, who is the head of the secret police, to be the architect of Saigon's repressions of Buddhists.

Henry Cabot Lodge, the United States Ambassador in Saigon, was said to have told President Ngo Dinh Diem Monday that Washington regarded Ngo Dinh Nhu's removal as necessary to the solution of the situation. President Kennedy said, however, that "that sort of a matter really should be discussed by Ambassador Lodge and others."

Mr. Kennedy, who indicated earlier this month that Saigon's repressive acts against Buddhists had seriously damaged unity in the anti-Communist struggle, said "we are for" those things and policies that help to win the war in Vietnam and "we oppose" what interferes with the war. [Question 3.]

"We want the war to be won, the Communists to be contained and the Americans to go home," he said. "That is our policy. I am sure it's the policy of the people of Vietnam. But we are not there to see a war lost, and we will follow the policy which I've indicated today in advancing those causes and issues which help win the war."

The President spoke of "the people of Vietnam" and did not mention President Ngo Dinh Diem in his replies to the questions on Vietnam.

Mr. Kennedy seemed to indicate indirectly that he agreed that aid should be cut if the Saigon regime did not, in the long run, change its attitudes.

Notes Church Resolution

He implied this in commenting on the resolution placed before the Senate today by Senator Frank Church, Democrat of Idaho, and 21 other Senators, uring that further American aid to South Vietnam be "terminated" and American personnel "withdrawn" if "cruel repressions" are not stopped

Speaking of the Church resolution, Mr. Kennedy said, "I've indicated my feeling that we should stay there and continue to assist South Vietnam. But I also indicated the feeling that the assistance we give should be used in the most effective way possible. I think that seems to be Senator Church's view."

Senator Church's statement on the Senate floor in introducing the resolution was one of the sharpest attacks made here on the Saigon regime.

Senator Church said that as United States efforts to help Vietnam had increased, "the situation has worsened."

"The Diem regime in South Vietnam has adopted policies of cruel repression," he said. "We have been dismayed by its persecution of the Buddhists . . . by the desecration of their temples, and by the brutality of attacks upon them. Too horrified to look, we have turned our eyes away from the sacrificial protests of Buddhists monks burning themselves alive in the streets of Saigon. Such grisly scenes have not been witnessed since the Christian martyrs marched hand in hand into the Roman arenas.

He Sees Undermining

"We have been denounced by the very members of the ruling family we have helped to keep in power. To persist in the support of such a regime can only serve to identify the United States with the cause of religious persecution, undermining our moral position throughout the world."

There are no plans to seek an immediate vote on the Church resolution because as the Administration prefers to keep it as a lever in its negotiations with Saigon.

Mr. Lodge was reported to have warned President Ngo Dinh Diem Monday that Congressional pressures at home might in the end force the Administration to end all aid.

It was in this conversation that Mr. Lodge was said to have told the Vietnamese President that the United States wished to see Ngo Dinh Nhu depart from the political scene in Saigon. The State Department has issued a formal denial that Mr. Lodge said such a thing.

Reports from Saigon today showed that although Ngo Dinh Diem seemed to have been impressed with the argument that Congress might force a cut in aid, neither he nor his brother was prepared to give in.

Although the Administration was still seeking to manage the increasingly complicated situation with patient diplomacy, many officials were beginning to think that after three weeks of stalemate, a showdown may not be too far away.

Some officials even thought that the Saigon regime and Ngo Dinh Nhu in particular, might be hoping for such a showdown now.

This, officials said, was the significance of the President's hints today in the wake of a Senate resolution that the Administration was known to have encouraged.

Simultaneously, it was reported, officials are engaged in a study of when and how selective cuts in aid should be made.

Message and Draft Text in Congress

Special to The New York Times

WASHINGTON, Aug. 5—Following are the texts of President Johnson's special message to Congress today on Vietnam, and of a proposed joint Congressional resolution.

President's Message

Last night I announced to the American people that the North Vietnamese regime had conducted further deliberate attacks against U.S. naval vessels operating in international waters, and that I had therefore directed air action against gunboats and supporting facilities used in these hostile operations.

This air action has now been carried out with substantial damage to the boats and facilities. Two U.S. aircraft were lost in the action.

After consultation with the leaders of both parties in the Congress, I further announced a decision to ask the Congress for a resolution expressing the unity and determination of the United States in supporting freedom and in protecting peace in Southeast Asia.

These latest actions of the North Vietnamese regime have given a new and grave turn to the already serious situation in Southeast Asia. Our commitments in that area are well known to the Congress. They were first made in 1954 by President Eisenhower. They were further defined in the Southeast Asia collective defense treaty approved by the Senate in February, 1955.

Pledged to Meet Aggression

This treaty with its accompanying protocol obligates the United States and other members to act in accordance with their Constitutional processes to meet Communist aggression against any of the parties or protocol states.

Our policy in Southeast Asia has been consistent and unchanged since 1954. I summarized it on June 2 in four simple propositions:

1. America keeps her word. Here as elsewhere, we must and shall honor our commitments.

2. The issue is the future of Southeast Asia as a whole. A threat to any nation in that region is a threat to all, and a threat to us.

3. Our purpose is peace. We have no military, political or territorial ambitions in the area.

4. This is not just a jungle war, but a struggle for freedom on every front of human activity. Our military and economic assistance to South Vietnam and Laos in particular has the purpose of helping these countries to repel aggression and strengthen their independence.

The threat to the free nations of Southeast Asia has long been clear. The North Vietnamese regime has constantly sought to take over South Vietnam and Laos. This Communist regime has violated the Geneva accords for Vietnam.

It has systematically conducted a campaign of subversion, which includes the direction, training, and supply of personnel and arms for the conduct of guerrilla warfare in South Vietnamese territory.

In Laos, the North Vietnamese regime has maintained military forces, used Laotian territory for infiltration into South Vietnam, and most recently carried out combat operations—all in direct violation of the Geneva agreements of 1962.

In recent months, the actions of the North Vietnamese regime have become steadily more threatening. In May, following new acts of Communist aggression in Laos, the United States undertook reconnaissance flights over Laotian territory, at the request of the Government of Laos. These flights had the essential mission of determining the situation in territory where Communist forces were preventing inspection by the International Control Commission.

When the Communists attacked these aircraft, I responded by furnishing escort fighters with instructions to fire when fired upon. Thus, these latest North Vietnamese attacks on our naval vessels are not the first direct attack on armed forces of the United States.

As President of the United States I have concluded that I should now ask the Congress, on its part, to join in affirming the national determination that all such attacks will be met, and that the U.S. will continue in its basic policy of assisting the free nations of the area to defend their freedom.

As I have repeatedly made clear, the United States intends no rashness, and seeks no wider war. We must make it clear to all that the United States is united in its determination to bring about the end of Communist subversion and aggression in the area.

We seek the full and effective restoration of the international agreements signed in Geneva in 1954, with respect to South Vietnam, and again at Geneva in 1962, with respect to Laos.

I recommend a resolution expressing the support of the Congress for all necessary action to protect our armed forces and to assist nations covered by the SEATO treaty At the same time, I assure the Congress that we shall continue readily to explore any avenues of political solution that will effectively guarantee the removal of Communist subversion and the preservation of the independence of the nations of the area.

The resolution could well be based upon similar resolutions enacted by the Congress in the past — to meet the threat to Formosa in 1955, to meet the threat to the Middle East in 1957, and to meet the threat to Cuba in 1962.

It could state in the simplest terms the resolve and support of the Congress for action to deal appropriately with attacks against our armed forces and to defend freedom and preserve peace in Southeast Asia in accordance with the obligations of the United States under the Southeast Asia Treaty.

I urge the Congress to enact such a resolution promptly and thus to give convincing evidence to the aggressive Communist nations, and to the world as a whole, that our policy in Southeast Asia will be carried forward and that the peace and security of the area will be preserved.

The events of this week would in any event have made the passage of a Congressional resolution essential. But there is an additional reason for doing so at a time when we are entering on three months of political campaigning. Hostile nations must understand that in such a period the United States will continue to protect its national interests, and that in these matters there is no division among us.

Proposed Resolution

Resolved by the Senate and House of Representatives of the United States of America in Congress assembled,

Whereas naval units of the Communist regime in Vietnam, in violation of the principles of the Charter of the United Nations and of international law, have deliberately and repeatedly attacked United States naval vessels lawfully present in international waters, and have thereby created a serious threat to international peace;

Whereas these attacks are part of a deliberate and systematic campaign of aggression that the Communist regime in North Vietnam has been waging against its neighbors and the nations joined with them in the collective defense of their freedom;

Whereas the United States is assisting the peoples of Southeast Asia to protect their freedom and has no territorial, military or political ambitions in that area, but desires only that these peoples should be left in peace to work out their own destinies in their own way;

Now therefore, be it resolved, by the Senate and House of Representatives of the United States of America in Congress assembled:

Section 1—The Congress approves and supports the determination of the President, as Commander in Chief, to take all necesary measures to repel any armed attack against the forces of the United States and to prevent further aggression.

Section 2 — The United States regards as vital to its national interest and to world peace the maintenance of international peace and security in Southeast Asia. Consonant with the Constitution and the Charter of the United Nations and in accordance with its obligations under the Southeast Asia Collective Defense Treaty, the United States is, therefore, prepared, as the President determines, to take all necessary steps, including the use of armed force, to assist any member or protocol state of the Southeast Asia Collective Defense Treaty requesting assistance in defense of its freedom.

Section 3—This resolution shall expire when the President shall determine that the peace and security of the area is reasonably assured by international conditions created by action of the United Nations or otherwise, except that it may be terminated earlier by concurrent resolution of the Congress.

August 6, 1964

CONGRESS BACKS PRESIDENT ON SOUTHEAST ASIA MOVES

RESOLUTION WINS

Senate Vote Is 88 to 2 After House Adopts Measure, 416-0

By E. W. KENWORTHY
Special to The New York Times

WASHINGTON, Aug. 7—The House of Representatives and the Senate approved today the resolution requested by President Johnson to strengthen his hand in dealing with Communist aggression in Southeast Asia.

After a 40-minute debate, the House passed the resolution, 416 to 0. Shortly afterward the Senate approved it, 88 to 2. Senate debate, which began yesterday afternoon, lasted nine hours.

The resolution gives prior Congressional approval of "all necessary measures" that the President may take "to repel any armed attack" against United States forces and "to prevent further aggression."

The resolution, the text of which was printed in The New York Times Thursday, also gives advance sanction for "all necessary steps" taken by the President to help any nation covered by the Southeast Asia collective defense treaty that requests assistance "in defense of its freedom."

Johnson Hails Action

President Johnson said the Congressional action was "a demonstration to all the world of the unity of all Americans."

"The votes prove our determination to defend our forces, to prevent aggression and to work firmly and steadily for peace and security in the area," he said.

"I am sure the American people join me in expressing the deepest appreciation to the leaders and members of both parties in both houses of Congress for their patriotic, resolute and rapid action."

The debates in both houses, but particularly in the Senate, made clear, however, that the near-unanimous vote did not reflect a unanimity of opinion on the necessity or advisability of the resolution.

Except for Senators Wayne L. Morse, Democrat of Oregon, and Ernest Gruening, Democrat of Alaska, who cast the votes against the resolution, members in both houses uniformly praised the President for the retaliatory action he had ordered against North Vietnamese torpedo boats and their bases after the second torpedo boat attack on United States destroyers in the Gulf of Tonkin.

There was also general agreement that Congress could not reject the President's requested resolution without giving an impression of disunity and nonsupport that did not, in fact, exist.

There was no support for the thesis on which Senators Morse and Gruening based their opposition—that the resolution was "unconstitutional" because it was "a predated declaration of war power" reserved to Congress.

Nevertheless, many members said the President did not need the resolution because he had the power as Commander in Chief to order United States forces to repel attacks.

Several members thought the language of the resolution was unnecessarily broad and they were apprehensive that it would be interpreted as giving Congressional support for direct participation by United States troops in the war in South Vietnam.

Expansion Held Inevitable

Representative of these doubts and reservations were the brief remarks by Senator George D. Aiken, Republican of Vermont. Senator Aiken, a member of the Foreign Relations Committee, said:

"It has been apparent to me for some months that the expansion of the war in Southeast Asia was inevitable. I felt that it shouldn't occur, but the decision wasn't mine.

"I am still apprehensive of the outcome of the President's decision, but he felt that the interests of the United States required prompt action. As a citizen I feel I must support our President whether his decision is right or wrong.

"I hope the present action will prove to be correct. I support the resolution with misgivings."

In the House, Eugene Siler, Republican of Kentucky, who was absent, was paired against the resolution, but his opposition was not counted. His office said he regarded the resolution as "buck-passing" by the President with the intent of silencing any later criticism.

Reservations about the resolution took two principal forms. The first was that it might be interpreted as giving advance approval of a change in the United States mission in South Vietnam of providing a training cadre and matériel.

Senator Gaylord Nelson, Democrat of Wisconsin, made much of this question yesterday. Today he proposed an amendment to resolve all doubts about the meaning of the resolution.

Conflicting Views Noted

Mr. Nelson noted that some members had welcomed the resolution as authorizing the President "to act against the privileged sanctuary" of the Communists in North Vietnam while other members thought it did not envisage an extension of the present mission.

His amendment stated: "Our continuing policy is to limit our role to the provision of aid, training assistance, and military advice, and it is the sense of Congress that, except when provoked to a greater response, we should continue to attempt to avoid a direct military involvement in the Southeast Asian conflict."

Mr. Nelson asked Senator J. W. Fulbright, Democrat of Arkansas, whether as chairman of the Foreign Relations Committee and floor manager of the resolution he would accept the amendment. If not, Mr. Nelson said, he could not support the resolution.

Mr. Fulbright replied that he could not accept the amendment because the House had already voted and adoption of the amendment would require that the resolution go to conference with resulting delay.

'An Accurate Reflection'

However, Mr. Fulbright added that the amendment was "unobjectionable" as a statement of policy and was "an accurate reflection of what I believe is the President's policy."

With this reassurance, Mr. Nelson was satisfied that he had made a "legislative record" of Administration intent. He did not offer his amendment and voted for the resolution.

The second reservation arose from the possibility that Premier Nguyen Khanh of South Vietnam might extend the war into North Vietnam and that the United States would lose control of its freedom of action.

Senator Jacob K. Javits, Republican of New York, asked Mr. Fulbright: "Suppose that South Vietnam should be jeopardized by its own extension of the struggle beyond its own capacity to wage a successful war in North Vietnam. Then what would happen in terms of our commitment and the commitment which the President is empowered to undertake?"

Mr. Fullbright declared that he did not believe South Vietnam "could involve us beyond the point where we ourselves wished to be involved."

August 8, 1964

PRESIDENT MAKES OFFER TO START VIETNAM TALKS UNCONDITIONALLY; PROPOSES $1 BILLION AID FOR ASIA

FIGHT WILL GO ON

President Says Saigon Must Be Enabled to Shape Own Future

By CHARLES MOHR
Special to The New York Times

BALTIMORE, April 7—President Johnson said tonight that the United States was ready to begin, without prior conditions, diplomatic discussions to end the war in Vietnam.

In a speech at Johns Hopkins University that was carried on television and radio, Mr. Johnson also said he would ask Congress to approve a $1 billion American investment in a vast Southeast Asian regional development program that eventually could include North Vietnam.

The President made it clear that while he would begin "unconditional discussions" for peace, any settlement in Vietnam demanded "an independent South Vietnam—securely guaranteed and able to shape its own relationship to all others."

He said, however, that South Vietnam could be a neutral state, "tied to no alliance, a military base for no country."

Two Months of Air Attacks

The speech, which came two months after the start of intensive American air strikes against North Vietnam, was the first statement of willingness by the United States to enter negotiations on Vietnam without prior conditions. Heretofore the Administration has said that negotiations could begin only after some "signal" from North Vietnam that it was willing to end aggression against its southern neighbor.

Government officials indicated that they had had no indication that either Hanoi or Peking would accept an invitation to unconditional talks.

High officials said that Mr. Johnson's use of the word "unconditional" meant "exactly what it says," and that the United States would be willing to enter into any kind of diplomatic contact with such Communist powers as North Vietnam and China even while the Vietcong continued to fight in South Vietnam.

The officials hinted that the United States might insist on continuing air strikes on North Vietnam during the discussions.

The only "condition" mentioned by these sources was that the United States would not engage in diplomatic talks with the National Liberation Front, the political arm of the Vietcong, on the ground that the front was only an "agent of North Vietnam."

Mr. Johnson, speaking on invitation at Shriver Hall auditorium, made it clear that his willingness to negotiate did not mean that the United States would give up the fight.

He said the air strikes had been launched "to convince the leaders of North Vietnam—and all who seek to share their conquest—of a simple fact: We will not be defeated. We will not grow tired. We will not withdraw, either openly or under the cloak of a meaningless agreement."

The speech was partly the American answer to an appeal last Thursday by 17 nonaligned nations that asked for quick negotiations without conditions. A formal answer will be made by the United States soon.

A crowd of about 1,300 people applauded Mr. Johnson's statement of willingness to negotiate. It applauded equally his firm statement that the United States would not accept defeat. He was interrupted by applause 15 times.

Mr. Johnson said he hoped that "all other industrialized countries, including the Soviet Union," would join in his plan for regional development in Southeast Asia.

He said he hoped that the United Nations Secretary General, U Thant, "could use the prestige of his great office, and his deep knowledge of Asia to initiate as soon as possible with the countries of the area a plan for cooperation in increased development."

Mr. Johnson added that he intended to expand and speed up programs to use American farm surpluses to help feed and clothe the needy in Asia.

He said that very shortly he would name a special team of Americans, headed by Eugene R. Black, former president of the International Bank for Reconstruction and Development, "to inaugurate our participation in these programs."

"We cannot and must not wait for peace" to begin these economic efforts, Mr. Johnson said.

"We would hope that North Vietnam would take its place in the common effort just as soon as peaceful cooperation is possible."

The President first mentioned the possibility that the United States would support a regional economic plan for Southeast Asia in a statement to his Cabinet last month. It was made public March 25.

"We often say how impressive power is," the President remarked. "But I do not find it impressive at all. The guns and the bombs, the rockets and the warships, are all symbols of human failure. They are necessary symbols. They protect what we cherish. But they are witness to human folly."

New Accords a Possibility

The President said that once it became clear to the Communist powers that American "patience and determination" in prosecuting the war were unending, "then it should also be clear that the only path for reasonable men is the path of peaceful settlement."

"We will never be second in the search for such a peaceful settlement in Vietnam," he said.

"There may be many ways to this kind of peace: in discussion or negotiation with the governments concerned, in large groups or small ones; in the reaffirmation of old agreements or their strengthening with new ones."

With those words he indicated that the United States might be willing to help write a new agreement to replace the Geneva accords of 1954, which ended the Indochina war and led to the partition of Vietnam.

In recent weeks Administration spokesmen have been saying that new agreements were not necessary but that a return to the "essentials" of the 1954 accords was necessary for peace. Mr. Johnson said:

"We have stated this position over and over again 50 times and more to friend and foe alike. And we remain ready, with this purpose, for unconditional discussions."

Government sources maintained, as did the President, that the offer to talk unconditionally was not "a marked change in policy." However, the emphasis had been on the futility of negotiations and there had been nothing like tonight's clear offer.

North Vietnamese support for the Vietcong is "the heartbeat" of the war, the President declared. He justified the aerial warfare against the North by saying:

"In recent months attacks on South Vietnam were stepped up. Thus it became necessary for us to increase our response and to make attacks by air. This is not a change of purpose. It is a change in what we believe that purpose requires."

The President said that "we know that air attacks alone will not accomplish" all of the United States purposes in defending South Vietnam, "but it is our best and prayerful judgment that they are a necessary part of the surest road to peace."

"We hope that peace will come swiftly," said Mr. Johnson, but "we must be prepared for a long-continued conflict. It will require patience as well as bravery—the will to endure as well as the will to resist."

Noting that some 400 Americans "have ended their lives on Vietnam's steaming soil," Mr. Johnson said:

"Why must this nation hazard its ease and its interests and its power for the sake of a people so far away?"

"We fight," he explained "because we must fight if we are to live in a world where every country can shape its own destiny."

The auditorium was picketed by pacifist groups urging an American withdrawal from Vietnam and carrying such signs as: "End the war—Not the world."

Mr. Johnson, who returned to Washington after the speech, was accompanied by Mrs. Johnson and their daughters, and by Vice President and Mrs. Hubert H. Humphrey.

April 8, 1965

PRESIDENT URGES WORLDWIDE DRIVE TO CURB DISEASE

Also Asks for Joint Effort to Spread Education—Cost of Plan Is $524-Million

By FELIX BELAIR Jr.
Special to The New York Times

WASHINGTON, Feb. 2—President Johnson asked Congress today for a global attack on ignorance and disease and called on all nations—"friend and foe alike"—to join in the battle.

In a special message read to the House and Senate, the President said that improving the education and health of mankind would be "the first work of the world for generations to come."

He urged prompt passage of international health and education acts of 1966 to give new purpose to continuing efforts and to blaze new trails in research and enlightenment.

The President proposed to devote $524-million of funds already budgeted to the combined undertaking, a 60 per cent increase over the $331-million voted by Congress for similar objectives in the current fiscal year, which ends June 30. Most of the money, about $354-million, would come from foreign aid funds.

Goals Are Restated

Recalling that last year Congress had shown by its actions that the nation's foremost task was to improve the health and education of the people, the President declared:

"We would be shortsighted to confine our vision to this nation's shorelines. The same rewards we count at home will flow from sharing in a worldwide effort to rid mankind of the slavery of ignorance and the scourge of disease.

"We bear a special role in this liberating mission. Our resources will be wasted in defending freedom's frontiers if we neglect the spirit that makes men want to be free."

"We call on rich nations and poor nations to join with us—to help each other and to help themselves," the President said.

Poses a Choice

He offered the legislative program as the American response to the declaration of William James half a century ago that mankind must seek "a moral equivalent to war."

"The choice between light and darkness, between health and sickness, between knowledge and ignorance is not one that we can ignore," the President said. "The light that we generate can be the brightest hope of history. It can illuminate the way toward a better life for all.

"But the darkness—if we let it gather — can become the final, terrible midnight of mankind."

The President acknowledged that many of the proposals under the heading of education had not been tested, but he said they were worth a trial.

The main effect of the President's educational proposals would be to give the Department of Health, Education and Welfare a role on international educational affairs for the first time since its creation in 1953. He proposed to create within the department a Center for Educational Cooperation, a focal point for leadership in international education.

Would Formulate Policy

This agency would be engaged mainly in policy formulation and would act as a channel for communication between United States missions abroad and the educational community here, would provide direction for programs assigned to the department and assist public and private agencies conducting international programs.

His educational proposals included:

¶An exchange program under the Peace Corps with an initial goal of 5,000 volunteers from 46 foreign countries where corpsmen now serve who would teach their language and culture in United States schools.

¶An educational placement service to recruit and assign United States teachers to posts overseas and lead to a world teacher exchange to bring classrooms of all nations into closer relation with each other.

Among his health objectives were:

¶On increase in the number of children receiving diet supplements in underdeveloped countries from 70-million to 150-million in the next five years.

¶The eradication of smallpox throughout the world by 1975 and malaria from the Western Hemisphere and other endemic areas within a decade.

¶The creation of an international career service in health.

The President's message today was a companion piece to his request yesterday for nearly $3.4-billion for foreign aid, including $2.4-billion to attack the root causes of poverty" in underdeveloped countries.

A third message tomorrow will deal with the world food crisis and outline a plan to harness the nation's agricultural abundance to the objectives of world peace.

In addition to the Center for Educational Cooperation, he asked for a Council on International Education, a corps of education officers in the United States Foreign Service, grants to develop new courses in world affairs in elementary and secondary schools and to finance development of new techniques for teaching basic education and fighting illiteracy.

In this connection, officials said a pilot program of elementary and adult educational television now operating in Colombia would be extended to six other countries, Ethiopia, Chile, Peru, Jamaica, Venezuela and Nigeria.

The Colombia project is using 1,500 television sets provided by the Agency for International Development in school classrooms.

Other grants were proposed by the president for universities to promote "centers of excellence" in dealing with particular problems and particular regions of the world, to develop administrative staffs and facilities for long-term overseas commitments, and to assist research and educational agencies dealing with social and economic development abroad.

The President also recommended a goal of 1,000 school-to-school partnerships through which United States schools help in construction of s sister school in developing countries.

These eventually would include books and equipment and teacher and student visits. They would be administered by the Peace Corps but financed mainly by participating schools.

"We are ready to serve as host to international gatherings," the President said. "I have therefore called on the Secretary of State and the Attorney General to explore ways to remove unnecessary hindrances in granting visas to guests invited from abroad."

Removal of tariff and other barriers to the free importation of educational materials was also urged, including the duty-free entry of visual and auditory materials of an educational scientific or cultural nature.

Another proposal was that for grants among the 90,000 foreign students now enrolled in United States institutions of learning for special courses and summer institutes. The President said many of such students "will someday play leading roles in their own countries."

To cooperate in worldwide efforts to deal with population problems, the President proposed expanded research in human reproduction and population dynamics, the training of more American and foreign specialists in this field, and assistance to the family planning programs in nations requesting such help.

Officials said research in human reproduction would include studies to improve the accuracy of the rhythm method of birth control.

In addition to funds for contraceptive devices, research grants would be made for studying the problem of timing of ovulation and to more accurately identify the safe periods when conception will not occur.

February 3, 1966

PRESIDENT VOWS TO PRESS PUNISHING OF AGGRESSORS; HANOI AREA BOMBED AGAIN

TALKS IN MIDWEST

Johnson Again Urges Foe to Set a Time for Peace Parley

By JOHN D. POMFRET
Special to The New York Times

OMAHA, June 30—President Johnson said today that United States air strikes on military targets in North Vietnam "will continue to impose a growing burden and a high price on those who wage war against the freedom of their neighbors."

The resolute tone of Mr. Johnson's remarks, made in a speech, indicated no wavering in his decision to step up the tempo of the war to convince North Vietnam that it cannot win and should seek to negotiate a settlement.

It was the President's first pronouncement alluding to the important escalation of the war signaled by the United States bombing raids yesterday on fuel dumps close to Hanoi and Haiphong. The tenor of the President's remarks made it plain that he was unswayed by criticism of the raids in Congress and abroad.

Support for Policy Urged

In a broad-ranging speech, Mr. Johnson emphasized the perils posed by developing world food shortages and his hope that nations, no matter what their ideologies, could cooperate to end poverty, ignorance and disease.

He also urged Americans to stand fast behind his policy in Vietnam.

"If you are too busy and not inclined to help, please count 10 before you hurt," the President asked.

[In a later speech in Des Moines, Mr. Johnson said that if the leaders of North Vietnam "will only let me know when and where they would like to ask us directly what can be done to bring peace to South Vietnam, I will have my closest and most trusted associates there in a matter of hours." He said there need be no agenda or commitments, Page 11.]

The President chose for his earlier speech a site calculated to underscore the peaceful intentions of the United States: The Omaha Municipal Dock on the Missouri River.

Tied up there was a barge loaded with the five-millionth ton of grain to be sent to India since emergency shipments began in January. Mr. Johnson gave the signal to start the barge downriver to Baton Rouge, La., where the grain will be reloaded.

Mr. Johnson declared that he was convinced that "after decades of war and threats of war, peace is more within our reach than at any time in this century."

This is so, he said, because "we have made up our mind to deal with the two most common threats to the peace of the world." These he said, are the desire of most people to win a better way of life and the design of some to force their way of life on others.

"Now if we ignore these theats or if we attempt to meet them only by the rhetoric of visionary intentions instead of good works of determination, I am certain that tyranny and not peace will be our ultimate fate," Mr. Johnson declared.

"If the strong and the wealthy turn from the needs of the weak and the poor, frustration is sure to be followed by force. No peace and no power is strong enough to stand for long against the restless discontent of millions of human beings who are without any hope."

Food for Freedom

The President said that most of the world's population was losing the battle to feed itself. In underdeveloped countries, he said, the population is growing at a more rapid rate than the food supply.

"If the present trend continues," he warned, "we can now see the point at which even our own vast productive resources, including millions of acres in reserve, will not be sufficient."

The program proposed in his Food for Freedom message to Congress to help underdeveloped nations expand their food production is only a beginning, Mr. Johnson said.

"We must work for a global effort," he said. "Hunger knows no ideology. Hunger knows no single race or nationality. We recognize the contributions of the Soviet Union [and] of Yugoslavia."

"We welcome the support of every nation of the world," he continued. "I long for the day when we and others—whatever their political creed—will turn our joint resources to the battle against poverty, ignorance and disease."

The President devoted a major portion of his speech to outlining the basic reasons for the United States commitment in Vietnam. He presumably was trying to allay the growing discontent reflected by public-opinion polls.

Reasons for U.S. Presence

He cited these basic reasons for the United States presence in Vietnam:

¶The United States is obligated to help those whose rights are threatened by force.

¶South Vietnam is important to the security of the rest of "free Asia," where, shielded by the courage of the South Vietnamese, other nations "are driving toward economic and social development in a new spirit of regional cooperation."

¶The outcome in South Vietnam will determine whether "ambitious and aggressive nations can use guerrilla warfare to take over their weaker neighbors."

President Johnson dealt with the last point at considerable length, reflecting the Administration's view that the war, waged without traditional military fronts, was a difficult one for the American people to understand.

In 1965, the President said, the Communists killed or kidnapped 12,000 South Vietnamese civilians.

"If, by such methods, the agents of one nation can go out and hold and seize power where turbulent change is occurring in another nation," he declared, "our hope for peace and order will suffer a crushing blow all over the world and it will be an invitation to the would-be conquerer to keep on marching. And that is why the problem of guerrilla warfare, the problem of Vietnam, is a very critical threat to peace not just in South Vietnam but in all of this world in which we live."

The purpose of the United States, Mr. Johnson said, "is to convince North Vietnam that this kind of aggression is too costly and cannot succeed."

He said that the tide of war had started to turn against the North Vietnamese, but added this sober warning:

"No one knows how long it will take. Only Hanoi can be the judge of that. No one can tell you how much effort it will take. No one can tell you how much sacrifice it will take. No one can tell you how costly it will be. But I can and I do here and now tell you this: The aggression they are conducting will not succeed. The people of South Vietnam will be given the chance to work out their own destiny, in their own way, and not at the point of a bayonet."

The Communists have shown no sign of wanting to negotiate peace, he said, and they believe that political disagreement in Washington and confusion and doubt in the United States will give them victory.

"They are wrong," the President added.

NIXON WOULD LINK POLITICAL ISSUES TO MISSILE TALKS

Seeks to Promote Gains on Mideast, Perhaps Vietnam, in Meeting With Soviet

HIS FIRST NEWS PARLEY

President Eases Campaign Demand for a 'Clear-Cut' Military Superiority

By HEDRICK SMITH
Special to The New York Times

WASHINGTON, Jan. 27 — President Nixon proposed today that arms talks with the Soviet Union be linked with progress on political issues of concern to both nations, particularly on the Middle East.

In his first news conference as President, Mr. Nixon indicated that he saw the Middle East, strategic arms control, and possibly Vietnam as part of a range of issues to be approached simultaneously in discussions between his Administration and the Soviet Union.

"What I want to do," he said, "is to see to it that we have strategic arms talks in a way and at a time that will promote, if possible, progress on outstanding political problems at the same time—for example, on the problem of the Mideast, and on other outstanding problems in which the United States and the Soviet Union, acting together, can serve the cause of peace."

Demands Softened

The President made a point of toning down his campaign demands for a "clear-cut military superiority" over the Soviet Union, conceding that words like "superiority" might mistakenly serve to spur the arms race.

"Our objective," he said in reply to a question, "is to be sure that the United States has sufficient military power to defend our interests and to maintain the commitments which this Administration determines are in the interest of the United States around the world."

"I think sufficiency is a better term, actually, than either superiority or parity," Mr. Nixon said.

Warns of 'Next Explosion'

He underscored his concern over the "powder keg" in the Middle East with a warning that the "next explosion" there could involve a confrontation between the nuclear powers. To avert this, he recommended what he termed new initiatives by the United States, but he did not go into detail.

Four hundred fifty-six newsmen and technicians, most of them standing, crammed the White House East Room for the news conference.

At first Mr. Nixon, in a medium blue suit, seemed a bit nervous, clasping his hands behind his back and having trouble clearing his throat during an early answer.

But he relaxed fairly quickly and was soon gesturing and smiling at the reporters, who broke into laughter at a remark he made about turning on the lights at the White House —an allusion to President Johnson's order to turn off unnecessary lights at the mansion.

Foreign policy dominated the substance of the conference, as Mr. Nixon said it had dominated his first week in office. On various issues, these are some of the points he made:

¶He favors Senate ratification of the treaty to halt the spread of nuclear weapons, and hopes for such action at "an early time." The decision on when the Administration will put the treaty before Congress will be taken up later this week by the National Security Council, possibly tomorrow.

¶The Vietnam talks in Paris are "going to take time" and it would be a mistake to put a timetable on them or make "overly optimistic statements." He said the United States had put forward specific proposals for restoring the demilitarized zone, mutual troop withdrawals and prisoner exchanges, which he thought were a better approach than seeking a cease-fire.

¶His Administration will continue United States opposition to Communist China's admission to the United Nations, but looks forward to a meeting with Peking's negotiators in Warsaw on Feb. 20 to see "whether new changes of attitude on their part on major, substantive issues may have occurred."

Mr. Nixon, who refrained during the Presidential campaign from giving a detailed prescription for peace in Vietnam, sidestepped a direct question on that subject today. But he emphasized later that his Administration was reviewing the entire problem and that it offered a new approach, without going into specifics.

"We have a new team in Paris, with some old faces, but a new team," Mr. Nixon asserted. "We have new direction from the United States. We have a new sense of urgency with regard to the negotiations. There will be new tactics. We believe that those tactics may be more successful than the tactics of the past."

'Semantics' Revised

Differing with such Congressional critics of the war as Senator J. W. Fulbright, chairman of the Foreign Relations Committee, and apparently reflecting the opinion of civilian and military aides in Saigon, the President brushed aside the prospects of an early cease-fire. Mr. Fulbright recently said it was the first logical order of business at the talks in Paris.

"When you have a guerrilla war, in which one side may not even be able to control many of those who are responsible for the violence in the area, the cease-fire may be meaningless,' Mr. Nixon said.

Some officials later were worried that he might have left himself open to eventual contentions by the enemy that they could not control their forces once hostilities had been formally stopped.

President Nixon, saying he anticipated many questions, made no opening statement. He was questioned several times by reporters about past Republican insistence on American arms "superiority." He took the opportunity to revise his campaign semantics, as he put it.

Last Oct. 24, in one of his major campaign speeches, Mr. Nixon warned of a developing "security gap" with the Russians. At Senate hearings on confirmation of Melvin R. Laird as Secretary of Defense, Mr. Laird emphasized the need for American arms "superiority" before the missile talks begin.

A questioner asked Mr. Nixon to explain his position, and to compare it with the idea of "sufficiency," which was ascribed to Henry A. Kissinger, Mr. Nixon's special assistant for national security affairs.

President Nixon replied that Dr. Kissinger's suggestion of sufficiency "would meet, certainly, my guideline and I think Secretary Laird's guideline, with regard to superiority." Later, the White House acknowledged that it could find no point at which Mr. Kissinger had used the term "sufficiency."

In an article on United States foreign policy published last December by the Brookings Institution, Dr. Kissinger spoke critically of "slogans" like superiority or parity unless given precise meaning.

President Nixon said today that parity tempted each side to believe "it has a chance to win" and does "not necessarily assure that a war may not occur." Public emphasis on superiority, he said, could make the Russians feel "in an inferior position" and therefore spur them to new arms development.

NIXON ASKS TROOP PULLOUT IN A YEAR AND WOULD JOIN VIETNAM POLITICAL TALKS

SPEAKS TO NATION

Hints Partial Cutback of U.S. Forces Will Come in Any Case

By ROBERT B. SEMPLE Jr.
Special to The New York Times

WASHINGTON, May 14—President Nixon proposed tonight a phased, mutual withdrawal of the major portions of United States, allied and North Vietnamese forces from South Vietnam over a 12-month period.

Then, according to Mr. Nixon's proposal, the remaining non-South Vietnamese forces would withdraw to enclaves, abide by a cease-fire and complete their withdrawals.

The President made the proposal in a nationwide television address in which he gave his first full-length report to the country on the war in Vietnam.

Although the President indicated that such full-scale withdrawals would probably require lengthy negotiations, he hinted strongly that "the time is approaching" when some partial reductions of combat troops could be accomplished regardless of what happens in the negotiations in Paris.

Prepared to Negotiate

Mr. Nixon said further that the United States was prepared to participate in negotiations leading to a political settlement, rather than continue to insist that Saigon and the Vietcong conduct political negotiations while Hanoi and Washington dealt only with military issues.

White House sources sought to contrast Mr. Nixon's offer of a "simultaneous start on withdrawal" with the last formal United States proposal.

That proposal, offered at the Manila conference of the United States and its allies in Vietnam in October, 1966, said that American withdrawals would be completed within six months after North Vietnamese withdrawls. The implication of the Manila proposal was that there would be some American troops left in the country after all of Hanoi's forces had withdrawn.

Supervised Elections Offered

The President also offered, for the first time, internationally supervised elections to insure "each significant group in South Vietnam a real opportunity to participate in the political life of the nation."

The proposal for internationally supervised elections was regarded as reflecting a concession by Saigon to the extent that such outside supervision would infringe on the sovereignty of the Saigon regime.

The President said that the proposals were made on the basis of full consultation with President Nguyen Van Thieu of South Vietnam, and White House sources said that President Thieu had agreed to them.

The President delivered the speech from a small theater in the east wing of the White House. His demeanor was solemn, as he hurried through his complicated, 3,000-word text.

Much of Mr. Nixon's address was familiar, carrying echoes of his own campaign and of President Johnson's speeches on Vietnam. He declared that the right of the South Vietnamese people to determine their own destiny remained a nonnegotiable point at the bargaining table and he ruled out any settlement that could be construed as a disguised defeat.

Wants to End War

"I want to end this war," Mr. Nixon declared. "The American people want to end this war. The people of South Vietnam want to end this war. But we want to end it permanently so that the younger brothers of our soldiers in Vietnam will not have to fight in the future in another Vietnam someplace in the world."

The President rejected the idea of a one-sided pullout of American troops as demanded by Hanoi and the National Liberation Front, or Vietcong. In its 10-point peace proposal offered last week, the Vietcong called for the unconditional withdrawal of American forces.

At the same time, however, he held out the promise of an early, partial reduction in allied forces because of what he described as Saigon's increasing military strength. He emphasized that this might be accomplished quite apart from what occurred in the negotiations in Paris.

"The time is approaching," the President declared, "when South Vietnamese forces will be able to take over some of the fighting fronts now being manned by Americans."

White House sources said that such withdrawals, when they occurred, would very definitely involve combat troops and would not be confined to supply forces behind the lines.

The President offered Hanoi a face-saving method of removing its troops, by dropping the Johnson Administration's insistence that Hanoi admit it had regular troops fighting in South Vietnam.

In a paragraph dropped, possibly inadvertently, from his prepared text, but which the White House said the President stood by, he declared:

"If North Vietnam wants to insist that it has no forces in South Vietnam, we will no longer debate the point—provided that its forces cease to be there, and that we have reliable assurances that they will not return," he declared.

This was one of several places in the speech where the President offered a flexible negotiating technique, or ambiguous language, that could be developed in future secret bargaining.

Two Tones Are Noted

He emphasized that none of the American proposals was being put forward on a "take-it-or-leave-it basis," and that he was "quite willing to consider other approaches," including Hanoi's or the Vietcong's.

On the subject of withdrawals, Mr. Nixon insisted on one point. If North Vietnam agreed to withdraw its forces on the basis of a phased timetable, he said, it would be required to withdraw them not only from South Vietnam but from Cambodia and Laos as well. The Cambodian border is only 35 miles from Saigon, the Laotian border only 25 miles from Hue, and the allies would not accept withdrawals that left those two major South Vietnamese centers exposed to renewed war.

The speech sounded to some observers as if it had been written in two parts and by two hands. Observers found the flexibility of Mr. Nixon's specific proposals in decided contrast to his rather stern rhetoric.

He asserted that the credibility of the United States would be badly damaged if Saigon were abandoned, and added:

"If Hanoi were to succeed in taking over South Vietnam by force—even after the power of the United States had been engaged—it would greatly strengthen those leaders who scorn negotiation, who advocate aggression and who minimize the risks of confrontation with the United States. It would bring peace now, but it would enormously increase the danger of a bigger war later.

"If we are to move successfully from an era of confronttation to an era of negotiation, then we have to demonstrate—at the point at which confrontation is being tested—that confrontation with the United States is costly and unrewarding."

An Apparent Warning

At another point, the President appeared to be warning the enemy that these proposals represented genuine concessions, a conciliatory position that could be ignored or repudiated only at some risk.

"I must also make it clear, in all candor, that of the needless suffering continues, this will affect other decisions. Nobody has anything to gain by delaying," Mr. Nixon declared.

Pressed for an explanation of this sentence, White House sources said simply that it ought to be self-explanatory.

White House officials refused to characterize the address as another element in the Administration's accelerating effort to assure the American public that progress was being made and, thus, to purchase additional time in which to carry out negotiations free of heavy public pressure.

At the same time, however, the President made what appeared to be a direct bid for continued patience. He conceded that he could not legitimately demand "unlimited patience from a people whose hopes for peace have too often been raised and cruelly dashed over the past four years," but added:

"Tonight, all I ask is that you consider these facts and, whatever our differences, that you support a program which can lead to a peace we can live with and a peace we can be proud of.

"Nothing could have a greater effect in convincing the enemy he should negotiate in good faith than to see the American people united behind a generous and reasonable peace offer."

The White House also rejected speculation that the speech had been scheduled as a response to the Vietcong's 10-point plan. The White House explanation for the timing was that quite apart from recent developments it was a "propitious moment" for "developing momentum" in the Paris peace talks.

May 15, 1969

NIXON CALLS FOR PUBLIC SUPPORT AS HE PURSUES HIS VIETNAM PLAN ON A SECRET PULLOUT TIMETABLE

POLICY UNCHANGED

President Says Hasty Withdrawal Would Be a 'Disaster'

By MAX FRANKEL

Special to The New York Times

WASHINGTON, Nov. 3—President Nixon pleaded tonight for domestic support as he persisted in his effort to find peace in Vietnam and as he unfolded what he said was a plan to bring home all United States ground combat forces on an orderly but secret timetable.

It was the first time Mr. Nixon had spoken of a plan to recall "all" combat infantry units, though he set no deadline, and the first time he had referred to a private timetable, though he did not commit himself to a definite pace.

He made clear that his policies on Vietnam remained the same as the ones he outlined last May, the only difference being that a recent enemy restraint on the battlefield had rendered the withdrawal timetable "more optimistic."

Hasty Withdrawal Rejected

Delivering his long-awaited report on Vietnam policy by television and radio from the White House, Mr. Nixon rejected a "precipitate withdrawal," which he said would be a prescription for "a disaster of immense magnitude."

He said the enemy alone bore responsibility for the deadlock in the peace negotiations and offered in evidence some of his hitherto private diplomatic initiatives, including an exchange of letters with the late President of North Vietnam, Ho Chi Minh.

If a settlement cannot be negotiated, Mr. Nixon reiterated, then the nation's responsibility to its allies and to the peace of the world requires a measured pace of disengagement. That pace, the President said again, will be geared to the ability of the South Vietnamese forces to take over combat duties and to the level of combat imposed by the enemy.

Critics' Advice Resisted

Though the emphasis on a deliberate plan to find a lasting peace was clearly addressed to impatient critics of his tactics in Congress and around the country, the President resisted most of the critics' advice for a bold new initiative or announcement, such as a unilateral cease-fire or a public timetable for withdrawal.

In fact, the President placed some of the burden for success of his plan on the cooperation of his critics.

"I pledged in my campaign for the Presidency to end the war in a way that we could win the peace," he said. "I have initiated a plan of action which will enable me to keep that pledge.

"The more support I can have from the American people, the sooner that pledge can be redeemed, for the more divided we are at home, the less likely the enemy is to negotiate in Paris.

"Let us be united for peace. Let us also be united against defeat. Because let us understand: North Vietnam cannot defeat or humiliate the United States. Only Americans can do that."

Taking only oblique notice of the Oct. 15 moratorium and other massive demonstrations for peace, Mr. Nixon said he would be untrue to his oath and obligations if he allowed national policy "to be dictated by the minority" who he said counsel defeat in Vietnam and "who attempt to impose it on the nation by mounting demonstrations in the street."

As a White House aide remarked, in advising reporters that Mr. Nixon was holding to his deliberate course in Vietnam, the President had decided to try to do "what was right and not what was new."

The President began his speech by citing reasons why he had decided after assuming office not to end the war by withdrawing all forces from Vietnam, though he said it would have been easy to attribute the blame for military defeat to his predecessor, Lyndon B. Johnson.

He then cited some of his efforts to explore "every possible private avenue" to peace, including the letter to President Ho, which was sent in mid-July. Mr. Nixon said that President Ho's reply, received three days before the North Vietnamese leader died on Sept. 3, "flatly rejected" his initiative.

Future Course Described

Mr. Nixon cited the new orders to prepare the South Vietnamese to assume full responsibility for their own security, disclosed a 20 per cent reduction in air operations in South Vietnam — since August, aides said—noted the recent signs of enemy restraint and then described his future course in these words:

"We have adopted a plan that we have worked out in cooperation with the South Vietnamese for the complete withdrawal of all United States ground combat forces and their replacement by South Vietnamese forces on an orderly scheduled timetable.

"This withdrawal will be made from strength and not from weakness. As South Vietnamese forces become stronger, the rate of American withdrawal can become greater."

The President said he could not divulge the timetable because disclosure would deprive him of necessary flexibility and would also eliminate Hanoi's incentive to negotiate in good faith.

Other informed officials here have given as a further reason the feeling that a definite timetable ran the risk of either provoking domestic dissent or undermining the confidence and stability of the South Vietnamese, or both. But Mr. Nixon did not allude to this reasoning.

"We must retain the flexibility to base each withdrawal decision on the situation as it is at that time," Mr. Nixon said. He noted that he would be influenced not only by the capacities of the South Vietnamese forces but also by possible progress in the Paris talks and the level of enemy combat activity.

For example, the President explained, his timetable for the withdrawal of ground combat troops—which had been previously estimated to number about 250,000—is "more optimistic" now than it was in June because enemy infiltration into South Vietnam and the rate of American casualties have markedly decreased in recent months.

But if the infiltration or casualty rates should increase again, he added, this would reflect a "conscious decision" by the enemy and require an adjustment in his own policy.

Warning Given to Hanoi

Mr. Nixon asserted that Hanoi could make no greater mistake than to increase the violence again. An increase, he said, would not only affect his withdrawal timetable but, to the extent that it jeopardized the remaining American forces in Vietnam, would evoke "strong and effective measures" by the United States.

He cited efforts to enlist the help of the Soviet Union and other governments that maintain diplomatic relations with Hanoi, and the exchange of letters with President Ho Chi Minh through a personal friend of the North Vietnamese leader. Aides said the intermediary had refused to be identified.

Mr. Nixon's letter, dated July 15, reaffirmed a desire to work for a just peace and said there was nothing to be gained by delay. President Ho Chi Minh's reply, dated Aug. 25 but received in Paris on Aug. 30, only three days before his death, demanded a complete withdrawal of American troops.

"It has become clear that the obstacle in negotiating an end to the war is not the President of the United States," Mr. Nixon said. "And it is not the South Vietnamese Government."

Hanoi's intransigence would continue, the President predicted, as long as it is convinced "that all it has to do is to wait for our next concession and the next until it gets everything it wants."

In summarizing the choices available to him at this stage of the war, Mr. Nixon expressed the conviction that they were basically only two:

"I can order an immediate precipitate withdrawal of all Americans from Vietnam without regard to the effects of that action," he said, citing the risk of massacre in Vietnam, the risk of new threats to the peace in many parts of the world and the danger of "remorse and divisive recrimination" among the American people.

"Or we can persist in our search for a just peace through a negotiated settlement if possible," he said, "or through continued implementation of our plan for Vietnamization if necessary—a plan in which we will withdraw all of our forces from Vietnam on a schedule in accordance with our program, as the South Vietnamese become strong enough to defend their own freedom."

Contradiction Denied

This reference to "all of our forces" as opposed to an earlier reference to "all U.S. ground combat forces" represented no contradiction, aides explained. They said the first, and more concrete portion of the President's program dealt with combat troops whereas his reference to all troops covered a still longer time span.

The President's repeated use of the word "plan" appeared to be a semantic innovation, but it corresponded almost exactly to his use of the word "program" for peace in his first major Vietnam address. Mr. Nixon indicated at several points that his plan was a continuing policy, not a new one.

His first Vietnam report, on May 14, laid out a program to end the war that involved neither a "purely military" solution nor a "one-sided withdrawal." If offered negotiations for the mutual withdrawal of all non-South Vietnamese forces and for arrangements that would give the people of South Vietnam a "free choice" or political future.

Although Mr. Nixon's address tonight covered much of the same ground—often in strikingly similar phrases—as his first Vietnam policy address on May 14, he gave new emphasis to his hopes for "Vietnamization" of the war effort, spoke more critically of the policies of former President Johnson and stressed at length his disappointment over what he said was Hanoi's refusal to bargain for a settlement.

He cited "two private offers" for a rapid settlement that he said he had made even before his inauguration January 20 through a person who he said was in contact with the leaders of North Vietnam. To these, he said, Hanoi replied in effect with calls "for our surrender," Mr. Nixon said.

Mr. Nixon indicated in May that even without negotiation some American troops could begin to come home as the South Vietnamese forces proved themselves capable of assuming a larger combat burden. In June the President announced a first reduction of 25,000 men by Aug. 31. In September, after a month's delay due to disagreement in the Administration and the threat of enemy offensives, he scheduled a further reduction, of 35,000 men, to be completed by Dec. 15.

The whole approach had two distinct facets: either negotiation for a political solution and fairly swift withdrawal of most American troops or "Vietnamization" of the war to give the South Vietnamese an increasing share of the combat burden while the Americans withdrew gradually.

The President and his associates were disappointed in two respects.

First, their negotiating package failed to energize the Paris talks. They received hints that Hanoi and the Vietcong might be willing to deal separately with Washington, but the President refused to negotiate behind the back of the Saigon Government.

Second, the domestic support that had greeted the President's speech began to erode through the summer. Demands for a more rapid withdrawal were pressed on him by members of Congress, former officials of the Johnson Administration and commentators.

During this period of accelerating public pressure, and two days before Moratorium Day, Mr. Nixon took the unusual step of scheduling his address three weeks in advance.

The White House never explained why he left so much time for more debate and more pressure. His aides insisted that the timing was unrelated to elections tomorrow in several states and many municipalities.

The White House said that the South Vietnamese Government had been briefed on the speech through normal diplomatic channels. But Congressional leaders were given only a brief outline this evening. Reporters were unabled to write from a text only half an hour before the President went on the air, at 9:30 P.M.

NIXON GIVES 'DURABLE PEACE' PLAN WITH GREATER RELIANCE ON ALLIES; CAUTIONS RUSSIANS ON MIDDLE EAST

3 PRINCIPLES SET

Stress Put on Strong Partners, Defense and Negotiation

By ROBERT B. SEMPLE Jr.
Special to The New York Times

WASHINGTON, Feb. 18 — President Nixon set forth today the fundamentals of a foreign policy designed to achieve a "durable peace" in the seventies. The policy commits the United States to a major role in world affairs, sharply qualified, however, by the President's judgment that the United States should carry less of the burden and its allies more.

In the first "annual report" submitted by an American President on the state of the world, Mr. Nixon offered a compromise between the momentum of history and the realities of the present—between two decades of accumulated cold-war commitments and the limitations on the commitments imposed by changing conditions overseas and competing domestic priorities.

Deterrent Big Factor

To that end, he outlined a foreign policy based on three principles: partnership with allies who now "have the ability . . . to deal with local disputes which once might have required our intervention"; the preservation of a defensive capability sufficient to deter would-be aggressors, and a readiness to negotiate with friend and foe to resolve conflicts and reduce arms.

Of the three, the principle that a lasting peace would henceforth require "a more responsible participation by our foreign friends in their own defense and progress" dominated the 119-page document and helped to tie together its sections. This principle flavored discussions of joint allied efforts to defend Europe, the proposed efforts to assist Latin America, future security arrangements in Asia, and pleas to other countries to share the burden of foreign aid to underdeveloped regions.

Henry Alfred Kissinger

In what was essentially a general philosophical exercise, Mr. Nixon occasionally gave more detailed estimates of matters of current concern.

His assessment of the Soviet missile threat, for example, appeared no less serious today than when he first announced his plans to proceed with an antiballistic missile system last spring. "I believed then, and I am even more convinced today, that there is a serious threat to our retaliatory capacity," he said, noting that by the end of this year it was estimated that the Soviet Union would have 1,590 missiles, against 1,710 projected for the United States. The Soviet missile force, he insisted, raises grave questions about Soviet intentions.

Addressing himself to other current crises, Mr. Nixon gave an optimistic report on the progress of pacification of the Vietnamese countryside and the training of the South Vietnamese Army, but offered little hope for an immediate breakthrough in the Paris negotiations.

He warned the Soviet Union on the Middle East and to refrain from exploiting Arab-Israeli tensions to enlarge its sphere of influence in the area.

Avoids Retreat

Inevitably, however, Mr. Nixon found himself returning to the theme of shared responsibilities in a changing world. What he appeared to be setting forth was a global version of the so-called Nixon doctrine first expounded on Guam, in which he promised Asia a nuclear shield against massive attack but asserted that in cases of lesser forms of aggression, the United States would expect the threatened nation to provide the manpower for its defense.

The President carefully said that he was not proposing to retreat from the world stage—"America cannot live in isolation if it expects to live in peace," he declared—and he stressed that the United States would not hesitate to furnish assistance "where it makes a real difference and is considered in our interest."

But he left little doubt that future decisions to intervene would be carefully weighed and that, generally, the United States would seek to move, without swift disengagement or a return to isolationism, from "dominance to partnership" in world affairs.

The document was transmitted to Congress at noon after weeks of fanfare. It was divided into four sections: a brief summary of the foreign policy-making machinery devised by the President and his national security adviser, Henry A. Kissinger; a long middle section dealing with American policy toward Europe, the hemisphere, Asia and the Pacific, Vietnam, the Middle East, Africa, international economic problems, and the United Nations; and two shorter sections summarizing defense positions and planning and the prospects for negotiation with the Communist world on arms-control and other issues of mutual concern.

Proud of Achievement

In a brief appearance before reporters the other day, shortly before a background session provided by high Administration officials, Mr. Nixon expressed obvious pleasure and pride in his achievement. He said it was "the most comprehensive statement ever made," and while he did not mean by these words to fault his predecessors, he said he thought it was not only useful but unique to have pulled together "in one place" an account of the Administration's successes, failures, strategies and hopes in foreign policy.

The policy paper was largely the work of Mr. Kissinger, who

in turn drew on the resources of the State and Defense Departments, the National Security Council staff, and a speechwriter, William Safire, who gave it a final polish. Mr. Nixon has acknowledged his own limited role by remarking: "I even read it myself." But the thoughts were his; indeed, he had expressed many of them during his trips to Europe and Asia, and the document was filled with quotations from his earlier declarations.

'My Best View'

"It is my best view," he said, "of where we've been and where we're going."

Around the central theme of self-help and shared responsibilities revolved a number of subsidiary themes. One prominent subtheme involved Mr. Nixon's efforts to measure foreign - policy commitments against other national priorities.

"We are not involved in the world because we have commitments," Mr. Nixon said, "we have commitments because we are involved. Our interests must shape our commitments, rather than the other way around."

Mr. Nixon asserted with some pride that he had "established procedures for the intensive scrutiny of defense issues in the light of over-all national priorities." While he did not describe these procedures in detail, he conceded that the United States did not have "unlimited means" to pursue "every worthwhile national objective," and said he had tried to develop means to insure the "consistency" of domestic and defense needs.

Still another prominent characteristic of the document was Mr. Nixon's attitude of confidence in the "system" of policy making formulated under Mr. Kissinger, which he described in some detail. He said the system—anchored by the National Security Council, through which all policy choices flow—had replaced the old system of "crisis management" with what he called a more intelligent way of "shaping the future."

A third prominent strain was Mr. Nixon's repeated emphasis on fundamental changes in global conditions. In his comments a few days ago, he said that the world as he knew it as a Congressman and Vice President no longer existed, and in the report he reflected this with the assertion that "the postwar period in international relations has ended" and in his now-familiar judgment, first expressed at the Republican convention in 1968, that the time had come to move "from an era of confrontation to an era of negotiation."

Europe has made remarkable strides since the days of the Marshall Plan, he said, which explained and justified his appeal to Europeans to "play a greater role in our common policies." No less dramatic were the changes he noted in the Communist world, once a "unified bloc," now a schismatic and uneasy alliance.

From this fundamental upheaval, he suggested, have sprung new-found hopes for eased tensions. While he did not claim too much for these hopes—"we are under no illusions. We know that there are enduring national differences" — he noted that the United States and the Soviet Union had engaged in discussions on a number of issues without propagandizing and recrimination.

At the same time, he conceded that relations with the Soviet Union were "far from satisfactory," and said that Soviet leaders had displayed alarming ambitions in the Middle East and had refused to exert a "helpful influence" in the Paris peace negotiations.

Accordingly, he suggested, long-range hopes of détente should not obscure the need for immediate measures to guard against the possibility of Communist aggression.

His report on battlefield conditions conveyed considerable optimism. He claimed "tangible progress" for Vietnamization—strengthening the South Vietnamese forces—as well as pacification of the countryside and the isolation of enemy troops from their traditional sources of intelligence, food, money and manpower.

Yet even here Mr. Nixon expressed caution, noting that "claims of progress" had often turned out wrong and that there were many good reasons why Hanoi might wish to continue the struggle and avoid a genuine settlement.

The chapters on America's relations with its allies varied in length and specificity. Africa received general treatment. The United Nations got a modest compliment as a "forum for crisis diplomacy," an energetic if underrated promoter of human rights, technical assistance and relief, and peace-keeping body as yet incapable of solving "fundamental international disputes, especially among the superpowers."

If the political future of Europe should be left to Europeans, Mr. Nixon said, so too should fundamental decisions regarding the economic development of Latin America be left to Latin Americans. In a chap- Latin-American policy statement of Oct. 31, the President again offered aid, tariff preferences, and other incentives to Latin-American growth, but asserted that the United States would not seek to define the programs and would henceforth proceed on the belief that "the principal future pattern of this assistance must be U.S. support for Latin-American initiatives."

Similarly, on foreign aid, Mr. Nixon noted that "multilateral institutions must play an increasing role in the provision of aid." And he said that while the United States would increase its contributions to them he hoped other countries would do the same. He also said "our bilateral aid must carry fewer restrictions," such as the requirement that all goods be purchased in the United States.

February 19, 1970

NIXON SAYS SOVIET AND U.S. DEFINED PACT ON MISSILES

A WARNING TO MOSCOW

President Declares He Will Increase Arms Outlays if Russian Build-Up Goes On

By BERNARD GWERTZMAN
Special to The New York Times

WASHINGTON, Feb. 9 — President Nixon, in his third annual foreign policy message to Congress, said today that the United States and the Soviet Union had reached an accord on the outline—if not yet the details — of an interim agreement on the limitation of strategic arms. He said such an agreement could restrain the arms race without jeopardizing either side's security.

Mr. Nixon warned that if, in the absence of an accord, the Russians continued their intensified missile deployment and threatened to upset the current balance of power, he would not hesitate to increase spending on American strategic weapons.

The major focus in Mr. Nixon's 95,000-word State of the World report was on United States relations with the Soviet Union and China. The document also covered nearly every area of international life, sometimes with only a broad-brush approach but often in significant detail.

'Civilized Discourse'

Major points in the report, which bears the title "United States Foreign Policy for the 1970's: The Emerging Structure of Peace," included these:

¶There are "serious grounds" for believing that a fundamental shift in Soviet-American relations may occur, but Mr. Nixon said it was unclear whether the Russians, engaged in a vast arms build-up, had undertaken a major policy shift or were making tactical moves for their own advantage.

¶In the meeting with Soviet leaders in May, the President said, he hopes for concrete agreements beyond arms control and bilateral matters, including an understanding on limits on the arms flow to the Middle East and on curbs on big-power rivalry in such areas as South Asia, plus a discussion of measures to reduce tensions in Europe.

¶The President conceded that Japan had every reason to be shocked by his unilateral economic and diplomatic initiatives last summer, but he did not apologize for the moves, which he said were necessary. He said that by the end of last year confidence had been restored and he applauded Japan's assumption of greater responsibility in Asia commensurate with her economic power.

¶Mr. Nixon reported continued progress on all fronts

—pacification, Vietnamization and economic reform — in Vietnam, while noting that the enemy might be preparing for a major offensive. He stressed the flexibility of his eight-point peace proposal, but insisted that he would not abandon the Saigon Government or prisoners of war to the enemy. He pledged to secure the return of the P.O.W.'s through negotiations or "other means."

Mr. Nixon said there were serious grounds for believing that "a fundamental improvement in the U.S.-Soviet relationship may be possible." But he said that it was unclear whether there had been a permanent change in Soviet policy "or only a passing phase concerned more with stactic than with a fundamental commitment to a stable international system."

'Concrete Arrangements'

In his meeting with Soviet leaders in May, Mr. Nixon said he hopes for "concrete arrangements of benefit," which, besides arms control and bilateral matters, would include an understanding on avoiding an inflammation of the situation in the Middle East, a curb on big-power rivalry in such areas as South Asia and discussion of measures to reduce tensions in Europe further.

Summing up the "watershed year" that had just passed, the President said that the United States, despite sharp problems with Japan and with its Western European allies, had achieved "a more balanced alliance" with its friends. The forthcoming trips to Peking and Moscow are evidence of "a more creative connection" with America's adversaries, he added.

A sense of achievement pervaded the document—an attitude underscored in Mr. Nixon's brief radio address to the nation this morning on the message.

He said in the radio address that various "breakthroughs toward peace" took place last year because his Administration had consistently "stopped reacting on the basis of yesterday's habits and started acting to deal with the realities of today and the oportunities of tomorow."

In an example of his rhetoric, he said that his current eight-point Vietnam peace plan was "the most generous peace offer in the history of warfare."

The report also contained a section on "disappointments" during the year. The most important, Mr. Nixon said, was the failure to end the Vietnam war. He also noted the inability to prevent the war between India and Pakistan, the continued tension in the Middle East, continued disagreements in Latin America, the diminishing foreign aid available for Africa and the inability of the United States to keep Nationalist China in the United Nations.

The report's discussion of the status of the 27-month-old talks on the limitation of strategic arms—the so-called SALT talks—was closely linked to the current balance of power in the world and to the determined Soviet effort to accelerate its deployment of land-based and submarine-launched missiles.

Crucial Milestone Foreseen

After noting that the Soviet Union had improved its forces "in virtually every category of strategic offensive and defensive weapons," Mr. Nixon said the United States was "approaching a crucial turning point in our strategic arms programs."

"If the Soviet Union continues to expand strategic forces, compensating United States programs will be mandatory," he said. "The preferable alternative would be a combination of mutual restraint and an agreement in SALT."

"But under no circumstances will I permit the further erosion of the strategic balance with the U.S.S.R." he added. "I am confident that the Congress shares these sentiments."

He said that the Russians were undertaking either "major improvements or the deployment of a totally new missile system" and that two new or greatly modified land-based intercontinental ballistic missile systems were being developed.

The Russians have built silos for additional giant 23-megaton SS-9 missiles that could destroy American offensive missile sites, the President said, also noting that in the near future they would have more missile submarines than the United States' current 41.

With this as a background, Mr. Nixon noted that "a consensus is developing on certain essential elements" of a strategic arms agreement.

He said both sides agreed that there should be a comprehensive limitation of the number of antiballistic missile (ABM) defensive systems. Deployments of ABM's should neither provide a defense for the entire country nor threaten the strategic balance, he said.

Agreement on a limitation on ABM's has not been reached, he explained, because the existing Soviet ABM defense network of 64 missile launchers surrounds Moscow while the initial American Safeguard program is geared to protect offensive missiles in less populated areas.

The Americans have proposed an asymmetric formula under which the Russians could have 100 missiles for Moscow's defense while the United States would have more for ICBM protection.

Mr. Nixon said that the two sides had agreed that once an accord was reached on details, the ABM agreement would be formalized in a treaty that would require Senate aproval.

Throughout the talks the United States has pressed for a comprehensive limitation on offensive weapons as well, but Mr. Nixon indicated that a freeze was unlikely and that there should be only an interim arrangement on the halt of "certain offensive weapons."

Focus on Land Missiles

Informed sources have said that the two sides have decided to postpone action on submarine-launched missiles and are concentrating on land-based ones. Because of that, Mr. Nixon, in his budget, authorized further work on a long-range submarine-launched missile system to keep ahead of Soviet submarine construction.

In his report Mr. Nixon did not rule out an early submarine agreement, assering that it was "still under intensive negotiation." In an apparent rejoinder to those in the Senate who have argued for a comprehensive treaty or none at all, Mr. Nixon said:

"We must weigh the advantages of prolonging the current stage of negotiations in order to reach agreements on every offensive system against the consequences of allowing the current Soviet build-up to continue, perhaps for a considerable period."

He said that an interim agreement would not impair American security, adding: "Moreover, Soviet willingness to limit the size of its offensive forces would reflect a desire for longer-term solutions rather than unilateral efforts to achieve marginal advantages."

Stressing his preference for the interim agreement, he said it "will be a major step in constraining the strategic arms race without compromising the security of either side." On the other hand, he said, if the negotiations are protracted, that would inevitably lead to an acceleration of the arms race.

"This is a reality of our competitive relationship," he said.

An Agenda for Moscow

On his proposed agenda for the Moscow talks in May, the President listed either an accord on the initial arms agreement or on the issues to be addressed in the second stage—a sign of confidence that an interim agreement would be worked out in the next three months.

Somewhat unexpectedly, Mr. Nixon placed Middle Eastern problems as the second most important item on the proposed agenda. Administration spokesmen have long expressed a desire to get an agreement with Moscow on limiting the flow of arms to the area. In his report Mr. Nixon gave an assessment of the scope of Soviet involvement in Egypt.

In 1970, he related, the Russians deployed some 80 antiaircraft missiles, several squadrons of Soviet-manned combat aircraft, 5,000 missile crewmen and technicians, and about 11,000 other advisers. Since then, he said, they have introduced mobile antiaircraft missiles, the advanced MIG-23 fighter and other aircraft. Most recently they have sent TU-16 bombers, equipped with long-range missiles, he added.

President Nixon said that the Soviet Union and the United States could encourage a Middle East settlement by furthering negotiation.

Tensions in Europe

Mr. Nixon said he also expected to discuss in Moscow the prospects for further easing of tensions in Europe. He said the United States favored participation in a carefully prepared European conference on security and cooperation, long proposed by the Soviet bloc. He reiterated that he opposed a unilateral cut in United States forces in Europe.

In summarizing the year's events, the President laid heavy stress on still-secret correspondence he had with Soviet leaders. He indicated that it helped facilitate the agreement on an improved status for West Berlin and the understanding on the arms talks announced last May 20.

CHAPTER 8

Administration Scandals

In retrospect, it is astonishing that the scandals touching the White House have been so few. The federal government of the United States is history's greatest plum. It administers 3,000,000 jobs all of which in modern times are well paid. It lets contracts routinely which run into hundreds of millions of dollars. It has control of levers which can send the stock and commodities markets shooting up or down to garner fat profits for traders. All of these powers ultimately center in the president's mansion.

Even the most vigilant president would be unable to guarantee a scandal-free administration in modern times. The apparatus is simply too huge to be controlled. Furthermore, the majority of our presidents have had problems on their minds which were much more pressing than police work. Nevertheless, there has been some remarkable carelessness on the part of some of our chief executives who did not profit personally from the chicanery of their subordinates but who could have stopped it with little effort.

The outstanding example was Warren G. Harding. Although no evidence has ever linked him to Teapot Dome, the record is clear that those involved included his closest personal friends, the poker-playing buddies with whom he spent his relaxed hours and whose characters should have been open books to him. To a lesser extent, the same observations could be made about Harry S Truman who had a remarkable weakness for coming to the defense of men who can only be described as ''sleazy.'' It would be unfair to Truman, however, not to note that he fought with the same fierce passion for men who were *not* cronies, but whom he regarded as good Americans under partisan attack—such as Dean Acheson and Gen. George C. Marshall.

At this distance, the ''mess in Washington'' seems rather trivial and it is doubtful that Mr. Truman will go down in history as a scandal-ridden president. The stakes were not large—mink coats and Polaroid cameras—and none of them touched the men to whom he turned for substantial advice on national policy. The furor aroused at the time has faded against the larger issues of his administration. Whatever the final verdict, it will almost certainly turn on the Truman doctrine, the Marshall plan and his prosecution of the Cold War.

In contrast, the major scandal of the Eisenhower administration involved his closest personal aide and advisor—Sherman Adams. Yet, neither then nor later, did the president suffer from public blame. The Eisenhower personality was too obviously above petty graft, and Adams was looked upon as a man who had betrayed the presidential trust. It is doubtful whether history will grant more than a footnote to the episode.

Richard M. Nixon

The New York Times

The John F. Kennedy and Lyndon B. Johnson administrations were relatively free of financial scandals but Johnson was plagued by lingering suspicions from his days as a Texas senator and Senate Majority Leader. Most of these centered around Bobby Baker, who had been the Secretary to the Senate Majority under the Texan's leadership. Baker was convicted for his wheeling and dealing while Johnson was president. There was never any evidence that the Texan had been the beneficiary of any of the Baker shenanigans. But Baker had unquestionably been a Johnson protege and the two could not be disassociated in the public mind.

The scandal of the twentieth century that really changed history was Richard M. Nixon's Watergate. Only this revelation of wrongdoing cut so deeply that a president was driven from office before the end of his term. There is every reason to believe that it will remain in the public consciousness long after the others have been forgotten. This rests upon the fact that it was outside the pattern of classic White House or governmental chicanery.

All of the other scandals, from the "embalmed beef" that opens this chapter to Bobby Baker, were centered on money. They were primarily efforts by second-rate men to use the federal government to make a quick buck. As Watergate unfolded, it became apparent that money was a secondary consideration to the conspirators. Their primary objective was to remain in power by any means whatsoever with no regard to the traditional live-and-let-live standards that have characterized Americans politics throughout most of our history.

The American people have long since become inured to thievery in government. They do not condone it but they can understand it and are unlikely to go on an emotional binge when it is revealed. The use of undercover operatives, wire-tapping and burglary as instruments for political struggle was something else again. There was a sinister ring to Watergate that had been missing in the past.

The result was a changed attitude toward the presidency. Other chief executives may appear who can evoke adulation from the American people, but it is unlikely that we will again have a man who is the object of popular idolatry merely because he is president. Whatever happens, the myth of the presidency as an ennobling institution has been destroyed.

GER

THE PRESIDENT'S DESIRE.

He Tells the War Investigators that They Must Point Out Those Guilty of Mismanaging.

WASHINGTON, Sept. 25.—The commission appointed by President McKinley to investigate the administration of the War Department in relation to its conduct of the Spanish-American war will begin its labors formally to-morrow.

In addressing the commission yesterday, when it had its first meeting, the President said, among other things:

"Gentlemen: Before suggesting the matters which shall come before you for investigation, I desire to express my appreciation to each of you for your willingness to accept the patriotic service to which you have been invited. You are to perform one of the highest public duties that can fall to a citizen, and your unselfishness in undertaking it makes me profoundly grateful.

"There has been in many quarters severe criticism of the conduct of the war with Spain. Charges of criminal neglect of the soldiers in camp and field and hospital and in transports have been so persistent that, whether true or false, they have made a deep impression upon the country. It is my earnest desire that you shall thoroughly investigate these charges and make the fullest examination of the administration of the War Department in all of its branches, with the view to establishing the truth or falsity of these accusations. I put upon you no limit to the scope of your investigation. Of all departments connected with the army I invite the closest scrutiny and examination, and shall afford every facility for the most searching inquiry. The records of the War Department and the assistance of its officers shall be subject to your call.

"I cannot impress upon you too strongly my wish that your investigation shall be so thorough and complete that your report when made will fix the responsibility for any failure or fault by reason of neglect, incompetency, or maladministration upon the officers and bureaus responsible therefor—if it be found that the evils complained of have existed.

"The people of the country are entitled to know whether or not the citizens who so promptly responded to the call of duty have been neglected or misused or maltreated by the Government to which they so willingly gave their services. If there have been wrongs committed the wrong-doers must not escape conviction and punishment."

September 26, 1898

A DEADLY PARALLEL.

An official of the Government has lately given out a statement which he thinks it an extremely favorable showing of the care taken in the Spanish war of the health and life of our soldiers. It is to the effect that of 2,906 deaths reported, 300 were in battle or from wounds, and 2,606 were from disease, while he quotes the deaths in battle or from wounds during the civil war as 40,000 out of a total of 360,000, leaving 320,000 due to disease. According to these figures, it will be seen that the ratio of deaths from disease is almost exactly the same in the two records.

If the statement were correct, what would it prove? At most, that in thirty-three years, during which the country has advanced enormously in population, in wealth, in industrial development, and in the spread of education, the War Department has not advanced at all. Even this contention would not cover the facts, because the United States undertook the war for the Union absolutely unprepared, with an empty Treasury, without an adequate organization, and literally spent a longer time than was consumed in the whole Spanish war in securing the safety of the National capital. Everything had to be done in desperate haste, and often at a terrible cost of life. If, for instance, the last year of the civil war should be taken for comparison, when the War Department had had its lessons and had the resources to apply their teachings, the comparison would be far more just and far less favorable to the department of to-day.

But the statement we have quoted, so far as the statistics of the civil war are concerned, is all wrong. The figures of the Adjutant General's office covering the four years of the war are as follows:

Killed in battle	67,058
Died from wounds	43,012
	110,070

Died from disease	199,720	
Died from accident, murder, in Confederate prisons, &c.	40,154	
		239,874
Total		349,944

It will be seen from this that, so far from disease being eight times as fatal as battle and wounds, it was not twice as fatal. And even if we add the deaths from accident, in prison, &c., to those from disease, the ratio to deaths in battle and from wounds is but a trifle over two to one.

In fact, the ratio of the efficiency of the War Department in the civil war to that of the War Department of to-day is, roughly, the ratio of STANTON to ALGER. Does the statistician of the Government care to figure that out?

November 4, 1898

MILES'S BAD BEEF INQUIRY

Meat Sent to Cuba and Puerto Rico Equally Condemned.

"EXPERIMENT" WAS PRETENSE

The Army's Commander Insists that Chemicals Used Were Responsible for Much Sickness.

CINCINNATI, Ohio, Dec. 23.—Gen. Miles returned to Washington to-day after being the guest of honor here last night at the New England banquet. The Commercial Tribune to-day has the following interview with him:

"When asked as to the investigation into the beef ration scandal he is now making, to which he referred in his testimony Wednesday, Gen. Miles said:

"'My suspicions were aroused several months ago and I at once instituted an investigation into the matter of sending beef to the army in the West Indies. The item in my testimony of Wednesday relating to 337 tons of refrigerator beef and 198,000 pounds of canned fresh beef, which was unfit for food, is only an item. This quantity was sent to one town in Puerto Rico alone. How much more was sent to Puerto Rico I do not know.'

"'How was the beef supply for the army in Cuba?'

"'It was just as bad. The conditions there were no better than they were in Puerto Rico, as I indicated in my testimony.'

"'How about rations before the army embarked? Was the supply no better before the transports sailed than after the army was established in Cuba?'

"'It was the same at Tampa and the same at Jacksonville.'

"'Will you give a little more light as to what you meant by this assertion in your testimony before the War Investigating Commission Wednesday?'

"Gen. Miles had suggested that the food was sent to his large army under pretense of an experiment.

"'I think,' continued Gen. Miles, 'that that sentence is sufficiently plain. Pretense is the precise term to use. It is absurd to pretend that these enormous quantities of beef were sent to an entire army simply as an experiment. To expect that the beef can be exposed to a tropical sun for sixty hours without mortifying is out of the question.'

"'How about the chemicals used in preparing this beef?'

"'As I stated in my testimony, I believe that the action of these chemicals was largely responsible for the sickness in the army. I have medical authority for this statement, and I believe it to be true.'

"'How far along has your own investigation into this subject progressed?'

"'It began several months ago. I have the testimony of a large number of officers and men upon this matter, some of which I gave in my testimony before the commission. My inquiry is still in progress, and some of the most important information I have received has been acquired in the last few days.'

"'What channel will this investigation take upon its conclusion?'

"'I will not discuss that. It is my duty to investigate any wrong existing in the army, and that I am now doing in the regular military manner. The work is not completed yet, and until it is done I will have nothing more to add to the statement made before the commission.'

"'What was the matter with the tents?'

"'There were not enough of them. They were not suited to stand the weather, and some of them were poor.'"

December 24, 1898

ALGER MAY RETIRE FROM THE CABINET

Angered by the President's Order to Court-Martial Eagan.

PREFERRED COURT OF INQUIRY

This Course Would Have Made Gen. Miles Also a Defendant.

The Commissary General Likely to be Relieved from Duty and Put Under Arrest To-day.

WASHINGTON, Jan. 17.—The air is full of surmise to-night concerning Secretary Alger and Commissary General Eagan. Gen. Eagan is surely to be court-martialed, and Alger possibly is to resign from the Cabinet. The two things are made to hang together, the decision by the President and the Cabinet to have Gen. Eagan brought directly to court-martial, without the preliminary of a court of inquiry, being the alleged cause of Secretary Alger's determination to get out. Neither Eagan nor Alger will discuss the developments of the day, and the silence of the two affords a great deal of opportunity for surmise and conjecture.

President McKinley decided yesterday that Gen. Eagan should be court-martialed, every member of the Cabinet except one being of the opinion that his offense could not be permitted to pass unnoticed. Secretary Alger alone stood out for a court of inquiry. Early to-day, before the hour for the meeting of the Cabinet, Secretary Alger and Adjt. Gen. Corbin went to the White House and remained there in conversation with the President until the Cabinet assembled. Secretary Alger and Gen. Corbin then left, the Secretary going to his home, and the Adjutant General to his office.

As soon as the Cabinet adjourned the announcement was made that the court-martial had been ordered to be constituted, and that Gen. Corbin would find a list of officers having the necessary rank to serve and who are convenient of access for immediate service. Gen. Corbin was back at the White House soon after the dissolution of the Cabinet council, and after his second visit it was learned that the list he offered to the President had been revised, substitutions being made for some of the names submitted by the Adjutant General. It was at this time that the report began to be whispered that Secretary Alger, profoundly dissatisfied with the course taken by the President in ordering a court-martial, instead of the court of inquiry which the Secretary and Gen. Corbin preferred, had thrown out an intimation, if it were not a distinct affirmation, of his purpose to resign if his views were thus overruled.

Varying shades of opinion about the case were entertained by members of the Cabinet when it first came to their notice, and several members were open to conviction about the proposition to convene a court of inquiry. Secretary Alger, it seems, could find no reason for anything except a court of inquiry. He preferred that sort of investigation, it is asserted, because the court of inquiry would lay the foundation for a trial of Gen. Miles, putting him on his defense before Eagan. A court-martial, on the other hand, will bring Eagan to book to answer for conduct unbecoming an officer and a gentleman, and for conduct prejudicial to good order and military discipline. The court of inquiry would be an annoyance to the Commanding General. The only anxious man about the result of a court-martial will be Gen. Eagan.

ALGER DISLIKED BY THE ARMY.

Unless common report turns out to have misrepresented the feelings and position of Gen. Alger, his resignation on account of Gen. Eagan will not cause widespread grief. In the army there is no other opinion than that the presence of Alger at the head of the War Department has been the cause of much of the confusion, inefficiency, mismanagement, suffering, and lack of discipline that have culminated in this crowning act of insubordination which the Secretary appears anxious to excuse. Unless the President makes some concession to Alger, which the public cannot be expected to agree to, there seems to be a chance that he may unload the heaviest burden which his Administration has persisted in carrying.

Army officers who talk to-night about the gossip of the day express the hope that a new Secretary of War will at once break up the cliques that now devote themselves to keeping the department divided, and that the President will find a man to succeed Alger who will understand military matters well enough to exact respect between the line and staff, to choke off the ambitious designs of high officers to crowd down those above and below them, and to put a stop to the course that has resulted in Eagan's assumption that he could insult the Major General commanding without incurring the censure of the Secretary of War.

There can be no doubt in the estimation of army officers that unless Eagan had had good reason to believe Alger agreed with the views he expressed about Gen. Miles the former would never have ventured to assail him as he did. That the Secretary of War is not above cherishing and expressing his dislikes was shown in the treatment he extended to Col. Roosevelt. It is true that Gen. Corbin has assumed a large share of the blame for the use made by Secretary Alger of Col. Roosevelt's letter, and that Gen. Corbin shares the dislike of Gov. Roosevelt entertained by the Secretary of War. But the reply suggested to that by army officers who discuss this matter is that no self-respecting Secretary of War, with an ounce of brains with which to do his own thinking, would permit his opinions to be supplied to him ready made by his Adjutant General.

THE EAGAN COURT-MARTIAL.

Secretary Alger to-night confirmed the announcement made earlier in the day that a court-martial for the trial of Commissary General Eagan would be ordered. He made this statement as he was leaving the White House with Adjt. Gen. Corbin after a conference of half an hour with the President. As to the charges to be preferred against the Commissary General, the Secretary declined to say anything, nor would he talk respecting the personnel of the court, adding that this would be announced to-morrow night about 9 o'clock.

Gen. Eagan has not yet been relieved of his duties in anticipation of his prospective trial, but it is understood that the order for his arrest preparatory to trial will of itself carry with it his relief from official duties. It was said at the War Department to-day that the order for arrest might be served on Gen. Eagan by an officer of the army some time during the official day to-morrow. This will enable him to make formal application for the privilege of going beyond the limits in which ordinarily he would be confined, and permit him to visit the department or any other place to which he may find it necessary to go.

In the absence of the announcement of the detail for the court-martial, there is a good deal of speculation as to its composition. General practice is for a majority of the court to consist of the peers or superiors in rank of the defendant. This would make the task of selecting a court a hard one, because it is not easy to find a sufficient number of general officers ranking with a Brigadier General to make up a desirable quota. But latitude is permitted the appointing authority in such selections, as the ninth article of war reads: "No officers shall, when it can be avoided, be tried by officers inferior in rank." It will be noticed that the phrase "if it can be avoided" leaves opportunity for the appointment of junior officers.

Major Gen. Wesley Merritt has been mentioned as likely to be appointed President of the court-martial. This, perhaps, is due to the fact that he is the only available Major General of the regular army, the others being Gen. Brooke in Cuba and Gen. Miles here. The friends of Gen. Merritt are hoping that he will not be selected, fearing that he will be accused of prejudice by one or perhaps both sides.

The penalty for the offense with which Gen. Eagan probably will be tried—conduct unbecoming an officer and a gentleman—is one of the most severe known in the army, being dismissal. Article 61 reads as follows:

"Any officer who is convicted of conduct unbecoming an officer and a gentleman shall be dismissed from the service."

If the court shall find Gen. Eagan guilty, even with extenuating circumstances, it must attach this sentence and then the only hope for the officer would be in the exercise of clemency by the President, based perhaps upon the court's recommendations.

January 18, 1899

EAGAN AND THE BEEF CANNERS.

Reticence in Washington About a Report of an Agreement Between Them.

WASHINGTON, Jan. 27.—Gen. Eagan and the officers at the War Department were adamant to-day when questioned concerning the publication of a Chicago dispatch containing the intimation that there was an improper understanding between Eagan and the canners of beef in Chicago. Gen. Eagan will not talk about any publication in the paper in which this dispatch appeared, and no one else could be found who would admit that it had any applicability to the War Department.

J. G. Brine, the representative here of the Chicago beef canners, has been sought for diligently by many reporters. He is said to be still living at the Arlington, but it is certain that he has not been in the hotel since very early to-day. The assertion is made by a very much interested man who has been looking for him that he left the city this morning simply to get out of the way of the newspaper men and the War Department. Whatever his business has been, he has employed prominent counsel, but W. W. Dudley, who is understood to be the man, could not be found to-night.

While not much credence is given to the story at the War Department, it is considered highly probable that the War Investigating Commission will be obliged to look into the matter, as the information it might gain would be valuable to the President in considering the findings and recommendations of the Eagan court-martial. All the testimony given thus far by the representatives of the beef producers has been to the effect desired by the packers and canners. Until the report is probed that there has been some sort of understanding between Gen. Eagan and the agent here of some of the beef handlers, the War Investigating Commission can scarcely be comfortable or convinced that it has searched for every essential fact.

January 28, 1899

THE PRESIDENT AND ALGERISM.

In another column we reproduce parts of what seems to us a very weighty and important article printed in yesterday's Evening Post. It is an appeal against the President to the people of the United States, and it is quite possible that the fact of its appearance in The Evening Post would disincline the President to attend to it. No wonder. A considerable number of persons in private stations who formerly found it necessary to attend to what The Evening Post said have lately found its editorial utterances negligible. But this is for reasons which have nothing to do with the merits of the appeal it makes to the public against the President.

The mistake of this appeal we believe to be precisely that it is directed to the public against the President. Our readers know that THE TIMES has never insulted the President by putting him in the same class with the Secretary of War. We believe Mr. MCKINLEY to be an honest, loyal American citizen, sincerely desirous of serving his party by serving his country. What we believe of Mr. ALGER, our readers know, and it is unnecessary and might be unseemly just now to repeat. It is not perhaps easily credible that the President has not perceived what injury the Secretary of War has done to the Administration. But when we consider in what an atmosphere of flattery and courtiership a President of the United States must live who has so many good things to give away it becomes credible. If old and brave and faithful officers of the United States Army talked to the President with the freedom with which it seems they talk to the editors of The Evening Post, with the freedom with which we know that they talk to other editors, the President would know that the army is demoralized. Here we are, at the close of a victorious war, which has raised the United States Army to a very proud position not only in the eyes of Americans but in the eyes of all the world. This is the time when one might expect the gallant and faithful officers who have been working through long years of darkness and neglect to bring our little army to that condition of efficiency which it so proudly proved, in a few radiant weeks of struggle and glory, to be happy over the result of their long and obscure labors. Yet the state of mind of these men, when it should be satisfaction and elation over great tasks well performed, is one of dejection and disgust. The honor of the army has been soiled. The morale of the army has been lowered. It could not make over again the brilliant campaign which it made in Cuba. It would not "have the heart." And all because a petty and pushing politician, who, as a volunteer soldier, was recommended for dismissal for shirking his duty, but who is now supposed to be in a position to control the Electoral vote of Michigan, (let not the President forget that!) has been injecting and has been allowed by the President to inject the methods and even the men he has employed in Michigan politics into an honorable and gallant service.

Why does the President keep ALGER in the place in which he has displayed an incompetence so abysmal, a spirit so small? This is the question which every officer of the United States Army who stands upon his merits and not upon his "pull" has been asking for months. It is the question which a body of civilians and Republicans that is daily growing larger is asking with increasing urgency and getting no answer. Moreover, every faithful and deserving officer, and every civilian who knows anything about the conditions of the army, look with fresh horror at the proposal to add two or three thousand commissioned officers to the United States Army, simply and solely by favor and not with the least pretense of any test or guarantee of fitness. They look forward to a perfect debauch of Algerism when the new Army bill is enacted. It is for the President to disappoint their doleful expectations and to reassure them. He can do it, first, by dismissing Secretary ALGER from a place which a man of self-respect would not have consented to hold for twenty-four hours after his efforts to screen his subordinate had failed, and, next, by making public an assurance that the new appointments to the army will be made not by favor, but by the application of some fair and impartial test of "the promise and potency" of professional competency. If the President does these things he will shew an honest intention to undo the mischief which ALGER has done, and which he could not have done without the acquiescence of the President. If he does not do this, he should be plainly told that he is doing what in him lies to consummate the ruin of the United States Army.

January 31, 1899

THE REAL ALGER PERIL.

From The Evening Post, Jan. 30.

Some people profess not to understand the heat with which the Alger scandals are discussed. Why should distinguished officers of the army grow white with rage as they talk of the Secretary of War? Why should officers of the navy take so deep an interest in the affairs of a department not their own, and speak, as they do, with mingled contempt and dread of Mr. Alger? He is but one example more of incompetence in office. Maladministration and the smirch of politics on public business are not such startling novelties. * * *

The answer is that there is far more than a question of personality involved. Alger and his methods and his backers stand for an assault upon the army more deadly than any armed enemy could ever deliver. They are for breaking down its prestige and morale. For their own personal and partisan ends, they would prostitute the one trained service the country has. That is why regular army officers are roused to indignation at the mention of the name of Alger. He has trampled on the most cherished traditions of their profession. For merit he has substituted favoritism. He has stuffed the service with civilians. Boys he has put over gray-haired veterans, just as used to be the case when commissions in the army were openly sold. Assignments to duty are made under the Alger system, orders are given, not to get the work done in the best military manner, but to make places for dependents, to pay political debts and create political obligations. Alger's is the dirty hand of politics fouling a profession that has been peculiarly the home of educated gentlemen. No wonder the gentlemen display some heat when speaking of one who is their official superior, but whose intrigues and tricks and deceptions and base uses of the army fill them with loathing for the man and with fears for the future of the service.

The very judicial processes of the army, the attempts of its officers to keep the honor of their ranks unsullied and to punish and expel black sheep, are meddled with and thwarted by the political bias and motives of the head of the War Office. * * * But the court-martial of Capt. Carter has already become a public scandal, so outrageously have the President and Secretary Alger, in connection with it, interfered with the regular course of military justice. That officer was tried by court-martial in December, 1897; he was found guilty of corruption in engineering contracts, was sentenced to dismissal from the army, the court also recommending that criminal proceedings be brought against him. What has been the result? The President and Secretary of War have kept the papers in their possession all these months, and have been straining every nerve to find some way of letting the inculpated officer escape full punishment. Reason? Political and social "pull." * * * In a desperate hope to save so well-connected an offender, the President employed Mr. Edmunds to review the proceedings to see if some legal flaws might not be found. Mr. Edmunds's bill of $5,400 the President then had the effrontery to order paid out of the National Defense Fund! This was too much even for a friendly Controller of the Treasury. * * * Yet people wonder that under such a President and such a Secretary and such debauching and dishonoring methods regular army officers should not think everything for the best.

Why navy officers should also make forcible remarks about Alger is now getting to be plain. They fear that his slimy methods will soon invade the navy. Already the first step has been taken or attempted. The Senate has amended the Navy Personnel bill so as to permit the Secretary to appoint civilians direct. Officers of the navy are frantic at the proposal. They would rather see the whole bill fail. It is a plan to Algerize the navy. This is the sort of thing which makes the real Alger peril apparent. Nothing is too fine, no traditions or system too sacred, for his sprawling hand to seize upon and subdue to partisan schemes. He is ready to take the last step in political degradation and corruption, and make of both army and navy a politician's machine instead of an honorable and secure profession. And when anybody says Alger, he means, of course, Alger's master. The President is reported to have said that he and the Secretary must stand or fall together. So they must; and it will not be long before the indignation of army and navy at the demoralizing and defiling work of Alger will begin to burn hotly against the man who is both legally and morally responsible for what his underling does.

January 31, 1899

THE ARMY MEAT SCANDAL

Gen. Miles Reiterates His Assertions About Embalmed Beef.

CANNED ROAST BEEF NO BETTER

Was Nothing More than the Pulp Left by the Process of Making Extract —Gen. Merritt Reticent.

Besides reiterating his previous assertions regarding the serving of embalmed, or chemically treated, beef to the United States soldiers during the war with Spain, Major Gen. Nelson A. Miles said last evening that he had evidence that certain "canned roast beef" supplied to the soldiers was nothing more than the pulp left after making extract of beef. The commanding General of the United States Army was seen at the Waldorf-Astoria, and, while disinclined to say anything more publicly about the "army beef scandal," he replied to some specific questions with explicit frankness.

"These facts that have come out about the kind of canned beef furnished to our soldiers during the late war," said Gen. Miles, "are the result of investigations made by regimental commanders. They cannot be successfully disputed. I don't care what set of men deny them. By my order a circular was sent out on Sept. 20 to the commanding officers of the regiments which were in service during the late war, to investigate and report on the complaints that bad meat had been furnished as rations to the men. Reports of regimental commanders have been coming in since last Fall. I had received fourteen of these reports when I testified befor the commission of inquiry. Now I have about thirty reports, and they all tell the same story.

"The men of the different regiments reported to their commanding officers that meat served out to them as canned roast beef nauseated them. They did not know what was the matter with it, but they could not keep it on their stomachs. I know now what the trouble was. There was no life or nourishment in the meat. It had been used to make beef extract, and after the juice was squeezed out of it the pulp was put back in the cans and labeled 'roast beef.' I have the evidence of men who have seen this thing done. You have observed the advertisements of how a pound of beef extract contains the essence of several pounds of beef. Well, the soldiers got, as roast beef, some of the meat from which beef extract had been made. From all parts of the country the reports of regimental commanders are coming in confirming these facts.

"The 'embalmed beef' matter is entirely different from that of the canned 'roast beef.' What I have said about the 'embalmed beef,' however, is abundantly substantiated by evidence. I have the affidavits of men who have seen the process of embalming beef or treating it chemically for the purpose of preserving it.

"Yes, I received a telegram from Col. Albert A. Pope authorizing me to draw on him for $1,000 to be used in proving that chemicals were used to embalm beef furnished to our soldiers. I replied to Col. Pope's telegram and told him that I appreciated his patriotism and public spirit, but that I did not think it would be necessary to spend $1,000 to prove that the beef was embalmed. With regard to my suggestion that a thousand-dollar guarantee of good faith be required from the men who were reported as having offered to give $100,000 if proof could be furnished that the beef was embalmed, I can only say that I regarded that offer of $100,000 as pure bluff. I shall take no steps in the matter one way or the other, and I have nothing to say about any further investigations that may be made of complaints concerning the treatment of soldiers in camps, hospitals, or elsewhere."

Asked if he felt disposed to make any comment on the result of the court-martial of Gen. Eagan, the commanding General said:

"Certainly not. With regard to Gen. Eagan, or his trial I have nothing whatever to say."

Gen. Miles spent nearly all of the forenoon yesterday in his room at the Waldorf-Astoria attending to his correspondence. In the afternoon he made a few social calls. He expects to return to Washington to-day.

Major Gen. Wesley Merritt, in command of this department of the United States Army, was also at the Waldorf-Astoria yesterday. He returned from Washington on Monday and resumed his duties on Governors Island. He spent a part of yesterday at headquarters on the island attending to routine matters, but, pending some alterations in his residential quarters there, he will make his home at the Waldorf-Astoria. He declined last evening to speak of the Eagan court-martial, over which he presided, and he was equally reticent regarding the army beef scandals.

There was a noticeably large representation of the military element in the Waldorf-Astoria, and in other up-town hotels as well, yesterday afternoon. Several regimental officers who were engaged in active service during the recent war are now here on business, and will remain here for some time. Other officers came on from Washington partly in attendance on Gen. Miles and Gen. Merritt, and partly for the purpose of attending the Charity Ball. Col. James Allen of Gen. Miles's staff is at the Holland House. Major L. H. Strother of Gen. Merritt's staff was a guest at the Waldorf-Astoria yesterday, and at the Grand Hotel were Gen. J. F. Weston, United States Army; Col. Peter D. Vroom, United States Army; Col. W. P. Hall, United States Army, and Lieut. Col. J. L. Donovan of the Sixty-ninth Regiment.

February 1, 1899

WAR COMMISSION'S REPORT

Miles's Strictures on Army Beef Severely Criticised.

GENERAL'S CHARGES DISMISSED

Mass of Expert Testimony Offsetting Them Held to be Conclusive —Alger Sustained.

WASHINGTON, Feb. 8.—The War Investigating Commission has now completed its labors and its report will be in the hands of the President to-morrow. The commission held a session to-day that extended well into the afternoon, going over details. To-morrow the members of the commission will meet at their old offices, formally attach their signatures to the original document, and proceed in a body to the Executive Mansion to inform the President that they have completed their mission and present their report. The commission then will cease to exist. The commission's quarters will be vacated immediately, and will be taken possession of by Gen. Kennedy and Major Watkins, who hold the newly created offices of Advisers to the War Department on Colonial Affairs.

The report of the War Commission is a voluminous document of 150 printed pages. Each member has been provided with a printed copy to retain, and arrangements have been made so that the President will have as many printed copies as he wishes when he makes the document public.

The report makes an important feature of the beef issue, and dismisses as a general proposition the charges that have been made against the beef furnished the army. It finds, it is understood, that most of the beef was such as could be properly furnished as an emergency ration, pointing out that the evidence showed it never was intended to be anything but an emergency ration. It says there were only two witnesses who really testified against the beef, Gen. Miles and Major Daly, the Chief Surgeon who made the report regarded as the most sensational forwarded to the commission by Gen. Miles. As to the testimony of these two witnesses the commission, it is understood, goes on to point out the mass of evidence submitted to the contrary as offsetting it.

As to such of the canned beef as was found to be objectionable, the commission points out the effect of the tropical climate in producing liquefaction of the fat in the meat and the consequent rendering of the contents unpalatable. Most of the beef, though, is found to have been satisfactory for emergency use, where fresh beef or beef on the hoof could not be procured.

The strictures of Gen. Miles made publicly on the beef and his public expressions in other ways, it is understood, are subjected to a severe criticism. The methods and manner of loading the transports in Gen. Shafter's Cuban expedition are also discussed, and responsibility placed for the results.

The report finds that the statements of chemical treatment made by Gen. Miles on the authority of Major Daly are not borne out by the chemical experts, who were also placed on the stand. It quotes from Major Daly's testimony, and then takes up the testimony of Chemists Clarke of the Geological Survey and Bigelow of the Agricultural Department, who examined analyses of the beef submitted, and find that as a chemical expert Major Daly is not supported by other chemical authorities, and that, therefore, his testimony is regarded as not worthy of credence.

There are also said to be some recommendations as to organization of certain branches of the army, but, it is stated, the recommendations are not radical.

As to the administration and conduct of the war the conclusions of the commission are understood to be that everything possible was done by the department in the limited time it had at its command in making its preparations for the war, and the report says that the conduct of the war not only worked out in the end successfully but in such a way as to be worthy of great commendation.

The report says that the evidence before the commission shows that Secretary Alger exercised proper diligence and supervision, and that his subordinates also were efficient, experienced, and faithful. The commission is a unit on its report, and there is no minority report.

At the outset the commission divided itself into sub-committees for the separate consideration of designated branches of the main subject of inquiry. These sub-reports will be added to the principal statement of conclusions handed to the Chief Executive.

February 9, 1899

ALGER RESIGNS FROM THE CABINET

Retires, Under Fire, from Secretary of War's Office.

SUCCUMBS TO CRITICISM

Special to The New York Times.

WASHINGTON, July 19. — Secretary of War Alger has retired under fire.

Having shut his ears for more than a year to the storm of public criticism that has been directed against him from the beginning of the war with Spain, refusing to accept either hints or open advice to surrender a position held by him with dissatisfaction on the part of the people and annoyance to the Administration, he has at last, apparently with a sudden change of mind, asked to be relieved from furtner occupation of his office.

He offered his resignation to the President during an early morning call at the White House. At the moment he declared his determination to serve no longer. He expressed the hope that his services might cease at once. Before the conversation between the Secretary and the President closed it was understood that while the resignation was to be accepted at the pleasure of the President, a successor to Mr. Alger would be named before the close of the month.

The information sent to THE NEW YORK TIMES that Secretary Alger had gone to Long Branch to talk with Vice President Hobart about his resignation was correct. It is learned that it was not the first time that Vice President Hobart and Mr. Alger had talked about the withdrawal of Alger from the Cabinet. When the President and his party were at Thomasville, Ga., last Spring, and Alger was in the South, he had a conversation with Mr. Hobart on the way back concerning the ceaseless criticism from which he was suffering.

Alger was then determined to "face it out," and insisted that he would be able to disprove the assertions which held him responsible for the many shortcomings charged against his management of the army. Mr. Hobart, it is related, declared to the Secretary that he would not remain for a day in office if so much censure was lodged against him, and that he would, by resigning, prove that it was the fault of the system and not the man that put the army in such a light.

The inference drawn by those persons at the War Department who to-day sought to discover the facts, was that since the story of his alliance with Pingree became public he had become convinced, helped by the feeling of embarrassment shown by the Administration, that he had staid too long, and that he must revise his determination of a few months ago. So he concluded to go again to Mr. Hobart and hear from him his opinion at this time about the propriety and desirability of his withdrawal from office.

From the promptness with which Alger acted, it is assumed that Mr. Hobart repeated, with some additional reasons to those given on the way home from Thomasville, his advice that Secretary Alger, for his personal comfort and for the good of his party, offer his resignation to the President. He had no doubt of the acceptance of it.

Alger could scarcely wait from last night until this morning to make his last official call at the White House.

The news of his action did not get out quickly. It was stated immediately after his departure for the War Department that he had talked about official matters relating to the campaign in the Philippines. That account was good until about the lunch hour, when it began to be whispered about the War Department that Alger had resigned.

He was in his office later on, but did not appear to be interested in the current business. When he was asked an hour after the resignation had become generally known if the report was true he promptly denied it, and at 5 o'clock admitted it, and declared that he would not give the reasons for his resignation, nor write a statement to convey the reason at length.

AS TO HIS SUCCESSOR.

If the Secretary had been able to hear the discussion about the department immediately after his resignation became generally known he would have learned that the interest in the War Department was no longer attached to him but was in learning the name of his successor. It has been assumed here for weeks that his successor would have to be named soon. The President, it is believed, has considered the necessity of having a candidate ready for appointment.

Reviving an old report, the name of Ambassador Porter was brought up first, and it has been positively asserted that the President has addressed Gen. Horace Porter with the view of preparing him to accept the office.

One of the reports from the White House to-night is that the President is desirous of having a good lawyer as his Secretary of War. The talk is that he considers that with so experienced an officer as Gen. Corbin as his military adviser he would be helped to a greater extent by a civilian Secretary conversant with law than by a military officer alone.

One report has connected the name of Gen. F. V. Greene with the War Department, and for the reason of his experience as a business man and a commander of forces in the Philippines he would be especially useful as an adviser about the campaign in the Philippines. This suggestion does not arouse great interest in the minds of those men who are satisfied with their status in the department and with the share they enjoy of power there.

The recommendation has been heard by some officers that if the President desires the services and advice of a lawyer as well as a good military man, he will choose Gen. J. H. Wilson, now in command at Matanzas. To that suggestion is generally returned the reply that the President must select a New York man, as that State has no member of the Cabinet, and not a man from Delaware.

Gen. Anson G. McCook has sometimes been suggested as likely to be an acceptable Secretary of War, but it cannot be ascertained that he has ever had anything more than a chance of getting the office.

TALK OF ROOSEVELT.

Gov. Roosevelt is sometimes mentioned, but the impression here is that he could not be prevailed upon to give up his present honorable and important position to take a Cabinet office for a short time. Still, there are persons here who recall his recent visit as significant of something more than a desire on the part of the President to consult him about appointments.

The transfer of Attorney General Griggs from the Department of Justice to the War Department has been suggested by those who are figuring on Secretary Alger's successor to-night.

In this same connection the name of Elihu Root, the well-known New York lawyer, is mentioned.

Secretary Alger's plans for the future have already been defined. Mr. Meiklejohn, the Assistant Secretary of War, is at present supposed to be in Wisconsin, whither he went two weeks ago to make a personal inspection of the Fox River improvements, a scheme which has given the Engineering Bureau endless trouble, and which now requires some positive recommendation at the hands of the Secretary to Congress at the next session. He has been notified of what has happened and is expected to return to Washington to assume charge of the War Department until such time as the President shall name a permanent Secretary.

Probably that will be by the end of the present month and by Aug. 1 Secretary Alger will be at liberty to lay down his task. He is much wearied by the weight of responsibility he has borne for nearly two years and a half; he has aged many years, in the opinion of his personal friends, and is in need of rest. He proposes to depart for the Northwest, and spend some time in the lumber camps belonging to him, and then to pay visits to his children. This will occupy his time until well along into next Fall. About political matters, the Secretary does not speak now, but it may be fairly surmised that he then will be ready, in view of his already announced decision, to take such part in the Michigan Senatorial contest as conditions at the time will warrant.

Notwithstanding Gen. Alger's declaration that he will not make a statement, it is said by those who have talked with him to-day that his temper is none of the best, that he is smarting from the sense of being permitted to be the victim of a system that he was unable to run or reform, and that when he is fully released from the constraints that now hold him he will unload a confession that will be in the nature of an accusation

A BUZZ OF COMMENT.

The news of the resignation caused a buzz of comment this evening in all public places, but at the White House there was no evidence throughout the evening that any unusual event had occurred. The President went for a drive with his niece, Miss Duncan, late in the afternoon, handling the reins himself. There were no callers of importance during the early part of the evening, but about 9 o'clock Secretary Hay, accompanied by Senator Fairbanks of Indiana, who is just back from an inspection of the Alaska boundary seat of difficulty, came over for a talk on this subject.

Secretary Hitchcock and Controller Dawes called socially for a few minutes. There was no evidence of a Cabinet conference and no suggestion of anything in that line. There was nothing to give out for publication, it was said. An evening round of the Cabinet officers still in town showed the same unwillingness to talk of the resignation. Some of them said that they had felt that the resignation was likely to come at any time, but they were so surprised at the published announcement that it was actually in hand that they were at first inclined to regard it as premature.

Adjt. Gen. Corbin was seen during the evening, and while not wishing to discuss any of the facts connected with the resignation expressed his personal regret at the turn of affairs. He said:

"I feel great sympathy and great respect for the Secretary. History will show that if he has erred it has been on the side of the soldier, on the side of those who were fighting the battles. No man in that position has ever had more at heart the interests of the soldiers, their comfort, and, their welfare. Time and again he has said to us that everything must yield before the requirements of the men in the field, and if the funds were lacking he would pay for it himself. He will leave the department with the respect and esteem of every one in it."

Secretary Alger's departure from the Cabinet will leave in it only three of those members who entered it at the beginning of the Administration, namely, Messrs. Gage, Long, and Wilson. The number of changes that have occurred in the two and a half years of its life has been very unusual.

Six Cabinet officers in all have resigned their portfolios, either to retire to private life or to accept other positions of honor and trust at the hands of the President. These include Secretaries of State Sherman, who went out because of ill-health and advanced age, and Day, who accepted a United States Judgeship; Attorney General McKenna, who accepted a position on the Supreme Court bench of the United States; Postmaster General Gary, who retired because of ill-health, and Secretary Bliss of the Interior Department, who returned to New York and resumed active connection with business affairs.

July 20, 1899

GEN. MILES'S STATUS NOW.

He Has Been Practically Restored to the Command of the Army.

Special to The New York Times.

WASHINGTON, Aug. 11.—The rehabilitation of Gen. Miles is practically complete. Nothing has been apparently said or done to change the conditions of semi-warfare which existed at Army Headquarters during Secretary Alger's régime; there has been no blare of trumpets and no public reinstallation of the commanding officer of the army, but he has simply assumed his proper place as commander, and his position as such is recognized. That the restoration has taken place is proved by the desire to see him of persons who have propositions to lay before the War Department. It has been many months since any one who had any suggestions to make thought it worth while to consult the Major General in command.

Another significant incident was the discussion over Secretary Alger's order taking the Inspector General's office away from Gen. Miles's jurisdiction. The chief argument advanced to Secretary Root for the amendment of that order was that it was necessary to have reports relating to the condition of the army pass through the Commanding General's office, so that he could be officially informed of it and be prepared to perform his duties intelligently. A month ago Gen. Miles had no duties to perform, and it was not necessary for him to have any such information. Now it is regarded as a matter of course that he should be placed in possession of it.

August 12, 1899

DEMOCRATS ATTACK FALL ON OIL LEASES AS A NEW BALLINGER

National Committee Calls Teapot Dome a Parallel to Scandal in Taft Administration.

DENBY ALSO IS ASSAILED

'Sluice Gates Were Apparently Opened' Under Two Secretaries, 'Says Statement.

FRAUD INQUIRY TALKED OF

Investigating Senators Reported to Want It—Administration Exercised Over Developments.

Special to The New York Times.

WASHINGTON, Jan. 20.—Characterizing the recent leasing of naval oil reserves as another Ballinger scandal, the Democratic National Committee issued today a statement in which the activities of Albert B. Fall, former Secretary of the Interior, and Secretary Denby of the Navy Department were bitterly attacked as an exploitation of the Government.

Some members of the Senate Committee on Public Lands, which has been investigating the oil leases for six months, are reported to be convinced that fraud existed in some respects in connection with the transfer. An inquiry into this phase of the matter seems likely to follow the movement which starts in the Senate tomorrow to cancel the lease of the Teapot Dome reserve to Harry F. Sinclair and that of the naval reserve in California to the Doheny group.

According to some of the investigators, the whole affair seems likely to develop into one of the greatest Government scandals in recent years. Administration officials are reported to be much concerned over developments in connection with the oil reserve leases.

Secret Connivance Charged.

The statement issued for the Democratic National Committee said:

"The Teapot Dome scandal has its direct parallel in the Ballinger scandal, which shook the Taft Administration to its very foundation. In the Ballinger case the Morgan and Guggenheim interests were stopped short of making billions of dollars in exploiting Alaska's resources, by the employment of pitiless publicity as a weapon of attack.

"In the Teapot Dome and other kindred cases, occurring under the present Administration, the Sinclair-Doheny-Standard Oil group was fortunate enough to get in its wizard work before the spotlight of publicity was turned in its direction. In secret connivance with amiable and exceedingly generous administrative officials in charge of the public domain, Mr. Harry F. Sinclair apparently has succeeded in depriving the nation of the sum total of its naval oil reserves and in thriftily lining his own pockets with something like $106,000,000.

"This, according to his own testimony before the Congressional investigation committee, was the sum paid to him for the stock of the Mammouth Oil Company, organized to take over the Government oil property, which Albert B. Fall, public servant, surrendered to him, and for which the citizen-owners will receive, in the long run, only about 1,600,000 barrels of oil out of an estimated total of 26,000,000 which the Teapot Dome is now said to hold; the ownership of some surface oil storage tanks scattered along the coasts, for the building of which they are to be called upon to pay to these companies large royalties of oil; and, in case of emergency or threatened danger to the country demanding large use of oil, the doubtful privilege of buying back from the Sinclair interests, at their own prices, oil that should by right belong to them now."

The review tells of the efforts of Presidents Roosevelt, Taft and Wilson to conserve the oil supply, and how their efforts to prevent exploitation of public lands were set aside in the Harding Administration under Secretary Fall.

"From the minute Senator Albert Bacon Fall took office as Secretary of the Interior and Edwin Denby was made Secretary of the Navy the sluice gates were apparently opened to unrestrained exploitation of the nation's resources by private interests," the review continues.

Refers to Fall and Alaska.

Continuing, it speaks of unsuccessful efforts by Secretary Fall to take over control of the Forest Service and "then throw open Alaska for exploitation of the pulp and wood forests." This fight precipitated a breach between himself and the Department of Agriculture and friends of the conservation such as Gifford Pinchot, the statement declares.

"When Secretary Fall went into office," it continues, "the United States was the proud possessor of five oil reserves acquired by the Government during the Taft and Wilson Administrations—Reserves 1 and 2 in California; Reserve 3 (Teapot Dome) in Wyoming, and Reserves 4 and 5 in Utah, made up of what is called 'Shale' oil deposits, which have not yet been fully or satisfactorily developed.

"When Secretary Fall went out of office, Reserve 1 in California, had been turned over bodily to the Doheney oil interests, this company being allowed to extend their operations until today they are said to hold, through the unexampled generosity of the Interior Department, combined with the amazing acquiescence of the Navy Department, a lease which authorizes them to drill wells and drain out oil on tracts covering a large part of the whole reserve. Reserve 2, also in California, had been obligingly parceled out between the Southern Pacific Railroad and the Honolulu Oil Company, and reserves in Utah had been, in part, leased to other enterprising oil companies.

"This, with the later giving away of the Teapot Dome reserve in Wyoming, practically wiped out the oil supply of the United States Navy.

"Secretary Denby testified that he had approved the transfer of the leasing powers of the navy to the Department of the Interior, and declared that when he had heard the reserves were being depleted by neighboring oil wells he had reached the conclusion they should be leased and believed the Interior Department better fitted to handle the oil supply than the Navy Department. He admitted, however, referring the matter to other navy officials, and acknowledged under questioning that he did not know whether the President had the right to divest the Navy Department of the leasing authority conferred on it by Congress and that many naval officers had protested against the transfer."

Summarizes Results of Hearing.

The Democratic statement reviewed the developments in the hearing before the Senate committee, but was prepared too early to include a reference to Senator Fall's testimony that he had obtained a $100,000 loan from E. B. McLean, the Washington publisher, which Mr. McLean later denied, saying that Mr. Fall had returned his checks to him with the statement that he (Fall) had obtained the loan from another source. The statement's summary of what was developed in the hearing follows:

"That, notwithstanding the purpose of Congress to exclude the Interior Department from any control over the Naval Reserves except to the limited extent already existing, the entire administration of the reserves was by an executive order dated May 31, 1921, turned over to that department.

"That, armed with this new authority, Secretary of the Interior Fall had negotiated and put through this colossal oil deal in secret, without advertising for competitive bids, and with the question at least an open one whether he had any legal right to sign such a lease.

"That the amount of drainage made the excuse for leasing Teapot Dome, as asserted by the experts of the Geological Survey, was inconsequential.

"That the lease disposing of the Teapot Dome reserves was executed on April 7, 1922, but that it probably did not receive the signature of Secretary Denby until about April 12; that The Wall Street Journal carried a notice of the lease in its issue of April 14, but that official admission was not made of the deal until April 21, when simultaneous announcements, in identical language, were made by the Navy and Interior Departments in response to letters from Senator Kendrick demanding such information.

"That Secretary Denby concurred in this apparently illegal disposition of the naval oil reserves, and signed important papers involved in the transaction without even knowing what they contained, his strange excuse being that these papers were "too technical.'

"That the Secretary of the Navy also failed to consult the opinions of his own staff officers and experts in regard to the transfer of the oil reserves to the Interior Department; that he had taken neither the General Board of the Navy nor the council of bureau chiefs into his confidence in this matter; and that upon examination by the committee he was unable to give the name of any officer who had expressed approbation of his course.

"That, owing to the rocky formation of the Wyoming soil, no serious damage to the Teapot Dome holding had been or was ever likely to be done; and that the alleged drainage in this field, pleaded by Mr. Fall as an excuse for turning over this vast property to the oil interests, had all been caused—if caused at all—by the deliberate digging of wells on adjacent properties by the very interests to whom Fall himself had leased this property.

Calls Sinclair the Chief Beneficiary.

"That the chief beneficiary of the deal was Harry F. Sinclair.

"That the chief loser in the deal was the United States Government, which, according to expert calculations made before the committee, will get out of the whole reserve only about five million barrels of oil (out of a calculated total of about 26,000,000 barrels), two-thirds of this to be turned back in royalties to the Sinclair interests in payment for construction of surface storage tanks—leaving the total amount of Government-owned oil in storage of about 1,666,000 barrels. Even with the estimated losses by leakage, 22,000,000 barrels would have remained to the United States if this lease had not been executed. The question presented is whether 22,000,000 barrels of Government-owned oil safe in the ground is to be preferred to 1,666,000 barrels in surface tanks at the seaboard.

"That, following the Teapot Dome exposure and Mr. Fall's resignation from the Cabinet, the former Secretary accepted employment with the Sinclair interests, journeyed to London on an oil mission for Sinclair, meeting him there and going with him to Russia on a trip of several months' duration in connection with the latter's Russian oil deals; and that Mr. Fall claimed on the witness stand that he could see no impropriety in such action.

"That Mr. Fall, though seemingly in financial difficulties in 1920, and with unpaid taxes on his Western lands dating back eight years, was, following the Teapot Dome lease, in sufficiently affluent circumstances to meet his tax obligations, to add materially to his ranch acreage and to finance extensive improvements on those lands already in his possession.

"That Mr. Sinclair, a few weeks after the oil deal, shipped to Secretary Fall at his New Mexican ranch blooded cattle from his New Jersey farms, and that Mr. Fall's payment for the cattle had been $5 less than the freight which had been paid by Sinclair for the shipment.

"That every naval officer specially detailed to investigate conditions on the oil reserves who had become practically well informed on this subject, or who supported former Secretary of the Navy Daniels to conserve the oil fields for use of the navy, had, after Mr. Fall began his campaign to get possession of the navy's oil supply, been either ordered to sea or for duty in some foreign country, it being openly charged that these changes in personnel detail had been adopted by the Interior Department in administering the affairs of the naval reserves.

"Commander H. A. Stuart, in charge of the naval reserves of the Navy Department from 1918 until April 5, 1921, testified before the committee that Secretary Fall insisted that Secretary Denby should detach him and Commander Shafroth, who was also connected with the naval reserves, and send them out of Washington, the demand being made, it was explained, after these two officers had presented to Mr. Fall their objection to the granting of certain leases to one of the big oil companies."

January 21, 1924

COOLIDGE DEFIES SENATE ON DENBY; IGNORES CALL FOR HIS RESIGNATION; WILL ACT ONLY ON COUNSEL'S REPORT

COOLIDGE STANDS ON RIGHTS

Power to Dismiss, Except By Impeachment, Rests With Him, He Says.

INSISTS ON THE FULL FACTS

He Will Then, He Declares, Ask for Any Resignations That the Evidence Warrants.

REASSURES THE PUBLIC

People's Interests Will Be Safeguarded and All Wrongdoing Punished, He Asserts.

Special to The New York Times.

WASHINGTON, Feb. 11.—President Coolidge defied the United States Senate tonight, issuing a statement in which he declined to act upon the resolution of the Senate passed late this afternoon by a vote of 47 to 34, requesting him to call for the resignation of Secretary Denby.

In his statement issued four hours after the Robinson resolution was received at the White House from a special Senate messenger, the President issued his statement declining to take official recognition of the action of the Senate.

The President declared that he would call for the resignation of any official when such action is warranted, and that he did not propose to sacrifice "any innocent man for my own welfare, nor do I propose to retain in office any unfit man for my own welfare."

Mr. Coolidge's statement included a defense of his stand, quoting from President Madison and President Cleveland on the necessity of the Executive maintaining his rights inviolate and of the three branches of the Government—executive, legislative and judicial—being kept separate and distinct.

The statement concluded by reassuring the people that he would act as the facts warrant, and that he would safeguard the public interest and punish any wrongdoing.

Leaves Responsibility to Coolidge.

Senator Robinson, Democrat l ;der and author of the resolution which the Senate today adopted to the effect that "It is the sense of the United States Senate that the President of the United States immediately request the resignation" of Secretary Denby when he read Mr. Coolidge's statement said:

"The Senate having expressed emphatically its own advice in the matter the President can, of course, take such action as he sees fit. Nobody questions the President's power either to dismiss or retain Secretary Denby and the full responsibility is upon him."

Senator Pepper of Pennsylvania, who opposed the Robinson resolution, commenting on the President's decision, said:

"If the American theory of Government is to be maintained there must be a division of functions between the legislative, executive and judicial branches. If any branch invades the territory of another the invasion must be repelled with decisiveness and dignity. It is in this spirit that the President's statement is conceived and uttered. I feel sure that his stand will be approved by all right-thinking people."

Senator Walsh of Montana, who more than any other man in public life, has been responsible for bringing out the facts in connection with the oil leases said:

"It seems to me that the President appears to be relying on counsel to advise him what to do in the case of Secretary Denby. The counsel will rather advise the President whether the leases are valid or invalid. Whether they are or not, affects very slightly, if at all, the question as to whether Mr. Denby is or is not the right man for Secretary of the Navy, or whether the great public interests entrusted to that office are not placed in his hands. I apprehend counsel will scarcely venture to advise him on that question. And as to the legality of the leases, the President might reasonably act upon the unanimous opinion of both houses of Congress."

Senator W. Cabell Bruce, Democrat, of Maryland, who opposed the Robinson resolution, said:

"I think the President has taken the right position, and one that is sound legally and in every way. His action is such as I anticipated, and one that any President, who was properly advised and desired to maintain the dignity of his office, would assume.

"I voted against the resolution because I could not in conscience support it. Of course, I am glad that the President has made such a manly and courageous statement."

Senator Lenroot, Chairman of the Public Lands Committee investigating the oil leases, said:

"That is a very good statement of the President's. Of course, he is correct. It is exclusively an executive function."

Coolidge Confers With Weeks.

Over the noonday meal at the White House today President Coolidge and Secretary Weeks conferred about the Robinson resolution. Earlier in the day C. Bascom Slemp, the President's secretary, had gone to the War Department for a conference with Mr. Weeks, at which the luncheon engagement was made.

As the Secretary of War left the main entrance of the executive mansion he was surrounded by a group of newspaper men.

"Do you look for any developments this afternoon following the Senate's action on the Robinson resolution?" he was asked.

"No, I do not," he replied.

"Then do you look for the present Cabinet to remain intact?"

"In my opinion, yes."

"Even in event of passage of the Robinson resolution?"

"The only function the Senate has in connection with Cabinet officers is to confirm their nominations. I cannot see what difference any action by the Senate would make."

Mr. Weeks then was questioned as to whether he thought Mr. Denby's position was somewhat untenable because he has defended publicly the making of the oil leases as legal and stated he "would do it over again" if necessary, whereas against this the President had appointed special counsel to prosecute the leases in court. This viewpoint previously had been expressed in another official quarter.

"Do you think these two facts make necessary a decision as to which is the official Administration attitude?" he was asked.

"No," he replied. "In my opinion that is a matter for the courts to decide, not the Administration."

The War Secretary explained he believed that President Coolidge was not necessarily expressing an opinion when he appointed special counsel, but had taken this step rather that the courts might finally settle the controversy.

Mr. Weeks is admitted to be very close to Mr. Coolidge politically, and his opinions on a matter of such major political importance are believed to add great weight to the White House decision.

Furthermore Mr. Weeks and Mr. Denby had a long conference on Saturday, following which Mr. Weeks talked with the President.

Hubert Work, Secretary of the Interior, also had a long conference with Mr. Weeks today.

One of the campaign managers for Mr. Coolidge, however, said earlier in the day that Mr. Denby would have to get out because of his defense of the leases. With Mr. Denby remaining in the Cabinet, it was said, his defense would be construed as the Administration's attitude, and the President had repudiated that through his appointment of Mr. Strawn and Mr. Pomerene as special prosecutors.

February 12, 1924

ADMITS HARDING NAMEDSOME UNWORTHY

Senator Pepper Declares Party Must Accept Responsibility for These Errors.

Special to The New York Times.

PHILADELPHIA, March 1.—The Republican Party, in the opinion of Senator George Wharton Pepper, must accept responsibility for a "fruitage of unworthiness," resulting from the fact that "some unworthy men" passed the scrutiny of former President Warren G. Harding.

Speaking at a testimonial given to him and Senator David A. Reed tonight, Senator Pepper amazed his audience by his frank discussion of what he described as "the faults of Mr. Harding's virtues." He said:

"President Harding, as adequately interpreted by Secretary Hughes, was the embodiment of love for his fellowmen. His temperament was what the country needed at a time when the world was filled with bitterness.

"But love of mankind, like other virtues, has certain corresponding dangers—the faults of a virtue—and it came to pass that some unworthy men passed his scrutiny, whom a more penetrating and impersonal executive would have detected and there is a fruitage of unworthiness of which the party must accept responsibility."

Senator Reed caustically criticized the spirit which prevails in the Senate, which, he asserted, was less dependable at the moment than the House and less likely to give constructive consideration to any problem.

"The thing we are confronted with at Washington," Senator Pepper said, "is the problem of trying to find out what is the right and square thing to do. We see before us the faults of taking people at their face value too readily, and whenever you have that kind of a situation it is easy for men to pass the sentinel, set there as the appointing power, and then men who are unworthy get into office."

Of Mr. Fall he said:

"We see the spectacle of a Secretary of the Interior who yielded to a temptation which none of us can estimate. He must be regarded as a betrayer of his party and his chief."

March 2, 1924

SEES LOSS OF WORLD FAITH.

CLEVELAND, March 8.—The world is in its worst situation in several hundred years, Newton D. Baker, former Secretary of War, said, in an address made here yesterday.

Loss in confidence in Government and public officials, following disclosures in the Teapot Dome leases was a reflex of the loss of faith throughout the world, he declared.

The Veterans' Bureau investigation was necessary, but that of the Bok peace plan was an evidence of inflammation, he said.

"Recently I have had occasion to travel and talk to all sorts of people," he continued, "and I have not found any one generous enough to concede there may be one honest man in Washington."

March 9, 1924

DAUGHERTY IS OUSTED BY COOLIDGE; TURNS ON PRESIDENT AND ACCUSERS; INQUIRY ON MELLON IS ASKED IN SENATE

PRESIDENT TAKES ACTION

Tells Attorney General He Embarrasses the Administration.

AT ODDS ON SECRET FILES

Coolidge Could Not Agree to Refusal to Give Them to the Senate Committee.

DAUGHERTY DEFIES FOES

Declares 'Cowardice' and 'Surrender of Principle' Should Not Dictate Expediency.

Special to The New York Times.

WASHINGTON, March 28.—Harry M. Daugherty, storm centre of the Harding and the Coolidge Administrations, resigned to-day as Attorney General at the request of President Coolidge.

Mr. Daugherty's resignation, which became effective at once and makes the second Cabinet casualty resulting from the oil scandal and the flood of charges following in its wake, was handed in only after the President formally demanded it, declaring that Mr. Daugherty could not give disinterested attention to his duties while at the same time combating the accusations made before the Senate investigating committee. Mr. Coolidge pointed specifically to the matter of turning over the confidential files of the Department of Justice to the committee, and declared that his continuance in office must of necessity be a source of "ever-increasing embarrassment."

Mr. Daugherty formally resigned in a letter of three terse sentences, asserting that he was doing so "solely out of deference to your request," but followed this up with an open letter to the President in his best fighting manner, denouncing his Senatorial accusers and declaring that "cowardice" and "surrender of principle" should never be allowed to dictate "party expediency." He brushed aside the reasons advanced by the President as "hardly warranted by the facts," and warned of the danger of "government by slander, by terrorism and by fear."

On making this letter public Mr. Daugherty boarded a train at Washington as a "private citizen" and left for Atlantic City.

William J. Burns, Chief of the Bureau of Investigation, is expected to resign upon the appointment of a new Attorney General, and other important changes in the Department of Justice, which has not been functioning well in the last few months, will follow the induction into office of Mr. Daugherty's successor.

Harlan Fiske Stone, who recently resigned as Dean of the Columbia Law School, and Arthur Prentice Rugg, Chief Justice of the Supreme Court of Massachusetts, are known to be under serious consideration by the President for the new Cabinet vacancy. Charles E. Hughes, Secretary of State, is mentioned in the gossip as also under consideration along with Senator Borah and Senator Pepper, Judge William S. Kenyon, Governor Baxter of Maine and Governor Grosbeck of Michigan.

It is declared, however, in informed circles, that the selection rests between Mr. Stone and Judge Rugg.

Solicitor General James M. Beck is now Acting Attorney General.

Mr. Daugherty is a candidate for Coolidge delegate at large in the Ohio primaries April 29. The placing of Mr. Daugherty's name on the ticket was approved by the President himself on Feb. 23 while the storm clouds were gathering about the head of the Attorney General, and there is some speculation in Washington tonight as to whether Mr. Daugherty will go before the Ohio electors as a Coolidge delegate at large.

President Coolidge decided definitely yesterday to force Attorney General Daugherty out of office, although he had indicated his attitude on the previous day when he declined to approve Mr. Daugherty's course in refusing the Department of Justice files to the Senate Investigating Committee. President Coolidge's letter was sent to Mr. Daugherty before noon yesterday and Mr. Daugherty left his office then to consult with his friends. The White House expected to receive Mr. Daugherty's resignation last night.

The resignation came just before 10 o'clock this morning and was delivered to the White House by Warren F. Martin, Assistant to Mr. Daugherty. Within ten minutes after its arrival the White House made public President Coolidge's request and Attorney General Daugherty's compliance therewith.

President Coolidge had steadfastly declined to be forced into hasty action in the case of Mr. Daugherty. Within a few days after Edwin Denby resigned as Secretary of the Navy as the result of Senate attacks, the demand became insistent for the retirement of Mr. Daugherty. This demand came not only from Democrats, but also came strongly from leading Republican Senators.

Late in last month Senator Lodge and Senator Pepper, acting for the conservative wing of the Republican Party, conferred with the President and urged that he ask Mr. Daugherty to retire. This the President declined to do, although he made it very clear in talks with Mr. Daugherty that he desired to have his resignation.

Mr. Coolidge then summoned Senator Borah and told him he wanted suggestions for a successor to Mr. Daugherty. Senator Borah, at that time, on the last Sunday in February, in the presence of Mr. Daugherty, presented reasons to the President why Mr. Daugherty should resign.

Inside information following this conference was that Mr. Daugherty would resign within forty-eight hours or be forced out of office. But when the forty-eight hours expired Mr. Daugherty issued a defiant statement in which he said, "It is not my purpose to even consider tendering my resignation as Attorney General until a fair hearing on charges preferred against me." This ultimatum was delivered to the President by Mr. Daugherty on the afternoon of Feb. 27, after which the Attorney General left the city, going to Chicago and later to Florida to visit his sick wife.

Senator Wheeler's resolution to investigate the Attorney General was held up for several days during these conferences in the hope that Mr. Daugherty would resign and make unnecessary the inquiry. It is understood that Senator Wheeler so informed Senator Borah and others who conferred with the President and that the President had been so informed.

After the Republican Senators failed to get Mr. Daugherty's resignation by political arguments and personal persuasion, the Wheeler resolution was passed and within a few days after that, early in March, the investigation began. This brought out sensational ex parte accusations which led to the door of Mr. Daugherty, but did not involve him personally in wrongdoing. In the past four weeks the Administration point of view has been that Mr. Daugherty should have his opportunity of replying to his assailants and that the President would not disturb him until this investigation had ended.

The assurance given to Mr. Daugherty by the President on Feb. 27 that he would not demand his resignation while the inquiry was in progress had to be broken because of the sudden development over the request for the Department of Justice files by the investigating committee. Mr. Daugherty refused these files and the President found it impossible to support him in such a course.

* * * * *

March 29, 1924

BORAH PUTS BLAME FOR FEDERAL EVILS ON CAMPAIGN GIFTS

Declares Corruption Will Exist So Long as Parties Accept Vast Contributions.

BUT SEES BRIGHT FUTURE

Americans Are Sound, Senator Says, and Will Cleanse Their Own Government.

UPHOLDS THE DEMOCRATS

Not Exposure of Wrongdoing, but Agreement to Conceal It, the Greatest Danger.

Special to The New York Times.

WASHINGTON, April 6.—What **appears** to be the first attempt of any **notable** public man to appraise the testimony given to committees of the Senate engaged in investigation into alleged corruption in the Government service was made this afternoon in an address by Senator Borah of Idaho before the College Men's Law Enforcement League in Calvary Baptist Church. He did not mince words in referring to the situation, which he regarded as deplorable, but at the same time there was a note of optimism for the future throughout his address. In his opinion the American people are sound, and he expressed confidence in the soundness of the American Government, and looked to its citizens to purge it of "the slinking, secret, sordid enemy which has been at work in our midst."

Seeking to find a reason for conditions revealed by the Congressional committees of inquiry, Senator Borah attributed these conditions in part to the practice of political parties—and he blamed both Republicans and Democrats— in accepting campaign contributions from commercial interests in these days, when "the Government deals with all the vast concerns of business—coal, ships, oil, tariffs." He instanced one person with large business interests giving $50,000 to the Democratic Party and $75,000 to the Republican Party.

"Both political parties," said Mr. Borah, "have for years placed themselves in an indefensible position in these matters. It all leads to that sinister and subtle influence which does more to break down representative government than any specific instance or open bribe."

Still lower down in the foundation of **present** unsatisfactory conditions, Mr. Borah found the heritage of war, with its "wastes and extravagance, and then corruption." The "exchange of honor and place for gain" was one of war's inevitable consequences, he held.

The efforts of men to gain control of Government through contributions to party campaign funds fitted into this state of affairs, according to Senator Borah's argument, and he expressed the belief that "so long as the present system and standards prevail in American politics, regardless of party, you will have conditions no less deplorable than those which now confront us."

Mr. Borah made known that he was not of those who complained of the part played by the Democrats in the current investigations. It was one of the advantages of party government, he said, that one political party vigilantly watched and criticized the other. The danger arose, he asserted, out of a tacit truce between the great political parties that each would not criticize or expose evil practices. That, he asserted, was exactly what happened with reference to campaign contributions through both parties accepting and pursuing the practice.

In the view of Senator Borah, the revelations should not be accepted "as an impeachment either of our form of Government or of the capacity of the people to rule, but rather as a call to duty to preserve and hand on to posterity that inheritance which our forbears gave into our keeping." He expressed confidence that the people would turn "the agony" of the present situation "into the glory of a truly great and self-governing people."

The conditions which have prevailed here at the capital during the last few months," said Senator Borah, "have caused many people to wonder and to ask if a Government lige ours can stand against corruption, against the evil use of money in public affairs. We must not, of course, underestimate the significance of these revelations, but neither should we underestimate the intelligence, the character and the loyalty of our people.

"I recognize that venality in public place is the most subtle, the most elusive and one of the most deadly foes with which a people who seek to govern themselves have to contend. But I also recognize — I think I know — that the American people, when aroused, when warned, have both the capacity and the courage to purge the nation of the slinking, secret, sordid enemy which has been at work in our midst.

"Can and Will Cleanse Government."

"We should not for a moment lose faith in the ability of the people to govern. They can, and they will, cleanse their Government. They can, and they will, vindicate the faith of the fathers and justify the principles of government upon which they built.

"These revelations must not be accepted as an impeachment either of our form of government or of the capacity of the people to rule, but rather as a call to duty to preserve and hand on to posterity that inheritance which our forbears gave into our keeping. Through constitutional and lawful means, with due regard for orderly methods under a government of law, but in searching and remorseless fashion, let us make the hour of reckoning a memorable one. The days through which we are passing are the agony, but they may also be made the glory of a truly great and self-governing people.

"War brings waste and extravagance, and then corruption. One of its slippery, slimy spawn is corruption in public office—the exchange of honor and peace for gain, the heritage of a good name, the esteeem of your fellow-men, the future happiness and success of your own children—all bartered and sold for gold. This is one of the inevitable fruits of war. It has been so from Pericles to this hour.

"But the people of this country are sound, nevertheless. The Government, as a Government, is not corrupt. There are honest and faithful public servants and loyal and patriotic constituents. There are men and women, thousands and millions of them, just as willing to sacrifice for the honor of their country and just as capable of serving the cause of clean government as were their forbears. We do not doubt that at all.

"Instead of doubt and discouragement, instead of talking about Government breaking down and institutions caving in because some men have betrayed their trust, let's put our faith in that reserve of character, that sturdy, faithful, incorruptible and unpurchasable manhood and womanhood found throughout this land in every precinct, village and town, and, relying upon that incalculable force, let us face the future with faith and courage.

Holds American Honor Untouched.

"War has taken thousands of our youth, it has put a great burden upon us, it has left its fetid slime here and there upon the public service, but it has not corrupte and shall not corrupt American honor. That is in the keeping of the American people and they will safely guard it and preserve it. The revelations have uncovered rottenness, but they have also uncovered the high purpose and the incorruptible patriotism of 110,000,000 people.

"I do not underestimate, I trust, the potency of our great wealth as a nation, our vast areas, our undeveloped natural riches; I know the part they play in giving us prestige and power and permanency; but I know, as we all know, that in the last analysis it is not these upon which we rely for the success and preservation of our Government and our institutions, but upon the character of the people, and that is untainted.

"You young men need only lead the way; the people will support you. Cut your way through the labyrinth waste of extravagance and rottenness, fight back to an economic and clean Government, and the people will support you and honor you. It is a task worthy of your youth and your energy, your capacity and your courage.

"But the demoralization consequent upon the war does not tell the whole story. I venture to believe that so long as the present system and standards prevail in American politics, regardless of party, you will have conditions no less deplorable than those which now confront us.

"The country was shocked to learn that a very large sum of money was given to a high official by a party having business with the Government. Well, what have we to say about an individual having business, or expecting to have business, with the Government giving a very large sum of money to the political party which is in control, or is seeking control, of the entire machinery of the Government? And this is a practice which prevails in this country, not as to one party but as to all political parties.

Buying Influence Accepted Practice.

"These stupendous sums contributed to a political party do not simply measure the individual's patriotic interest in his party. Such large sums are asked for or given because of a desire to go beyond the ordinary interests of the individual in his party. You can buy influence with a political party quite as effectively as you can an individual. In the latter instance it is still denounced, in the former instance it has become an accepted practice.

"It appears, for instance, that one individual gave $50,000 to the Democratic Party and another $75,000 to the Republican Party, and both were expecting to do business with the Government. Now, these gentlemen do not stand alone. They did not initiate that kind of practice. They were doing what has become an accepted practice and system in this country. So long as political parties seeking power or control of the Government accept vast contributions from those who are interested in matters of legislation or administration, you will have sinister and corrupt and controlled Government.

"In these days the Government deals with all the vast concerns of business, coal, railroads, ships, oil, tariffs, and it is simply intolerable that political parties accept vast contributions from those vitally interested in these matters. It is still morse for the parties to go out and solicit contributions from such individuals. For, I repeat, these unusual sums are not given merely because of the common interest which partisans have in their parties.

"Both political parties have for years placed themselves in an indefensible position in these matters. It all leads to that sinister and subtle influence which does more to break down representative government than any specific instance or open bribe. Besides, the open bribe follows inevitably as a result of the former practice.

"I am not one of those who complain of the Democrats because of anything they have contributed to the revelations which have been brought about. It is one of the advantages of party government that one political party vigilantly watches and criticizes the other. I hope that will always be so. The conditions would soon be intolerable in this country if it were not so. The danger arises not out of criticism and exposure, but out of a tacit truce between the great parties that they will not criticize or expose the evil practices.

"That is exactly what has happened with reference to campaign contributions. Both parties accept the system and pursue the practice. So long as they do this, these specific instances of exposure may help to put one party in and the other party out, but the cause of clean government, of disinterested and wise legislation and uncontrolled administration will not be greatly served. The people are greatly interested, naturally, in any individual dereliction of public duty, but they are far more interested in having a government at Washington, regardless of which party is in power, uncontrolled and uninfluenced by sinister and selfish interests."

April 7, 1924

SENATE, 40 TO 30, CONDEMNS LEASING OF NAVY OIL FIELDS

Adopts the Majority Report, Written by Walsh, Scoring Fall, Doheny and Sinclair.

SPENCER DEFENDS THEM

Administration Senators Back His Minority Report, but Are Defeated, 42 to 28.

DEMOCRATIC IRE IS ROUSED

Reed Denounces His Missouri Colleague as Seeing No Wrong and Defending Every Infamy.

Special to The New York Times.

WASHINGTON, Jan. 20.—By a vote of 40 to 30 the Senate this afternoon disposed of the Teapot Dome scandal, so far as the Senate's investigation of it is concerned, by adopting the majority report of the Senate investigating committee, scoring the granting of leases of the naval oil reserve lands to E. L. Doheny and Harry F. Sinclair. Prior to taking that action the Senate rejected, by a vote of 42 to 28, the minority report, signed by five Republican members, which defended the granting of the oil lease.

No Democrat voted for the minority report. A few Republicans and others classified politically as Republicans who supported Senator La Follette in last year's election joined in defeating the minority report and adopting the majority report. Senator La Follette himself was absent.

Walsh Wrote Majority Report.

The reports were presented by the Committee on Public Lands and Surveys which conducted the oil lease investigation. Senator Walsh, Democrat, of Montana, "chief prosecutor" of the committee, wrote the majority report, which is mainly a review of the testimony taken by the committee, with condemnatory references to Albert B. Fall's part in the leasing arrangements and criticism of the secret manner in which the leases were awarded and of the policy involved in leasing Government oil reserves to private interests. The majority promises to make recommendations for legislation affecting naval oil lands as soon as the courts have finished with the Sinclair and Doheny cases.

A feature of the debate which preceded the adoption of the majority report was the severe criticism of Senator Spencer, Republican, of Missouri, who was sponsor for the minority report, signed by him and four other Republican members of the investigating committee, Senators Smoot of Utah, Stanfield of Oregon, Cameron of Arizona and Bursum of New Mexico. Mr. Spencer was attacked in a satirical speech by his colleague from Missouri, Senator Reed, who found sympathetic assistance from other Democrats in the brief comments they contributed.

Senator Walsh characterized the Spencer report as a "tissue of half truths," and Senator Reed declared of Senator Spencer that "with unblushing countenance he can defend any infamy."

The Votes on the Reports.

The record vote by which the Spencer report was rejected follows:

FOR THE MINORITY REPORT—28.

Republicans—28.

Bingham, Gooding, Phipps,
Bursum, Hale, Smoot,
Butler, Jones (Wash.) Spencer,
Cameron, Keyes, Sterling,
Capper, McKinley, Wadsworth,
Cummins, McLean, Warren,
Curtis, Means, Watson,
Ernst, Metcalf, Willis.
Fernald, Oddie,
Fess, Pepper.

Democrats—None.

AGAINST THE MINORITY REPORT—42.

Republicans—7.

Borah, Frazier, Norris.
Brookhart, Johnson (Cal)
Couzens, Norbeck,

Democrats—34.

Broussard, Harrison, Reed (Mo.),
Bruce, Heflin, Sheppard,
Caraway, Kendrick, Shields,
Copeland, King, Simmons,
Dial, McKellar, Smith,
Dill, Mayfield, Stanley,
Edwards, Neely, Swanson,
Ferris, Overman, Underwood,
Fletcher, Pittman, Walsh (Mass)
George, Ralston, Walsh (Mon.),
Glass, Ransdell, Wheeler.
Harris,

Farmer-Labor—1.

Shipstead.

The roll call on the adoption of the Walsh report follows:

FOR THE MAJORITY REPORT—40.

Republicans—6.

Borah, Frazier, Norbeck,
Brookhart, Johnson (Cal.) Norris.

Democrats—33.

Broussard, Harris, Ransdell,
Bruce, Harrison, Reed (Mo.),
Caraway, Heflin, Sheppard,
Copeland, Kendrick, Shields,
Dial, King, Simmons,
Dill, McKellar, Smith,
Edwards, Mayfield, Swanson,
Ferris, Neely, Underwood,
Fletcher, Overman, Walsh (Mass.)
George, Pittman, Walsh (Mont.)
Glass, Ralston, Wheeler.

Farmer-Labor—1.

Shipstead.

AGAINST THE MAJORITY REPORT—30.

Republicans—30.

Bingham, Fess, Oddie,
Bursum, Gooding, Pepper,
Butler, Hale, Phipps,
Cameron, Jones (Wash.) Smoot,
Capper, Keyes, Spencer,
Couzens, McCormick, Sterling,
Cummins, McKinley, Wadsworth,
Curtis, McLean, Warren,
Ernst, Means, Watson,
Fernald Metcalf, Willis.

Democrats—None.

When Senator Spencer, in addressing the Senate in behalf of the adoption of the minority report, contended that the leasing of Government oil fields to private interests was legal and predicted that the courts would so determine, and justified them on the ground that they would double the strength of the navy through providing reserve oil for storage at Pearl Harbor, Hawaii, he was questioned ironically by Senators Johnson of California and Caraway of Arkansas as to why he did not show consistency by demanding the withdrawal of prosecutions against those who had benefited by the leases.

"Absurd," said Caraway of the Spencer report.

"A cross-word puzzle," amended Walsh of Massachusetts.

"Don't slander the cross-word puzzle because some people think there is sense in them," remarked Caraway.

Reed Assails Spencer.

"I rise to congratulate the State of Missouri," said Senator Reed, "upon possessing a representative so amiable and innocent that, like the three Japanese apes, he sees no evil, he hears no evil and he speaks no evil, and consequently is duly qualified to defend all evil—an innocent abroad, in the intellectual and political world, who finds virtue in every act and with unblushing confidence can defend every infamy.

"That is a rare and unusual trait of character and parliamentary rules forbid me giving direct application.

"I recall, however, that when the country was startled by the story of Newberry's bribery and corruption, when a shiver of horror went over the land at the knowledge that an electorate had been bought and sold, and that the second highest office within the gift of the greatest people on earth—a position in the United States Senate—had been placed in substance and effect upon the auction block and knocked down to the highest bidder, the distinguished Senator from Missouri saw no evil, heard no evil, spoke no evil. But he rose in eulogy and defense of that man who afterward, with bowed and shamed face, resigned from the Senate to escape a further investigation."

Senator Reed said that in the case of former Attorney General Daugherty Senator Spencer had shown the innocence described by Shakespeare in his first stage of man, and had placed "a halo of virtue surrounding the head of that gentleman who afterward was compelled by the President to yield his resignation and to vanish from public life."

Again, said Senator Reed, Senator Spencer had assisted Mr. Daugherty by expressing "a legal doubt" as to whether the Senate could examine the bank records of moneys placed to the credit of the Attorney General in his brother's bank in Ohio.

Recalls Defense of Denby.

"I recall," continued Senator Reed, "how he stood then in the defense of Denby, seeing no evil, hearing no evil, thinking no evil, and yet I recall that Denby was forced from office and yielded his resignation.

"All this is of the past, but I never expected to see the day when in this Senate any man would arise in his place and endeavor by perfervid oratory to create a halo of patriotism and place it on the brow of Albert B. Fall and to give him that glorification in connection with the very transactions which took place coincident with, and are interlocked with, the payment to Fall of $100,000 as the price of his official soul.

"I read from the minority report: 'Secretaries Denby and Fall with equal patriotism—' "

"That is," explained Senator Reed, "patriotism equal to that of Mr. Daniels—with 'equal patriotism had a different conception of preparedness.'

"Again: 'Patriotically Denby and Fall sought to effect what would avoid the possibility of World War experiences.'

"Patriotically!" exclaimed Senator Reed. "Yet, interwoven with these contracts which are interlocked with each by time and circumstances, and were all part and parcel of the warp and web of this infamy that blackened the character of the republic, was the payment of a $100,000 bribe; and in the mystery that followed was the development of misuse by Government agents of secret telegraphic code of the Government; the obstruction of the processes of justice; the horrible flood of scandal which was finally developed into fact before a Senate committee; and even now as we sit here and deliberate we find that apparently the records of a Canadian corporation organized for the purpose of paying further moneys to Fall have disappeared and the officers and agents of that corporation are conveniently in Paris or hunting wild animals in Africa and unable to answer the subpoenas of this Government.

"Now, when the Government is engaged in a struggle to recover that of which it was defrauded, we find a Senator of the United States who voted for the prosecutions which charged fraud, fraud in the execution of these leases, fraud upon our Government through the corrupt hands of Fall, writing a eulogy of Fall's patriotism and declaring on the floor of the Senate, as he has in the last ten minutes, that he doubted the illegality or the corruption of the leases at the very time he voted to make these charges.

"Further comment is not necessary. The eloquence of Demosthenes could not, in words, paint a halo for the brow of Albert Fall that would not be so manifestly fraud itself that all the people of the United States could see through that halo the fraudulent hand of the man who sought to portary it."

Spencer Quotes the Bible.

"I want to make one statement," said Senator Spencer in reply. "Somewhere in the Good Book I think it is written that when a man speaketh first his cause seemeth to be just; then cometh his neighbor and searcheth it.' "

In rejoinder to that statement, Senator Reed likewise quoted the Bible, saying:

"The Senator is fond of the Scriptures, devoted to the Holy Writ, and let me say to him he reminds me of a passage as I consider him in connection with his minority criticisms: 'Deal gently, for my sake, with the young man Absalom.' "

"My distinguished colleague," said Senator Spencer, "has seen fit to make reflection about me. I want to read one sentence from the minority report. He speaks of my placing a halo upon the brow of Fall. This is from the report of the minority, which I wrote:

" 'The minority concur in full measure of criticism, which the majority indulged, upon the conduct of a Cabinet officer who is shown to have accepted a loan of $100,000 and certain other favors while in office.'

"That is my own language and, further:

" 'Such acts cannot be tolerated and are not to be condoned. If the claim that these favors were in the nature of bribes is sustained in the criminal proceedings already begun, punishment adequate and prompt will follow. Crime is individual and guilt is personal. Under the Constitution men are presumed to be innocent until proved guilty, but whether the participants be in fact guilty under the law, or innocent, the act itself is most reprehensible, causes national humiliation and cannot be overlooked.'

"That is the halo around the brow of Mr. Fall. I want to repeat all I said about Secretary Denby. No fairer, more patriotic, abler man has been in the Cabinet during my acquaintance with public life and I am glad to say everything I have said in praise of his patriotism, integrity and character."

Walsh Wants "Abler" Withdrawn.

Senator Walsh suggested that Senator Spencer withdraw the word "abler," but the Missouri Senator did not respond.

Senator Spencer said the reference to former Attorney General Daugherty by Senator Reed was "gratuitous, for there is no mention of Daugherty's name in the minority report from beginning to end."

In replying to Senator Spencer, Senator Reed pointed out that the minority referred to "the loan of money to Fall," but asked "who but a fool believes it was a loan?"

After the Biblical quotation "Deal gently, for my sake, with the young man Absalom," Senator Reed said of his colleague:

"Truly he has been gentle in reading the eulogy of Fall's patriotism and referring to the loan."

"Some day," concluded Senator Reed, "we will erect a monument to him that will be of the purest white marble and inscribed on it the legend of the culprits he has defended on the floor of the Senate, and we will proclaim the new doctrine, 'not that there is nothing new under the sun,' but 'there is nothing wrong under the sun.' "

January 21, 1925

TEAPOT DOME IS WON BACK; SUPREME COURT DENOUNCES SINCLAIR LEASE AS FRAUD

FALL CALLED FAITHLESS

Conspired to Beat Law and Naval Oil Policy, Says Bench.

HIS LIBERTY BONDS SINISTER

Continental Trading Company Is Assailed as 'Created for Illegitimate Purpose."

GOVERNMENT GETS TANKS

Only Congress Can Repay Sinclair the Millions He Spent on Property.

Special to The New York Times.

WASHINGTON, Oct. 10.—The Teapot Dome Naval Reserve oil fields of Wyoming were restored to the complete ownership and control of the United States Government today by a sweeping decision handed down by the Supreme Court, no members dissenting.

The Court also declared that when former Secretary of the Interior Albert B. Fall of Three Rivers, N. M., leased the Wyoming reserve to Harry F. Sinclair it was the culmination of a conspiracy between the former head of the Interior Department and the New York oil man, the purpose of which was "to circumvent the law and to defeat public policy."

The decision was written by Associate Justice Pierce Butler, and in the opinion of Government counsel is an even stronger expression than was the decision, also written by Justice Butler, which ruled that the Elk Hills (Cal.) transaction between Fall and Edward L. Doheny was tainted with fraud and ordered that property restored to the Government.

Government Wins All Points.

Every contention of the Government was upheld in today's decision. There was no comfort anywhere in the decision's more than 9,000 words for either Fall, Sinclair or their lawyers. As for Fall, the Court bluntly declared that the facts disclosed in the famous Continental Trading Company, Ltd., incidents were such as to confirm "the belief, generated by other circumstances in the case, that he was a faithless public officer."

"It is a wonderful decision," said Owen J. Roberts of Government counsel, talking over the telephone from Philadelphia to THE NEW YORK TIMES Bureau in Washington, "and it is even more sweeping than was the other splendid decision in the Elk Hills case. It is a great victory for the Government, and all that I care to say now is that the people of the United States, in view of these two decisions of their highest court, should be very happy this night."

Former Senator Atlee Pomerene of Ohio, Mr. Roberts's colleague in the prosecution of the oil cases, was just as emphatic. The two outstanding questions decided, said Mr. Pomerene, were, first, that the transaction was fraudulent in nature, and, secondly, that there was no authority in law for the making of the leases and contracts.

Neither Mr. Roberts nor Mr. Pomerene would say anything about the possible effect of the decision in the trial of the criminal conspiracy charge against Fall and Sinclair, which begins in the Criminal Branch of the Supreme Court of the District of Columbia at 10 o'clock next Monday morning.

Estimate Cost to Sinclair.

Just what the decision means in dollars to Mr. Sinclair and his associates is largely a matter of conjecture, the estimate of the navy being that the amount may be in the neighborhood of $10,000,000.

In the Elk Hills transaction, the losses to Doheny and his associates have been placed as high as $24,000,000. In the matter of the Elk Hills property, a recent survey has indicated, it is said, that there are more than 700,000,000 barrels of oil in the reserve. When it was transferred to Doheny the ground content was estimated at less than one-third of that amount and Doheny, before the Senate Committee, testified he expected to clear $100,000,000. It would appear in view of the latest r ports that had the deal been upheld b the courts the ultimate return would have been nearer three times that sum.

Today's decision puts an end to the civil phase of the oil lease transactions. These cases have traveled through six United States courts and in five instances the Government has been upheld. The one victory for the opposition was in the District Court of Wyoming, where Judge Blake Kennedy held that the Teapot Dome transaction was within the law and that the Continental Trading Company phase was not a controlling issue in determining the question of fraud.

That an effort will be made to get the fact of today's court decision before the jury before which Fall and Sinclair will be tried for conspiracy is considered fairly certain. It is just as certain that the defense lawyers will fight to the last ditch to keep out any reference to it by the prosecution.

Reimbursement Up to Congress.

Whether Sinclair or his associates will be reimbursed for the great fortune they have expended under the provisions of the Teapot Dome lease and the pipe line contract is a question, the court held today, which can be answered only by Congress. The Court ordered that the property be restored to the Government, and added that Sinclair must abide by the judgment of Congress "as to the use or removal of the improvements or other relief claimed by them."

The first part of the decision handed down by Justice Butler is a description of the property involved in the Fall-Sinclair transaction, including the proposed storage facilities, tankage and other items of expense incurred after control passed from the navy to the Mammoth Oil Company, which Sinclair organized to take over the oil fields and exploit them.

"So far as concerns the power under the act of June 4, 1920, to make them, the lease and agreement now before the Court cannot," said Justice Butler, "be distinguished from those held to have been made without authority of law in Pan-American Petroleum and Transport Company vs. the United States, and the United States is entitled to have them canceled."

Coming to the question as to whether the transaction was fraudulent in nature, the Court said the question to be answered was whether or not the evidence as disclosed proved the charge that the whole thing was a conspiracy, the purpose of which was to defraud the Government.

Finds Fall Keen to Control.

The decision said that, from the beginning, Fall was "keen to control the leasing of the naval petroleum reserves" and that he was "eager" to have the administration of the reserves given to him.

As for former Secretary of the Navy Denby, the Court took the position that the circumstances indicated that Denby "intended to be passive and let Fall dominate," and that instead of personally participating, he was largely represented at the various oil lease conferences by the then Rear Admiral, but now Captain, John K. Robison, U. S. N., retired, at the time Engineer-in-Chief of the navy and the chief supporter of the leasing policies advocated by Fall.

The decision gave a detailed recital of events from the time that Sinclair visited Three Rivers in Christmas week of 1921 up to the return of Fall to Washington in the latter part of January, 1922, when he sent for Sinclair and the late Colonel J. W. Zevely and had "Robison tell them what would be necessary in any proposal for a lease"; and Robison, it was pointed out, told them that the entire Teapot Dome reserve should be developed and a pipe line constructed.

Reference was made to a statement by Fall to a representative of a prospective bidder for the Teapot Dome that he was not ready to consider the leasing of the reserve. This was in March, 1922. On another occasion, on April 10, three days after the lease was signed, Fall, the Court pointed out, told another prospective bidder that he would entertain a bid and would "be glad to see a representative of the company at Three Rivers."

Assails Drainage Argument.

Commenting on the secrecy which marked the negotiations, Justice Butler said there never was any legitimate reason for secrecy.

As for the drainage argument advanced by Fall and by Sinclair as justification for leasing the reserve, the Court declared that the evidence warranted the finding that these expressions were made in bad faith to make it appear that there was a reason for the exhaustion of the reserve and the proposed disposition of its products; while Fall's failure to submit the lease to the Attorney General or to any lawyer in the Interior Department indicated, the Court declared, that Fall "knew the transaction was liable to be condemned as illegal, and that, without regard to the law, he intended to put it through."

Coming to the Continental Trading Company phase of the case, Justice Butler pointed out that "shortly after the making of the lease Fall received from a hidden source a large amount of Liberty bonds and that others were used for his benefit."

In some detail the career of the Continental Trading Company was traced up to May, 1923, when it was dissolved, and, to use the language of the Court, "all its records destroyed."

The departure from this country for Europe in January, 1924, of H. M. Blackmer of the Midwest Refining Company and James E. O'Neil of the Prairie Oil and Gas Company, and the absence from American jurisdiction of Colonel Robert W. Stewart of the Standard Oil Company of Indiana at the time of the trial of the case before the District Court in Cheyenne, Wyo., were cited by the Court.

Condemns Continental Company.

"The creation of the Continental Company, the purchase and resale of contracts," the decision continued, "enabling it to make more than $8,000,000 without capital, risk or effort, the assignment of the contract to the resale purchasers for a small fraction of its probable value, and the purpose to conceal the disposition of its assets make it plain that the company was created for some illegitimate purpose. And the clandestine and unexplained acquisition of these bonds by Fall confirms the belief, generated by other circumstances in the case, that he was a faithless public officer. There is nothing in the record that tends to mitigate the sinister significance attaching to that enrichment."

The Court decided that it required no discussion "to make it plain that the facts and circumstances above referred to require a finding that, pending the making of the lease and agreement, Fall and Sinclair, contrary to the Government's policy for the conservation of oil reserves for the navy and in disregard of law, conspired to procure for the Mammoth Compaany all the products of the reserve on the basis of exchange of royalty oil for construction work, fuel oil, &c.; that Fall so favored Sinclair in the making of the lease and agreement that it was not possible for him loyally or faithfully to serve the interests of the United States, or impartially to consider the applications of others for leases in the reserve, and that the leases and agreement were made fraudulently by means of collusion and conspiracy between them."

Says Lessee Has No Equity.

The tanks, pipe line and other improvements put upon the reserve for the purpose of taking away its products were not, the Court ruled, authorized by Congress.

"The lease and supplemental agreement," the decision concluded, "were fraudulently made to circumvent the law and to defeat public policy. No equity arises in favor of the lessee or the other petitioners to prevent or condition the granting of the relief directed by the Circuit Court of Appeals. Petitioners are bound to restore title and possession of the reserve to the United States, and must abide by the judgment of Congress as to the use or removal of the improvements, or other relief, claimed by them."

Navy Department's Plans.

The decision was described at the Navy Department as very similar in effect to that in the Pan-American case. The policy of the department in operating the reserve, according to Secretary Wilbur, will be the same as for Reserve No. 1 in California—namely, to conserve as much of the oil in the ground as possible. Detailed arrangements for administering the property are to be decided upon quickly.

The department estimated that loss to Mr. Sinclair growing out of the decision would be at least $10,000,000. The receivers appointed by the courts have impounded, as accumulated receipts from the sale of products of Teapot Dome since they took office on March 13, 1924, a total of $3,000,000. The value of oil taken from the property by the Mammoth Company from the date of the lease on April 7, 1922, until the receivers took over the property for the courts, amounted to $2,220,787.52, on which $342,278.83 was paid to the Government in royalty.

From the receipts during the period of Mr. Sinclair's operation he constructed under his contract with the Government two 150,000-gallon oil tanks and several smaller gas and oil tanks at Portsmouth, N. H., at a cost of $1,000,000. These tanks, in which no oil was ever stored for the Government, now revert to the navy.

In addition, the Mammoth Company spent large sums in developing the facilities of the Teapot Dome reserve, including the drilling of sixty-two producing oil wells, twelve gas wells and ten dry wells. These ran as deep at 3,000 feet and are estimated to have cost about $3,000,000.

Since the receivership the gas wells have been shut down and the receivers have had constructed only two wells, the latter as offsets to meet drainage. Other developments by the Mammoth Company included the construction on the leasehold of twenty-seven oil tanks, with capacities from 55,000 to 80,000 barrels, involving an estimated outlay of $1,500,000. The navy now obtains all this improved property.

WASHINGTON FEES TO BE INVESTIGATED

Secretary Johnson and Others Act on Report an Ex-Colonel With 'Influence' Got $1,000

WASHINGTON, June 21 (AP)—A three-pronged investigation was ordered today after a report that a wartime lieutenant colonel got a $1,000 fee as a down payment on work he said he would do helping a client get a Government contract.

The report was in today's issue of The New York Herald Tribune.

Jack Steele, in a copyrighted story, said that James V. Hunt, a so-called management counselor here, had accepted a $1,000 fee from Paul Grindle, president of a furniture factory in Framingham, Mass.

Mr. Grindle was quoted as saying that Mr. Hunt was an official in the War Assets Administration after he left the Army, had implied he had considerable influence around Washington.

Prominent Names Mentioned

According to Mr. Grindle, Mr. Hunt mentioned the names of several prominent Washingtonians, as if he were on friendly terms with them.

Among those mentioned, Mr. Grindle said, were Maj. Gen. Harry H. Vaughan, military aide to President Truman; Louis Johnson, Secretary of Defense, and Jess Larson, former War Assets Administrator who recently was named Federal Works Administrator.

Mr. Grindle said he gave Mr. Hunt $1,000, and agreed to supply an additional $500 a month for expense money plus 5 per cent of the gross amount of any contract he received. The agreement was signed May 9, 1949.

But, the story said, Mr. Grindle kept a record of all conversations, and turned these records over to The Herald Tribune.

As a result, investigations were ordered by these persons:

Secretary Johnson. He said he wanted to see whether anyone had received "percentage" contracts with the National Military Establishment.

Admiral Paul Mather, who succeeded Mr. Larson as head of the War Assets Administration. He said the story would be investigated thoroughly. (The WAA has the job of disposing of war surplus supplies which originally had cost billions.)

Senator Clyde R. Hoey, Democrat, of North Carolina, chairman of the Senate Investigations Subcommittee of the Committee on Expenditures in the Executive Departments, also called for "a complete investigation of all the facts."

Secretary Johnson issued a statement saying that buying by the armed forces was conducted "openly, without favoritism, and under established procedures." He said he hoped business men would help expose those who claimed to have lots of influence.

Hunt Is Silent on Story

At the offices of J. V. Hunt & Co. here a secretary said that Colonel Hunt would make no comment until he had had a chance to talk with his lawyer.

She added that he had canceled plans to leave for Cambridge, Mass., to attend the graduation of his son from Harvard.

In a Senate speech today Senator Charles W. Tobey, Republican, of New Hampshire, demanded that Congress take action at once against "these grafters" who used or claimed influence to get Government contracts during the war.

Senator Joseph R. McCarthy, Republican, of Wisconsine, told the Senate that he had full confidence in Mr. Larson, the former head of war assets.

Mr. McCarthy recalled that he had headed a subcommittee which investigated Mr. Larson and war surplus disposal last year. He said Republicans and Democrats agreed that Mr. Larson "topped all" Federal officials for efficiency and freedom from influence.

All the persons mentioned by Colonel Hunt who could be reached denied they had ever been influenced by him.

June 22, 1949

FEDERAL CONTRACTS ARE BIG BUSINESS

Hence the Small Business Man Looking for One Often Runs Into Many Difficulties

By H. WALTON CLOKE

WASHINGTON, Aug. 13—Because the Federal Government has billions of dollars' worth of contracts to let every year, Washington has become the mecca of the "five percenters" and the "influence peddlers." But for the little business man seeking a contract, it is the most confused place in the world.

To get a Government contract, many a small business man feels that it is necessary to be on the scene. However, he finds himself in a labyrinth about which he knows virtually nothing. That is when he becomes a sitting duck for a "five percenter."

Dependence on "Insiders"

If he does not decide then that he needs someone to guide him, someone who "knows the ropes" and the "insiders," he will get the general impression after he has visited various Government agencies and departments. The Government is cognizant of the fact that the small business man encounters difficulties, and it is trying to remedy the situation.

At present there is no specific Government agency to which a business man can go in Washington for advice on how to apply for a Government contract. For instance, if he is interested in obtaining a part of the $5,000,000 of contracts let every year by the Maritime Commission, he can obtain as much information by writing a letter to the agency as he can by making a trip to Washington and being shunted from office to office. If he does come to Washington the chances are he looks up a "five percenter."

The Investigations subcommittee of the Senate Committee on Expenditures in the Executive Departments which is inquiring into the activities of the "five percenters" and the "influence peddlers" has discovered that selling influence may be unethical, but it is not always illegal.

Committee Objective

Nevertheless, the fact remains that no one condones the misuse of Government influence for a price. If the subcommittee keeps its sights on its declared objective, there necessarily must be a continuous effort to prevent the drama and the "big-name" personalities now involved from obscuring the fundamental purpose of the inquiry. That purpose is to make it easier for a small business man to get a contract.

Indicative of the changes that are being planned in this system is the new Military Procurement Information Center which the Munitions Board has set up at the direction of Secretary Johnson. Its purpose is to provide a central directing service to business men seeking military contracts.

The center maintains offices in the Pentagon, Room 3D773, and is staffed by Army, Navy and Air Force personnel. Copies of all invitations to bid, abstracts of bids and other pertinent documents are available at the center, except when security precludes. This system is expected to be a tremendous aid in eliminating the middleman or the "influence peddler" who can get a business man a contract for 5 per cent of its value because he "knows the ropes."

Routine on Sealed Bids

For instance, if an electrical appliance dealer from New Bedford, Mass., walks into the Pentagon looking for a military contract he is referred immediately to the information center. There he tells a clerk the type of material he has for sale and he is told, in turn, what branch of the service might be buying those items. Then he receives a list of what is being purchased and is told how to bid.

When this process is completed the business man is on his own. Under the sealed competitive bid routine used by the Government in the majority of cases, Government officials contend that the New Bedford business man will have an equal chance with all others.

'GET TO THE BOTTOM'

Bishop in The St. Louis Star-Times

August 14, 1949

TRUMAN REQUESTS PUBLIC TO SUSPEND JUDGING VAUGHAN

President Says Senate Group Releases Adverse Testimony, Holds Up Favorable Data

HOEY DENIES UNFAIRNESS

In Answer, He Makes Public Secret Material Contradicting General on Freeze Units

By H. WALTON CLOKE
Special to THE NEW YORK TIMES.

WASHINGTON, Aug. 18—Maj. Gen. Harry H. Vaughan, President Truman's military aide, was defended again by the Chief Executive today who urged the press "in common fairness" to suspend judgment on the General until he had testified before the Senate "five percenter" inquiry.

The President at his news conference was critical of the methods used to conduct the inquiry. He stressed that hearings that had been unfavorable to General Vaughan had been held in public, while those favorable to his aide were conducted behind closed doors.

Mr. Truman's remarks drew an immediate reply from Senator Clyde R. Hoey, Democrat, of North Carolina, who is chairman of the investigations subcommittee of the Senate Committee on Expenditures in the Executive Departments. The subcommittee is conducting the inquiry to determine whether "five percenters," or "influence peddlers," have any effect on the letting of Government contracts.

Mr. Hoey said that the subcommittee had attempted at all times "to be fair"—and in certain instances "scrupulously fair." Senator Joseph R. McCarthy, Republican, of Wisconsin, a member of the subcommittee, demanded that the President "fire General Vaughan as Coordinator of Veterans Affairs."

As a result of the President's statement, the subcommittee made public this afternoon sixty-six pages of testimony taken in private session. It deals in part with the deep-freeze units that General Vaughan received from the president of a Chicago perfume manufacturing company and contradicts statements made by the General about the refrigerators.

Senator Hoey said that the subcommittee "regrets that this effort to be scrupulously fair in this instance may have appeared to be an attempt to unfairly withhold testimony."

When the President began his press conference he read rapidly from a prepared statement and notified reporters that they could quote him. With General Vaughan and his other aides standing behind him, Mr. Truman stated:

"Gentlemen, before we start, I have a statement I want to make to you. At the outset I want to say to you that I do not intend to answer any questions pertaining to testimony that has been given before Senator Hoey's committee.

"General Vaughan has already said he would go before the committee and make a full statement on all matters with which his name has been connected, and I suggest, as has the chairman of the committee, that you gentlemen and your editors, in common fairness, suspend judgment on General Vaughan until he has been heard by the committee."

Adverse Stories Laid to "Leaks"

The President said that most of the unfavorable stories about General Vaughan came from the private sessions held by the subcommittee and were the direct result of "leaks." He added with a big smile that when the general did go to Capitol Hill to testify, it undoubtedly would be a field day. That session, he predicted, would not take place behind closed doors.

A reporter objected, saying that a great many of the hearings were open to the public. The President said that all he knew about the investigation was what he read in the newspapers.

This marked the second time since the "five percenters" inquiry began that Mr. Truman has spoken in defense of General Vaughan. He had said previously that the testimony had not changed his opinion of his aide.

The subcommittee conducting the inquiry is the successor to the War Investigating Committee that the President headed during World War II as a Senator from Missouri.

Discussing the hitherto secret testimony concerning General Vaughan, Senator Hoey said that yesterday the President's aide notified the subcommittee that he desired a transcript of the private session.

"It was decided," the Senator added, "that the executive (private) testimony would be furnished the general for his personal use upon the condition that the subcommittee would release it to the public at the same time."

General Vaughan's office was told of this decision, Mr. Hoey continued, and at that time his office "informed us that the general did not desire the subcommittee to release the testimony in question."

Deny Faults in Freeze Units

The testimony, received last Monday, contained remarks by Harry Hoffman, president of Hoffman & York, Inc., Milwaukee advertising agency; Albert J. Gross of Milwaukee, former head of his own company that made the deep-freeze units, and Robert L. Quirk, vice president of the Quirk Company, Cudahy, Wis., manufacturer of the cases for the refrigerators.

Other testimony has shown that David Bennett, president of the Albert Verley Company, perfume manufacturer of Chicago, paid for seven deep-freeze units in the summer of 1945, two of which General Vaughan received.

The others were delivered to Mrs. Harry S. Truman at the summer White House in Independence, Mo.; Chief Justice Fred M. Vinson, then director of the Office of War Mobilization and Reconversion; John W. Snyder, Secretary of the Treasury; James K. Vardaman Jr., now a governor of the Federal Reserve Board, but then President Truman's naval aide, and Matthew J. Connelly, a White House secretary.

In a statement issued last Saturday, General Vaughan said that in 1945 "I had a talk with two old friends of mine * * * Mr. Harry Hoffman and Mr. David Bennett."

"The subject of deep-freeze units came up," he recalled, "and I said that I would like to have one for my house, and that I also would like to send one to the little White House in Independence."

General Vaughan went on to say that Mr. Hoffman told him he was associated with a company that was beginning to manufacture deep-freeze units, and he believed that he could get hold of some "factory rejects." Later, the general added, Mr. Hoffman told him that he could obtain some deep-freeze units that "did not have commercial value, as they were experimental models."

The testimony released today presented a different version. Mr. Gross testified at Monday's private session that there was nothing wrong with the refrigerators sent to the general and his friends.

Sales of Units Stressed

William P. Rogers, chief counsel of the subcommittee, asked Mr. Gross:

"It was not an experimental model; you had been making them for some time. It was not a reject."

"That is right," the witness replied. "There was nothing obsolete in the refrigeration line at that time, nothing at all. I would say that we sold approximately $18,000 to $20,000 of those prior to the time this shipment was made."

Senator Karl E. Mundt, Republican of South Dakota, a member of the subcommittee, asked Mr. Gross if he were sure the refrigerators were not rejects.

"We had no such animal," Mr. Gross replied.

Mr. Quirk testified that his company had built some of the cabinets for the Gross company's freezers, and that the material that went into them was the best obtainable.

"Was there anything about the work that you did that was experimental or defective in any way," Mr. Rogers asked.

"No," Mr. Quirk said, "there was nothing defective on our part."

Mr. Hoffman also had a slightly different version of how Mr. Bennett decided to send the refrigerators to the General and his friends. The advertising executive, whose company handles an account of the Verley company, testified that he was in the White House, in General Vaughan's office, and "I happened to overhear a telephone conversation of General Vaughan and somebody else."

They were discussing "the matter of a deep-freeze unit that was needed at Independence, Mo.," Mr. Hoffman said, then added:

"They were trying to locate something that would serve that purpose. In fact, they were trying to get a Coca Cola freezer somewhere and I mentioned to General Vaughan the fact that I had seen a freezer on display in the window of a small shop in a little community I live in outside Milwaukee."

"But I made no offer to ship a freezer to Independence, Mo.," he testified.

Later in the day, however, he said that he telephoned Mr. Bennett and told him of the conversation he overheard. Mr. Bennett, according to Mr. Hoffman, said that "Well, I will be glad to ship one down there."

Mr. Hoffman told the subcommittee that he was then authorized by Mr. Bennett to have a refrigerator shipped to the Little White House.

"I telephoned back to Milwaukee," Mr. Hoffman said, "and made the arrangements, and I do not recall if it was in that conversation or shortly after that, that Mr. Bennett, on his own suggestion, said: 'I would also like to ship some to a number of other Administration leaders whom I like and admire.'"

Says Bennett Spends Freely

"I think you should know something about Mr. Bennett," Mr. Hoffman said. **"You see I have worked for him since 1933. He has always been a very wealthy man, a very prosperous man. He has always had big cars and chauffeurs and big apartments.**

"He has had yachts and he has always had an extremely profitable business. He is one of those people, one of those fellows to whom gifts like that just do not mean anything. Money was spent very freely.

"He sent those freezers without the knowledge of the people who received them, and I am sure that in most cases they probably were completely surprised to get them, but he just wanted to do it."

Senator Mundt asked Mr. Hoffman if General Vaughan "ever asked you to send a deep-freeze unit to anybody else?"

"No," the witness answered.

"There was never any discussion between yourself and General Vaughan that these were reject models or experimental models or anything like that, was there?" Mr. Rogers asked.

Mr. Hoffman replied: "No, although——"

Senator Mundt interposed to say that "you are not trying to convey the idea that Mr. Bennett was just giving second-hand junk to the summer White House, were you?"

"No," Mr. Hoffman replied.

He testified that General Vaughan was an old friend of his, adding that he had known him for perhaps fifteen years or so. He said that he had introduced Mr. Bennett to the general, and that the perfume manufacturer knew him "pretty well."

Maragon Plane Trip Bared

Members of the subcommittee asked Mr. Gross how much Mr. Bennett paid for the refrigerators. The manufacturer of the units said that four of the freezers sold for $390 each and three for $520. The more expensive units were later models, he added, but they were sold at a 35 per cent discount.

The testimony taken at the private session also showed that a military transport plane was used in 1945 to take John Maragon, a prominent figure in the inquiry, and two associates to Europe. Mr. Maragon was at the time employed by the Verley company.

Yesterday, Senator McCarthy demanded that Mr. Maragon be indicted for perjury on the basis of testimony received by the subcommittee.

Mr. Hoffman testified on the trip to Europe. He said that he and Mr. Maragon were accompanied by a lawyer representing Mr. Bennett. Asked who made the arrangements for them to go by "Air Transport Command," Mr. Hoffman said: "Mr. Maragon." They paid their own fares, he added.

Mr. Rogers asked Mr. Hoffman if he knew that Mr. Maragon had trouble getting through customs when they returned from Europe. He replied that he did not know "that John had trouble with the customs people until after we left the Customs Department."

Mr. Hoffman acknowledged, however, that he knew Mr. Maragon was carrying "a canister of oil" for use in perfume manufacture, and that the latter was in the customs inspector's office quite a long time.

"He (Mr. Maragon) did not tell you that on the declaration he had declared this essential oil as four bottles of champagne, did he?" Mr. Rogers asked.

"No," the witness replied.

"Then he did not tell you later on, that when they asked him about this, he said that these four bottles of champagne were for Mr. George Drescher (then a secret service man) of the White House, did he?" the subcommittee lawyer asked.

"No, sir, he did not," Mr. Hoffman said.

"Did you have a talk with Mr. Bennett about a fine or a penalty that was imposed on Mr. Maragon for attempting to bring in this essential oil as champagne?" Mr. Rogers asked.

Says Bennett Was "Upset"

Mr. Hoffman said that he did not know about any fine until, perhaps, a year later "when Mr. Bennett mentioned it to me rather casually."

He added that he believed Mr. Bennett was rather "upset" about the matter and had said of Mr. Maragon: "The damned fool, the stuff could have come in duty free anyway."

Senator McCarthy called attention to the fact that it was when Mr. Maragon was subject to "very severe penalties" as a result of bringing in the perfume oil that the Verley company arranged to send "very valuable gifts" to General Vaughan and other prominent persons in the Administration.

Senator Mundt tried to connect the freezer gifts with the arrangements that Mr. Maragon made for the men to go to Paris on an ATC plane. Business men, he said, were being denied the right to go abroad at that time and that "somebody had to sort of grease the skids if you were going to be among the selected few who went."

August 19, 1949

NO VAUGHAN OUSTER; TRUMAN BACKS AIDE

Special to THE NEW YORK TIMES.

WASHINGTON, Jan. 19—Amid renewed demands for the removal of Maj. Gen. Harry H. Vaughan, the President's military aide, Mr. Truman asserted today that he would be retained and in his present status.

In a report yesterday a Senate investigatings subcommittee criticized General Vaughan for accepting seven home freezer as gifts from the Albert Verley Company, a perfume concern.

Asked during his news conference whether there would be "any change in the status of General Vaughan," Mr. Truman replied that there would be none.

The demand for General Vaughan's removal was renewed today by Senators Joseph R. McCarthy of Wisconsin and Karl E. Mundt of South Dakota, Republicans. Senator Clyde R. Hoey, Democrat, of North Carolina, however, declared:

"It should be borne in mind that the criticisms of General Vaughan do not reflect on his character or integrity, but relate instead to customs and practices engaged in by him. The committee did not suggest that the President take any action."

WASHINGTON, Jan. 19 (UP)—Maj. Gen. Harry H. Vaughan received tonight the award of the distinguished service medal of the American Legion's National Guard of Honor for his work in rehabilitating veterans of the second World War. The award was made at the guard's annual ball.

January 20, 1950

MARAGON IS GUILTY OF LYING TO SENATE; DENIED BAIL, JAILED

Friend of Gen. Vaughan Faces Eight Months to Ten Years on Each of Two Counts

CLEARED ON ONE CHARGE

Jury Convicts Him of Perjury at Five Percenter Inquiry on Bank Account and Job

By The Associated Press.

WASHINGTON, April 26—John Maragon, once a hanger-on around the White House, was convicted today of criminally lying to Senators.

He was found guilty of perjuring himself about his bank accounts and employment and sent to jail until time for sentencing—perhaps a week from Friday.

But he was cleared of one of the Government's main charges, that he lied about business deals with Federal departments. He was accused of doing the lying when he testified last year to Senators investigating influence peddlers and five percenters.

Five percenters are persons who charge a fee, usually 5 per cent, for representing others in business matters with the Government.

Maragon, 57 years old, is a one-time Kansas City shoe-shine boy who became a figure around Washington and a friend of the Presidential military aide, Maj. Gen. Harry H. Vaughan.

He wilted a little in his chair but did not change expression when the jury brought in the verdict. It had considered the case an hour and thirty-six minutes.

The Government accused Maragon of going around town saying he represented General Vaughan or came from the White House and of trying to influence or coerce Federal employes into helping various business concerns.

But the defense, and Federal District Judge Jennings Bailey, emphasized that what Maragon did, right or wrong, was not the issue—what the jury had to determine was whether he lied about what he did.

The specific charges on which Maragon was convicted were that he lied when he said:

1. His only bank account in 1945-1946 was in a Washington bank. The trial brought out evidence he had another account in San Antonio, Tex.
2. At the time he took a temporary job with the State Department in Greece in 1945, he had ended his employment with a Chicago importing concern, Albert Verley & Co. The Government produced evidence he was on the departmental and Verley payrolls at the same time.

Maragon could be sentenced on each of these two counts to as little as eight months to two years in prison or to as long as forty months to ten years. The courts rarely impose the maximum penalty.

But Judge Bailey refused to release Maragon on bail until he was sentenced.

Maragon's lawyer, Irvin Goldstein, announced he would try for a new trial and carry the case as far as possible. Mr. Goldstein said he might be able to argue his motion for a new trial a week from Friday. If Judge Bailey rejects the motion, Maragon could be sentenced immediately afterward. Then the case could be appealed to a higher court.

April 27, 1950

R. F. C. HEARING WEIGHED FOR POLITICAL EFFECTS

Democrats Discount Its Importance But G.O.P. Revives an Old Slogan

By W. H. LAWRENCE

Special to THE NEW YORK TIMES.

WASHINGTON, March 10—Republicans are borrowing for use in 1952 an 80-year-old Democratic battle cry, "Turn the Rascals Out." It was first used nationally by Samuel J. Tilden in his campaign against the excesses of the Republican Administration of President Grant.

Republican leaders see its applicability to the next Presidential campaign in the scandals disclosed or hinted at by a series of Congressional investigations, including those now in progress into the Reconstruction Finance Corporation and into organized crime throughout the country.

The Republicans will admit, if pressed, that the revelations about how a White House secretary got her mink coat or how the White House military aide accepted a present of several home freezer machines are not exactly in the category of major scandals.

But it is part of the Republican strategy to use these and other incidents to create in the minds of the American people a question as to whether there are many other and bigger instances of improper official misconduct or corruption during the last eighteen years the Democrats have been in power in Washington.

"How deep these and other scandals go, nobody knows," said Guy G. Gabrielson, Republican National chairman, in an Elgin, Ill., speech tonight. "Nobody is likely to know so long as the present Administration is in power. * * *

"There is only one way to clean up this mess. A campaign slogan shouted during the early history of the Republic applies with equal force today. It consists of four plain, blunt words—'Turn the Rascals Out.'"

What Mr. Gabrielson argued was that the cumulative effect of the revelations at R. F. C. hearings, the crime inquiries, the 5 per center investigation and others must convince the American people that the moral climate of the Truman Administration is low.

Republican strategists believe that charges of coddling communism and corruption can be major factors in 1952 as things now stand.

They are, therefore, enjoying immensely the big headlines that have grown out of the R. F. C. hearings conducted by Senator J. William Fulbright, Arkansas Democrat, and the assertions of organized crime links with politics brought out by another Senatorial committee headed by Senator Estes Kefauver, Tennessee Democrat.

So far, President Truman has carried the burden of defending his Administration without too much help from other Democrats, and practically none from the Democratic National Committee as such.

The President made a spirited defense of the R. F. C. board and of his administrative aide, Donald Dawson, when the Fulbright Committee first rendered its report. That report strongly implied that there had been too much influence brought by Mr. Dawson and the Democratic National Committee to bear on R. F. C. members considering loans.

But since public hearings began and some of the evidence the committee had was brought out publicly, the White House, for the most part, has said "no comment."

One of the charges in the Fulbright report was that William M. Boyle Jr., Democratic national chairman, intervened to obtain hearings for R. F. C. loan applicants. Mr. Boyle replied that of course he did, that this was routine procedure for a political party, and that it did not constitute improper influence.

When the President obtained from the R. F. C. all the letters in its files from Congressmen dealing with loans, Senator Fulbright angrily asserted that it looked like an attempt to discredit his investigation by implying that Congressmen also used their influence to help constituents get loans. But the President never made the letters public. He said that he had no evidence of improper influence used by members either of the executive or legislative branch of the Government.

The Fulbright committee did score a major political victory on the basic point of R. F. C. organization. The President adopted its reorganization proposal and sent it along to Congress for approval.

The principal industry of Washington is, of course, politics, and there always are discussions here of how great or lasting an impact a single event will have on the American public. Much of the reasoning in these discussions springs from wishful thinking. That is true today when politicians try to measure the effect in 1952 of 1951's "scandals."

The Republicans believe they have a good issue, but the most impressive rebuttal to this theory is the fact that the Republicans were able to retain the White House in the 1924 election despite the Teapot Dome scandal. There is nothing yet turned up by any of the current investigations that even approaches the magnitude of the corruption and bribery proved in connection with that oil lease.

It is the feeling of the Democrats that the present "scandals" are too picayune to be remembered by the voter twenty-one months from now. One of the reasons the Democratic National Committee is not more active in combating the present Republican arguments about the "scandals" is that it would just as soon not add fuel to the fire, letting it go out so the voter will forget about it completely.

It is true, of course, that Thomas E. Dewey of New York rode into the Governor's Mansion at Albany on his record as a "gang-buster," but he never was able in his two campaigns for the White House to make charges of corruption convince enough voters he should be President.

Charges of corruption often are very effective in local political campaigns. Former Senator Scott Lucas of Illinois, the Senate's majority leader who was beaten for re-election in 1950, is convinced that one of the factors that militated against him was the Kefauver investigation in Chicago of Dan Gilbert, whom the Democrats had nominated for Sheriff of Cook County.

But, on the national level, past experience indicates that votes are decided by more basic considerations than a few mink coats or home freezer machines. In 1948, for example, when nearly all the experts and pollsters foresaw an easy victory for Governor Dewey, an on-the-spot inquiry in the Middle West, where there was a genuine last-minute change of votes, indicated that a basic cause for Democratic gains was a sharp drop in the price of corn in mid-October. The "pocketbook nerve" convinced the farmer that Democrats were more likely than Republicans to keep the farm prices high.

March 11, 1951

TWO OBSERVATIONS ON THE R. F. C. INQUIRY

Morris, A. P. Newsfeatures

"Dear taxpayer—"

Messner in The Rochester Times-Union

"On the spot."

TRUMAN DECLARES HIS HOUSE IS CLEAN; DEFENDS CONDUCT

In Intimate, Informal Interview the President Asks History, Not Press, to Judge Him

STRESSES PEACE EFFORTS

Refuses Comment on Details of Exposures on R. F. C.—Dodges Queries on '52

By ANTHONY LEVIERO
Special to THE NEW YORK TIMES

MR. TRUMAN MEETS THE PRESS ON WINTER WHITE HOUSE LAWN

The President, wearing a two-tone, open-necked shirt, holding conference at Key West yesterday
Associated Press Wirephoto

KEY WEST, Fla., March 15—President Truman defended today his conduct as an office holder, praised his staff as honorable men and expressed the hope that in the perspective of history he would be remembered as an apostle of peace who had prevented World War III.

The exposures in the Senate's investigation of the Reconstruction Finance Corporation, the Gallup Poll reporting his prestige at lowest ebb and adverse newspaper comment were encompassed in Mr. Truman's views.

His house has always been clean, the President said calmly in a half-hour press conference on the lawn of the winter White House here.

He ranged up through the line of his predecessors, mentioning several, and stating that George Washington had suffered most of all at the hands of the press.

Jefferson, Jackson, Lincoln and Cleveland have at last attained their place in history, too, he said, and Wilson and Franklin D. Roosevelt will find theirs.

As for himself he did not expect to be judged properly for twenty-five or thirty years and he advised the reporters not to try now.

The news conference moved at an easier and more informal pace than in Washington and President Truman appeared unruffled by all manner of questions that sought for tarnished spots in the armor of his Administration.

He said he was feeling fine but was finding it awfully hard to reduce here because the food was so good. His face wore an even tan, acquired during his morning swims. He wore a handsome coat-type sport shirt. Its collar was white and the edge along the buttons and of the short sleeves were also white. He wore gray trousers and white shoes.

Mr. Truman sat in an elaborate wicker chair facing reporters and photographers wearing all sorts of informal attire. Behind the President stood several members of his staff. The setting for the conference was the secluded lawn of his cottage on the naval reservation. Exotic subtropical trees were all around.

As the President warmed to his subject, commenting readily on most issues raised by the reporters, they tried to have the transcript of the entire conference put on the record for direct quotation. Mr. Truman would not have it so, however. He allowed them to quote two passages directly and the rest was to be paraphrased, according to the rules that prevail in Washington.

Here is what Mr. Truman said when asked what he would like to have his Administration remembered for:

"I hope it will be remembered for its sincere effort for world peace, and if we accomplish that, if we get through this era without a third World War, I think that probably is what it will be remembered for."

And when he was reminded that his sixth anniversary in office—April 12—was drawing near, he was asked what he would like to say about that. He gave permission to quote this from the record:

"I will make this comment, though, Bert" (Andrews of The New York Herald Tribune), "that all a President of the United States can do is to endeavor to make the Government—the executive branch—run in the public interest. I have striven very hard to accomplish that purpose. The Administration of no President can be correctly evaluated during his term, or within twenty-five or thirty years after that term. Thomas Jefferson has just now come into his own as a President.

"The same is true of Jackson, Lincoln, Grover Cleveland. And the same thing will be true of Wilson and Franklin Roosevelt. It takes an objective survey of what has happened and what was (sic) trying to be accomplished to decide whether the President has been a success or not. And you can't decide that now, or here, and neither can I."

Calls House Always Clean

The discussion was touched off when a reporter asked Mr. Truman if he had anything to say about the demand last week by Senator William F. Knowland, Republican of California, that the President return to Washington and clean house.

His house was always clean; what was he talking about? Mr. Truman replied.

Then he was asked if this was his reply to editorials and cartoons suggesting there was a lack of ethical and moral responsibility in some of the people around him. This, of course, was an indirect approach to the disclosures in the R. F. C. inquiry—an approach that got most direct later.

He would answer point-blank and categorically that this was not true, Mr. Truman said.

Next he was asked if he still stood on the statement he had made in Washington that no illegality had been found in efforts in the executive branch or in Congress to influence the granting of loans by the Government lending agency. This had particular reference to a file of 300 or 400 letters written by Senators and Representatives to the R. F. C. in connection with loans.

Mr. Truman replied that his statement referred only to the letters he had read. They simply requested loans and there was nothing illegal in them, he said.

The President said he had never written a letter asking for anything in the ten years he was a Senator.

No Comment on Dawson

There was a question next about Donald Dawson, his administrative assistant. Mr. Dawson has been named in the R. F. C. inquiry as one of those who tried to influence the directors in the issuing of loans. The reporter wanted to know if it was proper for Mr. Dawson to have stayed as a free guest at the Hotel Saxony in Miami Beach, which had received a substantial loan from the R. F. C. Mr. Truman declined to comment on that.

The questioning returned to his time as a Senator and the President reiterated that he had never written letters to Government departments urging them to do anything. Then he recalled that he had written to urge the Interstate Commerce Commission and the Securities and Exchange Commission to place railroad securities on sale in the open market. He had succeeded in getting that done, he explained.

A reporter asked a question about the integrity of the people associated with the President. Part of the question and the answer was lost to most of the circle of reporters and Mr. Truman repeated himself.

He (the reporter) was trying to find out if the people around him (the President) were honest or not, the President explained.

His people were honorable and he would not have them if they were not, he declared.

Mr. Truman replied "no comment" to further questions about Mr. Dawson, and about Mrs. E. Merl Young, who received an expensive fur coat at the time of her husband's connections with R. F. C. directors. The coat came from a borrower assisted by Mr. Young, whose wife is a stenographer at the White House.

As for the Gallup Poll, which this week showed that only 26 per cent of the voters now approve of Mr. Truman's "handling of his job as President," with 57 per cent disapproving and 17 per cent having no opinion, Mr. Truman said he had expressed himself on polls in 1949.

He would say no more about the Gallup Poll, which had predicted the election of his rival, Governor Dewey, in 1948, or of a recent United Press poll of Democratic state leaders that showed he was still their No. 1 candidate, but that if Mr. Truman chose not to run in 1952 Senator Paul Douglas, Democrat of Illinois, was the second choice.

Mr. Truman dodged questions about the Presidential race in 1952, laughingly saying that if he answered them the reporters would no longer be able to speculate and draw their own conclusions.

When a reporter brought up the sixth anniversary and Mr. Truman replied he hoped the second six years would not be so hard, the reporter thought he had trapped the President.

"So you're going to run again," demanded the reporter.

Mr. Truman laughed and said he had made no such implication.

He was asked if he considered the press had abused him. He responded that the press had been just as good as could be to him. This might have been a facetious remark, because Mr. Truman has blamed parts of the press for unfairness to him. But when the question was repeated later he difinitely reiterated that he was not implying he had been abused.

He closed the discussion in a broad gesture of goodwill. He said that if the supreme goal of peace was attained he did not mean that he alone would be responsible. The whole Government —the legislative, the executive and the judiciary—will have done their part, he declared. He said he hoped that the peace could be assured because two generations of youngsters had been slaughtered in two big wars and that was a hard gap to fill.

March 16, 1951

Ethics Inquiry Bluntly Scores Executive, Congress, Public

By C. P. TRUSSELL

Special to The New York Times.

WASHINGTON, Oct. 17—A Senate subcommittee assigned last spring to look into the ethics and moral standards prevailing in the running of the National Government called on the executive branch today to take a lion's share of the blame for dark public conclusions drawn from scandals turned up by Congressional investigations.

In a report viewed on Capitol Hill as being shocking at points, and bluntly frank and realistic throughout, the subcommittee, headed by Senator Paul H. Douglas, Democrat of Illinois, warned, at the same time, that Congress should not hold itself aloof from censure. And, going beyond Washington, the report admonished the public at large to restrain itself from putting a halo above its own head.

The report carried many recommendations for legislative action to bring about corrections and all the recommendations, it declared, were found to be needed in the face of disclosures brought to light by Congressional investigations.

"No group in society," the report stated, "is in a position to point the finger of scorn at others. Influence peddlers can exist only as long as business men or others are willing to patronize them. Favoritism can be a problem only when individual men and women seek favors of the Government.

"Gifts, improper pressure and bribes come from outside the Government, from individuals, from organizations, and from groups which are part of what we call the 'public'."

In some quarters the report was called "brutal." There was speculation whether it would cause explosions—dismissals of officials or lesser personnel—or, instead, draw official ridicule.

HIS GROUP REPORTS

Senator Paul H. Douglas
The New York Times

The report was signed by Democrats and Republicans usually found in the listings of "liberals." Besides Senator Douglas, they were Senators Matthew M. Neely of West Virginia and Hubert H. Humphrey of Minnesota, Democrats, and George D. Aiken of Vermont and Wayne Morse of Oregon, Republicans. They were assisted by Frank W. McCulloch and George A. Graham, as consultants, and Philip A. Willkie, son of the 1940 Republican Presidential nominee, the late Wendell Willkie, as counsel.

At great issue was what was "proper" or "improper" in the exchange of favors—in and out of Congress—when an official decision was pending.

The subcommittee was somewhat stumped to find a dividing line. It considered the proffer of a cigarette, a sociable luncheon, and then up to a mink coat. It refused to take the slide rule of one witness at a Congressional hearing who contended that, on the receipt of gifts, no ham weighing less than twelve pounds was "improper" to receive from seekers of governmental favors.

Urges Special Commission

The subcommittee urged that a special commission, having spokesmen from every walk of American life, be created to serve as a watchdog of official conduct and recommend, for legal enforcement, punishment of abuses.

The group, a unit of the Senate Committee on Labor and Public Welfare, was assigned to its job as a result of a resolution introduced by Senator J. William Fulbright, Democrat of Arkansas, after the start of public hearings on favoritism and political influence in lending operations of the Reconstruction Finance Corporation. Senator Fulbright headed that investigation.

The inquiry by the Douglas group reached into findings concerning "influence peddling" in general, abuses of subsidy programs, irregularities in multi-billion-dollar procurement programs, lobbying in and out of Congress and recent resignations, suspensions and indictments of personnel charged with the honest collection of taxes. It also went into many signs of questionable actions at lower-than-executive levels.

It reported that it had not, by any means, completed its assignment. From what it had found, it urged for Congressional action a long list of remedies aimed at bad spots which those who had followed Congressional investigations could identify.

These included, first, proposed amendments to the Administrative Procedures Act that might spell the summary dismissal from service of those who:

1. Engaged in any personal business transaction or private arrangement for personal profit which accrued from or was based on an official position, authority or confidential information.
2. Accepted any valuable gifts, favor or service directly or indirectly from any person or organization with which the official or employe transacted business for the Government.
3. Discussed future employment outside the Government with a person or organization with which there was pending official business.
4. Divulged valuable commercial or economic information of a confidential character to unauthorized persons or released such information in advance of its authorized release date.
5. Became unduly involved—to give one example—through frequent luncheons, dinners, parties or other expensive social engagements with persons outside the Government with whom they did official business.

The subcommittee proposed further that the Administrative Procedures Act be amended to prohibit Federal officials who participated in the making of loans, granting of subsidies, negotiation of contracts, fixing of rates or the issuance of valuable permits from acting in any official transaction or decision which concerned chiefly a person or organization by which they had been employed in the preceding two years or with which they had had a valuable economic interest.

Restrictions Advocated

The law, the subcommittee stated, also should be toughened to provide that:

1. Former Federal officials and employes not be allowed to appear before agencies in which they were formerly employed in cases which they previously handled or of which they had direct knowledge. Nor, it added, should they be permitted to assist in the preparation of such cases.
2. For a period of two years afterward Federal agents and employes of a rank of $10,000-a-year or above who leave the government shall not appear before the Federal agencies in which they were formerly employed as a representative of a person or organization doing business with the government.

The penalties of disbarment from practice before a Federal agency and of cancellation of contracts would be imposed in cases where it was found that persons had sought to corrupt or had been corrupted. Full publicity would be given to such findings.

The subcommittee proposed that a law be passed to force a reporting annually by all members of Congress and Federal officials of income they received in excess of $10,000 a year. As an aside, subcommittee members asserted that this proposal already had been drafted for submittal to Congress before President Truman asked for the same thing in a recent message.

"Erroneous Assumption"

"Veneration for the principle of government according to law," the subcommittee stated, "has its inverse side—an erroneous assumption that what is lawful is right. Although this is an untruth which authoritarian governments of all varieties have demonstrated vividly and recently, representative governments also must be on guard lest they make the same mistakes . . . Legality is not enough."

The formation of a citizens committee of nationwide scope and jurisdiction was urged to help the policing of official ethics and many problems were offered for further study, some being problems suggested by congressional inquiry but not analyzed sufficiently to warrant specific recommendation now.

The most serious problems of public officials, the subcommittee concluded, were the products of four factors, stated as follows:

"1. There is much at stake in public policies which directly affect the income and welfare of individuals, industries and groups.

"2. Members of Congress have almost free discretion in making these policies and administrative officials have great discretion in administering them.

"3. The great authority vested in elected officials is justified by the principle that they, as representatives of the public, will exercise their authority in the public interest and for public purposes; similarly, the discretionary authority delegated to administrators is based on (similar) assumption.

"4. * * * But in a great variety of ways * * * interested parties not willing to let the wheels of government turn unassisted * * * bring pressure to bear upon legislators and administrators in order to secure favorable decisions."

The subcommittee declared that the morals of officials could be distinguished but "certainly not separated" from public morals generally.

"The moral standards of the country, indeed," it added, "provide the ethical environment which in turn conditions the standard of behavior of public officials."

The subcommittee found that influence peddling by government personnel was a phenomenon that could "not be ignored." Reports about it might have been exaggerated, the group added, and "the gullible have been defrauded by men whose influence was fictitious."

"On the record," it said, "we in Congress must also seem unduly complacent. Neither house has acted vigorously to tighten its discipline in moral matters or to raise its ethical standards. In recent years some members have been convicted of crime and sent to prison, but they have not been expelled.

"Neither house has been particularly diligent in searching out and punishing questionable conduct on the part of its members."

October 18, 1951

PRESIDENT PLEDGES A DRASTIC PROGRAM TO END CORRUPTION

Indicates He May Name Board of Inquiry in Day or Two—Plans No Cabinet Change

MURPHY SEEN IN KEY ROLE

Former New York Police Head Is Said to Have Accepted Post in Investigation

By W. H. LAWRENCE

Special to THE NEW YORK TIMES.

WASHINGTON, Dec. 13—President Truman today pledged continued drastic efforts to expose and punish faithless Federal employes as reports circulated that Judge Thomas F. Murphy of New York soon would be named to a special Presidential commission to investigate corruption charges.

Mr. Truman told his news conference that "wrongdoers have no house with me, no matter who they are or how big they are," and indicated he would set up his own board of inquiry, with broad powers to sift the scandal charges, soon—perhaps within the next day or two.

The President maintained, however, that a prime purpose of his extraordinary inquiry would be to show that the vast majority of Governmental employes were honest people, trying to do their duty and not to be smeared by the acts of a few who were not faithful to their trust.

Reports of Judge Murphy's selection for the post of investigating corruption came from well-informed sources a few hours after the Presidential news conference. He was said to be slated for a key role in this inquiry, bringing into play the talents that first won him fame when he successfully prosecuted Alger Hiss for perjury, and later led to his appointment as New York Police Commissioner, where he conducted the clean-up of a major police scandal. He was promoted last summer to a lifetime post as United States Judge for the Southern District of New York.

"Impartial and Fearless"

"Hard-hitting, conscientious, impartial and fearless" were the words used by New York's independent Mayor Vincent R. Impellitteri when he first named Judge Murphy as Police Commissioner in 1950—and these are all qualities that will be tested severely in the new job to which the President is reported to have summoned the 45-year-old, 6-foot-4-inch jurist.

Judge Murphy was said in informed quarters to have accepted the President's bid on condition that it would not be necessary for him to resign from the bench. He is expected in Washington soon for a White House conference at which detailed plans for the inquiry will be made.

There was no solid information available here tonight about the identity of the other members of the commission.

There have been recurring reports that J. Edgar Hoover, director of the Federal Bureau of Investigation, would be a member. He accompanied Attorney General J. Howard McGrath to a secret White House meeting with Mr. Truman yesterday, at which the corruption issue was discussed.

There also have been reports that Mr. Hoover might replace Mr. McGrath as Attorney General, but Mr. Truman denied these today, saying he did not anticipate any changes in his Cabinet. Mr. Hoover, the President said, would continue to do his duty in the manner he always has done it as the chief investigator for the Government.

Outside Activities Face Ban

Speaking to a standing-room-only crowd of 168 reporters at his first press conference since his Florida vacation, Mr. Truman insisted that there was nothing new or unusual, except the widespread publicity, about the recent flood of stories of scandal in Government.

The President expressed personal anger at officials involved, and said one of the first reforms would be a flat prohibition against responsible Government officials engaging in outside activities, such as the practice of law.

He declared that all the cases of wrong-doing in Government, now being publicized from Capitol Hill, first had been discovered and punished by the Executive Branch of Government and that the Congressional investigating committees had come along after the fact to capture the headlines.

In response to questions, he said he did not anticipate the voluntary or requested resignations of Attorney General McGrath, any other member of his Cabinet, any top Governmental bureau head, or of Frank McKinney, the new Democratic National Chairman.

Mr. McKinney has been under newspaper attack recently for his investments in the Empire Tractor Corporation, which netted him a $68,000 profit on a $26,000 investment over a ten-month period. But the President said that Mr. McKinney suited him right down to the ground, and he was inclined to think his actions must be right if they were criticized by newspapers.

It was a rough-and-tumble news conference, in which the President was subjected to unusually sharp questioning by reporters. His answers often were caustic, and particularly so when he voiced criticism of The St. Louis Post-Dispatch, which he accused of particular bias against Democrats.

He also told Bert Andrews, chief of the Washington Bureau of The New York Herald Tribune, who had confessed that he was puzzled about some aspects of the scandal story, that he was easily puzzled because he always was speculating about something about which he did not know anything.

Asked by a reporter for comment on the prediction of Mr. McKinney on Tuesday, after a White House conference, that there would be drastic action looking toward a Government house-cleaning, the President said he preferred a different verb. The right way to say it, he said, was to refer to continued drastic action, because whenever drastic action had been required in the past, the President had taken it.

"A Truman Committee"

He said he had not made up his mind whether to set up a special investigatory body or to conduct the inquiry through regular channels, but that, if there was a special commission, it would not resemble anything in the past, such as the special Roberts-Pomerene Commission that looked into the Teapot Dome scandal, but would be an original plan of his own.

A reporter wanted to know if it might be called "A Truman Committee," and the President said it might, adding he had had such a committee once that worked very well. This was a reference to his special investigating committee that studied problems of production and the armed forces during World War II when he was a Senator.

When the President declared repeatedly that all the cases of scandal now in the public spotlight had been uncovered first by the Executive, and not by the Congress, reporters asked him to name some instances in the past when he had taken drastic action.

Mr. Truman replied that he had dispensed with several Cabinet officers, but he did not name them nor indicate why they had been dismissed. He also said he had dismissed or obtained the resignations of Collectors of Internal Revenue at Boston, St. Louis and San Francisco before any Congressional committees had looked into their affairs.

Raymond P. Brandt, Washington correspondent for The St. Louis Post - Dispatch, questioned the President about the removal of James Finnegan as Internal Revenue Collector, declaring that Mr. Finnegan had not resigned until a grand jury was looking into his activities.

The President said Mr. Finnegan's resignation had been requested long before, but had been hard to obtain, and that he had not wished to dismiss him. Mr. Brandt said Mr. Finnegan had testified that the White House had asked him to defer his resignation and Mr. Truman said this was a misstatement.

Mr. Brandt wanted to know why Mr. Finnegan was allowed to resign, and the President asked him what he would have done under the circumstances, adding quickly that he knew what the St. Louis Post-Dispatch would have done to any Democrat. That paper, he said, would cut off the head of a Democrat any time it had the chance.

Queried for comment on Mr. McKinney's description of him as angry because some faithless employes had sold him down the river, Mr. Truman asked who would not feel angry under the circumstances. He said that a man who had taken an oath to defend and support the Constitution of the United States and who had not done it, would make any executive angry, and ought to make any newspaper angry.

The President returning to the White House after meeting newsmen in the old State Department Building.

Discusses Caudle Case

Discussing the case of Theron Lamar Caudle, who was ousted by the President as Assistant Attorney General in charge of the Tax Division for oustide activities incompatible with his official position, Mr. Truman said that he did not think it was right for any Government employe in a responsible position to have outside interests.

In connection with Mr. Caudle's ouster and subsequent testimony before a special House Ways and Means subcommittee, reporters quizzed the President about the continued defense of Mr. Caudle by his superior, Mr. McGrath.

The President said he had investigated Mr. Caudle and was ready to dismiss him some time back, before the Congressional committee had started its inquiry. A reporter observed that Mr. McGrath had testified yesterday that he did not know anything wrong with Mr. Caudle.

To this the President replied coldly, maybe so, that he did not keep books for the Attorney General when he was Attorney General, but kept books only for himself.

The President said it was his desire to take action as promptly as possible to clean up the situation in government, because nobody believed more than he did in clean government. That, he said, had been his record and theory ever since he became a public officeholder back in 1922, and he invited the reporters to check his record on that point.

It was here that he underlined his seriousness by authorizing direct quotation of this statement:

"Wrongdoers have no house with me, no matter who they are or how big they are."

He told his aides, later, that the phrase was an old Southern colloquialism, which could be roughly translated as meaning he had no use for, and did not like, wrongdoers.

Several times Mr. Truman made the point that there was nothing unusual or new about the current crop of Government scandals.

A reporter suggested that perhaps there were just more of them now, but the President challenged him, declaring that, if he would look over the records of the Internal Revenue Bureau, the reported would find that the average number of people who had been dismissed eevry year had been about the same. He said that, perhaps, scandal reached a little higher up now than it did before, but the number of cases was not larger.

Every time a Federal employe goes wrong, the President declared, he has complete and hearty cooperation by some fellow on the outside who wants to profit by it, and that fellow is just as guilty.

A CHRONOLOGY OF THE CORRUPTION ISSUE

Figures indicate number of Internal Revenue employes removed in the clean-up drive.

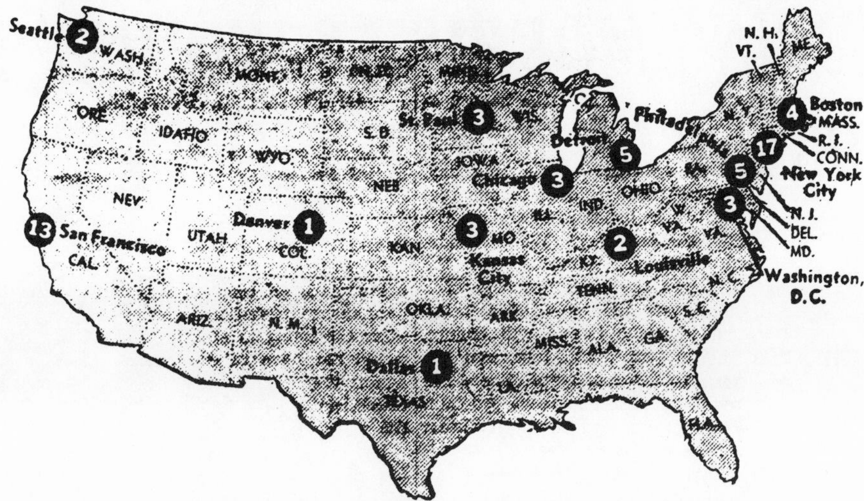

The issue of corruption in the Federal Government, which has reached a climax in recent weeks, has been building up more than a year. These are the high points in its development:

AUGUST, 1950—Secretary of the Treasury John W. Snyder asks resignation of James P. Finnegan, St. Louis Collector of Internal Revenue, because of Finnegan's outside activities. (Finnegan has said President Truman advised him not to resign; Mr. Truman has said he did not force the issue because Finnegan's resignation was "hard to get.")

NOV. 14—California Commission on Organized Crime accuses San Francisco revenue office of links with underworld. Federal Bureau of Internal Revenue follows up with investigation.

NOV. 20—Special agents of Revenue Bureau begin investigation of irregularities in St. Louis office.

FEB. 2, 1951—House resolution establishes Ways and Means subcommittee under Representative Cecil R. King, Democrat of California, to investigate administration of tax laws.

MARCH 10—Finnegan named before Senate Banking Committee as link in R. F. C. influence chain.

APRIL 24—Finnegan announces resignation to give more time to private law practice. (He has since been indicted on charges of using his office for private gain.)

JUNE 27—Denis W. Delaney, Boston Collector of Internal Revenue, suspended pending investigation. (Later fired and indicted for bribery.)

JULY 31—George J. Schoeneman, Commissioner of Internal Revenue, resigns; Mr. Truman names John B. Dunlap to replace him.

SEPT. 10—King subcommittee begins open hearings in New York on tax fraud charges.

SEPT. 28—Collector James G. Smyth and eight employes in San Francisco office suspended. (Smyth has since been indicted.)

OCT. 23—Joseph P. Marcelle, Brooklyn Collector of Internal Revenue, resigns under fire.

NOV. 1—Mr. Truman says he will ask for a law placing Internal Revenue collectors under civil service.

NOV. 17—Mr. Truman forces resignation of T. Lamar Caudle, Assistant Attorney General in charge of the Justice Department's Tax Division, for engaging in "outside activities * * * incompatible with the duties of his office."

NOV. 28—President fires thirty-one Revenue Bureau officials and employes.

DEC. 4—Abraham Teitelbaum, Chicago attorney, tells King subcommittee that names of high officials, including Caudle and Charles Oliphant, chief counsel of the Revenue Bureau, were mentioned in connection with an offer to "fix" his tax delinquency for $500,000. (Both Caudle and Oliphant subsequently denied any part in such a shakedown.)

DEC. 5—Oliphant resigns as chief counsel of Revenue Bureau.

DEC. 6—Attorney General J. Howard McGrath orders grand jury investigation of Teitelbaum's charges of tax shakedown.

DEC. 11—Attorney General McGrath tells King subcommittee Caudle had failed to give him full details on his outside business dealings. He says President Truman has not told him why Caudle was fired.

DEC. 12—Oliphant testifies he accepted favors from individuals involved in tax cases.

DEC. 15—President Truman confers with Federal Judge Thomas F. Murphy of New York on plans for rooting out corruption in the Federal Government.

Since John B. Dunlap took over as Commissioner of Internal Revenue last summer, sixty-two officials and employes have been removed. The map above shows how many have been removed in each district.

M'GRATH IS OUT AS ATTORNEY GENERAL AFTER FIRING MORRIS AS INQUIRY HEAD; U. S. JUDGE M'GRANERY PUT IN CABINET

UPSETS COME FAST

Resignation of McGrath Follows Quickly His Ousting of Morris

TRUMAN CONFIRMS ACTION

F.B.I. May Take Over the Data Assembled or Successor May Follow the Leads

By ANTHONY LEVIERO
Special to THE NEW YORK TIMES.

WASHINGTON, April 3—President Truman snapped up the resignation of Attorney J. Howard McGrath today shortly after Mr. McGrath had dismissed Newbold Morris, the Administration's corruption investigator.

The President immediately named his friend, Federal District Court Judge James Patrick McGranery of Philadelphia, to succeed Mr. McGrath and take over the stewardship of the Justice Department at a time when it is under heavy fire for alleged malfeasance among its officials.

The double-action removal of the officials exploded Mr. Morris' plans to wipe out corruption in the Federal establishment and ended two days of extreme tension in the White House.

The dismissal and the resignation cleared the air for the time, but the President was back at the beginning in facing the formidable problem of trying to make good on a pledge to eliminate misconduct in public office.

Mr. Morris thus has not been allowed to fulfill his mission. But he claimed one great victory—the removal of Mr. McGrath—and he declared that if he could have remained six months instead of two he could have unseated many more office-holders.

Back to New York

Tonight Mr. Morris was packing his bags for his return to New York tomorrow without so much as a thank you or a good-by from President Truman. His career as an investigator was ended as he was preparing to begin in about two weeks grand jury investigations here and in New York.

Mr. Morris contended in a farewell news conference that Attorney General McGrath had ousted him because he had finally realized that Mr. Morris meant business.

"Everything was cozy, comfortable and cordial until Howard McGrath discovered I meant business," said Mr. Morris. "I guess we can draw the conclusion from the action of Mr. McGrath that Washington doesn't want to be investigated. That makes it even, because I didn't enjoy being an investigator."

The Attorney General dismissed Mr. Morris in a short, sharp letter that began with "Sir" and said:

"Please be informed that your appointment as a Special Assistant to the Attorney General is hereby terminated and your services as an employe of the Department of Justice shall cease at the close of business today.

"You are hereby requested to deliver all files, records and documents in your offices to the Federal Bureau of Investigation. Very truly yours, J. Howard McGrath, Attorney General."

President Truman was equally expeditious in evicting Mr. McGrath from his Cabinet. He said in his news conference that he had read about Mr. McGrath's ouster of Mr. Morris in an afternoon newspaper. Soon after there was a telephone call between Mr. McGrath and himself in which the Attorney General resigned. Mr. Truman would not say whether he had placed the call and requested the resignation.

Mr. Truman said he knew that Mr. McGrath planned to discharge Mr. Morris but was not informed when the action was to take place. In his tone and words was a plain inference that he was displeased with the action, or at least with the timing of it.

Whether Mr. McGrath resigned or was forced out the White House would not make clear, but the Attorney General in a farewell message of his own viewed his retirement as a "penalty." He said:

"I have done my duty as I saw it. I have stood up for what I believe to be great principles of personal liberty and the fundamental rights of employes of the Federal Government. I gladly accept the penalty which in this instance attaches to the performance of this duty."

Morris Without Rancor

Mr. Morris declared that, if he had been allowed to do his job, by Labor Day he would have presented "a package to the President of the United States and the people of this country which would have made sense and shown a pattern of conduct in government." He recalled without show of rancor that Mr. Truman had alloted him $450,000 of his emergency fund to carry on his work.

This correspondent, in an interview earlier in the day with Morton Baum, right-hand man to Mr. Morris, learned that the investigator's staff of fifty persons already had collected substantial leads in about a score of cases of official wrong-doing.

These had come from Government officials, the general public and newspaper men, and were to have provided the basis of the grand jury investigations.

An ironic touch was the fact that one of the dossiers concerned a certain Republican Senator who has been one of the most prominent opponents of the Truman Administration.

The files in these cases now will have to be turned over to the Federal Bureau of Investigation, as Mr. McGrath directed Mr. Morris to do in his curt letter of dismissal.

A question arose whether any of the officials or private citizens would feel compromised to have their material taken out of the hands of investigators who, while they worked within the framework of the Justice Department, had received a Presidential franchise to operate independently.

Bitterness, tenseness, a lack of amenities and a rough kind of formality, more military than anything else, marked the swift sequence of the day's astonishing events. The atmosphere around the White House, the Morris headquarters and the Justice Department seemed electric, the more so because of the goodwill that had prevailed before.

For Mr. McGrath at 48 years of age it was the end of a high career in the Administration. Had he not heeded Mr. Truman's call to party service two and a half years ago when he became Attorney General, he would still be an untouchable United States Senator from Rhode Island until his term ended in November.

Before he took the job of Attorney General he had served dually as Senator and chairman of the Democratic National Committee, directing Mr. Truman's political campaign from the time that the President's stock was very low in 1948.

Morris Seems Finished

Mr. Morris came to Washington two months ago confident that he had the backing of the President. In his case the paradox was that it was Attorney General McGrath himself who had called him to Washington to take the difficult task.

Now Judge McGranery has been assigned by the President to take up where Mr. McGrath and Mr. Morris left off. President Truman said in a news conference this afternoon that the new Attorney General would assume responsibility for the corruption inquiry.

Mr. Truman also gave this answer when asked if Mr. Morris might be reinstated, but it appeared to be a foregone conclusion that Mr. Morris was finished. It has been apparent for some two weeks that the White House no longer felt that Mr. Morris was the man for the job.

Judge McGranery will have to be confirmed by the Senate before he can assume office. President Truman said he would take office as soon as the formalities could be completed. Political observers noted that Judge McGranery is, like Mr. McGrath, a prominent Catholic layman and to some of them it appeared as if the Administration was trying to minimize any political losses from the unceremonious departure of Mr. McGrath, who long had been a party stalwart.

* * * * *

April 4, 1952

EISENHOWER HAILED IN TOUR OF SOUTH; PLEDGES END OF 'TOP-TO-BOTTOM MESS'; TRUMAN SAYS G. O. P. RISKS ATOMIC WAR

GENERAL HITS HARD

Crowds Yell 'Pour It On' as Candidate Charges Corruption in Capital

HE REVIEWS TAX SCANDAL

By W. H. LAWRENCE
Special to THE NEW YORK TIMES.

MIAMI, Sept. 2—Gen. Dwight D. Eisenhower struck hard today on the issue of corruption in Washington and scored an impressive personal triumph on the first campaign invasion of the deep South by any Republican Presidential nominee.

On flying visits to Atlanta, Jacksonville and Miami, General Eisenhower was greeted by large, cheering crowds and drew a cordial welcome from Georgia's Gov. Herman Talmadge, a Democrat who considered bolting his party earlier this year but later agreed to run as a Presidential elector pledged to the candidacy of Gov. Adlai E. Stevenson of Illinois, the Democratic nominee. During the day the Republican candidate addressed three audiences estimated to total 62,000.

Beginning a sustained campaign for the Presidency that will not end until Election Day, Nov. 4, General Eisenhower took off the gloves today and dealt with the asserted sins of the Democrats in down-to-earth language that brought cries of "Yahoo" and "Pour it on" from the crowds that gathered to hear him.

Describing the "mess" in Washington, whose existence he said had been admitted by Governor Stevenson, General Eisenhower declared that it was "the inevitable and sure-fire result of an Administration by too many men who are too small for their jobs, too big for their breeches and too long in power." He asserted that the cost of this mess came out of "the hide" of every American citizen.

Called Friend of South

"This Washington mess," the general said, "is not a one-agency mess, or a one-bureau mess or a one-department mess. It is a top-to-bottom mess."

Before an audience estimated at 35,000 in the heart of Atlanta at midday, Governor Talmadge welcomed General Eisenhower as a "friend" of the South, who probably could have had the Democratic Presidential nomination for the asking in either 1948 or 1952.

The Georgia Governor complained bitterly that his state too long had been taken for granted by the national leadership of the Democratic party, and that its delegation had been "subjected to insults and ridicule" from the Democratic convention that picked Governor Stevenson for the Presidency.

While Governor Talmadge did not urge the crowd to vote for General Eisenhower, he certainly did nothing to discourage it, and he went on to wish the Republican nominee "continued godspeed."

With obvious reference to Governor Stevenson, whom he has called the hand-picked candidate of the Truman Administration, the General declared that "no change of goods in the showcase can make the rotten goods back in the warehouse any better."

"No man, however honest, can clean up this mess if he is elected as the nominee of the Administration which created the mess," he aserted. "No man can set out to restore honesty to government if he owes his election in any degree to those who have condoned corruption. He could have no real freedom to put his house in order if he was in that kind of debt to that kind of officials."

Charges Cover-Up of Crooks

The present Administration, he charged, is conducted by men "who are busy covering up their own crooks" and who are, therefore, "too busy to look after the welfare, the housing, the jobs and the security of the American people" and too busy "to think through the hard decisions and provide the leadership which is necssary to build the peace of this world."

He promised if elected to replace the "whitewash brush" with a "scoop-shovel" to throw the rascals out of Washington, and he promised Federal workers that "they will have no more crooked bosses."

"* * * Why should we Americans any longer tolerate the doubtful, the fearful, the corrupt in high places?" General Eisenhower asked his Atlanta audience, and the cry came back, "We shouldn't."

September 3, 1952

ADAMS BILLS PAID BY INDUSTRIALIST

Boston Concern Involved in F.T.C. and S.E.C. Cases Picked Up Hotel Charges

By WILLIAM M. BLAIR
Special to The New York Times.

WASHINGTON, June 10—House investigators introduced records today to show that a Boston industrialist had paid nearly $2,000 in hotel bills for Sherman Adams, the Assistant to President Eisenhower, and his family.

The hotel bills were presented with allegations that Bernard Goldfine of Brookline, Mass., had been able to get preferred treatment before Federal regulatory agencies because of his friendship with Mr. Adams.

A staff investigator for the House Subcommittee on Legislative Oversight made public photostatic copies of the hotel bills. All were for suites at the Sheraton-Plaza Hotel in Boston. They ranged over a period starting Nov. 24, 1955, to May 5-6 of this year.

James C. Hagerty, White House press secretary, said Mr. Adams was out of town and probably was fishing in New England after making commencement addresses. He said he would have no comment until he got in touch with Mr. Adams.

The hotel bills were detailed after Miss Mildred Paperman, bookkeeper for Mr. Goldfine, branded as illegal a subcommittee subpoena for her employer's records. Roger Robb, Washington attorney and counsel for Miss Paperman and Mr. Goldfine, told reporters the hotel bills were a "smear."

The subcommittee brushed aside their protests. Representative Oren Harris, Democrat of Arkansas and subcommittee chairman, gave her until next Tuesday to produce Mr. Goldfine's records. "And I must tell you," Mr. Harris added, "that failure to do so probably will bring contempt proceedings by the House of Representatives."

The subcommittee has been conducting a broad inquiry to determine whether the Federal regulatory agencies have been carrying out their functions as Congress intended. It has dwelt long on the Federal Communications Commission and allegations that political and other pressures dominated commission decisions in television channel awards.

Bernard Goldfine

Associated Press

Sherman Adams

The Goldfine case involved the Federal Trade Commission and the Securities and Exchange Commission. Mr. Goldfine's past troubles with the F.T.C. cover violations of the Federal Wool Labeling Act. His difficulties with the S. E. C. cover failure to file annual reports on two Boston real estate companies that he controls.

Outside the subcommittee's hearing room, Mr. Robb asserted that the subcommittee had demonstrated "exactly what we said they were going to do in conducting a smear session." He said "you can see that if we fail to produce they will smear us."

Mr. Adams and Mr. Goldfine, he said, are "intimate friends" and have known each other for twenty years, dating back to before Mr. Adams was Governor of New Hampshire.

"When Adams passed through Boston, Goldfine would entertain him," Mr. Robb said. "Adams understood that the suite at the hotel was maintained by Stratmore Woolen Mills." The textile company is one of three involved in a 1955 case before the F. T. C. The mills are controlled by Mr. Goldfine.

Mr. Robb indicated that his clients would stand firm on deciding what was relevant to the inquiry rather than let the subcommittee make that determination, as it has insisted.

Asked what would happen if they failed to comply with the subpoena, he replied: "Then it will wind up in the courts. That's what they build court houses for. We are not going to let them go on a fishing expedition into Mr. Goldfine's records."

Francis X. McLaughlin, subcommittee investigator, who testified on the hotel bills, said he had been told by the manager of the Boston hotel that Mr. Goldfine did not regularly maintain a suite.

The bills for eleven separate visits, most of them for two days for Governor and Mrs. Adams, actually totaled $1,642.28. Mr. McLaughlin testified they bore notations such as "entire bill to be charged to Mr. Goldfine" or "charge complete bill to Bernard Goldfine." The cost of the suites, he said, ranged from $37 a day to $65 a day.

On one occasion, the bills showed that Mr. Adams' daughter, Sarah, was a guest, and another time, the Adams' son, Samuel, stayed in a suite.

Following is the list of hotel bills listed by the records of the House subcommittee as having been paid by Mr. Goldfine, for Mr. Adams and members of his family.

Nov. 24-26, 1955, Governor and Mrs. Adams, $220.56.

Dec. 27-28, 1955, Governor and Mrs. Adams, $151.11.

Dec. 27-28, 1955, Sarah Adams, Lincoln, N. H., $9.37.

March 10-12, 1956, Governor and Mrs. Adams, $164.60.

April 24-25, 1956, Governor and Mrs. Adams (with address "White House, Washington"), $187.85.

March 8-9, 1957, Governor and Mrs. Adams, $170.30.

No date, Sherman Adams, $50.

June 7-8, 1957, Governor and Mrs. Adams, $106.83.

Sept. 21-26, 1957, Governor and Mrs. Adams, $361.13.

Dec. 6-8, 1957, Governor and Mrs. Adams, $161.27.

May 5-6, Governor and Mrs. Adams, $59.26.

The last bill was dated May 5-6, 1958, he said, "the day before the subpoena was served" for the Goldfine records. The subpoena called for all manner of records "including, but not limited to, expenditures made in behalf of all officials, employes, or representatives of the Executive, Legislative and Judicial branches of the Federal and state governments" from Jan. 1, 1950, to date.

It also called for all kinds of stock records from Jan. 1, 1925, to the present of the East Boston Company and its subsidiary, the East Boston Port Development Corporation.

Joseph T. Conlon, another subcommittee attorney, presented a long history of the companies before the S. E. C., which requires annual financial and other reports from companies listed on stock exchanges. East Boston has been listed on the Boston Stock Exchange.

Robert W. Lishman, subcommittee counsel, in contending that the subpoena was valid to the inquiry, asserted that "it appears that throughout the years there has been lavish entertainment of various high public officials." He continued: "We're not making any accusations but we believe the public is entitled to know the facts of the fraternization of these officials in trying to determine whether this was related to companies able to insulate themselves from the law."

It was then that he called Mr. McLaughlin and Mr. Conlon to testify and establish the relevancy of the records to the possibility of political pressure on regulatory agencies.

Mr. McLaughlin said the "allegations" that Mr. Goldfine had received "preferred treatment" from the F. T. C. and S. E. C. had been made "in part by Mr. John Fox." Mr. Fox was publisher of the defunct Boston Post and has been attorney for a group of minority stockholders of the East Boston Company in a Federal court suit in Boston.

Mr. McLaughlin also said the allegations had come from "employes of the F. T. C. who were present at the time of a telephone conversation between Bernard Goldfine and Sherman Adams."

This was a reference to a 1955 meeting in the office of Edward E. Howrey, then F. T. C. chairman, after Mr. Goldfine's textile mills had been cited for mislabeling woolen-blend fabrics.

The testimony on the hotel bills and other matters was spread on the record after the subcommittee had voted to open and make public what had occurred in an executive session. The executive session was asked by Mr. Robb to prevent "wild accusations" such as he asserted were thrown around at a Boston hearing last week on the Goldfine case.

The transcript, read on orders of the subcommittee, showed that several members had protested the futility of the executive session because Miss Paperman did not have any records with her.

June 11, 1958

ADAMS DENIES USING HIS INFLUENCE BUT ADMITS MISTAKES OF JUDGMENT; PRESIDENT VOICES FULL CONFIDENCE

DEMOCRATS WARY

White House Aide, on Stand, Agrees Calls Carry Weight

By WILLIAM M. BLAIR
Special to The New York Times.

WASHINGTON, June 17 — Sherman Adams swore today that he had never used his White House position to influence the decisions of Government agencies for anyone.

But in hindsight, he said, he would have acted "a little more prudently" in approaching Federal agencies in behalf of his long-time friend and New England industrialist, Bernard Goldfine, if he had to do it over again.

Almost immediately after his return to the White House from his two hours of questioning before the Special House Subcommittee on Legislative Oversight, Mr. Adams conferred with President Eisenhower and returned to his duties.

The President Approves

James C. Hagerty, White House press secretary, said Mr. Adams had no intention of resigning and that "the President still has full confidence" in his chief of staff. The White House considers the matter a closed book, Mr. Hagerty said.

President Eisenhower knew of Mr. Adams' testimony and approved, Mr. Hagerty said.

The subcommittee also heard that Mr. Goldfine had lent $400,000 to the now defunct Boston Post at the behest of Gov. Paul A. Dever, a Democrat. Governor Dever has since died.

Mr. Adams, the Assistant to the President, confirmed under oath that Mr. Goldfine had paid hotel bills for him and Mrs. Adams in Boston, New York and Plymouth, Mass. He acknowledged that Mr. Goldfine had given him a vicuña coat. And he testified that Mr. Goldfine had presented the $2,400 Oriental rug now on his living room floor as a loan, not as a gift.

Challenged by Democrats

He told the subcommittee that he had come before it voluntarily but not to apologize. His errors, if any, he said, "were mistakes of judgment and not of intent," a point sharply challenged by Democrats. The White House counsel, Gerald D. Morgan, accompanied Mr. Adams to the hearing room.

Under questioning by Democrats on the subcommittee, Mr. Adams acknowledged that telephone calls from him to Government agencies would carry some weight.

And in answer to the direct question of whether he thought he had overstepped the "bounds of propriety" in dealing with Mr. Goldfine, he soberly conceded that he could "not wholly disagree with the implications" of the question.

He also said he had not known that information supplied to him in his inquiries for Mr. Goldfine had been confidential material and that disclosure had been contrary to Federal law and regulations of the Federal Trade Commission and the Securities and Exchange Commission.

After the hearing, Representative Oren Harris, the subcommittee chairman, asserted he regarded Mr. Adams' actions as "highly improper for a party in his position."

Asked whether he believed Mr. Adams should resign or be dismissed, the Arkansas Democrat replied:

"Mr. Adams will have to search his own conscience and Mr. Eisenhower should do likewise."

In addition to Mr. Morgan, the former Governor of New Hampshire went before the subcommittee accompanied by his wife. Mr. Morgan sat at his right as he faced the subcommittee.

It was the first time Mr. Adams had gone before a Congressional committee since he came to the White House despite invitations and appeals that he appear to explain various Administration actions. He attracted some 600 spectators, who taxed the capacity of the caucus room in the Old House Office Building. Spectators stood three and four deep around the room.

Although major party officials were pictured as reserving judgment, two Republican members of Congress called for Mr. Adams' resignation despite the White House announcement that he would stay.

Representative John B. Bennett of Michigan, a member of the House subcommittee that heard Mr. Adams, commented that the Assistant to the President might not have intended any impropriety.

"But wittingly or unwittingly he has caused his integrity to be brought into question under circumstances of his own making and his continued tenure in high position he holds does not seem justifiable," he said.

On the Senate side of the Capitol, Senator John J. Williams of Delaware said he could not accept Mr. Adams' explanations and that his "resignation is in order."

He asserted that he saw no difference between Mr. Adams' acceptance of an oriental rug and a vicuña coat and the home freezers given to officials of the Truman Administration.

"The Adams case" was raised at the President's regular meeting with legislative leaders in the White House this morning, but not until it was about to break up.

Then, it was learned, the President, who was described as somewhat grim, told them he would get a copy of the statement Mr. Adams had made to the subcommittee.

Senator William F. Knowland of California, who is among those who called for a full explanation from Mr. Adams, said party leaders were reserving judgment until all the facts were in. Some have said they believed Mr. Adams had undercut the party in its political campaign cry of "clean up the mess in Washington."

President Gets Vicuña

Before he went to Capitol Hill this morning Mr. Adams made his statement for the benefit of television and newsreel cameras. And also an hour before the subcommittee appearance, Mr. Hagerty announced that President Eisenhower had once received vicuña material from Mr. Goldfine but had given it away to some unremembered person. The President wrote a letter of thanks to Mr. Goldfine, who had given similar material to many political figures, including Mr. Adams.

Mr. Adams' recital before the subcommittee covered his relationship with Mr. Goldfine, "a poor immigrant who made a success of his enterprise and himself," of gifts exchanged by the families over the years, and the difficulties of "drawing the line" in making requests to Federal agencies on behalf of others.

He said that two years ago, the "White House staff had "counseled together" on the problem of requests made from many sources. Since that time, he said, he had concluded that "sensitive to the implications that might accrue from instances" such as related to the subcommittee, it was "desirable that the staff of the President of the United States should refrain from doing anything which might possibly lead" to overstepping the bounds of propriety.

Mr. Harris posed the questions of whether Mr. Adams had gone beyond the bounds of propriety in accepting gifts, hotel bills and other favors from Mr. Goldfine.

Mr. Adams stated that his errors "perhaps" had stemmed from inexperience although he disclaimed any intention of being a "fledgling in this business of politics."

Nevertheless, he went on, "there are lessons to be learned, and I think perhaps somewhat more prudence would undoubtedly have perhaps obviated some of the questions that have come before your committee."

He said he could not "wholly disagree with some of the implications contained" in Mr. Harris' question.

Mr. Adams testified that he had never sought any preferred treatment for Mr. Goldfine from the F. T. C. when he asked the chairman of that agency to give him a memorandum on a Goldfine case. That case involved Goldfine companies called by the commission for misbranding of textile fabrics.

Nor had he sought favors from the S. E. C., he said, when Mr. Goldfine had been cited for the failure of two of his real estate companies to file any reports and other pertinent financial information.

Violations Charged

Robert W. Lishman, the subcommittee counsel, called his attention to the fact that the disclosure by the agencies of the material he had sought in the Goldfine cases had been contrary to Federal statutes and rules and regulations of the independent commissions.

Mr. Adams responded that he was not familiar with rules governing confidential information. He said that "all I did was to send the inquiry to the man who was responsible as chairman of the commission for a reply." He said he knew nothing of the "merits" of the case.

"I never attempted to advise myself concerning these rules and regulations," he said.

In his usual dry manner, he told Representative John E. Moss, Democrat of California, that "I've heard it rumored" that a mere telephone call from him carried considerable influence. But disclaiming any intention of being facetious he said:

"I am sensitive to the fact that implications can be drawn as the result of any call which I make."

He said his calls were "legion" and that he 'routinely" made them in answer to requests.

Mr. Moss recalled that he, like other Democrats, had come under the "whiplash of a very critical judgment imposed" by the Republicans upon the conduct of the Truman Administration.

And, he said, he had heard during the "Adams case" some prominent people say the affair was a matter of judgment and not of intent.

"I think we must apply at all times, the same rules and the same standards to all persons who occupy similar positions," Mr. Moss said.

Adams Says 'No'

In his opening statement, Mr. Adams said he had tried to see to it that the President's staff had made every effort to deal with "every proper request" that had been presented.

The concern of the subcommittee, he said, was "did Bernard Goldfine benefit in any way in his relations with any branch of the Federal Government because he was a friend of Sherman Adams?"

"Did Sherman Adams seek to secure favors or benefits for Bernard Goldfine because of this relationship?

"The answer to both questions is 'No.'"

The subcommittee could also ask, he said, whether it was proper for any public official to accept gifts from a friend. His own answer was that this was a question for "every man in public life to answer for himself." But he denied that in his public life he had ever permitted any personal relationship to affect his actions.

The $2,400 Oriental rug now on the living room floor of the Adams' rented house in Washington still is Mr. Goldfine's property, Mr. Adams testified. In 1954 Mr. Goldfine told the Adamses during a visit here that they ought to have a "less shabby" rug than they had at that time and he sent one to them.

"Anytime you move from these premises or go back to New Hampshire, I will reclaim it," Mr. Adams quoted his friend as saying.

Harris Sees Violation

WASHINGTON, June 17 (UPI)—Mr. Harris said tonight that Mr. Adams had technically violated the law by passing certain information to Mr. Goldfine.

"I think the proceedings which we have developed here have shown that there was a technical violation of the laws regulating Federal agencies," Mr. Harris said.

June 18, 1958

SHERMAN ADAMS RESIGNS; SEES 'VILIFICATION' DRIVE; PRESIDENT VOICES SADNESS

AIDE GOES ON TV

Tells Nation He Was Innocent of Wrong in Goldfine Case

By RUSSELL BAKER

Special to The New York Times.

WASHINGTON, Sept. 22—Sherman Adams resigned his White House post today under heavy political pressure.

Mr. Adams, the Assistant to the President since early 1953, told a national radio and television audience that the decision had been forced upon him through a "campaign of vilification" calculated to destroy him and embarrass President Eisenhower and his Administration.

Rather than let this happen and endanger Republican chances for gaining control of Congress this November, Mr. Adams said, he decided to quit.

Resignation Accepted

President Eisenhower accepted the Adams resignation "with sadness." A letter from him to Mr. Adams was made public as the staff chief began speaking to the radio-TV audience.

In it the President deplored "the circumstances that have decided you to resign." Mr. Adams, he went on, showed "selfless and tireless devotion" to his White House job.

"Your total dedication to the nation's welfare," he wrote, "has been of the highest possible order."

The President called Mr. Adams' five-and-a-half-year performance in the White House "brilliant" and "unselfish."

"You will be sorely missed," he added.

Adams Defends Record

In his speech, Mr. Adams depicted himself as the innocent victim of elements—only partly identified—engaged in a "calculated and contrived effort" to discredit him.

Although he and the President earlier this year had both conceded that there might have been imprudence in his relationship with the New England textile magnate, Bernard Goldfine, Mr. Adams made no such concession tonight.

"I have done no wrong," he said.

He insisted that his own testimony and that of "every responsible official" had clearly exonerated him of any wrongdoing.

Despite the fact that this testimony to his innocence was "wholly undisputed," he said, an effort to 'attack and discredit" him had continued incessantly.

He accused the House Special Subcommittee on Legislative Oversight, which investigated the Goldfine matter, with being a party to this effort. The subcommittee, he asserted, listened to "completely irresponsible testimony and, without conscience, gave ear to rumor, innuendo and even unsubstantiated gossip."

The committee produced evidence last June that Mr. Adams had made inquiries at two Federal regulatory agencies in behalf of Mr. Goldfine. It also showed that Mr. Goldfine had paid more than $3,000 in hotel bills for Mr. Adams and had presented him a vicuña coat and an oriental rug.

Violations Charged

Mr. Adams insisted that his inquiries to the agencies in-

Associated Press Wirephoto

CONFERENCE IN NEWPORT: President Eisenhower accompanies Sherman Adams to helicopter after talk at summer White House. The Assistant to the President had flown there early yesterday to confer on his resignation.

volved had been merely routine checks he would have made for any business man seeking similar information. The sub-committee contended, however, that Mr. Adams had violated the law and the regulations of the Federal Trade Commission in one instance.

President Eisenhower told a news conference at that time that Mr. Adams might have been "imprudent." But, he added, "I respect him because of his personal and official integrity. I need him."

Many Republican candidates facing election campaigns this fall publicly took the position that Mr. Adams was a political liability that would endanger their prospects. Until the Maine election on Sept. 8, however, it appeared that Mr. Adams had ridden out the storm.

The Maine vote, a Democratic triumph that overwhelmed one Republican—Senator Frederick G. Payne—who had associated with Mr. Goldfine, renewed Republican pressure for Mr. Adams's removal.

It was this renewal of Republican pressure that brought the final decision. This morning Mr. Adams flew from Washington to Newport, R. I., where the President is vacationing.

He and the President talked for an hour and fifteen minutes. Mr. Adams spent twenty-five more minutes with James C. Hagerty, White House Press secretary. Then he conferred again briefly with the President.

Resignation Submitted

It was during these conferences, Mr. Adams said tonight, that he submitted his resignation. To the outside world, however, his decision remained a mystery.

Mr. Hagerty announced only that the radio and television networks had been asked for radio and television time so that Mr. Adams might speak tonight. The Presidential Assistant, accompanied by Mr. Hagerty, flew back to Washington, arriving shortly after 1 P. M. Newsmen and photographers, contrary to White House custom, were barred from Anacostia Naval Air Station where their plane landed.

The question that had been bothering Republican politicians for the last week was whether Mr. Adams' resignation, coming this late in the political season, would have any appreciable effect on the outcome of the November elections. Some felt that the long period over which the Adams story had been in the headlines had already damaged the Republicans' chances.

In his explanation to the people tonight, Mr. Adams said:

"A campaign of vilification by those who seek personal advantage by my removal from public life has continued up to this very moment.

"These efforts, it is now clear, have been intended to destroy me and, in so doing, to embarrass the Administration and the President of the United States."

The 'Easy Way'

The "easy way," he said, would have been to resign at the outset—"to remove the target."

But, he went on, he ignored this course. It was not his nature, he said, "to run in the face of adversity." And, he explained, "since I have done no wrong," to have resigned earlier could have been construed as an admission that he had.

However, he continued, he was forced also to consider the effect of his continuing in office upon the President's future programs and upon his party's chances for regaining control of Congress in November.

In both instances, he indicated, he decided that to continue would be harmful. He said he had reached this decision within the last few days.

Mr. Adams will continue at his desk until a successor can be appointed in what Mr. Adams made the most powerful job in the White House, short of the President's own.

Mr. Adams spoke at 6:35 P. M. from the Washington studio of the Columbia Broadcasting System, but his address was also carried live by the National Broadcasting Company. The American Broadcasting Company repeated his statement later on its networks. It lasted about eight minutes.

Mr. Adams drove to the studio in his green Oldsmobile station wagon, accompanied only by a White House policeman who rode in the passenger's seat.

September 23, 1958

KICKBACK LINKED TO JOHNSON AIDE

Assistant Denies Soliciting Ads From Baker Friend

By CABELL PHILLIPS
Special to The New York Times

WASHINGTON, Jan. 21—An aide to President Johnson and a Maryland insurance man have given conflicting testimony about an alleged advertising kickback to a Texas television station owned by the President's family.

The conflict was revealed today in testimony taken privately earlier this month by the Senate Rules Committee. The panel is investigating possible conflicts of interest involving Robert G. Baker, while he was secretary to the Senate Democratic majority.

At closed sessions Jan. 9 and 17, the committee heard Don B. Reynolds, an insurance broker in suburban Silver Spring, Md., who is a friend and business associate of Mr. Baker. He testified that, with Mr. Baker's help, he sold Mr. Johnson $200,000 worth of life insurance from 1957 to 1961.

He told the committee under oath that a Johnson aide, Walter Jenkins, had induced him to buy $1,200 worth of advertising on station KTBC of Austin, Tex., owned by the LBJ Company, a Johnson family enterprise. At the time of the alleged conversation, Mr. Jenkins was an aide in the office of Mr. Johnson, then a Senator; he is now on the White House staff.

In an affidavit submitted to the committee, Mr. Jenkins denied that he had ever talked to Mr. Reynolds about buying advertising time.

The testimony also showed that, at Mr. Baker's insistence, Mr. Reynolds gave Senator Johnson a $542 stereophonic phonograph in 1959 and paid $42.50 for its installation in the Senator's Spring Valley home. Mr. Reynolds said he had never received any acknowledgment from the Johnsons.

Senator Robert C. Byrd, Democrat of West Virginia, asked if Mr. Johnson knew at the time the phonograph was installed that it was Mr. Reynolds who had given it to him.

His Name on Invoice

"I don't think there would have been any question about it, sir, because, this set, the invoice was billed from the Magnavox Company directly to Senator Johnson,' Mr. Reynolds said.

"But that would not necessarily connect you with the transaction,' Senator Byrd said.

"It showed that the charges were to be sent to Don Reynolds, sir," Mr. Reynolds replied.

A copy of the invoice was included in the transcript. It showed that the phonograph had been billed to Mr. Reynolds, but it gave Senator Johnson's name and address on the same line under "shipping instructions."

In his sworn statement, Mr. Jenkins said he had been informed that "the alleged gift of the record player to Mr. and Mrs. Johnson was a present from Robert G. Baker."

At the White House today, Mr. Johnson's press secretary, Pierre Salinger, said that Mr. Jenkins's statement to the committee "makes it clear that the President never had any communication with Mr. Reynolds about the record player, and considered it a gift from a long-time employe"—Baker.

Mr. Salinger was asked if the President still had the set. He replied, "I believe he gave it to one of his household employes some time ago."

He was not asked to comment on the statement about the television advertising.

Among other things that Mr. Reynolds told the committee were the following:

¶Mr. Baker helped him get a $10,000 commission in obtaining a performance bond for the construction of the District of Columbia Stadium.

¶Mr. Baker, Thomas Webb Jr. and Representative Abraham J. Multer, Democrat of Brooklyn, were instrumental in getting the Mortgage Guarantee Insurance Company a hospitable hearing in Washington.

¶Mr. Baker and Scott I. Peek, former assistant to Senator George A. Smathers, Democrat of Florida, were involved in a Florida shopping center and motel that were principally financed by teamsters' union funds.

¶Mr. Reynolds referred a pregnant unmarried young woman to Mr. Baker for advice about an abortion. The testimony did not make clear whether the abortion ever took place.

¶Mr. Reynolds was recently "threatened" by Mr. Baker's law partner, Ernest C. Tucker, because of his testimony before the committee.

Committee Is Divided

The release of Mr. Reynolds's testimony has caused a sharp partisan split in the nine-man Rules Committee.

In announcing last week that the transcript would be made public, the chairman, Senator B. Everett Jordan, Democrat of North Carolina, said that Mr. Reynolds would not be recalled unless "new information is developed requiring his testimony."

Republican members of the panel have argued that the Reynolds testimony should have been further explored in public hearings.

The Democratic members are believed to be wary about looking too deeply into areas that impinge upon the relationship between Mr. Baker and the President. For the decade while Mr. Johnson was Senate Democratic leader and Vice President, Mr. Baker was regarded as his protégé.

An aide to Senator Jordan said he knew of no plans by the committee to ask Mr. Jenkins to testify. The Senator was out of the city today.

The testimony released today provided fresh insight into the scope and intricacy of Mr. Baker's business affairs while he was a $19,600-a-year Senate employe.

Mr. Reynolds and Mr. Baker are fellow South Carolinians. When Mr. Reynolds set up his insurance agency in 1955, Mr. Baker agreed to become a partner and officer by purchasing 10 shares at $25 a share.

Mr. Baker never paid for any stock but retained title in the company. What he did contribute was the influence of his name and his contacts with people of power in the capital, Mr. Reynolds said.

Paid Baker $15,000

This was a first-rate bargain for the agency, because Mr. Baker brought in a lot of good business, including that of Senator Johnson, Mr. Reynolds said. Over the years, he paid Mr. Baker a total of $15,000, in various sums, for "services rendered," he said.

Mr. Reynolds said he was puzzled a few years ago when Mr. Baker insisted that he take promissory notes for each payment tendered. Mr. Reynolds indicated that he regarded these payments as fees for services rendered by Mr. Baker and thus did not expect to be paid back. Presumably, the promissory notes made it possible for Mr. Baker to show the payments on his own books as loans rather than earnings.

Among the business opportunities that Mr. Baker turned up for him, Mr. Reynolds said, was that of intermediary in writing a $14,000,000 performance bond for the construction of the District of Columbia Stadium in 1960.

Mr. Baker introduced him to Matthew M. McCloskey, the Philadelphia contractor who for many years was treasurer of the Democratic National Committee, Mr. Reynolds said. When Mr. McCloskey got the stadium contract, Mr. Reynolds's companies wrote the preformance bond and Mr. Reynolds got a $10,000 commission.

Mr. Reynolds testified he had given $4,000 of the commission to Mr. Baker and $1,500 to William W. McLeod Jr., clerk of the House District Committee, which was the legislative guardian of the stadium project.

Mr. Baker also put him in touch with Mr. Webb, a Washington lawyer who represented Clint Murchison, the Texas oil millionaire, and had close connections with James R. Hoffa, president of the International Brotherhood of Teamsters, Mr. Reynolds said.

In 1959, Mr. Reynolds told the committee, he joined with Mr. Webb, Mr. Baker, Mr. Peek and four Jacksonville, Fla., businessmen to erect a motel and shopping center at Jacksonville Beach.

They formed a corporation known as the WERT Company, each participant contributing $600 to its capitalization. Mr. Baker gave Mr. Reynolds $1,200 in cash to cover his own purchase and that of Mr. Peek, the witness said. He said that the stock of Mr. Baker and Mr. Peek had been held in the name of Mr. Webb and that they had never appeared as owners of record.

Through Mr. Webb, the group obtained a $100,000 mortgage loan from the teamsters' union welfare and retirement fund to complete the purchase of the property and to clear it, Mr. Reynolds said. Later the group got a commitment from the fund for an additional loan of $400,000 for construction, he said.

The motel project failed a year ago and the teamsters' union has begun court action to recover from the stockholders.

Mr. Reynolds testified at greater length about the life insurance policy for Senator Johnson than about any other subject.

Because of his heart attack, the Senator was regarded as a poor insurance risk in 1957, but one of Mr. Reynolds's companies was willing to write a policy on him, the witness said. Mr. Reynolds told Mr. Baker of this, and Mr. Baker put him in touch with Mr. Jenkins, the witness said.

Shortly thereafter, a $50,000 policy was issued, and this was later increased to $100,000. The applicant, Mr. Reynolds said, was Mrs. Johnson, who is chairman of the board of the LBJ Company, and the company was named as beneficiary.

Buys Second Policy

In 1961, Mr. Johnson, then Vice President, bought another $100,000 policy through the same company, making his daughters the beneficiaries.

Mr. Reynolds said that sometime before the second policy was placed he was called to Mr. Jenkins's office. He was shown a letter from a rival Texas insurance man saying that if he, the rival, could write insurance on Mr. Johnson, he would be willing to buy advertising time on station KTBC, Mr. Reynolds said.

The questioning went this way:

Q. Now, the injection of the purchase of advertising was something new. You never had that pointed out to you before, had you? A. No, sir.

Q. Did you agree to purchase the advertising? A. I made the statement that, consistent with having the privilege of writing the insurance for the then Vice

President, that I would do my best to buy the comparable advertising time.

Q. Did you buy the advertising at the cost of $1,208? A. Yes, sir. I purchased it for the name of the Mid-Atlantic Stainless Steel Corporation.

Senator Carl T. Curtis, Republican of Nebraska, pursued the point further in a later exchange.

Q. Did you buy this advertising time to advertise your insurance company? A. No, sir; because it was expected of me.

Q. Who conveyed that thought to you? A. Mr. Walter Jenkins, sir, in his office.

Q. Are you sure you did not volunteer to buy the advertising? A. Yes, sir. But I hoped that by doing this it would develop goodwill.

Mr. Jenkins had submitted an affidavit to the committee covering this point. In it he stated that he had no knowledge "of any arrangements whereby Reynolds purchased advertising time on the TV station."

"He emphatically denies ever suggesting to Robert G. Baker or to Reynolds the LBJ Company should get any sort of rebate from the commissions earned by Reynolds," the affidavit said.

Senator Curtis read portions of the affidavit aloud and asked Mr. Reynolds, "You would disagree with that?"

"Completely, sir," Mr. Reynolds answered.

Mr. Reynolds added that he had sold his $1,200 advertising rights to Mid-Atlantic Stainless Steel for $160.

January 22, 1964

JOHNSON ASSERTS HE TOOK STEREO AS INNOCENT GIFT

Explains Phonograph Was Only One of Presents He and Baker Exchanged

By TOM WICKER
Special to The New York Times

WASHINGTON, Jan. 23 — President Johnson pictured as innocent today his receipt of an expensive stereophonic phonograph from Robert G. Baker, the former secretary of the Senate majority whose business dealings are under investigation here.

Referring to the stereophonic set as a gift of "the Baker family," the President said that "we had exchanged gifts before."

The President also gave an account of the purchase of $200,000 of insurance on his life after his heart attack in 1955. But he did not comment on charges that have been made in the Baker investigation that the agent who sold the insurance was forced to buy advertising on the Johnson family television station.

First Remarks on Case

Mr. Johnson, turning from a foreign policy statement on Panama to the Baker case, surprised White House reporters with his remarks. He left the room where he was speaking before they could question him.

Mr. Johnson's unexpected remarks were the first that he has made on the Baker case, a major topic of conversation in Washington since last fall. Mr. Baker was the Democratic secretary while Mr. Johnson was the Senate majority leader, and was widely regarded at that time as Mr. Johnson's protégé.

Mr. Baker was forced to resign his post when charges of improper use of his influence were raised against him.

Today, the Senate Rules Committee, which is investigating Mr. Baker, heard testimony of a temporary bank credit of $100,000 that he had obtained. He used the credit to aid in getting a Federal storm damage loan of $54,000 for a motel in which he had an interest.

The committee released testimoney last Monday that brought the President publicly into the picture. The testimony was that of Don B. Reynolds, the insurance agent, who told the committee about the stereo set and the television advertising.

Mr. Johnson appeared at 5:04 P.M. in the White House Fish Room near his office, ostensibly to make a policy statement on the situation in Panama. Television and newsreel cameras were present but Mr. Johnson was not being televised "live."

The room was jammed with reporters. As Mr. Johnson concluded the Panama statement, Merriman Smith of United Press International spoke up.

"Mr. President," he said, "before you go I wonder if you could entertain another question or so. For example, how do you think things are going up on the Hill?"

Mr. Johnson answered readily enough. First he spoke of legislative accomplishments since he became President. He mentioned his hopes that the civil rights bill might be passed in the House before the break for Lincoln's Birthday. Then he said that Senator Harry F. Byrd of Virginia had just called to tell him that the tax reduction bill had been acted upon favorably by the Senate Finance Committee.

Then Mr. Johnson offered his surprise, and to many reporters it seemed that he had been waiting for a suitable opportunity.

"You are also writing some other stories," he said, "I think about an insurance policy that was written on my life some seven years ago and I am still here. The company in which Mrs. Johnson and my daughters have a majority interst, along with some other stockholders, were somewhat concerned when I had a heart attack in 1955 and in 1957 they purchased insurance on my life made payable to the company.

This was a reference to the LBJ Company, which operates the only television station in Austin, Tex.

Mr. Reynolds had told the investigating committee that he sold a $50,000 insurance policy on Mr. Johnson's life in 1957 and that it was later raised to $100,000. A further $100,000 policy was issued on Mr. Johnson when he had become Vice President, Mr. Reynolds said.

The President mentioned none of those figures.

"The insurance premiums were never included as a business expense" of the LBJ Company, he said, but the insurance was considered "good business practice in case something happened to me so Mrs. Johnson and the children wouldn't have to sell their stock on the open market and lose control of the company."

Pierre Salinger, the White House news secretary, said Mr. Johnson had made the point about the insurance premiums because it had been alleged in some newspapers that the premiums had been deducted from the LBJ Company's income tax. That left the inference, Mr. Salinger said, that the company actually was owned by Mr Johnson rather than by his wife and daughters.

The premiums were paid by the company with "after-tax money," Mr. Salinger said.

Mr. Johnson also said of the insurance controversy:

"That insurance was purchased here in Washington and on a portion of the premiums paid Mr. Don Reynolds got a small commission. Mr. George Sampson, the general agent for the Manhattan Insurance Company, handled it and we have paid some $78,000 in premiums up to date and there is another $11,800 due next month, which the company will probably pay to take care of that insurance."

Mr. Johnson made no mention of the charge made by Mr. Reynolds concerning advertising. The agent told the Senate surance sale had been made, Walter Jenkins, a Johnson aide, had induced him to buy $1,200 worth of advertising on station KTBC of Austin, the station owned by the LBJ Company.

Mr. Jenkins, now on the White House staff, denied the allegation in a sworn statement to the committee.

Mr. Johnson did not deal with Mr. Reynold's contention that the insurance sale had been arranged with the help of Mr. Baker. He discussed at some length, however, his receipt of a $542 stereophonic phonograph in 1959.

That, Mr. Johnson said, was a gift "that an employe of mine made to me and Mrs. Johnson."

"The Baker family gave us a stereo set," Mr. Johnson said, referring to Mr. Baker by name for the first and only time.

"We used it for a period and we had exchanged gifts before. He was an employe of the public and had no business pending before me and was asking for nothing and so far as I knew expected nothing in return any more than I did when I had presented him with gifts."

Thus, Mr. Johnson referred to Mr. Baker both as an "employe of mine" and as an "employe of the public."

In fact, as a member of the Senate staff, Mr. Baker was paid his $19,600 yearly salary by the Federal Government, justifying one description. As secretary of the Democratic majority, of which Mr. Johnson was leader, however, Mr. Baker was largely responsible to Mr. Johnson.

Mr. Reynolds, in telling the investigating committee about the stereo, said he had paid for the set and had paid the $42.50 installation charge. This was done, he said, at Mr. Baker's insistence.

Mr. Jenkins's affidavit to the committee said he had been informed that the phonograph was "a present from Robert G. Baker."

January 24, 1964

SENATE REFUSES TO WIDEN SCOPE OF BAKER INQUIRY

Mansfield and Case Engage in Angry Dispute Before Resolution Is Defeated

G.O.P. LOSES A BATTLE

42-33 Vote Rejects a Call for Investigating Improper Activities of Senators

By CABELL PHILLIPS

Special to The New York Times

WASHINGTON, May 11—In one of the angriest debates in recent Congressional history, the Senate defeated today a Republican proposal to broaden the Robert G. Baker investigation to include improper activities by Senators.

The critical vote came on a motion by the Democratic leader, Mike Mansfield of Montana, to table, and thus kill, a resolution by Senator John J. Williams, Republican of Delaware. The resolution, to extend the scope of the investigation, was tabled by a 42-to-33 vote.

But the substantive issue was virtually lost sight of in a tempestuous shouting match between Mr. Mansfield and Senator Clifford P. Case, Republican of New Jersey, a co-sponsor of the resolution.

The Republicans have been attempting to force the Rules Committee to reopen its investigation into the private business dealings of Mr. Baker, who resigned under fire in October as secretary to the Senate's Democratic majority.

9 Democrats Back Move

In the voting today, nine Democrats joined 24 Republicans in voting against tabling. All who voted for tabling were Democrats.

Ordinarily two of the most courteous and restrained members of the chamber, Senators Case and Mansfield were engaged for almost 15 minutes in an angry dispute over an issue of parliamentary privilege.

The Democratic leader had denounced the Williams-Case resolution as politically inspired and as "impugning the integrity of the whole Senate with sly innuendo."

Mr. Case leaped to his feet asking Mr. Mansfield to yield the floor to him. Mr. Mansfield refused and Mr. Case cried to the chair: "Mr. President, a point of personal privilege." He said that Mr. Mansfield had accused him of improper conduct.

Case Repeats Demand

As Mr. Mansfield continued to speak, Mr. Case appealed to the chair again, his voice rising with anger. He repeatedly shouted his demand of parliamentary privilege while Mr. Mansfield shouted his denial that Mr. Case's privilege had been breached by anything he had said.

At one point Senator Mansfield, his normally pale face flushed and his voice shaking with emotion, cried out:

"This is the first time in my 12 years in the Senate that I have been subjected to such treatment, and I do not like it."

Senator Case, equally shaken, protested:

"This is the most shocking overriding of a Senator's rights I have ever experienced."

The presiding officer throughout the fray was one of the Senate's most junior members, Edward M. Kennedy, Democrat of Massachusetts, younger brother of President Kennedy.

He banged his gavel futilely and shouted for first one and then the other antagonist to take his seat. He was being advised by the Senate parliamentarian, Charles L. Watkins.

But in the turmoil, even the scholarly Mr. Watkins appeared to be confused.

At one point he apparently advised the presiding officer to honor Mr. Case's point of privilege. But in a moment he appeared to reconsider and advised that the Democratic leader had not transgressed the Senate's rules and should not be made to take his seat.

As Mr. Case continued to protest, and other members added their voices to the general uproar, Mr. Mansfield demanded a vote on his tabling motion and the chair ordered the roll called.

Senate observers said they could not recall a similar outburst of passion and acrimony on the Senate floor in many years.

Some of these observers felt that Mr. Case had been unfairly dealt with both by Mr. Mansfield and Mr. Kennedy. The rules of the Senate are, in general, generous in their deference to a member pleading a point of personal privilege, which is a claim of injury to his dignity or his integrity.

His Appeal Is Denied

By custom at least, the chair will usually order the offending Senator to stop talking and be seated while it hears the other's complaint. If the complaint is not sustained by the chair, the aggrieved party, under certain circumstances, can appeal such a decision to the Senate as a whole.

Mr. Case repeatedly demanded that this rule be invoked today. When he was denied, he demanded the right to appeal the chair's ruling to the Senate.

Mr. Mansfield contended that he had not maligned Mr. Case in anything he had said. He also argued that, because his motion was being considered under a rigid 40-minute time limit, it was necessary to press the matter to a vote without delay.

Although the Senate is considering the civil rights bill, it was able to get into the proposal stemming from the Baker investigation in this manner:

Senator Mansfield asked Senator Spessard L. Holland, Democrat of Florida, who was speaking on the rights measure, to give way for 40 minutes to the other proposal. Mr. Holland agreed, and continued his speech later.

Afterwards, both Mr. Mansfield and Mr. Case talked separately to reporters. While each man displayed the effects of an unsettling emotional experience each declared there had been "nothing personal" in the exchange between them.

The consequence of the incident, from a legislative standpoint, was that the scope of the Rules Committee's inquiry into Mr. Baker's affairs remained unchanged.

Mr. Mansfield, contending that the Rules Committee had all the authority it needed, said today that he saw no justice in adopting a new resolution that would permit "any Senator to impugn the character of any or all of his colleagues on the basis of vague suspicions."

"I say to all Senators present," he declared, "let us have done with the sly innuendo . . ."

Case Interrupts Speaker

Mr. Case broke in at this point and the following colloquy ensued:

MR. CASE: Mr. President, will the Senator yield.

MR. MANSFIELD: . . . the intemperate inference . . .

MR. CASE: Mr. President, a point of personal privilege.

MR. MANSFIELD: Mr. President, I do not yield the floor for any purpose. I ask that the Senator be instructed to take his seat.

PRESIDING OFFICER: The Senator from Montana has the floor.

MR. CASE: Mr. President, a point of order. The majority leader is out of order . . .

Mr. MANSFIELD: I say to all Senators, let us have done with the sly innuendo. . . .

MR. CASE: The Senator from Montana is not entitled to speak out of order.

PRESIDING OFFICER: In the opinion of the chair, the Senator from Montana has not violated any personal brivilege. . . .

MR. MANSFIELD: I have the floor. I will not yield.

Mr. Kennedy then ruled that the time had expired and directed that the roll be called on the motion to table the resolution.

May 15, 1964

Rules Panel Softens Code On Finances of Senators

By CABELL PHILLIPS
Special to The New York Times

WASHINGTON, June 29—The Senate Rules Committee approved today a limited and carefully worded resolution requiring Senators and Senate employes to disclose certain facts about their financial holdings. The action was taken at the end of a heated two-and-a-half-hour session following the rejection of a more strongly worded substitute offered by Senator Joseph S. Clark, Democrat of Pennsylvania.

Carried 8 to 1, the winning resolution obviously failed to satisfy a number of members of both parties. Its sponsor was the committee chairman, Senator B. Everett Jordan, Democrat of North Carolina, who later described the resolution as "a very good compromise of many points of view."

Senator Carl T. Curtis of Nebraska, senior Republican on the panel, cast the solitary vote against the measure. He did so, he said, because the resolution does not involve a disclosure of income; does not cover the holdings of spouses, and carries no enforcement features.

'Better Than Nothing'

A Democrat who did vote favorably said he had done so only because it was "a better-than-nothing compromise."

Today's action represents the first—and possibly the only—legislative outcome of the committee's eight-month-long investigation into the outside business activities of Robert G. Baker, former secretary to the Senate Democratic majority. A final report on the committee's findings—and other legislative recommendations, if any—is expected late this week or early in the next.

Mr. Jordan followed the unusual practice of rushing the disclosure resolution to the Senate floor ahead of its supporting committee report in order, he said, to head off a similar measure that will be offered as an amnedment to the Federal pay bill tomorrow by Senator Kenneth B. Keating, Republican of New York.

The Keating proposal is more stringent in its disclosure requirements than the Rules Committee version. It would make enactment of a salary increase for members of Congress contingent upon adoption of the disclosure amendment.

The resolution approved today requires only that Senate members and employes make annual reports to the secretary of the Senate identifying all businesses, partnerships, trusts "or other legal entity" operated for profit in which they hold a pecuniary interest.

The rule would be applicable only to persons whose Senate salaries exceed $10,000, and reporting would be required only when the value of the outside holdings exceeds 50 per cent of the holder's Senate salary.

The proposal does not require reports of income from these holdings, or from outside fees, honorariums and gifts. Nor does it require the reporting of holdings by members of the principal's family.

"This has nothing to do with income," Mr. Jordan explained. "Its purpose is to show what stocks or bonds or other financial interests a Senator or a Senate employe has.

"If we had had this kind of reporting while Bobby Baker was here we would have known that he was a vice president in the Reynolds Insurance Agency. He would have had to report his beneficial interest in the Carousel Motel and the Serv-U Company."

In addition to outside holdings, Senators and employes would be required to give the name and address of any "professional firm" in which he has an interest that engages in practice before agencies of the Federal Government.

The resolution would also prohibit Senate employes taking any part in the allocation of political campaign funds between members of the Senate.

Mr. Clark's resolution, which was reportedly defeated by a 5-to-3 vote (Senator Hugh Scott, Pennsylvania Republican, was not present when the vote was taken), called for disclosure not only of all outside holdings, but also of all outside earnings from whatever sources, including capital gains, in excess of $100.

It would also have required disclosure of assets held by spouses and "strawmen" in which a Senator or employe enjoyed a beneficial interest.

To enforce the new rules, the Clark proposal would have given the Rules Committee authority to investigate alleged violations to recommend disciplinary action up o expulsion from the Senate.

The resolution adopted by the committee today is also less stringent than the disclosure provision originally proposed by the committee's chief counsel, Maj. Lennox P. McClendon.

In a draft of his first report, which was disclosed in May, the counsel recommended that members and employes be required to report both their outside holdings and their outside earnings.

Observers consider it unlikely that Congress will accept the discipline of a strict reporting procedure on members' outside business and financial activities. Past experience has shown that Senators and Representatives are willing to impose such restrictions upon the executive branch, and to a lesser extent upon their own employes. But they have consistently declined to give serious consideration to applying those restrictions to themselves.

For this reason, it is believed that Mr. Jordan has attempted to find a formula that Congress will accept rather than one to satisfy the advocates of Congressional reform.

June 30, 1964

Reynolds Says Baker Got '60 Funds to Aid Johnson

By CABELL PHILLIPS
Special to The New York Times

WASHINGTON, Dec. 1—Don B. Reynolds told the Senate Rules Committee today that he acted as a "bag man" in 1960 in the transfer of an allegedly illegal campaign contribution of $25,000 from Matthew H. McCloskey to Robert G. Baker.

Mr. Reynolds said Mr. Baker had told him that $15,000 of this money was to go to the campaign of John F. Kennedy for President and Lyndon B. Johnson for Vice President. The Maryland insurance man said he had no knowledge of where the money had actually gone.

His testimony was supported by copies of invoices and a canceled check. These indicated that Mr. McCloskey, builder of the $20 million D.C. Stadium, had overpaid the premium on his company's performance bond, with most of the excess going to Mr. Baker for political purposes.

Mr. Johnson was then the Senate Democratic leader and, thus, Mr. Baker's superior.

Partisan Dispute Arises

The hearing today was a resumption of an investigation, begun more than a year ago, into the business affairs of Mr. Baker, former secretary of the Senate's Democratic majority. Almost immediately, the proceedings were bogged down in partisan dispute among committee members.

Repeatedly, Senator Carl T. Curtis of Nebraska, the senior Republican on the committee, accused the committee counsel, Lennox P. McLendon, of trying to impeach the testimony of Mr. Reynolds rather than trying to extract information from him.

Seated next to Senator Curtis as a guest of the committee was Senator John J. Williams, Republican of Delaware, who touched off the initial Baker inquiry and has accused the committee of a lack of zeal and courage. At one point, he tangled with the chairman, Senator B. Everett Jordan, Democrat of North Carolina, over material in the Reynolds testimony that Senator Williams said he, himself, had given the committee months ago.

After another exchange between Senator Williams and

Mr. McLendon, Senator Curtis turned to the counsel and said angrily:

"You have called Senators down when they are asking questions, and I resent it. And I resent the sandbagging of a colleague."

Mr. Reynolds, a husky six-footer with gray hair and a pronounced Southern accent, is an insurance broker in nearby Silver Spring, Md. Mr. Baker was briefly associated with him in business three or four years ago.

Mr. Reynolds said that the entire purpose of his serving as "bag man" between Mr. McCloskey and Mr. Baker was to divert money from the stadium project into political channels. The Corrupt Practices Act makes it illegal for a corporation to make political contributions. It also imposes a limit of $5,000 on the contribution of an individual.

The witness said that he first became interested in the D. C. Stadium contract in the spring of 1959. He said that Mr. Baker invited him to have breakfast at the Mayflower Hotel with a small group that included former President Harry S. Truman and Mr. McCloskey.

Discuss Stadium Bill

Mr. McCloskey, who later became Ambassador to Ireland, was at that time treasurer of the Democratic National Committee.

At the end of the breakfast, Mr. Reynolds said, Mr. Baker took him and Mr. McCloskey aside to discuss a bill then pending in Congress to authorize the construction of the stadium. Mr. Baker said that he and William L. McLeod, then chief counsel for the House District of Columbia Committee, could assure passage of the bill, Mr. Reynolds said. The understanding was that Mr. McCloskey would get the contract for the stadium and that Mr. Reynolds would write the insurance for the project, he said.

The witness then quoted Mr. Baker as saying to Mr. McCloskey: "The additional funds we have discussed can be channeled through Don."

This, Mr. Reynolds told the committee, related to a proposed overpayment on the insurance contracts that could be used as concealed political contributions.

Mr. Truman was not a party to any of this conversation, Mr. Reynolds said.

Subsequently, the witness continued, he was awarded only the performance bond in the stadium project. Copies of two invoices and a canceled check covering this transaction were then introduced into the record by the committee.

Money Is Deposited

The first invoice was addressed to Mr. Reynolds from the insurance brokers through whom he had placed the bond, Hutchinson, Rivinus & Co., of Philadelphia. This was in the sum of $73,631.28 and was dated Sept. 13, 1960.

The second invoice was from Mr. Reynolds to the McCloskey company, dated Sept. 14, and was in the sum of $109,205.60. This invoice was made out for the larger sum, the witness said, on instructions from Mr. Baker.

The third document was a photostat of a canceled check drawn by the McCloskey company to the order of Don Reynolds Associates, Inc., dated Oct. 17, 1960, for $109,205.60.

Associated Press Wirephoto

DESCRIBES HIS ROLE: Don B. Reynolds, insurance man, arriving for Senate Rules Committee hearing in the Robert G. Baker case.

Mr. Reynolds said that, at Mr. Baker's suggestion, he deposited this check in a savings and loan company with which he did not usually do business. From the proceeds, he paid the proper premium on the performance bond to Hutchinson, less his commission of $10,000. Out of the remainder, approximately $35,000, he kept $10,000 as "my fee for acting as bag man" and gave the rest to Mr. Baker over a period of time as he called for it in sums of $5,000, always in cash.

Mr. Reynolds said it was his understanding that Mr. Baker and Mr. McCloskey had agreed that $15,000 of this sum was to go to the Kennedy-Johnson campaign fund, and that Mr. Baker was to distribute the remaining $10,000 to other Democratic campaign funds as he saw fit.

Public Session Delayed

The public session, originally scheduled for this morning, was delayed until 2:30 o'clock while the committee was locked in a three-hour debate in an executive session attended both by Mr. Reynolds and Senator Williams. The subject under debate was reportedly whether the committee should investigate allegations that party girls had been involved in some of Mr. Baker's business activities while he was a Senate employe.

After the closed session, the chairman indicated that "the call girl angle" would not be taken up for the present. He did not rule out the possibility that it might come up later.

At one point, when Senator Curtis accused Mr. McLendon of trying to discredit Mr. Reynold's testimony, the counsel replied, "I'm after the truth."

Mr. Reynolds produced a Bible and opened it, saying, "I refer the committee to read the 32d verse of St. John and stop using semantics to misinterpret what I say."

He said later that he had referred to John 8:32, which says: "And ye shall know the truth, and the truth shall make you free."

Mr. McCloskey and members of his company will be called later this week to give their side of the story. The contractor previously denied any wrongdoing in the matter.

December 2, 1964

JENKINS DENIES USING PRESSURE

Former Johnson Aide Gives Replies in Baker Inquiry

By BEN A. FRANKLIN
Special to The New York Times

WASHINGTON, Feb. 24 — Walter W. Jenkins denied for a second time today that he had ever used coercion or pressure on Don B. Reynolds, an insurance salesman, to buy advertising time on a Texas television station owned by President Johnson's family.

Mr. Jenkins, former special assistant to the President, also denied other assertions by Mr. Reynolds, who sold two $100,000 policies on Mr. Johnson's life before he became President. Mr. Reynolds was once a business associate of Robert G. Baker, former secretary to the Senate's Democratic majority.

Mr. Jenkins's denials were made in answers to 40 written questions submitted to him Feb. 10 by the Senate Rules Committee, which is investigating Mr. Baker's private business affairs. A transcript of the questions and answers was made public by the committee today.

Mr. Jenkins was excused from appearing personally before the committee earlier this month. He has been under intensive psychiatric treatment for "severe depression" since resigning from the White House staff last October after his two arrests on morals charges were disclosed. His statement today said two psychiatrists had informed him his appearance would be "injurious to my health."

Mr. Reynolds, a key witness in the Baker investigation, testified before the committee in January, 1964. He said that Mr. Jenkins had indicated it was "expected" of him, in return for receiving the Johnson life insurance business, to buy commercial advertising time on KTBC, an Austin television station owned by the Johnson family.

Mr. Reynolds said he sold the first policy in 1957, when Mr. Johnson was Senate Democratic leader, about two years after Mr. Johnson's heart attack, and sold the second one in 1961. After selling the first policy, he bought $1,208 worth of KTBC advertising time for which he had no use, he testified.

Mr. Jenkins, in his sworn statement to the committee, denied that he had "at any time" attempted "to force, compel, coerce or require" Mr. Reynolds to buy the television time by "duress or compulsion."

However, Mr. Jenkins said he did "communicate to Mr. Reynolds" the fact that a Texas insurance salesman who was a regular buyer of KTBC advertising time was also seeking the Johnson life insurance business. "I am reasonably sure, although not certain, that I did it through Mr. Baker," he said.

Cousin Sold Insurance

Mr. Baker was then an officer of Mr. Reynolds's insurance agency in Silver Spring, Md. Mr. Jenkins was treasurer of the Johnson broadcasting enterprise, the LBJ Company, now the Texas Broadcasting Company.

Mr. Jenkins said that he had met Mr. Reynolds through Mr. Baker.

Mr. Reynolds's Texas competitor, Mr. Jenkins said, was Huff Baines, a cousin of Mr. Johnson, who "not only had been an advertiser on the [Johnson] radio and television stations for many years, but also had always related the amount of his advertising to the amount of his business done with the station."

"I merely communicated directly to him [Mr. Reynolds] or through Mr. Baker that the station had found another source for the insurance, that the source was a long-time advertiser and, accordingly, the LBJ Company planned to buy its insurance from that source," Mr. Jenkins declared.

"At that time, Mr. Reynolds offered to purchase advertising for the purpose of meeting the competition from the Texas agent," Mr. Jenkins said. "Certainly I did not 'pressure' him to do so."

Reynolds Wanted Business

"I received word soon from either Mr. Reynolds or Mr. Baker—and I think it was Mr. Baker—that Mr. Reynolds wished very much to sell the policies and would like to purchase advertising time in the event he sold them," Mr. Jenkins went on.

The insurance rates offered by Mr. Reynolds's company, the Manhattan Life Insurance Company of New York, were lower and Manhattan was willing to write a larger policy than Mr. Baines's company would offer, Mr. Jenkins said. For these reasons, he concluded the sale with Mr. Reynolds, he said.

Mr. Reynolds testified that he subsequently resold the television time for $160.

In his statement today, Mr. Jenkins said he relayed word of Mr. Reynolds's willingness to buy the television time to J. C. Kellam, then the general manager of KTBC.

The committee asked Mr. Jenkins to comment on an assertion he made in an interview with the committee staff in December, 1963. At that time he said, that he had "no knowledge of any arrangements by which Reynolds purchased advertising time on the TV station."

Knew About Purchase

Mr. Jenkins's reply today said: "I meant that I did not have knowledge of any arrangements or the specifics for the advertising. I did know Mr. Reynolds planned to purchase the advertising time and I have never asserted the contrary."

The beneficiary of the insurance policies was the LBJ Company, which paid the premiums. Mr. Jenkins said the purpose was to allow the company to buy up outstanding shares of stock in the event of Mr. Johnson's death and to retain control of the company for the Johnson family.

Mr. Jenkins contradicted Mr. Reynolds's testimony that the former White House aide had instructed him to "pay in cash to Baker" a kickback on the Johnson life insurance commissions.

Mr. Baker resigned his $19,600-a-year Senate post under fire in October, 1963, after Republicans demanded to know how he had built a fortune estimated at $2 million. The course of the Rules Committee's investigation of him remains uncertain. The Democratic majority has shown increasingly open skepticism of many of Mr. Reynolds's allegations.

The committee chairman, Senator B. Everett Jordan, Democrat of North Carolina, said that the committee, meeting at 10 A.M. Tuesday, would review a report from the Justice Department on a number of Mr. Reynolds's assertions.

February 25, 1965

Report Denouncing Baker Closes Inquiry by Senators

By CABELL PHILLIPS

Special to The New York Times

WASHINGTON, June 30—The Senate Rules Committee passed today another milestone, and possibly its last one, in its long investigation of the business affairs of Robert G. Baker, former secretary to the Senate's Democratic majority.

The committee chairman, Senator B. Everett Jordan, Democrat of North Carolina, filed with the Senate today what the committee called its final report on the Baker case. The report used sharper language to attack Mr. Baker's behavior, and urged stronger remedial action by the Senate, than did the previous "final" report, filed almost a year ago.

The report suggested that consideration be given indicting Mr. Baker for violation of the conflict-of-interest laws in connection with an alleged payment of $5,000 to him by a lobbyist backing legislation concerning the licensing of Ocean Freight Forwarders.

Senate Rule Urged

Recommendations made in the report included adopting a rule that would require Senators and Senate employes earning more than $10,000 a year to make periodic reports of their outside income. The report also proposed restricting outside employment of Senate employes to activities that did not interfere with their regular duties.

During his tenure as secretary to the Senate Democrats and earlier, Mr. Baker was regarded as an intimate of Lyndon B. Johnson, then the Democratic leader of the Senate. In 1957, Mr. Johnson termed Mr. Baker "one of my most trusted, most loyal and most competent friends."

The report today did not mention this former relationship. President Johnson was mentioned only in a minority report by the Republicans, and there only in testimony quoted from the hearing transcript.

This quoted Don B. Reynolds, a Maryland insurance broker, as saying that from 1952 until Mr. Johnson became Vice President in 1961, "I saw Mr. Baker generally once or twice a week—sometimes more, sometimes less."

Protests by Republicans

The investigation began in October, 1963, when Mr. Baker resigned his $19,600-a-year Senate job after it was disclosed that he was engaging in multimillion-dollar business activities in his spare time.

Last July 8 the committee reported it had found Mr. Baker guilty of "many gross improprieties" and closed the books on the affair over the vehement protest of Republican Senators. The case became a cause célèbre in the Presidential campaign that year.

Last October the case was reopened to investigate charges that Mr. Baker had been involved in a political payoff involving the construction of the $20 million D.C. Stadium here in 1960.

The report on this phase of the investigation was delayed for months while Democratic and Republican members of the committee argued over the conclusions to be drawn from the inquiry and the recommendations to be made.

In effect, the report filed today wrapped up both phases of the investigation. It served to emphasize again the wide and acrimonious difference in viewpoint between the six Democrats on the committee and the three Republicans.

As he has done many times in the last 12 months, the senior Republican on the panel, Senator Carl T. Curtis of Nebraska, characterized the investigation as "a whitewash."

Still to be heard from was Senator John J. Williams, Republican of Delaware, who has been the sharpest and most effective critic of the committee's handling of the case. He is not a member of the Rules Committee but supplied the initiative, and much of the evidence, to open both phases of the investigation.

Senator Jordan said that the 67-page report had been approved by a majority of the committee. However, the Republican members used almost as many pages as the Democrats to express their reservations and objections.

'A Disturbing Picture'

In substance, the report reiterated the earlier findings on the first phase of the investigation, saying, "A disturbing, if confused, picture emerged of the scope and the ethical propriety of Baker's business activities."

The first phase of the investigation was confined to discovering possible conflicts of interest in which Mr. Baker may have been involved in amassing a business fortune estimated at more than $2 million while he was on the Senate payroll. Among the major incidents in Mr. Baker's career that the committee looked into were the following:

¶A charge that he had used political influence in trying to obtain a vending machine franchise in the nearby plant of Melpar, Inc., an electronics subcontractor for the Government. (Mr. Baker was a defendant in a $300,000 civil damage suit from which this charge grew. The suit was subsequently settled out of court, reportedly for $30,000.)

¶His 50 per cent partnership in the Carousel Motel, a $1

Associated Press Wirephoto

'FINAL' REPORT: Senator B. Everett Jordan, Democrat of North Carolina, chairman of Senate Rules Committee, studies material relating to committee's investigation of private business life of Robert G. Baker, former secretary of Senate Democratic majority.

million vacation resort on the Maryland seashore.

¶His dealings in the stock of the Mortgage Guaranty Insurance Corporation, from which Mr. Baker and a number of his friends made substantial profits.

¶His dealings with Mr. Reynolds. It was through Mr. Reynolds that Mr. Baker was allegedly able to give a $584 stereophonic phonograph to the then Democratic leader of the Senate, Mr. Johnson. Mr. Reynolds told the committee that, with Mr. Baker's help, he had sold two life insurance policies aggregating $200,000 to Mr. Johnson while Mr. Johnson was Democratic leader and, later, Vice President. Mr. Reynolds testified he had subsequently been induced by Walter W. Jenkins, a Johnson aide, to buy advertising time he did not need on the Johnson-owned television station in Austin, Tex. Mr. Jenkins denied this allegation.

¶Mr. Baker's acquisition of a controlling interest in the Serv-U Corporation, a vending machine company with more than $3 million of contracts with concerns doing business with the Government.

After hearings extending from December, 1963, through March, 1964, with testimony from 66 witnesses, the committee said that Mr. Baker was "guilty of many gross improprieties" but did not accuse him of any specific violation of the law.

Reynolds Testimony Doubted

The second phase of the investigation arose from charges by Senator Williams, based on information supplied him by Mr. Reynolds. Mr. Reynolds alleged that Matthew H. McCloskey, builder of the D.C. Stadium, had made, through Mr. Baker, an illegal contribution of $25,000 to the Democratic campaign fund of 1960.

Mr. Reynolds's story was that the McCloskey company had intentionally overpaid him $35,000 in premiums for a performance bond. The understanding, he said, was that he was to keep $10,000 and give the rest to Mr. Baker for use in the Democratic campaign. He produced a canceled check for $109,205 from the McCloskey company in settlement of a premium billing of $73,631.

Mr. McCloskey testified that the overpayment had been made, but he insisted that it was a bookkeeping "goof" and that, if any of the money went to Mr. Baker or the Democratic committee, he had no knowledge of it.

The Rules Committee said it had only Mr. Reynolds's testimony of this transaction to rely upon, and that this testimony contained so many contradictions and loopholes that he could not be believed. In this connection, the report stated:

"It continued to be Reynolds's allegations alone which provided the focus for our investigation. In the absence of corroborative testimony, everything hinged on the credibility of Reynolds. Reynolds's credibility was destroyed, and out of his own mouth."

The committee, in effect, absolved the McCloskey company of any wrongdoing in the stadium case, and it was unable to implicate Mr. Baker in the manner alleged by Mr. Reynolds.

Payment by Lobbyist Scored

But in a corollary case that evolved from the stadium investigation, the committee denounced Mr. Baker more sharply than it had previously done. This involved an alleged payment of $5,000 to Mr. Baker by a lobbyist, Myron Weiner, in connection with legislation concerning the licensing of Ocean Freight Forwarders. The payment was made two days after the bill became law.

"This case," the report states, "furnishes evidence of the most flagrant of all Baker's activities in the use of his office and the prestige of his position for his personal financial profit.

"Although it presents legal technicalities, which it is not appropriate to discuss in this report, it justifies careful consideration looking to an indictment for violation of the conflict-of-interest statute."

In their separate statement of views, the Republicans levelled their sharpest criticism at the Democrats' attitude toward Mr. Reynolds.

"A disturbing aspect of the Baker investigation," the Republicans said, "was the continuing effort to discredit witnesses who were willing to testify before the committee and whose testimony extended the investigation into new fields.

"This was the case with respect to Don B. Reynolds. As contrasted with the treatment of other witnesses, the practice of discrediting the testimony of Reynolds is striking."

The Republicans attacked the Democrats for not pursuing Mr. Reynolds's allegations about Mr. Jenkins and the advertising contract more vigorously and accused them of lagging in investigating Mr. Reynolds's charges concerning Mr. McCloskey.

They were also sharply critical of the committee for not delving more deeply into information given by Mr. Reynolds concerning Mrs. Ellen Rometsch, an alien who has returned to Germany, and other alleged call girls who Mr. Reynolds insisted were involved in some of Mr. Baker's business activities.

The committee disposed of the call-girl issue by referring Mr. Reynolds's information to the Federal Bureau of Investigation. The F.B.I. report to the committee, which was also released today, led the committee majority to conclude that no useful purpose would be served by following that line of inquiry.

Motive Is Big Mystery In Raid on Democrats

By WALTER RUGABER

Special to The New York Times

WASHINGTON, June 25 — Moving through the basement after midnight, the guard found strips of tape across the latches of two doors leading to the underground garage.

It was an altogether fit beginning for a first-rate mystery — the raid on the Democratic National Committee headquarters.

In the eight days since, the White House and the Republican party have been embarrassed, the Democrats have sensed a big election-year issue and a major Federal investigation has begun.

The mystery has involved Republican officials, former agents of the Central Intelligence Agency, White House aides and bewildering assortments of anti-Castro Cubans.

Guard Not Alarmed

There has been talk of telephone taps, spy cameras and stolen files; of obscure corporations and large international financial transactions; of an unsolved raid on a chancery office and on an influential Washington law firm.

The guard, Frank Wills, a tall, 24-year-old bachelor who earned $80 a week patrolling one of the office buildings in the Watergate complex for General Security Services, Inc., was not greatly alarmed when he found the tape.

The high-priced hotel rooms, prestigious offices and elegant condominium apartments within the Watergate development had been favorite targets of Washington's burglars and sneak thieves for several years.

Along with three present or former Cabinet officers and various other Republican leaders, the tenants included the Democratic National Committee. Its offices had been entered at least twice within the last six weeks. But Mr. Wills assumed that the office building's maintenance men had immobilized the latches. He tore off the strips of tape, allowing the two doors to lock, and returned to his post in the lobby.

Ten minutes later, acting on what he now calls a "hunch," he returned to the basement. The latches were newly taped. So were two others, on a lower level, that had been unobstructed only minutes before.

"Somebody was taping the doors faster than I was taking it off," Mr. Mills said in an interview later. "I called the police." His alarm was logged at the central station at 1:52 A.M. on Saturday, June 17.

It took less than 48 hours for the authorities to clamp a fairly tight lid on things. Much of the information that emerged afterward, even on the most pedestrian points, was unofficial or leaked by unnamed sources.

And none of it established motive. Washington went on a speculative binge, but even those running the investigation were said to be confused and uncertain. The available facts offered many possible interpretations.

More Tape Found

First to reach the Watergate were plainclothes members of the Second District Tactical Squad. They went first to the eighth and top floor, where tape was found on a stairway door. Nothing else was amiss, however.

Working their way down, they found more tape on the sixth floor. With guns drawn, they entered the darkened offices of the Democratic National Committee. Crouched there were five unarmed men, who surrendered quietly.

"They didn't admit what they were doing there," said John Barret, one of the plainclothes men who handcuffed the five and lined them up against a wall. "They were very polite, but they wouldn't talk."

Presumably, there was plenty to talk about—the taped latches, for example.

For one thing, taping the doors was a dead giveaway. Ordinarily, burglars use wooden match sticks. Also, why did anyone bother with the door on the eighth floor?

Furthermore, once the tampering had been discovered, it was risky in the extreme to repeat it. Who did it? And why were two separate basement entrances taped the second time?

Why, in fact, were any? All of the doors open freely from the inside, and once entrance to the building had been gained, an intruder could have left without keys and without setting off an alarm.

Too Many Men

Five men were found in the Democratic offices, which struck those informed in such matters as three or four too many.

The five men were charged with burglary and led off to the District of Columbia jail, where they all gave false names to the booking officer. After a routine fingerprint check, they were identified as follows:

Bernard L. Barker, 55 years old, a native of Havana who fled the Fidel Castro regime and became an American citizen. He is president of Barker Associates, a Miami real estate concern.

James Walter McCord Jr., 53, a native of Texas. He is now president of McCord Associates, Inc. of suburban Rockville, Md., a private security agency.

Frank Sturgis, 48, who lost his American citizenship for fighting in the Castro army but regained it later. He has changed his name from Frank Fiorini but is still known under both names. He works at the Hampton Roads Salvage Company, Miami.

Eugenio R. Martinez, 51, a man with $7,199 in his savings account and who works as a notary public and as a licensed real estate operator. He now works for Mr. Barker's agency and is said to earn $1,000 a month.

Virgilio R. Gonzalez, 45, a locksmith at the Missing Link Key Shop, Miami. He is reported to have been a house painter and a barber in Cuba, which he fled after Mr. Castro's takeover in 1959.

All except Mr. McCord left Miami Friday afternoon, apparently on Eastern Airlines Flight 190, which arrived at Washington National Airport at 3:59 P.M. Mr. Barker used his American Express credit card to rent a car at that time.

The four men checked into two rooms—214 and 314—at the Watergate Hotel. They are understood to have dined that evening in the hotel restaurant. The hotel connects with the office building through the underground garage.

What Police Seized

The police collected what the five men had with them at the time of their arrest and obtained warrants to search the two hotel rooms and the rented automobile. An inventory included:

¶Two 35-mm. cameras equipped with close-up lens attachments, about 40 rolls of unexposed 35-mm. film, one roll of film from a Minox "spy" camera and a high intensity lamp—all useful in copying documents.

¶Two or three microphones and transmitters. Two ceiling panels had been removed in an office adjacent to that of the party chairman, Lawrence F. O'Brien, and it was theorized that the equipment was being installed, replaced or removed.

¶An assortment of what were described as lock picks and burglary tools, two walkie-talkie radios, several cans and pen-like canisters of Chemical Mace and rubber surgical gloves, which all five men had been wearing.

¶Nearly $6,000 in cash. The money, found in the possession of the five and in the two hotel rooms, included some $5,300 in $100 bills bearing consecutive serial numbers.

Parts of the Democratic headquarters had been ransacked. Mr. O'Brien subsequently said that the party's opponents could have found an array of sensitive material, but no pattern to the search has been disclosed.

Last Sunday, the Associated Press discovered from Republican financial records filed with the Government that Mr. McCord worked for both the Comittee to Re-Elect the President and the Republican National Committee.

'Security Coordinator'

The records showed that since January Mr. McCord had received $1,209 a month as "security coordinator" for the Nixon organization, and that since October he was paid more than $600 a month for guard services for the Republican unit.

The following day it was learned that in address books taken by the police from Mr. Barker and Mr. Martinez the name of E. (for Everette) Howard Hunt appeared. Mr. Hunt had worked, as recently as March 29, as a White House consultant.

The police also turned up in the belongings of the five suspects an unmailed envelope that contained Mr. Hunt's check for $6, made out to the Lakewood Country Club in Rockville, and a bill for the same amount.

Both Mr. Hunt and Mr. McCord were members of the Rockville Club, and there were published reports that Mr. Hunt met with Mr. Barker in Miami two weeks before the break-in.

The White House said that Mr. Hunt worked 87 days in 1971 and 1972 under Charles W. Colson, special counsel to the President. Mr. Colson has frequently handled sensitive political assignments.

The consultant, who is the author of 42 novels under several pen names, works full time as a writer for Robert R. Mullen & Co., a Washington public relations firm with long-standing Republican connections.

The firm's president, Robert F. Bennett, quoted Mr. Hunt as saying he "was nowhere near that place [the Watergate] Saturday." The writer has declined public comment, however, and Mr. Bennett has suspended him.

Security Man Dropped

The Republicans quickly discharged Mr. McCord as their security man and denied emphatically that they had had any connection with the raid on the Democratic headquarters.

"We want to emphasize that this man [Mr. McCord] and the other people involved were not operating either on our behalf or with our consent," said John N. Mitchell, the former Attorney General who is now head of the Nixon committee.

Ronald L. Ziegler, the White House press secretary, said that "a third-rate burglary attempt" was unworthy of comment by him and asserted that "certain elements may try to stretch this beyond what it is."

The White House pointed out that there was no evidence that either Mr. Colson or Mr. Hunt had been involved in any way in the raid on the Democrats, and several high-ranking police officials privately advanced the same view.

The Democratic National Committee, however, filed a $1-million civil suit against the five accused raiders and against the Committee to Re-Elect the President, charging that the Democrats' civil rights and privacy had been violated.

Mr. Mitchell described this as "another example of sheer demagoguery on the part of Mr. O'Brien." Mr. O'Brien said that there was "a developing clear line to the White House."

Stories About Spies

More or less simultaneously with the political exchanges, the reports about former spies began to come in. All five of the arreested men were said to have had ties to the Central Intelligence Agency.

Mr. Hunt, operating under the code name "Eduardo," was described as the man in direct charge of the abortive invasion of the Bay of Pigs in Cuba in 1961. He is known to have worked for the C.I.A. from 1949 to 1970.

Mr. Barker also worked for the C.I.A. He was reported to have been Mr Hunt's "paymaster" for the Cuban landing and, under the code name "Macho," to have established the secret invasion bases in Guatemala and Nicaragua.

Mr. McCord, too, was a C.I.A. agent. After three years with the Federal Bureau of Investigation, he joined the intelligence unit in 1951 and resigned in 1970. His role in the Bay of Pigs was understood to be relatively minor.

The spy angles led directly to the Cuban refugee angle. It was disclosed that on the weekend of May 26-29, eight men who described themselves as representatives of an organization called "Ameritas", registered at the Watergate Hotel.

The eight included those arrested in Democratic headquarters except Mr. McCord. It was also disclosed that during that May weekend there was a burglary of the Democratic offices.

"Ameritas" turned out to be an obscure real estate concern in Miami. One of the principals was a close friend of Mr. Barker but none of the arrested men ever owned an interest in the company.

A man who does, Miguel A. Suarez, a prominent lawyer in the Cuban community, said that Mr. Barker had made "unauthorized" use of the Ameritas letterheads in making reservations at the Watergate for the eight men.

Search Is On For Four

The F.B.I. began a nationwide search for the four others who stayed there, and the theory grew that if "Ameritas" was not, as the police had speculated, a right-wing, anti-Castro paramilitary unit, there must be one somewhere..

The Chilean chancery, representing a left-wing Government, was mysteriously searched during the night of May 13-14, and the door of a law firm with several prominent Democrats as members was tampered with on the night of May 15-16.

Some of the $100 bills found by the police appear to have been withdrawn from Mr. Barker's Miami bank. The money had been deposited there in the form of checks drawn on the Banco Internacional, S.A., Mexico City.

There are countless anti-Castro organizations in the Miami area, ranging in size from one member to hundreds, and many of them are devoted to plotting. Among those cited in connection with the break-in was one involving veterans of the Bay of Pigs.

While it was conjectured that a Cuban group might have been seeking to curry favor with the Republicans or to battle leftists, this theory, like all the others, was uncertain.

June 26, 1972

NIXON BELITTLES M'GOVERN CHARGE

Says 'Responsible' Persons Will Be 'Turned Off' by Corruption Allegation

By ROBERT B. SEMPLE Jr.

Special to The New York Times

WASHINGTON, Oct. 5—Striking back after weeks of silence, President Nixon dismissed with calculated contempt today Senator George McGovern's charge that his Administration was the most corrupt and deceitful in history.

Mr. Nixon, who appeared before a news conference in his Oval Office this morning, addressed the corruption issue in measured and at times almost inaudible tones that seemed deliberately designed to contrast with what he suggested was the shrill and irresponsible campaign tactics of his opponent.

First Since Aug. 19

"I think the responsible members of the Democratic party will be turned off by this kind of campaigning," he said, "and I would suggest that responsible members of the press, following the single standard to which they are deeply devoted, will also be turned off by it."

The news conference was Mr. Nixon's first since Aug. 19, when he met newsmen in California. Whether by coincidence or by design, both news conferences have come on days when Mr. McGovern, the Democratic Presidential nominee, has been making major campaign statements, first on taxes and welfare and, today, on foreign policy.

October 6, 1972

AIDE TERMS NIXON WILLING TO ASSIST BUGGING INQUIRIES

Says White House May Let Senate Panel Query Staff Members in Private

RESPONSE TO CRITICISM

President Tells Associates to Go Before Watergate Grand Jury if Called

Special to The New York Times

WASHINGTON, March 30—Responding to mounting criticism, the White House indicated today its readiness to compromise with the Senate's investigation of the Watergate case on the issue of furnishing witnesses and information from President Nixon's personal staff.

Ronald L. Ziegler, the White House press secretary, announced at the same time that the President had issued an affirmative order to all members of his staff to testify if called before a Federal grand jury that is continuing to look into the Watergate raid.

With respect to both the court and Congressional inquiries into political espionage, Mr. Ziegler said that Mr. Nixon was willing to cooperate in any way that did not do "violence to the separation of powers." In either investigation, however, appearances by members of the White House staff would be limited to sessions closed to the public.

Two Linked to Planning

H.R. Haldeman, the President's chief of staff, and John

W. Dean 3d, the White House Counsel, recently connected by hearsay to the planning of the Watergate raid, are believed never to have appeared before the grand jury investigating the case.

But last summer and fall the grand jury called, and heard from, other senior advisers to the President, including John N. Mitchell, the former Attorney General; Jeb Stuart Magruder, a onetime White House aide and later deputy manager of the Nixon re-election campaign, and Charles W. Colson, a former special counsel to the President.

Mr. Nixon has invoked the doctrine of executive privilege to prevent his staff from testifying before the Senate's Watergate investigators, but he has never applied the doctrine to judicial proceedings. The President himself is legally immune from being required to appear in a judicial proceeding, but whether his aides could be required to appear is legally unclear.

Restatement of Policy

Mr. Ziegler presented his statements today as reaffirmation of old policy to clear up certain "misunderstandings" about the White House position.

But, for the first time, the White House appeared to be showing concern about the bipartisan attacks on the Administration's conduct in the case. Also for the first time, Mr. Ziegler's remarks, made after long White House meetings, had a conciliatory tone.

The change was believed to be at least in part a result of concern, expressed by a number of Republicans in Congress and elsewhere, that the White House might be covering up involvement of Presidential aides and others close to the President in the operations of the men who broke into and bugged the headquarters of the Democratic National Committee in the Watergate complex here last June.

Mr. Ziegler delivered a long oral statement on the subject at midday shortly before Mr. Nixon departed for his home in San Clemente, Calif., where he is scheduled to remain for about 10 days.

He said he wished to "dispel the myth" that "we seek to cover up."

The statement was made at Mr. Ziegler's daily press briefing, which was two hours late, presumably because of the "meetings" concerned with the Watergate investigations.

Mr. Ziegler, who almost never mentions the Watergate case unless asked about it, said he was speaking out because of concern over a "series of unsubstantiated charges" that have been emerging from the select Senate committee headed by Senator Sam J. Ervin, Democrat of North Carolina, that have linked White House staff members to the case.

Denying that staff members were involved, Mr. Ziegler said, "The personal rights of individual members have been abused by procedures that are less than orderly and judicial."

"The public media and the White House news briefings are not the place to make an evaluation of these charges," Mr. Ziegler said.

Two men who were connected with Mr. Nixon's re-election campaign organization have been convicted in the Watergate burglary and bugging and five other men, one a former White House consultant, have pleaded guilty.

James W. McCord Jr., one of those convicted, has testified under oath before the Ervin committee that his fellow conspirators gave him the impression that they had cleared their clandestine operations with ranking officials in the Administration, several sources have said.

Mr. Ziegler insisted that the White House position all along has been one of cooperation on the Watergate matter. The President has said that, in order to preserve the separation of powers between the legislative and executive branches, he would not let Mr. Dean or other staff members appear before a formal meeting of a Congressional committee, and Mr. Ziegler said today that this policy was unchanged. However he went on to say:

"Any member of the White House staff called by the grand jury will be required by the President to testify. That is a restatement of policy in effect."

'Ready to Cooperate'

As to the Ervin committee, Mr. Ziegler said, "We are ready to cooperate, to work out procedures to meet the needs of the committee without doing violence to the separation of powers."

Mr. Ziegler would not specify what procedure might be acceptable to the President, but he clearly indicated a willingness to reach some compromise between the committee's desire to have Mr. Dean and other officials appear as sworn witnesses in open session and the White House's offer, made separately to the Senate Judiciary committee, to accept written questions and supply written answers.

One possibility is an appearance of White House officials before closed, informal committee sessions. Disputes over the use of executive privilege to prevent testimony by Presidential aides, on the ground that it would disrupt the orderly functioning of the Government, have frequently been resolved in this manner.

Mr. Ziegler was asked why, if the White House was interested in preserving the separation of powers between the branches of government, the President would order his aides to appear as sworn witnesses before a judicial body but not a legislative body. The question was not answered.

Testimony before a grand jury is secret and is carried out under the direction of Justice Department officials. Testimony before a Congressional committee is usually open.

The White House statement came as Republicans in Congress continued to voice concern about the case.

Hugh Scott of Pennsylvania, the Senate minority floor leader, said he was "deeply disturbed at any developments which taint the political process," adding, "I think the concern is simply that the facts should all be ascertained and made public." Last week, after a meeting with the President, Mr. Scott said he had been assured that Mr. Nixon "had nothing to hide."

Senators Charles McC. Mathias Jr. of Maryland and Jacob K. Javits of New York made floor speeches warning that the Watergate affair threatened to damage public confidence in the American political process.

Senator Robert W. Packwood of Oregon called the Watergate case "the most odious issue since the Teapot Dome" and joined other Republicans in urging Mr. Nixon to appoint former Senator John J. Williams, Republican of Delaware, to conduct a new investigation.

Senator Williams was known as a one-man, nonpartisan investigator of waste and corruption when he was in the Senate.

March 31, 1973

NIXON WITHDRAWS GRAY NOMINATION AS F.B.I. DIRECTOR

Official, Involved in Bitter Struggle for Confirmation, Requested the Move

2 CONSIDERED FOR POST

Justice Department Lawyer and Ellsberg Trial Judge Said to Be Under Study

By JOHN M. CREWDSON

Special to The New York Times

WASHINGTON, April 5 — President Nixon accepted today a request from L. Patrick Gray 3d that his nomination to become director of the Federal Bureau of Investigation be withdrawn.

A spokesman at the San Clemente, Calif., White House, where Mr. Nixon is spending the week, said that Mr. Gray had conveyed his wish to step aside in a telephone call to the President, who had "regretfully agreed."

Gerald L. Warren, the deputy White House press secretary, said he had "no word" on when a new directer might be nominated, or who it might be. However, the list of possible successors under consideration is reliably reported to contain only two names.

They are Henry E. Petersen, a career Justice Department lawyer who is now in charge of its Criminal Division, and William Matthew Byrne Jr., a Federal district judge who is presiding over the Pentagon papers trial in Los Angeles.

The Gray nomination became the focus of a bitter, partisan struggle in the Senate almost from the moment it was announced by the White House six weeks ago.

Only a few hours before Mr. Gray disclosed that he was withdrawing his name, the Senate Judiciary Committee met in a surprise session with the intent of deciding his fate.

A motion was introduced to kill the nomination by indefinitely postponing it, but the committee adjourned without taking a vote because two members were absent.

In a statement, the President said that "in view of the action of the Senate Judiciary Committee" this afternoon, it was now "obvious that Mr. Gray's nomination will not be confirmed by the Senate."

Mr. Nixon continued:

"In fairness to Mr. Gray, and out of my overriding concern for the effective conduct of the vitally important business of the F.B.I., I have regretfully agreed to withdraw Mr. Gray's nomination."

The President added that he had asked Mr. Gray to stay on as the bureau's acting director, a post he has held since the death of J. Edgar Hoover last May, until a new nominee was confirmed.

Mr. Gray's office declined to say whether he had decided to remain and released only this brief statement on his behalf:

"I have asked the President to withdraw my nomination for the position of director of the Federal Bureau of Investigation. The basis for this decision is my deep conviction that the F.B.I.—a great and unique American institution of vital service to the President and to the American people—is entitled to permanent leadership at the earliest possible time."

As recently as last weekend, Mr. Nixon had insisted that Mr. Gray continued to enjoy the President's full confidence and support, and he termed "totally false" reports that a decision had been made to withdraw Mr. Gray's name.

'The Right Thing'

In reply to a newsman's question, Mr. Warren said tonight that, as far as he knew, the President was not aware of Mr. Gray's intentions before he received his call at about o'clock this afternoon, the same hour the Senate Judiciary Committee was convening.

The two Democratic members of the committee who were the most uncompromising opponents of Mr. Gray's nomination said within minutes of his withdrawal that they welcomed the move.

Senator Robert C. Byrd of West Virginia, who introduced the motion in the committee today to postpone the nomination indefinitely, said in a statement that he believed that Mr. Gray had done "the right thing under the circumstances."

Mr. Byrd, who had announced even before the confirmation hearings began that he would vote against Mr. Gray, called on the President to choose a successor who had had previous experience in law enforcement and "no connections whatsoever" with the Watergate case.

Senator John V. Tunney of California called the withdrawal "in the best interest of a nonpartisan and independent F.B.I., which he identified as "the crucial issue" in the nomination.

Mr. Gray's handling of the bureau's investigation of the Watergate break-in and bugging case were repeatedly characterized by Mr. Byrd, Mr. Tunney and other Democrats as less ambitious and impartial than would be necessary to qualify him for the traditionally nonpartisan post.

The Democrats insisted that Mr. Gray's most damaging revelation to the committee was that he had sent numerous investigative files on the Watergate case to John W. Dean 3d, President Nixon's chief legal counsel.

Mr. Gray told the committee that the files had included information from interviews with employes of the Committee for the Re-election of the President who had met with Federal agents in confidence to tell them of the alleged destruction of campaign records following the Watergate break-in.

One employe said later that Nixon campaign officials had somehow learned afterward of her "confidential" interview.

Mr. Gray also acknowledged that he had sent the records to Mr. Dean directly, despite advice from the F.B.I.'s legal counsel that he should pass them through the Attorney General, and after concluding that Mr. Dean had "probably" lied to F.B.I. agents investigating the case.

In his statement tonight, Mr. Nixon said that Mr. Gray's "compliance with this completely proper and necessary request" from Mr. Dean had exposed the nominee to "totally unfair innuendo and suspicion, and thereby seriously tarnished his fine record as acting director and promising future at the bureau."

The President called Mr. Gray, whom he first met at a party in 1947 while a young Representative "an able, honest and dedicated American."

United Press International

L. Patrick Gray 3d

Mr. Gray told the Senators that he had sent the files to Mr. Dean because he was conducting a special investigation for the President to determine whether any White House employes had been involved in the Watergate case, and that Mr. Dean was therefore "in the chain of command."

Mr. Gray was also criticized during his eight days of testimony for making what some Democrats labeled "political" speeches during last year's Nixon campaign and for his relative lack of experience in law enforcement.

The 56-year-old Mr. Gray, who retired from the Navy as a captain in 1960, practiced trust and tax law in Connecticut for eight years before joining the first Nixon Administration in 1969.

He worked first as an executive assistant to the then Secretary of Health, Education and Welfare Robert H. Finch, and later moved to the Justice Department, where he was Deputy Attorney General-designate when Mr. Nixon asked him to replace Mr. Hoover last year.

The White House denied on Saturday a report in a Minnesota newspaper that the nomination had been offered to Mr. Petersen ,and a source involved in the situation said today that there was no indication that a decision had yet been made between Mr. Petersen and Judge Byrne.

According to Senate committee sources, the Nixon Administration began to search in earnest for a replacement nominee more than a week ago, ultimate settling on the two men, both of whom have Democratic backgrounds.

However, those sources noted that Mr. Petersen, who as head of the Justice Department's Criminal Division directed the prosecution in the Watergate trial, could expect to be asked a number of questions about the scope of the Watergate case if he was nominated.

Investigation Criticized

In particular, the sources said, the committee would be certain to ask Mr. Petersen about his decision not to prosecute Donald H. Segretti, a California lawyer who reportedly headed a political espionage and sabotage effort for the Republicans during the Presidential campaign.

Mr. Gray disclosed to the Judiciary Committee three weeks ago that Herbert W. Kalmbach, President Nixon's personal lawyer, had told F.B.I. agents that he paid Mr. Segretti up to $40,000 in Republican campaign contributions for unspecified "services" to the party.

Mr. Kalmbach told the agents, Mr. Gray said, that he had been directed to do so by Dwight L. Chapin, who resigned in January as the White House appointments secretary.

The criminal investigation and prosecution in the Watergate case have also been criticized by Democrats for not answering the questions of who authorized and financed the bugging and other clandestine operations.

However, one Democratic committee aide said that although Mr. Petersen would not "sail through" confirmation hearings, "I think he'd probably get through."

"I don't think he'd receive the same kind of grilling [that Mr. Gray got]," said another aide. "He hasn't given any political speeches."

A man who was Mr. Petersen's superior at the Justice Department a few years ago added that "everybody up there [on the committee] knows him, and has the same opinion of him—Mr. Integrity."

Mr. Petersen is said to want the F.B.I. job if he can be assured beforehand that his confirmation is likely. "He just isn't about to risk a 26-year career in a two-week hearing," said an associate.

Committee sources say that Judge Byrne would be likely to encounter even less opposition from the Senate than would Mr. Petersen, but little is known about Judge Byrne's desire for the post.

A 42-year-old bachelor, he served as the United States Attorney in Los Angeles during the Johnson and Nixon Administrations and was appointed to the Federal bench by President Nixon in 1970.

NIXON REPORTS 'MAJOR' FINDINGS IN WATERGATE INQUIRY HE MADE; NEW INDICTMENTS ARE EXPECTED

IMMUNITY BARRED

President to Let White House Aides Testify Before Senators

By R. W. APPLE Jr.
Special to The New York Times

WASHINGTON, April 17—President Nixon announced today that "major developments" had come to light in the Watergate case as a result of a new investigation that he himself had conducted.

Appearing before a hurriedly summoned gathering of the White House press corps, Mr. Nixon read two announcements promising limited testimony from his aides before a Senate investigating committee and asserting that "real progress" had been made in getting to the bottom of the case.

The President, who answered no questions, took the unusual step of raising the prospect of indictments. He said he would suspend any Government employe indicted in connection with the Watergate break-in and discharge immediately anyone who was convicted.

Condemns Cover-Up

"No individual holding, in the past or at present, a position of major importance in the Administration should be given immunity from prosecution," he said. "I condemn any attempt to cover up in this case, no matter who is involved."

A few moments after the President's dramatic appearance, Ronald L. Ziegler, the White House press secretary, declared that Mr. Nixon's past statements denying any involvement by White House staff members were now "inoperative."

Mr. Ziegler said that what the President had said in the past was based on "investigations prior to the developments announced today," and thus no longer applied. Because of the new information since developed, he said, the President had restated the situation.

New Indictments Seen

Early tonight, Government sources said that further indictments would be issued within a week. But Earl J. Silbert, the principal United States Attorney prosecuting the case, declined to comment.

In yet another development that indicated a change in White House posture, a lawyer for the Democratic National Committee said late tonight that it had received "some serious offers" from the Committee for the Re-election of the President to settle civil damage suits arising from the Watergate incident.

Sheldon S. Cohen, the party's counsel, said that the Nixon organization had offered "significant amounts" to the Democrats if the suits were dropped. According to some reports, the offers involved as much as $500,000.

Comment Not Repeated

Mr. Ziegler specifically refused to repeat his comment of March 24 in which he said that the President retained full confidence in his counsel, John W. Dean 3d.

Mr. Dean had conducted an investigation on the basis of which the President asserted at a news conference last Aug. 29 that he could "say categorically that no one in the White House staff, no one in this Administration, presently employed, was involved in this very bizarre incident."

Mr. Nixon and his spokesmen had clung to that position through the 1972 electoral campaign, through thousands of newspaper and television reports questioning it and through increasingly critical comments by officeholders of both parties—until the President, calm and somber, appeared in the West Wing press room this afternoon with his statements.

Mr. Nixon indicated, and the White House subsequently confirmed, that Mr. Dean had been involved neither in negotiations with the Senate Watergate committee, headed by Senator Sam J. Ervin Jr., Democrat of North Carolina, nor in the investigation that led to the major new development of which the President spoke.

That, together with Mr. Ziegler's refusal to reiterate Presidential support for the counsel, led White House sources to speculate that the grand jury's attention might be centering on him.

Administration sources said it did not appear that H. R. Haldeman, the White House chief of staff, who is usually considered Mr. Nixon's most important aide, was involved in the new developments.

Mr. Haldeman is not known to have testified before the grand jury. Among those have done so are Mr. Dean, former Attorney General John N. Mitchell, Jeb S. Magruder, Dwight L. Chapin and Gordon C. Strachan — all of whom worked at the White House or at the Committee for the Re-election of the President at the time of the Watergate burglary.

In a brief interview in his New York apartment house lobby tonight, Mr. Mitchell was asked whether he might be the target of the President's statements in the case.

"I can't imagine why," he replied.

Asked why he thought Mr. Nixon was moving now on the unfolding case, Mr. Mitchell said, "I think he always was No doubt about it."

The President, who said at a news conference on March 15 that no member of his staff would be permitted to testify before Senator Ervin's committee, retreated somewhat from that posture today.

In March, he said flatly, "Members of the White House still will not appear before a committee of Congress in any formal session." Today, however, he said "all members of the White House staff will appear voluntarily"—but under certain restrictions.

As indicated by the President, the committee meetings will be formal, but they may be "in the first instance" in executive session—that is, in secret—"if appropriate." Further, as he stated things, staff members may reassert executive privilege "as to any question" during the meetings.

Thus it appeared that if there were any conflict it would come when specific questions that the White House did not wish to answer were asked.

Mr. Nixon said that he thought an agreement had been reached which was satisfactory to him and to the committee because it contained "ground rules which would preserve the separation of powers without suppressing the facts."

However, there were ambiguities in the President's statement. He said that witnesses might appear in executive session "in the first instance"—but he did not say that testimony would then be repeated in open session, or who would decide whether it could.

He also said that staff members "will answer fully all proper questions"—but he did not reconcile that with the reserved right to executive privilege, nor did he say who would decide which questions were proper and which not.

Mr. Nixon said at the outset of his second statement—the one that dealt with the possibility of indictments—that he had begun "intensive new inquiries" into the Watergate case on March 21 as the result of "serious charges which came to my attention, some of which were publicly reported."

His charges have led to a revival of interest in the case.

Congressional sources reported, however, that Mr. Nixon had swung into action after L. Patrick Gray 3d, who was at that time the President's nominee for director of the Federal Bureau of Investigation, testified on March 22 before the Senate Judiciary Committee.

Mr. Gray said on that day that Mr. Dean, the White House counsel, had "probably" lied to F.B.I. agents investigating the case. Two weeks later, Mr. Nixon withdrew the nomination of Mr. Gray.

The President, Mr. Ziegler said today, had taken personal command of the new investigation. He said that Henry E. Petersen, Assistant Attorney General in charge of the Criminal Division, had carried out much of the inquiry along with several of his associates.

At about the same time, two White House staff members who have never been accused of involvement with the Watergate case, John D. Ehrlichman and Leonard Garment, began negotiations with Senators Ervin and Howard H. Baker Jr. of Tennessee, the committee's ranking Republican, and their aides.

According to a senior White House official, strategy meetings, in which Mr. Haldeman was involved, were held last Thursday and Friday. On Saturday, Mr. Mitchell, who for a time managed Mr. Nixon's 1972 campaign, paid an unannounced visit to the White House.

After three days of White House silence — including a news briefing this morning when Gerald L. Warren, the deputy press secretary, turned aside about 50 Watergate questions from angry reporters — Mr. Ziegler disclosed tonight that Mr. Mitchell had come to talk with Mr. Ehrlichman.

Finally, on Sunday afternoon, in another unannounced meeting, Mr. Nixon conferred in his hideaway office in the Executive Office Building next door to the White House with Attorney General Richard G. Kleindienst and Mr. Petersen.

This afternoon, reporters were called back to the White House. An hour and a half later, at 4:37 P.M., Mr. Nixon walked into the press room, dressed in a blue suit, a sheaf of typescript in hand, and read it. It took three minutes.

Associated Press

President Nixon talking to reporters at the White House yesterday about Watergate case

April 18, 1973

DEAN IS REBUKED

Ziegler Disputes His Statement on Trying to Find Scapegoat

By R. W. APPLE Jr.

Special to The New York Times

WASHINGTON, April 19 — The White House abandoned today all show of support for the embattled Presidential counsel, John W. Dean 3d, who has been accused of complicity in the Watergate case.

Mr. Dean, a 34-year-old lawyer who conducted the investigation on which President Nixon based his original denials of White House involvement in the break-in, issued a statement this morning declaring that no one would succeed in making him "a scapegoat."

Mr. Dean, heretofore considered one of the stanchest "team players" in the Administration, bypassed the White House chain of command in issuing the statement, notifying neither Mr. Nixon nor the press office in advance. Instead, his secretary, her voice trembling, phoned it to newspaper offices.

Ziegler Rebukes Dean

Ronald L. Ziegler, the White House press secretary, appeared for the regular morning news briefing about an hour later and reiterated his statement of yesterday that he would answer no questions whatever about the Watergate episode.

Then, in response to the first question, he rebuked Mr. Dean, declaring that Mr. Nixon's statement on Tuesday "made it quite clear that the process now under way is not one to find scapegoats but one to get at the truth."

In a major reversal of his previous position, Mr. Nixon said on Tuesday that he would permit his aides to testify before a Senate committee investigating the bugging of Democratic National Committee headquarters last June and that he had ordered that no major Administration official be given immunity from prosecution.

No New Backing Given

Mr. Dean's stock began to drop immediately after the President's statement, when Mr. Ziegler refused to repeat earlier expressions of Mr. Nixon's support for the counsel. Furthermore, the President had made it clear that Mr. Dean was involved in neither the latest investigation of the case nor in negotiations with the Senate committee over new ground rules.

In response to a barrage of further questions today, Mr. Ziegler expressed no enthusiasm for him at all.

Had Mr. Dean been fired? No. Had he resigned? No. Was he in his office today? Yes.

When had the President last talked to Mr. Dean on the phone? I don't know.

At one point, Mr. Ziegler was asked just what Mr. Dean was doing these days.

"He's in his office," he replied. "I don't know what he's doing. Attending to business, I assume" — here he chuckled audibly — "business of some sort."

Finally, he was asked whether Mr. Dean was still a functioning member of the staff, whether he was still trusted, whether he was still given responsible tasks. Mr. Ziegler replied that he could say only that Mr. Dean had not resigned or been dismissed.

'Isolated, Cut Off'

Another White House staff member said, "John has been isolated, cut off."

The mood at the White House, insofar as it could be established from the few junior aides willing to talk, was one of apprehension. One aide said he was trying to work, "but most people seem to be running around in a state of panic."

Mr. Ziegler was good-natured during the briefing, and even said he loved his job. But he seemed to betray nervousness when he "misspoke" himself, to use his phrase, three times in a single sentence when discussing Mr. Nixon's conference with a group of Jewish leaders.

Asked why Mr. Dean had been treated as he had, one Administration official, not in the White House, suggested that the Nixon inner circle felt betrayed by what he called Mr. Dean's "inadequate" initial investigation, conducted last summer.

John W. Dean 3d

Mr. Ziegler confirmed today that Mr. Dean had never submitted a written report. He said that he did not know whether the oral report was delivered directly to Mr. Nixon or through an intermediary.

Named by Magruder

Mr. Dean was named by Jeb Stuart Magruder in the conversations with Federal prosecutors on Saturday as one of the participants in a meeting in February 1972, in which the Watergate bugging and a political espionage campaign were planned.

Early this week, Mr. Dean hired a new lawyer, Robert C. McCandless, an Oklahoma Democrat who ran Senator Hubert H. Humphrey's field organization in the 1968 Presidential campaign. Mr. Dean and Mr. McCandless married, and subsequently divorced, daughters of the late Senator Thomas C. Hennings of Missouri, but remained close.

Mr. Dean has told friends in the last two days that he is ready to implicate other White House aides in testimony to the grand jury, and his reference in his statement to his determination to avoid being a scapegoat bore this out.

One friend acknowledged today that Mr. Dean's status was awkward, but commented, "He's still counsel to the President. They haven't taken away his desk or anything."

Mr. Dean's statement in full was as follows:

"To date I have refrained from making any public comment whatsoever about the Watergate case. I shall continue that policy in the future because I believe that the case will be fully and justly handled by the grand jury and by the Ervin select committee.

"It is my hope, however, that those truly interested in seeing that the Watergate case is completely aired and that justice will be done will be careful in drawing any conclusions as to the guilt or involvement of any persons until all the facts are known and until each person has had an opportunity to testify under oath in his own behalf.

"Finally, some may hope or think that I will become a scapegoat in the Watergate case. Anyone who believes this does not know me, know the true facts, nor understand our system of justice."

Mr. Ziegler could shed no light on who the "some" to whom Mr. Dean referred might be. Mr. Dean was unavailable.

April 20, 1973

Two Angry Factions Clash in White House

Haldeman-Ehrlichman Team Reported Battling Mitchell-Dean Circle

By CHRISTOPHER LYDON
Special to The New York Times

WASHINGTON, April 22—Experts on the White House now discern, in the new outburst of recriminations on the Watergate affair, a clear pattern of factional strife that threatens the top command of the executive branch.

"The Haldeman-Ehrlichman side of the White House is in open warfare with the Mitchell-Dean side," said a senior adviser to President Nixon over the weekend. "It is a brutal battle."

Some of the angry principals openly admit a spirit of "every man for himself." Yet observers also see a rallying of allies along two main lines of power and loyalty within Mr. Nixon's top staff.

One part of the executive structure, as Presidential confidants now describe it, was recruited, led and protected by former Attorney General John N. Mitchell. The other side looked to the White House chief of staff, H. R. Haldeman, as its captain, and to John D. Ehrlichman, a Presidential counselor, as his deputy.

After more than five years of cordial rivalry, the two groups are in a struggle that some White House insiders say could bring down both factions.

A scorecard line-up of the two Nixon groups, as compiled by ranking officials and former officials, sheds considerable light on last week's charges and countercharges.

Last week, a Haldeman man, Jeb Stuart Magruder, told Federal prosecutors that Mr. Mitchell and John W. Dean 3d, a young Mitchell protégé, had been in on the original planning to bug the Democratic National Committee offices in the Watergate complex during the Presidential campaign last year.

The 38-year-old Mr. Magruder—a Californian and a marketing man, like many in the Haldeman faction—first served the Nixon Administration as deputy to Herbert G. Klein, the director of communications for the executive branch and an old friend of the President's.

During the summer of 1971. after Mr. Mitchell appointed one of his own young lieutenants, Harry S. Flemming, to organize a Nixon re-election committee, Mr. Haldeman countered by sending Mr. Magruder in to help run the early operation. By the spring of 1972, Mr. Magruder was understood to have cut off most of Mr. Flemming's influence.

Immediately after news leaked out that Mr. Magruder was implicating Mr. Mitchell and Mr. Dean in the Watergate plot, Mr. Dean's friends put out the story that Mr. Haldeman had helped to conceal the truth about the bugging by intercepting and distoring the results of the investigation that Mr. Dean, as White House counsel, conducted for the President.

Mr. Dean, now 34, had been called "Mitchell's fair-haired boy" since 1969 when he was the Attorney General's trouble-shooter in the Justice Department.

One Presidential aide recalls the dramatic scene that marked Mr. Dean's appointment to the White House: President Nixon was on the verge of announcing that Leonard Garment, his former law partner and still a member of the White House staff, would become the chief counsel. At the last minute, the aide says Mr. Mitchell came into the President's office to insist on the choice of Mr. Dean.

In Touch With Mitchell

In managing White House legal business, Mr. Dean stayed in close touch with Mr. Mitchell and the Justice Department.

Mr. Dean warned last week that he would not be made a "scapegoat" in the Watergate scandal. He drafted a statement himself and had his secretary phone it to news offices after Ronald L. Ziegler, the White House press secretary, reportedly refused to put it out through the normal channels. Mr. Ziegler, who once worked for Mr. Haldeman at the J. Walter Thompson advertising agency, has always been considered a part of the Haldeman White House machinery.

Mr. Mitchell confirmed last week, in response to Mr. Magruder's charge, that he had participated in discussions about bugging the Democrats, though he insisted he had repeatedly vetoed plans suggested by Mr. Magruder and G. Gordon Liddy, one of seven convicted conspirators.

At a news conference Friday, in what some sources interpreted as a thrust at Mr. Haldeman, Mr. Mitchell added: "I would like to know who it was that kept bringing them back and back and back."

William G. Hundley, Mr. Mitchell's lawyer in the case, said over the weekend that Mr. Mitchell had not meant to implicate Mr. Haldeman. But other Mitchell associates rejected that disclaimer.

'The Only Person'

'Who else but Haldeman was in a position to challenge Mitchell on something like that?" a Mitchell confidant asked. "Haldeman is the only person he could be pointing at."

In the Nixon Administration's happier days, the Mitchell and Haldeman groups shared responsibility and credit for the President's domestic success. But members of both groups now say that there were always latent tensions between them and a clear sense of their different identities.

The "hard-core Mitchell group," according to one of its members, was assembled on the organizational side of the 1968 campaign, which Mr. Mitchell managed, and much of its strength was later concentrated in the Justice Department.

Robert S. Mardian, for example, now working with his family construction company in Phoenix, Ariz., was Mr. Mitchell's campaign lieutenant in the Western states in 1968, and later served as counsel to the Department of Health, Education and Welfare and as Assistant Attorney General in the Internal Security Division. Mr. Mardian has denied all suggestions that he was involved in planning or covering up the Watergate raid.

Worked with Magruder

Frederick C. Larue, another member of the Mitchell group, is a wealthy Mississippian who helped run the 1968 campaign in the South and handled special assignments for the White House later, Mr. LaRue, who worked closely with Mr. Magruder in last year's campaign, has repeatedly been mentioned in news accounts as a conduit of Republican funds to the Watergate defendants. He has recently been unavailable for comment.

Harry S. Flemming, 32, is a Virginian, the son of Arthur S. Flemming, who was Secretary of Health, Education and Welfare in the Eisenhower Administration. He describes himself as a "Mitchell man" in the first phase of the Nixon re-election campaign, but concedes he was jostled out of power even before it got started.

The Mitchell men, according to one of them, considered themselves the organizers and the grass-roots politicians in the Administration. The Haldeman group "tended to be advance men and image guys," he said. "You never heard the Mitchell group talk media, but that talk dominated the other crowd. I always had the impression that their group tolerated the political side but had no feel for politics."

The "hard-core Haldeman group" came from the world of advertising and, directly or indirectly, from California.

Mr. Magruder, who had a background in merchandising cosmetics and women's hosiery, was considered the Haldeman crowd's most versatile administrator.

Dwight L. Chapin, who worked with Mr. Haldeman in Mr. Nixon's 1962 campaign for the California Governor's office, was the chief of staff's personal aide in the White House. He had also brought Gordon C. Strachan, a classmate at the University of Southern California, into the Haldeman orbit at the White House.

Mr. Chapin recruited still another U.S.C. friend, Donald H. Segretti, to run an espionage and sabotage branch of the Nixon re-election campaign. The Segretti operation has not yet been closely associated with any member of the Mitchell group.

In relatively gentle give-and-take years ago, there were other differences between the Mitchell and Haldeman groups. Mr. Mitchell's allies tended to identify somewhat with the Cabinet against the White House; it was Hugh W. Sloan Jr., a Haldeman man, who refused to let Walter J. Hickel, Secretary of the Interior, see President Nixon in the summer of 1970, precipitating an angry letter from Mr. Hickel and Mr. Hickel's dismissal from the Government.

Some members of the Haldeman group snickered privately when Mr. Nixon's first two nominees to the Supreme Court, Clement F. Haynsworth Jr. and G. Harrold Carswell, were first cleared by Attorney General Mitchell and then rejected by the Senate.

Mr. Mitchell snickered in return at the substantial failure of the hard-hitting White House campaign for Republican Senate and House candidates in 1970. He told friends that Mr. Haldeman had designed the 1970 strategy.

In many enterprises the Mitchell and Haldeman groups overlapped or were indistinguishably intertwined.

The key to the Watergate affair and other mysteries, sources close to the case suggest, may be Liddy, who declined to take the stand at his own trial and has maintained silence on the Watergate episode ever since.

Liddy's standing with the Haldeman-Mitchell divide is not yet clear. After being dismissed from the Treasury Department in 1971, he applied for a job at the Justice Department but was turned down by Mr. Mardian, among others.

It was Mr. Dean, a Mitchell man, who recommended Liddy for a job at the Nixon re-election committee. But it was Mr. Magruder, a Haldeman man, who hired him and was supposed to supervise his work.

NIXON ACCEPTS ONUS FOR WATERGATE, BUT SAYS HE DIDN'T KNOW ABOUT PLOT; HALDEMAN, EHRLICHMAN, DEAN RESIGN; RICHARDSON PUT IN KLEINDIENST POST

NEW DATA CITED

President Tells How He Changed Mind About Charges

By JOHN HERBERS
Special to The New York Times

WASHINGTON, April 30 — President Nixon told the nation tonight that he accepted the responsibility for what happened in the Watergate case even though he had had no knowledge of political espionage or attempts to cover it up.

The President went on nationwide television and radio to discuss the case after he received the resignations of three top staff members who have been implicated—H. R. Haldeman, John D. Ehrlichman and John W. Dean 3d. He also accepted the resignation of Attorney General Richard G. Kleindienst.

Wrongdoing Alleged

While the President accepted the responsibility and pledged every effort to achieve justice in the case, he alleged wrongdoing or cover-up attempts on the part of those he had delegated to run his 1972 Presidential campaign and those he appointed to investigate the matter during the campaign.

And he implied that his own election officials, in the Watergate espionage, were attempting to stop wrongdoing by the Democrats.

Mr. Nixon also said that hereafter the investigation of the Watergate matters would be delegated to his new Attorney General, Elliot L. Richardson, while he, the President, turned his attention to grave foreign and domestic matters. He added that he would leave it up to Mr. Richardson whether to appoint a special prosecutor.

Weeks of Tension

The speech, which came after weeks of growing tension at the White House as developments in the Watergate scandal implicated Administration figures, was an emotional appeal to save the integrity of the Presidency for the 1,361 days, by Mr. Nixon's count, that remain in his term. This was the 100th day of his second term.

"Tonight I ask for your prayers to help me in everything that I do," Mr. Nixon said at the end. "God bless America, and God bless each and every one of you."

He accepted responsibility for Watergate with these words:

"In any organization the man at the top must bear the responsibility. That responsibility, therefore, belongs here in this office. I accept it."

Tonight Mr. Nixon was tense and grave. At the start of the speech he stumbled several times as he shuffled the pages from which he read. Afterward, technicians in the room said, the President brushed tears from his eyes and said, "It wasn't easy."

He gave the country the explanation that Republican leaders had been urging him to do for months.

First, he sought to establish his own innocence. For the first time in his long political career last year, he said, he had not run his own campaign. He said he had delegated that responsibility because he, as a candidate for re-election, had more important duties — the running of his office and the seeking of peace in Vietnam.

Last June, when he heard of the burglary and bugging of the Democratic National Committee he was appalled, he said, and appointed officials to look into it for any wrongdoing. Until March this year, he believed no one in the White House was involved. Since learning that members of his staff were implicated, Mr. Nixon said, he has spent much of his time attempting to get to learn the truth.

Bars Cowardly Way

"For specific criminal actions by specific individuals who committed those actions, those who committed those actions must of course bear the liability and pay the penalty," he said. "For the fact that alleged improper actions took place within the White House or within my campaign organization, the easiest course would be for me to blame those whom I delegated the responsibility to run the campaign. But that would be the cowardly thing to do."

"I will not place the blame on subordinates," he continued, his voice breaking slightly, "on people whose zeal exceeded their judgment and who may have done wrong in a cause they deeply believed to be right." He then said that he would assume the responsibility.

The President did not specify in what way he would accept the responsibility. But he made it clear that the guilty should be punished and he would not stand in the way.

"There can be no whitewash at the White House," he said.

Mr. Nixon suggested that his own investigators had lied to him. He said there had been "an effort to conceal the facts both from the public—from you—and from me."

The President's highly emotional appeal was characteristic of Nixon speeches of the past in which he has sought to defend himself from attacks. While accepting the blame, he said there had been "campaigning excesses" in both major parties and he left the implication that, in the Watergate case, one side, the Republicans, may have been trying to prevent the excesses of the other, the Democrats.

"Two wrongs do not make a right," Mr. Nixon said.

After accepting the responsibility, Mr. Nixon sought to elevate himself above the Watergate issue in order to better conduct his office. He said the prosecution of the case would be delegated to Mr. Richardson.

"I know that, as Attorney General, Elliot Richardson will be both fair and he will be fearless in pursuing this case wherever it leads," he said. "There is vital work to be done toward our goal of a lasting structure of peace in the world, work that cannot wait—work that I must do."

The President, having accepted the resignation of some top assistants, thus became faced with having to reshape the White House staff and find a way for the Administration to maintain its credibility.

The President was urged by Republican leaders around the country to name a chief of staff who has been in no way implicated in the allegations of political sabotage and who has an impeccable record for public service.

Mr. Nixon's decision to accept the resignations of his two aides was made over the weekend **in the isolation of his mountaintop retreat at Camp David, Md., as both his friends and foes waited and wondered what he would do.**

It was a typical performance for the 60-year-old President, who has prided himself on his handling of many crises in his long political career. There was evidence that this one was filled with as much personal trauma as any in the past.

Mr. Nixon began his retreat Friday evening after the Watergate disclosures rocked the White House all week, culminating in the resignation of L. Patrick Gray 3d as acting director of the Federal Bureau of Investigation and the President's hurried appointment of William D. Ruckelshaus as a temporary replacement.

Key Aides Left Behind

The President went by helicopter with his usual security force and his Irish setter, King Timahoe. Among those left behind were his close confidants of his four and a half years in the Presidency—Mr. Haldeman and Mr. Ehrlichman, men he characterized today as "two of my closest friends and most trusted assistants."

All week there had been indications that Mr. Nixon hoped to ride out the scandals of political espionage with Mr. Haldeman and Mr. Ehrlichman in place. They accompanied him on a trip to Mississippi on Friday, and several White House sources said that the two men had been attempting to hold their jobs.

But the pressures from Republican leaders around the country for dismissal of all major officials who had been mentioned in the Watergate case or were responsible for White House involvement had become great.

For much of the weekend, the President was reported to be in seclusion at the wooded retreat in the Catoctin Mountains, 70 miles from the White House, with only King Timahoe for company.

Then, on Saturday evening, things began to happen. The President called for his personal secretary, Rose Mary Woods, an indication that he might be preparing a statement in the Watergate case.

Yesterday, the helicopter traffic was heavy between the White House and Camp David. First, Mr. Haldeman and Mr. Ehrlichman flew up and conferred with the President. So did Mr. Kleindienst, who had not been implicated in the scandals but who had personal and professional relations with some who were. Mr. Richardson, who had been Secretary of Defense, was called off a Washington tennis court and whisked to the mountaintop.

Then this morning, shortly before noon, Ronald L. Ziegler, the White House press secretary, appearing harried and shaken, announced that the President had accepted the resignations of Mr. Haldeman, Mr. Ehrlichman, Mr. Kleindienst and Mr. Dean, the White House counsel; that he had appointed Mr. Richardson as Attorney General; and that the President was going on radio and television to discuss the matter.

The White House left the impression that, while Mr. Dean had been dismissed outright, Mr. Haldeman and Mr. Ehrlichman had agreed in their meeting with the President to resign with Mr. Nixon's good wishes. It was understood, however, that Mr. Ehrlichman was more agreeable to leaving than was Mr. Haldeman, the man who had directed the White House staff with stern efficiency and had wielded more influence there than any other aide.

May 1, 1973

Pentagon Papers Charges Are Dismissed by Court

NEW TRIAL BARRED

But Decision Does Not Solve Constitutional Issues in Case

By MARTIN ARNOLD
Special to The New York Times

LOS ANGELES, May 11—Citing what he called "improper Government conduct shielded so long from public view," the judge in the Pentagon papers trial dismissed today all charges against Dr. Daniel Ellsberg and Anthony J. Russo Jr.

And he made it clear in his ruling that the two men would not be tried again on charges of stealing and copying the Pentagon papers.

"The conduct of the Government has placed the case in such a posture that it precludes the fair, dispassionate resolution of these issues by a jury," he said.

David R. Nissen, the chief prosecutor, said, "It appears that the posture is such that no appeal will be possible."

Defendants Not Vindicated

But the decision by United States District Court Judge William Matthew Byrne Jr. did not vindicate the defendants; it chastised the Government. Nor did it resolve the important constitutional issues that the case had raised.

The end of the trial, on its 89th day, was dramatic. The courtroom was jammed; the jury box was filled with news reporters; defense workers in the Ellsberg-Russo cause, mostly young people, sat in chairs lining the courtroom wall.

Dr. Ellsberg and Mr. Russo, surrounded by their lawyers, stared intently as Judge Byrne quickly read his ruling.

The Government's action in this case, he said, "offended a sense of justice," and so "I have decided to declare a mistrial and grant the motion for dismissal." The time was 2:07 P.M.

The courtroom erupted in

United Press International

Judge William Matthew Byrne Jr., above, threw out the Pentagon papers case and, left, defendants were freed. They are Anthony J. Russo Jr., left, and Dr. Daniel Ellsberg.

loud cheering and clapping. The judge, barely hiding a smile, quickly strode out the door behind his bench.

Tension had been building for two days, since the sudden disclosure by the Government yesterday that telephone conversations of Dr. Ellsberg were picked up by wiretapping in late 1969 and early 1970, and that all records and logs of those conversations had disappeared from the Federal Bureau of Investigation.

When this morning the Government was still unable to produce either the records or a legal authorization for the taps, it was evident that the case had ended.

The jury was not present when the judge read his decision. It had been sent home until Monday morning.

Before rendering his decision, the judge offered the defendants the opportunity to go to the jury for a verdict. He said that he would withhold his ruling on their motion to dismiss if they wanted. He indicated that if they did decide to go to the jury, he would probably dismiss some of the counts—six for espionage, six for theft and one for conspiracy.

He said that he believed enough of the case was left to litigate before the jury, if the defendants so desired. They did not, and then he read his ruling.

"A judgment of acquittal goes to all the facts," he said, but he added that if he ruled on that defense motion, "it would not dispose of all the issues." That, he said, "can only be done by going to the jury."

He did say, however, that his ruling was based not only on the wiretap disclosures, "or based solely on the break-in" of the office of Dr. Ellsberg's psychiatrist on Sept. 3, 1971, by agents in the employ of the White House.

NIXON CONCEDES WIDE WHITE HOUSE EFFORT TO CONCEAL SOME ASPECTS OF WATERGATE; CITES HIS CONCERN OVER NATIONAL SECURITY

PRESIDENT'S VIEW

He Implies Illegalities by Aides—Asserts He Will Not Quit

By JOHN HERBERS

Special to The New York Times

WASHINGTON, May 22 — President Nixon conceded today that there had been "wide-ranging efforts" in the White House to conceal some aspects of the Watergate case, but he said those actions had stemmed from his legitimate interest in protecting national security.

In the 4,000-word statement, Mr. Nixon both apologized for and defended his actions. He declared in a supplementary statement that he had no intention of resigning the Presidency, saying: "I will not abandon my responsibilities. I will continue to do the job I was elected to do."

As for his own part, the President reiterated his own innocence in the burglary of the Democratic National Committee offices on June 17, 1972, and its cover-up, but he said that he had asked his associates not to let the investigation of the case disclose covert intelligence operations conducted in the interest of national security.

To Avert Compromise

"I wanted justice done with regard to Watergate," the President said, "but in the scale of national priorities with which I had to deal — and not at that time having any idea of the extent of political abuse which Watergate reflected — I also had to be deeply concerned with insuring that neither the covert operations of the C.I.A. nor the operations of the special investigations unit should be compromised."

And he suggested that his closest associates, H. R. Haldeman and John D. Ehrlichman, who resigned April 30, may well have carried his instructions on protecting the national security to illegal attempts to cover up the episode.

"With hindsight," the President said, "It is apparent that I should have given more heed to the warning signals I received along the way about a Watergate cover-up and less to the reassurances.

'Beyond My Directives'

"It now appears that there were persons who may have gone beyond my directives, and sought to expand on my efforts to protect the national security operations in order to cover up any involvement they or certain others might have had in Watergate."

As evidence of his determination to have wrongdoing exposed, the President softened his previous positions on executive privilege. The right to remain silent will not be claimed, he said, in regard "to any testimony concerning possible criminal conduct or discussions of possible criminal conduct."

The statement was released late this afternoon in an atmosphere of great tension that has been building in the White House as the Watergate disclosures have mounted. It was issued, the President said, because of "grossly misleading impressions of many of the facts as they relate both to my own role and to certain unrelated activities involving national security."

The President's statement went much further than he had before in conceding White House involvement; it presented a marked contrast to the White House posture of flat "no involvement" of only one and one-half months ago, and it contained new, and more humble, acceptance of responsibility. He said:

"It is clear that unethical, as well as illegal, activities took place in the course of that campaign. None of these took place with my specific approval or knowledge. To the extent that I may in any way have contributed to the climate in which they took place, I did not intend to; to the extent that I failed to prevent them, I should have been more vigilant."

Ronald L. Ziegler, the White House press secretary, in a heated session with reporters following the release of the statement, said the President would appear before the press in "the very near future" to answer further to the Watergate charges.

Leonard Garment, the new White House counsel, said one reason for releasing a detailed statement today was to meet "the legitimate concerns" of political leaders of both parties that the President should be less seclusive and secretive.

The President and his aides seemed to be signaling an end to a period of passiveness on Mr. Nixon's part in the Watergate affair, a posture uncharacteristic of Richard Nixon in past crises. Mr. Garment said so complicated and involved was the Watergate case and related matters that it had taken a long time to sort out the facts and, in effect, build a legal case for the White House.

Today's statement constituted an outline, with some of the details still vague, that is expected to be followed in building a defense for Mr. Nixon in the weeks and months ahead.

First, the President sought to separate his own moves in protecting national security from the Watergate burglary and other illegal activities that stemmed from both Watergate and the investigative efforts for security.

He acknowledged that in 1969 "a special program of wiretaps" had been set up to prevent leaks of secret information important to the new President's foreign policy initiatives. He said there were "fewer than 20 taps" and these were terminated in February, 1971.

In 1970, the Administration was concerned about a wave of bombings, explosions, campus disruptions and other violence sweeping the nation in connection with antiwar protests and decided a better intelligence operation was needed, he said. He appointed J. Edgar Hoover, then director of the Federal Bureau of Investigation, as chairman of an interagency in-

John J. Caulfield at Watergate hearing.

out all it could about Mr. Ellsberg's associates and his motives."

"Because of the extreme gravity of the situation, and not then knowing what additional national secrets Mr. Ellsberg might disclose," he said, "I did impress upon Mr. Krogh the vital importance to the national security of his assignment. I did not authorize and had no knowledge of any illegal means to be used to achieve this goal.

"However, because of the emphasis I put on the crucial importance of protecting the national security, I can understand how highly motivated individuals could have felt justified in engaging in specific activities that I would have disapproved had they been brought to my attention."

There have been reports that Mr. Nixon, citing national security, twice opposed the release to the Ellsberg trial court of information regarding the burglary of the Los Angeles psychiatrist. The President said today that when the matter was brought to his attention he directed that the information be transmitted to the court.

On the Watergate break-in, President Nixon said once again that it came to him as "a complete surprise" and he had no inkling that any such illegal activity had been planned by anyone connected with his campaign.

"Within a few days, however, I was advised that there was a possibility of C.I.A. involvement in some way," he said. Mr. Garment and other aides would not say who so advised the President.

"It did seem to me possible that, because of the involvement of former C.I.A. personnel, and because of some of their apparent associations, the investigation could lead to the uncovering of covert C.I.A. operations totally unrelated to the Watergate break-in," the President said.

telligence committee to prepare recommendations, he recalled.

On June 25 of that year, Mr. Nixon said, the committee submitted a report that included recommendations for resuming "certain intelligence operations that had been suspended in 1966." "These in turn had included authorization for surreptitious entry—breaking and entering, in effect—on specified categories of targets in specified situations related to national security," he went on.

But he said that on reconsideration Mr. Hoover opposed the plan and it was never put in effect.

"It was this unused plan and related documents that John Dean [former White House counsel] removed from the White House and placed in a safe deposit box," he said.

The White House has asked for the document back on the ground it contains top secret matters on national security.

The President also acknowledged that in 1971, amid concern about continued leaks in foreign policy matters, a small intelligence unit called "the plumbers" was set up. It was this unit that was responsible for the burglarizing of the office of Dr. Daniel Ellsberg's psychiatrist.

Mr. Nixon said his decision to set up the unit came during the week following the publication of the Pentagon papers by The New York Times. "There was every reason to believe this [publication of the papers] was a security leak of unprecedented proportions," he said.

"It created a situation in which the ability of the Government to carry on foreign relations even in the best of circumstances could have been severely compromised," he added.

He said he "looked to John Ehrlichman for the supervision of this group."

Mr. Nixon said he told a member of the unit, Egil Krogh Jr., "that as a matter of first priority, the unit should find

McCord, convicted in Watergate break-in,

He noted at this point that one of the suspects, later convicted, was E. Howard Hunt Jr., who had been a member of "the plumbers."

"Therefore, I was also concerned that the Watergate investigation might well lead to an inquiry into the activities of the special investigations unit itself," he went on.

He felt it was important, Mr. Nixon said, "to avoid disclosure of the details of the national security matters with which the group was concerned. I knew that once the existence of the group became known, it would lead inexorably to a discussion of these matters, some of which remain, even today, highly sensitive."

His aides would not expand on what those matters were.

He continued, "I instructed Mr. Haldeman and Mr. Ehrlichman to insure that the investigation of the break-in not expose either an unrelated covert operation of the C.I.A. or the activities of the White House investigations unit.

"It was certainly not my intent, nor my wish, that the investigation of the Watergate break-in or of related acts be impeded in any way."

This was a reference to statements of officials of the Central Intelligence Agency, released in Congressional hearings, that the White House aides asked that C.I.A. involvement be used as a cover-up of the collecting and "laundering" of campaign funds through Mexico, later used to finance the Watergate burglary. Mr. Haldeman was quoted as saying "it is the President's wish" that the cover-up proceed. Mr. Haldeman, however, has denied that Mr. Nixon was involved.

May 23, 1973

DEAN TELLS INQUIRY THAT NIXON TOOK PART IN WATERGATE COVER-UP FOR EIGHT MONTHS; HE ALSO NAMES HALDEMAN AND EHRLICHMAN

ON STAND ALL DAY

Ex-Counsel Says He Warned President of a 'Cancer'

By JAMES M. NAUGHTON

Special to The New York Times

WASHINGTON, June 25 — John W. Dean 3d, asserting that President Nixon had failed to heed a warning that the Watergate case was "a cancer growing on the Presidency," testified today that the President had taken part in the Watergate cover-up for as long as eight months.

Mr. Dean, the dismissed White House legal counsel, told the Senate's investigating committee that he still clung to a belief that Mr. Nixon "did not realize or appreciate at any time the implications of his involvement."

Nonetheless, in a day-long, matter-of-fact recitation of Mr. Dean's own involvement in the Watergate cover-up and in 47 documents that he submitted to the Senate committee, he described a widespread effort to mask the extent of the conspiracy that he said spread from the White House staff, the Committee for the Re-election of the President, the Department of Justice and, ultimately, to the oval office of the White House.

Explosive Testimony

The testimony was explosive, yet tamped down in its immediate impact by the somber demeanor of the witness. The caucus room of the Old Senate Office Building, where Presidential candidacies have begun, was hushed as the Senators and audience waited to learn whether Mr. Dean's recitation might point toward the President's undoing. As he read his long statement, Senators turned pages simultaneously to keep up with the text and the five previous weeks of hearings became a prelude to Mr. Dean's declarations.

His head bowed as he read calmly from a 245-page prepared account, Mr. Dean publicly detailed for the first time the following allegations of Mr. Nixon's own involvement:

¶The President complimented him last September for having helped to assure that the Government's investigation of the Watergate case "had stopped with [G. Gordon] Liddy," one of the convicted Watergate conspirators.

¶In February, the President asked him to report directly to Mr. Nixon on what he learned of the continuing investigations because H. R. Haldeman and John D. Ehrlichman, the two senior domestic aides to the President, "were principals in the matter," and also meeting with Mr. Dean was taking up too much of their time.

¶The President discussed with him on March 13 the demands by the Watergate conspirators for large sums of money to maintain their silence and that when Mr. Dean told him it could cost more than $1-million, Mr. Nixon "told me that was no problem." A month later, Mr. Dean said, the President sought to pass off the remark as a joke.

¶The President had told him of discussions early this year with Mr. Ehrlichman and Charles W. Colson, a former special counsel to the President, about a promise to grant executive clemency to E. Howard Hunt Jr., another of the Watergate defendants.

¶The President directed that the Administration try to curtail the Senate investigation and block an attempted inquiry into Watergate by the House Banking and Currency Committee last September. The President also ordered aides to make sure that L. Patrick Gray 3d, the former acting director of the Federal Bureau of Investigation, would be "pulled up short" in his testimony last spring to the Senate Judiciary Committee.

¶At one point, in a meeting on March 21, the President discussed with his aides the possibility that the cover-up might be kept secret if John N. Mitchell, the former Attorney General and director of Mr. Nixon's re-election campaign, could be persuaded to assume publicly responsibility for the burglary and wiretapping of the Democratic headquarters at Watergate a year ago.

¶After he (Dean) had resolved to try to "end the mess without mortally wounding the President" by giving information to Government prosecutors, the President apparently tape recorded an April 15 meeting with him and asked a number of "leading questions" in an evident effort to create a record that would "protect himself."

¶The President tried to get him, in a "tense conversation" on April 16, to sign two letters of resignation that tended to incriminate Mr. Dean, but he "looked the President squarely in the eyes and told him I would not sign the letters" or become a "White House scapegoat."

Mr. Dean's recital to the Senate Select Committee on Presidential Campaign Activities consumed the entire hearing today. Members of the committee will interrogate him tomorrow and Wednesday and they plan to call Mr. Mitchell as the next witness on Thursday.

Mr. Dean did not provide any firsthand information to link the President to prior knowledge of the Watergate burglary and the arrests of five men inside the Democratic National Committee offices. But he told, in a fourth-hand account, of having been advised in February that Mr. Haldeman had "cleared" with the President Liddy's $250,000 master plan to gather information on the Democratic opposition in the 1972 campaign.

Furthermore, he said he was told last Nov. 15 by Mr. Haldeman and Mr. Ehrlichman that Mr. Nixon had decided he must obtain the resignation of Dwight L. Chapin, the former White House appointments secretary, because of Mr. Chapin's involvement with Donald H. Segretti, the alleged director of a broad campaign of sabotage of Democratic Presidential candidacies.

Reports Burglary Order

The former White House counsel said that another aide to Mr. Nixon, Egil Krogh Jr., had told him on March 29 that the authority for a September, 1971, burglary of the office of a psychiatrist treating Dr. Daniel Ellsberg had come "right out of the oval office."

Mr. Dean's account was the first before the Senate committee to accuse Mr. Nixon categorically of involvement in the cover-up. He sat alone at the witness table, his wife, Maureen, and his lawyers seated one row behind him, to dramatize what he had said last week was the loneliness of his plight in making accusations about the President.

He acknowledged to the committee—before which he appeared only after obtaining a grant of partial immunity from prosecution—that he had been involved himself in "obstructing justice," arranging for "perjured testimony" and in making personal use of $4,850 of campaign funds.

As he began his appearance before the Senators, Mr. Dean said that he hoped that when all the facts were known "the President is forgiven." He apologized for having to describe illegal acts of "friends" and of individuals he said he admired, but he went on to recount, calmly, without passion and in narrative form, the involvement of several score Government and campaign officials in the Watergate case.

Cites Kalmbach Role

He said that within 10 days after the Watergate arrests, Herbert W. Kalmbach, formerly Mr. Nixon's personal secretary, had consented to arrange to gather "silence money" to keep the Watergate trial defendants from talking. He described his own contacts with Mr. Kalmbach to arrange the payoffs, saying that he had been acting at the direction of Mr. Mitchell, with the "approval" of Mr. Haldeman and Mr. Ehrlichman.

Mr. Dean said that the White House Congressional relations staff had helped to prevail on members of the House Banking and Currency Committee last year to vote against subpoenas of key White House and re-election committee officials.

He told of an attempted cover-up of the activities of Mr. Segretti, including his participation in arrangements to have Mr. Segretti keep traveling around the country last fall to avoid newsmen.

On Oct. 13, after details of Mr. Segretti's alleged sabotage activities appeared in print, Mr. Dean said, he took part in a White House meeting with Mr. Ehrlichman; Richard A. Moore, a special counsel to the President; Patrick A. Buchanan, a speech writer for Mr. Nixon, and Ronald L. Ziegler, the White House press secretary. The meeting was to prepare Mr. Ziegler to handle questions about the Segretti matter at news briefings, Mr. Dean said.

Arranging Payments

Mr. Dean tied Mr. Colson to negotiations in the White House to arrange for payments to Hunt and other Watergate defendants of a $350,000 fund of "surplus money" left over from the 1968 campaign and the 1970 Congressional campaign.

After the election last November, he asserted, Mr. Colson recorded a telephone conversation in which Hunt demanded more money. Mr. Colson gave a copy of the tape to Mr. Dean, who said today he had played the recording—in Mr. Nixon's own lodge at Camp David, Md., when the President was not there—for Mr. Haldeman and Mr. Ehrlichman.

Mr. Dean said that after initially trying to arrange for Mr. Mitchell to provide funds for the Watergate defendants, Mr. Haldeman had reluctantly consented to use of the $350,000 fund and said, "send the entire damn bundle" to Frederick C. LaRue, who had been Mr. Mitchell's chief deputy on the re-election committee.

At one point, Mr. Dean said that from the beginning of the attempted cover-up a year ago, "a pattern had developed where I was carrying messages" from officials at the campaign committee—Mr. Mitchell, Maurice H. Stans, the finance chairman, and Robert C. Mardian, the former political adviser—to Mr. Haldeman and Mr. Ehrlichman in the White House and back. He said these contacts concerned "how each quarter was handling the cover-up and relevant information as to what was occurring."

But he said that he had gradually become persuaded that the Watergate stain was spreading throughout the Administration and that he began, earlier this year, trying to persuade Mr. Nixon that it was "time for surgery" on the Watergate "cancer."

He said that it became clear from his contacts with the President that he "had not really made the President understand" the risks, including possible impeachment, that might result from a continued cover-up.

According to Mr. Dean's testimony, the effort of the Nixon Administration to limit the investigation of the Watergate break-in to those immediately arrested and to cover up any involvement of White House officials in surveillance operations against the Democratic National Committee and Democratic Presidential candidates began within two days of the June 17 break-in.

Dean's Story

This, in brief, is the story Mr. Dean told today of the mounting efforts, at times approaching the frenetic, to prevent the investigation of the Watergate episode from engulfing the White House:

Landing in San Francisco on June 18, 1972, from Manila, Mr. Dean said, he learned of the break-in in a call from Fred Fielding, his assistant, and immediately departed for Washington.

He said that on Monday, the 19th, he had a succession of meetings and telephone conversations with Jack Caulfield, then with the Treasury; Jeb Stuart Magruder, deputy director of the re-election committee, who volunteered that the whole thing was "all Liddy's fault"; Mr. Ehrlichman, who told him to find out what he could; Gordon Strachan of the White House staff and Mr. Colson, the latter assuring him that he had "no involvement in the matter whatsoever" but expressing concern about "the contents" in the safe of Hunt; Liddy, who said Mr. Magruder "had pushed him into doing it" and apologized for his men being caught, and Attorney General Richard G. Kleindienst, who said the F.B.I. and the District of Columbia police were investigating.

The most important developments on that day, he related, were (1) that Mr. Strachan said to Mr. Dean that Mr. Haldeman had instructed him to winnow the Haldeman files of "damaging materials" such as "Wirefax information from the DNX" and destroy them, and (2) that Mr. Ehrlichman ordered Mr. Dean to "call Liddy to have him tell Hunt to get out of the country," and also to remove the contents of Hunt's safe.

At Mitchell's Place

On the evening of the 19th or 20th, Mr. Dean said, he went to Mr. Mitchell's apartment. Mr. Mardian and Mr. Magruder were there, and Mr. Dean recalled only that there was a discussion of "how to handle the matter from a public relations standpoint."

At a meeting with Mr. Kleindienst—Mr. Dean could not

remember whether it was the 19th or the 20th—he said, "I told him that I did not know if the President was involved, but I was concerned" because if the investigation led to the White House "the chances of re-electing the President would be severely damaged."

At this point, Mr. Dean related, Mr. Kleindienst sent for Henry E. Petersen, Assistant Attorney General, and left the two men together.

"I told him I had no idea where this thing might end," Mr. Dean said, "but I told him I didn't think the White House could withstand a wide-open investigation [and] I had reason — without being specific with him — to suspect the worst."

At mid-morning of June 20, he said, men from the General Services Administration who had opened Hunt's safe brought the contents to him. He said the contents included a hand gun; a large briefcase containing electronic equipment; a large batch of classified State Department cables from the early years of the Vietnam war, a "bogus cable" implicating the Kennedy Administration in the fall of the Diem regime in 1963; "a number of materials relating to Daniel Ellsberg," who made the Pentagon study of the Vietnam war available to the press; "some materials relating to an investigation Hunt had conducted for Colson at Chappaquiddick," and many memorandums to Mr. Colson on the performance of the "plumbers unit" under Mr. Krogh that had been formed on the President's orders to investigate leaks.

Mr. Dean said that, on his orders, Mr. Fielding separated out the "politically sensitive documents" which were then placed in Mr. Dean's safe. The briefcase was put in a locked closet in his office, he said, and the State Department documents stored in an aide's office pending their return to the department.

Later, he said, when he reported to Mr. Ehrlichman on the contents of Hunt's safe, Mr. Ehrlichman told him "to shred" the bogus cable, the documents relating to Dr. Ellsberg and other politically sensitive material, and to "deep six" the briefcase with the electronic equipment. Then, Mr. Dean testified:

"I asked him what he meant by 'deep six.' He leaned back in his chair and said, 'You drive across the river on your way home at night, don't you?' I said yes. He said, 'Well, when you cross over the bridge on your way home, just toss the briefcase into the river.'"

Mr. Dean said that he suggested to Mr. Ehrlichman that he get rid of the bugging equipment since he also crossed the river. "He said, no thank you," said Mr. Dean.

He said he was "very troubled" about Mr. Ehrlichman's instruction, and Mr. Fielding shared his feeling that it would be "an incredible action to destroy potential evidence." Therefore, he said, he decided not to follow the instructions.

June 26, 1973

ADMINISTRATION 'POLITICAL ENEMIES' LISTED

SCORES OF NAMES

Politicians, Newsmen, Labor and Business Officials Included

By **DAVID E. ROSENBAUM**

Special to The New York Times

WASHINGTON, June 27—John W. Dean 3d told the Senate Watergate committee today that the White House lists of political enemies filled a file "several inches thick."

The former Presidential counsel turned over to the committee several different lists, compiled in mid-1971, containing the names of scores of prominent and obscure politicians, journalists, labor officials, entertainers, academicians, Democratic campaign contributors and businessmen.

Purpose Outlined

Mr. Dean also gave the committee several documents outlining the purpose of the lists. He said that the lists and the documents came from a file entitled "Opponents List and Political Enemies Project."

In one of the documents—a memorandum written by Mr. Dean in August, 1971, to President Nixon's top advisers, H. R. Haldeman and John D. Ehrlichman—Mr. Dean suggested "how we can use the available Federal machinery to screw our political enemies."

Another memorandum that Mr. Dean said he prepared recommended using Internal Revenue Service machinery to harass political opponents of the President.

Two of the lists in the file contained the names of contributors, large and small, to the campaign of Senator Edmund S. Muskie of Maine, who was then a candidate for the Democratic Presidential nomination. Senator Muskie had voluntarily made public the names of his donors.

Ervin Is Amused

As Mr. Dean recounted to the committee this afternoon how the lists were prepared and constantly updated, Senator Sam J. Ervin Jr., the committee's chairman, began to smile.

When Mr. Dean paused, the North Carolina Democrat, his eyebrows jumping, remarked, "I can't forbear observing, when I see the list of opponents, why the Democratic vote was so light in the election."

What appeared to be a master list of political opponents ran to several hundred names. It included 10 Democratic Senators, all 12 black House members, more than 50 newspaper and television reporters and executives and celebrities such as Joe Namath, Steve McQueen and Barbra Streisand.

Mr. Namath, the quarterback of the New York Jets, was

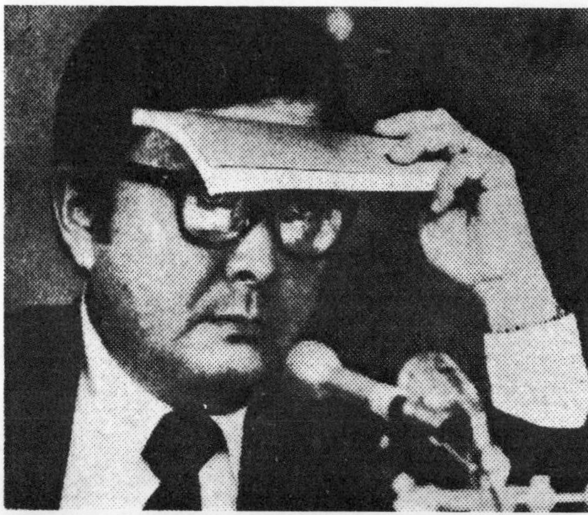

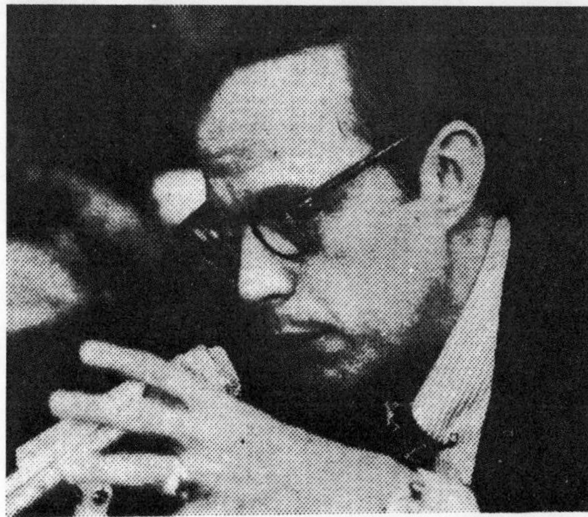

The New York Times/Barton Silverman

Senator Daniel K. Inouye, Democrat of Hawaii, shades his eyes while questioning John W. Dean 3d.

identified as "New York Giants; businessman; actor." There are a number of other inaccuracies in the list.

The businessmen ranged in prominence from Thomas J. Watson Jr., board chairman of International Business Machines Corporation, and Sargent Shriver, who was to become the Democratic Vice Presidential nominee, to Arthur R. Taylor, identified as executive of the International Paper Company who is now president of the Columbia Broadcasting System, and George H. Talbot, identified as president of Charlotte Liberty Mutual Insurance Company.

The master list included several organizations that were considered political enemies, including three newspapers, The New York Times, The Washington Post and The St. Louis Post-Dispatch.

Mr. Dean said that the master list was prepared in the office of Charles W. Colson, then a Presidential counselor.

That list was not dated. But, in his August memorandum to Mr. Haldeman and Mr. Ehrlichman, Mr. Dean suggested "a small list of names as our targets for concentration." He went on to say in the memorandum:

"I feel it is important that we keep our targets limited for several reasons: (1) A low visibility of the project is imperative; (2) It will be easier to accomplish something real if we don't overexpand our efforts; and (3) We can learn more about how to operate such an activity if we start small and build."

Subsequently, the list was reduced to about 20 names. Periodically, names were added to and removed from this smaller list.

One condensed list of 20 names was prepared by Mr. Colson, according to Mr. Dean. Mr. Colson said tonight he believed the lisst had been prepared by a member of his staff.

He said a list was also kept of Administration supporters. "The purpose was very simple and straightforward," Mr. Colson said. "To keep the social office, the personnel office, the press office, the counsel's office, and other offices in the White House advised of persons who had been particularly supportive of the President or persons who had been particularly critical of the President.

One such critical list contained pointed comments about the persons who were included.

For instance, following the name of John Conyers Jr., a Democratic Representative from Detroit, was the following comment:

"Coming on fast. Emerging as a leading black anti-Nixon spokesman. Has known weakness for white females."

Following the name of Sidney Davidoff, an aide to Mayor Lindsay, were these remarks:

"A first-class S.O.B., wheeler-dealer and suspected bagman. Positive results would really shake the Lindsay camp and Lindsay's plans to capture youth vote. Davidoff in charge."

Following the name of Dr. Morton Halperin, once an aide to Henry A. Kissinger and a supporter of antiwar causes, was the comment, "A scandal would be most helpful here."

There was no evidence of action taken against many of those on the list. But one man, Daniel Schorr, a newsman for the Columbia Broadcasting System, was investigated by the Federal Bureau of Investigation. And it has been disclosed that Mr. Halperin's telephone had been tapped.

Another list, containing some of the names on Mr. Colson's list, included the names of Dr. Eugene Carson Blake, general secretary of the World Council of Churches, and Leonard Bernstein, the composer and conductor. After both names was the notation "per request." It was not clear who made the request.

This list was prepared by Mr. Dean and forwarded to Mr. Haldeman's office.

Teamster Aide on List

One name on many of the lists was that of Harold J. Gibbons, a Teamsters Union vice president. In June, 1972, Mr. Colson wrote Mr. Dean that he had learned "on good authority" that there were "discrepancies in Mr. Gibbons's tax returns. Mr. Colson told Mr. Dean to "see if this one can be started at once."

Mr. Colson went on to say that "if there is an informer's fee, let me know. There is a good cause at which it can be donated."

Mr. Colson is known to have a close relationship with the hierarchy of the Teamsters Union. Mr. Gibbons is considered a maverick by other officials of the union.

PRESIDENT REFUSES TO RELEASE TAPES

COURT TEST SEEN

Separation-of-Powers Doctrine Is the Basis of Nixon's Stand

By R. W. APPLE Jr.
Special to The New York Times

WASHINGTON, July 23—President Nixon refused today to release tape recordings of his conversation about the Watergate case. Both his special prosecutor and the Senate Watergate committee moved at once to subpoena the tapes.

Three subpoenas — one each from the prosecutor, Archibald Cox, and the Senate committee covering the tapes and one from the committee covering other documents—were served shortly after 6 P.M. They were accepted by Leonard Garment, the acting White House counsel, and J. Fred Buzhardt, a special counsel.

Gerald L. Warren, the deputy Presidential press secretary, said that he could not predict whether they would be honored or not, but other White House officials said that the decision had already been made to ignore them, thus implicitly inviting a test in the Federal courts.

Response Sought Thursday

The subpoenas call for a response on Thursday.

And so the constitutional struggle between the President and those charged with investigating the Watergate and allied scandals was finally joined, more than 13 months after the break-in at the Democratic National Committee.

Mr. Nixon took his firm stand behind the doctrine of separation of powers, despite the prevailing view among politicians outside the White House that to do so would convince the public that he had something to hide.

He also took the risk that the battle could result in his being the first President to be impeached—put on trial before the Senate—since Andrew Johnson in 1868. But the White House inner circle believes, and many Senators and Representatives agree, that the Congress will hesitate before forcing the issue to that extreme.

Letter to Ervin

In a letter to Senator Sam J. Ervin Jr., Democrat of North Carolina, the Senate committee chairman, the President argued that "the tapes are entirely consistent with what I know to be the truth and what I have stated to be the truth." But he insisted that "the tapes would not finally settle" the question of his involvement.

"As in any verbatim recording of informal conversations," Mr. Nixon added, "they contain comments that persons with different perspectives and motivations would inevitably interpret in different ways."

"If you will notice," Senator Ervin said to general laughter in the hearing room, the President says he has heard the tapes or some of them, and they sustain his position. But he says he's not going to let anybody else hear them for fear they might draw a different conclusion."

The Senate committee received the President's letter at lunchtime and went into executive session. When the open hearing resumed, Senator Ervin, looking grim, announced before the hushed room and a national television audience that the committee had decided unanimously to subpoena the tapes. He spoke of the Watergate affair as "the greatest tragedy this country has ever suffered."

Senator Howard H. Baker Jr., Republican of Tennessee, the vice chairman, also spoke briefly about the committee's decision, expressing his "disappointment" over a "confrontation" with the White House.

2d Letter To Ervin

Mr. Nixon also sent a second, private letter to Mr. Ervin, which the Senator made public. In it, he said that he knew of "no useful purpose that will be served" by a meeting between himself and Senator Ervin, which he promised on July 12. The President said that he was willing to go through with a meeting if Mr. Ervin insisted, but Mr. Ervin said he would not.

The committee's subpoenas were delivered by Rufus L. Edmisten, deputy counsel, and Terry F. Lenzner, assistant chief counsel of the committee. The subpoena from Mr. Cox was delivered by two of his aides, Philip Lacovara and Peter Kreindler.

The rejection of the requests of the special prosecutor, Mr. Cox, was stated not by the President or by any permanent member of his staff but by Charles Alan Wright, a law professor at the University of Texas who has been serving as a $150-a-day consultant to the White House on Watergate matters.

In a letter couched in unusually blunt language, Mr. Wright dismissed Mr. Cox's contention that, because he was appointed by the President, he is a part of the executive branch and thus not involved in any separation-of-powers question.

"If you are an ordinary prosecutor, and thus a part of the executive branch as well as an officer of the court," Mr. Wright wrote, "you are subject to the instructions of your superiors, up to and including the President, and you can have access to Presidential papers only as and if the President sees fit to make them available to you."

Mr. Wright argued further that the separation-of-powers doctrine applied to Mr. Cox because release of the tapes to him "would lead to their use in the courts, and questions of separation of powers are in the forefront when the confidential documents of the Presidency are sought for use in the judicial branch."

Mr. Cox replied in a statement that Mr. Wright's arguments were "without foundation." The prosecutor, a law professor at Harvard University who served as Solicitor General under President Kennedy, has made it clear from the start that he would demand all relevant documents, and has told some friends that he would resign if he was unable to obtain them.

White House officials have said privately in recent days that the loss of Mr. Cox would be a further blow to the credibility of the President. But the tone of the Wright letter led some observers to wonder whether Mr. Nixon wanted him to quit.

Today, however, Mr. Cox said that he had no intention whatever of resigning.

Questions Turned Aside

Mr. Warren turned aside almost all questions at a special 3 P.M. briefing. He would not say where the tapes were being kept, when the secret listening devices that produced them had been disconnected or who has had access to the recordings.

The spokesman did disclose that Mr. Nixon had listened to some of the tapes early in June.

That was about the time that the first bits of what John W. Dean 3d, the deposed White House counsel, planned to tell the Senate committee later in the month began to become public. Mr. Dean's testimony heavily implicated the President in the Watergate cover-up, and the committee had hoped to discover whether he was telling the truth by listening to tapes of his numerous conversations with Mr. Nixon.

The existence of the tapes was made public a week ago when Alexander P. Butterfield, a former White House aide, told the Senate committee that Mr. Nixon had taped nearly all of his meetings and telephone conversations at the White House, in the Executive Office Building next door and at the Presidential retreat at Camp David, Md.

Mr. Nixon cited the volume of material contained on the tapes as one reason that they could not be released.

"The tapes could be accurately understood or interpreted only by reference to an enormous number of other documents and tapes, so that to open them at all would begin an endless process of disclosure of private Presidential records," he said.

The President concluded that "the tapes, which have been under my sole personal control, will remain so." He said that none had been transcribed and that none would be.

July 24, 1973

NIXON ASKS WATERGATE BE LEFT TO COURTS AND NATION 'GET ON WITH URGENT BUSINESS'; DENIES ANY PART IN BREAK-IN OR COVER-UP

REPORT TO NATION

President Offers His Reply to Charges on the Scandal

By R. W. APPLE Jr.

Special to The New York Times

WASHINGTON, Aug. 15 — President Nixon said tonight "the time has come to turn Watergate over to the courts" and "for the rest of us to get on with the urgent business of our nation."

In his long-awaited address to the nation on the scandal that has bedeviled his Administration, he asserted that confidence in the American economy, currency and foreign policy "is being sapped by uncertainty." He said "we cannot let an obsession with the past destroy" the future.

Mr. Nixon asserted once again that he had no prior knowledge of the Watergate burglary, and that he was unaware of subsequent efforts to cover it up until last March 21.

Origins Are Traced

And he traced the origins of what critics have called "the Watergate mentality" in the White House to violence and acts of civil disobedience in the nineteen-sixties that led "a few over-zealous persons" to resort to similar extremism in 1972.

"Both are wrong," the President declared. "Both should be condemned. No individual, no group and no political party has a corner on the market on morality in America."

But Mr. Nixon provided, in the televised speech and an accompanying 2,500-word statement, almost no additional information on the dozens of questions raised by testimony before the Senate Watergate committee. Instead, he traversed familiar ground and defended at length his refusal to release tape recordings of his meetings and telephone conversations.

The President, who recently recovered from a siege of viral pneumonia, appeared to have lost weight. He seemed earnest, almost somber, as he made his way through his 28-minute address, but he betrayed no signs of tension.

Many Questions Unanswered

"I recognize that this statement does not answer many of the questions and contentions raised during the Watergate hearings," Mr. Nixon said. "It has not been my intention to attempt any such comprehensive and detailed response.

"Neither do I believe I could enter upon an endless course of explaining and rebutting a complex of point-by-point claims and charges . . . and still be able to carry out my duties."

A far more detailed rejoinder had been expected in view of Mr. Nixon's long silence — he last issued a Watergate statement on May 22 — and the repeated promises by his spokesmen that he would speak out in full.

The tone of his remarks and his written statement tonight were similar to that of his May 22 statement. He took a hard line on the tapes and toward the Senate committee, but he admitted error on the part of some of his aides. He explained, he drew morals, he warned of the dangers ahead.

In sum, he seemed to have sided with those of his aides who urged conciliation but also to have taken a thought or two from the hard liners.

The political strategy underlying the speech was implicit in Mr. Nixon's closing appeal. The White House believes, along with some other observers, that the country is tiring of the scandal and is therefore ripe for the argument that its own self-interest lies in putting Watergate out of mind.

"Legislation vital to your health and well-being sits unattended on the Congressional calendar," Mr. Nixon told the nation. "Confidence at home and abroad in our economy, our currency and our foreign policy is being sapped by uncertainty.

Security Issues

"Critical negotiations are taking place on strategic weapons and troop levels in Europe that can affect the security of this nation and our allies long after Watergate is forgotten. Vital events are taking place in Southeast Asia which could lead to a tragedy for the cause of peace.

These are matters that will not wait. They cry out for action now. Either we, your elected representatives here in Washington, ought to get on with the jobs that need to be done—for you—or every one of you ought to be demanding to know why."

In effect, Mr. Nixon was appealing over the heads of his Capitol Hill critics and the commentators to the people. He chose not to reply to specific allegations, therefore, and instead replied to the whole concept of extended muckraking on Watergate.

In the statement, which was designed to give slightly more detail than possible in the speech, Mr. Nixon asserted that he had not used the Central Intelligence Agency to obstruct the Federal Bureau of Investigation's inquiry into the case; that no member of his staff had ever offered any defendant clemency; that he had never authorized the burglary of Dr. Daniel Ellsberg's former psychiatrist, and that he had relied heavily on the assurances of his since-deposed counsel, John W. Dean 3d, that no White House staff members were implicated.

"I had no prior knowledge of the Watergate operation," the President said. "I neither took part in nor knew about any of the subsequent cover-up activities. I neither authorized nor encouraged subordinates to engage in illegal or improper campaign tactics. That was—and is—the simple truth.

"In all the millions of words of testimony, there is not the slightest suggestion that I had any knowledge of the planning for the Watergate break-in. As for the cover-up, my statement has been challenged by only one of the 35 witnesses who appeared—a witness who offered no evidence beyond his own impressions, and whose testimony has been contradicted by every other witness in a position to know the facts."

Mr. Nixon's reference was to Mr. Dean.

But the President was silent on a number of key points, including the following:

¶The warning that L. Patrick Gray 3d, then the acting F.B.I. director, allegedly gave Mr. Nixon on July 6, 1972, that some of his aides were out to "mortally wound" him.

¶Mr. Dean's testimony that on Sept. 15, 1972, Mr. Nixon indicated indirectly to him that he knew of a cover-up.

¶The whole question of the disbursement of huge sums of money to the original defendants in the Watergate case.

Mr. Nixon briefly attacked the Senate committee, arguing that "both the hearings themselves and some of the commentaries on them have become increasingly absorbed in the effort to implicate the President personally in the illegal activities that took place."

The President accepted—as he had previously — "full responsibility" for illegal acts and promised that in the future his Administration would be "more vigilant in insuring that such abuses do not take place." He added, "No political campaign ever justifies obstructing justice or harassing individuals or compromising those great agencies of government that should and must be above politics."

Linked to Violence

Remarking that "the notion that the end justifies the means proved contagious," Mr. Nixon sought to link the violence of the nineteen sixties with Watergate. It was "deplorable," he said, that "some persons in 1972" emulated the nineteen sixties protesters.

The ultimate lesson of Watergate, the President argued in a key passage, requires "that we learn once again to work together, if not united in all of our purposes, then at least united in respect for the system by which our conflicts are peacefully resolved and our liberties are maintained."

Mr. Nixon put the final touches to his speech, drafted with the assistance of his two top writers, Raymond K. Price Jr. and Patrick Buchanan, late this afternoon at the White House. The President returned at midday from the last of a series of stays at Camp David, his retreat in the Catoctin Mountains.

As he has done so often in the past, Mr. Nixon chose the seclusion of Camp David in which to do most of the thinking that went into his address tonight—perhaps the most important of a political career that stretches back a quarter of a century to a postwar campaign for the House of Representatives.

He spoke against a gloomy political backdrop.

In trouble with the electorate not only because of Watergate but also because of economic problems, Mr. Nixon had watched his standing in the public opinion polls plummet since his inauguration for a second term on Jan. 20, only seven months ago.

The latest Gallup survey, published yesterday, showed that his popularity had sunk to 31 per cent. That was the lowest figure in two decades—lower than President Johnson's in the grimmest days of Vietnam protest and equal to that of President Truman's at the end of his tenure.

Mr. Nixon's speech ended a period of silence on the Watergate case. Not since May 22 had he made any detailed comment on the matter, although he had indirectly attacked his critics for what he described as their tendency to "wallow" in scandal.

More comments on the case may be forthcoming next week. Mr. Nixon will fly to New Orleans on Monday for a major speech to a convention of the Veterans of Foreign Wars, then continue to his oceanside estate at San Clemente, Calif., for a stay of two weeks.

During that time, according to Presidential aides, he is likely to hold his first news conference in five months. He last answered reporters' questtions on March 15.

Since that time, the 37 days of national televised hearings have not only uncovered new evidence of chicanery in the Watergate case and allied cases, but they have also brought the details of the scandal into the living rooms of America on an immense scale.

Mr. Dean was the principal witness who linked Mr. Nixon directly to the Watergate case and the cover-up. Some of the other witnesses suggested Presidential involvement, and some denied it; only Mr. Dean offered specific evidence.

August 16, 1973

JUDGE SIRICA ORDERS NIXON TO YIELD TAPES TO HIM FOR A DECISION ON GRAND JURY USE; PRESIDENT DECLARES HE 'WILL NOT COMPLY'

President First Since Jefferson Directed to Give Up Records

By WARREN WEAVER Jr.
Special to The New York Times

WASHINGTON, Aug. 29—President Nixon was ordered today by Judge John J. Sirica to make tape recordings of White House conversations involving the Watergate case available to him for a decision on their use by a grand jury.

Presidential aides announced, however, that Mr. Nixon "will not comply with the order."

A White House statement said that the President's lawyers, led by Prof. Charles Alan Wright, were considering appealing the decision by Judge Sirica, who is chief judge of the United States District Court here, but it also hinted that they might find some other method of sustaining the President's legal position.

If faced with a refusal by Mr. Nixon to accept the court's ruling or to challenge it by an appeal, Archibald Cox, the special prosecutor, might initiate contempt proceedings or begin an appeal of his own, based on the court's refusal to give him the tapes directly.

Serious Consequences

It was only the second time in the nation's history that a court had required a President, against his will, to produce his personal records as evidence, and the decision was certain to have serious political, governmental and legal consequences,

The New York Times/George Tames

Judge John J. Sirica, who ruled on the Presidential tapes, in his chambers

both immediate and long-range. The first case involved President Jefferson.

At San Clemente, where President Nixon is vacationing, officials announced that he would not comply with the court order on the ground that inspection of the tapes by a judge "is inconsistent with the President's position relating to the question of separation of powers as provided by the Constitution and the necessity of maintaining precedents of confidentiality of private Presidential conversations . . ."

The White House statement said that the President's lawyers were considering an appeal "or how otherwise to sustain" Mr. Nixon's legal position.

The last phrase raised the possibility that the President might ignore the order rather than appeal it, thus precipitating another constitutional clash between the executive and judical branches.

Authority Upheld

Judge Sirica said that he was "simply unable" to decide whether the President's refusal to release the tapes and related documents was valid without inspecting the recordings himself. He upheld the authority of the court to take such action.

If he finds evidence relating to criminal activity in the tapes, and it can be successfully separated from the privileged statements dealing with the President's official duties, the judge said, he will excise the privileged portions and pass the unprivileged portions along to the Watergate grand jury. Archibald Cox, the special prosecutor, is presiding over the panel.

"If privileged and unprivileged evidence are so inextricably connected that separation becomes impossible," he continued, "the whole must be privileged and no disclosure made to the grand jury."

Only once before, in 1807, had a Federal court ordered a President to produce a document from his records, and Judge Sirica relied heavily on the decision by Chief Justice John Marshall that required President Jefferson to furnish a letter for the treason trial of Aaron Burr. Burr was found not guilty of the treason charge.

President Nixon's lawyers, led by Professor Wright of the University of Texas Law School, had argued a week ago that he was not willing to permit a secret inspection of the tapes by the court because the President was the sole judge of what material should be withheld as privileged.

If the Watergate tapes "may be important in the investigation, if they may be safely heard by the grand jury," Judge Sirica asked in his opinion today, "would it not be a blot on the page which records the judicial proceedings of this country, if, in a case of such serious import as this, the court did not at least call for an inspection of the evidence in chambers?"

Judge Sirica based his decision to a considerable extent on the need for all citizens, regardless of their social or political position, to cooperate with a grand jury investigation.

"In all candor," he said, "the court fails to perceive any reason for suspending the power of courts to get evidence and rule on questions of privilege in criminal matters simply because it is the President of the United States who holds the evidence."

He called it "immaterial" whether the court had the "physical power" to enforce an order against the President, because the court "has a duty to issue appropriate orders" under any circumstances.

Relies on Good Faith

He said that court decisions "have always enjoyed the good faith of the executive branch," even when the Supreme Court invalidated President Truman's seizure of the steel industry in 1952, "and there is no reason to suppose that the courts in this instance cannot again rely on that same good faith."

"Indeed," he added, "the President himself has publicly so stated."

What Mr. Nixon said, in response to a question at his televised news conference last week, was that he would comply with "a definitive order of the Supreme Court," leaving open the question of precisely what that phrase meant.

If the President decided not to appeal Judge Sirica's ruling, as tonight's White House statement hinted, he might then argue that he had only promised to obey the Supreme Court, which has not spoken on the disputed issues involved.

Mr. Cox and his legal staff, advised of the President's statement, went into conference to discuss how they might counter a Nixon strategy that did not follow the traditional route of an appeal to the United States Court of Appeals and then, if unsuccessful, to the Supreme Court.

The prosecutor had asked Judge Sirica to turn the tapes over directly to the grand jury, and some lawyers regarded it as theoretically possible that he could appeal the decision, insofar as it fell short of the full relief he had sought.

Ordinarily, when a defendant in a lawsuit refuses to obey a court order, the plaintiff can go back to the judge and ask that the defendant be cited for contempt. On the basis of such a citation, the judge can levy a fine or impose a jail sentence, with either or both to run until the defendant complies with the order. In a Federal court, such orders are normally enforced by United States marshals.

In the Watergate tape cases, however, both Mr. Cox and the Senate investigating committee have been extremely reluctant to invoke a legal procedure charging the President with contempt, although both could have done so when Mr. Nixon refused to honor their subpoenas weeks ago.

Earlier, before the White House refusal to comply had been announced, a spokesman for Mr. Cox said, "Naturally, we are very pleased by Judge Sirica's decision. If appellate review is sought, we will do everything possible to expedite the proceedings."

Validity Recognized

Judge Sirica said that he recognized the validity of "an evidentiary privilege based on the need to protect Presidential privacy," the legal doctrine the Nixon attorneys called "executive privilege" and said extended to any information the President wished to keep secret "in the public interest."

But, he added, he could not agree with the President "that it is the executive that finally determines whether its privilege is properly invoked."

"The availability of evidence, including the validity and scope of privileges, is a judicial decision," he said.

He rejected as "unpersuasive" the contention of Mr. Nixon's lawyers that the President could not be served with legal process, such as a subpoena, because this would violate the constitutional doctrine of separation of powers.

He said that the courts had not hesitated to rule on acts of both the legislative and executive branches, in cases like the Truman steel seizure and the House of Representatives' exclusion of Adam Clayton Powell, later overruled by the Supreme Court.

4th Branch of Government

Judge Sirica said that giving the President special immunity from court rulings "tends to set the White House apart as a fourth branch of government." The Constitution provides for interaction between the branches, he said, and never intended to establish separate watertight governmental divisions.

In the Aaron Burr case, the defendant asked the Federal court, where he was on trial in Richmond, to subpoena President Jefferson to produce a letter from one of his co-conspirators to the White House. Chief Justice Marshall was presiding in the lower court, as Supreme Court Justices often did in those days.

The prosecution opposed Burr's motion for a subpoena, saying that the letter was a private one to Jefferson, probably contained confidential material that the President should not be compelled to disclose, perhaps even "state secrets" that might endanger "the national safety."

But Chief Justice Marshall ruled that the President, unlike the King of England, could be subpoenaed to provide essential information for a trial. At the same time, however, he expressed some passing doubt as to whether the court that issued such a subpoena could properly then compel compliance if the subject was the President.

Marshall Ruling Cited

The Nixon attorneys used this last statement to support their argument that the President was not subject to legal process as long as he occupied his office.

President Jefferson declined to appear in the court in Richmond on the ground that that would take too much time away from his official duties, but he agreed to provide the letter and offered to testify by deposition if he could be questioned in Washington.

As a result, the question of whether the President could be compelled to produce records was never tested further in the courts, making Mr. Nixon the first President to refuse to comply with a subpoena.

In his 23-page opinion today, Judge Sirica said the he had found it necessary to answer only two questions: "(1) whether the court has jurisdiction to decide the issue of privilege, and (2) whether the court has authority to enforce the subpoena . . . by way of an order requiring production for inspection in camera [that is, in a private chamber]. . . . The court concludes that both of the questions must be answered in the affirmative."

August 30, 1973

AGNEW QUITS VICE PRESIDENCY AND ADMITS TAX EVASION IN '67

Judge Orders Fine, 3 Years' Probation

By JAMES M. NAUGHTON
Special to The New York Times

WASHINGTON, Oct. 10—Spiro T. Agnew resigned as Vice President of the United States today under an agreement with the Department of Justice to admit evasion of Federal income taxes and avoid imprisonment.

The stunning development, ending a Federal grand jury investigation of Mr. Agnew in Baltimore and probably terminating his political career, shocked his closest associates and precipitated an immediate search by President Nixon for a successor.

"I hereby resign the office of Vice President of the United States, effective immediately," Mr. Agnew declared in a formal statement delivered at 2:05 P.M. to Secretary of State Kissinger, as provided in the Succession Act of 1792.

Minutes later, Mr. Agnew stood before United States District Judge Walter E. Hoffman in a Baltimore courtroom, hands barely trembling, and read from a statement in which he pleaded nolo contendere, or no contest, to a Government charge that he had failed to report $29,500 of income received in 1967, when he was Governor of Maryland. Such a plea, while not an admission of guilt, subjects a defendant to a judgment of conviction on the charge.

Spiro T. Agnew

Tells Court Income Was Taxable

"I admit that I did receive payments during the year 1967 which were not expended for political purposes and that, therefore, these payments were income taxable to me in that year and that I so knew," the nation's 39th Vice President told the stilled courtroom.

Judge Hoffman sentenced Mr. Agnew to three years' probation and fined him $10,000. The judge declared from the bench that he would have sent Mr. Agnew to prison had not Attorney General Elliot L. Richardson personally interceded, arguing that "leniency is justified."

In his dramatic courtroom statement, Mr. Agnew declared that he was innocent of any other wrongdoing but that it would "seriously prejudice the national interest" to involve himself in a protracted struggle before the courts or Congress.

Mr. Agnew also cited the national interest in a letter to President Nixon saying that he was resigning.

"I respect your decision," the President wrote to Mr. Agnew in a "Dear Ted" letter made public by the White House. The letter hailed Mr. Agnew for "courage and candor," praised his patriotism and dedication, and expressed Mr. Nixon's "great sense of personal loss." But it agreed that the decision was "advisable in order to prevent a protracted period of national division and uncertainty."

The resignation automatically set in motion, for the first time, the provisions of the 25th Amendment to the Constitution, under which the Republican President must nominate a successor who will be subject to confirmation by a majority vote in both houses of Congress, where Democrats predominate. Until a successor is confirmed and sworn in, the Speaker of the House, Carl Albert, Democrat of Oklahoma, will be first in line of succession to the Presidency.

Mr. Agnew's sudden resignation came only 11 days after he made an emotional declaration to a Los Angeles audience: "I will not resign if indicted! I will not resign if indicted!" It marked the second time in the nation's history that the Vice-Presidency was vacated by resignation. The first occasion was in 1832, when John C. Calhoun stepped down after he was chosen to fill a Senate seat from South Carolina.

Mr. Agnew's decision appeared to have been based on personal, rather than political or historic, considerations.

Close and authoritative associates of Mr. Agnew said that, contrary to official White House denials, Mr. Nixon at least twice asked him to resign after it was disclosed on Aug. 6 that the Vice President was under investigation

The requests were said to have been spurned by Mr. Agnew until sometime in the last week. According to some associates, Mr. Agnew was advised by his defense attorneys that the Department of Justice and the Internal Revenue Service had obtained "uncontrovertible evidence" of unreported income while he held office in Maryland.

Even so, the Vice President's closest associates had expected him to fight the accusations or at least to continue to seek a forum to try, as he did in his courtroom statement today, to place the accusations within the context of "a long-established pattern of political fund raising" in his home state.

Said to Have Accepted Reluctantly

Yesterday, the defense attorneys and officials at the Justice Department reportedly reached agreement on the plan under which Mr. Agnew would resign, plead no contest to the single tax-evasion charge and accept the department's pledge to seek a light sentence.

According to the sources, Mr. Agnew reluctantly accepted the proposal when he returned to Washington from a speaking engagement yesterday in New York and then told the President of his reluctant decision at 6 o'clock last night.

Shortly after 2 P.M. today, Mr. Agnew's staff was assembled in his office in the Executive Office Building next to the White House. As the Vice President was addressing the court in Baltimore, his military advisor, Maj. Gen. John M. Dunn, informed the staff of his decision.

Some of the aides wept. Others, stunned by the announcement, asked such things as how they should answer the telephone. And a number of them privately and bitterly denounced the President.

One of Mr. Agnew's stanchest supporters, Senator Barry Goldwater, Republican of Arizona, declared publicly that Mr. Agnew had been "treated shamefully by persons in responsible Government positions."

Justice Department Is Assailed

As Mr. Agnew had done until today, Senator Goldwater accused the Justice Department of having "convicted" the Vice President "by headlines and newscasts based on leaks of official information before a single legal charge had been filed."

Until today, Mr. Agnew had waged a determined campaign to halt the investigation of his Maryland political career, in which he was Baltimore County Executive before he became Governor. His attorneys had argued in preliminary legal skirmishes that the Constitution forbade the indictment of an incumbent Vice President and that the leaks of information about the charges against Mr. Agnew had destroyed any prospect for a fair hearing.

Thus, Mr. Agnew's surprise appearance this afternoon in the Baltimore courtroom marked a swift abandonment of his campaign for vindication. Judge Hoffman had been scheduled to hear in the courtroom arguments by reporters and news organizations seeking to quash subpoenas served on them by the Vice President's attorneys.

Feared Effort Would Take Years

At the same time, Mr. Agnew insisted that he was innocent of any other wrongdoing. But he said that his attorneys had advised him it might take years to establish his innocence and that he had been compelled to decide that "the public interest requires swift disposition of the problems which are facing me."

Some of Mr. Agnew's associates said later today that the signals of his momentous decision had been there but that they had not wished to accept them for what they became.

After the Vice President's emotional speech to the National Federation of Republican Women on Sept. 29 in Los Angeles, his aides described plans for subsequent speeches in which Mr. Agnew would reiterate the charge that the Justice Department had selected him as a "big trophy" to use in restoring reputations blemished by "ineptness" in the investigation of the Republican burglary of the Democrats' headquarters in the Watergate complex here.

But last Wednesday, President Nixon declared at a White House news conference that the charges against Mr. Agnew were "serious" and he defended the Justice Department's conduct of the case.

One Associate Is 'Flabbergasted'

The next night, in Chicago, Mr. Agnew delivered a speech marked by the absence of the accusations against the Justice Department and he asserted to assembled newsmen that "a candle is only so long, and eventually it burns out."

His press spokesman, J. Marsh Thompson, and other Agnew associates were reportedly ordered to make themselves unavailable to newsmen beginning early last week.

As one stunned Agnew associate remarked this afternoon, "I felt things were beginning to close in, but I still don't understand it. I'm flabbergasted."

A White House official familiar with previous discussions between Mr. Nixon and Mr. Agnew said, significantly, that the decision was "not altogether unexpected here—I think the initiative, this time, was from [Mr. Agnew's] side."

The shock of the announcement of Mr. Agnew's resignation had barely worn off when the White House and leaders in Congress began deliberating about both the politics and the mechanics of Vice Presidential succession.

Mr. Nixon was said to have begun consultation with leaders "both within and outside the Administration" on the nominee to succeed Mr. Agnew.

Mike Mansfield, Democrat of Montana, the Senate majority leader, assembled bipartisan Congressional officials to discuss the selection process and prepare for hearings to assess the qualifications of the nominee.

Speculation About Successor

The White House has repeatedly denied that it had a "contingency" list of potential successors. Published reports, and renewed speculation today, centered on the possibility that Mr. Nixon would nominate Attorney General Richardson, Governor Rockefeller of New York, former Secretary of the Treasury John B. Connally, Deputy Attorney General William D. Ruckelshaus or Senator Goldwater.

But Democratic leaders in the House have hinted privately that they would oppose a nominee who could be expected to confront their party three years from now as a Presidential candidate. Thus, others said to be under active consideration were such Republican elder statesmen as former Gov. William W. Scranton of Pennsylvania, former Senator John Sherman Cooper of Kentucky and former Secretary of State William P. Rogers.

Mr. Agnew, his career ended at the age of 54 years, was said to have begun telephoning friends to thank them for their past support. He disappeared from public view this afternoon as the limousine in which he was riding pulled away from the Baltimore courthouse and the former Vice President waved to spectators.

NIXON DISCHARGES COX FOR DEFIANCE; ABOLISHES WATERGATE TASK FORCE; RICHARDSON AND RUCKELSHAUS OUT

BORK TAKES OVER

Duties of Prosecutor Are Shifted Back to Justice Dept.

By DOUGLAS E. KNEELAND

Special to The New York Times

WASHINGTON, Oct. 20 — President Nixon, reacting angrily tonight to refusals to obey his orders, dismissed the special Watergate prosecutor, Archibald Cox, abolished Mr. Cox's office, accepted the resignation of Elliot L. Richardson, the Attorney General, and discharged William D. Ruckelshaus, the Deputy Attorney General.

The President's dramatic action edged the nation closer to the constitutional confrontation he said he was trying to avoid.

Senior members of both parties in the House of Representatives were reported to be seriously discussing impeachment of the President because of his refusal to obey an order by the United States Court of Appeals that he turn over to the courts tape recordings of conversations about the Watergate case, and because of Mr. Nixon's dismissal of Mr. Cox.

The President announced that he had abolished the Watergate prosecutor's office as of 8 o'clock tonight and that the duties of that office had been transferred back to the Department of Justice, where his spokesman said they would be "carried out with thoroughness and vigor."

Events Listed

These were the events that led to the confrontation between the President and Congress and the Government's top law enforcement officers:

¶Mr. Cox said in a televised news conference that he would return to Federal court in defiance of the President's orders to seek a decision that Mr. Nixon had violated a ruling that the tapes must be turned over to the courts.

¶Attorney General Richardson, after being told by the President that Mr. Cox must be dismissed, resigned.

¶Deputy Attorney General Ruckelshaus was ordered by Mr. Nixon to discharge Mr. Cox. Mr. Ruckelshaus refused and was dismissed immediately.

¶The President informed Robert H. Bork, the Solicitor General, that under the law he was the acting Attorney General and must get rid of Mr. Cox and the special Watergate force.

¶Mr. Bork discharged Mr. Cox and had the Federal Bureau of Investigation seal off the offices of the special prosecutor, which Mr. Cox had put in a building away from the Department of Justice to symbolize his independence. Some members of the Cox staff were still inside at the time.

¶The F.B.I. also sealed off the offices of Mr. Richardson and Mr. Ruckelshaus.

Mr. Richardson had no comment tonight, but he scheduled a news conference for Monday. Mr. Ruckelshaus said, "I'm going fishing tomorrow."

Mr. Cox's reaction was brief: "Whether we shall continue to be a government of laws and not of men is now for Congress and ultimately the American people [to decide]," he said.

The President's decisions today raised new problems.

For one, he must seek his third Attorney General in a year, now that Mr. Richardson has followed Richard G. Kleindienst as a victim of the Watergate affair.

Moreover, he has risked the possibility of a public and Congressional outcry over disbanding the Watergate force assembled last spring under Mr. Cox to allay suspicions that a Justice Department responsible to the President might not have been prosecuting those responsible for the Watergate break-in and cover-up with enough vigor.

Ford Backs Nixon

In addition, the confirmation of Representative Gerald R. Ford, the Michigan Republican who was designated by Mr. Nixon as his choice for Vice President after Spiro T. Agnew resigned, may run into trouble in Congress. Mr. Ford issued a statement tonight supporting Mr. Nixon's actions.

The announcement of the President's decisions came at 8:24 P.M. at an unusual Saturday night briefing by Ronald L. Ziegler, the White House press secretary.

By late this evening, some public reaction was already visible at the White House. Crowds of young people gathered at the northwest gate, some shouting anti-Nixon slogans. One youth held up a large sign saying, "Resign."

All evening, the White House switchboard was so swamped with calls that it was almost impossible to get through. Lights in the offices in the West Wing burned late into the night.

All day, newsmen in unusual numbers for a weekend wandered aimlessly through the press area of the White House, waiting for Mr. Cox's televised news conference from the National Press Buiding, and then for the President's reaction.

What Mr. Cox said when he appeared, relaxed and amiable as he slouched at a table, was that the President's proposal to make an edited summary of the tapes available to the Senate Watergate committee and the grand jury had created "insuperable difficulties" for him in conducting a criminal investigation.

"I think it is my duty as the special prosecutor, as an officer of the court and as the representative of the grand jury, to bring to the court's attention what seems to me to be noncompliance with the court's order," he declared.

Making it clear that he would defy the President's order "not to seek to invoke the judicial process further to compel production of recordings, notes or memoranda regarding private Presidential conversations," Mr. Cox added:

"I'm going to go about my duties on the terms of which I assumed them."

No Official Reaction

But for hours after Mr. Cox's news conference, there was no official reaction from the White House.

During the day, White House sources continued to provide background briefings to small groups of newsmen on Mr. Nixon's reasons for not appealing the appellate court's ruling on the Watergate tapes, but seeking instead to provide a summary that would be verified by Senator John C. Stennis, Democrat of Mississipp.

About 4:45 P.M., Mr. Richardson's limousine appeared in the driveway, and disappeared a half-hour later. But for hours, no one would even confirm that Mr. Richardson had seen the President.

Then, shortly before 8:30 P.M., a grim-faced Mr. Ziegler appeared at the podium in the press room with his deputy, Gerald Warren.

Reading from a prepared statement and later refusing to take questions, Mr. Ziegler reported that the President had discharged Mr. Cox and broken up the special Watergate prosecutor force.

Mr. Ziegler said the President had sought by his move tonight "to avoid a constitutional confrontation by an action that would give the grand jury what it needs to proceed with its work with the least possible intrusion of Presidential privacy."

"That action taken by the President in the spirit of accommodation that has marked American constitutional history was accepted by responsible leaders in Congress and the country," Mr. Ziegler added. "Mr. Cox's refusal to proceed in the same spirit of accommodation, complete with his announced intention to defy instructions from the President and press for further confrontation at a time of serious world crisis, made it necessary for the President to discharge Mr. Cox and to return to the Department of Justice the task of prosecuting those who broke the law in connection with Watergate."

Then, in four brief paragraphs, he announced the resignation of Mr. Richardson and the dismissal of Mr. Ruckelshaus.

The New York Times

Ex-Deputy Attorney General William D. Ruckelshaus.

United Press International

Attorney General Elliot L. Richardson introducing Archibald Cox, left, as special Watergate prosecutor last May.

Cox News Conference

By WARREN WEAVER Jr.

Special to The New York Times

WASHINGTON, Oct. 20—Archibald Cox, defying limits imposed on him by President Nixon, said today that he would return to Federal court in search of a decision that the President had violated valid orders to surrender nine tape recordings of White House conversations.

The embattled special prosecutor told a news conference that Mr. Nixon's proposal to make an edited summary of the tapes available to the Senate Watergate Committee and the grand jury had created "insuperable difficulties" for him in conducting a criminal investigation.

"I think it is my duty as the special prosecutor, as an officer of the court and as the representative of the grand jury, to bring to the court's attention what seems to be noncompliance with the court's order," Mr. Cox declared.

Resignation Is Barred

Mr. Cox also complained that the President had withheld White House documents he requested and the court had ordered be produced.

The special prosecutor made it clear that he had no intention of resigning in protest over the President's attempt to curb his activity. On the contrary, by ignoring the Nixon instructions, he appeared ready to test the President's willingness to accept the political responsibility for dismissing him.

In fact, Mr. Cox questioned whether anyone other than Attorney General Elliot L. Richardson had the right to give him instructions or to discharge him for failure to carry them out. He indicated that, throughout the last week's controversy with the White House, his relations with Mr. Richardson had remained good.

Mr. Nixon was reported today to have been urged by senior political advisers over recent weeks to dismiss Mr. Cox and face serious political criticism, rather than endure the prospect of a long series of indictments of former White House and Administration aides.

Mr. Cox indicated at his news conference today that he thought the White House had deliberately submitted to him a series of proposals for a compromise on the tapes controversy that were known to be unacceptable to him.

For more than an hour before an unusual Saturday crowd of reporters at the National Press Club, the former Harvard law professor put on a relaxed, low-key performance that belied his new status as a prime Presidential target.

He protested that he disliked confrontations, expressed worry that he was getting "too big for my britches," sidestepped inquiries that invited sharply critical replies and generally assumed the role of a homespun Yankee trying to do his legal duty.

"I'm not looking for a confrontation," Mr. Cox said. "I've worried a good deal through my life about problems of imposing too much strain upon our constitutional institutions, and I'm certainly not out to get the President of the United States."

'Repeated Frustration'

But he complained of difficulty in obtaining cooperation from the White House, declaring, "My efforts to get information, beginning in May, have been the subject of repeated frustration."

In a statement issued last night, Mr. Nixon said he would not comply with a week-old Court of Appeals decision requiring him to make the tapes available to Federal District Judge John J. Sirica, who would screen them in private and determine what potential Watergate evidence could be passed on to the grand jury.

The President said he would not appeal that decision to the Supreme Court, and he ordered Mr. Cox, as an employe of the executive branch, to take no further part in that court action and not to attempt any other legal moves aimed to obtain White House documents.

Instead, Mr. Nixon said he would edit a summary of the tapes himself and ask Senator John C. Stennis, as an independent authority, to listen to the recordings and verify the President's summary as full and accurate. Then the summary would go to the grand jury through Judge Sirica and to the Senate Watergate Committee, Mr. Nixon said.

Mr. Cox said that he could not accept the President's plan for the following reasons:

¶In a criminal investigation, "It is simply not enough to make a compromise in which the real evidence is available only to two or three men operating in secrecy, all but one of them aides to the President and men who have been associated with those who are the subject of the investigation."

¶The President's procedures would not establish what standards might be used for cutting "national security" information out of the summary and could result in deletion of material such as that dealing with the burglary of the office of Dr. Daniel Ellsberg's former psychiatrist or the tapping of telephones of White House aides with no foreign affairs responsibilities.

¶The President's instructions to Mr. Cox were "inconsistent" with pledges made by the Attorney General to the Senate "and through the Senate to the American people" that the special prosecutor would have independence.

¶It would be "most unlikely" that trial courts involved with any Watergate defendants would accept the Nixon-Stennis summaries as evidence, "and I would be left without the evidence with which to prosecute people whom I had used the summaries, perhaps, to indict."

¶Prosecution of some Watergate defendants might have to be abandoned if they argued they needed the tapes to make their defense.

Mr. Cox said, however, he had heard that the White House might release some tapes sought by John N. Mitchell and Maurice H. Stans for their defense in the New York trial involving illegal campaign contributions by Robert L. Vesco.

The tapes in question include private conversations in the President's Oval Office with John W. Dean 3d, his former counsel, and other witnesses who told frequently conflicting stories before the Senate Watergate panel about their involvment and Mr. Nixon's knowledge of the matters.

It was Dean who told the panel that members of the White House staff had been involved in a cover-up of the facts surrounding the June, 1972, burglary of Democratic National Committee headquarters in the Watergate complex here. His testimony was contradicted by a number of other White House aides.

Mr. Cox said that many White House papers that he wanted had been taken out of their regular files and "put in something special called Presidential files." He said he had been told he would receive other papers he requested but that "the delays have been extraordinary."

Among the documents he mentioned were notes he said had been made by John D. Ehrlichman, former chief domestic adviser to Mr. Nixon, dealing with "every conversation in which he participated." Another was a memorandus he said he had reason to believe had been dictated by Mr. Nixon after his conversation with Mr. Dean about the cover-up.

October 21, 1973

NIXON AGREES TO GIVE TAPES TO SIRICA IN COMPLIANCE WITH ORDERS OF COURT

ABRUPT REVERSAL

Crisis Over Watergate Appears Deflated for the Moment

By LESLEY OELSNER
Special to The New York Times

WASHINGTON, Oct. 23—President Nixon, in a stunning reversal, abruptly agreed today to turn over the Watergate tape recordings to Federal District Judge John J. Sirica.

He made his decision as he was confronted with the possibility of impeachment by the House of Representatives and with the likelihood of a contempt citation from Judge Sirica.

The move ended three months of his insistence that the tapes remain in the White House and that he, as President, maintain absolute control over them.

It appeared to deflate, at least for the moment, the constitutional crisis that erupted full-blown last weekend when the President announced that he would not appeal any further two court rulings ordering him to turn over the tapes; but also that he would not comply with them, either, and that he would give the district court only a "summary" of the tapes' contents.

Lawyers Disclose Move

Mr. Nixon's decision was announced by his lawyers this afternoon before Judge Sirica, the chief judge of the Federal District Court here, who issued the original order for the tapes last Aug. 29. Yesterday the same lawyers informed Judge Sirica in writing that Mr. Nixon would provide only the summary.

The recordings of conversations in the President's office had been sought in an attempt to learn who had been telling the truth about the Republican break-in last year at the Democratic headquarters in the Watergate complex here and the subsequent cover-up.

Standing before Judge Sirica shortly after 2 o'clock this afternoon, Charles Alan Wright, the Texas law professor who has headed the President's legal defense in the Watergate affair, said that "the President of the United States would comply in all respects with the order of Aug. 29 as modified by the order of the Court of Appeals."

The total capitulation came just a few hours after the House began taking its first tentative steps toward impeachment and just a day after the leaders of the legal profession began mobilizing to rebuff what they considered an unprecedented attack by Mr. Nixon on the system of law.

Wright View of Problem

But even while giving in, the President, through his lawyer, continued to insist that he acted correctly all along and that the "summary" would have satisfied the court's needs.

The problem, Mr. Wright said, was that, even if Judge Sirica agreed with the President, "there would have been those who would have said the President is defying the law."

"This President does not defy the law, and he has authorized me to say he will comply in full with the orders of the court," he went on.

A few minutes later, when the brief proceedings were over and Mr. Wright went outside to meet the waiting television camera crews, he repeated the point. "The President," he said again, his voice firm and his face solemn, "does not defy the law."

Unsettled Questions

The action today does not settle all the questions about the scope and effectiveness of future prosecutions of Watergate-related crimes.

For one thing, the President's agreement to turn over the disputed tapes to Judge Sirica in a few days does not mean that the grand jury will automatically or necessarily get to hear all the tapes.

Judge Sirica's original order specified that Mr. Nixon should present the tapes to the court so that Judge Sirica could examine them in private and decide which portions, if any, should be kept confidential under the doctrine of executive privilege. Under this doctrine, Presidents have long held certain information confidential to protect the orderly operation of the Government.

When the United States Court of Appeals for the District of Columbia Circuit upheld Judge Sirica's action Oct. 12, it modified the order somewhat to specify the procedure by which the President could continue to assert his privilege. The appeals court said that it was rejecting Mr. Nixon's "all-embracing claim of prerog ative" but that the President nevertheless "will have an opportunity to present more particular claims of privilege if accompanied by an analysis in manageable segments."

Directions to Prosecutor

It also specified that Mr. Nixon would be able to appeal the district court's decision on these particularized claims.

Another unanswered question is whether the prosecution will be able to obtain any other Presidential tape recordings, or any other material such as memorandums and reports.

When the President announced his "summary" plan last week, he said that he was directing Archibald Cox, the special Watergate prosecutor, "to make no further attempts by judicial process to obtain tapes, notes or memoranda of Presidential conversations." Mr. Cox's refusal to abide by this order led to his dismissal by the President on Saturday.

Immediately after the court proceedings this afternoon, Henry Ruth, Mr. Cox's second-in-command, remarked that it was unclear whether the Nixon agreement today erased all the implications of the Presidential order Friday.

At a White House briefing later, Gen. Alexander M. Haig Jr., Mr. Nixon's chief of staff, said that he was not yet in a position to answer whether the White House would continue to fight efforts to obtain these other materials.

However, he indicated that the President still felt strongly that his personal papers should not be turned over to the prosecution.

Henry E. Petersen, the Assistant Attorney General who has now been placed in charge of the prosecution of Watergate-related crimes, a task he had before Mr. Cox's appointment last summer, is known to believe that the prosecution may need some more White House documents. They could become vital, he feels, to respond to defendants' contentions that the Government has possession of exculpatory evidence — material that might tend to show their innocence.

The subpoena that led to the action today originally called for memorandums as well as tape recordings. Two specific memorandums were turned over.

Options Open to Court

The question of how Judge Sirica would deal with the President's refusal to comply with a court order had caused great speculation over the weekend, both inside and out of the legal profession. The judge had several options, including citing the President for contempt of court.

Judge Sirica indicated earlier today that he had no intention of letting the Watergate prosecutions lapse.

At 10 A.M. he called in the members of the two grand juries that have been investigating the Watergate affair and told them that the juries were still "operative and intact" and that he himself would "safeguard" their rights.

"These two grand juries will continue to function and pursue their work," the judge told the 42 men and women assembled before him, 21 on each jury. "You are not dismissed and will not be dismissed except as provided by law upon the completion of your work or the conclusion of your term."

Recent Events Cited

He had summoned them to court, he told them, to "alleviate" the anxiety that they had perhaps been feeling in the wake of "events that have recently transpired."

"In due course, the questions which now plague us will be answered," he assured them, "and you may rely on the court to safeguard your rights and to preserve the integrity of your proceedings."

After the jurors left the courtroom, to resume their deliberations elsewhere in the building, a professor from George Washington University's Law School asked the court to appoint a special counsel to represent the jurors' interest. The professor, John F. Banzhaf 3d, was rebuffed.

"If the court feels it necessary to appoint a special counsel," Judge Sirica said, it would not need "any outside guidance."

October 24, 1973

NIXON DECLARES HE DIDN'T PROFIT FROM PUBLIC LIFE

Tells A.P. Managing Editors 'I've Earned Every Cent, I'm Not a Crook'

By R. W. APPLE Jr.

Special to The New York Times

DISNEY WORLD, Fla., Nov. 17 — President Nixon told a group of newspaper executives tonight that he had never "profited from public service." He added: "I've earned every cent. I'm not a crook."

In a one-hour question-and-answer session with 400 participants in The Associated Press Managing Editors annual convention Mr. Nixon defended himself against all charges of wrongdoing and attempted to regain the political offensive.

After months of torment over the Watergate and allied scandals, the President gave detailed answers to more than a dozen questions. Among his disclosures were the following:

¶That he paid only "nominal amounts" of taxes in 1970 and 1971, principally because of deductions available to him for the donation of his Vice-Presidential papers. He gave no figures, but did not dispute those reported recently by The Providence, R.I., newspapers—$792 for 1970 and $878 for 1971.

¶That an increase in milk prices in 1972 had come about not because of promised campaign contributions from milk producers but because of what he called Congressional pressure from, among others Senator George McGovern of South Dakota, the President's Democratic opponent that year.

¶That a recording of his reminiscences for June 20, the contents of which had not previously been disclosed, showed that former Attorney General John N. Mitchell on that date gave him no details of the Watergate case, but merely "expressed his chagrin to me that the organization over which he had control could have gotten out of hand in this way." Later, Mr. Nixon said that "looking back, perhaps I should have cross-examined" Mr. Mitchell about Watergate.

¶That the system that produced the tape recordings of Mr. Nixon's Watergate conversations at the White House, many of which are of marginal quality, cost only $2,500 and consisted of "a little Sony" tape recorder and some "little lapel-mikes in my desk."

¶That he believed that when all legal proceedings had been completed, his former key associates, H. R. Haldeman and John D. Ehrlichman, "will come out all right" but that "they've already been convicted in the minds of millions of Americans because of what happened before the Senate Watergate committee."

¶That the Secret Service had, as previously reported, but never confirmed, placed a tap on the telephone of the President's brother, Donald, in an effort to learn of the activities of foreigners "who were trying to get him to use improper influence."

¶That after he retires he perhaps would write and would like to try to improve campaign financing.

Mr. Nixon dealt only briefly with non-Watergate topics during the nationally televised interview from the editors' convention at this vast entertainment complex near Orlando. But he did say that a system of gasoline rationing "would be something that the American people would resent very much," and added that his Administration's goal "is to make it not necessary."

The President seemed composed and on top of the subject throughout the session, faltering perceptibly only during the discussion of his taxes. In contrast with some of his recent appearances, he did not berate his critics or his political enemies.

He even had a bit of humor for one of the harshest of these. Harry Rosenfeld, the metropolitan editor of The Washington Post, which carried some of the most damaging early Watergate revelations, asked a question. The President answered it and added: "I like your sports page."

Only once did bitterness emerge. Discussing measures he had taken to alleviate the energy shortage, Mr. Nixon noted that he had left behind the backup plane that usually accompanies his personal jet, the Spirit of '76. If his plane "goes down," he said, "it goes down and then they don't have to impeach."

The editors, who came here from 43 states, clapper tepidly when the President entered the meeting room at the Contemporary Hotel on the Disney World grounds. But they, and particularly their families, responded much more warmly at the conclusion.

Impressed by Skill

A number of the news executives said that they had been impressed by Mr. Nixon's skill in fielding their questions.

The political importance of the occasion and the sober comportment of the editors was in sharp contrast to the setting. Mr. Nixon spoke in a gaudily modern room — blue draperies, orange chairs, mirrors on the ceiling — near the monorail line that passes through the hotel and leads to the "Magic Kingdom."

Invited here for "some straight talk," the President got down to the questions at once, with almost no introductory remarks. Some of his responses were as long as 12 minutes, some as short as one. He kept the session going beyond the allotted hour, remarking that that would not bother the television audience very much because "it's a lousy movie anyway."

Asked at one point what he planned to do when he retired, Mr. Nixon wisecracked, "That depends upon when I leave." But then he continued, more seriously. He would not make any speeches, he would not serve on any boards of directors ("boring"), he would not practice law, the President said.

Perhaps he would write, he added, and then, almost wistfully, said he might try to improve campaign financing. He would like to be remembered, Mr. Nixon remarked, as "a President that did his best to bring peace" to the world.

Discussing the nonexistence of two of the crucial Watergate tape recordings, the President said that he knew that, to most people, "it appears that it's impossible that when we have an Apollo system" that the White House taping facilities could have failed at a key moment.

But he insisted that his was "not a sophisticated system." He has said that President Johnson had used a much better one. Johnson assistants have denied that any such system existed.

The President prodded his new special Watergate prosecutor, Leon Jaworski, to get on with his investigation, commenting that Assistant Attorney General Henry E. Petersen, in charge of the Criminal Division, told him six months ago that the inquiry was already 90 per cent complete.

'Reputation Damaged'

"Now it's time that the case be brought to a conclusion," Mr. Nixon said. "The reputations of men, who are maybe not guilty, have been irreparably damaged."

But perhaps the most vivid comment came when Mr. Nixon told the editors he was not "a crook"—unusual language from a President, even one under fire. "I've made my mistakes," the President said, "but in all my years of public life I've never profited from public service. I've earned every cent. I'm not a crook."

Again, discussing the milk case, Mr. Nixon used pungent language. The Congress, he said, had "put a gun to our head" by signing petitions and introducing bills calling for better prices for milk producers.

According to White House officials, the President entered the meeting hoping to demonstrate that he could field the toughest Watergate queries with aplomb. At one point, he even asked himself a question—about the 1972 increase in milk prices—that none of the editors had asked.

Much the same goal lay behind Mr. Nixon's meetings with Republicans and conservative Democratic members of Congress at the White House this week. An aide described the latest Presidential counter-offensive as an effort to show that Mr. Nixon was "walking, talking, thinking and very much in command."

This evening's session with the editors was the first of three public appearances in a four-day period. Tomorrow, after spending a second straight night at his home in Key Biscayne, Mr. Nixon will continue his comeback campaign in Macon, Ga., where he plans to speak at Mercer University and at a 90th birthday celebration for former Representative Carl M. Vinson, once the chairman of the House Armed Services Committee.

On Tuesday, on the way back to Washington, the President will meet the Republican Governors at their conference in Memphis.

Even before the President began taking questions at random from the floor at the editors' meeting, it was apparent that the session would not be a no-holds-barred grilling.

For one thing, the White House press corps, whose daily responsibilities include coverage of the minutiae of the Watergate affair, was excluded from the questioning.

Moreover, Presidential aides have made it clear that Mr. Nixon still did not feel he could speak publicly with total candor, although they continued to promise that he would do so at an unspecified time.

According to Gerald L. Warren, the deputy White House press secretary, the President still feels constrained by at least three circumstances, as follows:

¶His desire to "protect the rights of all individuals" in the case, including those who might be mentioned in an adverse light on the much-disputed, still-secret Watergate tapes.

¶Court orders, which Mr. Warren did not identify, that Mr. Nixon feels inhibited by, despite a memorandum by Judge John J. Sirica that seemed to authorize him to do as he liked.

¶"National security" issues that still bother him.

JURY NAMED NIXON A CO-CONSPIRATOR BUT DIDN'T INDICT

St. Clair Confirms Action —He Asserts President Calls It 'Inappropriate'

KEY IMPACT FORESEEN

Defense Aide Says Court Is Likely to Admit More Tapes as Evidence

By ANTHONY RIPLEY
Special to The New York Times

WASHINGTON, June 6—President Nixon was named last February by a Watergate grand jury as an unindicted co-conspirator in the alleged attempt to cover up the Watergate burglary, his lawyer, James D. St. Clair, confirmed today.

The disclosure, which had been closely guarded in secret court hearings on the case, completes the circle of conspiracy alleged in the indictment handed up March 1 by the grand jury and explains what was contained in the mysterious briefcase handed to Federal Judge John J. Sirica at that time.

It is expected to have a significant impact on the upcoming trials, tying in the President's remarks and meetings with aides in the Watergate matter as possible evidence in the case, rather than excluding them as merely comments of an outsider whose aides were conspiring.

Effect of the Action

"If they tie him into these crucial meetings, this means there's an umbilical between him and us," said one defense attorney for the six men charged in the cover-up conspiracy. "That's what troubles me."

The report of the grand jury's action regarding the President was first published today in The Los Angeles Times — although numerous other news articles had suggested what the jury had done. Mr. St. Clair confirmed the report when newsmen asked him about the Los Angeles article.

Mr. St. Clair late today asked Judge Sirica to make the list of co-conspirators public, arguing that since the matter of the President's role had already been published there seemed no need for further secrecy.

The news is expected to have a political impact on the President and on his chances both at the impeachment hearings in the House and in his efforts to resist turning over further tape-recorded conversations sought in the case.

Surprise for Committee

"It is going to have a hell of an impact on the Hill," said another defense attorney speaking of impeachment efforts on Capitol Hill.

"What it means in terms of our defense is that a lot of those conversations that they held are admissible in evidence. And it makes the White House position far weaker in resisting tapes requests."

House Judiciary Committee members were caught by surprise by the disclosure. Though committee staff members apparently knew of Mr. Nixon's status as an unindicted co-conspirator, they had not yet informed the committee members.

Several members asked about it said it had little bearing on their duty to judge the evidence for impeachment. However, some said it might hurt the President politically.

Defense attorneys who have seen the list of unindicted co-conspirators said today that there were "no big surprises" on it. It is believed that the other names include those who have already pleaded guilty in the case and agreed to cooperate with the special Watergate prosecutor, Leon Jaworski.

Judge Sirica had issued a protective order sealing the names of co-conspirators. He said he would discuss the matter tomorrow in Federal District Court at an open hearing with lawyers for both sides.

Mr. St. Clair, who spoke to reporters this morning as he was entering the Judiciary Committee room for the impeachment hearings, said Mr. Nixon had been informed of the grand jury's action three or four weeks ago.

The President, he said, "regretted" the grand jury's action and considered it "inappropriate."

He also said the President thought the grand jury did not have all the evidence in the case and had come to a wrong conclusion.

Gerald L. Warren, the President's deputy press secretary, said at a news briefing that all the evidence taken together "proves the President's innocence."

In a meeting April 17, 1973, with Henry E. Petersen, head of the Criminal Division of the Justice Department, Mr. Nixon discussed the possibility of his aides being named unindicted co-conspirators and said that if this occurred they "would then be immediately put on leave." The remark is in the edited transcripts of tapes released by the White House.

Mr. Warren was asked if the President might be considering such action for himself.

"I'm not going to accept questions such as that relating to the President of the United States," he said, obviously irritated.

The possibility that the President might actually be a co-conspirator though unindicted was underscored May 24 when Mr. Jaworski asked the United States Supreme Court for access to tapes of 64 conversations, all but one of them including Mr. Nixon as a participant.

At that time Mr. Jaworski said that the 64 conversations had occurred in the course of "the criminal conspiracy."

The defendants in the cover-up case are John N. Mitchell, former Attorney General; H. R. Haldeman, John D. Ehrlichman and Gordon C. Strachan, former White House aides; Robert C. Mardian, a former aide to Mr. Mitchell, and Kenneth Wells Parkinson, lawyer for the Committee for the Re-election of the President.

Colson Off the List

Charles W. Colson, also named in the original indictment, was dropped following his plea of guilty Monday to charges in another Watergate-related case. Mr. Colson is to be sentenced later this month and has agreed to work with the special prosecutor.

The Watergate grand jury, empaneled on June 5, 1972, and still going, brought the first indictments against seven men for the burglary June 17, 1972, of the Democratic national headquarters at the Watergate office building.

Associated Press
James D. St. Clair, President Nixon's lawyer, discussing action of the Watergate grand jury.

On March 1, the grand jury handed up indictments to Judge Sirica along with the sealed briefcase that the jury instructed should go to the House impeachment investigators.

Judge Sirica, after a court hearing, agreed to turn it over.

The grand jurors at the time were reported to have voted unanimously to send the material to the House.

It appeared from the indictment itself that a central figure was missing.

In counts 40 through 44, the alleged payment of hush money to E. Howard Hunt Jr. was discussed, then apparently acted upon. Although some of the discussion took place in the President's office, there is no mention of it.

However, at that meeting, according to the White House transcripts, Mr. Nixon, talking about the payment of money to Mr. Hunt, said, "Would you agree that that's the prime thing that you damn well better get that done?"

"Obviously," Mr. Dean replied.

Mr. Jaworski has said publicly that he does not believe a sitting President can be indicted in a criminal action.

June 7, 1974

NIXON MUST SURRENDER TAPES, SUPREME COURT RULES, 8 TO 0; HE PLEDGES FULL COMPLIANCE

OPINION BY BURGER

Name of President Is Left in Indictment as Co-Conspirator

By WARREN WEAVER Jr.

Special to The New York Times

WASHINGTON, July 24—The Supreme Court ruled today, 8 to 0, that President Nixon must provide potential evidence for the criminal trial of his former subordinates, rejecting flatly the President's contention that he had absolute authority to withhold such material.

Eight hours later in California, the President announced through his attorney that he would accept the high court ruling and comply fully. Until today, White House spokesmen had strongly indicated that Mr. Nixon might choose to defy the Justices.

64 Conversations Cited

As a result of the historic Court decision, announced by Chief Justice Warren E. Burger in a tense, packed chamber, the President will surrender tape recordings and other data involving 64 White House conversations for use in the Watergate cover-up trial, and possibly in impeachment proceedings as well.

In a broader perspective, the Supreme Court reaffirmed with today's ruling its position, carved out in the early days of the republic, that the judicial branch decides what the law is and the executive branch is bound by that determination.

Not since its refusal in 1952 to permit President Truman to seize the nation's steel mills had the Supreme Court dealt so serious a blow to a President who read broader powers into his constitutional mandate than the Court was willing to recognize.

Possible Vote Effect

As an immediate consequence, today's one-sided decision appeared likely to sway some undecided Republicans on the House Judiciary Committee to vote in support of articles of impeachment.

Over a somewhat longer range, the ruling was expected to increase the number of Republicans and conservative Democrats in the House who were willing to vote against the President if the impeachment issue reaches the floor, as is now expected, late in August or early in September.

The special Watergate prosecutor, Leon Jaworski, had sought the data on the conversations as evidence to use in the September trial of six former Nixon aides accused of conspiring to conceal the 1972 burglary of Democratic national headquarters in the Watergate complex here.

Today's ruling was made with three of President Nixon's appointees joining in the vote against him. The fourth, Associate Justice William H. Rehnquist, had disqualified himself. The high court took the following actions:

¶Told the President to comply "forthwith" with Judge Sirica's order to turn over the tape recordings and other documents for screening and subsequent submission to Mr. Jaworski of all portions that provide relevant and admissible evidence for the cover-up trial.

¶Left standing the Watergate grand jury action naming President Nixon as an unindicted co-conspirator in the cover-up. The Justices ruled that the question whether the jury could name him was irrelevant and that they should not have agreed to review Judge Sirica's refusal to strike the President's name from the indictment.

¶Denied a motion by James D. St. Clair, the President's chief defense counsel, that the Justices examine the records of the Watergate grand jury to determine whether there was enough evidence to warrant the naming of Mr. Nixon as a co-conspirator.

Reading a condensed version of his 31-page opinion, Chief Justice Burger rejected every legal defense that the White House had attempted to erect in defense of the President's refusal to deliver the tape recordings to Judge Sirica.

The Court concluded unanimously, the Chief Justice said, that the President did not have an absolute constitutional right to keep his records confidential and that the interests of fairness in administering criminal justice outweighed the qualified privilege Mr. Nixon did enjoy.

"The allowance of the privilege to withhold evidence that is demonstrably relevant in a criminal trial would cut deeply into the guarantee of due process of law and gravely impair the basic function of the courts," Mr. Burger declared.

Court Effect Feared

"Without access to specific facts, a criminal prosecution may be totally frustrated," he continued, adding, "The President's broad interest in confidentiality of communications will not be vitiated by disclosure of a limited number of conversations preliminarily shown to have some bearing on the pending criminal cases."

The tapes, transcripts or memorandums that President Nixon was ordered to deliver to Judge Sirica will be screened by the District Court for any information considered relevant to the conspiracy trial of six former Nixon aides who are charged with covering up the Watergate burglary. The evidence will then be passed on by the court to the special prosecutor.

Mr. Jaworski expressed hope after the Court session that any evidence involved would be available in time for the scheduled trial opening on Sept. 9.

It appeared unlikely, however, that any material on the tapes would become available for the purposes of impeachment before the full House votes on charges against Mr. Nixon that the Judiciary Committee is expected to adopt within the next few days.

The Supreme Court cautioned in its decision that Judge Sirica's screening must involve "scrupulous protection against any release or publication of material not found by the court, at that stage, probably admissible in evidence and relevant to the issues of the trial for which it is sought."

Justice Burger also cautioned Judge Sirica to "discharge his responsibility to see to it that, until released to the special prosecutor, no in camera [privately examined secret] material is revealed to anyone."

Once relevant excerpts of the White House tapes have been delivered to Mr. Jaworski, it is up to him to decide what information, if any, should be forwarded to the House Judiciare Committee for impeachment purposes, and whether any such transmittal should be delayed because of the cover-up trial.

Some Judiciary Committee members were arguing that the impeachment proceedings be held up to take into consideration whatever evidence the new tapes may provide, but that would clearly require a postponement of six weeks to two months.

The Supreme Court decision did not recognize the interrelation between the Watergate trial evidence, officially before the Justices, and its possible applicability to impeachment, a connection that Mr. St. Clair had repeatedly urged it to weigh.

Voting against the White House position, in addition to Chief Justice Burger, were two other appointees of the President: Associate Justices Harry A. Blackmun and Lewis F. Powell Jr. The fourth Nixon appointee, Justice Rehnquist, declined to sit on the case, apparently because of his prior service in the Justice Department under Attorney General John N. Mitchell, one of the defendants in the cover-up trial.

Also concurring in the unanimous decision were Associate Justices William O. Douglas, William J. Brennan Jr., Potter Stewart, Byron R. White and Thurgood Marshall.

Pressure for Unanimity

Some Supreme Court observers had predicted that there would be strong pressure for a unanimous ruling by the Justices, in an institutional effort to discourage President Nixon from refusing to obey the Court.

For the second time in three weeks, the Court chamber was packed with lawyers, newsmen and spectators, many of whom had waited in line on the marble steps for hours. The palpable suspense was ended almost immediately, as Chief Justice Burger began announcing the ruling.

Observers had predicted that the Chief Justice would write the opinion in this politically sensitive case only if the decision was unanimous, and that the only unanimous decision possible, based on the July 8 arguments before the Court, would involve a ruling against the President.

For 17 minutes, Mr. Burger read carefully and unemotionally from the opinion. Only occasionally did he nod to emphasize a point, such as his assertion that "it is 'emphatically the province and the duty' of this Court 'to say what the law is' with respect to the claim of privilege presented in this case."

The Justices had obviously reacted negatively to Mr. St. Clair's argument that the high court had no authority to review a unilateral decision by the President that certain material was legally privileged.

Name Stays on Indictment

As a result of the Justices' decision that they should not have considered reviewing the unindicted co-conspirator question, Mr. Nixon's name will remain on the indictment, pursuant to Judge Sirica's refusal to expunge it.

The court held that Judge Sirica's ruling upholding the subpoena of the material was appealable because, otherwise, it could be reviewed only by citing the President for contempt and appealing that order, a method the Justices called "peculiarly inappropriate" under the circumstances.

Also rejected unanimously was Mr. St. Clair's contention that Mr. Jaworski did not have legal standing to sue the President. The special prosecutor's guarantees of independence upon his appointment, the Court ruled, made this "the kind of controversy courts traditionally resolve."

Chief Justice Burger pointedly denied the White House contention that the President, not the courts, had the ultimate right to make some legal determinations.

"The judicial power of the United States vested in the Federal courts by the Constitution can no more be shared with the executive branch than the chief executive, for example, can share with the judiciary the veto power, or the Congress share with the judiciary the power to override a Presidential veto."

The Court summed up its holding that Mr. Nixon does not have independent authority to decide which evidence he should withhold from the criminal justice system this way:

"To read the powers of the President as providing an absolute privilege as against a subpoena essential to enforcement of criminal statutes on no more than a generalized claim of the public interest in confidentiality of nonmilitary and nondiplomatic discussions would upset the constitutional balance of 'a workable government' and gravely impair the role of the courts."

It is standard Supreme Court procedure for the Justice who wrote the majority opinion in any case to deliver a brief synopsis of it from the bench, at the call of the Chief Justice. Mr. Burger's presentation today was much longer than is normal for less prominent cases.

Mr. Jaworski sat at one of the counsel tables with two of his assistants. Mr. St. Clair was not present, having flown to California over the weekend to confer with the President. He was represented by three White House staff attorneys.

HOUSE PANEL, 21 TO 17, CHARGES NIXON WITH DEFYING SUBPOENAS; ENDS ITS IMPEACHMENT DEBATE

3D COUNT IS VOTED

But Motions on Taxes and Cambodia War Are Defeated

By JAMES M. NAUGHTON
Special to The New York Times

WASHINGTON, July 30 — The House Judiciary Committee voted narrowly today to charge President Nixon with unconstitutional defiance of committee subpoenas, completing the draft of the bill of impeachment.

Before ending the long inquiry into the President's conduct and adjourning the deliberations at 11:08 tonight, the committee rejected proposals that it formally accuse Mr. Nixon of usurping Congressional war powers and of conducting his personal financial affairs in a manner demeaning his high office.

Thus, the 38-member committee, after nine months of intensive investigation and a week of anguished judgments, drew the following outline of the case on which the full House and, if the House votes impeachment, the Senate will ultimately decide Mr. Nixon's fitness to complete his second term in the White House:

¶Article I, approved Saturday by a 27-to-11 bipartisan committee vote, accused Mr. Nixon of having personally engaged in a course of conduct designed to obstruct justice in the Watergate case.

¶Article II, recommended to the House last night by a 28-to-10 roll-call vote, charged the President with a persistent effort to abuse his authority in violation of his constitutional oath to uphold and defend the nation's laws.

¶Article III, added today to the bill of impeachment on a near-party-line vote of 21-to-17, alleged that Mr. Nixon sought to impede the impeachment process by defying eight subpoenas for 147 recorded White House conversations and a variety of other evidence.

Approval of any of the three central charges by a majority of the House would result in the second impeachment of a President of the United States, the first since the Senate trial, and acquittal, of Andrew Johnson in 1868. A two-thirds majority vote of the Senate to convict Mr. Nixon on any of the accusations would strip him of his office.

The Judiciary Committee decisively defeated, early this evening, a motion to add an article to try the President for having conducted a bombing campaign over Cambodia in secrecy, beginning in 1969. Nine Democrats, including some liberal opponents of the Vietnam war, joined all 17 Republicans in the 26-to-12 vote to reject the proposed charge.

Late tonight, in the panel's final substantive vote on Mr. Nixon's conduct, Republicans and some Democrats combined too stave off 26 to 12, a charge of misconduct based on Mr. Nixon's underpayment of Federal income taxes and acceptance of Government-paid improvements to his personal homes in Florida and California.

Finally, in the pro forma statement signifying the end of the inquiry that had its roots in the Watergate burglary two years ago, the committee chairman announced that the article of impeachment would be "reported to the House."

House Debate Next

The resoultion in its final draft included the preamble and its stark proposal:

"Resolved, that Richard M. Nixon, President of the United States, is impeached for high crimes and misdemeanors, and that the following articles of impeachment be exhibited to the Senate."

Of the three charges adopted by the committee, the last appeared least likely to command an eventual majority when the 435-member House begins its formal impeachment debate next month.

Only three of the 10 republicans and conservative Southern Democrats who had endorsed one or both of the two other articles joined the majority to day in approving the subpoena charge.

The narrow margin, along with the warning of some Republican advocates of impeachment that the majority was bent on "political overkill," foreshadowed a bitter debate on the subpoena issue in the House.

But some impeachment proponents said privately that, if the third article survived House consideration, it might be among the most powerful charges in the Senate, where the 100 members are more prone to hold the White House to account for disregard of Congressional actions.

Republicans Shift

Two Republicans—Representative Robert McClory of Illinois, who sponsored the third article, and Representative Lawrence J. Hogan of Maryland—joined 19 Democrats in approving the formal accusation of defying committee subpoenas on a roll-call vote that ended at 3:28 P.M.

But four other Republicans, who voted Saturday to accuse Mr. Nixon of obstruction of justice in the Watergate case and again last night to charge him with repeated violations of his oath to uphold the law, contended today that no additional articles would be warranted in the bill of impeachment.

The four Republicans, who had helped to draft the first two articles, were Representatives Tom Railsback of Illinois, Hamilton Fish Jr. of upstate New York, M. Caldwell Butler of Virginia and William S. Cohen of Maine.

The third article, Mr. Railsback said, would represent "political overkill." Add a fourth and fifth centered on the Cambodian bombing and the President's personal finances, he warned the committee's Democratic majority, "and you watch what's going to happen to your fragile bipartisan coalition."

Move Held 'Too Much'

Two of the three conservative Southern Democrats, Representative Walter Flowers of Alabama and James R. Mann of South Carolina, agreed that, as Mr. Flowers put it, "I just think this is too much."

A committee majority pressed ahead, nonetheless, with the third charge, agreeing, in effect, with Representative Don Edwards, Democrat of California, that it would "destroy this safety valve" of impeachment if Mr. Nixon was permitted to defy subpoenas for recorded White House conversations and other impeachment evidence.

All 17 committee Republicans and 9 of the 21 Democrats combined, 26 to 12, to reject the article proposing to impeach Mr. Nixon for having concealed the Cambodian bombing campaign from the public and all but a few members of Congress.

The article, offered by Representative John Conyers Jr., Democrat of Michigan, charged that Mr. Nixon had deliberately violated the "power of the Congress to declare war, to make appropriations and to raise and support armies."

Mr. Conyers contended that the President's concealment of the bombing was of a piece with "all of the acts that have been debated thus far."

But even some Democrats who had opposed Mr. Nixon's Vietnam policies acknowledged that Congress was unlikely to remove Mr. Nixon because of them. Representative John F.

Peter W. Rodino Jr., left, chairman, and Edward Hutchinson, ranking Republican, at session of impeachment panel

Seiberling, Democrat of Ohio, added that, even though four of his constituents had died at Kent State University while opposing the President's policies, "we should not use our impeachment power to impeach this President for acts that others have done and for which this Congress is partly responsible."

On Mr. Nixon's personal finances, the most pungent criticism of the President came from one of his inveterate critics, Representative Jack Brooks, Democrat of Texas.

He charged that Mr. Nixon knew, in signing income tax returns for the years 1969 through 1972, that he "attested to false information" about his deductions and sought to "defraud the American people" of more than $400,000.

Moreover, Mr. Brooks contended that the Internal Revenue Service, in ruling last March that Mr. Nixon had $94,679 in unreported income from Government expenditures on his homes and as travel reimbursements to his family, made a clear case for a charge that Mr. Nixon violated the "emoluments" clause of the Constitution.

Under that clause, Presidents are expressly barred from receiving any personal income from the Government other than the salary set by statute.

Representative Charles E. Wiggins, Republican of California, asserting that willful fraud must be shown to take Mr. Nixon to task for his tax returns, said that the issue had "nothing to do with innocent mistake" on the President's tax deductions.

Mr. Railsback said that the attempt to insert the issue in the impeachment articles was "another case where we have impeachment-itis."

White House Acts

The committee's decision to include the third article occurred shortly before the White House turned over to Judge John J. Sirica of the United States District Court here the first 20 of 64 recorded White House conversations that the Supreme Court ruled last week could not be withheld by Mr. Nixon from the Watergate special prosecutor.

Mr. McClory said that Congress had at least as powerful a legal argument as the prosecutor had for requiring the President to comply with its subpoenas in a matter where Congress was attempting to judge the President's conduct in office.

If Mr. Nixon is to be the "sole arbiter" of what evidence shall be used to assess his conduct, Mr. McClory asked, "then how in the world could we conduct a thorough and complete and fair investigation?"

"Well, we just could not," he answered.

He called the President's disregard of the impeachment inquiry's subpoenas "the prime example of 'stonewalling'" by the White House in the scandals bred by the Watergate case.

But opponents of the third article asserted that it would weaken the Presidency to impeach Mr. Nixon on the subpoena issue, and that the committee had failed, in any event, to seek redress either through the courts or by seeking a House citation for contempt of Congress.

"This really is overkill at its worst," charged Representative Charles W. Sandman Jr., the New Jersey Republican who had sought unsuccessfully to block the adoption of the two earlier articles.

"There are enough votes here to pass anything," he said. "I know it, and you know it."

Representative Henry P. Smith 3d, Republican of upstate New York, said that it would have been preferable for the committee to seek the assistance of the Supreme Court as an "umpire" in the collision with the President over the subpoenaed tapes and documents.

Fairness Questioned

Moreover, he asked, "is it fair" to ask Mr. Nixon "to hand over what we hoped will be your confession?"

Several Republican opponents of the subpoena article charged that adoption of it by the committee and the House, or conviction on it by the Senate, would lead to constant peril to future Presidents if they tried to withhold material from an opposition Congress on proper grounds.

The committee voted, 24 to 14, to adopt an amendment refining the language of the third article to make clear that a President might be held impeachable only if he withheld evidence in an inquiry into his own conduct.

The amendment was sponsored by Representative Ray Thornton of Arkansas, the only one of the three conservative Southern Democrats to vote, later, for adoption of the article.

"What this really comes down to," insisted Representative John F. Seiberling, Democrat of Ohio, "is, does this committee mean what it says about conducting an impeachment inquiry, and mean it about the powers of Congress—or, when we are really faced by a stonewall in the White House do we just say 'poof' and collapse?"

Representative Wayne Owens, Democrat of Utah, opposed the restrictive language of the Thornton amendment, asserting that the Constitution gave the House the "sole power" of impeachment but no way to enforce it against a recalcitrant President save through impeachment itself.

"The President is the only individual in this country who can refuse to honor a subpoena," Mr. Owens said calmly, "and that is quite simply because he is the commander in chief of the armed forces, and he is the head of the executive branch, and we have not the physical ability to overcome his resistance to a Congressional subpoena."

Some of the advocates of impeachment who opposed the third article said that they believed Mr. Nixon's refusal to honor the subpoenas ought to be included among the matters to come to trial in the Senate but not as a separate article.

Will Seek Amendment

Representative Cohen said that he would try on the House floor to amend the obstruction-of-justice article, or the omnibus article, alleging a number of abuses of Presidential power, to guarantee that the issue come before the Senate if the third article was deleted by a House majority.

Mr. Thornton said that he would join in Mr. Cohen's effort. Mr. Flowers said that, while he would give some thought to inclusion of the subpoena issue in other broad charges against the President, he could not endorse it by itself.

"Let's not kid ourselves," he said. "If this article were standing alone, would we seriously be thinking about impeaching a President of the United States for this alone? I honestly think not."

Reconsideration Urged

"Perhaps we've been too infused with our newfound power," Mr. Flowers told his colleagues. "Please," he implored, "reconsider what you're doing here."

Minutes later, however, after accelerated degate the committee chairman, Representative Peter W. Rodino Jr., Democrat of New Jersey, called for the ayes and noes.

When the roll-call was ended—and both Mr. Fish and Mr. Mann, who had been undecided on the issue, voted against the third article—the tally was announced: 21 to 17.

And the case against the President, the product of a nine-month-long inquiry into the aftermath of the June 17, 1972, Watergate break-in, had apparently been drawn.

The House will begin debate around Aug. 19 before deciding whether to accept the committee's judgment. The Senate, to which the articles of impeachmen will go if approved by the House, will determine the duration of the 37th Presidency.

July 31, 1974

Transcript of President Nixon's Address to the Nation Announcing His Resignation

Following is a transcript of President Nixon's address last night as recorded by The New York Times:

Good evening.

This is the 37th time I have spoken to you from this office in which so many decisions have been made that shape the history of this nation.

Each time I have done so to discuss with you some matters that I believe affected the national interest. And all the decisions I have made in my public life I have always tried to do what was best for the nation.

Throughout the long and difficult period of Watergate, I have felt it was my duty to persevere; to make every possible effort to complete the term of office to which you elected me.

In the past few days, however, it has become evident to me that I no longer have a strong enough political base in the Congress to justify continuing that effort.

Deliberately Difficult

As long as there was such a base, I felt strongly that it was necessary to see the constitutional process through to its conclusion; that to do otherwise would be unfaithful to the spirit of that deliberately difficult process, and a dangerously destabilizing precedent for the future.

But with the disappearance of that base, I now believe that the constitutional purpose has been served. And there is no longer a need for the process to be prolonged.

I would have preferred to carry through to the finish whatever the personal agony it would have involved, and my family unanimously urged me to do so.

But the interests of the nation must always come before any personal considerations. From the discussions I have had with Congressional and other leaders I have concluded that because of the Watergate matter I might not have the support of the Congress that I would consider necessary to back the very difficult decisions and carry out the duties of this office in the way the interests of the nation will require.

I have never been a quitter.

To leave office before my term is completed is opposed to every instinct in my body. But as President I must put the interests of America first.

Full-Time President

America needs a full-time President and a full-time Congress, particularly at this time with problems we face at home and abroad.

To continue to fight through the months ahead for my personal vindication would almost totally absorb the time and attention of both the President and the Congress in a period when our entire focus should be on the great issues of peace abroad and prosperity without inflation at home.

Therefore, I shall resign the Presidency effective at noon tomorrow.

Vice President Ford will be sworn in as President at that hour in this office.

As I recall the high hopes for America with which we began this second term, I feel a great sadness that I will not be here in this office working on your behalf to achieve those hopes in the next two and a half years.

But in turning over direction of the Government to Vice President Ford I know, as I told the nation when I nominated him for that office 10 months ago, that the leadership of America will be in good hands.

In passing this office to the Vice President I also do so with the profound sense of the weight of responsibility that will fall on his shoulders tomorrow, and therefore of the understanding, the patience, the cooperation he will need from all Americans.

As he assumes that responsibility he will deserve the help and the support of all of us. As we look to the future, the first essential is to begin healing the wounds of this nation. To put the bitterness and divisions of the recent past behind us and to rediscover those shared ideals that lie at the heart of our strength and unity as a great and as a free people.

By taking this action, I hope that I will have hastened the start of that process of healing which is so desperately needed in America.

'The Best Interests'

I regret deeply any injuries that may have been done in the course of the events that led to this decision. I would say only that if some of my judgments were wrong—and some were wrong—they were made in what I believed at the time to be the best interests of the nation.

To those who have stood with me during these past difficult months, to my family, my friends, the many others who've joined in supporting my cause because they believed it was right, I will be eternally grateful for your support.

And to those who have not felt able to give me your support, let me say I leave with no bitterness toward those who have opposed me, because all of us in the final analysis have been concerned with the good of the country however our judgments might differ.

So let us all now join together in affirming that common commitment and in helping our new President succeed for the benefit of all Americans.

I shall leave this office with regret at not completing my term but with gratitude for the privilege of serving as your President for the past five and a half years.

These years have been a momentous time in the history of our nation and the world. They have been a time of achievement in which we can all be proud—achievements that represent the shared efforts of the administration, the Congress and the people. But the challenges ahead are equally great.

And they, too, will require the support and the efforts of a Congress and the people, working in cooperation with the new Administration.

We have ended America's longest war. But in the work of securing a lasting peace in the world, the goals ahead are even more far-reaching and more difficult. We must complete a structure of peace, so that it will be said of this generation—our generation of Americans—by the people of all nations, not only that we ended one war but that we prevented future wars.

We have unlocked the doors that for a quarter of a century stood between the United States and the People's Republic of China. We must now insure that the one-quarter of the world's people who live in the People's Republic of China will be and remain, not our enemies, but our friends.

Breakthroughs With Russia

In the Middle East, 100 million people in the Arab countries, many of whom have considered us their enemies for nearly 20 years, now look on us as their friends. We must continue to build on that friendship so that peace can settle at last over the Middle East and so that the cradle of civilization will not become its grave.

Together with the Soviet Union we have made the crucial breakthroughs that have begun the process of limiting nuclear arms. But we must set as our goal not just limiting but reducing and finally destroying these terrible weapons so that they cannot destroy civilization.

And so that the threat of nuclear war will no longer hang over the world and the people, we have opened a new relation with the Soviet Union. We must continue to develop and expand that new relationship so that the two strongest nations of the world will live together in cooperation rather than confrontation.

Around the world—in Asia, in Africa, in Latin America, in the Middle East—there are millions of people who live in terrible poverty, even starvation. We must keep as our goal turning away from production for war and expanding production for peace so that people everywhere on this earth can at last look forward, in their children's time if not in our time, to having the necessities for a decent life.

Here in America we are fortunate that most of our people have not only the blessings of liberty but also the means to live full and good, and by the world's standards, even abundant lives.

We must press on, however, toward a goal not only of more and better jobs but of full opportunity for every man, and of what we are striving so hard right now to achieve—prosperity without inflation.

For more than a quarter of a century in public life, I have shared in the turbulent history of this evening.

I have fought for what I believe in. I have tried, to the best of my ability, to discharge those duties and meet those responsibilities that were entrusted to me.

Sometimes I have succeeded. And sometimes I have failed. But always I have taken heart from what Theodore Roosevelt said about the man in the arena whose face is married by dust and sweat and blood. who strives valiantly, who errs and comes short again and again because there is not effort without error and shortcoming, but who does actually strive to do the deed, who knows the great enthusiasm, the great devotion, who spends himself in a worthy cause, who at the best knows in the end the triumphs of high achievements and with the worst if he fails, at least fails while daring greatly.

Dedication Pledged

I pledge to you tonight that as long as I have a breath of life in my body I shall continue in that spirit. I shall continue to work for the great causes to which I have been dedicated throughout my years as a Congressman, a Senator, Vice President and President, the cause of peace—not just for America but among all nations—prosperity, justice and opportunity for all of our people.

There is one cause above all to which I have been devoted and to which I shall always be devoted for as long as I live.

When I first took the oath of office as President five and a half years ago, I made this sacred commitment: to consecrate my office, my energies and all the wisdom I can summon to the cause of peace among nations.

I've done my very best in all the days since to be true to that pledge.

As a result of these efforts, I am confident that the world is a safer place today, not only for the people of America but for the people of all nations, and that all of our children have a better chance than before of living in peace rather than dying in war.

This, more than anything, is what I hoped to achieve when I sought the Presidency. This, more than anything, is what I hope will be my legacy to you, to our country, as I leave the Presidency.

To have served in this office is to have felt a very personal sense of kinship with each and every American. In leaving it, I do so with this prayer: May God's grace be with you in all the days ahead.

The Sediment After Watergate's Tide Recedes

By George E. Reedy

MILWAUKEE—It is too early for a total assessment of Watergate's long-range impact on the Presidency. But there is a strong possibility that as Richard M. Nixon's successors put the pieces back together again they will find a few holes have been blasted through the walls that have isolated Presidents from political reality.

Washington is a city where memories persist long after they have faded in other parts of the nation. The mischief allegedly caused by the Committee on the Conduct of the War is still discussed in the House and Senate more than a century after the Civil War, which gave it birth. Recollections of the Teapot Dome scandal still serve to keep some people honest.

On this basis, it is safe to predict that Presidents and their staffs will be haunted by the Watergate scandal for decades to come. They may not recall the specifics but they will remember that highly placed heads toppled largely through arrogance. A note of humility has been introduced into the White House; nothing could be healthier.

Of even greater importance, however, is the precedent of a President resigning under fire. Too much can be made of it. The idea cannot be sustained that this in any manner resembled the departure from office of a prime minister after a vote of no-confidence. It was much closer to an abdication, and the circumstances were so unusual that a repetition is unlikely.

Nevertheless, every future President must include in his calculations the possibility that a chief executive can be forced to leave office because he has overreached himself. It may never happen again, but there are some powers that are potent even though they are never exercised; it has now been proved that the people do have the power to change their Government between elections.

Mr. Nixon stated that he was resigning because he had lost his "political base" in the Congress. But no man can lose his base there unless he has lost it in the electorate. It is obvious that even though a sizable minority of Americans still support him and will continue to believe that he was railroaded out of office, he could no longer govern. He had lost his ability to lead.

To a large extent, the isolation of past Presidents has arisen from the conviction that a chief executive cannot be dislodged from office during his term short of the use of the agonizingly clumsy machinery of impeachment. This circumstance fostered an indifference to public pressure.

Mr. Nixon, of course, faced the virtual certainty of impeachment and conviction. Nevertheless, it was the force of public opinion, as expressed through the House and Senate, that forced the abdication.

Those who have opposed Mr. Nixon from the beginning complain that the process took too long. In retrospect, however, it is fortunate that it proved to be a difficult undertaking. We would be in real trouble had a precedent been set whereby a President could be dismissed because public favor had swung against him temporarily. From a pragmatic standpoint, the outcome represented a good balance: The chief executive can be removed, but only under extreme circumstances.

The basic problem of isolation, however, still remains even though it may have been diminished. What has really been established is that there are limits beyond which a President must not go.

Within those limits, he is still a man without peers who is called upon to make fundamental decisions without going through the grueling, adversary debate out of which political reality emerges. The limits depend upon the will of the people, which is difficult to mobilize and even more difficult to record until it is white hot.

The problem may not be immediately apparent under President Ford. He is the successor closest to Watergate; he appears to have the kind of personality best adapted to resisting the forces of isolation. But even he is going to find it difficult to elicit from those around him the blunt, harsh adversary dialogue that has been the lifeblood of our democracy.

As a partisan leader in the House of Representatives, he was surrounded by men and women who called him Jerry and told him what they thought in simple direct English. He is now "Mr. President," and no one, not even people like me who think such treatment is bad for Presidents, is going to approach him other than respectfully. It will be lonely.

For the time being, little can be done about widening the breach that has been made in the ramparts of Presidential isolation. Too much must be done to restore confidence in the Presidency to permit tinkering at the moment. But even though the problem has been partly alleviated it has not been solved, and considerable thought is still necessary.

George E. Reedy was press secretary for President Johnson.

August 15, 1974

For the first time in our history, we are serving under both a president and a vice president who owe their positions to appointment rather than to election. It is obvious that the consequences of such a condition are tremendous. We are much too close to draw even the most tentative conclusions on what lies ahead.

It is an historic moment. But historic moments produce little in contemporaries other than bewilderment. There is no point in an effort to determine the meaning. Therefore, this volume closes with a bare statement of the facts as seen by journalists.

GER

A Celebration Along the Path of Least Resistance

WASHINGTON — President Nixon proclaimed it "a new beginning for America" and his announcement on Friday that Gerald R. Ford was the ideal choice to become Vice President of the United States had the staged exuberance—the rhetorical flourish, the televised gaiety, the pretense of suspense—of a political convention moving confidently toward national triumph.

But this nominating convention took place on short notice in the East Room of the White House and, for all the surreal efforts to portray it as a venture toward manifest political destiny, there was no way to mask the fact that it was a product of the latest traumatic jolt to the Nixon Administration and national stability.

Two days earlier, Spiro T. Agnew surrendered the Vice Presidency to become a convicted felon. In one dramatic afternoon, Mr. Agnew resigned, pleaded no contest to one charge of Federal income tax evasion and was sentenced in a Baltimore courtroom to three years probation and fined $10,000 in the stunning climax to the Government's investigation of bribery, extortion and tax fraud during his 10 years in Maryland and United States politics.

The President made no reference to the bitter departure of the nation's 39th Vice President as he went before political leaders in the East Room and a nationwide television audience at 9 P.M. Friday to designate Mr. Ford, the Republican leader in the House of Representatives, as his nominee to be the 40th Vice President. The President offered no explanation of Mr. Agnew's tragedy. The President gave no rationale for his own role in arranging the bartered agreement by which Mr. Agnew escaped imprisonment in exchange for disclosure of detailed evidence assuring his public disgrace.

Instead, the President praised his Administration for achieving "peace with every nation of the world" and arranging "a rising expansion of our economy." He conceded—in referring to "a time in which we face great dangers but also a time of very great opportunity" that has become his stock definition of crisis—only that war in the Middle East threatened the peace and inflation imperiled the economy.

Thus, as if the unmentioned Agnew scandal had been a piece of good fortune, Mr. Nixon declared that he was ready to "share with all of you" the decision to nominate as Vice President a veteran of 25 years in the Congress, a man who shared the President's views on "the critical issues of foreign policy and national defense" and an understudy capable of taking over "if the responsibilities of the great office I hold should fall upon him."

The criteria seemed tailored, for the most part, to fit Gerald Rudolph Ford, the 60-year-old Michigan Congressman whose eight years as House Minority Leader bore the stamp of stanch opposition to the Johnson Administration's social activism and even more firm loyalty to the fiscal and foreign policies of the Nixon Administration.

If Mr. Ford was not regarded by his colleagues as an intellectual (Lyndon Johnson once groused that "Jerry's the only man I ever knew who can't chew gum and walk at the same time" and Mr. Nixon remarked several years ago that Mr. Ford had starred on the University of Michigan football team when there was no padded helmets to cushion the blows) he has been liked and even admired as a pragmatist.

His mid-term nomination is unprecedented and certain to undergo thorough, if friendly, study first in the House Judiciary Committee and then in the Senate Rules Committee before he can be sworn in. The wrangling had already begun over how to proceed under the 25th Amendment to the Constitution, which took effect in 1967, in the uncharted task of confirming the nomination by majority vote of both Houses of Congress. But the Democratic leaders favored Mr. Ford's choice

and had kept it a secret from Friday morning until Friday night.

All that was interesting, but at variance with an authoritative report from an associate of Mr. Ford that he was told of his selection before noon on Friday and that the possibility was first mentioned to him by Mr. Nixon 10 days earlier, just after then Vice President Agnew vowed he would not resign even if indicted.

Moreover, the President is known to have deliberated for some time about the seriousness of the threat by Congressional Democrats to oppose any nominee who wanted to seek the Presidency in 1976. The Democrats, and some Senate Republicans with White House ambitions, had no desire to be faced with a vote of approval on an individual they would have to campaign against three years later. They were particularly opposed to John B. Connally, the Democrat-turned-Republican who was widely believed to be the President's first choice.

Mr. Nixon was said to have prepared two basic lists even before he asked for suggestions Wednesday from a wide assortment of political and civil leaders. The first, representing what was called the "high-risk option," contained three likely 1976 candidates: Governors Rockefeller of

New York and Reagan of California, and Mr. Connally. The second list, the "low-risk option," had on it the names of five men believed certain to win swift confirmation: Senators Barry Goldwater of Arizona, Robert P. Griffin of Michigan, and Hugh Scott of Pennsylvania, White House counselor Melvin R. Laird, and Mr. Ford.

The request for nominations apparently was less a charade, as widely suspected, than a method to test support for the "high-risk" list and Mr. Connally especially. The predictable result was almost no support for Mr. Connally, a respectable showing for Governor Rockefeller, the favorite of most party professionals, but a Capitol Hill groundswell for Gerry Ford.

Mr. Nixon's choice of Mr. Ford thus meant, in one sense, a capitulation to Congress. At the same time, there was a fundamental attraction in it. Mr. Ford knows as well as anyone on Capitol Hill where to find the levers to power and influence among Democrats whose votes will be crucial in coming legislative brawls. The first test will be soon, on a measure Congress enacted Friday, setting limits on a President's authority to commit armed forces to undeclared war. It would require Congressional approval in 60 days for any combat venture and permit Congress to order withdrawal of troops from battle by a concurrent resolution, not subject to a Presidential veto. The bill itself is certain to be vetoed, and Mr. Ford's familiar role will be to make sure the veto is not overridden.

A second attraction in Mr. Ford's nomination is his likely role as the White House point man in the 1974 Congressional elections. He knows the territory, and his presence on the campaign circuit in key districts could have a decisive impact.

The basic shortcoming in Mr. Ford's designation is that hardly anyone knows much about him outside Washington and his home state. His nomination seems to do little, at least immediately, to enhance the President's effort to lift the thick fog of mistrust that Watergate has lowered on the Nixon White House.

More significant, three hours before Gerry Ford's nomination was announced on Friday, the United States Court of Appeals for the District of Columbia circuit upheld a lower court order compelling Mr. Nixon to release the secret White House tape recordings of his Watergate conversations. A few members of Congress already are suggesting that the Vice Presidential nomination be held up until the Supreme Court rules on the tapes case and, if the verdict goes against him, Mr. Nixon indicates whether he will obey.

The excruciating irony of Mr. Ford's nomination is that it was his unsuccessful 1970 effort to unseat Supreme Court Justice William O. Douglas, which established some of the modern House procedures for an impeachment case. Justice Douglas was represented by Simon H. Rifkind, a partner of the New York law firm whose most famous recent client was Spiro T. Agnew.

As one Democratic strategist in the House put it: "The Agnew thing has stirred up some feeling that we ought to get to the central question of Presidential succession. Gerry Ford won't have any trouble getting confirmed, but we're going to do it carefully. It's possible we could be picking a man who will be President nine months from now."

—JAMES M. NAUGHTON

October 14, 1973

A Plea to Bind Up Watergate Wounds

By MARJORIE HUNTER
Special to The New York Times

WASHINGTON, Aug. 9—Gerald Rudolph Ford became the 38th President of the United States today, declaring that "our long national nightmare is over."

Calling upon the nation to "bind up the internal wounds of Watergate," he said, "Our Constitution works. Our great Republic is a government of laws and not of men. Here the people rule."

And then, his voice filled with emotion, he urged the nation to pray for his predecessor and friend of a quarter century, Richard Milhous Nixon.

"May our former President, who brought peace to millions, find it for himself," he said.

Mr. Ford assumed the powers of the Presidency at 11:35 A.M., the moment that Mr. Nixon's letter of resignation was handed to Secretary of State Kissinger.

Then, at 12:03 P.M., he was administered the oath of office in the historic East Room of the White House by Chief Justice Warren E. Burger before an overflow crowd of friends, the Cabinet and former Congressional colleagues from both parties.

Wife Holds Bible

It was in that same room, scarcely two hours earlier, that Mr. Nixon said an emotional good-by to his Cabinet and top aides.

Raising his right hand, Mr. Ford rested his left hand on a Bible held by his wife and opened to one of his favorite passages, the fifth and sixth verses of the third chapter of Proverbs: "Trust in the Lord with all thine heart; and lean not unto thine own understanding. In all thy ways acknowledge Him, and He shall direct thy paths."

Then, in a firm voice, he took the oath of office: "I, Gerald R. Ford, do solemnly swear that I will faithfully execute the office of President of the United States and will to the best of my ability preserve, protect and defend the Constitution of the United States."

As the heavy applause ended, the 61-year-old President began perhaps the most moving speech of his career. Speaking in his flat, Middle Western tone, but with what appeared to be a new sense of self-assurance, he said that he was assuming the Presidency under circumstances never before experienced by Americans.

Minds Are Troubled

"This is an hour of history that troubles our minds and hurts our hearts," he said.

"Therefore," he continued, "I feel it is my first duty to make an unprecedented compact with my countrymen. Not an inaugural address, not a fireside chat, not a campaign speech. Just a little straight talk among friends. I intend it to be the first of many."

As the first American to assume the office after the resignation of a President, Mr. Ford said that he was "acutely aware that you have not elected me as your President by your ballots."

"So I ask you to confirm me as your President with your prayers," he added.

He declared that he had not gained office by secret promises, that he had not campaigned either for the Presidency or the Vice-Presidency.

"I have not subscribed to any partisan platform," he said. "I am indebted to no man and only to one woman, my dear wife."

This was reminiscent of his earlier "I am my own man," a declaration that he repeated frequently in recent months as he sought to remain loyal to Mr. Nixon and at the same time hold himself above the spreading taint of the Watergate affair.

He said that while he had not sought the responsibility, he would not shirk it. He said that those who nominated him and confirmed him just eight months ago as Vice President were his friends from both parties.

"It is only fitting then that I should pledge to them and to you that I will be the President of all the people," he said.

He said that he would address a joint session of Congress Monday night "to share with my former colleagues and with you, the American people, my views on the priority business of the nation and to solicit your views and theirs."

The joint session, it was disclosed later, will begin at 9 P.M. Monday.

Search for Peace

Seeking to reassure the nation and the world that the United States had not been permanently damaged by the events of recent days, the new President pledged an uninterrupted and sincere search for peace.

"America will remain strong and united," he said, "but its strength will remain dedicated to the safety and sanity of the entire family of man as well as to our own precious freedom."

Repeating words that he first used in his confimation hearings for Vice President last fall, Mr. Ford said:

"I believe that truth is the glue that holds governments together, not only our Government, but civilization itself. That bond, though strained, is unbroken at home and abroad."

He pledged candor in all his public and private acts as President and then, with simple eloquence, spoke the words that Americans had once despaired of ever hearing:

"My fellow Americans, our long national nightmare is over."

In his only direct reference to Watergate, the new President said:

"As we bind up the internal wounds of Watergate, more painful and more poisonous than those of foreign wars, let us restore the Golden Rule to our political process, and let brotherly love purge our hearts of suspicion and hate."

Asking for the nation's prayers for the Nixon family, he spoke feelingly of Mr. Nixon's wife and daughters "whose love and loyalty will forever be a shining legacy to all who bear the lonely burdens of the White House."

"I can only guess at those burdens," he continued, "although I have witnessed at close hand the tragedies that befell three Presidents and the lesser trials of others."

As he spoke his final words —"God helping me, I will not let you down" — the several hundred persons present gave him a standing ovation.

Plans for the simple inauguration were coordinated by Gen. Alexander M. Haig Jr., who was Mr. Nixon's chief of staff.

General Haig, accompanied by Mr. Nixon's longtime personal secretary, Rose Mary Woods, sat with members of Mr. Ford's Vice-Presidential staff during the ceremony.

The guest list, compiled largely by Mr. and Mrs. Ford, reflected the new President's popularity among Democrats as well as members of his own party.

It was predominantly a Congressional assembly, a gathering of those to whom Mr. Ford felt closest during his long years in the House.

Former Speaker John W. McCormack, a Democrat, came down from Boston and was warmly greeted upon his entrance into the room by two friendly adversaries, Melvin R. Laird and John W. Byrnes, both former Republican members of the House.

House Speaker Carl Albert of Oklahoma, a Democrat, arrived with a newly acquired Secret Service escort. Again, as he did 10 months ago after Spiro T. Agnew resigned as Vice President, Mr. Albert stands next in line to the Presidency until Mr. Ford selects and Congress confirms a new Vice President.

Rises About Dawn

Among others in the gathering were several who have been mentioned as possible Vice-Presidential choices. They included George Bush, chairman of the Republican National Committee, and Representative John B. Anderson of Illinois, the third-ranking Republican leader in the House.

Mr. Ford showed little of the strain of the last few days as he arrived for his inauguration. He wore a navy blue suit and a red, white and blue necktie.

He rose about dawn today, after only a few hours' sleep, and, wearing a robe, retrieved the morning newspaper—emblazed with black headlines, "Nixon Resigns"—from his front steps.

While the rest of the family slept, he prepared breakfast for himself and his youngest son, 18-year-old Steve, then conferred for nearly an hour at home with two of his close advisers, Mr. Byrnes and Philip W. Buchen of Grand Rapids, his former law partner.

Later, on the White House lawn, he bade an emotional farewell to his old friend, Mr. Nixon. The two men embraced just before Mr. Nixon stepped aboard a waiting helicopter.

Aides to the President said late today that it would be at least several days before the Fords moved into the White House.

President Nixon on TV as he announced his resignation

Associated Press
President Ford speaking at the White House yesterday

Proclamation of Pardon

Richard Nixon became the thirty-seventh President of the United States on January 20, 1969, and was re-elected in 1972 for a second term by the electors of forty-nine of the fifty states. His term in office continued until his resignation on August 9, 1974.

Pursuant to resolutions of the House of Representatives, its Committee on the Judiciary conducted an inquiry and investigation on the impeachment of the President extending over more than eight months. The hearings of the committee and its deliberations, which received wide national publicity over television, radio, and in printed media, resulted in votes adverse to Richard Nixon on recommended Articles of Impeachment.

As a result of certain acts or omissions occurring before his resignation from the office of President, Richard Nixon has become liable to possible indictment and trial for offenses against the United States. Whether or not he shall be so prosecuted depends on findings of the appropriate grand jury and on the discretion of the authorized prosecutor. Should an indictment ensue, the accused shall then be entitled to a fair trial by an impartial jury, as guaranteed to every individual by the Constitution.

It is believed that a trial of Richard Nixon, if it became necessary, could not fairly begin until a year or more has elapsed. In the meantime, the tranquility to which this nation has been restored by the events of recent weeks could be irreparably lost by the prospects of bringing to trial a former President of the United States. The prospects of such trial will cause prolonged and divisive debate over the propriety of exposing to further punishment and degradation a man who has already paid the unprecedented penalty of relinquishing the highest elective office in the United States.

NOW, THEREFORE, I, Gerald R. Ford, President of the United States, pursuant to the pardon power conferred upon me by Article II, Section 2, of the Constitution, have granted and by these presents do grant a full, free, and absolute pardon unto Richard Nixon for all offenses against the United States which he, Richard Nixon, has committed or may have committed or taken part in during the period from January 20, 1969, through August 9, 1974.

IN WITNESS WHEREOF, I have hereunto set my hand this 8th day of September in the year of our Lord nineteen hundred seventy-four, and of the independence of the United States of America the 199th.

History Played Out On Familiar Stage

By JAMES M. NAUGHTON
Special to The New York Times

WASHINGTON, Oct. 17—John M. Doar was there. The television cameras were on again, the 28 klieg lights dazzling. The President's conduct was in question once more. But the drama was enacted differently today before members of the House Judiciary Committee.

President Ford's voluntary appearance as a Congressional witness, to explain and defend the pardon he granted to his predecessor, took place in the same Room 2141 of the Rayburn House Office Building, where the votes were cast hardly three months ago to demand Richard M. Nixon's removal from the White House.

But this time Mr. Doar was on hand, not as the special counsel on impeachment but as a silent spectator. This time it was the President, not those on the Judiciary Committee, who made history, with an appearance for which only legend provided precedent. And this time the tone of the confrontation between Chief Executive, appearing in person, and members of Congress was strikingly different: civility replaced choler, deference supplanted hostility.

"Yes, sir," the President said to questioners.

"Thank you, Mr. President," the questioners said to Mr. Ford.

It was as if "Love Story" had been presented as a sequel to "Crime and Punishment."

Mr. Ford sat, alone, at the huge wooden witness table, where Mr. Doar and a battery of aides had constructed the case against Mr. Nixon. He crossed his ankles, relaxed, as he read a statement for 44 minutes in response to the questions posed in two formal resolutions of inquiry about the pardon.

The pardon's purpose, Mr. Ford insisted, was not to assist the man who had chosen him to be heir to the White House but to remove the nation's focus from Watergate and thus pursue "domestic tranquility." Whether the objective had been attained remained in question, but having said so, Mr. Ford tranquilly stacked the loose leaves of his text into a neat rectangle, laid them aside, sipped a third of a glass of water and scratched his left knee.

His calm demeanor was matched by most, but not all, of those seated before Mr. Ford at the double-decker dais of the Judiciary Committee.

The hearing was technically before a subcommittee, and its chairman, Representative William L. Hungate, Democrat of Missouri, began the proceeding by declaring, "The Subcommittee on Criminal Justice of the House Committee on the Judiciary today welcomes the President of the United States, Gerald R. Ford," and then promising not to keep the panel's guest past noon.

Mr. Ford made the point that he was there to answer only those questions relevant to the pardon—and not, for instance, to such matters as the controversial agreement giving the former President custody and eventual control of the Watergate tape recordings—and the subcommittee did not press for exceptions to the stipulation.

Although 22 of the 38 members of the full committee were present, only the none on the subcommittee were permitted to interrogate the witness. They did so, with one exception, gently.

The exception was Representative Elizabeth Holtzman, Democrat of Brooklyn, who voiced "dismay" that she would be permitted only five minutes to question Mr. Ford and that the panel had not agreed with her that the president's appearance should follow interrogation of White House subordinates who took part in the pardon arrangements.

Miss Holtzman spoke of "dark suspicions" in the land that the pardon was part of a "deal" with Mr. Nixon and read off eight separate questions at once, winding up with "would you be willing turn over to the subcommittee all tape recordings of conversations between yourself and Richard Nixon?" Mr. Ford responded to only one of the questions, but appeared to answer none. Miss Holtzman's time expired.

Representative Lawrence J. Hogan, Republican of Maryland, chided Miss Holtzman for "her accusatory opening speech" and used most of his five minutes to hail Mr. Ford "for the statement and your openness and candor in coming in this very historic event" and to describe the "absolute power" of Presidents to issue pardons.

Mr. Hungate's most salient question was whether Mr. Ford had consulted, as he suggested in his opening statement, with his wife, Betty, after being told in early August that he was likely to become President soon.

"I certainly did, Mr. Chairman," the Presaident replied

The two members of the House who had precipitated the event by introducing their separate resolutions of inquiry could not take part. One of them, Representative John Conyers Jr., Democrat of Michigan, a member of the Judiciary Committee but not the subcommittee, sat mute at the dais doing a slow, but silent, burn. He caressed his thick mustache while Mr. Ford was present and complained as the President departed that the hearing had been unsatisfactory.

The other sponsor of a formal resolution of inquiry, Representative Bella S. Abbzug, Democrat of Manhattan, is not a member of the Judiciary Committee. Despite a characteristic brown print dress and broad-brimmed brown hat, she was uncharacteristically inconspicuous in a rear corner of the spectators' gallery.

"A certain amount of reverential deference was shown," Mrs. Abzug remarked later of the proceeding. But she said "the whole subject has just begun to be discussed, and I think we have to unravel it."

The Judiciary Committee spent nine months attempting to unravel Watergate and, this morning, 120 minutes in reflection on the pardon. Former President Nixon spent at least four months withholding subpoenaed tapes and other evidence from the Judiciary Committee. President Ford went before the panel voluntarily.

Mr. Ford's last words before erturning to the White House were: "I thank you very, very much."

October 18, 1974

Mr. Ford Acts Like a President

IN THE NATION

By Tom Wicker

Gerald Ford is beginning to look more like a President, which is not necessarily a good thing. In dealing with the energy crisis, he has acted unilaterally, challenged rather than consulted Congress, and proclaimed one true religion.

There is much to be said for this reversion to the Lyndon Johnson-Richard Nixon style. Among other things, it provides an object lesson to those in and out of Congress who, in the wake of Vietnam and Watergate, have too glibly assumed that Congressional government is the proper alternative to an imperial Presidency. For after its opening spasms of reform, this Congress, too, is beginning to look more like a Congress.

The simple fact is that Mr. Ford has an energy program and Congress doesn't. Neither do the Democrats. And the basic reason for that is that the President—any President—has a policy-making apparatus that he can bring to a point of decision. Neither Congress nor the Democrats have that, either; the best they can offer is a balancing out of interests that can and usually does take months or even years to effect.

So, as nearly always happens on complex and controversial issues, the President has taken the initiative. His bureaucrats and computers have produced a program to deal with the energy crisis, and he has put it before Congress with the flat demand that its 535 members either pass it or come up with a program of their own. This means at the least that the Ford program will be at the center of debate, that the President has effectively set the terms of that debate, and that the Democratic majority in Congress will have to run to catch up with him.

Mr. Ford also may have forced action that Congress otherwise would have delayed or fudged. By unilaterally proclaiming an excise tax on imported oil—$1 a barrel, rising later

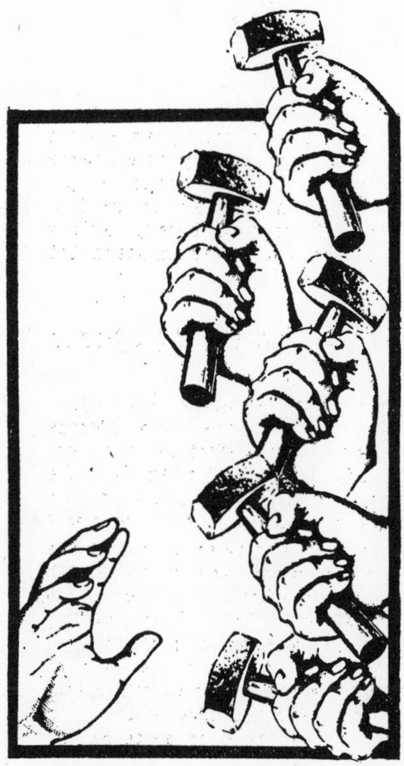

to $2, then $3—he has put the first stage of his plan into effect, which means that Congress either has to go along with much of the rest of it, or repeal the excise tax, sustaining the repeal over Mr. Ford's veto. The latter course, even if successful, would still leave Congressional Democrats the necessity to develop their own energy program, which they have not shown the will, the unity or the ability to do.

So throwing around some Presidential weight has its merits. Mr. Ford has cut through all the hot air about energy and brought the country to grips with the energy problem, which is just what a President is supposed to do. But he is not supposed to dictate solutions, and Congress is certainly not required to rubber-stamp them when he tries to. In fact, while the politicians on Capitol Hill may not be well-equipped for proposing, they can be pretty good at disposing, and they just might know a few things that Mr. Ford's bureaucrats and computers don't.

By proclaiming the oil excise without even consulting Congress, moreover, Mr. Ford has started taking money out of an economy in recession, thus diluting the effect of the stimulus that both he and they agree should be put into it.

The offsetting tax reductions by which Mr. Ford means to repay the higher costs of energy to the public cannot go into effect before mid-year at the earliest. The Ford tax rebate program, or any of the Congressional alternatives for stimulating the economy, will have to start putting purchasing power into the economy far more quickly than seems likely if they are to counteract the effects of the oil excise tax in the coming crucial months.

Proclaiming the excise tax as he did also presents Congress with the Ford energy plan as something of a fait accompli, when it is by no means certain that it is the best plan available, or even a good one. Mr. Ford himself has been heard to refer to his action as "putting a gun to Congress's head." In politics as in crime, that is playing rough, indeed, and while Mr. Ford may have forced action, he has not necessarily forced the right action at the right time.

The comprehensive energy plan Mr. Ford recommends has the great virtue of giving Congress something solid to work with. It sets goals and provides means of reaching them, but both the goals and the means need to be evaluated by people other than those who devised them. They may need to be improved or modified. Actual dollar costs per American family are in serious dispute; so is the long-term inflationary effect. Secondary and tertiary consequences need to be calculated as best they can be. Congressional hearings might be particularly helpful in achieving necessary public understanding. But if Congress has to weigh the energy program while under the gun of Mr. Ford's excise tax and its on-rushing economic effects, the country may well be hastened into action more easily regretted than redeemed.

January 31, 1975

Suggested Reading

Biographies and Studies of Individual Presidents

Beale, Howard K. *Theodore Roosevelt and the Rise of America to World Power.* Baltimore, Johns Hopkins, 1956.

Harbaugh, William Henry. *Power and Responsibility: The Life and Times of Theodore Roosevelt.* New York, Farrar, Straus and Cudahy, 1961.

Pringle, Henry Fowles. *The Life and Times of William Howard Taft.* 2 vols. New York and Toronto: Farrar & Rinehart, 1939. Pb, ShoeString, 1965.

Link, Arthur S. *Wilson.* 5 vols published. Princeton, Princeton University Press, 1947-.

Russell, Francis. *The Shadow of Blooming Grove: Warren G. Harding in His Times.* New York, McGraw-Hill, 1968.

White, William Allen. *A Puritan from Babylon: The Story of Calvin Coolidge.* New York, Macmillan, 1938.

Lyons, Eugene. *Herbert Hoover.* Garden City, N.Y., Doubleday, 1964.

Baker, Leonard. *Roosevelt and Pearl Harbor.* New York, Macmillan, 1970.

Burns, James MacGregor, *Roosevelt.* 2 vols. New York, Harcourt-Brace, 1956-70. Pb.

Freidel, Frank B. *Franklin D. Roosevelt.* 3 vols of a projected 6. Boston, Little Brown, 1952-.

Phillips, Cabell. *The Truman Presidency: The History of a Triumphant Succession.* New York, Macmillan, 1966.

Albertson, Albert, ed. *Eisenhower as President.* New York, Hill and Wang, 1963.

Hughes, Emmet John. *The Ordeal of Power: A Political Memoir of the Eisenhower Years.* New York, Atheneum, 1963.

Schlesinger, Arthur M., Jr. *A Thousand Days: John F. Kennedy in the White House.* Boston, Houghton, Mifflin, 1965.

Sorenson, Theodore C. *Kennedy.* New York, Harper & Row, 1965.

Goldman, Eric F. *The Tragedy of Lyndon Johnson.* New York, Knopf, 1968. Pb, Dell, 1969.

Safire, William. *Before the Fall.* Garden City, N.Y., Doubleday, 1975.

Wills, Garry. *Nixon Agonistes.* Boston, Houghton Mifflin, 1969. Pb

Evans, Rowland, Jr., and Robert D. Novak. *Nixon in the White House.* New York, Random House, 1972.

The Office of the Presidency

Corwin, E. S. *The President: Office and Powers, 1787-1957.* 4th rev. ed. New York, New York University Press, 1957.

Johnson, Richard T. *Managing the White House: An Intimate Study of the Presidency.* New York, Harper & Row, 1974.

Reedy, George E. *The Twilight of the Presidency.* New York, New American Library and World Publishing, 1970. Pb

Schlesinger, Arthur M., Jr. *The Imperial Presidency.* Boston, Houghton Mifflin, 1973.

Presidential Elections

Rosebloom, Eugene H. *A History of Presidential Elections.* 3rd ed. New York, Macmillan, 1970.

The Broadcast Media and the President

Minow, Newton N., John Bartlow Martin, and Lee M. Mitchell. *Presidential Television.* A Twentieth Century Fund Report. New York, Basic Books, 1973.

Administration Scandals

Bates, J. Leonard. *The Origins of Teapot Dome.* Urbana, University of Illinois Press, 1963.

Noggle, Burl. *Teapot Dome: Oil and Politics in the 1920's.* Baton Rouge, Louisiana State University Press, 1962.

Woodward, Bob, and Carl Bernstein. *All the President's Men.* New York, Simon and Schuster, 1974. Pb

NOTE—Pb indicates availability in paperback.

Index